# Law of Commercial Transactions

## &

## Business Associations

### Concepts and Cases

# Law of Commercial Transactions

## & 

## Business Associations

### Concepts and Cases

THOMAS BOWERS

JANE P. MALLOR

A. JAMES BARNES

MICHAEL J. PHILLIPS

ARLEN LANGVARDT

*all of*
*Indiana University*

**IRWIN**

Chicago  •  Bogotá  •  Boston  •  Buenos Aires  •  Caracas
London  •  Madrid  •  Mexico City  •  Sydney  •  Toronto

**IRWIN**
**Concerned About Our Environment**
In recognition of the fact that our company is a large end-user of fragile yet replenishable resources, we at IRWIN can assure you that every effort is made to meet or exceed Environmental Protection Agency (EPA) recommendations and requirements for a "greener" workplace.

To preserve these natural assets, a number of environmental policies, both companywide and department-specific, have been implemented. From the use of 50% recycled paper in our textbooks to the printing of promotional materials with recycled stock and soy inks to our office paper recycling program, we are committed to reducing waste and replacing environmentally unsafe products with safer alternatives.

Senior sponsoring editor: *Craig Beytien*
Marketing manager: *Cindy L. Ledwith*
Project editor: *Ethel Shiell*
Production supervisor: *Laurie Kersch*
Designer: *Mercedes Santos*
Manager, graphics and desktop services: *Kim Meriwether*
Compositor: *Carlisle Communications, Ltd.*
Typeface: *10/12 Times Roman*
Printer: *R. R. Donnelley & Sons Company*

**Library of Congress Cataloging-in-Publication Data**
Law of commercial transactions and business associations : concepts
  and cases  /  Thomas Bowers . . . [et al.].
    p.  cm.—(Irwin legal studies in business series)
    Includes index.
    ISBN 0-256-17864-X
    1. Commercial law—United States.  2. Sales—United States.
  3. Business enterprises—Law and legislation—United States.
  I.  Bowers, Thomas.  II. Series.
  KF889.L389  1995
  346.73'07—dc20
  [347.3067]                                      94–38814

*Printed in the United States of America*

1 2 3 4 5 6 7 8 9 0 DO 1 0 9 8 7 6 5 4

# ABOUT THE AUTHORS

**Thomas Bowers** joined the faculty of Indiana University's School of Business after working for the Brooklyn District Attorney and the Enforcement Division of the United States Securities and Exchange Commission in New York City. He has received 10 outstanding teaching awards at Indiana, and is the only two-time recipient of the Indiana University Student Choice Award for outstanding teaching. He has published extensively in legal, business, and professional journals. Bowers graduated Summa Cum Laude from the Ohio State University and earned his J.D. at New York University.

**Jane P. Mallor** has taught business law at Indiana University since 1976. During that time, she has received several teaching awards, including the Student Alumni Council Senior Faculty Award, the Faculty Colloquium for Excellence in Teaching, and the Amoco Foundation Award for Distinguished Teaching. Mallor received her B.A. from Indiana University and her J.D. from Indiana University School of Law.

**A. James Barnes** currently is Dean and Professor of Public and Environmental Affairs at Indiana University. He previously won a distinguished teaching award from Indiana University's School of Business. Barnes's government positions include Deputy Administrator of EPA, General Counsel of EPA, General Counsel of the Department of Agriculture, and trial attorney in the Department of Justice. Barnes received his B.A. with honors from Michigan State University and J.D. Cum Laude from Harvard Law School.

**Michael J. Phillips** has been teaching business law at Indiana University's School of Business since 1977. During that period, he has won eight best article or comment awards from the *American Business Law Journal*. After filling various editorial board positions, Phillips also served as editor-in-chief of the *Journal* from 1988 to 1990. In addition, he has twice chaired the business law department at Indiana University's School of Business. Phillips received his B.A. from Johns Hopkins University, earned a J.D. from Columbia University, and received L.L.M. and S.J.D. degrees from George Washington University.

**Arlen W. Langvardt**, currently Associate Professor of Business Law, joined the Indiana University Graduate School of Business after private practice as a trial attorney involved in a variety of legal areas. Langvardt has received several teaching awards at both the undergraduate and M.B.A. levels, and in 1989, he received the Holmes/Cardozo Award from the Academy of Legal Studies in Business. He has published 15 articles in law and business journals and delivered the 1992 Boal Memorial Lecture at Georgetown University Law Center. Langvardt received his B.A. with highest honors from Hastings College and J.D. with distinction from the University of Nebraska.

This textbook is devoted to the law affecting commercial transactions and business associations. While the textbook is a newcomer to the business law field, its authors are not, having accumulated over 45 years of textbook writing experience. Most of the author team has written the last four editions of this textbook's sister publication, *Business Law and the Regulatory Environment,* a leader in the fields of business law and the regulatory environment for 60-odd years. With the publication of this textbook—which we believe is the only business law casebook of its kind—the authors continue the pioneering legacy of their colleagues and former co-authors, Harold Lusk, Charles M. Hewitt, John D. Donnell, and Michael B. Metzger.

## COURSES USING THIS TEXTBOOK

We envision instructors using this book in a variety of courses. For students who have already completed a legal environment course, this book's emphasis on the law of contracts, Uniform Commercial Code topics such as sales and commercial paper, and business organizations enables a student taking a second business law course to complete his legal studies education. The classic example of such a second course is the required or elective course for finance and accounting majors that, in part, prepares students for the business law portion of the CPA Examination. In addition, a course covering only UCC topics may utilize this text, as may a course devoted to partnerships, corporations, other business organizations, and securities regulation. The theory behind this textbook is to offer students coverage of relevant business and commercial law topics without the surplusage of topics found in traditional business law textbooks. Of course, there may be other uses of this textbook we have not anticipated.

## IMPORTANT FEATURES IN THIS TEXTBOOK

### Clear and Comprehensive Coverage

Above all things, we take pride in our thorough and up-to-date coverage of business law. This text excels in its depth and clarity of treatment of each topic.

**Style and Presentation**   Our goal has been to write this text in a direct, lucid, and organized, yet relatively relaxed and conversational style. For this reason, we believe an instructor may cover certain topics by assigning them as reading without lecturing on them. We employ italics and boldface to emphasize key points and terms. Each chapter contains numerous examples of the law's application. Moreover, the textbook makes considerable use of numbered paragraphs, often introduced by italics or boldface, to list elements of a legal claim or applications of legal concepts.

**Case Selection**   We have made great efforts to find cases that clearly illustrate important points made in the text. Whenever possible, we also have tried to select cases that are of interest to students and are fun to teach. Our collective in-class teaching experience with the cases has helped us determine which of those cases best meet these criteria, and has influenced our selection decisions. We have attempted to select an appropriate mix of landmark and new cases. Except where older decisions are landmarks or best illustrate particular concepts, we have selected recent cases.

We have restated the facts of each case to ease students' understanding of the factual issues. The legal reasoning of each case is the actual language of the court, carefully edited to maximize student comprehension. In addition, we have placed the cases near the textual points they illustrate and provided textual lead-ins to them.

**Figures and Concept Reviews**    Aiding students' comprehension of difficult subjects is the use of charts, figures, and concept reviews. An instructor may use the concept reviews—such as the one on page 844 of Chapter 38, Liability Sections of the 1933 Act and 1934 Act—as the basis for class lectures and discussions.

**CPA Exam Coverage**    This book is not and does not purport to be a CPA Exam review textbook. Our objective is to inform students of the legal rules and problems they are likely to face in their commercial and business dealings. Nonetheless, the textbook addresses all the topics covered by the Business Law portion of the CPA Exam. The authors have analyzed every CPA Exam since 1974. Nearly every rule of law tested by the CPA Exam is in the textbook or the Instructor's Manual. Thus, we believe that this textbook offers a unique opportunity for an instructor to cover material essential to students' future business planning decisions and yet fairly prepare students for the CPA Exam.

## Capstone Questions

We have prepared capstone questions appearing at the end of each textbook chapter. Capstone questions are modeled after essay questions on the CPA Exam. However, the capstone questions are more than merely CPA Exam review questions. They provide instructors an excellent vehicle to determine students' understanding and ability to apply the law. The capstone questions typically address many issues, requiring students to manipulate a complex fact pattern, pick out the important facts, find the

applicable law, and come to a well-reasoned conclusion. Instructors may use the capstone questions as a means of teaching the material or reinforcing student learning of material presented in class.

## Up-to-Date Coverage

The authors are dedicated to keeping readers apprised of current changes in business laws. While the high number of recent legal developments incorporated in this textbook makes listing all of them impossible, the following deserve special mention:

· Chapter 19, Estates and Trusts, integrates the Uniform Probate Code.

· Chapters 23 to 26, the commercial paper chapters, incorporate Revised Article 3 of the Uniform Commercial Code and the concomitant amendments to Articles 1 and 4 of the UCC. The revision and the amendments have been adopted by a majority of the states.

· The characteristics of the important new business form, the Limited Liability Company, are summarized in Chapter 29, Introduction to Forms of Business and Formation of Partnerships, and covered extensively in Chapter 32, Limited Partnerships and Limited Liability Companies.

· Another important new business form, the Limited Liability Partnership, is discussed throughout the partnership chapters, Chapters 29 to 31, and in Chapter 38, Legal Responsibilities of Accountants.

· The corporations chapters, Chapters 33 to 36, comprehensively cover the regulation of nonprofit corporations. We believe that this book is the only business law textbook that covers nonprofit corporations in detail.

· Chapter 35, Management of Corporations, includes the 1994 amendments to the Revised Model Business Corporation Act regarding indemnification of directors and officers. Chapter 35 also covers the 1994 decision of the Supreme Court of Delaware, *Paramount Communications, Inc. v. Time, Inc.,* which considered the validity of takeover defenses.

- Chapter 37, Securities Regulation, incorporates the Securities and Exchange Commission's changes in Regulation D and Regulation A.
- Chapter 38, Legal Responsibilities of Accountants, includes as a text case the most important Rule 10b-5 case in many years, the Supreme Court's decision in *Central Bank of Denver v. First Interstate Bank of Denver,* which held that Rule 10b-5 does not impose liability on aiders and abettors.
- Chapter 40, Employment Law, includes the Family Medical and Leave Act of 1993, the Americans with Disabilities Act, changes made by the Civil Rights Act of 1991, and two 1993 decisions of the Supreme Court, *Harris v. Forklift Systems, Inc.* and *Hazen Paper Co. v. Biggins.*

## THE PACKAGE

This textbook is complemented by a most extensive, innovative package of student and instructor support material. Video and computerized supplements provide methods of applying, updating, and maximizing text materials. Traditional support materials for both students and instructors enhance daily classroom instruction and foster learning.

### Irwin's Legal Studies in Business Video Series

Adopters of this textbook may obtain Irwin's new case videos for classroom use. These videos, which number 20 in all, are contemporary dramatizations that portray recurrent business law issues. Some of the videos concern an issue or tightly focused group of issues that fit within a single chapter. Most, however, raise multiple issues spanning two or more chapters.

Portions of the case videos are integrated as problem cases in many of this book's chapters. They are designated by a video cassette icon—[ 📼 ]— and the term *Video Case.* The title of the video follows immediately.

Supplementary Video Case Notes, prepared by Richard Finkley of Governors State University, outline the facts, issues, and decision for each video segment. You will note that with each identified issue, there is an annotation directing you to the appropriate chapter in this text.

## Instructor's Manual

The author team has prepared the Instructor's Manual for this text. Each chapter in the manual contains teaching objectives, outlined suggestions for structuring your presentation of corresponding text chapter material, additional material and examples not mentioned in the text, and discussions of each text case, providing points for discussion with students. Each Instructor's Manual also contains answers to the Problems and Problem Cases, including case citations where appropriate. Detailed answers to the end-of-chapter capstone questions are also included. To help instructors preparing CPA candidates, we include a list of topics emphasized by the CPA Exam.

## Manual of Tests

The Manual of Tests, prepared by the authors, tests a full range of issues addressed by the textbook. Most questions are modeled after the Business Law portion of the CPA Exam. In addition, adopters of the textbook may obtain the Manual of Tests for the 9th edition of *Business Law and the Regulatory Environment,* which has additional questions testing the same material in corresponding chapters.

## Computest

A computerized version of the Manual of Tests is available. It allows instructors to generate random tests and to add their own questions.

## ACKNOWLEDGMENTS

We would like to recognize and thank the many people at Richard D. Irwin, Inc., who have assisted in the preparation of this text: Laurie Kersch, production supervisor; Mercedes Santos, cover designer; Ethel Shiell, project editor; and editors Karen Mellon and Craig Beytien.

We would also like to recognize Pam Davis Smoot, Becky Snedegar, and John Yarger of Indiana University, who assisted in the preparation of the manuscript.

**Thomas Bowers**
**Jane P. Mallor**
**A. James Barnes**
**Michael J. Phillips**
**Arlen W. Langvardt**

# Contents in Brief

## CORPORATIONS

## SPECIAL TOPICS

# CONTENTS

**PART 2**

# SALES

**PART**

**3**

# PROPERTY

**P A R T**

**4**

# DEBTORS' AND CREDITORS' RIGHTS

**PART 5**

# COMMERCIAL PAPER

**PART 6**

# AGENCY

**PARTNERSHIPS**

**PART**

**9**

## SPECIAL TOPICS

# LIST OF CASES

# PART 1

# CONTRACTS

# CHAPTER 1

# INTRODUCTION TO CONTRACTS

**INTRODUCTION**

*Scholars and courts have formulated numerous definitions of the term* contract. *The* Restatement (Second) of Contracts *defines a contract as "a promise or set of promises for the breach of which the law gives a remedy, or the performance of which the law in some way recognizes as a duty."[1] The essence of this definition for our purposes is that a contract is a legally enforceable promise or set of promises. In other words, parties to contracts are entitled to call on the state to force those with whom they have contracted to honor their promises. However, not all of the promises that people make attain the status of contracts. We have all made and broken numerous promises without fear of being sued by those to whom our promises were made. If you promise to take a friend out to dinner but fail to do so, you do not expect to be sued for breaching your promise. What separates such social promises from legally enforceable contracts?*

## THE NATURE OF CONTRACTS

Over the years, the common law courts have developed several basic tests that a promise must meet before it is treated as a contract. These tests comprise the basic elements of contract. Contracts are *agreements* (an *offer*, made and *accepted*) that are *voluntarily* created by persons with the *capacity* to contract. The objectives of the agreement must be *legal* and, in most cases, the agreement must be supported by some *consideration* (a bargained-for exchange of legal value). Finally, the law requires *written* evidence of the existence of some agreements before enforcing them (see Figure 1). The following chapters discuss each of these elements and other points that are necessary to enable you to distinguish contracts from unenforceable, social promises.

## THE SOCIAL UTILITY OF CONTRACT

Contracts enable persons acting in their own interests to enlist the support of the law in furthering their personal objectives. Contracts enable us to enter into agreements with others with the confi-

---

[1] *Restatement (Second) of Contracts* § 1 (1981).

**FIGURE 1    Getting to Contract**

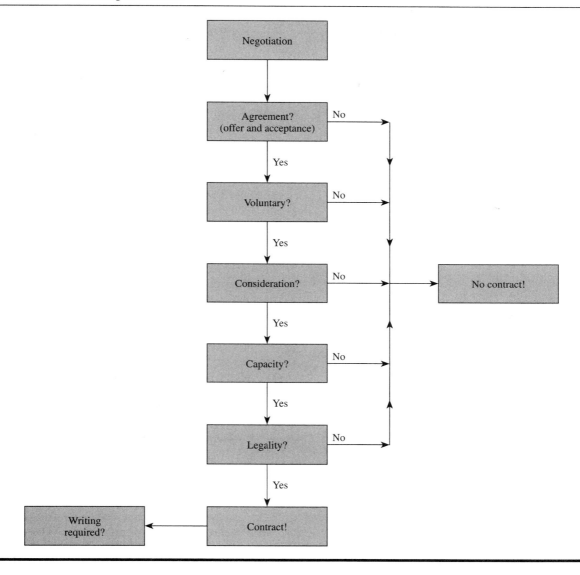

dence that we may call on the law, and not merely the good faith of the other party, to ensure that those agreements will be honored. Within broad limits defined by contract doctrine and public policy, the contract device enables us to create the private law that governs our relations with others—the terms of the agreements we make.

Contracts facilitate the private planning that is necessary in a modern, industrialized society. Few people would invest in a business enterprise if they could not rely on the builders and suppliers of their facilities and equipment, the suppliers of the raw materials necessary to manufacture products, and the customers who agree to purchase those products to honor their commitments. How could we make loans, sell goods on credit, or rent property unless loan agreements, conditional sales agreements, and leases were backed by the force of the law? Contract, then, is an inescapable and valuable part of the world as we know it. Like that world, its particulars tend to change over time, while its general characteristics remain largely stable.

## The Evolution of Contract Law

### Classical Contract Law

The contract idea is ancient. Thousands of years ago, Egyptians and Mesopotamians recognized devices like contracts; by the 15th century, the common law courts of England had developed a variety of theories to justify enforcing certain promises. Contract law did not, however, assume major importance in our legal system until the 19th century, when numerous social factors combined to shape the common law of contract. Laissez-faire (free market) economic ideas had a profound influence on public policy thinking during this period, and the Industrial Revolution created a perceived need for private planning and certainty in commercial transactions. The typical contract situation in the early decades of the 19th century involved face-to-face transactions between parties with relatively equal bargaining power who dealt with relatively simple goods.

The contract law that emerged from this period was strongly influenced by these factors. Its central tenet was *freedom of contract*: Contracts should be enforced because they are the products of the free wills of their creators, who should, within broad limits, be free to determine the extent of their obligations. The proper role of the courts in such a system of contract was to enforce these freely made bargains but otherwise to adopt a hands-off stance. Contractual liability should not be imposed unless the parties clearly agreed to assume it, but once an agreement had been made, liability was near absolute. The fact that the items exchanged were of unequal value was usually legally irrelevant. The freedom to make good deals carried with it the risk of making bad deals. As long as a person voluntarily entered a contract, it would generally be enforced against him, even if the result was grossly unfair. And since equal bargaining power tended to be assumed, the courts were usually unwilling to hear defenses based on unequal bargaining power. This judicial posture allowed the courts to formulate a pure contract law consisting of precise, clear, and technical rules that were capable of general, almost mechanical, application. Such a law of contract met the needs of the marketplace by affording the predictable and consistent results necessary to facilitate private planning.

### Modern Contract Law Development

As long as most contracts resembled the typical transaction envisioned by 19th-century contract law, such rules made perfect sense. If the parties dealt face-to-face, they were likely to know each other personally or at least to know each other's reputation for fair dealing. Face-to-face deals enabled the parties to inspect the goods in advance of the sale, and since the subject matter of most contracts was relatively simple, the odds were great that the parties had relatively equal knowledge about the items they bought and sold. If the parties also had equal bargaining power, it was probably fair to assume that they were capable of protecting themselves and negotiating an agreement that seemed fair at the time. Given the truth of these assumptions, there was arguably no good reason for judicial interference with private contracts.

America's Industrial Revolution, however, undermined many of these assumptions. Regional, and later national, markets produced longer chains of distribution. This fact, combined with more efficient means of communication, meant that people often contracted with persons whom they did not know for goods that they had never seen. And rapidly developing technology meant that those goods were becoming increasingly complex. Thus, sellers often knew far more about their products than did the buyers with whom they dealt. Finally, the emergence of large business organizations after the Civil War produced obvious disparities of bargaining power in many contract situations. These large organizations found it more efficient to standardize their numerous transactions by employing standard form contracts, which could also be used to exploit disproportionate bargaining power by dictating the terms of their agreements. Figure 2 summarizes the factors that shaped modern contract law.

The upshot of all this is that many contracts today no longer resemble the stereotypical agreements envisioned by the common law of contract. It has been estimated that over 90 percent of all contracts today are form contracts.[2] How should courts respond to contracts where the terms have been dictated by one party to another party who may not have read or understood them, and who, in

---

[2]Slawson, "Standard Form Contracts and Democratic Control of Lawmaking Power," 84 *Harv. L. Rev.* 529 (1971).

**FIGURE 2   Factors that Shaped Modern Contract Law**

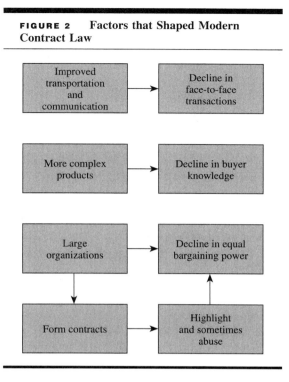

any event, may have lacked the power to bargain for better terms? Contract law is changing to reflect these changes in social reality. The 20th century has witnessed a dramatic increase in public intervention into private contractual relationships. Think of all the statutes governing the terms of what were once purely private contractual relationships. Legislatures commonly dictate many of the basic terms of insurance contracts. Employment contracts are governed by a host of laws concerning maximum hours worked, minimum wages paid, employer liability for on-the-job injuries, unemployment compensation, and retirement benefits. In some circumstances, product liability statutes impose liability on the manufacturers and sellers of products regardless of the terms of their sales contracts. The avowed purpose of much of this public intervention has been to protect persons who lack sufficient bargaining power to protect themselves.

Nor have the legislatures been the only source of public supervision of private agreements. Twentieth-century courts have been increasingly concerned with creating contract rules that produce just results. The result of this concern has been an increasingly hands-on posture by courts that often feel compelled to intervene in private contractual relationships to protect weaker parties. In the name of avoiding injustice, some modern contract doctrines impose contractual liability, or something quite like it, in situations where traditional contract rules would have denied liability. Similarly, other modern contract doctrines allow parties to avoid contract liability in cases where traditional common law rules would have recognized a binding agreement and imposed liability.

In the process of evolving to accommodate changing social circumstances, the basic nature of contract rules is changing. The precise, technical rules that characterized traditional common law contract are giving way to broader, imprecise standards such as good faith, injustice, reasonableness, and unconscionability. The reason for such standards is clear. If courts are increasingly called on to intervene in private contracts in the name of fairness, it is necessary to fashion rules that afford the degree of judicial discretion required to reach just decisions in the increasingly complex and varied situations where intervention is needed.

This heightened emphasis on fairness, like every other choice made by law, carries with it some cost. Imprecise, discretionary modern contract rules do not produce the same measure of certainty and predictability that their precise and abstract predecessors afforded. And because modern contract rules often impose liability in the absence of the clear consent required by traditional common law contract rules, one price of increased fairness in contract cases has been a diminished ability of private parties to control the nature and extent of their contractual obligations.

This change in the nature of contract law is far from complete, however. The idea that a contract is an agreement freely entered into by the parties still lies at the heart of contract law today, and contract cases may be found that differ very little in their spirit or ultimate resolution from their 19th-century predecessors. It is probably fair to say, however, that these are most likely to be cases where 19th-century assumptions about the nature of contracts are still largely valid. Thus, these cases involve contracts between parties with relatively equal bargaining power and relatively equal knowledge about the subject of the contract. Despite the existence of such cases, it is evident that contract law is in the process of significant change. Subsequent chapters highlighting the differences between modern contract rules and their traditional common law forebears render this conclusion inescapable. Before discussing particular examples of this new thrust in contract law, however, we should familiarize ourselves with the basic contract terminology that is used throughout the text.

## BASIC CONTRACT CONCEPTS AND TYPES

### Bilateral and Unilateral Contracts

Contracts have traditionally been classified as **bilateral** or **unilateral,** depending on whether one or both of the parties has made a promise. In unilateral contracts, only one party makes a promise. For example, if a homeowner says to a painter, "I will pay you $1,000 if you paint my house," the homeowner has made an offer for a unilateral contract, a contract that will be created only if and when the painter paints the house. If the homeowner instead says to the painter, "If you promise to paint my house, I will promise to pay you $1,000," he has asked the painter to commit to painting the house rather than just to perform the act of painting. This offer contemplates the formation of a bilateral contract. If the painter makes the requested promise to paint the house, a bilateral contract is created at that point.

In succeeding chapters, you will learn that unilateral contracts cause some particular problems related to offer and acceptance and to mutuality of obligation. These problems have caused many commentators to argue that the unilateral-bilateral contract distinction should be abandoned. The *Restatement (Second) of Contracts* and the Uniform Commercial Code, both of which are discussed later in this chapter, do not expressly use unilateral-bilateral terminology. However, both of these important sources of modern contract principles contain provisions for dealing with typical unilateral contract problems. Despite this evidence of disfavor, the courts continue to use unilateral contract terminology, in part because it enables them to do justice in some cases by imposing contractual liability on one party without the necessity of finding a return promise of the other party. For example, many recent employment cases have used unilateral contract analyses to hold employers liable for promises relating to pension rights, bonuses or incentive pay, and profit-sharing benefits, though the employees in question did not make any clear return promise to continue their employment for any specified time or to do anything else in exchange for the employer's promise.[3]

### Valid, Unenforceable, Voidable, and Void Contracts

A **valid contract** is one that meets all of the legal requirements for a binding contract. Valid contracts are, therefore, enforceable in court.

An **unenforceable contract** is one that meets the basic legal requirements for a contract but may not be enforceable due to some other legal rule. Chapter 8, Writing, discusses the statute of frauds, which requires written evidence of certain contracts. An otherwise valid oral contract that the statute of frauds requires to be in writing, for example, may be unenforceable due to the parties' failure to reduce the contract to written form. Another example of an unenforceable contract is an otherwise valid contract whose enforcement is barred by the applicable contract statute of limitations.

**Voidable contracts** are those in which one or more of the parties have the legal right to cancel their obligations under the contract. They are enforceable against both parties unless a party with the power to void the contract has exercised that power. Chapter 5, Reality of Consent, for example, states that contracts induced by misrepresentation, fraud, duress, or undue influence are voidable at the election of the injured party.

**Void contracts** are agreements that create no legal obligations because they fail to contain one or more of the basic elements required for enforceability. A void contract is, in a sense, a contradiction in terms. It would be more accurate to say that no contract was created in such cases. Chapter 7, Illegality, for example, mentions that a contract to commit a crime, such as an agreement for the sale of cocaine, does not create a binding legal obligation. Nonetheless, practical constraints may some-

---

[3]See Petit, "Modern Unilateral Contracts," 63 *B.U.L. Rev.* 551 (1983).

times encourage a party to such a contract to perform his agreement rather than raise an illegality defense.

## Express and Implied Contracts

In an **express contract,** the parties have directly stated the terms of their contract orally or in writing at the time the contract was formed. As the following *Cook v. Cook* case illustrates, however, the mutual agreement necessary to create a contract may also be demonstrated by the conduct of the parties. When the surrounding facts and circumstances indicate that an agreement has in fact been reached, an **implied contract** (also called a contract implied in fact) has been created. When you go to a doctor for treatment, for example, you do not ordinarily state the terms of your agreement in advance, although it is clear that you do, in fact, have an

agreement. A court would infer a promise by your doctor to use reasonable care and skill in treating you and a return promise on your part to pay a reasonable fee for her services.

## Executed and Executory Contracts

A contract is **executed** when all of the parties have fully performed their contractual duties, and it is **executory** until such duties have been fully performed.

Any contract may be described using one or more of the above terms. For example, Eurocars, Inc., orders five new Mercedes-Benz 500 SLs from Mercedes. Mercedes sends Eurocars its standard acknowledgment form accepting the order. The parties have a *valid, express, bilateral* contract that will be *executory* until Mercedes delivers the cars and Eurocars pays for them.

---

## COOK V. COOK
### 691 P.2d 664 (Ariz. Sup. Ct. 1984)

Intending to marry as soon as Donald's divorce became final, Rose Elsten and Donald Cook moved to Tucson in 1969 and lived there together until 1981. Although they did not marry, Rose used Donald's last name and they represented themselves to the community as husband and wife. Both parties worked throughout most of the relationship, pooling their income in two joint accounts and acquiring a house, two cars, and a number of shares of stock, all owned as joint tenants with right of survivorship. Rose left Donald in 1981. Of their joint assets, she received only one car and a few hundred dollars; Donald retained the balance.

Rose filed suit against Donald, arguing that he had breached their agreement to share their assets equally. In her deposition she said: "[E]verything we did and purchased, whether it be a vacuum cleaner or a car, was together as husband and wife. It was just something *that we agreed on,* that is how we were going to do it." When the trial court ruled against her, she appealed.

---

**Feldman, Justice**   The *sine qua non* of any contract is the exchange of promises. From this exchange flows the obligation of one party to another. Although it is most apparent that two parties have exchanged promises when their words express a spoken or written statement of promissory intention, mutual promises need not be express in order to create an enforceable contract. Indeed, a promise "may be inferred wholly or partly from conduct," and "there is no distinction in the effect of the promise whether it is expressed

in writing, or orally, or in acts, or partly in one of these ways and partly in others." *Restatement (Second) of Contracts.*

Thus, two parties may by their course of conduct express their agreement, though no words are ever spoken. From their conduct alone the finder of fact can determine the existence of an agreement. Although isolated acts of joint participation such as cohabitation or the opening of a joint account may not suffice to create a contract, the fact finder may infer an exchange of promises, and the existence of the contract, from the entire course of conduct between the parties.

The conduct of the parties certainly demonstrates such an agreement and intent. Rose and Donald maintained two joint accounts, a checking account and a credit union savings account, in the names of "Rose and Don Cook" and held them as joint tenants with right of survivorship. Neither Rose nor Donald maintained a separate account. Both deposited portions of their paychecks into the accounts and used the funds to pay for household expenses and various assets they purchased. In addition, Rose and Donald held jointly a number of shares of Southwest Gas stock purchased with funds from the credit union account. In 1972 they purchased a house, taking the deed as husband and wife in joint tenancy with right of survivorship. Both signed the mortgage, incurring liability for the full purchase price of the house, and payments on the mortgage were made out of the joint checking account. There is ample evidence to support a finding that Rose and Donald agreed to pool their resources and share equally in certain accumulations; their course of conduct may be seen as consistently demonstrating the existence of such an agreement.

**Judgment reversed in favor of Rose; case remanded for further proceedings.**

## QUASI–CONTRACT

The traditional common law insistence on the presence of all the elements required for a binding contract before contractual obligation is imposed can cause injustice in some cases. One person may have provided goods or services to another person who benefited from them but has no contractual obligation to pay for them because no facts exist that would justify a court in implying a promise to pay for them. Such a situation can also arise in cases where the parties contemplated entering into a binding contract but some legal defense exists that prevents the enforcement of the agreement. Consider the following examples:

**1.** Jones paints Smith's house by mistake, thinking it belongs to Reed. Smith knows that Jones is painting his house but does not inform him of his error. There are no facts from which a court can infer that Jones and Smith have a contract, because the parties have had no prior discussions or dealings.

**2.** Thomas Products fraudulently induces Perkins to buy a household products franchise by grossly misstating the average revenues of its franchisees. Perkins discovers the misrepresentation after he has resold some products that he has received but before he has paid Thomas for them. Perkins elects to rescind (cancel) the franchise contract on the basis of the fraud.

In the preceding examples, both Smith and Perkins have good defenses to contract liability; however, enabling Smith to get a free paint job and Perkins to avoid paying for the goods he resold would *unjustly enrich* them at the expense of Jones and Thomas. To deal with such cases and to prevent such unjust enrichment, the courts imply *as a matter of law* a promise by the benefited party to pay the *reasonable value* of the benefits he received. This idea is called **quasi-contract** (or contract implied in law) because it represents an obligation imposed by law to avoid injustice, not a contractual obligation created by voluntary consent. Quasi-contract liability has been imposed in situations too numerous and varied to detail. In general, however, quasi-contract liability is imposed when one party *confers a benefit* on another who *knowingly accepts it* and *retains it* under circumstances that make it *unjust* to do so without paying for it. So, if Jones painted Smith's house while Smith was away on vacation, Smith would probably not be liable for the reasonable value of the paint job because he did *not* knowingly accept it and because he has no way to return it to Jones. The following *Corrado* case highlights the centrality of the unjust enrichment idea to quasi-contract liability.

## ANTHONY CORRADO, INC. V. MENARD & CO.
### 589 A.2d 1201 (R.I. Sup. Ct. 1991)

Hart Engineering Company (Hart) was the general contractor for the construction of the Fields Point Waste Water Treatment Facility. Hart posted the necessary bond for the project, and Seaboard Surety Company (Seaboard) wrote the bond. Hart subcontracted with Menard & Co. Building Contractors (Menard) to do the masonry work. Menard purchased certain building materials for the project from Corrado, who supplied the materials but was never paid by either Menard or Hart. Corrado later sued Hart, Seaboard, and Menard. He won a summary judgment against Menard, but the trial court granted summary judgments in favor of Seaboard and Hart because Menard, not Hart or Seaboard, had ordered the materials. Corrado appealed.

**Per Curiam**   Corrado argues that under quasi-contract, he had a cause of action against Hart and Seaboard for unjust enrichment. In order to recover under quasi-contract, a plaintiff is required to prove three elements: (1) a benefit must be conferred upon the defendant by the plaintiff, (2) there must be appreciation by the defendant of such a benefit, and (3) there must be an acceptance of such benefit in such circumstances that it would be inequitable for a defendant to retain the benefit without paying the value thereof.

In reviewing a motion for summary judgment, a trial justice must determine, after an examination of the pleadings, affidavits, admissions, and answers to interrogatories, viewed in the light most favorable to the opposing party, whether there is a genuine issue regarding any material fact that must be resolved.

In his affidavit Frank Rampone, president of Hart, avers that from time to time Menard would submit an application for payment and that periodic payments were made to Menard. He further averred that Hart had no contractual relationship with Corrado and that it was Menard's obligation to pay Corrado directly from the periodic payments made to it. Hart never agreed to pay Corrado directly.

It is obvious from the record that there is no genuine issue regarding any material fact that must be resolved. No conflicting evidence was introduced to establish that Menard was not paid in full by Hart. Moreover, there was no evidence that would establish that Hart received any unjust enrichment from Corrado's building materials since Hart made periodic payments to Menard.

**Judgment for Hart and Seaboard affirmed.**

## PROMISSORY ESTOPPEL

Another very important idea that 20th-century courts have developed to deal with the unfairness that would sometimes result from the strict application of traditional contract principles is the doctrine of **promissory estoppel**. In numerous situations, one person may *rely* on a promise made by another even though the promise and surrounding circumstances are not sufficient to justify the conclusion that a contract has been created because one or more of the required elements is missing.

To allow the person who made such a promise (the promisor) to argue that no contract was created would sometimes work an injustice on the person who relied on the promise (the promisee). For example, in *Ricketts v. Scothorn,* a grandfather's promise to pay his granddaughter interest on a demand note he gave her so that she would not have to work was enforced against him after she had quit her job in reliance on his promise.[4] The

---

[4]57 Neb. 51, 77 N.W. 365 (1898).

Nebraska Supreme Court acknowledged that such promises were traditionally unenforceable because they were gratuitous and not supported by any consideration, but held that the granddaughter's reliance prevented her grandfather from raising his lack of consideration defense. In the early decades of this century, many courts began to extend similar protection to relying promisees. They said that persons who made promises that produced such reliance were *estopped,* or equitably prevented, from raising any defense they had to the enforcement of their promise. Out of such cases grew the doctrine of promissory estoppel. Section 90 of the *Restatement (Second) of Contracts* states:

A promise which the promisor should reasonably expect to induce action or forbearance on the part of the promisee or a third person and which does induce such action or forbearance is binding if injustice can be avoided only by enforcement of the promise. The remedy granted for breach may be limited as justice requires.

Thus, the elements of promissory estoppel are a *promise* that the *promisor should foresee is likely to induce reliance, reliance* on the promise by the promisee, and *injustice* as a result of that reliance.

When you consider these elements, it is obvious that promissory estoppel is fundamentally different from traditional contract principles. Contract is traditionally thought of as protecting *agreements* or bargains. Promissory estoppel, on the other hand, protects *reliance.* Early promissory estoppel cases applied the doctrine only to donative or gift promises. As subsequent chapters demonstrate, however, promissory estoppel is now being used by the courts to prevent offerors from revoking their offers, to enforce indefinite promises, and to enforce oral promises that would ordinarily have to be in writing. Given the basic conceptual differences between estoppel and contract, and the judicial tendency to use promissory estoppel to compensate for the absence of the traditional elements of contract, its growth as a new device for enforcing promises is one of the most important developments in modern contract law. Figure 3 summarizes the ways in which contract differs from quasi-contract and promissory estoppel.

**FIGURE 3    Contract and Contractlike Theories of Recovery**

| Theory | Key Concept | Remedy |
| --- | --- | --- |
| **Contract** | Voluntary agreement | Enforce promise |
| **Quasi-Contract** | Unjust enrichment | Reasonable value of services |
| **Promissory Estoppel** | Foreseeable reliance | Enforce promise or recover reliance losses |

## THE UNIFORM COMMERCIAL CODE

### Origins and Purposes of the Code

The Uniform Commercial Code (UCC) was created by the American Law Institute and the National Conference of Commissioners on Uniform State Laws. All of the states have adopted it except Louisiana, which has adopted only part of the Code. The drafters of the Code had several purposes in mind, the most obvious of which was to establish a uniform set of rules to govern commercial transactions, which are often conducted across state lines in today's national markets. Despite the Code's almost national adoption, however, complete uniformity has not been achieved. Many states have varied or amended the Code's language in specific instances, and some Code provisions were drafted in alternative ways, giving the states more than one version of particular Code provisions to choose from. Also, the various state courts have reached different conclusions about the meaning of particular Code sections. Work is currently under way to revise many basic sections of the Code, so uniformity will continue to be a problem as states adopt the revised sections at different rates and to different degrees.

In addition to promoting uniformity, the drafters of the Code sought to create a body of rules that would realistically and fairly solve the common problems occurring in everyday commercial transactions. Finally, the drafters tried to formulate rules that would promote fair dealing and higher standards in the marketplace.

## Scope of the Code

The Code contains nine substantive articles, most of which are discussed in detail in Parts 2, 4, and 5 of this book. The most important Code article for our present purposes is Article 2, the Sales article of the Code.

## Nature of Article 2

Many of the provisions of Article 2 exhibit the basic tendencies of modern contract law discussed earlier in this chapter. Accordingly, they differ from traditional contract law rules in a variety of important ways. The Code is more concerned with rewarding people's legitimate expectations than with technical rules, so it is generally more flexible than contract law. A court that applies the Code is more likely to find that the parties had a contract than is a court that applies contract law [2–204] (the numbers in brackets refer to specific Code sections). In some cases, the Code gives less weight than does contract law to technical requirements such as consideration [2–205 and 2–209].

The drafters of the Code sought to create practical rules to deal with what people actually do in today's marketplace. We live in the day of the form contract, so some of the Code's rules try to deal fairly with that fact [2–205, 2–207, 2–209(2), and 2–302]. The words *reasonable, commercially reasonable,* and *seasonably* (within a reasonable time) are found throughout the Code. This reasonableness standard is different from the hypothetical reasonable person standard in tort law. A court that tries to decide what is reasonable under the Code is more likely to be concerned with what people really do in the marketplace than with what a nonexistent reasonable person would do.

The drafters of the Code wanted to promote fair dealing and higher standards in the marketplace, so they imposed a **duty of good faith** [1–203] in the performance and enforcement of every contract under the Code. Good faith means "honesty in fact," which is required of all parties to sales contracts [1–201(19)]. In addition, merchants are required to observe "reasonable commercial standards of fair dealing" [2–103(1)(b)]. The parties cannot alter this duty of good faith by agreement [1–102(3)]. Finally, the Code expressly recognizes the concept of an **unconscionable contract,** one that is grossly unfair or one-sided, and it gives the courts broad discretionary powers to deal fairly with such contracts [2–302].[5]

The Code also recognizes that buyers tend to place more reliance on professional sellers and that professionals are generally more knowledgeable and better able to protect themselves than nonprofessionals. So, the Code distinguishes between **merchants** and nonmerchants by holding merchants to a higher standard in some cases [2–201(2), 2–205, and 2–207(2)]. The Code defines the term *merchant* [2–104(1)] on a case-by-case basis. If a person regularly deals in the kind of goods being sold, or pretends to have some special knowledge about the goods, or employed an agent in the sale who fits either of these two descriptions, that person is a merchant for the purposes of the contract in question. So, if you buy a used car from a used-car dealer, the dealer is a merchant for the purposes of your contract. But, if you buy a refrigerator from a used-car dealer, the dealer is probably not a merchant.

## Application of the Code

Article 2 expressly applies only to *contracts for the sale of goods* [2–102]. The Code contains a somewhat complicated definition of *goods* [2–105], but the essence of the definition is that *goods* are *tangible, movable, personal property.* So, contracts for the sale of such items as motor vehicles, books, appliances, and clothing are covered by Article 2. But Article 2 does *not* apply to contracts for the sale of real estate, stocks and bonds, or other intangibles. Article 2 also does not apply to *service* contracts. This can cause confusion because, although contracts of employment or other personal services are clearly not covered by Article 2, many contracts involve elements of both goods and services. As the

---

[5]Chapter 7 discusses unconscionability in detail.

following *Advent* case illustrates, the test that the courts most frequently use to determine whether Article 2 applies to such a contract is to ask which element, goods or services, *predominates* in the contract. Is the major purpose or thrust of the agreement the rendering of a service, or is it the sale of goods, with any services involved being merely incidental to that sale? This means that contracts calling for services that involve significant elements of personal skill or judgment in addition to goods probably are not governed by Article 2. Construction contracts, remodeling contracts, and auto repair contracts are all examples of mixed goods and services contracts that may be considered outside the scope of the Code.

Two other important qualifications must be made concerning the application of Code contract principles. First, the Code does not change *all* of the traditional contract rules. Where no specific Code rule exists, traditional contract law rules apply to contracts for the sale of goods. Second, and ultimately far more important, the courts have demonstrated a significant tendency to apply Code contract concepts by analogy to contracts not specifically covered by Article 2. For example, the Code concepts of good faith dealing and unconscionability have enjoyed wide application in cases that are technically outside the scope of Article 2. Thus, the Code is an important influence in shaping the evolution of contract law in general, and if this trend toward broader application of Code principles continues, the time may come when the dichotomy between Code principles and traditional contract rules is a thing of the past.

---

## ADVENT SYSTEMS LTD. v. UNISYS CORPORATION
### 925 F.2d 670 (3d Cir. 1991)

Advent Systems Limited (Advent), a British company engaged primarily in the production of computer software, developed an electronic document management system (EDMS), a process for transforming engineering drawings and similar documents into a computer database. Unisys Corporation (Unisys), an American computer manufacturer, decided to market Advent's EDMS in the United States. In 1987, Advent and Unisys signed two documents, one labeled "Heads of Agreement" and the other "Distribution Agreement," in which Advent agreed to provide the software and hardware making up the EDMS, as well as sales and marketing material and the technical personnel to work with Unisys employees in building and installing the document systems. The agreement was to continue for two years, subject to automatic renewal or termination on notice.

During the summer of 1987, Unisys attempted to sell the document system to a large oil company but was unsuccessful. Nevertheless, progress on the sales and training programs in the United States was satisfactory. But Unisys, then in the throes of restructuring, decided it would be better off developing its own document system, and in December 1987, it told Advent that the agreement was ended. Advent filed suit, alleging breach of contract, among other things. Unisys argued that the agreement with Advent was covered by the UCC and that it failed to contain an express quantity provision that the UCC statute of frauds requires. The trial court ruled, however, that the agreements were not covered by the Code because their services aspect predominated. When the jury awarded Advent $4,550,000 for breach of contract, Unisys appealed.

---

**Weis, Circuit Judge**    As the district court appraised the transaction, provisions for services outweighed those for products and, consequently, the arrangement was not predominantly one for the sale of goods. The agreements provided that Advent was to modify its software and hardware interfaces to run initially on equipment not manufactured by Unisys but eventually on Unisys hardware. "In so far as Advent has successfully completed [some of the processing] of software and hardware interfaces," Unisys promised to reimburse Advent to the extent of $150,000 derived from a "surcharge" on products purchased.

Advent agreed to provide twelve man-weeks of marketing manpower, but with Unisys bearing certain expenses. Advent also undertook to furnish an experienced systems builder to work with Unisys personnel at Advent's prevailing rates, and to provide sales and support training for Unisys staff as well as its customers.

The Distribution Agreement begins with the statement "Unisys desires to purchase, and Advent desires to sell, on a nonexclusive basis, certain of Advent hardware products and software licenses for resale worldwide." Following a heading "Subject Matter of Sales," appears this sentence, "Advent agrees to sell hardware and license software to Unisys, and Unisys agrees to buy from Advent the products listed in Schedule A." Schedule A lists twenty products, such as computer cards, plotters, imagers, scanners and designer systems.

Because software was a major portion of the "products" described in the agreement, this matter requires some discussion. Computer systems consist of "hardware" and "software." Hardware is the computer machinery, its electronic circuitry and peripheral items such as keyboards, readers, scanners and printers. Software is a more elusive concept. Generally speaking, "software" refers to the medium that stores input and output data as well as computer programs. The medium includes hard disks, floppy disks, and magnetic tapes.

In simplistic terms, programs are codes prepared by a programmer that instruct the computer to perform certain functions. When the program is transposed onto a medium compatible with the computer's needs, it becomes software. The increasing frequency of computer products as subjects of commercial litigation has led to controversy over whether software is a "good" or intellectual property. The Code does not specifically mention software.

In the absence of express legislative guidance, courts interpret the Code in the light of commercial and technological developments. The Code is designed "to permit the continued expansion of commercial practices" [1–102(2)(b)]. The Code applies to "transactions in goods" [2–102], which are defined as "all things (including specially manufactured goods) which are moveable at the time of the identification for sale" [2–105(1)].

Our Court has addressed computer package sales in other cases, but has not been required to consider whether the UCC applied to software per se. Computer programs are the product of an intellectual process, but once implanted in a medium are widely distributed to computer owners. An analogy can be drawn to a compact disc recording of an orchestral rendition. The music is produced by the artistry of musicians and in itself is not a "good," but when transferred to a laser-readable disc becomes a readily merchantable commodity. Similarly, when a professor delivers a lecture, it is not a good, but, when transcribed as a book, it becomes a good.

That a computer program may be copyrightable as intellectual property does not alter the fact that once in the form of a floppy disc or other medium, the program is tangible, moveable and available in the marketplace. The fact that some programs may be tailored for specific purposes need not alter their status as "goods" because the Code definition includes "specially manufactured goods." The topic has stimulated academic commentary with the majority espousing the view that software fits with the definition of a "good" in the UCC.

The relationship at issue here is a typical mixed goods and services arrangement. The services are not substantially different from those generally accompanying package sales of computer systems consisting of hardware and software. Although determining the applicability of the UCC to a contract by examining the predominance of goods or services has been criticized, we see no reason to depart from that practice here. We consider the purpose or essence of the contract. Comparing the relative costs of the materials supplied with the costs of the labor may be helpful in this analysis, but not dispositive. In this case the contract's main objective was to transfer "products." The specific provisions for training of Unisys personnel by Advent were but a small part of the parties' contemplated relationship.

The compensation structure of the agreement also focuses on "goods." The projected sales figures introduced during the trial demonstrate that in the contemplation of the parties the sale of goods clearly predominated. The payment provision of $150,000 for developmental work which Advent had previously completed was to be made through individual purchases of software and hardware rather than through the fees for services and is further evidence that the intellectual work was to be subsumed into tangible items for sale.

Applying the UCC to computer software transactions offers substantial benefits to litigants and the courts. The Code offers a uniform body of law on a wide range of questions likely to arise in computer software disputes: implied warranties, consequential damages, disclaimers of liability, the statute of limitations, to name a few. The importance of software to the commercial world and the advantages to be gained by the uniformity inherent in the UCC are strong policy arguments favoring inclusion. The contrary arguments are not persuasive, and we hold that software is a "good" within the definition of the Code.

**Judgment reversed and remanded for further proceedings consistent with the Court's opinion.**

---

Figure 4 illustrates when the Uniform Commercial Code applies.

## RESTATEMENT (SECOND) OF CONTRACTS

### Nature and Origins

In 1932, the American Law Institute published the first *Restatement of Contracts,* an attempt to codify and systematize the soundest principles of contract law gleaned from thousands of often conflicting judicial decisions. As the product of a private organization, the *Restatement* did not have the force of law, but as the considered judgment of some of the leading scholars of the legal profession, it was highly influential in shaping the evolution of contract law. The *Restatement (Second) of Contracts,* issued in 1979, is an attempt to reflect the significant changes that have occurred in contract law in the years following the birth of the first *Restatement of Contracts.* The tone of the *Restatement (Second) of Contracts* differs dramatically from that of the first *Restatement,* which is often characterized as a positivist attempt to formulate a system of black letter rules of contract law. The *Restatement (Second),* in contrast, reflects the "shift from rules to standards" in modern contract law—the shift from precise, technical rules to broader, discretionary principles that produce just results.[6] The *Restatement (Second)* has been heavily influenced by the UCC. In fact, many *Restatement (Second) of Contracts* provisions are virtually identical to their Code analogues. For example, the *Re-*

---

[6]Speidel, "Restatement Second: Omitted Terms and Contract Method," 67 *Cornell L. Rev.* 785, 786 (1982).

---

**FIGURE 4    When the Uniform Commercial Code Applies**

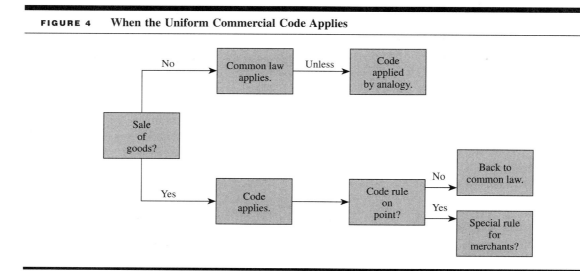

*statement (Second)* has explicitly embraced the Code concepts of *good faith*[7] and *unconscionability.*[8]

## Impact

The *Restatement (Second) of Contracts,* like its predecessor, does not have the force of law, and its relative newness prevents any accurate assessment of its impact on contemporary contract cases. Nonetheless, given the influential role played by the first *Restatement* and the previously mentioned tendency of the courts to employ Code principles by analogy in contract cases, it seems fair to assume that the *Restatement (Second)* will serve as a major inspiration for contract developments in the decades to come. For this reason, we give significant attention to the *Restatement (Second) of Contracts* in the following chapters.

### PROBLEMS AND PROBLEM CASES

**1.** In 1973, Baker and Ratzlaff entered a contract requiring Ratzlaff to grow 380 acres of popcorn and Baker to buy it at $4.75 per hundredweight. The contract gave Ratzlaff the right to terminate if Baker failed to pay for any of the popcorn on delivery. Early in 1974, Ratzlaff made the first two deliveries under the contract to Baker's plant. Baker's plant manager gave Ratzlaff weight tickets acknowledging receipt of the popcorn. Ratzlaff was not given payment and did not ask for it. Nor did he stop by Baker's business office, which was on a direct route between his farm and Baker's plant, to ask for payment. When Baker called to ask for further deliveries, Ratzlaff offered excuses, but did not mention payment. Ratzlaff later told Baker he was terminating due to Baker's failure to pay upon delivery, selling the remaining 1.6 million pounds of popcorn elsewhere for $8.00 per hundredweight. After hearing evidence that Baker's normal practice was to make payments at its office on the basis of copies of weight tickets sent from the plant, and that Baker would have paid promptly had Ratzlaff requested payment, the trial court ruled that Ratzlaff's termination was a breach of his duty to act in good faith. Was this ruling proper?

**2.** In April 1988, Reifschneider, a farmer since 1957, orally agreed to sell Grain Company 12,500 bushels of corn for $2.25 per bushel. The corn was to be delivered as harvested in October 1988. Shortly thereafter, Grain Company mailed Reifschneider a written confirmation of the oral agreement, with instructions to sign it and return the original. Reifschneider neither signed nor returned the confirmation, and in late June he told Grain Company that he felt no contract existed and would not deliver the corn. Reifschneider continued to refuse to acknowledge the contract, and ultimately sold his crop elsewhere. To cover his default, Grain Company bought 12,500 bushels of corn from another farmer, paying $8,425 more for it than it had agreed to pay Reifschneider. When Grain Company sued Reifschneider for breach of contract, he raised the Code statute of frauds [2–201] as a defense, arguing that his failure to sign the confirmation meant that it could not satisfy the writing requirement against him. Grain Company countered by arguing that he was a merchant, and pointing to Code section 2–201(2), which says that merchants who fail to object in writing to written confirmations they receive from other merchants within 10 days of receipt lose their statute of frauds defense. Was the trial court justified in ruling in favor of Grain Company?

**3.** When Thomas and Sandra Cole were divorced in 1983, Sandra received a judgment against Thomas of $36,556. In May and June 1985, Thomas incurred a hospital bill of $5,985. After discussing the matter with him, Sandra paid the bill with her own funds even though he still owed her $11,884 on the marriage dissolution judgment. When Thomas died in April 1986, Sandra filed claims against his estate for the balance due her under the marriage dissolution judgment and for the hospital bill. The estate challenged Sandra's claim for the hospital payment, arguing that she had paid it voluntarily and had no contractual right to recover the amount she paid. Was the trial court right in ruling in Sandra's favor?

**4.** First National Bank filed suit against Jessie Ordoyne and Patricia Ordoyne Bordelon for failure to pay sums due on a Visa card account. Ordoyne argued that he did not know that the account existed until the bank called him to inquire about his failure to make payments. He then told the bank that he and Patricia were divorced and that she must have

---

[7]*Restatement (Second) of Contracts* § 205 (1981).
[8]*Restatement (Second) of Contracts* § 208 (1981).

forged his signature to the account application form. The bank argued that he was nonetheless liable on a quasi-contractual basis, although it failed to prove that he had received any of the merchandise charged to the card. Was the trial court's decision in Jessie's favor correct?

**5.** Chow arranged through a travel agent to fly from Indianapolis to Singapore on June 27, 1986. Singapore Airlines gave him a round-trip ticket that included a TWA flight to Los Angeles. Shortly before the trip, Chow's flight was rerouted so that he had to fly to St. Louis first and then to San Francisco. During the St. Louis stopover, the flight developed engine trouble, causing a substantial delay. TWA personnel assured Chow that if he missed his connecting flight, TWA would arrange for him to take the next Singapore flight out of San Francisco. After the engine problem was fixed, TWA delayed the flight's departure an additional two hours to board additional passengers. Chow was again assured that if he missed his scheduled flight, TWA would make arrangements for him. Chow missed his Singapore flight by minutes, and was housed overnight at TWA's expense in San Francisco after once more being assured that TWA would make arrangements to get him on the next Singapore flight. When he called Singapore Airlines the next morning to see whether TWA had made him a reservation, Chow was told that no arrangements had been made. When he contacted TWA, he was told TWA would make the arrangements immediately. After waiting several hours, Chow learned TWA had still not made the arrangements and was told that TWA could no longer help him. Because Singapore Airlines no longer had economy class seats available, Chow had to buy a business class seat at an additional cost of $928. When he filed suit against TWA for that amount, TWA argued that the Conditions of Contract printed on Chow's ticket disclaimed any liability for failure to make connections. Did Chow have a valid claim against TWA?

**6.** Commercial Cornice, a subcontractor, entered a contract with Camel Construction, a general contractor, to furnish labor and materials for a construction project owned by Malarkey's, Inc. Commercial completed its obligations under the contract but only received $78,000 of the $177,773. When Commercial filed suit against Camel and Malarkey's for the remaining $99,773, Malarkey's moved to dismiss Commercial's claims against it on the ground that Commercial's only contract was with Camel. The trial court granted Malarkey's motion, despite the fact that the evidence indicated that Malarkey's had never paid Camel for the work. Was the dismissal of Commercial's claim against Malarkey's proper?

**7.** Early in 1986, Gray Communications contacted various television tower builders concerning the manufacture and erection of a television tower. After several discussions with Kline Iron & Steel, Gray received a signed written proposal from Kline to build and install the tower for $1,485,368. The proposal said that it could be revoked or modified by Kline prior to acceptance by Gray, and it required Kline's approval after acceptance by Gray. Gray refused to sign the proposal after Kline would not lower its bid to meet a competitor's lower bid, and Kline filed suit for breach of contract. At trial, Gray argued that no contract existed, and that even if a contract existed it was unenforceable because Gray had never signed the writing the UCC requires for all contracts for $500 or more. Kline argued that the contract was not covered by the UCC because it was a services contract. The evidence at trial indicated that the service component of the agreement amounted at most to 26 percent of the total cost. Should the court apply the UCC?

**8.** Dr. Monteleone, a neurologist, entered into a lease-purchase agreement for a turnkey computer system from Neilson Business Equipment Center, Inc. The system included both hardware and software recommended by Neilson after two Neilson representatives studied Dr. Monteleone's manual billing system. When the computer was delivered in July 1982, serious problems immediately developed. Neilson's attempts to modify the software, which it had acquired elsewhere and renamed the "Neilson Medical Office Management System," were unsuccessful. Dr. Monteleone notified Neilson that he was terminating the lease for cause and later filed suit against Neilson. The trial court awarded him $34,983.42 in damages for breaches of the implied warranties of merchantability and fitness for a particular purpose. Did the trial court err in holding that the case was governed by the UCC?

**9.** Stephen Gall and his family became ill after drinking contaminated water supplied to their home by the McKeesport Municipal Water Authority. They filed suit against the utility, arguing, among other things, that the utility had breached the UCC implied warranty of merchantability when it sold them contaminated water. The utility moved to dismiss their complaint, arguing that since water was not "goods," the UCC did not apply. Should the Galls' complaint be dismissed?

**10.** In February of 1981, Salamon, a builder, entered into written agreements to buy two lots owned by Terra for $9,000 each. The agreement provided that Salamon would take possession of the lots by April 15, 1981, but would not have to pay the bulk of the purchase price ($8,500 per lot) until delivery of the deeds in August 1981. Salamon intended to build a house on each lot and then sell the houses to third parties, paying off Terra with the proceeds of the house sales. Salamon partially completed the two houses but was unable either to obtain financing to complete them or to find purchasers for them. Terra extended the date of performance under the purchase agreements by several months, but because Salamon was never able to pay for the lots, he retained ownership of them. Salamon filed a quasi-contract suit against Terra to recover the value of the partially completed houses. The trial judge ruled that Terra had been unjustly enriched in the amount of $15,000. Had Terra been unjustly enriched?

**11.** 📼 *Video Case.* See "Car Deals." Jeff went to look at a car owned by Acme Motors. He wanted to buy the car and tentatively agreed on a price with Marx, but he asked if he could wait until his wife could see the car that evening. Acme agreed, promising in writing not to sell the car to anyone else in the interim. When Jeff and his wife returned to Acme that evening, however, they found that Acme had sold the car to another buyer. Jeff filed a breach of contract suit against Acme, pointing to a section of the UCC that provides that merchants can't revoke signed written offers. Should Jeff win?

## CAPSTONE QUESTIONS

Hanks, a professor of English, was involved in the following disputes:

· Hanks solicited a bid for a new central air conditioner for his home from Pierce Service Company, a retailer of residential heating and

cooling systems. After measuring the house, Pierce's representative recommended a particular brand and model of air conditioner. On May 1, 1994, relying on Pierce's selection, Hanks entered into a written contract in which he promised to purchase the unit recommended by Pierce and Pierce promised to sell it to Hanks for $2,200. On June 1, 1994, the air conditioner was delivered and installed. The air conditioner was not adequate to cool all of the rooms of the house to a desirable temperature. After unsuccessfully seeking adjustments from Pierce, Hanks sued Pierce for damages for breach of warranty under the UCC. Pierce maintains that the Uniform Commercial Code does not apply to this transaction because Hanks is not a merchant.

· Ronn Roofing entered into a contract with Fox, Hanks's next-door neighbor, to replace the roof on Fox's house for $2,500. On May 5, while Hanks was on vacation, Ronn Roofing's crew mistakenly went to Hanks's house instead of Fox's and replaced the roof on Hanks's house. Hanks did not know anything about this until he arrived home at the end of the week and found the job completed. Ronn Roofing invoiced Hanks for $2,500. Ronn Roofing claims that Hanks is obligated to pay for the roof under an implied contract, quasi-contract, or promissory estoppel.

**Required:**

Answer the following and give reasons for your conclusions.

**1.** State whether Pierce is correct in its position that the UCC does not apply to this case.

**2.** Assess whether Ronn Roofing's claims are likely to succeed.

**3.** State whether, as of May 2, 1994, Hanks's contract with Pierce Service would be classified as bilateral or unilateral, express or implied, executed or executory, and valid, voidable, unenforceable, or void.

# CHAPTER

## 2

# THE AGREEMENT:

# OFFER

**INTRODUCTION**

*The concept of mutual agreement lies at the heart of traditional contract law. Courts faced with deciding whether two or more persons entered into a contract look first for an* agreement *between the parties. Because the formation of an agreement is normally a two-step process by which one party makes a proposal and the other responds to the proposal, it is customary to analyze the agreement in two parts: offer and acceptance. This chapter, which concerns itself with the offer, and the next chapter, which covers acceptance, focus on the tools used by courts to determine whether the parties have reached the kind of agreement that becomes the foundation of a contract.*

## THE OBJECTIVE THEORY OF CONTRACT

At the outset, it is important to clarify one aspect of what is meant by the word *agreement.* In determining whether the parties reached an agreement, should courts look at what each party actually, in his own mind (*subjectively*) intended? Or should an agreement be dependent on the impression that each party has given to the rest of the world through words, acts, and circumstances that *objectively* indicate that intent? Early American courts took a subjective approach to contract formation, asking whether there was truly a "meeting of the minds" between the parties. This subjective standard, however, created uncertainty in the enforcement of contracts because it left every contract vulnerable to disputes about actual intent. The desire to meet the needs of the marketplace by affording predictable and consistent results in contracts cases dictated a shift toward an *objective theory of contracts.* By the middle of the 19th century, the objective approach to contract formation, which judges agreement by looking at the parties' outward manifestations of intent, was firmly established in American law. Judge Learned Hand once described the effect of the objective contract theory as follows:

A contract has, strictly speaking, nothing to do with the personal, or individual, intent of the parties. A contract is an obligation attached by the mere force of law to certain acts of the parties, usually words, which ordinarily accompany and represent a known intent. If however, it were proved by twenty bishops that either party when he used the words intended something else than the usual meaning which the law imposes on them, he would still be held, unless there were mutual mistake or something else of that sort.[1]

## What Is an Offer?

The *Restatement (Second) of Contracts* defines an **offer** as "the manifestation of willingness to enter into a bargain, so made as to justify another person in understanding that his assent to that bargain is invited and will conclude it."[2] An offer says, in effect, "This is it—if you agree to these terms, we have a contract." An offer is a critically important first step in the contract formation process. The person who makes an offer (the **offeror**) gives the person to whom she makes the offer (the **offeree**) the power to bind her to a contract simply by accepting the offer. If no offer was ever made, however, there was nothing to accept and no contract results.

Traditional contract law rules on contract formation are designed to ensure that persons are never bound to contracts unless they clearly intend to be bound. Therefore, the basic thing that the courts require for the creation of an offer is some objective indication of a *present intent to contract* on the part of the offeror. Two of the most important things from which courts infer an intent to contract are the *definiteness* of the alleged offer and the fact that it has been *communicated to the offeree*.

---

[1]*Hotchkiss v. National City Bank*, 200 F. 287, 293 (S.D.N.Y. 1911).

[2]*Restatement (Second) of Contracts* § 24 (1981).

## Definiteness of Terms

If Smith says to Ford, "I'd like to buy your house," and Ford responds, "You've got a deal," has a contract been formed? An obvious problem here is the parties' lack of specificity. A proposal that fails to state specifically what the offeror is willing to do and what he asks in return for his performance is unlikely to be considered an offer. One reason for the requirement of definiteness is that definiteness and specificity in an offer tend to indicate an intent to contract, whereas indefiniteness and lack of specificity tend to indicate that the parties are still negotiating and have not yet reached agreement. In the conversation between Smith and Ford, Smith's statement that he'd like to buy Ford's house is merely an invitation to offer or an invitation to negotiate. It indicates a willingness to contract in the future if the parties can reach agreement on mutually acceptable terms, but not a present intent to contract. If, however, Smith sends Ford a detailed and specific written document stating all of the material terms and conditions on which he is willing to buy the house and Ford writes back agreeing to Smith's terms, the parties' intent to contract would be objectively indicated and a contract would probably be created.

A second reason definiteness is important is that courts need to know the terms on which the parties agreed in order to determine if a breach of contract has occurred and calculate a remedy if it has. Keep in mind that the offer often contains all the terms of the parties' contract. This is so because all that an offeree is allowed to do in most cases is to accept or reject the terms of the offer. If an agreement is too indefinite, a court would not have a basis for giving a remedy if one of the parties alleged that the "contract" was breached. The following case, *Vian v. Carey*, presents an example of a situation in which the terms of the alleged contract were too indefinite.

---

## Vian v. Carey
### 1993 U.S. Dist. LEXIS 5460 (U.S. Dist. Ct. S.D.N.Y. 1993)

Mariah Carey is a famous, successful, and apparently wealthy entertainer. Joseph Vian, Carey's stepfather before she achieved stardom, was in the business of designing, producing, and marketing gift and novelty items. He claimed that Carey agreed orally to give him a license to produce "Mariah dolls," which would be statuettes of the singer that would play her most popular songs. Vian asserted that this right was given in exchange for his financial and emotional support of Carey, including picking her up from late-night recording sessions, providing her with the use of a car, paying for dental care, allowing her to use his boat for business meetings and rehearsals, and giving her various items to help furnish her apartment. Vian based his claim of an oral contract on three conversations, twice in the family car and once on Vian's boat. Vian said to Carey, "Don't forget about the Mariah dolls," and "I get the Mariah dolls." According to Vian, on one occasion, Carey responded "Okay"; on other occasions, she merely smiled and nodded. Although Carey admits that Vian mentioned the dolls two or three times, she testified that she thought it was a joke. Claiming that Carey breached the contract to license dolls in her likeness, Vian brought this action for breach of contract. Carey moved for summary judgment.

**Mukasey, District Judge**   An oral contract can form a binding contract. However, the prerequisites to contract formation must be satisfied. In determining whether a contract exists, what matters are the parties' expressed intentions, the words and deeds which constitute objective signs in a given set of circumstances. The issue is whether the objective circumstances indicate that the parties intended to form a contract. Without such an intent, neither a contract nor a preliminary agreement to negotiate in good faith can exist. In making such a determination, a court may look at whether the terms of the contract have been finally resolved. In addition, a court may consider the context of the negotiations. Vian has adduced no evidence that Carey ever intended by a nod of her head or the expression "okay" to enter into a complex commercial licensing agreement involving dolls in her likeness playing her copyrighted songs. The context in which this contract between an 18-year-old girl and her stepfather allegedly was made was an informal family setting, either in the car or on Vian's boat, while others were present. Vian's own version of events leads to the conclusion that there was no reason for Carey to think Vian was entirely serious, let alone that he intended to bind her to an agreement at that time.

There can be no meetings of the minds, required for the formation of a contract, where essential material terms are missing. Thus, even if the parties both believe themselves to be bound, there is no contract when the terms of the agreement are so vague and indefinite that there is no basis or standard for deciding whether the agreement had been kept or broken, or to fashion a remedy, and no means by which such terms may be made certain. As the New York Court of Appeals has held, "definiteness as to material matters is of the very essence of contract law. Impenetrable vagueness and uncertainty will not do."

Licensing contracts such as the one Vian claims a right to exploit normally are intricate business. They involve details. Even if the agreement was merely to agree on terms at some future time, under New York law, a mere agreement to agree, in which a material term is left for future negotiations, is unenforceable. The word "license" was not even used. As Carey points out, no price nor royalty term was mentioned, nor was the duration or geographic scope of the license, nor was Carey's right to approve the dolls. Vian has not raised a triable issue of fact as to the existence of a contract.

**Summary judgment granted in favor of Carey.**

**Definiteness: Traditional Approach**   Classical contract law took the position that courts are contract enforcers, not contract makers. The prospect of enforcing an agreement in which the parties had omitted terms or left terms open for later agreement was unthinkable to courts that took a traditional, hands-off approach to contracts. Traditionally, contract law required a relatively high standard of definiteness for offers, requiring that all the essential terms of a proposed contract be stated in the offer. The traditional insistence on definiteness can serve useful ends. It can prevent a person from being held to an agreement when none was reached or from being bound by a contract term to which he never assented. Sometimes, however, it can operate to frustrate the expectations of parties who intend to contract but, for whatever reason, fail to procure an agreement that specifies all the terms of the contract. Although vague agreements such as the one alleged in the *Vian* case are too indefinite to constitute a contract, the trend of modern contract law is to tolerate a lower degree of specificity in agreements than did classical contract law.

**Definiteness and Modern Contract Law**
Modern contract principles, with their increased emphasis on furthering peoples' justifiable expectations and their encouragement of a hands-on approach by the courts, often create contractual liability in situations where no contract would have resulted at common law. Perhaps no part of the Code better illustrates this basic difference between modern contract principles and their classical counterparts than does the basic Code section on contract formation [2–204]. Sales contracts under Article 2 can be created "in any manner sufficient to show agreement, including conduct which recognizes the existence of a contract" [2–204(1)]. So, if the parties are acting as though they have a contract by delivering or accepting goods or payment, for example, this may be enough to create a binding contract, even if it is impossible to point to a particular moment in time when the contract was created [2–204(2)]. The fact that the parties left open one or more terms of their agreement does not necessarily mean that their agreement is too indefinite to enforce. A sales contract is created if the court finds that the parties intended to make a contract and that their agreement is complete enough to allow the court to reach a fair settlement of their dispute ("a reasonably certain basis for giving an appropriate remedy" [2–204(3)]). The Code contains a series of gap-filling rules to enable courts to fill in the blanks on matters of price [2–305], quantity [2–306], delivery [2–307, 2–308, and 2–309(1)], and time for payment [2–310] when such terms have been left open by the parties.[3] Of course, if a term was left out because the parties were *unable* to reach agreement about it, this would indicate that the intent to contract was absent and no contract would result, even under the Code's more liberal rules. Intention is still at the heart of these modern contract rules;

the difference is that courts applying Code principles seek to further the parties' *underlying* intent to contract even though the parties have failed to express their intention about specific aspects of their agreement.

The *Restatement (Second) of Contracts* takes an approach to the definiteness question that is quite similar to the Code approach. It seeks to further the intent of the parties and, where intent to contract is indicated but some essential terms are left open, "a term which is reasonable in the circumstances is supplied by the court."[4] Unlike the Code, however, the *Restatement (Second)* indicates that a party's reliance on an indefinite agreement may justify its full or partial enforcement.[5] This provision highlights one of the most intriguing recent developments in contract law—the use of **promissory estoppel** to enforce indefinite agreements.[6]

**Promissory Estoppel and Indefinite Agreements**
It has long been the rule that promissory estoppel could not be used to enforce indefinite agreements because their indefiniteness meant that the court was left with no promise capable of being enforced. Sometimes people do, however, act in reliance on indefinite agreements, and to protect that reliance a few courts have deviated from the general rule. In such cases, it is common for courts to overcome the indefiniteness problem by awarding damages based on the promisee's losses due to reliance rather than by attempting to enforce the indefinite agreement.

*Hoffman v. Red Owl Stores, Inc.,* is probably the most famous case of this type.[7] Hoffman wanted to acquire a Red Owl franchised convenience store and, in reliance on Red Owl's promises during their negotiations, sold his bakery at a loss, bought a small grocery to gain experience, moved his family, and bought an option on a proposed site for the franchised store. The negotiations fell through, and when Hoffman sued, Red Owl argued that no contract resulted because the parties had never reached agreement on the essential terms governing their relationship. The Supreme Court of Wisconsin agreed, but nonetheless allowed Hoffman to recover

---

[3]Chapter 11 discusses these Code provisions in detail.

[4]*Restatement (Second) of Contracts* § 204 (1981).

[5]*Restatement (Second) of Contracts* § 34(3) (1981).

[6]See the general discussion of promissory estoppel in Chapter 1.

[7]26 Wis.2d 683, 133 N.W.2d 267 (Wis. Sup. Ct. 1965).

his reliance losses on the basis of promissory estoppel. In doing so, the court noted that nothing in the language of section 90 of the *Restatement* required that a promise serving as the basis of promissory estoppel be "so comprehensive in scope as to meet the requirements of an offer." Another example of both modern standards regarding definiteness and the use of promissory estoppel is seen in the following *AROK Construction Co. v. Indian Construction Services* case.

---

## AROK CONSTRUCTION CO. V. INDIAN CONSTRUCTION SERVICES
### 848 P.2d 870 (Ariz. Ct. App. 1993)

Indian Construction Services (ICS) is a general contractor. AROK Construction Co. is a drywall and stucco contractor. AROK and the principal owners of ICS had entered into contracts on three occasions prior to this case, using in all three situations identical standard form contracts.

In 1985, Window Rock Unified School District solicited bids for the services of a general contractor on its construction project. ICS submitted a bid to act as the general contractor, listing AROK in its bid as subcontractor for the drywall and stucco portions of the project. AROK had first submitted its bid over the telephone to ICS for $1.549 million. Before bid closing, however, ICS asked AROK to reduce its bid to $1.42 million. AROK's president told ICS's project manager that AROK would reduce its bid even further to $1.4 million if, as a result, ICS would agree to contract with AROK if the school district awarded the job to ICS. ICS's project manager stated that in exchange for AROK's further reduction to $1.4 million, "If [ICS] gets the job, [AROK] gets a job." AROK sent a letter to ICS confirming the $1.4 million quote and enclosed a detailed bid confirmation. The school district awarded the contract to ICS. After receiving notice to proceed with the project from the school district, ICS requested that AROK perform "value engineering" services with regard to its bid. (Value engineering involves changing the bid structure to lower the overall bid price without changing the profit structure for either the general contractor or the subcontractor). AROK complied and worked approximately 8 to 10 hours further reducing the subcontract price. Several months later, a dispute arose between ICS and AROK over the amount of the contract price, and ICS entered into subcontracts with two other companies to perform the drywall and stucco work. AROK brought suit for breach of contract. The trial court granted summary judgment in favor of ICS, and AROK appealed.

---

**Lankford, Judge** The old "formalist" view limited the agreement to written terms and emphasized rules of contract, such as the requirement that the agreement include all material terms. This has long since given way to the "realist" approach exemplified by the Uniform Commercial Code and the Second Restatement of Contracts. The latter emphasizes standards rather than rules, and assigns to courts the task of upholding the agreements parties intended to make.

ICS concedes for purposes of this appeal that its conditional promise, "If we get the job, you get the job," is an acceptance of AROK's promise to perform the work for a reduced price. ICS contends, however, that the parties failed to specify other terms essential to indicate their intent to be bound: the manner and time of payments, penalty provisions, time for completion, and bonding. ICS argues that as a result of the missing terms, no enforceable contract exists as a matter of law.

Is the agreement too uncertain to enforce? *Restatement (Second) of Contracts* section 33 establishes "reasonable certainty" as the standard for enforcement. The Restatement rule exemplifies the policy of the law to uphold agreements. Courts are never eager to undo agreements. Only when courts ensure that promises create obligations do promises have real meaning. Only then can those in the marketplace rely on their bargains to allocate their resources and plan for the future. For example, AROK presented evidence that it did not bid for other jobs because it had a contract with ICS. If that contract is not enforced, and AROK's resources were idled as a result of ICS's promise and breach, then one of the goals of contract law—economic efficiency—would be thwarted.

The enforcement of incomplete agreements is a necessary fact of economic life. Business people are not soothsayers, and can neither provide in advance for every unforeseen contingency nor answer every unasked question regarding a commercial agreement. This is especially so with a complex contract for a major construction project. Nor are entrepreneurs perfect at drafting legal documents. Finally, parties may want to bind themselves and at the same time desire to leave some matters open for future resolution in order to maintain flexibility. Thus, courts are often presented with incomplete bargains when the parties intend and desire to be bound. Refusing the enforcement of obligations the parties intended to create and that marketplace transactions require hardly seems the solution.

The standard for contract enforceability is not whether the agreement included a resolution of every matter and anticipated every contingency. "The terms of a contract are reasonably certain if they provide a basis for determining the existence of a breach and for giving an appropriate basis for determining the existence of a breach and for giving an appropriate remedy." *Restatement (Second) of Contracts* section 33(2). If a court can determine the existence of a breach by ICS and fashion an appropriate remedy for AROK, then the terms of their agreement are reasonably certain and enforceable. Thus, "gaps" or omitted terms, or vague and indefinite terms, are not invariably fatal to the rights of the parties to obtain enforcement of their bargain.

The terms of this contract are sufficiently certain for two independent reasons. First, ICS breached the contract at a point when the only terms necessary to determine the existence of the breach (scope of the work) and for giving an appropriate remedy (agreed-upon price) were present. Second, there was evidence of a course of dealing involving a standard form contract which could be used to supply any missing terms. We hold that the agreement is sufficiently definite to be enforceable.

AROK also claims that it is entitled to relief based upon promissory estoppel. We hold that this is a proper claim for relief as an alternative to the contract claim. If AROK can show that it acted or detrimentally relied upon ICS's promise to award the contract, then promissory estoppel is available. For example, AROK performed "value engineering" allegedly in reliance upon ICS's promise. AROK may also have forgone other work because it anticipated employing its resources in performing this contract. *Restatement (Second) of Contracts* section 90(1) states:

A promise which the promisor should reasonably expect to induce action or forbearance on the part of the promisee or a third person and which does induce such action or forbearance is binding if injustice can be avoided only by enforcement of the promise.

However, the remedy under this theory may be more limited than damages for breach of contract. In particular, relief may sometimes be limited to restitution or to damages or specific relief measured by the extent of the promisee's reliance rather than by the terms of the promise. Thus, AROK may be entitled to recover only the value of its work in "value engineering" unless it can show greater loss due to its reliance.

**Reversed and remanded in favor of AROK.**

---

## Communication to Offeree

When an offeror communicates the terms of an offer to an offeree, he objectively indicates an intent to be bound by those terms. The fact that an offer has *not* been communicated, on the other hand, may be evidence that the offeror has not yet decided to enter into a binding agreement. For example, assume that Stevens and Meyer have been negotiating over the sale of Meyer's restaurant. Stevens confides in his friend, Reilly, that he plans to offer Meyer $150,000 for the restaurant. Reilly goes to Meyer and tells Meyer that Stevens has decided to offer him $150,000 for the restaurant and has drawn up a written offer to that effect. After learning the details of the offer from Reilly, Meyer telephones Stevens and says, "I accept your offer." Is Stevens now contractually obligated to buy the restaurant? No. Since *Stevens* did not communicate the proposal to Meyer, there was no offer for Meyer to accept.

## SPECIAL OFFER PROBLEM AREAS

### Advertisements

Generally speaking, advertisements for the sale of goods at specified prices are *not* considered to be offers. Rather, they are treated as being invitations to offer or negotiate. The same rule is generally applied to signs, handbills, catalogs, price lists, and price quotations. This rule is based on the presumed intent of the sellers involved. It is not reasonable to conclude that a seller who has a limited number of items to sell intends to give every person who sees her ad, sign, or catalog the power to bind her to contract. Thus, if Customer sees Retailer's advertisement of Whizbang XL laptop computers for $2,000 and goes to Retailer's store indicating his intent to buy the computer, Customer is making an offer, which Retailer is free to accept or reject. This is so because Customer is manifesting a present intent to contract on the definite terms of the ad.

In some cases, however, particular ads have been held to amount to offers. Such ads are usually highly specific about the nature and number of items offered for sale and what is requested in return. This specificity precludes the possibility that the offeror could become contractually bound to an infinite number of offerees. In addition, many of the ads treated as offers have required some special performance by would-be buyers or have in some other way clearly indicated that immediate action by the buyer creates a binding agreement. The potential for unfairness to those who attempt to accept such ads and their fundamental difference from ordinary ads justify treating them as offers. *Jackson v. Investment Corporation of Palm Beach* presents an example of an advertisement that was held to constitute an offer.

---

## JACKSON V. INVESTMENT CORP. OF PALM BEACH
### 585 So.2d 949 (Fla. Ct. App. 1991)

John Jackson read an ad in the *Miami Herald* stating that the Pic-6 Jackpot for the last evening of the dog track racing season would be $825,000. Jackson went to the track on that date, picked the winner in the six designated races, and won the jackpot. However, Investment Corporation of Palm Beach, the owner of the dog track, contended that it should not have to pay more than $25,000 because it had intended the amount of the jackpot to be $25,000, not $825,000. The mix-up occurred when Investment submitted to the newspaper a prior ad with the following words written on the face of it: "Guaranteed Jackpot $25,000 must go tonight," and the newspaper employee who prepared the final draft of the ad mistook the dollar sign with only one slash-mark to be the number 8. Investment paid Jackson $25,000 on the night of the races, but Jackson later brought suit to claim the balance. At trial, the judge instructed the jury that it should find for Investment unless the evidence supported the claim that Investment intended by its newspaper advertisement to make an offer to pay a guaranteed jackpot of $825,000. The jury returned a verdict in favor of Investment and the trial judge entered judgment on the verdict. Jackson appealed, claiming that this instruction to the jury was erroneous.

---

**Downey, Judge**     There was no evidence adduced that Investment intended the jackpot to be $825,000. Jackson concedes that Investment never intended the jackpot to be the larger amount. The point is that Investment's subjective intent was not material in determining what the contract was between the parties. As the Florida Supreme Court said in

*Gendzier v. Bielecki,* quoting from Justice Oliver Wendell Holmes:

The making of a contract depends not on the agreement of two minds in one intention, but on the agreement of two sets of external signs—not on the parties having meant the same thing but on their having said the same thing.

Professor Williston, in his work on Contracts, describes the test as:

[T]he test of the true interpretation of an offer or acceptance is not what the party making it thought it meant or intended it to mean, but what a reasonable person in the position of the parties would have thought it meant. 1 *Williston on Contracts* sec. 94, 339–40.

It appears to us that the law, applicable to offers of a reward, is also applicable to the type of advertisement involved in this case. The offer is a mere proposal or conditional promise which, if accepted before it is revoked, creates a binding contract. We have given due consideration to Investment's argument regarding the advertisement as an "invitation to bargain," but find it inapposite here. The "invitation to bargain" rule appears to be applied in advertising wherein:

Neither the advertiser nor the reader of his notice understands that the latter is empowered to close the deal without further expression by the former. Such advertisements are understood to be mere requests to consider and examine and negotiate; and no one can reasonably regard them otherwise unless the circumstances are exceptional and the words used are very plain and clear. 1 *Corbin on Contracts* sec. 25 (1963).

Here there are no further negotiations indicated. If a member of the public buys a winning ticket on six races, he has accepted the offer and the parties have a contract. We thus hold that the trial court erred in instructing the jury as it did and we reverse the judgment appealed from and remand the cause for a new trial.

**Judgment reversed in favor of Jackson.**

## Rewards

Advertisements offering rewards for lost property, for information, or for the capture of criminals are generally treated as offers for unilateral contracts. To accept the offer and be entitled to the stated reward, offerees must perform the requested act—return the lost property, supply the requested information, or capture the wanted criminal. Some courts have held that only offerees who started performance with knowledge of the offer are entitled to the reward. Other courts, however, have indicated the only requirement is that the offeree know of the reward before completing performance. In reality, the result in most such cases probably reflects the court's perception of the equities of the particular case at hand.

## Auctions

Sellers at auctions are generally treated as making an invitation to offer. Those who bid on offered goods are, therefore, treated as making offers that the owner of the goods may accept or reject. Acceptance occurs only when the auctioneer strikes the goods off to the highest bidder; the auctioneer may withdraw the goods at any time before acceptance. However, when an auction is advertised as being "without reserve," the seller is treated as having made an offer to sell the goods to the highest bidder and the goods cannot be withdrawn after a call for bids has been made unless no bids are made within a reasonable time.[8]

## Bids

The bidding process is a fertile source of contract disputes. Advertisements for bids are generally treated as invitations to offer. Those who submit bids are treated as offerors. According to general contract principles, bidders can withdraw their bids at any time prior to acceptance by the offeree inviting the bids, and the offeree is free to accept or reject any bid. The previously announced terms of the bidding may alter these rules, however. For example, if the advertisement for bids unconditionally states that the contract will be awarded to the lowest responsible bidder, this will be treated as an offer that is accepted by the lowest bidder. Only proof by the offeror that the lowest bidder is not responsible can prevent the formation of a contract.

---

[8]These rules and others concerned with the sale of goods by auction are contained in § 2–328 of the UCC.

Also, under some circumstances discussed later in this chapter, promissory estoppel may operate to prevent bidders from withdrawing their bids.

Bids for governmental contracts are generally covered by specific statutes rather than by general contract principles. Such statutes ordinarily establish the rules governing the bidding process, often require that the contract be awarded to the lowest bidder, and frequently establish special rules or penalties governing the withdrawal of bids.

## WHICH TERMS ARE INCLUDED IN THE OFFER?

After making a determination that an offer existed, a court must decide which terms were included in the offer so that it can determine the terms of the parties' contract. Put another way, which terms of the offer are binding on the offeree who accepts it? Should offerees, for example, be bound by fine print clauses or by clauses on the back of the contract? Originally, the courts tended to hold that offerees were bound by all the terms of the offer on the theory that every person had a duty to protect himself by reading agreements carefully before signing them.

In today's world of lengthy, complex form contracts, however, people often sign agreements that they have not fully read or do not fully understand. Modern courts tend to recognize this fact by saying that offerees are bound only by terms of which they had actual or reasonable notice. If the offeree actually read the term in question, or if a reasonable person should have been aware of it, it will probably become part of the parties' contract. A fine-print provision on the back of a theater ticket would probably not be binding on a theater patron, however, because a reasonable person would not expect such a ticket to contain contractual terms. By contrast, the terms printed on a multipage airline or steamship ticket might well be considered binding on the purchaser if such documents would be expected to contain terms of the contract.

This modern approach to deciding the terms of a contract gives courts an indirect, but effective, way of promoting fair dealing by refusing to enforce unfair contract terms on the ground that

the offeree lacked reasonable notice of them. Disclaimers and exculpatory clauses (contract provisions that seek to relieve offerors of some legal duty that they would otherwise owe to offerees) are particularly likely to be subjected to close judicial scrutiny. Additional ways of analyzing unexpected and unfair contract terms are discussed in Chapter 7.

## TERMINATION OF OFFERS

After a court has determined the existence and content of an offer, it must determine the duration of the offer. Was the offer still in existence when the offeree attempted to accept it? If not, no contract was created and the offeree is treated as having made an offer that the original offeror is free to accept or reject. This is so because, by attempting to accept an offer that has terminated, the offeree has indicated a present intent to contract on the terms of the original offer though he lacks the power to bind the offeror to a contract due to the original offer's termination.

### Terms of the Offer

The offeror is often said to be "the master of the offer." This means that offerors have the power to determine the terms and conditions under which they are bound to a contract. As the following *Newman* case indicates, an offeror may include terms in the offer that limit its effective life. These may be specific terms, such as "you must accept by December 5, 1994" or "this offer is good for five days," or more general terms, such as "for immediate acceptance," "prompt wire acceptance," or "by return mail." General time limitation language in an offer can raise difficult problems of interpretation for courts trying to decide whether an offeree accepted before the offer terminated. Even more specific language, such as "this offer is good for five days," can cause problems if the offer does not specify whether the five-day period begins when the offer is sent or when the offeree receives it. Not all courts agree on such questions, so wise offerors should be as specific as possible in stating when their offers terminate.

## NEWMAN V. SCHIFF
**778 F.2d 460 (8th Cir. 1985)**

Irwin Schiff, a self-styled tax rebel who had made a career out of his tax protest activities, appeared live on the February 7, 1983, CBS News "Nightwatch" program. During the course of the program, which had a viewer participation format, Schiff repeated his longstanding position that "there is nothing in the Internal Revenue Code which says anyone is legally required to pay the tax." Later in the program, Schiff stated: "If anybody calls this show and cites any section of this Code that says an individual is required to file a tax return, I will pay them $100,000."

Attorney John Newman failed to see Schiff live on "Nightwatch," but saw a two-minute taped segment of the original "Nightwatch" interview several hours later on the "CBS Morning News." Certain that Schiff's statements were incorrect, Newman telephoned and wrote "CBS Morning News," attempting to accept Schiff's offer by citing Internal Revenue Code provisions requiring individuals to pay federal income tax. CBS forwarded Newman's letter to Schiff, who refused to pay on the ground that Newman had not properly accepted his offer. Newman sued Schiff for breach of contract. The trial court ruled in Schiff's favor, and Newman appealed.

---

**Bright, Senior Circuit Judge**   It is a basic legal principle that mutual assent is necessary for the formation of a contract. Courts determine whether the parties expressed their assent to a contract by analyzing their agreement process in terms of offer and acceptance. An offer is the "manifestation of willingness to enter into a bargain, so made as to justify another person in understanding that his assent to that bargain is invited and will conclude it." *Restatement (Second) of Contracts* § 24 (1981). Schiff's statement on "Nightwatch" that he would pay $100,000 to anyone who called the show and cited any section of the Internal Revenue Code "that says an individual is required to file a tax return" constituted a valid offer for a reward. If anyone had called the show and cited the code sections that Newman produced, a contract would have been formed and Schiff would have been obligated to pay the $100,000 reward.

Newman, however, never saw the live CBS "Nightwatch" program on which Schiff appeared and this lawsuit is not predicated on Schiff's "Nightwatch" offer. Newman saw the "CBS Morning News" rebroadcast of Schiff's "Nightwatch" appearance. This rebroadcast served not to renew or extend Schiff's offer, but rather only to inform viewers that Schiff had made an offer on "Nightwatch." An offeror is the master of his offer and it is clear that Schiff by his words, "If anybody calls this show," limited his offer in time to remain open only until the conclusion of the live "Nightwatch" broadcast. A reasonable person listening to the news rebroadcast could not conclude that the above language constituted a new offer rather than what it actually was, a news report of the offer previously made, which had already expired.

Although Newman has not "won" his lawsuit in the traditional sense of recovering a reward that he sought, he has accomplished an important goal in the public interest of unmasking the "blatant nonsense" dispensed by Schiff. For that he deserves great commendation from the public. Perhaps now CBS and other communication media who have given Schiff's mistaken views widespread publicity will give John Newman equal time in the public interest.

**Judgment for Schiff affirmed.**

## Lapse of Time

Offers that fail to provide a specific time for acceptance are valid for a reasonable time. What constitutes a reasonable time depends on the circumstances surrounding the offer. How long would a reasonable person in the offeree's position believe she had to accept the offer? Offers involving things subject to rapid fluctuations in value, such as stocks, bonds, or commodities futures, have a very brief duration. The same is true for offers involving goods that may spoil, such as produce.

The context of the parties' negotiations is another factor relevant to determining the duration of an offer. For example, most courts hold that when parties bargain face-to-face or over the telephone, the normal time for acceptance does not extend past the conclusion of their conversation unless the offeror indicates a contrary intention. Where negotiations are carried out by mail or telegram, the time for acceptance would ordinarily include at least the normal time for communicating the offer and a prompt response by the offeree. Finally, in cases where the parties have dealt with each other on a regular basis in the past, the timing of their prior transactions would be highly relevant in measuring the reasonable time for acceptance.

## Revocation

**General Rule: Offers are Revocable**   As the masters of their offers, offerors can give offerees the power to bind them to contracts by making offers. They can also terminate that power by revoking their offers. The general common law rule on revocations is that offerors may revoke their offers at any time prior to acceptance, *even if they have promised to hold the offer open for a stated period of time.* In the following situations (summarized in Figure 1), however, offerors are *not* free to revoke their offers.

**1.** *Options.* An **option** is a separate contract in which an offeror agrees not to revoke her offer for a stated time in exchange for some valuable consideration.[9] You can think of it as a contract in which an offeror sells her right to revoke her offer. For example, Jones, in exchange for $5,000, agrees to give Dewey Development Co. a six-month option to

purchase her farm for $550,000. In this situation, Jones would not be free to revoke the offer during the six-month period of the option. The offeree, Dewey Development, has no obligation to accept Jones's offer. In effect, it has merely purchased the right to consider the offer for the stated time without fear that Jones will revoke it. The traditional common law rule on options requires the actual payment of the agreed-on consideration before an option contract becomes enforceable. Therefore, in the above example, if Dewey Development never, in fact, paid the $5,000, no option was created and Jones could revoke her offer at any time prior to its acceptance by Dewey Development.

**2.** *Firm offers for the sale of goods.* The Code makes a major change in the common law rules governing the revocability of offers by recognizing the concept of a **firm offer** [2–205]. Like an option, a firm offer is irrevocable for a period of time. In contrast to an option, however, a firm offer does not require consideration to be given in exchange for the offeror's promise to keep the offer open. Not all offers to buy or sell goods qualify as firm offers, however. To be a firm offer, an offer must:

· Be made by an offeror who is a *merchant.*
· Be contained in a signed[10] writing.
· Give assurances that the offer will be kept open.

An offer to buy or sell goods that fails to satisfy these three requirements is governed by the general common law rule and is revocable at any time prior to acceptance. If an offer *does* meet the requirements of a firm offer, however, it will be irrevocable for the time stated in the offer. If no specific time is stated in the offer, it will be irrevocable for a *reasonable* time. Regardless of the terms of the firm offer, the outer limit on a firm offer's irrevocability is *three* months. For example, if Worldwide Widgets makes an offer in a signed writing in which it proposes to sell a quantity of its XL7 Turbo Widgets to Howell Hardware and gives assurances that the offer will be kept open for a year, the offer is a firm offer, but it can be revoked after three months if Howell Hardware has not yet accepted it.

---

[9]Chapter 4 discusses consideration in detail.

[10]Under UCC § 1–201(39), the word *signed* includes any symbol that a person makes or adopts with the intent to authenticate a writing.

In some cases, however, offerees are the true originators of an assurance term in an offer. When offerees have effective control of the terms of the offer by providing their customers with preprinted purchase order forms or order blanks, they may be tempted to take advantage of their merchant customers by placing an assurance term in their order forms. This would allow offerees to await market developments before deciding whether to fill the order, while their merchant customers, who may have signed the order without reading all of its terms, would be powerless to revoke. To prevent such unfairness, the Code requires that assurance terms on forms provided by offerees be separately signed by the offeror to effect a firm offer. For example, if Fashionable Mfg. Co. supplies its customer, Retailer, with preprinted order forms that contain a fine-print provision giving assurances that the customer's offer to purchase goods will be held open for one month, the purported promise to keep the offer open would not be enforceable unless Retailer separately signed that provision.

**3.** *Offers for unilateral contracts.* Suppose Franklin makes the following offer for a unilateral contract to Waters: "If you mow my lawn, I'll pay you $25." Given that an offeree in a unilateral contract must fully perform the requested act to accept the offer, can Franklin wait until Waters is almost finished mowing the lawn and then say "I revoke!"? Obviously, the application of the general rule that offerors can revoke at any time before acceptance creates the potential for injustice when applied to offers for unilateral contracts because it would allow an offeror to revoke after the offeree has begun performance but before he has had a chance to complete it. To prevent injustice to offerees who rely on such offers by beginning performance, two basic approaches are available to modern courts.

Some courts have held that once the offeree has begun to perform, the offeror's power to revoke is suspended for the amount of time reasonably necessary for the offeree to complete performance. Section 45 of the *Restatement (Second)* takes a similar approach for offers that unequivocally require acceptance by performance by stating that once the offeree begins performance, an option contract is created. The offeror's duty to perform his side of the bargain is conditional on full performance by the offeree.

| FIGURE 1 | When Offerors Cannot Revoke |
|---|---|
| **Options** | Offeror has promised to hold offer open and has received consideration for that promise |
| **Firm Offers** | Merchant offeror makes written offer to buy or sell goods, giving assurances offer will be held open |
| **Unilateral Contract Offers** | Offeree has started to perform requested act before offeror revokes |
| **Promissory Estoppel** | Offeree foreseeably and reasonably relies on offer being held open, and will suffer injustice if it is revoked |

Another approach to the unilateral contract dilemma is to hold that a bilateral contract is created once the offeree begins performance. This is essentially the position taken by section 62 of the *Restatement (Second),* which states that when the offer invites acceptance either by a return promise or performance, the beginning of performance operates as an acceptance and a promise by the offeree to render complete performance.

**4.** *Promissory estoppel.* In some cases in which the offeree *relies* on the offer being kept open, the doctrine of promissory estoppel can operate to prevent offerors from revoking their offers prior to acceptance. Section 87(2) of the *Restatement (Second)* says:

An offer which the offeror should reasonably expect to induce action or forbearance of a substantial character on the part of the offeree before acceptance and which does induce such action or forbearance is binding as an option contract to the extent necessary to avoid injustice.

Many of the cases in which promissory estoppel has been used successfully to prevent revocation of offers involve the bidding process. For example, Gigantic General Contractor seeks to get the general contract to build a new high school gymnasium for Shadyside School District. It receives bids from subcontractors. Pliny Electric submits the lowest bid to perform the electrical work on the job, and Gigantic uses Pliny's bid in preparing its bid for the general contract. Here, Pliny has made an offer to

Gigantic, but Gigantic cannot accept that offer until it knows whether it has gotten the general contract. The school district awards the general contract to Gigantic. Before Gigantic can accept Pliny's offer, however, Pliny attempts to revoke it. In this situation, a court could use the doctrine of promissory estoppel to hold that the offer could not be revoked.

**Effectiveness of Revocations**    The question of *when* a revocation is effective to terminate an offer is often a critical issue in the contract formation process. For example, Davis offers to landscape Winter's property for $1,500. Two days after making the offer, Davis changes his mind and mails Winter a letter revoking the offer. The next day, Winter, who has not received Davis's letter, telephones Davis and attempts to accept. Contract? Yes. As the following *Lyon* case indicates, the general rule on this point is that revocations are effective only when they are actually *received* by the offeree.

The basic idea behind this rule is that the offeree is justified in relying on the intent to contract manifested by the offeror's offer until she actually knows that the offeror has changed his mind. This explains why many courts have also held that if the offeree receives reliable information indicating that the offeror has taken action inconsistent with an intent to enter the contract proposed by the offer, such as selling the property that was the subject of the offer to someone else, this terminates the offer. In such circumstances, the offeree would be unjustified in believing that the offer could still be accepted.

The only major exception to the general rule on effectiveness of revocations concerns offers to the general public. Because it would be impossible in most cases to reach every offeree with a revocation, it is generally held that a revocation made in the same manner as the offer is effective when published, without proof of communication to the offeree.

## Lyon v. Adgraphics
### 540 A.2d 398 (Conn. Ct. App. 1988)

Edward Sherman engaged V. R. Brokers as listing agent for the sale of Adgraphics, his business. On December 5, 1985, William Lyon made a written offer to purchase the business for $75,000 and attached certain conditions to the offer. Later the same day, Sherman signed a written counteroffer offering to sell for $80,000 and rejecting two of the conditions contained in Lyon's offer. On December 7, at 11:35 A.M., Lyon signed the counteroffer before a notary public and then brought it to the office of V. R. Brokers around noon on that day. Before Lyon could hand the signed counteroffer to Robert Renault, the principal of V. R. Brokers, Renault told him that Sherman wanted to cancel his counteroffer. Lyon filed a breach of contract suit, and, when the trial court ruled in his favor, Sherman appealed.

**Borden, Judge**    It is a basic principle of contract law that in order to form a binding contract there must be an offer and acceptance based on a mutual understanding of the parties. The counteroffer by Sherman created a power of acceptance in Lyon. That counteroffer, however, was revocable by Sherman at any time prior to acceptance by Lyon.

The trial court's conclusion that Lyon's acceptance of the counteroffer was effective when he signed it was contrary to our law. Revocation of an offer in order to be effectual must be received by the

offeree before he has exercised his power of creating a contract by acceptance of the offer. Acceptance is operative, if transmitted by means which the offeror has authorized, as soon as its transmission begins and it is put out of the offeree's possession. Lyon's act of signing the written counteroffer failed to communicate the acceptance to Sherman or his agent and failed to put the acceptance out of Lyon's possession. It was, therefore, ineffective to create a contract.

When Sherman, through his agent, informed Lyon that the counteroffer was withdrawn, Lyon's power to accept the counteroffer no longer existed. This was done before Lyon had properly accepted the counteroffer by transmitting the signed counteroffer to Renault. Accordingly, no enforceable contract between the parties was ever created. **Judgment reversed in favor of Sherman.**

---

## Rejection

An offeree may expressly reject an offer by indicating that he is unwilling to accept it. He may also impliedly reject it by making a counteroffer, an offer to contract on terms materially different from the terms of the offer.[11] As a general rule, either form of rejection by the offeree terminates his power to accept the offer. This is so because an offeror who receives a rejection may rely on the offeree's expressed desire not to accept the offer by making another offer to a different offeree.

One exception to the general rule that rejections terminate offers concerns offers that are the subject of an option contract. Some courts hold that a rejection does not terminate an option contract and that the offeree who rejects still has the power to accept the offer later, so long as the acceptance is effective within the option period.[12]

**Effectiveness of Rejections**    As a general rule, rejections, like revocations, are effective only when actually received by the offeror. This is because there is no possibility that the offeror can rely on a rejection by making another offer to a different offeree until she actually has notice of the rejection. Therefore, an offeree who has mailed a rejection could still change her mind and accept if she communicates the acceptance before the offeror receives the rejection.[13]

## Death or Insanity of Either Party

The death or insanity of either party to an offer automatically terminates the offer without notice. A meeting of the minds is obviously impossible when one of the parties has died or become insane.[14]

## Destruction of Subject Matter

If, prior to an acceptance of an offer, the subject matter of a proposed contract is destroyed without the knowledge or fault of either party, the offer is terminated.[15] So, if Marks offers to sell Wiggins his lakeside cottage and the cottage is destroyed by fire before Wiggins accepts, the offer was terminated on the destruction of the cottage. Subsequent acceptance by Wiggins would not create a contract.

## Intervening Illegality

An offer is terminated if the performance of the contract it proposes becomes illegal before the offer is accepted. So, if a computer manufacturer offered to sell sophisticated computer equipment to another country, but two days later, before the offer was accepted, Congress placed an embargo on all sales to that country, the offer was terminated by the embargo.[16]

---

[11]Chapter 3 discusses counteroffers in detail.

[12]Section 37 of the *Restatement (Second) of Contracts* adopts this rule.

[13]Chapter 3 discusses this subject in detail.

[14]Death or insanity of a party that occurs after a contract has been formed can excuse performance in contracts that call for personal services to be performed by the person who has died or become insane. This is discussed in Chapter 10.

[15]In some circumstances, destruction of the subject matter can also serve as a legal excuse for a party's failure to perform his obligations under an existing contract. Chapter 10 discusses this subject.

[16]In some circumstances, intervening illegality can also serve as a legal excuse for a party's failure to perform his obligations under an existing contract. Chapter 10 discusses this subject.

---

---

### PROBLEMS AND PROBLEM CASES

⬥

**1.** In 1989, the New Jersey Highway Authority increased its tolls from 25 cents to 35 cents. In connection with this increase, it authorized the sale of tokens for a discounted price—$10 for a roll of 40 tokens, a savings of $4 per roll for customers— for a limited time. The authority advertised this sale through several media, including signs on the parkway itself. Shortly after the discount sale began, complaints were made that the tokens were not available. The authority explained that the shortage probably resulted from an unanticipated demand for the tokens resulting from purchasers hoarding them. The authority then began limiting the sales to certain days of the week, but even with that limitation, the demand could not be satisfied. Schlictman, a motorist who used the toll roads, sued the authority for breach of contract after trying unsuccessfully, on five different occasions within the authorized sale dates and times, to buy the discounted tokens. What should the result be?

**2.** In 1985, First Colonial Savings Bank ran a newspaper advertisement that stated in part:

**You Win 2 Ways**

WITH FIRST COLONIAL'S

**Savings Certificates**

1 Great Gifts                                    2 & High Interest

Saving at First Colonial is a very rewarding experience. In appreciation for your business we have Great Gifts for you to enjoy **NOW**—and when your investment matures you get your entire principal back **PLUS GREAT INTEREST.**

Plan B: 3½ Year Investment

Deposit $14,000 and receive two gifts: a Remington Shotgun and GE CB Radio, OR an RCA 20" Color-Trac TV, and $20,136.12 upon maturity in 3½ years.

Relying on this ad, the Changs deposited $14,000 with First Colonial on January 3, 1986. They received a color television that day from First Colonial and expected to receive the sum of $20,136.12 upon maturity of the deposit in three and one-half years. First Colonial also gave the Changs a certificate of deposit when they made their deposit. When the Changs returned to liquidate the certificate of deposit upon its maturity, they were informed that the advertisement contained a typographical error and that they should have deposited $15,000 in order to receive the sum of $20,136.12 upon maturity of the certificate of deposit. First Colonial did not inform the Changs, nor were the Changs aware, that the advertisement contained an error until after the certificate of deposit had matured. First Colonial did display in its lobby pamphlets that contained the correct figures when the Changs made their deposit. The Changs sued First Colonial to recover the $1,312.19 difference between the $20,136.12 amount in the advertisement and the $18,823.93 that First Colonial actually paid to the Changs. Should they prevail?

**3.** On August 4, 1980, Normile made a written offer to buy property owned by Miller. Miller signed and returned the offer after making several substantial changes in its terms and initialing those changes. The executed form was delivered to Normile by Byer, the real estate agent who had shown him the property. In the early afternoon of August 5, 1980, Miller accepted an offer by Segal to buy her property on terms similar to those in the modified offer she had returned to Normile. At 2:00 P.M. that day, Byer told Normile: "You snooze, you lose; the property has been sold." Shortly thereafter, Normile attempted to accept Miller's proposal. Was the trial court correct in ruling that Normile and Miller had no contract?

**4.** In April 1981, Action Ads, Inc., hired Judes as a salesperson. The employment contract provided that: "Sixty days from your date of hire, Action Ads will provide a medical insurance program for you and your dependents." Judes was not very successful as a salesperson for Action, earning only $580.09 in commissions during the entire tenure of his employment with the company. Action never provided the promised medical insurance, a fact

Judes learned when he inquired about whether he was covered in August of 1981. Judes did little or no solicitation for Action after August, and the last order he placed with Action was in October 1981. During the period in which he was purportedly working for Action, Judes held himself out as unemployed, collecting $2,448 in unemployment benefits. In November 1981, Judes was seriously burned in a gas explosion at a mobile home. He filed suit against Action to recover his medical expenses, arguing that Action had breached the employment contract by failing to provide insurance coverage for him. Action Ads asserted that the agreement to provide "a medical insurance program" was too indefinite to be enforceable because the parties' agreement did not cover anything specific about the nature of the insurance coverage. What should the result be?

**5.** Less than an hour before his estranged wife underwent emergency surgery for an ectopic pregnancy caused by another man, McAdoo was asked to sign a standard form contract prepared by St. John's Episcopal Hospital. McAdoo testified that at the time he signed the form his wife's physical appearance and declared mental state convinced him that she was near death. Further, he stated that, under such circumstances, it did not occur to him to read carefully or question the implications of the papers he was being asked to sign. The form contained a provision that read as follows:

ASSIGNMENT OF INSURANCE BENEFITS: I hereby authorize payment directly to the above named hospital of the hospital expense benefits otherwise payable to me but not to exceed the hospital's regular charges for this period of hospitalization. I understand that I am financially responsible to the hospital for the charges not covered by my group insurance plan.

McAdoo's wife survived and was discharged from St. John's eight days later. McAdoo did not visit her after the day of the operation and had not had any further contact with her when the hospital filed suit against him to collect her hospital bill. Should St. John's be able to enforce the agreement against McAdoo?

**6.** Phyllis Chaplin filed a class action suit against Consolidated Edison (Con Ed) for allegedly discriminating against epileptics in violation of the Rehabilitation Act of 1973. In August 1981, Con Ed's lawyer sent Chaplin's lawyer a settlement

offer. Chaplin's lawyer replied by saying that Chaplin had "objections" to the proposed settlement. On September 16, 1981, Con Ed's lawyer replied, saying: "Any further negotiation is an impossibility; if this agreement is not satisfactory to your client in its present form, I must withdraw all offers of settlement." In a letter dated September 17, 1981, Chaplin's lawyer answered that "after careful consideration" Chaplin still had "objections" to Con Ed's offer. Later on September 17, a federal appellate court ruled that private suits such as Chaplin's were not allowed under the Rehabilitation Act. On September 30, 1981, Chaplin's lawyer told Con Ed's lawyer that Chaplin had had "a change of heart" and was accepting the settlement offer. Con Ed's lawyer replied that the settlement was no longer acceptable. Was Con Ed bound by the settlement offer?

**7.** In October 1981, Christy and Andrus were involved in an automobile accident. On November 8, 1982, Aetna Casualty and Surety Company, Andrus's insurer, sent a letter to Christy and his insurer, The Travelers Insurance Company, offering to settle Christy's claim against Andrus for $8,507. Neither Christy nor The Travelers responded to this letter until February 4, 1984, when an attorney for The Travelers sent Aetna a letter attempting to accept the settlement offer. Aetna then responded that any claim Christy had against Andrus was barred by the state's two-year statute of limitations and that The Travelers' attempt to accept was not timely. Christy filed suit against Andrus and Aetna, arguing that they were bound by the settlement. At trial, Aetna introduced uncontradicted testimony that customary practice in the insurance industry was to respond to settlement offers within a few weeks. Was the trial court decision in Aetna's favor correct?

**8.** In March 1985, Cagle, a potato farmer, entered into a written agreement to buy seed potatoes from H. C. Schmieding Produce Company. The terms of the contract obligated Cagle to pay a portion of the purchase price immediately, with the balance to be paid when the crop to be raised from the seed potatoes was harvested. Cagle paid the preharvest portion of the price and proceeded to cultivate the potatoes. He failed to harvest most of the resulting crop, however, or to pay Schmieding the postharvest portion of the purchase price. When Schmieding sued him for breach of contract, Cagle filed a counterclaim arguing that Schmieding had breached a second contract, which obligated him to purchase Cagle's crop. According to Cagle, this second contract resulted from two telephone conversations with Schmieding's employees, occurring in late February 1985 and in May 1985. Cagle introduced evidence to show that Schmieding had agreed in those conversations to pay him $5.50 per bag for approximately 10,000 bags of white potatoes and to pay him market price at harvest time for all of his red potatoes grown on 30 acres of land. Cagle also introduced a letter from Schmieding, dated May 26, 1985, which said: "We are looking forward to working with you on the shipment of your crop," and asked him to "give us a week notice before you are ready to ship, in order for us to prepare our sales orders." Was this contract sufficiently definite to be enforceable?

**9.** In June 1973, Berryman signed an agreement giving Kmoch, a real estate broker, a 120-day option to purchase 960 acres of Berryman's land in exchange for "$10.00 and other valuable consideration," which was never paid. Kmoch hired two agricultural consultants to produce a report that he intended to use in order to interest other investors in joining him to exercise the option. In late July 1973, Berryman telephoned Kmoch and asked to be released from the option agreement. Nothing definite was agreed to, and Berryman later sold the land to another person. In August, Kmoch decided to exercise the option and contacted the local Federal Land Bank representative to make arrangements to buy the land. After being told by the representative that Berryman had sold the property, Kmoch sent Berryman a letter attempting to exercise the option. Kmoch argued that the option was still in effect and that, in any event, Berryman was estopped from revoking it. Was Kmoch right?

**10.** Warner Electric, an electrical subcontractor, submitted a bid to the Utah Subcontractors Bid Depository Service for the electrical subcontract on the construction of the General Services Administration (GSA) Metallurgy Research Center in Salt Lake City, Utah. Warner based its bid on specifications and bid forms supplied by the GSA. John Price Associates, a general contractor, used Warner's subcontract bid, which was the lowest submitted, in preparing its bid for the general contract. Price was the lowest bidder and was awarded the contract for the project. A few days after Price had signed a contract with the GSA, Warner told Price that it had a problem with its subcontract bid because the bid did not include certain laboratory work described in section 11600 of the GSA plans, work which Warner had thought would be performed by the general contractor. Warner refused to sign the subcontract without a promise of additional payment for the section 11600 work. Price notified Warner by mailgram that it was accepting Warner's bid. Later that day, Warner's attorney delivered a letter to Price withdrawing Warner's bid. Price then contacted the other subcontractors and ultimately hired another subcontractor for $94,845 more than Warner's bid price. Was Warner free to revoke its offer?

**11.** 📼    *Video Case.* See "Too Good to Be True." A couple read three advertisements: The first was a newspaper ad for a new Mark 12 Luxury Automobile for $9,999. Although they thought the ad might be a typographical mistake, there was no fine print in the ad and the two decided to go to the dealership and see if it would "make good on the offer." Once there, they learned that the price of the car was $29,999, not $9,999. The salesperson stated that the advertised price was an obvious typo. Is the dealership obligated to sell the car for $9,999?

The second was a flyer from a supermarket inviting customers to "Come celebrate good old-fashioned values for our 25th anniversary." The flyer advertised New York strip steak for $.99 per pound. Upon arrival at the store, however, the couple learned that the ad was an error and the price was intended to be $7.99 per found, not $.99. The employee pointed to a memo posted in the store that announced that the ad was an error. Was the ad an offer? If it had been an offer, would the memo posted in the store be a valid revocation?

The third ad was a flyer from an electronics superstore that stated, "Dear Preferred Customer: special close-out of Ubachi VCRs. Only three available at this unbelievable price, first come, first served, no rain checks." The couple camped outside the store all night to be first in line, but the store refused to sell the advertised item and tried to sell them a different, higher-priced model instead. Was this ad an offer?

**12.** 📼    *Video Case.* See "Roof Repair." Roofer had submitted a bid to resurface a roof on the Bobco factory in Industrial Park. He had gotten encouraging signals about getting the job and was just about to get a signed contract to do the work when the Bobco factory burned to the ground. What is the status of Roofer's offer to resurface the roof?

See also "Car Deals" and "Martin Manufacturing."

## CAPSTONE QUESTIONS

On September 1, 1995, DuPont, who wanted to sell his property, placed the following advertisement in the classified section of the local newspaper:

Beautiful country home sited privately on 5 acres on prestigious Bluebird Lake with gatehouse secured. Outstanding lakefront views. Features main-level master bedroom suite, professional chef's kitchen, heated pool & jacuzzi, tennis court, large dock. One-of-a-kind offering! $1,700,000.

The following events then occurred:

- On September 6, DuPont delivered a letter to Burnside, in which he proposed to sell the property to Burnside for a "fair price." Burnside wrote back on September 8 and stated that he accepted DuPont's offer. Burnside claims that DuPont is contractually bound to sell the property to him.

- On September 7, having learned that Margulis was interested in buying the property, DuPont made a written offer to sell the property to Margulis for $1,659,000. This offer stated that it would remain open until September 10. However, on September 8, DuPont delivered to Margulis a revocation of the offer that he had made to Margulis. On September 9, Margulis delivered a written acceptance to DuPont.

Margulis asserts that DuPont's offer was irrevocable and that a valid contract to sell the property exists between the parties.

- On September 8, DuPont delivered an offer to sell the property to Powell for $1,670,000. On September 9, DuPont received from Powell a counteroffer in which Powell stated that he would buy the property for $1,650,000. DuPont did not respond to this. On September 10, Powell delivered to DuPont a written acceptance of DuPont's offer to sell the property for $1,670,000. Powell asserts that DuPont is contractually obligated to sell the property to him.

- On September 11, Bell, who had read DuPont's advertisement, sent DuPont a registered letter stating that he accepted DuPont's offer and would buy the house at the advertised price. On September 12, however, after DuPont received this letter but before he replied to it, Bell died suddenly. Not knowing that Bell had died, DuPont sent a letter to Bell on September 13, affirming that he would sell the property to Bell for $1,700,000. DuPont claims that a contract was formed and Bell's estate must purchase the property.

## Required:

Answer the following and give reasons for your conclusions.

1. State whether Burnside's claim is correct.
2. State whether Margulis's claims are correct.
3. State whether Powell's claim is correct.
4. State whether DuPont is correct in his claim.

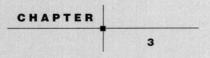

# CHAPTER
## 3

# THE AGREEMENT:

# ACCEPTANCE

**INTRODUCTION**

*The preceding chapter discussed the circumstances under which a proposal would constitute the first stage of formation of an agreement: the offer. This chapter focuses on the final stage of forming an agreement: the acceptance. The acceptance is vitally important because it is with the acceptance that the contract is formed. This chapter discusses the requirements for making a valid acceptance as well as the rules concerning the time at which a contract comes into being.*

## WHAT IS AN ACCEPTANCE?

An **acceptance** is "a manifestation of assent to the terms [of the offer] made by the offeree in the manner invited or required by the offer."[1] In determining if an offeree accepted an offer, thus creating a contract, a court will look for evidence that the offeree intended to enter the contract on the terms proposed by the offeror and that he communicated his acceptance to the offeror.

### Intention to Accept

In determining whether an offeree accepted an offer, the court is looking for the same *present intent to contract* on the part of the offeree that it found on the part of the offeror. The difference is that the offeree must objectively indicate a present intent to contract on the terms of the offer before a contract results. As the master of the offer, the offeror may specify in detail what behavior is required of the offeree to bind him to a contract. If the offeror does so, the offeree must ordinarily comply with all the terms of the offer before a contract results.

### Intent and Acceptance on the Offeror's Terms

**Traditional Mirror Image Rule**     The traditional contract law rule is that an acceptance must be the *mirror image* of the offer. As the following *Benya* case indicates, attempts by offerees to change the terms of the offer or to add new terms to it are

---

[1]*Restatement (Second) of Contracts* § 50(1) (1981).

treated as counteroffers because they impliedly indicate an intent by the offeree to reject the offer instead of being bound by its terms. However, if an offeree merely asks about the terms of the offer without indicating its rejection (an *inquiry regarding terms*), or accepts the offer's terms while complaining about them (a *grumbling acceptance*), no rejection is implied. Also, recent years have witnessed a judicial tendency to apply the mirror image

rule in a more liberal fashion by holding that only *material* (important) variances between an offer and a purported acceptance result in an implied rejection of the offer. Distinguishing among a counteroffer, an inquiry regarding terms, and a grumbling acceptance is often a difficult task. The fundamental issue, however, remains the same: Did the offeree objectively indicate a present intent to be bound by the terms of the offer?

## Benya v. Stevens and Thompson Paper Co.
### 468 A.2d 929 (Vt. Sup. Ct. 1983)

On September 24, 1979, Vincent Benya's agent presented Stevens and Thompson Paper Company (S&T) with a sales agreement to purchase 5,243 acres of timber land owned by S&T for $605,366.50. S&T's lawyer made several modifications to the agreement, raising the cash to be paid at closing from $5,000 to $10,000, raising the interest rate on the mortgage S&T would hold on the property until it was fully paid for from 9 percent to 10 percent, providing for quarterly rather than annual payments on the mortgage, and changing the deed S&T was to provide from a warranty to a special warranty deed. S&T's vice president then initialed each change and signed the document, which was mailed back to Benya's agent. In early November, S&T received a new sales agreement from Benya, which differed from the two previous versions in a number of ways. S&T neither signed this agreement nor responded to it in any way. On November 7, S&T sold the property to someone else. Benya filed suit for breach of contract, and, when the trial court ruled in his favor, S&T appealed.

**Billings, Chief Justice**    The trial court found that the September 24th sales agreement constituted a binding contract as both parties had signed it. The court concluded that the changes made by S&T to Benya's sales agreement were minor since the purchase price, closing date and deposit were substantially the same, and therefore did not constitute a counteroffer.

The law relative to contract formation has long been well settled in Vermont and elsewhere. For an acceptance of an offer to be valid, it must substantially comply with the terms of the offer. An acceptance that modifies or includes new terms is not an acceptance of the original offer; it is a counteroffer by the offeree that must be accepted or rejected by the original offeror. The offeror's acceptance of the offeree's counteroffer may be accomplished either expressly or by conduct.

On the record before us it is clear that the September 24th purchase and sales agreement was

an offer from Benya to S&T that S&T never accepted. Instead, S&T significantly altered the terms of Benya's offer. These changes were not, as characterized by the trial court, minor and therefore of no effect on Benya's offer. Taken together, they constitute S&T's proposal for a new deal, or, more precisely, a counteroffer. Also clear from the record is that Benya never accepted, either expressly or otherwise, S&T's counteroffer. After Benya and his agent discussed S&T's counteroffer, the decision was made to draft a third proposal, which in turn altered the deposit and time of payment terms of S&T's counteroffer. S&T never signed or in any other way expressed its assent to this proposal. Additionally, the conduct of the parties demonstrates their understanding that agreement had not yet been reached.

**Judgment reversed in favor of S&T.**

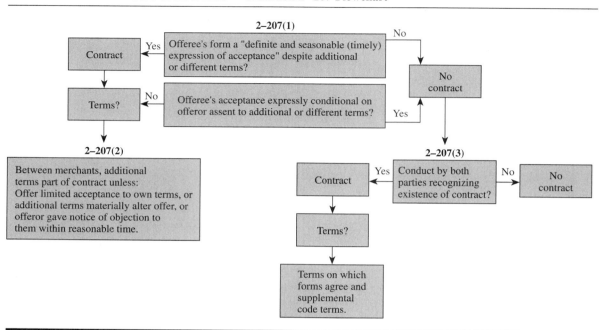

**FIGURE 1**   The "Battle of the Forms"—A Section 2–207 Flowchart

## The UCC and the "Battle of the Forms"

Strictly applying the mirror image rule to modern commercial transactions, most of which are carried out by using preprinted form contracts, would often result in frustrating the parties' true intent. Offerors use standard order forms prepared by their lawyers, and offerees use standard acceptance or acknowledgment forms drafted by their counsel. The odds that these forms will agree in every detail are slight, as are the odds that the parties will read each other's forms in their entirety. Instead, the parties to such transactions are likely to read only crucial provisions concerning the goods ordered, the price, and the delivery date called for, and if these terms are agreeable, believe that they have a contract.

If a dispute arose before the parties started to perform, a court strictly applying the mirror image rule would hold that no contract resulted because the offer and acceptance forms did not match exactly. If a dispute arose after performance had commenced, the court would probably hold that the offeror had impliedly accepted the offeree's counteroffer and was bound by its terms.

Because neither of these results is very satisfactory, the Code, in a very controversial provision often called the "Battle of the Forms" section [2–207] (see Figure 1), has changed the mirror image rule for contracts involving the sale of goods. As you will see in the following *Union Carbide* case, section 2–207 allows the formation of a contract even when there is some variance between the terms of the offer and the terms of the acceptance. It also makes it possible, under *some* circumstances, for a term contained in the acceptance form to become part of the contract. The Code provides that a *definite and timely expression of acceptance* creates a contract, even if it includes terms that are *different from those stated in the offer* or even if it states *additional terms* that the offer did not address [2–207(1)]. An attempted acceptance that *was expressly conditioned* on the offeror's agreement to the offeree's terms would *not* be a valid acceptance, however [2–207(1)].

What are the terms of a contract created by the exchange of standardized forms? The *additional* terms contained in the offeree's form are treated as "proposals for addition to the contract." If the parties are both *merchants*, the additional terms become part of the contract *unless*:

1. The offer *expressly limits acceptance* to its own terms,
2. The new terms would *materially alter* the offer, or
3. The offeror gives notice of objection to the new terms within a reasonable time after receiving the acceptance [2–207(2)].

The *Union Carbide* case shows how courts analyze whether a term contained in the acceptance has become part of the contract.

When the offeree has made his acceptance expressly conditional on the offeror's agreement to the new terms or when the offeree's response to the offer is clearly not "an expression of acceptance" (e.g., an express rejection), no contract is created under section 2–207(1). A contract will only result in such cases if the parties engage in conduct that "recognizes the existence of a contract," such as an exchange of performance. Unlike his counterpart under traditional contract principles, however, the offeror who accepts performance in the face of an express rejection or expressly conditional acceptance is not thereby bound to all of the terms contained in the offeree's response. Instead, the Code provides that the terms of a contract created by such performance are those on which the parties' writings *agree*, supplemented by appropriate gap-filling provisions from the Code [2–207(3)].

---

## Union Carbide Corp. v. Oscar Mayer Foods Corp.
### 947 F.2d 1333 (7th Cir. 1991)

Union Carbide sold Oscar Mayer plastic casings that Oscar Mayer uses in manufacturing sausages. The prices in Union Carbide's invoices to Oscar Mayer included two 1 percent sales taxes that are applicable to sales that originate in Chicago. In 1980, another one of Oscar Mayer's suppliers of plastic sausage casings began charging a price that was 1 percent lower than Union Carbide's. This supplier had begun accepting orders at an office outside of Chicago and had decided that therefore it did not have to pay one of the sales taxes. When Oscar Mayer informed Union Carbide of this, Union Carbide instructed its customers to send their orders to an address outside Chicago, too, and it stopped paying both sales taxes and therefore deleted them from the invoices it sent Oscar Mayer. Thus Union Carbide had met and indeed beat the other supplier's discount by lowering its price 2 percent compared to the other supplier's reduction of 1 percent.

In 1988, the Illinois tax authorities decided that the two sales taxes were due notwithstanding the change of address and assessed Union Carbide $88,000 in back taxes on sales to Oscar Mayer and $55,000 in interest on those sales. Union Carbide paid this and then brought this suit to recover what it had paid from Oscar Mayer, claiming that Oscar Mayer had agreed to indemnify it for all sales tax liability. It relied on the following provision printed on the back of its invoices to Oscar Mayer and also in a "price book" that it sent its customers:

In addition to the purchase price, Buyer shall pay Seller the amount of all governmental taxes . . . that Seller may be required to pay with respect to the production, sale or transportation of any materials delivered hereunder.

The trial court granted a summary judgment in favor of Oscar Mayer, and Union Carbide appealed.

---

**Posner, Circuit Judge**    The common law rule was that if the purported acceptance of an offer was not identical to the offer, the acceptance was a fresh offer and had to be expressly accepted by the original offeror for the parties to have a contract. This "mirror image" rule was widely believed to take insufficient account of the incorrigible fallibility of human beings engaged in commercial as in other dealings, and is changed by the Uniform Commercial Code, which allows an acceptance to make a contract even if it adds terms to the offer. Moreover, if it is a contract between "merchants" (in the sense of "pros," UCC section 2–104(1)—as Union Carbide and Oscar Mayer are), the additional terms become part of the contract. But not any additional terms; only those to which the offeror would be unlikely to object, because they fill out the contract in an expectable fashion, and hence do not alter it materially. If a term added by the offeree in his acceptance works a material alteration of the offer, the acceptance is still effective, but the term is not; that is, the contract is enforceable minus the term the offeree tried to add. An alteration is material if consent to it cannot be presumed. What is expectable, hence unsurprising, is okay; what is unexpected, hence surprising, is not.

This is not the end of the analysis, however. Even if the alteration is material, the other party can, of course, decide to accept it. Put differently, consent can be inferred from other things beside the unsurprising character of the new term: even from silence, in the face of a course of dealings that makes it reasonable for the other party to infer consent from a failure to object. An offeror can protect himself against additional terms, material or not, by expressly limiting acceptance to the terms of the offer.

The record does not reveal the origins of Union Carbide's dealings with Oscar Mayer. All we know is that in 1980 the parties' method of dealing was as follows. Oscar Mayer would from time to time send large purchase orders to Union Carbide which would not be filled immediately but instead would be filed for future reference. When Oscar Mayer actually needed casings it would phone Union Carbide and tell it how many it needed and Union Carbide would ship the casings the next day. After the casings arrived Oscar Mayer would send Union Carbide a purchase order for the shipment on the same form used for the standing orders. These "release orders," as the specific purchase orders were called, were like checks written against a bank account—only this was a sausage-casings account. At about the same time that Oscar Mayer sent Union Carbide a release order, Union Carbide would send Oscar Mayer an invoice for the shipment—and the so-called indemnity clause was on the back of the invoice and also in a price book that Union Carbide sent its customers from time to time. So every actual purchase of sausage casings involved an exchange of four documents: the standing order, the price book, the release order, the invoice. Such a pattern of sequential exchange of documents governing a single sale is a prototypical situation for the application of UCC section 2–207. Union Carbide does not question that for purposes of our decision the purchase orders by Oscar Mayer are the offers and Union Carbide's invoices are the acceptances, and that the price book, if it be assumed to be an offer, was never accepted. So the indemnity clause was binding on Oscar Mayer only if the clause did not work a material alteration of the terms in the purchase orders.

Those orders don't exactly *discuss* taxes, but they contain a space for sales tax to be added into the purchase price, and Union Carbide points out that, consistent with this indication of willingness to pay sales tax, Oscar Mayer paid uncomplainingly all sales taxes that appeared on Union Carbide's invoices. If the sales tax rates had risen, Oscar Mayer would have had to pay the higher rates. What difference does it make, asks Union Carbide, if the increase took the form of an assessment of back taxes? It makes a big difference, amounting to a material alteration to which Oscar Mayer did not consent either explicitly or implicitly. If a tax increase showed up on an invoice, Oscar Mayer would have to pay but might then decide to cease buying casings from Union Carbide, as it had every right to do; it did not have a requirements contract with Union Carbide but could switch at will to other suppliers some of whom might not be subject to the tax. To assume responsibility for taxes shown on an individual invoice is quite different from assuming an open-ended, indeed incalculable, liability for back taxes. The tax clause altered the contract materially; and since the clause was at best ambiguous, this is not a case where consent can realistically be inferred from Oscar Mayer's silence in the face of a succession of acceptances (Union Carbide's invoices) containing the new term. There was no breach of contract.

**Judgment affirmed in favor of Oscar Mayer.**

## Acceptance in Unilateral Contracts

A unilateral contract involves the exchange of a promise for an act. To accept an offer to enter such a contract, the offeree must perform the requested act. As you learned in the last chapter, however, courts applying modern contract rules may prevent an offeror from revoking such an offer once the offeree has begun performance. This is achieved by holding either that a bilateral contract is created by the beginning of performance or that the offeror's power to revoke is suspended for the period of time reasonably necessary for the offeree to complete performance.

## Acceptance in Bilateral Contracts

A bilateral contract involves the exchange of a promise for a promise. As a general rule, to accept an offer to enter such a contract, an offeree must *make the promise requested by the offer*. This may be done in a variety of ways. For example, Wallace sends Stevens a detailed offer for the purchase of Stevens's business. Within the time period prescribed by the offer, Stevens sends Wallace a letter that says, "I accept your offer." Stevens has *expressly* accepted Wallace's offer, creating a contract on the terms of the offer. Acceptance, however, can be *implied* as well as express. Offerees who take action that objectively indicates agreement risk the formation of a contract. For example, offerees who act in a manner that is inconsistent with an offeror's ownership of offered property are commonly held to have accepted the offeror's terms. So, if Arnold, a farmer, leaves 10 bushels of corn with Porter, the owner of a grocery store, saying, "Look this corn over. If you want it, it's $5 a bushel," and Porter sells the corn, he has impliedly accepted Arnold's offer. But what if Porter just let the corn sit and, when Arnold returned a week later, Porter told Arnold that he did not want it? Could Porter's failure to act ever amount to an acceptance?

**Silence as Acceptance**   Since contract law generally requires some objective indication that an offeree intends to contract, the general rule is that an offeree's silence, without more, is *not* an acceptance. In addition, it is generally held that an offeror cannot impose on the offeree a duty to respond to the offer. So, even if Arnold made an offer to sell corn to Porter and said, "If I don't hear from you in three days, I'll assume you're buying the corn," Porter's silence would still not amount to acceptance.

On the other hand, the circumstances of a case sometimes impose a duty on the offeree to reject the offer affirmatively or be bound by its terms. These are cases in which the offeree's silence objectively indicates an intent to accept. Customary trade practice or prior dealings between the parties may indicate that silence signals acceptance. So, if Arnold and Porter had dealt with each other on numerous occasions and Porter had always promptly returned items that he did not want, Porter's silent retention of the goods for a week would probably constitute an acceptance. Likewise, an offeree's silence can also operate as an acceptance if the offeree has indicated that it will. For example, Porter (the *offeree*) tells Arnold, "If you don't hear from me in three days, I accept."

Finally, it is generally held that offerees who accept an offeror's performance knowing what the offeror expects in return for his performance have impliedly accepted the offeror's terms. So, if Apex Paving Corporation offers to do the paving work on a new subdivision being developed by Majestic Homes Corporation, and Majestic fails to respond to Apex's offer but allows Apex to do the work, most courts would hold that Majestic is bound by the terms of Apex's offer.

**Acceptance When a Writing Is Anticipated**
Frequently, the parties to a contract intend to prepare a written draft of their agreement for both parties to sign. This is a good idea not only because the law requires written evidence of some contracts,[2] but also because it provides written evidence of the terms of the agreement if a dispute arises at a later date. If a dispute arises before such a writing has been prepared or signed, however, a question may arise concerning whether the signing of the agreement was a necessary condition to the creation of a contract. A party to the agreement who now wants out of the deal may argue that the parties did not intend to be bound until both parties signed the writing. As the following *Texaco* case indicates, a clear expression of such an intent by the parties

---

[2]Chapter 8 discusses this subject in detail.

during the negotiation process prevents the formation of a contract until both parties have signed. However, in the absence of such a clear expression of intent, the courts ask whether a reasonable person familiar with all the circumstances of the parties' negotiations would conclude that the parties intended to be bound only when a formal agreement was signed. If it appears that the parties had concluded their negotiations and reached agreement on all the essential aspects of the transaction, most courts would probably find a contract at the time agreement was reached, even though no formal agreement had been signed.

---

### Texaco, Inc. v. Pennzoil Co.
**729 S.W.2d 768 (Tex. Ct. App. 1987)**

On December 28, 1983, in the wake of well-publicized dissension between the board of directors of Getty Oil Company and Gordon Getty, Pennzoil announced an unsolicited, public tender offer for 16 million shares of Getty Oil at $100 each. Gordon Getty was a director of Getty Oil and the owner, as trustee of the Sarah C. Getty Trust, of 40.2 percent of the 79.1 million outstanding shares of Getty Oil. Shortly thereafter, Pennzoil contacted both Gordon Getty and a representative of the J. Paul Getty Museum, which held 11.8 percent of the shares of Getty Oil, to discuss the tender offer and the possible purchase of Getty Oil.

The parties drafted and signed a Memorandum of Agreement providing that Pennzoil and the Trust (with Gordon Getty as trustee) were to become partners on a 3/7ths to 4/7ths basis, respectively, in owning and operating Getty Oil. The museum was to receive $110 per share for its 11.8 percent ownership, and all other outstanding public shares were to be cashed in by the company at $110 per share. The memorandum provided that it was subject to the approval of Getty Oil's board. On January 2, 1984, the board voted to reject the memorandum price as too low and made a counterproposal to Pennzoil of $110 per share plus a $10 debenture. On January 3, the board received a revised Pennzoil proposal of $110 per share plus a $3 "stub" that was to be paid after the sale of a Getty Oil subsidiary. After discussion, the board voted 15 to 1 to accept Pennzoil's proposal if the stub price was raised to $5. This counteroffer was accepted by Pennzoil later the same day. On January 4, Getty Oil and Pennzoil issued identical press releases announcing an agreement in principle on the terms of the Memorandum of Agreement. Pennzoil's lawyers began working on a formal transaction agreement describing the deal in more detail than the outline of terms contained in the Memorandum of Agreement and press release.

On January 5, the board of Texaco, which had been in contact with Getty Oil's investment banker, authorized its officers to make an offer for 100 percent of Getty Oil's stock. Texaco first contacted the Getty Museum, which, after discussion, agreed to sell its shares to Texaco. Later that evening, Gordon Getty accepted Texaco's offer of $125 per share. On January 6, the Getty Board voted to withdraw its previous counteroffer to Pennzoil and to accept Texaco's offer. Pennzoil later filed suit against Texaco for tortious interference with its contract with the Getty entities. At trial, Texaco argued, among other things, that no contract had existed between Pennzoil and the Getty entities. The jury disagreed, awarding Pennzoil $7.53 billion in actual damages and $3 billion in punitive damages. Texaco appealed.

---

**Warren, Justice**  Texaco contends that there was insufficient evidence to support the jury's finding that at the end of the Getty Oil board meeting on January 3, the Getty entities intended to bind themselves to an agreement with Pennzoil. Pennzoil contends that the evidence showed that the parties intended to be bound to the terms in the Memorandum of Agreement plus a price term of $110 plus a $5 stub, even though the parties may have contemplated a later, more formal document to memorialize the agreement already reached.

If parties do not intend to be bound to an agreement until it is reduced to writing and signed by both parties, then there is no contract until that event occurs. If there is no understanding that a signed writing is necessary before the parties will be bound, and the parties have agreed upon all substantial terms, then an informal agreement can be binding, even though the parties contemplated evidencing their agreement in a formal document later. It is the parties' expressed intent that controls which rule of contract formation applies. Only the outward expressions of intent are considered—secret or subjective intent is immaterial to the question of whether the parties were bound.

Several factors have been articulated to help determine whether the parties intended to be bound only by a formal, signed writing: (1) whether a party expressly reserved the right to be bound only when a written agreement is signed; (2) whether there was any partial performance by one party that the party disclaiming the contract accepted; (3) whether all essential terms of the alleged contract had been agreed upon; and (4) whether the complexity or magnitude of the transaction was such that a formal, executed writing would normally be expected.

Any intent of the parties not to be bound before signing a formal document is not so clearly expressed in the press release to establish, as a matter of law, that there was no contract at that time. The press release does refer to an agreement "in principle" and states that the "transaction" is subject to execution of a definitive merger agreement. But the release as a whole is worded in indicative terms, not in subjunctive or hypothetical ones. The press release describes what shareholders will receive, what Pennzoil will contribute, that Pennzoil will be granted an option, etc.

We find little relevant partial performance in this case that might show that the parties believed that they were bound by a contract. However, the absence of relevant part performance in this short period of time does not compel the conclusion that no contract existed.

There was sufficient evidence for the jury to conclude that the parties had reached agreement on all essential terms of the transaction with only the mechanics and details left to be supplied by the parties' attorneys. Although there may have been many specific items relating to the transaction agreement draft that had yet to be put in final form, there is sufficient evidence to support a conclusion by the jury that the parties did not consider any of Texaco's asserted "open items" significant obstacles precluding an intent to be bound.

Although the magnitude of the transaction here was such that normally a signed writing would be expected, there was sufficient evidence to support an inference by the jury that that expectation was satisfied here initially by the Memorandum of Agreement, signed by a majority of shareholders of Getty Oil and approved by the board with a higher price, and by the transaction agreement in progress that had been intended to memorialize the agreement previously reached.

**Judgment for Pennzoil affirmed.**

*Note:* The court's decision was contingent on a reduction in the punitive damages awarded by the jury from $3 billion to $1 billion. Texaco ultimately sought reorganization under the protection of the Bankruptcy Court and the parties finally settled the case for $3 billion.

## Acceptance of Ambiguous Offers

Although offerors have the power to specify the manner in which their offers can be accepted by requiring that the offeree make a return promise (a bilateral contract) or perform a specific act (a unilateral contract), often an offer is unclear about which form of acceptance is necessary to create a contract. In such a case, both the Code [2–206(1)(a)] and the *Restatement (Second)*[3] suggest that the offer may be accepted in any manner that is *reasonable* in light of the circumstances surrounding the offer. Thus, either a promise to perform or performance, if reasonable, creates a contract.

**Acceptance by Shipment**    The Code specifically elaborates on the rule stated in the preceding section by stating that an order requesting prompt or current shipment of goods may be accepted either by a *prompt promise to ship* or by a *prompt or current shipment* of the goods [2–206(1)(b)]. So, if

---

[3]*Restatement (Second) of Contracts* § 30(2) (1981).

Ampex Corporation orders 500 IBM personal computers from Marks Office Supply, to be shipped immediately, Marks could accept either by promptly promising to ship the goods or by promptly shipping them. If Marks accepts by shipping, any subsequent attempt by Ampex to revoke the order will be ineffective.

What if Marks did not have 500 IBMs in stock and Marks knew that Ampex desperately needed the goods? Marks might be tempted to ship another brand of computers (that is, *nonconforming goods*— goods different from what the buyer ordered), hoping that Ampex would be forced by its circumstances to accept them because by the time they arrived it would be too late to get the correct goods elsewhere. Marks would argue that by shipping the wrong goods it had made a counteroffer because it had not performed the act requested by Ampex's order. If Ampex accepts the goods, Marks could argue that Ampex has impliedly accepted the counteroffer. If Ampex rejects the goods, Marks would arguably have no liability since it did not accept the order.

The Code prevents such a result by providing that prompt shipment of either conforming goods (what the order asked for) or nonconforming goods (something else) operates as an acceptance of the order [2–206(1)(b)]. This protects buyers such as Ampex because sellers who ship the wrong goods have simultaneously accepted their offers and breached the contract by sending the wrong merchandise.[4]

But what if Marks is an honest seller merely trying to help out a customer that has placed a rush order? Must Marks expose itself to liability for breach of contract in the process? The Code prevents such a result by providing that no contract is created if the seller notifies the buyer within a reasonable time that the shipment of nonconforming goods is intended as an accommodation (an attempt to help the buyer) [2–206(1)(b)]. In this case, the shipment is merely a counteroffer that the buyer is free to accept or reject and the seller's notification gives the buyer the opportunity to seek the goods he needs elsewhere.

## Who Can Accept an Offer?

As the masters of their offers, offerees have the right to determine who can bind them to a contract. So, the only person with the legal power to accept an offer and create a contract is the *original offeree*. An attempt to accept by anyone other than the offeree is treated as an offer, because the party attempting to accept is indicating a present intent to contract on the original offer's terms. For example, Price offers to sell his car to Waterhouse for $5,000. Berk learns of the offer, calls Price, and attempts to accept. Berk has made an offer that Price is free to accept or reject.

## COMMUNICATION OF ACCEPTANCE

### Communication Required for Valid Acceptance

To accept an offer for a bilateral contract, the offeree must make the promise requested by the offer. In the Offer chapter, you learned that an offeror must communicate the terms of his proposal to the offeree before an offer results. This is so because communication is a necessary component of the present intent to contract required for the creation of an offer. For similar reasons, it is generally held that an offeree must communicate his intent to be bound by the offer before a contract can be created. To accept an offer for a unilateral contract, however, the offeree must perform the requested act. The traditional contract law rule on this point assumes that the offeror will learn of the offeree's performance and holds that no further notice from the offeree is necessary to create a contract unless the offeror specifically requests notice. The traditional rule can sometimes cause hardship to offerors who may not, in fact, know that the offeree has commenced performance. Neither the Code [section 2–206(2)] nor the *Restatement (Second)* will enforce such a contract against an offeror who has no way of learning of the offeree's performance with reasonable promptness and certainty.[5]

### Manner of Communication

The offeror, as the master of the offer, has the power to specify the precise time, place, and manner in which acceptance must be communicated. This is called a *stipulation*. If the offeror stipulates a particular manner of acceptance, the offeree must respond in this way to form a valid acceptance. Suppose Prompt Printing makes an offer to Jackson

---

[4]Chapter 13 discusses the rights and responsibilities of the buyer and seller following the shipment of nonconforming goods.

[5]*Restatement (Second) of Contract* § 54 (2) (1981).

and the offer states that Jackson must respond by certified mail. If Jackson deviates from the offer's instructions in any significant way, no contract results unless Prompt Printing indicates a willingness to be bound by the deviating acceptance. If, however, the offer merely *suggests* a method or place of communication or is *silent* on such matters, the offeree may accept within a *reasonable time* by *any reasonable means* of communication. So, if Prompt Printing's offer did not *require* any particular manner of accepting the offer, Jackson could accept the offer by any reasonable manner of communication within a reasonable time.

## When Is Acceptance Communicated?

### Acceptances by Instantaneous Forms of Communication

When the parties are dealing face-to-face, by telephone, or by other means of communication that are virtually instantaneous, there are few problems determining when the acceptance was communicated. As soon as the offeree says, "I accept," or words to that effect, a contract is created, assuming that the offer was still in existence at that time.

### Acceptances by Noninstantaneous Forms of Communication

Suppose the circumstances under which the offer was made reasonably lead the offeree to believe that acceptance by some noninstantaneous form of communication is acceptable, and the offeree responds by using mail, telegraph, or some other means of communication that creates a time lag between the dispatching of the acceptance and its actual receipt by the offeror. The practical problems involving the timing of acceptance multiply in such transactions. The offeror may be attempting to revoke the offer while the offeree is attempting to accept it. An acceptance may get lost and never be received by the offeror. The time limit for accepting the offer may be rapidly approaching. Was the offer accepted before a revocation was received or before the offer expired? Does a lost acceptance create a contract when it is dispatched, or is it totally ineffective?

Under the so-called "mailbox rule," properly addressed and dispatched acceptances can become effective when they are *dispatched*, even if they are lost and never received by the offeror. The mailbox rule, which is discussed further in the following *Casto v. State Farm Mutual Insurance Co.* case,

protects the offeree's reasonable belief that a binding contract was created when the acceptance was dispatched. By the same token, it exposes the offeror to the risk of being bound by an acceptance that she has never received. The offeror, however, has the ability to minimize this risk by stipulating in her offer that she must actually receive the acceptance for it to be effective. Offerors who do this maximize the time that they have to revoke their offers and ensure that they will never be bound by an acceptance that they have not received.

### Operation of the Mailbox Rule: Traditional Rules

Under traditional contract law, the mailbox rule makes acceptances effective upon dispatch when the offeree used a manner of communication that was expressly or impliedly **authorized** (invited) by the offeror. Any manner of communication *suggested* by the offeror (e.g., "You may respond by mail") would be *expressly* authorized, resulting in an acceptance sent by the suggested means being effective on dispatch. Unless circumstances indicated to the contrary, a manner of communication *used by the offeror in making the offer* would be *impliedly* authorized (e.g., an offer sent by mail would impliedly authorize an acceptance by mail), as would a manner of communication common in the parties' trade or business (e.g., a trade usage in the parties' business that offers are made by mail and accepted by telegram would authorize an acceptance by telegram). Conversely, an improperly dispatched acceptance or one that was sent by some means of communication that was *nonauthorized* would be effective when *received*, assuming that the offer was still open at that time. This placed on the offeree the risk of the offer being revoked or the acceptance being lost.

### Operation of the Mailbox Rule: Modern Rules

Under both the UCC and the *Restatement (Second) of Contracts*, an offer that does not indicate otherwise is considered to invite acceptance by *any reasonable means* of communication, and a properly dispatched acceptance sent by a reasonable means of communication within a reasonable time is effective on dispatch. What is reasonable depends on the circumstances in which the offer was made. These include the speed and reliability of the means used by the offeree, the nature of the transaction (e.g., does the agreement involve goods subject to rapid price fluctuations?), the existence of any trade usage governing the transaction, and the existence of prior dealings between the parties (e.g., has the offeree previously used the mail to accept telegraphed offers from the offeror?). So, under proper circumstances, a mailed response to a telegraphed offer or a telegraphed response to a mailed offer might be considered reasonable and therefore effective on dispatch.

What if an offeree attempts to accept the offer by some means that is *unreasonable* under the circumstances or if the acceptance is not properly addressed or dispatched (e.g., misaddressed or accompanied by insufficient postage)? Modern contract law rejects the traditional rule that such acceptances cannot be effective until received. Under both the Code [1–201(38)] and section 67 of the *Restatement (Second)*, an acceptance sent by an unreasonable means would be effective on dispatch *if* it is received within the time that an acceptance by a reasonable means would normally have arrived. The *Casto* case shows what happens when an improperly dispatched acceptance is not received within the time that a properly dispatched acceptance would have been.

---

## Casto v. State Farm Mutual Insurance Co.

### 594 N.E.2d 1004 (Ct. App. Ohio 1991)

In 1985, State Farm issued Deborah Casto an automobile insurance policy on her Jaguar. Casto also insured a second car, a Porsche, with State Farm. Sometime in September or early October 1987, Casto received two renewal notices, indicating that the next premium was due on October 10, 1987. State Farm sent a notice of cancellation on October 16, indicating that the policy would be canceled on October 29. Casto denied having received this notice. On October 20, Casto placed two checks, one for the Jaguar and one for the Porsche, in two preaddressed envelopes that had been supplied by State Farm. She gave these envelopes to Donald Dick, who mailed them on the same day. The envelope containing the Porsche payment was timely delivered to State Farm, but State Farm never received the Jaguar payment, and that policy was canceled.

Casto was involved in an accident on November 20 while driving the Jaguar. When she made a claim with State Farm, she learned that the policy had been canceled. After the accident, the envelope containing the Jaguar payment was returned to her stamped "Returned for postage." Casto brought this declaratory judgment action seeking a declaration that her insurance policy was in effect as of the date of the accident. The trial court rendered a judgment for State Farm and Casto appealed.

---

**Reilly, Presiding Judge** The facts indicate that while the payment was mailed before October 29, it was not received by the insurance company. The issue then is whether the insurance premium is effectively paid on the day it was mailed or the day it is received by the company.

An insurance policy is a contract and the relationship between the insurer and its insured is contractual in nature. The renewal of an insurance policy is generally considered a new contract of insurance to which the requirements of offer and acceptance apply. The well-established general rule of contract formation is that an acceptance transmitted in a form invited by the offer is operative as soon as it is put out of the offeree's possession, regardless of whether it ever reaches the offeror. This is the so-called "mailbox rule" which states that in the absence of any limitation to the contrary in the offer, an acceptance is effective when mailed. One of the parties must bear the risk of loss. As the offeror has the power to condition acceptance of the offer on actual receipt, the courts have uniformly held that, in the absence of language to the contrary, an acceptance is effective when mailed.

To be effective upon mailing, however, the acceptance must be properly dispatched. The offeree must properly address the acceptance and take whatever other precautions as are ordinarily observed in the transmission of similar messages. It is undisputed that State Farm provided Casto with pre-addressed envelopes and thus authorized her to mail her premium payments. Furthermore, the renewal notices contain no language requiring actual receipt before payment is deemed effective. Finally, Casto and Donald Dick testified in their depositions that the Jaguar and Porsche payments were mailed on October 20, 1987, nine days before the cancellation date. Their testimony is further supported by the fact that the Porsche payment was actually received by State Farm before the cancellation date. Thus, the only remaining question is whether the payment was properly dispatched.

Casto testified that the check and renewal notice were placed in a pre-addressed and stamped envelope. Donald Dick also testified that both envelopes were stamped when he mailed them. Nevertheless, the envelope did not bear any postage when it was returned to Casto. Casto bore the burden of proving that the envelope was stamped when it was mailed. When the findings of fact leave some material fact undetermined, a reviewing court will presume that the issue of fact was not proved by the party having the burden of proof. We thus presume that the trial court concluded that the envelope was not stamped when mailed, and there is sufficient evidence in the record to support such a finding. As the envelope was not properly dispatched, the payment was not effective upon mailing under the facts of this case.

**Judgment affirmed in favor of State Farm.**

**Stipulated Means of Communication** As we discussed earlier, an offer may stipulate the means of communication that the offeree must use to accept by saying, in effect: "You must accept by mail." An acceptance by the stipulated means of communication is effective on dispatch, just like an acceptance by any other reasonable or authorized means of communication (see Figure 2). The difference

**FIGURE 2** Time of Acceptance

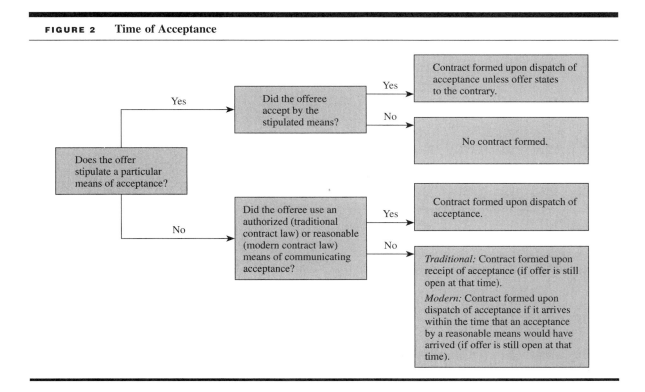

is that an acceptance by other than the stipulated means does not create a contract because it is an acceptance at variance with the terms of the offer.

**Contradictory Offeree Responses**    How do these rules work when the offeree sends mixed signals to the offeror? Suppose Case mails a counteroffer to White, impliedly rejecting an offer that White has made to him, and then, before White receives the rejection, Case mails a letter of acceptance. Is a contract formed? In the last chapter, you learned that Case's counteroffer (that is, rejection) would not be effective to terminate White's offer until White actually *receives* it. If we applied the normal rules of offer and acceptance to these facts, we might conclude that the parties had a contract because Case's acceptance by mail was effective on dispatch. White, however, might receive Case's counteroffer and sell the house to a third party before he receives Case's acceptance. To prevent

such an unfair result, most courts hold that when an offeree dispatches an acceptance after first dispatching a rejection, the acceptance does not create a contract unless it is received before the rejection. Therefore, if White receives the counteroffer before he receives the acceptance, no contract results. If, on the other hand, he receives the acceptance before receiving the counteroffer, a contract results.

What is the result if Case had first mailed White an acceptance, then changed his mind and shortly thereafter mailed White a rejection? Applying normal offer and acceptance rules to these facts, we would conclude that Case's acceptance was effective on dispatch and that Case no longer had the power to reject the offer. But the application of these rules would result in unfairness if White received Case's rejection first and relied on it by selling to someone else. In such a situation, Case would be *estopped* from enforcing the contract due to White's reliance.

### CONCEPT REVIEW
### CONTRADICTORY OFFEREE RESPONSES

| Offeree Sends First | Offeree Sends Second | Offeror Receives First | Result |
|---|---|---|---|
| Rejection | Acceptance | Rejection | No contract |
| Rejection | Acceptance | Acceptance | Contract |
| Acceptance | Rejection | Rejection | If offeror relied on rejection, offeree is estopped from enforcing the contract |
| Acceptance | Rejection | Acceptance | Contract |

### PROBLEMS AND PROBLEM CASES

**1.** Since 1974, Lone Star Donut Company had placed orders for its sugar requirements with Great Western Sugar Co. (GWS) through a sugar broker. In October 1980, GWS adopted a new policy of requiring a letter agreement for each order. The first such letter was forwarded from GWS to Lone Star

by the broker on October 9, 1980. It concluded with the following language:

This letter is a written confirmation of our agreement, and unless it is signed by the buyer and returned to Great Western within 15 days of the date hereof, the agreement shall be deemed breached by Buyer and automatically terminated. Please sign and return to me the enclosed counterpart of this letter signalling your acceptance of the above agreement.

Lone Star signed and returned this letter. On December 2, Lone Star again ordered sugar. GWS initially neglected to send a letter agreement, finally doing so in late January 1981, in response to prodding by the broker. This letter concluded as follows:

This letter is a written confirmation of our agreement. Please sign and return to me the enclosed counterpart of this letter signalling your acceptance of the above agreement.

Lone Star, angered over the delay, refused to sign and subsequently refused to purchase sugar. Was a contract formed?

**2.** First Texas Savings Association promoted a "$5,000 Scoreboard Challenge" contest. Contestants who completed an entry form and deposited it with First Texas were eligible for a random drawing. The winner was to receive an $80 savings account with First Texas, plus four tickets to a Dallas Mavericks home basketball game chosen by First Texas. If the Mavericks held their opponent in the chosen game to 89 or fewer points, the winner was to receive an additional $5,000 money market certificate. In October 1982, Jergins deposited a completed entry form with First Texas. On November 1, 1982, First Texas tried to amend the contest rules by posting notice at its branches that the Mavericks would have to hold their opponent to 85 or fewer points before the contest winner would receive the $5,000. In late December, Jergins was notified that she had won the $80 savings account and tickets to the January 22, 1983, game against the Utah Jazz. The notice contained the revised contest terms. The Mavericks held the Jazz to 88 points. Was Jergins entitled to the $5,000?

**3.** In April 1973, in response to a request from Mobil Chemical for a bid on a two-sided precoater, Egan Machinery submitted a "quotation" describing the components of the precoater and the details of its operation. The quotation stated a price for the precoater but did not contain conditions of sale. In May 1973, Mobil sent Egan a purchase order for the precoater. The purchase order contained the following language:

Important—this order expressly limits acceptance to terms stated herein, and any additional or different terms proposed by the seller are rejected unless expressly agreed to in writing.

Egan responded with an order acknowledgment in May 1973, which provided that:

This order is accepted on the condition that our Standard Conditions of Sale, which are attached hereto and made a part hereof, are accepted by you, notwithstanding any modifying or additive conditions contained on your purchase order. Receipt of this acknowledgment by you without prompt written objection thereto shall constitute an acceptance of these terms and conditions.

One of the terms included in Egan's Standard Conditions required Mobil to indemnify Egan against any liability Egan might incur to persons injured by the precoater if the injury resulted from Mobil's failure to require its employees to follow safety procedures and/or use safety devices while operating it. When a Mobil employee who was injured while operating the precoater later won a $75,000 judgment against Egan, Egan filed suit against Mobil seeking indemnity. Did the indemnity clause become part of the contract?

**4.** Atwood bought a new pickup truck from Best Buick. When he took it home, his wife objected to the purchase. Atwood returned the car to Best, which agreed to take the truck back as a trade-in on another vehicle. Atwood traded for a new station wagon, which he registered and insured and sought to title in his name. When he took the car home, however, his wife objected to the color of its interior. Atwood returned the car to Best, but refused to accept any of the numerous other vehicles Best made available to him. He also refused to sign an application that would allow Best to retrieve the title to the car so it could sell it to someone else. Best then told him that unless he removed the car from its premises it would charge him a $5 per day storage fee. The Atwoods later sued Best for the return of the purchase price. Best counterclaimed for the storage fee. Should the Atwoods prevail?

**5.** Western Tire, Inc., had a lease on a building owned by the Skredes that was due to expire on April 30, 1978. The lease gave Western the right to renew the lease for an additional five-year term if the Skredes were given written notice of Western's intent to renew at least 30 days prior to the expiration date. It also specifically provided that notice would only be effective when it was deposited in a U.S. Post Office by registered or certified mail. On February 27, Western's attorney sent the Skredes a notice of Western's intent to renew by ordinary mail, which the Skredes did not receive until after April 1, 1978. On April 5, 1978, Western's lawyer, discovering his mistake, sent a second notice by certified mail. On April 14, 1978, the Skredes told Western that the lease was canceled. Did they have the right to cancel?

**6.** On January 16, 1987, Koop, an employee of Professional Search, Inc., called Renner, the director of systems software for Northwest Airlines, to inquire about possible job openings in Renner's department. Koop explained to Renner that if Northwest Airlines hired a candidate recommended by Professional Search, Professional Search would be entitled to charge Northwest Airlines 30 percent of the candidate's starting salary. Renner told Koop that a systems analyst position was open and described the job. Renner also stated that Northwest Airlines was not currently interviewing for that position and that Koop should direct further inquiries to Northwest Airlines's human resources department. Later, Koop and Wawrzyniak discussed Wawrzyniak's desire to be placed as a systems analyst and Wawrzyniak signed a placement contract. On January 20, 1987, Koop sent Wawrzyniak's résumé to Renner. Koop later called Renner, who told him the résumé "looked good." On February 19, Wawrzyniak filled out an application for a systems position with Northwest Airlines, claiming he heard of the opening through a friend. On April 13, Northwest Airlines hired Wawrzyniak. Professional Search claimed that a placement contract had been formed between it and Northwest Airlines, and sought to recover its $12,000 commission. Will Professional Search prevail?

**7.** In 1986, Mercy Memorial Hospital decided to open an outpatient family practice clinic in Petersburg. It retained a recruiter to identify a private family practitioner. The recruiter brought the hospital and Dr. Kamalnath together. In June 1986, Iacoangeli, the hospital's director of planning and development, wrote Dr. Kamalnath a letter in which he made an offer to her that proposed terms regarding salary, office rental, line of credit for professional and operational expenses, home relocation, and other matters. Dr. Kamalnath did not accept this written offer. Instead, she suggested various changes and additions, principally an increase in the term of employment to three years and a provision that the hospital handle marketing. On June 30, Iacoangeli sent Dr. Kamalnath a second letter incorporating the longer period of employment, subject to annual performance reviews, and proposing other terms. Iacoangeli also prepared several drafts of a proposed contract, but none of these proved satisfactory to Dr. Kamalnath. Dr. Kamalnath nevertheless moved to Petersburg and began work, although she had no signed contract, the parties still differed as to some contractual duties such as the responsibility for certain major expenses, and the clinic was not yet complete. The Petersburg clinic was not as successful as the parties had hoped. Relations between them deteriorated, and the hospital notified Dr. Kamalnath to vacate the clinic in November 1987. Was there a contract between the hospital and Dr. Kamalnath?

**8.** On March 30, Cushing, a member of an antinuclear protest group, applied to the New Hampshire adjutant general's office for permission to hold a dance in the Portsmouth armory. On March 31, the adjutant general mailed a signed contract offer agreeing to rent the armory to the group. The agreement required Cushing to accept by signing a copy of the agreement and returning it to the adjutant general within five days after its receipt. On April 3, Cushing received the offer and signed it. At 6:30 P.M. on April 4, Cushing received a call from the adjutant general attempting to revoke the offer. Cushing told the adjutant general that he had signed the contract and placed it in the office outbox on April 3, customary office practice being to collect all mail from outboxes at the end of the day and deposit it in the U.S. mail. On April 6, the adjutant general's office received the signed contract in the mail, dated April 3 and postmarked April 5. Assuming Cushing was telling the truth, did the parties have a contract?

**9.** Krack Corporation bought steel tubing from Metal-Matic for 10 years. The parties' usual practice was for Krack to send Metal-Matic purchase orders to which Metal-Matic would respond by sending an acknowledgment form and shipping the requested tubing. Metal-Matic's form provided that its acceptance was "expressly made" conditional on Krack's assent to the acknowledgment's terms, which included a clause limiting Metal-Matic's liability for consequential damages due to breach of warranty. Krack sold a cooling unit it had made with Metal-Matic's tubing to Diamond Fruit. The tubing was defective, causing losses to Diamond's fruit. When Diamond sued Krack, Krack sought indemnity from Metal-Matic. Metal-Matic argued that it was not responsible, citing the consequential damages clause in its acknowledgment. Was that clause part of the contract between Krack and Metal-Matic?

**10.** Soldau was fired by Organon, Inc. He received a letter from Organon offering to pay him double the normal severance pay if he would sign a release giving up all claims against the company. The letter incorporated the proposed release, which Soldau signed, dated, and deposited in a mailbox outside a post office. When he returned home, Soldau found that he had received a check from Organon in the amount of the increased severance pay. He returned to the post office and persuaded a postal employee to open the mailbox and retrieve the release. Soldau cashed Organon's check and subsequently filed an age discrimination suit against Organon. Was Soldau bound by the release?

## CAPSTONE QUESTIONS

Bylow Corporation, a clothing manufacturer, is involved in the following disputes:

- Bylow received a signed purchase order from Zippi & Company, a retailer of men's clothing, for 50 of a particular style of white cotton shirt. The purchase order requested rush delivery. Bylow did not have that particular style in stock, so it shipped another style of white cotton shirt along with a memorandum stating that it was shipping the different style of shirt as an accommodation to Zippi. Zippi rejected the shirts shipped by Bylow and now claims that Bylow is in breach of contract.
- Using its standard purchase order form, Bylow ordered a stated quantity of buttons from a button manufacturer, Kenyon Corporation. Kenyon promptly sent back an acknowledgment form stating unconditionally that it would ship the buttons to Bylow under the terms proposed by Bylow. The acknowledgment form that Kenyon sent to Bylow also contained a provision requiring Bylow to obtain a written return authorization from Kenyon before returning any goods in order to receive full

credit for returned goods. Bylow was dissatisfied with the buttons and returned them without first receiving a return authorization from Kenyon. Kenyon has invoiced Bylow for part of the cost of the buttons. Bylow claims that no contract was formed because Kenyon's acceptance added a new term, or, if a contract was formed, the return authorization provision did not become part of the contract.

- On October 1, 1995, Bylow made a written offer to sell one of its warehouses to Samson Foods Corporation for $250,000. The offer stated that acceptance must be made by certified mail and must be received by Bylow by October 8, 1995. The following events then occurred:
  a. On October 2, Samson mailed a letter of acceptance by regular first-class mail.
  b. On October 4, Bylow received an offer to purchase the warehouse from Cutko Corporation for $325,000. This offer stated that "Your failure to reject this offer by October 7 will signify your acceptance." Bylow did not respond to this offer.
  c. On October 4, Bylow telephoned Samson and notified it that Bylow's offer to sell the warehouse to Samson was revoked.
  d. On October 5, Bylow received a written offer to purchase the warehouse for $335,000 from Deadbolt Security and immediately accepted this offer.
  e. The U.S. Postal Service misplaced Samson's letter of acceptance for several weeks and delivered it to Bylow on October 16.
  f. Both Samson and Cutko claim to have enforceable contracts to purchase the warehouse.

## Required:

Answer the following and give reasons for your conclusions.

1. Assess Zippi's claim that Bylow is in breach of contract.
2. State whether Bylow's claims in relation to its contract with Kenyon are correct.
3. State whether Samson's and Cutko's claims are correct.

# CHAPTER
## 4

# CONSIDERATION

**INTRODUCTION**

*One of the things that separates a contract from an unenforceable social promise is that a contract requires voluntary agreement by two or more parties. Not all agreements, however, are enforceable contracts. At a fairly early point in the development of classical contract law, the common law courts decided not to enforce gratuitous (free) promises. Instead, only promises supported by consideration were enforceable in a court of law. This was consistent with the notion that the purpose of contract law was to enforce freely made bargains. As one 19th-century work on contracts put it: "The common law . . . gives effect only to contracts that are founded on the mutual exigencies of men, and does not compel the performance of any merely gratuitous agreements."[1] The concept of consideration distinguishes agreements that the law will enforce from gratuitous promises, which are normally unenforceable. This chapter focuses on the concept of consideration.*

## THE IDEA OF CONSIDERATION

A common definition of **consideration** is *legal value, bargained for and given in exchange for an act or a promise*. Thus, a promise generally cannot be enforced against the person who made it (the *promisor*) unless the person to whom the promise was made (the *promisee*) has given up something of legal value in exchange for the promise. In effect, the requirement of consideration means that a promisee must pay the price that the promisor asked to gain the right to enforce the promisor's promise. So, if the promisor did not ask for anything in exchange for making her promise or if what the promisor asked for did not have legal value (e.g., because it was something to which she was already entitled), her promise is not enforceable against her because it is not supported by consideration. Figure 1 graphically illustrates the elements of consideration.

Consider the early case of *Thorne v. Deas*, in which the part owner of a sailing ship named the *Sea Nymph* promised his co-owners that he would insure the ship for an upcoming voyage.[2] He failed

[1]T. Metcalf, *Principles of the Law of Contracts* (1874), p. 161.
[2]4 Johns. 84 (N.Y. 1809).

## FIGURE 1    The Elements of Consideration

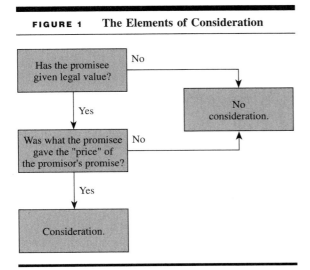

to do so, and when the ship was lost at sea, the court found that he was not liable to his co-owners for breaching his promise to insure the ship. Why? Because his promise was purely gratuitous; he had neither asked for nor received anything in exchange for making it. Therefore, it was unenforceable because it was not supported by consideration.

This early example illustrates two important aspects of the consideration requirement. First, the requirement *tended to limit the scope of a promisor's liability for his promises* by insulating him from liability for gratuitous promises and by protecting him against liability for reliance on such promises. Second, the mechanical application of the requirement *often produced unfair results*. This potential for unfairness has produced considerable dissatisfaction with the consideration concept. As the rest of this chapter indicates, the relative importance of consideration in modern contract law has been somewhat eroded by numerous exceptions to the consideration requirement and by judicial applications of consideration principles designed to produce fair results.

## LEGAL VALUE

Consideration can be an act in the case of a unilateral contract or a promise in the case of a bilateral contract. An act or a promise can have legal value in one of two ways. If, in exchange for the promisor's promise, the promisee does, or agrees to

do, something he had no prior legal duty to do, that provides legal value. If, in exchange for the promisor's promise, the promisee refrains from doing, or agrees not to do, something she has a legal right to do, that also provides legal value. Note that this definition does not require that an act or a promise have monetary (economic) value to amount to consideration. Thus, in a famous 19th-century case, *Hamer v. Sidway*,[3] an uncle's promise to pay his nephew $5,000 if he refrained from using tobacco, drinking, swearing, and playing cards or billiards for money until his 21st birthday was held to be supported by consideration. Indeed, the nephew had refrained from doing any of these acts, even though he may have benefited from so refraining. He had a legal right to indulge in such activities, yet he had refrained from doing so at his uncle's request and in exchange for his uncle's promise. This was all that was required for consideration. *Lyon v. Reames Foods, Inc.*, which appears later in this chapter, elaborates on the different forms that legal value can take.

## Adequacy of Consideration

The point that the legal value requirement is not concerned with actual value is further borne out by the fact that the courts generally will not concern themselves with questions regarding the adequacy of the consideration that the promisee gave. This means that as long as the promisee's act or promise satisfies the legal value test, the courts do not ask whether that act or promise was worth what the promisor gave, or promised to give, in return for it. This rule on adequacy of consideration reflects the laissez-faire assumptions underlying classical contract law. Freedom of contract includes the freedom to make bad bargains as well as good ones, so promisors' promises are enforceable if they got what they asked for in exchange for making their promises, even if what they asked for was not nearly so valuable in worldly terms as what they promised in return. Also, a court taking a hands-off stance concerning private contracts would be reluctant to step in and second-guess the parties by setting aside a transaction that both parties at one time considered satisfactory. Finally, the rule against considering the adequacy of consideration can promote certainty and predictability in commercial transactions by

[3]27 N.E. 256 (N.Y. Ct. App. 1891).

denying legal effect to what would otherwise be a possible basis for challenging the enforceability of a contract—the inequality of the exchange.

Several qualifications must be made concerning the general rule on adequacy of consideration. First, if the inadequacy of consideration is apparent on the face of the agreement, most courts conclude that the agreement was a disguised gift rather than an enforceable bargain. Thus, an agreement calling for an unequal exchange of money (e.g., $500 for $1,000) or identical goods (20 business law textbooks for 40 identical business law textbooks) and containing no other terms would probably be unenforceable. Gross inadequacy of consideration may also give rise to an inference of fraud, duress,[4] lack of capacity,[5] unconscionability,[6] or some other independent basis for setting aside a contract. However, inadequacy of consideration, standing alone, is never sufficient to prove lack of true consent or contractual capacity. Although gross inadequacy of consideration is not, by itself, ordinarily a sufficient reason to set aside a contract, the courts may refuse to grant specific performance or other equitable remedies to persons seeking to enforce unfair bargains.

Finally, some agreements recite "$1," or "$1 and other valuable consideration," or some other small amount as consideration for a promise. If no other consideration is actually exchanged, this is called *nominal consideration*. Often, such agreements are attempts to make gratuitous promises look like true bargains by reciting a nonexistent consideration. Most courts refuse to enforce such agreements unless they find that the stated consideration was truly bargained for.

## Illusory Promises

For a promise to serve as consideration in a bilateral contract, the promisee must have promised to do, or to refrain from doing, something at the promisor's request. It seems obvious, therefore, that if the promisee's promise is illusory because it really does not bind the promisee to do or refrain from doing anything, such a promise could not serve as consideration. Such agreements are often said to lack the

mutuality of obligation required for an agreement to be enforceable. So, a promisee's promise to buy "all the sugar that I want" or to "paint your house if I feel like it" would not be sufficient consideration for a promisor's return promise to sell sugar or hire a painter. In neither case has the promisee given the promisor anything of legal value in exchange for the promisor's promise. Remember, though: So long as the promisee has given legal value, the agreement will be enforceable even though what the promisee gave is worth substantially less than what the promisor promised in return.

**Cancellation or Termination Clauses**    The fact that an agreement allows one or both of the parties to cancel or terminate their contractual obligations does not necessarily mean that the party (or parties) with the power to cancel has given an illusory promise. Such provisions are a common and necessary part of many business relationships. The central issue in such cases concerns whether a promise subject to cancellation or termination actually represents a binding obligation. A right to cancel or terminate at any time, for any reason, and without any notice would clearly render illusory any other promise by the party possessing such a right. However, limits on the circumstances under which cancellation may occur, such as a dealer's failure to live up to dealership obligations, or the time in which cancellation may occur (such as no cancellations for the first 90 days), or a requirement of advance notice of cancellation (such as a 30-day notice requirement) would all effectively remove a promise from the illusory category. This is so because in each case the party making such a promise has bound himself to do *something* in exchange for the other party's promise.

Of course, some parties to agreements may not want their agreements to amount to binding contracts. For example, a manufacturer selling through a system of independent retail dealers may want to retain maximum flexibility by giving itself a unilateral right to terminate a dealer at any time, for any reason, without notice. Such an "intentional no contract" strategy relies on the fact that the manufacturer's greater bargaining power may allow it to impose such terms on its dealers. This kind of business strategy is very difficult, if not impossible, to pursue today, however, given the numerous "dealer day in court" statutes that past abuses have

---

[4]Fraud and duress are discussed in Chapter 5.

[5]Lack of capacity is discussed in Chapter 6.

[6]Chapter 7 discusses unconscionability in detail.

produced and the fact that many courts have stricken down unilateral cancellation clauses as unconscionable. As you will see in the following *Lyon* case, a party's duty of good faith and fair dealing can limit the right to terminate and prevent its promise from being considered illusory.

---

## LYON v. REAMES FOODS, INC.
### 1992 U.S. Dist. LEXIS 4184 (U.S. Dist. Ct. Kan. 1992)

William Reames, president and sole shareholder of Reames Foods, recruited and hired Donald Lyon to be a salesperson for the company. Before joining Reames Foods, Lyon had been employed by and was a part owner in the Certified Meat Company. Lyon claims that when Reames approached him about joining the company, he had been concerned about the possibility that Reames might decide to sell the company in the future. Lyon did not want to help build the company's sales over time and then be subject to termination by a new owner after the company was sold. Lyon claimed that he received from Reames and Reames Foods an oral agreement guaranteeing him employment for five years after a change in ownership of the company, but the existence of such an agreement was denied by Reames Foods. Lyon asserted that, in reliance on this oral contract, he sold his ownership interest in the Certified Meat Company, quit his old job, and joined Reames Foods in April 1976.

Lyon attempted to get the terms of the alleged oral contract with Reames Foods reduced to writing, but Reames continually put off his requests. Finally, at a meeting in November 1977, after several discussions between Reames and Lyon, Reames handed to Lyon a copy of a document entitled "Work Agreement." This document, which Lyon claims sets forth the terms of the earlier oral agreement, was typed on Reames Foods's letterhead, and was signed by Reames as president and agent of Reames Foods. The document provided in part that:

it is agreed that in event of the sale of the company . . . we of REAMES FOODS, INC. do guarantee and assure Donald F. Lyon of five (5) years continued employment at a minimum of his current salary effective at such time. . . . Donald Lyon agrees that he will, during such period of time, maintain all of his efforts in working for the company and will be employed by no other party during said period of time and said employment may be discontinued at any time if said Donald F. Lyon fails to perform his work in a manner satisfactory to the Board of Directors.

The document was signed by Reames, but was not signed by Lyon. Reames and Reames Foods claim that this document was merely one of many proposals and counterproposals considered by Lyon and Reames, and that it does not amount to an enforceable contract in itself.

Reames sold Reames Foods to the T. Marzetti Company in October 1989. In December 1989, Lyon was terminated. Lyon sued Reames and Reames Foods for breach of contract, among other claims. Lyon sought summary judgment asking the court to determine whether there was an enforceable contract and whether various defenses asserted by the defendants, including lack of consideration, could be maintained.

---

**Lungstrom, District Judge**    It is elementary that, as a general rule, in order for a promise to be legally enforceable as a contract there must be consideration. Consideration can be either a benefit given or to be given to the promisee, a forbearance experienced or to be experienced by the promisor, or mutual promises. Reames Foods contends that the agreement did not require Lyon to give anything of value to Reames Foods in consideration for his alleged employment guarantee. Yet, assuming that an agreement between the parties was reached, the written memorialization, signed by William Reames, requires that Lyon give up his right to work for another employer during the five years that his employment would be guaranteed. If the condition contained in the agreement occurred, i.e., if Reames Foods was sold, Lyon promised to work exclusively for that company in exchange for

Reames Foods's promise to assure Lyon of a job for five years. Lyon's promised forbearance would be consideration for Reames Foods's promised employment. In addition, however, Lyon gave up a job and an ownership interest in his former employer in order to join Reames Foods. Therefore, Reames Foods's contention that any alleged agreement was not supported by sufficient consideration is unfounded.

Reames Foods argues that, even if the alleged agreement was supported by consideration, it is unenforceable because it is illusory. According to Reames Foods, it could have terminated Lyon just before a sale of the company was finalized and thereby avoided all liability to him. If a promise is illusory it cannot be sufficient consideration to support a contract. Professor Farnsworth has recognized that promises which allow the promisor to terminate its rights and duties at any time will, without more, have been held to be illusory. He notes, however, that when the promisor retains the power to terminate, but only within a period of time after which it loses this power, the promise is not illusory "if the period expires without either party manifesting an intention not to be bound." E. Farnsworth, Contracts, section 2.14, at 81 (2d ed. 1990). This is exactly the case here. Although Reames Foods may have had the ability to terminate the alleged contract before ownership of the company was transferred, it failed to do so. After this triggering event came and passed without Reames Foods exercising its option to fire Lyon, it became bound to fulfill its obligations under the contract.

Moreover, it also appears that the promise was not illusory from its original making. Lyon argues that Reames Foods was not free to fire him at any time before the company was sold. The court agrees. Iowa law recognizes an implied obligation in all contracts requiring that the party for whom performance will be done will not obstruct, hinder, or delay the other party to the contract from completing his or her obligations under the contract. The current trend among courts is to read such obligations into allegedly illusory promises in order to make them enforceable. Contrary to its assertion, Reames Foods did not possess an unbridled right to terminate Lyon before a sale of the company in order to avoid liability to him. There were sufficient legal constraints on Reames Foods's ability to fire Lyon that this alleged agreement is not illusory.

Reames Foods contends that Lyon never signed [the written document] or otherwise manifested the intention to accept it. It is obvious that genuine issues of fact remain regarding whether the written document delivered to Lyon constitutes an enforceable contract. Resolution should be by the trier of fact, not by the court on a motion for summary judgment. If the trier of fact determines that the parties intended to enter into a contract and that sufficient assent was manifested, the agreement between the parties would be enforceable.

**Summary judgment granted in part in favor of Lyon and denied in part.**

*Note:* The case was tried several months later, and the court found in favor of Lyon, awarding him $234,144.82 in damages.

---

**Output and Requirements Contracts**   Contracts in which one party to the agreement agrees to buy all of the other party's production of a particular commodity (*output* contracts) or to supply all of another party's needs for a particular commodity (*requirements* contracts) are common business transactions that serve legitimate business purposes. They can reduce a seller's selling costs and provide buyers with a secure source of supply. Prior to the enactment of the UCC, however, many common law courts used to refuse to enforce such agreements on the ground that their failure to specify the quantity of goods to be produced or purchased rendered them illusory. The courts also feared that a party to such an agreement might be tempted to exploit the other party. For example, subsequent market conditions could make it profitable for the seller in an output contract or the buyer in a requirements contract to demand that the other party buy or provide more of the particular commodity than the other party had actually intended to buy or sell. The Code legitimizes requirements and output contracts. It addresses the concern about the potential for exploitation by limiting a party's demands to those quantity needs that occur in *good faith* and are not unreasonably disproportionate to any quantity estimate contained in the contract, or to any normal prior output or requirements if no estimate is stated [2–306(1)]. Chapter 11, Formation and Terms of Sales Contracts, discusses this subject in greater detail.

**Exclusive Dealing Contracts**    When a manufacturer of goods enters an agreement giving a distributor the exclusive right to sell the manufacturer's products in a particular territory, does such an agreement impose sufficient obligations on both parties to meet the legal value test? Put another way, does the distributor have any duty to sell the manufacturer's products and does the manufacturer have any duty to supply any particular number of products? Such agreements are commonly encountered in today's business world, and they can serve the legitimate interests of both parties. The Code recognizes this fact by providing that, unless the parties agree to the contrary, an exclusive dealing contract imposes a duty on the distributor to use her best efforts to sell the goods and imposes a reciprocal duty on the manufacturer to use his best efforts to supply the goods [2–306(2)].

## Preexisting Duties

The legal value component of our consideration definition requires that promisees do, or promise to do, something in exchange for a promisor's promise that they had no prior legal duty to do. Thus, as a general rule, performing or agreeing to perform a preexisting duty is not consideration. This seems fair because the promisor in such a case has effectively made a gratuitous promise, since she was already entitled to the promisee's performance.

**Preexisting Public Duties**    Every member of society has a duty to obey the law and refrain from committing crimes or torts. Therefore, a promisee's promise not to commit such an act can never be consideration. So, Thomas's promise to pay Brown $100 a year in exchange for Brown's promise not to burn Thomas's barn would not be enforceable against Thomas. Since Brown has a preexisting duty not to burn Thomas's barn, his promise lacks legal value.

Similarly, public officials, by virtue of their offices, have a preexisting legal duty to perform their public responsibilities. For example, Smith, the owner of a liquor store, promises to pay Fawcett, a police officer whose beat includes Smith's store, $50 a week to keep an eye on the store while walking her beat. Smith's promise is unenforceable because Fawcett has agreed to do something that she already has a duty to do.

**Preexisting Contractual Duties**    The most important preexisting duty cases are those involving preexisting *contractual* duties. These cases generally occur when the parties to an existing contract agree to *modify* that contract. As the *Gross* case (which follows shortly) indicates, the general common law rule on contract modification holds that an agreement to modify an existing contract requires some *new consideration* to be binding.

For example, Turner enters into a contract with Acme Construction Company for the construction of a new office building for $350,000. When the construction is partially completed, Acme tells Turner that due to rising labor and materials costs it will stop construction unless Turner agrees to pay an extra $50,000. Turner, having already entered into contracts to lease office space in the new building, promises to pay the extra amount. When the construction is finished, Turner refuses to pay more than $350,000. Is Turner's promise to pay the extra $50,000 enforceable against him? No. All Acme has done in exchange for Turner's promise to pay more is build the building, something that Acme had a preexisting contractual duty to do. Therefore, Acme's performance is not consideration for Turner's promise to pay more.

Although the result in the preceding example seems fair (why should Turner have to pay $400,000 for something he had a right to receive for $350,000?) and is consistent with consideration theory, the application of the preexisting duty rule to contract modifications has generated a great deal of criticism. Plainly, the rule can protect a party to a contract such as Turner from being pressured into paying more because the other party to the contract is trying to take advantage of his situation by demanding an additional amount for performance. However, mechanical application of the rule could also produce unfair results when the parties have freely agreed to a fair modification of their contract. Some critics argue that the purpose of contract modification law should be to enforce freely made modifications of existing contracts and to deny enforcement to coerced modifications. Such critics commonly suggest that general principles such as good faith and unconscionability, rather than technical consideration rules, should be used to police contract modifications.

Other observers argue that most courts in fact apply the preexisting duty rule in a manner calculated to reach fair results, because several exceptions to the rule can be used to enforce a fair modification agreement. For example, any new consideration furnished by the promisee provides sufficient consideration to support a promise to modify an existing contract. So, if Acme had promised to finish construction a week before the completion date called for in the original contract, or had promised to make some change in the original contract specifications such as to install a better grade of carpet, Acme would have done something that it had no legal duty to do in exchange for Turner's new promise. Turner's promise to pay more would then be enforceable because it would be supported by new consideration.

Many courts also enforce an agreement to modify an existing contract if the modification resulted from *unforeseen circumstances* that a party could not reasonably be expected to have foreseen, and which made that party's performance far more difficult than the parties originally anticipated. For example, if Acme had requested the extra payment because abnormal subsurface rock formations made excavation on the construction site far more costly and time-consuming than could have been reasonably expected, many courts would enforce Turner's promise to pay more.

Courts can also enforce fair modification agreements by holding that the parties mutually agreed to terminate their original contract and then entered a new one. Because contracts are created by the will of the parties, they can be terminated in the same fashion. Each party agrees to release the other party from his contractual obligations in exchange for the other party's promise to do the same. Because such a mutual agreement terminates all duties owed under the original agreement, any subsequent agreement by the parties would not be subject to the preexisting duty rule. A court is likely to take this approach, however, only when it is convinced that the modification agreement was fair and free from coercion.

---

## Gross v. Diehl Specialties International

### 776 S.W.2d 879 (Mo. Ct. App. 1989)

In 1977, Dairy Specialties, Inc. (Dairy), hired George Gross to develop nondairy products for customers allergic to milk and to serve as general manager. The employment contract was for a term of 15 years and provided for annual wages of $14,400 plus cost-of-living increases. It also provided that when 10 percent of Dairy's gross profits exceeded Gross's annual salary, he would receive the difference between the two figures. In addition, Gross would receive a royalty of 1 percent of the selling price of all products Dairy produced using one or more of Gross's inventions or formulae. This royalty increased to 2 percent after the expiration of the agreement, at which time ownership of the inventions and formulae (which were jointly held during the term of the agreement) would revert to Gross.

In 1982, Dairy was bought from its original owner by the Diehl family. The Diehls insisted on renegotiation of Gross's contract with Dairy as a condition of the purchase. Although he was not a party to the sale and received nothing tangible from it, Gross agreed to a new contract that had the same expiration date as the first one but that eliminated his cost-of-living increases, gave Dairy exclusive ownership of his inventions and formulae during and after the term of the agreement, and eliminated his right to royalties after the agreement expired. After the sale, Gross was given additional duties but no additional compensation. In 1984, after a business downturn, Gross was fired. He filed suit, arguing that his termination benefits should be calculated under his original contract. When the trial court ruled in the company's favor, he appealed.

———————————————■———————————————

**Smith, Presiding Judge**   A modification of a contract constitutes the making of a new contract and such new contract must be supported by consideration. Where a contract has not been fully performed at the time of the new agreement, the substitution of a new provision, resulting in a modification of the obligation of both sides, for a provision in the old contract still unperformed is sufficient consideration for the new contract. A promise to carry out an existing contractual duty does not constitute consideration.

Under the 1982 agreement the company undertook no greater obligations than it already had. Gross on the other hand received less than he had under the original contract. His base pay was reduced back to its 1977 amount despite the provision in the 1977 contract calling for cost of living adjustments. He lost his equal ownership in his formulae during the term of the agreement and his exclusive ownership after the termination of the agreement. He lost all royalties after termination of the agreement. In exchange for nothing, the company acquired exclusive ownership of the formulae during and after the agreement, eliminated royalties after the agreement terminated, and achieved a reduction in Gross's base salary. The company did no more than promise to carry out an already existing contractual duty. There was no consideration for the 1982 agreement.

**Judgment reversed in favor of Gross; case remanded for recalculation of damages.**

**Code Contract Modification**   The drafters of the Code sought to avoid many of the problems caused by the consideration requirement by dispensing with it in two important situations: As discussed in the Offer chapter, the Code does not require consideration for firm offers [2–205]. The Code also provides that an agreement to modify a contract for the sale of goods needs *no consideration* to be binding [2–209(1)]. For example, Electronics World orders 200 XYZ televisions at $150 per unit from XYZ Corp. Electronics World later seeks to cancel its order, but XYZ refuses to agree to cancellation. Instead, XYZ seeks to mollify a valued customer by offering to reduce the price to $100 per unit. Electronics World agrees, but when the televisions arrive, XYZ bills Electronics World for $150 per unit. Under classical contract principles, XYZ's promise to reduce the price of the goods would not be enforceable because Electronics World has furnished no new consideration in exchange for XYZ's promise. Under the Code, no new consideration is necessary and the agreement to modify the contract is enforceable.

Several things should be made clear about the operation of this Code rule. First, XYZ had no duty to agree to a modification and could have insisted on payment of $150 per unit. Second, as the following *Roth Steel Products* case illustrates, modification agreements under the Code are still subject to scrutiny under the general Code principles of good faith and unconscionability, so unfair agreements or agreements that are the product of coercion are unlikely to be enforced. Finally, the Code contains two provisions to protect people from fictitious claims that an agreement has been modified. If the original agreement requires any modification to be in writing, an oral modification is unenforceable [2–209(2)]. Regardless of what the original agreement says, if the price of the goods in the modified contract is $500 or more, the modification is unenforceable unless the requirements of the Code's statute of frauds section [2–201] are satisfied [2–209(3)].[7]

---

[7]Chapter 8 discusses § 2–201 of the Code in detail.

## ROTH STEEL PRODUCTS V. SHARON STEEL CORPORATION
### 705 F.2d 134 (6th Cir. 1983)

In November 1972, when conditions in the steel industry were highly competitive and the industry was operating at about 70 percent of its capacity, Sharon Steel Corporation agreed to sell Roth Steel Products several types of steel at prices well below Sharon's published book prices for such steel. These prices were to be effective from January 1 until December 31, 1973.

In early 1973, however, several factors changed the market for steel. Federal price controls simultaneously discouraged foreign steel imports and encouraged domestic steel producers to export a substantial portion of their production to avoid domestic price controls, sharply reducing the domestic steel supply. In addition, the steel industry experienced substantial increases in labor, raw material, and energy costs, compelling steel producers to increase prices. The increased domestic demand for steel and the attractive export market caused the entire industry to operate at full capacity; as a consequence, nearly every domestic steel producer experienced substantial delays in delivery.

On March 23, 1973, Sharon notified Roth that it was discontinuing all price discounts. Roth protested, and Sharon agreed to continue to sell at the discount price until June 30, 1973, but refused to sell thereafter unless Roth agreed to pay a modified price that was higher than that agreed to the previous November but still lower than the book prices Sharon was charging other customers. Because Roth was unable to purchase enough steel elsewhere to meet its production requirements, it agreed to pay the increased prices. When a subsequent dispute arose between the parties over late deliveries and unfilled orders by Sharon in 1974, Roth filed a breach of contract suit against Sharon, arguing, among other things, that the 1973 modification agreement was unenforceable. When the trial court ruled in favor of Roth, Sharon appealed.

---

**Celebrezze, Senior Circuit Judge**    The ability of a party to modify a contract which is subject to Article Two of the UCC is broader than common law, primarily because the modification needs no consideration to be binding. [UCC Sec. 2–209(1)]. A party's ability to modify an agreement is limited only by Article Two's general obligation of good faith. In determining whether a particular modification was obtained in good faith, a court must make two distinct inquiries: whether the party's conduct is consistent with "reasonable commercial standards of fair dealing in the trade," and whether the parties were in fact motivated to seek modification by an honest desire to compensate for commercial exigencies.

The first inquiry is relatively straightforward; the party asserting the modification must demonstrate that his decision to seek modification was the result of a factor, such as increased costs, which would cause an ordinary merchant to seek a modification of the contract. The second inquiry, regarding the subjective honesty of the parties, is less clearly defined. Essentially, this requires the party asserting the modification to demonstrate that he was, in fact, motivated by a legitimate commercial reason and that such a reason is not offered merely as a pretext. Moreover, the trier of fact must determine whether the means used to obtain the modification are an impermissible attempt to obtain a modification by extortion or overreaching.

The single most important consideration in determining whether the decision to seek a modification is justified is whether, because of changes in the market or other unforeseeable conditions, performance of the contract has come to involve a loss. In this case, the district court found that Sharon suffered substantial losses by performing the contract as modified. We are convinced that unforeseen economic exigencies existed which would prompt an ordinary merchant to seek a modification to avoid a loss on the contract.

The second part of the analysis, honesty in fact, is pivotal. The district court found that Sharon "threatened not to sell Roth any steel if Roth refused to pay increased prices after July 1, 1973" and, consequently, that Sharon acted wrongfully. We believe that the district court's conclusion that

Sharon acted in bad faith by using coercive conduct to extract the price modification is not clearly erroneous. Therefore, we hold that Sharon's attempt to modify the November 1972 contract, in order to compensate for increased costs which made performance come to involve a loss, is ineffective because

Sharon did not act in a manner consistent with Article Two's requirement of honesty in fact when it refused to perform its remaining obligations under the contract at 1972 prices.

**Judgment affirmed in favor of Roth.**

## Debt Settlement Agreements

One special variant of the preexisting duty rule that causes considerable confusion occurs when a debtor offers to pay a creditor a sum less than the creditor is demanding in exchange for the creditor's promise to accept the part payment as full payment of the debt. If the creditor later sues for the balance of the debt, is the creditor's promise to take less enforceable? The answer depends on the nature of the debt and on the circumstances of the debtor's payment.

**Liquidated Debts**    A **liquidated debt** is a debt that is both due and certain; that is, the parties have no good faith dispute about either the existence or the amount of the original debt. If a debtor does nothing more than pay less than an amount he clearly owes, how could this be consideration for a creditor's promise to take less? Such a debtor has actually done less than he had a preexisting legal duty to do—namely, to pay the full amount of the debt. For this reason, the creditor's promise to discharge a liquidated debt for part payment of the debt at or after its due date is *unenforceable* for lack of consideration.

For example, Connor borrows $10,000 from Friendly Finance Company, payable in one year. On the day payment is due, Connor sends Friendly a check for $9,000 marked: "Payment in full for all claims Friendly Finance has against me." Friendly cashes Connor's check, thus impliedly promising to accept it as full payment by cashing it, and later sues Connor for $1,000. Friendly is entitled to the $1,000 because Connor has given no consideration to support Friendly's implied promise to accept $9,000 as full payment.

However, had Connor done something he had no preexisting duty to do in exchange for Friendly's promise to settle for part payment, he could enforce Friendly's promise and avoid paying the $1,000. For

example, if Connor had paid early, before the loan contract called for payment, or in a different medium of exchange than that called for in the loan contract (such as $4,000 in cash and a car worth $5,000), he would have given consideration for Friendly's promise to accept early or different payment as full payment.

**Unliquidated Debts**    A good faith dispute about either the existence or the amount of a debt makes the debt an **unliquidated debt**. The settlement of an unliquidated debt is called an **accord and satisfaction**.[8] When an accord and satisfaction has occurred, the creditor cannot maintain an action to recover the remainder of the debt that he alleges is due. For example, Computer Corner, a retailer, orders 50 personal computers and associated software packages from Computech for $75,000. After receiving the goods, Computer Corner refuses to pay Computech the full $75,000, arguing that some of the computers were defective and that some of the software it received did not conform to its order. Computer Corner sends Computech a check for $60,000 marked: "Payment in full for all goods received from Computech." A creditor in Computech's position obviously faces a real dilemma. If Computech cashes Computer Corner's check, it will be held to have impliedly promised to accept $60,000 as full payment. Computech's promise to accept part payment as full payment would be enforceable because Computer Corner has given consideration to support it: Computer Corner has given up its right to have a court determine the amount it owes Computech. This is something that Computer Corner had no duty to do; by giving up this right and the $60,000 in exchange for Computech's implied promise, the consideration require-

---

[8]Accord and satisfaction is also discussed in Chapter 10.

ment is satisfied. The result in this case is supported not only by consideration theory but also by a strong public policy in favor of encouraging parties to settle their disputes out of court. Who would bother to settle disputed claims out of court if settlement agreements were unenforceable?

Computech could refuse to accept Computer Corner's settlement offer and sue for the full $75,000, but doing so involves several risks. A court may decide that Computer Corner's arguments are valid and award Computech less than $60,000. Even if Computech is successful, it may take years to resolve the case in the courts through the expensive and time-consuming litigation process. In addition, there is always the chance that Computer Corner may file for bankruptcy before any judgment can be collected. Faced with such risks, Computech may feel that it has no practical alternative other than to cash Computer Corner's check.[9]

**UCC Section 1–207 and Accord and Satisfaction**
In some states, a creditor such as Computech has a third, and much more desirable, alternative course of action to either returning the debtor's full-payment check or cashing it and entering an accord and satisfaction. The original version of section 1–207 of the UCC states that:

A party who with explicit reservation of rights assents to performance in a manner offered by the other party does not thereby prejudice the rights reserved. Such words as "without prejudice," "under protest" or the like are sufficient.

Some state courts have interpreted this language to mean that the Code has changed the common law accord and satisfaction rule by allowing a creditor to accept a full-payment check "under protest" or "without prejudice" without giving up any rights to sue for the balance due under the contract. However, the majority of courts that have considered the issue have held that 1–207 does *not* supersede accord and satisfaction rules. In addition, a recent

revision of 1–207 that has been enacted in a growing number of states specifically provides that 1–207 does not apply to accord and satisfaction.

**Composition Agreements** Composition agreements are agreements between a debtor and two or more creditors who agree to accept as full payment a stated percentage of their liquidated claims against the debtor at or after the date on which those claims are payable. Composition agreements are generally enforced by the courts despite the fact that enforcement appears to be contrary to the general rule on part payment of liquidated debts. Many courts have justified enforcing composition agreements on the ground that the creditors' mutual agreement to accept less than the amount due them provides the necessary consideration. The main reason why creditors agree to compositions is that they fear that their failure to do so may force the debtor into bankruptcy proceedings, in which case they might ultimately recover a smaller percentage of their claims than that agreed to in the composition.

### Forbearance to Sue

An agreement by a promisee to refrain, or forbear, from pursuing a legal claim against a promisor can be valid consideration to support a return promise—usually to pay a sum of money—by a promisor. The promisee has agreed not to file suit, something that she has a legal right to do, in exchange for the promisor's promise. The courts do not wish to sanction extortion by allowing people to threaten to file spurious claims against others in the hope that those threatened will agree to some payment to avoid the expense or embarrassment associated with defending a lawsuit. On the other hand, we have a strong public policy favoring private settlement of disputes. Therefore, it is generally said that the promisee must have a good faith belief in the validity of his or her claim before forbearance amounts to consideration.

### Bargained–For Exchange

Up to this point, we have focused on the legal value component of our consideration definition. But the fact that a promisee's act or promise provides legal value is not, in itself, a sufficient basis for finding that it amounted to consideration. In addition, the promisee's act or promise must have been bargained

---

[9]A new provision of Article 3 of the Uniform Commercial Code, section 3–311, covers accord and satisfaction by use of an instrument such as a "full payment" check. With a few exceptions, the basic provisions of section 3–311 parallel the common law rules regarding accord and satisfaction that are described in this chapter and Chapter 10.

for and given in exchange for the promisor's promise. In effect, it must be the price that the promisor asked for in exchange for making his promise. Over a hundred years ago, Oliver Wendell Holmes, one of our most renowned jurists, expressed this idea when he said, "It is the essence of a consideration that, by the terms of the agreement, it is given and accepted as the motive or inducement of the promise."[10]

## Past Consideration

*Past consideration*—despite its name—is not consideration at all. Past consideration is an act or other benefit given in the past that was *not* given in exchange for the promise in question. Because the past act was not given in exchange for the present promise, it cannot be consideration. Consider again the facts of the famous case of *Hamer v. Sidway*, discussed earlier in this chapter. There, an uncle's promise to pay his nephew $5,000 for refraining from smoking, drinking, swearing, and other delightful pastimes until his 21st birthday was supported by consideration because the nephew had given legal value by refraining from participating in the prohibited activities. However, what if the uncle

---

[10]O. W. Holmes, *The Common Law*, p. 239 (1881).

had said to his nephew on the eve of his 21st birthday: "Your mother tells me you've been a good lad and abstained from tobacco, hard drink, foul language, and gambling. Such goodness should be rewarded. Tomorrow, I'll give you a check for $5,000." Should the uncle's promise be enforceable against him? Clearly not, because although his nephew's behavior still passes the legal value test, in this case it was not bargained for and given in exchange for the uncle's promise.

## Moral Obligation

As a general rule, promises made to satisfy a preexisting moral obligation are unenforceable for lack of consideration. The fact that a promisor or some member of the promisor's family, for example, has received some benefit from the promisee in the past (e.g., food and lodging, or emergency care) would not constitute consideration for a promisor's promise to pay for that benefit, due to the absence of the bargain element. Some courts find this result distressing and enforce such promises despite the absence of consideration. In addition, a few states have passed statutes making promises to pay for past benefits enforceable if such a promise is contained in a writing that clearly expresses the promisor's intent to be bound.

---

**CONCEPT REVIEW**

## CONSIDERATION

| Consideration* | Not Consideration |
|---|---|
| Doing something you had no preexisting duty to do | Doing something you had a preexisting duty to do |
| Promising to do something you had no preexisting duty to do | Promising to do something you had a preexisting duty to do |
| Paying part of a liquidated debt prior to the date the debt is due | Nominal consideration (unless actually bargained for) |
| Paying a liquidated debt in a different medium of exchange than originally agreed to | Paying part of a liquidated debt at or after the date the debt is due |
| Agreeing to settle an unliquidated debt | Making an illusory promise |
| Agreeing not to file suit when you have a good faith belief in your claim's validity | Past consideration |
| | Preexisting moral obligation |

*Assuming bargained for.

## EXCEPTIONS TO THE CONSIDERATION REQUIREMENT

The consideration requirement is a classic example of a traditional contract law rule. It is precise, abstract, and capable of almost mechanical application. It can also, in some instances, result in significant injustice. Modern courts and legislatures have responded to this potential for injustice by carving out numerous exceptions to the requirement of consideration. Some of these exceptions (for example, the Code firm offer and contract modification rules) have already been discussed in this and preceding chapters. In the remaining portion of this chapter, we focus on several other important exceptions to the consideration requirement.

### Promissory Estoppel

As discussed in Chapter 9, Introduction to Contracts, the doctrine of promissory estoppel first emerged from attempts by courts around the turn of this century to reach just results in donative (gift) promise cases. Classical contract consideration principles did not recognize a promisee's reliance on a donative promise as a sufficient basis for enforcing the promise against the promisor. Instead, donative promises were unenforceable because they were not supported by consideration. In fact, the essence of a donative promise is that it does not seek or require any bargained-for exchange. Yet people continued to act in reliance on donative promises, often to their considerable disadvantage.

Refer to the facts of *Thorne v. Deas*, discussed earlier in this chapter. The co-owners of the *Sea Nymph* clearly relied to their injury on their fellow co-owner's promise to get insurance for the ship. Some courts in the early years of this century began to protect such relying promisees by *estopping* promisors from raising the defense that their promises were not supported by consideration. In a wide variety of cases involving gratuitous agency promises (as in *Thorne v. Deas*), promises of bonuses or pensions made to employees, and promises of gifts of land, courts began to use a promisee's detrimental (harmful) reliance on a donative promise as, in effect, a *substitute for* consideration.

In 1932, the first *Restatement of Contracts* legitimized these cases by expressly recognizing promissory estoppel in section 90. The elements of promissory estoppel were then essentially the same as they are today: a *promise* that the promisor should reasonably expect to induce reliance, *reliance* on the promise by the promisee, and *injustice* to the promisee as a result of that reliance. As the following *Niehaus* case illustrates, promissory estoppel is now widely used as a consideration substitute, not only in donative promise cases but also in cases involving commercial promises contemplating a bargained-for exchange. The construction contract bid cases discussed in Chapter 10 are another example of this expansion of promissory estoppel's reach. In fact, although promissory estoppel has expanded far beyond its initial role as a consideration substitute into other areas of contract law, it is probably fair to say that it is still most widely accepted in the consideration context.

---

## NIEHAUS V. DELAWARE VALLEY MEDICAL CENTER
### 631 A.2d 1314 (Super. Ct. Pa. 1993)

Patricia Niehaus was an employee of Delaware Valley Medical Center. The medical center distributed an employee handbook that stated that if an employee were granted an approved leave of absence, that employee, at the end of the leave, would be guaranteed the same position or one similar to the position occupied prior to the leave of absence. The handbook also stated, however, that the provisions in the handbook were not to be interpreted as a contract of employment and that either party could terminate the employment relationship at any time. Niehaus made a written request for a nine months' leave, and her request was approved. At the end of her leave, however, Delaware Valley refused to rehire Niehaus for any position. Niehaus sued the medical center for breach of contract and promissory estoppel, and the trial court dismissed her complaint. Niehaus appealed.

---

**Wieand, Judge**   The presumption under Pennsylvania law is that all employment is at will and, therefore, an employee may be discharged for any reason or no reason. The medical center contends in this case that because Niehaus was an employee at will, she could be terminated for any reason or no reason, and that it would be absurd to require a rehiring of Niehaus when she could thereafter be discharged immediately. In any event, suggests the employer, there was no consideration for an agreement to rehire Niehaus following an approved leave of absence. It is argued, therefore, that the provision in the handbook is unenforceable.

In the instant case, whether or not there was consideration, the employer's promise is enforceable under principles of promissory estoppel. "A promise which the promisor should expect to induce action or forbearance on the part of the promisee or a third person and which does induce such action or forbearance is binding if injustice can be avoided only by enforcement of the promise." *Restatement (Second) of Contracts* section 90(1). Where an employer expects, if not demands, that its employees abide by a policy expressed with particularity in an employee handbook, an employee may justifiably rely thereon and expect justifiably that the employer will do the same.

Here, the medical center, by its handbook, had guaranteed its employees that if a leave of absence were requested and approved by the employer, then the employee could return at the end of the leave of absence and would be restored to the same or similar position as that occupied by the employee prior to the leave of absence. Under this policy, the employer had a right to expect a stable work force, where employees would take leave of absence only with the employer's consent and approval. An employee who was granted an approved leave of absence, however, could also rely upon the employer's promise that the employee would be rehired. The employer's promise was not illusory. When the employee was induced in fact to seek and obtain an approved leave of absence without pay on the assurance that she could return to the same or similar employment at the expiration of her leave, enforcement of the promise was essential to avoid injustice.

The medical center argues, however, that a cause of action for breach of contract of employment cannot be based on the provisions of the handbook where other language disclaims an intent to form a contract. In this case, Niehaus was initially employed at will. When the employee requested a leave of absence without pay, the employer could have refused to approve it or, indeed, could have revoked its promise of renewed employment at the end of the leave of absence. This it did not do. Instead, it approved the leave of absence in accordance with its handbook promise. It is this approval which thereupon gave rise to an implied contract and not the mere language in the handbook.

We conclude that the trial court erred when it summarily dismissed Niehaus's amended complaint. The complaint is sufficient to allege a cause of action for breach of a contract to rehire.

**Reversed in favor of Niehaus and remanded for further proceedings.**

## Debts Barred by Statutes of Limitations

Statutes of limitations set an express statutory time limit on a person's ability to pursue any legal claim. A creditor who fails to file suit to collect a debt within the time prescribed by the appropriate statute of limitations loses the right to collect it. Many states, however, enforce a new promise by a debtor to pay such a debt, even though technically such promises are not supported by consideration because the creditor has given nothing in exchange for the new promise. Most states afford debtors some protection in such cases, however, by requiring that the new promise be in writing to be enforceable.

## Debts Barred by Bankruptcy Discharge

Once a bankrupt debtor is granted a discharge,[11] creditors no longer have the legal right to collect discharged debts. Most states enforce a new promise by the debtor to pay (reaffirm) the debt regardless of whether the creditor has given any consideration to support it. To reduce creditor attempts to pressure debtors to reaffirm, the Bankruptcy Reform Act of 1978 made it much more difficult for debtors to reaffirm debts discharged in bankruptcy proceedings.

---

[11]Chapter 22 discusses bankruptcy in detail.

The act requires that a reaffirmation promise be made prior to the date of the discharge and gives the debtor the right to revoke his promise within 30 days after it becomes enforceable. This act also requires the Bankruptcy Court to counsel individual (as opposed to corporate) debtors about the legal effects of reaffirmation and requires Bankruptcy Court approval of reaffirmations by individual debtors. In addition, a few states require reaffirmation promises to be in writing to be enforceable.

## Charitable Subscriptions

Promises to make gifts for charitable or educational purposes are often enforced, despite the absence of consideration, when the institution or organization to which the promise was made has acted in reliance on the promised gift. This result is usually justified on the basis of either promissory estoppel or public policy.

### PROBLEMS AND PROBLEM CASES

**1.** Grouse, a recently graduated pharmacist who was working as a retail pharmacist for Richter Drug, applied for a job with Group Health Plan, Inc. Grouse was interviewed at Group Health by Elliott, chief pharmacist, and Shoberg, general manager. On December 4, 1975, Elliott telephoned Grouse at work and offered him a job as a pharmacist at Group Health's St. Louis Park Clinic. Grouse accepted, informing Elliott that he would give Richter two weeks' notice. That afternoon, Grouse received an offer from a Veterans Administration Hospital in Virginia, which he declined because of Group Health's offer. Elliott called back to confirm that Grouse had resigned. Sometime in the next few days, Elliott mentioned to Shoberg that he had hired, or was thinking of hiring, Grouse. Shoberg told him that company hiring requirements included a favorable written reference, a background check, and approval of the general manager. Elliott contacted two faculty members at the University of Minnesota School of Pharmacy, who declined to give references. He also contacted an internship employer and several pharmacies where Grouse had done relief work. Their responses were that they had not had enough exposure to Grouse's work to form a judgment about his capabilities. Because Elliott was unable to supply a favorable reference for

Grouse, Shoberg hired another person to fill the position. On December 15, 1975, Grouse called Group Health and reported that he was free to begin work. Elliott informed Grouse that someone else had been hired. Grouse had difficulty regaining full-time employment and suffered wage loss as a result. Does he have any recourse against Group Health?

**2.** Omni Group, Inc., signed an earnest money agreement offering Mr. and Mrs. John Clark $2,000 per acre for a piece of property the Clarks owned, which was thought to contain about 59 acres. The agreement provided that Omni's obligation was subject to receipt of a satisfactory engineer's and architect's feasibility report assessing the property's development potential. The Clarks signed the earnest money agreement, but later refused to proceed with the sale. When Omni filed suit for breach of contract, the Clarks argued that their promise to sell was unenforceable because Omni's promise to buy was illusory due to the fact that it was conditioned on a satisfactory feasibility report. Was Omni's promise illusory?

**3.** When Nancy and Gerald Harrington were divorced in 1981, they executed a property settlement agreement giving him ownership of their farm. In return, he agreed to pay her $150,000; a $10,000 down payment and 15 annual payments. He gave her two mortgages on the farm to secure the debt. Gerald paid Nancy the initial $10,000, but was able to pay her only $3,000 in subsequent payments due to financial difficulties. Late in 1981, Gerald asked Nancy to execute satisfactions of the two mortgages so he could obtain refinancing of previous bank loans, which lenders were unwilling to provide as long as the farm was encumbered by the mortgages she held. At that time Nancy and Gerald's son, Ronn, was farming the land with Gerald. Nancy was afraid that Ronn would not inherit the farm because Gerald had remarried and his wife had become pregnant. In exchange for Gerald's promise to will the farm to Ronn, Nancy promised to execute satisfactions of the mortgages and to release Gerald from liability on his debt to her under their original agreement. Gerald subsequently made a will leaving his land to Ronn, but Nancy did not execute satisfactions of the mortgages. Instead, in 1983, she filed a foreclosure suit against Gerald. She asserted that her promise to execute satisfactions of the mortgages was unenforceable for lack of consideration. Is she correct?

**4.** In November 1981, C. F. Wooding Co. (Wooding) ordered a number of metal doors and door frames from County Fire Door Corporation (County) for a construction project Wooding was working on. After County was allegedly late in delivering the goods to the work site, Wooding told County that it would only pay $416.88 of the $2,618.88 that County claimed was the balance due because the delays in delivery caused Wooding additional installation expenses. County denied the validity of Wooding's claim and insisted that the full amount was due. Wooding then sent County a check for $416.88. On its face was a notation stating that it was final payment for the project, and on its reverse side the check stated: "By its endorsement, the payee accepts this check in full satisfaction of all claims against the C. F. Wooding Co. arising out of or relating to Purchase Order #3302, dated 11/17/81." County cashed the check, but only after crossing out the conditional language on the reverse side and adding the following language: "This check is accepted under protest and with full reservation of rights to collect the unpaid balance for which this check is offered in settlement." County filed suit against Wooding for the unpaid balance. In a state that follows the majority view about the effect of UCC section 1–207 on the common law doctrine of accord and satisfaction, can County prevail?

**5.** Roland and Leslie lived together for four years and had a child together. In June 1983, Roland filed suit to evict Leslie from his house in Duxbury, Massachusetts, and to obtain custody of their child. Leslie then filed a breach of contract action against Roland arguing that she had a right to a share of the property. In September 1983, Leslie and Roland agreed to settle both actions. She and his child were to return to live with him and he was to support them. Roland also promised to pay her legal fees from both actions. Roland and Leslie later separated again, and he refused to pay her legal fees, arguing that his promise was not supported by consideration because Massachusetts does not recognize "palimony" actions by unmarried cohabitants. Is Roland right?

**6.** Marna Balin, who had suffered two automobile accidents in 1972, hired Norman Kallen, an attorney, to represent her. Kallen did not do much work on the cases and urged Balin to settle for $25,000. She became dissatisfied with his representation, and in 1974 she asked Samuel Delug, another attorney, to take over the cases and get her files from

Kallen. Delug wrote and called Kallen several times, but Kallen refused to forward the files or sign a Substitution of Attorney form (things he was obligated to do by the California rules of professional conduct) because he was afraid Balin would not pay him for the work he had done. Only when Delug promised to give him 40 percent of his attorney's fee did Kallen forward the files and sign the form. Delug negotiated a settlement of $810,000, and the attorney's fees amounted to $324,000. When he refused to pay Kallen 40 percent, Kallen filed suit. Is Delug's promise enforceable?

**7.** The Larabees owned a farm in Dearborn County, Indiana, subject to a life estate held by Mrs. Larabee's mother. In the autumn 1971, the Larabees gave their friends, the Booths, permission to build a summer cottage on the farm. Construction began in the spring of 1972. Shortly thereafter, the Booths asked if they could build a permanent home there, and Mrs. Larabee agreed. In September 1972, she and her husband signed an agreement promising to convey a piece of the farm to the Booths on the expiration of Mrs. Larabee's mother's life estate. The agreement specifically provided that the land was to be conveyed for "no consideration." When the house was completed and Mrs. Larabee's mother had died, however, the Larabees refused to convey the land as promised. Is their promise to convey enforceable?

**8.** Passander was executive vice president of Spickelmier Industries. Because Spickelmier was facing financial difficulties, a committee of creditors had been formed to oversee its operations. In November 1971, the committee projected a small profit for the year and recommended that bonuses be given to certain key employees if the profit materialized. This recommendation was adopted by Spickelmier's board of directors in late December, and Passander was promised a $1,500 bonus. In January 1972, however, the board's executive committee discovered that the earlier profit estimates had been overly optimistic and that insufficient funds were available to pay the bonuses. Instead of taking the board's recommendation that the bonuses not be paid, the chairman of the board negotiated a compromise whereby one half of the originally specified bonus would be paid as planned, with the balance to be paid when funds were available. Passander accepted the half bonus, and later in the month his contract with Spickelmier was renegotiated to provide for a 25 percent salary increase and guaranteed quarterly bonuses of $500. In June 1972, Passander quit his job, later filing suit against Spickelmier for the remaining half of his 1971 bonus. Can he recover it?

**9.** Kaufmann was employed by Fiduciary Management, Inc. (FMI). In September 1988, Lanier, president and sole shareholder of FMI, signed and gave a letter to Kaufmann, which stated in part:

If your employment is terminated without cause before July 1, 1990, Fiduciary Management, Inc. agrees that within one month of the date on which your full salary ceases to be paid you will receive an additional payment of $150,000.

The context of this letter was that several projects serviced by FMI were experiencing financial difficulties and Lanier's sons advised him that Kaufmann was distracted, that he may have been considering leaving FMI, and that he needed to focus on his work. The letter was intended to help him focus on his work, presumably by giving him a sense of job security. After receiving the letter, Kaufmann undertook a secret and systematic search for another job. In January 1990, Kaufmann's employment with FMI ceased. He was not paid the $150,000 that had been promised in the letter, and he sued Lanier and FMI to recover the money. Was Lanier's promise to pay $150,000 enforceable?

**10.** ▣ *Video Case.* See "California Dreaming." Jensen offered Judy, a resident of Chicago, a position in a company in Los Angeles. Jensen gave Judy an employee handbook, extolled the low turnover of his firm's work force, and told her that there was a "no-cut policy." Jensen told Judy that if she decided to relocate within a year, the job was hers. After deciding to accept the job, Judy called Jensen and informed him. She also told him that she did not know how long it would take to sell her house in Chicago, but Jensen told her to give him a call as soon as she arrived in Los Angeles and said, "We're really looking forward to having you on board." Six months later, Judy and her husband quit their jobs, sold their house in Chicago, and moved to Los Angeles. When Judy called Jensen, however, he said that the position they had discussed was not available and the company had no openings. Was the company's promise to hire Judy enforceable?

**11.** ▣ *Video Case.* See "A Christmas Story." Tinker Construction had a contract with Scroge to build a factory addition for Scroge by a particular

date. The contract contained a penalty clause exacting daily penalties for late performance, and Tinker was working hard to complete the building on time. Because prompt completion of the addition was so important to Scroge, however, Scroge offered Tinker a bonus if it completed the factory addition on time. Scroge also learned that the supplier of parts for machinery that he had contracted for had called and said that it could not deliver the parts on Scroge's schedule for the price it had agreed to. Because there was no other supplier, Scroge promised to pay the requested higher price. The factory addition was completed on time and the parts arrived on time. Scroge then refused to pay both the bonus to Tinker and the higher price for the parts. Were these promises enforceable?

See also "The Stock Option" and "A Bedtime Story."

## CAPSTONE QUESTIONS

Rust Construction Company, a general contractor, entered into a written contract with Rooney to build an addition on Rooney's house according to architect's specifications for $55,000. Rust agreed to complete the construction by June 1, 1995. Among the materials specified by the architect were a number of windows, which Rust ordered from Knight-Mayer Window and Door Company for a total of $5,900. The following then occurred:

· Knight-Mayer contacted Rust and stated that it had experienced an unanticipated price increase from its supplier and was requesting that Rust pay an increased price of $6,500 for the windows. Rust agreed to this and confirmed the conversation with a written memorandum in which it agreed to pay $6,500 for the windows. After the windows were delivered, however, Rust refused to pay more than the $5,900 originally agreed on for the windows. Rust claimed that the modification was unenforceable because it was not supported by consideration.

· Lawson, one of Rust's best finish carpenters, resigned in order to move to a distant state. At a party held in Lawson's honor the day after his resignation, Rust's president, Don Rust, stated that in appreciation for Lawson's excellent performance during the 10 years he had worked for Rust, Rust would pay him a bonus of $200 per month for the next year. Lawson accepted this offer. In reliance on the promise of an additional $200 per month income, Lawson signed a lease for an apartment that was more expensive by $150 than the one he had planned to rent. Rust paid the $200 for one month but made no further payments to Lawson. Lawson claims that he gave legal value in exchange for Rust's promise to pay the $200 per month and that the agreement is a legally enforceable contract or, in the alternative, that it is legally enforceable under the doctrine of promissory estoppel.

· Rooney promised to pay Rust a bonus of $500 if it completed the construction three days early. Rust did complete the construction three days early and claimed that it had earned the bonus. Rooney ultimately refused to pay it, however. She asserted that Rust's completing the work three days early was not adequate consideration to support her promise to pay an additional $500.

· Within several days of completing the addition, Rust invoiced Rooney for $15,000, which was the balance of the contract price—not including the promised bonus—that remained to be paid at the time of completion. Rooney was dissatisfied with the manner in which some of the roofing and finish work had been done and refused to pay Rust anything. Rust contended that nothing was wrong with the work and that Rooney owed it $15,000. After a prolonged dispute, the parties agreed that Rooney would pay Rust $9,000 in total satisfaction of her debt. Rooney gave Rust a check for $9,000 and Rust accepted it. Rust then continued to invoice Rooney for $6,000 and is now threatening litigation.

## Required:

Answer the following and give reasons for your conclusions.

1. State whether Rust's claim is correct.
2. State whether Lawson's claims are correct.
3. State whether Rooney's assertion is correct.
4. Assess whether Rust is likely to win this lawsuit.

**CHAPTER**

**5**

# REALITY OF CONSENT

**INTRODUCTION**

*In a complex economy that depends on planning for the future, it is crucial that the law can be counted on to enforce contracts. In some situations, however, there are compelling reasons for permitting people to escape or avoid their contracts. An agreement obtained by force, trickery, unfair persuasion, or error is not the product of mutual and voluntary consent. A person who has made an agreement under these circumstances will be able to avoid it, because his consent was not real.*

*This chapter discusses five doctrines that permit people to avoid their contracts because of the absence of real consent: misrepresentation, fraud, mistake, duress, and undue influence. Doctrines that involve similar considerations will be discussed in Chapter 6, Capacity to Contract, and Chapter 7, Illegality.*

## EFFECT OF DOCTRINES DISCUSSED IN THIS CHAPTER

Contracts induced by misrepresentation, fraud, duress, mistake, or undue influence are generally considered to be **voidable**. This means that the person whose consent was not real has the power to **rescind** (cancel) the contract. A person who rescinds a contract is entitled to the return of anything he gave the other party. By the same token, he must offer to return anything he has received from the other party.

**Necessity for Prompt and Unequivocal Rescission**   Suppose Johnson, who recently bought a car from Sims Motors, learns that Sims Motors made fraudulent statements to her to induce her to buy the car. She believes the contract was induced by fraud and wants to rescind it. How does she act to protect her rights? To rescind a contract based on fraud or any of the other doctrines discussed in this chapter, she must act promptly and unequivocally. She must object promptly upon learning the facts that give her the right to rescind and must clearly express her intent to cancel the contract. She must also avoid any behavior that would suggest that she affirms or **ratifies** the contract. (Ratification of a voidable contract means that a person who had the right to rescind has elected not to do so. Ratification ends the right to rescind.) This means that she should avoid unreasonable delay in notifying the other party of her rescission, because unreasonable delay communicates that she has ratified the contract. She should also avoid any conduct that would send a "mixed message," such as continuing to accept benefits from the other party or behaving in any other way that is inconsistent with her expressed intent to rescind.

## MISREPRESENTATION AND FRAUD

### Nature of Misrepresentation

A misrepresentation is an assertion that is not in accord with the truth. When a person enters a contract because of his justifiable reliance on a misrepresentation about some important fact, the contract is voidable.

It is not necessary that the misrepresentation be intentionally deceptive. Misrepresentations can be either *innocent* (not intentionally deceptive) or *fraudulent* (made with knowledge of falsity and intent to deceive). A contract may be voidable even if the person making the misrepresentation believes in good faith that what he says is true. Either innocent misrepresentation or fraud gives the complaining party the right to rescind a contract.

### Nature of Fraud

Fraud is the type of misrepresentation that is committed knowingly, with the intent to deceive. The legal term for this knowledge of falsity, which distinguishes fraud from innocent misrepresentation, is **scienter**. A person making a misrepresentation would be considered to do so "knowingly" if she knew that her statement was false, if she knew that she did not have a basis for making the statement, or even if she just made the statement without being confident that it was true. The intent to deceive can be inferred from the fact that the defendant knowingly made a misstatement of fact to a person who was likely to rely on it.

Traditionally, courts have distinguished two forms of fraud: **fraud in the inducement** and **fraud in the execution.** Fraud in the inducement is fraud about some fact involved in the contract that is used for the purpose of obtaining a person's consent to

enter a contract—for example, fraudulent statements about the condition of property being sold. Fraud in the execution is fraud regarding the nature of a written instrument—for example, Morrison gets Twomey to sign a contract by tricking him into believing that he is signing a job application. Unlike fraud in the inducement, fraud in the execution makes a contract *void*. Because fraud in the inducement is much more common than fraud in the execution, the remaining discussion will concentrate on fraud in the inducement.

As is true for innocent misrepresentation, the contract remedy for fraudulent misrepresentation is rescission. The tort liability of a person who commits fraud is different from that of a person who commits innocent misrepresentation, however. A person who commits fraud may be liable for damages, possibly including punitive damages, for the tort of **deceit**. As you will learn in following sections, innocent misrepresentation and fraud share a common core of elements.

**Election of Remedies**    In some states, a person injured by fraud cannot rescind the contract *and* sue for damages for deceit; he must elect (choose) between these remedies. In other states, however, an injured party may pursue both rescission and damage remedies and does not have to elect between them.[1]

## REQUIREMENTS FOR RESCISSION ON THE GROUND OF MISREPRESENTATION

The fact that one of the parties has made an untrue assertion does not in itself make the contract voidable. Courts do not want to permit people who have exercised poor business judgment or poor common sense to avoid their contractual obligations, nor do they want to grant rescission of a contract when there have been only minor and unintentional misstatements of relatively unimportant details. A drastic remedy such as rescission should be used only when a person has been seriously misled about a fact important to the contract by someone he had the right to rely on. A person seeking to rescind a contract on the ground of innocent or fraudulent

---

[1]Under every state's law, however, a person injured by fraud in a contract for the *sale of goods* can both rescind the contract and sue for damages. This is made clear by section 2–721 of the Uniform Commercial Code, which specifically states that no election of remedies is required in contracts for the sale of goods.

misrepresentation must be able to establish each of the following elements:

1. An untrue assertion of fact was made.
2. The fact asserted was material *or* the assertion was fraudulent.
3. The complaining party entered the contract because of his reliance on the assertion.
4. The reliance of the complaining party was reasonable.

In tort actions in which the plaintiff is seeking to recover damages for deceit, the plaintiff would have to establish a *fifth* element: injury. He would have to prove that he had suffered actual economic injury because of his reliance on the fraudulent assertion. In cases in which the injured person seeks only rescission of the contract, however, proof of economic injury is usually not required.

### Untrue Assertion of Fact

To have misrepresentation, one of the parties must have made an untrue assertion of fact or engaged in some conduct that is the equivalent of an untrue assertion of fact. The fact asserted must be a *past or existing fact*, as distinguished from a promise or prediction about some future happening.

The **concealment** of a fact through some active conduct intended to prevent the other party from discovering the fact is considered to be the equivalent of an assertion. Like a false statement of fact, concealment can be the basis for a claim of misrepresentation or fraud. For example, if Summers is offering his house for sale and paints the ceilings to conceal the fact that the roof leaks, his active concealment constitutes an assertion of fact. Under some circumstances, **nondisclosure** also can be the equivalent of an assertion of fact. Nondisclosure differs from concealment in that concealment involves the active hiding of a fact, while nondisclosure is the failure to offer information.

**Problem Area: Nondisclosure**    Suppose you are a prospective home buyer who inspects a house for possible purchase. The seller of the house knows that there is a hidden but serious structural defect in the house that will cost approximately $30,000 to correct, but does not mention this to you. Neither you nor the professional inspector you hire to examine the house for defects observes any evidence of structural defects, and you contract to purchase the house based on your assumption that it is in good condition. You later learn about the existence of this defect. Do you have the right to rescind the contract? The issue raised by this problem is whether the seller's silence about the defect was misrepresentation. In other words, was his nondisclosure the equivalent of an assertion that the structural defect did not exist?

Under traditional contract law, the answer to this question would probably have been no. Under the traditional view of nondisclosure, the circumstances under which the law required disclosure were very limited. (These are the first three circumstances described in the next section.) Mere silence on the part of a contracting party generally did not amount to misrepresentation. One reason for this treatment of nondisclosure was that unlike concealment and outright statements of fact, which are active forms of misconduct, nondisclosure is passive. Fundamentally, though, the traditional view of nondisclosure expressed the highly individualistic philosophy expressed in the well-known phrase *caveat emptor* ("let the buyer beware"): Each contracting party is responsible for taking care of himself and is not his "brother's keeper."

In recent years, however, courts and legislatures have expanded the circumstances under which a person has the duty to take affirmative steps to disclose relevant information. This is consistent with modern contract law's emphasis on influencing ethical standards of conduct and achieving fair results. Some duties of disclosure have been created by statutes, such as the Truth in Lending Act[2] and the federal securities laws,[3] but courts also have been increasingly active in expanding the duty to disclose. In addition to the circumstances in which federal or state statutes would require a contracting party to disclose facts, there are four circumstances in which most courts today require disclosure. In these situations, the person's failure to disclose a fact would be the equivalent of an assertion that the fact did not exist.

1. *Fiduciary relationship.* If a fiduciary relationship (a relationship of trust and confidence) exists between the parties to the contract, a party who knows of an important fact that the other person does not know about would have the duty to disclose it.

---

[2]See Chapter 20 for a discussion of the Truth in Lending Act.
[3]These laws are discussed in Chapter 37.

This makes sense, because a person who has good reason to believe that the other party is looking out for his welfare will not approach the contract with the same degree of vigilance as the person who is dealing at arm's length with a stranger. This sort of duty to disclose would not apply to ordinary contracting parties who are bargaining at arm's length.

**2.** *Correcting "half-truths."* When a person makes a statement about a situation, he has the duty to disclose any facts that would be necessary to correct a half-truth. For example, Carlson, a car salesperson who is trying to sell a used car, knows that the previous owner of the car used it exclusively for drag racing on Sundays. If Carlson tells a customer that the previous owner of the car "drove it only on Sundays," he would have the legal duty to disclose the additional material fact that the car had been used exclusively for drag racing.

**3.** *Correcting statements made false by later events.* A person has the duty to disclose information that will be necessary to correct a previous statement that may have been true when made but that has become false because of later events. For example, White, who wants to sell her house, tells a prospective purchaser truthfully that the roof of the house has never leaked. Several days later, the roof leaks after a heavy storm. White has the legal duty to make the disclosure that is necessary to correct her previous statement.

**4.** *Good faith and fair dealing require disclosure.* In the hypothetical case with which we began this discussion of nondisclosure—the case of the seller who failed to disclose the existence of a hidden structural defect in the house he was selling—the home buyer entered into the contract under the mistaken assumption that the house was free of structural defects. The *Restatement (Second)* *of Contracts* provides for a duty to disclose that would be applicable in this situation. Under section 161 of the *Restatement (Second)*, a person must disclose facts necessary to correct the other party's mistake about a basic assumption of the contract when nondisclosure amounts to a failure to act in good faith and in accordance with reasonable standards of fair dealing. Most states today apply a duty to disclose along these lines.

Note that this sort of duty to disclose has broader application than the first three circumstances described above because it can apply even when the parties are dealing at arm's length and no partial disclosures have been made. Note also that this duty to disclose is intertwined with concepts of good faith and fair dealing. The *Restatement (Second)* does *not* say that a person who possesses information always has the obligation to educate the other party. Rather, the duty to speak arises only when failing to do so would constitute a failure to behave in a way that is in accord with prevailing concepts of good faith and reasonable standards of dealing. Nondisclosure is most likely to constitute a failure to act reasonably and in good faith when a party has access to information that is not readily available to the other party. In addition, sellers are more likely to be required to disclose information than are buyers.

Transactions involving the sale of real estate are among the most common situations in which this duty to disclose arises. Most states now hold that a seller who knows about a latent (hidden) defect that materially affects the value of the property he is selling has the obligation to speak up about this defect. *Stambovsky v. Ackley*, which follows, involves an interesting application of the duty to disclose in the context of a sale of real estate.

---

## STAMBOVSKY V. ACKLEY
### 572 N.Y.S.2d 672 (N.Y. Sup. Ct., App. Div. 1991)

Jeffrey Stambovsky, a resident of New York City, contracted to purchase a house in the Village of Nyack, New York, from Helen Ackley. The house was widely reputed to be possessed by poltergeists, which Ackley and members of her family had reportedly seen. Ackley did not tell Stambovsky about the poltergeists before he bought the house. When Stambovsky learned of the house's reputation, however, he promptly commenced this action for rescission. The trial court dismissed his complaint, and Stambovsky appealed.

**Rubin, Justice**    The unusual facts of this case clearly warrant a grant of equitable relief to the buyer who, as a resident of New York City, cannot be expected to have any familiarity with the folklore of the Village of Nyack. Not being a "local," Stambovsky could not readily learn that the home he had contracted to purchase is haunted. Whether the source of the spectral apparitions seen by Ackley are parapsychic or psychogenic, having reported their presence in both a national publication ("Readers' Digest") and the local press (in 1977 and 1982, respectively), Ackley is estopped to deny their existence and, as a matter of law, the house is haunted. More to the point, however, no divination is required to conclude that it is Ackley's promotional efforts in publicizing her close encounters with these spirits which fostered the home's reputation in the community. In 1989, the house was included in a five-home walking tour of Nyack and described in a November 27th newspaper article as a "riverfront Victorian (with ghost)." The impact of the reputation thus created goes to the very essence of the bargain between the parties, greatly impairing both the value of the property and its potential for resale.

[*The court discussed the fact that New York law does not recognize a remedy for damages incurred as a result of the seller's mere silence, applying instead the doctrine of caveat emptor. The court then proceeded to discuss the availability of rescission.*]

From the perspective of a person in the position of the plaintiff, a very practical problem arises with respect to the discovery of a paranormal phenomenon: "Who you gonna call?" as the title song to the movie "Ghostbusters" asks. Applying the strict rule of *caveat emptor* to a contract involving a house possessed by poltergeists conjures up visions of a psychic or medium routinely accompanying the structural engineer and Terminix man on an inspection of every home subject to a contract of sale. The doctrine of *caveat emptor* requires that a buyer act prudently to assess the fitness and value of his purchase. It should be apparent, however, that the most meticulous inspection and the search would not reveal the presence of poltergeists at the premises or unearth the property's ghoulish reputation in the community. Therefore, there is no sound policy reason to deny Stambovsky relief for failing to discover a state of affairs which the most prudent purchaser would not be expected to even contemplate.

Where a condition which has been created by the seller materially impairs the value of the contract and is peculiarly within the knowledge of the seller or unlikely to be discovered by a prudent purchaser exercising due care, nondisclosure constitutes a basis for rescission as a matter of equity. Any other outcome places upon the buyer not merely the obligation to exercise care in his purchase but rather to be omniscient with respect to any fact which may affect the bargain. No practical purpose is served by imposing such a burden upon a purchaser. To the contrary, it encourages predatory business practice and offends the principle that equity will suffer no wrong to be without a remedy.

In the case at bar, Ackley deliberately fostered the public belief that her home was possessed. Having undertaken to inform the public at large, to whom she has no legal relationship, about the supernatural occurrences on her property, she may be said to owe no less a duty to her contract vendee. Application of the remedy of rescission is entirely appropriate to relieve the unwitting purchaser from the consequences of a most unnatural bargain.

**Judgment modified in favor of Stambovsky, reinstating his action seeking rescission of the contract.**

**Problem Area: Statements of Opinion**    In holding that only untrue statements of *fact* give a relying person the right to rescind a contract, contract law traditionally has distinguished between assertions of *fact* and assertions of *opinion*. Although it can be difficult to separate fact from opinion, there is an important distinction between a statement that communicates a person's knowledge and a statement that communicates only his uncertain belief about a fact or his personal judgment about such matters as quality or value. The latter sort of statement usually cannot be the basis of a misrepresentation claim because the person to whom such a statement of opinion is made is not justified in relying on it. This is especially true when the statement relates to something about which the parties have relatively equal knowledge and peoples' points of view are likely to differ. In such a case, each party is expected to form his own opinion. A classic example of this sort of statement of opinion is a seller's "puff" (salestalk or general praise of an item being sold), such as "This suit will look terrific on you."

Even when the statement is clearly one of opinion, there are three situations in which the statement of opinion can be the basis of a misrepresentation claim because reliance is justifiable under the circumstances.[4] These include:

**1.** *Relationship of trust and confidence.* A person can be justified in relying on a statement of opinion if it is reasonable to do so because of a relationship of trust and confidence between him and the speaker. For example, if Madison, the long-time financial adviser of the elderly Holden, persuades Holden to invest her money in Madison's failing business by telling her that it is a wise investment, Holden would be justified in relying on Madison's statement of opinion.

**2.** *Relying party is unusually susceptible.* Reliance on a statement of opinion can be justifiable when the relying party is someone who is particularly susceptible to the particular type of misrepresentation involved. This sort of case would be likely to involve relying parties who are vulnerable to being misled because of some obvious disadvantage such as illiteracy or lack of intelligence or experience.

**3.** *Reliance on person who has superior skill or judgment.* Reliance on an assertion of opinion can also be justifiable when the relying party reasonably believes that the person on whose opinion he is relying has superior skill or judgment about the subject matter of the contract. This would apply when the opinion relates to some matter about which superior training or experience is necessary to form the opinion. For example, Buyer, who knows that Salesperson is an experienced auto mechanic, would be justified in relying on Salesperson's statement that a particular used car is "in A-1 condition."

---

[4]*Restatement (Second) of Contracts* § 169.

## Materiality

If the misrepresentation was innocent, the person seeking to rescind the contract must establish that the fact asserted was **material**. A fact will be considered to be material if it is likely to play a significant role in inducing a reasonable person to enter the contract or if the person asserting the fact knows that the other person is likely to rely on the fact. For example, Rogers, who is trying to sell his car to Ferguson and knows that Ferguson idolizes professional bowlers, tells Ferguson that a professional bowler once rode in the car. Relying on that representation, Ferguson buys the car. Although the fact Rogers asserted might not be important to most people, it would be material here because Rogers knew that his representation would be likely to induce Ferguson to enter the contract.

Even if the fact asserted was not material, the contract may be rescinded if the misrepresentation was *fraudulent*. The rationale for this rule is that a person who fraudulently misrepresents a fact, even one that is not material under the standards previously discussed, should not be able to profit from his intentionally deceptive conduct.

## Actual Reliance

Reliance means that a person pursues some course of action because of his faith in an assertion made to him. For misrepresentation to exist, there must have been a causal connection between the assertion and the complaining party's decision to enter the contract. If the complaining party knew that the assertion was false or was not aware that an assertion had been made, there has been no reliance.

## Justifiable Reliance

Courts also scrutinize the reasonableness of the behavior of the complaining party by requiring that his reliance be *justifiable*. A person does not act justifiably if he relies on an assertion that is obviously false or not to be taken seriously.

**Problem Area: The Relying Party's Failure to Investigate the Accuracy of an Assertion**    One problem involving the justifiable reliance element is determining the extent to which the relying party is responsible for investigating the accuracy of the statement on which he relies. Classical contract law held that a person who did not attempt to discover readily discoverable facts was generally not justified in relying on the other party's statements about them. For example, under traditional law, a person would not be entitled to rely on the other party's assertions about facts that are a matter of public record or that could be discovered through a reasonable inspection of available documents or records.

The extent of the responsibility placed on a relying party to conduct an independent investigation has declined in modern contract law, however. For example, section 172 of the *Restatement* states that the complaining party's fault in not knowing or

discovering facts before entering the contract does not make his reliance unjustifiable unless the degree of his fault was so extreme as to amount to a failure to act in good faith and in accordance with reasonable standards of fair dealing. Recognizing that the traditional rule operated to encourage misrepresentation, courts in recent years have tended to decrease the responsibility of the relying party and to place a greater degree of accountability on the person who makes the assertion. The case of *Cousineau v. Walker*, which follows, is an excellent example of this trend.

---

## COSINEAU V. WALKER
### 613 P.2d 608 (Alaska Sup. Ct. 1980)

Devin and Joan Walker owned property in Eagle River, Alaska. In 1976, they listed the property for sale with a real estate broker. They signed a multiple listing agreement that described the property as having 580 feet of highway frontage and stated, "ENGINEER REPORT SAYS OVER 1 MILLION IN GRAVEL ON PROP." A later listing contract signed with the same broker described the property as having 580 feet of highway frontage, but listed the gravel content as "minimum 80,000 cubic yds of gravel." An appraisal prepared to determine the property's value stated that it did not take any gravel into account but described the ground as "all good gravel base."

Wayne Cousineau, a contractor who was also in the gravel extraction business, became aware of the property when he saw the multiple listing. After visiting the property with his real estate broker and discussing gravel extraction with Mr. Walker, Cousineau offered to purchase the property. He then attempted to determine the lot's road frontage, but was unsuccessful because the property was covered with snow. He was also unsuccessful in obtaining the engineer's report allegedly showing "over 1 million in gravel." Walker admitted at trial that he had never seen a copy of the report, either. Nevertheless, the parties signed and consummated a contract of sale for the purchase price of $385,000. There was no reference to the amount of highway frontage in the purchase agreement.

After the sale was completed, Cousineau began developing the property and removing gravel. Cousineau learned that the description of highway frontage contained in the real estate listing was incorrect when a neighbor threatened to sue him for removing gravel from the neighbor's adjacent lot. A subsequent survey revealed that the highway frontage was 410 feet—not 580 feet, as advertised. At about the same time, the gravel ran out after Cousineau had removed only 6,000 cubic yards.

Cousineau stopped making payments and informed the Walkers of his intention to rescind the contract. Cousineau brought an action against the Walkers, seeking the return of his money. The trial court found for the Walkers, and Cousineau appealed.

---

**Boochever, Justice**    An innocent misrepresentation may be the basis for rescinding a contract. There is no question that the statements made by Walker and his real estate agent in the multiple listing were false.

The bulk of the Walkers' brief is devoted to the argument that Cousineau's unquestioning reliance on Walker and his real estate agent was imprudent and unreasonable. Cousineau failed to obtain and review the engineer's report. He failed to obtain a survey or examine the plat available at the recorder's office. He failed to make calculations that would have revealed the true frontage of the lot. Although the property was covered with snow, the buyer, according to Walker, had ample time to inspect it. The buyer was an experienced businessman who frequently bought and sold real estate. Discrepancies existed in the various property descriptions which should have alerted Cousineau to potential problems. In short, the Walkers urge that the doctrine of *caveat emptor* precludes recovery.

There is a split of authority regarding a buyer's duty to investigate a vendor's fraudulent statements, but the prevailing trend is toward placing a minimal duty on a buyer. The recent draft of the *Restatement of Contracts* allows rescission for an innocent material misrepresentation unless a buyer's fault was

so negligent as to amount to "a failure to act in good faith and in accordance with reasonable standards of fair dealing." We conclude that a purchaser of land may rely on material representations made by the seller and is not obligated to ascertain whether such representations are truthful. A buyer of land, relying on an innocent misrepresentation, is barred from recovery only if the buyer's acts in failing to discover defects were wholly irrational, preposterous, or in bad faith.

Although Cousineau's actions may well have exhibited poor judgment for an experienced businessman, they were not so unreasonable or preposterous in view of Walker's description of the property that recovery should be denied.

**Judgment reversed in favor of Cousineau.**

---

### CONCEPT REVIEW
## MISREPRESENTATION AND FRAUD

|  | Innocent Misrepresentation | Fraud |
|---|---|---|
| **Remedy** | Rescission | Rescission *and/or* tort action for damages |
| **Elements** | 1. Untrue assertion of fact (or equivalent)<br>2. Assertion relates to material fact<br>3. Actual reliance<br>4. Justifiable reliance | 1. Untrue assertion of fact (or equivalent)<br>2. Assertion made with knowledge of falsity (scienter) and intent to deceive<br>3. Actual reliance<br>4. Justifiable reliance<br>5. Economic loss (in a tort action for damages) |

---

## MISTAKE

### Nature of Mistake

Anyone who enters a contract does so on the basis of his understanding of the facts that are relevant to the contract. His decision about what he is willing to exchange with the other party is based on this understanding. If the parties are wrong about an important fact, the exchange that they make is likely to be quite different than what they contemplated when they entered the contract, and this difference is due to simple error rather than to any external events such as an increase in market price. For example, Fox contracts

to sell to Ward a half-carat stone, which both believe to be a tourmaline, at a price of $65. If they are wrong and the stone is actually a diamond worth at least $2,500, Fox will have suffered an unexpected loss and Ward will have reaped an unexpected gain. The contract would not have been made at a price of $65 if the parties' belief about the nature of the stone had been in accord with the facts. In such cases, the person adversely affected by the mistake can avoid the contract under the doctrine of mistake. The purpose of the doctrine of mistake is to prevent unexpected and unbargained for losses that result when the parties are mistaken about a fact central to their contract.

**What Is a Mistake?** In ordinary conversation, we may use the term *mistake* to mean an error in judgment or an unfortunate act. In contract law, however, a mistake is a *belief* about a fact that is *not in accord with the truth*.[5] The mistake must relate to facts as they exist at the time the contract is created. An erroneous belief or prediction about facts that might occur in the future would not qualify as a mistake.

As in misrepresentation cases, the complaining party in a mistake case enters a contract because of a belief that is at variance with the actual facts. Mistake is unlike misrepresentation, however, in that the erroneous belief is not the result of the other party's untrue statements.

The *Wilkin v. 1st Source Bank* case, which follows, illustrates the concept and effect of mistake in contract law.

[5]*Restatement (Second) of Contracts* § 151.

---

## Wilkin v. 1st Source Bank
### 548 N.E.2d 170 (Ind. Ct. App. 1990)

Olga Mestrovic, the widow of internationally known sculptor and artist Ivan Mestrovic, owned a large number of works of art created by her late husband. Mrs. Mestrovic died, leaving a will in which she directed that all the works of art created by her husband were to be sold and the proceeds distributed to surviving members of the Mestrovic family. Mrs. Mestrovic also owned real estate at the time of her death. 1st Source Bank, as the personal representative of Mrs. Mestrovic's estate, entered into a contract to sell this real estate to Terrence and Antoinette Wilkin. The purchase agreement provided that certain personal property on the premises would be sold to the Wilkins, too: specifically, the stove, refrigerator, dishwasher, drapes, curtains, sconces, and French doors in the attic.

After taking possession of the property, the Wilkins complained to the bank that the property was left in a cluttered condition and would require substantial cleaning effort. The trust officer of the bank offered the Wilkins two options: Either the bank would obtain a rubbish removal service to clean the property, or the Wilkins could clean the property and keep any items of personal property they wanted. The Wilkins opted to clean the property themselves. At the time these arrangements were made, neither the bank nor the Wilkins suspected that any works of art remained on the premises.

During the clean-up efforts, the Wilkins found eight drawings apparently created by Ivan Mestrovic. They also found a plaster sculpture of the figure of Christ with three small children. The Wilkins claimed ownership of these works of art by virtue of their agreement with the bank. The probate court ruled that there was no agreement for the purchase of the artwork, and the Wilkins appealed.

---

**Hoffman, Judge** Mutual assent is a prerequisite to the creation of a contract. Where both parties share a common assumption about a vital fact upon which they based their bargain, and that assumption is false, the transaction may be avoided if because of the mistake a quite different exchange of values occurs from the exchange of values contemplated by the parties. *J. Calamari & J. Perillo, The Law of Contracts* section 9-26 (1987).

The necessity of mutual assent is illustrated in the classic case of *Sherwood v. Walker* (1887). The owners of a blooded cow indicated to the purchaser that the cow was barren. The purchaser appeared to believe that the cow was barren. Consequently, a bargain was made to sell at a price per pound at which the cow would have brought approximately $80.00. Before delivery, it was discovered that the cow was with calf and that she was, therefore, worth from $750.00 to $1,000.00 The court ruled that the transaction was voidable: "[T]he mistake . . . went to the very nature of the thing. A barren cow is substantially a different creature than a breeding one."

Like the parties in *Sherwood*, the parties in the instant case shared a common presupposition as to the existence of certain facts which proved false. The bank and the Wilkins considered the real estate which the Wilkins had purchased to be cluttered with items of personal property variously characterized as "junk," "stuff," or "trash." Neither party suspected that works of art created by Ivan Mestrovic remained on the premises.

As in *Sherwood*, one party experienced an unexpected, unbargained-for gain while the other experienced an unexpected, unbargained-for loss. Because the bank and the Wilkins did not know that the eight drawings and the plaster sculpture were included in the items of personalty that cluttered the real property, the discovery of those works of art by the Wilkins was unexpected. The resultant gain to the Wilkins and loss to the Bank were not contemplated by the parties when the bank agreed that the Wilkins could clean the premises and keep such personal property as they wished.

The following commentary on *Sherwood* is equally applicable to the case at bar:

"Here the buyer sought to retain a gain that was produced, not by a subsequent change in circumstances, nor by the favorable resolution of known uncertainties when the contract was made, but by the presence of facts quite different from those on which the parties based their bargain." *Palmer, Mistake and Unjust Enrichment* 16–17 (1962).

The probate court properly concluded that there was no agreement for the purchase, sale, or other disposition of the eight drawings and plaster sculpture.

**Judgment for 1st Source Bank affirmed.**

---

## Mistakes of Law

A number of the older mistake cases state that mistake about a principle of law will not justify rescission. The rationale for this view was that everyone was presumed to know the law. More modern cases, however, have granted relief even when the mistake is an erroneous belief about some aspect of law.

## Negligence and the Right to Avoid for Mistake

Although courts sometimes state that relief will not be granted when a person's mistake was caused by his own negligence, they have often granted rescission even when the mistaken party was somewhat negligent. Section 157 of the *Restatement (Second) of Contracts* focuses on the *degree* of a party's negligence in making the mistake. It states that a person's fault in failing to know or discover facts before entering the contract will not bar relief unless his fault amounted to a failure to act in good faith.

## Effect of Mistake

The mere fact that the contracting parties have made a mistake is not, standing alone, a sufficient ground for avoidance of the contract. The right to avoid a contract because of mistake depends on several factors that are discussed in following sections. One important factor that affects the right to avoid is whether the mistake was made by just one of the parties (**unilateral mistake**) or by both parties (**mutual mistake**).

## Mutual Mistake

A mutual mistake exists when both parties to the contract have erroneous assumptions about the same fact. When *both* parties are mistaken, the resulting contract can be avoided if the three following elements are present:

1. The mistake relates to a basic assumption on which the contract was made.
2. The mistake has a material effect on the agreed-on exchange.
3. The party adversely affected by the mistake does not bear the risk of the mistake.[6]

**Mistake about a Basic Assumption**    Even if the mistake is mutual, the adversely affected party will not have the right to avoid the contract unless the mistake concerns a basic assumption on which the

---

[6]*Restatement (Second) of Contracts* § 152.

contract was based. Assumptions about the identity, existence, quality, or quantity of the subject matter of the contract are among the basic assumptions on which contracts typically are founded. It is not necessary that the parties be consciously aware of the assumption; an assumption may be so basic that they take it for granted. For example, if Peterson contracts to buy a house from Tharp, it is likely that both of them assume at the time of contracting that the house is in existence and that it is legally permissible for the house to be used as a residence.

An assumption would not be considered a basic assumption if it concerns a matter that bears an indirect or collateral relationship to the subject matter of the contract. For example, mistakes about matters such as a party's financial ability or market conditions usually would not give rise to avoidance of the contract.

**Material Effect on Agreed-On Exchange**   It is not enough for a person claiming mistake to show that the exchange is something different from what he expected. He must show that the imbalance caused by the mistake is so severe that it would be unfair for the law to require him to perform the contract. He will have a better chance of establishing this element if he can show not only that the contract is *less* desirable for him because of the mistake, but also that the other party has received an unbargained-for advantage.

**Adversely Affected Party Does Not Bear the Risk of Mistake**   Even if the first two elements are present, the person who is adversely affected by the mistake cannot avoid the contract if he is considered to bear the risk of mistake.[7] Courts have the power to allocate the risk of a mistake to the adversely affected person whenever it is reasonable under the circumstances to do so.

One situation in which an adversely affected person would bear the risk of mistake is when he has expressly contracted to do so. For example, if Buyer contracted to accept property "as is," he may be considered to have accepted the risk that his assumption about the quality of the property may be erroneous.

---

[7]*Restatement (Second) of Contracts* § 154.

The adversely affected party also bears the risk of mistake when he contracts with *conscious awareness* that he is ignorant or has limited information about a fact—in other words, he *knows that he does not know* the true state of affairs about a particular fact, but he binds himself to perform anyway. Suppose someone gives you an old, locked safe. Without trying to open it, you sell it and "all of its contents" to one of your friends for $25. When your friend succeeds in opening the safe, he finds $10,000 in cash. In this case, you would not be able to rescind the contract because, in essence, you gambled on your limited knowledge . . . and lost.

## Mutual Mistakes in Drafting Writings

Sometimes, mutual mistake takes the form of erroneous *expression* of an agreement, frequently caused by a clerical error in drafting or typing a contract, deed, or other document. In such cases, the remedy is *reformation* of the writing rather than avoidance of the contract. Reformation means modification of the written instrument to express the agreement that the parties made but failed to express correctly. Suppose Arnold agrees to sell Barber a vacant lot next to Arnold's home. The vacant lot is "Lot 3, block 1;" Arnold's home is on "Lot 2, block 1." The person typing the contract strikes the wrong key, and the contract reads, "Lot 2, block 1." Neither Arnold nor Barber notices this error when they read and sign the contract, yet clearly they did not intend to have Arnold sell the lot on which his house stands. In such a case, a court will reform the contract to conform to Arnold and Barber's true agreement.

## Unilateral Mistake

A unilateral mistake exists when only one of the parties makes a mistake about a basic assumption on which he made the contract. For example, Plummer contracts to buy from Taylor 25 shares of Worthright Enterprises, Inc., mistakenly believing that he is buying 25 shares of the much more valuable Worthwrite Industries. Taylor knows that the contract is for the sale of shares of Worthright. Taylor (the nonmistaken party) is correct in his belief about the identity of the stock he is selling;

only Plummer (the mistaken party) is mistaken in his assumption about the identity of the stock. Does Plummer's unilateral mistake give him the right to avoid the contract? Courts are more likely to allow avoidance of a contract when both parties are mistaken than when only one is mistaken. The rationale for this tendency is that in cases of unilateral mistake, at least one party's assumption about the facts was correct, and allowing avoidance disappoints the reasonable expectations of that nonmistaken party.

It is possible to avoid contracts for unilateral mistake, but to do so, proving the elements necessary for mutual mistake is just a starting point. *In addition to* proving the elements of mistake discussed earlier, a person trying to avoid on the ground of unilateral mistake must show *either* one of the following:

**1.** *The nonmistaken party caused or had reason to know of the mistake.* Courts permit avoidance in cases of unilateral mistake if the nonmistaken party caused the mistake, knew of the mistake, or even if the mistake was so obvious that the nonmistaken party had reason to realize that a mistake had been made.[8] For example, Ace Electrical Company makes an error when preparing a bid that it submits to Gorge General Contracting. If the mistake in Ace's bid was so obvious that Gorge knew about it when it accepted

Ace's offer, Ace could avoid the contract even though Ace is the only party who was mistaken. The reasoning behind this rule is that the nonmistaken person could have prevented the loss by acting in good faith and informing the person in error that he had made a mistake. It also reflects the judgment that people should not take advantage of the mistakes of others or

**2.** *It would be unconscionable to enforce the contract.* A court could also permit avoidance because of unilateral mistake when the effect of the mistake was such that it would be unconscionable to enforce the contract. To show that it would be unconscionable to enforce the contract, the mistaken party would have to show that the consequences of the mistake were severe enough that it would be unreasonably harsh or oppressive to enforce the contract.[9] In the example above, Ace Electrical Company made an error when preparing a bid that it submits to Gorge General Contracting. Suppose that Gorge had no reason to realize that a mistake had been made, and accepted the bid. Ace might show that it would be unconscionable to enforce the contract by showing that not only will its profit margin not be what Ace contemplated when it made its offer, but also that it would suffer a grave loss by having to perform at the mistaken price.

---

[8] *Restatement (Second) of Contracts* § 153.

[9] The concept of unconscionability is developed more fully in Chapter 7.

---

**CONCEPT REVIEW**

## AVOIDANCE ON THE GROUND OF MISTAKE

|  | Mutual Mistake | Unilateral Mistake |
| --- | --- | --- |
| **Description** | Both parties mistaken about same fact | Only one party mistaken about a fact |
| **Needed for Avoidance** | Elements of mistake:<br>1. Mistake about basic assumption on which contract was made<br>2. Material effect on agreed exchange<br>3. Person adversely affected by mistake does not bear the risk of the mistake | Same elements as mutual mistake<br>*Plus*<br>*a.* Nonmistaken party caused mistake or had reason to know of mistake<br>*Or*<br>*b.* Effect of mistake is to make it unconscionable to enforce contract |

## DURESS

### Nature of Duress

Duress is wrongful coercion that induces a person to enter or modify a contract. One kind of duress is physical compulsion to enter a contract. For example, Thorp overpowers Grimes, grasps his hand, and forces him to sign a contract. This kind of duress is rare, but when it occurs, a court would find that the contract was *void*. A far more common type of duress occurs when a person is induced to enter a contract by a *threat* of physical, emotional, or economic harm. In these cases, the contract is considered *voidable* at the option of the victimized person. This is the form of duress addressed in this chapter.

The elements of duress have undergone dramatic changes. Classical contract law took a very narrow view of the type of coercion that constituted duress, limiting duress to threats of imprisonment or serious physical harm. Today, however, courts take a much broader view of the types of coercion that will constitute duress. For example, modern courts recognize that threats to a person's economic interests can be duress.

### Elements of Duress

To rescind a contract because of duress, one must be able to establish both of the following elements:

1. The contract was induced by an improper threat.
2. The victim had no reasonable alternative but to enter the contract.[10]

**Improper Threat**   It would not be desirable for courts to hold that every kind of threat constituted duress. If they did, the enforceability of all contracts would be in question, because every contract negotiation involves at least the implied threat that a person will not enter into the transaction unless her demands are met. What degree of wrongfulness, then, is required for a threat to constitute duress? Traditionally, a person would have to threaten to do something she was not legally entitled to do—such as threaten to commit a crime or a tort—for that threat to be duress. Many courts today follow the

*Restatement (Second)* position that, to be duress, the threat need not be wrongful or illegal but must be *improper*—that is, improper to use as leverage to induce a contract.

Under some circumstances, threats to institute legal actions can be considered improper threats that will constitute duress. A threat to file either a civil or a criminal suit without a legal basis for doing so would clearly be improper. What of a threat to file a well-founded lawsuit or prosecution? Generally, if there is a good faith dispute over a matter, a person's threat to file a lawsuit to resolve that dispute is *not* considered to be improper. Otherwise, every person who settled a suit out of court could later claim duress. However, if the threat to sue is made in bad faith and for a purpose unrelated to the issues in the lawsuit, the threat can be considered improper. In one case, for example, duress was found when a husband who was in the process of divorcing his wife threatened to sue for custody of their children—something he had the right to do—unless the wife transferred to him stock that she owned in his company.[11]

The *Restatement (Second)* takes the position that a threat to institute a criminal prosecution is always impermissible pressure to induce a contract, even if the person making the threat has good reason to believe that the other person has committed a crime. It also provides that it is improper for a contracting party to make a threat that would constitute a breach of the duty of good faith and fair dealing under his contract with the person who is the recipient of the threat.[12] This provision is relevant to the many duress cases that arise in the context of coerced modifications of existing contracts or settlements of existing debts.

**Victim Had No Reasonable Alternative**   The person complaining of duress must be able to prove that the coercive nature of the improper threat was such that he had no reasonable alternative but to enter or modify the contract. Classical contract law applied an objective standard of coercion, which required that the degree of coercion exercised had to be sufficient to overcome the will of a person of ordinary courage. The more modern standard for coercion focuses on the alternatives open to the

---

[10]*Restatement (Second) of Contracts* § 175.

[11]*Link v. Link*, 179 S.E.2d 697 (1971).
[12]*Restatement (Second) of Contracts* § 176.

complaining party. For example, Barry, a traveling salesperson, takes his car to Cheatum Motors for repair. Barry pays Cheatum the full amount previously agreed on for the repair, but Cheatum refuses to return Barry's car to him unless Barry agrees to pay substantially more than the contract price for the repair. Because of his urgent need for the return of his car, Barry agrees to do this. In this case, Barry technically had the alternative of filing a legal action to recover his car. However, this would not be a *reasonable alternative* for someone who needs the car urgently because of the time, expense, and uncertainty involved in pursuing a lawsuit. Thus, Barry could avoid his agreement to pay more money under a theory of duress.

**Problem Area: Economic Duress**   Today, the doctrine of duress is often applied in a business context. *Economic duress*, or *business compulsion*, are terms commonly used to describe situations in which one person induces the formation or modification of a contract by threatening another person's economic interests. A common coercive strategy is to threaten to breach the contract unless the other party agrees to modify its terms. For example, Moore, who has contracted to sell goods to

Stephens, knows that Stephens needs timely delivery of the goods. Moore threatens to withhold delivery unless Stephens agrees to pay a higher price. Another common situation involving economic duress occurs when one of the parties offers a disproportionately small amount of money in settlement of a debt and refuses to pay more. Such a strategy exerts great economic pressure on a creditor who is in a desperate financial situation to accept the settlement because he cannot afford the time and expense of bringing a lawsuit.

Classical contract law did not recognize economic duress because this type of hard bargaining was considered neither improper nor coercive. After all, the victim of the sorts of economic pressure described above had at least the theoretical right to file a lawsuit to enforce his rights under the contract. Modern courts recognize that improper economic pressure can prevent a resulting contract or contract modification from being truly voluntary, and the concept of economic duress is well-accepted today. Even in recent cases, however, it is not always clear how much hard bargaining is tolerated. *Eulrich v. Snap-On Tools Corp.*, which follows, presents an example of hard bargaining that a court found to have gone too far.

## EULRICH V. SNAP-ON TOOLS CORP.
### 853 p.2d 1350 (Or. Ct. App. 1993)

Snap-On manufactures and sells hand tools to a nationwide network of dealers, each of whom is assigned a marketing territory. The dealers, in turn, resell the tools to professional mechanics. Dan Eulrich, an auto body mechanic who had never before operated a business, entered into a dealership agreement and became a Snap-On dealer in 1986. Eulrich initially invested $22,000 from his savings and promised to pay a balance of $22,500 from the sale of inventory. The dealership agreement included a provision allowing termination of the dealership by either party. It further provided that upon termination, if Snap-On consented, Eulrich could resell to Snap-On any new tools remaining in his possession.

From the very beginning, Eulrich's dealership was not profitable. In early 1987, he tried to get a more profitable territory because his territory was not supporting him, but he was told to work the territory harder. Eulrich's supervisors, Tim Kash and Ray Park, insisted that anyone could succeed as a dealer by following Snap-On's sales program. (However, there was evidence that Snap-On's marketing system was designed to provide a maximum number of potential dealers and profit for Snap-On, while providing inadequate revenue to support dealers. As a result, dealers quickly failed and were replaced by new recruits.) By the spring of 1987, Eulrich was financially ruined and informed Kash and Park that he wanted to exercise his rights under the dealership agreement and terminate his dealership.

Beginning in April, he attempted to get Kash and Park to "check in" his truck, which he understood would allow him to receive a refund for the tools and the equity in his van. He needed this money to pay his household bills because his dealership had depleted his personal finances. Kash and Park repeatedly put off this check-in until June 1. By that time, as they knew, Eulrich was in serious financial difficulty and could not pay his living expenses, a situation that was aggravated by the fact that Eulrich's wife was ill and required hospitalization but had no medical insurance.

On the day of the check-in, after having worked five or six hours to unload the van under trying circumstances, Kash and Park had Eulrich come into Park's office to "do paperwork." Eulrich was physically tired and emotionally drained. In the office, Kash and Park berated Eulrich for his poor business practices. They also presented Eulrich with a number of documents, none of which had been sent to him in advance to review, and told him to sign them. Kash told Eulrich that he would have to sign the papers before he could get any money. When he asked when he would get a check, Park told him that there would be no checks until the inventory was done and all of the papers were signed. Eulrich signed the papers.

Included in the papers that he signed was a "Termination Agreement," which included an agreement by Snap-On to repurchase Eulrich's tool inventory at current dealer cost. Also included in the document was a release of claims which provided that "each party to this Agreement waives any and all claims it may have against the other arising out of the Dealership terminated by this Agreement. . . ." Eulrich was not aware that a release was included in the Termination Agreement, nor was he aware that he had any legal claims against Snap-On.

Eulrich later filed a lawsuit against Snap-On, Kash, Park, and another Snap-On supervisor to recover damages for fraud, breach of good faith and fair dealing, and breach of contract arising out of the original dealership contract. The defendants asserted that the release barred these claims. Eulrich sought to rescind the release on a number of grounds, including economic duress. The trial judge allowed the rescission and the jury awarded general and punitive damages to Eulrich on his damage claims in the amount of $8,912,000. Snap-On appealed.

---

**Riggs, Judge**    Eulrich acknowledges that, if the release is not rescinded, all of his claims for damages are barred. He asserts that the release should be rescinded because it was executed under economic duress. The gravamen of a claim of economic duress is that, as a result of some wrongful act by one party, the other party is deprived of free will in entering in the agreement.

Defendants argue that we should look only at their threat not to repurchase the tools and that, because the dealership agreement did not require defendants to buy back Eulrich's tools, there was nothing legally wrongful in that conduct. That inquiry is too narrow. Even if we look only at defendants' acts at the time that the termination agreement was executed, requiring Eulrich to sign the termination agreement in order to receive payment for the tools was a wrongful act. The contract conditioned repurchase of the tools on Snap-On's consent, but defendants' performance of that contract term is subject to the duty of good faith and fair dealing. A threat may be a breach of the duty of good faith and fair dealing under the contract even if the threatened act is not itself a breach of the contract. "In the context of duress, an act or threat

is wrongful if it is 'an abuse of the powers of the party making the threat; that is, any threat the purpose of which was not to achieve the end for which the right, power, or privilege was given.' " *Calamari & Perillo, Contracts section 9-3 (3d ed. 1987).* Defendants had no right to abuse their power to consent under the contract by threatening to withhold consent unless Eulrich executed another contract releasing all claims.

In determining whether there was economic duress, a court must consider all surrounding factors and circumstances. Here, there was evidence that defendants' actions, up to the time the termination agreement was signed, were fraudulent and caused Eulrich's economic distress. Defendants knowingly engaged in an ongoing scheme to induce Eulrich into the business, to deny him an adequate sales territory to support his business, to browbeat and demoralize him into believing that the failure of the business was his fault rather than that of the inadequate design of the marketing system, and by depleting all of his financial resources. Defendants knew that their ongoing scheme was causing Eulrich financial distress, resulting in a lack of resources to meet daily household needs and his wife's medical needs. Despite this knowledge, and the provision in the dealer agreement that allowed either party to terminate the agreement on written notification, and despite Eulrich's numerous attempts to return the van and tools for a refund, defendants made Eulrich wait six or seven weeks to terminate the agreement. In the light of all the circumstances leading to the signing of the termination agreement, we conclude that defendants' conduct was wrongful.

Nevertheless, defendants argue that there was no economic duress because Eulrich had reasonable alternatives to signing the release. They contend that, under the dealership agreement, Eulrich had the option of keeping the inventory and selling it outside the dealership, which would have allowed him to recoup his inventory investment, or that he could have refused to sign the agreement, reserving his rights, or could have taken the termination agreement home with him and sought legal advice before he signed it. Under the coercive circumstances present here, those were not reasonable alternatives.

Eulrich had tried in vain for nearly two months to check in his van and tools and obtain the refund that defendants had promised for the tools. During that time, his poor financial situation deteriorated further. Selling Snap-On's product was a losing proposition; it would not have been a reasonable alternative for him to continue that course as a way of recouping his investment. Neither was refusing to sign the termination agreement and seeking a legal remedy a reasonable alternative. By the time defendants finally allowed Eulrich to check in the tools for the promised refund, Eulrich needed money immediately, and defendants knew it. For a legal remedy to be a reasonable alternative, it must be an "immediate and adequate remedy" and [this] is tested by a practical standard that takes into consideration the exigencies of the situation. Refusing to sign defendants' termination agreement and commencing legal action against them was not a reasonable alternative, because such a course would have taken time and Eulrich's financial condition was perilous. Faced with the choice between complying with defendants' demand and receiving the badly needed funds, or refusing to sign and facing financial disaster, Eulrich had no reasonable alternative and thus found himself deprived of the exercise of his free will. Accordingly, we conclude that his agreement to the release was a result of economic duress and that the trial court did not err in allowing the rescission.

**Judgment allowing rescission affirmed in favor of Eulrich. [The case was also remanded for the correction of an error in the damages awarded to Eulrich.]**

## Undue Influence

### Nature of Undue Influence

**Undue influence** is unfair persuasion. Like duress, undue influence involves wrongful pressure exerted on a person during the bargaining process. In undue influence, however, the pressure is exerted through *persuasion* rather than through coercion. The doctrine of undue influence was developed to give relief to persons who are unfairly persuaded to enter a contract while in a position of weakness that makes them particularly vulnerable to being preyed on by those they trust or fear. A large proportion of undue influence cases arise after the death of the person who has been the subject of undue influence, when his relatives seek to set aside that person's contracts or wills.

**Determining Undue Influence**   All contracts are based on persuasion. There is no precise dividing line between permissible persuasion and impermissible persuasion. Nevertheless, several hallmarks of undue influence cases can be identified. Undue influence cases normally involve both of the following elements:

1. The relationship between the parties is either one of trust and confidence or one in which the person exercising the persuasion dominates the person being persuaded.
2. The persuasion is unfair.[13]

---

[13]*Restatement (Second) of Contracts* § 177.

**Relation between the Parties**    Undue influence cases involve people who, though they have capacity to enter a contract, are in a position of particular vulnerability in relationship to the other party to the contract. This relationship can be one of trust and confidence, in which the person being influenced justifiably believes that the other party is looking out for his interests, or at least that he would not do anything contrary to his welfare. Examples of such relationships would include parent and child, husband and wife, or lawyer and client.

The relationship can also be one in which one of the parties holds dominant psychological power that is not derived from a confidential relationship. For example, Royce, an elderly man, is dependent on his housekeeper, Smith, to care for him. Smith persuades Royce to withdraw most of his life savings from the bank and make an interest-free loan to her. If the persuasion Smith used was unfair, the transaction could be avoided because of undue influence.

**Unfair Persuasion**    The mere existence of a close or dependent relationship between the parties that results in economic advantage to one of them is not sufficient for undue influence. It must also appear that the weaker person entered the contract because he was subjected to unfair methods of persuasion. In determining this, a court will look at all of the surrounding facts and circumstances. Was the person isolated and rushed into the contract, or did he have access to outsiders for advice and time to consider his alternatives? Was the contract discussed and consummated in the usual time and place that would be expected for such a transaction, or was it discussed or consummated at an unusual time or in an unusual place? Was the contract a reasonably fair one that a person might have entered voluntarily, or was it so lopsided and unfair that one could infer that he probably would not have entered it unless he had been unduly influenced by the other party? The answers to these and similar questions help determine whether the line between permissible and impermissible persuasion has been crossed.

---

**CONCEPT REVIEW**

**WRONGFUL PRESSURE IN THE BARGAINING PROCESS**

|  | Duress | Undue Influence |
|---|---|---|
| **Nature of Pressure** | Coercion | Unfair persuasion of susceptible individual |
| **Elements** | 1. Contract induced by improper threat<br>2. Threat leaves party no reasonable alternative but to enter or modify contract | 1. Relationship of trust and confidence or dominance<br>2. Unfair persuasion |

---

**PROBLEMS AND PROBLEM CASES**

**1.** King Chevrolet provided a 1982 Chevrolet Cavalier to one of its salespeople, Stein. During the eight months Stein drove the car, it was repaired or adjusted 10 times. There were repairs to the carburetor, choke, speedometer, door moldings, seat belt buzzer alarm, and spark plugs as well as a complete paint job. Of the 36 demonstrators Stein had driven over the years as a car salesperson, this was the worst. Stein finally complained to the service de-

partment about the car, and asked Lewis, King Chevrolet's sales manager, if he could have another demonstrator because his car was so unreliable. Not long afterward, Muzelak, who had purchased her previous car from Lewis, contacted Lewis about buying a new car. Lewis told her that the "right car for her" was the 1982 Chevrolet Cavalier demonstrator that Stein had used. Lewis did tell Muzelak that the car was a demonstrator, but he did not mention any of the previous repair problems with the car. (Stein later testified that Lewis told him it took someone with his sales ability to "get rid of" that car.) Muzelak bought the car. Over the course of the next eight months, Muzelak's car was in King Chevrolet's service department for repairs 13 times. Some of the problems were never corrected. The car was so unreliable that Muzelak did not drive it after the first eight months of use. Does Muzelak have grounds for an action for fraud?

**2.** On May 17, Cobaugh was playing in the East End Open Golf Tournament. When he arrived at the ninth tee, he found a new Chevrolet Beretta, together with signs which proclaimed: "HOLE-IN-ONE Wins this 1988 Chevrolet Beretta GT Courtesy of KLICK-LEWIS Buick Chevy Pontiac $49.00 OVER FACTORY INVOICE in Palmyra." Cobaugh aced the ninth hole and attempted to claim his prize. Klick-Lewis refused to deliver the car, however. Klick-Lewis had offered the car as a prize for a charity golf tournament sponsored by the Hershey-Palmyra Sertoma Club two days earlier and had neglected to remove the car and signs prior to Cobaugh's hole-in-one. Cobaugh sued to compel delivery of the car. Would the doctrine of mistake provide a ground for Klick-Lewis to avoid the contract?

**3.** West Branch Land Co. owned a tract of land, which it listed for sale. The listing that was published in the local Multiple Listing Service listing sheet and distributed to all subscribing real estate agencies described the property as being "zoned multi for 35 townhouses" when in fact it was really zoned for only 30. Acleson, a licensed real estate broker, received a copy of the listing and, after calculating the costs per unit on the basis of 35 units, submitted an offer to purchase the property. The parties ultimately contracted for the sale of the property for $65,000. The final contract made no mention of the acreage of the land or of its zoning status. Acleson could have determined the true acreage and zoning status by checking the plat map that was available at the local city planner's office. Almost two years after the sale, Acleson learned that the property was really zoned for only 30 units. Will Acleson's failure to investigate the zoning of the land prevent him from obtaining a remedy for misrepresentation or fraud?

**4.** Odorizzi, an elementary school teacher, was arrested on criminal charges involving illegal sexual activity. After having been arrested, questioned by police, booked, and released on bail, and going 40 hours without sleep, he was visited in his home by the superintendent of the school district and the principal of his school. They told him that they were trying to help him and that they had his best interests at heart. They advised him to resign immediately, stating that there was no time to consult an attorney. They said that if he did not resign immediately, the district would dismiss him and publicize the proceedings, but that if he resigned at once, the incident would not be publicized and would not jeopardize his chances of securing employment as a teacher elsewhere. Odorizzi gave them a written letter of resignation, which they accepted. The criminal charges against Odorizzi were later dismissed, and he sought to resume his employment. When the school district refused to reinstate him, Odorizzi attempted to rescind his letter of resignation on several grounds, including undue influence. (He also alleged duress, but the facts of his case did not constitute duress under applicable state law.) Can Odorizzi avoid the contract on the ground of undue influence?

**5.** The O'Connors entered into a contract with the Kings in 1986 to lease their townhouse to the Kings with an option to purchase. Prior to leasing the townhouse, Mr. King noticed a crack in a retaining wall near the house's driveway, and Mr. O'Connor showed him an area along the east foundation wall where there was a separation of the earth and foundation. The O'Connors agreed to pay for dirt to be brought in and placed along the east foundation. Both parties believed this would eliminate potential water problems in the basement. At some point prior to the time the Kings leased the townhouse, water seeped into the basement of the townhouse, but the O'Connors did not tell the Kings about this because there was no apparent water damage. Furthermore, when Ms. King explicitly questioned the O'Connors about the existence of water in the basement, the O'Connors denied any existence of water in the basement. The Kings exercised their option to purchase the townhouse in June of 1987. By the fall of that year, the Kings began experiencing problems with doors sticking and interior walls cracking. They later discovered that the retaining wall crack had widened and that there was water damage in the basement bathroom. When the O'Connors refused their demand to pay for the repairs, the Kings moved out of the townhouse. The O'Connors sued the Kings for breach of contract, and the Kings counterclaimed for rescission of the contract. Can the Kings rescind the contract?

**6.** Boskett, a part-time coin dealer, paid $450 for a dime purportedly minted in 1916 at Denver and two additional coins of relatively small value. After carefully examining the dime, Beachcomber Coins, a retail coin dealer, bought the coin from Boskett for $500. Beachcomber then received an offer from a third party to purchase the dime for $700, subject to certification of its genuineness from the American Numismatic Society. That organization labeled the coin a counterfeit. Can Beachcomber rescind the contract with Boskett on the ground of mistake?

**7.** Robert & Wendy Pfister asked Foster & Marshall, a stock brokerage firm, to evaluate some stocks that they owned, including 100 shares of Tracor Computing Corporation. The stock was no longer traded on the New York Stock Exchange. The Pfisters did not know the value of the stock, but they believed it to be of little value. They were surprised when Foster & Marshall told them that the stock was trading at $49.50 under its new name, Continuum Co., Inc., so that the value of the Pfisters' stock was $4,950. They asked Foster & Marshall to recheck the figures and brought their stock certificates in for verification. Based on Foster & Marshall's reassurances that they owned 100 shares of Continuum and that these were worth $4,950, the Pfisters sold the stock to Foster & Marshall. As a result of receiving this money for the stock, the Pfisters made a commitment to build a new home, which before the sale had been a "borderline decision." A year after the transaction, Foster & Marshall discovered that the Tracor Computing stock had been exchanged for Continuum stock at a 10-to-1 ratio and that the Pfisters had owned only 10 shares of Continuum. Foster & Marshall claimed relief under the doctrine of mistake and sued the Pfisters to recover the $4,466.25 it had overpaid them. Will Foster & Marshall win?

**8.** Mrs. Gossinger slipped and fell on soapy water that had flooded the bathroom floor of the apartment that she and her husband rented from Sutherland, a member of the Apartment Owners Association of the Regency of Ala Wai. She immediately drove herself to the hospital, where the physician examined her, performed tests, and concluded that she had suffered a back strain, which he advised her "would take a long time to heal." He advised her to have a follow-up examination at the beginning of the following week—or sooner if her condition worsened. The next day, the Gossingers wrote to the Association demanding compensation for personal injury and property damage caused by the flooding incident. Three days later, an insurance adjuster for State Farm Insurance Company met with the Gossingers to settle their claims. As a result of the meeting, the Gossingers settled their claims for $1,100 and signed a release that purported to discharge the Association and all other persons who might be liable for her injuries from all liability for any personal injury or property damage resulting from her fall. Approximately one year after signing the release, Mrs. Gossinger's back pain had not subsided. Upon examination by a physician, she was diagnosed as suffering from a herniated disc, requiring surgery and leading to more than $20,000 in medical expenses. The Gossingers filed a negligence suit against Sutherland and the Association. The Gossingers asserted that the release is invalid because of unilateral or mutual mistake. Was it?

**9.** Ashton Development hired Rich & Whillock, Inc., to do grading and excavating work on a construction project. The contract specified that removal of any rock encountered would be considered an "extra." After a month's work, Rich & Whillock encountered rock on the project site. Ashton agreed that the rock would have to be blasted and that this would involve extra costs. It directed Rich & Whillock to go ahead with the blasting and bill for the extra cost. Rich & Whillock did so, submitting separate invoices for the regular contract work and the extra blasting work and receiving payment every two weeks. After completing the work, Rich & Whillock submitted a final billing for an additional $72,286.45. This time Ashton refused to pay. Rich & Whillock communicated that it would "go broke" without this final payment because it was a new business with rented equipment and had numerous subcontractors waiting to be paid. Ashton replied that it would pay $50,000 or nothing. Stating, "I have a check for you, and just take it or leave it, this is all you get. If you don't want this, you have got to sue me," Ashton's agent presented Rich & Whillock with an agreement for a final compromise payment of $50,000. Rich & Whillock signed the settlement agreement and received a $25,000 check after communicating that the agreement was "blackmail" and that it was signing the agreement only because it was necessary in order to survive. Rich & Whillock later signed a release form and received a second check for $25,000. Several months afterward, however, Rich & Whillock sued Ashton for breach of contract, maintaining that the settlement agreement and release should not be enforced. Are the settlement agreement and release voidable?

**10.** Reed purchased a house from King. Neither King nor his real estate agents told Reed before the sale that a woman and her four children had been murdered there 10 years earlier. Reed learned of the gruesome episode from a neighbor after the sale. She sued King and his real estate agents, seeking rescission and damages on the ground that King should have disclosed the history of the house to her. Can Reed rescind the contract?

**11.** 📼 *Video Case.* See "In the Cards." Johnson owned a new baseball card store that had been very busy during its first week of operation. Not wanting to close the store while he went out for dinner, he got a temporary clerk who knew nothing about baseball cards to staff the store in his absence. He instructed the clerk that the prices on the cards were marked and if anyone wanted to negotiate for the more expensive cards in the glass case, she was to tell them to return and talk to Johnson. While Johnson was out, a boy came in and asked to look at the Ernie Banks rookie card, which was in the glass case. The card was marked "1200." The boy asked whether the card was really worth $12 and the clerk replied, "Yeah, I guess it is" and sold the card to him for $12. When Johnson returned and looked through the sales, he saw that the card had been sold for $12, when its true price was $1,200. Is the contract voidable on the ground of any reality of consent doctrine?

**12.** 📼 *Video Case.* See "The Stock Option." As part of an employee benefit plan, Famco gave stock options to its employees. There were two restrictions on the sale of stock to employees, however. First, if the employee terminated employment for any reason, Famco had the right to buy the stock at book value (often less than market value). Second, if an employee wanted to sell the stock while employed, Famco had a right of first refusal. Famco's CEO called a meeting with three employees who had purchased stock. During this meeting, the CEO reminded the employees that if their employment terminated, the company could repur-

chase the stock at book value. The employees felt that they had to sell their stock back to Famco or they would lose their jobs, in which case they would have to sell their stock anyway. Two employees agreed to resell the stock to Famco. Were these agreements to sell the stock to Famco voidable?

See also "Car Deals."

## CAPSTONE QUESTIONS

**1.** Wiley Motors advertised a 1992 Cornerstone minivan for sale. The van had previously been purchased new but had been returned to the dealership by its initial owner because of its extremely poor service record. The van had been returned for service 20 times between the spring of 1992 and the fall of 1994. It had been especially unreliable in the winter months, when it frequently did not start in weather colder than 35 degrees. Trusting came to Wiley to inspect and test-drive the van in response to Wiley's ad. On the day that Trusting test-drove the van, however, it was a warm spring day and the van operated perfectly. Wiley's salesperson did not mention any of the previous repair problems to Trusting because he wanted to mislead Trusting into buying the van. Trusting asked the salesperson if the van had ever been involved in an accident, and the salesperson responded that it had not. The salesperson believed in all good faith that this statement was true. In fact, the van had been involved in an accident and had incurred some frame damage, but Wiley (and its salesperson) did not know this. Trusting purchased the van. Within a short time, Trusting began having trouble with the van both from the frame damage and from some of the same conditions that had caused the van's service problems for its original owner. Trusting seeks to rescind the purchase and is considering suing Wiley for damages for fraud as well.

### Required:

Answer the following and give reasons for your conclusions.

1. Assess whether Trusting has a legal right to rescind the purchase.

2. State whether Trusting has the right to seek both rescission and damages if he is able to prove fraud.

**2.** Grey, age 70, was in the hospital suffering from a terminal illness that caused him a great deal of pain but did not interfere with his mental faculties. Charles, a real estate broker and developer who had long served as Grey's real estate broker, visited Grey daily at the hospital. During these visits, Charles urged Grey repeatedly to sell a tract of undeveloped land that Grey owned to him (Charles) at a price substantially below fair market value. After several weeks of this persuasion, Grey finally agreed because he was concerned that Charles would be angry or hurt if he did not sell the property to him. A contract of sale was signed by both of the parties in Grey's hospital room. At the time of contracting, Grey assumed that the property was zoned for single family use only. Charles, however, knew that the property was zoned for commercial uses, which made it more valuable. The contract did not describe the zoning and neither party spoke of it. Grey later regretted entering the contract and seeks to rescind it.

**Required:**

Answer the following and give reasons for your conclusions.

Assess whether Grey has the right to avoid the contract on the ground of duress, undue influence, and/or mistake.

# CHAPTER 6

# CAPACITY TO CONTRACT

## INTRODUCTION

*One of the major justifications for enforcing a contract is that the parties* voluntarily consented *to be bound by it. It follows, then, that a person must have the* ability *to give consent before he can be legally bound to an agreement. For truly voluntary agreements to exist, this ability to give consent must involve more than the mere physical ability to say yes or shake hands or sign one's name. Rather, the person's maturity and mental ability must be such that it is fair to presume that he is capable of representing his own interests effectively. This concept is embodied in the legal term* capacity.

## LACK OF CAPACITY

**Capacity** means the ability to incur legal obligations and acquire legal rights. Today, the primary classes of people who are considered to lack capacity are minors (who, in legal terms, are known as *infants*), persons suffering from mental illnesses or defects, and intoxicated persons.[1] Contract law gives them the right to *avoid* (escape) contracts that they enter during incapacity. This rule provides a means of protecting people who, because of mental impairment, intoxication, or youth and inexperience, are disadvantaged in the normal give and take of the bargaining process.

Usually, lack of capacity to contract comes up in court in one of two ways. In some cases, it is asserted by a plaintiff as the basis of a lawsuit for the money or other benefits that he gave the other party under their contract. In others, it arises as a defense to the enforcement of a contract when the defendant is the party who lacked capacity. The responsibility for alleging and proving incapacity is placed on the person who bases his claim or defense on his lack of capacity.

### Effect of Lack of Capacity

Normally, a contract in which one or both parties lacks capacity because of infancy, mental impairment, or intoxication is considered to be voidable.

---

[1]In times past, married women, convicts, and aliens were also among the classes of persons who lacked capacity to contract. These limitations on capacity have been removed by statute and court rule, however.

People whose capacity is impaired in any of these ways are able to enter a contract and enforce it if they wish, but they also have the right to avoid the contract. There are, however, some individuals whose capacity is so impaired that they do not have the ability to form even a voidable contract. A bargain is considered to be void if, at the time of formation of the bargain, a court had already **adjudicated** (adjudged or decreed) one or more of the parties to be mentally incompetent or one or more of the parties was so impaired that he could not even manifest assent (for example, he was comatose or unconscious).

## MINORS' CONTRACTS

### Minors' Right to Disaffirm

Courts have long recognized that minors are in a vulnerable position in their dealings with adults. Courts granted minors the right to avoid contracts as a means of protecting against their own improvidence and against overreaching by adults. The exercise of this right to avoid a contract is called **disaffirmance**. The right to disaffirm is personal to the minor. That is, only the minor or a legal representative such as a guardian may disaffirm the contract. No formal act or written statement is required to make a valid disaffirmance. Any words or acts that effectively communicate the minor's desire to cancel the contract can constitute disaffirmance.

If, on the other hand, the minor wishes to enforce the contract instead of disaffirming it, the adult party must perform. You can see that the minor's right to disaffirm puts any adult contracting with a minor in an undesirable position: He is bound on the contract unless it is to the minor's advantage to disaffirm it. The right to disaffirm has the effect of discouraging adults from dealing with minors.

#### Exceptions to the Minor's Right to Disaffirm

Not every contract involving a minor is voidable, however. State law often creates statutory exceptions to the minor's right to disaffirm. These statutes prevent minors from disaffirming such transactions as marriage, agreements to support their children, educational loans, life and medical insurance contracts, contracts for transportation by common carriers, and certain types of contracts approved by a court (such as contracts to employ a child actor).

### Period of Minority

At common law, the age of majority was 21. However, the ratification in 1971 of the 26th Amendment to the Constitution giving 18-year-olds the right to vote stimulated a trend toward reducing the age of majority. The age of majority has been lowered by 49 states. In almost all of these states, the age of majority for contracting purposes is now 18.

### Emancipation

**Emancipation** is the termination of a parent's right to control a child and receive services and wages from him. There are no formal requirements for emancipation. It can occur by the parent's express or implied consent or by the occurrence of some events such as the marriage of the child. In most states, the mere fact that a minor is emancipated does *not* give him capacity to contract. A person younger than the legal age of majority is generally held to lack capacity to enter a contract, even if he is married and employed full time.

### Time of Disaffirmance

Contracts entered during minority that affect title to *real estate* cannot be disaffirmed until majority. This rule is apparently based on the special importance of real estate and on the need to protect a minor from improvidently disaffirming a transaction (such as a mortgage or conveyance) involving real estate. All other contracts entered during minority may be disaffirmed as soon as the contract is formed. The minor's power to avoid his contracts does not end on the day he reaches the age of majority. It continues for a period of time after he reaches majority.

How long after reaching majority does a person retain the right to disaffirm the contracts he made while a minor? A few states have statutes that prescribe a definite time limit on the power of avoidance. In Oklahoma, for example, a person who wishes to disaffirm a contract must do so within one year after reaching majority.[2] In most states, however, there is no set limit on the time during which a person may disaffirm after reaching majority. In determining whether a person has the right to

---

[2]Okla. Stat. Ann. tit. 15 sec. 18 (1983).

**FIGURE 1**    **Time Line Showing Effect of Ratification**

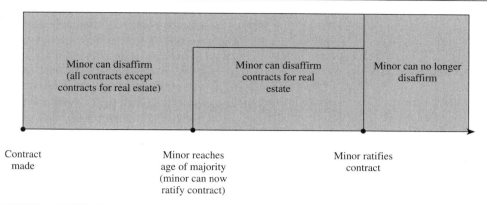

disaffirm, a major factor that courts consider is whether the adult has rendered performance under the contract or relied on the contract. If the adult has relied on the contract or has given something of value to the minor, the minor must disaffirm within a reasonable time after reaching majority. If he delays longer than a period of time that is considered to be reasonable under the circumstances, he will run the risk of *ratifying* (affirming) the contract. (The concept and consequences of ratification are discussed in the next section.) If the adult has neither performed nor relied on the contract, however, the former minor is likely to be accorded a longer period of time in which to disaffirm, sometimes even years after he has reached majority.

## Ratification

Though a person has the right to disaffirm contracts made during minority, this right can be given up after the person reaches the age of majority. When a person who has reached majority indicates that he intends to be bound by a contract that he made while still a minor, he surrenders his right to disaffirm. This act of affirming the contract and surrendering the right to avoid the contract is known as **ratification**. Ratification makes a contract valid from its inception. Because ratification represents the former minor's election to be bound by the contract, he cannot later disaffirm. Ratification can be done effectively only after the minor reaches

majority. Otherwise, it would be as voidable as the initial contract. The effect of ratification is illustrated in Figure 1.

There are no formal requirements for ratification. Any of the former minor's words or acts after reaching majority that indicate with reasonable clarity his intent to be bound by the contract are sufficient. Ratification can be *expressed* in an oral or written statement, or, as is more often the case, it can be *implied* by conduct on the part of the former minor. Naturally, ratification is clearest when the former minor has made some express statement of his intent to be bound. Predicting whether a court will determine that a contract has been ratified is a bit more difficult when the only evidence of the alleged ratification is the conduct of the minor. A former minor's acceptance or retention of benefits given by the other party for an unreasonable time after he has reached majority can constitute ratification. Also, a former minor's continued performance of his part of the contract after reaching majority has been held to imply his intent to ratify the contract.

## Duty to Return Consideration upon Disaffirmance

If neither party has performed his part of the contract, the parties' relationship will simply be canceled by the disaffirmance. Since neither party has given anything to the other party, no further adjustments are necessary. But what about the situation where, as is often the case, the minor has paid money to the adult and the adult has given property to the minor? Upon disaffirmance, each party has the duty to return to the other any consideration that the other has given. This means that the minor must return any consideration given to him by the adult that remains in his possession. However, if the minor is unable to return the consideration, most states will still permit him to disaffirm the contract.

The duty to return consideration also means that the minor has the right to recover any consideration he has given to the adult party. He even has the right to recover some property that has been transferred to third parties. One exception to the minor's right to recover property from third parties is found in section 2–403 of the Uniform Commercial Code, however. Under this section, a minor cannot recover *goods* that have been transferred to a good faith purchaser. For example, Simpson, a minor, sells a 1980 Ford to Mort's Car Lot. Mort's then sells the car to Vane, a good faith purchaser. If Simpson disaffirmed the contract with Mort's, he would *not* have the right to recover the Ford from Vane.

## Must the Disaffirming Minor Make Restitution? A Split of Authority

If the consideration given by the adult party has been lost, damaged, destroyed, or simply has depreciated in value, is the minor required to make restitution to the adult for the loss? The traditional rule is that the minor who cannot fully return the consideration that was given to her is *not* obligated to pay the adult for the benefits she has received or to compensate the adult for loss or depreciation of the consideration. Some states still follow this traditional rule. (As you will read in the next section, however, a minor's misrepresentation of age can, even in some of these states, make her responsible for reimbursing the other party upon disaffirmance). The rule that restitution is not required is designed to protect minors by discouraging adults from dealing with them. After all, if an adult knew that he might be able to demand the return of anything that he transferred to a minor, he would have little incentive to refrain from entering into contracts with minors.

The traditional rule, however, can work harsh results for innocent adults who have dealt fairly with minors. It strikes many people as unprincipled that a doctrine intended to protect against unfair exploitation of one class of people can be used to unfairly exploit another class of people. As courts sometimes say, the minor's right to disaffirm was designed to be used as a "shield rather than as a sword." For these reasons, a growing number of states have rejected the traditional rule. The courts and legislatures of these states have adopted rules that require minors who disaffirm their contracts and seek refunds of purchase price to reimburse adults for the use or depreciation of their property. The following case, *Dodson v. Shrader*, follows this approach.

## Dodson v. Shrader
**824 S.W.2d 545 (Tenn. Sup. Ct. 1992)**

Joseph Dodson, age 16, bought a 1984 Chevrolet truck from Burns and Mary Shrader, owners of Shrader's Auto Sales, for $4,900 cash. At the time, Burns Shrader, believing Dodson to be 18 or 19, did not ask Dodson's age and Dodson did not volunteer it. Dodson drove the truck for about eight months, when he learned from an auto mechanic that there was a burned valve in the engine. Dodson did not have the money for the repairs, so he continued to drive the truck without repair for another month until the engine "blew up" and stopped operating. He parked the car in the front yard of his parents' house. He then contacted the Shraders, rescinding the purchase of the truck and requesting a full refund. The Shraders refused to accept the truck or to give Dodson a refund. Dodson then filed an action seeking to rescind the contract and recover the amount paid for the truck. Before the court could hear the case, a hit-and-run driver struck Dodson's parked truck, damaging its left front fender. At the time of the circuit court trial, the truck was worth only $500. The Shraders argued that Dodson should be responsible for paying the difference between the present value of the truck and the

$4,900 purchase price. The trial court found in Dodson's favor, ordering the Shraders to refund the $4,900 purchase price upon delivery of the truck. The Tennessee Court of Appeals affirmed this judgment, and the Shraders appealed.

———————————■———————————

**O'Brien, Justice**   The law on the subject of the protection of infants' rights has been slow to evolve. The underlying purpose of the "infancy doctrine" is to protect minors from their lack of judgment and from squandering their wealth through improvident contracts with crafty adults who would take advantage of them in the marketplace.

There is, however, a modern trend among the states, either by judicial action or by statute, in the approach to the problem of balancing the rights of minors against those of innocent merchants. As a result, two minority rules have developed which allow the other party to a contract with a minor to refund less than the full consideration paid in the event of rescission. The first of these minority rules is called the "Benefit Rule." This rule holds that, upon rescission, recovery of the full purchase price is subject to a deduction for the minor's use of the merchandise. This rule recognizes that the traditional rule in regard to necessaries has been extended so far as to hold an infant bound by his contracts, where he failed to restore what he has received under them to the extent of the benefit actually derived by him from what he has received from the other party to the transaction. The other minority rule holds that the minor's recovery of the full purchase price is subject to a deduction for the minor's "use" of the consideration he or she received under the contract, or for the "depreciation" or "deterioration" of the consideration in his or her possession.

We are impressed by the statement made by the Court of Appeals of Ohio:

At a time when we see young persons between 18 and 21 years of age demanding and assuming more responsibilities in their daily lives; when we see such persons charged with the responsibility for committing crimes; when we see such persons being sued in tort claims for acts of negligence; when we see such persons subject to military service; when we see such persons engaged in business and acting in almost all other respects as an adult, it seems timely to re-examine the case law pertaining to contractual rights and responsibilities of infants to see if the law as pronounced and applied by the courts should be redefined.

We state the rule to be followed hereafter, in reference to a contract of a minor, to be where the minor has not been overreached in any way, and there has been no undue influence, and the contract is a fair and reasonable one, and the minor has actually paid money on the purchase price, and taken and used the article purchased, that he ought not to be permitted to recover the amount actually paid, without allowing the vendor of the goods reasonable compensation for the use of, depreciation, and willful or negligent damage to the article purchased, while in his hands. If there has been any fraud or imposition on the part of the seller or if the contract is unfair, or any unfair advantage has been taken of the minor inducing him to make the purchase, then the rule does not apply. This rule will fully and fairly protect the minor against injustice or imposition, and at the same time it will be fair to a business person who has dealt with such minor in good faith.

This rule is best adapted to modern conditions under which minors are permitted to, and do in fact, transact a great deal of business for themselves, long before they have reached the age of legal majority. Many young people work and earn money and collect it and spend it oftentimes without any oversight or restriction. The law does not question their right to buy if they have the money to pay for their purchases. It seems intolerably burdensome of everyone concerned if merchants cannot deal with them safely, in a fair and reasonable way. Further, it does not appear consistent with practice of proper moral influence upon young people, tend to encourage honesty and integrity, or lead them to a good and useful business future if they are taught that they can make purchases with their own money, for their own benefit, and after paying for them, and using them until they are worn out and destroyed, go back and compel the vendor to return to them what they have paid upon the purchase price. Such a doctrine can only lead to the corruption of principles and encourage young people in habits of trickery and dishonesty.

**Reversed and remanded in favor of the Shraders.**

## Effect of Misrepresentation of Age

It is not unheard of for a minor to occasionally pretend to be older than he is. The normal rules dealing with the minor's right to disaffirm and his duties upon disaffirmance can be affected by a minor's misrepresentation of his age.[3] Suppose, for example, that Jones, age 17, wants to lease a car from Acme Auto Rentals, but knows that Acme rents only to people who are at least 18. Jones induces Acme to lease a car to him by showing a false identification that represents his age to be 18. Acme relies on the misrepresentation. Jones wrecks the car, attempts to disaffirm the contract, and asks for the return of his money. What is the effect of Jones's misrepresentation? State law is not uniform on this point.

The traditional rule was that a minor's misrepresentation about his age did not affect his right to disaffirm and did not create any obligation to reimburse the adult for damages or pay for benefits received. The theory behind this rule is that one who lacks capacity cannot acquire it merely by claiming to be of legal age. As you can imagine, this traditional approach does not "sit well" with modern courts, at least in those cases in which the adult has dealt with the minor fairly and in good faith, because it creates severe hardship for innocent adults who have relied on minors' misrepresentations of age.

State law today is fairly evenly divided among those states that take the position that the minor who misrepresents his age will be *estopped* (prevented) from asserting his infancy as a defense and those that will allow a minor to disaffirm regardless of his misrepresentation of age. Among the states that allow disaffirmance despite the minor's misrepresentation, most hold the disaffirming minor responsible for the losses suffered by the adult, either by allowing the adult to counterclaim against the minor for the tort of deceit or by requiring the minor to reimburse the adult for use or depreciation of his property.

## Minors' Obligation to Pay Reasonable Value of Necessaries

Though the law regarding minors' contracts is designed to discourage adults from dealing with (and possibly taking advantage of) minors, it would be undesirable for the law to discourage adults from selling minors the items that they need for basic survival. For this reason, disaffirming minors are required to pay the reasonable value of items that have been furnished to them that are classified as **necessaries.** A necessary is something that is essential for the minor's continued existence and general welfare that has not been provided by the minor's parents or guardian. Examples of necessaries include food, clothing, shelter, medical care, tools of the minor's trade, and basic educational or vocational training.

A minor's liability for necessaries supplied to him is **quasi contractual**. That is, the minor is liable for the *reasonable value* of the necessaries that she actually receives. She is not liable for the entire price agreed on if that price exceeds the actual value of the necessaries, and she is not liable for necessaries that she contracted for but did not receive. For example, Joy Jones, a minor, signs a one-year lease for an apartment in Mountain Park at a rent of $300 per month. After living in the apartment for three months, Joy breaks her lease and moves out. Because she is a minor, Joy has the right to disaffirm the lease. If shelter is a necessary in this case, however, she must pay the reasonable value of what she has actually received—three months' rent. If she can establish that the actual value of what she has received is less than $300 per month, she will be bound to pay only that lesser amount. Furthermore, she will not be obligated to pay for the remaining nine months' rent, because she has not received any benefits from the remainder of the lease.

Whether a given item is considered a necessary depends on the facts of a particular case. The minor's age, station in life, and personal circumstances are all relevant to this issue. As is emphasized in the *Webster Street Partnership* case, which follows, an item sold to a minor is not considered a necessary if the minor's parent or guardian has already supplied him with similar items. For this reason, the range of items that will be considered necessaries is broader for married minors and other emancipated minors than it is for unemancipated minors.

---

[3]You might want to refer back to Chapter 5 to review the elements of misrepresentation.

## WEBSTER STREET PARTNERSHIP V. SHERIDAN
### 368 N.W.2d 439 (S. Ct. Neb. 1985)

Webster Street owns real estate in Omaha, Nebraska. On September 18, 1982, Webster Street entered into a written contract to lease an apartment to Matthew Sheridan and Pat Wilwerding for one year at a rental of $250 per month. Although Webster Street did not know this, both Sheridan and Wilwerding were younger than the age of majority (which was 19) when the lease was signed.

Sheridan and Wilwerding paid $150 as a security deposit and rent for the remainder of September and the month of October, for a total of $500. They failed to pay their November rent on time, however, and Webster Street notified them that they would be required to move out unless they paid immediately. Unable to pay rent, Sheridan and Wilwerding moved out of the apartment on November 12. Webster Street later demanded that they pay the expenses it incurred in attempting to rerent the property, rent for the months of November and December (apparently the two months it took to find a new tenant), and assorted damages and fees, amounting to $630.94. Sheridan and Wilwerding refused to pay any of the amount demanded on the ground of minority, and demanded the return of their security deposit. Webster Street then filed this lawsuit. The district court found that the apartment was a necessary and that Sheridan and Wilwerding were liable for the 12 days in November in which they had actually possessed the apartment without paying rent, but that they were entitled to the return of their security deposit. Webster Street appealed from this ruling.

---

**Krivosha, Chief Justice**   The privilege of infancy will not enable an infant to escape liability under all circumstances. For example, it is well established that an infant is liable for the value of necessaries furnished him. Just what are necessaries, however, has no exact definition. The term is flexible and varies according to the facts of each individual case. A number of factors must be considered before a court can conclude whether a particular product or service is a necessary. The articles must be useful and suitable. To be necessaries the articles must supply the infant's personal needs, either those of his body or those of his mind. However, the term "necessaries" is not confined to merely such things as are required for bare subsistence. What may be considered necessary for one infant may not be necessaries for another infant whose state is different as to rank, social position, fortune, health, or other circumstances. To enable an infant to contract for articles as necessaries, he must have been in actual need of them, and obliged to procure them for himself. They are not necessaries as to him, however necessary they may be in their nature, if he was already supplied with sufficient articles of the kind, or if he had a parent or guardian who was able and willing to supply them. The burden of proof is on the plaintiff to show that the infant was destitute of the articles and had no way of procuring them except by his own contract.

The undisputed testimony is that both tenants were living away from home, apparently with the understanding that they could return home at any time. It would appear that neither Sheridan nor Wilwerding was in need of shelter but, rather, had chosen to voluntarily leave home, with the understanding that they could return whenever they desired. One may at first blush believe that such a rule is unfair. Yet, on further consideration, the wisdom of such a rule is apparent. If landlords may not contract with minors, except at their peril, they may refuse to do so. In that event, minors who voluntarily leave home but who are free to return will be compelled to return to their parents' home—a result which is desirable. We therefore hold that the district court erred in finding that the apartment was a necessary.

Because the rental of the apartment was not a necessary, the minors had the right to avoid the contract, either during their minority or within a reasonable time after reaching their majority. Disaffirmance by an infant completely puts an end to the contract's existence both as to him and as to the adult with whom he contracted. Because the parties then stand as if no contract had ever existed, the infant can recover payments made to the adult, and the adult is entitled to the return of whatever was received by the infant.

The record shows that Wilwerding clearly disaffirmed the contract during his minority. Moreover, when Webster Street ordered the minors out for failure to pay rent and they vacated the premises, Sheridan likewise disaffirmed the contract. The record indicates that Sheridan reached majority on November 5. To suggest that a lapse of 7 days was not disaffirmance within a reasonable time would be foolish. Once disaffirmed, no contract existed between the parties and the minors were entitled to recover all of the moneys which they paid and to be relieved of any further obligation under the contract. The judgment of the district court is therefore reversed and the cause remanded with directions to vacate the judgment in favor of Webster Street and to enter a judgment in favor of Matthew Sheridan and Pat Wilwerding in the amount of $500, representing September rent in the amount of $100, October rent in the amount of $250, and the security deposit in the amount of $150.

**Judgment reversed in favor of Sheridan and Wilwerding.**

## CAPACITY OF MENTALLY IMPAIRED PERSONS

### Theory of Incapacity

Like minors, people who suffer from a mental illness or defect are at a disadvantage in their ability to protect their own interests in the bargaining process. Contract law makes their contracts either void or voidable to protect them from the results of their own impaired perceptions and judgment and from others who might take advantage of them.

### Test for Mental Incapacity

Incapacity on grounds of mental illness or defect, which is often referred to in cases and texts as "insanity," encompasses a broad range of causes of impaired mental functioning, such as mental illness, brain damage, mental retardation, or senility. The mere fact that a person suffers from some mental illness or defect does not necessarily mean that he lacks capacity to contract, however. He could still have full capacity unless the defect or illness affects the particular transaction in question.

The usual test for mental incapacity is a *cognitive* one; that is, courts ask whether the person had sufficient mental capacity to understand the nature and effect of the contract. Some courts have criticized the traditional test as unscientific because it does not take into account the fact that a person suffering from a mental illness or defect might be unable to *control* his conduct. Section 15 of the *Restatement (Second) of Contracts* provides that a person's contracts are voidable if he is unable to *act* in a reasonable manner in relation to the transaction and the other party has reason to know of his condition. Where the other party has reason to know of the condition of the mentally impaired person, the *Restatement (Second)* standard would provide protection to people who understood the transaction but, because of some mental defect or illness, were unable to exercise appropriate judgment or to control their conduct effectively. This standard is employed by the court in the following case, *Farnum v. Silvano*.

## FARNUM V. SILVANO
### 540 N.E.2d 202 (App. Ct. of Mass. 1989)

Viola Farnum was 90 years old when she sold her real estate in South Yarmouth to Joseph Silvano, age 24. Farnum knew and trusted Silvano because he had done mowing and landscape work on her property. Although the fair market value of Farnum's property was $115,000 at the time of the sale, she agreed to sell it as well as the furniture and other furnishings in the house for $64,900. Silvano had reason to know of the inadequacy of the purchase price. Farnum's nephew had warned Silvano not to proceed with the sale. In addition, Silvano was able to get a mortgage for $65,000 from the bank to finance the purchase.

Farnum's mental competence had begun to fail seriously three years before the sale to Silvano. She began to engage in aberrant conduct such as lamenting not hearing from her sisters, who were dead, and she would wonder where the people upstairs in her house had gone, when there was no upstairs to her house. She offered to sell her house to a neighbor for $35,000. She became abnormally forgetful, locking herself out of her house and breaking into it rather than calling on a neighbor with whom she had left a key. She hid her cat to protect it from "the cops." She would express the desire to return to Cape Cod although she was on Cape Cod. She easily became lost. Her sister and nephew had to pay her bills and balance her checkbook. She was hospitalized several times during the three-year period preceding the sale to Silvano. Medical tests revealed organic brain disease.

During the transaction in question, Farnum was represented by a lawyer selected and paid by Silvano. That lawyer and a lawyer for the bank that was making a loan to Silvano attended the closing at Farnum's house. At the closing, Farnum was cheerful, engaged in pleasantries, and made instant coffee for those present. After the transaction, however, Farnum insisted to others, including her sister and nephew, that she still owned the property. Six months after the conveyance, Farnum was admitted to the hospital for treatment of dementia and seizure disorder. She was discharged to a nursing home.

Farnum's nephew, who was ultimately appointed her guardian, brought this suit on Farnum's behalf to rescind the sale on the ground of Farnum's mental impairment. The trial judge concluded that Farnum had been "aware of what was going on," and denied the rescission. Farnum appealed.

---

**Kass, Judge**   On the basis of a finding that Farnum enjoyed a lucid interval when she conveyed her house to Silvano, for approximately half its market value, a Probate Court judge decided that Farnum had capacity to execute the deed. A different test measures competence to enter into a contract and we, therefore, reverse the judgment.

Competence to enter into a contract presupposes something more than a transient surge of lucidity. It involves not merely comprehension of what is "going on," but an ability to comprehend the nature and quality of the transaction, together with an understanding of its significance and consequences. In the act of entering into a contract there are reciprocal obligations, and it is appropriate, when mental incapacity, as here, is manifest, to require a baseline of reasonableness.

In *Krasner v. Berk*, the court cited with approval the synthesis of those principles now appearing in the *Restatement (Second) of Contracts* section 15(1), which regards as voidable a transaction entered into with a person who, "by reason of mental illness or defect (a) . . . is unable to understand in a reasonable manner the nature and consequences of the transaction, or (b) . . . is unable to act in a reasonable manner in relation to the transaction and the other party has reason to know of [the] condition."

Applied to the case at hand, Farnum could be aware that she was selling her house to Silvano for much less than it was worth, while failing to understand the unreasonableness of doing so at a time when she faced serious cash demands for rent, home care, or nursing care charges. That difference between awareness of the surface of a transaction, *i.e.*, that it was happening, and failure to comprehend the unreasonableness and consequences of the transaction by a mentally impaired person was recognized and discussed in *Ortolere v. Teachers' Retirement Bd.* In the Ortolere case, a teacher who was enrolled in a retirement plan suffered a psychotic break. Her age was sixty and she also suffered from cerebral arteriosclerosis. While thus afflicted, Grace Ortolere changed her selection of benefit to choose the maximum retirement allowance during her lifetime with nothing payable after her death—this in the face of severely diminished life expectancy and her husband having given up his employment to care for her full time. The court observed that her selection was so unwise and foolhardy that a fact finder might conclude that it was explainable only as a product of psychosis.

We think Farnum did not possess the requisite contextual understanding. She suffered mental disease which had manifested itself in erratic and irrational conduct and was confirmed by diagnostic test. Her physician did not think she was competent to live alone. Relatively soon after the transaction, Farnum's mental deficits grew so grave that it became necessary to hospitalize her. The man to whom she sold her property for less than its value was not a member of her family or someone who had cared for her for long duration. Farnum was not represented by a lawyer who knew her and considered her overall interests as a primary concern. The mission of the lawyer secured by Silvano, and paid by him, was to effect the transaction. As we have observed, Farnum was faced with growing cash demands for her maintenance, and, in her circumstances, it was not rational to part with a major asset for a cut-rate price.

The decisive factor which we think makes Farnum's delivery of her deed to Silvano voidable was his awareness of Farnum's inability to act in a reasonable manner. Silvano knew or had reason to know of Farnum's impaired condition from her conduct, which at the times material caused concern to her relatives, her neighbors, and her physician. Silvano was aware that he was buying the house for about half its value. He had been specifically warned by Farnum's nephew about the unfairness of the transaction and Farnum's mental disability.

Farnum is entitled to rescission of the conveyance.

**Judgment reversed in favor of Farnum.**

---

## The Effect of Incapacity Caused by Mental Impairment

The contracts of people who are suffering from a mental defect at the time of contracting are usually considered to be *voidable*. In some situations, however, severe mental or physical impairment may prevent a person from even being able to manifest consent. In such a case, no contract could be formed.

As mentioned at the beginning of this chapter, contract law makes a distinction between a contract involving a person who has been *adjudicated* (judged by a court) incompetent at the time the contract was made and a contract involving a person who was suffering from some mental impairment at the time the contract was entered but whose incompetency was not established until *after* the contract was formed. If a person is under guardianship at the time the contract is formed—that is, if a court has found a person mentally incompetent after holding a hearing on his mental competency and has appointed a guardian for him—the contract is considered *void*. On the other hand, if *after* a contract has been formed, a court finds that the person who manifested consent lacked capacity on grounds of mental illness or defect, the contract is usually considered *voidable* at the election of the party who lacked capacity (or his guardian or personal representative).

## The Right to Disaffirm

If a contract is found to be voidable on the ground of mental impairment, the person who lacked capacity at the time the contract was made has the right to disaffirm the contract. A person formerly incapacitated by mental impairment can ratify a contract if he regains his capacity. Thus, if he regains capacity, he must disaffirm the contract unequivocally within a reasonable time, or he will be deemed to have ratified it.

As is true of a disaffirming minor, a person disaffirming on the ground of mental impairment must return any consideration given by the other party that remains in his possession. A person under this type of mental incapacity is liable for the reasonable value of necessaries in the same manner as are minors. Must the incapacitated party reimburse the other party for loss, damage, or depreciation of non-necessaries given to him? This is generally said to depend on whether the contract was basically fair and on whether the other party had reason to be aware of his impairment. If the contract is fair, bargained for in good faith, and the other party had no reasonable cause to know of the incapacity, the contract cannot be disaffirmed unless the other party is placed in *status quo* (the position she was in before the creation of the contract). However, if the other party had reason to know of the incapacity, the incapacitated party is allowed to disaffirm without placing the other party in status quo. This distinction discourages people from attempting to take advantage of mentally impaired people, but it spares those who are dealing in good faith and have no such intent.

## CONTRACTS OF INTOXICATED PERSONS

### Intoxication and Capacity

Intoxication (either from alcohol or the use of drugs) can deprive a person of capacity to contract. The mere fact that a party to a contract had been drinking when the contract was formed would *not* normally affect his capacity to contract, however. Intoxication is a ground for lack of capacity only when it is so extreme that the person is unable to understand the nature of the business at hand. Section 16 of the *Restatement (Second) of Contracts* further provides that intoxication is a ground for lack of capacity only if *the other party has reason to know* that the affected person is so intoxicated that he cannot understand or act reasonably in relation to the transaction.

The rules governing the capacity of intoxicated persons are very similar to those applied to the capacity of people who are mentally impaired. The basic right to disaffirm contracts made during incapacity, the duties upon disaffirmance, and the possibility of ratification upon regaining capacity are the same for an intoxicated person as for a person under a mental impairment. In practice, however, courts traditionally have been less sympathetic with a person who was intoxicated at the time of contracting than with minors or those suffering from a mental impairment. It is rare for a person to actually escape his contractual obligations on the ground of intoxication. A person incapacitated by intoxication at the time of contracting might nevertheless be bound to his contract if he fails to disaffirm in a timely manner.

### PROBLEMS AND PROBLEM CASES

1. Smith, age 17, purchased a car from Bobby Floars Toyota, signing an agreement to pay the balance of the purchase price in 30 monthly installments. Ten months after he reached majority (which was 18 in that state), Smith voluntarily returned the car to Floars and stopped making payments. At this point, he had made 11 monthly payments, 10 of which were made after his 18th birthday. Floars sold the car at public auction and sued Smith for the remaining debt. Will Smith be required to pay?

2. Robertson, while a minor, contracted to borrow money from his father for a college education. His father mortgaged his home and took out loans against his life insurance policies to get some of the money he lent to Robertson, who ultimately graduated from dental school. Two years after Robertson's graduation, his father asked him to begin paying back the amount of $30,000 at $400 per month. Robertson agreed to pay $24,000 at $100 per month. He did this for three years before stopping the payments. His father sued for the balance of the debt. Could Robertson disaffirm the contract?

3. Green, age 16, contracted to buy a Camaro from Star Chevrolet. Green lived about six miles from school and one mile from his job, and used the Camaro to go back and forth to school and work. When he did not have the car, he used a car pool to get to school and work. Several months later, the car became inoperable due to a blown head gasket, and Green gave notice of disaffirmance to Star Chevrolet. Star Chevrolet refused to refund the purchase price, claiming, in part, that the car was a necessary. Was it?

4. Clardy had suffered from a manic depressive condition for 15 years, for which he took medication. On April 1, 1989, Clardy first spoke to Shoals Ford about the purchase of a truck and filled out the initial papers. On that same day, while visiting his daughter, he had become agitated and out of control, throwing his medicine into a burning pile of leaves. On April 3, he signed the necessary documents, but was advised that, because of a poor credit rating, a down payment of $10,500 would be required rather than the $5,000 down payment that had been previously discussed. Early in the morning of April 5, Clardy banged on the doors and windows of his daughter's household until he awakened everyone there. He threatened their lives and forced his daughter to write him a check for $500. After Clardy left, his daughter went to her attorney's office and asked that he prepare a petition to have Clardy involuntarily committed. She then called Shoals Ford to notify it that Clardy would be coming in to purchase a particular truck and to tell it of his condition. Clardy's wife also spoke with Shoals Ford's sales representatives and told them

that Clardy was not working, that he was ill and would be committed, that "buying sprees" were a symptom of his disease, and that the truck could not be insured. She asked them not to sell the truck to him. Shoals Ford's representative merely stated that if Clardy had the money to buy the truck it was "none of her concern." That same day, Clardy returned to Shoals Ford with the down payment and picked up the truck. Clardy was admitted to the hospital later that night. The psychiatrist who saw him the next day found him to be incompetent and testified that he could not visualize Clardy being otherwise on April 5. A month later, his wife was appointed conservator and guardian for him. She brought an action to set aside the purchase on the ground of lack of capacity and recover the money that Clardy had paid Shoals Ford. Will she win?

**5.** At a time when the age of majority in Ohio was 21, Lee, age 20, contracted to buy a 1964 Plymouth Fury for $1,552 from Haydocy Pontiac. Lee represented herself to be 21 when entering the contract. She paid for the car by trading in another car worth $150 and financing the balance. Immediately following delivery of the car to her, Lee permitted one John Roberts to take possession of it. Roberts delivered the car to someone else, and it was never recovered. Lee failed to make payments on the car, and Haydocy Pontiac sued her to recover the car or the amount due on the contract. Lee repudiated the contract on the ground that she was a minor at the time of purchase. Can Lee disaffirm the contract without reimbursing Haydocy Pontiac for the value of the car?

**6.** In 1955, the Probate Court of Franklin County adjudged Beard to be mentally incompetent and appointed a guardian for him. Thereafter, in 1978, a successor guardian was appointed for Beard. On February 22, 1989, while still under guardianship, Beard executed a promissory note for $10,254.60 to Huntington National Bank in order to finance the purchase of a 1987 Nissan pickup truck. The flexible interest rate for the note was to be paid over a five-year period, with monthly installments of $170.91. Beard made only a few payments on the note before dying on July 31, 1989. In the four- or five-year period prior to his death, Beard had had several dealings with the bank, including the financing of two other truck purchases. He had maintained a sparkling credit rating, fully repaying his previous loans. Toland was appointed administrator of

Beard's estate. When she learned of the outstanding debt to the bank, she returned the car to the bank. The bank sold it and sought to have the estate pay the outstanding debt left after crediting the proceeds of the car and Beard's payments. Toland rejected the bank's claim, contending that the promissory note was invalid because of Beard's lack of capacity. Is she right?

**7.** Randy Hyland owed money to the First State Bank of Sinai on two promissory notes that had already become due. The bank agreed to extend the time of payment if Randy's father, Mervin, acted as a cosigner. Mervin had executed approximately 60 promissory notes with the bank and was a good customer. A new note was prepared for Mervin's signature. Buck, the bank employee with whom Randy dealt, knew that Mervin drank, but later testified that he was unaware of any alcohol-related problems. Mervin had been drinking heavily from late summer through the early winter of 1981. During this period, his wife and son managed the farm, and Mervin was weak, unconcerned with family and business matters, uncooperative, and uncommunicative. When he was drinking, he spent most of his time at home, in bed. He was involuntarily committed to hospitals twice during this period. He was released from his first commitment on September 19 and again committed on November 20. Between the periods of his commitments, he did transact some business himself, such as paying for farm goods and services, hauling his grain to storage elevators, and making decisions concerning when grain was to be sold. When Randy brought this note home, Mervin was drunk and in bed. On October 20 or 21, he rose from the bed, walked into the kitchen, and signed the note. Later, Randy returned to the bank with the note, which Mervin had properly signed, and added his own signature. The due date on this note was April 20, 1982. On April 20, the note was unpaid. Buck notified Randy of the overdue note, and on May 5, Randy brought to the bank a blank check signed by Mervin with which the interest on the note was to be paid. Randy filled in the check for the amount of interest owing. No further payments were made on the note, and Randy filed for bankruptcy in June 1982. After unsuccessfully demanding the note's payment from Mervin, the bank ultimately filed suit against Mervin. Mervin asserted incapacity on the ground of intoxication, claiming that he had no recollection of seeing the note, discussing it with his son, or signing it. Can Mervin now avoid the contract?

**8.** In 1984, when Kavovit was 12 years old, he and his parents entered into a contract with Scott Eden Management whereby Scott Eden became the exclusive personal manager to supervise and promote Kavovit's career in the entertainment industry. This agreement ran from February 8, 1984 to February 8, 1986, with an extension for another three years. It entitled Scott Eden to receive a 15 percent commission on Kavovit's gross compensation. It specifically provided that, with respect to contracts entered by Kavovit during the term of the agreement, Scott Eden was entitled to its "commission from the residuals or royalties of such contracts, the full term of such contracts, including all extensions or renewals thereof, notwithstanding earlier termination of this agreement." In 1986, Kavovit signed an agency contract with the Andreadis Agency, a licensed agent selected by Scott Eden pursuant to industry requirements. Thereafter, Kavovit signed several contracts for his services. The most important contract secured a role for him on "As the World Turns." Income from this contract began in 1987 and continued through 1990 with a possibility of renewal. In February 1989, one week before Kavovit's contract with Scott Eden was to expire, Kavovit's attorney notified Scott Eden that Kavovit was disaffirming the contract on the ground of infancy. Scott Eden sued Kavovit to recover its commissions for Kavovit's performances prior to the date of disaffirmance and its commissions on Kavovit's contracts in the entertainment or promotion fields that were executed during the term of the agreement between Scott Eden and Kavovit. Must Kavovit pay these commissions even though he disaffirmed the contract?

**9.** ▣ *Video Case.* See "In the Cards." A boy bought an Ernie Banks rookie card for $12 from an inexperienced clerk in a baseball card store owned by Johnson. The card had been marked "1200," and Johnson, who had been away from the store at the time of the sale, had intended the card to be sold for $1,200, not $12. Can Johnson get the card back by asserting the boy's lack of capacity?

## CAPSTONE QUESTIONS

**1.** On November 1, 1995, Mullins Motors, Inc., and Waxman entered into a written contract for the sale of a used car for $1,600 cash. Waxman planned to use the car to drive to and from school and in his part-time job as a newspaper carrier. After six months of driving the car, Waxman brought the car back, stated that he was disaffirming the contract, and requested a refund in full. At this time, the car had a value of $900. Mullins has refused to refund Waxman's money and accept the return of the car. It makes the following arguments:

- Waxman waited too long to disaffirm the contract. By driving the car for six months, Waxman ratified the contract and cannot now disaffirm.
- The car is a necessary and Waxman is obligated to pay the contract price for it.
- At the very least, Mullins is entitled to withhold $700 to reflect the depreciation of the car.

**2.** On December 1, 1995, Platt contracted to purchase a new car, a Cornerstone Tia, from Mullins Motors at the "sticker price." Platt had had three alcoholic drinks at lunch immediately before entering the contract. At the time he entered the contract, he understood the transaction but he was mildly intoxicated. Two weeks later, Platt sought to rescind the purchase on the ground of lack of capacity.

## Required:

Answer the following and give reasons for your conclusions.

1. Assess the validity of Mullin Motors's three arguments in regard to its contract with Waxman.
2. State whether Platt can disaffirm the contract with Mullins Motors.

# CHAPTER

## 7

# ILLEGALITY

**INTRODUCTION**

*Although the public interest normally favors the enforcement of contracts, there are times when the interests that usually favor the enforcement of an agreement are subordinated to conflicting social concerns. As you read in Chapter 5, Reality of Consent, and Chapter 6, Capacity to Contract, for example, people who did not truly consent to a contract or who lacked the capacity to contract have the power to cancel their contracts. In these situations, concerns about protecting disadvantaged persons and preserving the integrity of the bargaining process outweigh the usual public interest in enforcing private agreements. Similarly, when an agreement involves an act or promise that violates some legislative or court-made rule, the public interests threatened by the agreement outweigh the interests that favor its enforcement. Such an agreement will be denied enforcement on the ground of* illegality, *even if there is voluntary consent between two parties who have capacity to contract.*

## MEANING OF ILLEGALITY

When a court says that an agreement is illegal, it does not necessarily mean that the agreement violates a criminal law, although an agreement to commit a crime is one type of illegal agreement. Rather, an agreement is illegal either because the legislature has declared that particular type of contract to be unenforceable or void or because the agreement violates a **public policy** that has been developed by courts or that has been manifested in constitutions, statutes, administrative regulations, or other sources of law.

The term *public policy* is impossible to define precisely. Generally, it is taken to mean a widely shared view about what ideas, interests, institutions, or freedoms promote public welfare. For example, in our society, there are strong public policies favoring the protection of human life and health, free competition, and private property. Judges' and legislators' perceptions of desirable public policy influence the decisions they make about the resolution of cases or the enactment of statutes. Public policy may be based on a prevailing moral code, on an economic philosophy, or on the need to protect a valued social institution such as the family or the judicial system. If the enforcement of an agreement would create a threat to a public policy, a court may determine that it is illegal.

## Determining Whether an Agreement Is Illegal

If a statute states that a particular type of agreement is unenforceable or void, courts will apply the statute and refuse to enforce the agreement. Relatively few such statutes exist, however. More frequently, a legislature will forbid certain conduct but will not address the enforceability of contracts that involve the forbidden conduct. In such cases, courts must determine whether the importance of the public policy that underlies the statute in question and the degree of interference with that policy are sufficiently great to outweigh any interests that favor enforcement of the agreement.

In some cases, it is relatively easy to predict that an agreement will be held to be illegal. For example, an agreement to commit a serious crime is certain to be illegal. However, the many laws enacted by legislatures are of differing degrees of importance to the public welfare. The determination of **illegality** would not be so clear if the agreement violated a statute that was of relatively small importance to the public welfare. For example, in one Illinois case,[1] a seller of fertilizer failed to comply with an Illinois statute requiring that a descriptive statement accompany the delivery of the fertilizer. The sellers prepared the statements and offered them to the buyers but did not give them to the buyers at the time of delivery. The court enforced the contract despite the sellers' technical violation of the law because the contract was not seriously injurious to public welfare.

Similarly, the public policies developed by courts are rarely absolute; they, too, depend on a balancing of several factors. In determining whether to hold an agreement illegal, a court will consider the importance of the public policy involved and the extent to which enforcement of the agreement would interfere with that policy. They will also consider the seriousness of any wrongdoing involved in the agreement and how directly that wrongdoing was connected with the agreement.

For purposes of our discussion, illegal agreements will be classified into three main categories: (1) agreements that violate statutes, (2) agreements that violate public policy developed by courts, and (3) unconscionable agreements and contracts of adhesion.

## AGREEMENTS IN VIOLATION OF STATUTE

### Agreements Declared Illegal by Statute

State legislatures occasionally enact statutes that declare certain types of agreements unenforceable, void, or voidable. In a case in which a legislature has specifically stated that a particular type of contract is void, a court need only interpret and apply the statute. These statutes differ from state to state. Some are relatively uncommon. For example, an Indiana statute declares surrogate birth contracts to be void.[2] Others, such as *usury statutes* and *wagering statutes*, are common.

**Usury Statutes**    Federal law and the law of most states set limits on the amount of interest that can be charged for a loan or forbearance (refraining from making a demand for money that is already due). *Usury* means obtaining interest beyond the amount that is authorized by law for these transactions. The statutes that define usury and set the maximum permissible limit for interest are not uniform in their prohibitions or their penalties. When a transaction is covered by usury laws and the rate of interest charged for the use of money exceeds the statutory limit, the contract to pay that interest rate is unenforceable.

**Wagering Statutes**    All states either prohibit or regulate wagering, or gambling. There is a thin line separating wagering, which is illegal, from well-accepted, lawful transactions in which a person will profit from the happening of an uncertain event. The hallmark of a wager is that neither party has any financial stake or interest in the uncertain event except for the stake that he has created by making the bet. The person making a wager *creates* the risk that he may lose the money or property wagered upon the happening of an uncertain event. Suppose Ames bets Baker $20 that the Cubs will win the pennant this year. Ames has no financial interest in a

---

[1]*Amoco Oil Co. v. Toppert*, 56 Ill. App. 3d 1294 (Ill. Ct. App. 1978).

[2]Ind. Code 31-8-2-2 (1988).

Cubs victory other than that which he has created through his bet. Rather, he has created the risk of losing $20 for the sole purpose of bearing that risk. If, however, people make an agreement about who shall bear an existing risk in which one of them has an actual stake or interest, that is a legal, risk-shifting agreement. Property insurance contracts are classic examples of risk-shifting agreements. The owner of the property pays the insurance company a fee (premium) in return for the company's agreement to bear the risk of the uncertain event that the property will be damaged or destroyed. If, however, the person who takes out the policy had no legitimate economic interest in the insured property (called an **insurable interest** in insurance law), the agreement is an illegal wager.

## Agreements that Violate the Public Policy of a Statute

As stated earlier, an agreement can be illegal even if no statute specifically states that that particular sort of agreement is illegal. Legislatures enact statutes in an effort to resolve some particular problem. If courts enforced agreements that involve the violation of a statute, they would frustrate the purpose for which the legislature passed the statute. They would also promote disobedience of the law and disrespect for the courts.

**Agreements to Commit a Crime**   For the reasons stated above, contracts that require the violation of a criminal statute are illegal. If Grimes promises to pay Judge John Doe a bribe of $5,000 to dismiss a criminal case against Grimes, for example, the agreement is illegal. Sometimes the very formation of a certain type of contract is a crime, even if the acts agreed on are never carried out. An example of this is an agreement to murder another person. Naturally, such agreements are considered illegal under contract law as well as under criminal law.

**Agreements that Promote Violations of Statutes**
Sometimes a contract of a type that is usually perfectly legal—say, a contract to sell goods—is deemed to be illegal under the circumstances of the case because it promotes or facilitates the violation of a statute. Suppose Davis sells Sims goods on

credit. Sims uses the goods in some illegal manner and then refuses to pay Davis for the goods. Can Davis recover the price of the goods from Sims? The answer depends on whether Davis knew of the illegal purpose and whether he intended the sale to further that illegal purpose. Generally speaking, such agreements will be legal unless there is a direct connection between the illegal conduct and the agreement in the form of active, intentional participation in or facilitation of the illegal act. Knowledge of the other party's illegal purpose, standing alone, is generally not sufficient to render an agreement illegal. When a person is aware of the other's illegal purpose *and* actively helps to accomplish that purpose, an otherwise legal agreement—such as a sale of goods—might be labeled illegal.

**Licensing Laws: Agreement to Perform an Act for Which a Party Is Not Properly Licensed**
Congress and the state legislatures have enacted a variety of statutes that regulate professions and businesses. A common type of regulatory statute is one that requires a person to obtain a license, permit, or registration before engaging in a certain business or profession. For example, state statutes require lawyers, physicians, dentists, teachers, and other professionals to be licensed to practice their professions. In order to obtain the required license, they must meet specified requirements such as attaining a certain educational degree and passing an examination. Real estate brokers, stockbrokers, insurance agents, sellers of liquor and tobacco, pawnbrokers, electricians, barbers, and others too numerous to mention are also often required by state statute to meet licensing requirements to perform services or sell regulated commodities to members of the public.

What is the status of an agreement in which one of the parties agrees to perform an act regulated by state law for which she is not properly licensed? This will often be determined by looking at the purpose of the legislation that the unlicensed party has violated. If the statute is **regulatory**—that is, the purpose of the legislation is to protect the public against dishonest or incompetent practitioners—an agreement by an unlicensed person is generally held to be unenforceable. For example, if Spencer, a first-year law student, agrees to draft a will for Rowen for a fee of $150, Spencer could not enforce the agreement and collect a fee from Rowen for drafting the will because she is not licensed to practice law. This result makes sense, even though it imposes a hardship on Spencer. The public interest in ensuring that people on whose legal advice others rely have an appropriate educational background and proficiency in the subject matter outweighs any interest in seeing that Spencer receives what she bargained for.

On the other hand, where the licensing statute was intended primarily as a **revenue-raising** measure—that is, as a means of collecting money rather than as a means of protecting the public—an agreement to pay a person for performing an act for which she is not licensed will generally be enforced. For example, suppose that in the example used above, Spencer is a lawyer who is licensed to practice law in her state and who met all of her state's educational, testing, and character requirements but neglected to pay her annual registration fee. In this situation, there is no com- pelling public interest that would justify the harsh measure of refusing enforcement and possibly inflict- ing forfeiture on the unlicensed person.

Whether a statute is a regulatory statute or a revenue-raising statute depends on the intent of the legislature, which may not always be expressed clearly. Generally, statutes that require proof of character and skill and impose penalties for viola- tion are considered to be regulatory in nature. Their requirements indicate that they were intended for the protection of the public. Those that impose a significant license fee and allow anyone who pays the fee to obtain a license are usually classified as revenue raising. The fact that no requirement other than the payment of the fee is imposed indicates that the purpose of the law is to raise money rather than to protect the public. Because such a statute is not designed for the protection of the public, a violation of the statute is not as threatening to the public interest as is a violation of a regulatory statute.

---

**CONCEPT REVIEW**

## CONTRACTS THAT VIOLATE A LICENSING STATUTE

| Type of Licensing Statute | Regulatory | Revenue Raising |
|---|---|---|
| **Purpose of Statute** | Protect the public welfare | Provide source of revenue |
| **Typical Characteristics of Statute** | Require proof of character, skill, and training, and impose penalties for violation | Impose fee with no or few other requirements |
| **Status of Contracts that Violate Statute** | Contracts violating statute usually illegal | Contracts violating statute still legal (validity of contract not affected by statute) |

---

It would be misleading to imply that cases involving unlicensed parties always follow such a mechanical test. In some cases, courts may grant recovery to an unlicensed party even where a regu- latory statute is violated. If the public policy pro- moted by the statute is relatively trivial in relation to the amount that would be forfeited by the unli- censed person and the unlicensed person is neither dishonest nor incompetent, a court may conclude that the statutory penalty for violation of the regu- latory statute is sufficient to protect the public interest and that enforcement of the agreement is appropriate. Under section 181 of the *Restatement (Second) of Contracts*, an agreement to pay an unlicensed person for doing an act for which a license is required is unenforceable only if the licensing statute has a regulatory purpose *and* if the interest in enforcement of the promise is clearly outweighed by the public policy behind the statute.

The following case, *Ransburg v. Haase*, shows how courts treat contracts that violate licensing statutes designed to protect the public interest.

---

## RANSBURG V. HAASE
### 586 N.E.2d 1295 (Ill. Ct. App. 1992)

David and Alexandra Ransburg, residents of Peoria, Illinois, orally hired David William Haase Associates, a Peoria business that designs and decorates houses, to act as the architect, construction manager, designer, and decorator of a house that the Ransburgs wanted to have built in Vail, Colorado. The parties discussed this project both in Peoria and in Colorado. The parties agreed that Haase would provide budgetary control and monitor every aspect of the design, construction, and furnishing of the house. They also agreed to a construction budget of $838,000 and a furnishing budget of $107,500, for a total project cost of $949,500. The scheduled completion date was December 18, 1988. Haase was to receive $80,000, including travel and other expenses, as compensation for his services. The Ransburgs ultimately sued Haase, alleging that he failed to complete the project on time, failed to ensure compliance with applicable building codes and easements, and failed to control the budget so that the total cost of the project exceeded $1.2 million. Count II of this suit stated an alternative cause of action in which the Ransburgs alleged that Haase had held himself out as an architect but is not a registered architect in Illinois or any other state. Claiming that the contract for architectural services was against public policy, they sought recovery of the fees paid to Haase. The trial court dismissed this count, and the Ransburgs appealed.

---

**Barry, Justice**   The initial question is whether Haase acted in violation of the Illinois Architecture Act when he represented to the Ransburgs that he is an architect and undertook to provide architectural services in connection with the construction of a residence in Colorado. The allegations in the complaint plainly charge Haase with offering professional services as an architect in Peoria where he operated a design and decorating business. Regardless of where the services were ultimately furnished, holding himself out to the Ransburgs as an architect in Illinois was a violation of the Illinois Architecture Act.

As a general rule, courts will not enforce a contract involving a party who does not have a license called for by legislation that expressly prohibits the carrying on of the particular activity without a license where the legislation was enacted for the protection of the public, not as a revenue measure. In other words, a person practicing a profession without a license cannot recover fees for services rendered. The purposes of the Illinois statute prohibiting the practice of architecture without the required registration has long been held to be for the protection of the public. In *Hattis Associates, Inc. v. Metro Sports Inc.*, the court said:

The statute was not intended to protect architects by limiting the work to licensed architects. Rather, its real purpose was to protect the public from damage caused by the work of incompetent and unlicensed architects.

Applying the general rule to the case before us, it does not appear that the contract would be enforceable.

Do Illinois courts recognize a cause of action to recover money previously paid to defendant for architectural services which have been rendered but for which defendant was not licensed? Although it is a general rule that parties to a void contract will be left where they have placed themselves with no recovery of money paid for illegal services, exceptions to that rule have been recognized under two different rationales: (1) that the person who paid for the services is not in *pari delicto* [equally at fault] with the unlicensed person, and (2) that the law in question was passed for the protection of the person who paid and it appears that the purposes of the law would be better effectuated by granting relief than by denying it.

We believe the public policy of Illinois to be better served by recognizing a cause of action here. To allow the unlicensed architect to retain the fees paid is to allow him to practice architecture in the state of Illinois without a license and to reap the rewards thereof. The purpose of the Illinois licensing act can best be effectuated by recognizing the Ransburgs' right to recovery.

**Dismissal of Count II reversed in favor of the Ransburgs, and case remanded for further proceedings.**

## AGREEMENTS IN VIOLATION OF PUBLIC POLICY ARTICULATED BY COURTS

Courts have broad discretion to articulate public policy and to decline to lend their powers of enforcement to an agreement that would contravene what they deem to be in the best interests of society. There is no simple rule for determining when a particular agreement is contrary to public policy. Public policy may change with the times; changing social and economic conditions may make behavior that was acceptable in an earlier time unacceptable today, or vice versa. The following are examples of agreements that are frequently considered vulnerable to attack on public policy grounds.

### Agreements in Restraint of Competition

The policy against restrictions on competition is one of the oldest public policies declared by the common law. This same policy is also the basis of federal and state antitrust statutes. The policy against restraints on competition is based on the economic judgment that the public interest is best served by free competition. Nevertheless, courts have long recognized that some contractual restrictions on competition serve legitimate business interests and should be enforced. Therefore, agreements that limit competition are scrutinized very closely by the courts to determine whether the restraint imposed is in violation of public policy.

If the *sole* purpose of an agreement is to restrain competition, it violates public policy and is illegal. For example, if Martin and Bloom, who own competing businesses, enter an agreement whereby each agrees not to solicit or sell to the other's customers, such an agreement would be unenforceable. Where the restriction on competition was part of (*ancillary to*) an otherwise legal contract, the result may be different because the parties may have a legitimate interest to be protected by the restriction on competition.

For example, if Martin had *purchased* Bloom's business, the goodwill of the business was part of what she paid for. She has a legitimate interest in making sure that Bloom does not open a competing business soon after the sale and attract away the very customers whose goodwill she paid for. Or suppose that Martin hired Walker to work as a salesperson in her business. She wants to assure herself that she does not disclose trade secrets, confidential information, or lists of regular customers to Walker only to have Walker quit and enter a competing business.

To protect herself, the buyer or the employer in the above examples might bargain for a contractual clause that would provide that the seller or employee agrees not to engage in a particular competing activity in a specified *geographic area* for a specified *time* after the sale of the business or the termination of employment. This type of clause is called an **ancillary covenant not to compete**, or as it is more commonly known, a **non-competition clause**. They most frequently appear in *employment contracts, contracts for the sale of a business, partnership agreements*, and *small-business buy-sell agreements*. In an employment contract, the non-competition clause might be the only part of the contract that the parties put in writing.

**Enforceability of Non-Competition Clauses** Although non-competition clauses restrict competition and thereby affect the public policy favoring free competition, courts enforce them if they meet the following three criteria.

**1.** *Clause must serve a legitimate business purpose.* This means that the person protected by the clause must have some justifiable interest—such as an interest in protecting goodwill or trade secrets—that is to be protected by the non-competition clause. It also means that the clause must be *ancillary* to, or part of, an otherwise valid contract. For example, a non-competition clause that is one term of an existing employment contract would be ancillary to that contract. By contrast, a promise not to compete would not be enforced if the employee made the promise *after* he had already resigned his job, because the promise not to compete was not ancillary to any existing contract.

**2.** *The restriction on competition must be reasonable in time, geographic area, and scope.* Another way of stating this is that the restrictions must not be any greater than necessary to protect a legitimate interest. It would be unreasonable for an employer or buyer of a business to restrain the other party from engaging in some activity that is not a competing activity or from doing business in a territory in which the employer or buyer does not do business, because this would not threaten his legitimate interests.

**3.** *The non-competition clause should not impose an undue hardship.* A court will not enforce a non-competition clause if its restraints are unduly burdensome either on the public or on the party whose ability to compete would be restrained. In one case, for example, the court refused to enforce a non-competition clause against a gastroenterologist because of evidence that the restriction would have imposed a hardship on patients and other physicians requiring his services.[3] Non-competition clauses in employment contracts that have the practical effect of preventing the restrained person from earning a livelihood are unlikely to be enforced as well. This is discussed further in the next section.

**Non-Competition Clauses in Employment Contracts**    Restrictions on competition work a greater hardship on an employee than on a person who has sold a business. For this reason, courts tend to judge non-competition clauses contained in employment contracts by a stricter standard than they judge similar clauses contained in contracts for the sale of a business. In some states, statutes limit or

even prohibit non-competition clauses in employment contracts. In others, there is a trend toward refusing enforcement of these clauses in employment contracts unless the employer can bring forth very good evidence that he has a protectible interest that compels enforcement of the clause. The employer can do this by showing that he has entrusted the employee with trade secrets or confidential information, or that his goodwill with "near-permanent" customers is threatened. In the absence of this kind of proof, a court might conclude that the employer is just trying to avoid competition with a more efficient competitor and refuse enforcement because there is no legitimate business interest that requires protection. You will see this approach in the case of *Steamatic of Kansas City, Inc. v. Rhea,* which follows.

Furthermore, many courts refuse to enforce non-competition clauses if they restrict employees from engaging in a "common calling." A common calling is an occupation that does not require extensive or highly sophisticated training but instead involves relatively simple, repetitive tasks. Under this common calling restriction, various courts have refused to enforce non-competition clauses against salespersons, a barber, and an auto trim repairperson.

---

[3]*Iredell Digestive Disease Clinic, P.A. v. Petrozza*, 373 S.E.2d 449 (N.C. Ct. App. 1988).

---

## Steamatic of Kansas City, Inc. v. Rhea
**763 S.W.2d 190 (Mo. Ct. App. 1988)**

Steamatic of Kansas City, Inc., specialized in cleaning and restoring property damaged by fire, smoke, water, or other elements. It employed Samuel Rhea as a marketing representative. His duties included soliciting customers, preparing cost estimates, supervising restoration work, and conducting seminars. At the time of his employment, Rhea signed a non-competition agreement prohibiting him from entering into a business in competition with Steamatic within six counties of the Kansas City area for a period of two years after the termination of his employment with Steamatic.

Late in 1987, Rhea decided to leave Steamatic. In contemplation of the move, he secretly extracted the agreement restricting his postemployment activity from the company's files and destroyed it. Steamatic learned of this and discharged Rhea. Steamatic filed suit against Rhea to enforce the non-competition agreement when it learned that he was entering a competing business. The trial court enforced the non-competition agreement and granted an injunction against Rhea. Rhea appealed.

---

**Clark, Presiding Judge**    Covenants not to compete restrain commerce and limit the freedom of an employee to pursue his trade. Enforcement of such

agreements is, therefore, carefully restricted. An employer cannot extract a restrictive covenant from an employee merely to protect himself from competition but a limited time and geographical restraint may be deemed reasonable and enforceable if a legitimate protectible interest of the employer is served. An employer has a protectible and proprietary right in his ''stock of customers'' and their good will.

In the present case, before Steamatic may claim to enforce the agreement prohibiting Rhea from engaging in a competing business, it must appear that Steamatic has a stock of customers who regularly deal with Steamatic. A customer in this sense is one who repeatedly has business dealings with a particular tradesman or business. Unless the proponent of the restrictive covenant has a trade following, that is, a group of customers who regularly patronize the business of the particular employer, there can be no stock of customers and no protectible interest.

In this case the facts showed that disaster victims engaged Steamatic to provide restoration services only on a single occasion after the event of a fire or other casualty. The only possible repeat business which Steamatic could anticipate would be in those rare instances when a second casualty befell the same victim. No evidence was adduced to show that such had occurred in the past, or, indeed, that Steamatic enjoyed any repeat business at all. Steamatic was not shown to have had any contact with the customer before the casualty gave rise to a need for restoration services. After the services were performed, there was no repeat business. Prospects for restoration services were not contacted and solicited through any confidential or privileged source, but merely upon knowledge generally available to the public at large that a casualty had occurred. There was, therefore, no ongoing customer relationship between Steamatic and any identifiable persons or companies.

The evidence did show that Rhea was careful to maintain a good reputation for Steamatic with the [insurance] adjustors as a company which ''got the job done'' and satisfied the insured. The purpose was to procure a favorable recommendation for Steamatic by the adjustor if the latter's advice were sought by a disaster victim. The evidence was that the owner of the damaged property decided whether to employ Steamatic, or some other company, and it was the owner's responsibility to pay the charges even though the proceeds of an insurance claim would defray the expense in whole or in part. The insurance companies were not Steamatic customers and therefore Steamatic had no protectible interest in the good will of the adjustors.

It is apparent Rhea set about to enter employment competitive with Steamatic under the impression that he would be in violation of his agreement. His conduct in surreptitiously removing and destroying the agreements leads to this conclusion. Guilty conduct, however, is not the test by which the availability of injunctive relief is measured. The question is whether Steamatic had a protectible interest in a stock of customers. It did not and therefore Rhea's conduct in removing his papers from Steamatic's files is not relevant. The trial court erred when it enjoined Rhea from engaging in the damage restoration business.

**Judgment reversed in favor of Rhea.**

## The Effect of Overly Broad Non-Competition Clauses

The courts of different states treat unreasonably broad non-competition clauses in different ways. Some courts will strike the entire restriction if they find it to be unreasonable and will refuse to grant the buyer or employer any protection. Others will refuse to enforce the restraint as written, but will adjust the clause and impose such restraints as would be reasonable. In case of breach of an enforceable non-competition clause, the person benefited by the clause may seek damages or an injunction (a court order preventing the promisor from violating the covenant).

## Exculpatory Clauses

An **exculpatory clause** is a provision in a contract that purports to relieve one of the parties from tort liability. Exculpatory clauses are suspect on public policy grounds for two reasons. First, courts are concerned that a party who can contract away his liability for negligence will not have the incentive to use care to avoid hurting others. Second, courts are concerned that an agreement that accords one party such a powerful advantage might have been the result of the abuse of superior bargaining power rather than truly voluntary choice. Although exculpatory agreements are often said to be "disfavored" in the law, courts do not want to prevent parties who are dealing on a fair and voluntary basis from determining how the risks of their transaction shall be borne if their agreement does not threaten public health or safety.

Courts enforce exculpatory clauses in some cases and refuse to enforce them in others, depending on the circumstances of the case, the identity and relationship of the parties, and the language of the agreement. A few ground rules can be stated. First, an exculpatory clause cannot protect a party from liability for any wrongdoing greater than negligence. One that purports to relieve a person from liability for fraud or some other willful tort will be considered to be against public policy. In some cases, in fact, exculpatory clauses have been invalidated on this ground because of broad language stating that one of the parties was relieved of "all liability." Second, exculpatory clauses will not be effective to exclude tort liability on the part of a party who owes a duty to the public (such as an airline) because this would present an obvious threat to the public health and safety.

A third possible limitation on the enforceability of exculpatory clauses arises from the increasing array of statutes and common law rules that impose certain obligations on one party to a contract for the benefit of the other party to the contract. Workers' compensation statutes and laws requiring landlords to maintain leased property in a habitable condition are examples of such laws. Sometimes the person on whom such an obligation is placed will attempt to escape it by inserting an exculpatory or waiver provision in a contract. Such clauses are often—though not always—found to be against public policy because, if enforced, they would frustrate the very purpose of imposing the duty in question. For example, an employee's agreement to relieve her employer from workers' compensation liability is likely to be held illegal as a violation of public policy.

Even if a clause is not against public policy on any of the above three grounds, a court may still refuse to enforce it if a court finds that the clause was **unconscionable**, a **contract of adhesion**, or some other product of abuse of superior bargaining power. (Unconscionability and contracts of adhesion are discussed later in this chapter.) This determination depends on all of the facts of the case. Facts that tend to show that the exculpatory clause was the product of *knowing* consent will increase the likelihood that it will be enforced. For example, a clause that is written in clear language and conspicuous print is more likely to be enforced than one written in "legalese" and presented in fine print. Facts that tend to show that the exculpatory clause was the product of *voluntary* consent increase the likelihood of enforcement of the clause. For example, a clause contained in a contract for a frivolous or unnecessary activity, such as the Ironman Decathlon in *Milligan v. Big Valley Corporation*, is more likely to be enforced than is an exculpatory clause contained in a contract for a necessary activity such as medical care.

---

## Milligan v. Big Valley Corporation
### 754 P.2d 1063 (Sup. Ct. Wyo. 1988)

Dean Griffin, an expert skier and certified ski instructor, entered the Ironman Decathlon held at the Grand Targhee ski resort, which was owned and operated by Big Valley Corporation. The decathlon was held for fun rather than profit. It consisted of several events, including swimming five pool laps, bowling one line, drinking a quart of beer, throwing darts, and skiing in both downhill and cross-country races. The downhill ski race was the first event in the decathlon. It was held early in the morning before the resort was opened to the public. Prior to the race, Griffin and all of the other downhill contestants were required to sign a document entitled "General Release of Claim." This provided in part:

In consideration of my being allowed to participate in IRONMAN DECATHLON at Targhee Resort, Alta, Wyoming, I irrevocably and forever hereby release and discharge any and all of the employees, agents, or servants and owners of Targhee Resort and the other sponsors of IRONMAN DECATHLON officially connected with this event of and from any and all legal claims or legal liability of any kind involving bodily injury or death sustained by me during my stay at Targhee Resort. I hereby personally assume all risks in connection with said event and I further release the aforementioned resort, its agents, and operators, for any harm which might befall me as a participant in this event, whether foreseen or unforeseen and further save and hold harmless said resort and persons from any claim by me or my family, estate, heirs or assigns. /s/ Dean Griffin 4/13/84

About 10 minutes after the race began, Griffin was found unconscious approximately three quarters of the way down the mountain. He died a few hours later. No one witnessed the incident that caused his death, but it was speculated that he lost control of his skis and hit a tree.

Elizabeth Milligan, as personal representative for Griffin's estate, filed this wrongful death action against Big Valley on behalf of Griffin's son. The trial court granted a summary judgment in favor of Big Valley on the ground that the exculpatory agreement signed by Griffin released Big Valley from all liability. Milligan appealed.

———————————————■———————————————

**Cardine, Justice** Exculpatory agreements releasing parties from negligence liability for damages or injury are valid and enforceable in Wyoming if they do not violate public policy. Generally, agreements absolving participants and proprietors from negligence liability during hazardous recreational activities are enforceable, subject to willful misconduct limitations.

To determine whether this type of release is valid and enforceable, we consider:

1. Whether there exists a duty to the public;
2. The nature of the service performed;
3. Whether the contract was fairly entered into;
4. Whether the intention of the parties is expressed in clear and unambiguous language.

A duty to the public exists if the nature of the business or service affects the public interest and the service performed is considered an essential service. Types of services thought to be subject to public regulation and therefore demanding a public duty or considered essential have included common carriers, hospitals and doctors, public utilities, innkeepers, public warehousemen, employers, and services involving extra-hazardous activities. Generally, a private recreational business does not qualify as a service demanding a special duty to the public, nor are its services of a special, highly necessary or essential nature. The Ironman Decathlon can best be labeled a recreational type of activity of no great public import.

The agreement in question does not involve severe disparity of bargaining power. A disparity of bargaining power will be found when a contracting party with little or no bargaining strength has no reasonable alternative to entering the contract at the mercy of the other's negligence. For example, a member of the public contracting with a public utility, common carrier, hospital, or employer often has no real choice or alternative and is, therefore, at the mercy of the other. Such is not the case here. Grand Targhee did not force Griffin to ski in the race. Skiing in the race was not a matter of practical necessity for the public, and putting on the race was not an essential service. Thus, no decisive bargaining advantage existed. No evidence suggests that Griffin was unfairly pressured into signing the agreement or that he was deprived of an opportunity to understand its implications.

Milligan argues that the release was entered into unfairly because it contained boilerplate language prepared solely by the resort and was an adhesive contract. The argument is without merit. The mere fact that a contract is on a printed form prepared by one party and offered on a "take it or leave it" basis does not automatically establish it as an adhesive contract. There must be a showing that the parties were greatly disparate in bargaining power and that there was no opportunity for negotiation for services which could not be obtained elsewhere. Here no such showing was made. Indeed, the evidence is to the contrary. The release was fairly executed and satisfies the first three criteria.

The final factor requires us to determine whether the release agreement evidences the parties' intent to release Big Valley from liability for negligent acts in clear and unambiguous language. The language could not be clearer. Examining the release in light of the purpose of the contract, it is clear that the parties intended to release the ski resort and all those involved in the Ironman Decathlon from liability. It is clear that the intent was to release Big Valley from negligence liability. The absence of the word "negligence" is not fatal to an exculpatory clause if the terms of the contract clearly show intent to extinguish liability.

We conclude that the release is not void as a matter of public policy and that Big Valley was entitled to judgment as a matter of law.

**Judgment for Big Valley affirmed.**

---

**Family Relationships and Public Policy** In view of the central position of the family as a valued social institution, it is not surprising that an agreement that unreasonably tends to interfere with family relationships will be considered illegal. Examples of this type of contract include agreements whereby one of the parties agrees to divorce a spouse or agrees not to marry.

In recent years, courts have been presented with an increasing number of agreements between unmarried cohabitants that purport to agree upon the manner in which the parties' property will be shared or divided upon separation. It used to be widely held that contracts between unmarried cohabitants were against public policy because they were based on an immoral relationship. As unmarried cohabitation has become more widespread, however, the law concerning the enforceability of agreements between unmarried couples has changed. For example, in the 1976 case of *Marvin v. Marvin*, the California Supreme Court held that an agreement between an unmarried couple to pool income and share property could be enforceable.[4] Today, most courts hold that agreements between unmarried couples are not against public policy unless they are explicitly based on illegal sexual relations as the consideration for the contract or unless one or more of the parties is married to someone else.

## Unfairness in Agreements: Contracts of Adhesion and Unconscionable Contracts

Under classical contract law, courts were reluctant to inquire into the fairness of an agreement. Because the prevailing social attitudes and economic philosophy strongly favored freedom of contract, American courts took the position that so long as there had been no fraud, duress, misrepresentation, mistake, or undue influence in the bargaining process, unfairness in an agreement entered into by competent adults did not render it unenforceable.

As the changing nature of our society produced many contract situations in which the bargaining positions of the parties were grossly unequal, the classical contract assumption that each party was capable of protecting himself was no longer persuasive. The increasing use of standardized contracts (preprinted contracts) enabled parties with superior bargaining power and business sophistication to virtually dictate contract terms to weaker and less sophisticated parties.

Legislatures responded to this problem by enacting a variety of statutory measures to protect individuals against the abuse of superior bargaining power in specific situations. Examples of such legislation include minimum wage laws and rent control ordinances. Courts became more sensitive to the fact that superior bargaining power often led to **contracts of adhesion** (contracts in which a stronger party is able to determine the terms of a contract, leaving the weaker party no practical choice but to "adhere" to the terms). Some courts responded by borrowing a doctrine that had been

---

[4]134 Cal. Rptr. 815 (1976).

developed and used for a long time in courts of equity, the doctrine of **unconscionability**. Under this doctrine, courts would refuse to grant the equitable remedy of specific performance for breach of a contract if they found the contract to be oppressively unfair. Courts today can use the concepts of unconscionability or adhesion to analyze contracts that are alleged to be so unfair that they should not be enforced.

## UNCONSCIONABILITY

One of the most far-reaching efforts to correct abuses of superior bargaining power was the enactment of section 2–302 of the Uniform Commercial Code, which gives courts the power to refuse to enforce all or part of a contract for the sale of goods or to modify such a contract if it is found to be unconscionable. By virtue of its inclusion in Article 2 of the Uniform Commercial Code, the prohibition against unconscionable terms applies to every contract for the sale of goods. The concept of unconscionability is not confined to contracts for the sale of goods, however. Section 208 of the *Restatement (Second) of Contracts,* which closely resembles the unconscionability section of the UCC, provides that courts may decline to enforce unconscionable terms or contracts. The prohibition of unconscionability has been adopted as part of the public policy of many states by courts in cases that did not involve the sale of goods, such as banking transactions and contracts for the sale or rental of real estate. It is therefore fair to state that the concept of unconscionability has become part of the general body of contract law.

## Consequences of Unconscionability

The UCC and the *Restatement* (Second) sections on unconscionability give courts the power to manipulate a contract containing an unconscionable provision so as to reach a just result. If a court finds that a contract or a term in a contract is unconscionable, it can do one of three things: it can refuse to enforce the entire agreement; it can refuse to enforce the unconscionable provision but enforce the rest of the contract; or it can "limit the application of the unconscionable clause so as to avoid any unconscionable result." This last

alternative has been taken by courts to mean that they can make adjustments in the terms of the contract.

## Meaning of Unconscionability

Neither the UCC nor the *Restatement (Second) of Contracts* attempts to define the term *unconscionability.* Though the concept is impossible to define with precision, unconscionability is generally taken to mean the *absence of meaningful choice* together with *terms unreasonably advantageous* to one of the parties.

The facts of each individual case are crucial to determining whether a contract term is unconscionable. Courts will scrutinize the process by which the contract was reached to see if the agreement was reached by fair methods and whether it can fairly be said to be the product of knowing and voluntary consent.

**Procedural Unconscionability**  Courts and writers often refer to unfairness in the bargaining process as *procedural unconscionability.* Some facts that may point to procedural unconscionability include the use of fine print or inconspicuously placed terms, complex, legalistic language, and high-pressure sales tactics. One of the most significant facts pointing to procedural unconscionability is the lack of voluntariness as shown by a marked imbalance in the parties' bargaining positions, particularly where the weaker party is unable to negotiate more favorable terms because of economic need, lack of time, or market factors. In fact, in most contracts that have been found to be unconscionable, there has been a serious inequality of bargaining power between the parties. It is important to note, however, that the mere existence of unequal bargaining power does not make a contract unconscionable. If it did, every consumer's contract with the telephone company or the electric company would be unenforceable. Rather, in an unconscionable contract, the party with the stronger bargaining power *exploits* that power by driving a bargain containing a term or terms that are so unfair that they "shock the conscience of the court." You will see several examples of procedural unconscionability in the following case, *John Deere Leasing Company v. Blubaugh.*

## JOHN DEERE LEASING COMPANY V. BLUBAUGH
### 636 F. Supp. 1569 (U.S. Dist. Ct., D. Kan. 1986)

Reuben Blubaugh, a farmer, leased a Model 6620 combine from John Deere Leasing (JDL). The lease, which was printed on very lightweight paper, provided that Blubaugh would pay four annual rentals of $15,991.37 and at the end of the lease term would have the option to purchase the equipment for $27,191.25. On the reverse side of the lease, printed in light-colored fine print, were several terms that spelled out what JDL's remedies would be if Blubaugh failed to make a rental payment. These provisions gave JDL the right to repossess the combine, sell it, and keep the proceeds of such a sale. Even though Blubaugh was only agreeing to rent the combine rather than to buy it, these default provisions also made Blubaugh responsible for an additional amount of money that represented the difference between the "termination value" of the combine (as defined in a complicated formula on the reverse side of the lease) and any money received by JDL if it repossessed and sold the combine.

Blubaugh read and signed the front of the contract but did not read the back. His understanding was that he had entered a basic lease with an option to purchase arrangement. His potential liability under the lease was not explained to him by anyone from JDL. Blubaugh paid $30,939.16 toward the first two rental payments, then made no further payments. JDL repossessed the combine and sold it for $42,000. JDL then sued Blubaugh for an additional $12,054.63, which was the amount due under the default clauses on the reverse side of the lease. Blubaugh defended on the ground that the default clauses were unconscionable.

---

**Kelly, District Judge**    Before turning to the discussion of the legal principles which are controlling in this case, the court makes the following observations. The terms in question herein are on the back of the lease, and are written in such fine, light print as to be nearly illegible. In fact, the print is so light that neither party was able to obtain a satisfactory photocopy. The court was required to use a magnifying glass to read the reverse side. The court found the wording to be unreasonably complex. It is as if the scrivener intended to conceal the thrust of the agreement in the convoluted language and fine print. The term which provides for the addition of the option price to the lessee's liability on default is a term quite outside the norm. JDL's contention that Blubaugh had a duty to ascertain the meaning of all terms, in the face of the near concealment of this unusually harsh remedy, is inexcusably inadequate and need not be tolerated by any court. This court is surprised that a reputable company such as Deere would stoop to this.

The term "unconscionability" is not defined in the UCC. Courts, in attempting to define "unconscionability" under UCC 2–302, have distinguished between "procedural" and "substantive" unconscionability. An illustrative case is *Bank of Indiana, N.A. v. Holyfield*, wherein the court stated:

The indicators of procedural unconscionability generally fall into two areas: (1) lack of knowledge, and (2) lack of voluntariness. A lack of knowledge is demonstrated by a lack of understanding of the contract terms arising from inconspicuous print or the use of complex, legalistic language, disparity in sophistication of parties, and lack of opportunity to study the contract and inquire about contract terms. A lack of voluntariness is demonstrated in contracts of adhesion when there is a great imbalance in the parties' relative bargaining power, the stronger party's terms are unnegotiable, and the weaker party is prevented by market factors, timing or other pressures from being able to contract with another party on more favorable terms or to refrain from contracting at all.

Substantive unconscionability is found when the terms of the contract are of such an oppressive character as to be unconscionable. It is present when there is a one-sided agreement whereby one party is deprived of all the benefits of the agreement or left without a remedy for another party's nonperformance or breach, a large disparity between the cost and price or a price far in excess of that prevailing in the market price, or terms which bear no reasonable relationship to business risks assumed by the parties.

In the case at bar, *both* procedural and substantive unconscionability are present. First, the lease was procedurally unconscionable because Blubaugh agreed to terms of which he had no knowledge, and his agreement was not "voluntary." While it is true that Blubaugh failed to read the back of the lease, he probably did not read it because he did not see it. On the first try here the court did not! Moreover, the court is convinced that even if he had read it, he would not have understood it. The lease was preprinted and so complex by virtue of its legalistic language that a party with no training in law or finance could not possibly decipher the potential for disadvantage. Further, there was clearly a disparity in sophistication between JDL and Blubaugh, a farmer. Therefore, Blubaugh lacked knowledge of his risk of liability when he signed the lease.

Additionally, the surrounding circumstances indicate Blubaugh's agreement to the detrimental term was not voluntary. The lease was an "adhesion" contract that was obviously drafted by JDL for its benefit and presented to Blubaugh in a manner that did not leave room for negotiations. JDL was clearly in a superior bargaining position. Because Blubaugh lacked knowledge and voluntariness, the contract was procedurally unconscionable.

The clause was also substantively unconscionable in that it exacted a penalty on Blubaugh for terminating the lease. In this case, the lessor's remedies allowed JDL to add the "purchase option" amount to the rental deficiency, and then to set this amount off against the sale proceeds. Here, however, no binding contract of sale existed. Allowing JDL to recoup the option to purchase price from Blubaugh is a penalty and would allow JDL to reap a windfall. Accordingly, the court finds the provision to be substantively unconscionable.

**Judgment entered in favor of Blubaugh.**

## Substantive Unconscionability

In addition to looking at facts that might indicate procedural unconscionability, courts will scrutinize the contract terms themselves to determine whether they are oppressive, unreasonably one-sided, or unjustifiably harsh. This aspect of unconscionability is often referred to as *substantive unconscionability*. Examples include situations in which a party to the contract bears a disproportionate amount of the risk or other negative aspects of the transaction and situations in which a party is deprived of a remedy for the other party's breach. In some cases, unconscionability has been found in situations in which the contract provides for a price that is greatly in excess of the usual market price.

There is no mechanical test for determining whether a clause is unconscionable. Generally, in cases in which courts have found a contract term to be unconscionable, there are elements of *both* procedural and substantive unconscionability. Though courts have broad discretion to determine what contracts will be deemed to be unconscionable, it must be remembered that the doctrine of unconscionability is designed to prevent oppression and unfair surprise—not to relieve people of the effects of bad bargains.

The cases concerning unconscionability are quite diverse. Some courts, such as the court in the following case, *Murphy v. McNamara*, have found unconscionability in contracts involving grossly unfair sales prices. Although the doctrine of unconscionability has been raised primarily by victimized consumers, there have been cases in which businesspeople in an inherently weak bargaining position have been successful in asserting unconscionability.

### MURPHY V. MCNAMARA
#### 416 A.2d 170 (Conn. Super. Ct. 1979)

Carolyn Murphy, a welfare recipient with four minor children, saw an advertisement in the local newspaper that had been placed by Brian McNamara, a television and stereo dealer. It stated the following:

Why buy when you can rent? Color TV and stereos. *Rent to own!* Use our Rent-to-own plan and let TV Rentals deliver either of these models to your home. *We feature*—Never a repair bill—No deposit—No credit needed—No long term obligation—Weekly or monthly rates available—Order by phone—Call today—Watch color TV tonight.

As a result of this advertisement, Murphy leased a 25-inch Philco color console television set from McNamara under the "Rent to Own" plan. The lease agreement provided that Murphy would pay a $20 delivery charge and 78 weekly payments of $16. At the end of this period, Murphy would own the set. The agreement also provided that the customer could return the set at any time and terminate the lease as long as all rental payments had been made up to the return date. Murphy entered the lease because she believed that she could acquire ownership of a television set without first establishing credit, as was stressed in McNamara's ads. At no time did McNamara inform Murphy that the terms of the lease required her to pay a total of $1,268 for the set. The retail sales price for the same set was $499.

After making $436 in payments over a period of about six months, Murphy read a newspaper article criticizing the lease plan and realized the amount that the agreement required her to pay. She stopped making payments, and McNamara sought to repossess the set, threatening to file a criminal complaint against her if she failed to return it. Murphy, claiming that the agreement was unconscionable, filed suit for an injunction barring McNamara from repossessing the TV set or filing charges against her.

---

**Berdon, Judge**   An excessive price charged a consumer with unequal bargaining power can constitute a violation of 2–302 of the Uniform Commercial Code. In the case of *Jones v. Star Credit Corp.*, the plaintiffs, welfare recipients, purchased a home freezer unit for $900.00. The freezer had a retail value of approximately $300.00. The court held the contract was unconscionable under 2–302 of the Uniform Commercial Code and reformed the contract by excusing further payments over the $600.00 already paid by the plaintiffs. There have been similar holdings by other courts. The failure on the part of McNamara to advise Murphy of the total price she would be required to pay under the terms of the contract further compounded the unfairness of his trade practices.

In sum, an agreement for the sale of consumer goods entered into with a consumer having unequal bargaining power and which calls for an unconscionable purchase price, constitutes an unfair trade practice. By unequal bargaining power, the court means that at the time the contract was made there was such an inequality of bargaining power (for example, because of the consumer's need for credit) that the merchant could insist on the inclusion of unconscionable terms in the contract which were not justifiable on the grounds of commercial necessity. The intent of this rule is not to erase the doctrine of freedom of contract, but to make realistic the assumption of the law that the agreement has resulted from real bargaining between parties who had freedom of choice and understanding and ability to negotiate in a meaningful fashion. Viewed in that sense, freedom to contract survives but the marketers of consumer goods are brought to an awareness that the restraint of unconscionability is always hovering over their operations and that courts will employ it to balance the interests of the consumer public and those of the seller.

**Injunction granted, prohibiting McNamara from repossessing the TV set, using harassing collection techniques, or filing criminal charges against Murphy, but permitting McNamara to file suit for the difference between the amount Murphy paid and the value of the set.**

---

## CONTRACTS OF ADHESION

A contract of adhesion is a contract, usually on a standardized form, offered by a party who is in a superior bargaining position on a "take it or leave it" basis. The person presented with such a contract has no opportunity to negotiate the terms of the contract; they are imposed on him if he wants to receive the goods or services offered by the stronger party. In addition to not having a "say" about the terms of the contract, the person who signs a standardized contract of adhesion may not even know or understand the terms of the contract that he is signing. When these factors are present, the objective theory of contracts and the normal duty to read contracts before signing them may be modified.

All of us have probably entered contracts of adhesion at one time or another. The mere fact that a contract is a contract of adhesion does not, in and of itself, mean that the contract is unenforceable. Courts will not refuse enforcement to such a contract unless the term complained of is either unconscionable or is a term that the adhering party could not reasonably expect to be included in the form that he was signing.

Unenforceable contracts of adhesion can take different forms. The first is seen when the contract of adhesion contains a term that is harsh or oppressive. In this kind of case, the party offering the contract of adhesion has used his superior bargaining power to dictate unfair terms. Here the concepts of unconscionability and adhesion overlap. A court—as you saw in the *Blubaugh* case—may use the word adhesion when describing procedural unconscionability.

The second situation in which contracts of adhesion are refused enforcement occurs when a contract of adhesion contains a term that, while it may not be harsh or oppressive, is a term that the adhering party could *not* be expected to have been aware that he was agreeing to. This type of case relates to the fundamental concept of agreement in an era in which lengthy, complex, standardized contracts are common. If a consumer presented with a contract of adhesion has no opportunity to negotiate terms and signs the contract without knowing or fully understanding what he is signing, is it fair to conclude that he has consented to the terms? It is reasonable to conclude that he has consented at least to the terms that he could have expected to be in the contract, but *not* to any terms that he could not have expected to be contained in the contract. The following case, *Broemmer v. Abortion Services, Inc.*, presents an example of a contract of adhesion that was held to be unenforceable.

---

## BROEMMER V. ABORTION SERVICES OF PHOENIX, LTD.
### 840 P.2d 1013 (Sup. Ct. Ariz. 1992)

In December 1986, Melinda Broemmer was 21 years old, unmarried, and 16 or 17 weeks pregnant. She was a high school graduate earning less than $100 a week and had no medical benefits. The father-to-be insisted that she have an abortion, but her parents advised against it. Broemmer later described the time as one of considerable confusion and turmoil for her. Broemmer's mother contacted Abortion Services of Phoenix and made an appointment for Broemmer for December 29, 1986. When they arrived at the clinic, Broemmer was escorted into an adjoining room and asked to complete three forms: a consent to treatment form, a questionnaire asking for a detailed medical history, and an agreement to arbitrate. The agreement to arbitrate stated that "any dispute arising between the Parties as a result of the fees and/or services" would be settled by binding arbitration and that "any arbitrators appointed by the AAA [American Arbitration Association] shall be licensed medical doctors who specialize in obstetrics/gynecology." No one made any effort to explain this to Broemmer and she was not provided with a copy of the agreement. She completed all three forms in less than five minutes. After Broemmer returned the forms to the front desk, she was taken into an examination room where preoperation procedures were performed. She was then instructed to return at 7:00 A.M. the next morning. She returned the following day and a physician performed the abortion. As a result of this procedure, Broemmer suffered a punctured uterus, which required medical treatment. Broemmer later filed a malpractice lawsuit against Abortion Services. Abortion Services moved to dismiss the suit on the ground that arbitration was required under the agreement. The trial court granted a summary judgment to Abortion Services. Although the Court of Appeals found that the agreement to arbitrate was a contract of adhesion, it still affirmed the trial court's judgment because the arbitration agreement was neither unconscionable nor beyond Broemmer's reasonable expectations. Broemmer appealed.

---

**Moeller, Justice**    The enforceability of the agreement to arbitrate is determined by principles of general contract law. Under those principles, the contract in this case was one of adhesion. An adhesion contract is typically a standardized form offered to consumers of goods and services on essentially a "take it or leave it" basis without affording the consumer a realistic opportunity to bargain and under such conditions that the consumer cannot obtain the desired product or services except by acquiescing in the form contract.

The printed form agreement signed by Broemmer in this case possesses all the characteristics of a contract of adhesion. The form is a standardized contract offered to Broemmer on a "take it or leave it" basis. In addition to removing from the courts any potential dispute concerning fees or services, the drafter inserted additional terms potentially advantageous to itself requiring that any arbitrator appointed by the American Arbitration Association be a licensed medical doctor specializing in obstetrics/gynecology. The contract was not negotiated but was, instead, prepared by Abortion Services and presented to Broemmer as a condition of treatment. Staff at the clinic neither explained its terms to Broemmer nor indicated that she was free to refuse to sign the form; they merely represented that she had to complete three forms. Applying general contract law to the undisputed facts, the court of appeals correctly held that the contract was one of adhesion.

Our conclusion that the contract was one of adhesion is not, of itself, determinative of its enforceability. To determine whether this contract of adhesion is enforceable, we look to two factors: the reasonable expectations of the adhering party and whether the contract is unconscionable. As the court stated in *Graham v. Scissor-Tail, Inc.*:

Generally speaking, there are two judicially imposed limitations on the enforcement of adhesion contracts. The first is that such a contract or provision which does not fall within the reasonable expectations of the weaker or "adhering" party will not be enforced against him. The second is that a contract or provision, even if consistent with the reasonable expectations of the parties, will be denied enforcement if, considered in its context, it is unduly oppressive or "unconscionable."

Clearly, the issues of knowing consent and reasonable expectations are closely related and intertwined. Although customers typically adhere to standardized agreements and are bound by them without even appearing to know the standard terms in detail, they are not bound to unknown terms which are beyond the range of reasonable expectation. The *Restatement* focuses our attention on whether it was beyond plaintiff's reasonable expectations to expect to arbitrate her medical malpractice claims, which includes waiving her right to a jury trial, as part of the filling out of the three forms. Clearly, there was no conspicuous or explicit waiver of the fundamental right to a jury trial or any evidence that such rights were knowingly, voluntarily, and intelligently waived. The only evidence presented compels a finding that waiver of such fundamental rights was beyond the reasonable expectations of Broemmer. In this case failure to explain to Broemmer that the agreement required all potential disputes, including malpractice disputes, to be heard only by an arbitrator who was a licensed obstetrician/gynecologist requires us to view the "bargaining process" with suspicion. It would be unreasonable to enforce such a critical term against Broemmer when it is not a negotiated term and Abortion Services failed to explain it to her or call her attention to it.

Broemmer was under a great deal of emotional stress, had only a high school education, was not experienced in commercial matters, and is still not sure "what arbitration is." The contract fell outside Broemmer's reasonable expectations and is, therefore, unenforceable. Because of this holding, it is unnecessary for us to determine whether the contract is also unconscionable.

**Judgment reversed in favor of Broemmer.**

---

## EFFECT OF ILLEGALITY

### General Rule

As a general rule, courts will refuse to give any remedy for the breach of an illegal agreement. A court will refuse to enforce an illegal agreement and will also refuse to permit a party who has fully or partially performed her part of the agreement to recover what she has parted with. The reason for this rule is to serve the public interest, not to punish the parties.

In some cases, the public interest is best served by allowing some recovery to one or both of the parties. Such cases constitute exceptions to the "hands off" rule. The following discussion concerns the most common situations in which courts will grant some remedy even though they find the agreement to be illegal.

## Excusable Ignorance of Facts or Legislation

Though it is often said that ignorance of the law is no excuse, courts will, under certain circumstances, permit a party to an illegal agreement who was excusably ignorant of facts or legislation that rendered the agreement illegal to recover damages for breach of the agreement. This exception is used where only *one* of the parties acted in ignorance of the illegality of the agreement and the other party was aware that the agreement was illegal. For this exception to apply, the facts or legislation of which the person claiming damages was ignorant must be of a relatively minor character—that is, it must not involve an immoral act or a serious threat to the public welfare. Finally, the person who is claiming damages cannot recover damages for anything that he does after learning of the illegality. For example, Warren enters a contract to perform in a play at Craig's theater. Warren does not know that Craig does not have the license to operate a theater as required by statute. Warren can recover the wages agreed on in the parties' contract for work that he performed before learning of the illegality.

When *both* of the parties are ignorant of facts or legislation of a relatively minor character, courts will not permit them to enforce the agreement and receive what they had bargained for, but they will permit the parties to recover what they have parted with.

## Rights of Parties Not Equally in the Wrong

The courts will often permit a party who is not equally in the wrong (in technical legal terms, not *in pari delicto*) to recover what she has parted with under an illegal agreement. One of the most common situations in which this exception is used involves the rights of "protected parties"—people who were intended to be protected by a regulatory statute—who contract with parties who are not properly licensed under that statute. Most regulatory statutes are intended to protect the public. As a general rule, if a person guilty of violating a regulatory statute enters into an agreement with another person for whose protection the statute was adopted, the agreement will be enforceable by the party whom the legislature intended to protect. You saw an example of this in *Ransburg v. Haase*, which appeared earlier in this chapter.

Another common situation in which courts will grant a remedy to a party who is not equally in the wrong is one in which the less guilty party has been induced to enter the agreement by misrepresentation, fraud, duress, or undue influence.

## Rescission before Performance of Illegal Act

Obviously, public policy is best served by any rule that encourages people not to commit illegal acts. People who have fully or partially performed their part of an illegal contract have little incentive to raise the question of illegality if they know that they will be unable to recover what they have given because of the courts' hands-off approach to illegal agreements. To encourage people to cancel illegal contracts, courts will allow a person who rescinds such a contract before any illegal act has been performed to recover any consideration that he has given. For example, Dixon, the owner of a restaurant, pays O'Leary, an employee of a competitor's restaurant, $1,000 to obtain some of the competitor's recipes. If Dixon has second thoughts and tells O'Leary the deal is off before receiving any recipes, he can recover the $1,000 he paid O'Leary.

## Divisible Contracts

If part of an agreement is legal and part is illegal, the courts will enforce the legal part so long as it is possible to separate the two parts. A contract is said to be *divisible*—that is, the legal part can be separated from the illegal part—if the contract consists of several promises or acts by one party, each of which corresponds with an act or a promise by the other party. In other words, there must be a separate consideration for each promise or act for a contract to be considered divisible.

Where no separate consideration is exchanged for the legal and illegal parts of an agreement, the agreement is said to be *indivisible*. As a general rule, an indivisible contract that contains an illegal part will be entirely unenforceable unless it comes within one of the exceptions discussed above. However, if the major portion of a contract is legal, but the contract contains an illegal provision that does not affect the primary, legal portion, courts will often enforce the legal part of the agreement and simply decline to enforce the illegal part. For example, suppose Alberts sells his barbershop to Bates. The contract of sale provides that Alberts will not engage in

**FIGURE 1** Effect of Illegality

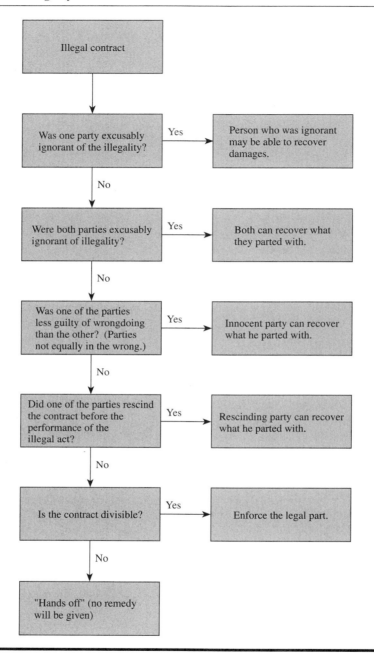

barbering anywhere in the world for the rest of his life. The major portion of the contract—the sale of the business—is perfectly legal. A provision of the contract—the ancillary covenant not to compete—is overly restrictive, and thus illegal. A court would enforce the sale of the business but modify or refuse to enforce the restraint provision. See Figure 1.

**1.** Isokappacase, a product manufactured by PTX Corp., is used as a starter medium and bacteriophage preventative medium in the production of cheese. Because of its high protein content, Isokappacase can also be used as a yield enhancer by adding it directly into cheese milk. When the product is used in this way, however, federal law requires that the resulting product be labeled as an imitation cheese and that the label list the ingredients in the end product to reflect the characteristics of imitation cheese. Podell, a salesman for Blossom Farm Products, was the sole U.S. distributor of Isokappacase. Over the course of three years, Blossom sold a large volume of Isokappacase to Kasson Cheese. Kasson used Isokappacase as a yield enhancer, introducing it directly into cheese milk to enhance cheese yields from the milk, but it did not label its final product as imitation cheese as required by federal standards. Had Kasson labeled its end product as an imitation cheese, it would have been able to sell the end product for only $.70 per pound rather than the $1.40 per pound it received for selling it as real cheese. Blossom was aware of the fact that Kasson's extremely large volume purchases of the product could only be accounted for by Kasson's use of Isokappacase as a yield enhancer. Podell acknowledged that once he recognized that Kasson was ordering about 100 times more Isokappacase than would be needed if it were using the products as a starter medium, he realized that such large volume orders could only mean that Kasson was using the product as a yield enhancer. Blossom also tacitly knew that Kasson was mislabeling its product. Both Kasson and Blossom benefited economically from this volume purchase and use. Kasson failed to pay Blossom $138,306 for its last order of Isokappacase, and Blossom brought suit to collect the money. Kasson defended on the ground that the contract was illegal. Was it? Must Kasson pay for the Isokappacase?

**2.** Moorehead & Associates is an "heir locating" business. In 1987, Arkules, Moorehead's brother, was doing a random review of probate files for Moorehead & Associates, when he discovered the estate of Yelverton, who had died apparently leaving no known heirs. After some genealogical research and a tip from a third party, the existence of Landi, the son of Yelverton, eventually became known to Moorehead & Associates. It located Landi and entered into a contract with him to do "all things necessary to obtain the inheritance" in exchange for 40 percent of the inheritance. The contract provided that Moorehead would retain an attorney and pay the expenses for researching and proving the validity of Landi's claim of inheritance, including attorney's fees. Moorehead's father, a licensed attorney, later contacted Landi by telephone and agreed to send him genealogical materials. He also sent a letter to Landi on his legal stationery in which he provided Landi with Yelverton's family history and gave Landi advice regarding probating the Yelverton estate. Landi later hired his own attorney and filed an action to rescind or reform the heir locator agreement, claiming that the agreement was illegal because a state statute limits fees charged for assistance in recovering escheated property (property going to the state because the deceased died without heirs) to 30 percent of the value of the property and because the defendants were acting as private investigators without first having obtained a private investigator license. Will the agreement be upheld?

**3.** Stern and Whitehead entered into a surrogacy contract in New Jersey. The contract provided that in exchange for $10,000, Whitehead would become pregnant through artificial insemination using Stern's sperm, carry the child to term, bear it, and surrender her parental rights to the child so that the child could be adopted by Stern's wife. A New Jersey criminal statute prohibits paying or accepting money in connection with any placement of a child for adoption. New Jersey also has a comprehensive statutory scheme regulating the termination of parental rights. This law provides that parental rights can be terminated only in cases of voluntary, written surrender of a child to an approved agency or where there has been a showing of parental abandonment or unfitness.

Whitehead did become pregnant with Stern's child and carried it to term. After the child's birth, however, she resisted surrendering the child. Stern sued to enforce the surrogacy contract, but Whitehead asserted that it was illegal. Should the surrogacy contract be enforced?

**4.** Strickland attempted to bribe Judge Sylvania Woods to show leniency toward one of Strickland's friends who had a case pending before the judge. Judge Woods immediately reported this to the state's attorney and was asked to play along with Strickland until the actual payment of money occurred. Strickland gave $2,500 to the judge, who promptly turned it over to the state's attorney's office. Strickland was indicted for bribery, pled guilty, and was sentenced to a four-year prison term. Three months after the criminal trial, Strickland filed a motion for the return of his $2,500. Will the court order the return of his money?

**5.** Sadri, a California resident, incurred $22,000 in gambling debts over a two-day period in 1991 while gambling at Caesar's Tahoe casino in Nevada, where gambling is legal. On January 13 and 14, he wrote the casino two personal checks for $10,000 and $2,000. On January 14, he executed two memoranda of indebtedness for $5,000 each. In exchange for the checks and memoranda, Sadri received chips, which he lost playing baccarat. Sadri later stopped payment on the checks and memoranda, which had been drawn on his bank in California. Caesar's Tahoe could have sought a judgment in Nevada courts, where gambling debts may legally be recovered. Instead, it assigned its claim to Metropolitan Creditors Service (MCS) for collection. MCS sued Sadri in a California trial court to collect the gambling debts. California courts historically have refused to enforce gambling debts—even those incurred in a state in which gambling was legal—on the public policy ground that gambling is contrary to good morals. California also has a strong public policy against gambling on credit. In recent years, California has demonstrated increasing tolerance of gambling by enacting a state lottery and allowing forms of gambling such as pari-mutuel horse racing, draw poker clubs, and charitable bingo games. Will the California court allow MCS to recover the gambling debt from Sadri?

**6.** Ben Lee Wilson had been licensed to practice architecture in the state of Hawaii, but his license lapsed in 1971 because he failed to pay a required $15 renewal fee. A Hawaii statute provides that any person who practices architecture without having been registered and "without having a valid unexpired certificate of registration . . . shall be fined not more than $500 or imprisoned not more than one year, or both." In 1972, Wilson performed architectural and engineering services for Kealakekua Ranch, for which he billed the Ranch $33,994.36. When the Ranch failed to pay Wilson's fee, he brought an action for breach of contract. What will the result be?

**7.** Ralph contracted to purchase a business, American Horse Enterprises, from Bovard. He executed promissory notes to Bovard in connection with this purchase. American Horse Enterprises was primarily in the business of manufacturing drug paraphernalia such as "roach clips" and "bongs" used to smoke marijuana. At the time of the sale of American Horse Enterprises, the manufacture of drug paraphernalia was not itself illegal, but state criminal statutes made it illegal to possess, use, and transfer marijuana. Both Ralph and Bovard knew that the products produced by American Horse

Enterprises were used for illegal purposes. Ralph defaulted on the promissory notes and Bovard sued to recover on them. Ralph defends on the ground that the sale of the business was illegal. Was it?

**8.** Dr. Ellis, an orthopedic surgeon, entered into a contract of employment with the Elko Clinic. Among other provisions, the contract of employment contained a non-competition clause in which Dr. Ellis agreed not to practice medicine within a distance of five miles from the city limits of Elko, Nevada, for a period of two years from the termination date of his employment. During Dr. Ellis's employment, he treated patients who would otherwise have had to travel to Reno, Salt Lake City, or elsewhere to seek the services of an orthopedic surgeon. At the expiration of his employment contract, Dr. Ellis gave notice to the Clinic that he intended to establish his own office in Elko for the practice of his specialty. The Clinic sued Dr. Ellis to enforce the non-competition clause. Should the non-competition clause be enforced as written?

**9.** Hohe, a 15-year-old student at Mission Bay High School, was injured during an annual campus hypnotism show sponsored by the PTSA (Parent, Teacher, and Student Association) as a fundraiser. Hohe was one of 18 or 20 subjects selected at random from a group of many volunteers. Her participation in the "Magic of the Mind Show" was conditioned on signing two release forms. Hohe's father signed a form entitled "Mission Bay High School PTSA Presents Dr. Karl Santo," which stated that he waived "all liability" against the PTSA, high school, and school district. Hohe and her father both signed a second form entitled "KARL SANTO HYPNOTIST," in which they agreed to "indemnify and hold you and any third parties harmless from any and all liability, loss or damage . . . caused by or arising in any manner from my participation in the Magic of the Mind Show." During the course of the show, Hohe was injured when she slid from her chair and also fell to the floor about six times. Hohe sued the school district and the PTSA for her injuries. She argues that the releases she and her father signed are contrary to public policy. Are they?

**10.** Gianni Sport was a New York manufacturer and distributor of women's clothing. Gantos was a clothing retailer headquartered in Grand Rapids, Michigan. In 1980, Gantos's sales total was 20 times greater than Gianni Sport's, and in this industry, buyers were "in the driver's seat." In June 1980, Gantos submitted to Gianni Sport a purchase order for women's holiday clothing to be delivered on October 10, 1980. The purchase order contained the following clause:

Buyer reserves the right to terminate by notice to Seller all or any part of this Purchase Order with respect to Goods that have not actually been shipped by Seller or as to Goods which are not timely delivered for any reason whatsoever.

Gianni Sport made the goods in question especially for Gantos. This holiday order comprised 20 to 22 percent of Gianni Sport's business. In late September 1980, before the goods were shipped, Gantos canceled the order. Was the cancellation clause unconscionable?

**11.** On September 29, 1987, Guido, a practicing lawyer, visited Koopman's Academy of Equestrian Arts to inquire about taking horseback riding lessons. At that time, she signed an agreement stating that she agreed to release the owners and managers of the Academy for liability for any injury, loss, or damage that she might suffer as a result of negligence by any of them. Prior to signing, Koopman told Guido that the form "didn't mean anything. It is something that I need to have you sign, because my insurance company won't let me give lessons unless I have people sign this. . . ." Guido went ahead and signed the form without reading it because she did not think it was enforceable. Guido took lessons from Koopman as often as twice a week until June 1988, when she was thrown from one of Koopman's horses and injured. Guido sued Koopman for negligence and Koopman asserted the release as a defense. Guido claimed that the release is illegal and unenforceable. Was it?

**12.** Kansas City Community Center (KCCC), a not-for-profit provider of drug and alcohol rehabilitation services, contracted with Heritage Industries, a manufacturer of prefabricated modular housing, to plan, design, and construct KCCC's new rehabilitation facility for $477,300. As part of its contract, Heritage agreed to complete architectural plans and engineering work for the facility. KCCC paid Heritage $9,546 to begin architectural drawing and site engineering. Soon after Heritage began designing the facility, however, KCCC learned that Heritage lacked a corporate certificate of authority to practice either architecture or engineering in the state of Missouri. KCCC filed suit to terminate the contract and get restitution of the $9,546 that it had paid Heritage as a down payment. Heritage argued that

rather than voiding the entire contract, the court should treat as unenforceable only the provisions dealing with architectural and engineering services. Is this a good argument?

## CAPSTONE QUESTIONS

**1.** Glenn posed as a lawyer and entered into a contract to represent Hood in his divorce. Hood had no idea that Glenn was not a licensed lawyer. Glenn represented Hood and obtained a divorce and a favorable financial settlement for Hood. Glenn then sent Hood a bill for $10,000, which reflected the fee that she and Hood had agreed on in their contract. (Assume the $10,000 would be a reasonable fee for a licensed lawyer to charge for the services that Hood received.) Hood learned that Glenn was not a licensed lawyer and refused to pay her. Glenn argues that Hood received the benefit of her services and she is entitled to recover the $10,000.

**Required:**

Answer the following and give reasons for your conclusion.

State whether Glenn has the right to recover her fee from Hood.

**2.** Donahue entered into an employment contract to work as a chef in Morris's restaurant in Westborough, New York. The only written part of his contract was a provision prohibiting him from owning, operating, or being employed by another restaurant in Westborough, New York, for two years after leaving his employment with Morris. In his position, Donahue learned a number of secret recipes that Morris closely guarded. After working for six months for Morris, Donahue resigned to accept a position as a chef in a competing restaurant in Westborough. Donahue claims that the non-competition provision is illegal and unenforceable.

**Required:**

Answer the following and give reasons for your conclusion.

Evaluate the enforceability of the non-competition provision.

# CHAPTER

**8**

# WRITING

**INTRODUCTION**

*Your study of contract law so far has focused on the requirements for the formation of a valid contract. You should be aware, however, that even when all the elements of a valid contract exist, the enforceability of the contract and the nature of the parties' obligations can be greatly affected by the form in which the contract is set out and by the language that is used to express the agreement. An otherwise valid contract can become unenforceable if it does not comply with the formalities required by state law. A person may be unable to offer evidence about promises and agreements made in preliminary negotiations because the parties later adopted a written contract that did not contain those terms. And, of course, the legal effect of any contract is determined in large part by the way in which a court interprets the language it contains. This chapter discusses the ways in which the enforceability of a contract and the scope of contractual obligations can be affected by the manner in which people express their agreements.*

## THE STATUTE OF FRAUDS

Despite what many people believe, there is no general requirement that contracts be in writing. In most situations, oral contracts are legally enforceable, assuming that they can be proven. Still, oral contracts are less desirable than written contracts in many ways. They are more easily misunderstood or forgotten than written contracts. They are also more subject to the danger that a person might fabricate terms or fraudulently claim to have made an oral contract where none exists.

In 17th-century England, the dangers inherent in oral contracts were exacerbated by a legal rule that prohibited parties to a lawsuit from testifying in their own cases. Since the parties to an oral contract could not give testimony, the only way they could prove the existence of the contract was through the testimony of third parties. As you might expect, third parties were sometimes persuaded to offer false testimony about the existence of contracts. In an attempt to stop the widespread fraud and perjury that resulted, Parliament enacted the Statute of Frauds in 1677. It required written evidence before certain classes of contracts would be enforced.

Although the possibility of fraud exists in every contract, the statute focused on contracts in which the potential for fraud was great or the consequences of fraud were especially serious. The legislatures of American states adopted very similar statutes, also known as statutes of frauds. These statutes, which require certain kinds of contracts to be evidenced by a signed writing, are exceptions to the general rule that oral contracts are enforceable.

Statutes of frauds have produced a great deal of litigation, due in part to the public's ignorance of their provisions. It is difficult to imagine an aspect of contract law that is more practical for businesspeople to know about than the circumstances under which an oral contract will not suffice.

## Effect of Failure to Comply with the Statute of Frauds

The statute of frauds applies only to executory contracts. If an oral contract has been completely performed by both parties, the fact that it did not comply with the statute of frauds would not be a ground for rescission of the contract.

What happens if an executory contract is within the statute of frauds but has not been evidenced by the type of writing required by the statute? It is not treated as an illegal contract because the statute of frauds is more of a formal rule than a rule of substantive law. Rather, the contract that fails to comply with the statute of frauds is *unenforceable.* Although the contract will not be enforced, a person who has conferred some benefit on the other party pursuant to the contract can recover the reasonable value of his performance in an action based on *quasi-contract.*

## Contracts within the Statute of Frauds

A contract is said to be "within" the statute of frauds if the statute requires that sort of contract to be evidenced by a writing. In almost all states, the following types of contracts are within the statute of frauds:

1. Collateral contracts in which a person promises to perform the obligation of another person.
2. Contracts for the sale of an interest in real estate.
3. Bilateral contracts that cannot be performed within a year from the date of their formation.
4. Contracts for the sale of goods for a price of $500 or more.
5. Contracts in which an executor or administrator promises to be personally liable for the debt of an estate.
6. Contracts in which marriage is the consideration.

Of this list, the first four sorts of contracts have the most significance today, and our discussion will focus primarily on them.

The statutes of frauds of the various states are not uniform. Some states require written evidence of other contracts in addition to those listed above. For example, a number of states require written evidence of contracts to pay a commission for the sale of real estate. Others require written evidence of ratifications of infants' promises or promises to pay debts that have been barred by the statute of limitations or discharged by bankruptcy.

The following discussion examines in greater detail the sorts of contracts that are within most states' statute of frauds.

### Collateral Contracts

A **collateral contract** is one in which one person (the *guarantor*) agrees to pay the debt or obligation that a second person (the *principal debtor*) owes to a third person (the *obligee*) if the principal debtor fails to perform. For example, Cohn, who wants to help Davis establish a business, promises First Bank that he will repay the loan that First Bank makes to Davis if Davis fails to pay it. Here, Cohn is the guarantor, Davis is the principal debtor, and First Bank is the obligee. Cohn's promise to First Bank must be in writing to be enforceable.

Figure 1 shows that a collateral contract involves at least three parties and at least two promises to perform (a promise by the principal debtor to pay the obligee and a promise by the guarantor to pay the obligee). In a collateral contract, the guarantor promises to pay *only if the principal debtor fails to do so.* As you will read in the following case, *Crozier and Gudsnuk, P.C. v. Valentine,* the essence of the collateral contract is that the debt or obligation is owed primarily by the principal debtor and the guarantor's debt is *secondary.* Thus, not all three-party transactions are collateral contracts.

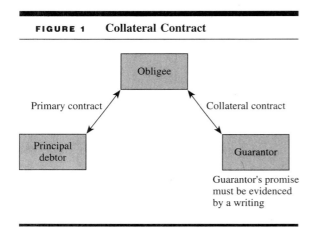

**FIGURE 1   Collateral Contract**

Obligee

Primary contract / Collateral contract

Principal debtor          Guarantor

Guarantor's promise must be evidenced by a writing

When a person undertakes an obligation that is *not* conditioned on the default of another person, and the debt is his own rather than that of another person, his obligation is said to be *original,* not collateral. For example, when Timmons calls Johnson Florist Company and says, "Send flowers to Elrod," Timmons is undertaking an obligation to pay *her own*—not someone else's—debt.

## CROZIER AND GUDSNUK, P.C. v. VALENTINE
### 1992 Conn. Super. LEXIS 1179 (Super. Ct. Conn. 1992) No. CV-91-0036504

Michael Valentine, Jr., an adult over the age of 18, was charged with criminal assault. His parents, Lorraine and Michael Valentine, Sr., contacted the law firm of Crozier and Gudsnuk about representing their son in the criminal action. In October 1990, attorney Barbara DeGennaro, an associate in the law firm, agreed to represent Valentine. The law firm claims that Valentine's parents orally agreed to guarantee payment for the legal fees incurred by their son. Approximately 10 days after DeGennaro had agreed to represent Valentine, Mrs. Valentine paid the firm's retainer by signing a check for $250. The law firm represented Valentine in the criminal assault charge until February 25, 1991, when its representation ended at the request of the Valentines. The law firm claims that the reasonable value of the legal services it performed was $4,200. It brought suit against Valentine's parents to recover the legal fees owed to the firm. It asked the court for a prejudgment attachment of the Valentines' home. A hearing was held on this issue.

**Jones, Judge**   The present case involves an alleged oral contract made between a law firm and the parents of an adult child charged in a criminal action. The Statute of Frauds provides that:

No civil action may be maintained in the following cases unless the agreement, or a memorandum of the agreement, is made in writing and signed by the party, or the agent of the party, to be charged . . . (2) against any person upon any special promise to answer for the debt, default or miscarriage of another.

The Valentines have raised the Statute of Frauds as a defense, claiming that the oral agreement of guarantee made between the parents and the law firm was a separate, collateral undertaking independent of the law firm's representation of Michael Valentine, Jr. In *Adamowicz v. Stevens,* the court held:

The statute is not a defense if the promise was an original undertaking. Fundamentally the distinction between a contract which falls within the condemnation of the statute of frauds and one which does not is that the former is a collateral undertaking to answer in case of a default on the part of the obligor in the contract, upon whom still rests the primary liability to perform; whereas, in the latter, the obligation assumed is a primary one that the contract shall be performed.

Further, an undertaking by a party not before liable, for the purpose of securing the performance of a duty for which the party for whom the undertaking is made continues liable, is a special promise to answer for the debt, default or miscarriage of another and is within the statute of frauds.

In the present case, only the adult son of the Valentines was legally represented by the law firm.

The parents were not charged in any criminal action and received no material benefit from the law firm's representation of Michael Valentine, Jr. If the oral agreement between the parents and the law firm was in fact a separate, collateral undertaking, then the agreement will be within the statute of frauds. From the facts before this court, the parents cannot be seen as principal parties in the legal services agreement between the law firm and their adult son. The record indicates that the oral agreement to guarantee payment for legal fees constitutes a separate and

collateral undertaking and as such, it falls within the statute of frauds.

For the foregoing reasons, this Court denies the plaintiff's application for prejudgment remedy. The Court notes in passing that [the statute of frauds] was adopted by the legislature in order to encourage certain contracting parties to put their agreements into writing so as to avoid certain pitfalls.

**Plaintiff's application denied in favor of the Valentines.**

**Exception: Main Purpose or Leading Object Rule** There are some situations in which a contract that is technically collateral is treated like an original contract because the person promising to pay the debt of another does so for the primary purpose of securing some personal benefit. Under the **main purpose** or **leading object** rule, no writing is required where the guarantor makes a collateral promise for the main purpose of obtaining some personal economic advantage. When the consideration given in exchange for the collateral promise is something the guarantor seeks primarily for his own benefit rather than for the benefit of the primary debtor, the contract is outside the statute of frauds and does not have to be in writing. Suppose, for example, that Penn is a major creditor of Widgetmart, a retailer. To help keep Widgetmart afloat and increase the chances that Widgetmart will repay the debt it owes him, Penn orally promises Rex Industries, one of the Widgetmart's suppliers, that he will guarantee Widgetmart's payment for goods that Rex sells to Widgetmart. In this situation, Penn's oral agreement could be enforced under the main purpose rule if the court finds that Penn was acting for his own personal financial benefit.

### Interest in Land

Any contract that creates or transfers an interest in land is within the statute of frauds. The inclusion of real estate contracts in the statute of frauds reflects the values of an earlier, agrarian society in which land was the primary basis of wealth. Our legal system historically has treated land as being more important than other forms of property. Courts have

interpreted the land provision of the statute of frauds broadly to require written evidence of any transaction that will affect the ownership of an interest in land. Thus, a contract to sell or mortgage real estate must be evidenced by a writing, as must an option to purchase real estate or a contract to grant an easement or permit the mining and removal of minerals on land. A lease is also a transfer of an interest in land, but most states' statutes of frauds do not require leases to be in writing unless they are long-term leases, usually those for one year or more. On the other hand, a contract to erect a building or to insure a building would not be within the real estate provision of the statute of frauds because such contracts do not involve the transfer of interests in land.[1]

**Exception: Full Performance by the Vendor** An oral contract for the sale of land that has been completely performed by the vendor (seller) is "taken out of the statute of frauds"—that is, is enforceable without a writing. For example, Peterson and Lincoln enter into an oral contract for the sale of Peterson's farm at an agreed-on price and Peterson, the vendor, delivers a deed to the farm to Lincoln. In this situation, the vendor has completely performed and most states would treat the oral contract as being enforceable.

**Exception: Part Performance (Action in Reliance) by the Vendee** When the vendee (purchaser of land) does an act in clear reliance on an oral contract for the sale of land, an equitable

---

[1]Note, however, that a writing might be required under state insurance statutes.

doctrine commonly known as the "part performance doctrine" permits the vendee to enforce the contract notwithstanding the fact that it was oral. The part performance doctrine is based on both evidentiary and reliance considerations. The doctrine recognizes that a person's conduct can "speak louder than words" and can indicate the existence of a contract almost as well as a writing can. The part performance doctrine is also based on the desire to avoid the injustice that would otherwise result if the contract were repudiated after the vendee's reliance.

Under section 129 of the *Restatement (Second) of Contracts,* a contract for the transfer of an interest in land can be enforced even without a writing if the person seeking enforcement:

1. Has *reasonably relied* on the contract and on the other party's assent.
2. Has changed his position to such an extent that *enforcement of the contract is the only way to prevent injustice.*

In other words, the vendee must have done some act in reliance on the contract and the nature of the act must be such that restitution (returning his money) would not be an adequate remedy. The part performance doctrine will not permit the vendee to collect damages for breach of contract, but it will permit him to obtain the equitable remedy of **specific performance,** a remedy whereby the court orders the breaching party to perform his contract.[2]

A vendee's reliance on an oral contract could be shown in many ways. Traditionally, many states have required that the vendee pay part or all of the purchase price and either make substantial improvements on the property or take possession of it. For example, Contreras and Miller orally enter into a contract for the sale of Contreras's land. If Miller pays Contreras a substantial part of the purchase price and either takes possession of the land or begins to make improvements on it, the contract would be enforceable without a writing under the part performance doctrine. These are not the only sorts of acts in reliance that would make an oral contract enforceable, however. Under the *Restatement (Second)* approach, if the promise to transfer land is clearly proven or is admitted by the breaching party, it is not necessary that the act of reliance

include making payment, taking possession, or making improvements.[3] It still is necessary, however, that the reliance be such that restitution would not be an adequate remedy. For this reason, a vendee's payment of the purchase price, standing alone, is usually *not* sufficient for the part performance doctrine.

## Contracts that Cannot Be Performed within One Year

A bilateral, executory contract that cannot be performed within one year from the day on which it comes into existence is within the statute of frauds and must be evidenced by a writing. The apparent purpose of this provision is to guard against the risk of faulty or willfully inaccurate recollection of long-term contracts. Courts have tended to construe it very narrowly.

One aspect of this narrow construction is that most states hold that a contract that has been fully performed by *one* of the parties is "taken out of the statute of frauds" and is enforceable without a writing. For example, Nash enters into an oral contract to perform services for Thomas for 13 months. If Nash has already fully performed his part of the contract, Thomas will be required to pay him the contract price.

In addition, this provision of the statute has been held to apply only when the terms of the contract make it impossible for the contract to be completed within one year. If the contract is for an indefinite period of time, it is not within the statute of frauds. This is true even if, in retrospect, the contract was not completed within a year. Thus, Weinberg's agreement to work for Wolf for an indefinite period of time would not have to be evidenced by a writing, even if Weinberg eventually works for Wolf for many years. As demonstrated by *Hodge v. Evans Financial Corporation,* which follows, the mere fact that performance is unlikely to be completed in one year does not bring the contract within the statute of frauds. In most states, a contract "for life" is not within the statute of frauds because it is possible—since death is an uncertain event—for the contract to be performed within a year. In a few states such as New York, contracts for life are within the statute of frauds.

---

[2]Specific performance is discussed in more detail in Chapter 10.

[3]*Restatement (Second) of Contracts* § 129, comment *d.*

## HODGE v. EVANS FINANCIAL CORPORATION
### 823 F.2d 559 (D.C. Cir. 1987)

On two occasions in 1980, Albert Hodge met with John Tilley, president and chief operating officer of Evans Financial Corporation, to discuss Hodge's possible employment by Evans. Hodge was 54 years old at that time and was assistant counsel and assistant secretary of Mellon National Corporation and Mellon Bank of Pittsburgh. During these discussions, Tilley asked Hodge what his conditions were for accepting employment with Evans, and Hodge replied, "No. 1, the job must be permanent. Because of my age, I have a great fear about going back into the marketplace again. I want to be here until I retire." Tilley allegedly responded, "I accept that condition." Regarding his retirement plans, Hodge later testified, "I really questioned whether I was going to go much beyond 65." Hodge subsequently accepted Evans's offer of employment as vice president and general counsel. He moved from Pittsburgh to Washington, D.C., in September 1980 and worked for Evans from that time until he was fired by Tilley on May 7, 1981.

Hodge brought a breach of contract suit against Evans. The case was tried before a jury, which rendered a verdict in favor of Hodge for $175,000. Evans appeals.

---

**Wald, Chief Justice**    Evans argues that the oral employment agreement between Evans and Hodge is unenforceable under the statute of frauds. Because the agreement here contemplated long-term employment for a number of years, Evans argues that the statute requires it to have been in writing in order to be enforceable.

Despite its sweeping terms, the one-year provision of the statute has long been construed narrowly and literally. Under prevailing interpretation, the enforceability of a contract under the statute does not depend on the actual course of subsequent events or on the expectations of the parties. Instead, the statute applies only to those contracts whose performance could not possibly or conceivably be completed within one year. The statute of frauds is thus inapplicable if, at the time the contract is formed, any contingent event could complete the terms of the contract within one year.

Hodge argues that, under this interpretation of the statute of frauds, a permanent or lifetime employment contract does not fall within the statute because it is capable of full performance within one year if the employee were to die within the period. Hodge's view of the statute's application to lifetime or permanent employment contracts has, in fact, been accepted by an overwhelming majority of courts and commentators.

The employment contract in this case cannot reasonably be interpreted as a contract for a specified period of time. Hodge unequivocally alleged a contract for permanent employment, not a contract until he reached age sixty-five or for any other stated period of time. The fact that Hodge expected to retire at some point does not mean that his contract could not possibly be performed within one year. All employment contracts of permanent, lifetime, or indefinite duration undoubtedly contemplate retirement; such contracts certainly do not mean that employees are bound to work until the moment they drop dead. Hodge's permanent employment contract with Evans could therefore be fully performed, according to its terms, upon Hodge's retirement or upon his death. Under the conventional view the latter possibility is sufficient to take the contract out of the statute. That Hodge expected to retire before he died is completely irrelevant to this case so long as the contract was legally susceptible of performance within one year. The applicability of the statute of frauds does not depend on the expectations of the parties.

We recognize that the conventional view of the statute is somewhat "legalistic." Yet the statute of frauds itself is widely understood as a formal device that shields promise breakers from the consequences of otherwise enforceable agreements. The conventional, narrowing interpretation overwhelmingly adopted by courts and commentators is designed to mollify the often harsh and unintended consequences of the statute. Here the jury concluded, despite Evans's vigorous defense, that Hodge was promised permanent employment and that he was nonetheless fired without cause. Under the traditional, narrow view of the statute, the

statute of frauds does not bar the enforcement of such jury verdicts.

**Judgment for Hodge affirmed.**

---

**Computing Time**     In determining whether a contract is within the one-year provision, courts begin counting time on the day when the contract comes into existence. If, under the terms of the contract, it is possible to perform it within one year from this date, the contract does not fall within the statute of frauds and does not have to be in writing. If, however, the terms of the contract make it impossible to complete performance of the contract (without breaching it) within one year from the date on which the contract came into existence, the contract falls within the statute and must meet its requirements to be enforceable. Thus, if Hammer Co. and McCrea agree on August 1, 1993, that McCrea will work for Hammer Co. for one year, beginning October 1, 1993, the terms of the contract dictate that it is not possible to complete performance until October 1, 1994. Because that date is more than one year from the date on which the contract came into existence, the contract falls within the statute of frauds and must be evidenced by a writing to be enforceable.

### Sale of Goods for $500 or More

The original English Statute of Frauds required a writing for contracts for the sale of goods for a price of 10 pounds sterling or more. In the United States today, the writing requirement for the sale of goods is governed by section 2–201 of the Uniform Commercial Code. This section provides that contracts for the sale of goods for the price of $500 or more are not enforceable without a writing or other specified evidence that a contract was made. There are a number of alternative ways of satisfying the requirements of section 2–201. These will be explained later in this chapter.

**Modifications of Existing Sales Contracts**     Just as some contracts to extend the time for performance fall within the one-year provision of the statute of frauds, agreements to modify existing

sales contracts can fall within the statute of frauds if the contract as modified is for a price of $500 or more.[4] UCC section 2–209(3) provides that the requirements of the statute of frauds must be satisfied if the contract as modified is within its provisions. For example, if Carroll and Kestler enter into a contract for the sale of goods at a price of $490, the original contract does *not* fall within the statute of frauds. However, if they later modify the contract by increasing the contract price to $510, the modification falls within the statute of frauds and must meet its requirements to be enforceable.

### Promise of Executor or Administrator to Pay a Decedent's Debt Personally

When a person dies, a personal representative is appointed to administer his estate. One of the important tasks of this personal representative, who is called an executor if the person dies leaving a will or an administrator if the person dies without a will, is to pay the debts owed by the decedent. No writing is required when an executor or administrator—acting in his representative capacity—promises to pay the decedent's debts from the funds of the decedent's estate. The statute of frauds requires a writing, however, if the executor, acting in her capacity as a private individual rather than in her representative capacity, promises to pay one of the decedent's debts out of her own (the executor's) funds. For example, Thomas, who has been appointed executor of his Uncle Max's estate, is presented with a bill for $10,500 for medical services rendered to Uncle Max during his last illness by the family doctor, Dr. Barnes. Feeling bad that there are not adequate funds in the estate to compensate Dr. Barnes for his services, Thomas promises to pay Dr. Barnes from his own funds. Thomas's promise would have to be evidenced by a writing to be enforceable.

---

[4]Modifications of sales contracts are discussed in greater detail in Chapter 4.

## Contract in which Marriage Is the Consideration

The statute of frauds also requires a writing when marriage is the consideration to support a contract. The marriage provision has been interpreted to be inapplicable to agreements that involve only mutual promises to marry. It can apply to any other contract in which one party's promise is given in exchange for marriage or the promise to marry on the part of the other party. This is true whether the promisor is one of the parties to the marriage or a third party. For example, if Hicks promises to deed his ranch to Everett in exchange for Everett's agreement to marry Hicks's son, Everett could not enforce Hicks's promise without written evidence of the promise.

Prenuptial (or antenuptial) agreements present a common contemporary application of the marriage provision of the statute of frauds. These are agreements between couples who contemplate marriage. They usually involve such matters as transfers of property, division of property upon divorce or death, and various lifestyle issues. Assuming that marriage or the promise to marry is the consideration supporting these agreements, they are within the statute of frauds and must be evidenced by a writing.[5]

---

[5]Note, however, that "nonmarital" agreements between unmarried cohabitants who do not plan marriage are not within the marriage provision of the statute of frauds, even though the agreement may concern the same sorts of matters that are typically covered in a prenuptial agreement. The legality of agreements between unmarried cohabitants is discussed in Chapter 7.

---

CONCEPT REVIEW

## CONTRACTS WITHIN THE STATUTE OF FRAUDS

| Provision | Description | Exceptions (situations in which contract does not require a writing) |
|---|---|---|
| **Marriage** | Contracts, other than mutual promises to marry, where marriage is the consideration | — |
| **Year** | Bilateral contracts that, *by their terms,* cannot be performed within one year from the date on which the contract was formed | Full (complete) performance by one of the parties |
| **Land** | Contracts that create or transfer an ownership interest in real property | 1. Full performance by vendor (vendor deeds property to vendees)<br><br>or<br><br>2. "Part performance" doctrine: Vendee relies on oral contract—for example, by:<br>   *a.* Paying substantial part of purchase price, and<br>   *b.* Taking possession or making improvements |
| **Executor's Promise** | Executor promises to pay estate's debt out of his own funds | — |
| **Sale of Goods at Price of $500 or More (UCC § 2–201)** | Contracts for the sale of goods for a contract price of $500 or more; also applies to modifications of contracts for goods where price as modified is $500 or more | See alternative ways of satisfying statute of frauds under UCC |
| **Collateral Contracts, Guaranty** | Contracts where promisor promises to pay the debt of another if the primary debtor fails to pay | "Main purpose" or "leading object" exception: Guarantor makes promise primarily for her own economic benefit |

## Meeting the Requirements of the Statute of Frauds

### Nature of the Writing Required

The statutes of frauds of the various states are not uniform in their formal requirements. However, most states require only a *memorandum* of the parties' agreement; they do not require that the entire contract be in writing. The memorandum must provide written evidence that a contract was made, but it need not have been created with the intent that the memorandum itself would be binding.

In fact, in some cases, written offers that were accepted orally have been held sufficient to satisfy the writing requirement. As you will see in the following *Putt v. City of Corinth* case, a memorandum may be in any form. Typical examples include letters, telegrams, receipts, or any other writing indicating that the parties had a contract. The memorandum need not be made at the same time the contract comes into being; in fact, the memorandum may be made at any time before suit is filed. If a memorandum of the parties' agreement is lost, its loss and its contents may be proven by oral testimony.

---

## Putt v. City of Corinth
### 579 So. 2d 534 (Sup. Ct. Miss. 1991)

John Putt owned commercial real estate known as the King Tractor Building, which was located in Corinth, Mississippi. Putt had most recently used it to operate a used car business. In the fall of 1984, the Corinth Gas and Water Department, which is an arm of the City of Corinth, was seeking a building suitable for housing its maintenance department and storing equipment and spare parts. Putt learned about this and approached Wayne McGee, department manager, and Dennis Coleman, a department employee, telling them his building was for sale for $100,000. McGee appeared at the regular monthly meeting of the Utilities Commission and reported his conversation with Putt. The commission authorized the inspection of Putt's building and, after receiving a favorable inspection report, authorized commissioner Leland Martin to negotiate a purchase agreement with Putt. There was a metal shed or building on the property that the commission saw no use for. Putt agreed to remove it and reduce the purchase price to $95,000. The parties then reached an agreement for the purchase of the building for $95,000. On March 11, 1985, the commission formally approved the purchase as evidenced by the following minute entry:

*WAREHOUSE:* Commissioner Martin reported that they had obtained the agreement of John Putt to sell the building on Old Highway 45 (Tate Street) to the City for $95,000.00 with him to retain the shed immediately north of the building. After discussion, the Commission found that the appraisal by Lou Miller was $100,000.00 and that the shed would be of little value to the Gas and Water Department and that the reasonable market value of the property was $95,000.00 and should be purchased for the use of the Water and Gas Departments. The purchase to be made with funds from the Gas Department and the Water Department to pay rent on the building.

These minutes were signed by the chairman of the commission and attested by the secretary of the commission.

Putt removed the shed from the land and moved his used car business to another location. He also terminated the tenancy of some at-will renters on the property from whom he had been receiving $250 and $450 a month, respectively. He also cleaned up the warehouse in preparation for the closing. A dispute arose between Putt and the City about matters involved in the closing of the sale and the City refused to purchase Putt's property. In July 1985, the City purchased other property. Putt sued the City for breach of contract. The City moved for summary judgment on the ground that the contract did not comply with the statute of frauds, and the trial court granted a summary judgment in favor of the City and dismissed Putt's complaint. Putt appealed.

**Robertson, Justice** People are able to contract for the purchase and sale of real property and have their contracts given effect because the law allows such. As with the other facilities our law affords persons for realizing their wishes, land sales contracts are attended by certain formalities which, if not met, may leave the agreement a nullity and legally unenforceable. As a general rule, Mississippi law does not require that contracts be made in writing. Put otherwise, oral contracts are ordinarily no less enforceable than others.

The legislature has enacted an exception to this general rule, to the end of reducing the risk that persons will be held to contracts they did not make. This exception performs an evidentiary function, and provides, in the present context, that

An action shall not be brought whereby to charge a defendant . . . upon any contract for the sale of lands . . . unless the promise or agreement upon which such action may be brought, *or some memorandum or note thereof,* shall be in writing, and signed by the party to be charged therewith.

It is commonly known as the statute of frauds.

What is central to our inquiry today is whether there is in fact an otherwise legally enforceable contract of sale between Putt and the City. Nothing in the statute of frauds requires that the contract itself be in writing. The statute is satisfied so long as there is "some memorandum or note thereof." For the prevention of frauds, the statute merely prescribes the form a part of the evidence must take. Oral testimony regarding the fact is admissible as well. The "memorandum or note" serves but to show a basis for believing that the offered oral evidence rests on a real transaction. *Gulf Refining Company v. Travis* suggests the memorandum "must contain words appropriate to, and indicating an intention thereby, to convey or lease land, must identify the land, [and] set forth the purchase price."

The minutes of the Utilities Commission unmistakably authorized an intent to buy, identify the land, set out the purchase price and otherwise meet *Gulf Refining's* indicia. These minutes are signed by the President and Secretary of the Utilities Commission and were, in fact, approved at a subsequent meeting. We hold that these minutes are a "memorandum or note" satisfying the statute. Beyond this, the present record provides an evidentiary basis upon which we may find that Putt and the City entered a valid and enforceable contract of sale.

**Reversed and remanded in favor of Putt.**

**Contents of the Memorandum** Although there is a general trend away from requiring complete writings to satisfy the statute of frauds, an adequate memorandum must still contain several things. Generally, the essential terms of the contract must be indicated in the memorandum, although states differ in their requirements concerning how specifically the terms must be stated. The identity of the parties must be indicated in some way, and the subject matter of the contract must be identified with reasonable certainty. This last requirement causes particular problems in contracts for the sale of land, since many statutes require a detailed description of the property to be sold.

**Contents of Memorandum under the UCC** The standard for determining the sufficiency of the contents of a memorandum is more flexible in cases concerning contracts for the sale of goods. This looser standard is created by the language of UCC section 2–201, which states that the writing must be sufficient to indicate that a contract for sale has been made between the parties, but a writing can be sufficient even if it omits or incorrectly states a term agreed on. However, the memorandum is not enforceable for more than the quantity of goods stated in the memorandum. Thus, a writing that does not indicate the *quantity* of goods to be sold would not satisfy the Code's writing requirement.

**Signature Requirement** The memorandum must be signed by the *party to be charged* or his authorized agent. (The party to be charged is the person using the statute of frauds as a defense— generally the defendant unless the statute of frauds is asserted as a defense to a counterclaim.) This means that it is not necessary for purposes of meeting the statute of frauds for both parties' signatures to appear on the document. It is, however, in the best interests of both parties for both signatures to appear on the writing; otherwise, the contract evidenced by the writing is enforceable only against the signing party. Unless the statute expressly provides that the memorandum or contract must be signed at the end, the signature may appear any place on the memorandum. Any writing, mark, initials, stamp, engraving, or other symbol placed or printed on a memorandum will suffice as a signature, as long as the party to be charged intended it to authenticate (indicate the genuineness of) the writing.

**Memorandum Consisting of Several Writings**
In many situations, the elements required for a memorandum are divided among several documents. For example, Wayman and Allen enter into a contract for the sale of real estate, intending to memorialize their agreement in a formal written document later. While final drafts of a written contract are being prepared, Wayman repudiates the contract. Allen has a copy of an unsigned preliminary draft of the contract that identifies the parties and contains all of the material terms of the parties' agreement, an unsigned note written by Wayman that contains the legal description of the property, and a letter signed by Wayman that refers to the contract and to the other two documents. None of these documents, standing alone, would be sufficient to satisfy the statute of frauds. However, Allen can combine them to meet the requirements of the statute, provided that they all relate to the same agreement. This can be shown by physical attachment, as where the documents are stapled or bound together, or by references in the documents themselves that indicate that they all apply to the same transaction. In some cases, it has also been shown by the fact that the various documents were executed at the same time.

## ALTERNATIVE MEANS OF SATISFYING THE STATUTE OF FRAUDS IN SALE OF GOODS CONTRACTS

As you have learned, the basic requirement of the UCC statute of frauds [2–201] is that a contract for the sale of goods for the purchase price of $500 or more must be evidenced by a written memorandum that indicates the existence of the contract, states the quantity of goods to be sold, and is signed by the

party to be charged. Recognizing that the underlying purpose of the statute of frauds is to provide more evidence of the existence of a contract than the mere oral testimony of one of the parties, however, the Code also permits the statute of frauds to be satisfied by any of four other types of evidence. These different methods of satisfying the UCC statute of frauds are depicted in Figure 2. Under the UCC, then, a contract for the sale of goods for a purchase price of $500 or more for which there is no written memorandum signed by the party to be charged can meet the requirements of the statute of frauds in any of the following ways:

1. *Confirmatory memorandum between merchants.* Suppose Gardner and Roth enter into a contract over the telephone for the sale of goods at a price of $5,000. Gardner then sends a memorandum to Roth confirming the deal they made orally. If Roth receives the memo and does not object to it, it would be fair to say that the parties' conduct provides some evidence that a contract exists. Under some circumstances, the UCC permits such confirmatory memoranda to satisfy the statute of frauds even though the writing is signed by the party who is seeking to enforce the contract rather than the party against whom enforcement is sought [2–201(2)]. This exception applies only when *both* of the parties to a contract are *merchants.* Furthermore, the memo must be sent within a reasonable time after the contract is made and must be sufficient to bind the person who sent it if enforcement were sought against him (that is, it must indicate that a contract was made, state a quantity, and be signed by the sender). If the party against whom enforcement is sought receives the memo, has reason to know its contents, and yet fails to give written notice of objection to the contents of the memo within 10 days after receiving it, the memo can be introduced to meet the requirements of the statute of frauds.

2. *Part payment or part delivery.* Suppose Rice and Cooper enter a contract for the sale of 1,000 units of goods at $1 each. After Rice has paid $600, Cooper refuses to deliver the goods and asserts the statute of frauds as a defense to enforcement of the contract. The Code permits part payment or part delivery to satisfy the statute of frauds, but only for the quantity of goods that have been delivered or paid for [2–201(3)(c)]. Thus, Cooper would be required to deliver only 600 units rather than the 1,000 units Rice alleges that he agreed to sell.

**FIGURE 2**   **Satisfying the Statute of Frauds for a Contract for the Sale of Goods for a Price of $500 or More**

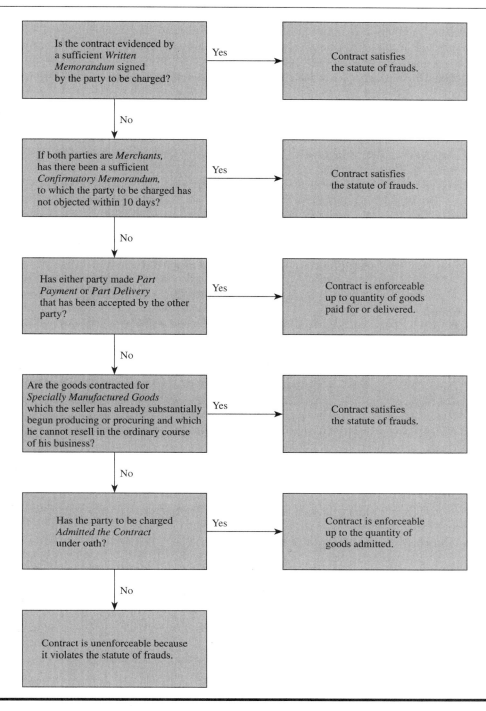

**3.** *Admission in pleadings or court.* Another situation in which the UCC statute of frauds can be satisfied without a writing occurs when the party being sued admits the existence of the oral contract in his trial testimony or in any document that he files with the court. For example, Nelson refuses to perform an oral contract he made with Smith for the sale of $2,000 worth of goods, and Smith sues him. If Nelson admits the existence of the oral contract in pleadings or in court proceedings, his admission is sufficient to meet the statute of frauds. This exception is justified by the strong evidence that such an admission provides. After all, what better evidence of a contract can there be than is provided when the party being sued admits under penalty of perjury that a contract exists? When such an admission is made, the statute of frauds is satisfied as to the quantity of goods admitted [2–201(3)(b)]. For example, if Nelson only admits contracting for $1,000 worth of goods, the contract is enforceable only to that extent.

**4.** *Specially manufactured goods.* Finally, an oral contract within the UCC statute of frauds can be enforced without a writing in some situations involving the sale of specially manufactured goods. This exception to the writing requirement will apply only if the nature of the specially manufactured goods is such that they are not suitable for sale in the ordinary course of the seller's business. Completely executory oral contracts are not enforceable under this exception. The seller must have made a substantial beginning in manufacturing the goods for the buyer, or must have made commitments for their procurement, before receiving notice that the buyer was repudiating the sale [2–201(3)(a)]. For example, Bennett Co. has an oral contract with Stevenson for the sale of $2,500 worth of calendars imprinted with Bennett Co.'s name and address. If Bennett Co. repudiates the contract before Stevenson has made a substantial beginning in manufacturing the calendars, the contract will be unenforceable under the statute of frauds. If, however, Bennett Co. repudiated the contract after Stevenson had made a substantial beginning, the oral contract would be enforceable. The specially manufactured goods provision is based both on the evidentiary value of the seller's conduct and on the need to avoid the injustice that would otherwise result from the seller's reliance.

## PROMISSORY ESTOPPEL AND THE STATUTE OF FRAUDS

The statute of frauds, which was created to prevent fraud and perjury, has often been criticized because it can create unjust results. One of the troubling features of the statute is that it can as easily be used to defeat a contract that was actually made as it can to defeat a fictitious agreement. As you have seen, courts and legislatures have created several exceptions to the statute of frauds that reduce the statute's potential for creating unfair results. In recent years, courts in some states have allowed the use of the doctrine of **promissory estoppel**[6] to enable some parties to recover under oral contracts that the statute of frauds would ordinarily render unenforceable.

Courts in these states hold that, when one of the parties would suffer serious losses because of her reliance on an oral contract, the other party is estopped from raising the statute of frauds as a defense. This position has been approved in the *Restatement (Second) of Contracts.* Section 139 of the *Restatement (Second)* provides that a promise that induces action or forbearance can be enforceable notwithstanding the statute of frauds if the reliance was foreseeable to the person making the promise and if injustice can be avoided only by enforcing the promise. The idea behind this section and the cases employing promissory estoppel is that the statute of frauds, which is designed to prevent injustice, should not be allowed to work an injustice. Section 139 and these cases also impliedly recognize the fact that the reliance required by promissory estoppel to some extent provides evidence of the existence of a contract between the parties, since it is unlikely that a person would materially rely on a nonexistent promise.

The use of promissory estoppel as a means of circumventing the statute of frauds is still controversial, however. Many courts fear that enforcing oral contracts on the basis of a party's reliance will essentially negate the statute. In cases involving the UCC statute of frauds, an additional source of concern involves the interpretation of section 2–201. Some courts have construed the provisions listing specific alternative methods of satisfying

---

[6]The doctrine of promissory estoppel is discussed in Chapters 9 and 12.

section 2–201's formal requirements to be *exclusive,* precluding the creation of any further exceptions by courts.

# THE PAROL EVIDENCE RULE

## Explanation of the Rule

In many situations, contracting parties prefer to express their agreements in writing even when they are not required to do so by the statute of frauds. Written contracts rarely come into being without some prior discussions or negotiations between the parties, however. Various promises, proposals, or representations are usually made by one or both of the parties before the execution of a written contract. What happens when one of those prior promises, proposals, or representations is not included in the terms of the written contract? For example, suppose that Jackson wants to buy Stone's house. During the course of negotiations, Stone states that he will pay for any major repairs that the house needs for the first year that Jackson owns it. The written contract that the parties ultimately sign, however, does not say anything about Stone paying for repairs, and, in fact, states that Jackson will take the house "as is." The furnace breaks down three months after the sale, and Stone refuses to pay for its repair. What is the status of Stone's promise to pay for repairs? The basic problem is one of defining the boundaries of the parties' agreement. Are all the promises made in the process of negotiation part of the contract, or do the terms of the written document that the parties signed supersede any preliminary agreements?

The **parol evidence rule** provides the answer to this question. The term *parol evidence* means written or spoken statements that are *not contained in the written contract.* The parol evidence rule provides that, when parties enter a *written contract* that they intend as a complete **integration** (a complete and final statement of their agreement), a court will not permit the use of evidence of *prior* or *contemporaneous* statements to add to, alter, or contradict the terms of the written contract. This rule is based on the presumption that when people enter into a written contract, the best evidence of their agreement is the written contract itself. It also reflects the idea that later expressions of intent are presumed to prevail over earlier expressions of intent. In the hypothetical case involving Stone and Jackson, assuming that they intended the written contract to be the final integration of their agreement, Jackson would not be able to introduce evidence of Stone's promise to pay for repairs. The effect of excluding preliminary promises or statements from consideration is, of course, to confine the parties' contract to the terms of the written agreement. The lesson to be learned from this example is that people who put their agreements in writing should make sure that all the terms of their agreement are included in the writing. The following case, *Slivinsky v. Watkins-Johnson Company,* illustrates the application of the parol evidence rule.

---

### SLIVINSKY V. WATKINS-JOHNSON COMPANY
**270 Cal. Rptr. 585 (Cal Ct. App. 1990)**

In July 1984, Sandra Slivinsky applied for a job as a materials scientist with Watkins-Johnson Company, a large aerospace manufacturer. Directly above the signature line on the application she signed was the statement: "I understand that employment by WATKINS-JOHNSON COMPANY is conditional upon . . . execution of an Employment Agreement. . . . I further understand that if I become employed by Watkins-Johnson Company, there will be no agreement, expressed or implied, between the company and me for any specific period of employment, nor for continuing or long-term employment." Over the next several months, Watkins-Johnson contacted Slivinsky's references, requested her transcripts, and set up a series of interviews. Slivinsky claims that at these interviews she was promised "long-term," "indefinite," and "permanent" employment, not dependent on business cycles, and subject to termination only for cause. Finally, Watkins-Johnson made a verbal offer of employment to Slivinsky and she accepted. On January 7, 1985, which was Slivinsky's first day at work, Slivinsky signed the employee agreement that had been referred to in her employment application. Set apart in bold type, the last paragraph of this agreement provided that there was no express or implied agreement between the parties regarding the duration of her employment and that the employment could be terminated at any time with or without cause.

As a result of the space shuttle *Challenger* disaster in January 1986, Watkins-Johnson experienced significant business losses and government contract cancellations. The management decided that employee cutbacks were essential to cope with the loss of business. Ultimately, 24 employees, including Slivinsky, were selected for the reduction in force program. Watkins-Johnson terminated her employment in June 1986.

Slivinsky brought suit against Watkins-Johnson for breach of the employment contract, asserting that she had been terminated without cause in violation of the parties' express and implied agreement. She also claimed that the reasons given for her termination were pretextual and that she was really fired for other reasons, such as her supervisor disliking her. The trial court granted Watkins-Johnson's motion for summary judgment, and Slivinsky appealed.

---

**Cottle, Associate Justice**    Slivinsky claims that the parties' employment agreement includes factors such as oral assurances of job security and Watkins-Johnson's personnel policies and practices not to terminate employees except for good cause. Watkins-Johnson [argues] that it is limited to the parties' express written contract defining the employment as at-will.

The dispositive issue, therefore, is whether we can look beyond the four corners of the parties' written agreements to ascertain the complete agreement of the parties. The answer to that question involves application of the parol evidence rule, a rule of substantive law precluding the introduction of evidence which varies or contradicts the terms of an integrated written instrument. If the parties intended that the Application and Employment Agreement constituted an integration, i.e., the final expression of their agreement with respect to grounds for termination, then those agreements may not be contradicted by evidence of any prior agreement or of a contemporaneous oral agreement. No particular form is required for an integrated agreement. When only part of the agreement is integrated, the parol evidence rule applies to that part.

Applying these standards, we conclude that the contract was integrated with respect to the grounds for termination. Slivinsky's employment application specifically conditioned employment upon execution of an employment agreement. It further provided that if Slivinsky were to become employed by Watkins-Johnson, there "will be no agreement, ex-

pressed or implied, . . . for any specific period of employment, nor for continuing or long-term employment." When Slivinsky executed the Employee Agreement, she acknowledged "that there is no agreement, express or implied, between employee and the Company for any specific period of employment, nor for continuing or long-term employment. Employee and the Company each have a right to terminate employment, with or without cause." Reading these documents together, the only reasonable conclusion that can be drawn is that the parties intended that there would be no other agreement regarding termination other than that set forth in the Employee Agreement. Consequently, evidence of an implied agreement which contradicts the terms of the written agreement is not admissible. There cannot be a valid express contract and an implied contract, each embracing the same subject, but requiring different results.

Because we hold that the contract is a contract for employment terminable at will, we do not reach the issues regarding whether good cause existed for Slivinsky's termination based on Watkins-Johnson's decision to reduce its work force. Even if the reduction in force were a pretextual ground for terminating Slivinsky's employment, it would not be actionable with an at-will employment contract unless the employer's motivation for a discharge contravenes some significant public policy principle. No such public policy violation is alleged here.

**Judgment for Watkins-Johnson affirmed.**

## Scope of the Parol Evidence Rule

The parol evidence rule is relevant only in cases in which the parties have expressed their agreement in a written contract. Thus, it would not apply to a case involving an oral contract or to a case in which writings existed that were not intended to embody the final statement of at least part of the parties' contract. The parol evidence rule has been made a part of the law of sales in the Uniform Commercial Code [2–202], so it is applicable to contracts for the sale of goods as well as to contracts governed by the common law of contracts. Furthermore, the rule excludes only evidence of statements made *prior to* or *during* the signing of the written contract. It does not apply to statements made after the signing of the contract. Thus, evidence of subsequent statements is freely admissible.

## Admissible Parol Evidence

In some situations, evidence of statements made outside the written contract is admissible notwithstanding the parol evidence rule. Parol evidence is permitted in the situations discussed below either because the writing is not the best evidence of the contract or because the evidence is offered, not to contradict the terms of the writing, but to explain the writing or to challenge the underlying contractual obligation that the writing represents.

**1.** *Additional terms in partially integrated contracts.* In many instances, parties will desire to introduce evidence of statements or agreements that would supplement rather than contradict the written contract. Whether they can do this depends on whether the written contract is characterized as *completely integrated* or *partially integrated*. A completely integrated contract is one that the parties intend as a *complete and exclusive statement* of their entire agreement. A partially integrated contract is one that expresses the parties' final agreement as to some but not all of the terms of their contract. When a contract is only partially integrated, the parties are permitted to use parol evidence to prove the *additional* terms of their agreement. Such evidence cannot, however, be used to contradict the written terms of the contract. To determine whether a contract is completely or partially integrated, a court must determine the parties' intent. A court judges intent by looking at the language of the contract, the apparent completeness of the writing, and all the

surrounding circumstances. It will also consider whether the contract contains a **merger clause** (also known as an **integration clause**). These clauses, which are very common in form contracts and commercial contracts, provide that the written contract is the complete integration of the parties' agreement. They are designed to prevent a party from giving testimony about prior statements or agreements and are generally effective in indicating that the writing was a complete integration. Even though a contract contains a merger clause, parol evidence could be admissible under one of the following exceptions.

**2.** *Explaining ambiguities.* Parol evidence can be offered to explain an ambiguity in the written contract. Suppose a written contract between Lowen and Matthews provides that Lowen will buy "Matthews's truck," but Matthews has two trucks. The parties could offer evidence of negotiations, statements, and other circumstances preceding the creation of the written contract to identify the truck to which the writing refers. Used in this way, parol evidence helps the court interpret the contract. It does not contradict the written contract.

**3.** *Circumstances invalidating contract.* Any circumstances that would be relevant to show that a contract is not valid can be proven by parol evidence. For example, evidence that Holden pointed a gun at Dickson and said, "Sign this contract, or I'll kill you," would be admissible to show that the contract was voidable because of duress. Likewise, parol evidence would be admissible to show that a contract was illegal or was induced by fraud, misrepresentation, undue influence, or mistake.

**4.** *Existence of condition.* It is also permissible to use parol evidence to show that a writing was executed with the understanding that it was *not to take effect until the occurrence of a condition* (a future, uncertain event that creates a duty to perform). Suppose Farnsworth signs a contract to purchase a car with the agreement that the contract is not to be effective unless and until Farnsworth gets a new job. If the written contract is silent about any conditions that must occur before it becomes effective, Farnsworth could introduce parol evidence to prove the existence of the condition. Such proof merely elaborates on, but does not contradict, the terms of the writing.

**5.** *Subsequent agreements.* As you read earlier, the parol evidence rule does not forbid parties to introduce proof of *subsequent agreements*. This is true even if the terms of the later agreement cancel, subtract from, or add to the obligations stated in the written contract. The idea here is that when a writing is followed by a later statement or agreement, the writing is no longer the best evidence of the agreement. You should be aware, however, that subsequent modifications of contracts may sometimes be unenforceable due to lack of consideration or failure to comply with the statute of frauds. In addition, contracts sometimes expressly provide that modifications must be written. In this situation, an oral modification would be unenforceable.

---

**CONCEPT REVIEW**

## PAROL EVIDENCE RULE

| Parol Evidence Rule | Applies when: | Provides that: |
|---|---|---|
| | Parties create a writing intended as a final and complete integration of at least part of the parties' contract. | Evidence of statements or promises made before or during the creation of the writing cannot be used to supplement, change, or contradict the terms of the written contract. |
| **But Parol Evidence *Can* Be Used to** | 1. Prove consistent, additional terms when the contract is *partially integrated*.<br>2. Explain an ambiguity in the written contract.<br>3. Prove that the contract is void, voidable, or unenforceable.<br>4. Prove that the contract was subject to a condition.<br>5. Prove that the parties subsequently modified the contract or made a new agreement. | |

---

## INTERPRETATION OF CONTRACTS

Once a court has decided what promises are included in a contract, it is faced with *interpreting* the contract to determine the *meaning* and *legal effect* of the terms used by the parties. Courts have adopted broad, basic standards of interpretation that guide them in the interpretation process.

The court will first attempt to determine the parties' *principal objective.* Every clause will then be determined in the light of this principal objective. Ordinary words will be given their usual meaning and technical words (such as those that have a special meaning in the parties' trade or business) will be given their technical meaning, unless a different meaning was clearly intended.

Guidelines grounded in common sense are also used to determine the relationship of the various terms of the contract. Specific terms that follow general terms are presumed to qualify those general terms. Suppose that a provision that states that the subject of the contract is "guaranteed for one year" is followed by a provision describing the "one-year guarantee against defects in workmanship." Here, it is fair to conclude that the more specific term qualifies the more general term and that the guarantee described in the contract is a guarantee of workmanship only, and not of parts and materials.

Sometimes, there is internal conflict in the terms of an agreement and courts must determine which term should prevail. When the parties use a form contract or some other type of contract that is partially printed and partially handwritten, the handwritten provisions will prevail. If the contract was drafted by one of the parties, any ambiguities will be resolved against the party who drafted the contract.

If both parties to the contract are members of a trade, profession, or community in which certain words are commonly given a particular meaning (this is called a *usage*), the courts will presume that the parties intended the meaning that the usage gives to the terms they use. For example, if the word dozen in the bakery business means 13 rather than 12, a contract between two bakers for the purchase of 10 dozen loaves of bread will be presumed to mean 130 loaves of bread rather than 120. Usages can also add provisions to the parties' agreement. If the court finds that a certain practice is a matter of common usage in the parties' trade, it will assume that the parties intended to include that practice in their agreement. If contracting parties are members of the same trade, business, or community but do not intend to be bound by usage, they should specifically say so in their agreement.

**1.** Golomb allegedly orally agreed to sell to Lee for $275,000 the Ferrari once owned by King Leopold of Belgium. Golomb ultimately refused to sell the car and Lee sued him. At trial, Golomb denied ever promising to sell the car to Lee. Can Lee enforce this alleged promise?

**2.** Boyd-Scarp, a building contractor, was building a new home for Rathmann. Rathmann paid Boyd-Scarp for appliances for the new home and Boyd-Scarp contracted with Al Booth's, an appliance supplier, for the purchase of the appliances. Al Booth's had heard that Boyd-Scarp was having financial problems. Before delivering the appliances to the Rathmanns' new home, it contacted Rathmann and asked him to guarantee payment. Al Booth's alleges that Rathmann orally promised to pay for the appliances if Boyd-Scarp failed to pay. Al Booth's then delivered the appliances. Boyd-Scarp became insolvent and did not pay Al Booth's for the appliances. Al Booth's turned to Rathmann for payment. Rathmann asserted the statute of frauds as a defense. Will he be successful in using this defense?

**3.** In January 1980, Mayer entered into an oral contract of employment with King Cola for a three-year term. Mayer moved from Chattanooga to St. Louis and began working. King Cola paid his moving expenses. In accordance with the parties' negotiations, Mayer awaited a written contract, but none was ever executed. The employment relationship soon began to deteriorate, and after several months King Cola's president told Mayer that he was not going to be given a contract. In May 1980, King Cola discharged Mayer. In a state that does not recognize the doctrine of promissory estoppel as an exception to the statute of frauds, will Mayer be able to enforce the contract?

**4.** Green owns a lot (Lot S) in the Manomet section of Plymouth, Massachusetts. In July 1980, she advertised it for sale. On July 11 and 12, the Hickeys discussed with Green purchasing Lot S and orally agreed to a sale for $15,000. On July 12, Green ac-cepted the Hickeys' check for $500. Hickey had left the payee line of the deposit check blank, because of uncertainty whether Green or her brother was to receive the check. Hickey asked Green to fill in the appropriate name. Green, however, held the check, did not fill in the payee's name, and neither cashed nor indorsed it. Hickey told Green that his intention was to sell his home and build on the lot he was buying from Green. Relying on the arrangements with Green, the Hickeys advertised their house in newspapers for three days in July. They found a purchaser quickly. Within a short time, they contracted with a purchaser for the sale of their house and accepted the purchaser's deposit check. On the back of this check, above the Hickeys' signatures indorsing the check, was noted: "Deposit on purchase of property at Sachem Rd. and First St., Manomet, Ma. Sale price, $44,000." On July 24, Green told Hickey that she no longer intended to sell her property to him and instead had decided to sell it to someone else for $16,000. Hickey offered to pay Green $16,000 for the lot, but she refused this offer. The Hickeys then filed a complaint against Green seeking specific performance. Green asserted that relief was barred by the statute of frauds. Is this correct?

**5.** In June 1976, Moore went to First National Bank and requested the president of the bank to allow his sons, Rocky and Mike, to open an account in the name of Texas Continental Express, Inc. Moore promised to bring his own business to the bank and orally agreed to make good any losses that the bank might incur from receiving dishonored checks from Texas Continental. The bank then furnished regular checking account and bank draft services to Texas Continental. Several years later, Texas Continental wrote checks totaling $448,942.05 that were returned for insufficient funds. Texas Continental did not cover the checks, and the bank turned to Moore for payment. When Moore refused to pay, the bank sued him. Does Moore have a good statute of frauds defense?

**6.** Mark and Barney Brownlee were farmers who, as a partnership doing business as Brownlee Brothers, grew and sold crops. In addition to farming, Barney Brownlee owned a gas station. On July 22, 1983, Barney Brownlee allegedly telephoned Goldkist and, after checking on the current price of soybeans, allegedly agreed to deliver 5,000 bushels of soybeans to Goldkist between August 22 and September 22, at $6.88 per pound. Although no written agreement signed by either of the Brownlees was created, Goldkist did send the Brownlees a written memorandum dated July 22, which confirmed the agreement to sell 5,000 bushels of soybeans on the terms described above. The Brownlees received the memorandum but did not respond to it. They also did not deliver the soybeans, and Goldkist was forced to "cover" the contract (buy soybeans from another source). Goldkist then brought this action to recover its losses arising out of the necessity to cover. The Brownlees asserted as a defense the fact that there was no writing signed by either of them as required by UCC section 2–201. Is this a good argument?

**7.** Dyer purchased a used Ford from Walt Bennett Ford for $5,895. She signed a written contract, which showed that no taxes were included in the sales price. Dyer contended, however, that the salesperson who negotiated the purchase with her told her both before and after her signing of the contract that the sales tax on the automobile had been paid. The contract Dyer signed contained the following language:

The above comprises the entire agreement pertaining to this purchase and no other agreement of any kind, verbal understanding, representation, or promise whatsoever will be recognized.

It also stated:

This contract constitutes the entire agreement between the parties and no modification hereof shall be valid in any event and Buyer expressly waives the right to rely thereon, unless made in writing, signed by Seller.

Later, when Dyer attempted to license the automobile, she discovered that the Arkansas sales tax had not been paid on it. She paid the sales tax and sued Bennett for breach of contract. What result?

**8.** Starry is a general contractor in the business of asphalt road construction. Murphy was one of its suppliers. In March 1990, a Murphy sales manager orally promised to sell Starry 20,000 tons of asphalt cement oil for $90 per ton. That agreement was confirmed with a written acknowledgment form that specifically stated that causes beyond the control of either party would be an excuse for delay or failure to perform if notice were given promptly. In April 1990, Starry determined that it would need more asphalt cement oil. It contacted Murphy and requested an additional 5,000 tons. Several days later, Murphy's sales manager orally agreed to sell the additional oil on the same terms and conditions as those initially agreed to. Starry neglected to send a confirmatory

memorandum of this oral modification. In August 1990, due to the war in the Persian Gulf, Murphy began experiencing an unprecedented demand for asphalt cement oil. Starry employees became concerned that Murphy might not supply the additional oil and contacted Murphy to request a written confirmation of the modification. Murphy's sales manager allegedly responded, "Don't worry about it. I'll take care of you. I've never cheated you in the past. You are a good customer, and I treat our good customers right." This sales manager, however, was subsequently promoted and replaced by another Murphy employee. In September, the new sales manager informed Starry that because of the oil crisis, Murphy would be forced to allocate its supply. Believing that Murphy would ultimately deliver the additional oil, Starry did not approach other suppliers until late September. At that time, it made arrangements to purchase the additional oil from other suppliers at a higher price. In October 1990, Starry sent a letter to Murphy discussing the agreement between it and Murphy for the sale of 25,000 tons of oil. Murphy was unable to deliver the additional oil and denied that the agreement was ever modified to include an additional 5,000 tons of oil. Starry sued it for breach of contract. Will Starry be able to enforce an agreement to sell the additional quantity of oil?

**9.** Lovely was living in Ann Arbor, Michigan, and working at two jobs there when Dierkes offered Lovely employment with the Real Food Company in Jackson, Michigan. Dierkes promised Lovely a three-year employment contract, a salary of $400 per week, and a percentage interest in Real Food. He also promised that Lovely would not be discharged without good cause. Lovely relocated his family to Jackson in reliance on Dierkes's promise. He began performing under the agreement and requested several times that Dierkes reduce the contract to writing. Dierkes allegedly assured Lovely that a writing was forthcoming. After two months of employment, Dierkes discharged Lovely. Lovely sued Dierkes and Real Food for breach of contract. Dierkes claims that the contract is unenforceable because of the statute of frauds. Can Lovely enforce this contract?

**10.** In 1981, Goodman was living in Oklahoma with her husband, who was suffering from a terminal illness. She and her husband traveled to the Connecticut home of her mother, Mayer, to discuss whether Goodman should return to Connecticut. Goodman and Mayer reached an oral agreement providing that Goodman would live in Mayer's house, would make certain refurbishments, and care for Mayer in return for which Mayer would convey the house to Goodman. Goodman also agreed to pay one half the value of the house to her sister, Savoy, upon the death of Goodman's husband. The Goodmans sold their Oklahoma home and moved to Connecticut. They contracted for renovations, which were paid from the proceeds of the Oklahoma house. In September 1981, Goodman and Mayer had an argument, after which the Goodmans vacated Mayer's house at her request. Shortly thereafter, Mayer changed her will, which had left one-half of her estate to each of her two daughters, and disinherited Goodman, leaving her entire estate on her death to Savoy. Mayer sued her mother's estate, claiming the existence of an enforceable oral contract. Will she prevail?

**11.** 📼 *Video Case.* See "Car Deals." Acme Used Cars Sales and Service sold a used car to Jones. Prior to the signing of a written purchase contract, Acme's salesperson told Jones that he "wouldn't find a car like this at any price" and "this car is a crown jewel." However, the purchase order that Jones signed stated that the car was being sold "as is" and that "no warranties or representations concerning the car have been made or given except as contained" in the contract. Jones later discovered that the brakes were defective and needed to be rebuilt. If Jones sued Acme, would the parol evidence rule prevent the admission of testimony about the salesperson's statements?

**12.** 📼 *Video Case.* See "Sour Grapes." Fred, a jelly manufacturer in Chicago, ordered grapes by telephone for a price of $800 from Gus, a grape grower in California. Gus sent a written purchase order confirmation. He also shipped the grapes, but they were spoiled when they arrived. Would the statute of frauds prevent this contract from being enforced?

See also "Software Horror Story" and "A Christmas Story."

---

## CAPSTONE QUESTIONS

---

Worthmore Industries, a manufacturer of goods, was involved in the following disputes:

· Shaw applied for a job at Worthmore. Worthmore orally offered Shaw a job at a specified salary for a period of three years, and Shaw orally accepted. After several months, Worthmore fired Shaw without just cause. Shaw claims that the contract to employ him for three years is enforceable.

· Worthmore sold a tract of land to Rosen. Rosen claimed that before the written contract was signed, Worthmore's representative had promised him that Worthmore would remove the gasoline tank that was buried on the property. Nothing in the written contract indicates that this promise was made, however.

· Rocky Road, Inc., a Worthmore customer who owed a debt to Worthmore for goods previously shipped, placed another order. Worthmore refused to sell other than C.O.D. to Rocky Road unless the debt was paid. Bart, the father of Rocky Road's president, orally promised to guarantee Rocky Road's debt. Worthmore released the goods to Rocky Road, however, without first obtaining a written guaranty from Bart. Rocky Road fails to pay its debt and Worthmore attempts to collect the money from Bart. Bart claims that the statute of frauds bars enforcement of his promise.

· Worthmore entered into an oral contract to sell a stated quantity of goods to Widgetech Industries, also a merchant, for a total contract price of $10,000. Worthmore immediately dispatched a memorandum confirming the agreement. Its authorized representative signed the memorandum. Three weeks later, the parties orally agreed to modify the contract to increase the price to $10,989. Shortly before delivery, Widgetech contacted Worthmore and repudiated the contract. Widgetech asserts that the contract is unenforceable because of the statute of frauds.

## Required:

Answer the following and give reasons for your conclusions.

1. State whether Shaw's claim is correct.
2. Assess whether a court would enforce Worthmore's alleged promise to remove the gasoline tank.
3. State whether Bart's claim is correct.
4. State whether Widgetech's argument is correct.

# Rights of Third Parties

### INTRODUCTION

*In preceding chapters, we have emphasized the way in which an agreement between two or more people creates legal rights and duties on the part of the contracting parties. Since a contract is founded on the consent of the contracting parties, it might seem to follow that they are the only ones who have rights and duties under the contract. Although this is generally true, there are two situations in which people who were not parties to a contract have legally enforceable rights under it: when a contract has been* assigned *(transferred) to a third party and when a contract is* intended to benefit a third person *(a* third-party beneficiary*). This chapter discusses the circumstances in which third parties have rights under a contract.*

## Assignment of Contracts

Contracts give people both rights and duties. If Murphy buys Wagner's motorcycle and promises to pay him $1,000 for it, Wagner has the *right* to receive Murphy's promised performance (the payment of the $1,000) and Murphy has the *duty* to perform the promise by paying $1,000. In most situations, contract rights can be transferred to a third person and contract duties can be delegated to a third person. The transfer of a *right* under a contract is called an **assignment.** The appointment of another person to perform a *duty* under a contract is called a **delegation.**

## Nature of Assignment of Rights

A person who owes a duty to perform under a contract is called an **obligor.** The person to whom he owes the duty is called the **obligee.** For example, Samson borrows $500 from Jordan, promising to repay Jordan in six months. Samson, who owes the duty to pay the money, is the obligor, and Jordan, who has the right to receive the money, is the obligee. An assignment occurs when the obligee transfers his right to receive the obligor's performance to a third person. When there has been an assignment, the person making the assignment—the original obligee—is then called the **assignor.** The person to whom the right has been transferred is called the **assignee.** Figure 1 summarizes these key terms.

## FIGURE 1 Assignment: Key Terms

| Obligor | Obligee | Assignment | Assignor | Assignee |
|---|---|---|---|---|
| Person who owes the duty to perform | Person who has the right to receive obligor's performance | Transfer of the right to receive obligor's performance | Obligee who transfers the right to receive obligor's performance | Person to whom the right to receive obligor's performance is transferred |

## FIGURE 2 Assignment

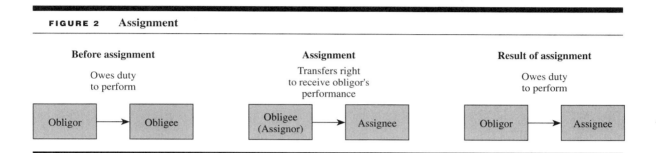

Suppose that Jordan, the obligee in the example above, assigns his right to receive Samson's payment to Kane. Here, Jordan is the assignor and Kane is the assignee. The relationship between the three parties is represented in Figure 2. Notice that the assignment is a separate transaction; it occurs after the formation of the original contract.

The effect of the assignment is to extinguish the assignor's right to receive performance and to transfer that right to the assignee. In the above example, Kane now owns the right to collect payment from Samson. If Samson fails to pay, Kane, as an assignee, now has the right to file suit against Samson to collect the debt.

People assign rights for a variety of reasons. A person might assign a right to a third party to satisfy a debt that he owes. For example, Jordan, the assignor in the above example, owes money to Kane, so he assigns to Kane the right to receive the $500 that Samson owes him. A person might also sell or pledge the rights owed to him to obtain financing. In the case of a business, the money owed to a business by customers and clients is called *accounts receivable.* A business's accounts receivable are an asset to the business that can be used to raise money in several ways. For example, the business may pledge its accounts receivable as collateral for a loan. Suppose Ace Tree Trimming Co. wants to borrow money from First Bank and gives First Bank a security interest (an interest in the debtor's property that secures the debtor's performance of an obligation) in its accounts receivable.[1] If Ace defaults in its payments to First Bank, First Bank will acquire Ace's rights to collect the accounts receivable. A person might also make an assignment of a contract right as a gift. For example, Lansing owes $2,000 to Father. Father assigns the right to receive Lansing's performance to Son as a graduation gift.

**Evolution of the Law Regarding Assignments**
Contract rights have not always been transferable. Early common law refused to permit assignment or delegation because debts were considered to be too personal to transfer. A debtor who failed to pay an honest debt was subject to severe penalties, including imprisonment, because such a failure to pay was viewed as the equivalent of theft. The identity of the creditor was of great importance to the debtor, since one creditor might be more lenient than another.

---

[1]Security interests in accounts and other property are discussed in Chapter 21.

Courts also feared that the assignment of debts would stir up unwanted litigation. In an economy that was primarily land-based, the extension of credit was of relatively small importance. As trade increased and became more complex, however, the practice of extending credit became more common. The needs of an increasingly commercial society demanded that people be able to trade freely in intangible assets such as debts. Consequently, the rules of law regarding the assignment of contracts gradually became more liberal. Today, public policy favors free assignability of contracts.

**Sources of Assignment Law Today**    Legal principles regarding assignment are found not only in the common law of contracts but also in Articles 2 and 9 of the Uniform Commercial Code. Section 2–210 of Article 2 contains principles applicable to assignments of rights under a contract for the sale of *goods*. Article 9 governs security interests in accounts and other contract rights as well as the outright sale of accounts. Article 9's treatment of assignments will be discussed in more detail in Chapter 21, Security Interests in Personal Property, but some provisions of Article 9 relating to assignments will be discussed in this chapter.

## Creating an Assignment

An assignment can be made in any way that is sufficient to show the assignor's intent to assign. No formal language is required, and a writing is not necessary unless required by a provision of the statute of frauds or some other statute. Many states do have statutes requiring certain types of assignments to be evidenced by a writing, however. Additionally, an assignment for the purposes of security must meet Article 9's formal requirements for security interests.[2]

It is not necessary that the assignee give any consideration to the assignor in exchange for the assignment. Gratuitous assignments (those for which the assignee gives no value) are generally revocable until such time as the obligor satisfies the obligation, however. They can be revoked by the

assignor's death or incapacity or by notification of revocation given by the assignor to the assignee.

## Assignability of Rights

Most, but not all, contract rights are assignable. Although the free assignability of contract rights performs a valuable function in our modern credit-based economy, assignment is undesirable if it would adversely affect some important public policy or if it would materially vary the bargained-for expectations of the parties. There are several basic limitations on the assignability of contract rights.

First, an assignment will not be effective if it is *contrary to public policy.* For example, most states have enacted statutes that prohibit or regulate a wage earner's assignment of future wages. These statutes are designed to protect people against unwisely impoverishing themselves by signing away their future incomes.

Second, an assignment will not be effective if it *adversely affects the obligor* in some significant way. An assignment is ineffective if it materially changes the obligor's duty or increases the burden or risk on the obligor. Naturally, any assignment will change an obligor's duty to some extent. The obligor will have to pay money or deliver goods or render some other performance to one party instead of to another. These changes are not considered to be sufficiently material to render an assignment ineffective. Thus, a right to receive money or goods or land is generally assignable. In addition, covenants not to compete are generally considered to be assignable to buyers of businesses. For example, Jefferson sells RX Drugstore to Waldman, including in the contract of sale a covenant whereby Jefferson promises not to operate a competing drugstore within a 30-mile radius of RX for 10 years after the sale. Waldman later sells RX to Tharp. Here, Tharp could enforce the covenant not to compete against Jefferson. The reason for permitting assignment of covenants not to compete is that the purpose of such covenants is to protect an asset of the business—goodwill—for which the buyer has paid.

An assignment could be ineffective because of its variation of the obligor's duty, however, if the contract right involved a *personal relationship* or an element of *personal skill, judgment,* or *character.* For this reason, contracts of employment in which an employee works under the direct and personal supervision of an employer cannot be assigned to a new

---

[2]These requirements are discussed in Chapter 21.

employer. An employer could assign a contract of employment, however, if the assignee-employer could perform the contract without adversely affecting the interests of the employee, such as would be the case when an employment relationship does not involve personal supervision by an individual employer. This point is illustrated by the following case, *Special Products Manufacturing, Inc. v. Douglass.*

A purported assignment is ineffective if it significantly increases the burden of the obligor's performance. For example, if Walker contracts to sell Dwyer all of its requirements of wheat, a purported assignment of Dwyer's rights to a corporation that has much greater requirements of wheat would probably be ineffective because it would significantly increase the burden on Walker.

---

## SPECIAL PRODUCTS MANUFACTURING, INC. v. DOUGLASS
### 553 N.Y.S.2d 506 (N.Y. S. Ct., App. Div. 1990)

Thaddeus Douglass was a highly trained servicer of hardness-testing machinery who was employed by Page-Wilson Corporation. In August and April 1983, Douglass signed two employment agreements governing the terms and conditions of his employment with Page-Wilson. The first agreement prohibited Douglass, while he was working for Page-Wilson and for one year after the termination of his employment, from using, to Page-Wilson's detriment, any of its customer lists or other intellectual property acquired from his job there. The second agreement, which applied to the same time period, prohibited Douglass from accepting employment from or serving as a consultant to any business that was in competition with Page-Wilson. In April 1987, Canrad Corporation purchased all assets and contractual rights of Page-Wilson, including Douglass's two employment contracts. Special Products Manufacturing (Special Products), a wholly owned subsidiary of Canrad, assumed plant operations. Douglass worked for Special Products until his resignation in February 1988.

Shortly after that, Special Products filed this lawsuit against Douglass, alleging that Douglass had affixed his name and home telephone number to the machines he serviced, so that the ensuing maintenance calls would reach him personally. It also alleged that, following his resignation, Douglass established a competing business and actively solicited Special Products's clientele. Douglass did not answer the complaint in a timely manner, and, after a long delay, the trial judge entered a default judgment in favor of Special Products. Douglass appealed this order, arguing in part that Special Products did not have the right to enforce the agreements not to compete.

---

**Yesawich, Justice**     We perceive no merit in the contention that because Douglass entered into the agreements with Page-Wilson, they are unenforceable by Special Products. In an uncontroverted affidavit based upon personal knowledge, Special Products's vice-president of sales avows that Special Products acquired all of Page-Wilson's contract rights, including Douglass's. Douglass's consent was not required to effectuate this transfer. When the original parties to an agreement so intend, a covenant not to compete is freely assignable. Here, such intent is unmistakably evident in the first employment agreement which expressly "inure[s] to the benefit of the successors and assigns of Page-Wilson." And, while the second document contains no similar provision, neither does it specifically forbid assignment. Because executory contracts, which do not involve exceptional personal skills on the part of the assignor and which the assignee can perform without adversely affecting the rights and interests of the adverse party, are freely assignable absent a contractual, statutory or public policy prohibition, a clear and unambiguous prohibition is essential to effectively prevent assignment. Accordingly, the assignment to Special Products perpetuated the restrictive covenant provision, the very terms of which Douglass violated without justification.

**Order in favor of Special Products affirmed.**

**Contract Clauses Prohibiting Assignment**   A contract right may also be nonassignable because the original contract expressly forbids assignment. For example, leases often contain provisions forbidding assignment or requiring the tenant to obtain the landlord's permission for assignment.[3]

Antiassignment clauses in contracts are generally enforceable. Because of the strong public policy favoring assignability, however, such clauses are often interpreted narrowly. For example, a court might view an assignment made in violation of an antiassignment clause as a breach of contract for which damages may be recovered, but not as an invalidation of the assignment. Another tactic is to interpret a contractual ban on assignment as prohibiting only the delegation of duties.

The UCC takes this latter position. Under section 2–210(2), general language prohibiting assignment of "the contract" or "all my rights under the contract" is interpreted as forbidding only the delegation of duties, unless the circumstances indicate to the contrary. Section 2–210 also states that a right to damages for breach of a whole sales contract or a right arising out of the assignor's performance of his entire obligation may be assigned even if a provision of the original sales contract prohibited assignment. In addition, UCC section 9–318(4) invalidates contract terms that prohibit (or require the debtor's consent to) an assignment of an account or creation of a security interest in a right to receive money that is now due or that will become due.

## Nature of Assignee's Rights

When an assignment occurs, the assignee is said to "step into the shoes of his assignor." This means that the assignee acquires all of the rights that his assignor had under the contract. The assignee has the right to receive the obligor's performance, and if performance is not forthcoming, the assignee has the right to sue in his own name for breach of the obligation. By the same token, the assignee acquires no greater rights than those possessed by the assignor.

Because the assignee has no greater rights than did the assignor, the obligor may assert any defense or claim against the assignee that he could have asserted against the assignor, subject to certain time limitations discussed below. A contract that is void, voidable, or unenforceable as between the original parties does not become enforceable just because it has been assigned to a third party. For example, if Richards induces Dillman's consent to a contract by duress and subsequently assigns his rights under the contract to Keith, Dillman can assert the doctrine of duress against Keith as a ground for avoiding the contract.

**Importance of Notifying the Obligor**   An assignee should promptly notify the obligor of the assignment. Although notification of the obligor is not necessary for the assignment to be valid, such notice is of great practical importance. One reason notice is important is that an obligor who does not have reason to know of the assignment could render performance to the assignor and claim that his obligation had been discharged by performance. An obligor who renders performance to the assignor without notice of the assignment has no further liability under the contract. For example, McKay borrows $500 from Goodheart, promising to repay the debt by June 1. Goodheart assigns the debt to Rogers, but no one informs McKay of the assignment, and McKay pays the $500 to Goodheart, the assignor. In this case, McKay is not liable for any further payment. But if Rogers had immediately notified McKay of the assignment and, after receiving notice, McKay had mistakenly paid the debt to Goodheart, McKay would still have the legal obligation to pay $500 to Rogers. Having been given adequate notice of the assignment, he may remain liable to the assignee even if he later renders performance to the assignor.

An assignor who accepts performance from the obligor after the assignment holds any benefits that he receives as a trustee for the assignee. If the assignor fails to pay those benefits to the assignee, however, an obligor who has been notified of the assignment and renders performance to the wrong person may have to pay the same debt twice.

An obligor who receives notice of an assignment from the assignee will want to assure himself that the assignment has in fact occurred. He may ask for written evidence of the assignment or contact the assignee and ask for verification of the assignment. Under UCC section 9–318(3), a notification of assignment is ineffective unless it reasonably identifies the rights assigned. If requested by the account debtor (an obligor who owes money for goods sold

---

[3]The assignment of leases is discussed further in Chapter 18.

or leased or services rendered), the assignee must furnish reasonable proof that the assignment has been made, and, unless he does so, the account debtor may disregard the notice and pay the assignor.

**Defenses against the Assignee**  An assignee's rights in an assignment are subject to the defenses that the obligor could have asserted against the assignor. Keep in mind that the assignee's rights are limited by the terms of the underlying contract between the assignor and the obligor. When defenses arise from the terms or performance of that contract, they can be asserted against the assignee even if they arise after the obligor receives notice of the assignment. For example, on June 1, Worldwide Widgets assigns to First Bank its rights under a contract with Widgetech, Inc. This contract obligates Worldwide Widgets to deliver a quantity of widgets to Widgetech by September 1, in return for which Widgetech is obligated to pay a stated purchase price. First Bank gives prompt notice of the assignment to Widgetech. Worldwide Widget fails to deliver the widgets and Widgetech refuses to pay. If First Bank brought an action against Widgetech to recover the purchase price of the widgets, Widgetech could assert Worldwide Widget's breach as a defense, even though the breach occurred after Widgetech received notice of the assignment.[4]

In determining what other defenses can be asserted against the assignee, the time of notification plays an important role. After notification, as we discussed earlier, payment by the obligor to the assignor will not discharge the obligor.

## Subsequent Assignments

An assignee may "reassign" a right to a third party, who would be called a **subassignee.** The subassignee then acquires the rights held by the prior assignee. He should give the obligor prompt notice of the subsequent assignment, because he takes his interest subject to the same principles discussed above regarding the claims and defenses that can be asserted against him.

## Successive Assignments

Notice to the obligor may be important in one other situation. If an assignor assigns the same right to two assignees in succession, both of whom pay for the assignment, a question of priority results. An assignor who assigns the same right to different people will be held liable to the assignee who acquires no rights against the obligor, but which assignee is entitled to the obligor's performance? Which assignee will have recourse only against the assignor? There are several views on this point.

In states that follow the "American rule," the first assignee has the better right. This view is based on the rule of property law that a person cannot transfer greater rights in property than he owns. In states that follow the "English rule," however, the assignee who first gives notice of the assignment to the obligor, without knowledge of the other assignee's claim, has the better right. The *Restatement (Second) of Contracts* takes a third position. Section 342 of the *Restatement (Second)* provides that the first assignee has priority unless the subsequent assignee gives value (pays for the assignment) and, without having reason to know of the other assignee's claim, does one of the following: obtains payment of the obligation, gets a judgment against the obligor, obtains a new contract with the obligor by novation, or possesses a writing of a type customarily accepted as a symbol or evidence of the right assigned (such as a passbook for a savings account).

## Assignor's Warranty Liability to Assignee

Suppose that Ross, a 16-year-old boy, contracts to buy a used car for $2,000 from Donaldson. Ross pays Donaldson $500 as a down payment and agrees to pay the balance in equal monthly installments. Donaldson assigns his right to receive the balance of the purchase price to Beckman, who pays $1,000 in cash for the assignment. When Beckman later attempts to enforce the contract, however, Ross disaffirms the contract on grounds of lack of capacity. Thus, Beckman has paid $1,000 for a worthless claim. Does Beckman have any recourse against

---

[4]Similarly, if the assignor's rights were subject to discharge because of other factors such as the nonoccurrence of a condition, impossibility, impracticability, or public policy, this can be asserted as a defense against the assignee even if the event occurs after the obligor receives notice of assignment. See *Restatement (Second) of Contracts* § 336(3). The doctrines relating to discharge from performance are explained in Chapter 10.

**FIGURE 3    Delegation: Key Terms**

| Obligor | Obligee | Delegation | Delegator | Delegatee |
|---|---|---|---|---|
| Person who owes the duty to perform | Person who has the right to receive obligor's performance | Appointment of another person to perform the obligor's duty to the obligee | Obligor who appoints another to perform his duty to obligee | Person who is appointed to perform the obligor's duty to the obligee |

Donaldson? When an assignor is paid for making an assignment, the assignor is held to have made certain implied warranties about the claim assigned.

The assignor impliedly warrants that the claim assigned is valid. This means that the obligor has capacity to contract, the contract is not illegal, the contract is not voidable for any other reason known to the assignor (such as fraud or duress), and the contract has not been discharged prior to assignment. The assignor also warrants that he has good title to the rights assigned and that any written instrument representing the assigned claim is genuine. In addition, the assignor impliedly agrees that he will not do anything to impair the value of the assignment. These guarantees are imposed by law unless the assignment agreement clearly indicates to the contrary. One important aspect of the assigned right that the assignor does not impliedly warrant, however, is that the obligor is solvent.

## DELEGATION OF DUTIES

### Nature of Delegation

A **delegation** of duties occurs when an obligor indicates his intent to appoint another person to perform his duties under a contract. For example, White owns a furniture store. He has numerous existing contracts to deliver furniture to customers, including a contract to deliver a sofa to Coombs. White is the *obligor* of the duty to deliver the sofa and Coombs is the *obligee*. White decides to sell his business to Rosen. As a part of the sale of the business, White assigns the rights in the existing contracts to Rosen and delegates to him the performance of those contracts, including the duty to deliver the sofa to Coombs. Here, White is the *delegator* and Rosen is the *delegatee*. White is

appointing Rosen to carry out his duties to the obligee, Coombs. Figure 3 summarizes the key terms regarding delegation.

In contrast to an assignment of a right, which extinguishes the assignor's right and transfers it to the assignee, the delegation of a *duty* does *not* extinguish the duty owed by the delegator. This point is made in *Rosenberg v. Son, Inc.*, which follows this discussion. The delegator remains liable to the obligee unless the obligee agrees to substitute the delegatee's promise for that of the delegator (this is called *a novation*, and will be discussed in greater detail later in this chapter). This makes sense because, if it were possible for a person to escape his duties under a contract by merely delegating them to another, any party to a contract could avoid liability by delegating duties to an insolvent acquaintance. The significance of an effective delegation is that performance by the delegatee will discharge the delegator. In addition, if the duty is a delegable one, the obligee cannot insist on performance by the delegator; he must accept the performance of the delegatee. The relationship between the parties in a delegation is shown in Figure 4.

### Delegable Duties

A duty that can be performed fully by a number of different persons is delegable. Not all duties are delegable, however. The grounds for finding a duty to be nondelegable resemble closely the grounds for finding a right to be nonassignable. A duty is nondelegable if delegation would violate public policy or if the original contract between the parties forbids delegation. In addition, both section 2–210(1) of the UCC and section 318(2) of the *Restatement (Second) of Contracts* take the position that a party to a contract may delegate his duty to

**FIGURE 4** Delegation

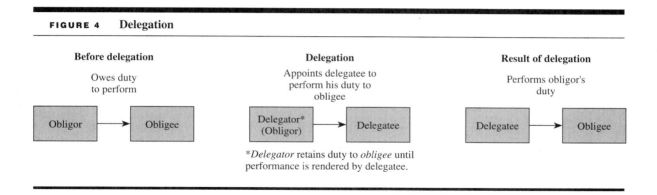

*Delegator* retains duty to *obligee* until performance is rendered by delegatee.

perform to another person unless the parties have agreed to the contrary or unless the other party has a *substantial interest* in having the original obligor perform the acts required by the contract. The key factor used in determining whether the obligee has such a substantial interest is the degree to which performance is dependent on the individual traits, skill, or judgment of the person who owes the duty to perform. For example, if Jansen hires Skelton, an artist, to paint her portrait, Skelton could not effectively delegate the duty to paint the portrait to another artist. Similarly, an employee could not normally delegate her duties under an employment contract to some third person, because employment contracts are made with the understanding that the person the employer hires will perform the work. The situation in which a person hires a general contractor to perform specific work is distinguishable, however. In that situation, the person hiring the general contractor would normally understand that at least part of the work would be delegated to subcontractors.

## Language Creating a Delegation

No special, formal language is necessary to create an effective delegation of duties. In fact, since parties frequently confuse the terms *assignment* and *delegation,* one of the problems frequently presented to courts is determining whether the parties intended an assignment only or both an assignment and a delegation. Unless the agreement indicates a contrary intent, courts tend to interpret assignments as including a delegation of the assignor's duties. Both the UCC 2–210(4) and section 328 of the *Restatement*

*(Second) of Contracts* provide that, unless the language or the circumstances indicate to the contrary, general language of assignment such as language indicating an assignment of "the contract" or of "all my rights under the contract" is to be interpreted as creating *both* an assignment and a delegation.

## Assumption of Duties by Delegatee

A delegation gives the delegatee the right to perform the duties of the delegator. The mere fact that duties have been delegated does not always place legal responsibility on the delegatee to perform. The delegatee who fails to perform will not be liable to either the delegator or the obligee unless the delegatee has assumed the duty by expressly or impliedly undertaking the obligation to perform. However, both section 2–210(4) of the UCC and section 328 of the *Restatement (Second)* provide that an assignee's acceptance of an assignment is to be construed as a promise by him to perform the duties under the contract, unless the language of the assignment or the circumstances indicate to the contrary. Frequently, a term of the contract between the delegator and the delegatee provides that the delegatee assumes responsibility for performance. A common example of this is the assumption of an existing mortgage debt by a purchaser of real estate. Suppose Morgan buys a house from Friedman, agreeing to assume the outstanding mortgage on the property held by First Bank. By this assumption, Morgan undertakes personal liability to both Friedman and First Bank. If Morgan fails to make the mortgage payments, First Bank has a cause of action against Morgan personally. An assumption does *not* release the delegator from liability, however. Rather, it creates a situation in which both the delegator and the assuming delegatee owe duties to the obligee. If the assuming delegatee fails to pay, the delegator can be held liable. Thus, in the example described above, if Morgan fails to make mortgage payments and First Bank is unable to collect the debt from Morgan, Friedman would have secondary liability. Friedman, of course, would have an action against Morgan for breach of their contract.

## Discharge of Delegator by Novation

As you have seen, the mere delegation of duties—even when the delegatee assumes those duties—does not release the delegator from his legal obligation to the obligee. A delegator can, however, be discharged from performance by **novation.**

A novation is a particular type of substituted contract in which the obligee agrees to discharge the original obligor and to substitute a new obligor in his place. The effects of a novation are that the original obligor has no further obligation under the contract and the obligee has the right to look to the new obligor for fulfillment of the contract. A novation requires more than the obligee's consent to having the delegatee perform the duties. In the example used above, the mere fact that First Bank accepted mortgage payments from Morgan would not create a novation. Rather, there must be some evidence that the obligee agrees to discharge the old obligor and substitute a new obligor. As you will see in the following *Rosenberg* case, this can be inferred from language of a contract or such other factors as the obligee's conduct or the surrounding circumstances.

---

## ROSENBERG V. SON, INC.
### 491 N.W.2d 71 (Sup. Ct. N.D. 1992)

In February 1980, Mary Pratt entered into a contract to buy a Dairy Queen restaurant located in Grand Forks's City Center Mall from Harold and Gladys Rosenberg. The terms of the contract for the franchise, inventory, and equipment were a purchase price totaling $62,000, a $10,000 down payment, and $52,000 due in quarterly payments at 10 percent interest over a 15-year period. The sales contract also contained a provision denying the buyer a right of prepayment for the first five years of the contract. In October 1982, Pratt assigned her rights and delegated her duties under this contract to Son, Inc. The assignment between Pratt and Son contained a "Consent to Assignment" clause, which was signed by the Rosenbergs. It also contained a "save harmless" clause, in which Son promised to indemnify Pratt for any claims, demands, or actions that might result from Son's failure to perform the agreement. After this transaction, Pratt moved to Arizona and had no further knowledge of or involvement with the Dairy Queen business. Also following the assignment, the Dairy Queen was moved from the mall to a different location in Grand Forks.

Son assigned the contract to Merit Corporation in June 1984. This assignment did not include a consent clause, but the Rosenbergs knew of the assignment and apparently acquiesced in it. They accepted a large prepayment from Merit, reducing the principal balance to $25,000. After the assignment, Merit pledged the inventory and equipment of the Dairy Queen as collateral for a loan from Valley Bank and Trust. Payments from Merit to the Rosenbergs continued until June 1988, at which time the payments ceased, leaving an unpaid principal balance of $17,326.24 plus interest. The Rosenbergs attempted collection of the balance from Merit, but Merit filed bankruptcy. The business assets pledged as collateral for the loan from Valley Bank and Trust were repossessed. The Rosenbergs brought this action for collection of the outstanding debt against Son and Pratt. The trial court granted summary judgment in favor of Son and Pratt and against the Rosenbergs, and the Rosenbergs appealed.

**Erickstad, Chief Justice**      It is a well-established principle in the law of contracts that a contracting party cannot escape its liability on the contract by merely assigning its duties and rights under the contract to a third party. This rule of law applies to all categories of contracts, including contracts for the sale of goods, which is present in the facts of this case.

Thus, when Pratt entered into the "assignment agreement" with Son, a simple assignment alone was insufficient to release her from any further liability on the contract. It is not, however, a legal impossibility for a contracting party to rid itself of an obligation under a contract. It may seek the approval of the other original party for release, and substitute a new party in its place. In such an instance, the transaction is no longer called an assignment; instead, it is called a novation. If a novation occurs in this manner, it must be clear from the terms of the agreement that a novation is intended by all parties involved. Both original parties to the contract must intend and mutually assent to the discharge of the obligor from any further liability on the original contract.

It is evident from the express language of the assignment agreement between Pratt and Son that only an assignment was intended, not a novation. The agreement made no mention of discharging Pratt from any further liability on the contract. To the contrary, the latter part of the agreement contained an indemnity clause holding Pratt harmless in the event of a breach by Son. Thus, it is apparent that Pratt contemplated being held ultimately responsible for performance of the obligation. Furthermore, the agreement was between Pratt and Son; they were the parties signing the agreement, not the Rosenbergs. An agreement between Pratt and Son cannot unilaterally affect the Rosenbergs' rights under the contract. The Rosenbergs did sign a consent to the assignment at the bottom of the agreement. However, by merely consenting to the assignment the Rosenbergs did not consent to a discharge of the principal obligor—Pratt. Nothing in the language of the consent clause supports such an allegation. A creditor is free to consent to an assignment without releasing the original obligor. Thus, the express language of the agreement and

intent of the parties at the time the assignment was made did not contemplate a novation by releasing Pratt and substituting Son in her stead.

The inquiry as to Pratt's liability does not end at this juncture. The trial court released Pratt from any liability on the contract due to the changes or alterations which took place following her assignment to Son. While it is true that Pratt cannot be forced to answer on the contract irrespective of events occurring subsequent to her assignment, it is also true that she cannot be exonerated for every type of alteration or change that may develop.

> The buyer can assign his right to the goods or land and can delegate performance of his duty to pay that price. But observe that he remains bound "as before"; the assignee and the seller cannot, by agreement or by waiver, make it the assignor's duty to pay a different price or on different conditions. If the seller is willing to make such a change, he must trust to the assignee alone.

4 *Corbin on Contracts* section 866 at 458–59.

The trial court decided that any alteration in the underlying obligation resulted in a release of Pratt on the contract. It appears that not every type of alteration is sufficient to warrant discharge of the assignor. As suggested by Professor Corbin in the language highlighted above, the alteration must "prejudice the position of the assignor." 4 *Corbin on Contracts* section 866 at 459.

If the changes in the obligation prejudicially affect the assignor, a new agreement has been formed between the assignee and the other original contracting party. More concisely, a novation has occurred and the assignor's original obligation has been discharged. Although we have previously determined that the terms of the assignment agreement between Pratt and Son did not contemplate a novation, there are additional methods of making a novation besides doing so in the express terms of an agreement. The question of whether or not there has been a novation is a question of fact. The trial court should not have granted summary judgment. There are questions of fact remaining as to the result of the changes in the contract. Thus, we reverse the summary judgment and remand for further proceedings.

**Reversed and remanded in favor of the Rosenbergs.**

**FIGURE 5**    **Third-Party Beneficiaries**

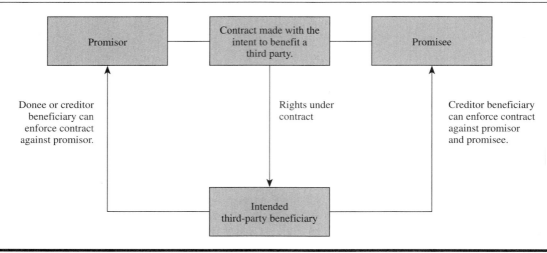

## THIRD–PARTY BENEFICIARIES

There are many situations in which the performance of a contract would constitute some benefit to a person who was not a party to the contract. Despite the fact that a nonparty may expect to derive advantage from the performance of a contract, the general rule is that no one but the parties to a contract or their assignees can enforce it. In some situations, however, parties contract for the purpose of benefiting some third person. In such cases, the benefit to the third person is an essential part of the contract, not just an incidental result of a contract that was really designed to benefit the parties. Where the parties to a contract *intended* to benefit a third party, courts will give effect to their intent and permit the third party to enforce the contract. Such third parties are called **third-party beneficiaries.** Figure 5 illustrates the relationship of third-party beneficiaries to the contracting parties.

### Intended Beneficiaries versus Incidental Beneficiaries

For a third person (other than an assignee) to have the right to enforce a contract, she must be able to establish that the contract was made with the intent to benefit her. A few courts have required that both parties must have intended to benefit the third party. Most courts, however, have found it to be sufficient if the person to whom the promise to perform was made (the *promisee*) intended to benefit the third party. In ascertaining intent to benefit the third party, a court will look at the language used by the parties and all the surrounding circumstances. One factor that is frequently important in determining intent to benefit is whether the party making the promise to perform (the *promisor*) was to render performance directly to the third party. For example, if Allison contracts with Jones Florist to deliver flowers to Kirsch, the fact that performance was to be rendered to Kirsch would be good evidence that the parties intended to benefit Kirsch. This factor is not conclusive, however. There are some cases in which intent to benefit a third party has been found even though performance was to be rendered to the promisee rather than to the third party. Intended beneficiaries are often classified as either *creditor* or *donee beneficiaries.* These classifications are discussed in greater detail below.

A third party who is unable to establish that the contract was made with the intent to benefit her is called an *incidental beneficiary.* A third party is classified as an incidental beneficiary when the benefit derived by that third party was merely an unintended by-product of a contract that was created for the benefit of those who were parties to it. Incidental beneficiaries acquire no rights under a contract. For example, Hutton contracts with Long

Construction Company to build a valuable structure on his land. The performance of the contract would constitute a benefit to Keller, Hutton's next-door neighbor, by increasing the value of Keller's land. The contract between Hutton and Long was made for the purpose of benefiting themselves, however. Any advantage derived by Keller is purely incidental to their primary purpose. Thus, Keller could not sue and recover damages if either Hutton or Long breaches the contract.

As a general rule, members of the public are held to be incidental beneficiaries of contracts entered into by their municipalities or other governmental units in the regular course of carrying on governmental functions. A member of the public cannot recover a judgment in a suit against a promisor of such a contract, even though all taxpayers will suffer some injury from nonperformance. A different result may be reached, however, if a party contracting with a governmental unit agrees to reimburse members of the public for damages or if the party undertakes to perform some duty for individual members of the public.

**Creditor Beneficiaries**   If the promisor's performance is intended to satisfy a legal duty that the promisee owes to a third party, the third party is a **creditor beneficiary.** The creditor beneficiary has rights against both the promisee (because of the original obligation) and the promisor. For example, Smith buys a car on credit from Jones Auto Sales. Smith later sells the car to Carmichael, who agrees to pay the balance due on the car to Jones Auto Sales. (Note that Smith is delegating his duty to pay to Carmichael, and Carmichael is assuming the personal obligation to do so.) In this case, Jones Auto Sales is a creditor beneficiary of the contract between Smith and Carmichael. It has rights against both Carmichael and Smith if Carmichael does not perform.

**Donee Beneficiaries**   If the promisee's primary purpose in contracting is to make a gift of the agreed-on performance to a third party, that third party is classified as a *donee beneficiary.* If the contract is breached, the donee beneficiary will have a cause of action against the promisor, but not against the promisee (donor). For example, Miller contracts with Perpetual Life Insurance Company, agreeing to pay premiums in return for which Perpetual agrees to pay $100,000 to Miller's husband when Miller dies. Miller's husband is a donee beneficiary and can bring suit and recover judgment against Perpetual if Miller dies and Perpetual does not pay. The following case, *Warren v. Monahan Beaches Jewelry Center, Inc.,* provides another example of a donee beneficiary. It also demonstrates the implications of a person's status as an intended beneficiary.

---

### WARREN V. MONAHAN BEACHES JEWELRY CENTER, INC.
#### 548 So. 2d 870 (Fla. Ct. App. 1989)

Jay Andreson went to Monahan Beaches Jewelry Center (Monahan) to shop for a diamond engagement ring for his fiancée, Laneya Warren. Andreson told Monahan that the ring was to be given to Warren. Andreson and a salesperson discussed several aspects of the size, type, and style of the ring, and the salesperson made suggestions about what would be likely to be pleasing to Warren. Shortly before Christmas, Monahan sold Andreson a ring, which Monahan represented as being a diamond ring, for $3,974.25. Andreson gave the ring to Warren for Christmas as a symbol of their engagement. Warren soon noticed a small chip in the stone under the setting. She returned the ring to Monahan shortly after the Christmas holidays, and Monahan agreed to replace the stone with one of equal or greater value at no charge to Warren. After making this agreement, Warren took the ring to another jeweler to have it appraised. There she learned for the first time that the alleged diamond that Monahan sold to Andreson was in fact nothing more than cut glass or cubic zirconia.

Warren filed suit against Monahan on several counts, including breach of contract and violation of the Florida Deceptive and Unfair Trade Practices Act. The trial court dismissed her complaint and Warren appealed.

---

**Booth, Judge**  The law is that a person not party to a contract may sue for breach of contract where the parties' dealings clearly express the parties' intent to create a right primarily and directly benefiting a third party. In the present case, the precontract dealings between Andreson and Monahan, and the subsequent dealings between Warren and Monahan, clearly establish Warren as an intended third party beneficiary of the contract at issue. The complaint properly alleges that Monahan breached the contract when he failed to deliver a diamond ring to Andreson. The alleged breach of contract deprived Warren of the benefit of owning a diamond ring, which was the purpose of the sale. Warren has a valid cause of action for breach of contract as an intended third party beneficiary.

The trial court also erred in dismissing Warren's claim brought pursuant to [the Florida Deceptive and Unfair Trade Practices Act]. One of the purposes of Florida's Deceptive and Unfair Trade Practices Act is to protect consumers from suppliers who commit deceptive and unfair trade practices. Nothing in the statute or case law limits causes of action to the immediate purchaser. The issue of whether the intended beneficiary of a gift may be classified as a "consumer" appears to be an issue of first impression in this state. We hold that [the Act] applies and that Warren, as the beneficiary of the consumer transaction is a "consumer" in her own right and entitled to the remedies afforded.

**Judgment reversed in favor of Warren and case remanded for further proceedings.**

## Vesting of Beneficiary's Rights

Another possible threat to the interests of the third-party beneficiary is that the promisor and the promisee might modify or discharge their contract so as to extinguish or alter the beneficiary's rights. For example, Gates, who owes $500 to Sorenson, enters into a contract with Connor whereby Connor agrees to pay the $500 to Sorenson. What happens if, before Sorenson is paid, Connor pays the money to Gates and Gates accepts it or Connor and Gates otherwise modify the contract? Courts have held that there is a point at which the rights of the beneficiary vest—that is, the beneficiary's rights cannot be lost by modification or discharge. A modification or discharge that occurs after the beneficiary's rights have vested cannot be asserted as a defense to a suit brought by the beneficiary. The exact time at which the beneficiary's rights vest differs from jurisdiction to jurisdiction. Some courts have held that vesting occurs when the contract is formed, while others hold that vesting does not occur until the beneficiary learns of the contract and consents to it or does some act in reliance on the promise.

The contracting parties' ability to vary the rights of the third-party beneficiary can also be affected by the terms of their agreement. A provision of the contract between the promisor and the promisee stating that the duty to the beneficiary cannot be modified would be effective to prevent modification. Likewise, a contract provision in which the parties specifically reserved the right to change beneficiaries or modify the duty to the beneficiary would be enforced. For example, provisions reserving the right to change beneficiaries are very common in insurance contracts.

### PROBLEMS AND PROBLEM CASES

**1.** In 1974, Spiklevitz loaned money to Vincent and Geraldine Heron. The Herons signed a promissory note agreeing to repay the debt by January 15, 1975. In April 1980, the Herons sold their business to Markmil Corp. At that time, $3,510 of their debt to Spiklevitz remained unpaid. Markmil executed an "Assumption of Obligation," which stated that as part of the purchase price of the Herons' business, Markmil agreed to pay the list of debts written on an attached sheet of paper labeled "Exhibit A." Spiklevitz was listed as a creditor in Exhibit A for the balance owed to him. In June 1981, Spiklevitz sued Markmil to recover the amount remaining due on the note. Is Markmil obligated to pay?

**2.** Peterson was employed by Post–Newsweek as a newscaster-anchorman on station WTOP–TV (Channel 9) under a three-year employment contract that was to end June 30, 1980, and could be extended for two additional one-year terms at the option of Post–Newsweek. In June 1978, Post–Newsweek sold its operating license to the Evening News Association (Evening News), and Channel 9 was then designated as WDVM–TV. The contract of sale between Post–Newsweek and Evening News provided for the assignment of all contracts, including Peterson's employment contract. Peterson continued working for the station for more than a year after the change of ownership and received all of the compensation and benefits provided by his contract with Post–Newsweek. In early August 1979, he negotiated a new contract with a competing television station and tendered his resignation to Evening News. Evening News sued Peterson. Peterson defended on the ground that his employment contract was not assignable. Is he correct?

**3.** In May 1978, John and Judith Brooks contracted with Hayes to construct a Windsor Home (a packaged, predesigned, and precut home) on a lot that they owned. Hayes was primarily a real estate broker but also sold Windsor Homes. The construction contract required Hayes to "provide all necessary labor and materials and perform all work of every nature whatsoever to be done in the erection of a residence for" the Brookses. The Brookses and Hayes contemplated that Hayes would hire subcontractors to perform much of the home construction work and Hayes, who had no personal experience in construction, would not control the method of construction. During the construction, the Brookses requested that a "heatilator" be installed as an extra to increase the efficiency of the fireplace. Marr, the mason hired by Hayes to do the fireplace and other masonry work, installed the heatilator. The Brookses moved into the house in the winter of 1978. When they used the fireplace, they smelled smoke in areas of the house remote from the fireplace. Both the Brookses and Hayes hired several masons to inspect the fireplace system, but none of the masons was able to discover the cause of the problem. The Brookses used the fireplace with some frequency until November 1980, when a fire in the home caused structural damage around the fireplace and smoke damage to the house and the couple's personal property. It was discovered that Marr's negligence in installing the heatilator had caused the fire. The Brookses sued both Marr and Hayes. The case against Marr was dismissed because Marr went bankrupt. Is Hayes liable to the Brookses?

**4.** On April 20, Chapman-Harkey Company ordered a quantity of toys known as hang-ups from A. G. Bond Company, at a total cost of $13,378.56. Under the agreement between Chapman-Harkey and A. G. Bond, the hang-ups were sold on a "guaranteed-sale" basis—that is, Chapman-Harkey could return to A. G. Bond any hang-ups that it could not sell and receive a credit. On May 17, Chapman-Harkey received notice that A. G. Bond had assigned the account for this sale to Equitable Factors. In a letter dated May 19, Chapman-Harkey received written confirmation from A. G. Bond's agent that the goods were being sold on a guaranteed-sale basis. Chapman-Harkey failed to pay for the hang-ups, and Equitable Factors brought suit against it to recover the purchase price of the goods sold. At this point, Chapman-Harkey still had in its possession $5,753.78 worth of hang-ups, which it had been unable to sell. Can the guaranteed-sale term be raised as a defense against Equitable Factors, even though the defense did not become available until after notification of the assignment?

**5.** Jones paid Sullivan, the chief of the Addison Police Department, $6,400 in exchange for Sullivan's cooperation in allowing Jones and others to bring marijuana by airplane into the Addison airport without police intervention. Instead of performing the requested service, Sullivan arrested Jones. The $6,400 was turned over to the district attorney's office and was introduced into evidence in the subsequent trial in which Jones was tried for and convicted of bribery. After his conviction, Jones assigned his alleged claim to the $6,400 to Melvyn Bruder. Based on the assignment, Bruder brought suit against the state of Texas to obtain possession of the money. Will he be successful?

**6.** Post, Lumber, and Samson were construction-related businesses owned and operated by DiPietro. In May 1984, Boynton contracted with DiPietro personally and with Post for the lease of Boynton's property, which contained a sawmill. Lumber and Samson used the millsite along with Post in related businesses. At the same time, Boynton entered into a separate contract with Post, giving it a one-year option to purchase the millsite for $60,000. This option provided that on payment of $6,000 at the time of exercising the option, Boynton would transfer title to the property, and the balance would be financed in a specified way. In October 1984, Post assigned its rights in the option agreement to Lumber. In January 1985, Lumber attempted to exercise the option by sending a $6,000 check to Boynton with a letter expressing its readiness to execute the agreement and advising Boynton that the payment of rent would stop. Boynton cashed Lumber's check but did not respond to the letter. Lumber sent Boynton two more letters seeking to exercise the option before it lapsed, but Boynton did not respond. In later litigation, Boynton contended that the assignment of the option agreement was invalid because he was not notified of it. Is this a good argument?

7. Jay Beard Trucks entered into a franchise Dealer Sales and Service Agreement with General Motors (GMC). The agreement contained a provision limiting the possible future transfer of ownership of the dealership. These provisions required Beard to give notice to GMC of any proposed sale of the dealership and gave GMC the right to select each successor and replacement dealer. The contract also provided that GMC "shall not arbitrarily refuse to agree to such proposed change or sale" and that, in determining whether the proposal is acceptable to it, "GMC will take into account the qualifications, personal and business reputation, and financial standing of the proposed dealer operator and owners." Noller, the owner-operator of a Ford dealership and a Toyota dealership and one of the top 100 Ford dealers in the country, entered into negotiations to purchase Beard's dealership. The parties worked out a proposed buy-sell agreement and submitted it to GMC. GMC never contacted Noller, sent dealership transfer applications to him, obtained any documentation or additional information from him, or made inquiries to Beard about Noller's qualifications. Without doing an investigation about these matters, GMC refused to grant the franchise to Noller, apparently because he was also a Ford dealer. As a result, the contract between Noller and Beard fell through and Beard sold the dealership to a third party. Noller brought suit against GMC, asserting that he was an intended beneficiary of the Dealer Sales and Service Agreement between GMC and Beard, wherein GMC had agreed to specifically consider the proposed dealer's qualifications, personal and business reputation, and financial standing. Was he an intended beneficiary?

8. Yellow Cab contracted with the Birmingham Board of Education to transport physically handicapped students in the Birmingham school system.

The contract provided that Yellow Cab would furnish all necessary vehicles and personnel as well as perform maintenance and make all repairs so as to keep the equipment in a safe and efficient operating condition at all times. Yellow Cab subcontracted with Metro Limousine and Leasing to provide the transportation called for by its contract with the Board. Thereafter, Metro purchased two buses from Yellow Cab to use in transporting the students. DuPont, an employee of Metro, was injured when the brakes on the bus that he was driving failed, causing the bus to collide with a tree. DuPont sued Yellow Cab for breach of contract, alleging that Yellow Cab breached a nondelegable duty to properly maintain the bus and that that duty flowed to DuPont as a third-party beneficiary of the contract between Yellow Cab and the Board. Should DuPont win?

9. Mercantile-Safe Deposit & Trust Company frequently advised its long-time customer, Chaplin, about the planning of her estate. Merrick, Chaplin's former son-in-law, maintained a close relationship with Chaplin, and this relationship was reflected in the wills that Chaplin executed. At Chaplin's request, one of Mercantile's trust officers visited her at her home to discuss making certain changes in her will. Without first consulting with Mercantile's attorneys or other estate planning personnel about the appropriateness of these changes, the trust officer instructed Chaplin's attorney to draft a new will reflecting the changes that Chaplin requested. Merrick would have benefited under this will. The will was executed and Chaplin died in 1981. Because of a technical problem overlooked by Mercantile's trust officer, the will provision benefiting Merrick and his children was held to be ineffective and Merrick lost the bequest that he would have had otherwise. Merrick brought suit against Mercantile because of its failure to advise Chaplin properly. Does Merrick have any rights under the contract between Chaplin and Mercantile?

10. 🎞 *Video Case.* See "Roof Repairs." Roofer contracted with Driscoll Industries to do a roofing job. The job was too big for Roofer to handle, so he delegated his duties under the contract to another company that claimed to do that kind of roofing work all the time. However, the other company did such a poor job that it damaged the heating and cooling systems of the building. Is Roofer liable to Driscoll for the damage done by its delegatee?

See also "TV Repair" and "The Student Loan."

Acme Corporation, a widget manufacturer, is involved in each of the following transactions and sets of circumstances:

- Acme owes Big National Bank a $20,000 payment on an operating loan extended to it by the bank. Bogus Hardware Company owes Acme $20,000 for widgets recently delivered by Acme as the last installment under a long-term contract between the two firms. Acme, therefore, assigns to Big National the right to receive payment from Bogus under the Acme–Bogus contract. Acme does this without seeking Bogus's consent to the assignment. Prior to receiving any notification of this assignment from Acme or Big National, Bogus pays the $20,000 to Acme.

- Pursuant to a contract between Acme and Compco, Inc., Acme delivers a large quantity of widgets to Compco, which has 30 days from the date of delivery to pay the purchase price of $27,000. One week after this delivery, Acme, with the knowledge of Compco, assigns to Infidelity Savings & Loan (another of Acme's creditors) the right to collect the $27,000 from Compco under the Acme–Compco contract. Two days after this assignment takes place, Compco discovers that certain latent defects—which existed as of the time of delivery by Acme—made most of the widgets unsuitable for resale to Compco's retail customers. Compco, therefore, informs Infidelity that because of the defective widgets, it will pay a portion of the $27,000 but not the full amount. Infidelity argues that because it is an assignee and not the manufacturer of the widgets, Compco cannot use the widgets' defective condition as a partial defense to Infidelity's claim for payment.

- Realizing that many pressing orders and its present widget production capabilities probably would make it unable to furnish the several thousand widgets it is contractually bound to furnish to Dudco, Inc., by October 1, Acme and another widget manufacturer, Excel Corporation, agree (on September 1) that Acme will delegate to Excel the duty to furnish the widgets contemplated by the Acme–Dudco contract. Excel is a well-established, reliable manufacturer of widgets of the same type, grade, and quality produced by Acme. On September 2, when Acme notifies Dudco of Acme's delegation to Excel, Dudco takes the position that it is not obligated to accept widgets from Excel or any firm other than Acme.

- After making most of the payments under an installment contract for the purchase of a piece of widget-manufacturing equipment from Furd Widgetworks, Inc., Acme entered into a agreement with Griede Company. Under the Acme–Griede agreement, Acme transferred to Griede its interest in the widget-manufacturing equipment covered by the Acme–Furd contract, and Griede agreed (among other things) to pay Furd the remaining $10,000 installment payment due from Acme under the Acme–Furd contract. Acme notified Furd of Acme's agreement with Griede. Furd made no objection. Griede later failed to make the $10,000 payment to Furd.

## Required:

Answer the following and give reasons for your conclusions.

1. Discuss whether the assignment from Acme to Big National is valid, the reasons why or why not, and the respective rights and obligations of Acme, Bogus, and Big National under the circumstances.
2. State whether Infidelity's argument is correct.
3. State whether the position taken by Dudco is correct.
4. Discuss the respective rights and obligations of Acme, Griede, and Furd with regard to the purchase of the widget-manufacturing equipment.

# CHAPTER 10

# PERFORMANCE AND

# REMEDIES

## INTRODUCTION

*Contracts are generally formed before either of the parties renders any actual performance to the other. A person may be content to bargain for and receive the other person's promise at the formation stage of a contract because this permits him to plan for the future. Ultimately, however, all parties bargain for the* performance *of the promises that have been made to them.*

*In most contracts, each party carries out his promise and is* discharged *(released from all of his obligations under the contract) when his performance is complete. Sometimes, however, a party fails to perform or performs in an unsatisfactory manner. In such cases, courts are often called on to determine the respective rights and duties of the parties. This frequently involves deciding such questions as whether performance was due, whether the contract was breached, to what extent it was breached, and whether performance was excused. This task is made more difficult by the fact that contracts often fail to specify the consequences of nonperformance or defective performance. In deciding questions involving the performance of contracts and remedies for breach of contract, courts draw on a variety of legal principles that attempt to do justice, prevent forfeiture and unjust enrichment, and effectuate the parties' presumed intent.*

*This chapter presents an overview of the legal concepts that are used to resolve disputes arising in the performance stage of contracting. It describes how courts determine whether performance is due and what kind of performance is due, the consequences of contract breach, and the excuses for a party's failure to perform. It also includes a discussion of the remedies that are used when a court determines that a contract has been breached.*

## CONDITIONS

### Nature of Conditions

One issue that frequently arises in the performance stage of a contract is whether a party has the duty to perform. Some duties are *unconditional* or *absolute*—that is, the duty to perform does not depend on the occurrence of any further event other than the passage of time. For example, if Root promises to pay Downing $100, Root's duty is unconditional. When a party's duty is unconditional, he has the duty to perform unless his performance is excused. (The various excuses for nonperformance will be discussed later in this chapter.) When a duty is unconditional, the promisor's failure to perform constitutes a *breach of contract.*

In many situations, however, a promisor's duty to perform depends on the occurrence of some event that is called a **condition.** A condition is an uncertain, future event that affects a party's duty to perform. For example, if Melman contracts to buy Lance's house on condition that First Bank approve Melman's application for a mortgage loan by January 10, Melman's duty to buy Lance's house is *conditioned* on the bank's approving his loan application by January 10. When a promisor's duty is conditional, his duty to perform is affected by the occurrence of the condition. In this case, if the condition does not occur, Melman has no duty to buy the house. His failure to buy it because of the nonoccurrence of the condition will *not* constitute a breach of contract. Rather, he is discharged from further obligation under the contract.

Almost any event can be a condition. Some conditions are beyond the control of either party, such as when Morehead promises to buy Pratt's business if the prime rate drops by a specified amount. Others are within the control of a party, such as when one party's performance of a duty under the contract is a condition of the other party's duty to perform.

## Types of Conditions

There are two ways of classifying conditions. One way of classifying conditions focuses on the effect of the condition on the duty to perform. The other way focuses on the way in which the condition is created.

**Classifications of Conditions Based on Their Effect on the Duty to Perform**  As Figure 1 illustrates, conditions vary in their effects on the duty to perform.

**1.** *Condition precedent.* A condition precedent is a future, uncertain event that creates the duty to perform. If the condition does not occur, performance does not become due. If the condition does

occur, the duty to perform arises. The condition at issue in *Beverly Way Associates v. Barham,* which follows this discussion, is an example of a condition precedent.

**2.** *Concurrent condition.* When the contract calls for the parties to perform at the same time, each person's performance is conditioned on the performance or tender of performance (offer of performance) by the other. Such conditions are called **concurrent conditions.** For example, if Martin promises to buy Johnson's car for $5,000, the parties' respective duties to perform are subject to a concurrent condition. Martin does not have the duty to perform unless Johnson tenders his performance, and vice versa.

**3.** *Condition subsequent.* A **condition subsequent** is a future, uncertain event that **discharges** the duty to perform. When a duty is subject to a condition subsequent, the duty to perform arises but is discharged if the future, uncertain event occurs. For example, Wilkinson and Jones agree that Wilkinson will begin paying Jones $2,000 per month, but that if XYZ Corporation dissolves, Wilkinson's obligation to pay will cease. In this case, Wilkinson's duty to pay is subject to being discharged by a condition subsequent. The major significance of the distinction between conditions precedent and conditions subsequent is that the plaintiff bears the burden of proving the occurrence of a condition precedent, while the defendant bears the burden of proving the occurrence of a condition subsequent.

**Classifications of Conditions Based on the Way in which They Were Created**  Another way of classifying conditions is to focus on the means by which the condition was created.

**1.** *Express condition.* An **express condition** is a condition that is specified in the language of the parties' contract. For example, if Grant promises to sell his regular season football tickets to Carson on condition that Indiana University wins the Rose Bowl, Indiana's winning the Rose Bowl is an express condition of Grant's duty to sell the tickets.

When the contract expressly provides that a party's duty is subject to a condition, courts take it very seriously. When a duty is subject to an express condition, that condition must be strictly complied with in order to give rise to the duty to perform.

---

**FIGURE 1** **Effect of Conditions**

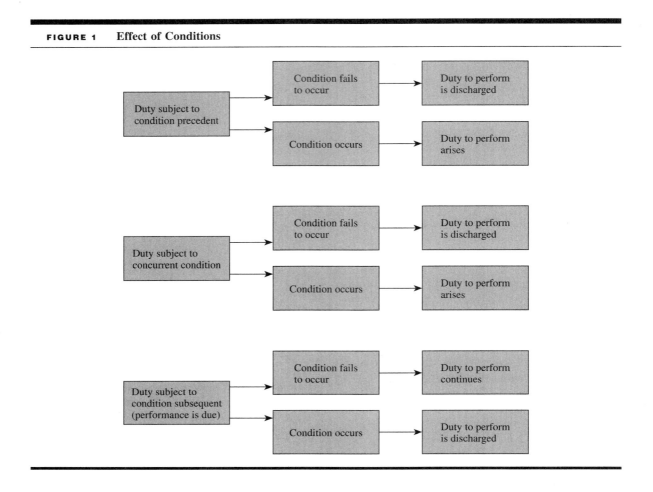

---

**2.** *Implied-in-fact condition.* An **implied-in-fact condition** is one that is not specifically stated by the parties but is *implied* by the nature of the parties' promises. For example, if Summers promises to unload cargo from Knight's ship, the ship's arrival in port would be an implied-in-fact condition of Summers's duty to unload the cargo.

**3.** *Constructive condition.* **Constructive conditions** (also known as *implied-in-law conditions*) are conditions that are imposed by law rather than by the agreement of the parties. The law imposes constructive conditions to do justice between the parties. In contracts in which one of the parties is expected to perform before the other, the law normally infers that that performance is a constructive condition of the other party's duty to perform. For example, if Thomas promises to build a house for King, and the parties' understanding is that King will pay Thomas an agreed-on price when the house

is built, King's duty to pay is subject to the constructive condition that Thomas complete the house. Without such a constructive condition, a person who did not receive the performance promised him would still have to render his own performance.

## Creation of Express Conditions

Although no particular language is required to create an express condition, the conditional nature of promises is usually indicated by such words as *provided that, subject to, on condition that, if, when, while, after,* and *as soon as.* The process of determining the meaning of conditions is not a mechanical one. Courts look at the parties' overall intent as indicated in language of the entire contract.

The following discussion explores two common types of express conditions.

**Example of Express Condition: Satisfaction of Third Parties**   It is common for building and construction contracts to provide that the property owner's duty to pay is conditioned on the builder's production of certificates to be issued by a specific architect or engineer. These certificates indicate the satisfaction of the architect or engineer with the builder's work. They are often issued at each stage of completion, after the architect or engineer has inspected the work done.

The standard usually used to determine whether the condition has occurred is a *good faith* standard. As a general rule, if the architect or engineer is acting honestly and has some good faith reason for withholding a certificate, the builder cannot recover payments due. In legal terms, the condition that will create the owner's duty to pay has not occurred.

If the builder can prove that the withholding of the certificate was fraudulent or done in bad faith (as a result of collusion with the owner, for example), the court may order that payment be made despite the absence of the certificate. In addition, production of the certificate may be excused by the death, insanity, or incapacitating illness of the named architect or engineer.

**Example of Express Condition: Personal Satisfaction**   Contracts sometimes provide that a promisee's duty to perform is conditioned on his personal satisfaction with the promisee's performance. For example, Moore commissions Allen to paint a portrait of Moore's wife, but the contract provides that Moore's duty to pay is conditioned on his personal satisfaction with the portrait.

How does a court determine whether the condition of personal satisfaction has occurred? If the court applies a standard of actual, subjective satis-

faction and Moore asserts that he is not satisfied, it would be very difficult for Allen to prove that the condition has occurred. If, on the other hand, the court applies an objective, "reasonable person" standard of satisfaction, Allen stands a better chance of proving that the condition has occurred.

In determining which standard of satisfaction to apply, courts distinguish between cases in which the performance bargained for involves personal taste and comfort and cases that involve mechanical fitness or suitability for a particular purpose. If personal taste and comfort are involved, as they would be in the hypothetical case described above, a promisor who is honestly dissatisfied with the promisee's performance has the right to reject the performance without being liable to the promisee. If, however, the performance involves mechanical fitness or suitability, the court will apply a reasonable person test. If the court finds that a reasonable person would be satisfied with the performance, the condition of personal satisfaction has been met and the promisor must accept the performance and pay the contract price. For example, Kitt Manufacturing Company hires Pace to design a conveyor belt system for use in its factory, conditioning its duty to pay on its personal satisfaction with the system. A court would be likely to find that this is a contract involving mechanical fitness and suitability for which an objective test of satisfaction could be used. These standards are illustrated in Figure 2 (see page 167). Because the "honest satisfaction" standard involves a danger of forfeiture by the performing party, courts prefer the objective test of satisfaction when objective evaluation is feasible. The following *Beverly Way Associates v. Barham* case discusses a further implication of personal satisfaction conditions.

---

## BEVERLY WAY ASSOCIATES V. BARHAM
### 276 Cal. Rptr. 240 (Ct. App. Cal. 1990)

On July 7, 1988, Phyllis Barham entered into a contract to sell her residential building in Long Beach, California, to Beverly Way Associates (Beverly Way) for $3.9 million. The contract provided for the opening of escrow (the procedure by which the sale would be consummated) and a closing within 60 days of that time. It also provided that Beverly Way's obligation to purchase the property "shall be conditioned upon" its approval of a number of specified inspections and documents and delivery of clear title. One of these items was a certified survey of the property that would show all improvements to the property and the location of all exceptions to the title. The contract gave Beverly Way 28 business days in which to inspect and approve documents after having been furnished them by Barham. On November 15, 1988, Barham furnished the material that Beverly Way required, and on December 2, Beverly Way wrote to Barham stating, "We reluctantly disapprove of the matters disclosed on the Survey and relating to the Property." This letter described in detail the reasons for its rejection. The letter expressed the hope that the parties could "keep the deal alive" and proposed two alternatives that would have changed the parties' arrangement substantially. There was no further communication between the parties until February 1989, when Beverly Way sent a second letter stating that it was prepared to waive its objections to the survey and to proceed to close the deal. Barham refused to sell the property and Beverly Way sued for specific performance. The trial court sustained a demurrer in favor of Barham, and Beverly Way appealed.

---

**Epstein, Judge**   Both sides to this appeal treat the buyer's right of approval under the contract as a condition precedent in favor of the buyer. They are quite correct in that characterization. "A condition is an event, not certain to occur, which must occur, unless its non-occurrence is excused, before performance under a contract becomes due." (*Rest. 2d, Contracts,* section 224).

We turn to an examination of the nature of the buyer's power to approve the condition precedent and to the effect of its disapproval. Most of the textual and case material on "satisfaction" conditions precedent turns on whether an objective or subjective standard is to be used in reviewing the reasonableness of its exercise. Neither party questions the reasonableness of the buyer's exercise of its approval authority in the December 2, 1988, letter.

The effect of a buyer's power to approve documentation required in a contract for the purchase of real estate "is to give the buyer an option not to consummate the purchase if it fails to meet the condition," at least so long as the buyer acts reasonably and in the exercise of good faith. Stated another way, the contract gives the buyer the power and privilege of termination in the event that it reasonably concludes that the condition has not been fulfilled. Except for the judicial gloss that the power of rejection must be exercised reasonably, the party having the power to approve or reject is in the same position as a contract offeree. It is hornbook law that an unequivocal rejection by an offeree, communicated to the offeror, terminates the offer; even if the offeror does no further act, the offeree cannot later purport to accept the offer and thereby create enforceable contractual rights against the offeror. There can be no question but that Beverly Way exercised its power of disapproval in this case. The December 2, 1988, letter said so expressly. This rejection, communicated to Barham, terminated the contract. It left Beverly Way with no power to create obligations against Barham by a late "waiver" of its objections and acceptance of the proffered documentation.

The fact that Beverly Way considered the existing contract to be at an end is reflected also by its effort to keep the "deal alive" by proposing two entirely new formulations that were novel to the agreement of the parties. It may be inferred that Beverly Way was hoping to find a way to acquire the property, but it cannot be doubted that it was unwilling to do so on the basis of what had been presented by Barham.

**Affirmed in favor of Barham.**

---

## Excuse of Conditions

In most situations involving conditional duties, the promisor does not have the duty to perform unless and until the condition occurs. There are, however, a variety of situations in which the occurrence of a condition will be excused. In such a case, the person whose duty is conditional will have to perform even though the condition has not occurred.

One ground for excusing a condition is that the occurrence of the condition has been *prevented* or *hindered* by the party who is benefited by the condition. For example, Connor hires Ingle to construct a garage on Connor's land, but when Ingle

**FIGURE 2** **Duty to Perform Conditioned on "Personal Satisfaction" (a form of express condition precedent)**

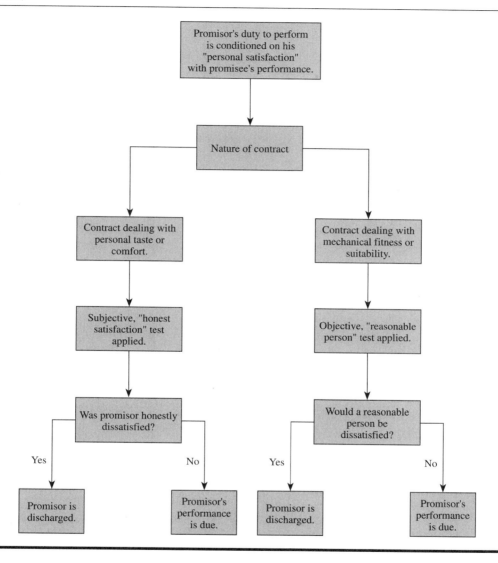

attempts to begin construction, Connor refuses to allow Ingle access to the land. In this case, Connor's duty to pay would normally be subject to a constructive condition that Ingle build the garage. However, since Connor prevented the occurrence of the condition, the condition will be excused, and Ingle can sue Connor for damages for breach of contract even though the condition has not occurred.

Other grounds for excuse of a condition include **waiver** and **estoppel.** When a person whose duty is conditional voluntarily gives up his right to the oc-

currence of the condition (waiver), the condition will be excused. Suppose that Buchman contracts to sell his car to Fox on condition that Fox pay him $2,000 by June 14. Fox fails to pay on June 14, but, when he tenders payment on June 20, Buchman accepts and cashes the check without reservation. Buchman has thereby *waived* the condition of payment by June 14.

When a person whose duty is conditional leads the other party to rely on his noninsistence on the condition, the condition will be excused because of estoppel. For example, McDonald agrees to sell his business to Brown on condition that Brown provide a credit report and personal financial statement by July 17. On July 5, McDonald tells Brown that he can have until the end of the month to provide the necessary documents. Relying on McDonald's assurances, Brown does not provide the credit report and financial statement until July 29. In this case, McDonald would be *estopped* (precluded) from claiming that the condition did not occur.

A condition may also be excused when performance of the act that constitutes the condition becomes *impossible*. For example, if a building contract provides that the owner's duty to pay is conditioned on the production of a certificate from a named architect, the condition would be excused if the named architect died or became incapacitated before issuing the certificate.

## PERFORMANCE OF CONTRACTS

When a promisor has performed his duties under a contract, he is discharged. Because his performance constitutes the occurrence of a constructive condition, the other party's duty to perform is also triggered, and the person who has performed has the right to receive the other party's performance. In determining whether a promisor is discharged by performance and whether the constructive condition of his performance has been fulfilled, courts must consider the standard of performance expected of him.

### Level of Performance Expected of the Promisor

In some situations, no deviation from the promisor's promised performance is tolerated; in others, less-than-perfect performance will be sufficient to discharge the promisor and give him the right to recover under the contract.

**1.** *Strict performance standard.* A **strict performance** standard is a standard of performance that requires virtually perfect compliance with the contract terms. Remember that, when a party's duty is subject to an express condition, that condition must be strictly and completely complied with in order to give rise to a duty of performance. Thus, when a promisor's performance is an express condition of the promisee's duty to perform, that performance

must strictly and completely comply with the contract in order to give rise to the other promisee's duty to perform. For example, if McMillan agrees to pay Jester $500 for painting his house "on condition that" Jester finish the job no later than June 1, 1994, a standard of strict or complete performance would be applied to Jester's performance. If Jester does not finish the job by June 1, his breach will have several consequences. First, since the condition precedent to McMillan's duty to pay has not occurred, McMillan does not have a duty to pay the contract price. Second, since it is now too late for the condition to occur, McMillan is discharged. Third, McMillan can sue Jester for breach of contract. The law's commitment to freedom of contract justifies such results in cases in which the parties have expressly bargained for strict compliance with the terms of the contract.

The strict performance standard is also applied to contractual obligations that can be performed either exactly or to a high degree of perfection. Examples of this type of obligation include promises to pay money, deliver deeds, and, generally, promises to deliver goods. A promisor who performs such promises completely and in strict compliance with the contract is entitled to receive the entire contract price. The promisor whose performance deviates from perfection is not entitled to receive the other party's performance if he does not render perfect performance within an appropriate time. He may, however, be able to recover the value of any benefits that he has conferred on the other party under a theory of quasi-contract.

**2.** *Substantial performance.* A **substantial performance** standard is a somewhat lower standard of performance that is applied to duties that are difficult to perform without some deviation from perfection *if* performance of those duties is *not* an express condition. A common example of this type of obligation is a promise to erect a building. Other examples include promises to construct roads, to cultivate crops, and to render some types of personal or professional services. Substantial performance is performance that falls short of complete performance in minor respects. As you will see in *Reale v. Linder,* it does not apply when a contracting party has been deprived of a material part of the consideration he bargained for. When a substantial performance standard is applied, the promisor who has substantially performed is discharged. His substantial performance triggers the other party's duty to pay the contract price less any damages resulting from the defects in his performance. The obvious purpose behind the doctrine of substantial performance is to prevent forfeiture by a promisor who has given the injured party most of what he bargained for. Substantial performance is generally held to be inapplicable to a situation in which the breach of contract has been *willful,* however.

---

## REALE V. LINDER
### 514 N.Y.S.2d 1004 (N.Y. Dist. Ct. 1987)

Thomas Linder hired Orlando Reale to build a 12 foot by 12 foot extension on his house with a raised wooden deck, sliding glass doors, and a gas-fired barbeque. Their written contract made no provision regarding obtaining a building permit or compliance with building codes, although it did contain a notation stating "plairs (sic) and permit $500 Dep." The agreed price for these improvements was $22,560.

It became evident that several features of the finished addition deviated from the state building code and the building plans that had been approved by the town. Reale had built the crawl space beneath the addition some 4 to 7 inches less than the 18 inches mandated by the state building code, which prevented inspection underneath the addition for structural defects. In addition, Reale sealed the framing of the addition, where substantial problems existed, without a prior inspection by the city building department or his own architect. Serious defects existed in the roof, and the plumbing work was not done by a licensed plumber, although it was later corrected. Improper or incomplete materials were used for the gas line for the barbeque, which caused a gas leak that had to be corrected. The steps leading down from the main dwelling to the addition are each 4 inches high rather than the 6 and 8 inches each that appear in the plan. In addition, Reale did no grade survey of the property before building, although expert witnesses testified that a grade survey was necessary to build the addition properly. The city building department initially denied a certificate of occupancy because the construction had been "closed up" and could not be inspected. It was issued only after Reale procured an architect's affidavit stating that he had inspected the location and that the work had been done in conformity with the approved plans and the state fire and building code, but this was apparently based on false information that Reale gave to the architect.

Linder made partial payment under the contract but withheld $5,855. Reale sued Linder to collect the unpaid balance. A trial was held and this is the trial court's opinion.

---

**Mogil, Judge**   The crux of Reale's argument in support of his complaint is that he substantially performed the contract. In order for a building contractor to be able to take advantage of the doctrine of substantial performance, he must not be guilty of a willful or intentional departure from the terms of his contract. This doctrine, however, permits compensation for all defects caused by the contractor's performance. Under this rule the party sued is protected as to any damages he may suffer due to the contractor's failure to strictly perform. The contractor must prove that the defects or omissions were insubstantial. This he has not done. Although the written agreement does not expressly provide that the contract be performed in conformance with state and local fire prevention and building code regulations, it must be presumed that the parties intended that the contract be performed in accordance with state and local laws. In every home improvement contract, the contractor has an implied duty to perform the contract in accordance with fire prevention and building code requirements. The consumer homeowner relies upon the contractor's skill and expertise to perform the improvements. Reale's failure to construct the extension to code requirements renders the alterations illegal and frustrates the purpose of the contract.

The doctrine of substantial performance is an equitable one intended to prevent injustice where a contractor inadvertently caused trivial, minor, non-essential deficiencies which may be easily and inexpensively remedied. Where the defect cannot be corrected without partially reconstructing the building, the doctrine of substantial performance does not apply. It has been shown that any request for a new or currently revised certificate of occupancy will be denied unless the defect of an improper crawl space is corrected. To correct the defect, the floor of the extension must be removed, the walls braced, excavations undertaken to remove additional earth, and the concrete and floor rebuilt. These corrections are tantamount to reconstructing the addition. Reale has not therefore shown either complete or substantial performance.

**Judgment entered in favor of Linder.**

---

### CONCEPT REVIEW
## SUBSTANTIAL PERFORMANCE

| Definition | Application | Effects | Limitation |
|---|---|---|---|
| Performance that falls short of complete performance in some minor respect but that does not deprive the other party of a material part of the consideration for which he bargained | Applies to performance that (1) is *not* an express condition of the other party's duty to perform and (2) is difficult to do perfectly | Triggers other party's duty to perform; requires other party to pay the contract price minus any damages caused by defects in performance | Breach cannot have been willful |

---

## Good Faith Performance

One of the most significant trends in modern contract law is that courts and legislatures have created a duty to perform in good faith in an expanding range of contracts.[1] The Uniform Commercial Code specifically imposes a duty of good faith in every contract within the scope of any of the articles of the Code [1–203]. A growing number of courts have applied the duty to use good faith in transactions between lenders and their customers as well as insurance contracts, employment contracts, and contracts for the sale of real property.

This obligation to carry out a contract in good faith is usually called the **implied covenant of good faith and fair dealing.** It is a broad and flexible duty that is imposed by law rather than by the agreement of the parties. It is generally taken to mean that neither party to a contract will do anything to prevent the other from obtaining the benefits that he has the right to expect from the parties' agreement or their contractual relationship. The law's purpose in imposing such a term in contracts is to prevent abuses of power and encourage ethical behavior.

Breach of the implied covenant of good faith gives rise to a contract remedy. In some states, it can also constitute a tort, depending on the severity of the breach. A tort action for breach of the implied covenant of good faith is more likely to be recognized in situations in which a contract involves a special relationship of dependency and trust between the parties or where the public interest is adversely affected by a contracting party's practices. Numerous cases exist, for example, in which insurance companies' bad faith refusal to settle claims or perform duties to their insured and lenders' failure to exercise good faith in their dealings with their customers have led to large damage verdicts. Likewise, in states in which the implied duty of good

---

[1] This trend is discussed in Chapter 1.

faith has been held applicable to contracts of employment, employers who discharge employees in bad faith have been held liable for damages.[2]

## BREACH OF CONTRACT

When a person's performance is due, any failure to perform that is not excused is a breach of contract. Not all breaches of contract are of equal seriousness, however. Some are relatively minor deviations, whereas others are so extreme that they deprive the promisee of the essence of what he bargained for. The legal consequences of a given breach depend on the extent of the breach.

At a minimum, a party's breach of contract gives the nonbreaching party the right to sue and recover for any damages caused by that breach. When the breach is serious enough to be called a **material breach,** further legal consequences ensue.

### Effect of Material Breach

A material breach occurs when the promisor's performance fails to reach the level of performance that the promisee is justified in expecting under the circumstances. In a situation in which the promisor's performance is judged by a substantial performance standard, saying that he failed to give substantial performance is the same thing as saying that he materially breached the contract.

The party who is injured by a material breach has the right to withhold his own performance. He is discharged from further obligations under the contract and may cancel it. He also has the right to sue for damages for total breach of contract.

### Effect of Nonmaterial Breach

By contrast, when the breach is not serious enough to be material, the nonbreaching party may sue for only those damages caused by the particular breach. In addition, he does not have the right to cancel the contract, although a nonmaterial breach can give him the right to suspend his performance until the breach is remedied. Once the breach is remedied, however, the nonbreaching party must go ahead and render his performance, minus any damages caused by the breach.

---

[2]This is discussed in Chapter 40.

### Determining the Materiality of the Breach

The standard for determining materiality is a flexible one that takes into account the facts of each individual case. The key question is whether the breach deprives the injured party of the benefits that he reasonably expected. For example, Norman, who is running for mayor, orders campaign literature from Prompt Press, to be delivered in September. Prompt Press's failure to deliver the literature until after the election in November deprives Norman of the essence of what he bargained for and would be considered a material breach.

In determining materiality, courts take into account the extent to which the breaching party will suffer forfeiture if the breach is held to be material. They also consider the magnitude (amount) of the breach and the willfulness or good faith exercised by the breaching party. The timing of the breach can also be important. A breach that occurs early on in the parties' relationship is more likely to be viewed as material than is one that occurs after an extended period of performance. Courts also consider the extent to which the injured party can be adequately compensated by the payment of damages.

**Time for Performance** A party's failure to perform on time is a breach of contract that may be serious enough to constitute a material breach, or it may be relatively trivial under the circumstances.

At the outset, it is necessary to determine when performance is due. Some contracts specifically state the time for performance, which makes it easy to determine the time for performance. In some contracts that do not specifically state the time for performance, such a time can be inferred from the circumstances surrounding the contract. In the Norman and Prompt Press hypothetical example, the circumstances surrounding the contract probably would have implied that the time for performance was some time before the election, even if the parties had not specified the time for performance. In still other contracts, no time for performance is either stated or implied. When no time for performance is stated or implied, performance must be completed within a "reasonable time," as judged by the circumstances of each case.

**Consequences of Late Performance** After a court determines when performance was due, it must determine the consequences of late performance. In some contracts, the parties expressly state that "time is of the essence" or that timely performance is "vital." This means that each party's timely performance by a specific date is an express condition of the other party's duty to perform. Thus, in a contract that contains a time is of the essence provision, any delay by either party normally constitutes a material breach. You will see an example of this in *F. J. Miceli and Slonim Development Corporation v. Dierberg,* which follows. Sometimes, courts will imply such a term even when the language of the contract does not state that time is of the essence. A court would be likely to do this if late performance is of little or no value to the promisee. For example, Schrader contracts with the local newspaper to run an advertisement for Christ-mas trees from December 15, 1994, to December 24, 1994, but the newspaper does not run the ad until December 26, 1994. In this case, the time for performance is an essential part of the contract and the newspaper has committed a material breach.

When a contract does not contain language indicating that time is of the essence and a court determines that the time for performance is not a particularly important part of the contract, the promisee must accept late performance rendered within a reasonable time after performance was due. The promisee is then entitled to deduct or set off from the contract price any losses caused by the delay. Late performance is not a material breach in such cases unless it is unreasonably late.

---

## F. J. MICELI AND SLONIM DEVELOPMENT CORPORATION V. DIERBERG
### 773 S.W.2d 154 (Mo. Ct. App. 1989)

Joanne and Louis Basso contracted with Mary Dierberg to purchase her property for $1,310,000. One term of the contract stated "The sale under this contract shall be closed . . . at the office of Community Title Company . . . on May 16, 1988 at 10:00 A.M. . . . Time is of the essence of this contract." After forming this contract, the Bassos assigned their right to purchase Dierberg's property to F. J. Miceli and Slonim Development Corporation.

At 10:00 A.M. on May 16, 1988, Dierberg appeared at Community Title Company for closing. No representative of Miceli and Slonim was there, nor did anyone from Miceli and Slonim inform Dierberg that there would be any delay in the closing. At 10:20 A.M., Dierberg declared the contract null and void because the closing did not take place as agreed, and she left the title company office shortly thereafter. Dierberg had intended to use the purchase money to close another contract to purchase real estate later in the day. At about 10:30 A.M., a representative of Miceli and Slonim appeared at Community Title Company to begin the closing procedures, but the representative did not have the funds for payment until 1:30 P.M. Dierberg refused to return to the title company to close, stating that Miceli and Slonim had breached the contract by failing to tender payment on time. She had already made alternative arrangements to finance her purchase of other real estate to meet her obligation under that contract.

Miceli and Slonim sued Dierberg for specific performance of the contract, claiming that the contract did not require closing exactly at 10:00 A.M., but rather some time on the day of May 16. Dierberg filed a motion for summary judgment, and the trial court granted it. Miceli and Slonim appealed.

---

**Karohl, Judge** Parties to a contract may provide that time is of the essence. A clause specifying time is of the essence ordinarily means a specific contractual provision fixing the time of performance is to be regarded as a vital element of the contract. If a contract specifies a certain time for performance, the contract must be performed at that time, even if time is specified by the hour. Custom will not alter express agreement of the parties.

Here, the contract clearly and precisely stated closing was to occur at 10:00 A.M. on May 16, 1988. Time and date were specifically referred to in three separate sections of the contract. It was agreed time was of the essence of the contract. This provision would relate to all three times and dates. Dierberg was obligated to close under another contract to purchase real estate later the same day. She relied on receiving the proceeds of her sale at 10:00 A.M. Because closing did not occur as agreed, Dierberg was required to make other arrangements to meet her obligation. These facts lend meaning to the judgment of the trial court that "10:00 A.M." was the agreement of Bassos and Dierberg, not a mere guideline.

When there is no ambiguity in a contract, it is the duty of the court to state its clear meaning. Here, the

court found there was no ambiguity in the contract and that the contract required closing at or reasonably near 10:00 A.M. We find no error in the judgment. Miceli and Slonim's failure to tender payment until 1:30 P.M. combined with its failure to inform Dierberg of the delay in closing, was a breach of contract. On undisputed facts, summary judgment was proper.

**Summary judgment for Dierberg affirmed.**

---

## TIME FOR PERFORMANCE

| Contract Language | Time for Performance | Consequences of Late Performance |
|---|---|---|
| "Time is of the essence" or similar language | The time stated in the contract | Material breach |
| Specific time is stated in or implied by the contract and late performance would have little or no value | The time stated in or implied by the contract | Material breach |
| Specific time is stated in or implied by the contract, but the time for performance is a relatively unimportant part of the contract | The time stated in or implied by the contract | Not a material breach unless performance is unreasonably late |
| No time for performance is stated in or implied by the contract | Within a reasonable time | Not material breach unless performance is unreasonably late |

---

**Anticipatory Repudiation**   One type of breach of contract occurs when the promisor indicates before the time for his performance that he is unwilling or unable to carry out the contract. This is called **anticipatory repudiation** or **anticipatory breach.** Anticipatory breach generally constitutes a material breach of contract that discharges the promisee from all further obligation under the contract.

In determining what constitutes anticipatory repudiation, courts look for some unequivocal statement or voluntary act that clearly indicates that the promisor cannot or will not perform his duties under the con-

tract. This may take the form of an express statement by the promisor. The promisor's intent not to perform could also be implied from actions of the promisor such as selling to a third party the property that the promisor was obligated to sell to the promisee. For example, if Ross, who is obligated to convey real estate to Davis, conveys the property to some third person instead, Ross has repudiated the contract.

When anticipatory repudiation occurs, the promisee is faced with several choices. For example, Marsh and Davis enter a contract in which Davis agrees to deliver a quantity of bricks to Marsh on

September 1, 1994, and Marsh agrees to pay Davis a sum of money in two installments. The agreement specifies that Marsh will pay 50 percent of the purchase price on July 15, 1994, and 50 percent of the purchase price within 30 days after delivery. On July 1, 1994, Davis writes Marsh and unequivocally states that he will not deliver the bricks. Must Marsh go ahead and send the payment that is due on July 15? Must he wait until September 1 to bring suit for total breach of contract? The answer to both questions is no.

When anticipatory repudiation occurs, the non-breaching party is justified in withholding his own performance and suing for damages right away, without waiting for the time for performance to arrive.[3] If he can show that he was ready, willing, and able to perform his part of the contract, he can recover damages for total breach of the contract. The nonbreaching party is not obligated to do this, however. If he chooses, he may wait until the time for performance in case the other party changes his mind and decides to perform.

### Recovery by a Party Who Has Committed Material Breach

A party who has materially breached the contract (that is, has not substantially performed) does not have the right to recover the contract price. If a promisor who has given some performance to the promisee cannot recover under the contract, however, the promisor will face forfeiture and the promisee will have obtained an unearned gain. There are two possible avenues for a party who has committed material breach to obtain some compensation for the performance he has conferred on the nonbreaching party.

1. *Quasi-contract.* A party who has materially breached a contract might recover the reasonable value of any benefits he has conferred on the promisee by bringing an action under quasi-contract.[4] This would enable him to obtain compensation for the value of any performance he has given that has benefited the nonbreaching party. Some

courts take the position that a person in material breach should not be able to recover for benefits he has conferred, however.

2. *Partial performance of a divisible contract.* Some contracts are divisible; that is, each party's performance can be divided in two or more parts and each part is exchanged for some corresponding consideration from the other party. For example, if Johnson agrees to mow Peterson's lawn for $20 and clean Peterson's gutters for $50, the contract is divisible. When a promisor performs one part of the contract but materially breaches another part, he can recover at the contract price for the part that he did perform. For example, if Johnson breached his duty to clean the gutters but fully performed his obligation to mow the lawn, he could recover at the contract price for the lawn-mowing part of the contract.

## EXCUSES FOR NONPERFORMANCE

Although nonperformance of a duty that has become due will ordinarily constitute a breach of contract, there are some situations in which nonperformance is excused because of factors that arise after the formation of the contract. When this occurs, the person whose performance is made impossible or impracticable by these factors is discharged from further obligation under the contract. The following discussion concerns the most common grounds for excuse of nonperformance.

### Impossibility

When performance of a contractual duty becomes impossible after the formation of the contract, the duty will be discharged on grounds of **impossibility.** This does not mean that a person can be discharged merely because he has contracted to do something that he is simply unable to do or that causes him hardship or difficulty. Impossibility in the legal sense of the word means "it cannot be done by anyone" rather than "I cannot do it." Thus, promisors who find that they have agreed to perform duties that are beyond their capabilities or that turn out to be unprofitable or burdensome are generally not excused from performance of their duties. Impossibility will provide an excuse for nonperformance, however, when some unexpected event arises after the formation of the contract and renders

---

[3]Uniform Commercial Code rules regarding anticipatory repudiation in contracts for the sale of goods are discussed in Chapter 13.

[4]Quasi-contract is discussed in Chapter 1. It involves the use of the remedy of restitution, which is discussed later in this chapter.

performance objectively impossible. The event that causes the impossibility need not have been entirely unforeseeable. Normally, however, the event will be one that the parties would not have reasonably thought of as a real possibility that would affect performance.

There are a variety of situations in which a person's duty to perform may be discharged on grounds of impossibility. The three most common situations involve illness or death of the promisor, supervening illegality, and destruction of the subject matter of the contract.

**Illness or Death of Promisor**   Incapacitating illness or death of the promisor excuses nonperformance when the promisor has contracted to perform personal services. For example, if Pauling, a college professor who has a contract with State University to teach for an academic year, dies before the completion of the contract, her estate will not be liable for breach of contract. The promisor's death or illness does not, however, excuse the nonperformance of duties that can be delegated to another, such as the duty to deliver goods, pay money, or convey real estate. For example, if Odell had contracted to convey real estate to Ruskin and died before the closing date, Ruskin could enforce the contract against Odell's estate.

**Supervening Illegality**   If a statute or governmental regulation enacted after the creation of a contract makes performance of a party's duties illegal, the promisor is excused from performing. Statutes or regulations that merely make performance more difficult or less profitable do not, however, excuse nonperformance. You will see an example of this form of impossibility in the following case, *Centex Corporation v. Dalton.*

---

## CENTEX CORPORATION V. DALTON
### 840 S.W.2d 952 (Sup. Ct. Tex. 1992)

Centex is a company engaged in residential and commercial construction and related financial services. John Dalton was an executive of a Texas thrift institution. In 1988, because the flagging Texas economy adversely affected the state's thrift institutions, the Federal Home Loan Bank Board (Bank Board) and other regulatory agencies decided to close, merge, liquidate, or sell several large thrift institutions. This plan was called the "Southwest Plan." In November 1988, Centex contacted Dalton to request that he help Centex acquire certain thrifts made available through the Southwest Plan. A few weeks later, Dalton traveled to Washington, D.C., where he made an unsuccessful bid to acquire a group of thrifts for Centex. While there, Dalton learned about the availability of four central Texas thrifts known as the "Lamb Package." Dalton informed Centex about this, and in December 1988, Centex entered into a letter agreement with Dalton in which it promised to pay Dalton $750,000 over a three-year period if Centex were successful in acquiring the Lamb Package. Before the parties signed this agreement, Centex met with the Bank Board and told it of its intention to pay fees to Dalton on completion of the purchase of the Lamb Package. The Bank Board told Centex that this would be acceptable as long as Centex—rather than any of the thrift institutions in the Lamb Package or any entity formed to acquire the Lamb Package—made the payment to Dalton. Arrangements were made to acquire the Lamb Package, but on December 28, 1988, the night before Centex's acquisition of the Lamb Package was to be finalized, Centex's representative learned that the Bank Board probably would not permit payment of the fees to Dalton. Centex nevertheless went ahead and finalized the purchase of the Lamb Package, forming a wholly owned subsidiary, Texas Trust Savings Bank, as the acquiring entity. At a meeting on December 28, 1988, the Bank Board approved the acquisition of the Lamb Package, conditioned on a prohibition against Texas Trust's direct or indirect payment of finder's fees. The transcript of the meeting shows that members of the Bank Board discussed Texas Trust's planned payment of fees to Dalton, made specific objection to the payment, and requested its general counsel to prepare an amendment to clarify that its prohibition against the payment of fees extended to affiliates of Texas Trust. On January 31, 1989, the Bank Board adopted the amendment proposed by its counsel.

Dalton performed the services required of him under the letter agreement, but Centex did not pay him because of the prohibition imposed by the Bank Board. Dalton brought suit against Centex for breach of contract. The trial court granted a summary judgment in favor of Dalton, awarding him $750,000 in damages plus interest, costs, and attorney's fees. Centex appealed, and the court of appeals affirmed the summary judgment. Centex appealed to the Texas Supreme Court. (In August 1989, while the case was on appeal, a federal statute called the Financial Institutions Reform Recovery and Enforcement Act became effective. This statute abolished the Bank Board, created the Office of Thrift Supervision (OTS), and gave OTS the powers formerly vested in the Bank Board. On December 11, 1990, OTS issued a cease-and-desist order to prevent Centex or Texas Trust from paying any fees to Dalton under the letter agreement.)

---

**Gammage, Justice**    Centex argues that, because its performance under the letter agreement has been made impracticable by having to comply with the Bank Board's order, its duty to render that performance is discharged. Congress gave the Bank Board power to regulate the acquisition and control of federally-insured thrifts by savings and loan holding companies. As a result, the Bank Board's prohibition makes it illegal for Centex to perform under the letter agreement. "Where a party's performance is made impracticable by the occurrence of an event the non-occurrence of which was a basic assumption on which the contract was made, his duty to render that performance is discharged." *Restatement (Second) of Contracts* section 261 (1981). A governmental regulation or order that makes impracticable the performance of a duty "is an event the non-occurrence of which was made a basic assumption on which the contract was made." Consequently, to avoid inconsistency with the Bank Board's prohibition and conflict with federal regulatory law, we must hold that Centex is excused from performance by the doctrine of impossibility.

When courts are asked to excuse a party's performance due to supervening circumstances which made performance impracticable or impossible, they sometimes attempt to allocate the burden of risk and decide who must pay for the unanticipated occurrence. Foreseeability is one factor used to decide which party assumed the risk of supervening impossibility. The foreseeability factor has, however, gradually decreased in importance. Here, one party,

Centex, cannot be required to pay, regardless of the foreseeability of the Bank Board's prohibition.

The court of appeals reasoned that the Bank Board's prohibition applied only to Texas Trust and not to Centex. We note, however, that the prohibition forbids not only the direct payment of finder's fees by Centex, which is an affiliate of Texas Trust, but also the indirect payments of such fees. We also note the court of appeals reasoned that, because the obligation of Centex to pay Dalton arose when the letter agreement was signed on December 23, 1988, before the Bank Board's adoption of its prohibition on December 29, 1988, the prohibition did not apply to the letter agreement. The court of appeals' reasoning was incorrect because the letter agreement is premised on a condition precedent. By the terms of the letter agreement, Dalton's right to enforce it could not accrue until the Bank Board approved the acquisition. Because the Bank Board, in approving the acquisition, prohibited the payment of the finder's fees, thereby invalidating the letter agreement, Dalton's right to enforce the letter agreement never accrued.

The Bank Board's order prohibits Centex's performance under the letter agreement, which otherwise would be enforceable under state contract law. Centex cannot pay Dalton and obey the governmental regulation, which has prohibited the proposed payment. Centex's duty to perform under the letter agreement is excused.

**Reversed in favor of Centex.**

---

**Destruction of the Subject Matter of the Contract**    If something that is essential to the promisor's performance is destroyed after the formation of the contract through no fault of the promisor, the promisor is excused from performing. For example, Woolridge contracts to sell his car to Rivkin. If an explosion destroys the car after the contract has been formed but before Woolridge has made delivery,

Woolridge's nonperformance will be excused. The destruction of nonessential items that the promisor intended to use in performing does not excuse nonperformance if substitutes are available, even though securing them makes performance more difficult or less profitable. Suppose that Ace Construction Company had planned to use a particular piece of machinery in fulfilling a contract to build a building for Worldwide Widgets Company. If the piece of machinery is destroyed but substitutes are available, destruction of the machinery before the contract is performed would *not* give Ace an excuse for failing to perform.

## Frustration of Venture

Closely associated with impossibility is the doctrine of **frustration of venture** (also known as **commercial frustration** or **frustration of purpose**). This doctrine provides an excuse for nonperformance when events that occur after the formation of the contract would deprive the promisor of the benefit of return performance. Although courts often include frustration cases within the general terminology of impossibility, frustration can be distinguished from impossibility and impracticability by the fact that the promisor in a frustration case is not necessarily prevented from performing. Rather, in frustration cases, the promisor is excused because the return performance by the other party has become worthless to him. For example, Boyd signs a contract for a one-year membership in an Eden Exercise Salon, for which he agrees to pay $50 per month. One week after signing the contract, Boyd is involved in a serious automobile accident and suffers injuries that cause him to be bedridden for a year. In such a case, the automobile accident and Boyd's resulting injuries did not prevent him from performing his duties under the contract (paying money each month), but this unexpected event does deprive Boyd of the benefit of receiving Eden's return performance. In such a case, a court might excuse Boyd's performance on the ground of frustration of venture.

## Commercial Impracticability

Section 2–615 of the Uniform Commercial Code has extended the scope of the common law doctrine of impossibility to cases in which unforeseen developments make performance by the promisor highly impracticable, unreasonably expensive, or of little value to the promisee. Rather than using a standard of impossibility, then, the Code uses the more relaxed standard of **impracticability.** Despite the less stringent standard applied, cases actually excusing nonperformance on grounds of impracticability are relatively rare. To be successful in claiming excuse based on impracticability, a promisor must be able to establish that the event that makes performance impracticable occurred without his fault and that the contract was made with the basic assumption that this event would not occur. This basically means that the event was beyond the scope of the risks that the parties contemplated at the time of contracting and that the promisor did not expressly or impliedly assume the risk that the event would occur.

Case law and official comments to UCC section 2–615 indicate that neither increased cost nor collapse of a market for particular goods is sufficient to excuse nonperformance, because those are the types of business risks that every promisor assumes. However, drastic price increases or severe shortages of goods resulting from unforeseen circumstances such as wars and crop failures can give rise to impracticability.

If the event causing impracticability affects only a part of the seller's capacity to perform, the seller must allocate production and deliveries among customers in a "fair and reasonable" manner and must notify them of any delay or any limited allocation of the goods. You can read more about commercial impracticability in Chapter 13, Performance of Sales Contracts.

The impracticability standard has been adopted in section 261 of the *Restatement (Second) of Contracts,* which closely resembles the provisions of section 2–615 of the UCC. States that follow the *Restatement (Second)* approach apply the impracticability standard to all types of contracts, not just those for the sale of goods.

## OTHER GROUNDS FOR DISCHARGE

Earlier in this chapter, you learned about several situations in which a party's duty to perform could be discharged even though that party had not himself performed. These include the nonoccurrence of a condition precedent or concurrent condition, the occurrence of a condition subsequent, material breach by the other party, and excuse from performance by impossibility, impracticability, or frustration. The following discussion deals with additional ways in which a discharge can occur.

### Discharge by Mutual Agreement

Just as contracts are created by mutual agreement, they can also be discharged by *mutual agreement.* An agreement to discharge a contract must be supported by consideration to be enforceable.

### Discharge by Accord and Satisfaction

An **accord** is an agreement whereby a promisee who has an existing claim agrees with the promisor that he will accept some performance different from that which was originally agreed on. When the promisor performs the accord, that is called a **satisfaction.**[5] When an accord and satisfaction occurs, the parties are discharged. For example, Root contracts with May to build a garage on May's property for $30,000. After Root has performed his part of the bargain, the parties then agree that instead of paying money, May will transfer a one-year-old Porsche to Root instead. When this is done, both parties are discharged.

### Discharge by Waiver

A party to a contract may voluntarily relinquish any right he has under a contract, including the right to receive return performance. Such a relinquishment of rights is known as a **waiver.** If one party tenders an incomplete or defective performance and the other party accepts that performance without objection, knowing that the defects will not be remedied, the party to whom performance was due will have discharged the other party from his duty of performance. For example, a real estate lease requires Long, the tenant, to pay a $5 late charge for late payments of rent. Long pays his rent late each month for five months, but the landlord accepts it without objection and without assessing the late charge. In this situation, the landlord has probably waived his right to collect the late charge.

To avoid waiving rights, a person who has received defective performance should give the

other party prompt notice that she expects complete performance and will seek damages if the defects are not corrected.

### Discharge by Alteration

If the contract is represented by a *written* instrument, and one of the parties intentionally makes a material alteration in the instrument without the other's consent, the alteration acts as a discharge of the other party. If the other party consents to the alteration or does not object to it when he learns of it, he is not discharged. Alteration by a third party without the knowledge or consent of the contracting parties does not affect the parties' rights.

### Discharge by Statute of Limitations

Courts have long refused to grant a remedy to a person who delays bringing a lawsuit for an unreasonable time. All of the states have enacted statutes known as **statutes of limitation,** which specify the period of time in which a person can bring a lawsuit.

The time period for bringing a contract action varies from state to state, and many states prescribe time periods for cases concerning oral contracts that are different from those for cases concerning written contracts. Section 2–725 of the Uniform Commercial Code provides for a four-year statute of limitations for contracts involving the sale of goods.

The statutory period ordinarily begins to run from the date of the breach. It may be delayed if the party who has the right to sue is under some incapacity at that time (such as minority or insanity) or is beyond the jurisdiction of the state. A person who has breached a contractual duty is discharged from liability for breach if no lawsuit is brought before the statutory period elapses.

### Discharge by Decree of Bankruptcy

The contractual obligations of a debtor are generally discharged by a decree of bankruptcy. Bankruptcy is discussed in Chapter 22.

## REMEDIES FOR BREACH OF CONTRACT

Our discussion of the performance stage of contracts so far has focused on the circumstances under which a party has the duty to perform or is excused

---

[5]Accord and satisfaction is also discussed in Chapter 4.

from performing. In situations in which a person is injured by a breach of contract and is unable to obtain compensation by a settlement out of court, a further important issue remains: What remedy will a court fashion to compensate for breach of contract?

Contract law seeks to encourage people to rely on the promises made to them by others. Contract remedies focus on the economic loss caused by breach of contract, not on the moral obligation to perform a promise. The objective of granting a remedy in a case of breach of contract is simply to compensate the injured party.

## Types of Contract Remedies

There are a variety of ways in which this can be done. The basic categories of contract remedies include:

1. Legal remedies (money damages).
2. Equitable remedies.
3. Restitution.

The usual remedy is an award of money damages that will compensate the injured party for his losses. This is called a **legal remedy** or **remedy at law,** because the imposition of money damages in our legal system originated in courts of law. Less frequently used but still important are **equitable remedies** such as specific performance. Equitable remedies are those remedies that had their origins in courts of equity rather than in courts of law. Today, they are available at the discretion of the judge. A final possible remedy is **restitution,** which requires the defendant to pay the value of the benefits that the plaintiff has conferred on him.

## Interests Protected by Contract Remedies

Remedies for breach of contract protect one or more of the following interests that a promisee may have:[6]

**1.** *Expectation interest.* A promisee's **expectation interest** is his interest in obtaining the objective or opportunity for gain that he bargained for and "expected." Courts attempt to protect this interest by formulating a remedy that will place the promisee in the position he would have been in if the contract had been performed as promised.

**2.** *Reliance interest.* A promisee's **reliance interest** is his interest in being compensated for losses that he has suffered by changing his position in reliance on the other party's promise. In some cases, such as when a promisee is unable to prove his expectation interest with reasonable certainty, the promisee may seek a remedy to compensate for the loss suffered as a result of relying on the promisor's promise rather than for the expectation of profit.

**3.** *Restitution interest.* A **restitution interest** is a party's interest in recovering the amount by which he has enriched or benefited the other. Both the reliance and restitution interests involve promisees who have changed their position. The difference between the two is that the reliance interest involves a loss to the promisee that does not benefit the promisor, whereas the restitution interest involves a loss to the promisee that does constitute an unjust enrichment to the promisor. A remedy based on restitution enables a party who has performed or partially performed her contract and has benefited the other party to obtain compensation for the value of the benefits that she has conferred.

## Legal Remedies (Damages)

### Limitations on Recovery of Damages in Contract Cases

An injured party's ability to recover damages in a contract action is limited by three principles:

**1.** *A party can recover damages only for those losses that he can prove with reasonable certainty.* Losses that are purely speculative are not recoverable. Thus, if Jones Publishing Company breaches a contract to publish Powell's memoirs, Powell may not be able to recover damages for lost royalties (her expectation interest), since she may be unable to establish, beyond speculation, how much money she would have earned in royalties if the book had been published. (Note, however, that Powell's reliance interest might be protected here; she could be allowed to recover provable losses incurred in reliance on the contract.)

**2.** *A breaching party is responsible for paying only those losses that were foreseeable to him at the time of contracting.* A loss is foreseeable if it would

---

[6]*Restatement (Second) of Contracts* § 344.

ordinarily be expected to result from a breach or if the breaching party had reason to know of particular circumstances that would make the loss likely. For example, if Prince Manufacturing Company renders late performance in a contract to deliver parts to Cheatum Motors without knowing that Cheatum is shut down waiting for the parts, Prince will not have to pay the business losses that result from Cheatum's having to close its operation.

**3.** *Plaintiffs injured by a breach of contract have the duty to mitigate (avoid or minimize) damages.* A party cannot recover for losses that he could have avoided without undue risk, burden, or humiliation. For example, an employee who has been wrongfully fired would be entitled to damages equal to his wages for the remainder of the employment period. The employee, however, has the duty to minimize the damages by making reasonable efforts to seek a similar job elsewhere.

## Compensatory Damages

Subject to the limitations discussed above, a person who has been injured by a breach of contract is entitled to recover **compensatory damages.** In calculating the compensatory remedy, a court will attempt to protect the expectation interest of the injured party by giving him the "benefit of his bargain" (placing him in the position he would have been in *had the contract been performed as promised*). To do this, the court must compensate the injured person for the provable losses he has suffered as well as for the provable gains that he has been prevented from realizing by the breach of contract. Normally, compensatory damages include one or more of three possible items: loss in value, any allowable consequential damages, and any allowable incidental damages.

**1.** *Loss in value.* The starting point in calculating compensatory damages is to determine the **loss in value** of the performance that the plaintiff had the right to expect. This is a way of measuring the expectation interest. The calculation of the loss in value experienced by an injured party differs according to the sort of contract involved and the circumstances of the breach. In contracts involving nonperformance of the sale of real estate, for example, courts normally measure loss in value by the difference between the contract price and the market price of the property. Thus, if Willis repudiates a contract with Renfrew whereby Renfrew was to purchase land worth $20,000 from Willis for $10,000, Renfrew's loss in value was $10,000. Where a seller has failed to perform a contract for the sale of goods, courts may measure loss in value by the difference between the contract price and the price that the buyer had to pay to procure substitute goods.[7] In cases in which a party breaches by rendering defective performance—say, by breaching a warranty in the sale of goods—the loss in value would be measured by the difference between the value of the goods if they had been in the condition warranted by the seller and the value of the goods in their defective condition.[8]

**2.** *Consequential damages.* **Consequential damages** (also called **special damages**) compensate for losses that occur as a consequence of the breach of contract. Consequential losses occur because of some special or unusual circumstances of the particular contractual relationship of the parties. For example, Apex Trucking Company buys a computer system from ABC Computers. The system fails to operate properly, and Apex is forced to pay its employees to perform the tasks manually, spending $10,000 in overtime pay. In this situation, Apex might seek to recover the $10,000 in overtime pay in addition to the loss of value that it has experienced.

Lost profits flowing from a breach of contract can be recovered as consequential damages if they are foreseeable and can be proven with reasonable certainty. It is important to remember, however, that the recovery of consequential damages is subject to the limitations on damage recovery discussed earlier.

**3.** *Incidental damages.* **Incidental damages** compensate for reasonable costs that the injured party incurs after the breach in an effort to avoid further loss. For example, if Smith Construction Company breaches an employment contract with Brice, Brice could recover as incidental damages those reasonable expenses he must incur in attempting to procure substitute employment, such as long-distance telephone tolls or the cost of printing new résumés.

---

[7]Remedies under Article 2 of the Uniform Commercial Code are discussed in detail in Chapter 14.

[8]See Chapter 12 for further discussion of the damages for breach of warranty in the sale of goods.

**Alternative Measures of Damages**     The foregoing discussion has focused on the most common formulation of damage remedies in contracts cases. The normal measure of compensatory damages is not appropriate in every case, however. When it is not appropriate, a court may use an alternative measure of damages. For example, where a party has suffered losses by performing or preparing to perform, he might seek damages based on his *reliance interest* instead of his expectation interest. In such a case, he would be compensated for the provable losses he suffered by relying on the other party's promise. This measure of damages is often used in cases in which a promise is enforceable under promissory estoppel.[9]

## Nominal Damages

**Nominal damages** are very small damage awards that are given when a technical breach of contract has occurred without causing any actual or provable economic loss. The sums awarded as nominal damages typically vary from 2 cents to a dollar.

## Liquidated Damages

The parties to a contract may expressly provide in their contract that a specific sum shall be recoverable if the contract is breached. Such provisions are

---

[9]Promissory estoppel is discussed in Chapters 1 and 4.

called **liquidated damages** provisions. For example, Murchison rents space in a shopping mall in which she plans to operate a retail clothing store. She must make improvements in the space before opening the store, and it is very important to her to have the store opened for the Christmas shopping season. She hires Ace Construction Company to construct the improvements. The parties agree to include in the contract a liquidated damages provision stating that, if Ace is late in completing the construction, Murchison will be able to recover a specified sum for each day of delay. Such a provision is highly desirable from Murchison's point of view because, without a liquidated damages provision, she would have a difficult time in establishing the precise losses that would result from delay. Courts scrutinize these agreed-on damages carefully, however.

If the amount specified in a liquidated damages provision is reasonable and if the nature of the contract is such that actual damages would be difficult to determine, a court will enforce the provision. When liquidated damages provisions are enforced, the amount of damages agreed on will be the injured party's exclusive damage remedy. If the amount specified is unreasonably great in relation to the probable loss or injury, however, or if the amount of damages could be readily determined in the event of breach, the courts will declare the provision to be a penalty and will refuse to enforce it. The issue of reasonableness of liquidated damages is presented in the *Luminous Neon, Inc. v. Parscale* case, which follows.

---

## LUMINOUS NEON, INC. V. PARSCALE
**836 P.2d 1201 (Ct. App. Kan. 1992)**

Rita Parscale, the owner of a restaurant, entered into negotiations to acquire outdoor advertising signs for her business from Luminous Neon. At the outset of the negotiations, Luminous Neon had offered to sell the signs to Parscale for $5,600 plus tax, but Parscale ultimately leased them. Under the terms of the lease, Parscale paid a rental of $191.75 plus tax per month for a term of five years. The lease also contained a liquidated damages clause that required Parscale, in the event of breach, to pay damages equal to 80 percent of the remaining payments due. That 80 percent represented Luminous Neon's expenses incurred in manufacturing, financing, and installing the signs, as well as profit. The 20 percent of the remaining payments that was not included as liquidated damages was for maintenance and service expenses that would not be incurred due to Parscale's breach.

Sometime after Parscale leased the signs, the City of Topeka began construction on a street that limited access to Parscale's business. That construction had an adverse effect on Parscale's business, and it ultimately closed. Parscale stopped making payments on the signs after making a total of 19 payments. Forty-one monthly payments of $191.75 remained due and payable, resulting in liquidated damages, including tax, of $6,651.04. Luminous Neon removed the signs from Parscale's business at her request. The removal added another $300 to the damages. Luminous Neon ultimately sued Parscale to collect this money. The trial court granted Luminous Neon's motion for summary judgment and awarded it $6,951.04. Parscale appealed.

---

**Bullock, Judge**    Parscale contends the court erred in granting summary judgment because a material fact existed relating to the liquidated damages claim of Luminous Neon. She argues that Luminous Neon's offer to sell the signs for $5,600 plus tax reveals that the liquidated damages were unreasonable. The contention that only the original sale price of the signs constitutes reasonable damages is not persuasive. There are advantages to be weighed when one considers leasing rather than purchasing an item. However, when one chooses to lease an item and then breaches that lease, it is unreasonable to believe damages should be based upon values attendant to a purchase of that item. By leasing rather than purchasing, Parscale avoided financing charges, insurance, repair, and maintenance expenses. Luminous Neon agreed to maintain the signs during the term of the lease.

The general rule is that courts will "refuse to enforce a liquidated damage provision which fixes damages in an amount grossly disproportionate to the harm actually sustained or likely to be sustained, and under certain circumstances indicative of gross proportion," such a provision will be deemed a penalty. 22 *Am. Jur. 2d, Damages* section 701, p. 758.

Luminous Neon custom designed the signs specifically for Parscale, and, notwithstanding her argument to the contrary, we are not persuaded that the signs are of particular value to Luminous Neon. Moreover, the trial court awarded the signs to Parscale. The damage clause of the lease was not a penalty, and the award did not unjustly enrich Luminous Neon.

**Judgment affirmed in favor of Luminous Neon.**

---

## Punitive Damages

**Punitive damages** are damages awarded in addition to the compensatory remedy that are designed to punish a defendant for particularly reprehensible behavior and to deter the defendant and others from committing similar behavior in the future. The traditional rule is that punitive damages are not recoverable in contracts cases unless a specific statutory provision (such as some consumer protection statutes) allows them or the defendant has committed *fraud* or some other independent tort. A few states will permit the use of punitive damages in contracts cases in which the defendant's conduct, though not technically a tort, was malicious, oppressive, or tortious in nature.

Punitive damages have also been awarded in many of the cases involving breach of the implied covenant of good faith. In such cases, courts usually circumvent the traditional rule against awarding punitive damages in contracts cases by holding that breach of the duty of good faith is an independent tort. The availability of punitive damages in such cases operates to deter a contracting party from deliberately disregarding the other party's rights. Insurance companies have been the most frequent target for punitive damages awards in bad faith cases, but employers and banks have also been subjected to punitive damages verdicts.

## EQUITABLE REMEDIES

In exceptional cases in which money damages alone are not adequate to fully compensate for a party's injuries, a court may grant an **equitable remedy** either alone or in combination with a legal remedy. Equitable relief is subject to several limitations, however, and will be granted only when justice is served by doing so. The primary equitable remedies for breach of contract are specific performance and injunction.[10]

---

[10]Another equitable remedy, *reformation,* allows a court to reform or "rewrite" a written contract when the parties have made an error in expressing their agreement. Reformation is discussed, along with the doctrine of mistake, in Chapter 5.

## Specific Performance

**Specific performance** is an equitable remedy whereby the court orders the breaching party to perform his contractual duties as promised. For example, if Barnes breached a contract to sell a tract of land to Metzger and a court granted specific performance of the contract, the court would require Barnes to deed the land to Metzger. (Metzger, of course, must pay the purchase price.) This remedy can be advantageous to the injured party because he is not faced with the complexities of proving damages, he does not have to worry about whether he can actually collect the damages, and he gets exactly what he bargained for. However, the availability of this remedy is subject to the limitations discussed below.

### The Availability of Specific Performance

Specific performance, like other equitable remedies, is available only when the injured party has no adequate remedy at law—in other words, when money damages do not adequately compensate the injured party. This generally requires a showing that the subject of the contract is unique or at least that no substitutes are available. Even if this requirement is met, a court will withhold specific performance if the injured party has acted in bad faith, if he unreasonably delayed in asserting his rights, or if specific performance would require an excessive amount of supervision by the court.

Contracts for the sale of real estate are the most common subjects of specific performance decrees because every tract of real estate is considered to be unique. Specific performance is rarely granted for breach of a contract for the sale of goods because the injured party can usually procure substitute goods. However, there are situations involving sales of goods contracts in which specific performance is given. These cases involve goods that are unique or goods for which no substitute can be found. Examples include antiques, heirlooms, works of art, and objects of purely sentimental value.[11] Specific performance is not available for the breach of a promise to perform a personal service (such as a contract for employment, artistic performance, or consulting services). A decree requiring a person to specifically perform a personal-services contract would probably be ineffective in giving the injured party what he bargained for. It would also require a great deal of supervision by the court. In addition, an application of specific performance in such cases would amount to a form of involuntary servitude.

## Injunction

Injunction is an equitable remedy that is employed in many different contexts and is sometimes used as a remedy for breach of contract. An **injunction** is a court order requiring a person to do something (**mandatory injunction**) or ordering a person to refrain from doing something (**negative injunction**). Unlike legal remedies that apply only when the breach has already occurred, the equitable remedy of injunction can be invoked when a breach has merely been *threatened*. Injunctions are available only when the breach or threatened breach is likely to cause *irreparable injury*.

In the contract context, specific performance is a form of mandatory injunction. Negative injunctions are appropriately used in several situations, such as contract cases in which a party whose duty under the contract is forbearance threatens to breach the contract. For example, Norris sells his restaurant in Gas City, Indiana, to Ford. A term of the contract of sale provides that Norris agrees not to own, operate, or be employed in any restaurant within 30 miles of Gas City for a period of two years after the sale.[12] If Norris threatens to open a new restaurant in Gas City several months after the sale is consummated, a court could *enjoin* Norris from opening the new restaurant.

## RESTITUTION

Restitution is a remedy that can be obtained either at law or in equity. Restitution applies when one party's performance or reliance has conferred a benefit on the other. A party's restitution interest is protected by compensating him for the value of benefits he has conferred on the other person.[13] This can be done through **specific restitution,** in

---

[11]Specific performance under § 2–716(1) of the UCC is discussed in Chapter 14.

[12]Ancillary covenants not to compete, or noncompetition agreements, are discussed in detail in Chapter 7.

[13]Quasi-contract is discussed in detail in Chapter 1.

which the defendant is required to return the exact property conferred on him by the plaintiff, or **substitutionary restitution,** in which a court awards the plaintiff a sum of money that reflects the amount by which he benefited the defendant. In an action for damages based on quasi-contract, substitutionary restitution would be the remedy.

Restitution can be used in a number of circumstances. Sometimes, parties injured by breach of contract seek restitution as an alternative remedy instead of damages that focus on their expectation interest. In other situations, a *breaching party* who has partially performed seeks restitution for the value of benefits he conferred in excess of the losses he caused. In addition, restitution often applies in cases in which a person rescinds a contract on the grounds of lack of capacity, misrepresentation, fraud, duress, undue influence, or mistake. Upon rescission, each party who has been benefited by the other's performance must compensate the other for the value of the benefit conferred. Another application of restitution occurs when a party to a contract that violates the statute of frauds confers a benefit on the other party. For example, Boyer gives Blake a $10,000 down payment on an oral contract for the sale of a farm. Although the contract is unenforceable (that is, Boyer could not get compensation for his expectation interest), the court would give Boyer restitution of his down payment.

### PROBLEMS AND PROBLEM CASES

**1.** In October 1984, the Gildeas put their house on the market. Kapenis met with the Gildeas' realtor, Murphy, to talk about making a bid on the Gildea home. Murphy prepared several purchase offers and, after some negotiation, both Kapenis and the Gildeas agreed to a contract that contained a clause stating that the contract was "subject to buyer obtaining suitable financing interest rate no greater than 12¾%." Kapenis and Murphy then began a search for financing. When Kapenis talked with an officer of First Federal Savings & Loan, he learned that under this mortgage his interest rate could be adjusted twice a year and that 2 percentage points could be added to the adjusted rate after the two-year fixed period. He was dissatisfied with this and asked that Murphy find additional forms of financing. Mur-

phy continued to inform Kapenis about various loan programs, but Kapenis rejected them because the monthly payments were too high. Another broker located a loan program of a 15-year term at 12½ percent interest with monthly payments of $419, but Kapenis stated that the monthly payments would be too high and not assumable and that these terms were unsatisfactory. Kapenis then informed the Gildeas that he could not find suitable financing and that he was withdrawing his offer. Is he legally entitled to do this?

**2.** Asphalt International chartered a tanker, the *Oswego Tarmac,* from Enterprise Shipping. The contract provided that Enterprise was obligated to maintain the vessel in good order but that it was absolved of responsibility for any loss or damage resulting from a collision and that, if the vessel should be lost, the contract would cease. While loading cargo alongside a pier, the *Oswego Tarmac* was rammed amidships by the bow of the motor vessel *Elektra* with such heavy impact that four of its tanks ruptured and heated asphalt spewed across the harbor. Expert appraisers estimated the cost of repair at not less than $1.5 million. The fair market value of the *Oswego Tarmac* prior to the collision was $750,000. Enterprise advised Asphalt International that the *Oswego Tarmac* was a complete loss. It refused Asphalt International's request to repair the vehicle. Asphalt International brought suit against Enterprise for breach of contract. Will it be successful?

**3.** Light contracted to build a house for the Mullers. After the job was completed, the Mullers refused to pay Light the balance they owed him under the contract, claiming that he had done some of the work in an unworkmanlike manner. When Light sued for the money, the Mullers counterclaimed for $5,700 damages for delay under a liquidated damages clause in the contract. The clause provided that Light must pay $100 per day for every day of delay in completion of the construction. The evidence indicated that the rental value of the home was between $400 and $415 per month. Should the liquidated damages provision be enforced?

**4.** The Warrens hired Denison, a building contractor, to build a house on their property. They executed a written contract in which the Warrens agreed to pay $73,400 for the construction. Denison's construction deviated somewhat from the specifications for the project. These deviations were presumably unintentional, and the cost of repairing them was $1,961.50. The finished house had a market value somewhat higher than the market value would have been without the deviations. The Warrens failed to pay the $48,400 balance due under the contract, alleging that Denison had used poor workmanship in constructing the house and that they were under no obligation to perform further duties under the contract. Are they correct?

5. Forman made a written offer to buy real estate from Benson under terms whereby Forman would pay the purchase price over a 10-year period. Benson did not know Forman and was concerned about his creditworthiness, so Forman's real estate agent suggested a term stating that the contract was "subject to seller's approving buyer's credit report." This term was agreed to by both parties and was inserted in the contract before it was signed. Forman then gave Benson a credit report and a personal financial statement. Benson said that the report "looks real good" and that he would have his attorney review it and begin the title work on the property. Over the course of the next six weeks, however, Benson met with Forman three times. During these meetings, he attempted to negotiate for a higher purchase price and interest rate. He also requested more financial information. Finally, Benson informed Forman that he rejected Forman's credit rating. Forman brought suit to enforce the contract. Will he prevail?

6. Kim, a homeowner, entered into a contract with Kilianek, an experienced contractor, to add an additional room onto his home. The architectural work in designing the room was to be done by Park & Associates. One provision of the contract between Kim and Kilianek stated that "Final payment . . . shall be paid by the Owner to the Contractor when the work has been completed, the contract fully performed, and a final Certificate for Payment has been issued by the Architect." Kim made periodic payments for a total of $14,100 toward the costs of construction. Although no final certificate for payment was issued by the architect, Kilianek demanded a final payment of $2,739. Is Kim obligated to make this payment?

7. Wolf Trap, an organization for the advancement of the performing arts, sponsors operas and other artistic programs at the Filene Center. The Filene Center is located in the Wolf Trap National Park, a national park owned by the U.S. government and operated by the National Park Service. The Center, which consists of a main stage tower, an auditorium, and an open lawn, provides both covered and uncovered seating for approximately 6,500 people. The park provides the parking space, which is separated from the Center and accessible by a number of pathways. Wolf Trap entered into a contract with the Opera Company of Boston whereby it agreed to pay the Opera Company $272,000 to perform four operas at the Filene Center on the nights of June 12, 13, 14, and 15, 1980. Among Wolf Trap's duties under the contract was the duty to provide lighting equipment as specified by the Opera Company's lighting designer. All four performances were sold out. Both parties performed their obligations for the first three performances. On June 15, the day of the last performance, however, there was a severe thunderstorm, which caused an electrical power outage that blacked out all electrical service in the park, its roadways, parking area, pathways, and auditorium. Representatives of the National Park Service and Wolf Trap held several conferences to decide what to do about the performance. The public utility advised that electrical service would not be resumed in the park until 11:00 P.M. or perhaps not even until the next morning. Various alternatives for supplying power were considered but none was regarded as being sufficient to resolve the problem. The Park Service was concerned about the safety of the 3,000 people who were already in the park; 3,500 more were expected before 8:00 P.M. The Park Service recommended the immediate cancellation of the performance and advised Wolf Trap that it disclaimed responsibility for the safety of the people who were to attend the performance. Wolf Trap agreed and the performance was canceled. A representative of the Opera Company was present at this meeting, but she neither took part in the decision nor voiced objection to the decision. Since the performance was canceled, Wolf Trap did not make the final payment called for in the contract to the Opera Company. The Opera Company sued Wolf Trap to recover the balance due under the contract. Was Wolf Trap's performance excused?

8. Shirley MacLaine Parker entered into a contract with Twentieth Century-Fox to play the female

lead in Fox's contemplated production of a movie entitled *Bloomer Girl.* The contract provided that Fox would pay Parker a minimum "guaranteed compensation" of $53,571.42 per week for 14 weeks, beginning May 23, 1966, for a total of $750,000. Fox decided not to produce the movie, and in a letter dated April 4, 1966, it notified Parker that it would not "comply with our obligations to you under" the written contract. In the same letter, with the professed purpose "to avoid any damage to you," Fox instead offered to employ Parker as the leading actress in another movie, tentatively entitled *Big Country, Big Man.* The compensation offered was identical. Unlike *Bloomer Girl,* however, which was to have been a musical production, *Big Country* was to be a dramatic "western type" movie. *Bloomer Girl* was to have been filmed in California; *Big Country* was to be produced in Australia. Certain other terms of the substitute contract varied from those of the original. Parker was given one week within which to accept. She did not, and the offer lapsed. Parker then filed suit against Fox for recovery of the agreed-on guaranteed compensation. Will she prevail?

**9.** Richmond Medical Supply (RMS) occupied commercial space that it leased from Clifton. When the lease was renewed, the parties included an addendum that required Clifton to make certain repairs, including "replacement and make in good working order the rear overhead door on or before the commencement of this lease, August 1, 1983." RMS continued in possession of the property even though Clifton failed to repair or replace the door. On November 8, 1983, thieves broke into the leased property by knocking out a wooden panel in the overhead door and removed cases, equipment, and inventory valued by RMS at $60,000, none of which was ever recovered. RMS brought an action for breach of contract, alleging that its loss was the direct consequence of Clifton's breach of his express promise to replace the door. Will Clifton be held liable for this loss?

**10.** Video Case. See "Roof Repair." Roofer had a contract to repair the roof on the Seaside Hotel. After the formation of the contract, however, extensive flood damage caused the hotel to be condemned. Are the parties' duties under the contract discharged?

See also "Sour Grapes" and "California Dreaming."

## CAPSTONE QUESTIONS

Hulk Company manufactures weight-lifting equipment and other exercise machines. It is involved in each of the following transactions and sets of circumstances:

· Exerco, Inc., owns and operates a sporting goods store in Dannyville, Indiana. A contract between Hulk and Exerco provides that on October 1, Hulk is to deliver a certain quantity of rowing machines to Exerco, and Exerco is to accept the machines and pay Hulk $12,000 at the time of delivery "if, as of October 1, the City of Dannyville has completed all resurfacing work on the street in front of Exerco's place of business and that street is then open to motorized traffic." Hulk delivers the rowing machines on October 1. As of that date, the City of Dannyville has completed the resurfacing of one of the two lanes of traffic on the street in front of Exerco's place of business. Although the other lane's resurfacing is not yet completed, the single resurfaced lane is open to cars, trucks, and other vehicles. Exerco refuses to accept and pay for the rowing machines.

· Under an October 1 contract between it and health spa owner Jacques Strappe, Hulk is to deliver certain Gargantuan brand weight-lifting equipment to Strappe on November 1 and Strappe is to pay Hulk $7,499 at the time of delivery. On October 10, Strappe notifies Hulk that he has no intention of performing his obligations under the contract.

· A contract between Hulk and Remod Company calls for Hulk to pay Remod $79,000 once Remod performs certain remodeling work in the office of Hulk's chief executive officer. Remod does the work according to all specifications set forth in the contract except for a specification calling for the placement of a round window with a 24-inch diameter in an office wall. The round window installed by Remod is only 21 inches in diameter. Hulk, therefore, takes the position that Remod breached the contract and that, accordingly, Hulk's obligation to pay Remod has not been triggered.

· Under a contract between Hulk and sporting goods wholesaler Markup Company, Hulk is to deliver 150 ski-style exercise machines to Markup in return for payment of $75,000 from Markup at the time of delivery. Hulk breaches the contract by failing to provide the machines at the agreed time of delivery or at any time thereafter. Markup therefore pays nothing to Hulk. Still needing the exercise machines Hulk was to have provided, Markup purchases 150 machines of the same type and quality from another manufacturer for $92,000 (the best price Markup could obtain under the circumstances). Markup then sues Hulk for breach of contract. In its complaint, Markup asks the court to grant judgment in its favor for $92,000 in compensatory damages plus an appropriate amount of punitive damages.

## Required:

Answer the following and give reasons for your conclusions.

1. Is Exerco obligated to accept the rowing machines and pay Hulk for them?
2. Must Hulk unsuccessfully attempt delivery on November 1 as a prerequisite to pursuing appropriate remedies against Strappe for breach of contract?
3. Is the position taken by Hulk concerning the Remod contract a correct position?
4. Is Markup's damages request correct?

# SALES

# CHAPTER

## 11

# FORMATION AND TERMS OF SALES CONTRACTS

**INTRODUCTION**

*In the contracts chapters, we introduced the common law rules that govern the creation and performance of contracts generally. Throughout much of history, special rules, known as the* law merchant, *were developed to control mercantile transactions in goods. Because transactions in goods commonly involve buyers and sellers located in different states—and even different countries—a common body of law to control these transactions can facilitate the smooth flow of commerce. To address this need, a Uniform Sales Act was drafted in the early 1900s and adopted by about two thirds of the states. Subsequently, the Uniform Commercial Code (UCC or Code) was prepared to simplify and modernize the rules of law governing commercial transactions.*

*This chapter reviews some Code rules that govern the formation of sales contracts previously discussed. It also covers some key terms in sales contracts, such as delivery terms, title, and risk of loss. Finally, it discusses the rules governing sales on trial, such as sales on approval and consignments.*

## SALE OF GOODS

The **sale of goods** is the transfer of ownership to tangible personal property in exchange for money, other goods, or the performance of services. The law of sales of goods is codified in Article 2 of the Uniform Commercial Code. While the law of sales is based on the fundamental principles of contract and personal property, it has been modified to accommodate current practices of merchants. In large measure, the Code discarded many technical requirements of earlier law that did not serve any useful purpose in the marketplace and replaced them with rules that are consistent with commercial expectations.

Article 2 of the Code applies only to *transactions in goods.* Thus, it does not cover contracts to provide services or to sell real property. However, some courts have applied the principles set out in the Code to such transactions. When a contract appears to call for the furnishing of both goods and services, a question may arise as to whether the Code applies. For example, the operator of a beauty parlor may use a commercial permanent solution intended to be used safely on humans that causes injury to a person's head. The injured person then might bring a lawsuit claiming that there was a breach of the Code's warranty of the suitability of the permanent solution. In such cases, the courts commonly assess whether the sale of goods is the *predominant* part of the transaction or merely an *incidental* part; where the sale of goods predominates, courts normally apply Article 2. The *Advent Systems Ltd. v. Unisys Corp.* case, which follows, illustrates the type of analysis courts use to determine whether a particular contract should be governed by the Code.

---

## ADVENT SYSTEMS LTD. V. UNISYS CORP.
### 925 F.2d 670 (3rd Cir. 1991)

Advent Systems Ltd. is a British company engaged primarily in the production of software for computers. As a result of its research and development efforts, by 1986 the company had developed an electronic document management system (EDMS), a process for transforming engineering drawings and similar documents into a computer database. Unisys Corp. manufactures a variety of computers. Unisys decided to market the Advent system in the United States. In June 1987, Unisys and Advent signed several agreements whereby Advent agreed to provide the software and hardware making up the document systems to be sold by Unisys in the United States. Advent was also obligated to provide sales and marketing material and staff as well as technical personnel to work with Unisys employees in building and installing the document systems. The agreement was to continue for two years, subject to automatic renewal or termination on notice.

During the summer of 1987, Unisys attempted to sell the document system to Arco, a large oil company, but was unsuccessful. Although the Unisys-Advent relationship was satisfactory initially, it soon came to an end. Unisys, which was in the throes of restructuring, decided it would be better served by developing its own document system. Accordingly, in December 1987, Unisys told Advent that their arrangement had ended. Advent filed a complaint against Unisys alleging, among other things, breach of contract and fraud. One of the issues in the lawsuit was whether the relationship between Advent and Unisys was one for the sale of goods—and hence subject to the statute of frauds provisions of the Uniform Commercial Code. The district court ruled that the UCC did not apply because although goods were to be sold, the services aspect of the contract predominated. Unisys appealed a judgment against it of $4,550,000 on the breach of contract claim.

---

**Weis, Circuit Judge**    The district court ruled that as a matter of law the arrangement between the two parties was not within the Uniform Commercial Code and, consequently, the statute of frauds was not applicable. As the district court appraised the transaction, provisions for services outweighed those for products and, consequently, the arrangement was not predominately one for the sale of goods.

The Code "applies to transactions in goods." Sec. 2–102. Goods are defined as "all things (including specially manufactured goods) which are moveable at the time of identification for sale." Sec. 2–105. The Pennsylvania courts have recognized that "goods" has a very expansive meaning under the UCC.

Our court has addressed computer package sales in other cases, but has not been required to consider whether the UCC applied to software per se.

Computer programs are the product of an intellectual process, but once implanted in a medium are widely distributed to computer owners. An analogy can be drawn to a compact disc recording of an orchestral rendition. The music is produced by the artistry of musicians and in itself is not a "good," but when transferred to a laser-readable disc becomes a readily merchantable commodity. Similarly, when a professor delivers a lecture, it is not a good, but, when transcribed as a book it becomes a good.

That a computer program may be copyrightable as intellectual property does not alter the fact that when in the form of a floppy disc or other medium, the program is tangible, moveable and available in the marketplace. The fact that some programs may be tailored for specific purposes need not alter their status as "goods" because the Code definition includes "specially manufactured goods."

Applying the UCC to computer software offers substantial benefits to litigants and the courts. The Code offers a uniform body of law on a wide range of questions likely to arise in computer software disputes: implied warranties, consequential damages, disclaimers of liability, the statute of limitations, to name a few.

The importance of software to the commercial world and the advantages to be gained by the uniformity in the UCC are strong policy arguments favoring inclusion. The contrary arguments are not persuasive, and we hold that software is a "good" within the definition in the Code.

The relationship at issue here is a typical mixed goods and services arrangement. The services are not substantially different from those generally accompanying package sales of hardware and software.

Although determining the applicability of the UCC to a contract by examining the predominance of goods or services has been criticized, we see no reason to depart from the practice here. As we pointed out in *De Flippo v. Ford Motor Co.,* segregating goods from non-goods and insisting that the Statute of Frauds apply only to a portion of the contract would be to make the contract divisible and impossible of performance within the intention of the parties.

We consider the purpose or essence of the contract. Comparing the relative costs of the materials supplied with the costs of the labor may be helpful in this analyis, but not dispositive. In this case the contract's main objective was to transfer "products." The specific provisions for training of Unisys personnel by Advent were but a small part of the parties' contemplated relationship.

The compensation structure of the agreement also focuses on "goods." The projected sales figures introduced during the trial demonstrate that in the contemplation of the parties the sale of goods clearly predominated.

We are persuaded that the transaction at issue here was within the scope of the Uniform Commercial Code.

**Judgment in favor of Advent reversed.**

Thus, the first question you should ask when faced with a contracts problem is: Is this a contract for the sale of goods? If it is not, then the principles of common law that were discussed in the contracts chapters apply. If the contract is one for the sale of goods, then the Code applies. This analysis is illustrated in Figure 1.

## LEASES

A lease of goods is a transfer of the right to possess and use goods belonging to another. Although the rights of one who leases goods (a lessee) do not constitute ownership of the goods, leasing is mentioned here because it is becoming an increasingly important way of acquiring the use of many kinds of goods, from automobiles to farm equipment. In some states, Article 2 and Article 9 of the UCC are applied to such leases by analogy. However, rules contained in these articles sometimes are inadequate to resolve special problems presented by leasing. For this reason, a new article of the UCC dealing exclusively with leases of goods, Article 2A, was written in 1987 and presented to state legislatures for possible adoption. Forty states have adopted Article 2A as of the time of this writing. Because of space limitations, this textbook does not cover Article 2A in detail.

## MERCHANTS

Many of the Code's provisions apply only to **merchants** or to transactions between merchants.[1] In addition, the Code sets a higher standard of conduct for merchants because persons who regularly deal in goods are expected to be familiar with the practices of that trade and with commercial law. Ordinary consumers and nonmerchants frequently have little knowledge of or experience in these matters.

---

[1]Under the Code, a "merchant" is defined as a "person who deals in goods of the kind or otherwise by his occupation holds himself out as having knowledge or skill peculiar to the practices or goods involved in the transaction or to whom such knowledge or skill may be attributed by his employment of an agent or broker or other intermediary who by his occupation holds himself out as having such knowledge or skill" [2–104(1)].

**FIGURE 1**   Choice of Law

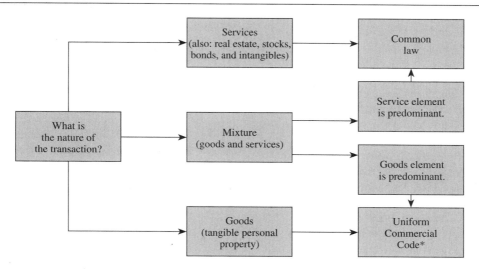

*If there is no specific Uniform Commercial Code provision governing the transaction, use the common law.

## Code Requirements

The Code requires that parties to sales contracts act in good faith and in a commercially reasonable manner. Further, when a contract contains an unfair or unconscionable clause, or the contract as a whole is unconscionable, the courts have the right to refuse to enforce the unconscionable clause or contract [2–302].[2] The Code's treatment of unconscionability is discussed in detail in Chapter 7, Illegality.

A number of the Code provisions concerning the sale of goods were discussed in the chapters on Contracts. The following is a list of some of the important provisions discussed earlier, together with the section of the Code and the chapters in the text where the discussion can be found.

**1.** *Firm offers.* Under the Code, an offer in writing by a merchant that gives assurance that the offer will be held open is not revocable for lack of consideration during the time stated, or for a reasonable time if no time is stated, up to a period of three months [2–205]. (See Chapter 2, The Agreement: Offer.)

**2.** *Formation.* Under the Code, a contract for the sale of goods may be made in any manner that shows that the parties reached agreement, even though no particular moment can be pointed to as the time when the contract was made. Where the parties intended to make a contract but left one or more terms open, the contract is valid despite the lack of definiteness so long as the court has a basis for giving a remedy [2–204]. (See Chapter 2.)

**3.** *Additional terms in acceptances.* The Code states that an expression of acceptance or written confirmation sent within a reasonable time operates as an acceptance even if it states terms additional to or different from those offered, unless acceptance is expressly conditional on assent to the additional or different terms [2–207]. (See Chapter 3, The Agreement: Acceptance.)

**4.** *Statute of frauds.* The statute of frauds in the Code applies to the sale of goods at a price of $500 or more. The Code makes special exceptions for written confirmations between merchants, part payment or part delivery, admissions in legal proceedings, and specially manufactured goods [2–201]. (See Chapter 8, Writing.)

---

[2]The numbers in brackets refer to sections of the Uniform Commercial Code.

## TERMS OF THE CONTRACT

### General Terms

Within broad limits, the parties to a contract to sell goods may include any terms on which they agree. Many practices have become common in the everyday transactions of business, and under the Code, if a particular matter is not covered specifically in a contract or is unclear, common trade practices are used to fill out the terms of the contract.

The Code sets out in some detail the rights of the parties when they use certain terms, and those meanings apply unless the parties agree otherwise. For example, if a contract includes an open-price clause where the price is to be determined later, or if a contract is silent about price, the price is what would be considered *reasonable* at the time of delivery. If the price is to be fixed by either the buyer or the seller, that person must act in *good faith* in setting the price. However, if it is clear from their negotiations that the parties do not intend to be bound unless they agree on a price, and the price is not agreed on or fixed, no contract results [2–305].

### Quantity Terms

In some cases, the parties may state the quantity of goods covered by their sales contract in an indefinite way. Contracts that obligate a buyer to purchase a seller's *output* of a certain item or all of the buyer's *requirements* of a certain item are commonly encountered. These contracts caused frequent problems under the common law because of the indefiniteness of the parties' obligations. If the seller decided to double its output, did the buyer have to accept the entire amount? If the market price of the item soared much higher than the contract price, could the buyer double or triple its demands?

### Output and Needs Contracts

In an "output" contract, one party is bound to sell its entire output of particular goods and the other party is bound to buy that output. In a "needs" or "requirements" contract, the quantity of goods is based on the needs of the buyer. In determining the quantity of goods to be produced or taken pursuant to an output or needs contract, the rule of *good faith* applies. Thus, the buyer may not demand or take a quantity that is unreasonably disproportionate to any stated estimate in the contract or to "normal" prior output or requirements if no estimate is stated [2–306(2)]. Similarly, the seller may not insist that the buyer take more than the estimate or prior output or requirements.

For example, Farmer contracts to supply Sam's Grocery with all of the apples Sam's requires for sale to customers. If Sam's has sold between 500 and 700 bushels of apples a year over the past 10 years, Sam could not require Farmer to deliver 5,000 bushels of apples to Sam's one year because Sam had an unusual demand for them. Similarly, it would not be reasonable for Sam to say he would take only 10 bushels in one year.

### Exclusive Dealing Contracts

The Code takes a similar approach to *exclusive dealing contracts*. Under the common law, these contracts were sources of difficulty due to the indefinite nature of the parties' duties. Did the dealer have to make any effort to sell the manufacturer's products, and did the manufacturer have any duty to supply the dealer? The Code provides that unless the parties make a different agreement, sellers have an obligation to use their best efforts to supply the goods to the buyer and buyers have obligations to use their best efforts to promote their sale [2–306(2)].

### Time for Performance

If no time for performance is stated in the sales contract, the Code implies a *reasonable time* for performance. If a contract requires successive performances over an indefinite period of time, the contract is valid for a reasonable time; however, either party can terminate it at any time upon the giving of reasonable notice unless the parties have agreed otherwise as to termination [2–309]. For example, Farmer Jack agrees to sell his entire output of apples each fall to a cannery at the then-current market price. If the contract does not contain a provision spelling out how and when the parties may terminate the contract, Farmer Jack can terminate it if he gives the cannery a reasonable time to make arrangements to acquire apples from someone else.

## Delivery Terms

Sales contracts customarily use standardized shipping terms that have specific commercial meanings. The terms **FOB (free on board)** and **FAS (free alongside ship)** are basic delivery terms. If the delivery term of the contract is FOB or FAS (and the contract also states the place at which the goods originate in connection with the FOB or FAS term), the seller must deliver to the carrier goods that (1) *conform to the contract* and (2) *are properly prepared for shipment* to the buyer. The seller also must make a *reasonable contract for transportation of the goods* on behalf of the buyer. Under such delivery terms, the goods are at the buyer's risk during transit and the buyer must pay the shipping charges. If the shipping term is *FOB destination,* the seller must deliver the goods to the designated destination and bears risk and expense during transit. These terms will be discussed in more detail later in this chapter.

## TITLE

### Passage of Title

Title to goods cannot pass from the seller to the buyer until the goods are identified to the contract [2–401(1)]. For example, if Seller agrees to sell Buyer 50 chairs and Seller has 500 chairs in his warehouse, title to 50 chairs will not pass from Seller to Buyer until Seller selects the 50 chairs that Buyer has purchased and identifies them as the chairs sold to Buyer.

The parties may agree between themselves when title to the goods will pass from the seller to the buyer. If there is no agreement, then the general rule is that the *title to the goods passes to the buyer when the seller completes his obligations as to delivery of the goods:*

1. If the contract requires the seller to "ship" the goods to the buyer, then title passes to the buyer when the seller delivers conforming goods to the carrier.
2. If the contract requires the seller to "deliver" the goods to the buyer, title does not pass to the buyer until the goods are delivered and tendered to the buyer.
3. If delivery is to be made without moving the goods, then title passes at the time and place of contracting. An exception is made if title to the goods is represented by a document of title such as a warehouse receipt; then, title passes when the document of title is delivered to the buyer.
4. If the buyer rejects goods tendered to him, title reverts to the seller [2–401(4)].

### Importance of Title

Common law determined most of the problems relating to risks, insurable interests in goods, remedies, and similar rights and liabilities on the basis of who was the technical title owner at the particular moment the right or liability arose. The Code, however, determines the rights of the seller and buyer and of third persons irrespective of the technicality of who has the title, unless the provision of the Code expressly refers to title.

Determination of who has title to the goods is important in instances in which the rights of the seller's or the buyer's creditors in the goods are an issue. The *Russell v. Transamerica Insurance Co.* case, which follows, illustrates another instance in which determination of the title holder may be important—whether the seller's insurance policy covers a particular loss.

## RUSSELL V. TRANSAMERICA INSURANCE CO.
### 322 N.W.2d 178 (Mich. Ct. App. 1982)

Russell, a full-service boat dealer and marine equipment service company, entered into an agreement to sell a 19-foot Kinsvater boat to Robert Clouser for $8,500. Pursuant to the agreement, Clouser made a down payment of $1,700, with the balance of the purchase price to be paid when he took possession of the boat. Under the agreement, Russell was to retain possession of the boat in order to transfer an engine and drive train from another boat. Upon the completion of these alterations, Clouser was to take delivery of the boat at Russell's marina.

While the boat was being tested by employees of Russell, prior to delivery to Clouser, it hit a seawall and was destroyed. Transamerica Insurance insured Russell under a policy that excluded watercraft hazards, except for damage to any watercraft under 26 feet in length not owned by Russell. Transamerica refused to honor a claim from Russell for the damage to Clouser's boat, contending that the policy excluded damage because Russell owned the boat at the time of the accident. Russell then brought suit against Transamerica Insurance. The trial court ruled in favor of Transamerica Insurance, and Russell appealed.

---

**Lambros, Judge**   The trial court, granting summary judgment in favor of Transamerica, stated: The facts reflect that the boat was in possession of Russell on August 4, 1977. Robert Clouser could not have taken delivery of the boat on the day in question. Under § 2–401(2), therefore, title had not passed to Clouser. . . . Effectively speaking, the risk of loss was, on August 4, 1977, on Russell's shoulders.

Under subsection (3)(b) of § 2–401, if delivery is to be made without moving the goods and no documents of title are involved, title passes at the time of contracting if the goods are already identified at the time of contracting. We note that goods need not be in a deliverable state to be identified to the contract.

In the instant case, because the 19-foot Kinsvater boat had been identified at the time the parties contracted for sale, because no documents of title were to be delivered by the sellers, there being no Michigan requirement for certificates of title for boats at that time, and because delivery of the boat was to be effected without its being moved, title

passed to the buyer at the time of contracting under § 2–401(3)(b). The fact that the boat was not outfitted with all the equipment specified in the contract did not prevent its identification to the contract nor did it prevent title from passing at that time.

In addition, we find that the trial court erred in its decision in equating risk of loss with title. Under § 2–509, risk of loss passes to the buyer on his receipt of the goods or on tender of delivery by the seller. Risk of loss, then, does not necessarily follow title. In the instant case, because Russell retained possession of the boat after title passed, he bore the risk of loss. Title in the buyer, however, triggered the policy exception to the watercraft hazard exclusion regardless of where risk of loss lay.

We hold that the trial court erred in granting summary judgment in favor of Transamerica because title in the boat at the time of the accident was in one other than Russell and the boat was, thus, covered under Russell's policy.

**Judgment reversed in favor of Russell.**

---

## TITLE AND THIRD PARTIES

### Obtaining Good Title

A fundamental rule of property law is that a buyer cannot receive better title to goods than the seller had. If Thief steals a television set from Adler and sells it to Brown, Brown does not get good title to the set, because Thief had no title to it. Adler would have the right to recover the set from Brown. Similarly, if Brown sold the set to Carroll, Carroll could get no better title to it than Brown had. Adler would have the right to recover the set from Carroll.

The Code provides several exceptions to the general rule that a buyer cannot get better title to goods than his seller had. The most important exceptions include the following: (1) a person who has a voidable title to goods can pass good title to a bona fide purchaser for value; (2) a person who buys goods in the regular course of a retailer's business takes free of any interests in the goods that the retailer has given to others; and (3) a person who buys goods in the ordinary course of a dealer's business takes free of any claim of a person who entrusted those goods to the dealer (such as a person who left his watch with a jeweler for repair).

## Transfers of Voidable Title

A seller who has a **voidable title** has the power to pass good title to a *good faith purchaser for value* [2–403(1)]. A seller has a voidable title to goods if he has obtained his title through fraudulent representations. For example, a person would have a voidable title if he obtained goods by impersonating another person or by paying for them with a bad check or if he obtained goods without paying the agreed purchase price when it was agreed that the transaction was to be a cash sale. Under the Code, **good faith** means "honesty in fact in the conduct or transaction concerned" [1–201(19)] and a buyer has given **value** if he has given any consideration sufficient to support a simple contract [1–201(44)].

For example, Jones goes to the ABC Appliance Store, convinces the clerk that he is really Clark, who is a good customer of ABC, and leaves with a stereo charged to Clark's account. If Jones sells the stereo to Davis, who gives Jones value for it and has no knowledge of the fraud that Jones perpetrated on ABC, Davis gets good title to the stereo. ABC cannot recover the stereo from Davis. Instead, ABC must look for Jones, the person who deceived it. In this situation, both ABC and Davis were innocent of wrongdoing, but the law considers Davis to be the more worthy of its protection for two reasons: (1) because ABC was in a better position to have prevented the wrongdoing by Jones and (2) because Davis bought the goods in good faith and for value. The Code would reach the same result if Jones had given ABC a check that later bounced and then sold the stereo to Davis, who was a good faith purchaser for value. Davis would have good title to the stereo, and ABC would have to pursue its right against Jones on the bounced check.

The *Charles Evans BMW, Inc. v. Williams* case, which follows, illustrates the importance of determining the identity and creditworthiness of a person to whom one sells goods. It also shows the importance of a subsequent buyer qualifying as a good faith purchaser for value so that it is able to get good title from a seller who had only a voidable title.

---

### CHARLES EVANS BMW, INC. V. WILLIAMS
**395 S.E.2d 650 (Ga. Ct. App. 1990)**

Williams agreed to sell his car to an individual named Hodge and accepted a cashier's check from Hodge as payment. Without indicating on the certificate of title that Hodge was the purchaser, Williams signed the title in his capacity as seller and delivered the document and the car to Hodge. The next day, Hodge, representing himself to be Williams, offered to sell the car to Charles Evans BMW. When a price was agreed on, Hodge presented the certificate of title containing Williams's signature as seller and received a check that named Williams as payee. Hodge cashed the check after he produced as identification a Kentucky driver's license bearing the same number as that issued to Williams. After the car had been purchased by Evans BMW from Hodge, Williams learned that the cashier's check he had accepted from Hodge was a forgery. By the time that Evans BMW became aware of the fact that it had not actually purchased the car from Williams, but rather from Hodge representing himself to be Williams, it had already resold the car.

At the direction of the local police authorities, the car and the certificate of title were returned to Evans BMW and it refunded the purchase price. Subsequently, the police directed Evans BMW to return the car to Williams. However, Evans BMW retained the certificate of title and then brought a lawsuit against Williams to determine who was the owner of the automobile. The trial court found in favor of Williams and Evans BMW appealed.

---

**Carley, Chief Judge** Section 2–403(1) provides in relevant part, that "[a] purchaser of goods acquires all title which his transferor had or had power to transfer. . . . A person with voidable title has power to transfer a good title to a good faith purchaser for value. When goods have been *delivered* *under a transaction of purchase* the purchaser has such power even though: (a) The transferor was deceived as to the identity of the purchaser, or (b) The delivery was in exchange for a check which was later dishonored; or . . . (d) The delivery was procured through fraud punishable as larcenous under the criminal law." (Emphasis supplied.)

Williams was not deprived of his car by a physical taking of which he was unaware. The undisputed evidence shows that Williams *delivered his car under a transaction of purchase* procured by the perpetration of a criminal fraud whereby he was deceived as to the identity of the purchaser who gave him a check that was later dishonored. In these circumstances, Williams conveyed *voidable title* to Hodge and Hodge, having voidable rather than void title, had the power to transfer *good title* to a good faith purchaser for value. Section 2–403(1) empowers a purchaser with a voidable title to confer good title upon a good faith purchaser for value where the good[s] were procured through fraud punishable as larcenous under the criminal law. The distinction between *theft* and *fraud* in this context is found in the statutory definitions of "delivery" and "purchase." Delivery concerns a voluntary transfer of possession and purchase refers to a voluntary transaction creating an interest in property. In the present case, Williams voluntarily relinquished possession to Hodge. As one commentator has pointed out, "a thief who wrongfully takes goods is not a purchaser . . . but a swindler who fraudulently induces the victim to voluntarily deliver them is a purchaser."

It follows that if Evans BMW was a good faith purchaser for value, it acquired good title to the car from Hodge. " 'Good faith' means honesty in fact in the conduct or transaction concerned." Sec. 1–201(19). " 'Good faith' in the case of a merchant

means honesty in fact and the observance of reasonable commercial standards of fair dealing in the trade." Sec. 2–103(1)(b). There is ample evidence of Evans BMW's "good faith" in its transaction with Hodge. Evans BMW's agent who actually negotiated the purchase neither knew nor had reason to know that Hodge's representations were false. When the agent noticed an error on the registration form, Hodge was told that he would have to obtain a corrected registration from the county. When Hodge left and returned with the corrected form, this gave additional credence to his representations that he was Williams and the owner of the car. Hodge also presented a certificate of title which bore William's unforged signature as seller. The price that Evans BMW agreed to pay for the car was not nominal. Evans BMW gave Hodge a check made out to Williams and Hodge was successful in cashing that check by using a driver's license bearing the same number of the license that had actually been issued to Williams. Thus, Hodge's scheme to impersonate Williams not only duped Evans BMW, but was also successful against the county and the bank.

In opposition, there was no evidence to show that, in negotiating and consummating the purchase from Hodge, Evans had been less than honest or had failed to observe reasonable commercial standards of fair dealing. Therefore, on the undisputed evidence of record, Evans BMW was, as a matter of law, a good faith purchaser for value when it bought the car from Hodge. It retains that good title as against Williams who conveyed voidable title to Hodge.

**Judgment reversed in favor of Charles Evans BMW.**

---

## Buyers in the Ordinary Course of Business

A person who buys goods in the ordinary course of business from a person dealing in goods of that type takes free of any security interest in the goods given by his seller to another person [9–307(1)]. A **buyer in ordinary course** is a person who in good faith, and without knowledge that the sale to him is in violation of the ownership rights of a third party, buys goods in the ordinary course of business of a

person selling goods of that kind, other than a pawnbroker [1–201(9)].

For example, Brown Buick may borrow money from Bank in order to finance its inventory of new Buicks; in turn, Bank may take a security interest in the inventory to secure repayment of the loan. If Carter buys a new Buick from Brown Buick, he gets good title to the Buick free and clear of the Bank's security interest if he is a buyer in the ordinary course of business. The basic purposes of this exception are (1) to protect those who innocently buy from merchants and (2) to promote confidence in such commercial transactions. The exception also reflects the fact that the bank is more interested in the proceeds from the sale than in the inventory. Security interests and the rights of buyers in the ordinary course of business are discussed in more detail in Chapter 28, Security Interests in Personal Property.

## Entrusting of Goods

A third exception to the general rule is that if an owner *entrusts* goods to a merchant who deals in goods of that kind, the merchant has the power to transfer all rights of the entruster to a buyer in the ordinary course of business [2–403(2)]. For example, Gail takes her watch to Jeweler, a retail jeweler, to have it repaired, and Jeweler sells the watch to Mary. Mary would acquire good title to the watch, and Gail would have to proceed against Jeweler for conversion of her watch. The purpose behind this rule is to protect commerce by giving confidence to buyers that they will get good title to the goods they buy from merchants in the ordinary course of business. However, a merchant-seller cannot pass good title to stolen goods even if the buyer is a buyer in the ordinary course of business. This is because the original owner did nothing to facilitate the transfer.

### CONCEPT REVIEW
### TITLE AND THIRD PARTIES

| | |
|---|---|
| **General Rule** | A seller cannot pass better title to goods than he has. |
| **Exceptions to General Rule** | 1. A person who has voidable title to goods can pass good title to a bona fide purchaser for value. <br> 2. A buyer in the ordinary course of a retailer's business takes free of any interests in the goods that the retailer has given to others. <br> 3. A person who buys goods in the ordinary course of a dealer's business takes free of any claims of a person who entrusted those goods to the dealer. |

## RISK OF LOSS

The transportation of goods from sellers to buyers can be a risky business. The carrier of the goods may lose, damage, or destroy them; floods, tornadoes, and other natural catastrophes may take their toll; thieves may steal all or part of the goods. If neither party is at fault for the loss, who should bear the risk? If the buyer has the risk when the goods are damaged or lost, the buyer is liable for the contract price. If the seller has the risk, he is liable for damages unless he can tender substitute performance.

The common law placed the risk on the party who had technical title at the time of the loss. The Code rejects this approach and provides specific rules governing risk of loss that are designed to provide certainty and to place the risk on the party best able to protect against loss and most likely to be insured against it. Risk of loss under the Code depends on the terms of the parties' agreement, on the moment the loss occurs, and on whether one of the parties was in breach of contract when the loss occurred.

### Terms of the Agreement

The contracting parties, subject to the rule of good faith, may specify who has the risk of loss in their agreement [2–509(4)]. This they may do directly or by using certain commonly accepted shipping terms in their contract. In addition, the Code has certain general rules on risk of loss that amplify specific shipping terms and control risk of loss in cases where specific terms are not used [2–509].

### Shipment Contracts

If the contract requires the seller to ship the goods by carrier but does not require their delivery to a specific destination, the risk passes to the buyer when the seller delivers the goods to the carrier [2–509(1)(a)]. Shipment contracts are considered to be the normal contract in which the contract requires the seller to send goods to the buyer but does not require the seller to guarantee delivery at a particular location.

The following are common shipping terms that create shipment contracts:

**1.** *FOB (free on board) point of origin.* This term calls for the seller to deliver the goods free of expense and at the seller's risk at the place *designated.* For example, a contract between a seller located in Chicago and a buyer in New York calls for delivery "FOB Chicago." The seller at his expense and at his risk must deliver the goods to a carrier in the place designated in the contract, namely Chicago, and arrange for their carriage to New York. Because the shipment term in this example is "FOB Chicago," the seller is not responsible for delivering the goods to a specific destination; for example, the buyer's place of business. If the term is "FOB vessel, car, or other vehicle," the seller must load the goods on board at his own risk and expense [2–319(1)].

**2.** *FAS (free alongside ship).* This term is common in maritime contracts and the contract normally specifies the name of a specific vessel and port—for example, "FAS Calgary [the ship],

Chicago Port Authority." The seller must deliver the goods alongside the vessel *Calgary* at the Chicago Port Authority at his own risk and expense [2–319(2)].

**3.** *CIF (cost, insurance, and freight).* This term means that the price of the goods includes the cost of shipping and insuring them. The seller bears this expense and the risk of loading the goods [2–320].

**4.** *C & F.* This term is the same as CIF except that the seller is not obligated to insure the goods [2–320].

The *Morauer v. Deak & Co., Inc.* case, which follows, provides an example of the risk borne by a buyer in a shipment contract.

---

## MORAUER V. DEAK & CO., INC.
### 26 UCC Rep. 1142 (D.C. Super. Ct. 1979)

On March 12, 1975, Raymond Morauer contracted with Deak & Co., a dealer in foreign currency, to purchase for investment purposes several bags of silver coins and a quantity of gold coins. He paid for his purchase with personal checks totaling $35,000. After his checks had cleared, he came to Deak's place of business to take delivery. Morauer had a discussion with Deak's assistant manager about the District of Columbia tax on the sale of gold. Both parties agreed that in order to avoid the tax, an admittedly legal endeavor, Deak would ship all of Morauer's gold coins to his residence in suburban Maryland. There was no District of Columbia tax on silver coins, so Morauer took possession of them.

Deak placed the gold coins in two packages and, as authorized by Morauer, sent the packages to his house by registered mail, return receipt requested. Deak did not insure the packages with the U.S. Postal Service but instead, in accordance with its custom, relied on its own insurance contract with its insurer to cover any risk of loss. Only one package was received by Morauer; however, he did not open it and thus did not realize at the time that he had received only a portion of his gold coins. More than two years later, while making an inventory of his collection, Morauer discovered the problem and notified Deak. By that time, the post office had destroyed its records of the shipment and Deak's insurance coverage for that shipment had expired. Morauer then brought a lawsuit asking the value at their time of purchase of the gold coins that he had not received.

---

**Smith, Judge**    The court must determine whether the risk of loss of the gold coins in question passed from the defendant Deak to Morauer upon Deak's delivery of the coins to the Post Office for shipment to Morauer. If so, then Deak is not liable to Morauer for the value of the lost shipment. If the risk of loss did not pass, however, then Deak is

liable for the full value of the coins at time of purchase.

The case is governed by § 2–509(1) of the UCC, and the court must determine whether paragraph (a) or paragraph (b) of subsection (1) controls. If the contract was a so-called "shipment" contract, then the risk of loss passed to

Morauer, the buyer, on Deak's delivery to the carrier, § 2–509(1)(a), provided, however, that Deak also satisfied the UCC's requirements for a valid "shipment" contract, § 2–504. If, on the other hand, the contract called for delivery at a particular destination, then the risk of loss never passed to Morauer, because the goods were never delivered, and Morauer must prevail, § 2–509(1)(b).

The fact that the parties had agreed that Deak would ship the coins to Morauer's residence in Maryland is not dispositive of this controversy. A "ship to" term in a sales contract has no significance in determining whether the agreement is a "shipment" or "destination" contract. Moreover, there is a preference in the UCC for "shipment" contracts. The drafters of the UCC state the preference and give the reasons for it in the following manner:

For the purposes of subsections (2) and (3) there is omitted from this Article the rule under prior uniform legislation that a term requiring the seller to pay the freight or cost of transportation to the buyer is equivalent to an agreement by the seller to deliver to the buyer or at an agreed destination. This omission is with the specific intention of negating the rule, for *under this Article the "shipment" contract is regarded as the normal one and the "destination" contract as the variant type. The seller is not obligated to deliver at a named destination and bear the concurrent risk of loss until arrival, unless he has specifically agreed so to deliver or the commercial understanding of the terms used by the parties contemplates such delivery.* Uniform Commercial Code Comment No. 5; § 2–503.

Here we have an order and payment by Morauer in person to Deak with receipts signed by Kirsch, Deak's agent, indicating Morauer's home address and, in one instance, including the further instruction, "c/o Mrs. Geraldine Morauer." Morauer and Kirsch discussed delivery of the coins, and Morauer decided that to avoid payment of the District of Columbia sales tax, he would have them shipped to his residence. Deak mailed the gold coins in two packages, both of which were properly addressed, stamped and deposited at the United States Post Office. Deak also included the cost of postage as part of Morauer's total bill. Therefore, we hold that Deak was authorized by the contract to ship the gold coins to Morauer by

carrier, and that the risk of loss passed from Deak to Morauer on delivery of the packages of coins to the Post Office.

Although the court's finding that the parties were operating under a "shipment" contract puts the risk of loss on Morauer from the time of Deak's delivery to the authorized carrier, there remains the question whether defendant Deak met all the statutory requirements of "shipment" contracts under the applicable UCC section 2–504. That section states:

Where the seller is required or authorized to send the goods to the buyer and the contract does not require him to deliver them at a particular destination, then unless otherwise agreed he must

(a) put the goods in the possession of such a carrier and make such a contract for their transportation as may be reasonable having regard to the nature of the goods and other circumstances of the case; and

(b) obtain and promptly deliver or tender in due form any document necessary to enable the buyer to obtain possession of the goods or otherwise required by the agreement or by usage of trade; and

(c) promptly notify the buyer of the shipment.

Failure to notify the buyer under paragraph (c) or to make a proper contract under paragraph (a) is a ground for rejection only if material delay or loss ensues.

In the case now before this court Deak followed its regular practice of insuring the shipments with its own insurance company, properly addressed each package and sent both by first-class, registered mail, with a return receipt requested. Deak therefore made all arrangements with the carrier, the United States Postal Service, as were "reasonable having regard to the nature of the goods and other circumstances of the case." § 2–504(a). Deak had no obligation under paragraph (b) of § 2–504, insofar as there were no documents necessary to enable Morauer to obtain possession of the goods, and none "otherwise required by the agreement or by usage of trade." And finally, Deak was in compliance with § 2–504(c) in that Kirsch notified Morauer of the mailing of the gold coins when Morauer went to Deak's office to take delivery personally of the silver coins he had also purchased.

**Judgment in favor of Deak.**

## Destination Contracts

If the contract requires the seller to deliver the goods to a specific destination, the seller bears the risk and expense of delivery to that destination [2−509(1)(b)]. The following are commonly used shipping terms that create destination contracts:

**1.** *FOB destination.* An FOB term coupled with the place of destination of the goods puts the expense and risk of delivering the goods to that destination on the seller [2−319(1)(b)]. For example, a contract between a seller in Chicago and a buyer in Phoenix might call for shipment FOB Phoenix. The seller must ship the goods to Phoenix at her own expense, and she also retains the risk of delivery of the goods to Phoenix.

**2.** *Ex-ship.* This term does not specify a particular ship, but it places the expense and risk on the seller until the goods are unloaded from whatever ship is used [2−322].

**3.** *No arrival, no sale.* This term places the expense and risk during shipment on the seller. If the goods fail to arrive through no fault of the seller, the seller has no further liability to the buyer [2−324]—that is, the buyer cannot sue for breach for nondelivery.

For example, a Chicago-based seller contracts to sell a quantity of shirts to a buyer FOB Phoenix, the buyer's place of business. The shirts are destroyed en route when the truck carrying the shirts is involved in an accident. The risk of the loss of the shirts is on the seller, and the buyer is not obligated to pay for them. The seller may have the right to recover from the trucking company, but between the seller and the buyer, the seller has the risk of loss. If the contract had called for delivery FOB the seller's manufacturing plant, then the risk of loss would have been on the buyer. The buyer would have had to pay for the shirts and then pursue any claims that he had against the trucking company.

## Goods in the Possession of Third Parties

If the goods are in the possession of a bailee and are to be delivered without being moved, the risk of loss passes to the buyer upon delivery to him of a *negotiable document of title* for the goods; if no negotiable document of title has been used, the risk of loss passes when the bailee indicates to the buyer that the buyer has the *right to the possession of the goods* [2−509(2)]. For example, if Farmer sells Miller a

quantity of grain currently stored at Grain Elevator, the risk of loss of the grain will shift from Farmer to Miller (1) when a negotiable warehouse receipt for the grain is delivered to Miller or (2) when Grain Elevator notifies Miller that it is holding the grain for Miller.

## Risk Generally

If the transaction does not fall within the situations discussed above, the risk of loss passes to the buyer upon *receipt* of the goods if the seller is a merchant; if the seller is not a merchant, then the risk of loss passes to the buyer upon the *tender of delivery* of the goods to the buyer [2−509(3)]. If Jones bought a television set from ABC Appliance on Monday, intending to pick it up on Thursday, and the set was stolen on Wednesday, the risk of loss remained with ABC. However, if Jones had purchased the set from his next-door neighbor and could have taken delivery of the set on Monday (i.e., delivery was tendered then), the risk of loss was Jones's.

## Effect of Breach on Risk of Loss

When a seller tenders goods that do not conform to the contract and the buyer has the right to reject the goods, the risk of loss remains with the seller until any defect is cured or until the buyer accepts the goods [2−510(1)]. Where the buyer rightfully revokes his acceptance of goods, the risk of loss is with the seller to the extent that any loss is not covered by the buyer's insurance [2−510(2)]. This rule gives the seller the benefit of any insurance carried by the buyer.

For example, if Adler bought a new Buick from Brown Buick that he later returned to Brown because of serious defects in it and if through no fault of Adler's the automobile was damaged while in his possession, then the risk of loss would be with Brown. However, if Adler had insurance on the automobile covering the damage to it and recovered from the insurance company, Adler would have to turn the insurance proceeds over to Brown or use them to fix the car before returning it to Brown.

When a buyer repudiates a contract for goods and those goods have already been set aside by the seller, the risk of loss stays with the buyer for a commercially reasonable time after the repudiation if the seller's insurance is not sufficient to cover any loss [2−510(3)]. Suppose Cannery contracts to buy Farmer's entire crop of peaches. Farmer picks the peaches, crates them, tenders delivery to Cannery, and stores them in his barn. Cannery then tells Farmer that it does not intend to honor the contract. Shortly thereafter, but before Farmer has a chance to find another buyer, the peaches are spoiled by a fire. If Farmer's insurance covers only part of the loss, Cannery must bear the rest of the loss.

## Insurable Interest

The Code recognizes the general commercial practice of insuring risks. A buyer may protect his interest in goods that are the subject matter of a sales contract before he actually obtains title. The buyer obtains an insurable interest in existing goods when they are identified as the goods covered by the contract even though they are in fact nonconforming. The seller retains an insurable interest in goods so long as he has either title or a security interest in them [2–501(2)]. The importance of the seller's retention of an insurable interest in goods he has sold is illustrated in the *Russell v. Transamerica Insurance Co.* case, which appeared earlier in this chapter.

---

## RISK OF LOSS

The point at which the risk of loss or damage to goods identified to a contract passes to the buyer is as follows:

1. If there is an agreement between the parties, the risk of loss passes to the buyer at the time they have agreed to.
2. If the contract requires the seller to ship the goods by carrier but does not require that the seller guarantee their delivery to a specific destination (shipment contract), the risk of loss passes to the buyer when the seller has delivered the goods to the carrier and made an appropriate contract for their carriage.
3. If the contract requires the seller to guarantee delivery of the goods to a specific destination (destination contract), the risk of loss passes to the buyer when the seller delivers the goods to the designated destination.
4. If the goods are in the hands of a third person and the contract calls for delivery without moving the goods, the risk of loss passes to the buyer when the buyer has the power to take possession of the goods—for example, when he receives a document of title.
5. In any situation other than those noted above where the seller is a merchant, the risk of loss passes to the buyer on his receipt of the goods.
6. In any situation other than those noted above where the seller is not a merchant, the risk of loss passes to the buyer on the tender of delivery to the buyer by the seller.
7. When a seller tenders goods that the buyer lawfully could reject because they do not conform to the contract description, the risk of loss stays on the seller until the defect is cured or the buyer accepts them.
8. When a buyer rightfully revokes acceptance of goods, the risk of loss is on the seller from the beginning to the extent it is not covered by the buyer's insurance.
9. If a buyer repudiates a contract for identified, conforming goods before risk of loss has passed to the buyer, the buyer is liable for a commercially reasonable time for any loss or damage to the goods that is not covered by the seller's insurance.

---

## SALES ON TRIAL

A common commercial practice is for a seller of goods to entrust possession of goods to a buyer to either give the buyer an opportunity to decide whether or not to buy them or to try to resell them to a third person. The entrusting may be known as a **sale on approval,** a **sale or return,** or a **consign-ment,** depending on the terms of the entrusting. Occasionally, the goods may be damaged, destroyed, or stolen, or the creditors of the buyer may try to claim them. On such occasions, the form of the entrusting will determine whether the buyer or the seller had the risk of loss and whether the buyer's creditors successfully can claim the goods.

## Sale on Approval

In a sale on approval, the goods are delivered to the buyer with an understanding that he may use or test them for the purpose of determining whether he wishes to buy them [2–326(1)(a)]. In a sale on approval, neither the risk of loss nor title to the goods passes to the buyer until he accepts the goods. The buyer has the right to use the goods in any manner consistent with the purpose of the trial, but any unwarranted exercise of ownership over the goods is considered to be an acceptance of the goods. Similarly, if the buyer fails to notify the seller of his election to return the goods, he is considered to have accepted them [2–327]. For example, if Dealer agrees to let Hughes take a new automobile home to drive for a day to see whether she wants to buy it and Hughes takes the car on a two-week vacation trip, Hughes will be considered to have accepted the automobile because she used it in a manner beyond that contemplated by the trial and as if she were its owner. If Hughes had driven the automobile for a day, decided not to buy it, and parked it in her driveway for two weeks without telling Dealer of her intention to return it, Hughes would also be deemed to have accepted the automobile.

Once the buyer has notified the seller of his election to return the goods, the return of the goods is at the seller's expense and risk. Because the title and risk of loss of goods delivered on a sale on approval remain with the seller, goods held on approval are not subject to the claims of the buyer's creditors until the buyer accepts them [2–326].

## Sale or Return

In a sale or return, the seller delivers goods to a buyer for resale with the understanding that the buyer has the right to return them [2–326(1)(b)]. Under a sale or return, the title and risk of loss are with the buyer. While the goods are in the buyer's possession, they are subject to the claims of his creditors [2–326 and 2–327]. For example, if Publisher delivers some paperbacks to Bookstore on the understanding that Bookstore may return any of the paperbacks that remain unsold at the end of six months, the transaction is a sale or return. If Bookstore is destroyed by a fire, the risk of loss of the paperbacks was Bookstore's and it is responsible to Publisher for the purchase price. Similarly, if Bookstore becomes insolvent and is declared a bankrupt, the paperbacks will be considered part of the bankruptcy estate. If the buyer elects to return goods held on a sale or return basis, the return is at the buyer's risk and expense.

## Sale on Consignment

Sometimes, goods are delivered to a merchant on consignment. If the merchant to whom goods are consigned maintains a place of business dealing in goods of that kind under a name other than that of the person consigning the goods, then the consignor must take certain steps to protect his interest in the goods or they will be subject to the claims of the merchant's creditors. The consignor must (1) make sure that a sign indicating the consignor's interest is prominently posted at the place of business, or (2) make sure that the merchant's creditors know that he is generally in the business of selling goods owned by others, or (3) comply with the filing provisions of Article 9 of the Code—Secured Transactions.

For example, Jones operates a retail music store under the name of City Music Store. Baldwin Piano Company delivers some pianos to Jones on consignment. If no notices are posted indicating Baldwin's interest in the pianos, if Jones is not generally known to be selling from a consigned inventory, and if Baldwin does not file its interest with the recording office pursuant to Article 9 of the Code, then the goods are subject to the claims of Jones's creditors. This is crucial to Baldwin because it may have intended to retain title. However, the Code treats a consignment to a person doing business under a name other than that of the consignor as a "sale or return" [2–326(3)]. If Jones did business as the Baldwin Piano Company, Baldwin's interest would be protected from the claims of Jones's creditors without the need for Baldwin to post a sign or to file under Article 9.

The case that follows, *In Re Auclair,* illustrates the risks borne by a person who makes goods available on a sale or return or consignment basis.

## In Re Auclair
## McGregor v. Jackson
### 131 BR 185 (Bankr. M.D. Ala. 1991)

Edd and Diane Auclair maintained a place of business in Covington County, Alabama, where they operated a gun shop and convenience store named Heath Grocery and Final Chapter Firearms. In November 1989, Luke Jackson delivered about 70 firearms to the Auclairs to sell on consignment. The consignment agreement provided as follows:

I, Edd Auclair, have received a number of guns, of which a list will be attached and I will sign. As I sell a gun I will pay James E. "Luke" Jackson or Betty King, with them giving me a receipt for that particular gun. If something should happen to Luke Jackson the guns are to be returned to Betty King or at that time Betty King and Edd Auclair can enter into an agreement. If something should happen to Edd Auclair, Diane agrees to return all guns that have not been paid for to Luke Jackson or Betty King and pay for any that has [sic] been sold.

The agreement was signed by Jackson, King, and the Auclairs.

On June 28, 1990, the Auclairs filed a petition in bankruptcy under Chapter 11 of the Bankruptcy Act. Shortly thereafter, Jackson removed the firearms he had consigned from the Auclairs' store. The bankruptcy trustee (McGregor) representing the Auclairs' creditors claimed that the firearms were the property of the bankruptcy estate.

---

**Gordon, Bankruptcy Judge** Both parties agree that Section 2–326(3) regarding consignments applies to the facts of this case. Under that subsection, goods delivered on consignment are "deemed to be on sale or return." Thus, by deeming the consignee a *purchaser* of the goods, the consignor is precluded from asserting an ownership claim to the goods vis-a-vis the consignee's creditors.

*Applying* that section to the instant case, Jackson is precluded from asserting his ownership of the firearms vis-a-vis the trustee. However, the subsection is not applicable to a consignor who—

**(a)** Complies with an applicable law providing for a consignor's interest or the like to be evidenced by a sign, or
**(b)** Establishes that the person conducting the business is generally known by his creditors to be substantially engaged in selling the goods of others, or
**(c)** Complies with the filing provisions of the article on secured transactions (Article 9). Section 2–326(3).

Jackson is not protected under (a) because Alabama does not have a sign law applicable to consignments. Jackson is not protected under (c) because he did not comply with the filing provisions of Article 9.

Jackson contends, but has failed to prove, that he is protected under (b). The evidence does not reflect that the debtors were "generally known by [their] creditors to be substantially engaged in selling the goods of others."

Jackson admitted that he did not notify any of the Auclairs' creditors that the firearms were placed with the Auclairs on consignment. The evidence reveals, *at best,* that only one of the Auclairs' eighteen creditors had knowledge of the consignment. The court concludes that the debtors were not "generally known by [their] creditors to be substantially engaged in selling" consigned firearms.

The court holds that the firearms in question are property of this bankruptcy estate which the trustee may sell. A separate order will be entered requiring Jackson to deliver the firearms to the trustee and to account for such property or its value. Jackson will have an unsecured claim for the value of the property returned to the trustee, for which he may file a proof of claim in this case.

**Judgment in favor of bankruptcy estate and against Jackson.**

# BULK TRANSFERS

## Bulk Transfer Legislation

There is one other situation where the creditors of a party to a sales contract may claim an interest (other than an Article 9 security interest) in the goods. This is in the case of a bulk transfer as covered by Article 6 of the Code. A **bulk transfer** occurs when a person whose main business is selling goods from stock (a retailer, a wholesaler, and in some cases a manufacturer) sells a major part of the materials, supplies, merchandise, or other inventory of the business in bulk and not in the ordinary course of business [6–102].

The danger in such cases is that financially troubled sellers may dispose of their assets secretly, pocket the proceeds, and disappear. In order to protect such a seller's creditors from being defrauded in this manner, Article 6 is designed to give them notice of the sale and enable them to file any claims they may have against the goods. The seller must give the buyer a sworn list of the seller's creditors and a schedule of the property to be transferred [6–104]. The buyer must keep this list available for inspection and copying by the seller's creditors for six months after the sale [6–104].

## Notice to Creditors

The buyer must notify all known creditors of the sale at least 10 days before taking possession of the goods [6–105]. Failure to comply with the requirements means that the buyer holds the goods in trust for the seller's creditors. In some states, an optional provision of the Code has been enacted requiring that the proceeds of the bulk transfer be paid to the seller's creditors [6–106].

## Statute of Limitations

Creditors have only six months from the time the transfer took place to enforce their rights under Article 6, unless the transfer was concealed from them. In such a case, they have six months after the transfer was discovered [6–111].

## Current Developments

For some time, there has been general dissatisfaction with the current bulk sales law. The National Conference of Commissioners on Uniform State Laws has prepared a draft revision to UCC Article 6 (Bulk Sales) for consideration by the states; at the same time, the commissioners have voted to recommend to the states that they repeal Article 6 and do without a bulk sales law. Thus, the future for bulk sales laws is in doubt.

---

**PROBLEMS AND PROBLEM CASES**

---

**1.** Mr. and Mrs. Abelman engaged the Capitol Termite and Pest Control Company to treat their home for a termite infestation. The chemical used by Capitol was Gold Crest Termide manufactured by Velsicol Chemical Corporation. Velsicol sold the Gold Crest Termide to a distributor, which in turn sold it to Capitol in bulk—in 55-gallon drums. Capitol did not buy materials specifically for each termite job. One 55-gallon drum would service many homes. Employees of Capitol pumped the chemical from the 55-gallon drums into a 5-gallon pail at Capitol's premises. Employees then poured the solution from the 5-gallon pail into a 1-gallon pail, which they filled half full. Next, they poured the half-gallon of Gold Crest Termide into a fixed 50-gallon tank on the back of Capitol's trucks and then filled the tank to capacity with water. Capitol's employees then applied this solution to the Abelman's residence. The Abelmans abandoned their home the day after Capitol completed treatment. Three years later, they brought suit against Capitol and Velsicol, contending that the termiticide had caused personal injuries and property damages. Among other things, they claimed there was a breach of express and implied warranties provided by the Uniform Commercial Code (discussed in Chapter 20). Velsicol and Capitol sought to dismiss these claims on the ground that there had not been a sale of goods and thus no warranties had arisen. Was the contract to obtain treatment for termites a sale of goods under the Uniform Commercial Code?

**2.** Suchy Funeral Home brought suit against Waldenmaier to recover the contracted price for a funeral, including the provision of a casket. Waldenmaier claimed that the lawsuit was commenced more than four years after the funeral and thus was barred by the Code's four-year statute of limitations. Suchy contended that the Code's statute of limitations did not apply because no ''sale of goods'' was involved. Should the court apply the Code's provisions to this contract?

**3.** Clive Lapp purchased a 1978 Chrysler Cordoba from Prospector Chevrolet on July 24, 1980. Lapp paid cash for the car, secured a temporary license sticker, and drove the car away. Three months after the sale, Prospector sent the title documents for the car to the County Treasurer's Office. When Lapp tried to pick up the title, the Treasurer informed him that the title could not be transferred to him because the application for title was in the name of Olive Lapp instead of Clive Lapp. Lapp did not notify Prospector of the error or take any other action to cause a valid title to be issued to him. Instead, he took the license plates from another car and illegally used them on the Cordoba. On September 16, 1981, Lapp was driving the Cordoba when he struck and killed Merlin Benjamin. Benjamin's estate sued Prospector, alleging that Prospector still had title to the Cordoba. Safeco Insurance, Prospector's insurer, argued that title had passed to Lapp. Did title pass to Lapp despite the fact that a certificate of title was not issued in his name?

**4.** Club Pro Golf Products was a distributor of golf products. It employed salesmen who called on customers to take orders for merchandise. The merchandise was sent by Club Pro directly to the purchaser, and payment was made by the purchaser directly to Club Pro. A salesman for Club Pro, Carl Gude, transmitted orders for certain merchandise to Club Pro for delivery to several fictitious purchasers. Club Pro sent the merchandise to the fictitious purchasers at the fictitious addresses, where it was picked up by Gude. Gude then sold the merchandise, worth approximately $19,000, directly to Simpson, a golf pro at a golf club. Gude retained the proceeds of sale for himself. Club Pro discovered the fraud and brought suit against Simpson to recover the merchandise. Club Pro alleged that Gude "stole" the merchandise from it "with intent to defraud it" and as a result had no authority to transfer title to Simpson. Did Gude have a void or a voidable title to the merchandise when he obtained it from Club Pro?

**5.** Lane, a dealer in new and used boats, sold a new boat and trailer to Johnson. Johnson paid for the boat and trailer by a check that the bank later dishonored. Johnson then resold the boat and

trailer to Honeycutt. Lane attempted to get the boat and trailer from Honeycutt. Can Lane recover them?

**6.** In June, Ramos entered into a contract to buy a motorcycle from Big Wheel Sports Center. He paid the purchase price of $893 and was given the papers necessary to register the cycle and get insurance on it. Ramos registered the cycle but had not attached the license plates to it. He left on vacation and told the salesperson for Big Wheel Sports Center that he would pick up the cycle on his return. While Ramos was on vacation, there was an electric power blackout in New York City and the cycle was stolen by looters. Ramos then sued Big Wheel Sports Center to get back his $893. Did Big Wheel Sports Center have the risk of loss of the motorcycle?

**7.** Debs, a dress manufacturer, sold Rose Stores 288 dresses. The order was on a Rose Stores printed form that stated, "Ship via Stuarts Express." Stuarts Express picked up the dresses at Debs, then one week later wrote Debs a letter informing it that the entire shipment was lost. Since Stuarts's liability is extremely limited by the shipping contract, who, between Debs and Rose, must absorb the risk of loss?

**8.** Legendary Homes, a home builder, purchased various appliances from Ron Mead T.V. & Appliance, a retail merchant selling home appliances. They were intended to be installed in one of Legendary Homes's houses and were to be delivered on February 1, 1984. At 5 o'clock on that day, the appliances had not been delivered. Legendary Homes's employees closed the home and left. Sometime between 5 and 6:30, Ron Mead delivered the appliances. No one was at the home so the deliveryman put the appliances in the garage. During the night, someone stole the appliances. Legendary Homes denied it was responsible for the loss and refused to pay Ron Mead for the appliances. Ron Mead then brought suit for the purchase price. Did Legendary Homes have the risk of loss of the appliances?

**9.** Collier, a retail store operator, accepted a delivery of stereo tapes, cartridges, and equipment from B & B Sales. The invoice noted that the goods had been "sold to" Collier and stated: "Terms 30-60-90; this equipment will be picked up if not sold in 90 days." Shortly thereafter, Collier's store was burglarized and all the merchandise was stolen.

B & B filed suit against Collier for the purchase price of the merchandise, claiming that the transaction was a sale and that Collier was liable to pay for the merchandise. Collier argued that the transaction was a consignment and that B & B had the risk of loss. Did Collier or B & B have the risk of loss of the merchandise?

10. Curtina International was a corporation engaged in the business of importing and distributing confectionery products, mainly varieties of wafers manufactured in Austria. From its inception in 1979, Curtina's business was not financially successful. By early 1981, Curtina was insolvent. Its largest unsecured creditor was one of its Austrian suppliers of wafers. In February 1981, Curtina's president approached Plymouth Enterprises, a corporation engaged in the business of buying and selling closeouts (excess, old, or out-of-season inventory) from manufacturers and wholesalers at a fraction of their normal selling prices. He offered to sell Plymouth Curtina's line of wafers. In March, Plymouth agreed to purchase substantially all of Curtina's inventory of wafers at approximately $12 per case, for a total of about $66,000; the wafers usually sold for about $50 a case to retail stores. Plymouth's representative was not aware that wafers constituted Curtina's entire inventory. At no time did Plymouth ask Curtina for a list of its creditors, and Plymouth did not furnish notice of the sale to Curtina's creditors. It took Plymouth approximately nine months to resell the wafers. Curtina was thrown into involuntary bankruptcy in April 1981. Murdock, the trustee in bankruptcy, sought to avoid the sale of the wafers to Plymouth, contending that it was made in violation of the state bulk sales law. Should the sale be voided for failing to comply with the bulk sales law?

11. ▣ *Video Case.* See "Software Horror Story." Chuck Mason, a computer consultant, was hired to develop customized software for a client, Ms. Clark. His plan was to purchase off-the-shelf software and to modify it to meet the customer's need. After identifying several software packages that might meet his need, he contacted a software retailer Bits and Bytes, by phone and explained that he needed to be able to modify the package at the source code level and to have the source code. He then asked Bits and Bytes to recommend a package that would meet these criteria and be easy to modify. After receiving the recommended software

(D-Base Hit) from Bits and Bytes, Chuck modified the software but was unable to get it to work as envisioned. Bits and Bytes refused to take it back because Chuck's modifications prevented it from being resold or returned to the software publisher. Chuck refused to pay Bits and Bytes for the package. Chuck then purchased a different software package (Customized Amazing Base) and customized it for his client. However, the customized software never functioned satisfactorily for the client, and she refused to pay Chuck for it. Does the UCC apply to the sale of the software by the retailer? Does it apply to the sale of the customized software by the consultant to the customer?

12. ▣ *Video Case.* See "TV Repair." Arnold took his old TV to an appliance store for repair. The appliance store developed financial problems and was unable to pay its debts to its creditors as they became due. Facing bankruptcy, the appliance store held a going-out-of-business sale and sold everything in the store, including Arnold's TV, to individual customers who had no knowledge of anyone else's interest in the goods. Does Arnold have the legal right to recover the TV from the person who bought it at the going-out-of-business sale?

13. ▣ *Video Case.* See "Sour Grapes." Jelly Manufacturer, a food processor in Chicago, placed a phone order with Grape Grower, a grower in California, for a quantity of perishable produce. The shipping term was *CIF* with payment to be made on delivery (COD). Grower delivered the goods called for in the contract to a carrier and contracted for their shipment. However, it neglected to provide that the goods be shipped under refrigeration. The goods were loaded on a nonrefrigerated boxcar, and as a result, the produce was spoiled when it reached Chicago. Who had the risk of loss, Grape Grower or Jelly Manufacturer?

---

## CAPSTONE QUESTIONS

Bloomington Corporation (BC), a wholesaler of medical devices and equipment, finds itself in the following disputes:

· On June 16, BC contracted with Sadler Computers, Inc., to design a new computer network, to select, provide, and install the equipment, and to maintain the network for BC.

The contract provided that BC would pay Sadler $500,000 for design, acquisition, and installation of the computer network and then $2,000 per month for a three-year period following installation for maintaining the system. The network was to be in place and operational by November 1. BC experienced problems with the system and by the middle of the following year concluded that, despite the efforts of Sadler to remedy the problems, the system did not meet the contract specifications and that it would have to bring suit against Sadler to try to recover the money it had paid for the system.

- On April 15, BC's facsimile machine malfunctioned. BC took it to Arthur's, an office supply company that was the local warranty agent for the machine's manufacturer, and Arthur's gave BC a receipt for the machine. Several days later, one of Arthur's employees mistook BC's machine for one of the used machines that Arthur's had available for sale and sold BC's to another customer. When BC's employee came for the machine, she learned the whole story. She immediately demanded its return from the purchaser but the purchaser refused.

- BC ordered a new laser printer from a mail-order supplier. The terms of the sale were FOB the seller's place of business and the seller agreed to ship the printer via United Parcel Service. The printer was badly damaged during shipment. BC has refused to pay for the damaged printer but the supplier insists that BC is obligated to pay for the printer and to pursue any remedies it may have against United Parcel Service for the damage.

- BC sent a shipment of 10 wheelchairs to a retail medical supply company on a "sale or return" basis that allowed the retailer to return any chairs that remained unsold at the end of a six-month period. Within the six-month period, a petition in bankruptcy was filed against the retailer. BC sought the return of the unsold wheelchairs for which it had not yet been paid but the bankruptcy trustee claimed that the wheelchairs were part of the retailer's bankruptcy estate and subject to the claims of its creditors.

## Required:

Answer the following and give reasons for your conclusions.

1. For the Sadler hypothetical, state whether the contract is governed by Article 2 (Sales) of the Uniform Commercial Code.

2. For the Arthur's hypothetical, state whether BC should expect to recover the machine.

3. For the mail-order supplier hypothetical, state whether the supplier's contention is correct.

4. For the retail medical supplier hypothetical, state whether the bankruptcy trustee's claim is correct.

# CHAPTER

## 12

# PRODUCT LIABILITY

## INTRODUCTION

*Suppose you are the president of a firm making products for sale to the public. One of your concerns would be the company's exposure to civil liability for defects in those products. As president, therefore, you would worry about changes in the law that make such liability more likely or more expensive. In other contexts, however, the same changes might appeal to you. This is especially true if* you *are harmed by defective products you purchase as a consumer. Such changes might also appeal to you if your firm wants to sue a supplier that has sold it defective products.*

*Each of these situations involves the law of* product liability. *Product liability law is the body of legal rules governing civil suits for losses resulting from defective goods.[1] After sketching product liability law's historical evolution, this chapter discusses the most important* theories of product liability recovery. *These theories are rules of law allowing plaintiffs to recover for losses resulting from defective goods once they prove certain facts. The second half of the chapter considers certain legal problems that are common to all the theories of recovery but that may be resolved differently from theory to theory.*

---

# THE EVOLUTION OF PRODUCT LIABILITY LAW

## The 19th Century

A century ago, the rules governing suits for defective goods were very much to sellers' and manufacturers' advantage. This was the era of *caveat emptor* (let the buyer beware). In contract suits, there was usually no liability unless the seller had made an express promise to the buyer and the goods did not conform to that promise. Some courts even required that the words *warrant* or *guarantee* accompany the promise before liability would exist. In negligence suits, the maxim of "no liability without fault" was widely accepted, and plaintiffs frequently had diffi-

---

[1]This chapter does not discuss the various federal consumer protection laws involving the payment and credit aspects of consumer transactions. Nor does it discuss product safety regulation. For these subjects, see Chapter 39.

culty proving negligence because the necessary evidence was under the defendant's control. In both contract and negligence cases, finally, the doctrine of "no liability outside privity of contract" often prevented plaintiffs from recovering against parties with whom they had not directly dealt.[2]

The social and economic conditions that prevailed for much of the 19th century help explain these prodefendant rules. At that time, laissez-faire values strongly influenced public policy and the law. One expression of those values was the belief that sellers and manufacturers should be contractually bound only when they deliberately assumed such liability by actually making a promise to someone with whom they dealt directly. Another factor limiting manufacturers' liability for defective products, some say, was the desire to promote industrialization by preventing potentially crippling damage recoveries against infant industries.

Certain features of the 19th-century economy, however, made that century's product liability rules less hard on plaintiffs than would otherwise have been the case. Chains of distribution tended to be short, so the no-liability-outside-privity defense was not always available. Because goods tended to be simple, buyers could sometimes inspect them for defects. Before the emergence of large corporations late in the 19th century, sellers and buyers were often of relatively equal size, sophistication, and bargaining power. This meant that they could deal on a relatively equal footing.

## The 20th Century

Today, many 19th-century social and economic tendencies are conspicuous by their absence. Laissez-faire values do not exercise the influence they did a century ago. Instead, a more protective, interdependent climate has emerged. With the development of a viable industrial economy, there has been less perceived need to protect manufacturers from liability for defective goods. The emergence of long chains of distribution has meant that consumers often do not deal directly with the parties respon-

sible for defects in the products they buy. Because sizable corporations tend to dominate the economy, consumers are less able to bargain equally with such parties in any event. Finally, the growing complexity of goods has made buyer inspections more difficult.

Due to such developments, product liability law has moved from its earlier *caveat emptor* emphasis to a stance of *caveat venditor* (let the seller beware). To protect consumers, modern courts and legislatures intervene in private contracts for the sale of goods and impose liability regardless of fault. As a result, sellers and manufacturers face greater liability and higher damage recoveries for defects in their products. Underlying the shift toward *caveat venditor* is the belief that sellers, manufacturers, and their insurers are best able to bear the economic costs associated with product defects and that they can usually pass on these costs through higher prices. Thus, the economic risk associated with defective products has been effectively spread throughout society, or socialized.

## The Current "Crisis" in Product Liability Law

Modern product liability law and its socialization-of-risk strategy have come under increasing attack over the past 15 to 20 years. Such attacks often focus on the difficulty sellers and manufacturers have encountered in obtaining product liability insurance and the increased costs of such insurance. Some observers blame the insurance industry for these problems, while others trace them to the increased liability and greater damage recoveries just discussed. Whatever their origin, the crisis in the liability insurance system has put sellers and manufacturers in a bind. Businesses unwilling or unable to buy expensive product liability insurance run the risk of being crippled by large damage awards unless they self-insure, which itself can be an expensive option today. Firms that purchase insurance, on the other hand, must pay a higher price for it. In either case, the resulting costs may be difficult to completely pass on. In addition, those costs may deter the development and marketing of innovative new products.

For these reasons and others, recent years have witnessed many efforts to scale back the proplaintiff thrust of modern product liability law. However,

---

[2]Privity of contract is the existence of a direct contractual relationship between two parties.

despite the introduction of several federal reform bills, Congress had not made any major changes in product liability law as of late 1994. As we note later in this chapter, however, tort reform efforts have occasionally been successful in the states.

## THEORIES OF PRODUCT LIABILITY RECOVERY

Technically, some theories of product liability recovery are contractual and some are tort-based. The contract theories involve a product **warranty**—a contractual promise about the nature of the product sold. In warranty cases, plaintiffs claim that the product failed to live up to the seller's promise. In tort cases, on the other hand, plaintiffs usually argue that the defendant was negligent or that strict liability should apply.

### Express Warranty

**Creating an Express Warranty**    UCC section 2–313(1) states that an **express warranty** is created in any of three ways.

**1.** Any *affirmation of fact or promise* regarding the goods creates an express warranty that the goods will conform to that affirmation. For instance, a computer seller's statement that a particular computer has a certain amount of memory creates an express warranty to that effect.

**2.** Any *description* of the goods creates an express warranty that the goods will conform to the description. This category includes: (1) statements that goods are of a certain brand, type, or model (e.g., an IBM dot-matrix computer printer); (2) descriptive adjectives characterizing the product (e.g., shatterproof glass); and (3) drawings, blueprints, and technical specifications.

**3.** A *sample* or *model* of goods to be sold creates an express warranty that the rest of the goods will conform to the sample or model. A sample is an object drawn from an actual collection of goods to be sold, while a model is a replica offered for the buyer's inspection when the goods themselves are unavailable.

The first two kinds of express warranties probably overlap; also, each can be either written or oral. In addition, magic words like *warrant* or *guarantee* no longer are needed to create an express warranty.

**Value, Opinion, and Sales Talk**    Statements of *value* ("This chair would bring you $2,000 at an auction") or *opinion* ("I think that this chair is a genuine antique Louis XIV") do not create an express warranty. The same is true of statements that amount to *sales talk* or *puffery* ("This chair is a good buy"). Of course, no sharp line separates such statements from express warranties. In close cases, a statement is more likely to be an express warranty if it is specific rather than indefinite, if it is stated in the sales contract rather than elsewhere,[3] or if it is unequivocal rather than hedged or qualified. The relative knowledge possessed by the seller and the buyer can also be an important factor. A car salesperson's statement about a used car, for instance, stands a greater chance of being an express warranty where the buyer knows little about cars than where the buyer is another car dealer. The following *Hall Farms* case discusses some of the points made in this paragraph.

**The Basis-of-the-Bargain Problem**    Under pre-Code law, there was no recovery for breach of an express warranty unless the buyer *relied* on that warranty in making the purchase. The UCC, however, ambiguously requires that the warranty be *part of the basis of the bargain*. Some courts read the Code's basis-of-the-bargain test as saying that full reliance is necessary. Others only require that the seller's warranty have been a *contributing factor* in the buyer's decision to purchase.

**Advertisements**    Statements made in advertisements, catalogs, or brochures *may* be express warranties. Such sources, however, are often filled with sales talk. Also, basis-of-the-bargain problems may arise if it is unclear whether or to what degree the statement really induced the buyer to make the purchase. For example, a buyer who reads an advertisement containing an express warranty one month before actually purchasing the product may or may not have been induced to purchase by the express warranty in the advertisement.

---

[3]Parol evidence rule problems can arise in express warranty cases. For example, a seller who used a written sale contract may argue that the rule excludes an alleged oral warranty. For the parol evidence rule, see Chapter 8.

**Multiple Express Warranties**    What happens when the seller gives two or more express warranties and those warranties arguably conflict? UCC section 2–317 says that such warranties should be read as consistent with each other and as cumulative if this is reasonable. If not, the parties' intention controls. In determining that intention: (1) exact or technical specifications defeat a sample, a model, or general descriptive language; and (2) a sample defeats general descriptive language.

---

## MARTIN RISPENS & SON V. HALL FARMS, INC.
### 601 N.E.2d 429 (Ind. Ct. App. 1992)

Hall Farms, Inc. ordered 40 pounds of Prince Charles watermelon seed from Martin Rispens & Son, a seed dealer. Rispens had obtained the seed from Petoseed Company, Inc., a seed producer. The label on Petoseed's can stated that the seeds are "top quality seeds with high vitality, vigor and germination." Hall Farms germinated the seeds in a greenhouse before transplanting the small watermelon plants to its fields. Although the plants had a few abnormalities, they grew rapidly. By mid-July, however, purple blotches had spread over most of the crop, and by the end of July the crop was ruined. It was later determined that the crop had been destroyed by "watermelon fruit blotch." Hall Farms's lost profits on the crop came to $180,000.

Hall Farms sued Petoseed for, among other things, breach of express warranty. Petoseed moved for summary judgment, but the trial court denied the motion. Petoseed appealed.

---

**Baker, Judge**    An express warranty is created by an affirmation of fact or promise made by the seller to the buyer which relates to the goods and becomes part of the basis of the bargain; it warrants that the goods shall conform to the affirmation or promise. It is not necessary that the seller use formal words such as "warrant" or "guarantee" or that he have a specific intention to make a warranty. On the other hand, an affirmation merely of the value of the goods or a statement purporting to be merely the seller's opinion or commendation of the goods does not create a warranty.

Whether a given representation is a warranty or merely an expression of the seller's opinion is determined in part by considering whether the seller asserts a fact of which the buyer is ignorant, or merely states an opinion or judgment on a matter of which the seller has no special knowledge and on which the buyer may be expected also to have an opinion and to exercise his judgment. Courts must also consider the degree of specificity expressed in the representation.

The label on Petoseed's can stated that the seeds are "top quality seeds with high vitality, vigor and germination." We consider the words "top quality seeds" as a classic example of puffery. The precise meaning of "top quality" is subject to considerably different interpretations.

Petoseed [also] claimed that its seeds possessed "high vitality, vigor and germination." Although reasonable people may differ as to the particular degree of vitality, vigor, and germination meant by the word "high," Petoseed did expressly warrant that its seeds would possess at least a modicum of vitality, vigor, and germination. If this affirmation became a basis of the bargain, an express warranty was created. We need not address this question, however, because even assuming Hall Farms relied on the affirmation, no breach occurred.

"Vitality" is the capacity to live, grow, or develop. "Vigor" is the capacity for natural growth and survival. "Germination" is the beginning of growth or sprouting. Here, there is no dispute that the watermelon seeds sprouted, grew, and developed a normal fruit set. Thus, the seeds conformed to the affirmation on Petoseed's labels; consequently, there was no breach. Partial summary judgment is appropriate when there is no conflict over facts dispositive of a portion of the litigation. Hall Farms may not recover from Petoseed based on an express warranty theory.

**Trial court decision denying Petoseed's motion for summary judgment on Hall Farms's express warranty claim reversed.**

## Implied Warranty of Merchantability

An **implied warranty** is a warranty created by *operation of law* rather than the seller's voluntary express statements. UCC section 2–314(1) creates the Code's **implied warranty of merchantability** by stating that "a warranty that the goods shall be merchantable is implied in a contract for their sale if the seller is a merchant with respect to goods of that kind." This is a clear example of the 20th-century tendency for government to intervene in private contracts to protect allegedly weaker parties.

In an implied warranty of merchantability case, the plaintiff argues that the seller breached the warranty by selling nonmerchantable goods. Under section 2–314, such claims can succeed only where the seller is a *merchant with respect to goods of the kind sold.*[4] A housewife's sale of homemade preserves or a hardware store owner's sale of a used car, for example, do not trigger the implied warranty of merchantability.

UCC section 2–314(2) states that, to be merchantable, goods must at least: (1) pass without objection in the trade; (2) be fit for the ordinary purposes for which such goods are used; (3) be of even kind, quality, and quantity within each unit (case, package, or carton) and among all units; (4) be adequately contained, packaged, and labeled; (5) conform to any promises or statements of fact made on the container or label; and (6) in the case of fungible goods, be of fair average quality. The most important of these requirements is that the goods must be *fit for the ordinary purposes for which such goods are used.* The goods need not be perfect to be fit for their ordinary purposes. Rather, they need only meet the reasonable expectations of the average consumer.

Such broad, flexible tests of merchantability are almost inevitable given the wide range of products sold in the United States today and the varied defects they can present. Still, a few generalizations about merchantability determinations are possible. Goods that fail to function properly or that have harmful side effects generally are not merchantable. A computer that fails to work properly or that destroys the owner's programs, for example, is not fit for the ordinary purposes for which computers are used. In cases involving allergic reactions to drugs or other products, courts frequently find the defendant liable if it was reasonably foreseeable that an appreciable number of consumers would suffer the reaction. As the following *Marriott* case reveals, there is some disagreement about the standard for food products that are alleged to be unmerchantable because they contain harmful objects or substances. Under the *foreign-natural* test, the defendant is liable if the object or substance is "foreign" to the product, but not liable if it is "natural" to that product. Increasingly, however, courts ask whether the food product met the consumer's *reasonable expectations.*

---

[4]The term *merchant* is defined in Chapter 1.

---

## YONG CHA HONG V. MARRIOTT CORPORATION
### 3 UCC Rep. Serv. 2d 83 (D. Md. 1987)

Yong Cha Hong bought some take-out fried chicken from a Roy Rogers Family Restaurant owned by the Marriott Corporation. While eating a chicken wing from her order, she bit into an object that she perceived to be a worm. Claiming permanent injuries and great physical and emotional upset from this incident, Hong sued Marriott for $500,000 in federal district court under the implied warranty of merchantability. After introducing an expert's report alleging that the object in the chicken wing was not a worm, Marriott moved for summary judgment. It claimed that the case involved no disputed issues of material fact, and that there was no breach of the implied warranty of merchantability as a matter of law.

———————————◼———————————

**Smalkin, District Judge**    It appears that the item encountered by plaintiff was probably not a worm or other parasite, although plaintiff, in her deposition, steadfastly maintains that it was a worm. If it was not a worm (i.e., if the expert analysis is correct), it was either one of the chicken's major blood vessels (the aorta) or its trachea, both of which would appear worm-like (although not meaty like a worm, but hollow). For [present] purposes, the court will assume that the item was not a worm. Precisely how the aorta or trachea wound up in this hapless chicken's wing is a fascinating, but as yet unanswered (and presently immaterial), question.

Does Maryland law provide a breach of warranty remedy for personal injury flowing from an unexpected encounter with an inedible part of the chicken's anatomy in a piece of fast food fried chicken? Marriott contends that there can be no recovery unless the offending item was a foreign object, i.e., not part of the chicken itself.

In many cases that have denied [implied] warranty recovery as a matter of law, the injurious substance was, as in this case, a natural (though inedible) part of the edible item consumed. Thus, in *Shapiro v. Hotel Statler Corp.* (1955), recovery was denied for a fish bone in "Hot Barquette of Seafood Mornay." But in all these cases the natural item was reasonably to be expected in the dish by its very nature, under the prevailing expectation of any reasonable consumer. Indeed, precisely this "reasonable expectation" test has been adopted in a number of cases. The reasonable expectation test has largely displaced the foreign-natural test adverted to by Marriott. This court is confident that Maryland would apply the reasonable expectation rule.

The court cannot conclude that the presence of a trachea or an aorta in a fast food fried chicken wing is so reasonably to be expected as to render it merchantable, as a matter of law. This is not like the situation [in a previous case] involving a one centimeter bone in a piece of fried fish. Everyone but a fool knows that tiny bones may remain in even the best filets of fish. This case is more like [another decision], where the court held that the issue was for the trier of fact, on a claim arising from a cherry pit in cherry ice cream. Thus, a question is presented that precludes the grant of summary judgment. The jury must determine whether a piece of fast food fried chicken is merchantable if it contains an inedible item of the chicken's anatomy. Of course, the jury will be instructed that the consumer's reasonable expectations form a part of the merchantability concept.

**Marriott's motion for summary judgment denied.**

══════════════════════════════════════

## Implied Warranty of Fitness

UCC section 2–315's **implied warranty of fitness for a particular purpose** arises where: (1) the seller has reason to know a particular purpose for which the buyer requires the goods, (2) the seller has reason to know that the buyer is relying on the seller's skill or judgment to select suitable goods, and (3) the buyer actually relies on the seller's skill or judgment in purchasing the goods. If these tests are met, there is an implied warranty that the goods will be fit for the buyer's *particular* purpose.

In many fitness warranty cases, buyers effectively put themselves in the seller's hands by making their needs known and saying that they are relying on the seller to select goods that will satisfy those needs. This may happen, for example, where a seller sells a computer system specially manufactured or customized for a buyer's particular needs. But sellers can also be liable where the circumstances reasonably indicate that the buyer has a particular purpose and is relying on the seller to satisfy that purpose, even though the buyer fails to make either explicit. However, buyers may have trouble recovering where they are more expert than the seller, submit specifications for the goods they wish to buy, inspect the goods, actually select them, or insist on a particular brand.

As the following *Dempsey* case makes clear, the implied warranty of fitness clearly differs from the implied warranty of merchantability. The tests for the creation of each warranty are plainly not the same. Under section 2–315, moreover, sellers only warrant that the goods are fit for the buyer's *particular* purposes, not the *ordinary* purposes for which such goods are used. If a 400-pound man asks a department store for a hammock that will support his weight but is sold a hammock that only can support normally sized people, there is a breach of the implied warranty of fitness but no breach of the implied warranty of merchantability. If the hammock cannot support *anyone's* weight, however, both warranties are breached.

---

## DEMPSEY V. ROSENTHAL
### 468 N.Y.S.2d 441 (N.Y. Civ. Ct. 1983)

Ruby Dempsey purchased a nine-week-old pedigreed male poodle from the American Kennels Pet Stores. She named the poodle Mr. Dunphy. Dempsey later testified that before making the purchase, she told the salesperson that she wanted a dog suitable for breeding purposes. Five days after the sale, she had Mr. Dunphy examined by a veterinarian, who discovered that the poodle had one undescended testicle. This condition did not seriously affect Mr. Dunphy's fertility, but it was a genetic defect that would probably be passed on to any offspring sired. Also, a dog with this condition could not be used as a show dog.

Dempsey demanded a refund from American Kennels, but her demand was denied. She then sued in small claims court, alleging that American Kennels had breached the implied warranty of fitness.

---

**Saxe, Judge**    UCC sections 2–314 and 2–315 make it clear that the warranty of fitness for a particular purpose is narrower, more specific, and more precise than the warranty of merchantability, which involves fitness for the *ordinary* purposes for which goods are used. The following are the conditions that are not required by the implied warranty of merchantability, but that must be present if a plaintiff is to recover on the basis of the implied warranty of fitness: (1) the seller must have reason to know the buyer's particular purpose, (2) the seller must have reason to know that the buyer is relying on the seller's skill or judgment to furnish appropriate goods, and (3) the buyer must, in fact, rely upon the seller's skill or judgment.

I find that the warranty of fitness for a particular purpose has been breached. Dempsey testified that she specified to the salesperson that she wanted a dog that was suitable for breeding purposes. Although this is disputed by the defendant, the credible testimony supports Dempsey's version of the event. Further, it is reasonable for the seller of a pedigreed dog to assume that the buyer intends to breed it. But it is undisputed by the experts here (for both sides) that Mr. Dunphy was as capable of siring a litter as a male dog with two viable and descended testicles. This, the defendant contends, compels a finding in its favor. I disagree. While it is true that Mr. Dunphy's fertility level may be unaffected, his stud value, because of this hereditary condition (which is likely to be passed on to future generations), is severely diminished.

**Judgment for Dempsey.**

## Negligence

Product liability suits based on the theory of **negligence** usually allege that the seller or manufacturer breached a duty to the plaintiff by failing to eliminate a reasonably foreseeable risk of harm associated with the product. Such suits typically claim one or more of the following: (1) improper *manufacture* of the goods (including improper materials and packaging), (2) improper *inspection,* (3) a failure to provide *adequate warnings* of hazards or defects, and (4) improper *design.*

**Improper Manufacture**    Negligence suits alleging the manufacturer's improper assembly, materials, or packaging often encounter problems because the evidence needed to prove a breach of duty is under the defendant's control.[5] However, liberal modern discovery rules and the doctrine of *res ipsa loquitur* can help plaintiffs establish a breach in such situations.

**Improper Inspection**    Manufacturers have a duty to inspect their products for defects that create a reasonably foreseeable risk of harm, if such an inspection would be practicable and effective. As before, *res ipsa loquitur* and modern discovery rules can help plaintiffs prove their case against the manufacturer.

Most courts have held that middlemen such as retailers and wholesalers have a duty to inspect the goods they sell only when they have actual knowledge or reason to know of a defect. In addition, such parties generally have no duty to inspect where this would be unduly difficult, burdensome, or time-consuming. Unless the product defect is obvious, for example, middlemen usually are not liable for failing to inspect goods sold in the manufacturer's original packages or containers.

On the other hand, sellers who prepare, install, or repair the goods they sell ordinarily have a duty to inspect those goods. Examples include restaurants, automobile dealers, and installers of household products. Usually, however, the scope of the inspec-tion need only be consistent with the preparation, installation, or repair work performed. Thus, it is unlikely that such sellers must unearth hidden or latent defects.

If there is a duty to inspect and the inspection reveals a defect, further duties can arise. For example, a seller or manufacturer may be required not to sell the product in its defective state, or at least to give a suitable warning.

**Failure to Warn**    Sellers and manufacturers have a duty to give an appropriate warning when their products pose a reasonably foreseeable risk of harm. But in determining whether there was a duty to warn and whether the defendant's warning was adequate, courts often consider other factors besides the reasonable foreseeability of the risk. These include the *magnitude or severity* of the likely harm, the *ease or difficulty of providing an appropriate warning*, and the likely *effectiveness of a warning*. As the following *Daniell* case makes clear, moreover, there is no duty to warn where the risk is *open and obvious.*

**Design Defects**    Manufacturers have a duty to design their products so as to avoid reasonably foreseeable risks of harm. Like failure-to-warn cases, however, design defect cases frequently involve other factors besides the reasonable foreseeability of harm. As before, one of these factors is the *magnitude or severity* of the foreseeable harm. Three others are *industry practices* at the time the product was manufactured, the *state of the art* (the state of existing scientific and technical knowledge) at that time, and the product's compliance or noncompliance with *government safety regulations.*[6]

Sometimes courts employ *risk-benefit analysis* when weighing these factors. In such analyses, three other factors—the design's *social utility,* the *effectiveness of alternative designs,* and the *cost of safer designs*—may figure in the weighing process. Even where the balancing process indicates that the design was not defective, courts may still require a suitable warning.

---

[5]Another problem concerns the negligence liability of computer designers and programmers. Some courts have held such parties to a higher standard of care when they develop custom application software, but others reject such claims.

[6]Some states have statutes stating that a product's compliance with state or federal product safety regulations creates a rebuttable presumption that it was not defective. Also, a few states have a statutory state-of-the-art defense.

---

## Daniell v. Ford Motor Company
### 581 F. Supp. 728 (D.N.M. 1984)

Connie Daniell attempted to commit suicide by locking herself inside the trunk of her 1973 Ford LTD. Daniell remained in the trunk for nine days, but survived after finally being rescued. Later, Daniell sued Ford in negligence to recover for her resulting physical and psychological injuries. She contended that the LTD was defectively designed because its trunk did not have an internal release or opening mechanism. She also argued that Ford was liable for negligently failing to warn her that the trunk could not be unlocked from within. Ford moved for summary judgment.

---

**Baldock, District Judge** As a general principle, a design defect is actionable only where the condition of the product is unreasonably dangerous to the user or consumer. Under negligence, a manufacturer has a duty to consider only those risks of injury which are foreseeable. A risk is not foreseeable where a product is used in a manner which could not reasonably be anticipated by the manufacturer and that use is the cause of the plaintiff's injury.

The purposes of an automobile trunk are to transport, stow, and secure the spare tire, luggage, and other goods and to protect those items from the weather. The design features of a trunk make it well near impossible that an adult intentionally would enter the trunk and close the lid. The dimensions of a trunk, the height of its sill and its load floor, and the efforts to first lower the lid and then to engage its latch, are among the design features which encourage closing and latching the trunk lid while standing outside the vehicle. The court holds that the plaintiff's use of the trunk compartment as a means to attempt suicide was an unforeseeable use as a matter of law. Therefore, the manufacturer had no duty to design an internal release or opening mechanism that might have prevented this occurrence.

Nor did the manufacturer have a duty to warn the plaintiff of the danger of her conduct, given the plaintiff's unforeseeable use of the product. Another reason why the manufacturer had no duty to warn the plaintiff of the risk inherent in crawling into an automobile trunk and closing the lid is [that] such a risk is obvious. There is no duty to warn of known dangers. Moreover, the potential efficacy of any warning, given the plaintiff's use of the trunk for a deliberate suicide attempt, is questionable.

Having held that the plaintiff's conception of the manufacturer's duty is in error, the court need not reach the issues of comparative negligence or other defenses such as assumption of risk.

**Ford's motion for summary judgment granted; Daniell loses.**

---

## Strict Liability

Strict products liability is a relatively recent development. Only in the 1960s did courts begin to impose such liability in significant numbers. The movement toward strict liability received a big boost when the American Law Institute promulgated section 402A of the *Restatement (Second) of Torts* in 1965. By now, the vast majority of the states have adopted some form of strict products liability. The most important reason is the socialization-of-risk strategy discussed earlier. Another common justification for strict products liability is that it stimulates manufacturers to design and build safer products. Strict liability also removes a problem that has long plagued plaintiffs in negligence suits—the need to prove a breach of duty.

**Section 402A's Requirements** Because it is the most common version of strict products liability, we limit our discussion of the subject to section 402A.

Section 402A provides that a "seller . . . engaged in the business of selling" a particular product is liable for physical harm or property damage suffered by the ultimate user or consumer of that product if the product was "in a defective condition unreasonably dangerous to the user or consumer or to his property." This rule applies even though "the seller has exercised all possible care in the preparation and sale of his product." Thus, section 402A states a rule of strict liability that eliminates the plaintiff's need to prove a breach of duty.

However, the liability imposed by section 402A is not absolute, for the section applies only if certain tests are met.

**1.** The seller must be *engaged in the business of selling the product that harmed the plaintiff.* Thus, section 402A only binds parties who resemble UCC merchants because they regularly sell the product at issue. For example, the section does not apply to a college professor's or a clothing store's sale of a used car.

**2.** The product must be in a *defective condition* when sold, and also must be *unreasonably dangerous* because of that condition. The usual test of a product's defective condition is whether the product meets the reasonable expectations of the average consumer. An unreasonably dangerous product is one that is dangerous to an extent beyond the reasonable contemplation of the average consumer. For example, good whiskey is not unreasonably dangerous even though it can cause harm, but whiskey contaminated with a poisonous substance qualifies. However, some courts balance the product's social utility against its danger when determining whether it is unreasonably dangerous.

Due to section 402A's unreasonably dangerous requirement, it covers a smaller range of product defects than the implied warranty of merchantability. A power mower that simply fails to operate, for instance, is not unreasonably dangerous, although it

would violate the merchantability standard. Some courts, however, blur the defective condition and unreasonably dangerous requirements, and a few have done away with the latter test.

**3.** Finally, defendants can avoid section 402A liability where the product was *substantially modified* by the plaintiff or another party after the sale, and the modification contributed to the plaintiff's injury or other loss.

**Applications of Section 402A**   As the following *Toney* case makes clear, design defect and failure-to-warn suits can be brought under section 402A. Even though section 402A is a strict liability provision, the standards applied in such cases often resemble the negligence standards discussed in the previous section.

Because it applies to sellers, section 402A covers retailers and other middlemen who market goods containing defects that they did not create and may not have been able to discover. Even though such parties often escape negligence liability, some courts have found them liable under section 402A's strict liability rule. However, other states have given middlemen some protection against 402A liability, and/or have required the manufacturer or other responsible party to indemnify them.

What about products (such as some drugs) that have great social utility, but that pose serious risks which cannot be eliminated? Imposing strict liability on such "unavoidably unsafe" products might deter manufacturers from developing and marketing them. Where products of this kind cause harm and a lawsuit follows, many courts follow comment *k* to section 402A. Comment *k* says that unavoidably unsafe products are neither defective nor unreasonably dangerous if they are properly prepared and accompanied by proper directions and a proper warning. For this rule to apply, of course, the product must be genuinely incapable of being made safer.

---

### TONEY V. KAWASAKI HEAVY INDUSTRIES, LTD.
#### 975 F.2d 162 (5th Cir. 1992)

Shortly after Billy Toney bought a used Kawasaki 750 motorcycle, he was struck from the side by a truck while riding the motorcycle on a highway. As a result, he suffered severe injuries to his left leg, leading to its eventual amputation. Toney sued Kawasaki in a Mississippi trial court, alleging that the motorcycle was improperly designed because it was not equipped with leg-protection devices, and that Kawasaki improperly failed to warn users about the dangers posed by the absence of such devices. After Kawasaki removed the case to federal district court, the district court granted Kawasaki's motion for summary judgment on Toney's section 402A claim. Toney appealed.

---

**Jolly, Circuit Judge**   To recover under Mississippi product strict liability law, the injured plaintiff must show that the product was "in a defective condition unreasonably dangerous." Mississippi has adopted the objective "consumer expectations" test to determine whether a product is unreasonably dangerous. The plaintiff must establish that the product was dangerous to an extent beyond that which would be contemplated by the ordinary consumer who purchases it, with the ordinary knowledge common to the community as to its characteristics. Furthermore, a product that has an open and obvious danger is not more dangerous than contemplated by the consumer, and hence cannot be unreasonably dangerous.

The ordinary consumer could see that [Toney's] motorcycle had no leg protection and, thus, could fully appreciate the motorcycle's design and its open and obvious dangers. An ordinary consumer would fully appreciate the danger that, if an automobile struck the side of the motorcycle, the rider's leg would be ruinously crushed. The danger of the product thus revealed and appreciated, it was not an unreasonably dangerous product for a manufacturer to market.

Toney next asserts that the district court erred in failing to consider his subjective state of mind in determining whether the danger presented by the design of his motorcycle was patent or latent. He testified that he did not appreciate the danger involved in riding a motorcycle without any leg protection features. Notwithstanding Toney's argument, the Mississippi Supreme Court has adopted an objective test of "consumer expectations" under section 402A. The test is the objective measure of the expectations of the generic consumer who has ordinary knowledge common to the community. The question in product strict liability cases is not whether the product is unreasonably dangerous to a given individual. Modern products are sold by the millions in markets comprising a cross section of the population and therefore are used by people with varying levels of education, experience, and ordinary common sense. The focus in product liability cases is on the product, not the individual purchaser.

**District court decision granting Kawasaki's motion for summary judgment affirmed.**

---

**CONCEPT REVIEW**

## COMPARING THE MAJOR PRODUCT LIABILITY THEORIES—THE BASICS

| Theory | Tort or Contract | Type of Defendant | Nature of Goods Sold | Remarks |
|---|---|---|---|---|
| **Express Warranty** | Contract | Seller of goods | Not as warranted by affirmation of fact or promise, description, sample, or model | Exemption for statements of value, opinion, or sales talk |
| **Implied Warranty of Merchantability** | Contract | Merchant for goods sold | Not merchantable; usually, not fit for ordinary purposes for which such goods used | Merchantability has other aspects |
| **Implied Warranty of Fitness** | Contract | Seller of goods | Not fit for buyer's particular purposes | Seller must have reason to know of buyer's needs and buyer's reliance, and buyer must actually rely |

| Theory | Tort or Contract | Type of Defendant | Nature of Goods Sold | Remarks |
|---|---|---|---|---|
| **Negligence** | Tort | Manufacturer or seller of goods | "Defective" due to improper manufacture, inspection, design, or failure to give suitable warning | Limited inspection duty for middlemen |
| **Section 402A** Strict Liability | Tort | Seller engaged in business of selling product sold | Defective and unreasonably dangerous | Strict liability; design defect and failure-to-warn suits possible |

## Other Theories of Recovery

**Warranty of Title**    Normally, a seller of goods impliedly warrants that: (1) the title he conveys is good and transfer of that title is rightful, and (2) the goods are free from any lien or security interest of which the buyer lacks knowledge. Thus, a buyer may recover damages against his seller where, for example, the seller has marketed stolen goods or goods that are subject to a third party's security interest. Also, a seller who is a merchant in goods of the kind sold normally warrants that the goods are free of any rightful patent or trademark infringement claim, or any similar claim, by a third party. The implied warranty of title can be excluded or modified only by: (1) specific language to that effect, or (2) circumstances that give the buyer reason to know that the seller does not claim title or purports only to sell the title he has.

**The Magnuson-Moss Act**    The relevant civil-recovery provisions of the federal Magnuson-Moss Warranty Act apply to sales of *consumer products* costing more than *$10 per item*.[7] A consumer product is tangible personal property normally used for personal, family, or household purposes. If a seller gives a *written warranty* for such a product to a *consumer,* the warranty must be designated full or limited. A seller who gives a full warranty promises to: (1) *remedy* any defects in the product and (2) *replace* the product or *refund* its

purchase price if, after a reasonable number of attempts, it cannot be repaired.[8] A seller who gives a limited warranty is bound to whatever promises it actually makes. However, neither warranty applies if the seller simply declines to give a written warranty.

**Misrepresentation**    Section 402B of the *Restatement (Second) of Torts* lets *consumers* recover for *personal injury* resulting from certain *misrepresentations* about goods they have purchased. The misrepresentation must: (1) be made by a party engaged in the business of selling goods of the kind purchased; (2) be made to the public by advertising, labels, or similar means; (3) concern a fact *material* to the goods purchased; and (4) be *actually and justifiably* relied on by the consumer. Suppose the manufacturer of a laxative states in its advertising that the laxative has no adverse side effects if used as directed. Smith, who has been influenced by the advertisements and has no reason to doubt their accuracy, buys a bottle of the laxative. If, after using it according to directions, Smith suffers injury to his digestive system, he can recover from the manufacturer for that injury.

---

[7]Other portions of the Magnuson-Moss Act are discussed later in this chapter and in Chapter 39.

[8]Also, many states have enacted so-called lemon laws that may apply only to motor vehicles, or to various other consumer products as well. The versions applying to motor vehicles generally require the manufacturer to replace the vehicle or refund its purchase price once certain conditions are met. These conditions may include the following: a serious defect covered by warranty, a certain number of unsuccessful attempts at repair or a certain amount of downtime due to attempted repairs, and the manufacturer's failure to show that the defect is curable.

## INDUSTRYWIDE LIABILITY

The development we call industrywide liability is a way for plaintiffs to bypass problems of causation that exist where several firms within an industry have manufactured a harmful standardized product, and it is impossible for the plaintiff to prove *which* firm produced the product that injured her. In such cases, each potential defendant can argue that the plaintiff should lose because she cannot show that *its* product caused the harm of which she complains. The usual reasons for the plaintiff's proof problems are the number of firms producing the product and the time lag between exposure to the product and the appearance of the injury. Many of the cases presenting this problem have involved DES (an antimiscarriage drug that has produced various ailments in daughters of the women to whom it was administered) or diseases resulting from long-term exposure to asbestos.

In such cases, some courts continue to deny recovery under traditional causation rules. However, using various theories whose many details are beyond the scope of this text, other courts have made it easier for plaintiffs to recover. Where recovery is allowed, some of these courts have *apportioned* damages among the firms that might have produced the harm-causing product. Typically, the apportionment is based on market share at some chosen time.

## DAMAGES IN PRODUCT LIABILITY SUITS

At this point, we begin to consider several problems that are common to each major theory of product liability recovery but that may be resolved differently from theory to theory.[9] The first such problem, the damages obtainable under each theory, strongly influences a plaintiff's strategy in a product liability suit. Here, we describe the major kinds of damages recoverable in products liability cases, along with the theories under which each can be recovered. One lawsuit can involve claims for all these sorts of damages.

**1. Basis-of-the-bargain damages**. Buyers of defective goods have not received full value for their purchase price. The resulting loss, usually called basis-of-the-bargain damages or direct economic loss, is the value of the goods as promised under the contract, minus the value of the goods actually received.

*Where awarded:*    Basis-of-the-bargain damages are usually not recoverable in *negligence* and *strict liability* cases. In *express* and *implied warranty* suits under the UCC, however, basis-of-the-bargain damages are recoverable where there was *privity of contract* (a direct contractual relation) between the plaintiff and the defendant. As discussed in the next section, however, only occasionally will a warranty plaintiff who lacks privity with the defendant obtain basis-of-the-bargain damages. Basis-of-the-bargain recoveries most often occur where an express warranty was made to a remote plaintiff through advertising, brochures, or labels.

**2. Consequential damages**. Consequential damages include: **personal injury, property damage** (damage to the plaintiff's other property), and **indirect economic loss** (e.g., lost profits or lost business reputation) resulting from a product defect. Consequential damages also include **noneconomic loss**—for example, pain and suffering, physical impairment, mental distress, loss of enjoyment of life, loss of companionship or consortium, inconvenience, and disfigurement. Noneconomic loss is usually part of the plaintiff's personal injury claim. Recently, several states have limited noneconomic loss recoveries, typically by imposing a dollar cap on them.

*Where awarded:*    Plaintiffs in *negligence* and *strict liability* cases normally can recover for personal injury and property damage. Recoveries for foreseeable indirect economic loss are sometimes allowed.

In UCC *express* and *implied warranty* suits where *privity exists* between the plaintiff and the defendant, the plaintiff can recover for: (1) personal injury and property damage, if either proximately resulted from the breach of warranty; and (2) indirect economic loss, if the defendant had reason to know that this was likely. As discussed in the next section, a UCC plaintiff who *lacks privity* with the defendant has a fairly good chance of recovering for personal injury or property damage. But recovery for indirect economic loss is rare because remote sellers usually cannot foresee such losses.

**3. Punitive damages**. Punitive (or exemplary) damages are intended to punish defendants who have acted in an especially outrageous fashion, and to deter them and others from so acting in the

---

[9]We generally do not consider how these problems are resolved under the warranty of title, the Magnuson-Moss Act, or section 402B.

future. Of the various standards for awarding punitive damages, perhaps the most common is the
defendant's conscious or reckless disregard for the
safety of those likely to be affected by the goods.
Examples include concealment of known product
hazards, knowing violation of government or industry product safety standards, failure to correct
known dangerous defects, and grossly inadequate
product testing or quality control procedures.

Due to their perceived frequency, size, and effect
on business and the economy, punitive damages have
been subjected to state tort reform regulation
throughout the 1980s. The approaches taken by these
statutes vary. Many set the standards for punitive
damage recovery and the plaintiff's burden of proof;
some articulate factors courts should consider when
ruling on punitive damage awards; and some create
special procedures for punitive damage determinations. Also, several states have limited the size of
punitive damage recoveries, usually by restricting
them to some multiple of the plaintiff's actual damages, or by putting a flat dollar cap on them.

*Where awarded:*    Assuming that the standards
just described have been met, punitive damages are
recoverable in *negligence* and *strict liability* cases.
Due to the traditional rule that punitive damages are
not available in contract cases, they are usually not
awarded in *express* and *implied warranty* suits.

Figure 1 summarizes the plaintiff's chances of
recovering the most important kinds of damages in
contract and tort cases.

## THE NO-PRIVITY DEFENSE

Today, defective products often move through long
chains of distribution before reaching the person
they harm. This means that a product liability
plaintiff often has not dealt directly with the party
ultimately responsible for his losses. Figure 2 depicts a hypothetical chain of distribution in which
goods defectively produced by a manufacturer of
component parts move vertically through the manufacturer of a product in which those parts are used,
a wholesaler, and a retailer, ultimately reaching the
buyer. The defect's consequences may move hori-
zontally as well, affecting members of the buyer's
family, guests in his home, and even bystanders. If
the buyer or one of these parties suffers loss due to
the defect in the component parts, can he successfully sue the component parts manufacturer or any
other party in the vertical chain of distribution with
whom he did not directly deal?

Because at that time there was no recovery for
defective goods without privity of contract between
the plaintiff and the defendant, such suits were
unlikely to succeed under 19th-century law. In the
preceding example the buyer would have been
required to sue his dealer. If the buyer was successful, the retailer might have sued the wholesaler, and
so on up the chain. For a variety of reasons (including a middleman's limited negligence liability for
failure to inspect), the party ultimately responsible
for the defect often escaped liability.

**FIGURE 1    When the Various Kinds of Damages Are Recoverable**

| Type of Damages | Express and Implied Warranty | Negligence and Section 402A |
|---|---|---|
| **Basis of the Bargain** | Within privity: Yes<br>Outside privity: Occasionally | Rarely |
| **Personal Injury and Property Damage** | Within privity: If proximate result of breach<br>Outside privity: Fairly good chance | Yes |
| **Indirect Economic Loss** | Within privity: If defendant has reason to know this likely<br>Outside privity: Rarely | Sometimes |
| **Punitive Damages** | Rarely | Yes, in appropriate cases |

**FIGURE 2    A Hypothetical Chain of Distribution**

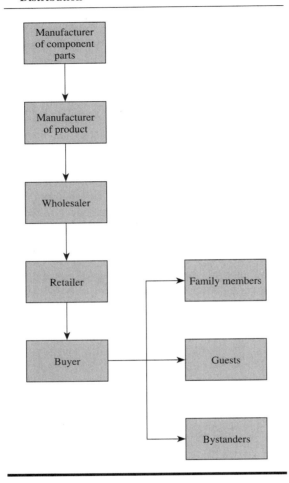

## Negligence and Strict Liability Cases

By now, the old no-liability-outside-privity rule has been severely eroded in tort suits. It has little, if any, effect in *strict liability* cases, where even bystanders can recover against remote manufacturers. In *negligence* cases, a plaintiff generally recovers against a remote defendant if the plaintiff's loss was a reasonably foreseeable consequence of the defect. Depending on the circumstances, therefore, bystanders and other distant parties might recover against a manufacturer in negligence as well.

## Warranty Cases

The no-privity defense still retains some vitality in UCC cases. Unfortunately, the "law" on this subject is complex and confusing. Under the Code, the privity question is formally governed by section 2–318, which comes in three alternative versions. Section 2–318's language, however, is a questionable guide to the courts' actual behavior in UCC privity cases.

**UCC Section 2–318**    Alternative A to section 2–318 says that a seller's express or implied warranty runs to natural persons in the family or household of *his* (the seller's) buyer and to guests in his buyer's home if they suffer personal injury and if it was reasonable to expect that they might use, consume, or be affected by the goods sold. On its face, Alternative A does little to undermine the traditional no-privity defense. In Figure 2, Alternative A would merely allow the buyer, his family, and guests in his home to sue the *retailer* for their personal injury.

Alternatives B and C go much further. Alternative B extends the seller's express or implied warranty to any natural person who has suffered personal injury, if it was reasonable to expect that this person would use, consume, or be affected by the goods. Alternative C is much the same, but it extends the warranty to any person (not just natural persons) and to those suffering injury in general (not just personal injury). If the reasonable-to-expect test is met, these two provisions should extend the warranty to many remote parties, including bystanders.

**Departures from UCC Section 2–318**    For various reasons, section 2–318's literal language is of questionable relevance in UCC privity cases. Some states have adopted privity statutes that differ from any version of section 2–318. Also, one of the comments to section 2–318 lets courts extend liability farther than the section expressly permits. Finally, versions B and C are fairly open ended as written. Thus, the plaintiff's ability to recover outside privity in warranty cases varies from state to state and situation to situation. The most important factors affecting resolution of this question include the following:

1. Whether it is *reasonably foreseeable* that a party such as the plaintiff would be harmed by the product defect in question.

2. The *status of the plaintiff.* On the average, consumers and other natural persons fare better outside privity than corporations and other business concerns.

3. The *type of damages* the plaintiff has suffered. In general, remote plaintiffs are: (a) most likely to recover for personal injury, (b) somewhat less likely to recover for property damage, (c) occasionally able to obtain basis-of-the-bargain damages, and (d) rarely able to recover for indirect economic loss. Recall from the previous section that a remote plaintiff is most likely to receive basis-of-the-bargain damages where an express warranty was made to him through advertising, brochures, or labels.

## DISCLAIMERS AND REMEDY LIMITATIONS

### Introduction

A product liability **disclaimer** is a clause in the sales contract whereby the seller tries to eliminate its *liability* under one or more theories of recovery. A **remedy limitation** is a clause attempting to block recovery of certain kinds of *damages.* Disclaimers attack the plaintiff's theory of recovery; if the disclaimer is effective, no damages of any sort are recoverable under that theory. A successful remedy limitation prevents the plaintiff from recovering certain types of damages but does not attack the plaintiff's theory of recovery. Damages not excluded may still be recovered, because the theory is left intact.

The main justification for enforcing disclaimers and remedy limitations is freedom of contract. Also, because goods accompanied by an effective disclaimer or remedy limitation are apt to be cheaper than other goods, enforcing such clauses gives buyers the flexibility to get a lower price by accepting a greater risk of uncompensated defects. For purchases by ordinary consumers and other unsophisticated buyers, however, these arguments are sometimes illusory. Often, the seller presents the disclaimer or remedy limitation in a standardized, take-it-or-leave-it fashion. In addition, it is doubtful whether many consumers read disclaimers and rem-

edy limitations at the time of purchase or would comprehend them if they were read. As a result, there usually is little or no genuine bargaining over disclaimers or remedy limitations in consumer situations. Instead, they are often effectively dictated by a seller with superior size and organization. These observations, however, are less valid where the buyer is a business entity with the capability to engage in genuine bargaining with sellers.

Because the realities surrounding the sale differ from situation to situation, and because some theories of recovery are more hospitable to contractual limitation than others, the law on product liability disclaimers and remedy limitations is complicated. We begin with a lengthy discussion of implied warranty disclaimers. Then we examine disclaimers of express warranty liability, negligence liability, and strict liability before considering remedy limitations separately.

### Implied Warranty Disclaimers

To determine the enforceability of implied warranty disclaimers, we must consider several sets of legal rules.[10] Figure 3 structures the steps in this analysis.

**The Basic Tests of UCC Section 2–316(2)** UCC section 2–316(2) apparently makes it easy for sellers to disclaim the implied warranties of merchantability and fitness for a particular purpose. The section states that to exclude or modify the implied warranty of merchantability, a seller must: (1) use the word *merchantability,* and (2) make the disclaimer conspicuous if it is written. To exclude or modify the implied warranty of fitness, a seller must: (1) use a writing, and (2) make the disclaimer conspicuous. A disclaimer is conspicuous if it is written so that a reasonable person ought to have noticed it. Capital letters, larger type, contrasting type, and contrasting colors usually suffice.

Unlike the fitness warranty disclaimer, a disclaimer of the implied warranty of merchantability can be oral. Also, while disclaimers of the latter warranty must always use the word *merchantability,*

---

[10]The same rules probably apply where a seller tries to modify an implied warranty or to limit its duration.

**FIGURE 3** The Enforceability of Implied Warranty Disclaimers

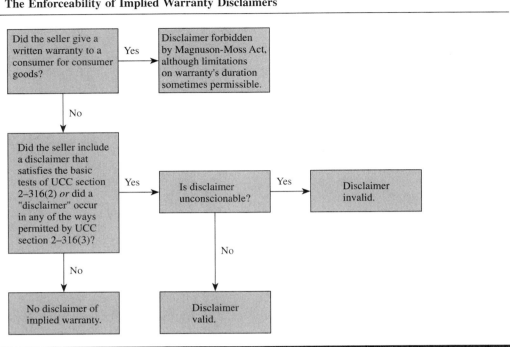

no special language is needed to disclaim the implied warranty of fitness. For example, a conspicuous written statement that "THERE ARE NO WARRANTIES WHICH EXTEND BEYOND THE DESCRIPTION ON THE FACE HEREOF" disclaims the implied warranty of fitness but not the implied warranty of merchantability.

**Other Ways to Disclaim Implied Warranties: UCC Section 2–316(3)** According to UCC section 2–316(3)(a), sellers can also disclaim either implied warranty by using such terms as "with all faults," "as is," and "as they stand." Some courts have held that these terms must be conspicuous to be effective as disclaimers.

UCC section 2–316(3)(b) describes two situations where the buyer's *inspection* of the goods or her *refusal to inspect* can act as a disclaimer. If a buyer examines the goods before the sale and fails to discover a defect that should have been reasonably apparent to her, there can be no implied warranty suit based on that defect. Also, if a seller requests that the buyer examine the goods and the buyer refuses, the buyer cannot base an implied

warranty suit on a defect that would have been reasonably apparent had she made the inspection. The definition of a reasonably apparent defect varies with the buyer's expertise. Unless the defect is blatant, ordinary consumers may have little to fear from section 2–316(3)(b).

Finally, UCC section 2–316(3)(c) says that an implied warranty can be excluded or modified by *course of dealing* (the parties' previous conduct), *course of performance* (the parties' previous conduct under the same contract), or *usage of trade* (any practice regularly observed in the trade). For example, if it is accepted in the local cattle trade that buyers who inspect the seller's cattle and reject certain animals must accept all defects in the cattle actually purchased, such buyers cannot mount an implied warranty suit for those defects.

**Unconscionable Disclaimers** From the previous discussion, it seems that any seller who retains a competent attorney can escape implied warranty liability at will. In fact, however, a seller's ability to disclaim implied warranties is restricted in various ways. One of these restrictions is the doctrine of

**unconscionability** established by UCC section 2–302 and discussed in Chapter 7.

By now, almost all courts apply section 2–302's unconscionability standards to implied warranty disclaimers even though those disclaimers satisfy UCC section 2–316(2). Despite a growing willingness to protect smaller firms that deal with corporate giants, courts still tend to reject unconscionability claims where business parties have contracted in a commercial context. However, implied warranty disclaimers are often declared unconscionable in personal injury suits by ordinary consumers.

**The Impact of Magnuson-Moss**   The Magnuson-Moss Act creates other important limitations on a seller's ability to disclaim implied warranties. If a seller gives a consumer a full warranty on consumer goods, the seller may not disclaim, modify, or limit the duration of any implied warranty. If a limited warranty is given, the seller may not disclaim or modify any implied warranty but may limit its duration to the duration of the limited warranty if this is done conspicuously and if the limitation is not unconscionable. Presumably, however, a seller can still disclaim by refusing to give a written warranty while placing the disclaimer on some other writing.

## Express Warranty Disclaimers

UCC section 2–316(1) says that an express warranty and a disclaimer should be read consistently if possible, but that the disclaimer must yield if such a reading is unreasonable. Because it is normally unreasonable for a seller to exclude with one hand what he has freely and openly promised with the other, it is very difficult to disclaim an express warranty.

## Negligence and Strict Liability Disclaimers

Disclaimers of negligence liability and strict liability are usually ineffective in cases involving ordinary consumers. However, some courts enforce such disclaimers where both parties are business entities that: (1) dealt in a commercial setting, (2) had relatively equal bargaining power, (3) bargained the product's specifications, and (4) negotiated the risk of loss from product defects (e.g., the disclaimer itself).

## Limitation of Remedies

Due to the expense they can create for sellers, consequential damages are the usual target of remedy limitations. Where a limitation of consequential damages succeeds, buyers of the product may suffer. For example, suppose that Dillman buys a computer system for $20,000 under a contract that excludes consequential damages and limits the buyer's remedies to the repair or replacement of defective parts. Suppose also that the system never works properly, causing Dillman to suffer $10,000 in lost profits. If the remedy limitation is enforceable, Dillman could only have the system replaced or repaired by the seller, and could not recover his $10,000 in consequential damages.

In negligence and strict liability cases, the tests for the enforceability of remedy limitations resemble the previous tests for disclaimers. Under the UCC, however, the standards for remedy limitations differ from those for disclaimers.

UCC section 2–719(3) allows the limitation of consequential damages in express and implied warranty cases, but also states that such a limitation may be unconscionable. The section adds that a limitation of consequential damages is quite likely to be unconscionable where the sale is for *consumer goods* and the plaintiff has suffered *personal injury*. Where the loss is "commercial," however, the limitation may or may not be unconscionable. The meaning of commercial loss is unclear. But in cases where it exists, courts must consider the many factors relevant to unconscionability determinations on a case-by-case basis.

## TIME LIMITATIONS

Traditionally, the main time limits on product liability suits have been the applicable contract and tort statutes of limitations. The usual UCC statute of limitations for express and implied warranty claims is four years after the seller offers the defective goods to the buyer (usually, four years after the sale).[11] In negligence and strict liability cases, the

---

[11]Also, in express and implied warranty cases, the buyer must notify the seller of the breach within a reasonable time after the buyer discovers or should have discovered it. There is no notice requirement for negligence and strict liability suits.

applicable tort statute of limitations is generally shorter. But it only begins to run when the defect was or should have been discovered—often, the time of the injury.

Due in part to tort reform, some states now impose various other limitations on the time within which product liability suits must be brought. Often, these limitations apply only to claims for death, personal injury, and property damage, but they override the states' other time limitations where they do apply. Among these additional time limitations are: (1) special statutes of limitations for product liability cases involving death, personal injury, or property damage (e.g., from one to three years after the time the injury or death occurred or should have been discovered); (2) special time limits for "delayed manifestation" injuries such as those resulting from exposure to asbestos; (3) useful safe life defenses (which prevent plaintiffs from suing once the product's "useful safe life" has passed); and (4) statutes of repose (whose aim is similar). Statutes of repose usually run for a 10- to 12-year period that begins when the product is sold to the first buyer not purchasing for resale—usually an ordinary consumer. In a state with a 10-year statute of repose, for example, such parties cannot recover for injuries that occur more than 10 years after they purchased the product causing the injury. This is true even when the suit is begun quickly enough to satisfy the applicable statute of limitations.

## DEFENSES

Many things—for example, the absence of privity or a valid disclaimer—can be considered defenses to a product liability suit. Here, however, our concern is with product liability defenses that involve the plaintiff's behavior.

### The Traditional Defenses

Traditionally, the three main defenses in a product liability suit have been the overlapping trio of product misuse, assumption of risk, and contributory negligence. **Product misuse** (or abnormal use) occurs when the plaintiff uses the product in some unusual, unforeseeable way, and this causes the loss for which she sues. Examples include ignoring the manufacturer's instructions, mishandling the product, and using the product for purposes for which it was not intended. But if the defendant had reason to

foresee the misuse and failed to take reasonable precautions against it, there is no defense. Product misuse is usually available in warranty, negligence, and strict liability cases.

**Assumption of risk** is the plaintiff's voluntary consent to a known danger. It can occur any time the plaintiff willingly exposes herself to a known product hazard—for example, by consuming obviously adulterated food. Like product misuse, assumption of risk ordinarily is a defense in warranty, negligence, and strict liability cases.

**Contributory negligence** is the plaintiff's failure to act with reasonable, prudent, self-protectiveness. In the product liability context, perhaps the most common example is the simple failure to notice a hazardous product defect. Contributory negligence is clearly a defense in a negligence suit, but courts disagree about whether or when it should be a defense in warranty and strict liability cases.

### Comparative Principles

Where they are allowed and proven, the three traditional product liability defenses completely absolve the defendant from liability. Dissatisfaction with this all-or-nothing situation has spurred the increasing use of *comparative* principles in product liability cases.[12] Rather than letting the traditional defenses completely absolve the defendant, courts and legislatures now apportion damages on the basis of relative fault. They do so by requiring that the fact finder establish the plaintiff's and the defendant's percentage shares of the total fault for the injury, and then award the plaintiff his total provable damages times the defendant's percentage share of the fault.

Unsettled questions persist among the states that have adopted comparative principles. First, it is not always clear what kinds of fault will reduce the plaintiff's recovery. However, some state comparative negligence statutes have been read as embracing assumption of risk and product misuse, and state comparative fault statutes usually define fault broadly. Second, comparative principles may assume either *pure* or *mixed* forms. In states that use

---

[12]Some of the newer state statutes, however, speak of comparative *fault*. Although courts and commentators often use the terms *comparative fault* and *comparative negligence* interchangeably, it is not always clear whether comparative negligence embraces forms of fault other than the plaintiff's negligence.

the mixed form, for example, the defendant has a complete defense where the plaintiff is more at fault than the defendant. Finally, there is some uncertainty about the theories of recovery and the types of damage claims to which comparative principles apply.

---

## States v. R. D. Werner Company
### 799 P.2d 427 (Colo. Ct. App. 1990)

Lloyd States was injured after falling from a step ladder at a construction site. He had placed the ladder's front feet (which are on the same side of the ladder as its steps) on a sidewalk, with its rear feet on the surface of an unfinished parking lot that was 6 to 9 inches below the front feet. This was contrary to the manufacturer's instructions for the use of the ladder, which were affixed to it. Then States climbed the ladder, turned on the steps so that his back was to them, and leaned over toward a building. He did so in order to attach a sign to the building with a power wrench while the sign was being held in place by an overhead crane. States pressed against the sign with one hand while using his other hand to apply pressure on the power wrench. As he did so, the ladder moved away from him and he fell.

States sued R. D. Werner Co., the manufacturer of the ladder, in a Colorado trial court under section 402A of the *Restatement (Second) of Torts*. He alleged that a defect in the ladder caused his fall and his injuries. After trial, the jury found for R. D. Werner. States appealed, attacking the trial court's instruction to the jury. The jury had been instructed that: (1) if both a defective product and the plaintiff's conduct contributed to his injury, the plaintiff's recovery must be reduced in proportion to his percentage share of the fault causing the injury; and (2) if the plaintiff's misuse of a product was the sole cause of his injuries, and the alleged product defect played no role in producing them, the seller or manufacturer of that product cannot be liable.

---

**Pierce, Judge**   Misuse of a product by the injured person is a recognized defense to a section 402A action. Misuse concerns an issue of causation and provides a complete defense to liability, regardless of any defective condition, if an unforeseeable and unintended use of the product, and not the alleged defect, caused the plaintiff's injuries. Plaintiff argues that the concept of comparative [fault] is to be applied to all product liability actions. He asserts that the [second] instruction [stated above] erroneously converts the statutory concept of comparative fault into a recovery bar, rather than a damage diminution remedy.

Section 13−21−406 [of the Colorado Revised Statutes] provides in pertinent part:

**Comparative fault as measure of damages.**
(1) In any product liability action, the fault of the person suffering the harm, as well as the fault of all others who are parties to the action for causing the harm, shall be compared by the trier of fact in accordance with this section. The fault of the person suffering the harm shall not bar such person . . . from recovering damages, but the award of damages to such person . . . shall be diminished in proportion to the amount of causal fault attributed to the person suffering the harm.

\* \* \* \* \*

(4) The provisions of [Colorado's comparative negligence statute] do not apply to any product liability action.

We interpret section 13−21−406 to mean that once it has been established that the product is defective, if both the defective product and the injured person's conduct contributed to the injury underlying plaintiff's claim, then the plaintiff's recovery must be reduced by a percentage representing the amount of fault attributable to his own conduct. Here, the jury was properly so instructed. Depending on the facts of the case, the injured person's misuse of the product could constitute comparative fault which would reduce the plaintiff's recovery. However, if the misuse is the *sole* cause of damages, and thus the alleged defect was not a cause thereof, then the plaintiff cannot recover under [section 402A]. Here, the instruction given to the jury provided that if Lloyd's misuse of the ladder, *rather than a defect*, caused Lloyd's injuries, R. D. Werner could not be held legally responsible for those injuries. The trial court did not err in giving this instruction.

**Trial court verdict for R. D. Werner affirmed.**

### PROBLEMS AND PROBLEM CASES

**1.** ▭ *Video Case.* See "TV Repair." Allen, a salesperson for an electronics store, is talking to Arnold, a customer, while Arnold picks up a portable TV and puts it on the counter preparatory to buying it. Allen tells Arnold that he "won't have any problems" with the set because he's "buying the best." He also tells Arnold that "I'm sure you'll enjoy your new set." After purchasing the set, taking it home, and plugging it in, Arnold finds that the set does not work. Assuming that Allen has the authority to bind the store, has the store breached an express warranty to Arnold? Assuming that the store is a merchant and has not disclaimed the implied warranty of merchantability, is it liable on that basis?

**2.** Ewers, who owns a saltwater aquarium with tropical fish, bought several seashells, a piece of coral, and a driftwood branch from the Verona Rock Shop. Just before the purchase, the salesclerk told Ewers that these items were "suitable for saltwater aquariums, if they [are] rinsed." After making the purchase, Ewers took the items home, rinsed them for 20 minutes in a saltwater solution, and put them in his aquarium. Within a week, 17 of his tropical fish died. The "rinsing" required to prevent their deaths is a week-long cleansing process that involves soaking the shells and the coral in boiling water. Suppose that you are Ewers's attorney in his express warranty suit against the shop. Make an argument that the clerk's statement is an express warranty. Make an argument that this warranty was breached.

**3.** Steven Taterka purchased a 1972 Ford Mustang from a Ford dealer in January 1972. In October 1974, after Taterka had put 75,000 miles on the car and Ford's express warranty had expired, he discovered that the tail-light assembly gaskets on his Mustang had been installed in such a way that water was permitted to enter the tail-light assembly, caus-

ing rust to form. Even though the rusting problem was a recurrent one of which Ford was aware, Ford did nothing for Taterka. Is Ford liable to Taterka under the implied warranty of merchantability?

**4.** Cathy Adelman-Tremblay purchased a "Nailene Nail Kit" at a drugstore. The kit included artificial fingernails, a nail sander file, and a tube of cyanoacrylate liquid glue (also known as Super Glue). After attaching the artificial nails to her fingernails with the glue, Adelman-Tremblay experienced pain and eventually suffered the permanent loss of all of her natural fingernails. The cause of the loss was an allergic reaction called "allergic contact dermatitis."

The manufacturer of the Nailene kit had sold more than 1 million such kits, and Adelman-Tremblay's reaction was the only known adverse reaction to the glue. Also, the relevant medical literature indicated that allergic reactions to the glue were virtually impossible. Nonetheless, a few cases of allergic contact dermatitis from exposure to the glue occurred after Adelman-Tremblay suffered her reaction. Is the manufacturer liable in negligence for failing to warn users of the possibility of such an allergic reaction? Can Adelman-Tremblay recover under the implied warranty of merchantability?

**5.** ▭ *Video Case.* See "Software Horror Story." Chuck contacts the Bits and Bites Computer Superstore to get a software package suitable for some customized computer program work he is performing for a client. He tells the store's salesperson that he needs a database management system that he can customize at the source code level. However, there is little discussion of his other needs, including the work Chuck is doing for the client. The salesperson recommends a system called "D-Base Hit" for $649, and Chuck relies on the salesperson's judgment in buying that package. As it turns out, D-Base Hit *can* be modified at the source code level, but it is otherwise unsuitable for the job Chuck is doing. Assuming that Article 2 of the UCC applies, has Bits and Bites breached the implied warranty of fitness for a particular purpose?

**6.** Gari West used Ovulen-28, a birth control medication manufactured by Searle & Company. She claimed that the Ovulen-28 caused her to develop a hepatic adenoma (a benign liver tumor), which eventually ruptured, causing a life-threatening situation. Assuming that the Ovulen-28 actually caused West's problem, what argument can Searle make to avoid the imposition of strict liability under section 402A? *Hint*: Assume that the Ovulen-28 has considerable social utility and cannot feasibly be made safer than it now is.

**7.** Curtis Hagans lost the ring finger of his left hand while operating an industrial table saw manufactured by the Oliver Machinery Company. The saw was originally equipped with a detachable blade guard assembly that would have prevented Hagans's injury had it been attached to the saw while Hagans was working. This assembly was detachable rather than permanently affixed to the saw because many common woodworking functions could not be performed with the assembly in place. Also, the saw exceeded industry safety practices and national and associational safety standards in effect at the time of its manufacture. In addition, few competing manufacturers included blade guards as standard equipment, and none offered a table saw with a permanently affixed blade guard.

Hagans sued Oliver in negligence and under *Restatement (Second) of Torts* section 402A, alleging that the saw was defectively designed because it did not include a permanent blade guard assembly. Did Hagans win? You can assume that injuries of the kind Hagans suffered were foreseeable consequences of manufacturing the saw without a permanent guard, and that Hagans was not careless in his operation of the saw.

**8.** Floyd Roysden had long smoked Camel and Winston cigarettes, both of which are products of the R. J. Reynolds Tobacco Company. In 1983, Roysden's severe peripheral atherosclerotic vascular disease became so severe that his left leg was amputated below the knee. Some medical evidence links this disease to cigarette smoking. Assuming that they were not improperly manufactured and did not contain any dangerous impurities, were the cigarettes Roysden smoked "defective" under section 402A? Were they "unreasonably dangerous?" Does it matter that there is little public knowledge about the link between cigarette smoking and the specific disease from which Roysden suffered (as opposed to the general health risks cigarette smoking creates)?

**9.** Joe Kysar purchased a baler built by the Vermeer Manufacturing Company after a Vermeer sales representative told him that the baler in question would produce bales weighing 3,000 pounds. In fact, the baler never produced a 3,000-pound bale. Kysar eventually sued Vermeer in a Wyoming trial court. The court found Vermeer liable under the UCC, but did not specify the exact basis of its holding. As a remedy, it ordered Vermeer to return the purchase price to Kysar, after which Kysar was to return the baler to Vermeer. Assuming that Vermeer breached either an express warranty or the implied warranty of fitness, was this the proper measure of recovery for defective goods under the UCC? Assume for the sake of argument that Kysar suffered no consequential damages of any kind.

**10.** Arlyn and Rose Spindler were dairy farmers who leased a feed storage silo from Agristor Leasing. The silo was supposed to limit the oxygen reaching the feed and thus to hinder its spoilage. The Spindlers alleged that the silo was defective and that the dairy feed it contained was spoiled as a result. They further alleged that due to the spoilage of the feed, their dairy herd suffered medically and reproductively and their milk production dropped. The Spindlers sued Agristor in negligence and under section 402A for their resulting lost income. What *type* of damages are they claiming? Under the majority rule, can they recover for such damages in negligence or under section 402A? Would your answer be different if the Spindlers had sued for the damage to the *dairy feed* itself? Assume for purposes of argument that both section 402A and negligence suits are possible under this equipment lease.

**11.** ▣ *Video Case.* See "Car Deals." Jake, a car salesman, is discussing a particular car with Jones, a customer at Jake's dealership. Jake tells Jones "you won't find a car like this at any price. This car is a crown jewel." Later, Jake says that he bought the car at an auction in Kentucky. Influenced by these statements, Jones buys the car. The bill of sale conspicuously says that the car is being sold "AS IS," and that no warranties or representations concerning the car have been made or given, except as stated in the bill of sale. Later,

Jones discovers that the car's brakes are so defective that the car is unsafe to drive.

Which, if any, of Jake's statements are express warranties? Which, if any, have been breached here? Does the language in the bill of sale disclaim any express warranties that might exist? Does the language in the bill of sale disclaim the implied warranty of merchantability? Assuming that the implied warranty of merchantability has not been disclaimed, is it breached here?

**12.** Duane Martin, a small farmer, placed an order for cabbage seed with the Joseph Harris Company, a large national producer and distributor of seed. Harris's order form included the following language:

NOTICE TO BUYER: Joseph Harris Company, Inc. warrants that seeds and plants it sells conform to the label descriptions as required by Federal and State seed laws. IT MAKES NO OTHER WARRANTIES, EXPRESS OR IMPLIED, OF MERCHANTABILITY, FITNESS FOR PURPOSE, OR OTHERWISE, AND IN ANY EVENT ITS LIABILITY FOR BREACH OF ANY WARRANTY OR CONTRACT WITH RESPECT TO SUCH SEEDS OR PLANTS IS LIMITED TO THE PURCHASE PRICE OF SUCH SEEDS OR PLANTS.

All of Harris's competitors used similar clauses in their contracts.

After Martin placed his order, and unknown to Martin, Harris stopped using a cabbage seed treatment that had been effective in preventing a certain cabbage fungus. Later, Martin planted the seed he had ordered from Harris, but a large portion of the resulting crop was destroyed by fungus because the seed did not contain the treatment Harris had previously used. Martin sued Harris for his losses under the implied warranty of merchantability.

Which portion of the notice quoted above is an attempted disclaimer of implied warranty liability, and which is an attempted limitation of remedies? Will the disclaimer language disclaim the implied warranty of merchantability under UCC section 2–316(2)? If Martin had sued under the implied warranty of fitness for a particular purpose, would the disclaimer language disclaim that implied warranty as well? Assuming that the disclaimer and the remedy limitation contained the correct legal boilerplate needed to make them effective, what argument could Martin still make to block their operation? What are his chances of success with this argument?

**13.** Moulton purchased a 1969 Ford LTD from Hull-Dobbs, a Ford dealer. His sales contracts with Ford and Hull-Dobbs contained valid disclaimers of the implied warranty of merchantability that satisfied UCC section 2–316(2). One year later, while Moulton was driving his car along an interstate highway, the Ford suddenly veered to the right, jumped the guardrail, and fell 26 feet to the street below. The accident was caused by a defect in the car's steering mechanism, and Moulton was seriously injured. Moulton sued Ford under the implied warranty of merchantability. Ford defended on the basis of its disclaimer. Moulton argued that the disclaimer was invalid in a personal injury case under UCC section 2–719(3), which makes the exclusion of consequential damages unconscionable in a case involving consumer goods and personal injury. Did Moulton's argument succeed?

## Capstone Questions

On February 1, 1994, Dillman & Solomon (D&S), a big, important New York investment firm, bought 10 Eclipse GS-20 computers for its investment analysts to use in their complex number-crunching exercises. The price was $100,000 for the 10 computers. D&S bought the computers from a wholesaler, who had purchased them from the manufacturer, Eclipse Electronics, Inc., an established computer manufacturer. The Eclipse warranty included with each computer contained the following language:

ECLIPSE DISCLAIMS ALL LIABILITY UNDER ANY EXPRESS OR IMPLIED WARRANTY, INCLUDING THE IMPLIED WARRANTY OF MERCHANTABILITY, AND UNDER ANY OTHER THEORY OF PRODUCT LIABILITY RECOVERY. The buyer's recovery for any defect in the computer is limited to the repair or replacement of parts which become defective before one year from the date of sale. ECLIPSE IS NOT LIABLE FOR ANY CONSEQUENTIAL DAMAGES ARISING FROM ANY DEFECT IN THE COMPUTER, WHETHER OCCURRING BEFORE OR AFTER THE ONE-YEAR PERIOD JUST DESCRIBED.

There was no bargaining between Eclipse and D&S over the language just quoted. Indeed, there never was any interaction between D&S and Eclipse over the computers D&S purchased.

On March 1, 1995, one of the computers (which had worked well until then) suffered a serious malfunction. This caused D&S to miscalculate the estimated future price of some bonds that it was planning to sell. As a result, D&S held the bonds when it should have sold them. The loss to the firm was approximately $1 million. D&S wants to sue Eclipse for its losses (the whole-saler has gone bankrupt).

## Required:

Answer the following and give reasons for your conclusions.

1. Is D&S likely to recover under section 402A?
2. Analyze D&S's ability to satisfy the elements of the following theories: express warranty, the implied warranty of merchantability, and the implied warranty of fitness for a particular purpose. For now, don't consider Eclipse's attempted disclaimer of these warranties.
3. Assuming that D&S could satisfy the elements of each of the three theories listed in question 2, does Eclipse's disclaimer negate those warranties?
4. Under which version(s) of UCC section 2–318 would Eclipse have a no-privity defense if a court stuck to the plain meaning of the relevant version? How would Eclipse's asserted no-privity defense fare under the privity *factors* discussed in the text?
5. Which language used by Eclipse is a remedy limitation rather than a disclaimer? Analyze its chances of success under the UCC.

CHAPTER

1 3

# PERFORMANCE OF

# SALES CONTRACTS

**INTRODUCTION**

*In the two previous chapters, we discussed the formation and terms of sales contracts, including those terms concerning express and implied warranties. In this chapter, the focus is on the legal rules that govern the performance of contracts. Among the topics covered are the basic obligations of the buyer and seller with respect to delivery and payment, the rights of the parties when the goods delivered do not conform to the contract, and the circumstances that may excuse the performance of a party's contractual obligations.*

## GENERAL RULES

The parties to a contract for the sale of goods are obligated to perform the contract according to its terms. The Uniform Commercial Code (UCC or Code) gives the parties great flexibility in deciding between themselves how they will perform a contract. The practices in the trade or business as well as any past dealings between the parties may supplement or explain the contract. The Code gives both the buyer and the seller certain rights, and it also sets out what is expected of them on points that they did not deal with in their contract. It should be kept in mind that the Code changes basic contract law in a number of respects.

### Good Faith

The buyer and seller must act in **good faith** in the performance of a sales contract [1–203].[1] Good faith is defined to mean "honesty in fact" in performing the duties assumed in the contract or in carrying out the transaction [1–201(19)]. Thus, if the contract requires the seller to select an assortment of goods for the buyer, the selection must be made in good faith; the seller should pick out a reasonable assortment [2–311]. It would not, for example, be good faith to include only unusual sizes or colors.

---

[1]The numbers in brackets refer to sections of the Uniform Commercial Code.

## Course of Dealing

The terms in the contract between the parties are the primary means for determining the obligations of the buyer and seller. The meaning of those terms may be explained by looking at any performance that has already taken place. For example, a contract may call for periodic deliveries of goods. If the seller has made a number of deliveries without objection by the buyer, the way the deliveries were made shows how the parties intended them to be made. Similarly, if there were any past contracts between the parties, the way the parties interpreted those contracts is relevant to the interpretation of the present contract. If there is a conflict between the express terms of the contract and the past course of dealing between the parties, the express terms of the contract prevail [1–205(4)].

## Usage of Trade

In many kinds of businesses, there are customs and practices of the trade that are known by people in the business and that are usually assumed by parties to a contract for goods of that type. Under the Code, the parties and courts may use these trade customs and practices—known as usage of trade—in interpreting a contract [2—202; 1–205]. If there is a conflict between the express terms of the contract and trade usage, the express terms prevail [1–205(4)].

The *Weisz Graphics v. Peck Industries* case illustrates how a court may consider the terms of a contract, the course of dealing between the parties, and trade usage in determining the interpretation of a contract between merchants.

---

## WEISZ GRAPHICS DIVISION OF THE FRED B. JOHNSON CO., INC. V. PECK INDUSTRIES, INC.
### 403 S.E.2d 146 (S.C. Ct. App. 1991)

Weisz Graphics is a custom manufacturer and seller of decals, markings, and other graphic materials and competes in a national market. Weisz manufactures its products to customer specifications based on blueprints, samples, art, or mechanical drawings. It manufactures only to order and does not maintain a general inventory. However, it regularly engages in what are known as "release programs" with its customer; such programs are common in the industry. Under a release program, Weisz manufactures a large quantity of goods to customer order, then warehouses the goods for the customer. As the customer needs the goods, Weisz releases them in specified lots and bills the buyer when it ships the goods. Release programs in the industry are generally limited to one year, due in part to the shelf life of the goods.

Peck Industries, a manufacturer of commercial signs for national and Memphis, Tennessee, accounts, uses pressure sensitive vinyl letters, numbers, and other products. Beginning in 1985, Peck began purchasing some of its requirements from Weisz; some contracts were for immediate manufacture and delivery while others were for extended delivery under a release program. A November 1985 order (P.O. 4426) provided: "BREAK UP INTO MULTIPLE SHIPMENTS." Weisz's acknowledgment contained the following shipment term: "On Releases Bill & Ship on release for 12 months." In April 1986, Peck sent a purchase order (P.O. 5885) for a quantity of goods that provided "TO BE BILLED AND SHIPPED AS RELEASED." Weisz sent back its standard acknowledgment form on which a clerk had typed "On Releases over 12 months." Other orders (P.O. 4037 and P.O. 4426)) were placed by Peck that stated on their face: "ORDER AS NEEDED FOR A PERIOD OF 1 YEAR." In each case, Weisz immediately manufactured the items ordered and over a period of a year released and billed shipments at Peck's request. At the end of the 12 months, Weisz refused to make further shipments until Peck paid in full the remaining balance on the shipment. Peck refused to pay, choosing instead to obtain its requirements from other manufacturers at higher prices. Weisz then brought suit for the balance due on the goods sold to Peck.

**Bell, Judge**     Section 1–205(3) states:

A course of dealing between parties and any usage of trade in the . . . trade in which they are engaged or should be aware [sic] give particular meaning to supplement or qualify terms of the agreement.

Similarly, section 2–208(1) provides that a course of performance between the parties which is accepted or acquiesced in without objection by a party with opportunity to object is relevant to determine the meaning of the agreement.

As to Purchase Order 4037, Peck itself specified that delivery was on release for one year. There is no evidence that Weisz's acknowledgment contained a similar notation. However, Weisz did not object and began delivering the goods on release.

Purchase Order 4426 specified multiple shipments, but no release period. Weisz's uncontradicted evidence showed that a time limitation is standard in the industry. It also showed that its prior course of dealing with Peck had been to ship on twelve-month release. None of its release contracts with Peck exceeded twelve months. Moreover, Peck accepted performance of Order 4426 without objection. Therefore, under sections 1–205(3) and 2–208(1), the twelve-month release period that supplemented the express provisions of the written form was part of the contract.

The same is true of Purchase Order 5885. Like Purchase Order 4426, it specified no release period. However, its express provisions were supplemented by trade usage and prior course of dealing which established the twelve month release period as a term of the contract.

In the alternative, the twelve-month release period became a term of the contract under section 2–207(2). In response to Purchase Order 4426 and 5885, Weisz's acknowledgment forms added a twelve-month release period. Neither of Peck's orders expressly limited Weisz's acceptance to the express terms of its standard form. Nor did Peck give Weisz a notification of objection to the acknowledgments. Instead, Peck began accepting performance of the contract without objection. Finally, the twelve-month limit was not a material alteration of the contract. Because it conformed to existing trade usage and prior course of dealing between the parties, it did not result in unreasonable surprise or hardship. Accordingly, both contracts incorporated a term for delivery on twelve-month release. Payment in full of the balance on the purchase price was due at the end of the twelfth month.

**Judgment for Weisz.**

## Modification

Under the Code, consideration is not required to support a modification or rescission of a contract for the sale of goods. However, the parties may specify in their agreement that modification or rescission must be in writing, in which case a signed writing is necessary for enforcement of any modification to the contract or its rescission [2–209].

## Waiver

In a contract that entails a number of instances of partial performance (such as deliveries or payments) by one party, the other party must be careful to object to any late deliveries or payments. If the other party does not object, it may waive its rights to cancel the contract if other deliveries or payments are late [2–208(3), 2–209(4)]. For example, a contract calls for a fish market to deliver fish to a supermarket every Thursday and for the supermarket to pay on delivery. If the fish market regularly delivers the fish on Friday and the supermarket does not object, the supermarket will be unable to cancel the contract for that reason. Similarly, if the supermarket does not pay cash but sends a check the following week, then unless the fish market objects, it will not be able to assert the late payments as grounds for later canceling the contract. A party that has waived rights to a portion of the contract not yet performed may retract the waiver by giving reasonable notice to the other party that strict performance will be required. The retraction of the waiver is effective unless it would be unjust because of a material change of position by the other party in reliance on the waiver [2–209(5)].

## Assignment

Under the Code, the buyer and/or the seller may generally delegate their duties to someone else. If there is a strong reason for having the original party perform the duties, perhaps because the quality of the performance might differ otherwise, the parties may not delegate their duties. Also, they may not delegate their duties if the parties agree in the contract that there is to be no assignment of duties. However, they may assign rights to receive performance—for example, the right to receive goods or payment [2–210].

## DELIVERY

### Basic Obligation

The basic duty of the seller is to deliver the goods called for by the contract. The basic duty of the buyer is to accept and pay for the goods if they conform to the contract [2–301]. The buyer and seller may agree that the goods are to be delivered in several lots or installments. If there is no such agreement, then a single delivery of all the goods must be made. Where delivery is to be made in lots, the seller may demand the price of each lot upon delivery unless there has been an agreement for the extension of credit [2–307].

### Place of Delivery

The buyer and seller may agree on the place where the goods will be delivered. If no such agreement is made, then the goods are to be delivered at the seller's place of business. If the seller does not have a place of business, then delivery is to be made at his home. If the goods are located elsewhere than the seller's place of business or home, the place of delivery is the place where the goods are located [2–308].

### Seller's Duty of Delivery

The seller's basic obligation is to tender delivery of goods that conform to the contract with the buyer. Tender of delivery means that the seller must make the goods available to the buyer. This must be done during reasonable hours and for a reasonable period of time, so that the buyer can take possession of the goods [2–503]. The contract of sale may require

the seller to merely ship the goods to the buyer but not to deliver the goods to the buyer's place of business. If this is the case, the seller must put the goods into the possession of a carrier, such as a trucking company or a railroad. The seller must also make a reasonable contract with the carrier to take the goods to the buyer. Then, the seller must notify the buyer that the goods have been shipped [2–504]. Shipment terms were discussed in Chapter 11, Formation and Terms of Sales Contracts.

If the seller does not make a reasonable contract for delivery or notify the buyer and a material delay or loss results, the buyer has the right to reject the shipment. Suppose the goods are perishable, such as fresh produce, and the seller does not ship them in a refrigerated truck or railroad car. If the produce deteriorates in transit, the buyer can reject the produce on the ground that the seller did not make a reasonable contract for shipping it.

In some situations, the goods sold may be in the possession of a bailee such as a warehouse. If the goods are covered by a negotiable warehouse receipt, the seller must indorse the receipt and give it to the buyer [2–503(4)(a)]. This enables the buyer to obtain the goods from the warehouse. Such a situation exists when grain being sold is stored at a grain elevator. The law of negotiable documents of title, including warehouse receipts, is discussed in Chapter 26, Checks and Documents of Title.

If the goods in the possession of a bailee are not covered by a negotiable warehouse receipt, then the seller must notify the bailee that it has sold the goods to the buyer and must obtain the bailee's consent to hold the goods for delivery to the buyer or release of the goods to the buyer. The risk of loss as to the goods remains with the seller until the bailee agrees to hold them for the buyer [2–503(4)(b)].

## INSPECTION AND PAYMENT

### Buyer's Right of Inspection

Normally, the buyer has the right to inspect the goods before he accepts or pays for them. The buyer and seller may agree on the time, place, and manner in which the buyer will inspect the goods. If no agreement is made, then the buyer may inspect the goods at any reasonable time and place and in any reasonable manner [2–513(1)].

If the shipping terms are cash on delivery (COD), then the buyer must pay for the goods before inspecting them unless they are marked "Inspection Allowed." However, if it is obvious even without inspection that the goods do not conform to the contract, the buyer may reject them without paying for them first [2–512(1)(a)]. For example, if a farmer contracted to buy a bull and the seller delivered a cow, the farmer would not have to pay for it. The fact that a buyer may have to pay for goods before inspecting them does not deprive the buyer of remedies against the seller if the goods do not conform to the contract [2–512(2)].

If the goods conform to the contract, the buyer must pay the expenses of inspection. However, if the goods are nonconforming, he may recover his inspection expenses from the seller [2–513(2)].

## Payment

The buyer and seller may agree in their contract that the price of the goods is to be paid in money or in other goods, services, or real property. If all or part of the price of goods is payable in real property, then only the transfer of goods is covered by the law of sales of goods. The transfer of the real property is covered by the law of real property [2–304].

The contract may provide that the goods are sold on credit to the buyer and that the buyer has a period of time to pay for them. If there is no agreement for extending credit to the buyer, the buyer must pay for them upon delivery. The buyer usually can inspect goods before payment except where the goods are shipped COD, in which case the buyer must pay for them before inspecting them.

Unless the seller demands cash, the buyer may pay for the goods by personal check or by any other method used in the ordinary course of business. If the seller demands cash, the seller must give the buyer a reasonable amount of time to obtain it. If payment is made by check, the payment is conditional on the check being honored by the bank when it is presented for payment [2–511(3)]. If the bank refuses to pay the check, the buyer has not satisfied the duty to pay for the goods. In that case, the buyer does not have the right to retain the goods and must give them back to the seller.

## ACCEPTANCE, REVOCATION, AND REJECTION

### Acceptance

**Acceptance** of goods occurs when a buyer, after having a reasonable opportunity to inspect them, either indicates that he will take them or fails to reject them. To **reject** goods, the buyer must notify the seller of the rejection and specify the defect or nonconformity. If a buyer treats the goods as if he owns them, the buyer is considered to have accepted them [2–606].

For example, Ace Appliance delivers a new color television set to Baldwin. Baldwin has accepted the set if, after trying it and finding it to be in working order, she says nothing to Ace or tells Ace that she will keep it. Even if the set is defective, Baldwin is considered to have accepted it if she does not give Ace timely notice that she does not want to keep it because it is not in working order. If she takes the set on a vacation trip even though she knows that it does not work properly, this is also an acceptance. In the latter case, her use of the television set would be inconsistent with its rejection and the return of ownership to the seller.

If a buyer accepts any part of a **commercial unit** of goods, he is considered to have accepted the whole unit [2–606(2)]. A commercial unit is any unit of goods that is treated by commercial usage as a single whole. It can be a single article (such as a machine), a set or quantity of articles (such as a dozen, bale, gross, or carload), or any other unit treated as a single whole [2–105(6)]. Thus, if a bushel of apples is a commercial unit, then a buyer purchasing 10 bushels of apples who accepts 8½ bushels is considered to have accepted 9 bushels.

### Effect of Acceptance

Once a buyer has accepted goods, he cannot later reject them unless at the time they were accepted, the buyer had reason to believe that the nonconformity would be cured. By accepting goods, the buyer does not forfeit or waive remedies against the seller for any nonconformities in the goods. However, if the buyer wishes to hold the seller responsible, he must give the seller *timely notice* that the goods are nonconforming.

The buyer is obligated to pay for goods that are accepted. If the buyer accepts all of the goods sold, she is, of course, responsible for the full purchase price. If the buyer accepts only part of the goods, she must pay for that part at the contract rate [2−607(1)].

## Revocation of Acceptance

Under certain circumstances, a buyer may **revoke** or undo the acceptance. A buyer may revoke acceptance of nonconforming goods where: (1) the nonconformity *substantially impairs* the value of the goods and (2) the buyer accepted them without knowledge of the nonconformity because of the difficulty of discovering the nonconformity, or the buyer accepted the goods because of the seller's *assurances* that it would cure the defect [2−608(1)].

The buyer must exercise her right to revoke acceptance within a reasonable time after the buyer discovers or should have discovered the nonconformity. Revocation is not effective until the buyer notifies the seller of the intention to revoke acceptance. After a buyer revokes acceptance, her rights are the same as they would have been if the goods had been rejected when delivery was offered [2−608].

The right to revoke acceptance could arise, for example, where Arnold buys a new car from Dealer. While driving the car home, Arnold discovers that it has a seriously defective transmission. When she returns the car to Dealer, Dealer promises to repair it, so Arnold decides to keep the car. If the dealer does not fix the transmission after repeated efforts to fix it, Arnold could revoke her acceptance on the grounds that the nonconformity substantially impairs the value of the car, that she took delivery of the car without knowledge of the nonconformity, and that her acceptance was based on Dealer's assurances that he would fix the car. Similarly, revocation of acceptance might be involved where a serious problem with the car not discoverable by inspection shows up in the first month's use.

Revocation must occur prior to any *substantial change* in the goods, however, such as serious damage in an accident or wear and tear from using them for a period of time. What constitutes a "substantial impairment in value" and when there has been a "substantial change in the goods" are questions that courts frequently have to decide when an attempted revocation of acceptance results in a lawsuit. The case below of *North River Homes, Inc. v. Bosarge* illustrates a number of the issues that arise in situations where a buyer is seeking to revoke her acceptance.

---

### North River Homes, Inc. v. Bosarge
**17 UCC Rep.2d 121 (Miss. Sup. Ct. 1992)**

On August 20, 1983, Elmer and Martha Bosarge purchased from J & J Mobile Home Sales a furnished mobile home manufactured by North River Homes. The mobile home, described by a J & J salesperson as the "Cadillac" of mobile homes, cost $23,900. Upon moving into their new home, the Bosarges immediately discovered defect after defect. The defects included a bad water leak that caused water to run all over the trailer and into the insulation, which in turn caused the trailer's underside to balloon downward, loose moldings, a warped dishwasher door, a warped bathroom door, holes in the walls, a defective heating and cooling system, cabinets with chips and holes in them, furniture that fell apart, rooms that remained moldy and mildewed, a closet that leaked rainwater, and spaces between the doors and windows and their frames that allowed the elements to come in. The Bosarges had not been able to spot the defects before taking delivery because they viewed the mobile home at night on J & J's lot and there was no light on in the mobile home.

The Bosarges immediately and repeatedly notified North River Homes of the defects, but it failed to repair the home satisfactorily. In November 1983, the Bosarges informed North River of their decision to revoke their acceptance of the defective home. On some occasions, repairmen came but did not attempt to make repairs, saying they would come back. Other times, the repairs were inadequate. For example, while looking for the water leak, a repairman cut open the bottom of the mobile home and then taped it back together with masking tape that failed to hold and resulted in the floor bowing out. Another repairman inadvertenly punctured a septic line and did not properly repair the puncture, resulting in a permanent stench. Other repairmen simply left things off at the home, such as a new dishwasher door and a countertop, saying they did not have time to make the repairs.

In June 1984, the Bosarges provided North River with an extensive list of problems that had not been corrected. When they did not receive a satisfactory response, they sent a letter on October 4, 1984, saying they would make no further payments. North River made no further efforts to correct the problems. In March 1986, the Bosarges's attorney wrote to North River formally revoking acceptance of the mobile home because of its substantially impaired value, tendering the mobile home back to it, and advising North River that it could pick the home up at its earliest convenience. They then brought a lawsuit requesting return of the purchase price and seeking damages for breach of various warranties.

---

**Prather, Justice**    When a consumer has accepted goods and subsequently discovers defects or a breach of implied merchantability, the consumer may invoke statutory and case law which conditions revocation of acceptance on:

(1) a nonconformity [or defect] which substantially impairs the value of the "lot or commercial unit;"
(2) an acceptance
    (a) (with discovery of the defect) on the reasonable assumption that the nonconformity [or defect] would be cured or
    (b) (without discovery) reasonably induced by the difficulty of the discovery or by the seller's assurances;
(3) revocation within a reasonable time after the nonconformity [or defect] was discovered or should have been discovered; and
(4) revocation before a substantial change occurs in the condition of the goods not caused by their own defects.

Once the consumer has properly notified the seller of his or her intent to revoke acceptance, the seller has a right to attempt to cure the alleged defect. This right is not unlimited; that is Mississippi law does not permit a seller to postpone revocation in perpetuity by fixing everything that goes wrong with the good. "There is a time when enough is enough"—when a consumer no longer must tolerate or endure a seller's repeated (though good faith) attempts to cure the defect. As aptly stated by a Florida Court of Appeals:

The buyer . . . is not bound to permit the seller to tinker with the article indefinitely in the hope it may ultimately be made to comply with the warranty. At some point in time, if major problems continue . . ., it must become obvious to all people that a particular [article] simply cannot be repaired or parts replaced so that the same is made free of defect.

When the "time has come," the consumer may revoke once and for all.

North River contends that the Bosarges' failure to move out of their mobile home after "rejecting it" constituted an exercise of ownership (or dominion) and waiver of their right to revoke acceptance. The Bosarges did not move out of their home in November 1983 and in October 1984—the dates when they notified North River of their intention to revoke acceptance—because they were repeatedly assured that the defects would be repaired. Their mistaken belief that North River would fulfill its assurances to repair the defects is but one reason why the Bosarges did not move out of their home. Another reason is simple and understandable:

When you tie up all your savings into purchasing a home, you cannot take it and park it somewhere. You have to live in it until you can get the people to clear your lot so you can put another one on it. Its just not like a car you can drive on the lot and hand them the keys and say, its yours. (Testimony of Martha Bosarge.)

North River's contention that the Bosarges should have moved out reflects ignorance of case law which requires a consumer, who expresses an intention to revoke acceptance, to provide a seller with a reasonable attempt to cure the defect. The evidence unequivocally shows that the Bosarges complied with this law; indeed, one could arguably contend that they complied to an unnecessary extent. But the Bosarges' great patience is not surprising in view of their financial inability to move elsewhere.

Any excessive or unreasonable use of the home by the Bosarges may be remedied through quantum meruit recovery—*not* through ineffectuation of revocation.

North River also contends that the Bosarges "failed to prove that the mobile home in question was substantially impaired." The Bosarges counter "that the evidence showed that their North River trailer was literally falling apart." The Bosarges

testimony revealed that each North River repairman who visited their home admitted to the Bosarges that their home was so defective that it "ought to be replaced." Notably, Ronnie Wilson, a HUD mobile home inspector provided testimony which is also supportive of the jury's finding; When asked if he would live in that kind of home (heating, cooling, leaking roof, mildew, ice), he answered "No, sir, my wife wouldn't let me, sir."

In sum the record is replete with evidence to support the jury's finding that the Bosarges' home was substantially impaired.

**Judgment for Bosarges affirmed.**

## Buyer's Rights on Improper Delivery

If the goods delivered by the seller do not conform to the contract, the buyer has several options. The buyer can (1) reject all of the goods, (2) accept all of them, or (3) accept any commercial units and reject the rest [2–601]. The buyer, however, cannot accept only part of a commercial unit and reject the rest. The buyer must pay for the units accepted at the price per unit provided in the contract.

Where the contract calls for delivery of the goods in separate installments, the buyer's options are more limited. The buyer may reject an installment delivery only if the nonconformity *substantially affects the value* of that delivery and *cannot be corrected* by the seller in a timely fashion. If the nonconformity is relatively minor, the buyer must accept the installment. The seller may offer to replace the defective goods or give the buyer an allowance in the price to make up for the nonconformity [2–612].

Where the nonconformity or defect in one installment impairs the value of the whole contract, the buyer may treat it as a breach of the whole contract but must proceed carefully so as not to reinstate the remainder of the contract [2–612(3)].

## Rejection

If a buyer has a basis for rejecting a delivery of goods, the buyer must act within a *reasonable time*

after delivery. The buyer must also give the seller *notice* of the rejection, preferably in writing [2–602]. The buyer should be careful to state all of the defects on which he is basing the rejection, including all of the defects that a reasonable inspection would disclose. This is particularly important if these are defects that the seller might cure (remedy) and the time for delivery has not expired. In that case, the seller may notify the buyer that he intends to redeliver conforming goods.

If the buyer fails to state in connection with his rejection a particular defect that is ascertainable by reasonable inspection, he cannot use the defect to justify his rejection if the seller could have cured the defect had he been given reasonable notice of it. In a transaction taking place between merchants, the seller has, after rejection, a right to a written statement of all the defects in the goods on which the buyer bases his right to reject, and the buyer may not later assert defects not listed in justification of his rejection [2–605].

In the case that follows, *Tai Wah Radio Manufactory Ltd. v. Ambassador Imports Ltd.,* the buyer kept a shipment of defective goods to use as leverage against the seller concerning a claim for damages on an earlier defective shipment. The court found that the buyer had accepted the shipment because it had not rejected it in a timely fashion.

## Tai Wah Radio Manufactory Ltd. v. Ambassador Imports Ltd.
### 3 UCC Rep.2d 117 (S.D.N.Y. 1987)

Tai Wah Manufactory Ltd., a Hong Kong company, is a manufacturer of electronic goods. Ambassador Imports Ltd., a New York company, is an importer and wholesale distributor of various products, including electronic goods. The two companies had been doing business with each other for about five years when in February 1985 Ambassador placed an order with Tai Wah for 2,000 stereo cassette recorders, which were delivered to and accepted by Ambassador in Los Angeles on April 15. On April 4, Ambassador placed another order for cassette recorders with Tai Wah, this time for 2,040 units.

Ambassador claimed that in May it began to receive complaints from its customers about the recorders from the first shipment, and several hundred units were returned to Ambassador before June 24. On May 31 and June 7, Ambassador sent telexes to Tai Wah advising it of problems with the quality of the plastic in the dial and with breakage of the cassette door, and asking that the problem be corrected for all future orders. On June 1, Tai Wah indicated that it was trying to improve the quality of the plastic and that future orders would be corrected. It also advised Ambassador that the second shipment had been sent on May 24. Despite the complaints about the quality of the recorders, Ambassador picked up the second shipment of recorders in Los Angeles on June 24. It made no effort to inspect the goods. On June 29, it notified Tai Wah that it did not want the second shipment, that it had picked it up only to hold as collateral to ensure that it would be compensated for its damages on the first shipment, and that it would return the second shipment when such compensation was arranged.

Tai Wah then brought a lawsuit against Ambassador to recover the contract price of the second shipment of recorders.

---

**Motley, District Judge**    Tai Wah asserts that it is entitled to judgment as a matter of law because Ambassador did not timely reject the second shipment of recorders as required by the Uniform Commercial Code. Ambassador contends that the notice of defects in the first shipment constituted notice of defects in the second shipment.

It is undisputed that Ambassador accepted the second shipment for the sole purpose of negotiating a settlement with Tai Wah concerning money owing on the first shipment. Ambassador obviously did not intend to pay for the second shipment with the knowledge that it would reject the recorders. In addition, it knew that the recorders were allegedly defective at the time of acceptance.

Section 2–608 of the UCC provides:

(1) The buyer may revoke his acceptance of a lot or commercial unit whose non-conformity substantially impairs its value to him if he has accepted it
    (a) on the reasonable assumption that its non-conformity would be cured and it has not been seasonably cured; or
    (b) without discovery of such non-conformity if his acceptance was reasonably induced either by the difficulty of discovery before acceptance or by the seller's assurances.

Thus, a buyer with knowledge that goods are defective when he accepts them does not lose his right to revoke the acceptance if the acceptance was based on the reasonable assumption that the non-conformity would be seasonably cured but the cure was not effected. In addition, acceptance may be revoked if the buyer, without discovering the non-conformity, was reasonably induced to accept the goods either by the difficulty of discovery before acceptance or by the seller's assurances. Neither of these exceptions is applicable to this case. When Ambassador accepted the second shipment of cassette recorders, it had knowledge of the recorder's allegedly defective nature. Ambassador did not assume Tai Wah would cure the nonconformity. Thus, Ambassador did not have the right to revoke the contract for the second shipment.

Although Ambassador may not have intended to keep the products when it took possession of the second shipment, this does not change the result. From the undisputed facts in this case, it is obvious that Ambassador was attempting to engage in a form of commercial "kidnapping" to compel Tai Wah to resolve its differences with Ambassador. Ambassador, instead of taking possession of the second shipment of recorders, should have rejected the second shipment. Tai Wah, in telexes, had advised Ambassador, prior to Ambassador's receipt of the second shipment, that the recorders had been shipped prior to Tai Wah's receipt of Ambassador's first complaints about the first shipment and prior to Tai Wah having the opportunity to make the needed corrections. Thus, Ambassador, with knowledge of the allegedly defective nature of the goods, should have rejected them. Accordingly, Tai Wah is entitled to payment for the second shipment.

However, if it is established at trial that Ambassador complained in a timely manner about the defects in the goods, Ambassador is entitled to damages for breach of warranty—the difference between the contract price of the recorders and their actual value. This would be an offset against the money Ambassador owes Tai Wah.

**Partial summary judgment awarded to Tai Wah.**

---

### CONCEPT REVIEW
## ACCEPTANCE, REVOCATION, AND REJECTION

| | |
|---|---|
| **Acceptance** | 1. Occurs when buyer, having had a reasonable opportunity to inspect goods, either (a) indicates he will take them or (b) fails to reject them.<br>2. If buyer accepts any part of a commercial unit, he is considered to have accepted the whole unit.<br>3. If buyer accepts goods, he cannot later reject them *unless* at the time they were accepted buyer had reason to believe that the nonconformity would be cured.<br>4. Buyer is obligated to pay for goods that are accepted. |
| **Revocation** | 1. Buyer may revoke acceptance of nonconforming goods where (a) the nonconformity *substantially impairs the value* of the goods and, (b) buyer accepted the goods without knowledge of the nonconformity because of the difficulty of discovering the nonconformity *or* buyer accepted because of assurances by the seller.<br>2. Right to revoke must be exercised within a *reasonable* time after buyer discovers *or* should have discovered the nonconformity.<br>3. Revocation must be invoked before there is any *substantial* change in the goods.<br>4. Revocation is not effective until buyer notifies seller of his intent to revoke acceptance. |
| **Rejection** | 1. Where the goods delivered do not conform to the contract, buyer may (a) reject all of the goods, (b) accept all of the goods, or (c) accept any commercial unit and reject the rest. Buyer must pay for goods accepted.<br>2. Where the goods are to be delivered in installments, an installment delivery may be rejected *only if* the nonconformity substantially affects the value of that delivery and cannot be corrected by the seller.<br>3. Buyer must act within a reasonable time after delivery. |

## Right to Cure

If the seller has some reason to believe that the buyer would accept nonconforming goods, then the seller can take a reasonable time to reship conforming goods. The seller has this opportunity even if the original time for delivery has expired. For example,

Ace Manufacturing contracts to sell 200 red baseball hats to Sam's Sporting Goods, with delivery to be made by April 1. On March 1, Sam's receives a package from Ace containing 200 blue baseball hats and refuses to accept them. Ace can notify Sam's that it intends to cure the improper delivery by supplying 200 red hats, and it has until April 1 to deliver the red hats to Sam's. If Ace thought that Sam's would accept the blue hats because on past shipments Sam's did not object to the substitution of blue hats for red, then Ace has a reasonable time even after April 1 to deliver the red hats [2–508].

If the buyer wrongfully rejects goods, she is liable to the seller for breach of the sales contract [2–602(3)].

## Buyer's Duties after Rejection

If the buyer is a merchant, then the buyer owes certain duties concerning the goods that he rejects. First, the buyer must follow any reasonable instructions that the seller gives concerning disposition of the goods. The seller, for example, might request that the rejected goods be shipped back to the seller. If the goods are perishable or may deteriorate rapidly, then the buyer must make a reasonable effort to sell the goods. The seller must reimburse the buyer for any expenses that the buyer incurs in carrying out the seller's instructions or in trying to resell perishable goods. In reselling goods, the buyer must act reasonably and in good faith [2–603(2) and (3)].

If the rejected goods are not perishable or if the seller does not give the buyer instructions, then the buyer has several options. First, the buyer can store the goods for the seller. Second, the buyer can reship them to the seller. Third, the buyer can resell them for the seller's benefit. If the buyer resells the goods, the buyer may keep his expenses and a reasonable commission on the sale. If the buyer stores the goods, the buyer should exercise care in handling them. The buyer also must give the seller a reasonable time to remove the goods [2–604].

If the buyer is not a merchant, then her obligation after rejection is to hold the goods with reasonable care for a sufficient time to give the seller an opportunity to remove them. The buyer is not obligated to ship the goods back to the seller [2–602]. The case that follows, *Lykins Oil Company v. Fekkos,* illustrates these principles.

---

### LYKINS OIL COMPANY V. FEKKOS

**507 N.E.2d 795 (Ohio Ct. Comm. Pl. 1986)**

Haralambos Fekkos purchased from Lykins Sales & Service a Yammar Model 165D, 16-horsepower diesel tractor and various implements. On Saturday, April 27, Fekkos gave Lykins a check for the purchase price, less trade-in, of $6,596, and had the items delivered to his residence. The next day, while attempting to use the tractor for the first time, Fekkos discovered it was defective. The defects included a dead battery requiring jump starts, overheating while pulling either the mower or the tiller, missing safety shields over the muffler and the power takeoff, and a missing water pump.

On Monday, Fekkos contacted Lykins's sales representative, who believed his claims to be true and agreed to have the tractor picked up from Fekkos's residence; Fekkos also stopped payment on his check. Fekkos placed the tractor with the tiller attached in his front yard as near as possible to the front door without driving it onto the landscaped area closest to the house. Fekkos left the tractor on his lawn because his driveway was broken up for renovation and his garage was inaccessible, and because the tractor would have to be jump started by Lykins's employees when they picked it up. On Tuesday, Fekkos went back to Lykins's store to purchase an Allis-Chalmers tractor and reminded Lykins's employees that the Yammar tractor had not been picked up and remained on his lawn.

On Wednesday, May 1, at 6:00 A.M., Fekkos discovered that the tractor was missing although the tiller had been unhitched and remained in the yard. Later that day, Lykins picked up the remaining implements. The theft was reported to the police. On several occasions, Fekkos was assured that Lykins's insurance would cover the stolen tractor, that it was Lykins's fault for not picking it up, and that Fekkos had nothing to worry about. However, Lykins subsequently brought suit against Fekkos to recover the purchase price of the Yammar tractor. Both Lykins and Fekkos moved for summary judgment in their favor.

---

**Watson, Judge**   Lykins argues in support of its motion for summary judgment that section 2–602 applies to this matter. Subsections 2(a) and (b) provide that:

Subject to the provisions of the two following sections on rejected goods:

(a) after rejection any exercise of ownership by the buyer with respect to any commercial unit is wrongful as against the seller; and

(b) if the buyer has before rejection taken physical possession of goods in which he does not have a security interest under the provisions of this Article (subsection (3) of Section 2–711), he is under a duty after rejection to hold them with reasonable care at the seller's disposition for a sufficient time to permit the seller to remove them.

Lykins argues that because Fekkos was already in possession of the tractor at the time he rejected it, he had the duty to hold it for a sufficient length of time for Lykins to remove it from Fekkos's premises. Lykins asserts that Fekkos breached this duty and is liable to Lykins because the tractor was unavailable to be picked up by Lykins on May 1, the day after the purchase order was cancelled and two days after Fekkos rejected the tractor.

On the other hand, Fekkos, in support of his motion for summary judgment argues that section 2–510 controls the matter. Section 2–510(1) provides:

(1) Where a tender or delivery of goods so fails to conform to the contract so as to give a right of rejection the risk of their loss remains on the seller until cure or acceptance.

Fekkos argues that because the tractor was of no use to him as delivered, it failed to conform to the contract so as to give him the right to reject it. Thus, Fekkos asserts, under section 2–510 the risk of loss remained on the seller at the point of the tractor's theft on May 1, 1985, because no cure or acceptance had been made at that point.

Alternatively, Fekkos argues that if section 2–602 is applicable to the case, he still is entitled to summary judgment because subsequent to his rejection he held the tractor with reasonable care, forced because of the necessity of jump starting, the impassibility of his driveway and inaccessibility of his garage. Fekkos argues that it would be unreasonable to assume that he could have anticipated that someone would "go to the trouble of removing the tiller, and then push or winch a 1,200-plus pound tractor onto a truck or drag or whatever."

The court in its research of Ohio sales law discovered no Ohio case law on the precise issue presented in this case. Indeed, there is little case law nationwide on this issue. However, the court sees no reason that the two aforementioned statutes are not to be read in *pari materia* to provide the law to be applied.

As to the instant case, while it may be said that Lykins retained the risk of loss of the nonconforming tractor, the liability for loss would fall on Fekkos if the facts show that Fekkos breached his duty to hold the tractor with reasonable care for sufficient time for removal, after notification of rejection to seller.

On the facts, the court finds that the actions taken by Fekkos were reasonable under all the circumstances and that Fekkos did not breach his duty to use reasonable care to hold the tractor until Lykins would retrieve it. The court notes that there is no evidence whatsoever that any of Lykins's employees indicated their dissatisfaction with Fekkos's decision to park the tractor on his front lawn when told by Fekkos that that was where he would leave it until they came. The evidence shows to this court's satisfaction that Fekkos acted reasonably because of the inaccessibility of his garage on account of the demolition of his driveway.

**Summary judgment for Fekkos.**

## ASSURANCE, REPUDIATION, AND EXCUSE

### Assurance

The buyer or seller may become concerned that the other party may not be able to perform his contract obligations. If there is a reasonable basis for that concern, the buyer or seller can demand **assurance** from the other party that the contract will be performed. If such assurances are not given within a reasonable time not exceeding 30 days, the party is considered to have repudiated the contract [2–609].

For example, a farmer contracts to sell 1,000 bushels of apples to a canner, with delivery to be made in September. In March, the canner learns that a severe frost has damaged many of the apple blossoms in the farmer's area and that 50 percent of the crop has been lost. The canner has the right to demand assurances in writing from the farmer that he will be able to fulfill his obligations in light of the frost. The farmer must provide those assurances within 30 days. Thus, he might advise the canner that his crop sustained only relatively light damage or that he had made commitments to sell only a small percentage of his total crop and expects to be able to fulfill his obligations. If the farmer does not provide such assurances in a timely manner, he is considered to have repudiated the contract. The canner then has certain remedies against the farmer for breach of contract. These remedies are discussed in the next chapter.

The *LNS Investment Company, Inc. v. Phillips 66 Company* case, which follows, illustrates a situation where a buyer became concerned about the seller's ability to perform and demanded assurances from the seller.

## LNS INVESTMENT COMPANY, INC. V. PHILLIPS 66 COMPANY
### 731 F.Supp. 1484 (D. Kansas 1990)

LNS Investment Company is the successor to the Compu-Blend Corporation (CBC), which blended, labeled, and packaged quart plastic bottles of motor oil for, among others, the Phillips 66 Company. On July 29, Peter Buhlinger, Phillips's manager of lubricants, wrote a letter to CBC that read as follows:

This will confirm our verbal agreement whereby Phillips will purchase additional quantities of plastic bottles from CBC during 1986.

CBC, in an effort to increase their packaging capacity, has committed to purchase several additional molds to blow the Phillips one-quart container. In order to amortize the cost of the additional equipment, Phillips has agreed to take delivery of a maximum of 4,000,000 bottles to be made available by December 31, 1986. This agreement includes the production available now and to be supplemented by the additional equipment. Should CBC be not able to produce the full 4,000,000 quarts by December 31, 1986, this agreement shall be considered satisfied.

Phillips' desire is to receive as many bottles packaged with Phillips motor oil in 1986 from CBC as possible. It is our intention to change to a different type of plastic one-quart container beginning in 1987 and therefore this agreement cannot extend past the December 31, 1986 deadline. All production would have to be of high resaleable [sic] plastic quarts filled with the appropriate Phillips products and labeled accordingly. The production would be required to be available on an even weekly basis in order to facilitate movement of the product to the warehouse and customers.

Although the agreement called for CBC to increase its production capacity, CBC experienced numerous problems in maintaining even its precontract capacity. Moreover, the quality of goods CBC was able to deliver was frequently unacceptable to Phillips. On September 18, a Phillips representative wrote to CBC complaining about the quality of goods Phillips was receiving, specifically mentioning neck finish and label application problems. The letter also noted that if Phillips had known how CBC would perform, it would not have committed to purchase CBC's hoped-for increase in production. CBC's chairman responded on September 29, acknowledging certain deficiencies, offering a number of reasons for the inability to perform, and stating that he was sure CBC would be showing "marked improvement in deliveries in the coming week and even more in another two or three weeks."

On October 15, the Phillips representative reiterated its continued dissatisfaction with CBC's products, indicating "we definitely do not want bottles on the shelf of the quality submitted." And, on December 16, he advised CBC that Phillips would not renew any commitments to purchase goods from CBC after March 31, 1987, because of CBC's poor performance under the July 29 agreement. In May 1987, CBC brought suit against Phillips, alleging that Phillips breached the July 29 agreement by failing to purchase CBC's full output of plastic bottles through December 31, 1986.

**O'Connor, Chief Judge** CBC's failure to provide either the quantity or quality of goods contemplated by the July 29 agreement entitled Phillips to suspend its performance. Section 2–609 of the Code states as follows:

Right to adequate assurance of performance.

(1) A contract for sale imposes an obligation on each party that the other's expectations will not be impaired. When reasonable grounds for insecurity arise with respect to the performance of either party, the other may in writing demand adequate assurance of due performance and until he receives such assurance may if commercially reasonable suspend any performance for which he has not already received the agreed return.

(2) Between merchants the reasonableness of grounds for insecurity and the adequacy of any assurance offered shall be determined according to commercial standards.

(3) Acceptance of any improper delivery or payment does not prejudice the aggrieved party's right to demand adequate assurance of future performance.

(4) After receipt of a justified demand failure to provide within a reasonable time not exceeding thirty days such assurance of due performance as is adequate under the circumstances of the particular case is a repudiation of the contract.

To suspend its performance pursuant to this section, Phillips must (1) have had reasonable grounds for insecurity regarding CBC's performance under the contract, (2) have demanded in writing adequate assurance of CBC's future performance and (3) have not received from CBC such assurances.

Phillips had reasonable grounds for insecurity regarding CBC's performance. The evidence conclusively demonstrated that CBC suffered numerous setbacks in its attempt to increase its capacity to produce plastic bottles for Phillips. Specifically, both the quantity and quality of the bottles were chronically poor. Indeed, Phillips was arguably entitled to cancel the contract soon after CBC's unacceptable performance began. Sec. 2–607(3)(a); 2–711(1). Although Phillips lost its right to cancel the contract by failing to elect that remedy within a reasonable time, the above circumstances were sufficient to establish Phillips' right to adequate assurance of CBC's future performance under Section 2–609.

Phillips demanded, in writing, assurance from CBC regarding CBC's future performance. Phillips notified CBC of the inadequacies of CBC's goods and requested assurance that CBC would take steps to rectify the same. Thus it was incumbent on CBC to provide adequate assurance of its future performance to Phillips.

CBC failed to provide Phillips with adequate assurance of its future performance. CBC's continual excuses for failing to perform, unaccompanied by corresponding remedial action, cannot be deemed adequate assurance under the Code. Accordingly, Phillips was entitled to suspend its own performance of the contract by refusing to place orders with CBC and/or cancelling orders already placed, thirty days after either or both the September 18, 1986, and October 15, 1986, letters. In view of this conclusion, Phillips did not breach the contract by suspending performance in December, 1986.

**Judgment for Phillips.**

## Anticipatory Repudiation

Sometimes, one of the parties to a contract *repudiates* the contract by advising the other party that he does not intend to perform his obligations. When one party repudiates the contract, the other party may suspend his performance. In addition, he may either await performance for a reasonable time or use the remedies for breach of contract that are discussed in the next chapter [2–610].

Suppose the party who repudiated the contract changes his mind. Repudiation can be withdrawn by clearly indicating that the person intends to perform his obligations. The repudiating party must do this before the other party has canceled the contract or has materially changed position by, for example, buying the goods elsewhere [2–611].

## Excuse

Unforeseen events may make it difficult or impossible for a person to perform his contractual obligations. The Code rules for determining when a person is excused from performing are similar to the general contract rules. General contract law uses the test of **impossibility.** In most situations, however, the Code uses the test of **commercial impracticability.**

The Code attempts to differentiate events that are unforeseeable or uncontrollable from events that were part of the risk borne by a party. If the goods required for the performance of a contract are destroyed without fault of either party prior to the time that the risk of loss passed to the buyer, the contract is voided [2–613]. Suppose Jones agrees to sell and deliver an antique table to Brown. The table is damaged when Jones's antique store is struck by lightning and catches fire. The specific table covered by the contract was damaged without fault of either party prior to the time that the risk of loss was to pass to Brown. Under the Code, Brown has the option of either canceling the contract or accepting the table with an allowance in the purchase price to compensate for the damaged condition [2–613].

If unforeseen conditions cause a delay or the inability to make delivery of the goods and thus make performance impracticable, the seller is excused from making delivery. However, if a seller's capacity to deliver is only partially affected, the seller must allocate production in any fair and reasonable manner among his customers. The seller has the option of including any regular customer not then under contract in his allocation scheme. When the seller allocates production, he must notify the buyers [2–615]. When a buyer receives this notice, the buyer may either terminate the contract or agree to accept the allocation [2–616].

For example, United Nuclear contracts to sell certain quantities of fuel rods for nuclear power plants to a number of electric utilities. If the federal government limits the amount of uranium that United has access to, so that United is unable to fill all of its contracts, United is excused from full performance on the grounds of commercial impracticability. However, United may allocate its production of fuel rods among its customers by reducing each customer's share by a certain percentage and giving the customers notice of the allocation. Then, each utility can decide whether to cancel the contract or accept the partial allocation of fuel rods.

In the absence of compelling circumstances, courts do not readily excuse parties from their contractual obligations, particularly where it is clear that the parties anticipated a problem and sought to provide for it in the contract.

## PROBLEMS AND PROBLEM CASES

**1.** Baker was a buyer and distributor of popcorn. Ratzlaff was a farmer who grew popcorn. In 1983, Baker and Ratzlaff entered into a written contract pursuant to which Ratzlaff agreed that in 1983 he would raise 380 acres of popcorn and sell the popcorn to Baker. Baker agreed to furnish the seed popcorn and to pay $4.75 per hundred pounds of popcorn. The popcorn was to be delivered to Baker as he ordered it, and Baker was to pay for the popcorn as it was delivered. At Baker's request, the first delivery was made on February 2 of the following year and the second on February 4. On neither occasion did Ratzlaff ask Baker to pay or Baker offer to pay. During that week, Ratzlaff and Baker had several phone conversations about further deliveries, but there was no discussion about payments. On February 11, Ratzlaff sent written notice to Baker that he was terminating the contract because Baker had not paid for the two loads of popcorn that had been delivered. In the meantime, Ratzlaff sold his remaining 1.6 million pounds of popcorn to another buyer at $8 per 100 pounds. Baker then sued Ratzlaff for breach of contract. Did Ratzlaff act in good faith in terminating the contract?

**2.** Ray Williams, a resident of Georgia, contracted to sell the "slaw cabbage" to be grown on 30 acres of farmland in Georgia to Thomas Curtin, a resident of New York, who intended to resell the cabbage to cole slaw manufacturers. The expected yield was 600 to 800 tons of cabbage, and the agreed price was $136 per ton. Large cabbages are generally preferable for making cole slaw, and Curtin orally advised Williams that he desired large cabbages (i.e., 12 heads or less per 50-pound bag); this request was not, however, incorporated into the written memorandum of agreement. Earlier agreements between Williams and Curtin had called for the sale of "large cabbage." The cabbage was planted in a way to provide the best assurance possible that the cabbage would be large cabbage as requested by Curtin. As a result of poor growing conditions, most of the cabbages grown on the acreage were small; moreover, prices for cabbage were generally higher than the price at which Williams had agreed to make the sale to Curtin. Curtin inspected the cabbage during the growing season and was aware of the small size of the cabbage. He advised Williams that he wanted all of the cabbage from the 30 acres, regardless of size. Williams, however, delivered only the large cabbages to Curtin (approximately 150 tons) and sold the smaller cabbages to other buyers at a price about three times higher than the price at which he had contracted to sell cabbage to Curtin. Williams claimed that in the trade in Georgia, "slaw cabbage" referred only to large cabbage with 12 cabbage heads or less per 50-pound bag. However, the other witnesses said that the term *slaw cabbage* was seldom used, that in their experience it had never been used to define a specific cabbage size, and that it meant simply cabbage suitable for processing into cole slaw. Did trade usage support Williams's contention that he was obligated to deliver only the large cabbages?

**3.** Harold Ledford agreed to purchase three used Mustang automobiles (a 1966 Mustang coupe, a 1965 fastback, and a 1966 convertible) from J. L. Cowan for $3,000. Ledford gave Cowan a cashier's check for $1,500 when he took possession of the coupe, with the understanding he would pay the remaining $1,500 on the delivery of the fastback and the convertible. Cowan arranged for Charles Canterberry to deliver the remaining vehicles to Ledford. Canterberry dropped the convertible off at a lot owned by Ledford and proceeded to Ledford's residence to deliver the fastback. He refused to unload it until Ledford paid him $1,500. Ledford refused to make the payment until he had an opportunity to inspect the convertible, which he suspected was not in the same condition that it had been in when he purchased it. Canterberry refused this request and returned both the fastback and the convertible to Cowan. Cowan then brought suit against Ledford to recover the balance of the purchase price. Was Ledford entitled to inspect the car before he paid the balance due on it?

**4.** Spada, an Oregon corporation, agreed to sell Belson, who operated a business in Chicago, two carloads of potatoes at "4.40 per sack, FOB Oregon shipping point." Spada had the potatoes put aboard railroad cars; however, it did not have floor racks placed under the potatoes, as was customary during the winter months. As a result, there was no warm air circulating and the potatoes were frozen while in transit. Spada claims that its obligations ended with the delivery to the carrier and that the risk of loss was on Belson. What argument would you make for Belson?

**5.** In April, Reginald Bell contracted to sell potatoes to Red Ball Potato Company for fall delivery. The contract specified that the potatoes were to be "85 percent U.S. 1's." In Red Ball's dealings with Bell and other farmers, potatoes were delivered and paid for in truckload quantities. In the fall, Bell delivered several truckloads of potatoes. Samples of each load were taken for testing, and most of the loads were determined to be below 85 percent U.S. No 1. What options are open to Red Ball?

**6.** In February 1988, Jeannie Fannin agreed to manufacture and install custom-made draperies in Mary Ann George's home for a total purchase price of $4,000. George selected an appropriate fabric from Fannin's swatch book and paid $1,500 on execution of the contract. In May, Fannin told George that she could not obtain the fabric initially selected, but that she could provide a substitute that was slightly different in color. After inspecting the substitute material, George agreed to the substitution. The draperies were completed and installed in July. George concluded that the draperies failed to close, did not hang right, failed to to keep out sunlight, heat, and cold, and had other deficiencies. She told Fannin that the workmanship was "shoddy" and Fannin agreed to make adjustments. When Fannin failed to return to make the adjustments, George refused to pay the $500 she owed on the drapes. In October, Fannin filed suit in small claims court to recover the balance, and George counterclaimed to recover the $3,500 she had already paid. At the time of the trial in July 1989, the drapes were still in use at George's house. Had George made an effective rejection of the drapes?

**7.** On May 23, 1978, Deborah McCullough, a secretary, purchased a 1978 Chrysler LeBaron from Bill Swad Chrysler-Plymouth. The automobile was covered by both a limited warranty and a vehicle service contract (extended warranty). Following delivery, McCullough advised the salesperson that she had noted problems with the brakes, transmission, air conditioning, paint job, and seat panels, as well as the absence of rustproofing. The next day, the brakes failed and the car was returned to the dealer for the necessary repairs. When the car was returned, McCullough discovered that the brakes had not been properly repaired and that none of the cosmetic work had been done. The car was returned several times to the dealer to correct these problems and others that developed subsequently. On June 26, the car was again returned to the dealer, who kept it for three weeks. Many of the defects were not corrected, however, and new problems with the horn and brakes arose. While McCullough was on a shopping trip, the engine abruptly shut off and the car had to be towed to the dealer. Then, while she was on her honeymoon, the brakes again failed. The car was taken back to the dealer with a list of 32 defects that needed correction. After repeated efforts to repair the car were unsuccessful, McCullough sent a letter to the dealer calling for rescission of the purchase, requesting return of the purchase price, and offering to return the car on receipt of shipping instructions. She received no answer and continued to drive it. McCullough then filed suit. In May 1979, the dealer refused to do any further work on the car, claiming that it was in satisfactory condition. By the time of the trial, in June 1980, it had been driven 35,000 miles, approximately 23,000 of which had been logged after McCullough mailed her notice of revocation. By continuing to operate the vehicle after notifying the seller of her intent to rescind the sale, did McCullough waive her right to revoke her original acceptance?

**8.** Walters, a grower of Christmas trees, contracted to supply Traynor with "top quality trees." When the shipment arrived and was inspected, Traynor discovered that some of the trees were not top quality. Within 24 hours, Traynor notified Walters that he was rejecting the trees that were not top quality. Walters did not have a place of business or an agent in the town where Traynor was. Christmas was only a short time away. The trees were perishable and would decline in value to zero by Christmas Eve. Walters did not give Traynor any instructions, so Traynor sold the trees for Walters's account. Traynor then tried to recover from Walters the expenses he incurred in caring for and selling the trees. Did Traynor act properly in rejecting the trees and reselling them for the seller?

**9.** Creusot-Loire, a French manufacturing and engineering concern, was the project engineer to construct ammonia plants in Yugoslavia and Syria. The design process engineer for the two plants—as well as a plant being constructed in Sri Lanka—specified burners manufactured by Coppus Engineering Corporation. After the burner specifications were provided to Coppus, it sent technical and service information to Creusot-Loire. Coppus expressly warranted that the burners were capable of continuous operation using heavy fuel oil with combustion air

preheated to 260 degrees Celsius. The warranty extended for one year from the start-up of the plant but not exceeding three years from the date of shipment. In January 1979, Creusot-Loire ordered the burners for the Yugoslavia plant and paid for them; in November 1979, the burners were shipped to Yugoslavia. Due to construction delays, the plant was not to become operational until the end of 1983. In 1981, however, Creusot-Loire became aware that there had been operational difficulties with the Coppus burners at the Sri Lanka and Syria plants and that efforts to modify the burners had been futile. Creusot-Loire wrote to Coppus expressing concern that the burners purchased for the Yugoslavia plant, like those in the other plants, would prove unsatisfactory and asking for proof that the burners would meet contract specifications. When subsequent discussions failed to satisfy Creusot-Loire, it requested that Coppus take back the burners and refund the purchase price. Coppus refused. Finally, Creusot-Loire indicated that it would accept the burners only if Coppus extended its contractual guarantee to cover the delay in the start-up of the Yugoslavia plant and if Coppus posted an irrevocable letter of credit for the purchase price of the burners. When Coppus refused, Creusot-Loire brought an action for breach of contract, seeking a return of the purchase price. Coppus claimed that Creusot-Loire's request for assurance was unreasonable. How should the court rule?

**10.** In July 1980, Alimenta (U.S.A.), Inc., and Gibbs, Nathaniel (Canada), Ltd., each an international dealer in agricultural commodities, entered into three separate contracts in advance of the 1980 peanut harvest. Each contract called for the delivery in installments by Gibbs to Alimenta of "1980 crop U.S. runner split peanuts." When Gibbs failed to make delivery of the quantities specified in the contract, and made some deliveries later than the scheduled dates, Alimenta brought suit against Gibbs seeking damages for breach of contract. Gibbs claimed that it was excused from full performance by the occurrence of a drought in the peanut-growing areas. The 1980 peanut crop had been planted in April and May. Rainfall was adequate in April, May, and June, and the crop came up in good condition. In the 25 years preceding 1980, the nation's peanut industry had experienced a steady growth in total production, with yield per acre increasing 250 percent over that period. In addition to Alimenta, Gibbs sold 1980 crop peanuts to 75 other customers and had contracted to purchase peanuts from 15 shellers in quantities 7 percent in excess of its sales. In early July, a hot and dry spell developed and became a full-fledged drought that did not break until late September. July and August were among the hottest and driest months on record in the last 100 years. In October, Gibbs received notices from 13 of its 15 shellers stating that because of the crop shortage, they were invoking Section 2–615 of the UCC and would be delivering only a portion of the peanuts they had contracted to deliver. Gibbs expected to receive only 52 percent of the peanuts it had contracted for, and in turn notified its customers, including, Alimenta, to expect reduced quantities. Alimenta ultimately received 87 percent of the contract quantity from Gibbs. Was Gibbs excused from full performance of its contract by the occurrence of the drought?

**11.** ▐▄█▌ *Video Case.* See "Sour Grapes." Jelly Manufacturer, a food processor in Chicago, placed a phone order with Grape Grower, a grower in California, for a quantity of perishable produce. The shipping term was CIF with payment to be made on delivery (COD). Grower delivered the goods called for in the contract to a carrier and contracted for their shipment. However, it neglected to provide that the goods be shipped under refrigeration. The goods were loaded on a nonrefrigerated boxcar, and as a result, the produce was spoiled when it reached Chicago. Jelly Manufacturer, as required by the COD term, paid for the produce by check before discovering the spoilage. By paying for the produce, has Jelly Manufacturer "accepted" the goods so that it cannot subsequently "reject" them as nonconforming?

When Jelly Manufacturer called Grower to complain, Grower offered to rush a replacement shipment. Jelly Manufacturer declined the offer, stating that it would not arrive in time for the produce to be processed and delivered to Grocery Chain in time to meet Jelly Manufacturer's contract with Grocery Chain. Was Jelly Manufacturer required to accept Grower's promise to make a replacement shipment?

## CAPSTONE QUESTIONS

Edgar's Fish, Inc., a large, generally reliable firm engaged in the wholesale fish trade, is periodically involved in disputes with customers and suppliers that Article 2 (Sales) may govern. The current disputes include the following:

· On October 1, Edgar's unintentionally shipped the wrong kind of crabs to Martha's Restaurant pursuant to an order that called for 30 bushels of Puget Sound Dungeness crabs, shipping instead 30 bushels of Chesapeake Bay blue crabs. Martha's accepted the crabs and began serving them to its customers. After serving about 4 bushels of the Chesapeake Bay crabs, it received some complaints that the crabs being served did not conform with the menu description. Martha's contacted Edgar's and told Edgar's that it was revoking its acceptance of the remaining crabs. Martha's claims that it has the right to do so because the crabs being delivered did not conform to the contract.

· On October 3, Edgar's shipped 200 bushels of mussels to a restaurant in Boston. Because of a delay in shipping, the mussels arrived a day later than the contract specified. The restaurant rejected all the mussels and immediately notified Edgar's of its decision. Edgar's asked the restaurant to return the mussels at Edgar's expense or to resell them in Boston. The restaurant refused, claiming that it had no obligations to Edgar's following rejection.

· On October 15, Edgar's contracted to sell to Royal Fine Foods 500 large Maine lobsters for $7,500 with delivery to be made on November 1. In late October, Maine lobster waters were infested by the "red tide"—a toxic bacterial phenomenon that renders contaminated sea life unsuitable for human consumption. Accordingly, Edgar's notified Royal on October 30 that it would not be able to deliver any Maine lobsters on November 1. Edgar's claimed that it was excused from performing the contract because of the unforeseen problem. Royal claimed that Edgar's was in breach of contract because it had made an unconditional promise to deliver the lobsters.

**Required:**

Answer the following and give reasons for your conclusions.

**1.** For the Martha's Restaurant hypothetical, state whether Martha's claim is correct.

**2.** For the Boston restaurant hypothetical, state whether the restaurant acted legally.

**3.** For the Royal Fine Foods hypothetical, state whether Royal's claim is correct.

# CHAPTER 14

# REMEDIES FOR
# BREACH OF
# SALES CONTRACTS

**INTRODUCTION**

*Usually, both parties to a contract for the sale of goods perform the obligations that they assumed in the contract. Occasionally, however, one of the parties to a contract fails to perform her obligations. When this happens, the Uniform Commercial Code (UCC or Code) provides the injured party with a variety of remedies for breach of contract. This chapter will set forth and explain the remedies available to an injured party, as well as the Code's rules that govern buyer-seller agreements as to remedies, and the Code's statute of limitations. The objective of the Code remedies is to put the injured person in the same position that he would have been in if the contract had been performed. Under the Code, an injured party may not recover consequential or punitive damages unless such damages are specifically provided for in the Code or in another statute [1–106].[1]*

■

## AGREEMENTS AS TO REMEDIES

The buyer and seller may provide their own remedies in the contract, to be applied in the event that one of the parties fails to perform. They may also limit either the remedies that the law makes available or the damages that can be covered [2–719(1)]. If the parties agree on the amount of damages that will be paid to the injured party, this amount is known as **liquidated damages.** An agreement for liquidated damages is enforced if the amount is *reasonable* and if *actual* damages would be *difficult to prove* in the event of a breach of the contract. The amount is considered reasonable if it is not so large as to be a *penalty* or so small as to be *unconscionable* [2–718(1)].

For example, Carl Carpenter contracts to build and sell a display booth for $5,000 to Hank Hawker for Hawker to use at the state fair. Delivery is to be made to Hawker by September 1. If the booth is not delivered on time, Hawker will not be able to sell his wares at the fair. Carpenter and Hawker might agree that if delivery is not made by September 1, Carpenter will pay Hawker $2,750 as liquidated damages. The actual sales that Hawker might lose without a booth would be very

---

[1]The numbers in brackets refer to sections of the Uniform Commercial Code.

hard to prove, so Hawker and Carpenter can provide some certainty through the liquidated damages agreement. Carpenter then knows what he will be liable for if he does not perform his obligation. Similarly, Hawker knows what he can recover if the booth is not delivered on time. The $2,750 amount is probably reasonable. If the amount were $500,000, it likely would be void as a penalty because it is way out of line with the damages that Hawker would reasonably be ex-pected to sustain. And if the amount were too small, say $1, it might be considered unconscionable and therefore not enforceable.

If a liquidated damages clause is not enforceable because it is a penalty or unconscionable, the injured party can recover the actual damages that he suffered. The *Baker v. International Record Syndicate, Inc.* case, which follows, illustrates a situation where a court enforced a liquidated damages clause in a contract.

---

## BAKER V. INTERNATIONAL RECORD SYNDICATE, INC.
### 812 S.W.2d 53 (Ct. App. Tex. 1991)

International Record Syndicate (IRS) hired Jeff Baker to take photographs of the musical group Timbuk-3. Baker mailed 37 "chromes" (negatives) to IRS via the business agent of Timbuk-3. When the chromes were returned to Baker, holes had been punched in 34 of them. Baker brought an action for breach of contract to recover for the damage done to the chromes.

A provision printed on Baker's invoice to IRS stated: "[r]eimbursement for loss or damage shall be determined by a photograph's reasonable value which shall be no less than $1,500 per transparency."

---

**Enoch, Chief Judge**    The Uniform Commercial Code provides:

Damages for breach by either party may be liquidated in the agreement but only at an amount which is reasonable in light of the anticipated harm caused by the breach, the difficulties of proof of loss, and the inconvenience or non-feasibility of otherwise obtaining an adequate remedy. A term fixing unreasonably large liquidated damages is void as a penalty.

Under Texas law a liquidated damages provision will be enforced when the court finds (1) the harm caused by the breach is incapable of estimation, and (2) the amount of liquidated damages is a reasonable forecast of just compensation. This might be termed the "anticipated harm" test. The party asserting that a liquidated damages clause is, in fact, a penalty provision has the burden of proof. Evidence related to the difficulty of estimation and the reasonable forecast must be viewed as of the time the contract was executed.

Baker testified that he had been paid as much as $14,000 for a photo session, which resulted in twenty-four photographs, and that several of these photographs had also been resold. Baker further testified that he had received as little as $125 for a single photograph. Baker also testified that he once sold a photograph for $500. Subsequently, he sold reproductions of the same photograph three additional times at various prices; the total income from this one photograph was $1,500. This particular photograph was taken in 1986 and was still producing income in 1990. Baker demonstrated, therefore, that an accurate demonstration of the damages from a single photograph is virtually impossible.

Timbuk-3's potential for fame was also an important factor in the valuation of the chromes. At the time of the photo session, Timbuk-3's potential was unknown. In view of the difficulty in determining the value of a piece of art, the broad range of values and long-term earning power of photographs, and the unknown potential for fame of the subject, $1,500 is not an unreasonable estimate of Baker's actual damages.

Additionally, liquidated damages must not be disproportionate to actual damages. If the liquidated damages are shown to be disproportionate to the actual damages, then the liquidated damages can be declared a penalty and recovery limited to actual damages proven. This might be called the "actual harm" test. The burden of proving this defense is upon the party seeking to invalidate the clause. The party asserting this defense is required to prove the amount of the other party's actual damages, if any, to show that the actual loss was not an approximation of the stipulated sum.

While evidence was presented that showed the value of several of Baker's other projects, this was not evidence of the photographs in question. The evidence clearly shows that photographs are unique items with many factors bearing on their actual value. Each of the thirty-four chromes may have had a different value. Proof of this loss is difficult; where damages are real but difficult to prove, injustice will be done the injured party if the court substitutes the requirements of judicial proof for the parties' own informed agreement as to what is a reasonable measure of damages. The evidence offered to prove Baker's actual damages lacks probative force. IRS failed to establish Baker's actual damages as to these particular photographs.

**Judgment reversed in favor of Baker.**

---

Liability for consequential damages resulting from a breach of contract (such as lost profits or damage to property) may also be limited or excluded by agreement. The limitation or exclusion is not enforced if it would be unconscionable. Any attempt to limit consequential damages for injury caused to a person by consumer goods is considered prima facie unconscionable [2–719(3)].

Suppose an automobile manufacturer makes a warranty as to the quality of an automobile that is purchased as a consumer good. It then tries to disclaim responsibility for any person injured if the car does not conform to the warranty and to limit its liability to replacing any defective parts. The disclaimer of consequential injuries in this case would be unconscionable and therefore would not be enforced. Exclusion of or limitation on consequential damages is permitted where the loss is commercial, as long as the exclusion or limitation is not unconscionable.

The *Hartzell v. Justus Co., Inc.* case, which follows, illustrates how the Code applies to a situation where circumstances cause a limited remedy agreed to by the parties to fail in its essential purpose. When this happens, the limited remedy is not enforced and the general Code remedies are available to the injured party.

---

### HARTZELL V. JUSTUS CO., INC.
**693 F.2d 770 (8th Cir. 1982)**

Dr. Allan Hartzell purchased a log home construction kit manufactured by Justus Homes. Hartzell purchased the package for $38,622 from Del Carter, who was Justus Homes's dealer for the Sioux Falls area. He also hired Carter's construction company to build the house, which eventually cost about $150,000. Hartzell was dissatisfied with the house in many respects. His chief complaints were that knotholes in the walls and ceilings leaked rain profusely and that the home was not weathertight because flashings were not included in the roofing materials and because the timbers were not kiln-dried and therefore shrank. He also complained that an undersized support beam, which eventually cracked, was included in the package. This defect resulted in floor cracks and in inside doors that would not close. Hartzell claimed that the structural defects were only partially remediable and that the fair market value of the house was reduced even after all practicable repairs had been made.

Hartzell brought suit against Justus Homes, alleging negligence and breach of implied and express warranties and seeking damages for loss in value and the cost of repairs. A jury awarded Hartzell a verdict of $34,794.67. Justus Homes appealed.

**Arnold, Circuit Judge**    Justus Homes contends the district court failed to adequately consider a limitation-of-remedies clause contained in its contract with Hartzell. Justus Homes relies on Clause 10c of the contract, which says that Justus will repair or replace defective materials, and Clause 10d, which states that this limited repair or replacement clause is the exclusive remedy available against Justus. These agreements, Justus asserts, are valid under the Uniform Commercial Code, § 2–719(1). Section 2–719(1) states:

(1) Subject to the provisions of subsections (2) and (3) of this section and of § 2–718 on liquidation and limitation of damages,

   (a) The agreement may provide for remedies in addition to or in substitution for those provided in this article and may limit or alter the measure of damages recoverable under this article, as by limiting the buyer's remedies to return of the goods and repayment of the price or to repair and replacement of nonconforming goods or parts; and

   (b) Resort to a remedy as provided is optional unless the remedy is expressly agreed to be exclusive, in which case it is the sole remedy.

Subsection (1) of § 2–719 is qualified by subsection (2): "Where circumstances cause an exclusive or limited remedy to fail of its essential purpose, remedy may be had as provided in this title." The jury's verdict for Hartzell in an amount almost exactly equal to Hartzell's evidence of cost of repairs plus diminution in market value means it must have found that the structural defects were not entirely remediable. Such a finding necessarily means that the limited warranty failed of its essential purpose.

Two of our recent cases support this conclusion. In *Soo Line R.R. v. Fruehauf Corp.*, the defendant claimed, relying on a limitation-of-remedies clause similar to the one involved here, that the plaintiff's damages should be limited to the reasonable cost of repairing the railroad cars that plaintiff had bought from defendant. The jury verdict included, among other things, an award for the difference between the value of the cars as actually manufactured and what they would have been worth if they had measured up to the defendant's representations. This court affirmed the verdict for the larger amount. We held, construing the Minnesota UCC, which is identical to 2–719 as adopted in South Dakota, that the limitation-of-

remedies clause was ineffective because the remedy as thus limited failed of its essential purpose. The defendant, though called upon to make the necessary repairs, had refused to do so, and the repairs as performed by the plaintiff itself "did not fully restore the cars to totally acceptable operating conditions."

Here, Justus Homes attempted to help with the necessary repairs, which is more than Fruehauf did in the *Soo Line* case, but after the repairs had been completed, the house was still, according to the jury verdict, not what Justus had promised it would be. The purpose of a remedy is to give to a buyer what the seller promised him—that is, a house that did not leak. If repairs alone do not achieve that end, then to limit the buyer's remedy to repair would cause that remedy to fail of its essential purpose.

An analogous case is *Select Port, Inc. v. Babcock Swine, Inc.*, applying 2–719 as adopted in Iowa. The defendant had promised to deliver to plaintiff certain extraordinary pigs known as Midwestern Gilts and Meatline Boars. Instead, only ordinary pigs were delivered. Plaintiff sued for breach of warranty, and defendant claimed that its damages, if any, should be limited to a return of the purchase price by an express clause to that effect in the contract. The district court held that the clause was unenforceable because it was unconscionable, see § 2–719(3), and because it failed of its essential purpose. We affirmed. "Having failed to deliver the highly-touted special pigs, defendants may not now assert a favorable clause to limit their liability."

So here, where the house sold was found by the jury to fall short of the seller's promises, and where repairs could not make it right, Justus Homes's liability cannot be limited to the cost of repairs. If the repairs had been adequate to restore the house to its promised condition, and if Dr. Hartzell had claimed additional consequential damages, for example, water damage to a rug from the leaky roof, the limitation-of-remedies clause would have been effective. But that is not this case.

The evidence in the record all demonstrates that the repair or replacement clause was a failure under the circumstances of this case. Some of the house's many problems simply could not be remedied by repair or replacement. The clause having failed of its essential purpose, that is, effective enjoyment of implied and express warranties, Dr. Hartzell was entitled, under UCC 2–719(2), to any of the buyer's remedies provided by the Code. Among these remedies are consequential damages as provided in 2–714 and 2–715(2).

**Judgment for Hartzell affirmed.**

## Statute of Limitations

The Code provides that a lawsuit for breach of a sales contract must be filed within four years after the breach occurs. The parties to a contract may shorten this period to one year, but they may not extend it for longer than four years [2–725]. Normally, a breach of warranty is considered to have occurred when the goods are delivered to the buyer. However, if the warranty covers future performance of goods (for example, a warranty on a tire for four years or 40,000 miles), then the breach occurs at the time the buyer should have discovered the defect in the product. If, for example, the buyer of the tire discovers the defect after driving 25,000 miles on the tire over a three-year period, he would have four years from that time to bring any lawsuit to remedy the breach.

In the *Wilson v. Hammer Holdings, Inc.* case, which follows, the court rejected the argument that a warranty given in connection with the sale of a painting extended to the future performance of the painting.

### WILSON V. HAMMER HOLDINGS, INC.
#### 6 UCC Rep.2d 321 (1st Cir. 1988)

In 1961, Dorothy and John Wilson purchased a painting entitled *Femme Debout* from the Hammer Galleries. They paid $11,000 for the work that was expressly guaranteed to be an original work of art by Edouard Vuillard. The purchase agreement stated that "the authenticity of this picture is guaranteed." In 1984, in preparation for selling it, the Wilsons had the picture examined by an expert. The expert determined that the painting was not done by the French artist Vuillard, and he refused to authenticate it.

The Wilsons returned the painting to the Hammer Galleries, and then brought a lawsuit seeking damages for breach of warranty. Hammer Galleries asserted that the claim was barred by the UCC's four-year statute of limitations. The district court held that the claim was barred by the statute of limitations, and Wilson appealed.

**Coffin, Circuit Judge**    The Massachusetts statute of limitations for breach of a sales contract is set out in section 2–725. That section provides that

(1) An action for breach of any contract for sale must be commenced within four years after the cause of action has accrued.
(2) A cause of action accrues when the breach occurs, regardless of the aggrieved party's lack of knowledge of the breach. A breach of warranty occurs when tender of delivery is made, except that where a warranty explicitly extends to future performance of the goods and discovery must await the time of such performance, the cause of action accrues when the breach is or should have been discovered.

There is no question that the Wilsons' action was untimely under this statute if it accrued at the time they purchased the painting and received the warranty because those events occurred twenty-six years before suit was filed. The Wilsons therefore contend that this case falls within the exception to section 2–725(2), and they argue that their cause of action accrued upon their discovery in 1985 that the painting was not authentic.

The district court found the exception in section 2–725(2) to be inapplicable because Hammer's warranty made no explicit reference to future performance as required by the statute. The Wilsons do not argue that the district court erred in reading the warranty to lack an explicit promise of future performance. Rather, they argue that a warranty of authenticity necessarily relates to the future condition of the artwork, despite the absence of explicit language to that effect, and for that reason, they claim that the exception in section 2–725(2) should apply to them. Section 2–725(2) refers to a warranty of "future performance," and so the Wilsons' theory depends first on extending the concept of a "performance" to a painting. They concede that paintings, unlike consumer goods like automobiles and washing machines, generally are not purchased based on how they "perform" or "function." They suggest, however, that a painting "performs" "by being what it is represented to be." In this case, they say, "Femme Debout" could "perform" only by being an authentic Vuillard.

Accepting at least for the sake of argument that a painting does "perform" by being genuine, the question then becomes whether Hammer's express warranty of authenticity not only guaranteed the present "being" of the painting as an authentic Vuillard but also extended, as required by section 2–725(2), to the future existence of a painting as a Vuillard. On this point, the Wilsons argue that because the authenticity of a painting does not change over time, Hammer's warranty necessarily guaranteed the present and future existence of the painting as an authentic Vuillard. Therefore, they contend, explicit words warranting future performance would be superfluous in this context.

One difficulty with this argument, however, is that it asks us to ignore the literal language of the statute requiring an explicit promise of future performance. The Wilsons argue essentially that because the statutory exception's requirement of an explicit prospective warranty does not make sense in the context of the sale of paintings, we should dispense with that requirement. We are reluctant, however, to waive the specific eligibility requirements established by the legislature for what, it must be remembered, is an exception to the general limitations rule.

Even if we were to accept the Wilsons' argument that Hammer's warranty necessarily extended to future performance of the painting, and thus met the prospective warranty requirement of section 2–725(2), we nevertheless would conclude that their action is time-barred. The statute also requires that discovery of the breach "must await" the time of such future performance. That is not the case here. Because of the static nature of authenticity, the Wilsons were no less capable of discovering that "Femme Debout" was a fake at the time of purchase than they were at a later time.

Our reluctance to enlarge the scope of the exception in section 2–725(2) is strengthened by the recognition that the statute of limitations for art buyers could run indefinitely. Indeed, in this case suit was filed 26 years after the purchase. Although Massachusetts legislators may choose to provide perpetual protection for consumers of artistic products, it would be presumptuous for us to assume they would. Moreover, we think it is more likely that, if Massachusetts chooses to extend protection to art buyers in the way the Wilsons suggest, the legislature would fix some endpoint to the seller's possible liability—perhaps similar to the 20-year limitations period for an action seeking the recovery of land.

**Judgment in favor of Hammer Galleries affirmed.**

---

## SELLER'S REMEDIES

### Remedies Available to an Injured Seller

A buyer may breach a contract in a number of ways. The most common are: (1) by wrongfully refusing to accept goods, (2) by wrongfully returning goods, (3) by failing to pay for goods when payment is due, and (4) by indicating an unwillingness to go ahead with the contract.

When a buyer breaches a contract, the seller has a number of remedies under the Code, including the right to:

· Cancel the contract [2−703(f)].

· Withhold delivery of undelivered goods [2−703(a)].

· Resell the goods covered by the contract and recover damages from the buyer [2−706].

· Recover from the buyer the profit that the seller would have made on the sale or the damages that the seller sustained [2−708].

· Recover the purchase price of goods delivered to or accepted by the buyer [2−709].

In addition, a buyer may become insolvent and thus unable to pay the seller for goods already delivered or for goods that the seller is obligated to deliver. When a seller learns of a buyer's insolvency, the seller has a number of remedies, including the right to:

· Withhold delivery of undelivered goods [2−703(a)].

· Recover goods from a buyer upon the buyer's insolvency [2−702].

· Stop delivery of goods that are in the possession of a carrier or other bailee [2−705].

## Cancellation and Withholding of Delivery

When a buyer breaches a contract, the seller has the right to cancel the contract and to hold up her own performance of the contract. The seller may then set aside any goods that were intended to fill her obligations under the contract [2−704].

If the seller is in the process of manufacturing the goods, she has two choices. She may complete manufacture of the goods, or she may stop manufacturing and sell the uncompleted goods for their scrap or salvage value. In choosing between these alternatives, the seller should select the alternative that will minimize the loss [2−704(2)]. Thus, a seller would be justified in completing the manufacture of goods that could be resold readily at the contract price. However, a seller would not be justified in completing specially manufactured goods that could not be sold to anyone other than the buyer who ordered them.

The purpose of this rule is to permit the seller to follow a reasonable course of action to mitigate (minimize) the damages. In *Madsen v. Murrey & Sons Co., Inc.,* which follows, the seller, who did not complete the manufacture of goods on the buyer's repudiation, but rather dismantled and largely scrapped the existing goods, was held not to have acted in a commercially reasonable manner.

---

### MADSEN V. MURREY & SONS CO., INC.
**743 P.2d 1212 (Utah Sup. Ct. 1987)**

Murrey & Sons Co., Inc. (Murrey), was engaged in the business of manufacturing and selling pool tables. Erik Madsen was working on an idea to develop a pool table that would, through the use of electronic devices installed in the rails of the table, produce lighting and sound effects in a fashion similar to a pinball machine. Murrey and Madsen entered into a written contract whereby Murrey agreed to manufacture 100 of its M1 4-foot by 8-foot six-pocket coin operated pool tables with customized rails capable of incorporating the electronic lighting and sound effects desired by Madsen. Under the agreement, Madsen would design the rails and provide the drawings to Murrey, who would manufacture them to Madsen's specifications. Madsen was to design, manufacture, and install the electronic components for the tables. Madsen agreed to pay $550 per table or a total of $55,000 for the 100 tables and made a $42,500 deposit on the contract.

Murrey began the manufacture of the tables while Madsen continued to work on the design of the rails and electronics. Madsen encountered significant difficulties and notified Murrey that he would be unable to take delivery of the 100 tables. Madsen then brought suit to recover the $42,500 he had paid Murrey.

Following Madsen's repudiation of the contract, Murrey dismantled the pool tables and used salvageable materials to manufacture other pool tables. A good portion of the material was simply used as firewood. Murrey made no attempt to market the 100 pool tables at a discount or at any other price in order to mitigate the damages. It claimed the salvage value of the materials it reused as $7,448. The trial court ordered Murrey to return $21,250 to Madsen and Murrey appealed.

---■---

**Howe, Justice**   Murrey contends that the trial court erred in concluding that it had failed to mitigate or minimize its damages in a commercially reasonable manner by not attempting to sell the 100 pool tables on the open market. It is a well-settled rule of the law of damages that "no party suffering a loss as the result of a breach of contract is entitled to any damages which could have been avoided if the aggrieved party had acted in a reasonably diligent manner in attempting to lessen his losses as a consequence of that breach." We have held:

Where a contractual agreement has been breached by a party thereto, the aggrieved party is entitled to those damages that will put him in as good a position as he would have been had the other party performed pursuant to the agreement. A corollary to this rule is that the aggrieved party may not, either by action or inaction, aggravate the injury occasioned by the breach, but has a duty actively to mitigate his damages.

Murrey asserts that it sufficiently mitigated its damages by dismantling the pool tables and salvaging various components that could be used to manufacture other pool tables. The salvage value to Murrey was claimed to be $7,448. Murrey presented testimony that selling the tables as "seconds" would damage its reputation for quality and that the various holes, notches and routings placed in the tables to accommodate the electrical components to be installed by buyer weakened the structure of the tables so as to submit seller to potential liability if they were sold on the market.

On the other hand, Ronald Baker, who had been involved with the manufacturing and marketing of pool tables for 25 years testified on behalf of the buyer that the notches, holes and routings made in the frame to accommodate electrical wiring would not adversely affect the quality or marketability of the 100 pool tables. According to Baker, the tables could have been sold at full value or at a discounted price. In addition to this testimony, the trial court had the opportunity to view the experimental table developed by Madsen and his associates and observe the holes, notches, and routings necessary for the electrical components.

The trial court found that Murrey's action in dismantling the tables and using the materials for salvage and firewood, rather than attempting to sell or market the tables at full or discounted price, was not commercially reasonable. The court then concluded that seller had a duty to mitigate its damages and failed to do so. The finding is supported by competent evidence.

Applying the trial court's finding that the pool tables, if completed, could have been sold for at least $21,250, Murrey's damages are the difference between the market price ($21,250) and the contract price ($55,000) or $33,750. The trial court found that Murrey was not entitled to any incidental damages. Under section 2−718(2), (3), Madsen's right to restitution of advance payments on the contract ($42,500) is subject to offset to the extent that seller establishes damages ($33,750), for a total recovery of $8,750.

**Judgment for Madsen affirmed, with the recovery set at $8,750.**

## Resale of Goods

If the seller sets aside goods intended for the contract or completes the manufacture of such goods, he is not obligated to try to resell the goods to someone else. However, he may resell them and recover damages. The seller must make any resale in good faith and in a commercially reasonable manner. If the seller does so, he is entitled to recover from the buyer as damages the difference between the resale price and the price the buyer agreed to pay in the contract [2−706].

If the seller resells, he may also recover incidental damages, but the seller must give the buyer credit for any expenses that the seller saved because of the buyer's breach of contract. Incidental damages include storage charges and sales commissions paid when the goods were resold [2–710]. Expenses saved might be the cost of packaging the goods and/or shipping them to the buyer.

If the buyer and seller have agreed as to the manner in which the resale is to be made, the courts will enforce the agreement unless it is found to be unconscionable [2–302]. If the parties have not entered into an agreement as to the resale of the goods, they may be resold at public or private sale, but in all events the resale must be made in good faith and in a commercially reasonable manner. The seller should make it clear that the goods he is selling are those related to the broken contract.

If the goods are resold at private sale, the seller must give the buyer reasonable notification of his intention to resell [2–706(3)]. If the resale is a public sale, such as an auction, the seller must give the buyer notice of the time and place of the sale unless the goods are perishable or threaten to decline in value rapidly. The sale must be made at a usual place or market for public sales if one is reasonably available; and if the goods are not within the view of those attending the sale, the notification of the sale must state the place where the goods are located and provide for reasonable inspection by prospective bidders. The seller may bid at a public sale [2–706(4)].

The purchaser at a public sale who buys in good faith takes free from any rights of the original buyer even though the seller has failed to conduct the sale in compliance with the rules set out in the Code [2–706(5)]. The seller is not accountable to the buyer for any profit that the seller makes on a resale [2–706(6)].

### Recovery of the Purchase Price

In the normal performance of a contract, the seller delivers conforming goods (goods that meet the contract specifications) to the buyer. The buyer accepts the goods and pays for them. The seller is entitled to the purchase price of all goods accepted by the buyer. She also is entitled to the purchase price of all goods that conformed to the contract and were lost or damaged after the buyer assumed the risk for their loss [2–709].

For example, a contract calls for Frank, a farmer, to ship 1,000 dozen eggs to Sutton, a grocer, with shipment "FOB Frank's Farm." If the eggs are lost or damaged while on their way to Sutton, she is

responsible for paying Frank for them. Risk of loss is discussed in Chapter 11, Formation and Terms of Sales Contracts.

In one other situation, the seller may recover the purchase or contract price from the buyer. This is where the seller has made an honest effort to resell the goods and was unsuccessful or where it is apparent that any such effort to resell would be unsuccessful. This might happen where the seller manufactured goods especially for the buyer and the goods are not usable by anyone else. Assume that Sarton's Supermarket sponsors a bowling team. Sarton's orders six green-and-red bowling shirts to be embroidered with "Sarton's Supermarket" on the back and the names of the team members on the pocket. After the shirts are completed, Sarton's wrongfully refuses to accept them. The manufacturer will be able to recover the agreed purchase price if it cannot sell the shirts to someone else.

If the seller sues the buyer for the contract price of the goods, she must hold the goods for the buyer. Then, the seller must turn the goods over to the buyer if the buyer pays for them. However, if resale becomes possible before the buyer pays for the goods, the seller may resell them. Then, the seller must give the buyer credit for the proceeds of the resale [2–709(2)].

### Damages for Rejection or Repudiation

When the buyer refuses to accept goods that conform to the contract or repudiates the contract, the seller does not have to resell the goods. The seller has two other ways of determining the damages that the buyer is liable for because of the breach of contract: (1) the difference between the contract price and the market price at which the goods are currently selling and (2) the "profit" that the seller lost when the buyer did not go through with the contract [2–708].

The seller may recover as damages the difference between the contract price and the market price at the time and place the goods were to be delivered to the buyer. The seller may also recover any incidental damages, but must give the buyer credit for any expenses that the seller has saved [2–708(1)]. This measure of damages most commonly is sought by a seller when the market price of the goods dropped substantially between the time the contract was made and the time the buyer repudiated the contract.

For example, on January 1, Toy Maker, Inc., contracts with the Red Balloon Toy Shop to sell the shop 100,000 hula hoops at $3.50 each, with delivery to be made in Boston on June 1. By June 1, the hula hoop fad has passed and hula hoops are selling for $1 each in Boston. If Toy Shop repudiates the contract on June 1 and refuses to accept delivery of the 100,000 hula hoops, Toy Maker is entitled to the difference between the contract price of $350,000 and the June 1 market price in Boston of $100,000. Thus, Toy Maker could recover $250,000 in damages plus any incidental expenses, but less any expenses saved by it in not having to ship the hula hoops to Toy Shop (such as packaging and transportation costs).

If getting the difference between the contract price and the market price would not put the seller in as good a financial position as the seller would have been in if the contract had been performed, the seller may choose an alternative measure of damages based on the lost profit and overhead that the seller would have made if the sale had gone through. The seller can recover this lost profit and overhead plus any incidental expenses. However, the seller must give the buyer credit for any expenses saved as a result of the buyer's breach of contract [2–708(2)].

Using the hula hoop example, assume that the direct labor and material cost to Toy Maker of making the hoops was 75 cents each. Toy Maker could recover as damages from Toy Shop the profit Toy Maker lost when Toy Shop defaulted on the contract. Toy Maker would be entitled to the difference between the contract price of $350,000 and its direct cost of $75,000. Thus, Toy Maker could recover $275,000 plus any incidental expenses and less any expenses saved.

## Seller's Remedies Where Buyer Is Insolvent

If the seller has not agreed to extend credit to the buyer for the purchase price of goods, the buyer must make payment on delivery of the goods. If the seller tenders delivery of the goods, he may with-hold delivery unless the agreed payment is made. Where the seller has agreed to extend credit to the buyer for the purchase price of the goods, but discovers before delivery that the buyer is insolvent, the seller may refuse delivery unless the buyer pays cash for the goods together with the unpaid balance for all goods previously delivered under the contract [2–702(1)].

At common law, a seller had the right to rescind a sales contract induced by fraud and to recover the goods unless they had been resold to a bona fide purchaser for value. Based on this general legal principle, the Code provides that where the seller discovers that the buyer has received goods while insolvent, the seller may reclaim the goods upon demand made within 10 days after their receipt. This right granted to the seller is based on constructive deceit on the part of the buyer. Receiving goods while insolvent is equivalent to a false representation of solvency. To protect his rights, all the seller must do is to make a demand within the 10-day period; he need not actually repossess the goods.

If the buyer has misrepresented his solvency to this particular seller in writing within three months before the delivery of the goods, the 10-day limitation on the seller's right to reclaim the goods does not apply. However, the seller's right to reclaim the goods is subject to the prior rights of purchasers in the ordinary course of the buyer's business, good faith purchasers for value, creditors with a perfected lien on the buyer's inventory [2–702(2) and (3)], and a trustee in bankruptcy. The relative rights of creditors to their debtor's collateral are discussed in Chapter 21, Security Interests in Personal Property.

The case that follows, *Conoco, Inc. v. Braniff, Inc.*, illustrates some of issues that may arise when a creditor seeks to reclaim goods from an insolvent buyer.

## CONOCO, INC. v. BRANIFF, INC.
**11 UCC Rep.2d 519 (Bankr. M.D. Fla. 1990)**

Braniff, an airline, had an agreement with Conoco whereby Conoco supplied Braniff with its needs for Jet A aviation fuel. The fuel was sent through an interstate common carrier pipeline used by numerous suppliers, including Conoco. The pipeline contained breakout points where fuel was directed out of the pipeline and into tank farm storage facilities operated by Ogden Allied Aviation Services, Braniff's designated fueling agent, at the Dallas–Fort Worth and Kansas City airports.

The agreement called for Braniff to make advance payments for its designated fuel needs for the following week, with settlement of overages or shortages on a monthly basis. Braniff made a payment of $320,000 on September 20, 1989, for its anticipated needs through September 27 and was scheduled to make a $420,000 payment on September 27, 1989. The payment was not made on September 27, and early the next morning Braniff filed a petition in bankruptcy under Chapter 11 of the Bankruptcy Code.

On September 29, 1989, Conoco sent Braniff a "Notice of Reclamation" seeking reclamation of unpaid fuel delivered into the tank farms at the Dallas–Fort Worth airports and Kansas City during the previous 10-day period. The reclamation notice identified the fuel it sought to reclaim by specifying 14 bills of lading representing unpaid shipments occurring from September 19 through September 27.

---

**Corcoran, Bankruptcy Judge**    In order to establish entitlement to reclamation from a debtor under section 2–702 of the UCC and section 546 of the Bankruptcy Code, a reclaiming seller must satisfy the following four-part test:

1. The debtor was insolvent at the time the goods were delivered by the seller;

2. A written demand was made on the debtor within ten days after the goods were delivered to the debtor;

3. The goods were identifiable at the time the demand was made; and

4. The goods were in the possession and control of the debtor at the time the demand was made.

Braniff contends that the fuel at issue here was neither identifiable nor in its possession and control at the time the reclamation demand was made because of the commingling that occurred in the common carrier pipelines and at the airport tank farms. Braniff points out that the fuel was pumped through a common carrier pipeline from Conoco's refineries with petroleum products belonging to numerous other suppliers. Once the fuel was received at the Ogden Allied tank farms, it was then commingled in large tanks with fuel supplied by other suppliers and allocated to and for the use of numerous users. At Dallas–Fort Worth, the commingled fuel allocated to Braniff had been supplied solely by Conoco. At Kansas City, the fuel allocated to Braniff had been supplied by four suppliers, including Conoco.

In the case of fungible, bulk petroleum products, such as jet fuel, the "identification" and "possession and control" requirements of the Code and the UCC mandate that the reclaiming party:

trace the [fuel] from its possession into an identifiable mass and to show that the mass contains only [fuel] of like kind and grade. If the mass of [fuel into which the fuel is traced] is subject to [the debtor's] control, then it is both "identifiable" and "in the possession of the debtor."

In this case the jet fuel type A was shipped from Conoco's refineries through a common carrier pipeline where it was commingled with other jet fuel type A refined by other suppliers and sold to other users. The commingling further occurred in the airport tank farms, from which many airlines withdrew the fuel that was ultimately pumped into airplanes. Plainly, on these facts, Conoco has traced its fuel into an identifiable mass containing only fuel of like grade and quality.

Likewise Conoco has shown that the mass of fuel in the airport tank farms was subject to Braniff's control. The tank farms were owned and operated by Braniff's fueling agent. The fueling agent would then draw down from the fuel in the storage tanks the amount needed to fuel Braniff aircraft. On this record, it is clear that the fueling agent abided by Braniff's instructions.

The fact that the tanks contained fuel allocated to other airlines, by itself, is irrelevant to the "identification" and "possession and control" issue. The inquiry here deals solely with the fuel in the tanks allocated to Braniff.

The fact that the fueling agent also served as fueling agent for other airlines and that other airlines controlled their allocable portion of the fuel in the tank farm storage tanks does not diminish the control Braniff exercised over its allocable portion. The point, of course, is that Braniff had the ability and authority to control the disposition of its fuel at the time the reclamation notice was received.

Conoco desires to reclaim 284,107 gallons for which it is unpaid from the ending pool of 397,735. In effect, Conoco wants the court to assume that Braniff used during the ten-day reclamation period the fuel that it had on hand before the period began, the fuel that Conoco supplied during the reclamation period for which payment was made, and the fuel provided by three other suppliers during the reclamation period. In other words, Conoco says only Conoco fuel for which payment had not been made was left in the tank at the end of the reclamation period and that Conoco can now claim this "identified" fuel.

Braniff, of course, contends just the opposite. Braniff would have the court assume that Braniff used during the ten-day reclamation period the Conoco fuel for which payment was not made so that the fuel remaining in the tank at the end of the period represents only fuel that was there before the reclamation period began, fuel supplied by Conoco for which payment was made during the reclamation period, and fuel supplied by other suppliers.

The court concludes that it is required to reject both approaches. Where, as here, there are several suppliers delivering fungible, bulk goods into a common tank, the supplier must do more than merely trace its fungible, bulk goods into the pool. The supplier must go further and show what quantity of goods was in the pool at the beginning of the relevant reclamation period. The supplier must also show when, and how much of the goods, each of the suppliers contributed to the pool during that period. Finally, the supplier must show how much of the total remained in the pool at the end of the relevant period. With that information the court can then determine the amount of each bulk shipment that was consumed by the debtor during the period. The court also can determine to which supplier the amount remaining in the tank at the end of the period should be attributed or the proportional way in which the amount remaining should be allocated among the suppliers. Implicit in the rule the court states here is a "first in, first out" theory of bulk fuel use to be used in cases such as this where fungible, bulk goods are pooled or commingled.

On the evidence presented, Conoco established its right to reclaim only the 100,002 gallons of fuel it delivered to Dallas–Fort Worth on September 26.

**Judgment for Conoco.**

---

## Seller's Right to Stop Delivery

If the seller discovers that the buyer is insolvent, he has the right to stop the delivery of any goods that he has shipped to the buyer, regardless of the size of the shipment. If a buyer repudiates a sales contract or fails to make a payment due before delivery, the seller has the right to stop delivery of any large shipment of goods, such as a carload, a truckload, or a planeload [2–705].

To stop delivery, the seller must notify the carrier or other bailee in time for the bailee to prevent delivery of the goods. After receiving notice to stop delivery, the carrier or other bailee owes a duty to hold the goods and deliver them as directed by the seller. The seller is liable to the carrier or other bailee for expenses incurred or damages resulting from compliance with his order to stop delivery. If a nonnegotiable document of title has been issued for the goods, the carrier or other bailee does not have a duty to obey a stop-delivery order issued by any person other than the person who consigned the goods to him [2–705(3)].

## Liquidated Damages

If the seller has justifiably withheld delivery of the goods because of the buyer's breach, the buyer may recover any money or goods he has delivered to the seller over and above the agreed amount of liquidated damages. If there is no such agreement, the seller may not retain an amount in excess of $500 or 20 percent of the value of the total performance for which the buyer is obligated under the contract, whichever is smaller. This right of restitution is subject to the seller's right to recover damages under other provisions of the Code and to recover the amount of value of benefits received by the buyer directly or indirectly by reason of the contract [2–718].

---

**CONCEPT REVIEW**

## SELLER'S REMEDIES (ON BREACH BY BUYER)

| Problem | Seller's Remedy |
|---|---|
| **Buyer Refuses to Go Ahead with Contract and Seller Has Goods** | 1. Seller may cancel contract, suspend performance, and set aside goods intended to fill the contract.<br>   *a.* If seller is in the process of manufacturing, he may complete manufacture or stop and sell for scrap, picking alternative that in his judgment at the time will minimize the seller's loss.<br>   *b.* Seller can resell goods covered by contract and recover difference between contract price and proceeds of resale.<br>   *c.* Seller may recover purchase price where resale is not possible.<br>   *d.* Seller may recover damages for breach based on difference between contract price and market price, or in some cases based on lost profits. |
| **Goods Are in Buyer's Possession** | 1. Seller may recover purchase price.<br>2. Seller may reclaim goods in possession of insolvent buyer by making a demand within 10 days after their receipt. If the buyer represented solvency to the seller in writing within three months before delivery, the 10-day limitation does not apply. |
| **Goods Are in Transit** | 1. Seller may stop any size shipment if buyer is insolvent.<br>2. Seller may stop carload, truckload, planeload, or other large shipment for reasons other than buyer's insolvency. |

---

## BUYER'S REMEDIES

### Buyer's Remedies in General

A seller may breach a contract in a number of ways. The most common are: (1) failing to make an agreed delivery, (2) delivering goods that do not conform to the contract, and (3) indicating that he does not intend to fulfill the obligations under the contract.

A buyer whose seller breaks the contract is given a number of alternative remedies. These include:

- Buying other goods (covering) and recovering damages from the seller based on any additional expense that the buyer incurs in obtaining the goods [2–712].
- Recovering damages based on the difference between the contract price and the current market price of the goods [2–713].
- Recovering damages for any nonconforming goods accepted by the buyer based on the difference in value between what the buyer got and what he should have gotten [2–714].

- Obtaining specific performance of the contract where the goods are unique and cannot be obtained elsewhere [2–716].

In addition, the buyer can in some cases recover consequential damages (such as lost profits) and incidental damages (such as expenses incurred in buying substitute goods).

### Buyer's Right to Cover

If the seller fails or refuses to deliver the goods called for in the contract, the buyer can purchase substitute goods; this is known as **cover.** If the buyer does purchase substitute goods, the buyer can recover as damages from the seller the difference between the contract price and the cost of the substitute goods [2–712]. For example, Frank Farmer agrees to sell Ann's Cider Mill 1,000 bushels of apples at $10 a bushel. Farmer then refuses to deliver the apples. Cider Mill can purchase 1,000 bushels of similar apples, and if it has to pay $11 a bushel, it can recover the difference ($1 a bushel) between what it paid ($11) and the contract price ($10). Thus, Cider Mill could recover $1,000 from Farmer.

The buyer can also recover any incidental damages sustained, but must give the seller credit for any expenses saved. In addition, he may be able to obtain consequential damages. The buyer is not required to cover, however. If he does not cover, the other remedies under the Code are still available [2–712].

The case that follows, *Saboundjian v. Bank Audi (USA)*, illustrates that a court will not allow an aggrieved party to speculate on the market at the defaulting party's expense.

---

## Saboundjian v. Bank Audi (USA)
**11 UCC Rep.2d 1165 (N.Y. Sup. Ct., App. Div. 1990)**

Vrej Saboundjian, a customer of Bank Audi, was a sophisticated international businessman well acquainted with the foreign exchange market. In April 1986, he began to speculate in foreign currency through the bank. The foreign currency trading market, which is global, operates without a central exchange and with individual banks throughout the world setting their own rates. Thus, a foreign exchange speculator like Saboundjian, by sending orders to Far East, Middle East, and European markets, is able to participate in foreign exchange trading even after the close of business at domestic banks.

On January 7, 1987, Saboundjian was holding a short position in deutsche marks. That afternoon, he asked the foreign exchange trader at Bank Audi (USA) to liquidate his short position when "deutsche marks reached 1.9360 per dollar." As was customary for the bank when an order was placed in the late afternoon or evening and the customer's price was not available in the domestic mark, Bank Audi relayed the order to a foreign bank, in this case, Investbank in the United Arab Emirates, to be executed. The bank's commission covering profit and expenses for performing the trade was added to the price requested by Saboundjian. Thus, the order placed at 3:24 P.M., eastern standard time, called for the bank to sell $2 million against deutsche marks at the rate of 1.9380 deutsche marks per dollar.

At 8 A.M. the following morning, the Bank Audi trader noticed that confirmation of the requested trade had not been received and telephoned Investbank and was advised that it had been unable to execute the requested trade. He was advised by Bank Audi (Paris) that the market had been very hectic and that the requested price had been quoted in the market only very briefly and thereafter dropped quickly.

At about 9 A.M., Saboundjian was advised that Investbank had been unable to effect the order; he was also advised of the current market price and that his order could be executed at that price if he desired. He indicated that he did not want the bank to execute at that price and that he was "bullish." At the time, he could have made a profit of approximately $4,700, somewhat less than the approximately $8,000 he would have made if his requested trade had been executed. He subsequently testified that "I thought if I wait maybe a couple of hours or one day, that I could see my price again and if I don't see the price, I said, you have to take the loss as the bank."

During the day, Saboundjian's position deteriorated to a small loss by the end of the day. He did not ask the bank to close out his position until February 6, 1987, at which time the value of the dollar in terms of deutsche marks had fallen to 1.8695. His losses exceeded $420,000. He subsequently brought an action against Bank Audi for failure to execute the January 6 trade and sought consequential damages in excess of $400,000. The bank filed a motion for partial summary judgment, seeking to limit its liability to the difference between Saboundjian's profit had the transaction been carried out as requested and the smaller profit he would have made had he acted to cover on January 8 when he learned of the failure of the January 7 trade. The trial court denied the motion and the bank appealed.

**Sullivan, Judge**    Even assuming the bank is liable for failing to execute the January 7, 1987, trade, liability is limited to the difference between the price at which Saboundjian could have executed the trade at issue were it not for the failure to carry it out, and the price at which he could have executed the transaction within a reasonable time after he learned that it had not been effected earlier. Since Saboundjian had a duty to act reasonably and mitigate any damages he may have sustained, the bank cannot be liable for his entire speculation, including losses realized on unrelated transactions. Thus, when a broker rightfully fails to purchase or sell a security as directed, the customer's damages are limited to the cost of covering or replacing the security. If the customer fails to cover within a reasonable time, damages are limited to the potential cost to cover as measured from the time he learns of the broker's failure and for a reasonable time thereafter in which he must decide on his course of action. A customer may not refuse to cover a transaction previously requested and thereby speculate on the market entirely at the risk of the broker.

Article 2 of the Uniform Commercial Code is instructive on the issue of damages. Under section 2−712(1), in the event of a breach, "the buyer may 'cover' by making in good faith and without unreasonable delay any reasonable purchase or contract to purchase goods in substitution for those due from the seller." The buyer may only recover from the seller "as damages the difference between the cost of cover and the contract price together with any incidental or consequential damages." Consequential damages are restricted, however, to those "which could not reasonably be prevented by cover or otherwise." Section 2−715(2). Thus Saboundjian is not entitled to consequential damages since he was in a position to effect cover immediately after having been notified of the bank's failure to execute the January 7 order.

Saboundjian's damages are therefore limited to no more than the difference between the profit he would have earned had the subject trade been executed on January 7, 1987, or approximately $8,000 as alleged in the complaint, and the profit that Saboundjian would have earned had he directed the execution of the trade within a reasonable time after he learned that his original order had not been executed.

**Judgment reversed in favor of Bank Audi.**

---

## Incidental Damages

Incidental damages include expenses that the buyer incurs in receiving, inspecting, transporting, and storing goods shipped by the seller that do not conform to those called for in the contract. Incidental damages also include any reasonable expenses or charges that the buyer has to pay in obtaining substitute goods [2−715(1)].

## Consequential Damages

In certain situations, an injured buyer is able to recover consequential damages such as the buyer's lost profits caused by the seller's breach of contract. The buyer must be able to show that the seller knew or should have known at the time the contract was made that the buyer would suffer special damages if the seller did not perform his obligations. The buyer must also show that he could not have prevented the damage by obtaining substitute goods [2−715(2)].

Suppose Knitting Mill promises to deliver 15,000 yards of a special fabric to Dorsey by September 1. Knitting Mill knows that Dorsey wants to acquire the material to make garments suitable for the Christmas season. Knitting Mill also knows that in reliance on the contract with it, Dorsey will enter into contracts with department stores to deliver the finished garments by October 1. If Knitting Mill fails to deliver the fabric or delivers the fabric after September 1, it may be liable to Dorsey for any consequential damages that she sustains if she is unable to acquire the same material elsewhere in time to fulfill her October 1 contracts.

Consequential damages can also include an injury to a person or property caused by a breach of warranty. For example, an electric saw is defective. Hanson purchases the saw, and while he is using it, the blade comes off and severely cuts his arm. The injury to Hanson is consequential damage resulting from a nonconforming or defective product.

## Damages for Nondelivery

If the seller fails or refuses to deliver the goods called for by the contract, the buyer has the option of recovering damages for the nondelivery. Thus, instead of covering, the buyer can get the difference between the contract price of the goods and their market price at the time he learns of the seller's breach. In addition, the buyer may recover any incidental damages and consequential damages, but must give the seller credit for any expenses saved [2–713].

Suppose Biddle agreed on June 1 to sell and deliver 1,500 bushels of wheat to a grain elevator on September 1 for $7 per bushel and then refused to deliver on September 1 because the market price was then $8 per bushel. The grain elevator could recover $1,500 damages from Biddle, plus incidental damages that could not have been prevented by cover.

The *Sun Maid Raisin Growers of California v. Victor Packing Co.* case, which follows, illustrates the application of the measure of damages for nondelivery. In this case, the market price of the goods at the time of delivery was significantly higher than the contract price, and the seller, who had gambled that the price would fall, had to pay substantial damages.

---

## SUN MAID RAISIN GROWERS OF CALIFORNIA V. VICTOR PACKING CO.

### 194 Cal. Rptr. 612 (Cal. Ct. App. 1983)

In November 1975, Victor Packing Company agreed to sell Sun Maid Raisin Growers 1,900 tons of raisins. The first 100 tons were sold at 39 cents per pound and the remainder at 40 cents per pound. No specific delivery date was agreed on. Victor indicated to Sun Maid on August 10, 1976, that it would not complete performance, being unable to deliver the last 610 tons. Sun Maid was able to purchase 200 tons at 43 cents per pound. Because of heavy rains in September 1976, the new crop of raisins suffered extensive damage and the price of raisins increased dramatically.

Sun Maid brought suit against Victor to recover damages. The trial court awarded $307,339 in damages to Sun Maid. Victor appealed, claiming that the increase in the lost profits due to the disastrous rain damage was not foreseeable.

---

**Franson, Acting Presiding Judge**    The basic measure of damages for a seller's nondelivery or repudiation is the difference between the market price and the contract price.

In addition to the difference between the market price and the contract price, the buyer can recover incidental damages such as expenses of cover and consequential damages such as lost profits to the extent that they could not have been avoided by cover. The inability to cover after a prompt and reasonable effort to do so is a prerequisite to recovery of consequential damages. If the buyer is only able to cover in part, he is entitled to the net cost of cover (the difference between the cover price and the contract price plus expenses) together with any consequential damages but less expenses saved in consequence of the seller's breach.

Under 2–715(2)(a), consequential damages include "any loss resulting from general or particular requirements and needs of which the seller at the time of contracting had reason to know and which could not reasonably be prevented by cover or otherwise." The "reason to know" language concerning the buyer's particular requirements and needs arises from *Hadley v. Baxendale*. The Code, however, has imposed an objective rather than a subjective standard in determining whether the seller should have anticipated the buyer's needs. Thus, actual knowledge by the seller of the buyer's requirements is not required. The only requirement under 2–715(2)(a) is that the seller reasonably should have been expected to know of the buyer's exposure to loss.

Furthermore, comment 6 to § 2–715 provides that if the seller knows that the buyer is in the business of reselling the goods, the seller is charged with knowledge that the buyer will be selling the goods in anticipation of a profit. "Absent a contractual provision against consequential damages a seller in breach will therefore always be liable for the buyer's resulting loss of profit."

Finally, a buyer's failure to take any other steps by which the loss could reasonably have been prevented bars him from recovering consequential damages. This is merely a codification of the rule that the buyer must attempt to minimize damages. In the present case, the evidence fully supports the finding that after Victor's breach of the contract on August 10, 1976, Sun Maid acted in good faith in a commercially reasonable manner and was able to cover by purchase only some 200 tons of substitute raisins at a cost of 43 cents per pound. There were no other natural Thompson seedless free tonnage raisins available for purchase in the market at or within a reasonable time after Victor's breach. Although the evidence indicates that Sun Maid actually was able to purchase an additional 410 tons of raisins after the September rainfall in its efforts to effect cover, these were badly damaged raisins which had to be reconditioned at a substantial cost to bring them up to market condition. According to Sun Maid, if the trial court had used the total cost of cover of the full 610 tons as the measure of damages rather than lost profits on resale, its damages would have totaled $377,720.

Although the trial court did not specify why it determined damages by calculating lost profits instead of the cost of cover, the court probably found that damages should be limited to the amount that would have put Sun Maid in "as good a position as if the other party had fully performed." Thus, Sun Maid was awarded the lesser of the actual cost of cover (treating the reconditioning of the 410 tons as a cost) and the loss of prospective profits.

In contending that the foreseeability requirement applies to the amount of the lost profits and not just to the fact of lost profits, Victor apparently acknowledges that it knew at the time of contracting that Sun Maid would be reselling the raisins to its customers in the domestic market. Victor has no alternative to this concession since it was an experienced packer and knew that Sun Maid marketed raisins year round in the domestic market. Further-

more, Victor must be presumed to have known that if it did not deliver the full quota of raisins provided under the contracts (1,900 tons) by the end of the crop year or before such reasonable time as thereafter might be agreed to, Sun Maid would be forced to go into the market to attempt to cover its then existing orders for sale of raisins. This is exactly what occurred.

Victor nonetheless contends it should not be liable for damages based on the extraordinarily high price of raisins in the fall of 1976 which was caused by the "disastrous" rains in September. These rains reportedly caused a 50 percent loss of the new crop which with the lack of a substantial carryover of 1975 raisins drove the market price from approximately $860 per packed weight ton to over $1,600 per packed weight ton. Victor does not assert the doctrine of impossibility or impracticability of performance as a defense [§ 2–615]. This is understandable since the nondelivery of raisins was not caused by the failure of a presupposed condition (continuance of the $860 per ton market price) but solely by Victor's failure to deliver the 610 tons of raisins during the 1975 crop year.

This is where the trial court's findings of Victor's bad faith becomes pertinent. A reasonable inference may be drawn that from early spring Victor was gambling on the market price of raisins in deciding whether to perform its contracts with Sun Maid. If the price would fall below the contract price, Victor would buy raisins and deliver them to Sun Maid. If the market price went substantially above the contract price, Victor would sit tight. While we cannot read Victor's mind during the late spring and summer months, we can surmise that it speculated that the market price would remain below the contract price after the current crop year so that it could purchase new raisins for delivery to Sun Maid at the contract price. It threw the dice and lost. The possibility of "disastrous" rain damage to the 1976 raisin crop was clearly foreseeable to Victor. Such rains have occurred at sporadic intervals since raisins have been grown in the San Joaquin Valley. Raisin packers fully understand the great risk in contracting to sell raisins at a fixed price over a period of time extending into the next crop year. The market price may go up or down depending on consumer demand and the supply and quality of raisins. If the seller does not have sufficient inventory to fulfill his delivery obligations within the time initially required or as subsequently modified by the parties, he will have to go into the market to purchase raisins. The fact that he may be surprised by an extraordinary rise in the market price does not mean that the buyer's prospective profits on resale are unforeseeable as a matter of law.

**Judgment for Sun Maid affirmed.**

## Damages for Defective Goods

If a buyer accepts defective goods and wants to hold the seller liable, the buyer must give the seller notice of the defect within a reasonable time after the buyer discovers the defect [2–607(3)]. Where goods are defective or not as warranted and the buyer gives the required notice, he can recover damages. The buyer is entitled to recover the difference between the value of the goods received and the value the goods would have had if they had been as warranted. He may also be entitled to incidental and consequential damages [2–714].

For example, Al's Auto Store sells Anders an automobile tire, warranting it to be four-ply construction. The tire goes flat when it is punctured by a nail, and Anders discovers that the tire is really only two-ply. If Anders gives the store prompt notice of the breach, she can keep the tire and recover from Al's the difference in value between a two-ply and a four-ply tire.

## Buyer's Right to Specific Performance

Sometimes, the goods covered by a contract are unique and it is not possible for a buyer to obtain substitute goods. When this is the case, the buyer is entitled to specific performance of the contract.

**Specific performance** means that the buyer can require the seller to give the buyer the goods covered by the contract [2–716]. Thus, the buyer of an antique automobile such as a 1910 Ford might have a court order the seller to deliver the specified automobile to the buyer because it was one of a kind. On the other hand, the buyer of grain in a particular storage bin could not get specific performance if he could buy the same kind of grain elsewhere.

## Buyer and Seller Agreements as to Remedies

As mentioned earlier in this chapter, the parties to a contract may provide remedies in addition to or as substitution for those expressly provided in the Code [2–719]. For example, the buyer's remedies may be limited by the contract to the return of the goods and the repayment of the price or to the replacement of nonconforming goods or parts. However, a court looks to see whether such a limitation was freely agreed to or whether it is unconscionable. In the latter case, the court does not enforce the limitation and the buyer has all the rights given to an injured buyer by the Code.

---

**CONCEPT REVIEW**

## Buyer's Remedies (on breach by seller)

| Problems | Buyer's Remedy |
| --- | --- |
| **Seller Fails to Deliver Goods or Delivers Nonconforming Goods that Buyer Rightfully Rejects or Justifiably Revokes Acceptance of** | 1. Buyer may cancel the contract and recover damages. <br> 2. Buyer may "cover" by obtaining substitute goods and recover difference between contract price and cost of cover. <br> 3. Buyer may recover damages for breach based on difference between contract price and market price. |

| Problems | Buyer's Remedy |
| --- | --- |
| **Seller Delivers Nonconforming Goods that Are Accepted by Buyer** | Buyer may recover damages based on difference between value of goods received and value of goods if they had been as warranted. |
| **Seller Has the Goods but Refuses to Deliver Them and Buyer Wants Them** | Buyer may seek specific performance if goods are unique and cannot be obtained elsewhere, or buyer may replevy goods identified to contract if buyer cannot obtain cover. |

### PROBLEMS AND PROBLEM CASES

**1.** Lobianco contracted with Property Protection, Inc., for the installation of a burglar alarm system. The contract provided in part:

Alarm system equipment installed by Property Protection, Inc., is guaranteed against improper function due to manufacturing defects of workmanship for a period of 12 months. The installation of the above equipment carries a 90-day warranty. The liability of Property Protection, Inc., is limited to repair or replacement of security alarm equipment and does not include loss or damage to possessions, persons, or property.

As installed, the alarm system included a standby battery source of power in the event that the regular source of power failed. During the 90-day warranty period, burglars broke into Lobianco's house and stole $35,815 worth of jewelry. First, they destroyed the electric meter so that there was no electric source to operate the system, and then they entered the house. The batteries in the standby system were dead, and thus the standby system failed to operate. Accordingly, no outside siren was activated and a telephone call that was supposed to be triggered was not made. Lobianco brought suit, claiming damage in the amount of her stolen jewelry because of the failure of the alarm system to work properly. Did the disclaimer effectively eliminate any liability on the alarm company's part for consequential damages?

**2.** On April 11, 1984, Neville Riley purchased a new Chevrolet Camaro from a Chevrolet dealer in Boston, Massachusetts. The car came equipped with a hydraulic jack that was designed, manufactured and sold by General Motors. The Camaro and jack subsequently changed hands several times and were sold to Jay Ronyak on July 24, 1989. While using the jack on August 29, 1989, to raise the Camaro, it malfunctioned, causing the car to fall on Ronyak.

He died several days later as a result of the accident. The administrator of Ronyak's estate brought suit against General Motors for breach of warranty. General Motors asserted that the lawsuit was barred by the statute of limitations, but the administrator contended that the warranties in this instance extended to the future performance of the automobile and the jack. She reasoned that "a person who purchases a jack as part of an automobile purchase will have no need for the jack at the time of the purchase, and indeed may not have needed the jack for months or even years after the purchase." Was the lawsuit barred by the four-year statute of limitations in the UCC?

**3.** Bechtel ordered an alabaster-colored mink coat from Pollock Furs. The coat had been specially made because she required an unusually large size and requested a particular styling. The coat cost $5,500, of which Bechtel paid $250. Several months later, she decided that she did not want the coat and canceled the order, even though Pollack Furs had completed the coat. Pollack Furs then filed suit for the balance of the purchase price. What can Bechtel argue in defense?

**4.** Cohn advertised a 30-foot sailboat for sale in *The New York Times*. Fisher saw the ad, inspected the sailboat, and offered Cohn $4,650 for the boat. Cohn accepted the offer. Fisher gave Cohn a check for $2,535 as a deposit on the boat. He wrote on the check, "Deposit on aux sloop, D'arc Wind, full amount $4,650." Fisher later refused to go through with the purchase and stopped payment on the deposit check. Cohn readvertised the boat and sold it for the highest offer he received, which was $3,000. Cohn then sued Fisher for breach of contract. He asked for damages of $1,679.50. This represented the $1,650 difference between the contract price and the sale price plus $29.50 in incidental expenses in reselling the boat. Is Cohn entitled to this measure of damages?

**5.** Dubrow, a widower, was engaged to be married. In October, he placed a large order with a furniture store for delivery the following January. The order included rugs cut to special sizes for the prospective couple's new house and many pieces of furniture for various rooms in the house. One week later, Dubrow died. When the order was delivered, his only heir, his daughter, refused to take the furniture and carpeting. The furniture store then sued his estate to recover the full purchase price. It had not tried to resell the furniture and carpeting to anyone else. Under the circumstances, was the seller entitled to recover the purchase price of the goods?

**6.** McCain Foods sold on credit and delivered a quantity of frozen french fries to Flagstaff Food Service Company. Several days later, when the potatoes had not yet been paid for, McCain discovered that Flagstaff was insolvent and had just filed a petition in bankruptcy. What would you advise McCain Foods to do?

**7.** Kneale bought two chairs from Modernage Furniture that were on sale for $97.50 apiece. The regular price of the chairs was $147.57 each, or $50.07 more than the sale price. Because the store had oversold that particular chair, it failed to deliver the items to Kneale, although she had paid the full purchase price in cash. She brought suit for breach of contract against Modernage Furniture. Modernage contended that its liability was limited to return of the purchase price. Was Modernage's liability for breach of contract limited to return of the purchase price?

**8.** Barr purchased from Crow's Nest Yacht Sales a 31-foot Tiara pleasure yacht manufactured by S-2 Yachts. He had gone to Crow's Nest knowing the style and type yacht he wanted. He was told that the retail price was $102,000 but that he could purchase the model they had for $80,000. When he asked about the reduction in price he was told that Crow's Nest had to move it because there was a change in the model and they had new ones coming in. He was assured that the yacht was new, that there was nothing wrong with it, and that it only had 20 hours on the engines. Barr installed a considerable amount of electronic equipment on the boat. When he began to use it, he experienced tremendous difficulties with equipment malfunctions. On examination by a marine expert it was determined that the yacht had earlier been sunk in salt water, resulting in significant rusting and deterioration in the engine,

equipment, and fixtures. Other experts concluded that significant replacement and repair was required, that the engines would have only 25 percent of their normal expected life, and that following its sinking, the yacht would have only half of its original value. Barr then brought suit against Crow's Nest and S-2 Yachts for breach of warranty. To what measure of damages is Barr entitled to recover for breach of warranty?

**9.** Certina USA is a watch manufacturer that sells its watches through traveling salespeople paid by it. Migerobe, Inc., owns and operates jewelry counters in McRae's department stores, which are located throughout the Southeast. In the summer of 1987, Migerobe contacted Gerald Murff, a Certina salesperson from whom it had previously purchased watches. It notified him that Migerobe was interested in buying Certina watches if the company decided to sell a large portion of its inventory at reduced prices. Migerobe had some reason to believe that Certina had excess inventory, and Certina in fact decided to eliminate its inventory as a result of a corporate decision to withdraw its watches from the U.S. market. Migerobe was hoping to acquire the Certina watches so that they could be used as "doorbusters" for an after-Thanksgiving sale. Doorbusters or "loss leaders" are items offered at a low price, which are designed to increase the traffic flow through a store and, thereby, increase corollary sales (the sale of nonadvertised items). On October 29, the parties agreed on the sale of over 2,000 watches at a price of $45 per watch. On November 4, the national accounts manager for Certina called Migerobe to say that Certina would not ship the watches. Migerobe brought suit against Certina to recover damages for breach of contract, including consequential damages in the form of lost profits on corollary sales. Migerobe asserted that the Certina salesperson was aware of its plan to use the watches as a loss leader by featuring them in a "doorbuster" Thanksgiving advertisement at a 50 percent discount. It also had data that showed it previously had increased its corollary sales by 69 to 87 percent when it had used similar doorbuster promotions. Was Migerobe entitled to recover the lost profits on corollary sales as consequential damages caused by Certina's breach of contract?

**10.** In 1972, Schweber contracted to purchase a certain black 1973 Rolls-Royce Corniche automobile from Rallye Motors. He made a $3,500 deposit on the car. Rallye later returned his deposit to him and told him that the car was not available. However, Schweber learned that the automobile was available to the dealer and was being sold to another customer. The dealer then offered to sell Schweber a similar car but with a different interior design. Schweber brought a lawsuit against the dealer to prevent it from selling the Rolls-Royce Corniche to anyone else and to require that it be sold to him. Rallye Motors claimed that he could get only damages and not specific performance. Approximately 100 Rolls-Royce Corniches were being sold each year in the United States, but none of the others would have the specific features and detail of this one. Is the remedy of specific performance available to Schweber?

**11.** 📼  *Video Case.* See "Sour Grapes." Jelly Manufacturer, a food processor in Chicago, placed a phone order with Grape Grower, a grower in California for a quantity of perishable produce. The shipping term was CIF with payment to be made on delivery (COD). Grape Grower delivered the goods called for in the contract to a carrier and contracted for their shipment. However, it neglected to provide that the goods be shipped under refrigeration. The goods were loaded on a nonrefrigerated boxcar, and as a result, the produce was spoiled when it reached Chicago. Jelly Manufacturer, as required by the COD term, paid for the produce by check before discovering the spoilage. When Jelly Manufacturer called Grape Grower to complain, Grower offered to rush a replacement shipment. Jelly Manufacturer declined the offer, stating that it would not arrive in time for the produce to be processed and delivered to Grocery Chain in time to meet Jelly Manufacturer's contract with Grocery Chain. Jelly Manufacturer arranged for a rush replacement shipment from a nearby source, but had to pay 150 percent of the prevailing market price for the produce. Even so, Jelly Manufacturer was unable to deliver the finished products to Grocery Chain and was required to pay a penalty for late delivery as provided in its contract with Grocery Chain. Can Jelly Manufacturer recover damages from Grape Grower for breach of contract? If so, what elements can be recovered? Can Grocery Chain recover the penalty from Jelly Manufacturer?

## CAPSTONE QUESTIONS

Perfect Sound, Inc. (PSI), is in the retail electronics business. It sells only products bearing its own brand name. PSI has a standard clause in its consumer retail sales agreements that provides:

You must inform our headquarters at 118 Main Street, Central City, Indiana, of any warranty claims you may have under the Perfect Sound, Inc., warranty for the product that you purchased. . . . During the period of one (1) year from the date of the original purchase, Perfect Sound, Inc., will repair the product without charge for parts or labor, or, at its option, replace the product. This repair or replacement is the purchaser's sole remedy. Perfect Sound, Inc., is not responsible for consequential damages that the purchaser may sustain including damage to cassettes, compact discs, CD-ROM, videos, or any other audio or video not part of the product sold. This limited warranty does not apply to any product damaged by accident, misuse, improper voltage, lightning, fire, or if you or anyone other than Perfect Sound, Inc., repairs or alters the product.

PSI makes hundreds of sales a day and has hired you to represent it in the occasional disputes with customers that it cannot resolve at the local managerial level. It recently sent you files that included the following:

- A buyer purchased a new home entertainment center. She immediately experienced difficulty with the speakers and made several complaints to her local store. The store had made several attempts to repair the speakers and to improve the sound quality. However, she waited 14 months after her purchase to complain about faulty sound to the home office. The buyer now insists on a full refund of her purchase price. PSI argues that its warranty obligations have expired and also asserts the exclusive remedy provision of the written warranty (above), which says that PSI will repair or replace but will not refund the price.

- PSI specially ordered a Danish television set for a long-standing customer who wanted a set with an ultramodern look. The set cost $3,500. When it arrived, the buyer refused to take delivery because he had decided he preferred a Swedish manufacturer's cabinetry. PSI tried to find another buyer for the specially ordered set but was unable to find anyone who would pay more than $1,300 for it.

· A customer who purchased a tape deck that admittedly was defective claimed that PSI should not only refund the purchase price of the tape deck but should also reimburse him for the loss of a number of original-recording tapes that the customer had made of performances of folksingers at folk festivals.

## Required:

Answer the following and give reasons for your conclusions.

1. With respect to the buyer who purchased the home entertainment center, advise PSI on the correctness of its position.

2. Advise PSI what remedies it has against the customer who rejected the Danish television set.

3. Advise PSI as to the damages that the aggrieved buyer of the tape deck would be entitled to recoup under the provisions of Article 2 of the Uniform Commercial Code.

**PART**

**3**

# PROPERTY

**CHAPTER 15**
Personal Property and Bailments

**CHAPTER 16**
Real Property

**CHAPTER 17**
Insurance

**CHAPTER 18**
Landlord and Tenant

**CHAPTER 19**
Estates and Trusts

# CHAPTER
## 15

# PERSONAL PROPERTY

# AND BAILMENTS

**INTRODUCTION**

*The concept of property is crucial to the organization of society. The essential nature of a particular society is often reflected in the way it views property, including the degree to which property ownership is concentrated in the state, the extent it permits individual ownership of property, and the rules that govern such ownership. History is replete with wars and revolutions that arose out of conflicting claims to, or views concerning, property. Significant documents in our own Anglo-American legal tradition, such as the Magna Carta and the Constitution, deal explicitly with property rights. This chapter will discuss the nature and classification of property. It will also examine the various ways that interests in personal property can be obtained and transferred, such as by production, purchase, or gift. The last half of the chapter explores the law of bailments. A bailment is involved, for example, when you check your coat in a coatroom at a restaurant or when you park your car in a public parking garage and leave your keys with the attendant.*

## NATURE OF PROPERTY

The word **property** is used in several distinct ways. The word is sometimes used to refer to a thing that is capable of being owned. It is also used to refer to a right or interest associated with a thing that gives the owner the ability to exercise dominion over that thing.

When we talk about ownership of property, we are talking about a bundle of rights that are recognized and enforced by the law. For example, ownership of a building includes the exclusive right to use, enjoy, sell, mortgage, or rent the building. If someone else tries to use the property without the owner's consent, the owner can use the courts and legal procedures to eject that person. Ownership of a patent includes the right to sell it, to license others to use it, or to produce the patented article personally.

In the United States, private ownership of property is protected by the Constitution, which provides that the government shall deprive no person of "life, liberty or property without due process of law." We recognize and encourage the rights of individuals to acquire, enjoy, and use property.

These rights, however, are not unlimited. For example, a person cannot use property in an unreasonable manner to the injury of others. Also, the state has **police power** through which it can impose reasonable regulations on the use of property, tax it, and take it for public use by paying the owner compensation for it.

Property can be divided into a number of categories based on its characteristics. The same piece of property may fall into more than one class. The following discussion explores the meaning of **personal property** and the numerous ways of classifying property.

## CLASSIFICATIONS OF PROPERTY

### Personal Property versus Real Property

Personal property is defined by process of exclusion. The term *personal property* is used in contrast to *real property*. Real property is the earth's crust and all things firmly attached to it.[1] For example, land, office buildings, and houses are all considered to be real property. All other objects and rights that can be owned are personal property. Clothing, books, bank accounts, and stock in a corporation are all examples of personal property.

Real property can be turned into personal property if it is detached from the earth. Similarly, personal property can be attached to the earth and become real property. For example, marble in the ground is real property. When the marble is quarried, it becomes personal property, but if it is used in constructing a building, it becomes real property again. Perennial vegetation that does not have to be seeded every year, such as trees, shrubs, and grass, is usually treated as part of the real property on which it is growing. When trees and shrubs are severed from the land, they become personal property. Crops that must be planted each year, such as corn, oats, and potatoes, are usually treated as personal property. However, if the real property on which they are growing is sold, the new owner of the real property also becomes the owner of the crops.

When personal property is attached to, or used in conjunction with, real property in such a way as to

be treated as part of the real property, it is known as a **fixture.** The law concerning fixtures is discussed in the next chapter.

### Tangible versus Intangible Personal Property

Personal property can be either tangible or intangible. Tangible property has a physical existence. Cars, animals, and computers are examples. Property that has no physical existence is called intangible property. For example, rights under a patent, copyright, or trademark would be intangible property.

The distinction between tangible and intangible property is important primarily for tax and estate planning purposes. Generally, tangible property is subject to tax in the state in which it is located, whereas intangible property is usually taxable in the state where its owner lives.

### Public and Private Property

Property is also classified as public or private based on the ownership of the property. If the property is owned by the government or a governmental unit, it is classified as public property. If it is owned by an individual, a group of individuals, a corporation, or some other business organization, it is private property.

## ACQUIRING OWNERSHIP OF PERSONAL PROPERTY

### Production or Purchase

The most common ways of obtaining ownership of property are by producing it or purchasing it. A person owns the property that she makes unless the person has agreed to do the work for someone else. In that case, the employer is the owner of the product of the work. For example, a person who creates a painting, knits a sweater, or develops a computer program is the owner unless she has been hired by someone to do the painting, knit the sweater, or develop the program. Another major way of acquiring property is by purchase. The law regarding the purchase of tangible personal property (that is, sale of goods) is discussed in Chapter 11.

---

[1]The law of real property is treated in Chapter 16.

## Possession of Unowned Property

In very early times, the most common way of obtaining ownership of personal property was simply by taking possession of unowned property. For example, the first person to take possession of a wild animal became its owner. Today, one can still acquire ownership of personal property by possessing it if the property is unowned. The two major examples of unowned property that can be acquired by possession are wild animals and abandoned property. Abandoned property will be discussed in the next section, which focuses on the rights of finders.

The first person to take possession of a wild animal property normally becomes the owner.[2] To acquire ownership of a wild animal by taking possession, a person must obtain enough control over it to deprive it of its freedom. If a person fatally wounds a wild animal, the person becomes the owner. Wild animals caught in a trap or fish caught in a net are usually considered to be the property of the person who set the trap or net. If a captured wild animal escapes and is caught by another person, that person generally becomes the owner. However, if that person knows that the animal is an escaped animal and that the prior owner is chasing it to recapture it, then he does not become the owner.

## RIGHTS OF FINDERS OF LOST, MISLAID, AND ABANDONED PROPERTY

The old saying "finders keepers, losers weepers" is not a reliable way of predicting the legal rights of those who find personal property that originally belonged—or still belongs—to another. The rights of the finder will be determined by whether the property he finds is classified as abandoned, lost, or mislaid.

**1.** *Abandoned property.* Property is considered to be abandoned if the owner intentionally placed the property out of his possession with the intent to relinquish ownership of it. For example, Norris takes his TV set to the city dump and leaves it there. The finder of abandoned property who takes

possession of it with intent to claim ownership becomes the owner of the property. This means he acquires better rights to the property than anyone else in the world, including the original owner. For example, if Fox finds the TV set, puts it in his car, and takes it home, Fox becomes the owner of the TV set.

**2.** *Lost property.* Property is considered to be lost when the owner did not intend to part with possession of the property. For example, if Barber's camera fell out of her handbag while she was walking down the street, it would be considered lost property. The person who finds lost property does not acquire ownership of it, but he acquires better rights to the lost property than anyone other than the true owner. For example, suppose Lawrence finds Barber's camera in the grass where it fell. Jones then steals the camera from Lawrence's house. Under these facts, Barber is still the owner of the camera. She has the right to have it returned to her if she discovers where it is—or if Lawrence knows that it belongs to Barber. As the finder of lost property, though, Lawrence has a better right to the camera than anyone else except Barber. This means that Lawrence has the right to require Jones to return it to him if he finds out that Jones has it.

If the finder does not know who the true owner is or cannot easily find out, the finder must still return the property if the real owner shows up and asks for the property. If the finder of lost property knows who the owner is and refuses to return it, the finder is guilty of conversion and must pay the owner the fair value of the property.

A finder who sells the property that he has found can only pass to the purchaser those rights that he has; he cannot pass any better title to the property than he himself has. Thus, the true owner could recover the property from the purchaser.

**3.** *Mislaid property.* Property is considered to be mislaid if the owner intentionally placed the property somewhere and accidentally left it there, not intending to relinquish ownership of the property. For example, Fields places her backpack on a coatrack at Campus Bookstore while shopping for textbooks. Forgetting the backpack, Fields leaves the store and goes home. The backpack would be considered to be mislaid rather than lost because Fields intentionally and voluntarily placed it on the coatrack. The consequences of property being classified as mislaid are that the finder acquires no rights to

---

[2]As wildlife is increasingly protected by law, however, some wild animals cannot be owned because it is illegal to capture them (e.g., endangered species).

the property. Rather, the person in possession of the real property on which the personal property was mislaid has the right to hold the property for the true owner and has better rights to the property than anyone other than the true owner. For example, if Stevens found Fields's backpack in Campus Bookstore, Campus Bookstore would have the right to hold the mislaid property for Fields. Stevens would acquire neither possession nor ownership of the backpack.

The rationale for this rule is that it increases the chances that the property will be returned to its real owner. A person who knowingly placed the property somewhere but forgot to pick it up might well remember later where she left the property and return for it.

Some states have a statute that allows finders of property to clear their title to the property. The statutes generally provide that the person must give public notice of the fact that the property has been found, perhaps by putting an ad in a local newspaper. All states have statutes of limitations that require the true owner of property to claim it or bring a legal action to recover possession of it within a certain number of years. A person who keeps possession of lost or unclaimed property for longer than that period of time will become its owner.

The following case, *Michael v. First Chicago Corporation,* presents an example of a conflict between a finder and an original owner over rights to personal property.

---

## MICHAEL V. FIRST CHICAGO CORPORATION
### 487 N.E.2d 403 (Ill. Ct. App. 1986)

First National Bank of Chicago (First Chicago) sold a number of used file cabinets on an "as is" basis to Zibton, a new and secondhand office supply and furniture dealer. Zibton had bought used furniture from First Chicago before. On this and previous occasions, Zibton bought the used furniture as a group even if some pieces were damaged or locked.

In the summer of 1983, Zibton sold some of these cabinets to Charles Strayve. Strayve gave one of the cabinets, a locked one with no keys, to his friend, Richard Michael. About six weeks later, Michael was moving the file cabinet in his garage when it fell over and several of the locked drawers opened. Inside were more than 1,600 certificates of deposit (CDs), including seven that had not been canceled or stamped paid and that were worth a total of $6,687,948.85, with maturity dates ranging from October 1982 to January 1983. Six of the CDs were payable to "Bearer."

First Chicago had placed the CDs in the cabinet between March and May 1983, when the responsibility for storing paid CDs was changed to a different unit of the bank. The CDs were moved from a vault to file cabinets at that time. Each drawer had been labeled with a card stating "Paid Negotiable CDs" and indicating the numbers of the CDs contained in the drawer. The new unit responsible for storing CDs determined that they could not use the file cabinets, so the CDs were transferred to tote boxes. First Chicago employees randomly checked to determine if the contents were gone and then transferred the file cabinets to the warehouse for sale.

Michael called the FBI, which took possession of all of the CDs. Michael and his wife then filed this declaratory judgment to determine who owned the CDs. The trial court ruled in favor of First Chicago, and the Michaels appealed.

---

**Reinhard, Justice**   The Michaels' primary argument is that they were entitled to possession of the CDs because the certificates were the subject of a sale from First Chicago. They maintain that First Chicago's actions in the handling and sale of the CDs showed an objective intent to transfer the certificates along with the used file cabinets in which the documents were stored.

Here, First Chicago was selling only used furniture to Zibton. Neither First Chicago nor Zibton suspected that CDs or any other type of valuable had been left in the file cabinet. The evidence clearly shows that the intention of the parties was for First Chicago to sell used furniture only, and Zibton was not speculating that other valuable items might be contained in the used furniture.

Where both buyer and seller were ignorant of the existence or presence of the concealed valuable, and the contract was not broad enough to indicate an intent to convey all the contents, known or unknown, the courts have generally held that as between the owner and purchaser, title to the hidden article did not pass by the sale. The evidence here is that used office furniture was being sold, and the possibility that something valuable might be in any of the used furniture had nothing to do with the sale. The fact that the sale of the used furniture was "as is" indicates the furniture was sold in its present condition, damaged or otherwise, and does not show an intent to sell the contents of the used furniture. Accordingly, the evidence does not support the Michaels' contention that the CDs as contents of the used furniture were intended by either party to the sale to be sold along with the furniture.

The Michaels' alternative contention is that the CDs are abandoned property, rather than lost or mislaid property, which the finder is entitled to keep. Mislaid property is that which is intentionally put in a certain place and later forgotten; property is lost when it is unintentionally separated from the dominion of its owner; and property is abandoned when the owner, intending to relinquish all rights to the property, leaves it free to be appropriated by any other person. A finder of property acquires no rights in mislaid property, is entitled to possession of lost property against everyone except the true owner, and is entitled to keep abandoned property.

For the purposes of this appeal, we need only determine whether the CDs are abandoned property. If otherwise, the owner is entitled to possession. Abandonment is generally defined as an intentional relinquishment of a known right. As a general rule, abandonment is not presumed and the party seeking to declare an abandonment must prove the abandoning party intended to do so.

The Michaels basically argue that the CDs were abandoned as shown by evidence that they were intentionally placed in the cabinets, they were not forgotten, and the cabinets were sold with no reservations. We disagree. It is readily apparent from the evidence that the CDs were to be transferred to other storage and some simply were overlooked and left in the file cabinets. The relinquishment of possession, under the circumstances here, without a showing of an intention to permanently give up all right to the CDs is not enough to show abandonment.

**Judgment for First Chicago affirmed.**

---

**CONCEPT REVIEW**

## RIGHTS OF FINDERS OF PERSONAL PROPERTY

| Character of Property | Description | Rights of Finder | Rights of Original Owner |
|---|---|---|---|
| **Lost** | Owner unintentionally parted with possession | Rights superior to everyone except the owner | Retains ownership; has the right to the return of the property |
| **Mislaid** | Owner intentionally put property in a place but unintentionally left it there | None; person in possession of real property on which mislaid property was found holds it for the owner, and has rights superior to everyone except owner | Retains ownership; has the right to the return of the property |
| **Abandoned** | Owner intentionally placed property out of his possession with intent to relinquish ownership of it | Finder who takes possession with intent to claim ownership acquires ownership of property | None |

## Leasing

A lease of personal property is a transfer of the right to possess and use personal property belonging to another.[3] Although the rights of one who leases personal property (a lessee) do not constitute ownership of personal property, leasing is mentioned here because it is becoming an increasingly important way of acquiring the use of many kinds of personal property, from automobiles to farm equipment.

In many states, Article 2 and Article 9 of the UCC are applied to personal property leases by analogy. However, rules contained in these articles are sometimes inadequate to resolve special problems presented by leasing. For this reason, a new article of the UCC dealing exclusively with leases of goods, Article 2A, was written in 1987. Article 2A has been presented to state legislatures for possible adoption. Approximately 40 states have adopted Article 2A as of the time of this writing.

## Gifts

Title to personal property can be obtained by **gift.** A gift is a voluntary transfer of property to the **donee** (the person who receives a gift), for which the **donor** (the person who gives the gift) gets no consideration in return. To have a valid gift, all three of the following elements are necessary:

1. The donor must *intend* to make a gift.
2. The donor must make *delivery* of the gift.
3. The donee must *accept* the gift.

The most critical requirement is delivery. The person who makes the gift must actually give up possession and control of the property either to the donee or to a third person to hold it for the donee. Delivery is important because it makes clear to the donor that he is voluntarily giving up ownership without getting something in exchange. A promise to make a gift is usually not enforceable;[4] the person must actually part with the property. In some cases, the delivery may be symbolic or constructive. For example, handing over the key to a strongbox can be symbolic delivery of the property in the strongbox.

There are two kinds of gifts: gifts *inter vivos* and gifts *causa mortis*. A gift *inter vivos* is a gift between two living persons. For example, when Tweedle's parents give her a car for her 21st birthday, that is a gift inter vivos. A gift *causa mortis* is a gift made in contemplation of death. For example, Uncle John, who is about to undergo a serious heart operation, gives his watch to his nephew, Sam, and tells Sam that he wants him to have it if he does not survive the operation.

A gift *causa mortis* is a conditional gift and is effective unless any of the following occurs:

1. The donor recovers from the peril or sickness under fear of which the gift was made, or
2. The donor revokes or withdraws the gift before he dies, or
3. The donee dies before the donor.

If one of these events takes place, ownership of the property goes back to the donor.

## Conditional Gifts

Sometimes a gift is made on condition that the donee comply with certain restrictions or perform certain actions. A conditional gift is not a completed gift, and it may be revoked by the donor before the donee complies with the conditions. Gifts in contemplation of marriage, such as engagement rings, are the primary example of a conditional gift. Such gifts are generally considered to have been made on an implied condition that marriage between the donor and donee take place. If the donee breaks the engagement without legal justification or if the engagement is broken by mutual consent, the donor will be able to recover the ring or other engagement gift. However, if the engagement is unjustifiably broken by the donor, he or she is generally not entitled to recover gifts made in contemplation of marriage. As is detailed in the case of *Fierro v. Hoel,* which follows, these rules are not uniformly applied in all states, however. Some states have enacted legislation prescribing the rules applicable to the return of engagement presents.

---

[3]A lease of personal property is a form of bailment, a "bailment for hire." Bailments are discussed later in this chapter.

[4]The idea is discussed in Chapter 4.

# FIERRO V. HOEL

### 465 N.W.2d 669 (Ct. App. Iowa 1990)

John Fierro and Janan Hoel became engaged to be married shortly before Thanksgiving in 1987. At the time of the proposal, Fierro presented Hoel with a 1.37 carat diamond in a platinum setting valued at approximately $9,000. The news of their engagement was shared with family and friends, and they started making wedding plans. After they located a condominium to purchase in New York City, Hoel refused to sign mortgage documents recognizing that Fierro's parents had loaned them money to make the purchase. Shortly thereafter, in March 1988, Fierro broke off the engagement. He asked Hoel to return the ring but she refused.

Fierro then filed a lawsuit seeking to establish ownership of the ring. He asserted that the ring was symbolic of the parties' intent to marry and inherently conditioned on their subsequent marriage. He contended that when a couple terminates their engagement, the ring must be returned to the donor. Hoel, on the other hand, took the position that Fierro had not expressly stated the condition when he gave the ring to her and that it should be viewed as a completed gift. The trial entered judgment for Hoel and Fierro appealed.

———————————————— ■ ————————————————

**Donielson, Judge**    The question before us is whether an engagement ring is a conditional gift or a completed gift upon delivery. The district court concluded that because John Fierro had placed no express conditions on the ring at the time possession was transferred to Janan Hoel, the engagement ring was a completed gift upon delivery. We hold an engagement ring is an inherently conditional gift and therefore reverse.

An engagement ring given in contemplation of marriage is an impliedly conditional gift. The jurisdictions which have considered cases dealing with the gift of an engagement ring uniformly hold that marriage is an implied condition of the transfer of title and that the gift does not become absolute until the marriage occurs. One court explained:

Where a gift of personal property is made with the intent to take place irrevocably, and is fully executed by unconditional delivery, it is a valid gift *inter vivos.* Such a gift is absolute and, once made, cannot be revoked. A gift, however, may be conditioned on the performance of some act by the donee, and if the condition is not fulfilled the donor may recover the gift. We find the conditional gift theory particularly appropriate when the contested property is an engagement ring. The inherent symbolism of this gift forecloses the need to establish an express condition that marriage will ensue. Rather the condition may be implied in fact or imposed by law in order to prevent unjust enrichment.

Once we recognize an engagement ring is a conditional gift, the question still remains: who gets the gift when the condition is not fulfilled. The obvious answer is the gift must be returned to the donor. However, an older majority line of cases follows the general principle that the donor of an engagement ring can recover the gift only if the engagement is dissolved by agreement or if the engagement is unjustifiably broken by the donee. The critical inquiry in cases following this principle is who was at "fault" for the termination of the relationship. The party to an engagement who was unjustifiably jilted became the owner of the ring—a type of "consolation prize."

What fact justifies the breaking of an engagement? The absence of a sense of humor? Differing musical tastes? Differing political views? The painfully learned fact is that marriages are made on earth, not in heaven. They must be approached with intelligent care and should not happen without a decent assurance of success. When either party lacks that assurance, for whatever reason, the engagement should be broken. No justificaiion is needed. Either party may act. Fault, impossible to fix, does not count. This court believes fault, in an engagement setting, is irrelevant.

This court adopts the "no fault" approach followed in a minority of jurisdictions. Since the major purpose of the engagement period is to allow a couple time to test the permanency of their feelings, it would seem highly ironic to penalize the donor for taking steps to prevent a possibly unhappy marriage.

In summary, we hold an engagement ring given in contemplation of marriage is an impliedly conditional gift; it is a completed gift only upon marriage. If the wedding is called off, for whatever reason, the gift is not capable of becoming a completed gift and must be returned to the donor.

**Reversed in favor of Fierro.**

---

**Hayden, Judge (dissenting)**   The additional factual background in this case is John had given Janan a pin that belonged to his grandmother. He told Janan explicitly the pin was to be returned to him if they ever broke up. Later when John gave her the ring he placed no conditions on it when she received it. The trial court weighed and considered this evidence. The trial court ruled John had ended the engagement and had placed no conditions on the ring as he had done on the heirloom pin.

The question before us in this case is was the ring a gift conditioned on marriage or was the ring an unconditional gift. The Iowa Supreme Court has stated what the appropriate burden of proof should be when it is claimed there is a conditional gift: If an unqualified transfer to the donee is proved, one asserting the delivery was made on some condition or trust has the burden of establishing such condition or trust. Thus, if the gift elements are proven, John has the burden of proof to show the gift was conditioned on marriage.

The three essential elements for an *inter vivos* gift are donative intent, delivery and acceptance. There is no question there has been a delivery and an acceptance. The remaining question is what was John's intent at the time he gave Janan the ring.

In this case the intention of John was evident from the testimony presented. Janan was responsible for the purchase and payment of the insurance on the ring. Also the ring was referred to by the parties at all times as "her ring." Finally, a demand for the ring was not made until nearly 30 days after John called off the engagement. Thus, it is evident the requirements for a gift were completed unless a condition was proved otherwise.

If John had imposed a condition of marriage on the gift of the ring, such a requirement must have been explicit and known. Thus, if John had wanted such a condition on the gift, he should have made this known and clearly understood at the time he gave possession of the ring to Janan.

There is evidence John was aware of the need to clearly express such a condition when giving this type of gift. John had made a condition of marriage a requirement for the previous gift of heirloom jewelry he had given to Janan. If the engagement was broken, the piece of heirloom jewelry would be returned. After the engagement was broken, the piece of heirloom jewelry was promptly returned. If John wanted the ring returned, he could have expressed such a condition as he did with the heirloom jewelry. Absent any such evidence of condition, I determine the giving of the ring is a valid completed gift.

I acknowledge parties are free to return engagement gifts. However, proper social etiquette does not demand their return, and neither should the courts as a matter of law.

---

## Uniform Transfers to Minors Act

The Uniform Transfers to Minors Act, which has been adopted in one form or another in every state, provides a fairly simple and flexible method for making gifts and other transfers of property to minors.[5] As defined in this act, a minor is anyone under the age of 21. Under the act, an adult may transfer money, securities, real property, insurance policies, and other property. The specific ways of doing this vary according to the type of property transferred. In general, however, the transferor (the person who gives or otherwise transfers the property) delivers, pays, or assigns the property to, or registers the property with, a custodian who acts for the benefit of the minor "under the Uniform Transfers

---

[5]This statute was formerly called, and is still called in some states, the Uniform Gift to Minors Act.

to Minors Act." The custodian is given fairly broad discretion to use the gift for the minor's benefit and may not use it for the custodian's personal benefit. The custodian may be the transferor himself, another adult, or a trust company, depending again on the type of property transferred. If the donor or other transferor fully complies with the Uniform Transfers to Minors Act, the transfer is considered to be irrevocable.

## Will or Inheritance

Ownership of personal property can also be transferred upon the death of the former owner. The property may pass under the terms of a will if the will was validly executed. If there is no valid will, the property is transferred to the heirs of the owner according to state laws. Transfer of property at the death of the owner will be discussed in Chapter 19, Estates and Trusts.

## Confusion

Title to personal property can be obtained by **confusion.** Confusion is the intermixing of goods that belong to different owners in such a way that they cannot later be separated. For example, suppose wheat belonging to several different people is mixed in a grain elevator. If the mixing was by agreement or if it resulted from an accident without negligence on anyone's part, each person owns his proportionate share of the entire quantity of wheat. However, a different result would be reached if the wheat was wrongfully or negligently mixed. Suppose a thief steals a truckload of Grade #1 wheat worth $8.50 a bushel from a farmer. The thief dumps the wheat into his storage bin, which contains a lower-grade wheat worth $4.50 a bushel, with the result that the mixture is worth only $4.50 a bushel. The farmer has first claim against the entire mixture to recover the value of his wheat that was mixed in. The thief, or any other person whose intentional or negligent act results in confusion of goods, must bear any loss caused by the confusion.

## Accession

Ownership of personal property can also be acquired by **accession.** Accession means increasing the value of property by adding materials or labor, or both. As a general rule, the owner of the original property becomes the owner of the improvements. This is particularly likely to be true if the improvement was done with the permission of the owner. For example, Hudson takes his automobile to a shop that replaces the engine with a larger engine and puts in a new four-speed transmission. Hudson is still the owner of the automobile as well as the owner of the parts added by the auto shop.

Problems can arise if materials are added or work is performed on personal property without the consent of the owner. If property is stolen from one person and improved by the thief, the original owner can get it back and does not have to reimburse the thief for the work done or the materials used in improving it. For example, a thief steals Rourke's used car, puts a new engine in it, replaces the tires, and repairs the muffler. Rourke is entitled to get his car back from the thief and does not have to pay him for the engine, tires, or muffler.

The result is less easy to predict, however, if property is mistakenly improved in good faith by someone who believes that he is the owner of the property. In such a case, a court must weigh the respective interests of two innocent parties: the original owner and the improver.

For example, Johnson, a stonecarver, finds a block of limestone by the side of the road and, assuming that it has been abandoned, takes it home and carves it into a sculpture. In fact, the block was owned by Hayes and, having fallen off a flatbed truck during transportation, is merely lost property, which Hayes ordinarily could recover from the finder. In a case such as this, a court could decide the case in one of two ways. The first alternative would be to give the original owner (Hayes) ownership of the improved property, but to allow the person who has improved the property in good faith (Johnson) to recover the cost of the improvements. The second alternative would be to hold that the improver, Johnson, has acquired ownership of the sculpture, but that he is required to pay the original owner the value of the property as of the time he obtained it. The greater the extent to which the improvements have increased the value of the property, the more likely it is that the court will choose the second alternative and permit the improver to acquire ownership of the improved property.

# BAILMENTS

## Nature of Bailments

A **bailment** is the delivery of personal property by its owner or one who has the right to possess it (the **bailor**) to another person (the **bailee**) who accepts it and is under an express or implied agreement to return it to the bailor or to someone designated by the bailor. Only personal property can be the subject of bailments.

Although the legal terminology used to describe bailments might be unfamiliar to most people, everyone is familiar with transactions that consti-tute bailments. For example, Lincoln takes his car to a parking garage where the attendant gives Lincoln a claim check and then drives the car down the ramp to park it. Charles borrows his neighbor's lawn mower to cut his grass. Carne, who lives next door to Axe, agrees to take care of Axe's cat while Axe goes on a vacation. These are just a few of the everyday situations that involve bailments. The case of *York v. Jones,* which follows, involves a bailment that is much more unusual but nevertheless illustrates the essential characteristics of a bailment.

---

## YORK V. JONES
### 717 F. Supp. 421 (E.D. Va. 1989)

Steven York and Risa Adler-York contacted the Jones Institute for Reproductive Medicine to determine if they were viable candidates for in vitro fertilization (IVF). This process involves removing one or more oocytes or eggs from the woman's body, fertilizing those eggs in vitro (outside of the womb) with the husband's sperm, and then depositing the developing masses into the woman's uterus. The Yorks were accepted into the Jones Institute's IVF program.

In May 1987, the Yorks signed a Cryopreservation Agreement outlining the procedure for cryopreservation or freezing of pre-zygotes and detailing the Yorks' rights in the frozen pre-zygote. The agreement explained that the cryopreservation procedure is available if more than five pre-zygotes are retrieved during the IVF treatment, so that the possibility for multiple births could be reduced while maintaining optimal chances for pregnancy. The agreement also provided in part:

We may withdraw our consent and discontinue participation at any time . . . and we understand our pre-zygotes will be stored only as long as we are active IVF patients at . . . Jones Institute. . . . We have the principal responsibility to decide the disposition of our pre-zygotes. Our frozen pre-zygotes will not be released from storage for the purpose of intrauterine transfer without the written consent of us both. In the event of divorce, we understand legal ownership of any stored pre-zygotes must be determined in a property settlement. . . . Should we for any reason no longer wish to attempt to initiate a pregnancy, we understand we may choose one of three fates for our pre-zygotes that remain in frozen storage. Our pre-zygotes may be: 1) donated to another infertile couple. . . . 2) donated for approved research investigation, and 3) thawed but not allowed to undergo further development.

The Yorks underwent IVF treatment on four occasions. Six eggs were removed from Mrs. York and fertilized with her husband's sperm, creating six embryos. Five of these embryos were transferred to Mrs. York's uterus, and the remaining embryo was cryogenically preserved in accordance with the procedures outlined in the Cryopreservation Agreement. None of the in vitro fertilization attempts resulted in pregnancy.

During the course of treatment, the Yorks moved to California. They sought to have the remaining frozen pre-zygote transferred from the Jones Institute in Norfolk, Virginia, to the Institute for Reproductive Research in Los Angeles, where the Yorks planned to attempt in vitro fertilization again. The Yorks arranged for proper transportation and handling of the pre-zygote, but the Jones Institute refused to allow such a transfer.

The Yorks brought suit against the Jones Institute and its physicians, claiming that its continued dominion and control over the pre-zygote was contrary to law and the parties' agreement. The Jones Institute filed a motion to dismiss, alleging that the Yorks' complaint did not state a claim on which relief could be granted. This is the trial court's ruling on that motion.

---

**Clarke, Jr., District Judge**    The Yorks' complaint in this case raises an issue of first impression in the rapidly developing field of human reproductive technology. The Jones Institute argues that the Yorks' proprietary rights in the pre-zygote are limited to the "three fates" enumerated in the [Cryopreservation Agreement] because there is no established protocol for the inter-institutional transfer of pre-zygotes.

The court begins its analysis by noting that the Cryopreservation Agreement created a bailor-bailee relationship between the Yorks and Jones Institute. While the parties in this case expressed no intent to create a bailment, under Virginia law, no formal contract or actual meeting of the minds is necessary. Rather, all that is needed is the element of lawful possession however created, and duty to account for the thing as the property of another that creates the bailment. The essential nature of a bailment relationship imposes on the bailee, when the purpose of the bailment has terminated, an absolute obligation to return the subject matter of the bailment to the bailor. The obligation to return the property is implied from the fact of lawful possession of the personal property of another.

In the instant case, the requisite elements of a bailment relationship are present. The Jones Institute consistently refers to the pre-zygote as the "property" of the Yorks. Although the Cryopreservation Agreement constitutes a bailment contract, the Agreement is nevertheless governed by the same principles as apply to other contracts.

The Cryopreservation Agreement should be more strictly construed against the Jones Institute, the parties who drafted the Agreement. The Jones Institute has defined the extent of its possession interest as bailee of the pre-zygote by the following provision of the Agreement: "We may withdraw our consent and discontinue participation at any time . . . and . . . our pre-zygote will be stored only as long as we are active IVF patients at the [Jones Institute.]" The Jones Institute has further defined the limits of its possessory interest by recognizing the Yorks' proprietary rights in the pre-zygote. The Agreement repeatedly refers to "our pre-zygote" and further provides that the Yorks have the "principal responsibility to decide the disposition" of the pre-zygote.

The Jones Institute takes the position that the plain language of the Cryopreservation Agreement limits the Yorks' proprietary right to the pre-zygote to the "three fates" listed in the Agreement. The Court finds, however, that the applicability of the three fates is limited by the following language, "Should we for any reason no longer wish to initiate a pregnancy, we understand we may choose one of three fates for our pre-zygotes. . . ." The allegations of the Yorks' complaint and the entire thrust of this litigation suggest that the Yorks continue to desire to achieve pregnancy. The Agreement does not state that the attempt to initiate a pregnancy is restricted to procedures employed at the Jones Institute. The "three fates" are therefore inapplicable to the case at bar. For the reasons stated, the Court finds that the Yorks' complaint states a claim upon which relief can be granted.

**Motion to dismiss denied in favor of the Yorks.**

---

## Elements of a Bailment

The essential elements of a bailment are:

**1.** The bailor must own or have the right to possess the property.

**2.** The bailor must deliver exclusive possession of and control over the property to the bailee.

**3.** The bailee must knowingly accept the property with the understanding that he owes a duty to return the property as directed by the bailor.

**FIGURE 1** Creation of a Bailment

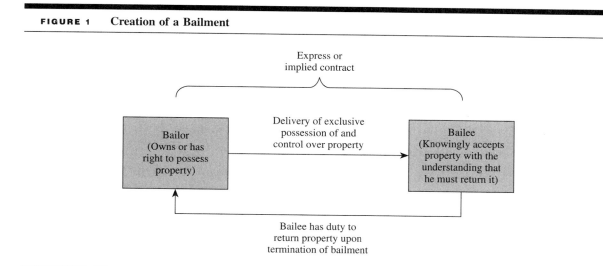

## Creation of a Bailment

A bailment is created by an express or implied contract. Whether the elements of a bailment have been fulfilled is determined by examining all the facts and circumstances of the particular situation. For example, a patron goes into a restaurant and hangs her hat and coat on an unattended rack. It is unlikely that this created a bailment, because the restaurant owner never assumed exclusive control over the hat and coat. However, if there is a checkroom and the hat and coat are checked with the attendant, a bailment will arise.

If a customer parks his car in a parking lot, keeps the keys, and can drive the car out himself whenever he wishes, a bailment has not been created. The courts treat this situation as a lease of space. Suppose he takes his car to a parking garage where an attendant gives him a claim check and then the attendant parks the car. There is a bailment of the car because the parking garage has accepted delivery and possession of the car. However, a distinction is made between the car and some packages locked in the trunk. If the parking garage was not aware of the packages, it would probably not be a bailee of them as it did not knowingly accept possession of them. The creation of a bailment is illustrated in Figure 1.

## Types of Bailments

Bailments are commonly divided into three different categories:

1. Bailments for the sole benefit of the bailor.
2. Bailments for the sole benefit of the bailee.
3. Bailments for mutual benefit.

The type of bailment involved in a case can be important in determining the liability of the bailee for loss of or damages to the property. As will be discussed later, however, some courts no longer rely on these distinctions for this purpose.

**Bailments for Benefit of Bailor**   A bailment for the sole benefit of the bailor is one in which the bailee renders some service but does not receive a benefit in return. For example, Brown allows his neighbor, Reston, to park her car in Brown's garage while she is on vacation and Brown does not ask for any compensation. Here, Reston, the bailor, has received a benefit from the bailee, Brown, but Brown has not received a benefit in return.

**Bailments for Benefit of Bailee**   A bailment for the sole benefit of the bailee is one in which the owner of the goods allows someone else to use them free of charge. For example, Anderson lends a lawn mower to her neighbor, Moss, so he can cut his grass.

**Bailments for Mutual Benefit**   If both the bailee and the bailor receive benefits from the bailment, it is a bailment for mutual benefit. For example, Sutton rents china for his daughter's wedding from E-Z Party Supplies for an agreed-on price. Sutton, the bailee, benefits by being able to use the china, while E-Z benefits from his payment of the rental charge. On some occasions, the benefit to the bailee is less tangible. For example, a customer checks a coat at an attended coatroom at a restaurant. Even if no charge is made for the service, it is likely to be treated as a bailment for mutual benefit because the restaurant is benefiting from the customer's patronage.

## Special Bailments

Certain kinds of professional bailees, such as inn-keepers and common carriers, are treated somewhat differently by the law and are held to a higher level of responsibility than is the ordinary bailee. The rules applicable to common carriers and innkeepers are detailed later in this chapter.

## Duties of the Bailee

The bailee has two basic duties:

1. To take care of the property that has been entrusted to her.
2. To return the property at the termination of the bailment.

The following discussion examines the scope of these duties.

## Duty of Bailee to Take Care of Property

The bailee is responsible for taking steps to protect the property during the time he has possession of it. If the bailee does not exercise proper care and the property is lost or damaged, the bailee is liable for negligence. The bailee would then be required to reimburse the bailor for the amount of loss or damage. If the property is lost or damaged without the fault or negligence of the bailee, however, the bailee is not liable to the bailor. The degree of care required of the bailee traditionally has depended in large part on the type of bailment involved.

**1.** *Bailment for the benefit of the bailor.* If the bailment is solely for the benefit of the bailor, the bailee is expected to exercise only a minimal, or slight, degree of care for the protection of the bailed property. He would be liable, then, only if he were grossly negligent in his care of the bailed property. The rationale for this is that if the bailee is doing the bailor a favor, it is not reasonable to expect him to be as careful as when he is deriving some benefit from keeping the goods.

**2.** *Bailment for mutual benefit.* Where the bailment is a bailment for mutual benefit, the bailee is expected to exercise ordinary or reasonable care. This degree of care requires the bailee to use the same kind of care a reasonable person would use to protect his own property in that situation. If the bailee is a professional that holds itself out as a professional bailee, such as a warehouse, it must use the degree of care that would be used by a person in that profession. This is likely to be more care than the ordinary person would use. In addition, there is usually a duty on a professional bailee to explain any loss or damage to property—that is, to show it was not negligent. If it cannot do so, it will be liable to the bailor.

**3.** *Bailment for the benefit of the bailee.* If the bailment is solely for the benefit of the bailee, the bailee is expected to exercise a high degree of care. A person who lends a sailboat to a neighbor would probably expect the neighbor to be even more careful with the sailboat than the owner might be, for example. In such a case, the bailee would be liable for damage to the property if he committed a relatively small degree of negligence.

A number of courts today view the type of bailment involved in a case as just one factor to be considered in determining whether the bailee should be liable for loss or damage to bailed goods. The modern trend appears to be moving in the direction of imposing a duty of reasonable care on bailees, regardless of the type of bailment. This flexible standard of care permits courts to take into account a variety of factors such as the nature and value of the property, the provisions of the parties' agreement, the payment of consideration for the bailment, and the experience of the bailee. In addition, the bailee is required to use the property only as was agreed between the parties. For example, Jones borrows Morrow's lawn mower to mow his lawn. If Jones uses the mower to cut the weeds on a trash-filled vacant lot and the mower is damaged, he would be liable because he was exceeding the agreed purpose of the bailment—to cut his lawn.

## Bailee's Duty to Return the Property

One of the essential elements of a bailment is the duty of the bailee to return the property at the termination of the bailment. If the bailed property is taken from the bailee by legal process, the bailee should notify the bailor and must take whatever action is necessary to protect the bailor's interest. In most instances, the bailee must return the identical property that was bailed. A person who lends a 1985 Volkswagen Rabbit to a friend expects to have that particular car returned. In some cases, the bailor does not expect the return of the identical goods. For example, a farmer who stores 1,500 bushels of Grade #1 wheat at a local grain elevator expects to get back 1,500 bushels of Grade #1 wheat when the bailment is terminated, but not the identical wheat he deposited.

The bailee must return the goods in an undamaged condition to the bailor or to someone designated by the bailor. If the goods have been damaged, destroyed, or lost, there is a rebuttable presumption of negligence on the part of the bailee. To overcome the presumption, the bailee must come forward with evidence showing that the accident, damage, or loss resulted from some cause consistent with the exercise of the relevant level of due care on his part. The operation of the rebuttable presumption can be seen in the *Magee v. Walbro* case, which follows. If the property is lost or damaged without the fault or negligence of the bailee, however, the bailee is not liable to the bailor.

---

### MAGEE V. WALBRO, INC.
**525 N.E.2d 975 (III. Ct. App. 1988)**

Walbro, Inc., doing business as Mysel Furs, was in the business of storing furs. It had arranged for United Parcel Service (UPS) to pick up furs from its customers and deliver them to Mysel's. In May 1982, Mysel's solicited Crella Magee's business to store her furs for the summer, and Magee agreed. Pursuant to an arrangement with Mysel's to pick up three furs from Magee, UPS delivered three empty boxes labeled with unique call numbers to Magee on May 25. Magee inserted a fur in each of the boxes, and UPS then picked up the three boxes, giving Magee's husband three tickets bearing call numbers identical to those marked on the boxes. UPS delivered the boxes to Mysel's on May 26. A Mysel's employee signed for the boxes but did not check to be sure that none of the boxes was empty. In July, Mysel's issued a storage receipt to Magee that showed only two furs. This storage receipt also contained a term that limited Mysel's liability for lost property to $100. Magee called Mysel's immediately and received assurances that the three furs were in storage.

When Magee went to pick up her three furs in October 1982, however, one of them—a blue fox jacket worth $3,400—was missing. Mysel's did not compensate Magee, arguing that its liability for lost articles was limited to $100. Magee then brought suit against Walbro, Mysel's, and UPS for breach of bailment and conversion. The trial court ruled for the defendants, and Magee appealed. (Magee voluntarily dismissed her case against UPS, so its liability is not involved in this appeal.)

---

**O'Connor, Justice**   Establishing a prima facie case of bailment raises a presumption of negligence by the defendant, which the defendant must rebut with evidence sufficient to support a finding of the nonexistence of the presumed fact. The trial court ruled that the evidence established a bailment between Magee and Walbro and Mysel's, thus raising the presumption of negligence. Walbro and Mysel produced no evidence, however, to rebut the presumption of negligence.

Based on the evidence presented, the trial court ruled that the lost jacket was delivered to Mysel Furs. Walbro and Mysel's argued that, assuming delivery of the jacket, any presumption of negligence was defeated by the procedures used in storing furs. The furs were placed in a locked, alarmed vault to which several, identifiable Mysel's employees had access. Mysel's then prepared and issued a storage receipt to the customer. Walbro presented no evidence to show that these procedures were followed for Magee's furs, and the storage receipt was not issued until six weeks after the jacket was delivered. It is reasonable to assume that the defendants' procedures and security precautions customarily resulted in the return of the customer's fur. Magee's fur was not returned; therefore, without showing more than the mere existence of safety and security measures, the defendants failed to rebut the presumption of negligence. Magee was therefore entitled to recover her damages.

Finally, the defendants asserted the defense of limitation of liability. Walbro and Mysel's argue that they effectively limited their liability to $100, citing *Schoen v. Wallace,* which upheld an agreement between a fur owner and fur storage company to limit the storage company's liability to $100. *Schoen* and [other cases] indicate, however, that the customer was aware of the limitation of liability before the furs were placed in storage. The *Schoen* decision was based in part on the fact that the plaintiff had dealt with the defendant before, knew of its insurance practices, [and] could have chosen another furrier had she found the limitation objectionable.

In the instant case, Magee testified that she was not told of the limitation until after the fur was lost. Defendants rely on the receipt of July 1982, which stated that liability was limited to $100. Magee should have known of the limitation after she received the receipt in July, but by that time her furs had been at Mysel's for six weeks.

The limitation does not apply in the instant case because Magee had no knowledge of the limitation before agreeing to store her furs. In *Schoen,* the court stated that it would be "unjust to permit the plaintiff to repudiate [the agreement to limit liability] because the coat was lost." In the instant case, it would be unjust to permit Mysel and Walbro to assert a limitation that was not made clear at the time that the bailment contract was made because the coat was lost. We therefore hold that the $100 limitation of liability is inapplicable in this case.

For the foregoing reasons, judgment in favor of the defendants is reversed, and this case is remanded to the trial court to enter judgment against Walbro and Mysel's and in favor of Magee in the amount of $3,400.

**Reversed and remanded in favor of Magee.**

---

### Bailee's Liability for Misdelivery

The bailee is also liable to the bailor if he misdelivers the bailed property at the termination of the bailment. The property must be returned to the bailor or to someone specified by the bailor.

If a third person claims to have rights in the bailed property that are superior to the rights of the bailor and demands possession of the bailed property, the bailee is in a dilemma. If the bailee refuses to deliver the bailed property to the third-person claimant and the third-person claimant is entitled to its possession, the bailee is liable to the claimant. If the bailee delivers the bailed property to the third-party claimant and the third-party claimant is not entitled to possession, the bailee is liable to the bailor. The circumstances may be such that the conflicting claims of the bailor and the third-person claimant can be determined only by judicial decision. In some cases, the bailee may protect himself by bringing the third-party claimant into a lawsuit

along with the bailor so that all the competing claims can be adjudicated by the court before the bailee releases the property, but this remedy is not always available.

### Limits on Liability

Bailees may try to limit or relieve themselves of liability for the bailed property. Some examples include the storage receipt purporting to limit liability to $100 in the *Magee v. Walbro, Inc.* case, signs near checkrooms, such as "Not responsible for loss of or damage to checked property," and disclaimers on claim checks, such as "Goods left at owner's risk." The standards used to determine whether such limitations and disclaimers are enforceable are discussed in detail in Chapter 7, Illegality.

Any attempt by the bailee to be relieved of liability for intentional wrongful acts is against public policy and will not be enforced. A bailee's ability to be relieved of liability for negligence is also limited. Courts look to see whether the disclaimer or limitation of liability was communicated to the bailor at the time of the bailment. Did the attendant point out the sign near the checkroom to the person when the coat was checked? Did the parking lot attendant call the person's attention to the disclaimer on the back of the claim check?

If not, as in the *Magee* case, the court may hold that the disclaimer was not communicated to the bailor and did not become part of the bailment contract. Even if the bailor was aware of the disclaimer, it still may not be enforced on the ground that it is contrary to public policy.

If the disclaimer was offered on a take-it-or-leave-it basis and was not the subject of arm's-length bargaining, it is less likely to be enforced than if it has been negotiated and voluntarily agreed on. A bailee may be able to limit liability to a certain amount or to relieve himself of liability for certain perils. Ideally, the bailee will give the bailor a chance to declare a higher value and to pay an additional charge to be protected up to the declared value of the goods. Common carriers, such as railroads and trucking companies, often take this approach. Courts do not look with favor on efforts by a person to be relieved of liability for negligence. For this reason, terms limiting the liability of a bailee stand a better chance of being enforced than do terms completely relieving the bailee of liability.

The bailor's knowledge of the bailee's facilities or of his method of doing business or the nature of prior dealings may give rise to an implied agreement as to the bailee's duties. The bailee may, if he wishes, assume all the risks incident to the bailment and contract to return the bailed property undamaged or to pay any damage to or loss of the property.

## Right to Compensation

The express or implied contract creating the bailment controls whether the bailee has the right to receive compensation for keeping the property or must pay for having the right to use it. If the bailment is made as a favor, then the bailee is not entitled to compensation even though the bailment is for the sole benefit of the bailor. If the bailment is the rental of property, then the bailee must pay the agreed rental rate. If the bailment is for the storage or repair of property, then the bailee is entitled to the contract price for the storage or repair services. If no

specific price was agreed on, yet compensation was contemplated by the parties, then the bailee gets the reasonable value of the services provided.

In many instances, the bailee will have a lien (a charge against property to secure the payment of a debt) on the bailed property for the reasonable value of the services. For example, Silver takes a chair to Ace Upholstery to have it recovered. When the chair has been recovered, Ace has the right to keep it until the agreed price—or, if no price was set, the reasonable value of the work—is paid. This is an example of an **artisan's lien,** which is discussed in greater detail in Chapter 21, Security Interests in Personal Property.

## Bailor's Liability for Defects in the Bailed Property

When personal property is rented or loaned, the bailor makes an implied warranty that the property has no hidden defects that make it unsafe for use. If the bailment is for the sole benefit of the bailee, then the bailor is liable for injuries that result from defects in the bailed property only if the bailor knew about the defects and did not tell the bailee. For example, Price lends his car, which he knows has bad brakes, to Sloan. If Price does not tell Sloan about the bad brakes and if Sloan is injured in an accident because the brakes fail, Price is liable for Sloan's injuries.

If the bailment is a bailment for mutual benefit, then the bailor has a larger obligation. The bailor must use reasonable care in inspecting the property and seeing that it is safe for the purpose for which it is intended. The bailor is liable for injuries suffered by the bailee because of defects that the bailor either knew about or should have discovered by reasonable inspection. For example, Friedman's Rent-All, which rents trailers, does not inspect the trailers after they are returned. A wheel has come loose on a trailer that Friedman's rents to Hirsch. If the wheel comes off while Hirsch is using the trailer and the goods Hirsch is carrying in it are damaged, Friedman's is liable to Hirsch.

In addition, product liability doctrines that apply a higher standard of legal responsibility have been applied to bailors who are commercial lessors of personal property.[6] Express or implied warranties of

---

[6]Product liability doctrines are discussed in Chapter 12.

quality under either Article 2 or Article 2A of the UCC may apply. Liability under these warranties does not depend on whether the bailor knew about or should have discovered the defect. The only question is whether the property's condition complied with the warranty. Some courts have also imposed strict liability on lessors-bailors of goods that cause personal injury or property damage to the lessee-bailee because they are defective and unreasonably dangerous. This liability is imposed regardless of whether the lessor was negligent.

---

**CONCEPT REVIEW**

## DUTIES OF BAILEES AND BAILORS

| Type of Bailment | Duties of Bailee | Duties of Bailor |
|---|---|---|
| **Sole Benefit of Bailee** | 1. Must use great care; liable for even slight negligence.<br>2. Must return goods to bailor or dispose of them at his direction.<br>3. May have duty to compensate bailor. | 1. Must notify the bailee of any known defects. |
| **Mutual Benefit** | 1. Must use reasonable care; liable for ordinary negligence.<br>2. Must return goods to bailor or dispose of them at his direction.<br>3. May have duty to compensate bailor. | 1. Must notify bailee of all known defects and any defects that could be discovered on reasonable inspection.<br>2. Commercial lessors may be subject to warranties of quality and/or strict liability in tort.<br>3. May have duty to compensate bailee. |
| **Sole Benefit of Bailor** | 1. Must use at least slight care; liable for gross negligence.<br>2. Must return goods to bailor or dispose of them at his direction. | 1. Must notify bailee of all known defects and any hidden defects that are known or could be discovered on reasonable inspection.<br>2. May have duty to compensate bailee. |

---

## SPECIAL BAILMENTS

### Common Carriers

Bailees that are common carriers are held to a higher level of responsibility than that to which bailees that are private carriers are held. Common carriers are licensed by governmental agencies to carry the property of anyone who requests the service. Airlines licensed by the Department of Transportation and trucks and buses licensed by the Interstate Commerce Commission are examples of common carriers. Private contract carriers carry goods only for persons selected by the carrier.

Both common carriers and private contract carriers are bailees. However, the law makes the common carrier an absolute insurer of the goods it carries. The common carrier is responsible for any loss of or damage to goods entrusted to it. The common carrier can avoid responsibility only if it can show that the loss or damage was caused by one of the following:

1. An act of God.
2. An act of a public enemy.
3. An act or order of the government.
4. An act of the person who shipped the goods.
5. The nature of the goods themselves.

The common carrier is liable if goods entrusted to it are stolen by some unknown person but not if the goods are destroyed when a tornado hits the warehouse. If goods are damaged because the shipper improperly packages or crates them, then the carrier is not liable. Similarly, if perishable goods are not in suitable condition to be shipped and deteriorate in the course of shipment, the carrier is not liable so long as it used reasonable care in handling them.

Common carriers are usually permitted to limit their liability to a stated value unless the bailor declares a higher value for the property and pays an additional fee.

## Hotelkeepers

Hotelkeepers are engaged in the business of offering food and/or lodging to transient persons. They hold themselves out to serve the public and are obligated to do so. Like the common carrier, the hotelkeeper is held to a higher standard of care than that of the ordinary bailee. The hotelkeeper is not a bailee in the strict sense of the word. The guest does not usually surrender the exclusive possession of his property to the hotelkeeper. However, the hotel-

keeper is treated as the virtual insurer of the guest's property. The hotelkeeper is not liable for loss of or damage to property if she can show that it was caused by one of the following:

1. An act of God.
2. An act of a public enemy.
3. An act of a governmental authority.
4. The fault of a member of the guest's party.
5. The nature of the goods.

Most states have passed laws that limit the hotelkeeper's liability, however. Commonly, the law requires the hotel owner to post a notice advising guests that any valuables should be checked into the hotel vault. The hotelkeeper's liability is then limited, usually to a fixed amount, for valuables that are not so checked. The following case, *Gooden v. Day's Inn,* illustrates the application of such a state statute.

## Gooden v. Day's Inn
### 385 S.E.2d 876 (Ct. App. Ga. 1990)

Marvin Gooden checked into a Day's Inn in Atlanta, Georgia, on March 3, 1988, paying in advance for two days' lodging. The next day he temporarily left his room, leaving a paper bag filled with approximately $9,000. Shortly thereafter, Mary Carter, a housekeeper, went into Gooden's room to clean it and found the bag of money. Seeing no other personal effects, she assumed that Gooden had checked out. Accordingly, she turned the bag over to her immediate supervisor, Vivian Clark, who in turn gave the bag of money to Dempsey Wilson who was responsible for general supervision and the maintenance of the grounds. Wilson had been employed by Day's Inn for approximately three years, and during that time he was occasionally given items of value to turn into the office. He always did so until this occasion, when he decided to abscond with the bag of money.

A safe was located on the premises of Day's Inn for the use of guests. Day's Inn posted a notice concerning the availability of the safe on the door of the room that Gooden occupied. Pursuant to this notice, Day's Inn disclaimed liability for guests' valuables unless they were placed in the safe. At no point did Gooden seek the use of the safe.

Georgia law (OCGA Sec. 43-21-10) provides in pertinent part that: "The innkeeper may provide a safe or other place of deposit for valuable articles and, by posting a notice thereof, may require the guests of the innkeeper to place such valuable articles therein or the innkeeper shall be relieved from responsibility for such articles."

Gooden brought a tort action against, among others, Day's Inn seeking damages in the amount of $9,000. Day's Inn contended that it could not be held responsible for the loss of Gooden's money since it posted notice concerning the availability of the safe and Gooden failed to take advantage of it. Gooden, in turn, argued that the Georgia statute could not insulate an innkeeper from liability where the loss of a guest's valuables is occasioned by the negligent or tortious conduct of the innkeeper's employees. The trial court granted summary judgment in favor of Day's Inn, Carter, and Clark, and Gooden appealed.

**McMurray, Presiding Judge**   The Georgia statute carves out no exception for losses occasioned by the negligence of the innkeeper. Thus, if the innkeeper posts notice of the availability of a safe pursuant to the statute, it is not liable for articles stolen from a guest's room even if its negligence contributed to the loss. Likewise, the statute carves out no exception for losses occasioned by the negligence or intentional torts of the innkeeper's employees. Thus, if the innkeeper posts notice in accordance with the statute, it is not liable for articles stolen from a guest's room even if its own employees were negligent in preventing the theft or were actually parties to the theft.

Gooden contends that, notwithstanding the protection afforded to innkeepers under OCGA Sec. 43-21-10, Day's Inn, Carter and Clark are liable under an implied "bailment" theory since they actually took possession of Gooden's bag of money for safekeeping. Assuming arguendo, the validity of Gooden's contention, we must conclude, nonetheless, that the trial court properly denied Gooden's motion for summary judgment and properly granted the defendants' motion for summary judgment.

"All bailees are required to exercise care and diligence to protect the thing bailed and to keep it safe. Different degrees of diligence are required according to the nature of the bailments." OCGA Sec. 44-12-43. If the bailment is for the exclusive benefit of the bailor, only slight diligence is required; if the bailment is for the mutual benefit of the parties, ordinary diligence is required; and if the bailment is for the exclusive benefit of the bailee, extraordinary diligence is required.

A bailee is discharged from liability when he shows the exercise of that degree of diligence required by his class of bailment. We assume, without deciding, that any bailment in this case was for the mutual benefit of the parties and that the degree of diligence required of Day's Inn, Carter and Clark was ordinary diligence. Even so, we find them to be discharged of liability. Why? Because they demonstrated that they acted with ordinary care and diligence concerning the bag of money. After all, Ms. Carter simply turned the bag of money over to her immediate supervisor, Ms. Clark, who in turn, gave the bag of money to the "senior technician," Dempsey Wilson, a person with general supervisory powers. Mr. Wilson had been entrusted with guests' valuables in the past and he always acted responsibly with regard to those valuables. The defendants had no way of knowing that Mr. Wilson would abscond with Gooden's bag of money and thus cannot be said to have acted negligently in turning the money over to him.

**Judgment affirmed.**

---

## Safe-Deposit Boxes

If a person rents a safe-deposit box at a local bank and places some property in the box, the box and the property are in the manual possession of the bank. However, it takes both the renter's key and the key held by the bank to open the box, and in most cases the bank does not know the nature, amount, or value of the goods in the box. Although a few courts have held the rental of a safe-deposit box not to be a bailment, most courts have found that the renter of the box is a bailor and the bank is a bailee. As such, the bank is not an insurer of the contents of the box. However, it is obligated to use due care and to come forward and explain loss of or damage to the property entrusted to it.

## Involuntary Bailments

Suppose a person owns a cottage on a beach. After a violent storm, a sailboat washed up on his beach. As the finder of lost or misplaced property, he may be considered the **involuntary bailee** or **constructive bailee** of the sailboat. This relationship may arise when a person finds himself in possession of property that belongs to someone else without having agreed to accept possession.

The duties of the involuntary bailee are not well defined. The bailee does not have the right to destroy the property or to use it. If the true owner shows up, the property must be returned to him. Under some circumstances, the involuntary bailee may be under an obligation to assume control of the property or to take some minimal steps to ascertain who the owner is, or both.

## PROBLEMS AND PROBLEM CASES

—————————————— ■ ——————————————

**1.** In 1945, Lieber was serving in the U.S. Army. He was one of the first soldiers to occupy Munich, Germany. He and some other soldiers entered Adolf Hitler's apartment and removed various items of Hitler's personal belongings. Lieber brought his share to his home in Louisiana. It included Hitler's uniform jacket and cap and some of his decorations and personal jewelry. Lieber's possession of these items was well known. There were several feature articles about them, and they were occasionally displayed to the public. Many years later, Lieber's chauffeur stole the collection and sold it to a dealer of historical material in New York. The dealer sold it to Mohawk Arms, which had no knowledge that it had been stolen. Lieber learned that Mohawk Arms had the collection and demanded that the company return it. Mohawk Arms claimed that it did not have to return the collection to Lieber because the collection properly belonged to the occupational military authority or to the Bavarian government and not to Lieber. Was Lieber entitled to the return of the collection that had been stolen from him?

**2.** The Kahrs put their silver (worth about $3,800), jewelry, and a wallet containing their credit cards in bags and stored them in their attic while they were on vacation. After they returned, they retrieved the bags containing the valuables and placed them on their dining room table along with bags containing some used clothing that they had decided to donate to Goodwill. Mr. Kahr mistakenly picked up the bags containing the silver and wallet and delivered them to Goodwill along with the bags of used clothing. He told Goodwill at that time that he was donating used clothing. A Goodwill employee who was marking the items for resale found the Kahrs' wallet in a bag and, realizing it was a mistake, called the Kahrs' residence about the wallet. She did not mention the silver, though, because she had not yet found it. Even when she did find it, she did not realize that it was sterling silver. The Kahrs realized the mistake about two hours later. They called Goodwill only to find that the silver had been sold for $15 to Markland. Markland refused to return the silver, and the Kahrs brought suit against Goodwill and Markland. Can the Kahrs get their silver back?

**3.** Bernice Paset, a customer of the Old Orchard Bank, found $6,325 in currency on the seat of a chair in an examination booth in the bank's safety-deposit vault. The chair was partially under a table. Paset notified officers of the bank and turned the money over to them. She was told by the bank officials that the bank would try to locate the owner and that she could have the money if the owner was not located within one year. The bank wrote to everyone who had been in the safety-deposit vault area either on the day of, or on the day preceding, the discovery, stating that some property had been found and inviting the customers to describe any property they might have lost. No one reported the loss of any currency, and the money remained unclaimed a year after it had been found. The bank refused to deliver the money to Paset, contending it was mislaid, not lost, property and that it had a better right to it. Was the money found on the chair in the safe-deposit vault mislaid property?

**4.** In October 1973, Richard Welton, a businessman in his late 60s, met Florence Gallagher, a widow in her late 40s. Welton subsequently underwent several operations for cancer. After he was released from the hospital, Gallagher devoted much time and attention to him. In 1975, she helped him operate an ice cream business he had purchased. Shortly thereafter, he moved into her house and spent considerable money fixing it up. Welton subsequently moved out to live with Gallagher's niece, Sandra Kwock, a woman in her 20s, who agreed to take care of him for the rest of his life in return for his giving her $25,000 in bearer bonds. Kwock left town with the bonds, much to Welton's dismay. In April 1976, Welton moved back in with Gallagher, gave her $20,000 in bearer bonds, and told her to place them in her safe-deposit box. Gallagher said that he told her he wanted her to have them as a gift because she was much more deserving than her niece. Later in 1976, Welton and Gallagher ended their relationship and he moved out of her house. He also demanded that she return the bonds, but she refused. Had Welton made a completed *inter vivos* gift of the bonds to Gallagher?

**5.** Ochoa's Studebaker automobile was stolen. Eleven months later, the automobile somehow found its way into the hands of the U.S. government, which sold it to Rogers at a "junk" auction for $85. At the time it was purchased by Rogers, no part of the car was intact. It had no top except a part of the frame; it had no steering wheel, tires, rims, cushions, or battery; the motor, radiator, and gears were out of the car; one wheel was gone, as was one axle; the fenders were partly gone; and the frame was broken. It was no longer an automobile but a pile of broken and dismantled parts of what was once Ochoa's car. Having purchased these parts, Rogers used them in the construction of a delivery truck at an expense of approximately $800. When the truck was completed, he put it to use in his furniture business. Several months later, Ochoa was passing Rogers's place of business and recognized the vehicle from a mark on the hood and another on the radiator. He discovered that the serial and engine numbers matched those on the car he had owned. Ochoa demanded the vehicle from Rogers, who refused to surrender it. Ochoa brought suit to recover possession of the property. In the alternative, he asked for the value of the vehicle at the time of the suit, which he alleged to be $1,000, and for the value of the use of the car from the time Rogers purchased it from the government. Was Ochoa entitled to recover possession of his property, which Rogers had substantially improved?

**6.** R. B. Bewley and his family drove to Kansas City to attend a week-long church convention. When they arrived at the hotel where they had reservations, they were unable to park their car and unload their luggage because of a long line of cars. They then drove to a nearby parking lot where they took a ticket, causing the gate arm to open, and drove in 15 or 20 feet. A parking attendant told them that the lot was full, that they should leave the keys with him, and that he would park the car. They told the attendant that they had reservations at the nearby hotel and that after they checked in they would come back for their luggage. Subsequently, someone broke into the Bewleys' car and stole their personal property from the car and its trunk. Was the parking lot a bailee of the property?

**7.** Georgie Simon entrusted 14 gold and silver coins to her ex-husband, Hardie Maloney, to take to a coin show in Atlanta, Georgia. He was to try to sell the coins, for which he would receive a 7 percent commission. Maloney traveled to the coin show along with his girlfriend, Ann Williams, and a male friend, Herbert Pellegrini, with whom he had previously traveled to 40 or 50 coin shows. Just before they got ready to leave the Waverly Hotel,

where the show had been held, Maloney and Williams went up to Pellegrini's room. Pellegrini would not permit Williams to use the bathroom because he wanted to check out before the deadline and avoid being charged for another day. Williams and Maloney helped Pellegrini carry his three pieces of luggage to the lobby. While Pellegrini checked out, Williams went to the ladies' room in the lobby of the hotel. While Williams was in the bathroom, Maloney went to get his car, on the suggestion and insistence of Pellegrini. He resisted the suggestion because he was carrying a briefcase containing Georgie Simon's coins, as well as the coins he had brought to, and purchased at, the show. Maloney wanted to wait until they could all walk over to the car together for protection. However, after being assured by Pellegrini that he would watch the briefcase, Maloney went to get the car. Maloney set the briefcase down beside Pellegrini's three bags in front of the hotel. When Maloney returned with the car, Pellegrini walked up to the vehicle carrying all three pieces of his luggage but left Maloney's briefcase in front of the hotel. When Maloney asked about the whereabouts of the briefcase, Pellegrini replied that he did not know where it was. It was never found. Georgie Simon brought suit against Maloney for $19,000, the value of the coins she had entrusted to him, and Maloney, in turn, filed a claim against Pellegrini for the loss of those coins as well as for the $12,300 in coins that he had entrusted to Pellegrini. Was Pellegrini liable for the loss of the coins entrusted to him?

**8.** Pringle, the head of the drapery department at Wardrobe Cleaners, went to the Axelrods' home to inspect some dining room draperies for dry-cleaning purposes. He spent about 30 minutes looking at the drapes and inspected both the drapes and the lining. He pointed out some roach spots on the lining that could not be removed by cleaning, but this was not of concern to the Axelrods. He did not indicate to them that the fabric had deteriorated from sunburn, age, dust, or air conditioning so as to make it unsuitable for dry cleaning. He took the drapes and had them dry cleaned. When the drapes were returned, they were unfit for use. The fabric had been a gold floral design on an eggshell-white background. When returned, it was a blotchy gold. Wardrobe Cleaners stated that it was difficult to predict how imported fabrics would respond to the dry-cleaning process and that the company was not equipped to pretest the fabric to see whether it was colorfast. The Axelrods sued Wardrobe Cleaners for $1,000, the replacement value of the drapes. Was Wardrobe Cleaners liable for the damage caused to the drapes during the dry-cleaning process?

**9.** In April, Carter brought her fur coat to Reichlin Furriers for cleaning, glazing, and storage until the next winter season. She was given a printed form of receipt, upon the front of which an employee of Reichlin had written $100 as the valuation of the coat. There was no discussion of the value of the coat, and Carter did not realize that such a value had been written on the receipt, which she did not read at the time. A space for the customer's signature on the front of the receipt was left blank. Below this space in prominent type appeared a notice to "see reverse side for terms and conditions." The other side of the receipt stated that it was a storage contract and that by its acceptance the customer would be deemed to have agreed to its terms unless notice to the contrary were given within 10 days. Fifteen conditions were listed. One of the conditions was as follows: "Storage charges are based upon valuation herein declared by the depositor, and amount recoverable for loss or damage to the article shall not exceed its actual value or the cost of repair or replacement with materials of like kind and quality or the depositor's valuation appearing in this receipt, whichever is less." In the fall of the year, after Carter had paid the bill for storage and other services on the coat, Reichlin informed her that the coat was lost. At that time, the fair market value of the coat was $450. Carter sued Reichlin for loss of the coat and sought $450 damages. Reichlin claimed that its liability was limited to $100. Is this correct?

**10.** On May 16, Mathilda Durandy, a resident of Paris, France, registered at the Fairmont Roosevelt Hotel in New Orleans. She was assigned to room 436 and to safe-deposit box 8. Over the next few days she used the box on numerous occasions, taking jewelry from it when she left for social engagements and replacing the jewelry in it on her return. At 5:30 A.M. on May 22, Durandy returned from a dinner dance and went to the front desk of the hotel to deposit her jewelry. She waited about 15 or 20 minutes but no hotel employer was visible and she could not see any call bell or telephone. Finally, she returned to her room, where she locked her door and secured the chain. She removed her jewelry, including a 16-carat diamond ring and other pieces

containing diamonds, rubies, and sapphires. Sometime thereafter, someone cut the chain, entered the room, cut the telephone cord, and stole Durandy's jewels. Under Louisiana law, an innkeeper is responsible for the effects of its guests and also must provide "an iron chest or other safe deposit for valuable articles." If the innkeeper provides safe-deposit procedures and appropriate notice to its guests, its liability is limited to $100. The Fairmont Roosevelt did have appropriate notices posted in its rooms. Was the hotel's liability for the stolen jewelry limited to $100?

## CAPSTONE QUESTIONS

Mindy Mork took her 1983 Chevrolet Chevette automobile to PDQ Auto Service, Inc.'s place of business to have new front brakes installed on the car. Because Mork did not arrive with the car until late afternoon and all PDQ mechanics were busy at that time, Mork and PDQ's service manager agreed that PDQ would keep possession of the car overnight and that the necessary work would be performed the following morning. Mork left the keys to the car with the service manager and proceeded to leave the PDQ premises. As she did so, Mork noticed a sign on the wall behind the service manager's desk. The sign read: "PDQ Auto Service, Inc., will not be liable for loss of or damage to any automobile or other item of property placed in PDQ's possession by a customer, regardless of the reason(s) for the loss or damage." PDQ's service manager parked Mork's car inside PDQ's repair shop, where the car was to be left for the night. Unbeknownst to the service manager and other PDQ personnel, the trunk of Mork's Chevette contained a rare item owned by Mork: an "Elvis on Black Velvet" (EOBV) picture autographed by the late Elvis Portly not long before the larger-than-life entertainer's untimely death from an overdose of jelly donuts. The presence of the autograph on the EOBV picture made the item worth approximately $5,000.

After leaving her car with the service manager, Mork began walking to her apartment. Approximately two blocks from the PDQ premises, Mork noticed something shiny in the grass next to the sidewalk. She picked up the item, which proved to be a silver money clip attached to 10 $100 bills and 10 $50 bills.

That night, long after PDQ's business hours ended, Phil Onious (a person unaffiliated with PDQ) entered PDQ's repair shop through a door that had been left open inadvertently by a PDQ mechanic. After discovering that the keys to Mork's Chevette had been left in the car's ignition, Onious drove the car away from the PDQ premises. While driving on a narrow, winding road a half-hour later, Onious lost control of the Chevette. The car left the road, went down an embankment, and collided with a tree. The car then exploded. As a result of the explosion, the car and all of its contents—including the autographed EOBV picture—were destroyed. Onious survived the incident. He has been criminally charged with various theft offenses. Mork has sued PDQ in an attempt to recover the value of her Chevette and the EOBV picture, on the theory that PDQ violated its duties as a bailee. PDQ makes these arguments: (1) no bailment was created as to Mork's car; (2) no bailment was created as to Mork's EOBV picture; and (3) even if some sort of bailment had been created, PDQ is not liable to Mork because (a) Onious, a thief unaffiliated with PDQ, caused the damage to Mork's property, and (b) the sign on the wall behind the service manager's desk operates to insulate PDQ from any liability it might otherwise have had.

## Required:

Answer the following and give reasons for your conclusions.

1. Evaluate Mork's chances of success in her lawsuit against PDQ. In doing so, analyze and discuss the arguments made by PDQ.

2. Discuss the nature and proper classification of the silver money clip and the $100 and $50 bills attached to it. State what rights, if any, Mork has with regard to the money clip and the money.

CHAPTER

16

# REAL PROPERTY

**INTRODUCTION**

*Land's special importance in the law has long been recognized. In the agrarian society of previous eras, land served as the basic measure and source of wealth. In today's industrialized society, land functions not only as a source of food, clothing, and shelter but also as an instrument of commercial and industrial development. It is not surprising, then, that a complex body of law—the law of* real property—*exists regarding the ownership, acquisition, and use of land.*

*This chapter discusses the scope of real property and the various ownership interests in it. In addition, the chapter examines the ways in which real property is transferred and the controls society places on an owner's use of real property.*

## SCOPE OF REAL PROPERTY

**Real property** includes not only land but also things firmly attached to or embedded in land. Buildings and other permanent structures thus are considered real property. The owner of a tract of real property also owns the air above it, the minerals below its surface, and any trees or other vegetation growing on the property.[1]

Unlike readily movable personal property, real property is immovable or attached to something immovable. Distinguishing between real and personal property is important because rules of law governing real property transactions such as sale, taxation, and inheritance are frequently different from those applied to personal property transactions.

### Fixtures

An item of personal property may, however, be attached to or used in conjunction with real property in such a way that it ceases being personal property and instead becomes part of the real property. This type of property is called a **fixture.**

Fixtures belong to the owner of the real property. One who provides or attaches fixtures to real property without a request to that effect from the owner of the real property is normally not entitled to

---

[1]Ownership of air above one's property is not an unlimited interest, however. Courts have held that the flight of aircraft above property does not violate the property owner's rights, so long as it does not unduly interfere with the owner's enjoyment of her land.

compensation from the owner. A conveyance (transfer of ownership) of real property also conveys the fixtures associated with that property, even if the fixtures are not specifically mentioned.

People commonly install items of personal property on the real property they own or rent. Disputes may arise regarding rights to such property. Suppose that Jacobsen buys an elaborate ceiling fan and installs it in his home. When he sells the house to Orr, may Jacobsen remove the ceiling fan, or is it part of the home Orr has bought? Suppose that Luther, a commercial tenant, installs showcases and tracklights in the store she leases from Nelson. May Luther remove the showcases and the lights when her lease expires, or do the items now belong to Nelson? If the parties' contracts are silent on these matters, courts will resolve the cases by applying the law of fixtures. As later discussion will reveal, Jacobsen probably cannot remove the ceiling fan because it is likely to be considered part of the real property purchased by Orr. Luther, on the other hand, may be entitled to remove the showcases and the lights under the special rules governing trade fixtures.

**Factors Indicating Whether an Item Is a Fixture**
There is no mechanical formula for determining whether an item has become a fixture. Courts tend, however, to consider these factors:

**1.** *Attachment.* One factor helping to indicate whether an item is a fixture is the degree to which the item is **attached** or **annexed** to the real property. If firmly attached to the real property so that it cannot be removed without damaging the property, the item is likely to be considered a fixture. An item of personal property that may be removed with little or no injury to the property is less likely to be considered a fixture.

Actual physical attachment to real property is not necessary, however. A close physical connection between the item of personal property and the real property may enable a court to conclude that the item is **constructively annexed**. For example, heavy machinery or remote control devices for automatic garage doors may be considered fixtures even though they are not physically attached to real property.

**2.** *Adaptation.* Another factor to be considered is **adaptation**—the degree to which the item's use is necessary or beneficial to the use of the real property. Adaptation is a particularly relevant factor when the item is not physically attached to the real property or is only slightly attached. When an item would be of little value except for use with certain real property, the item is likely to be considered a fixture even if it is unattached or could easily be removed. For example, keys and custom-sized window screens and storm windows have been held to be fixtures.

**3.** *Intent.* The third factor to be considered is the **intent** of the person who installed the item. Intent is judged not by what that person subjectively intended, but by what the circumstances indicate he intended. To a great extent, intent is indicated by the annexation and adaptation factors. An owner of real property who improves it by attaching items of personal property presumably intended those items to become part of the real estate. If the owner does not want an attached item to be considered a fixture, he must specifically reserve the right to keep the item. For instance, if a seller of a house wants to keep an antique chandelier that has been installed in the house, she should either replace the chandelier before the house is shown to prospective purchasers or specify in the contract of sale that the chandelier will be excluded from the sale.

*Ford v. Venard* presents a typical judicial analysis of whether an item of personal property has become a fixture.

FORD v. VENARD
**340 N.W.2d 270 (Iowa Sup. Ct. 1983)**

In 1973, Norman Van Sickle moved his double wide mobile home to a plot of land owned by Luelia Jedlicka. Van Sickle had the real estate landscaped, a foundation poured, concrete blocks set, and steel girders aligned on the blocks. After removing the hitches and wheels from the mobile home, he had the mobile home set on and hooked to the foundation. Thereafter, Van Sickle substantially modified his double-wide unit by welding it into a single unit, placing a roof over the entire building, and joining the exterior with siding. As a result, the structure could not be disassembled without tearing it apart and could not be moved as one unit except by a house mover.

Van Sickle had paid Jedlicka $500 as a down payment for the purchase of the land back in 1973, but had never made any further payments. He had never been asked to pay taxes and was told by Jedlicka that she paid them. Van Sickle had been told by the bank holding a security interest on the mobile home that the house would become part of Jedlicka's real estate after it was set on a foundation. Van Sickle did not consider himself the owner of the real estate; he believed the land belonged to Jedlicka.

In 1977, Henry Edsel Ford contracted with Jedlicka to buy the land. A clause in the Ford-Jedlicka contract specified that all "attached fixtures" were included as part of the real estate being sold. The question of ownership of the mobile home came to a head in 1982, when William Venard, a creditor of Van Sickle's, attempted to enforce a judgment against Van Sickle by attaching the mobile home and executing against it. Ford brought this action, claiming that he owned the mobile home and requesting an injunction to restrain Venard from executing against the mobile home. The trial court granted the injunction. Venard appealed.

---

**Harris, Justice**     The question is whether the mobile home was a fixture included under the terms of the land contract between Jedlicka and Ford. We think it plainly was. Under our common law rule, personal property becomes a fixture when:

**(1)** it is actually annexed to the realty, or to something appurtenant thereto;

**(2)** it is put to the same use as the realty with which it is connected; and

**(3)** the party making the annexation intends to make a permanent accession to the freehold.

The intention of the party annexing the improvement is the "paramount factor" in determining whether the improvement is a fixture. Physical attachment of the structure to the soil or to an appurtenance thereto is not essential to make the structure a part of the realty. On the other hand, a building which cannot be removed without destruction of a substantial part of its value becomes almost unavoidably an integral part of the real estate.

Venard argues that Van Sickle's home was not physically annexed to the realty and that Van Sickle never intended for his home to be permanently attached to the freehold. Ford, on the other hand, relies on these facts: the home's tongues and wheels have been removed; the home was set on a foundation and girders; it has been extensively remodeled into a single unit; and its removal would be expensive and damaging. He points out that the home was used as a homestead, which is the use for which the realty had been appropriated. He points to the bank's advice to Van Sickle that his home would become the property of Jedlicka when set on her land.

We have found buildings to be fixtures in a number of cases. We are convinced the home became attached to the land. It could not be removed from its present location except in the sense that any permanent home could be. We hold that it has become an integral part of the real estate. The trial court was correct in ordering the issuance of the permanent injunction.

**Affirmed in favor of Ford.**

---

**Express Agreement**     If the parties to an express agreement have clearly stated their intent about whether a particular item is to be considered a fixture, a court will generally enforce that agreement. For example, the buyer and seller of a house might agree to permit the seller to remove a fence or shrubbery that would otherwise be considered a fixture.

**Trade Fixtures**     An exception to the usual fixture rules is recognized when a *tenant* attaches personal property to leased premises for the purpose of carrying on her trade or business. Such fixtures, called **trade fixtures**, remain the personal property of the tenant and may normally be removed at the termination of the lease. This trade fixtures exception encourages commerce and industry. It recognizes that the commercial tenant who affixed the item of personal property did not intend a permanent improvement of the leased premises.

The tenant's right to remove trade fixtures is subject to two limitations. First, the tenant cannot remove the fixtures if doing so would cause substantial damage to the landlord's realty. Second, the tenant must remove the fixtures by the end of the lease if the lease is for a definite period; if the lease is for an indefinite period, the tenant usually has a reasonable time after the expiration of the lease to remove the fixtures. Trade fixtures not removed within the appropriate time become the landlord's property.

Leases may contain terms expressly addressing the parties' rights in any fixtures. A lease might give the tenant the right to attach items or make other improvements, and to remove them later. The reverse may also be true. The lease could state that any improvements made or fixtures attached will become the landlord's property at the termination of the lease. Courts generally enforce parties' agreements on fixture ownership.

**Security Interests in Fixtures**   Special rules apply to personal property subject to a lien or security interest at the time it is attached to real property. Assume, for example, that a person buys a dishwasher on a time-payment plan from an appliance store and has it installed in his kitchen. To protect itself, the appliance store takes a security interest in the dishwasher and perfects that interest by filing a financing statement in the appropriate real estate records office within the period of time specified by the Uniform Commercial Code. The appliance store then is able to remove the dishwasher if the buyer defaults in his payments. The store could be liable, however, to third parties such as prior real estate mortgagees for any damage removal of the dishwasher caused to the real estate. The rules governing security interests in personal property that will become fixtures are explained more fully in Chapter 21, Security Interests in Personal Property.

**CONCEPT REVIEW**

**FIXTURES**

| | |
|---|---|
| **Concept** | A *fixture* is an item of personal property attached to or used in conjunction with real property in such a way that it is treated as being part of the real property. |
| **Significance** | A conveyance of the real property will also convey the fixtures on that property. |
| **Factors Considered in Determining Whether Property Is a Fixture** | 1. Attachment: Is the item physically attached or closely connected to the real property?<br>2. Adaptation: How necessary or beneficial is the item to the use of the real property?<br>3. Intent: Did the person who installed the item manifest intent for the property to become part of the real property? |
| **Express Agreement** | Express agreements clearly stating intent about whether property is a fixture are generally enforceable. |
| **Trade Fixtures (Tenants' Fixtures)** | Definition of *trade fixture:* personal property attached to leased real property by a tenant for the purpose of carrying on his trade or business.<br>Trade fixtures can be removed and retained by the tenant at the termination of the lease except when one or more of the following apply:<br>1. Removal would cause substantial damage to the landlord's real property.<br>2. Tenant fails to remove the fixtures by the end of the lease (or within a reasonable time, if the lease is for an indefinite period of time).<br>3. An express agreement between the landlord and tenant provides otherwise. |

# Rights and Interests in Real Property

When we think of real property ownership, we normally envision one person owning all of the rights in a particular piece of land. Real property, however, involves a bundle of rights subject to ownership—sometimes by different people. This discussion examines the most common forms of present *possessory interests* (rights to exclusive possession of real property): **fee simple absolute** and **life estate**. It also explores the various ways in which two or more persons may share ownership of a possessory interest. Finally, it discusses the interests and rights one may have in another person's real property, such as the right to use the property or restrict the way the owner uses it.

## Estates in Land

The term **estate** is used to describe the nature of a person's ownership interest in real property. Estates in land are classified as either **freehold estates** or **nonfreehold estates**. Nonfreehold (or leasehold) estates are those held by persons who lease real property. They will be discussed in Chapter 18, which deals with landlord-tenant law. Freehold estates are ownership interests of uncertain duration. The most common types of freehold estates are fee simple absolute and life estates.

**Fee Simple Absolute**   The **fee simple absolute** is what we normally think of as "full ownership" of land. One who owns real property in fee simple absolute has the right to possess and use the property for an unlimited period of time, subject only to governmental regulations or private restrictions. She also has the unconditional power to dispose of the property during her lifetime or upon her death. A person who owns land in fee simple absolute may grant many rights to others without giving up fee simple ownership. For example, she may grant a mortgage on the property to a party who has loaned her money, lease the property to a tenant, or grant rights such as those to be discussed later in this section.

**Life Estate**   The property interest known as a **life estate** gives a person the right to possess and use property for a time measured by his or another person's lifetime. For example, if Haney has a life estate (measured by his life) in a tract of land known as Greenacre, he has the right to use Greenacre for the remainder of his life. At Haney's death, the property will revert to the person who conveyed the estate to him or will pass to some other designated person. Although a life tenant such as Haney has the right to use the property, he is obligated not to commit acts that would result in permanent injury to the property.

## Co-Ownership of Real Property

Co-ownership of real property exists when two or more persons share the same ownership interest in the same property. The co-owners do not have separate rights to any portion of the real property; each has a share in the whole property. Seven types of co-ownership are recognized in the United States.

**Tenancy in Common**   Persons who own property under a **tenancy in common** have undivided interests in the property and equal rights to possess it. When property is transferred to two or more persons without specification of their co-ownership form, it is presumed that they acquire the property as tenants in common. The respective ownership interests of the tenants in common may be, but need not be, equal. One tenant, for example, could have a two-thirds ownership interest in the property, with the other tenant having a one-third interest.

Each tenant in common has the right to possess and use the property. Individual tenants, however, cannot exclude the other tenants in common from also possessing and using the property. If the property is rented or otherwise produces income, each tenant is entitled to share in the income in proportion to her ownership share. Similarly, each tenant must pay her proportionate share of property taxes and necessary repair costs. If a tenant in sole possession of the property receives no rents or profits from the property, she is not required to pay rent to her cotenant unless her possession is adverse to or inconsistent with her cotenant's property interests.

A tenant in common may dispose of his interest in the property during life and at death. Similarly, his interest is subject to his creditors' claims. When a tenant dies, his interest passes to his heirs or, if he has made a will, to the person or persons specified in the will. Suppose Peterson and Sievers own

Blackacre as tenants in common. Sievers dies, having executed a valid will in which he leaves his Blackacre interest to Johanns. In this situation, Peterson and Johanns become tenants in common.

Tenants in common may sever the cotenancy by agreeing to divide the property or, if they are unable to agree, by petitioning a court for *partition*. The court will physically divide the property if that is feasible, so that each tenant receives her proportionate share. If physical division is not feasible, the court will order that the property be sold and that the proceeds be appropriately divided.

**Joint Tenancy**   A **joint tenancy** is created when equal interests in real property are conveyed to two or more persons by means of a document specifying that they are to own the property as joint tenants. The rights of use, possession, contribution, and partition are the same for a joint tenancy as for a tenancy in common. The joint tenancy's distinguishing feature is that it gives the owners the **right of survivorship**, which means that upon the death of a joint tenant, the deceased tenant's interest automatically passes to the surviving joint tenant(s). The right of survivorship makes it easy for a person to transfer property at death without making a will. For example, Devaney and Osborne purchase Redacre and take title as joint tenants. At Devaney's death, his Redacre interest will pass to Osborne even if Devaney did not have a will setting forth such an intent. By the same token, even if Devaney had a will that purported to leave his Redacre interest to someone other than Osborne, the will's Redacre provision would be ineffective.

A joint tenant may mortgage, sell, or give away her interest in the property during her lifetime. Her interest in the property is subject to her creditors' claims. When a joint tenant transfers her interest, the joint tenancy is severed and a tenancy in common is created as to the share affected by the transaction. When a joint tenant sells her interest to a third person, the purchaser becomes a tenant in common with the remaining joint tenant(s).

**Tenancy by the Entirety**   Approximately half of the states permit married couples to own real property under a **tenancy by the entirety**. This tenancy is essentially a joint tenancy with the added requirement that the owners be married. As does the joint tenancy, the tenancy by the entirety features the right of survivorship. Neither spouse can transfer the property by will if the other is still living. Upon the death of the husband or wife, the property passes automatically to the surviving spouse.[2]

A tenancy by the entirety cannot be severed by the act of only one of the parties. Neither spouse can transfer the property unless the other one also signs the deed. Thus, a creditor of one tenant cannot claim an interest in that person's share of property held in tenancy by the entirety. Divorce, however, severs a tenancy by the entirety and transforms it into a tenancy in common. Figure 1 compares the features of tenancy in common, joint tenancy, and tenancy by the entirety.

**Community Property**   A number of western and southern states recognize the **community property** system of co-ownership of property by married couples. This type of co-ownership assumes that marriage is a partnership in which each spouse contributes to the family's property base. Property acquired during the marriage through a spouse's industry or efforts is classified as *community* property. Each spouse has an equal interest in such property regardless of who produced or earned the property. Because each spouse has an equal share in community property, neither can convey community property without the other's joining in the transaction. Various community property states permit the parties to dispose of their interests in community property at death. The details of each state's community property system vary, depending on the specific provisions of that state's statutes.

Not all property owned by a married person is community property, however. Property a spouse owned before marriage or acquired during marriage by gift or inheritance is *separate* property. Neither spouse owns a legal interest in the other's separate property. Property exchanged for separate property also remains separately owned.

**Tenancy in Partnership**   When a partnership takes title to property in the partnership's name, the co-ownership form is called **tenancy in partnership**. This form of co-ownership is discussed in

---

[2]In states that do not recognize the tenancy by the entirety, married couples often own real property in joint tenancy, but they are not required to elect that co-ownership form.

**FIGURE 1**   Tenancy in Common, Joint Tenancy, and Tenancy by the Entirety

|  | Tenancy in Common | Joint Tenancy | Tenancy by the Entirety |
|---|---|---|---|
| **Equal Possession and Use?** | Yes | Yes | Yes |
| **Share Income?** | Yes | Yes | Presumably |
| **Contribution Requirement?** | Generally | Generally | Generally |
| **Free Conveyance of Interest?** | Yes; transferee becomes tenant in common | Yes, but joint tenancy is severed on conveyance and reverts to tenancy in common | Both must agree; divorce severs tenancy |
| **Effect of Death?** | Interest transferable at death by will or inheritance | Right of survivorship; surviving joint tenant takes decedent's share | Right of survivorship; surviving spouse takes decedent's share |

Chapter 29, Introduction to Forms of Business and Formation of Partnerships.

**Condominium Ownership**   Condominiums have become very common in the United States in recent years, even in locations outside urban and resort areas. Under condominium ownership, a purchaser takes title to her individual unit and becomes a tenant in common with other unit owners in shared facilities such as hallways, elevators, swimming pools, and parking areas. The condominium owner pays property taxes on her individual unit and makes a monthly payment for the maintenance of the common areas. She may generally mortgage or sell her unit without the other unit owners' approval. For federal income tax purposes, the condominium owner is treated as if she owned a single-family home, and is thus allowed to deduct her property taxes and mortgage interest expenses.

**Cooperative Ownership**   In a cooperative, a building is owned by a corporation or group of persons. One who wants to buy an apartment in the building purchases stock in the corporation and holds his apartment under a long-term, renewable lease called a *proprietary lease*. Frequently, the cooperative owner must obtain the other owners' approval to sell or sublease his unit.

## INTERESTS IN REAL PROPERTY OWNED BY OTHERS

In various situations, a person may hold a legally protected interest in real property owned by someone else. Such interests, to be discussed below, are not possessory because they do not give their holder the right to complete dominion over the land. Rather, they give him the right to use another person's property or to limit the way in which the owner uses the property.

### Easements

An **easement** is the right to make certain uses of another person's property (*affirmative easement*) or the right to prevent another person from making certain uses of his own property (*negative easement*). The right to run a sewer line across someone else's property would be an affirmative easement. Suppose an easement prevents Rogers from erecting, on his land, a structure that would block his neighbor McFeely's solar collector. Such an easement would be negative in nature.

If an easement qualifies as an **easement appurtenant**, it will pass with the land. This means that if the owner of the land benefited by an easement appurtenant sells or otherwise conveys the property, the new owner also acquires the right contemplated by the easement. An easement appurtenant is primarily designed to benefit a certain tract of land, rather than merely giving an individual a personal right. For example, Agnew and Nixon are next-door neighbors. They share a common driveway that runs along the borderline of their respective properties. Each has an easement in the portion of the driveway that lies on the other's property. If Agnew sells his property to Ford, Ford also obtains the easement in the driveway portion on Nixon's land. Nixon, of course, still has an easement in the driveway portion on Ford's land.

## Creation of Easements

Easements may be acquired in any of the following ways:

**1.** *By grant.* When an owner of property expressly provides an easement in his property to another while retaining ownership of the property, he is said to **grant** an easement. For example, Monroe may sell or give Madison, who owns adjoining property, the right to go across Monroe's land to reach an alley behind that land.

**2.** *By reservation.* When one transfers ownership of her land but retains the right to use it for some specified purpose, she is said to **reserve** an easement in the land. For example, Smythe sells land to Jones but reserves the mineral rights to the property as well as an easement to enter the land to remove the minerals.

**3.** *By prescription.* An easement by **prescription** is created when one person uses another's land openly, continuously, and in a manner adverse to the owner's rights for a period of time specified by state statute (the necessary period of time varying state to state). In such a situation, the property owner presumably is on notice that someone else is acting as if she possesses rights to use the property. If the property owner does not take action during the statutory period to stop the other person from making use of his property, he may lose his right to stop that use. Suppose, for instance, that State X allows easements by prescription to be obtained through 15 years of prescriptive use. Tara, who lives in State X, uses the driveway of her next-door neighbor, Kyle. Tara does this openly, on a daily basis, and without Kyle's permission. If this use by Tara continues for the 15-year period established by statute and Kyle takes no action to stop Tara within that time span, Tara will

obtain an easement by prescription. In that event, Tara will have the right to use the driveway not only while Kyle owns the property but also when Kyle sells the property to another party. Easements by prescription resemble *adverse possession*, a concept discussed later in this chapter.

**4.** *By implication.* Sometimes, easements are implied by the nature of the transaction rather than created by express agreement of the parties. Such easements, called **easements by implication**, take either of two forms: easements by prior use and easements by necessity.

An *easement by prior use* is created when land is subdivided and a path, road, or other apparent and beneficial use exists when part of the land is conveyed to another person. In this situation, the new owner of the conveyed portion of the land has an easement to continue using the path, road, or other prior use running across the nonconveyed portion of the land. Assume, for example, that a private road runs through Greenacre from north to south, linking the house located on Greenacre's northern portion to the public highway that lies south of Greenacre. Douglas, the owner of Greenacre, sells the northern portion to Kimball. On these facts, Kimball has an easement by implication to continue using the private road even where it runs across the portion of Greenacre retained by Douglas. To prevent such an easement from arising, Douglas and Kimball would need to have specified in their contract of sale that the easement would not exist.

An *easement by necessity* is created when real property once held in common ownership is subdivided in such a fashion that the only reasonable way a new owner can gain access to her land is through passage over another's land that was once part of the same tract. Such an easement is based on the necessity of obtaining access to property. Assume, for instance, that Tinker, the owner of Blackacre, sells Blackacre's northern 25 acres to Evers and its southern 25 acres to Chance. In order to have any reasonable access to her property, Chance must use a public road that runs alongside and just beyond the northern border of the land now owned by Evers; Chance must then go across Evers's property to reach hers. On these facts, Chance is entitled to an easement by necessity to cross Evers's land in order to go to and from her property.

**Easements and the Statute of Frauds**   As interests in land, easements are potentially within the coverage of the statute of frauds. To be enforceable, an express agreement granting or reserving an easement must be evidenced by a suitable writing signed by the party to be charged.[3] An express grant of an easement normally must be executed with the same formalities observed in executing the grant of a fee simple interest. However, easements not granted expressly (such as easements by prior use, necessity, or prescription) are enforceable despite the lack of a writing.

## Profits

A **profit** is a right to enter another person's land and remove some product or part of the land. Timber, gravel, minerals, and oil are among the products and parts frequently made the subject of profits. Generally governed by the same rules applicable to easements, profits are sometimes called *easements with a profit.*

## Licenses

A **license** is a temporary right to enter another's land for a specific purpose. Ordinarily, licenses are more informal than easements. Licenses may be created orally or in any other manner indicating the landowner's permission for the licensee to enter the property. Because licenses are considered to be personal rights, they are not true interests in land. The licensor may revoke a license at his will unless the license is coupled with an interest (such as the licensee's ownership of personal property located on the licensor's land) or the licensee has paid money or provided something else of value either for the license or in reliance on its existence. For example, Branch pays Leif $900 for certain trees on Leif's land. Branch is to dig up the trees and haul them to her own property for transplanting. Branch has an irrevocable license to enter Leif's land to dig up and haul away the trees.

## Restrictive Covenants

Within certain limitations, real estate owners may create enforceable agreements that restrict the use of real property. These private agreements are called

restrictive covenants. For example, Grant owns two adjacent lots. She sells one to Lee subject to the parties' agreement that Lee will not operate any liquor-selling business on the property. This use restriction appears in the deed Grant furnishes Lee. As another illustration, a subdivision developer sells lots in the subdivision and places a provision in each lot's deed regarding the minimum size of house to be built on the property.

The validity and enforceability of such private restrictions on the use of real property depend on the purpose, nature, and scope of the restrictions. A restraint that violates a statute or other expression of public policy will not be enforced. For example, the federal Fair Housing Act (discussed later in this chapter) would make unlawful an attempt by a seller or lessor of residential property to refuse to sell or rent to certain persons because of an existing restrictive covenant that purports to disqualify those prospective buyers or renters on the basis of their race, color, religion, sex, handicap, familial status, or national origin.

Public policy generally favors the unlimited use and transfer of land. A restrictive covenant therefore is unenforceable if it effectively prevents the sale or transfer of the property. Similarly, ambiguous language in a restrictive covenant is construed in favor of the less restrictive interpretation. A restraint is enforceable, however, if it is clearly expressed and neither unduly restrictive of the use and transfer of the property nor otherwise violative of public policy. Restrictions usually held enforceable include those relating to minimum lot size, building design and size, and maintenance of an area as a residential community.

An important and frequently arising question is whether subsequent owners of property are bound by a restrictive covenant even though they were not parties to the original agreement that established the covenant. Under certain circumstances, restrictive covenants are said to "run with the land" and thus bind subsequent owners of the restricted property. For a covenant to run with the land, it must have been *binding* on the original parties to it, and those parties must have *intended that the covenant bind their successors.* The covenant must also *"touch and concern"* the restricted land. This means that the covenant must involve the use, value, or character of the land, rather than being merely a personal obligation of one of the original parties. In addition,

---

[3]Chapter 8 discusses the statute of frauds and compliance with the writing requirement it imposes when it is applicable.

a covenant will not bind a subsequent purchaser unless she had notice of the covenant's existence when she took her interest. This notice would commonly be provided by the recording of the deed (a subject discussed later in this chapter) or other document containing the covenant.

Restrictive covenants may be enforced by the parties to them, by persons meant to benefit from them, and—if the covenants run with the land—by successors of the original parties to them. If restric-

tive covenants amounting to a general building scheme are contained in a subdivision plat (recorded description of a subdivision), property owners in the subdivision may be able to enforce them against noncomplying property owners.

*Mains Farm Homeowners Association v. Worthington* illustrates the difficult interpretation, enforceability, and public policy questions sometimes presented by litigation over restrictive covenants that run with the land.

## MAINS FARM HOMEOWNERS ASSOCIATION V. WORTHINGTON
### 854 P.2d 1072 (Wash. Sup. Ct. 1993)

A declaration of restrictive covenants for the platted Mains Farm subdivision was recorded in 1962. Worthington purchased a residential lot in Mains Farm in 1987. A house already existed on the property. Before purchasing, Worthington obtained and read a copy of the restrictive covenants, which stated, in pertinent part, that all lots in Mains Farm "shall be designated as 'Residence Lots' and shall be used for single family residential purposes only." Worthington later began occupying the residence along with four adults who paid her for 24-hour protective supervision and care. These four adults, who were not related to Worthington, were unable to do their own housekeeping, prepare their own meals, or attend to their personal hygiene. In providing this supervision and care on a for-profit basis, Worthington complied with the licensing and inspection requirements established by Washington law governing such enterprises.

The Mains Farm Homeowners Association (Association), which consisted of owners of property in the subdivision, filed suit against Worthington and asked the court to enjoin her from using her property as an adult family home business. Association asserted that Worthington's use violated the restrictive covenants quoted above. The trial court granted Association's motion for summary judgment and issued the requested injunction against Worthington's use. The Washington Court of Appeals affirmed. Worthington appealed to the Washington Supreme Court. Various organizations representing the interests of disabled adults submitted amicus curiae (friend of the court) briefs urging reversal.

**Brachtenbach, Justice**   *Before* defendant Worthington bought the premises, she *read* the restrictive covenants. Written opposition by other property owners was made known to her immediately after her purchase. Despite that knowledge, Worthington applied for a building permit to add a fifth bedroom to the house. She was advised by the county that her intended facility did not comply with applicable zoning. Worthington later obtained the permit by stating that only her family would be living with her. In her words: "I told them what they wanted to hear." These equitable considerations must be kept in mind when we interpret the restrictive covenants at issue here. Our analysis

leads to the conclusion that Worthington's commercial use is prohibited.

To reach this conclusion, we consider the meaning of "single family." The cases interpreting "family" are legion. Any of the cases must be used with caution. Some involve a state statute which bears a different relationship to zoning powers than to vested property rights embodied in a restrictive covenant. No purpose will be served by examining and comparing in detail the numerous cases which define "family." Because of the widely differing documents being interpreted, the contexts in which the word is used, and the fact-specific circumstances, it is impossible to arrive at a single, all-purpose definition of "family." The possibilities range from the traditional notion of persons related by blood, marriage, or adoption to the broader concept of a group of people who live, sleep, cook, and eat upon the premises as a single housekeeping unit. Likewise, attempting to use one of the many dictionary classifications solves nothing. For similar reasons, the use of a phrase or two out of a dictionary to define "residential" for purposes of this covenant is not acceptable.

Some reflection leads us to attribute certain characteristics to a concept of "family," even in an extended sense. These include: (1) a sharing of responsibilities among the members and a mutual caring whether physical or emotional, (2) some commonality whether it be friendship, shared employment, mutual social or political interest, (3) some degree of existing or contemplated permanency to the relationship, and (4) a recognition of some common purpose—persons brought together by reasons other than a referral by a state agency. Here, we have four persons, all strangers before arriving at this residence. By law, they cannot be related to Worthington by birth, adoption, or marriage. By law, they cannot be below the age of 18. By regulatory definition, they must require 24-hour protective supervision and care. Worthington could not form this "family" without a license from the State, which must approve the site and is free to inspect it. Worthington meets these qualifications and provides around-the-clock care as a means of making a living.

These are not the characteristics of a single family residence. Our primary goal is to ascertain the intent of the restrictive covenants and to accord the words their ordinary and common usage. The reasonable expectations of the other lot owners who bought their family houses in reliance on the long recorded covenants would not include a State-licensed, 24-hour operating business. In this case, Worthington's main use of her property is not to provide a single family residence, but to provide 24-hour protective care and supervision in exchange for money. It must therefore be concluded that the other lot owners are entitled in equity to the injunction granted by the trial court.

As an alternative ground for reversing the trial court, Worthington argues that the restrictive covenant violates a legislative declaration of public policy and is therefore void. The public policy question should not be resolved in this case, for various reasons. First, the record made in the trial court is not adequate to identify the facts and bases upon which such a significant public policy should be considered. It is true that the Legislature has found "that adult family homes are an important part of the state's long-term care system" [citation to statute omitted]. Unfortunately, this record shows little more. We know that the Legislature has not implemented this finding beyond declaring that such homes are considered residential for *zoning* purposes. We know nothing of the number of persons qualified for adult family homes or of whether that need is being met. We know nothing of the situation along those lines in the community or county in which the Mains Farm subdivision is located. We do not know whether there exists an adequate supply of adult family homes in areas not subject to restrictive covenants. We are unaware whether efforts by individual or governmental units have been successful in locating such homes either without neighborhood opposition or by successful negotiation with concerned owners. We have not been made aware of what coordinated efforts, if any, are being made by state or local agencies to establish adult family homes. All of these considerations would be relevant to any possible court finding that a significant public policy overrides the existing restrictive covenants at issue in this case.

In addition, the statute relied upon by Worthington as the source of a legislative declaration of public policy favoring adult family homes was not effective until after the written opinion of the trial court, and was not cited to the trial court. Moreover, the statute, in stating that an adult family home should be permitted in an area zoned for single-family dwellings, is by its very terms limited to *zoning*. When the Legislature intends to affect a *private land use restriction* (i.e., a covenant) as compared to *zoning*, it normally does so explicitly.

The cases from other jurisdictions cited by Worthington either do not reach the policy conflict presented here or are based upon entirely different statutory direction or even constitutional dictates. The various amici curiae raise a claimed violation of the federal Fair Housing Act. We do not consider issues raised first and only by amicus.

We hold that under the equities of these particular facts, the discretionary grant of an injunction was proper. We caution that the interpretation of a particular restrictive covenant is largely dependent upon the facts of the case at hand. Our holding should not be construed as an encompassing declaration concerning covenants and uses under other circumstances. Likewise, our rejection of the claimed public policy is limited to the facts herein, especially due to the record's lack of any comprehensive presentation of governmental goals, efforts, needs, and successes existing in fact.

**Injunction in favor of Association and against Worthington's use of property affirmed.**

---

**Termination of Restrictive Covenants** Restrictive covenants may be terminated in a variety of ways, including voluntary relinquishment or *waiver*. They may also be terminated *by their own terms* (such as when the covenant specifies that it is to exist for a certain length of time) or *by dramatically changed circumstances*. If Oldcodger's property is subject, for instance, to a restrictive covenant allowing only residential use, the fact that all of the surrounding property has come to be used for industrial purposes may operate to terminate the covenant. When a restrictive covenant has been terminated or held invalid, the deed containing the restriction remains a valid instrument of transfer but is treated as if the restriction had been removed from the document.

## ACQUISITION OF REAL PROPERTY

Title to real property may be obtained in various ways, including purchase, gift, will or inheritance, tax sale, and adverse possession. Original title to land in the United States was acquired either from the federal government or from a country that held the land prior to its acquisition by the United States. The land in the 13 original colonies had been granted by the king of England either to the colonies or to certain individuals. The states ceded the land in the Northwest Territory to the federal government, which in turn issued grants or patents of land. Original ownership of much of the land in Florida and the southwest came by grants from Spain's rulers.

### Acquisition by Purchase

Selling one's real property is a basic ownership right. Unreasonable restrictions on an owner's right to sell her property are considered unenforceable as against public policy. Most owners of real property acquired title by purchasing the property. Each state sets the requirements for proper conveyances of real property located in that state. The various elements of selling and buying real property are discussed later in this chapter.

### Acquisition by Gift

Real property ownership may be acquired by gift. For a gift of real property to be valid, the donor must deliver a properly executed deed to the property to the donee or to some third person who is to hold it for the donee. Neither the donee nor the third person needs to take actual possession of the property. The gift's essential element is delivery of the deed. Suppose that Fields executes a deed to the family farm and leaves it in his safe-deposit box for delivery to his daughter (the intended donee) when he dies. The attempted gift will not be valid, because Fields did not deliver the gift during his lifetime.

### Acquisition by Will or Inheritance

The owner of real property generally has the right to dispose of the property by will. The requirements for a valid will are discussed in Chapter 19, Estates and Trusts. If the owner of real property dies without a valid will, the property passes to his heirs as determined under the laws of the state in which the property is located.

### Acquisition by Tax Sale

If taxes assessed on real property are not paid when due, they become a *lien* on the property. This lien has priority over other claims to the land. If the taxes remain unpaid, the government may sell the land at a tax sale. Although the purchaser at the tax sale acquires title to the property, a number of states have statutes giving the original owner a limited time (such as a year) within which to buy the property from the tax sale purchaser for the price paid by the purchaser, plus interest.

## Acquisition by Adverse Possession

Each state has a statute of limitations that gives an owner of land a specific number of years within which to bring suit to regain possession of her land from someone who is trespassing on it. This period varies from state to state, generally ranging from 5 to 20 years. If someone wrongfully possesses land and acts as if he were the owner, the actual owner must take steps to have the possessor ejected from the land. If the owner fails to do this within the statutory period, she loses her right to eject the possessor.

Assume, for example, that Titus owns a vacant lot next to Holdeman's house. Holdeman frequently uses the vacant lot for a variety of activities and appears to be the property's only user. In addition, Holdeman regularly mows and otherwise maintains the vacant lot. He has also placed a fence around it. By continuing such actions and thus staying in possession of Titus's property for the statutory period (and by meeting each other requirement about to be discussed), Holdeman may position himself to acquire title to the land by **adverse possession.**

To acquire title by adverse possession, one must possess land in a manner that puts the true owner on notice of the owner's cause of action against the possessor. The adverse possessor's acts of possession must be (1) *open,* (2) *actual,* (3) *continuous,* (4) *exclusive,* and (5) *hostile* (or adverse) *to the owner's rights.* The hostility element is not a matter of subjective intent. Rather, it means that the adverse possessor's acts of possession must be inconsistent with the owner's rights. If a person is in possession of another's property under a lease, as a cotenant, or with the permission of the owner, his possession is not hostile. In some states, the possessor of land must also pay the property taxes in order to gain title by adverse possession.

It is not necessary that the same person occupy the land for the statutory period. The periods of possession of several adverse possessors may be "tacked" together when calculating the period of possession if each possessor claimed rights from another possessor. The possession must, however, be continuous for the requisite time.

## TRANSFER BY SALE

### Steps in a Sale

The major steps normally involved in the sale of real property are:

1. Contracting with a real estate broker to locate a buyer.
2. Negotiating and signing a contract of sale.
3. Arranging for the financing of the purchase and satisfying other requirements, such as having a survey conducted or acquiring title insurance.
4. Closing the sale, which involves payment of the purchase price and transfer of the deed, as well as other matters.
5. Recording the deed. *Very Important*

### Contracting with a Real Estate Broker

Although engaging a real estate broker is not a legal requirement for the sale of real property, it is common for one who wishes to sell his property to "list" the property with a broker. A listing contract empowers the broker to act as the seller's agent in procuring a ready, willing, and able buyer and in managing details of the property transfer. A number of states' statutes of frauds require listing contracts to be evidenced by a writing and signed by the party to be charged.

Real estate brokers are regulated by state and federal law. They owe *fiduciary duties* (duties of trust and confidence) to their clients. Chapter 27, The Agency Relationship, contains additional information regarding the duties imposed on such agents.

**Types of Listing Contracts**  Listing contracts specify such matters as the listing period's duration, the terms on which the seller will sell, and the amount and terms of the broker's commission. There are different types of listing contracts.

1. *Open listing.* Under an open listing contract, the broker receives a *nonexclusive* right to sell the property. This means that the seller and third parties (for example, other brokers) also are entitled to find a buyer for the property. The broker operating under an open listing is entitled to a commission only if he was the first to find a ready, willing, and able buyer.

2. *Exclusive agency listing.* Under an exclusive agency listing, the broker earns a commission if he *or any other agent* finds a ready, willing, and able buyer during the period of time specified in the contract. Thus, the broker operating under such a listing would have the right to a commission even if another broker actually procured the buyer. Under the exclusive agency listing, however, the seller has the right to sell the property himself without being obligated to pay the broker a commission.

3. *Exclusive right to sell.* An exclusive right to sell contract provides the broker the exclusive right to sell the property for a specified period of time and entitles her to a commission no matter who procured the buyer. Under this type of listing, a seller must pay the broker her commission even if it was the seller or some third party who found the buyer during the duration of the listing contract.

## Contract of Sale

The contract formation, performance, assignment, and remedies principles about which you read in earlier chapters apply to real estate sales contracts. Such contracts identify the parties and subject property, and set forth the purchase price, the type of deed the purchaser will receive, the items of personal property (if any) included in the sale, and other important aspects of the parties' transaction. Real estate sales contracts often make the closing of the sale contingent on the buyer's obtaining financing at a specified rate of interest, on the seller's procurement of a survey and title insurance, and on the property's passing a termite inspection. Because they are within the statute of frauds, real estate sales contracts must be evidenced by a suitable writing signed by the party to be charged in order to be enforceable.

## Fair Housing Act

The Fair Housing Act, enacted by Congress in 1968 and substantially revised in 1988, is designed to prevent discrimination in the housing market. Its provisions apply to real estate brokers, sellers (other than those selling their own single-family dwellings without the use of a broker), lenders, lessors, and appraisers. Originally, the act prohibited discrimination on the basis of race, color, religion, sex, and national origin. The 1988 amendments added handicap and "familial status" to this list. The familial status category was intended to prevent discrimination in the housing market against pregnant women and families with children.[4] "Adult" or "senior citizen" communities restricting residents' age do not violate the Fair Housing Act even though they exclude families with children, so long as the housing meets the requirements of the act's "housing for older persons" exemption.[5]

The act prohibits discrimination on the above-listed bases in a wide range of matters relating to the sale or rental of housing. These matters include refusals to sell or rent, representations that housing is not available for sale or rental when in fact it is, and discriminatory actions regarding terms, conditions, or privileges of sale or rental or regarding the provision of services and facilities involved in sale or rental.[6] The act also prohibits discrimination in connection with brokerage services, appraisals, and financing of dwellings.

Included within prohibited discrimination on the basis of handicap are refusals to permit a handicapped person to make (at his own expense) reasonable modifications to the property and refusals to make reasonable accommodations in property-related rules, policies, practices, or services when such modifications or accommodations are necessary to afford the handicapped person full enjoyment of the property. The act also outlaws the building of multifamily housing that is inaccessible to persons with handicaps.

A violation of the Fair Housing Act can result in a civil action brought by either the government or the aggrieved individual. If the aggrieved individual

---

[4]"Familial status" is defined as an individual or individuals under the age of 18 who is/are domiciled with a parent, some other person who has custody over him/her/them, or the designee of the parent or custodial individual. The familial status classification also applies to one who is pregnant or in the process of attempting to secure custody of a child or children under the age of 18.

[5]The Fair Housing Act defines "housing for older persons" as housing provided under any state or federal program found by the Secretary of HUD to be specifically designed and operated to assist elderly persons, housing intended for and solely occupied by persons 62 years old or older, or housing that meets the requirements of federal regulations and is intended and operated for occupancy by at least one person 55 years old or older.

[6]Chapter 18 discusses the Fair Housing Act's application to rentals of residential property.

brings suit and prevails, the court may issue injunctions, award actual and punitive damages, assess attorney's fees and costs, and grant other appropriate relief. Finally, the Fair Housing Act invalidates any state or municipal law requiring or permitting an action that would be a discriminatory housing practice under federal law.

**Financing the Purchase**   The various arrangements for financing the purchase of real property—such as mortgages, land contracts, and deeds of trust—are discussed in Chapter 20, Introduction to Credit and Secured Transactions.

## Deeds

Each state's statutes set out the formalities necessary to accomplish a valid conveyance of land. As a general rule, a valid conveyance is brought about by the execution and delivery of a **deed**, a written instrument that transfers title from one person (the grantor) to another (the grantee). Three types of deeds are in general use in the United States: *quitclaim deeds*, *warranty deeds*, and *deeds of bargain and sale* (also called *grant deeds*). The precise rights contemplated by a deed depend on the type of deed the parties have used.

**Quitclaim Deeds**   A **quitclaim deed** conveys whatever title the grantor has at the time he executes the deed. It does not, however, contain warranties of title. The grantor who executes a quitclaim deed does not claim to have good title—or any title, for that matter. The grantee has no action against the grantor under a quitclaim deed if the grantee does not acquire good title. Quitclaim deeds are frequently used to cure technical defects in the chain of title to property.

**Warranty Deeds**   A **warranty deed**, unlike a quitclaim deed, contains covenants of warranty. Besides conveying title to the property, the grantor who executes a warranty deed guarantees the title she has conveyed. There are two types of warranty deeds.

**1.** *General warranty deed.* Under a general warranty deed, the grantor warrants against (and agrees to defend against) all title defects and encumbrances (such as liens and easements), including those that arose before the grantor received her title.

**2.** *Special warranty deed.* Under a special warranty deed, the grantor warrants against (and agrees to defend against) title defects and encumbrances that arose after she acquired the property. If the property conveyed is subject to an encumbrance such as a mortgage, a long-term lease, or an easement, the grantor frequently provides a special warranty deed that contains a provision excepting those specific encumbrances from the warranty.

**Deed of Bargain and Sale**   In a **deed of bargain and sale** (also known as a **grant deed**), the grantor makes no covenants. The grantor uses language such as "I grant" or "I bargain and sell" or "I convey" property. Such a deed does contain, however, the grantor's implicit representation that he owns the land and has not previously encumbered it or conveyed it to another party.

## Form and Execution of Deed

Some states' statutes suggest a form for deeds. Although the requirements for execution of deeds are not uniform, they do follow a similar pattern. As a general rule, a deed states the *name of the grantee*, contains a *recitation of consideration and a description of the property conveyed,* and is *signed by the grantor*. Most states require that the deed be notarized (acknowledged by the grantor before a notary public or other authorized officer) in order to be eligible for recording in public records.

No technical words of conveyance are necessary for a valid deed. Any language is sufficient if it indicates with reasonable certainty the grantor's intent to transfer ownership of the property. The phrases "grant, bargain, and sell" and "convey and warrant" are commonly used. Deeds contain recitations of consideration primarily for historical reasons. The consideration recited is not necessarily the purchase price of the property. Deeds often state that the consideration for the conveyance is "one dollar and other valuable consideration."

The property conveyed must be described in such a manner that it can be identified. This usually means that the legal description of the property must be used. Several methods of legal description are used in the United States. In urban areas, descriptions are usually by lot, block, and plat. In rural areas where the land has been surveyed by the government, property is usually described by reference to

---

**FIGURE 2**    **Three Basic Types of Priority Systems for Recording Deeds**

---

| | |
|---|---|
| **Race Statutes** | Under a race statute—so named because the person who wins the race to the courthouse wins the property ownership "competition"—the first grantee who records a deed to a tract of land has superior title. For example, if Grantor deeds Blackacre to Kerr on March 1 and to Templin on April 1, Templin will have superior title to Blackacre if she records her deed before Kerr's is recorded. Race statutes are relatively uncommon today. |
| **Notice Statutes** | Under a notice system of priority, a later grantee of property has superior title if he acquired his interest without notice of an earlier grantee's claim to the property under an unrecorded deed. For example, Grantor deeds Greenacre to Jonson on June 1, but Jonson does not record his deed. On July 1, Marlowe purchases Greenacre without knowledge of Jonson's competing claim. Grantor executes and delivers a deed to Marlowe. In this situation, Marlowe would have superior rights to Greenacre even if Jonson ultimately records his deed before Marlowe's is recorded. |
| **Race-Notice Statutes** | The race-notice priority system combines elements of the systems just discussed. Under race-notice statutes, the grantee having priority is the one who *both takes his interest without notice* of any prior unrecorded claim and *records first*. For example, Grantor deeds Redacre to Frazier on September 1. On October 1 (at which time Frazier has not yet recorded his deed), Grantor deeds Redacre to Dixon, who is then unaware of any claim by Frazier to Redacre. If Dixon records his deed before Frazier's is recorded, Dixon has superior rights to Redacre. |

---

the government survey. It may also be described by a metes and bounds description that specifies the boundaries of the tract of land.

## Recording Deeds

Delivery of a valid deed conveys title from a grantor to a grantee. Even so, the grantee should promptly **record** the deed in order to prevent his interest from being defeated by third parties who may claim interests in the property. The grantee must pay a fee to have the deed recorded, a process that involves depositing and indexing the deed in the files of a government office designated by state law. A recorded deed operates to provide the public at large with notice of the grantee's property interest.

**Recording Statutes**    Each state has a **recording statute** that establishes a system for the recording of all transactions affecting real property ownership. These statutes are not uniform in their provisions. In general, however, they provide for the recording of all deeds, mortgages, land contracts, and similar documents.

**Types of Recording Statutes**    State recording statutes also provide for priority among competing claimants to rights in real property, in case conflicting rights or interests in property should be deeded to (or otherwise claimed by) more than one person. (Obviously, a grantor has no right to issue two different grantees separate deeds to the same property, but if this should occur, recording statutes provide rules to decide which grantee has superior title.) These priority rules apply only to grantees who have given value for their deeds or other interest-creating documents (primarily purchasers and lenders), and not to donees. A given state's recording statute will set up one of three basic types of priority systems: race statues, notice statutes, and race-notice statues. Figure 2 explains these priority systems. Although the examples used in Figure 2 deal with recorded and unrecorded deeds, recording statutes apply to other documents that create interests in real estate. Chapter 20, Introduction to Credit and Secured Transactions, discusses the recording of mortgages, as well as the adverse security interest–related consequences a mortgagee may experience if its mortgage goes unrecorded.

## Methods of Assuring Title

In purchasing real property, the buyer is really acquiring the seller's ownership interests. Because the buyer does not want to pay a large sum of money for something that proves to be of little or no value, it is important for her to obtain assurance that the seller has good title to the property. This is commonly done in one of three ways:

**1.** *Title opinion.* In some states, it is customary to have an attorney examine an **abstract of title**. An abstract of title is a history of what the public records show regarding the passage of title to (and other interests in) a parcel of real property. It is not a guarantee of good title. After examining the abstract, the attorney renders an opinion about whether the grantor has **marketable title** to the property. Marketable title is title free from defects or reasonable doubt about its validity. If the grantor's title is defective, the nature of the defects will be stated in the attorney's title opinion.

**2.** *Torrens system.* A method of title assurance available in a few states is the **Torrens system** of title registration. Under this system, one who owns land in fee simple obtains a certificate of title. When the property is sold, the grantor delivers a deed and a certificate of title to the grantee. All liens and encumbrances against the title are noted on the certificate, thus assuring the purchaser that the title is good except as to the liens and encumbrances noted on the certificate. However, some claims or encumbrances, such as those arising from adverse possession, do not appear on the records and must be discovered through an inspection of the property. In some Torrens states, encumbrances such as tax liens, short-term leases, and highway rights are valid against the purchaser even though they do not appear on the certificate.

**3.** *Title insurance.* Purchasing a policy of **title insurance** provides the preferred and most common means of protecting title to real property. Title insurance obligates the insurer to reimburse the insured grantee for loss if the title proves to be defective. In addition, title insurance covers litigation costs if the insured grantee must go to court in a title dispute. Lenders commonly require that a separate policy of title insurance be obtained for the lender's protection. Title insurance may be obtained in combination with the other previously discussed methods of assuring title.

## SELLER'S RESPONSIBILITIES REGARDING THE QUALITY OF RESIDENTIAL PROPERTY

Buyers of real estate normally consider it important that any structures on the property be in good condition. This factor becomes especially significant if the buyer intends to use the property for residential purposes. The rule of *caveat emptor* (let the buyer beware) traditionally applied to the sale of real property unless the seller committed misrepresentation or fraud or made express warranties about the property's condition. In addition, sellers had no duty to disclose hidden defects in the property. In recent years, however, the legal environment for sellers—especially real estate professionals such as developers and builder-vendors of residential property—has changed substantially. This section examines two important sources of liability for sellers of real property.

### Implied Warranty of Habitability

Historically, sellers of residential property were not regarded as making any **implied warranty** that the property was habitable or suitable for the buyer's use. The law's attitude toward the buyer-seller relationship in residential property sales began to shift, however, as product liability law underwent rapid change in the late 1960s. Courts began to see that the same policies favoring the creation of implied warranties in the sale of goods applied with equal force to the sale of residential real estate.[7] Both goods and housing are frequently mass-produced. The disparity of knowledge and bargaining power often existing between a buyer of goods and a professional seller is also likely to exist between a buyer of a house and a builder-vendor (one who builds and sells houses). Moreover, many defects in houses are not readily discoverable during a buyer's inspection. This creates the possibility of serious loss, because the purchase of a home is often the largest single investment a person ever makes.

For these reasons, courts in most states now hold that builders, builder-vendors, and developers make an implied warranty of habitability when they build or sell real property for residential purposes. An ordinary owner who sells her house—in other

---

[7]See Chapter 12 for a discussion of the development of similar doctrines in the law of product liability.

words, a seller who was neither the builder nor the developer of the residential property—does not make an implied warranty of habitability.

The implied warranty of habitability amounts to a guarantee that the house is free of latent (hidden) defects that would render it unsafe or unsuitable for human habitation. A breach of this warranty subjects the defendant to liability for damages, measured by either the cost of repairs or the loss in value of the house.[8]

A related issue that has led to considerable litigation is whether the implied warranty of habitability extends to subsequent purchasers of the house. For example, PDQ Development Co. builds a house and sells it to Johnson. If Johnson later sells the house to McClure, may McClure successfully sue PDQ for breach of warranty if a serious defect renders the house uninhabitable? Although some courts have rejected implied warranty actions brought by subsequent purchasers, many courts today hold that an implied warranty made by a builder-vendor or developer would extend to a subsequent purchaser.

May the implied warranty of habitability be *disclaimed* or *limited* in the contract of sale? It appears at least possible to disclaim or limit the warranty by a contract provision, subject to limitations imposed by the unconscionability doctrine, public policy concerns, and contract interpretation principles.[9] Courts

construe attempted disclaimers very strictly against the builder-vendor or developer, and often reject disclaimers that are not specific regarding rights supposedly waived by the purchaser.

## Duty to Disclose Hidden Defects

Traditional contract law provided that a seller had no duty to disclose to the buyer defects in the property being sold, even if the seller knew about the defects and the buyer could not reasonably find out about them on his own. The seller's failure to volunteer information, therefore, could not constitute misrepresentation or fraud. This traditional rule of nondisclosure was another expression of the prevailing *caveat emptor* notion. Although the nondisclosure rule was subject to certain exceptions,[10] the exceptions seldom applied. Thus, there was no duty to disclose in most sales of real property.

Today, courts in many jurisdictions have substantially eroded the traditional nondisclosure rule and have placed a duty on the seller to disclose any known defect that materially affects the property's value and is not reasonably observable by the buyer. The seller's failure to disclose such defects effectively amounts to an assertion that the defects do not exist—an assertion on which a judicial finding of misrepresentation or fraud may be based.[11] *Johnson v. Davis* illustrates the trend toward expansion of the duty to disclose.

---

[8]Measures of damages are discussed in Chapter 10.

[9]The unconscionability doctrine and public policy concerns are discussed in Chapter 7. Chapter 8 addresses contract interpretation.

[10]These exceptions are discussed in Chapter 5.

[11]Misrepresentation and fraud are discussed in Chapter 5.

---

## JOHNSON V. DAVIS
### 480 So. 2d 625 (Fla. Sup. Ct. 1985)

In May 1982, Morton and Edna Davis entered into a contract to buy a house from Clarence and Dana Johnson for $310,000. The house was three years old. The contract required a $5,000 initial deposit payment and an additional $26,000 deposit payment within five days. After the Davises had paid the initial $5,000 deposit but before they had paid the $26,000 deposit, Mrs. Davis noticed some buckling and peeling plaster around the corner of a window frame, as well as stains on ceilings in several rooms. When Mrs. Davis inquired about this, Mr. Johnson told her that the window had had a minor problem which was corrected long ago and that the stains were wallpaper glue. (The parties disagreed, at trial, about whether Mr. Johnson told Mrs. Davis at this time that there had never been any problems with the roof or ceilings.) The Davises then paid the remaining $26,000 deposit, and the Johnsons moved out of the house. Several days later, following a heavy rain, Mrs. Davis entered the house and discovered water gushing in from around the window frame, the ceiling of the family room, the light fixtures, the glass doors, and the stove in the kitchen. The Davises hired roofers, who reported that the roof was inherently defective and that any repairs would be temporary because the roof was "slipping." Only a new roof, at a cost of $15,000, could be watertight. The Davises then filed this action alleging breach of contract, fraud, and misrepresentation. They sought rescission of the contract and return of their deposit payments. The trial court awarded the Davises $26,000 plus interest but permitted the Johnsons to keep the initial $5,000 deposit plus interest. Both parties appealed to the District Court of Appeals, which held that the entire deposit should have been returned to the Davises. The Johnsons appealed.

---

**Adkins, Justice**   We agree with the district court's conclusions under a theory of fraud and find that the Johnsons' statements to the Davises regarding the condition of the roof constituted a fraudulent misrepresentation entitling the Davises to the return of the $26,000 deposit payment. The record reflects that the statement made by the Johnsons was a false representation of material fact, made with knowledge of its falsity, upon which the Davises relied to their detriment as evidenced by the $26,000 paid to the Johnsons. The fact that the false statements as to the quality of the roof were made after the signing of the purchase agreement does not excuse the seller from liability where the misrepresentations were made prior to the conveyance of the property.

In determining whether a seller of a home has a duty to disclose latent material defects to a buyer, the established tort law distinction between misfeasance and nonfeasance, action and inaction, must carefully be analyzed. The highly individualistic philosophy of the earlier common law consistently imposed liability upon the commission of affirmative acts of harm, but shrank from converting the courts into an institution for forcing men to help one another. Liability for nonfeasance has therefore been slow to receive recognition in the evolution of tort law.

In theory, the difference between misfeasance and nonfeasance is quite simple and obvious; however, in practice it is not always easy to draw the line and determine whether conduct is active or passive. That is, where failure to disclose a material fact is calculated to induce a false belief, the distinction between concealment and affirmative representations is tenuous. Both proceed from the same motives and are attended with the same consequences; both are violative of the principles of fair dealing and good faith.

Still there exists in much of our case law the old tort notion that there can be no liability for nonfeasance. The courts in some jurisdictions hold that where the parties are dealing at arm's length and the facts lie equally open to both parties, with equal opportunity of examination, mere nondisclosure does not constitute a fraudulent concealment.

These unappetizing cases are not in tune with the times and do not conform with current notions of justice, equity, and fair dealing. One should not be able to stand behind the impervious shield of caveat emptor and take advantage of another's ignorance. Our courts have taken great strides since the days when the judicial emphasis was on rigid rules and ancient precedents. Modern concepts of justice and fair dealing have given our courts the opportunity and latitude to change legal precepts in order to conform to society's needs. Thus, the tendency of the more recent cases has been to restrict rather than extend the doctrine of caveat emptor. The law appears to be working toward the ultimate conclusion that full disclosure of all material facts must be made whenever elementary fair conduct demands it.

The harness placed on the doctrine of caveat emptor in a number of other jurisdictions has resulted in the seller of a home being liable for failing to disclose material defects of which he was aware. We are of the opinion that the same philosophy regarding the sale of homes should also be the law in the state of Florida. Accordingly we hold that where the seller of a home knows of facts materially affecting the value of the property which are not readily observable and are not known to the buyer, the seller is under a duty to disclose them to the buyer. This duty is equally applicable to all forms of real property, new and used.

In the case at bar, the evidence shows that the Johnsons knew of and failed to disclose that there had been problems with the roof of the house. Mr. Johnson admitted during his testimony that the Johnsons were aware of roof problems prior to entering into the contract of sale and receiving the $5,000 deposit payment. Thus, we find that the Johnsons' fraudulent concealment also entitles the Davises to the return of the $5,000 deposit payment plus interest.

**Judgment for the Davises affirmed.**

## OTHER PROPERTY CONDITION–RELATED OBLIGATIONS OF REAL PROPERTY OWNERS AND POSSESSORS

In recent years, the law has increasingly required real property owners and possessors to take steps to further the safety of persons on the property and to make the property more accessible to disabled individuals. This section discusses two legal developments along these lines: the trend toward expansion of *premises liability* and the inclusion of property-related provisions in the *Americans with Disabilities Act.*

### Expansion of Premises Liability

**Premises liability** is the name sometimes used for negligence cases in which property owners or possessors (such as business operators leasing commercial real estate) are held liable to persons injured while on the property. Property owners and possessors face liability when their *failures to exercise reasonable care* to keep their property reasonably safe result in injuries to persons lawfully on the property. The traditional premises liability case was one in which a property owner's or possessor's negligence led to the existence of a potentially hazardous condition on the property (e.g., a dangerously slick floor or similar physical condition at a business premises), and a person justifiably on the premises (e.g., a business customer) sustained personal injury upon encountering that unexpected condition (e.g., by slipping and falling).

**Security Precautions against Foreseeable Criminal Acts**    Recent years have witnessed a judicial inclination to expand premises liability to cover other situations in addition to the traditional scenario. A key component of this expansion has been many courts' willingness to reconsider the once-customary holding that a property owner or possessor had no legal obligation to implement security measures to protect persons on the property from the wrongful acts of third parties lacking any connection with the owner or possessor. Today, courts frequently hold that a property owner's or possessor's duty to exercise reasonable care includes the obligation to take *reasonable security precautions* designed to protect persons lawfully on the premises from *foreseeable* wrongful (including criminal) acts by third parties.

This expansion has caused hotel, apartment building, and convenience store owners and operators to be among the defendants held liable—sometimes in very large damage amounts—to guests, tenants, and customers on whom violent third-party attackers inflicted severe physical injuries. In such cases, the property owners' or possessors' negligent failures to take security precautions restricting such wrongdoers' access to the premises served as at least a *substantial factor* leading to the plaintiffs' injuries. The security lapses amounting to a lack of reasonable care in a particular case may have been, for instance, failures to install deadbolt locks, provide adequate locking devices on sliding glass doors, maintain sufficient lighting, or employ security guards.

**Determining Foreseeability**    The security precautions component of the reasonable care duty is triggered only when criminal activity on the premises is foreseeable. It therefore becomes important to determine whether the foreseeability standard has been met. In making this determination, courts look at such factors as whether previous crimes had occurred on or near the subject property (and if so, the nature and frequency of those crimes), whether the property owner or possessor knew or should have known of those prior occurrences, and whether the property was located in a high-crime area. The fact-specific nature of the foreseeability and reasonable care determinations makes the outcome of a given premises liability case difficult to predict in advance. Nevertheless, there is no doubt that the current premises liability climate gives property owners and possessors more reason than ever before to be concerned about security measures.

### Americans with Disabilities Act

In 1990, Congress enacted the broad-ranging Americans with Disabilities Act (ADA). This statute was designed to eliminate longstanding patterns of discrimination against disabled persons in matters such as employment, access to public services, and access to business establishments and similar facilities open to the public. The ADA's Title III focuses on places of *public accommodation.*[12] It imposes on

---

[12]42 U.S.C. §§ 12181-12189 (1990). These sections examine only Title III of the ADA. Chapter 40 discusses the employment-related provisions set forth in Title I of the statute.

certain property owners and possessors the obligation to take reasonable steps to make their property accessible to disabled persons (individuals with a physical or mental impairment that substantially limits one or more major life activities).

**Places of Public Accommodation**　Title III of the ADA classifies numerous businesses and nonbusiness enterprises as places of **public accommodation**. These include hotels, restaurants, bars, theaters, concert halls, auditoriums, stadiums, shopping centers, stores at which goods are sold or rented, service-oriented businesses (running the gamut from gas stations to law firm offices), museums, parks, schools, social services establishments (day-care centers, senior citizen centers, homeless shelters, and the like), places of recreation, and various other enterprises, facilities, and establishments. Private clubs and religious organizations, however, are not treated as places of public accommodation for purposes of the statute.

**Modifications of Property**　Under the ADA, the owner or operator of a place of public accommodation cannot exclude disabled persons from the premises or otherwise discriminate against them in terms of their ability to enjoy the public accommodation. Avoiding such exclusion or other discrimination may require alteration of the business or nonbusiness enterprise's practices, policies, and procedures. Moreover, using language contemplating the possible need for physical modifications of property serving as a place of public accommodation, the ADA includes within prohibited discrimination the property owner's or possessor's "failure to take such steps as may be necessary to ensure that no individual with a disability is excluded" or otherwise discriminated against in terms of access to what nondisabled persons are provided. The failure to take these steps does not violate the ADA, however, if the property owner or possessor demonstrates that implementing such steps would "fundamentally alter the nature" of the enterprise or would "result in an undue burden."

Prohibited discrimination may also include the "failure to remove architectural barriers and communication barriers that are structural in nature," if removal is "readily achievable." When the removal of such a barrier is not readily achievable, the property owner or possessor nonetheless engages in prohibited discrimination if he, she, or it does not adopt "alter-

native methods" to ensure access to the premises and what it has to offer (assuming that the alternative methods are themselves readily achievable). The ADA defines *readily achievable* as "easily accomplishable and able to be carried out without much difficulty or expense." The determination of whether an action is readily achievable involves consideration of factors such as the action's nature and cost, the nature of the enterprise conducted on the property, the financial resources of the affected property owner or possessor, and the effect the action would have on expenses and resources of the property owner or possessor.

**New Construction**　Newly constructed buildings on property used as a place of public accommodation must contain physical features making the buildings *readily accessible* to disabled persons. The same is true of additions built on to previous structures. The ADA is supplemented by federal regulations setting forth property accessibility guidelines designed to lend substance and specificity to the broad legal standards stated in the statute. In addition, the federal government has issued technical assistance manuals and materials in an effort to educate public accommodation owners and operators regarding their obligations under the ADA.

**Remedies**　A person subjected to disability-based discrimination in any of the respects discussed above may bring a civil suit for injunctive relief. An injunction issued by a court must include "an order to alter facilities" to make the facilities "readily accessible to and usable by individuals with disabilities to the extent required" by the ADA. The court has discretion to award attorney's fees to the prevailing party. The U.S. Attorney General also has the legal authority to institute a civil action alleging a violation of Title III of the ADA. In such a case, the court may choose to grant injunctive and other appropriate equitable relief, award compensatory damages to aggrieved persons (when the Attorney General so requests), and assess civil penalties (up to $50,000 for a first violation and up to $100,000 for any subsequent violation) "to vindicate the public interest." When determining the amount of any such penalty, the court is to give consideration to any good faith effort by the property owner or possessor to comply with the law. The court must also consider whether the owner or possessor could reasonably have anticipated the need to accommodate disabled persons.

# LAND USE CONTROL

Although a real property owner generally has the right to use his property as he desires, society has placed certain limitations on this right. This section examines the property use limitations imposed by nuisance law and by zoning and subdivision ordinances. It also discusses the ultimate land use restriction—the eminent domain power—which enables the government to deprive property owners of their land.

## Nuisance Law

One's enjoyment of her own land depends to a great extent on the uses her neighbors make of their land. When the uses of neighboring landowners conflict, the aggrieved party frequently institutes litigation to resolve the conflict. A property use that unreasonably interferes with another person's ability to use or enjoy her own property may lead to an action for **nuisance** against the landowner or possessor engaging in the objectionable use.

The term *nuisance* has no set definition. It is often regarded, however, as encompassing any property-related use or activity that unreasonably interferes with the rights of others. Property uses potentially constituting nuisances include uses that are inappropriate to the neighborhood (such as using a vacant lot in a residential neighborhood as a garbage dump), bothersome to neighbors (such as keeping a pack of barking dogs in one's backyard), dangerous to others (such as storing large quantities of gasoline in 50-gallon drums in one's garage), or of questionable morality (such as operating a house of prostitution). To amount to a nuisance, a use need not be illegal. The fact that relevant zoning laws allow a given use does not mean that the use cannot be a nuisance. The

use's having been in existence before complaining neighbors acquired their property does not mean that the use cannot be a nuisance, though it does lessen the likelihood that the use would be held a nuisance.

The test for determining the presence or absence of a nuisance is necessarily flexible and highly dependent on the individual case's facts. Courts balance a number of factors, such as the social importance of the parties' respective uses, the extent and duration of harm experienced by the aggrieved party, and the feasibility of abating (stopping) the nuisance.

Nuisances may be private or public. To bring a *private nuisance* action, the plaintiff must be a landowner or occupier whose enjoyment of her own land is substantially lessened by the alleged nuisance. The remedies for private nuisance include damages and injunctive relief designed to stop the offending use. A *public nuisance* occurs when a nuisance harms members of the public, who need not be injured in their use of property. For example, if a power plant creates noise and emissions posing a health hazard to pedestrians and workers in nearby buildings, a public nuisance may exist even though the nature of the harm has nothing to do with any loss of enjoyment of property. Public nuisances involve a broader class of affected parties than do private nuisances. The action to abate a public nuisance must usually be brought by the government. Remedies generally include injunctive relief and civil penalties that resemble fines. Private parties may sue for abatement of a public nuisance or for damages caused by one only when they suffered unique harm different from that experienced by the general public.

*Wood v. Picillo* illustrates the application of nuisance law to a property owner who maintained a hazardous waste dump.

---

## WOOD V. PICILLO
### 443 A.2d 1244 (R.I. Sup. Ct. 1982)

The Picillos maintained a chemical dump site on a clearing on their land. The site was a huge trench about 200 feet long, 15 to 30 feet wide, and 15 to 20 feet deep. A thick layer of pungent, varicolored liquid covered the trench bottom. Along the periphery of the pit lay more than 100 55-gallon drums and 5-gallon pail containers. Some of these were upright and sealed, some were tipped, and some were partially buried. About 600 feet downhill from this site was a marshy wetland that drained into a river and several ponds. A witness testified that he saw the operator of a truck knock barrels marked "Combustible" off the truck's tailgate directly to the ground, where chemicals poured freely from the damaged barrels into the trench. Neighbors smelled "sickening," "heavy," and "terrible" odors that forced them to stay inside their homes. Several neighbors were made ill by the odors.

The attention of state officials was drawn to the site when an enormous explosion erupted into 50-foot flames in a trench on the Picillos' land, and the fire could not be extinguished. Investigators from the state environmental management department began an investigation of the site. The state fire marshal ordered the dumping to cease, but dumping operations continued. Edward Wood and other plaintiffs brought a nuisance action against the Picillos. The trial court found that the dumping operation was a nuisance. It issued an injunction against further chemical disposal operations on the Picillo property and ordered the Picillos to finance the cleanup and removal of the toxic wastes. The Picillos appealed.

---

**Weisberger, Judge**    The dump site proper might best be described in the succinct expression of the trial justice as "a chemical nightmare." At trial expert witnesses developed a scientific connection between the neighbors' experiences and the Picillos' operations. Laboratory analyses of samples taken from the trench, monitoring wells, and adjacent waters revealed the presence of five chemicals: toluene, xylene, chloroform, III trichloroethane, and trichloroethylene. According to the experts, the chemicals present on the Picillos' property and in the marsh, if left unchecked, would eventually threaten wildlife and humans well downstream from the dump site. Expert testimony further revealed that the chemicals had traveled and would continue to travel from the dump site into the marsh at the rate of about one foot per day. From the marsh, predicted the experts, the chemicals would flow into waters inhabited by fish and used by humans for recreational and agricultural purposes.

The Picillos contend that the evidence adduced at trial was insufficient to support a finding of public and private nuisance. We find this to be without merit. The essential element of an actionable nuisance is that persons have suffered harm or are threatened with injuries that they ought not to have to bear. Distinguished from negligence liability, liability in nuisance is predicated upon unreasonable injury rather than upon unreasonable conduct. Thus, plaintiffs may recover in nuisance despite the otherwise nontortious nature of the conduct which creates the injury.

The Picillos have accurately stated that the injury produced by an actionable nuisance "must be real and not fanciful or imaginary." The Picillos next suggest that the injuries in the case at bar are of the insubstantial, unactionable type. It is this statement, however, rather than the purported injuries, that is fanciful. The testimony to which reference is made in this opinion clearly establishes that the Picillos' dumping operations have already caused substantial injury to their neighbors and threaten to cause incalculable damage to the general public. The Picillos' neighbors have displayed physical symptoms of exposure to toxic chemicals and have been restricted in the reasonable use of their property. Moreover, expert testimony showed that the chemical presence on the Picillos' property threatens both aquatic wildlife and human beings with possible death, cancer, and liver disease. Thus, there was ample evidence at trial to support the finding of substantial injury.

For the reasons stated, the Picillos' appeal is dismissed.

**Judgment for Wood affirmed.**

---

## Eminent Domain

The Fifth Amendment to the Constitution provides that private property shall not be taken for public use without "just compensation." Implicit in this provision is the principle that the government has the power to take property for public use if it pays "just compensation" to the owner of the property. This power, called the power of **eminent domain**, makes it possible for the government to acquire private property for highways, water control projects, municipal and civic centers, public housing, urban renewal, and other public uses. Governmental units can delegate their eminent domain power to private corporations such as railroads and utility companies.

Although the eminent domain power is a useful tool of efficient government, there are problems inherent in its use. Determining when the power can be properly exercised presents an initial problem. When the governmental unit itself uses the property taken, as would be the case with property acquired for construction of a municipal building or a public highway, the exercise of the power is proper. The use of eminent domain is not so clearly justified, however, when the government acquires the property and resells it to a private developer. Although such acquisitions may be more vulnerable to challenge, recent cases have applied a very lenient standard in determining what constitutes a public use.

Determining *just compensation* in a given case poses a second and frequently encountered eminent domain problem. The property owner is entitled to receive the "fair market value" of his property. Critics assert, however, that this measure of compensation falls short of adequately compensating the owner for her loss, because *fair market value* does not cover such matters as the lost goodwill of a business or one's emotional attachment to his home.

A third problem sometimes encountered is determining when there has been a "taking" that triggers the government's just compensation obligation. The answer is easy when the government institutes a formal legal action to exercise the eminent domain power (often called an action to *condemn* property). In some instances, however, the government causes or permits a serious physical invasion of a landowner's property without having instituted formal condemnation proceedings. For example, the government's dam-building project results in persistent flooding of a private party's land. Courts have recognized the right of property owners in such cases to institute litigation seeking compensation from the governmental unit whose actions effectively amounted to a physical taking of their land. In these so-called **inverse condemnation** cases, the property owner sends the message that "you have taken my land; now pay for it." *Yee v. City of Escondido,*[13] which appears later in this chapter's discussion of other takings issues, involved an

unsuccessful attempt by landowners to stretch the *physical taking* concept further, however, than the Supreme Court was prepared to allow.

## Zoning and Subdivision Laws

State legislatures commonly delegate to cities and other political subdivisions the power to impose reasonable regulations designed to promote the public health, safety, and welfare (often called the *police power*). Zoning ordinances, which regulate real property use, stem from the exercise of the police power. Normally, zoning ordinances divide a city or town into various districts and specify or limit the uses to which property in those districts may be put. They also contain requirements and restrictions regarding improvements built on the land.

Zoning ordinances frequently contain direct restrictions on land use, such as by limiting property use in a given area to single-family or high-density residential uses, or to commercial, light industry, or heavy industry uses. Other sorts of use-related provisions commonly found in zoning ordinances include restrictions on building height, limitations on the portion of a lot that can be covered by a building, and specifications of the distance buildings must be from lot lines (usually called *setback* requirements). Zoning ordinances also commonly restrict property use by establishing population density limitations. Such restrictions specify the maximum number of persons who can be housed on property in a given area and dictate the amount of living space that must be provided for each person occupying residential property. In addition, zoning ordinances often establish restrictions designed to maintain or create a certain aesthetic character in the community. Examples of this type of restriction include specifications of buildings' architectural style, limitations on billboard and sign use, and designations of special zones for historic buildings.

Many local governments also have ordinances dealing with proposed subdivisions. These ordinances often require the subdivision developer to meet certain requirements regarding lot size, street and sidewalk layout, and sanitary facilities. They also require that the city or town approve the proposed development. Such ordinances are designed to further general community interests and to protect prospective buyers of property in the subdivision by ensuring that the developer meets minimum standards of suitability.

[13]112 S. Ct. 1522 (U.S. Sup. Ct. 1992).

**Nonconforming Uses**   A zoning ordinance has *prospective* effect. This means that the uses and buildings already existing when the ordinance is passed (**nonconforming uses**) are permitted to continue. The ordinance may provide, however, for the gradual phasing out of nonconforming uses and buildings that do not fit the general zoning plan.

**Relief from Zoning Ordinances**   A property owner who wishes to use his property in a manner prohibited by a zoning ordinance has more than one potential avenue of relief from the ordinance. He may, for instance, seek to have the ordinance **amended**—in other words, attempt to get the law changed—on the ground that the proposed amendment is consistent with the essence of the overall zoning plan.

A different approach would be to seek permission from the city or political subdivision to deviate from the zoning law. This permission is called a **variance**. A person seeking a variance usually claims that the ordinance works an undue hardship on her by denying her the opportunity to make reasonable use of her land. Examples of typical variance requests include a property owner's seeking permission to make a commercial use of her property even though it is located in an area zoned for residential purposes, or permission to deviate from normal setback or building size requirements.

Attempts to obtain variances and zoning ordinance amendments frequently clash with the interests of other owners of property in the same area—owners who have a vested interest in maintaining the status quo. As a result, variance and amendment requests often produce heated battles before local zoning authorities.

**Challenges to the Validity of the Zoning Ordinance**   A disgruntled property owner might also attack the zoning ordinance's validity on constitutional grounds. Litigation challenging zoning ordinances has become frequent in recent years, as cities and towns have used their zoning power to achieve social control. For example, assume that a city creates special zoning requirements for adult bookstores or other uses considered moral threats to the community. Such uses of the zoning power have been challenged as unconstitutional restrictions on freedom of speech. In *City of Renton v. Playtime Theatres, Inc.*, however, the Supreme Court upheld a zoning ordinance that prohibited the operation

of adult bookstores within 1,000 feet of specified uses such as residential areas and schools.[14] The Court established that the First Amendment rights of operators of adult businesses would not be violated by such an ordinance so long as the city provided them a "reasonable opportunity to open and operate" their businesses within the city. The reasonable opportunity test was satisfied in *City of Renton* even though the ordinance at issue effectively restricted adult bookstores to a small area of the community in which no property was then available to buy or rent. As lower court cases reveal, however, the fact-specific nature of the inquiry contemplated by the reasonable opportunity test means that the government is not guaranteed of passing the test in every case.[15]

Other litigation has stemmed from ordinances by which municipalities have attempted to "zone out" residential facilities such as group homes for mentally retarded adults. In a leading case, the Supreme Court held that the Constitution's Equal Protection Clause was violated by a zoning ordinance that required a special use permit for a group home for the mentally retarded.[16] (For a case indicating that similar issues nonetheless may be treated differently in the *restrictive covenant*—as opposed to zoning—setting, see *Mains Farm Homeowners Association v. Worthington*, which appears earlier in this chapter.) The Fair Housing Act, which forbids discrimination on the basis of handicap and familial status, has also been used as a basis for challenging decisions that

---

[14]475 U.S. 41 (U.S. Sup. Ct. 1986). A later case, *FW/PBS, Inc. v. City of Dallas,* 493 U.S. 215 (U.S. Sup. Ct. 1990), presented a different sort of restriction on adult businesses and resulted in a different outcome. There, the Court held that a comprehensive ordinance requiring licensing of adult cabarets and other adult entertainment establishments violated the First Amendment because the ordinance did not have appropriate procedural safeguards against arbitrary denials of licenses. The ordinance's chief defect was its failure to establish a time limit within which city authorities were required to act on license applications.

[15]See, for example, *Topanga Press, Inc. v. City of Los Angeles,* 989 F.2d 1524 (9th Cir. 1993). In that case, the Ninth Circuit Court of Appeals upheld the trial court's issuance of a preliminary injunction against the city's *City of Renton*-like zoning ordinance regarding adult businesses. The reasonable opportunity test was not passed by the city, given that much of the real estate supposedly still "available" for relocation of the adult businesses was submerged beneath the Pacific Ocean or was used as a landfill, for petroleum storage, for airport runways, or for some other purpose inconsistent with the notion that the property could somehow become available for use by adult businesses.

[16]*City of Cleburne v. Cleburne Living Centers,* 473 U.S. 432 (U.S. Sup. Ct. 1985).

zone out group homes. Such a challenge has a chance of success when the plaintiff demonstrates that the zoning board's actions were a mere pretext for discrimination.[17]

Many cities and towns have attempted to restrict single-family residential zones to living units of traditional families related by blood or marriage. In enacting ordinances along those lines, municipalities have sought to prevent the presence of groups of unrelated students, commune members, or religious cult adherents by specifically defining the term *family* in a way that excludes these groups. In *Belle Terre v. Boraas,*[18] the Supreme Court upheld such an ordinance as applied to a group of unrelated students. The Court later held, however, that an ordinance defining *family* so as to prohibit a grandmother from living with her grandsons was an unconstitutional intrusion on personal freedom regarding family life.[19] Restrictive definitions of *family* have been held unconstitutional under state constitutions in some cases but narrowly construed by courts in other cases.

## Land Use Regulation and Taking

Another type of litigation seen with increasing frequency in recent years centers around zoning laws and other land use regulations that make the use of property less profitable for development. Affected property owners have challenged the application of such regulations as unconstitutional takings of property without just compensation, even though these cases do not involve the actual physical invasions present in the inverse condemnation cases discussed earlier in this chapter.

States normally have broad discretion to use their police power for the public benefit, even when that means interfering to some extent with an owner's right to develop her property as she desires. Some regulations, however, may interfere with an owner's use of his property to such an extent that they constitute a taking. For instance, in *Nollan v. California Coastal Commission,*[20] the owners of a

beach-front lot (the Nollans) wished to tear down a small house on the lot and replace that structure with a larger house. The California Coastal Commission conditioned the grant of the necessary coastal development permit on the Nollans' agreeing to allow the public an easement across their property. This easement would have allowed the public to reach certain nearby public beaches more easily. The Nollans challenged the validity of the Coastal Commission's action. Ultimately, the Supreme Court concluded that the Coastal Commission's placing the easement condition on the issuance of the permit amounted to an impermissible regulatory taking of the Nollans' property. In reaching this conclusion, the Court held that the state could not avoid paying compensation to the Nollans by choosing to do by way of the regulatory route what it would have had to pay for if it had followed the formal eminent domain route.

**Regulations Denying Economically Beneficial Uses**  What about a land use regulation that allows the property owner no *economically beneficial use* of his property? *Lucas v. South Carolina Coastal Commission*[21] was brought by a property owner, Lucas, who had paid nearly $1 million for two residential beach-front lots before South Carolina enacted a coastal protection statute. This statute's effect was to bar Lucas from building any permanent habitable structures on the lots. The trial court held that the statute rendered Lucas's property "valueless" and that an unconstitutional taking had occurred, but the South Carolina Supreme Court reversed. The U.S. Supreme Court, however, held that when a land use regulation denies "all economically beneficial use" of property, there normally has been a taking for which just compensation must be paid. The exception to this rule, according to the Court, would be when the economically productive use being prohibited by the land use regulation was already disallowed anyway by nuisance law or other comparable property law principles. The Court therefore reversed and remanded the case for determination of whether there had been a taking under the rule crafted by the Court, or instead an instance in which the "nuisance" exception applied. On remand, the South Carolina Supreme Court concluded that a taking calling for compen-

---

[17]See, for example, *Baxter v. City of Nashville,* 720 F. Supp. 720 (S.D. Ill. 1989), which involved a challenge by a hospice for AIDS patients to a city's denial of a special use permit.

[18]416 U.S. 1 (U.S. Sup. Ct. 1974).

[19]*Moore v. City of East Cleveland,* 431 U.S. 494 (U.S. Sup. Ct. 1977).

[20]483 U.S. 825 (U.S. Sup. Ct. 1987).

[21]112 S. Ct. 2886 (U.S. Sup. Ct. 1992).

sation had occurred (and, necessarily, that the nuisance exception did not apply to Lucas's intended residential use).[22]

The mere fact that a land use regulation deprives the owner of the *highest and most profitable use* of his property does not mean, however, that there has been a taking. If the regulation still allows a use that is economically beneficial in a meaningful sense—even though not the most profitable use—the *Lucas* analysis would seem to indicate that an unconstitutional taking probably did not occur. At the same time, *Lucas* offered hints that less-than-total takings (in terms of restrictions on economically beneficial uses) may sometimes trigger a right of compensation on the land-owner's part. Thus, it appears that even as to land use regulations that restrict some but not all economically beneficial uses, property owners are likely to continue arguing (as they have in recent years) that the regulations go "too far" and amount to a taking.

There is no set formula for determining whether a regulation has gone too far. Courts look at the relevant facts and circumstances and weigh a variety of factors, such as the economic impact of the regulation, the degree to which the regulation interferes with the property owner's reasonable expectations, and the character of the government's invasion. The weighing of these factors occurs against the backdrop of a general presumption that state and local governments should have reasonably broad discretion to develop land use restrictions pursuant to the police power. As a result, the outcome of a case in which *regulatory taking* allegations are made is less certain than when a *physical taking* (a physical invasion of the sort addressed in the earlier discussion of inverse condemnation cases) appears to have occurred. *Yee v. City of Escondido*, which follows, illustrates an unsuccessful attempt by property owners to have an arguable case of regulatory taking (if any sort of taking at all) analyzed as if it were a physical taking.

---

[22]424 S.E.2d 484 (S.C. Sup. Ct. 1992).

---

## YEE V. CITY OF ESCONDIDO
### 112 S. Ct. 1522 (U.S. Sup. Ct. 1992)

Mobile home owners commonly place their mobile homes on small plots of land (often called *pads*) they have leased in a mobile home park. In 1978, California enacted the Mobilehome Residency Law. This statute prohibited mobile home park owners from evicting mobile home owners from leased pads unless the mobile home owner defaulted on rental payments or violated park rules, or the park owner decided to change the property from a mobile home park to a different land use. The statute also prohibited the park owner from requiring that a mobile home be removed from a pad when the mobile home was sold to a responsible purchaser who wished to lease the same pad from the park owner.

The City of Escondido later enacted a mobile home rent control ordinance. This ordinance rolled back rents charged by park owners to their 1986 levels and required park owners to obtain City Council approval before raising rents. John and Irene Yee owned two mobile home parks in Escondido. They and other park owners (referred to here collectively as "the Yees") sued the city. The Yees alleged that Escondido's rent control ordinance, when viewed against the backdrop of California's Mobilehome Residency Law, effected a *physical taking* of their property without just compensation. Specifically, the Yees asserted that the rent control ordinance "had the effect of depriving the plaintiffs of all use and occupancy of [their] real property and granting to the tenants of mobilehomes presently in [the plaintiffs' parks], as well as the successors in interest of such tenants, the right to physically permanently occupy and use the [plaintiffs'] real property." The Superior Court sustained the city's demurrer. The California Court of Appeal affirmed, concluding that the rent control ordinance could not constitute a *physical* taking. After the California Supreme Court denied review, the U.S. Supreme Court granted the Yees' petition for certiorari.

---

■

**O'Connor, Justice**     Most of our cases interpreting the Takings Clause of the Fifth Amendment fall within two distinct classes. Where the government authorizes a physical occupation of property (or actually takes title), the Takings Clause generally requires compensation. But where the government merely regulates the use of property, compensation is required only if considerations such as the purpose of the regulation or the extent to which it deprives the owner of the economic use of the property suggest that the regulation has unfairly singled out the property owner to bear a burden that should be borne by the public as a whole. The first category of cases requires courts to apply a clear rule; the second necessarily entails complex factual assessments of the purposes and economic effects of government actions.

The Yees' argument is predicated on the unusual economic relationship between park owners and mobile home owners. Park owners may no longer set rents or decide who their tenants will be. As a result, according to the Yees, any reduction in the rent for a mobile home pad causes a corresponding increase in the value of a mobile home, because the mobile home owner now owns, in addition to a mobile home, the right to occupy a pad at a rent below the value that would be set by the free market. Because (the argument goes) the California Mobilehome Residency Law makes it difficult to evict a mobile home owner or to require the mobile home's removal when it is sold to a purchaser who wishes to lease the same pad, the mobile home owner (or purchaser to whom he or she sells) is effectively a perpetual tenant of the park with a right to occupy a pad at below-market rent indefinitely. As a result, the Yees conclude, the rent control ordinance has transferred a discrete interest in land—the right to occupy the land indefinitely at a sub-market rent—from the park owner to the mobile home owner. The Yees contend that this transfer is no less than a right of physical occupation of the park owner's land.

This argument, while perhaps within the scope of our regulatory taking cases, cannot be squared easily with our cases on physical takings. The government effects a physical taking only where it *requires* the landowner to submit to the physical occupation of his land. Thus, whether the government floods a landowner's property or does no more than require the landowner to suffer the installation of a cable, the Takings Clause requires compensation if the government authorizes a compelled physical invasion of property.

But the Escondido rent control ordinance, even when considered in conjunction with the California Mobilehome Residency law, authorizes no such thing. The Yees voluntarily rented their land to mobile home owners. Neither the City nor the State compels park owners, once they have rented their property to tenants, to continue doing so forever. To the contrary, the Mobilehome Residency Law provides that the park owner who wishes to change the use of his land may evict his tenants, albeit with six or twelve months notice. Put bluntly, no government has required any physical invasion of the Yees' property. Their tenants were invited by them, not forced upon them by the government. While the right to exclude is doubtless one of the most essential sticks in the bundle of rights that are commonly characterized as property, we do not find that right to have been taken from the Yees on the mere face of the Escondido ordinance.

The state and local laws at issue here merely regulate *use* of land by regulating the relationship between landlord and tenant. This Court has consistently affirmed that States have broad power to regulate housing conditions in general and the landlord-tenant relationship in particular without paying compensation for all economic injuries that such regulation entails. When a landowner decides to rent his land to tenants, the government may place ceilings on the rents the landowner can charge, or require the landowner to accept tenants he does not like, without automatically having to pay compensation. Such forms of regulation are analyzed by engaging in the factual inquiries necessary to determine whether a regulation goes "too far" and thus constitutes a regulatory taking.

The Yees emphasize that the ordinance transfers wealth from park owners to incumbent mobile home owners. Other forms of land use regulation, however, can also be said to transfer wealth from the one who is regulated to another. The existence of the transfer in itself does not convert regulation into physical invasion. The ordinance does not have the effect of requiring park owners to submit to the physical occupation of their land.

The same may be said of the Yees' contention that the ordinance, when considered alongside the State's Mobilehome Residency Law, effectively amounts to compelled physical occupation because it deprives park owners of the ability to choose their incoming tenants [by removing park owners' ability to threaten disfavored would-be purchasers with higher pad rents]. Such an effect, however, does not convert regulation into the unwanted physical occupation of land. Because they voluntarily open their property to occupation by others, the Yees cannot assert a *per se* right to compensation based on this inability to exclude particular individuals.

We made this observation in *Loretto v. Teleprompter Manhattan CATV Corp.* (1982):

We affirm the traditional rule that a permanent physical occupation of property is a taking. In such a case, the property owner entertains a historically rooted expectation of compensation, and the character of the invasion is qualitatively more intrusive than perhaps any other

category of property regulation. We do not, however, question the equally substantial authority upholding a State's broad power to impose appropriate restrictions upon an owner's *use* of his property.

We continue to observe this distinction today. Because the Escondido rent control ordinance does not compel a landowner to suffer the physical occupation of his property, it does not effect a *per se* taking.

## Judgment for the City of Escondido affirmed.

In another portion of the opinion not set forth here, the Court declined to rule on the Yees' alternative claim of an impermissible *regulatory* taking. Because the Yees' petition for certiorari had referred only to the *physical* taking question, the Court concluded that it would be inappropriate to consider the regulatory taking issue.

---

### PROBLEMS AND PROBLEM CASES

**1.** In 1971, Swafford bought three metal buildings and installed them on his ranch. The buildings included (1) a horse barn with a dirt floor middle; (2) an office, a trophy room, and a tack room; and (3) an open-air hay shed with no siding. The buildings were prefabricated at a factory and were assembled at the ranch by Swafford's agent and bolted to concrete slabs. They were never moved after their assembly and installation. In 1973, Swafford mortgaged the property to Kerman. Swafford later defaulted on the debt, and Kerman instituted foreclosure proceedings. Kerman bought the ranch at the foreclosure sale. Swafford claims that the portable buildings belong to him and that he can remove them. Do they belong to Swafford?

**2.** In 1957 or 1958, the Hibbards cleared their land of overgrowth and set up a trailer park. There was no obvious boundary between their land and that of their neighbor to the east, so the Hibbards cleared the land up to a deep drainage ditch. They also built a road for use in entering and leaving the trailer park. In 1960, the Hibbards' neighbor, McMurray, discovered through a survey that the Hibbards had encroached on his land (the eastern parcel) by 20 feet. He so informed the Hibbards. The western parcel later changed hands several times until the Sanderses bought it in 1976.

The use of the western parcel changed little over the years. The road remained in continuous use in connection with the trailer park. The area between the road and the drainage ditch was also used by trailer park residents for parking, storage, garbage removal, and picnicking. Trailer personnel and tenants mowed grass up to the drainage ditch and planted flowers. The Sanderses installed underground wiring and surface power poles in the area between the road and the drainage ditch. In 1978, the Chaplins bought the eastern parcel. Shortly thereafter, they had a survey conducted. This survey revealed the Sanderses' encroachments. The Chaplins then sued to quiet title to the road and its shoulder (Parcel A) and the area between the road and the drainage ditch (Parcel B). With 10 years being the relevant possession period under state law, the Sanderses asserted that they owned Parcels A and B by virtue of adverse possession. Were the Sanderses correct?

**3.** The Wakes owned a tract of land. They used one part of the tract as a farm and the other part as a cattle ranch. Each spring and fall, the Wakes drove cattle from the ranch over an access road on the farm to Butler Springs, which was also located on the farm. From Butler Springs, they ranged the cattle eastward to adjacent government land, where they held grazing rights. In December 1956, the Wakes sold the farm portion of the land on contract to the Hesses. The contract of sale expressly reserved an easement in the Wakes to use the Butler Springs water and the right-of-way from Butler Springs across the property to the federal land. The contract described the Butler Springs area but did not describe the access road leading to Butler Springs from the county road. In 1963, the Hesses sold the farm to the Johnsons. These parties' contract referred to the Wakes' easement. The Wakes continued to use the access road and Butler Springs until 1964, when they sold their ranch and granted the Butler Springs easement to the purchasers. The ranch later changed hands several times, but each owner continued to use the access road and Butler Springs. In 1978, shortly after the Nelsons bought the ranch, the Johnsons sent them a letter "revoking permission" to use the access road. The Johnsons later placed locks on the gates across the access road. The Nelsons alleged that they had easement rights in the Butler Springs area and the access road leading to it. Were they correct?

**4.** Major developed a subdivision in which he built a number of houses and offered them for sale. The Rozells bought one of the houses. Upon the first rain, water entered under the crawl space of the house. Water then accumulated to a depth of 17 inches in a room where the furnace and water heater were located. This frequently caused the water heater not to work. Major's attempts to keep the water out were unsuccessful. Water continued to accumulate in the room whenever there was a rainfall of any consequence. As a result, the house was damp and had a peculiar odor. Mildew also became a problem. Did the Rozells have a cause of action against Major? If so, what cause of action?

**5.** A restrictive covenant applicable to most lots in an industrial park was recorded in 1957. The restrictive covenant prohibited property improvements taller than 45 feet. It also forbade billboards and advertising signs except those identifying the name, business, and products of the person or firm occupying the property on which the billboards or signs appeared. In other words, billboards or signs promoting businesses located elsewhere (off-premises advertising) were prohibited. The City of Rolling Meadows acquired property in the industrial park in 1960. Shortly thereafter, approximately one tenth of the park's 201 acres were condemned so that a new public highway, Route 53, could run through the park.

National Advertising Company and Universal Outdoor, Inc., leased industrial park property during the 1980s and began constructing billboards on their leased property. They intended these billboards to be between 49 and 56 feet tall and available for advertising use by other businesses (i.e., for off-premises advertising). The City of Rolling Meadows learned of the restrictive covenant shortly after construction of the billboards began. The city then filed suit against National and Universal in an effort to enforce the restrictive covenant and halt the billboard construction. National and Universal argued, among other things, that the character of the industrial park area had changed substantially and that the restrictive covenant therefore should no longer be enforceable. As of the time of the litigation, Route 53 was a six-lane highway carrying approximately 100,000 to 150,000 cars per day through the industrial park. Was there a sufficient change in circumstances to justify a conclusion that the restrictive covenant was no longer enforceable?

**6.** The Parkers used part of their property for housing, breeding, raising, and selling German shepherd dogs. As many as 25 dogs were on the Parkers' property at one time. Many of the dogs were trained as guard, protection, or attack dogs. The dogs' barking and offensive odors annoyed adjacent property owners. The Parkers sometimes let some of the dogs wander around the neighborhood unsupervised. This caused neighbors to be concerned about the safety of their children. The Parkers' property was subject to a restriction prohibiting noxious or offensive activity and providing that no animal could be raised, bred, or kept for any purpose other than serving as household pets. Three owners of adjacent homes brought suit against the Parkers, seeking to have them enjoined from keeping a number of dogs. The Parkers argued that the subdivision restriction did not prohibit them from keeping the dogs. Were the neighbors entitled to obtain an injunction against the Parkers? If so, on what grounds?

**7.** Davis bought a 12-acre tract of land in 1967. The tract was landlocked, although it had some frontage on Beaver Lake, a navigable watercourse. At one time, a single owner, Clark, had owned all the land now owned by Davis, her neighbors the Attaways, and others in the area. At first, Davis reached her property by using an old trail across the Attaways' property and another tract. In 1975, however, the Attaways put in a gate to obstruct the trail. After that, Davis walked to her land. She later filed suit to acquire a right-of-way giving her access from a public road (Walnut Road) to her land. Was Davis entitled to such access?

**8.** Elliot and Davis owned property in Athens, Georgia, where the University of Georgia is located. Their property was in an area whose residential-purpose zoning allowed an unlimited number of related persons to occupy the same residence but no more than four unrelated persons to occupy the same residence. Elliott and Davis sought to sell their property to The Potter's House, an entity that planned to operate an alcohol and drug rehabilitation center on the property. This center would house 12 rehabilitation program participants (all unrelated persons) plus an employee of The Potter's House. The rehabilitation center therefore would not have complied with applicable zoning. The sale from Elliott and Davis to The Potter's House was conditional on the ability to obtain zoning changes to accommodate the rehabilitation center. After the City of Athens refused requests that the area's zoning be altered to accommodate the rehabilitation center, Elliott, Davis, and The Potter's House sued the city on the theory that the city's refusal to make a zoning accommodation violated the federal Fair Housing Act's provisions prohibiting discrimination on the basis of handicap. All parties to the case agreed that the rehabilitation center's inhabitants would be considered handicapped for purposes of the Fair Housing Act. The city argued, however, that it qualified for an exemption set forth in the Fair Housing Act for reasonable maximum occupancy restrictions imposed by local law. According to the city, its ordinance restricting the number of unrelated persons who could live together was designed to regulate the large university student population in Athens and to guard against extreme density-oriented problems in areas near the University of Georgia. Was the zoning ordinance a reasonable maximum occupancy restriction exempting the city from responsibility under the Fair Housing Act?

**9.** Glover and Santangelo owned adjacent parcels of property in Oregon. Both lots were on a hillside allowing views of Mt. Shasta, Lake Ewana, and the downtown area of Klamath Falls. Santangelo's lot (Lot 10), which was on the downhill side of Glover's lot (Lot 9), was encumbered by a restrictive covenant executed at a time when Glover's house was almost completed and Lot 10 was bare. The covenant prohibited any second story from ever being erected on any building in a specified area of Lot 10. The covenant expressly stated that it was intended to run with the land and that it was executed "so that the value of Lot 9 as a 'view lot' would not be impaired" by future construction on Lot 10. Santangelo began construction on his house, a substantial proportion of which lay in the portion of Lot 10 that was covered by the restrictive covenant. The house consisted of a main level and a "daylight basement." On the uphill side of the house, approximately one third of the basement was constructed above what would have been the original grade of the property. This basement had windows on the uphill side. The main floor was raised several feet off the ground. The house substantially impaired Glover's western view, but did not disturb Glover's view to the south, across another neighbor's land. As it became apparent to Glover that the house would impair his western view, he attempted to halt the construction. With full knowledge of Glover's complaint, Santangelo proceeded to complete the house. What legal rights did Glover have in this case?

**10.** Emma Yocum was married to James Yocum as of the time of her death in 1990. She and James had begun living together in March 1959. In July 1959, by way of a warranty deed that referred to them as "husband and wife," Emma and James took ownership of a home. She and James, however, were not yet married. Emma was still married to Joseph Perez, from whom she was divorced in April 1960. Emma and James were married in July 1960. When they acquired their home in 1959, James had provided the down payment. A mortgage executed by Emma and James at that time also referred to them as husband and wife even though they were not then married. After Emma's death in 1990, her children by her marriage to Joseph Perez filed suit in an effort to have the court determine present ownership of the home Emma and James had owned during her lifetime. Had Emma and James owned the home as *tenants in common* (meaning that Emma's interest in the property would pass to her estate, in which her children were entitled to share), or instead as either *tenants by the entirety* or *joint tenants* (meaning that James would then solely own the home by virtue of the right of survivorship)?

**11.** The Duchaines leased their property to Southern Massachusetts Broadcasters for a five-year period. While occupying the leased property, Southern installed a radio tower, which it used to transmit radio broadcasts. The tower was a 390-foot steel-frame structure that stood on three legs and was attached by iron bolts to five-foot-square cement foundations. Although it was possible to remove the tower from the property, Southern neither attempted to remove it nor claimed the right to do so until two and one-quarter years after vacating the Duchaines' property. Southern then filed suit, claiming ownership of the tower. Was Southern entitled to prevail?

## CAPSTONE QUESTIONS

Ann Oldcodger is the sole proprietor of an Elderville, West Virginia, retail business that focuses on the clothing needs of elderly persons. She also owns or has interests in various parcels of real property located in or near Elderville. Oldcodger is involved in each of the following sets of circumstances:

· Oldcodger operates her retail business in a building she rents from Properties Unlimited, Inc. (PU), which owns numerous commercial properties. With the oral consent of PU's leasing manager, Oldcodger installed a considerable amount of shelving in the building. Oldcodger uses the shelves to hold and display the merchandise available for sale at her store. The shelves are firmly attached to the interior walls of the building by means of a combination of screws, bolts, and brackets. If the shelves were removed, they would leave small but "fillable" holes in the walls. Oldcodger's written lease with PU is about to expire. Oldcodger intends to move her business to another location. She has notified PU that she intends to remove the shelves from the leased premises upon expiration of the lease. PU has objected, contending that Oldcodger is obligated to leave the shelves in place. The Oldcodger-PU lease contains no provisions addressing this matter of dispute between the parties.

· Oldcodger and her elderly sister, Geri Atric, owned Greenacre (a parcel of farmland) in joint tenancy as of the time of Atric's recent death.

Atric's will, which met all legal requirements and was recently admitted to probate, contains a provision stating that "I hereby leave my interest in Greenacre to my nephew, Peter (Petie) Atric."

· Oldcodger owns a house that is located along one side of an alley. The alley is owned by the City of Elderville. On the other side of the alley is a vacant strip of ground that is 12 feet wide and 35 feet long. The strip sits adjacent to residential property owned by Don Dingleberry. Oldcodger has long assumed that she owned the strip, but potentially erroneous surveys done long ago, coupled with ambiguities in local property records, have led to uncertainty on this point. Dingleberry wished to buy the strip in order to increase the size of his yard. Because she did not use the strip and because Dingleberry had always been a good neighbor, Oldcodger charged Dingleberry only $250 in return for her quitclaim deed to him regarding the strip. Neither party was represented by an attorney in this transaction. A few weeks later, the City of Elderville acquired information enabling it to clear up the previous ambiguities in the property records pertaining to the strip. This information, plus further information obtained through a new survey, revealed that the city, not Oldcodger, owned the strip. Dingleberry has now sued Oldcodger on the theory that she breached her obligation to provide him good title to the strip.

· Oldcodger owns another house, which she has rented to tenants for a number of years. Oldcodger would like to tear down the house and construct a building from which she would operate a laundromat. She reasonably believes that use of the property for a laundromat would ultimately be more lucrative financially than is use of the property as a rental dwelling. The operation of a laundromat, however, would run afoul of Elderville's zoning ordinance, which allows only residential uses (and thus prohibits commercial uses) in the area where Oldcodger's property is located. Oldcodger has unsuccessfully sought a variance from the city. She has, therefore, sued Elderville, alleging that the zoning ordinance and the city's refusal to give her a variance amount to a taking for which she is entitled to compensation.

**Required:**

Answer the following and give reasons for your conclusions.

1. Is Oldcodger entitled to remove the shelves upon expiration of her lease, or is she obligated, as PU contends, to leave the shelves in place?
2. In view of the facts set forth above, who owns Greenacre?
3. Should Dingleberry win his suit against Oldcodger?
4. Should Oldcodger win her suit against the City of Elderville?

**CHAPTER**

**17**

# INSURANCE

**INTRODUCTION**

*Insurance serves as a frequent topic of discussion in various contexts in today's society. Advertisements for companies offering life, automobile, and property insurance appear daily on television and in the print media. Journalists report on issues of health insurance coverage and movements for reform. Persons engaged in business publicly and privately lament the excessive (from their perspective) costs of obtaining liability insurance. Insurance companies and insurance industry critics offer differing explanations for why those costs have reached their present levels.*

*Despite the frequency with which insurance matters receive public discussion and the perceived importance of insurance coverage, major legal aspects of insurance relationships remain largely unfamiliar to many persons. This chapter, therefore, examines important components of insurance law. We begin by discussing the nature of insurance relationships and exploring contract law's application to insurance policies in general. We then discuss other legal concepts and issues associated with specific types of insurance, most notably property insurance, liability insurance, and life insurance.[1] The chapter concludes with an examination of an important judicial trend—allowing insurers to be held liable for compensatory and punitive damages if they refuse in bad faith to perform their policy obligations.*

## NATURE AND BENEFITS OF INSURANCE RELATIONSHIPS

Insurance relationships arise from an agreement under which a risk of loss that one party (normally the **insured**) otherwise would have to bear is shifted to another party (the **insurer**). The ability to obtain insurance enables the insured to lessen or avoid the adverse financial effects that would be likely if certain happenings were to take place. In return for the insured's payment of necessary consideration

---

[1]This chapter's discussion of health insurance is limited in scope, primarily because at the time this book went to press, differing proposals for potentially sweeping federal legislation governing health insurance availability and coverage were being considered in Congress. Another frequently encountered type of insurance, title insurance, was discussed in Chapter 16.

(the **premium**), the insurer agrees to shoulder the financial consequences stemming from particular risks if those risks should materialize in the form of actual events.

Each party presumably benefits from the insurance relationship. The insured obtains a promise of coverage for losses that, if they materialize, could easily exceed the amounts of the premiums paid. Along with this promise, the insured acquires the supposed "peace of mind" that insurance companies and agents like to emphasize. By collecting premiums from many insureds over a substantial period of time, the insurer stands to profit despite its obligation to make payments covering financial losses that stem from insured-against risks. The insured-against risks, after all, are just that: risks. In some instances, events triggering the insurer's payment obligation to a particular insured may never occur (e.g., the insured's property never sustains damage from a cause contemplated by the property insurance policy). The insurer nonetheless remains entitled to the premiums collected during the policy period. Other times, events that call the insurer's payment obligation into play in a given situation may occur infrequently (e.g., a particular insured under an automobile insurance policy has an accident only every few years) or only after many years of premium collection (e.g., an insured paid premiums on his life insurance policy for 35 years prior to his death).

## INSURANCE POLICIES AS CONTRACTS

### Interested Parties

Regardless of the type of insurance involved, the insurance relationship is fundamentally contractual. This relationship involves at least two—and frequently more than two—interested parties. As noted earlier, the insurer (usually a corporation), in exchange for the payment of consideration (the premium), agrees to pay for losses caused by specific events (sometimes called *perils*). The insured is the person who acquires insurance on real or personal property or insurance against liability, or, in the case of life or health insurance, the person whose life or health is the focus of the policy. The person to whom the insurance proceeds are payable is the **beneficiary.** Except in the case of life insurance, the insured and the beneficiary will often be the same person. In most but not all instances, the insured

will also be the **owner** of the policy (the person entitled to exercise the contract rights set out in the insurance policy and in applicable law). In view of the contractual nature of the insurance relationship, insurance policies must satisfy all of the elements required for a binding contract.

### Offer, Acceptance, and Consideration

The insurance industry's standard practice is to have the potential insured make an offer for an insurance contract by completing and submitting an application (provided by the insurer's agent), along with the appropriate premium, to the insurer. The insurer may then either accept or reject this offer. If the insurer accepts, the parties have an insurance contract under which the insured's initial premium payment and future premium payments furnish consideration for the insurer's promises of coverage for designated risks, and vice versa.

What constitutes acceptance of the offer set forth in the application may vary somewhat, depending on the type of insurance requested and the language of the application. As a general rule, however, acceptance occurs when the insurer (or agent, if authorized to do so) indicates to the insured an intent to accept the application. It is important to know the precise time when an acceptance occurs, because the insurer's contractual obligations to the insured do not commence until acceptance has taken place. If the insured sustains losses after the submission of the application (the making of the offer) but prior to an acceptance by the insurer, those losses normally must be borne by the insured rather than the insurer.

With property insurance and sometimes other types of insurance, the application may be worded so that insurance coverage begins when the insured signs the application. This arrangement provides temporary coverage until the insurer either accepts or rejects the offer contained in the application. The same result may also be achieved by the use of a *binder*, an agreement for temporary insurance pending the insurer's decision to accept or reject the risk.

Figure 1 depicts the formation of an insurance contract.

**Insurer's Delay in Acting on Application**     A common insurance law problem is the effect of the insurer's delay in acting on the application. If the applicant suffers a loss after applying but before a

---

**FIGURE 1**   Creation of an Insurance Contract

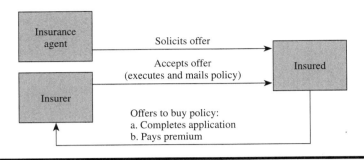

---

delaying insurer formally accepts, who must bear the loss? As a general rule, the insurer's delay does not constitute acceptance. Some states, however, have held that an insurer's retention of the premium for an unreasonable time constitutes acceptance and hence obligates the insurer to cover the insured's loss.

Other states have allowed negligence suits against insurers for delaying unreasonably in acting on an application. The theory of these cases is that insurance companies have a public duty to insure qualified applicants and that an unreasonable delay prevents applicants from obtaining insurance protection from another source. A few states have enacted statutes establishing that insurers are bound to the insurance contract unless they reject the prospective insured's application within a specified period of time.

## Effect of Insured's Misrepresentation

Applicants for insurance have a duty to reveal to insurers all the material (significant) facts about the nature of the risk so that the insurer may make an intelligent decision about whether to accept the risk. When an insurance application includes a false statement by the insured regarding a material matter, the insured's misrepresentation, if relied on by the insurer, has the same effect produced by misrepresentation in connection with other contracts—the contract becomes voidable at the election of the insurer. This means that the insurer may avoid its obligations under the policy. The same result is possible if the insured failed, in the application, to disclose known material facts to the insurer, which issued a policy it would not have issued if the

disclosures had been made. (As will be seen later in the chapter, however, certain clauses frequently appearing in life insurance policies may limit the ability of issuers of such policies to use the insured's misrepresentation as a way of avoiding all obligations under the policy.)

**Warranty/Representation Distinction**   It sometimes becomes important to distinguish between **warranties** and representations that the insured makes (usually in the application) to induce the insurer to issue an insurance policy. Warranties are *express terms in the insurance policy.* They are intended to operate as conditions on which the insurer's liability is based. The insured's breach of warranty terminates the insurer's duty to perform under the policy. For example, a property insurance policy on a commercial office building specifies that the insured must install and maintain a working sprinkler system in the building, but the insured never installs the sprinkler system. The sprinkler system requirement is a warranty, which the insured breached by failing to install the system. This means that the insurer may not be obligated to perform its obligations under the policy.

Traditionally, an insured's breach of warranty has been seen as terminating the insurer's duty to perform *regardless of whether the condition set forth in the breached warranty was actually material to the insurer's risk* (unlike the treatment given to the insured's misrepresentations, which do not make the insurance policy voidable unless they pertained to a material matter). In view of the potential harshness of the traditional rule concerning the effect of a breach of warranty, some states have refused to allow insurers to escape liability on breach of warranty grounds unless the condition contemplated by the breached warranty was indeed material.

## Capacity of Parties

Generally speaking, a contract is not enforceable unless both parties to it had the legal capacity to bind themselves to an agreement. This is seldom a problem in the insurance context, whose typical contracting parties—a corporation and an adult—clearly would have capacity in nearly all instances. An insurance policy taken out by a minor may sometimes be treated differently, due to the usual rule that a minor's lack of capacity makes the minor's contract voidable at the election of the minor.[2] For purposes of the insurance setting, however, many states have departed from the usual rule by enacting statutes that make the insurance contracts of minors enforceable against them.

## Legality

The law distinguishes between unlawful wagering contracts and valid insurance contracts. A wagering contract creates a new risk that did not previously exist. Such a contract is contrary to public policy and therefore illegal. An insurance contract, however, *transfers existing risks*—a permissible, even desirable, economic activity. A major means by which insurance law separates insurance contracts from wagering contracts is the typical requirement that the party who purchases a policy of property or life insurance must possess an **insurable interest** in the property or life being insured. Specific discussion of the insurable interest requirement appears in this chapter's later sections on property and life insurance.

## Form and Content of Insurance Contracts

**Writing**   State law governs whether insurance contracts are within the statute of frauds and must be evidenced by a writing. Some states require specific types of insurance contracts to be in writing. Contracts for property insurance are not usually within the statute of frauds, meaning that they may be either written or oral unless they come within some general provision of the statute of frauds—for example, the "one-year" provision.[3] Even when a writing is not legally required, however, wisdom dictates that the parties reduce their agreement to written form whenever possible.

**Reformation of Written Policy**   As one would expect, insurance companies' customary practice is to issue written policies of insurance regardless of whether the applicable statute of frauds requires a writing. An argument sometimes raised by insureds is that the written policy issued by the insurer did not accurately reflect the content of the parties' actual agreement. For instance, after the occurrence of a loss for which the insured thought there was coverage under the insurance contract, the insured learns that the loss-causing event was excluded from coverage by the terms expressly stated in the written policy. In such a situation, the insured may be inclined to argue that the written policy should be judicially **reformed**, so as to make it conform to the parties' supposed actual agreement.

Although reformation is available in appropriate cases, courts normally presume that the written policy of insurance should be treated as the embodiment of the parties' actual agreement. Courts consider reformation an extreme remedy. Hence, they usually refuse to grant reformation unless either of two circumstances is present. The first reformation-triggering circumstance exists when the insured and the insurer, through its agent or agents, were *mutually mistaken* about a supposedly covered event or other supposed contract term (i.e., both parties believed an event was covered by, or some other term was part of, the parties' insurance agreement but the written policy indicated otherwise). The alternative route to reformation calls for proof that the insurer committed fraud as to the terms contained in the policy or otherwise engaged in inequitable conduct. *Ridenour v. Farm Bureau Insurance Co.*, which follows, illustrates the judicial presumption that the written policy sets forth the parties' true agreement. The case also confirms that the insured's unilateral mistake—as opposed to the parties' mutual mistake—about policy terms will not warrant reformation.

---

[2]An insurance contract taken out on the life of a minor (the insured) *by an adult* (the owner) is not voidable, however. Only when the minor is the owner of the policy does the usual concern over the minor's lack of capacity come into play.

[3]The usual provisions of the statute of frauds are discussed in detail in Chapter 8.

## Ridenour v. Farm Bureau Insurance Company
### 377 N.W.2d 101 (Neb. Sup. Ct. 1985)

In August 1982, a hog confinement building owned by Charles Ridenour collapsed and was rendered a total loss. Some of Ridenour's hogs were killed as a further result of the collapse. Ridenour made a claim for these losses with his property insurer, Farm Bureau Insurance Company, whose Country Squire policy had been issued on Ridenour's property in July 1977 and had been renewed on a yearly basis after that. Farm Bureau denied the claim because the policy did not provide coverage for the collapse of farm buildings such as the hog confinement structure. Moreover, though the policy provided coverage for hog deaths resulting from certain designated causes, collapse of a building was not among the causes listed. Asserting that the parties' insurance contract was to have covered the peril of building collapse notwithstanding the terms of the written policy, Ridenour sued Farm Bureau. He asked the court to order reformation of the written policy so that it would conform to the parties' supposed agreement regarding coverage.

At trial, Ridenour testified about a February 1982 meeting in which he, his wife, and their son discussed insurance coverage with Farm Bureau agent Tim Moomey. Ridenour testified that he wanted to be certain there was insurance coverage if the hog confinement building collapsed because he had heard about the collapse of a similar structure owned by someone else. Therefore, he asked Moomey whether the Country Squire policy then in force provided such coverage. According to Ridenour, Moomey said that it did. Ridenour's wife, Thelma, testified that she asked Moomey (during the same meeting) whether there would be coverage if the floor slats of the hog confinement building collapsed and caused hogs to fall into the pit below the building. According to her testimony, Moomey responded affirmatively. The Ridenours' son, Tom, testified to the same effect. Mr. and Mrs. Ridenour both testified that they had not completely read the Country Squire policy and that because they did not understand the wording, they relied on Moomey to interpret the policy for them.

Moomey, who had ended his relationship with Farm Bureau by the time the case came to trial, testified that at no time did the Ridenours request that the hogs and the confinement building be insured so as to provide coverage for losses resulting from collapse of the building. Moomey knew that collapse coverage was not available from Farm Bureau for hog confinement buildings. In addition, Moomey testified that he met with Ridenour in April 1982 and conducted a "farm review" in which he discussed a coverage checklist and the Country Squire policy's declarations pages (which set forth the policy limits). This checklist, which Ridenour signed after Moomey reviewed it with him, made no reference to coverage for collapse losses. (Ridenour admitted in his testimony that he had signed the checklist after Moomey read off the listed items to him.) When Moomey was contacted by the Ridenours on the day the building collapsed, he had his secretary prepare a notice of loss report for submission to Farm Bureau. He also assigned an adjuster to inspect the property. Moomey and the adjuster discussed the fact that the Country Squire policy did not provide coverage for Ridenour's losses. Ridenour further testified that the day after the collapse occurred, Moomey told him he was sorry but that Farm Bureau's home office had said there was no coverage.

The trial court granted reformation, as Ridenour had requested. Farm Bureau appealed.

---

**Caporale, Judge**    The principle upon which Ridenour relies is that reformation is decreed in order to effectuate the real agreement of the parties when a written instrument does not represent their true intent. In this jurisdiction reformation may be decreed where there has been a mutual mistake or where there has been a unilateral mistake caused by the fraud or in-equitable conduct of the other party. To obtain reformation the evidence must be clear, convincing, and satisfactory. Such evidence is present when there has been produced in the trier of fact a firm belief or conviction that a fact to be proved exists. Moreover, there is a strong presumption that a written instrument correctly expresses the intention of the parties to it.

The record does not produce in us a firm belief or conviction that there was a mutual mistake of fact. Moomey was a trained and experienced insurance agent who, after he had no relationship with Farm Bureau, testified he knew the coverage claimed by Ridenour was not available from Farm Bureau and who denied representing that such coverage existed under the policy. Ridenour argues that Moomey's expression of sorrow over the fact that Farm Bureau's home office said there was no coverage, coupled with the facts that he caused a notice of loss report to be prepared and arranged for an adjuster to inspect the property, establishes that Moomey did think collapse coverage for the hog building existed. We conclude otherwise. Prudence dictated that Ridenour's claim be noted and investigated. Investigation of this claim to determine the facts does not imply a thought that coverage exists. Neither does an expression of regret that the home office said coverage does not exist necessarily imply an earlier belief by Moomey that there was coverage. It may as easily imply regret at the confirmation of what Moomey already knew.

Any mistake which may have existed was therefore one made only by Ridenour. Under such a circumstance he must, in order to recover, clearly, convincingly, and satisfactorily establish that the mistake was either the result of fraud on the part of Farm Bureau or due to Farm Bureau's inequitable conduct. Ridenour concedes in his brief that there was no fraud, but argues that Farm Bureau engaged in inequitable conduct by not delivering the declarations pages until after the loss. The late delivery of the declarations pages is more than adequately explained, however, by the fact that Ridenour was tardy in paying his premium. Moreover, since Ridenour admits that he did not read the policy, he cannot be heard to complain that not having the declarations pages deprived him of an opportunity to discover that he had no collapse coverage on his hog confinement building.

The nature of the conflict in the evidence in this case is not unlike that present in . . . earlier cases which resulted in a denial of reformation. [In addition,] the principal cases relied upon by Ridenour in which reformation was decreed are distinguishable from the case presently before us [because in each of the cases cited by Ridenour, the insured and the insurer's agent both testified that the agent made coverage assumptions and representations that were inconsistent with the terms of the written policy]. Indeed, in [those cases] there was no evidentiary conflict as to what the agent represented; consequently, the only conclusion which could have been reached was that there had been a mutual mistake. In the case before us, however, the evidence falls short of overcoming the presumption that the policy as written correctly expresses the intention of the parties at the time it was renewed.

**Judgment and decree of reformation reversed in favor of Farm Bureau.**

**Interpretation of Insurance Contracts** Modern courts realize that many persons who buy insurance do not have the training or background to fully understand the technical language often contained in insurance policies. As a result, courts tend to interpret insurance policy provisions as they would be understood by an average person. In addition, courts construe ambiguities in an insurance contract against the insurer, the drafter of the contract (and hence the user of the ambiguous language). This rule of construction means that if a word or phrase used in an insurance policy is equally subject to two possible interpretations, one of which favors the insurer and the other of which favors the insured, the court will adopt the interpretation that favors the insured.

A number of states purport to follow the *reasonable expectations of the insured* approach to interpretation of insurance policies. Analysis of judicial decisions reveals, however, that this approach's content and effect vary among the states ostensibly subscribing to it. Some states do little more than attach the reasonable expectations label to the familiar principles of interpretation set forth in the preceding paragraph. A few states give the reasonable expectations approach a much more significant effect by allowing courts to effectively read clauses into or out of an insurance policy, depending on whether reasonable persons in the position of the insured would have expected such clauses to be in a policy of the sort at issue. When applied in the latter manner, the reasonable expectations approach tends to resemble reformation in its effect.

**Clauses Required by Law**    The insurance business is highly regulated by the states, which recognize the importance of the interests protected by insurance and the difference in bargaining power that often exists between insurers and their insureds. In an attempt to remedy this imbalance, many states' statutes and insurance regulations require the inclusion of certain standard clauses in insurance policies. Many states also regulate such matters as the size and style of the print used in insurance policies. Laws in a growing number of states encourage or require the use of plain, straightforward language (rather than insurance jargon and legal terms of art) in policies whenever such language is possible to use.

**Notice and Proof of Loss-Causing Event**    The insured (or, in the case of life insurance, the beneficiary) who seeks to obtain the benefits or protection provided by an insurance policy must notify the insurer that an event covered by the policy has occurred. In addition, the insured (or the beneficiary) must furnish reasonable proof of the loss-causing event. Property insurance policies, for instance, ordinarily require the insured to furnish a sworn statement (called a *proof of loss*) in which the covered event and the resulting damage to the insured's property are described. Under life insurance policies, the beneficiary is usually expected to provide suitable documentation of the fact that the insured person has died. Liability insurance policies call for the insured to give the insurer copies of liability claims made against the insured.

**Time Limits**    Insurance policies commonly specify that notice and proof of loss must be given within a specified time. Policies sometimes state that compliance with these requirements is a condition of the insured's recovery and that failure to comply terminates the insurer's obligation. Other times, policies merely provide that failure to comply suspends the insurer's duty to pay until proper compliance occurs. Some courts require the insurer to prove it was harmed by the insured's failure to give notice before allowing the insurer to avoid liability on the ground of tardy notice.

**Cancellation and Lapse**    When a party with the power to terminate an insurance policy (extinguish all rights under the policy) exercises that power, **cancellation** has occurred. **Lapse** occurs at the end of the term specified in a policy written for a stated duration, unless the parties take action to renew the policy for an additional period of time. Alternatively, lapse may occur as a result of the insured's failure to pay premiums or some other significant default on the part of the insured. Special issues regarding cancellation and lapse of property and life insurance will be discussed later in the chapter.

**Third Parties and Insurance Contracts**    As a general rule, contracts are assignable only when the assignment will not materially alter the promisor's burden of performance. The insured's identity, character, and traits are important elements of the risk in property, life, health, and liability insurance policies. Therefore, such policies are generally nonassignable. It is also common for insurance policies to contain express restrictions on assignability. After a loss covered by an insurance policy has occurred, however, the insured may normally assign to another party the right to receive benefits under the policy. Such an assignment is permissible because it involves no change in the insurer's risk.

## Performance and Breach by Insurer

The insurer performs its obligations by paying out the sums (and taking other related actions) contemplated by the policy's terms within a reasonable time after the occurrence of an event that calls the duty to perform into play. If the insurer fails or refuses to pay despite the occurrence of a payment-triggering event, the insured of course may sue the insurer for breach of contract. By proving that the insurer's denial of the insured's claim for payment constituted a breach, the insured becomes entitled to recover compensatory damages in at least the amount that the insurer would have had to pay under the policy if the insurer had not breached.

What if the insurer's breach caused the insured to incur consequential damages that, when added to the amount due under the policy, would lead to a damages claim exceeding the dollar limits set forth in the policy? Assume that XYZ Computer Sales, Inc.'s store building is covered by a property insurance policy with Secure Insurance Co., that the building is destroyed by an accidental fire (a covered peril), and that the extent of the destruction makes the full $300,000 policy limit owing from Secure to XYZ. Secure, however, denies payment because it believes—erroneously—that XYZ officials committed arson (a cause, if it had been the actual one, that would have relieved Secure from any duty to pay). Because it needs to rebuild and take other related steps to stay in business but is short on available funds due to Secure's denial of its claim, XYZ borrows the necessary funds from a bank. XYZ thereby incurs substantial interest costs, which are consequential damages XYZ would not have incurred if Secure had performed its obligation under the policy. Assuming that XYZ's consequential damages would have been foreseeable to Secure, most states would allow XYZ to recover the consequential damages in addition to the amount due from Secure under the policy.[4] This is so even though the addition of the consequential damages would cause XYZ's damages recovery to exceed the dollar limit set forth in the parties' insurance policy. The breaching insurer's liability may exceed the policy limits despite the insurer's good faith (though incorrect) basis for denying the claim, because a good faith but erroneous refusal to pay is nonetheless a breach of contract. If the insurer could point to the policy limits as a maximum recovery in this type of situation, it would have an all-too-convenient means of avoiding responsibility for harms that logically flowed from its breach of contract.

Due to similar reasoning, many states' laws provide that if an insured successfully sues her insurer for amounts due under the policy, the insured may recover interest on those amounts (amounts that, after all, should have been paid by the insurer much sooner and without litigation). Some states also have statutes providing that insureds who successfully sue insurers are entitled to awards of attorney's fees. Punitive damages are *not* allowed, however, when the insurer's breach of contract consisted of a *good faith (though erroneous) denial* of the insured's claim. Later in this chapter, we will explore the recent judicial trend toward allowing punitive damages when the insurer's breach was in *bad faith* and thus amounted to the tort of bad faith breach of contract.

## PROPERTY INSURANCE

Owners of residential and commercial property always face the possibility that their property might be damaged or destroyed by any number of causes beyond their control. These causes include, to name a few notable ones, fire, lightning, hail, and wind. Although property owners may not be able to prevent harm to their property, they can secure some protection against resulting financial loss by contracting for property insurance and thereby transferring certain risks of loss to the insurer. Certain persons holding property interests that fall short of ownership may likewise seek to benefit, as will be seen, from the risk-shifting feature of property insurance.

### The Insurable Interest Requirement

As noted earlier in this chapter, in order for a property insurance contract not to be considered an illegal wagering contract, the person who purchases the policy (the policy owner) must have an **insurable interest** in the property being insured. One has an insurable interest if he, she, or it possesses a legal or equitable interest in the property and that interest translates into an economic stake in the continued existence of the property and the preservation of its condition. In other words, a person has an insurable interest if he would suffer a financial loss in the event of harm to the subject property. If no insurable interest is present, the policy is void.

**Examples of Insurable Interest**   The legal owner of the insured property would obviously have an insurable interest. So might other parties whose legal or equitable interests in the property do not rise to the level of an ownership interest. For example, mortgagees and other lienholders would have insurable interests in the property on which

---

[4]Even though the terms of the insurance policy almost certainly would state that Secure's payment obligation is limited to costs of repair or replacement or to the property's actual cash value—that is, without any coverage for consequential harms experienced by the insured—Secure cannot invoke this policy language as a defense. If Secure had performed its contract obligation, its payment obligation would have been restricted to what the policy provided in that regard. Having breached the insurance contract, however, Secure stands potentially liable for consequential damages to the full extent provided for by general contract law. For additional discussion of damages for breach of contract, see Chapter 10.

they hold liens.[5] A nonexhaustive list of other examples would also include holders of life estates in real property, buyers under as-yet unperformed contracts for the sale of real property, and lessees of real estate.[6] In the types of situations just noted, the interested party stands to lose financially if the property is damaged or destroyed. *Crowell v. Delafield Farmers Mutual Fire Insurance Company*, which follows shortly, provides a further example of a property interest substantial enough to amount to an insurable interest.

**Timing and Extent of Insurable Interest**    A sensible and important corollary of the insurable interest principle is that the requisite insurable interest must exist *at the time of the loss* (i.e., at the time the subject property was damaged). If an insurable interest existed when the holder thereof purchased the property insurance but the interest was no longer present when the loss occurred, the policy owner is not entitled to payment for the loss. This would mean, for example, that a property owner who purchased property insurance would not be entitled

to collect from the insurer for property damage that occurred after she had transferred ownership to someone else. Similarly, a lienholder who purchased property insurance could not collect under the policy if the loss took place after his lien had been extinguished by payment of the underlying debt or by another means.

The extent of a person's insurable interest in property is limited to the value of that interest. For example, Fidelity Savings & Loan extends Williams a $95,000 loan to purchase a home and takes a mortgage on the home as security. In order to protect this investment, Fidelity obtains a $95,000 insurance policy on the property. Several years later, the house is destroyed by fire, a cause triggering the insurer's payment obligation. At the time of the fire, the balance due on the loan is $84,000. Fidelity's recovery under the insurance policy is limited to $84,000, because that amount is the full extent of its insurable interest. (An alternative way by which mortgagees protect their interest is to insist that the property owner list the mortgagee as the *loss payee* under the property owner's policy. This means that if the property is destroyed, the insurer will pay the policy proceeds to the mortgagee. Once again, however, the mortgagee's entitlement to payment under this approach would be limited to the dollar value of its insurable interest, with surplus proceeds going to the insured property owner.)

---

[5]Chapter 20 contains a detailed discussion of security interests in real property. Chapter 21 addresses security interests in personal property.

[6]Chapter 16 contains a discussion of life estates and an examination of contracts for the sale of real property. Leases of real estate are explored in Chapter 18.

---

## CROWELL V. DELAFIELD FARMERS MUTUAL FIRE INSURANCE COMPANY
### 453 N.W.2d 724 (Minn. Ct. App. 1990)

Earl and Vonette Crowell owned and operated a farm in Cottonwood County, Minnesota. In 1980, the Crowells took out a mortgage on the property with Farm Credit Services. They also took out a fire insurance policy with Delafield Farmers Mutual Insurance Company. This policy ran from October 1985 until October 1988. The Crowells failed to make their mortgage payments and Farm Credit began foreclosure proceedings. Upon foreclosure, mortgagors such as the Crowells have a right of redemption for a specified time, during which they have the right to buy back their property after it has been sold to another. In November 1987, the Crowells' right of redemption ended. Under Minnesota law, however, farmers who lose their farms to corporate lenders are given an additional opportunity to repurchase their farms under a "right of first refusal." This right meant that Farm Credit was forbidden to sell the farm to anyone else before offering it to the Crowells at a price no higher than the highest price offered by a third party. Farm Credit allowed the Crowells to remain on the farm while they tried to secure financing to buy the property under their right of first refusal.

On November 27, 1987, the farmhouse was substantially destroyed by fire. The Crowells filed a claim for the loss with Delafield. Delafield paid the claim on the Crowells' personal effects inside the house, but denied the claim on the structure itself. It claimed that since the Crowells' period of redemption had expired, they no longer had an insurable interest in the farmhouse. The Crowells brought suit. When the trial court granted summary judgment for the Crowells, Delafield appealed.

---

**Kalitowski, Judge** To be entitled to recovery for a loss, an insured must have an insurable interest in the property covered by the policy. To have an insurable interest, the party must suffer a loss of property interest that is substantial and real. A person has an insurable interest in property when the relationship between him and the property is such that he has a reasonable expectation, based upon a real or legal right, of benefit to be derived from the continued existence of the property and of loss or liability from its destruction. The Minnesota Supreme Court has stated that it is not necessary that the insured should have an absolute right of property, and that he has an insurable interest if, by the destruction of the property, he will suffer a loss, whether he has or has not any title to, lien upon, or possession of the property itself.

Farm Credit foreclosed on the Crowells' farm mortgage. The Crowells remained on and continued to operate the farm. After the redemption period, Farm Credit became the absolute owner of the property. The record indicates Farm Credit allowed the Crowells to remain on the farm after the redemption period expired because it was involved in the Crowells' effort to secure financing to enable them to exercise their statutory right of first refusal. In addition, Farm Credit did not purchase and the Crowells did not cancel fire insurance on the property.

By creating a right of first refusal, the legislature gave financially distressed farmers who had lost their farms to corporate lenders an opportunity to repurchase the farms. The legislative purpose of this right of first refusal is to encourage and protect the family farm as a basic economic unit, to insure it as the most socially desirable mode of agricultural production, and to enhance and promote the stability and well-being of rural society in Minnesota and the nuclear family.

This right of first refusal gives family farmers some additional right or interest in the property they lost to corporate lenders. Based on this legal right in the property, the Crowells had a reasonable expectation to derive a benefit from the continued existence of the farmhouse. Although the Crowells no longer had title to the farm, they were allowed to remain on the land with all parties' knowledge and intention that they would exercise their right of first refusal and regain the farm. Therefore, they expected the benefit of living in the farmhouse until they exercised that right.

It is clear the Crowells suffered a loss from the destruction of the farmhouse. Since the fire the Crowells have been unable to live in the farmhouse. This situation forces the Crowells to live several miles from their farm and commute between their home and the farm, causing additional expenses and inconvenience. The advantage of living on the farm is clearly lost.

Under the facts of this case we hold the trial court was correct in holding this right gave the Crowells an insurable interest in the farm and its structures.

**Judgment for the Crowells affirmed.**

---

## Covered and Excluded Perils

Property insurers usually do not undertake to provide coverage for losses stemming from any and all causes of harm to property. Instead, property insurers tend to either specify certain causes (**covered perils**) as to which the insured *will* receive payment for resulting losses—meaning that there is no coverage regarding a peril not specified—or set forth a seemingly broad statement of coverage but then specify certain perils concerning which there will be *no* payment for losses (**excluded perils**). (Sometimes, property insurers employ a combination of these two approaches by specifying certain covered perils and certain excluded perils.)

**Typical Covered Perils** The effects of these approaches are essentially the same, as most property insurers tend to provide coverage for the same sorts of causes of harm to property. The perils concerning which property insurance policies typically provide benefits include fire, lightning, hail, and wind. In addition, property insurance policies often cover harms to property resulting from causes such as the impact of an automobile or aircraft (e.g., an automobile or aircraft crashes into an insured building), vandalism, certain collapses of buildings, and certain accidental discharges or overflows from pipes or heating and air-conditioning systems.

**Fire as a Covered Peril** Historically, the importance of coverage against the peril of fire made *fire insurance* a commonly used term. Various insurance companies incorporated the term into their official firm name; the policies these companies issued came to be called *fire insurance policies* even when they covered perils in addition to fire (as policies increasingly have done in this century). As a result, judges, commentators, and persons affiliated with the insurance industry will sometimes refer to today's policies as fire insurance policies despite the usual property insurer's tendency to cover not only fire but also some combination of the other perils mentioned in the preceding paragraph. Whether the term used is *property insurance* (generally employed in this chapter) or *fire insurance*, reference is being made to the same type of policy.

Fire-related losses covered by property insurance policies are those resulting from accidental fires. An accidental fire is one other than a fire deliberately set by, or at the direction of, the insured for the purpose of damaging the property. In other words, the insured obtains no coverage for losses stemming from the insured's act of arson. This commonsense restriction on an insurer's duty to pay for losses also applies to other harms the insured deliberately caused to his property.

For purposes of fire coverage, insurance contracts often distinguish between *friendly fires*, which are those contained in a place intended for a fire (such as fires in a woodstove or fireplace), and *hostile fires*, which burn where no fire is intended to be (such as fires caused by lightning, outside sources, electrical shorts, or those that began as friendly fires but escaped their boundaries). Losses caused by hostile fires are covered; those stemming from friendly fires tend not to be. As a general rule,

covered fire losses may extend beyond direct damage caused by the fire. Indirect damage caused by smoke and heat is usually covered, as is damage caused by firefighters in their attempts to put out the fire.

**"All-Risk" Policies and Property Contamination Claims** A so-called all-risk policy of property insurance takes the previously mentioned approach of setting forth a broad general rule of coverage and then specifying narrowly defined exclusions from that general rule. In recent years, public concern has intensified regarding problems of pollution and contamination of property due to the presence of hazardous wastes, leaking and seepage of toxic chemicals, and the like. The market value of property affected by such problems may be markedly reduced as a result. Pursuant to federal environmental law, the federal government sometimes requires the cleanup of contaminated real property. When property owners either are charged with the responsibility of conducting a cleanup or otherwise reach the conclusion that such action will be necessary, they have become increasingly inclined to make claims against their property insurers—particularly those offering all-risk coverage—for recovery of the clean-up costs. Alternatively, affected property owners sometimes make claims against their insurers for payment of a supposed loss that took the form of a reduced property value.

These claims are based on the theory that the release or accumulation of hazardous wastes or other toxic substances on the property constitutes a covered harm within the all-risk policy's broad coverage language (and does not come within an exclusion from coverage). When the pollution problem, hazardous waste accumulation, or toxic chemical contamination did not result from deliberate wrongful actions by the insured, courts sometimes rule that the insured is entitled to recover benefits from the all-risk insurer. Cases of this nature are complicated, however, by various issues that go beyond interpreting a policy's coverage and exclusion provisions. Other difficult issues include determining when the harm to the property took place (when the hazardous substance began accumulating on the property, when the problem first manifested itself, or when the problem became especially acute) and determining whether the harm occurred during the time the insurer at issue was insuring the property. Sometimes, these cases involve various insurers that insured the property at different times and are involved in a dispute as to which one of them must cover the loss. The potential exposure insurers offering all-risk policies may face regarding environmental harms and cleanup costs has caused some property insurers to insert specific "pollution exclusion" or "hazardous waste exclusion" clauses in new policies that they issue.

**Typical Excluded Perils** Although flood-related harm to property may seem similar to harm stemming from some of the weather-related causes listed earlier among the typical covered perils, it does not usually receive the same treatment. Property insurance policies frequently exclude coverage for flood damage. On this point, however, as with other questions regarding perils covered or excluded, the actual language of the policy at issue must always be consulted before a coverage issue is resolved in any given case.[7] Other typical exclusions include earthquake damage and harm to property stemming from war or nuclear reaction, radiation, or contamination. As previously indicated, property insurance policies exclude coverage for losses caused by the insured's deliberate actions that were intended to cause harm to the property.

**Additional Coverages** Even as to perils for which there may not be coverage in the typical property insurance policy, the property owner may sometimes be able to purchase a specialized policy (e.g., a flood insurance policy) that does afford coverage for such perils. Other times, even if coverage for a given peril is not provided by the terms of most standard property insurance policies, it may nonetheless be possible for the property owner to have coverage for that peril added to the policy by paying an additional premium. This is sometimes done, for example, by policy owners who desire earthquake coverage.

**Personal Property Insurance** Although the broad term *property insurance* is what has been employed, the discussion so far in this section has

---

[7]It may be that a type of peril frequently excluded in property insurance policies is in fact a covered peril under the language of the policy at issue. Alternatively, losses that at first glance appear to have resulted from an excluded peril may sometimes be characterized as having resulted, at least in part, from a covered peril. In the latter event, there may be some coverage for the losses.

centered around policies providing coverage for harm to *real* property. Items of *personal* property are, of course, insurable as well. Property insurance policies commonly known as homeowners' policies—because the real property serving as the policy's primary subject is the insured's dwelling—cover not only harm to the dwelling but also to personal property located inside the dwelling or otherwise on the subject real property. (Sometimes, depending on the policy language, there may be coverage even when the item of personal property was not located at the designated real property when the item was damaged.) Property insurance policies covering office buildings and other commercial real estate often provide some level of personal property coverage as well. When personal property coverage is included in a policy primarily concerned with real property coverage, the perils insured against in the personal property coverage tend to be largely the same as, though not necessarily identical to, those applicable to the real property coverage.

Lessees of residential or commercial real estate may obtain insurance policies to cover their items of personal property that are on the leased premises. Such policies are highly advisable, because the apartment or office building owner's insurance policy on the real property is likely to furnish little or no coverage for the tenant's personal property.

Automobile insurance policies are in part personal property insurance policies because they provide coverage (under what are usually called the *comprehensive* and *collision* sections) for car damage resulting from such causes as fire, wind, hail, vandalism, or collision with an animal or tree. (As will be seen, automobile insurance policies also contain significant features of another major type of insurance policy to be discussed later—liability insurance.) Other specialized types of personal property insurance are also available. For example, some farmers purchase crop insurance in order to guard against the adverse financial effects that would result if a hailstorm or other covered peril severely damaged a season's crop.

## Nature and Extent of Insurer's Payment Obligation

Property insurance policies are **indemnity** contracts. This means that the insurer is obligated to reimburse the insured for his actual losses associated with a covered harm to the insured property. The insured's recovery under the policy thus cannot exceed the extent of the loss sustained. Neither may it exceed the extent of the insured's insurable interest (as discussed earlier in this chapter) or the amount of coverage that the insured purchased (the **policy limits**).[8]

Policy provisions other than the policy limits also help define the extent of the insurer's obligation to pay. When covered real property is damaged but not destroyed, the **cost of repair** is normally the relevant measure. Many policies provide that when covered real property is destroyed, the insurer must pay the **actual cash value** (or *fair market value*) of the property. Some policies, however, establish **cost of replacement** as the payment obligation in this situation. The policies that call for payment of the actual cash value frequently give the insurer the option to pay the cost of replacement, however, if that amount would be less than the actual cash value. As to covered personal property, the controlling standard is typically the least of the following: cost of repair, cost of replacement, or actual cash value.[9]

Many property insurance policies supplement the above provisions by obligating the insurer to pay the insured's reasonable costs of temporarily living elsewhere if the insured property was her residence and the damage to the residence made it uninhabitable pending completion of repairs or replacement. Comparable benefits may sometimes be provided in policies covering business property. Lost profits and similar consequential losses resulting from harm to or destruction of one's insured property, however, do not normally fall within the insurer's payment obligation unless a specific provision obligates the insurer along those lines.[10] Regardless of whether the damaged or destroyed property is real or personal in nature, the particular language of the policy at issue must always be consulted before a definite determination can be made concerning what is and is not within the insurer's duty to pay.

**Valued and Open Policies**   When insured real property is destroyed as a result of fire or another covered peril, the amount to be paid by the insurer may be further influenced by the type of policy involved. Some property insurance contracts are **valued policies.** If real property insured under a valued policy is destroyed, the insured is entitled to recover the face amount of the policy regardless of the property's fair market value. For example, in 1985, Douglas purchased a home with a fair market value of $90,000. Douglas also purchased a valued policy with a face amount of $90,000 to insure the house against various risks, including fire. The home's fair market value decreased over the next several years because of deterioration in the surrounding neighborhood. In 1994, when the home had a fair market value of only $75,000, it was destroyed by fire. Douglas is entitled to $90,000 (the face amount of the valued policy) despite the reduction in the home's fair market value.

Most property insurance policies, however, are open policies. Open policies allow the insured to recover the fair market value (actual cash value) of the property at the time it was destroyed, up to the limits stated in the policy. Thus, if Douglas had had an open policy in the example presented in the previous paragraph, he would have been entitled to only $75,000 when the home was destroyed by fire. Suppose instead that Douglas's home had increased in value, so that at the time of the fire its fair market value was $105,000. In that event, it would not matter what type of policy (valued or open) Douglas had. Under either type of policy, his recovery would be limited to the $90,000 face amount of the policy.

**Coinsurance Clause**   Some property insurance policies contain a **coinsurance clause**, which may operate as a further limit on the insurer's payment obligation and the insured's right to recovery. A coinsurance clause provides that in order for the insured to be able to recover the full cost of partial losses, the insured must obtain insurance on the property in an amount equal to a specified percentage (often 80 percent) of the property's fair market value.

[8]Some insurers, however, provide (in exchange for a more substantial premium than would be charged for a policy without this feature) a homeowner's policy under which the insurer could become obligated to pay *more* than the policy limits if the insured's home was destroyed and the cost to replace it would actually exceed the policy limits.

[9]Concerning certain designated items of personal property such as furs or jewelry, policies often set forth a maximum insurer payout (such as $1,000) that is less than the general policy limits applicable to personal property. Such a payout limitation would operate as a further restriction on the extent of the insurer's obligation.

[10]Recall, however, that if the insurer violates its payment obligation by wrongfully failing or refusing to pay what the policy contemplates, the insurer has committed a breach of contract. As noted in this chapter's earlier discussion of insurance policies as contracts, fundamental breach of contract principles dictate that the breaching insurer is potentially liable for consequential damages.

**FIGURE 2   Operation of Coinsurance Clause**

| Fair Market Value at Time of Loss | Face Value of Policy | Amount of Insurance Required | Actual Loss | Recovery |
|---|---|---|---|---|
| $100,000 | $60,000 | $80,000 | $ 40,000 | $30,000 |
| 100,000 | 60,000 | 80,000 | 100,000 | 60,000 |

For example, PDQ Corporation has a fire insurance policy on its warehouse with Cooperative Mutual Insurance Group. The policy has an 80 percent coinsurance clause. The warehouse had a fair market value of $100,000, meaning that PDQ was required to carry at least $80,000 of insurance on the building. PDQ, however, purchased a policy with a face amount of only $60,000. A fire partially destroyed the warehouse, causing $40,000 worth of damage to the structure. Because of the coinsurance clause, PDQ will recover only $30,000 from Cooperative. This figure was arrived at by taking the amount of insurance carried ($60,000) divided by the amount of insurance required ($80,000) times the loss ($40,000).

The coinsurance formula for recovery for partial losses is stated as follows:

$$\frac{\text{Amount of insurance carried}}{\text{Coinsurance percent} \times \text{Fair market value}} \times \text{Loss} = \text{Recovery}$$

Remember that the coinsurance formula applies only to *partial* losses (i.e., damage to, but not complete destruction of, property). If PDQ's warehouse had been totally destroyed by the fire, the formula would not have been used. PDQ would have recovered $60,000—the face amount of the policy—for the total loss. If the formula had been used, it would have indicated that Cooperative owed PDQ $75,000—more than the face amount of the policy. This result would be neither logical nor in keeping with the parties' insurance contract. Whether the loss is total or partial, the insured is not entitled to recover more than the face amount of the policy. The examples just discussed are depicted in Figure 2.

**Pro Rata Clause**   With the limited exception of the valued policy (discussed above), the insured

cannot recover more than the amount of the actual loss. A rule allowing the insured to recover more than the actual loss could encourage unscrupulous persons to purchase policies from more than one insurer on the same property (thus substantially overinsuring it) and then intentionally destroy the property in a way that appears to be a covered peril (e.g., committing arson but making the fire look accidental). In order to make certain that the insured does not obtain a recovery that exceeds the actual loss, property insurance policies commonly contain a *pro rata clause*, which applies when the insured has purchased insurance policies from more than one insurer. The effect of the pro rata clause is to apportion the loss among the insurance companies. (Applicable state law sometimes contains a rule having this same effect.)

Under the pro rata clause, the amount any particular insurer must pay the insured depends on the percentage of total insurance coverage represented by that insurer's policy. For example, Mumford purchases two insurance policies to cover his home against fire and other risks. His policy from Security Mutual Insurance Corp. has a face amount of $50,000; his policy from Reliable Insurance Co. is for $100,000. Mumford's home is partially destroyed by an accidental fire, with a resulting loss of $30,000. As illustrated in Figure 3, Security Mutual must pay Mumford $10,000, with Reliable having to pay the remaining $20,000 of the loss.

The formula for determining each insurer's liability under a pro rata clause is stated as follows:

$$\frac{\text{Amount of insurer's policy}}{\text{Total coverage by all insurers}} \times \text{Loss} = \text{Liability of insurer}$$

Thus, Security Mutual's payment amount was calculated as follows:

---

**FIGURE 3    Operation of Pro Rata Clause**

| Policy A | Policy B | Total Insurance (Policy A plus Policy B) | Actual Loss | Liability of Insurer A | Liability of Insurer B |
|---|---|---|---|---|---|
| $50,000 | $100,000 | $150,000 | $30,000 | $10,000 | $20,000 |

---

$$\frac{\$50{,}000 \ (\text{Security Mutual's policy})}{\$150{,}000 \ (\text{Total of both policies})} \times \$30{,}000 \ (\text{Loss}) = \$10{,}000$$

Reliable's payment amount could be similarly calculated by substituting $100,000 (Reliable's policy amount) for the $50,000 (Security Mutual's policy amount) in the numerator of the equation. This formula may be used for both partial and total losses. However, each company's payment obligation is limited by the face amount of its policy. Thus, Security Mutual could never be liable for more than $50,000. Similarly, Reliable's liability is limited to a maximum of $100,000.

## Right of Subrogation

The insurer may be able in some instances to exercise a **right of subrogation** if it is required to pay for a loss under a property insurance contract. Under the right of subrogation, the insurer obtains all of the insured's rights to pursue legal remedies against anyone who negligently or intentionally caused the harm to the property. For example, Arnett purchased a property insurance policy on her home from Benevolent Insurance Company. Arnett's home was completely destroyed by a fire that spread to her property when her neighbor, Clifton, was burning leaves and negligently failed to control the fire. After Benevolent pays Arnett for her loss, Benevolent's right of subrogation entitles it to sue Clifton to recover the amount Benevolent paid Arnett. Arnett will be obligated to cooperate with Benevolent and furnish assistance to it in connection with the subrogation claim.

If the insured provides the liable third party a general release from liability, the insurer will be released from his payment obligation to the insured. Suppose that in the above scenario, Clifton per-suaded Arnett to sign an agreement releasing him from liability for the fire. Because this action by Arnett would interfere with Benevolent's right of subrogation, Benevolent would not have to pay Arnett for the loss. A partial release of Clifton by Arnett would relieve Benevolent of responsibility to Arnett to the extent of her release.

## Duration and Cancellation of Policy

Property insurance policies are usually effective for a designated period such as six months or a year. They are then extended for consecutive periods of like duration if the insured continues to pay the necessary premium and neither the insured nor the insurer elects to cancel the policy. The insured is normally entitled to cancel the policy at any time by providing the insurer written notice to that effect or by surrendering the policy to the insurer. Although property insurers usually have some right to cancel policies, terms of the policies themselves and/or governing law typically limit the grounds on which property insurers may do so. Permitted grounds for cancellation include the insured's nonpayment of the premium and, as a general rule, the insured's misrepresentation or fraud (see this chapter's discussion of contract law's applicability to insurance policies). Policy provisions and/or applicable law typically provide that if the property insurer intends to cancel the policy, the insured must be given meaningful advance written notice (often 30 days) of this intent before cancellation takes effect.

Another cancellation basis exists by virtue of the **increase of hazard** clauses that appear in many property insurance policies. An increase of hazard clause provides that the insurer's liability will be terminated if the insured takes any action materially increasing the insurer's risk. Some increase of hazard provisions also specify certain types of behavior that will cause termination. Common examples of such behavior include keeping highly explosive material on the property and allowing the premises to remain vacant for a lengthy period of time. *Good v. Continental Insurance Company*, which follows, illustrates the operation of an increase of hazard clause.

---

## GOOD V. CONTINENTAL INSURANCE COMPANY
### 291 S.E.2d 198 (S.C. Sup. Ct. 1982)

Sims and Dorothy Good purchased a standard fire insurance policy on their home from Continental Insurance Company. The policy contained an "increase of hazard" clause stating that the insurer would not be liable if the risk of fire was increased "by any means within the control or knowledge of the insured." A November 1977 fire almost completely destroyed the house. While putting out the fire, firefighters discovered an illegal liquor still concealed in a false closet under the eaves of the roof. The still, encased by bricks and mortar, consisted of a 90-gallon copper vat over an 8- to 10-inch butane gas burner. Firefighters also discovered 22 half-gallons of "moonshine" and many 55-gallon drums full or partially full of mash. A police department detective who dismantled and examined the still's burner after the fire offered the opinion that the still was in operation when the fire occurred. Good denied this, though he admitted installing the still two years earlier—after his insurance policy became effective. Continental refused to pay for the destruction on the ground that the still was an increased hazard.

The Goods sued Continental to recover proceeds under the policy. When the trial court awarded damages to the Goods, Continental appealed.

---

**Harwell, Justice**    In [previous cases], this court held that coverage under an insurance policy was suspended if the increased risk was permanent and continuous even though it did not produce the loss. However, if the increased risk caused the loss, an occasional, temporary increase of risk was sufficient to void a policy.

In addition to these guidelines, to void the policy the increase of hazard must be material and substantial such that the insurer could not reasonably be presumed to have contracted to assume it. Also, according to the policy, increased hazard must be accomplished by means solely within the control and knowledge of Good after the insurance contract was effected.

The evidence leads unmistakably to the following: the distillery was permanently installed; it was regularly used at least during the holiday season; Good installed the still after the insurance policy became effective; and only he operated the still. We conclude that the only reasonable inference from the evidence is that there had been an increase of hazard, thereby voiding the policy.

The use to which the Goods put their dwelling was so foreign to the normal uses of a dwelling as to become beyond the contemplation of the insurer. Surely the insurer did not contemplate providing insurance coverage on a residence which concealed an illegal still and the fruits of its operation.

**Judgment reversed in favor of Continental.**

---

## LIABILITY INSURANCE

As its name suggests, liability insurance provides the insured the ability to transfer liability risks to the insurer. Under policies of liability insurance, the insurer agrees, among other things, to pay sums the insured becomes legally obligated to pay to another party. This enables the insured to minimize the troublesome or even devastating financial effects that he could experience in the event of his liability to someone else.

## Types of Liability Insurance Policies

Liability insurance policies come in various types. These include, but are not limited to: **personal liability policies** designed to cover a range of liabilities an individual person could face; **business liability policies** (sometimes called *comprehensive general liability policies*) meant to apply to various liabilities that sole proprietors, partnerships, and corporations might encounter in their business operations; **professional liability policies** (sometimes called *malpractice insurance policies*) that cover physicians, attorneys, accountants, and members of other professions against liabilities to clients and sometimes other persons; and **workers' compensation policies** under which insurers agree to cover employers' statutorily required obligation to pay benefits to injured workers.

Some policies combine property insurance features with liability insurance components. Automobile insurance policies, for instance, afford property insurance when they cover designated automobiles owned by the insured against perils such as vandalism, hail, and collisions with animals, telephone poles, and the like. Other sections of automobile insurance policies provide liability insurance to the insured (the policy owner), members of her household, and sometimes other authorized drivers when their use of a covered automobile leads to an accident in which they face liability to another party. Typical homeowners' policies also combine property and liability insurance features. Besides covering the insured's home and contents against perils of the types discussed earlier in this chapter, these policies normally provide the insured coverage for a range of liabilities he may face as an individual.

## Liabilities Insured Against

Although the different types of liability insurance policies discussed above contain different terms setting forth the liabilities covered and not covered, liability policies commonly afford coverage against the insured's liability for negligence but not against the insured's liability stemming from deliberate wrongful acts (most intentional torts and most be-

havior constituting a crime).[11] Liability policies tend to reach this common ground in the same sorts of ways property insurance policies define the scope of coverage—by listing particular liabilities that are covered and stating that an unlisted liability is not covered, by setting forth a seemingly broad statement of coverage and then specifying exclusions from coverage, or by employing a combination of the previous approaches (e.g., specifying certain covered liabilities and certain excluded liabilities).

### Personal Liability and Homeowners' Policies

Personal liability policies and the liability sections of homeowners' policies often state that coverage is restricted to instances of "bodily injury" and "property damage" experienced by a third party as a result of an "occurrence" for which the insured faces liability. These sorts of policies normally define *occurrence* as an "accident" resulting in bodily injury or property damage. The provisions just noted lead to the conclusion that intentional torts and most criminal behavior, if committed or engaged in by the insured, would fall outside the coverage of the policy at issue because they are not accidents (whereas instances of the insured's negligence would be). This conclusion is underscored by typical clauses purporting to exclude coverage for bodily injury or property damage the insured intended to cause. The occurrence, bodily injury, and property damage references in these policies also indicate that liabilities stemming from, for example, breach of contract would not be covered either (no accident, no bodily injury, no property damage). In addition, personal liability policies and liability sections of homeowners' policies also tend to specify that if bodily injury or property damage results from the insured's business or professional pursuits, it is not covered.

**Business Liability Policies**   Business liability policies also feature coverage for bodily injury and property damage stemming from the insured's actions. The relevant range of actions, of course, is broadened to include the insured's business pursuits or "conduct of business." A major focus remains on unintentional wrongful conduct (usually negligence)

---
[11]Workers' compensation liability policies are somewhat different, as later discussion in this chapter will reveal.

of the insured, with the insured's deliberate wrongful acts normally being specifically excluded from coverage. These policies also tend to provide the insured coverage in instances where the insured would be liable for certain torts of his employees (normally under the *respondeat superior* doctrine).[12]

In addition, business liability policies sometimes afford coverage broader than instances of tortious conduct producing physical injury or property damage. Some policies, for instance, contain a clause that contemplates coverage for the insured's defa-

---

[28]The *respondeat superior* doctrine is discussed in Chapter 28. Although the insured's own intentional torts would not normally be covered, business liability policies sometimes provide that if the insured is liable on *respondeat superior* grounds for an employee's intentional tort such as battery, the insured will be covered unless the insured directed the employee to commit the intentional tort.

mation of another person or invasion of that person's privacy (though other policies specifically exclude coverage for those same torts). Furthermore, the broad "conduct of business" language in certain policies, as well as specialized clauses (in some policies) referring to liability stemming from advertising or unfair competition, may contemplate coverage for the insured's legal wrongs that cause others to experience economic harm. In the end, the particular liabilities covered by a business liability policy cannot be determined without a close examination of the provisions in the policy at issue. It may become necessary for a court to interpret a policy provision whose meaning is unclear or scope is uncertain. In the *Cope* case, which follows, the court addressed the scope of a conduct of business clause through the use of contract interpretation techniques introduced earlier in this chapter.

---

## PROPERTY OWNERS INSURANCE CO. v. COPE
### 772 F. Supp. 1096 (N.D. Ind. 1991)

Property Owners Insurance Co. (POI) was the insurer and Thomas Cope was the insured under a liability policy that excluded coverage except in instances of liability "with respect to the conduct of a business" owned by Cope. Cope owned a roofing business. While the policy was in force, Cope traveled to Montana with Edward Urbanski, a person with whom Cope did significant business. While on this trip, Cope snowmobiled with a group of persons that included Gregory Johnson, who died in a snowmobiling accident. Johnson's estate brought a wrongful death suit against Cope in a Montana court. POI then filed a declaratory judgment action against Cope and Johnson's estate in the U.S. District Court for the Northern District of Indiana. In this suit, POI sought a judicial determination that it had no obligations to Cope and Johnson's estate under the liability insurance policy. The parties agreed that Indiana law would control the case, which came before the court on POI's motion for summary judgment.

---

**Moody, District Judge**    POI maintains that the Montana snowmobiling trip was a recreational event rather than "the conduct of a business" owned by Cope. Thus, argues POI, the Montana trip was not covered by the insurance contract. Cope, however, maintains that he intended the Montana trip to advance both business and pleasure, thus bringing it under the policy.

The parties have not briefed, nor has the court found, any Indiana law interpreting the words "conduct of a business" in the context of an exclusion in a contract to provide liability insurance to a business owner. The closest reported case is apparently *Uni-*

*gard Mutual Insurance Co. v. Martin* (1982), [an Arizona Court of Appeals case] cited by POI. The evidence before the *Martin* court showed that the object of a large annual fishing trip was both recreation and the advancement of business. The *Martin* court . . . focused on the express terms of the [liability] insurance contract. [Noting that the fishing trip was heavily recreational but only incidentally business-connected, and stressing the policy's exclusion for "personal" activities that were not in "direct conduct of a business," the *Martin* court held that the policy at issue did not afford coverage.]

Applying *Martin* to this case, the court readily distinguishes the Arizona precedent on its facts. The *Martin* court relied heavily on [the] particular wording [of the policy involved there] in making its most important analytical point—namely, that the insurance contract was not ambiguous, but plainly excluded the fishing trip by its express terms. The *Martin* court focused especially on the words "direct conduct" in the exclusion before it, defining each word at length, and with particular emphasis on the word "direct." In the case at bar, the contract language is different, the limitation on coverage arising by negative implication from the words "only with respect to the conduct of a business." The word "direct" does not modify "conduct" in this case, nor does the contract expressly contrast personal and business activities. Accordingly, the *Martin* case does not present a perfect template for dealing with this action.

Whether or not the *Martin* court properly read the contract before it as unambiguous, the policy issue before this court is not resolved by the familiar Indiana rule that where an insurance contract is clear and unambiguous, the language therein must be given its plain meaning. [T]his court holds that the words "with respect to the conduct of a business" are, in this context, not sufficiently self-defining in their plain meaning. Rather, those words are ambiguous and require construction because reasonable persons might well differ on the question of whether they exclude coverage for activities furthering dual purposes of recreation and profit.

[U]nder settled principles for the interpretation of ambiguous insurance contracts . . . , this court construes the policy in favor of the insured. Thus, the court holds that the language of the contract before it does not exclude, as a matter of law, coverage for activities that serve dual purposes of recreation and profit. If insurance companies operating in Indiana desire the benefit of such an exclusion, it is a simple enough matter for them to draft their policies to unambiguously exclude coverage for recreational activities furthering business objectives.

In this case, the record on summary judgment reveals a genuine dispute over the factual nature of the Montana snowmobiling trip. This dispute is certainly material, for the factual nature of the trip will, under the express terms of the contract at issue, determine the applicability of the policy's limit on liability. It remains, however, for the court to further explore the materiality of that dispute by detailing the applicable legal standard for assessing the facts. The *Martin* court, in this regard, paints an alarming picture of insurer liability leaping up in extreme situations, perhaps even with chance meetings at Little League games. On the other hand, if hypotheticals are brought to bear, this court can readily imagine a far different situation at the other extreme, one in which a business executive who enjoys his solitude, loathes the boors to whom he must sell his product, and hopes to retire at the earliest possible moment, must nevertheless occasionally invite customers to cocktails or sporting events for the purely fictional purpose of having fun. The *Martin* court, apparently concerned with the dubious horrors of the slippery slope, seems inclined to create a bright line rule denying coverage in both situations. Given the ambiguity in the contract at issue here, however, this court is prepared to seek out a test in the law capable of discriminating among situations of mixed profit and recreation motives.

Cope advances the workmen's compensation test applied in Indiana law for many years: [whether] the activity at issue was "required by or incidental to" the insured's business. The *Martin* court rejected this type of test because the liberal coverage policy motivating workmen's compensation statutes is not at play in a private insurance contract. In this case, however, the contract is ambiguous, which brings to bear Indiana's policy of construing insurance exclusions against insurers. Thus, a significant policy of Indiana insurance law—already employed in construing the contract to cover mixed motive activities—parallels the expansive coverage policy motivating workmen's compensation, and justifies application of the same test. Accordingly, this court holds that the test for coverage under the "conduct of a business" policy at issue is whether Cope's Montana snowmobiling trip was necessary or incidental to the pursuit of profit through his business.

Of course, nothing in this opinion should be read as establishing that the Montana snowmobiling trip was sufficiently related to the insured's business to support a jury verdict of liability under the policy. Rather, this opinion merely establishes Cope's right to present evidence against exclusion at trial.

**POI's motion for summary judgment denied.**

**Other Liability Policies**   Professional liability policies also afford coverage for the insured's tortious conduct, this time in the practice of his or her profession. Negligent professional conduct producing harm to a third party (normally bodily injury in the medical malpractice setting but usually economic harm in the legal or other professional malpractice context) would be a covered liability. Wrongful professional conduct of an intentional nature typically would not be covered.

Automobile liability policies cover liability for physical injury and property damage stemming from the insured's (and certain other drivers') negligent driving. Once again, however, there is no coverage for liability arising from the insured's (or another driver's) deliberate vehicle operation acts of a wrongful nature.

Workers' compensation policies tend to approach coverage questions somewhat differently, primarily because injured employees need not prove negligence on the part of their employer in order to be entitled to benefits. Therefore, the insurer's obligation under a workers' compensation policy is phrased in terms of the liability the insured employer would face under state law.

## Insurer's Obligations

**Duty to Defend**   When another party makes a legal claim against the insured and the nature and allegations of the claim are such that the insurer would be obligated to cover the insured's liability if the claim were proven, the insurer has a **duty to defend** the insured. A commonsense precondition of this duty's being triggered is that the insured must notify the insurer that the claim has been made against her. The duty to defend means that the insurer must furnish, at its expense, an attorney to represent the insured in litigation resulting from the claim against her. If the insurer fails to perform its duty to defend in an instance where the duty arose, the insurer has breached the insurance contract. Depending on the facts, the breaching insurer would at least be liable for compensatory damages (as indicated in this chapter's earlier discussion of insurance policies as contracts)[13] and potentially for punitive damages as well under the *bad faith* doctrine examined later in this chapter.

---

[13]The compensatory damages in such an instance would normally be the reasonable costs incurred by the insured in retaining an attorney and paying him to represent her. Of course, if the insured ended up being held liable in the third party's suit and the insurer wrongfully refused to pay the damages assessed against the insured in that case, the insured's compensatory damages claim against the breaching insurer would be increased substantially.

Sometimes it is quite clear that the insurer's duty to defend applies or does not apply, given the nature of the claim made against the insured. Other times, however, there may be uncertainty as to whether the claim alleged against the insured would fall within the scope of the liability insurance policy. Such uncertainty, of course, means that it is not clear whether the insurer has a duty to defend. Insurers tend to take one of two approaches in an effort to resolve this uncertainty. Under the first approach, the insurer files a declaratory judgment suit against the insured. In this suit, the insurer asks the court to determine whether the insurer owes obligations to the insured under the policy (including the duty to defend as well as the payment obligation to be discussed shortly) in connection with the particular liability claim made against the insured by the injured third party. The other option insurers often pursue when it is unclear whether the liability policy applies is to retain an attorney to represent the insured in the litigation filed by the third party—thus fulfilling any duty to defend that may be owed—but to do so under a *reservation of rights* notice. By providing the reservation of rights notice to the insured, the insurer indicates that it reserves the right, upon acquisition of additional information, to conclude (or seek a later judicial determination) that it does not have the obligation to pay any damages that may be assessed against the insured as a result of the third party's claim. The insurer's reservation of rights also serves to eliminate an argument that by proceeding to defend the insured, the insurer waived the ability to argue that any actual liability would not be covered.

**Duty to Pay Sums Owed by Insured**   If a third party's claim against the insured falls within the liabilities covered by the policy, the insurer is obligated to pay the compensatory damages held by a judge or jury to be due and owing from the insured to the third party. In addition, the insured's obligation to pay such expenses as court costs would also be covered. These payment obligations are subject, of course, to the policy limits of the insurance contract involved. For example, if the insured is held liable for compensatory damages and court costs totaling $150,000 but the policy limits of the relevant liability policy are $100,000, the insurer's contractual obligation to pay sums owed by the insured is restricted to $100,000.

Is the insurer also obligated to pay any *punitive damages* assessed against the insured as a result of a covered claim? As a general rule, the insurer will have no such obligation, either because of an insurance contract provision to that effect or because of judicial decisions holding that notions of public policy forbid arrangements by which one could transfer his punitive damages liability to an insurer. Not all courts facing this issue have so held, however, meaning that in occasional instances the insured's punitive damages liability may also be covered if the insurance policy's terms specifically contemplate such a result.

The liability insurer need not wait until litigation has been concluded (and damages are awarded or not awarded) to attempt to dispose of a liability claim made against the insured. Insurance policy provisions, consistent with our legal system's tendency to encourage voluntary settlements of claims, allow insurers to negotiate settlements with third parties who have made liability claims against the insured. These settlements involve payment of an agreed sum of money to the third party, in exchange for the third party's giving up her legal right to proceed with litigation against the insured. Settlements may occur regardless of whether litigation has been formally instituted by the third party or whether the claim against the insured consists of the third party's prelitigation demand for payment by the insured. If settlements are reached—and they are reached much more often than not—the substantial costs involved in taking a case all the way to trial may be avoided. The same is also true, from the insurer's perspective, of the damages that might have been assessed against the insured if the case had been tried. Note, however, that even if the defendant (the insured) wins a suit that does proceed to trial, the costs to the insurer are still substantial even though there is no award of damages to pay. Those costs include a considerable amount for attorney's fees for the insured (the insurer's obligation regardless of the outcome of the case) as well as other substantial expenses associated with protracted litigation. Accordingly, even when the insurer thinks that the insured probably would prevail if the case went to trial, the insurer may be interested in pursuing a settlement with the third party claimant if a reasonable amount (an amount less than what it would cost the insurer to defend the case) can be agreed upon.

## Is There a Liability Insurance Crisis?

During roughly the past decade, the necessary premiums for liability insurance policies of various types (particularly business and professional liability policies) have risen considerably. Sometimes, the premiums charged by liability insurers have become so sub-

stantial that would-be insureds have concluded that they cannot afford liability insurance and therefore must go without it despite its importance. In addition, some insurers have ceased offering certain types of liability policies and/or have become much more restrictive in their decisions about which persons or firms to insure.

Insurance companies tend to blame the above state of affairs on what they see as a tort law regime under which plaintiffs win lawsuits too frequently and recover very large damage awards too often. As a result, insurers have been among the most outspoken parties calling for tort reform, a subject discussed earlier in this book. Plaintiffs' attorneys and critics of the insurance industry blame rising liability insurance premiums on, primarily, another alleged cause: questionable investment practices and other unsound business practices supposedly engaged in by insurance companies. The parties making these assertions thus oppose tort reform efforts as being unnecessary and unwise.

Liability insurance premiums in general may not be increasing as rapidly today as they did a few years ago, but they remain substantial in amount. So long as liability insurance remains unaffordable or otherwise difficult to obtain, there is a "crisis," given the adverse financial consequences that could beset an uninsured person. This is so regardless of which of the competing explanations set forth above bears greater legitimacy.

## LIFE INSURANCE

Life insurance provides a means of lessening the financial hardships that result from the death of a given person. A few basic life insurance concepts were alluded to in this chapter's section on insurance policies as contracts. This section builds on the earlier discussion by examining specialized legal topics and issues that arise in connection with life insurance.

### Parties Other than Insurer

Earlier in the chapter, we noted that in the property and liability insurance contexts, the same person will often be the insured (the purchaser of the insurance), the policy owner (the party entitled to enforce the contract rights set forth in the policy), and the beneficiary (the party entitled to payment under the policy). Life insurance, however, departs from this typical property and liability insurance model. In the life insurance setting, the insured is *the person whose life is insured* under the policy. That person may or may not have been the purchaser of the policy. Although the insured may also be the party entitled to enforce the policy's contract rights (the policy owner), it is not unusual for the policy owner to be someone other than the insured. The policy owner is typically the party who purchased the policy, but this is not always true.

Life insurance also departs from the property and liability model with regard to the identity of the beneficiary (the person entitled to payment when the insured dies). The beneficiary, who is designated by the policy owner, will often be one or more family members or friends of the insured, or sometimes business partners of the insured. Of course, the policy owner may double as the designated beneficiary. It is also possible that the insured's estate could be specified as the beneficiary instead of a particular individual (or individuals) being so designated. Life insurance policies often allow the policy owner to change the designated beneficiary prior to the insured's death. Some policies, however, contain terms under which the designation of a beneficiary is irrevocable, meaning that a different beneficiary cannot be substituted for the one already specified.

## Insurable Interest

As discussed earlier in this chapter, an insurable interest is required in order to keep an insurance contract from being an illegal wagering contract. In the life insurance context, the requisite insurable interest *must exist at the time the policy was issued* but need not exist at the time of the insured's death. Persons who stand to suffer a financial loss in the event of the insured's death have the insurable interest necessary to support the purchase of a life insurance policy on the insured. The insured and his or her spouse, parents, children, and other dependents thus possess an insurable interest in the insured's life.

In addition, the business associates of the insured may also have an insurable interest in his or her life. Such persons would include the insured's employer, business partners, or shareholders in a closely held corporation with which the insured is connected. Creditors of the insured also have an insurable interest, but only to the extent of the debt owed by the insured.

## Types of Life Insurance Policies

A life insurance contract is a valued policy because, upon the insured's death, the insurer must pay the beneficiary a set amount that equals the **face value** of the policy (the amount of insurance coverage purchased). The policy's face value helps determine the amount of the premiums that must be paid to keep the policy in force. A policy with a large face value will, of course, cost the purchaser of the policy more in premiums than will a policy with a smaller face value.

Two basic types of life insurance, **whole life policies** and **term policies,** merit discussion. Although both types are valued policies, they differ in important respects.

**Whole Life Policies**   *Whole life policies—* sometimes called *ordinary life* or *straight life* policies—contemplate that the insured (or the owner, if a person other than the insured) will pay a set premium for the remainder of his life or until a specified time when the obligation to pay further premiums will cease. The whole life policy does more than impose on the insurer the obligation to pay the policy's face value upon the insured's death. Such a policy possesses a savings feature, in that it develops a **cash surrender value** as premiums are paid. The insured policy owner may recover this value if the policy is terminated. In addition, whole life policies develop a loan value as premiums are paid. This sometimes enables the policy owner to borrow money from the insurer at favorable interest rates. Because of the investment feature and the potential for borrowing present in whole life policies, premiums that the policy owner must pay for such policies usually tend to be higher than the premiums required for term insurance—at least when the insured is in his 30s and perhaps his 40s.

**Term Policies**   *Term policies* are so named because they are designed to be in effect for a designated term or duration, such as one year. These policies provide insurance coverage only, without the cash surrender value and loan value features present in whole life insurance. In return for the payment of premiums during the term of the policy, the insurer agrees to pay the face amount of the policy if the insured dies during the term.

For many persons, having a suitable amount of insurance coverage in the event of the insured's death may be much more important than an added investment feature or the prospect of borrowing funds in the future. Term policies may be an economical way of obtaining coverage, because premiums for a term policy of a given face value often start lower than for a whole life policy of the same face value. This tends to be true if the term policy is purchased while the insured is in her 30s or early 40s. Although term policies are typically written for a one-year period, they frequently have a *guaranteed renewability* provision. This provision enables the insured (or the owner, if insured and owner are not one and the same) to renew the policy for successive additional terms up to a specified age, without having to undergo medical examinations designed to show that the insured is still in good health. Those desiring insurance coverage may thus keep the term policy in force.

In keeping a term policy in force year after year, however, they face the downside of term policies—annual premium increases. As the insured gets another year older, the premium necessary to keep the term policy in force rises. Although term insurance premiums typically begin lower than whole life premiums, term insurance premiums eventually will equal or exceed those for a whole life policy of the same face value. Therefore, owners of term policies may eventually face the need to decide whether to convert their term policies to whole life policies and thereby avoid the ever-increasing term premiums (plus acquire the added benefits of whole life policies). Term policies often contain a *guaranteed conversion option,* under which the insured may choose to convert the term policy to a whole life policy.

## Other Special Issues and Policy Provisions

**Misrepresentation Issues**    As explained earlier in this chapter, an insurance applicant's misrepresentations concerning material matters may cause a resulting insurance contract to become voidable at the option of the insurer. In the life insurance setting, misrepresentations regarding the proposed insured's health condition become the focus of considerable attention. Whether the insurer is able to avoid its policy obligations on the basis of the insurance applicant's health-related misstatements or failures to disclose will depend on the seriousness of the matter misstated or not disclosed by the applicant, and on the degree to which knowledge of the truth would have influenced the insurer's decision on whether to issue a policy. If the insurer

would not have issued the policy had it known the truth, the insurer is likely to be allowed to avoid its policy obligation.

**Misstatement of Age Clauses**    Two common provisions in life insurance policies help to offset the potentially harsh effect that might otherwise result from certain false representations by the insurance applicant. These provisions are *misstatement of age clauses* and *incontestability clauses.* Under a misstatement of age clause, the insurer is allowed to reduce the amount it must pay upon the insured's death if the insured's age listed in the application for insurance was lower than the insured's actual age at that time. The amount of the insurer's payment obligation will be lowered to reflect the amount of coverage that the premiums paid would have bought at the correct age's premium rates.

For example, having stated his age as 39, Wingfield purchases a $100,000 face-value policy on himself from Invincible Insurance Co. When Wingfield dies, Invincible learns he was actually 43 when he took out the policy. Because the premium rate for a 43-year-old would have been higher, the total amount of premiums actually paid by Wingfield would have purchased only $85,000 in coverage at the correct premium rate. Therefore, under the misstatement of age clause, Invincible would be obligated to pay Wingfield's beneficiary $85,000 rather than $100,000.

**Incontestability Clauses**    Under the incontestability clauses commonly seen in life insurance policies, insurers are barred from contesting their liability under the policy on the basis of certain misrepresentations by the insured if the policy has been in force for a specified period of time (frequently, two years). Incontestability clauses do not, however, prevent the insurer from contesting liability on the grounds that the requisite insurable interest was lacking, that an impostor filled in for the insured at the required medical exam, or that the policy purchaser took out the policy with the intent to kill the insured and collect the policy proceeds.

**Special Cancellation and Lapse Issues**    Insurers generally cannot cancel life insurance contracts as long as the necessary premiums are being paid. A contrary rule could tempt insurers to terminate policies covering seriously ill insureds and would thus poorly serve insureds, policy owners, and beneficiaries.

The policy owner may cancel a life insurance policy by surrendering it to the insurer. If the policy is a whole life policy, the owner is usually allowed under the policy provisions to recover the accumulated cash surrender value or to purchase a paid-up or extended policy. Under a paid-up policy, the owner acquires a fully paid-for policy on the insured. The policy's face value is the amount of coverage that the cash surrender value would purchase, in light of the insured's age. An extended policy is a term policy having the same face value as the original policy that was surrendered.

*Lapse* of a term insurance policy occurs upon the expiration of the stated duration, unless the policy is renewed. Any life insurance policy, whether term or whole life, lapses if the necessary premiums are not paid. When a whole life policy lapses due to nonpayment of premiums, the owner normally has the same rights to cash surrender value and a paid-up or extended policy as are made available to the owner who surrenders a whole life policy. The owner whose term insurance lapses because of nonpayment of premiums, however, has no such remedies.

In order to guard against the potentially harsh consequences stemming from lapsed life insurance policies (particularly lapsed term policies), many states have enacted statutes allowing policy owners a grace period within which they may pay past-due premiums and thereby avoid policy lapse or cancellation. A typical statutory grace period is 30 days. Life insurance policies themselves sometimes contain similarly motivated provisions, under which the owner whose life insurance policy has lapsed is given a limited time within which to pay past-due premiums and furnish proof of insurability (the insured's good health). By doing these things within the specified time, the owner obtains reinstatement of the policy.

# HEALTH INSURANCE

With the costs of medical treatment, hospitalization, and medications having increased dramatically in recent years, health insurance has become a critical means by which insureds minimize the adverse financial consequences associated with illness and injury. The costs of serious illness or injury may be financially crippling unless insurance coverage exists.[14] Health insurance has thus become a virtual necessity in today's society, as demonstrated by the fact that a very large percentage of the U.S. population does have some form of health coverage.

## Nature of Coverage

Health insurance policies typically provide coverage for medical expenses resulting from a broad range of illnesses and injuries experienced by the insured (or by the insured's family member, if family coverage was procured by the insured). In setting forth the illnesses or injuries covered under the policy, health insurers take approaches similar to the previously discussed methods used by property insurers when they stake out the scope of those policies' coverage. This means that health insurance policies tend to specify an exclusive list of covered illnesses and injuries, set forth a broad general statement of coverage but then specify certain excluded causes, or combine the two approaches by specifying certain covered illnesses and injuries and designating other causes as excluded.

Whichever approach is used, most illnesses and injuries tend to be covered in some fashion. The resulting expenses that stem from medically necessary treatment then become subject to the terms of the insurer's payment obligation, as discussed below. Excluded causes often include preexisting health conditions—the insured's (or family member's) illnesses or injuries that befell the insured (or family member) before the effective date of the policy.

## Insurer's Payment Obligation

As a general rule, health insurance policies require the insured to pay up to a certain amount in medical expenses per year before the insurer's payment obligation is triggered. This amount is known as the **deductible**. The specific amount varies from policy to policy. Once the insured has met his or her deductible, the insurer becomes obligated to pay all

---

[14]Disability insurance, under which insureds obtain coverage against loss of income resulting from long-term disabilities that interfere with one's ability to perform one's job, addresses the same sorts of financial concerns. Disability insurance will not be discussed further in this chapter.

or part of the insured's medically necessary expenses that result from a covered illness or injury. If the policy establishes a payment obligation that is a percentage of the medical expenses, 80 percent is fairly typical, though once again this differs from policy to policy. When the health insurer makes payment, it may either pay the insured if the insured has already paid the medical bill or pay the health care provider directly if the insured has not yet paid the bill.

Increasingly, policies tie the insurer's payment obligation to what the insurer establishes as the usual and customary cost of a particular medical procedure or treatment. If the health care provider's charge for a particular procedure or treatment exceeds this usual and customary cost, the excess is not covered. The insurer's payment obligation is then to pay all or the specified percentage (depending on the policy's provisions) of the usual and customary cost.

Health policies tend to make special provisions for covered conditions requiring long-term medical care or hospitalization. These special provisions establish somewhat different payment obligations for the insurer. Often, these provisions specify that the insurer will pay a designated percentage of hospital expenses up to a certain amount, and then all of the hospital expenses once that amount has been reached. The exact percentages and amounts in a given situation are determined by checking the terms of the particular policy at issue.

Special provisions defining the extent of the insurer's obligation to pay for prescription medication costs are not uncommon. In addition, health policies sometimes contain specifications of maximum dollar amounts that the insurer will pay for certain surgical procedures or other medical treatments. Often, policy provisions state that there is no payment obligation regarding experimental medical treatments (treatments that are not yet classifiable as generally accepted medical treatments).

## Group Policies

Most persons' health insurance coverage comes through group policies, under which an employer or an organization contracts with a health insurer for coverage to be made available to employees of that employer or members of that organization. From the perspective of insured employees or insured members of organizations, the chief advantage of group

policies is that the necessary premiums are significantly lower than the premiums one would have to pay in order to obtain a nongroup policy. The cessation of one's employee or group membership status may lead to a loss of her group insurance benefits and therefore significantly higher costs to her if she is forced to seek nongroup coverage. Sometimes these added costs will simply be prohibitively high. Other times, the typical policy exclusion for preexisting conditions will prove to be a problem when the insured must seek new health insurance coverage because she has lost her group insurance. Congress has attempted to deal with these sorts of problems by establishing limited rights to continued coverage in certain instances where the insured's employee status or organization membership has ended. Nevertheless, the problems persist.

## The Health Insurance Debate

Although most U.S. residents have health insurance coverage of some sort, millions do not. Access to affordable coverage has become a major concern in today's society. There has been ongoing debate in the federal and state political arenas concerning how to control spiraling health care costs and increase access to affordable health insurance. As this book went to press, differing proposals for potentially sweeping federal legislation governing health insurance availability and coverage were being proposed and considered in Congress. These competing proprosals advocated different approaches on such issues as whether there should be "universal" coverage (for all U.S. residents), whether employers should be required to make health insurance available to their employees, and whether large health insurance purchasing cooperatives should be instituted as a means of attempting to reduce premium costs. Another area of disagreement was the extent to which membership in health maintenance organizations (HMOs) should be encouraged by any federal legislation overhauling the health insurance business. HMOs offer insurance plans under which member patients are treated by HMO-affiliated physicians under arrangements designed to control medical costs and presumably lessen the premiums or fees that HMO members must pay for health care coverage.

Still other debated issues, as of the time this book went to press, included whether Medicare and Medicaid should also be overhauled as part of health care and health insurance reform, and if so, to what extent. Medicare is a government program under which many, but not all, of senior citizens' medical expenses are covered. Medicaid, another government program, handles medical expenses of low-income persons. Some of the proposals for health insurance reform also sought to address insurance access problems stemming from the loss of group insurance and the existence of preexisting health conditions. In addition, the competing proposals addressed whether (and the extent to which) alterations in the law of medical malpractice would be a useful aid in controlling the increases in health care costs and increases in insurance premiums.

As the above discussion suggests, any attempt at legislative reformation of health insurance as we know it is a significant undertaking that necessitates addressing many interrelated issues. If congressionally mandated changes—or even self-imposed changes chosen by the insurance industry—are to occur, they cannot be implemented overnight. Succeeding years will reveal not only the substance of the reform routes chosen but also the effectiveness or ineffectiveness of those routes.

## BAD FAITH BREACH OF INSURANCE CONTRACT

Earlier in this chapter, we discussed the liability that an insurer will face if it breaches its policy obligations by means of a good faith but erroneous denial of coverage. That liability is for compensatory damages—damages designed to compensate the insured for the losses stemming from the insurer's breach—just as in breach of contract cases outside the insurance setting. Punitive damages are not available, however, when the insurer's wrongful failure or refusal to perform stemmed from a good faith (though erroneous) coverage denial. What if the insurer's failure or refusal to perform exhibited a lack of good faith? In this section, we examine the recent judicial tendency to go beyond the conventional remedy of compensatory damages and to assess punitive damages against the insurer when the insurer's refusal to perform its policy obligations amounted to the tort of **bad faith breach of contract**.

The special nature of the insurer–insured relationship tends to involve a "we'll take care of you" message that insurers communicate to insureds—at least at the outset of the relationship. Recognizing

this, courts have displayed little tolerance in recent years for insurers' unjustifiable refusals to take care of insureds when taking care of them is clearly called for by the relevant policy's terms. When an insurer refuses to perform obvious policy obligations without a plausible, legitimate explanation for the refusal, the insurer risks more than being held liable for compensatory damages. If the facts and circumstances indicate that the insurer's refusal to perform stemmed not from a reasonable argument over coverage but from an intent to "stonewall," deny or unreasonably delay paying a meritorious claim, or otherwise create hardship for the insured, the insurer's breach may be of the bad faith variety. Because bad faith breach is considered an independent tort of a flagrantly wrongful nature, punitive damages—in addition to compensatory damages—have been held to be appropriate. The purposes of punitive damages in this context are the same as in other types of cases that call for punitive damages: to punish the flagrant wrongdoer and to deter the wrongdoer (as well as other potential wrongdoers) from repeating such an action.

The past decade has witnessed bad faith cases in which many millions of dollars in punitive damages have been assessed against insurers. The types of situations in which bad faith liability has been found have included a liability insurer's unjustifiable refusal to defend its insured and/or pay damages awarded against the insured in litigation that clearly triggered the policy obligations. Various cases of very large punitive damages assessments for bad faith liability have stemmed from property insurers' refusals to pay for the insured's destroyed property when the cause was clearly a covered peril and the insurer had no plausible rationale for denying coverage. Still other bad faith cases in which liability was held to exist have included malpractice or other liability insurers' refusals to settle certain probably meritorious claims against the insured within the policy limits. Bad faith liability in these cases tends to involve a situation in which the insured is held legally liable to a plaintiff for an amount well in excess of the dollar limits of the liability policy (meaning that the insured would be personally responsible for the amount of the judgment in excess of the policy limits), after the liability insurer, without reasonable justification, refused the plaintiff's offer to settle the case for an amount less than or equal to the policy limits.

Whether bad faith liability exists in a given case depends, of course, on all of the relevant facts and circumstances. Although bad faith liability is not established in every case in which insureds allege it, cases raising a bad faith claim are of particular concern to insurers.

### PROBLEMS AND PROBLEM CASES

**1.** Eighteen-year-old Arthur Smith became intoxicated at a New Year's Eve party. At 11:00 P.M., Smith left the party and began walking home. Police officer Don Czopek saw Smith walking down the center of a road and weaving from side to side. Because Smith was interfering with traffic and placing himself at risk of physical harm, Czopek pulled his patrol car alongside Smith and attempted to talk him into getting off the road. Smith refused, became argumentative, and started shouting. Czopek parked his patrol car, got out, and approached Smith in an effort to calm him down. Smith became increasingly hostile and grabbed Czopek by the lapels of his coat. Officer Herdis Petty then arrived on the scene to assist Czopek. A struggle occurred as the two officers attempted to handcuff Smith and put him into a patrol car. Smith kicked, hit, and bit the officers during this struggle, which continued for a substantial length of time. Czopek suffered frostbite on one of his hands. Petty sustained broken ribs as a result of being kicked by Smith (plus other less serious injuries). Smith was later convicted of assault and battery. He admitted that he intentionally resisted arrest but said that he did not recall hitting or kicking anyone. Officers Czopek and Petty filed a civil suit against Smith's parents, whose homeowners' policy with Group Insurance Company of Michigan (GICOM) provided liability coverage to the insureds—a status that, under the policy's terms, included Arthur Smith—for third parties' personal injury claims resulting from an "occurrence." The policy defined "occurrence" as "an accident, including injurious exposure to conditions, which results . . . in bodily injury or property damage." The policy contained an exclusion from coverage for "bodily injury or property damage which is either expected or intended from the standpoint of the insured." GICOM filed a declaratory judgment suit in which it asked the court to declare that it had no duty to

defend or indemnify Arthur Smith and his parents in connection with the litigation brought by Czopek and Petty. Was GICOM entitled to such a ruling by the court?

**2.** Herbert Prashker was a partner in a law firm. Pursuant to their partnership agreement, the firm's partners purchased two life insurance policies on Prashker's life. The partners were named as beneficiaries. These policies, whose face amounts totaled $1,350,000, were obtained because Prashker was the most significant partner in terms of business generation and size of capital account. Prashker later fell ill with cancer and could no longer practice law. The partners agreed to terminate the partnership business. Five months after the partnership ceased doing business, Prashker died. Prashker's former partners sought to recover the life insurance proceeds. So did Prashker's daughter. She argued that the former partners were not entitled to the insurance proceeds because their insurable interest ended when the partnership was terminated. Were Prashker's former partners entitled to the life insurance proceeds?

**3.** In a class action suit, the plaintiffs alleged that an automobile loan program instituted by Bank of the West (BOW) violated California's Unfair Business Practices Act. No common law unfair competition claim was made in the suit. The Unfair Business Practices Act did not allow courts to award compensatory or punitive damages, but did authorize courts to order "the disgorgement of money" wrongfully obtained. BOW settled the class action suit by paying $500,000 and agreeing to make changes in the operation of the loan program. BOW contended that the $500,000 payment was covered by the terms of a liability policy issued to BOW by Industrial Indemnity Co. The policy provided coverage for "all sums which the insured shall become legally obligated to pay as damages because of advertising injury to which this insurance applies." The policy went on to define "advertising injury" as "injury arising out of . . . libel, slander, defamation, violation of right of privacy, unfair competition, or infringement of copyright, title or slogan." Industrial filed a declaratory judgment action in which it asked the court to determine that the policy did not cover the $500,000 payment made by BOW to settle the class action suit. The trial court ruled in Industrial's favor, but the intermediate appellate court reversed. It concluded that the policy afforded coverage because the term "unfair competition" was ambiguous and thus could refer to either the common law of unfair competition or statutory claims such as those under the Unfair Business Practices Act. Was the intermediate appellate court correct?

**4.** Benjamin Born applied for a life insurance policy from Medico Life Insurance Company. The application form called for a health history, which Born provided. In addition, the application form asked specific questions about preexisting medical conditions. Born's wife, Adeline, answered these questions by stating that Born had no preexisting medical problems and was in good health. After issuing the policy, Medico discovered that Born had a history of heart disease, degenerative arthritis, and urinary system disorders. Medico then rescinded the policy and provided Born a check representing a refund of the premiums he had paid. Taking the position that he was still insured, Born refused the refund check. On these facts, was Medico entitled to rescind the policy?

**5.** The Pecks owned a lawn and garden supply store. Standard Marine was the insurer of the store and its contents. The Pecks placed a fireworks display in the store, where it was subsequently set off by a young boy. A resulting fire damaged or destroyed much of the Pecks' merchandise. Standard Marine refused to reimburse the Pecks for their loss, citing this clause in the policy: "The Company shall not be liable for loss occurring while the hazard is increased by any means within the control or knowledge of the insured." Was Standard Marine obligated to pay the Pecks for their loss?

**6.** The Plummers owned a commercial building in which they operated two businesses. The building and its contents were insured by Indiana Insurance Company (IIC). After an explosion and fire destroyed the building, the Plummers filed a claim and proof of loss with IIC. After an investigation, IIC denied the claim due to its conclusion that the Plummers had intentionally set the fire. IIC then filed a declaratory judgment action in which it asked for a determination that it had no obligation to cover losses stemming from the fire. The Plummers counterclaimed, seeking damages for breach of contract as well as punitive damages. The jury returned a verdict in favor of the

Plummers on all issues. The jury awarded the Plummers approximately $700,000 in compensatory damages (an amount that exceeded the policy limits set forth in the insurance policy at issue), plus $3.5 million in punitive damages. The $700,000 compensatory damages award included not only the value of the destroyed building and its contents (what would have been due under the policy) but also $200,000 in consequential damages allegedly incurred by the Plummers as a result of IIC's lengthy investigation of the fire and ultimate denial of the Plummers' claim. For the most part, the consequential damages represented interest costs and similar expenses incurred by the Plummers—costs and expenses they would not have incurred if IIC had paid their claim. Although the evidence IIC adduced at trial included experts' testimony that the fire had been intentionally set, the jury rejected that testimony and accepted the Plummers' contrary evidence. IIC appealed, arguing that its denial of the Plummers' claim was in good faith, that it therefore should have no liability for consequential damages and punitive damages, and that the damages awarded for breach of an insurance contract cannot exceed the policy limits set forth in the contract. Was IIC correct in these arguments?

**7.** In 1972, Betty DeWitt and her husband, Joseph, purchased a house. Title was taken in Betty's name. Seven years later, the DeWitts were divorced. Under the 1979 divorce decree, Joseph was given possession of the house and Betty was ordered to sign the deed over to him. Joseph died in January 1980. Soon thereafter, Betty moved into the house and purchased a fire insurance policy from American Family Mutual Insurance Company. The policy had a face value of $38,500. In August 1980, the house was completely destroyed by fire. At that time, American Family learned of her divorce and the decree ordering her to convey title to Joseph. American Family refused to pay on the policy, arguing that Betty did not have an insurable interest. Was American Family correct?

**8.** Robert Baer and Dareen Dahlstrom had been close friends for more than 20 years. Dahlstrom, who was in the process of separating from her husband, went to visit Baer in July 1988. On various occasions, Baer had used a recreational drug known as Ecstacy. For several years after its discovery, Ecstasy was not an illegal drug. It was, however, designated by federal law as a prohibited controlled substance beginning in March 1988. Baer believed that the use of Ecstasy had certain psychological and emotional benefits, and that using it might help Dahlstrom cope with the personal problems she was experiencing at the time of her July 1988 visit. After she and Baer discussed his beliefs regarding Ecstasy, Dahlstrom told him that she wanted to use the drug. Baer and Dahlstrom went through various rituals in preparation for use of the drug and recited a prayer that "this [may] bring harm to no one and blessing to all." Baer then removed some Ecstasy from his personal supply, which he had purchased prior to March 1988. Baer dissolved approximately one-half of his usual dose in a glass of water and gave it to Dahlstrom. She drank the mixture. Within approximately 30 minutes, she was dead. Dahlstrom's survivors filed a wrongful death suit against Baer, who asserted that the claim fell within the liability coverage provided to him by State Farm Insurance Company as part of his homeowner's policy. The policy afforded coverage for third parties' claims for physical injury resulting from an "occurrence," which was defined in terms of an "accident" that caused injury. The policy also contained an exclusion from coverage for injury that was either intended or expected by the insured. State Farm filed a declaratory judgment action in which it asked for a judicial determination that in light of the above provisions in the parties' insurance contract as well as public policy considerations, it owed Baer no coverage duties regarding the suit that stemmed from Dahlstrom's death. Was State Farm entitled to the relief it sought?

**9.** Jeffrey Lane was employed by Memtek, Inc. at its Arby's Restaurant. He was being trained as a cook. After 11:00 one evening, Lane finished work and clocked out. He remained in the restaurant's lobby, however, because he was waiting for the manager to complete her duties. As Lane waited, friends of other restaurant employees came to a door of the restaurant. Lane and the other employees became involved in a conversation with these persons, who included John Taylor. Lane told Taylor that he could not enter the restaurant because it was closed. Taylor did not attempt to force his way into the restaurant. Instead, he "dared" Lane to come outside. Lane left the restaurant "of [his] own

will" (according to Lane's deposition) for what he assumed would be a fight with Taylor. In the fight that transpired, Lane broke Taylor's nose and knocked out three of his teeth. Lane later pleaded guilty to a criminal battery charge. Taylor filed a civil suit against Lane and Memtek in an effort to collect damages stemming from the altercation with Lane. American Family Mutual Insurance Company provided liability insurance for Memtek in connection with its restaurant. The policy stated that for purposes of American Family's duties to defend and indemnify, "the insured" included not only Memtek but also Memtek's "employees, . . . but only for acts within the scope of their employment." American Family filed a declaratory judgment action in which it asked the court to determine that it owed Lane neither a duty to defend nor a duty to indemnify in connection with the incident giving rise to Taylor's lawsuit. American Family's theory was that for purposes of that incident, Lane was not an insured within the above-quoted policy provision. Was American Family correct?

**10.** In December 1988, Counihan purchased a property insurance policy under which Allstate Insurance Co. insured her house against all risks of loss. In February 1989, the U.S. government seized the house and sought its forfeiture under federal law due to its connection with illegal drug activity that occurred in July 1988. After two trials and an appeal, the Second Circuit Court of Appeals affirmed the forfeiture of the property in 1993. A fire had destroyed the house in 1990, while Counihan's policy with Allstate allegedly was in force. Counihan filed a claim with Allstate to recover the value of the destroyed house. The forfeiture statute under which the government had sought forfeiture of Counihan's property stated that "[a]ll right, title, and interest in property [to which the government has been held entitled to forfeiture due to the property's connection with illegal drug activity] shall vest in the United States upon commission of the act giving rise to forfeiture under this section." Arguing that this statute's retroactive effect would mean that Counihan did not possess an insurable interest when she purchased the policy and when the fire destroyed the house, Allstate asserted that its insurance contract with Counihan was void and unenforceable. Did Counihan have the necessary insurable interest at the times in question?

Andre Preneur and his twin sister, Andrea Preneur, are shareholders in the corporation known as A-P Enterprises, Inc. The two of them handle virtually all of the day-to-day management of the business of A-P Enterprises. On major business decisions, they solicit input from their friend, Dick Dolt, who is the only other shareholder in the firm. Dolt nearly always agrees with Andre and Andrea. A-P Enterprises owns various parcels of real property, which it uses in connection with its business. Andre separately and individually owns other real property. The same is true of Andrea. Consider each of the following insurance-related situations:

- Andre procured a standard property insurance policy on his home from Safehome Insurance Co. While the policy was in effect, Andre's home was destroyed by fire, a covered peril. Safehome denied Andre's claim and refused to pay him anything, however, because Safehome possessed a reasonably based, good faith belief that Andre had arranged for an unemployed chiropractic school graduate to burn down the house. Andre, who in reality did no such thing, sued Safehome over the claim denial. Andre sought compensatory and punitive damages. The court ruled in Andre's favor and awarded him compensatory damages. It refused, however, to assess punitive damages against Safehome. Andre has appealed the court's denial of punitive damages.

- After owning a summerhouse for several years, Andrea sold it to her cousin, Irving. Andrea loaned Irving $100,000 of the $200,000 purchase price in return for (1) his agreement to repay her by means of monthly payments of principal and interest, and (2) his granting her a mortgage on the summerhouse as security for the debt. Andrea then obtained, from Rocksolid Insurance Co., a property insurance policy on the summerhouse. While this policy was in effect and while Irving still owed Andrea the debt described earlier, the summerhouse was destroyed by a tornado (a covered peril).

Asserting that Andrea did not possess the necessary insurable interest because she was not the owner of the summerhouse, Rocksolid has denied Andrea's claim for payment under the policy.

- A-P Enterprises owns the building from which the firm does business. A-P purchased a property insurance policy on this building from Good Faith Insurance Co. The policy, which contained an 80 percent coinsurance clause, had a face amount of $200,000. The building's fair market value, however, was $400,000. A fire—a covered peril—caused $104,000 worth of damage to the building.

- A-P Enterprises also owns a warehouse, which A-P has insured under separate property insurance policies with Solitary Mutual Insurance Co. ($100,000 face amount) and Eastwestern Insurance Co. ($150,000 face amount). Each policy contained a pro rata clause. A tornado—a covered peril—caused $90,000 worth of damage to the warehouse.

- Dolt has taken out separate life insurance policies on the lives of Andre and Andrea.

## Required:

Answer the following and give reasons for your conclusions.

1. Should Andre win his appeal of the trial court's refusal to assess punitive damages against Safehome?

2. Is Rocksolid correct in its assertion that Andrea did not possess the necessary insurable interest in the summerhouse?

3. How much must Good Faith pay A-P Enterprises on A-P's claim under the policy covering the A-P building?

4. How much, respectively, must Solitary Mutual and Eastwestern pay A-P Enterprises on A-P's claims under the policies covering the A-P warehouse?

5. If Andre or Andrea dies, does Dolt possess a sufficient insurable interest to support recovery under the appropriate life insurance policy?

# CHAPTER

## 18

# LANDLORD AND TENANT

**INTRODUCTION**

*Landlord-tenant law has undergone dramatic change during the past two decades, due in large part to the changing nature of the relationship between landlords and tenants. In England and in early America, farms were the usual subjects of leases. The tenant's primary object was to lease land on which to grow crops or graze cattle. Accordingly, traditional landlord-tenant law viewed the lease as primarily a conveyance of land and paid relatively little attention to its contractual aspects.*

*In today's industrialized society, however, the landlord-tenant relationship is typified by the lease of property for residential or commercial purposes. The tenant occupies only a small portion of the total property. He bargains primarily for the use of structures on the land rather than for the land itself. He is likely to have signed a form lease provided by the landlord, the terms of which he may have had little opportunity to negotiate. In areas with a shortage of affordable housing, a residential tenant's ability to bargain for favorable lease provisions is further hampered. Because the typical landlord-tenant relationship can no longer fairly be characterized as one in which the parties have equal knowledge and bargaining power, it is not always realistic to presume that tenants are capable of negotiating to protect their own interests.*

*Although it was initially slow to recognize the changing nature of the landlord-tenant relationship, the law now tends to place greater emphasis than it once did on the contract components of the relationship. As a result, modern contract doctrines such as unconscionability, constructive conditions, the duty to mitigate damages, and implied warranties are applied to leases. Such doctrines may operate to compensate for tenants' lack of bargaining power. In addition, state legislatures and city councils have enacted statutes and ordinances that increasingly regulate leased property and the landlord-tenant relationship.*

*This chapter's discussion of landlord-tenant law will focus on the nature of leasehold interests, the traditional rights and duties of landlords and tenants, and recent statutory and judicial developments affecting those rights and duties.*

# LEASES AND TENANCIES

## Nature of Leases

A **lease** is a contract under which an owner of property, the **landlord** (also called the *lessor*), conveys to the **tenant** (also called the *lessee*) the exclusive right to possess property for a period of time. The property interest conveyed to the tenant is called a **leasehold estate.**

## Types of Tenancies

The duration of the tenant's possessory right depends upon the type of **tenancy** established by or resulting from the lease. There are four main types of tenancies.

**1.** *Tenancy for a term.* In a **tenancy for a term** (also called a *tenancy for years*), the landlord and tenant have agreed on a specific duration of the lease and have fixed the date on which the tenancy will terminate. For example, if Dudley, a college student, leases an apartment for the academic year ending May 30, 1995, a tenancy for a term will have been created. The tenant's right to possess the property ends on the date agreed upon without any further notice, unless the lease contains a provision permitting extension.

**2.** *Periodic tenancy.* A **periodic tenancy** is created when the parties agree that rent will be paid in regular successive intervals until notice to terminate is given, but do not agree on a specific lease duration. If the tenant pays rent monthly, the tenancy is from month to month; if the tenant pays yearly, as is sometimes done under agricultural leases, the tenancy is from year to year. (Periodic tenancies therefore are sometimes called *tenancies from month to month* or *tenancies from year to year.*) To terminate a periodic tenancy, either party must give advance notice to the other. The precise amount of notice required is often defined by state statutes. For example, to terminate a tenancy from month to month, most states require that the notice be given at least one month in advance.

**3.** *Tenancy at will.* A **tenancy at will** occurs when property is leased for an indefinite period of time and either party may choose to conclude the tenancy at any time. Generally, tenancies at will involve situations in which the tenant either does not pay rent or does not pay it at regular intervals. For example, Landon allows her friend Trumbull to live in the apartment over her garage. Although this tenancy's name indicates that it is terminable "at [the] will" of either party, most states require that the landlord give reasonable advance notice to the tenant before exercising the right to terminate the tenancy.

**4.** *Tenancy at sufferance.* A **tenancy at sufferance** occurs when a tenant remains in possession of the property (holds over) after a lease has expired. In this situation, the landlord has two options: (1) treating the holdover tenant as a trespasser and bringing an action to eject him; and (2) continuing to treat him as a tenant and collecting rent from him. Until the landlord makes her election, the tenant is a tenant at sufferance. Suppose that Templeton has leased an apartment for one year from Larson. At the end of the year, Templeton holds over and does not move out. Templeton is a tenant at sufferance. Larson may have him ejected or may continue treating him as a tenant. If Larson elects the latter alternative, a new tenancy is created. The new tenancy will be either a tenancy for a term or a periodic tenancy, depending on the facts of the case and any presumptions established by state law. Thus, a tenant who holds over for even a few days runs the risk of creating a new tenancy he might not want.

---

**CONCEPT REVIEW**

## TYPES OF TENANCIES

| Type of Lease | Characteristics | Termination |
|---|---|---|
| **Tenancy for a Term** | Landlord and tenant agree on a specific duration of the lease and fix the date on which the tenancy will end | Ends automatically on the date agreed upon; no additional notice necessary |
| **Periodic Tenancy** | Landlord and tenant agree that tenant will pay rent at regular, successive intervals (e.g., month to month) | Either party may terminate by giving the amount of advance notice required by state law |

| Type of Lease | Characteristics | Termination |
|---|---|---|
| **Tenancy at Will** | Landlord and tenant agree that tenant may possess property for an indefinite amount of time, with no agreement to pay rent at regular, successive intervals | May be terminated "at will" by either party, but state law requires advance notice |
| **Tenancy at Sufferance** | Tenant remains in possession after the termination of one of the leaseholds described above, until landlord has brought ejectment action against tenant or collected rent from him | Landlord has choice of:<br>1. Treating tenant as a trespasser and bringing ejectment action against him, or<br>2. Accepting rent from tenant, thus creating a new leasehold |

## Execution of a Lease

As transfers of interests in land, leases may be covered by the statute of frauds. In most states, a lease for a term of more than one year from the date it is made is unenforceable unless it is evidenced by a suitable writing signed by the party to be charged. A few states, however, require leases to be evidenced by a writing only when they are for a term of more than three years.

Good business practice demands that leases be carefully drafted to make clear the parties' respective rights and obligations. Care in drafting leases is especially important in cases of long-term and commercial leases. Lease provisions normally cover such essential matters as the term of the lease, the rent to be paid, the uses the tenant may make of the property, the circumstances under which the landlord may enter the property, the parties' respective obligations regarding the condition of the property, and the responsibility (as between landlord and tenant) for making repairs. In addition, leases often contain provisions allowing a possible extension of the term of the lease and purporting to limit the parties' rights to assign the lease or sublet the property. State or local law often regulates lease terms. For example, the Uniform Residential Landlord and Tenant Act (URLTA) has been enacted in a substantial minority of states. The URLTA prohibits the inclusion of certain lease provisions, such as a clause by which the tenant supposedly agrees to pay the landlord's attorney's fees in an action to enforce the lease. In states that have not enacted the URLTA, lease terms are likely to be regulated at least to a moderate degree by some combination of state statutes, common law principles, and local housing codes.

## RIGHTS, DUTIES, AND LIABILITIES OF THE LANDLORD

### Landlord's Rights

The landlord is entitled to receive the *agreed rent* for the term of the lease. Upon expiration of the lease, the landlord has the right to the *return of the property in as good a condition as it was when leased,* except for normal wear and tear and any destruction caused by an act of God.

**Security Deposits**   Landlords commonly require tenants to make security deposits or advance payments of rent. Such deposits operate to protect the landlord's right to receive rent as well as her right to reversion of the property in good condition. In recent years, many cities and states have enacted statutes or ordinances designed to prevent landlord abuse of security deposits. These laws typically limit the amount a landlord may demand and require that the security deposit be refundable, except for portions withheld by the landlord due to the tenant's nonpayment of rent or tenant-caused property damage beyond ordinary wear and tear. Some statutes or ordinances also require the landlord to place the funds in interest-bearing accounts when the lease is for more than a minimal period of time. As a general rule, these laws require landlords to provide tenants a written accounting regarding their security deposits and any portions being withheld. Such an accounting normally must be provided within a specified period of time (30 days, for example) after the termination of the lease. The landlord's failure to comply with statutes and ordinances regarding security deposits may cause the landlord to experience adverse consequences that vary state by state.

## Landlord's Duties

**Fair Housing Act**    As explained in Chapter 16, the Fair Housing Act prohibits housing discrimination on the basis of race, color, sex, religion, national origin, handicap, and familial status.[1] The Fair Housing Act prohibits discriminatory practices in various transactions affecting housing, including the rental of dwellings.[2] Included within the act's prohibited instances of discrimination against a protected person are refusals to rent property to such a person, discrimination against him or her in the terms, conditions, or privileges of rental, publication of any advertisement or statement indicating any preference, limitation, or discrimination operating to the disadvantage of a protected person, and representations that a dwelling is not available for rental to such a person when, in fact, it is available.

The act also makes it a discriminatory practice for a landlord to refuse to permit a tenant with a handicap to make—at his own expense—reasonable modifications to leased property. The landlord may, however, condition this permission on the tenant's

agreement to restore the property to its previous condition upon termination of the lease, reasonable wear and tear excepted. In addition, landlords are prohibited from refusing to make reasonable accommodations in rules, policies, practices, or services if such accommodations are necessary to afford a handicapped tenant equal opportunity to use and enjoy the leased premises. When constructing certain types of multifamily housing for first occupancy, property owners and developers risk violating the act if they fail to make the housing accessible to persons with handicaps.

Due to a perceived increase in the frequency with which landlords would refuse to rent to families with children, the act prohibits landlords from excluding families with children. If, however, the dwelling falls within the act's "housing for older persons" exception, this prohibition does not apply.[3]

In *Walker v. Crigler,* which follows, the court demonstrates the importance of the public policy notions underlying the Fair Housing Act by holding that a property owner may be held liable for his agent's discriminatory actions even if the property owner has instructed the agent to comply with applicable anti-discrimination laws.

---

[1]Familial status is defined in Chapter 16.

[2]The act provides an exemption for certain persons who own and rent single-family houses. To qualify for this exemption, owners must not use a real estate broker or an illegal advertisement and cannot own more than three such houses at one time. It also exempts owners who rent rooms or units in dwellings in which they themselves reside, if those dwellings house no more than four families.

---

[3]The "housing for older persons" exception is described in Chapter 16.

---

### WALKER v. CRIGLER
#### 976 F.2d 900 (4th Cir. 1992)

Alleging that the following facts amounted to discrimination on the basis of sex in the rental of housing and that the Fair Housing Act was therefore violated, Darlene Walker filed suit against property owner Frank Whitesell and his property manager, Constance Crigler. Walker, a single mother of one son, worked in Falls Church, Virginia and wished to rent an apartment there for herself and her son. In July 1989, Walker sought the assistance of the Town and Country Properties (TCP) firm. TCP agents showed Walker the Multiple Listing Service (MLS) listings of available rental properties in Falls Church. After reviewing these listings, Walker became interested in an apartment located at 124 Falls Avenue. Whitesell owned this property. Crigler, a professional realtor, served as Whitesell's property manager for 124 Falls Avenue and other rental properties owned by Whitesell. Crigler's responsibilities included finding financially qualified tenants for Whitesell's properties.

The MLS listing for 124 Falls Avenue specified $600 per month as the rent and described the property as a two-bedroom apartment that was "ideal for two men." Walker decided that she wanted to rent the apartment because it was close to a school for her son and was accessible to public transportation facilities. A TCP agent testified at trial that when he told Crigler he intended to submit the rental application of a financially qualified single mother (Walker), Crigler stated that she would not rent to a female applicant under any circumstances. Another TCP agent contacted Crigler on Walker's behalf; Crigler reiterated her policy of not renting to women. Walker testified that when she personally telephoned Crigler regarding the apartment, Crigler stated essentially the same thing and added that in the past, boyfriends of single female tenants had caused problems. Roughly two months after these conversations took place, the 124 Falls Avenue apartment was rented to two men who paid a total monthly rent of $580—$20 per month less than what Walker had been willing to pay.

Crigler testified that she never told anyone she would not rent the apartment to a single woman. The evidence revealed that in January 1989 (approximately six months before Walker's unsuccessful attempt to rent the apartment), Whitesell's awareness of housing discrimination suits against landlords caused him to send Crigler a memorandum instructing her to comply with applicable antidiscrimination laws in screening possible tenants for his rental properties.

An instruction given by the trial judge to the jury stated that if the jury found Fair Housing Act violations on Crigler's part, Whitesell would also be liable if Crigler was Whitesell's agent and was acting within the scope of her employment at the time she engaged in discrimination. The jury returned a verdict in Walker's favor against Crigler for $5,000 in compensatory damages. The jury ruled in Whitesell's favor, however, on Walker's claim against him. The trial judge denied Walker's motions for judgment notwithstanding the verdict and for a new trial. Walker appealed.

---

**Murnaghan, Circuit Judge**   The jury ruled in Whitesell's favor, holding, apparently, that Crigler [despite clearly being Whitesell's agent] was not acting in the scope of her employment when she denied Walker's attempts to rent the 124 Falls Avenue premises because Walker was a woman. The sole evidence to support the jury's conclusion that Whitesell was not liable for damages for the discrimination was the evidence indicating that Crigler was instructed not to refuse to rent on discriminatory grounds. In denying the motion for judgment notwithstanding the verdict, the trial judge concluded that the evidence of Whitesell's instruction was sufficient to support the jury's verdict. We find, however, that the court's conclusion is based on an erroneous theory of law. Since there is no unsettled question of fact to be submitted for decision by the jury, it is appropriate to reverse the judgment that Whitesell was not liable for compensatory damages and to direct entry of judgment against Whitesell in Walker's favor in the amount of $5,000.

The evidence is sufficient to support the conclusion that Whitesell specifically intended that Crigler not discriminate. In many cases involving issues other than housing discrimination, such a finding would refute the assertion that Crigler acted within the scope of employment and would concurrently shield Whitesell from any liability as principal. However, the arguable conclusion that Crigler acted outside the scope of employment is irrelevant in the present case, for Whitesell could not insulate himself from liability for sex discrimination in regard to living premises owned by him and managed for his benefit merely by relinquishing the responsibility for preventing such discrimination to another party. We adopt the general rule applied by other federal courts that the duty of a property owner not to discriminate in the leasing or sale of that property is nondelegable.

We are not unmindful of the arguable incongruity of applying liability to Whitesell and . . . similarly situated [property owners] who are apparently non-culpable in a housing discrimination instance but must still bear the burden of liability. The central question to be decided in a case such as this, however, is which innocent party—the owner whose agent acted contrary to his instruction, or the potential renter who felt the direct harm of the agent's discriminatory failure to offer the residence for rental—will ultimately bear the burden of the harm caused. It is clear that the overriding societal priority of the provision of "fair housing throughout the United States" (clearly set out in the Fair Housing Act) indicates that the one innocent party with the power to control the acts of the agent—the owner of the property or other responsible superior—must act to compensate the injured party for the harm and to ensure that similar harm will not occur in the future.

It must not be overlooked that although the property owner's duty to prevent discrimination is nondelegable, the owner [usually] will not be subjected to liability for the full amount of all successful claims, [because] contribution from other liable parties may offset some or all of the payment for which the owner is responsible. [Although Crigler, in a separate legal proceeding, filed for bankruptcy and obtained a discharge of her judgment debt to Walker and any contribution-related obligation to Whitesell,] we may assume in the great majority of cases that real estate agents will not turn bankrupt or otherwise [become] judgment-proof. They will remain liable for damages flowing from flaunting a principal's intentions.

Just as we feel no qualms in holding a property owner responsible for paying property taxes, meeting health code safety requirements, or ensuring that other responsibilities to protect the public are met—

and we refuse to allow the owner to avoid these responsibilities with an assertion that he conferred the duty to another—we must hold those who benefit from the sale and rental of property to the public to the specific mandates of antidiscrimination law if the goal of equal housing opportunity is to be reached. Whitesell, despite forbidding discrimination on the part of Crigler, cannot, under the Fair Housing Act, dispose of his duty to prevent sexual discrimination in the rental of 124 Falls Avenue, a property which he owned and which was operated for his benefit.

**Judgment in favor of Whitesell reversed; trial court ordered to enter judgment in favor of Walker and against Whitesell for $5,000 in compensatory damages.**

---

**Implied Warranty of Possession**  Landlords have certain obligations that are imposed by law whenever property is leased. One of these obligations stems from the landlord's **implied warranty of possession**. This warranty guarantees the tenant's right to possess the property for the term of the lease. Suppose that Turner rents an apartment from Long for a term to begin on September 1, 1994, and to end on August 31, 1995. When Turner attempts to move in on September 1, 1994, she finds that Carlson, the previous tenant, is still in possession of the property. In this case, Long has breached the implied warranty of possession.

**Implied Warranty of Quiet Enjoyment**  By leasing property, the landlord also makes an **implied warranty of quiet enjoyment** (or *covenant of quiet enjoyment*). This covenant guarantees that the tenant's possession will not be interfered with as a result of the landlord's act or omission. In the absence of an emergency that threatens the property or a contrary provision in the lease, the landlord may not enter the leased property during the term of the lease. If he does, he will be liable for trespass. In some cases, courts have held that the covenant of quiet enjoyment was violated when the landlord failed to stop third parties, such as trespassers or other tenants who make excessive noise, from interfering with the tenant's enjoyment of the leased premises.

**Constructive Eviction**  The doctrine of **constructive eviction** may aid a tenant when property becomes unsuitable for the purposes for which it was leased because of the landlord's act or omission, such as the breach of a duty to repair or the covenant of quiet enjoyment. Under this doctrine, which applies both to residential and commercial property, the tenant may terminate the lease because he has effectively been evicted as a result of the poor condition or the objectionable circumstances there. Constructive eviction gives a tenant the right to vacate the property without further rent obligation if he does so *promptly* after giving the landlord reasonable notice and an opportunity to correct the problem. Because constructive eviction requires the tenant to vacate the leased premises, it is an unattractive option, however, for tenants who cannot afford to move or do not have a suitable alternative place to live.

## Landlord's Responsibility for Condition of Leased Property

The common law historically held that landlords made no implied warranties regarding the *condition* or *quality* of leased premises. As an adjunct to the landlord's right to receive the leased property in good condition at the termination of the lease, the common law imposed on the *tenant* the duty to make repairs. Even when the lease contained a

368 Part 3 Property

landlord's express warranty or express promise to make repairs, a tenant was not entitled to withhold rent if the landlord failed to carry out his obligations. This was because a fundamental contract performance principle—that a party is not obligated to perform if the other party fails to perform—was considered inapplicable to leases. In recent years, however, changing views of the landlord-tenant relationship have resulted in dramatically increased legal responsibility on the part of landlords for the condition of leased residential property.

**Implied Warranty of Habitability**     The legal principle that landlords made no implied warranty regarding the condition of leased property arose during an era when tenants used land primarily for agricultural purposes. Buildings existing on the property were frequently of secondary importance. They also tended to be simple structures, lacking modern conveniences such as plumbing and wiring. These buildings were fairly easily inspected and repaired by the tenant, who was generally more self-sufficient than today's typical tenant. In view of the relative simplicity of the structures, landlord and tenant were considered to have equal knowledge of the property's condition upon commencement of the lease. Thus, a rule requiring the tenant to make repairs seemed reasonable.

The position of modern residential tenants differs greatly from that of an earlier era's agricultural tenants. The modern residential tenant bargains not for the use of the ground itself, but for the use of a building (or portion thereof) as a dwelling. The structures on land today are complex, frequently involving systems (such as plumbing and electrical systems) to which the tenant does not have physical access. Besides decreasing the likelihood of perceiving defects during inspection, this complexity compounds the difficulty of making repairs—something at which today's tenant already tends to be less adept than his grandparents were. Moreover, placing a duty on tenants to negotiate for express warranties and duties to repair is no longer feasible. Residential leases are now routinely executed on standard forms provided by landlords.

For these reasons, statutes or judicial decisions in most states now impose an **implied warranty of habitability** on landlords leasing residential property. According to the vast majority of cases, this warranty is applicable only to *residential* property, and not to property leased for commercial uses. The implied warranty of habitability's content in lease settings is basically the same as in the sale of real estate—the property must be safe and suitable for human habitation. In lease settings, however, the landlord not only must deliver a habitable dwelling at the beginning of the lease but also must *maintain* the property in a habitable condition during the term of the lease. Various statutes and judicial decisions provide that the warranty includes an obligation that the leased property comply with any applicable housing codes. From a tenant's point of view, the implied warranty of habitability is superior to constructive eviction because a tenant does not have to vacate the leased premises in order to seek a remedy for breach of the warranty.

**Remedies for Breach of Implied Warranty of Habitability**     The particular remedies for breach of the implied warranty of habitability differ from state to state. Some of the remedies a tenant may pursue include:

**1.** *Action for damages.* The breach of the implied warranty of habitability violates the lease and renders the landlord liable for damages. The damages generally are measured by the diminished value of the leasehold. The landlord's breach of the implied warranty of habitability may also be asserted by the tenant as a counterclaim and defense in the landlord's action for eviction and/or nonpayment of rent.

**2.** *Termination of lease.* In extreme cases, the landlord's breach of the implied warranty of habitability may justify the tenant's termination of the lease. For this remedy to be appropriate, the landlord's breach must have been substantial enough to constitute a material breach.

**3.** *Rent abatement.* Some states permit rent abatement, a remedy under which the tenant withholds part of the rent for the period during which the landlord was in breach of the implied warranty of habitability. Where authorized by law, this approach allows the tenant to pay a reduced rent that reflects the *actual* value of the leasehold in its defective condition. There are different ways of computing this value. State law determines the amount by which the rent will be reduced.

**4.** *Repair-and-deduct.* A growing number of states have statutes permitting the tenant to have defects repaired and to deduct the repair costs from her rent. The repairs authorized in these statutes are usually limited to essential services such as electricity and plumbing. They also require that the tenant give the landlord notice of the defect and an adequate opportunity to make the repairs himself.

**Housing Codes**  Many cities and states have enacted housing codes that impose duties on property owners with respect to the condition of leased property. Typical of these provisions is Section 2304 of the District of Columbia Housing Code, which provides: "No person shall rent or offer to rent any habitation or the furnishing thereof unless such habitation and its furnishings are in a clean, safe and sanitary condition, in repair and free from rodents or vermin." Such codes commonly call for the provision and maintenance of necessary services such as heat, water, and electricity, as well as suitable bathroom and kitchen facilities. Housing codes also usually require that specified minimum space-per-

tenant standards be met, that windows, doors, floors, and screens be kept in repair, that the property be painted and free of lead paint, that keys and locks meet certain specifications, and that the landlord issue written receipts for rent payments. A landlord's failure to comply with an applicable housing code may result in a fine or in liability for injuries resulting from the property's disrepair. The noncompliance may also result in the landlord's losing part or all of his claim to the agreed-upon rent. Some housing codes establish that tenants have the right to withhold rent until necessary repairs have been made and the right to move out in cases of particularly egregious violations of housing code requirements. As revealed by the following *Breezewood Management* case, the violation of an applicable housing code may also give rise to or strengthen a tenant's claim that the implied warranty of habitability was breached.

## BREEZEWOOD MANAGEMENT COMPANY V. MALTBIE
### 411 N.E.2d 670 (Ind. Ct. App. 1980)

On August 2, 1978, Dan Maltbie and John Burke, students at Indiana University, entered into a one-year written lease with Breezewood Management Company for the rental of an apartment in an older house in Bloomington, Indiana. The agreed rent was $235 per month. When Burke and Maltbie moved in, they discovered numerous defects: rotting porch floorboards, broken and loose windows, an inoperable front door lock, leaks in the plumbing, a back door that would not close, a missing bathroom door, inadequate water pressure, falling plaster, exposed wiring over the bathtub, and a malfunctioning toilet. Later, they discovered more leaks in the plumbing, a leaking roof, the absence of heat and hot water, cockroach infestation, and pigeons in the attic.

The City of Bloomington had a housing code in effect at that time. Code enforcement officers inspected the apartment and found over 50 violations, 11 of which were "life-safety" violations (defined as conditions that might be severely "hazardous to health of the occupant"). These conditions remained largely uncorrected after notice by the code officers and further complaints by Burke and Maltbie.

On May 3, 1979, Maltbie vacated the apartment, notified Breezewood, and refused to pay any further rent. Breezewood agreed to let Burke remain and pay $112.50 per month. Breezewood then filed suit against Burke and Maltbie for $610.75, which was the balance due under the written rental contract plus certain charges. Burke and Maltbie each filed counterclaims against Breezewood, claiming damages and abatement of the rent for breach of the implied warranty of habitability. At trial, Burke and Maltbie presented evidence showing that the reasonable rental value of the apartment in its defective condition was only $50 per month during colder weather and $75 per month during warmer weather. The trial court entered judgment against Breezewood on its claim and awarded Burke and Maltbie a total of $1,030 in damages on their counterclaims. Breezewood appealed.

**Robertson, Presiding Judge**    Over time, many exceptions have eroded the common law doctrine of *caveat lessee*. In most circumstances, the modern tenant lacks the skill and "know-how" to inspect and repair housing to determine whether it is fit for its particular purpose. In *Boston Housing Authority v. Hemingway*, the court treated the lease agreement as a contract in which the landlord promised to deliver premises suitable to the tenant's purpose in return for the tenant's promise to pay rent. In *Javins v. First National Realty Corporation*, the United States Court of Appeals for the District of Columbia found an implied warranty of habitability in the lease agreement, the minimum habitability standards being established by the Housing Regulations for the District of Columbia. The court stated that landlord-tenant law should be governed by the same implied warranty of fitness which covers a sale of goods under the Uniform Commercial Code. The court said:

In the case of the modern apartment dweller, the value of the lease is that it gives him a place to live. The city dweller who seeks to lease an apartment on the third floor of a tenement has little interest in the land 30 or 40 feet below, or even in the bare right to possession within the four walls of his apartment. When American city dwellers seek shelter today, they seek a well known package of goods and services—a package which includes not merely walls and ceilings, but also adequate heat, light, and ventilation, serviceable plumbing facilities, secure windows and doors, proper sanitation, and proper maintenance.

In the case at bar, the Bloomington Housing Code was in effect at the time of the lease agreement, and, by law, was incorporated into it. Burke and Maltbie had a reasonable expectation that their basic housing needs would be met: heating, plumbing, electricity, and structural integrity of the premises. For the reasons that a housing code was in effect and the premises violated many of its provisions, we hold that Breezewood breached an implied warranty of habitability.

**Judgment for Burke and Maltbie affirmed.**

---

**Americans with Disabilities Act**    Landlords leasing property constituting a *place of public accommodation* (primarily commercial property as opposed to private residential property) must pay heed to Title III of the Americans with Disabilities Act. Under Title III, owners and possessors of real property that is a place of public accommodation may be expected to make reasonable accommodations, including physical modifications of the property, in order to allow disabled persons to have access to the property. Chapter 16 contains a detailed discussion of Title III's provisions.

## Landlord's Tort Liability

**Traditional No-Liability Rule**    There were two major effects of the traditional rule that a landlord had no legal responsibility for the condition. The first effect—that the uninhabitability of the premises traditionally did not give a tenant the right to withhold rent, assert a defense to nonpayment, or terminate a lease—has already been discussed. The second effect was that landlords normally could not be held liable in tort for injuries suffered by tenants on leased property. This state of affairs stemmed from the notion that the tenant had the ability and responsibility to inspect the property for defects before leasing it. By leasing the property, the tenant was presumed to take it as it was, with any existing defects. As to any defects that might arise during the term of the lease, the landlord's tort immunity was seen as justified by his lack of control over the leased property once he had surrendered it to the tenant.

**Traditional Exceptions to No-Liability Rule**    Even before the current era's pro-tenant legal developments, however, courts created exceptions to the no-liability rule. In the following situations, landlords have traditionally owed the tenant (or an appropriate third party) a duty, the breach of which could constitute a tort:

1. *Duty to maintain common areas.* Landlords have a duty to use reasonable care to *maintain the common areas* (such as stairways, parking lots, and elevators) over which they retain control. If a tenant or a tenant's guest sustains injury as a result of the landlord's negligent maintenance of a common area, the landlord is liable.

2. *Duty to disclose hidden defects.* Landlords have the duty to disclose hidden defects about which they

know, if the defects are not reasonably discoverable by the tenant. The landlord is liable if a tenant or appropriate third party suffers injury because of a hidden danger that was known to the landlord but undisclosed.

**3.** *Duty to use reasonable care in performing repairs.* If a landlord repairs leased property, he must *exercise reasonable care in making the repairs.* The landlord may be liable for the consequences stemming from negligently performed repairs, even if he was not obligated to perform them.

**4.** *Duty to maintain property leased for admission to the public.* The landlord has a duty to suitably maintain property that is leased for *admission to the public.* A theater would be an example.

**5.** *Duty to maintain furnished dwellings.* The landlord who rents a *fully furnished dwelling* for a short time impliedly warrants that the premises are safe and habitable.

Except for the above circumstances, the landlord traditionally was not liable for injuries suffered by the tenant on leased property. Note that none of these exceptions would apply to one of the most common injury scenarios—when the tenant was injured by a defect in her own apartment and the defect resulted from the landlord's failure to repair rather than from negligently performed repairs.

**Current Trends in Landlord's Tort Liability**
Today, there is a strong trend toward abolition of the traditional rule of landlord tort immunity. The proliferation of housing codes and the development of the implied warranty of habitability have persuaded a sizable number of courts to impose on landlords the duty to use *reasonable care* in their maintenance of the leased property. As discussed earlier, a landlord's duty to keep the property in repair may be based on an express clause in the lease, the implied warranty of habitability, or provisions of a housing code or statute.

The landlord now may be liable if injury results from her negligent failure to carry out her duty to make repairs. As a general rule, a landlord will not be liable unless she had *notice* of the defect and a reasonable opportunity to make repairs.

The duty of care landlords owe tenants has been held to include the duty to take reasonable steps to protect tenants from substantial risks of harm created by other tenants. Courts have held landlords liable for tenants' injuries resulting from dangerous conditions (such as vicious animals) maintained by other tenants when the landlord knew or had reason to know of the danger.

It is not unusual for landlords to attempt to insulate themselves from negligence liability to tenants by including an *exculpatory clause* in the standard form leases they expect tenants to sign. An exculpatory clause purports to relieve the landlord from legal responsibility that the landlord could otherwise face (on negligence or other grounds) in certain instances of premises-related injuries suffered by tenants. In recent years, a number of state legislatures and courts have frowned upon exculpatory clauses when they are included in leases of residential property. The *Crawford v. Buckner* case, which follows shortly, illustrates the increasing judicial tendency to limit the effect of exculpatory clauses or declare them unenforceable on public policy grounds when they are included in residential leases.

Another area of possible future expansion of landlords' liability could be the application of product liability principles to the residential lease setting. The California Supreme Court, for instance, has held a landlord strictly liable for a tenant's physical injuries that resulted from a hidden defect present when the tenant leased the property.[4]

---

[4]*Becker v. IRM Corp.,* 213 Cal. Rptr. 213 (Cal. Sup. Ct. 1985).

---

## CRAWFORD v. BUCKNER
**839 S.W.2d 754 (Tenn. Sup. Ct. 1992)**

In order to rent an apartment in a building owned by Tobe McKenzie and McKenzie Development Corporation (MDC), Linda Crawford was required to sign a standard form lease provided by McKenzie and MDC. This lease contained an exculpatory clause stating that McKenzie and MDC "shall not be liable" to Crawford "for any injury to [Crawford's] person or loss of or damage to property for any cause." Two months after Crawford rented the apartment (which was located on the building's second floor), a fire broke out in the first-floor apartment of Debra and Larry Buckner. The fire spread to Crawford's apartment and blocked Crawford from escaping through the front (and only) door of her apartment. To escape the fire, Crawford jumped from a second-story window. When she landed, she sustained numerous injuries, partly due to debris on the ground behind the apartment building.

Crawford filed a negligence suit against the Buckners, McKenzie, and MDC. She alleged that McKenzie and MDC were negligent in failing to maintain the building's fire alarm system, in failing to maintain the ground area behind the apartment building, and in continuing to allow the Buckners to reside in the apartment complex despite numerous complaints to McKenzie and MDC about the Buckners' behavior. McKenzie and MDC asserted that the exculpatory clause in their lease with Crawford barred her negligence claim against them. The trial court agreed and granted those defendants' motion for summary judgment. When Tennessee's intermediate court of appeals affirmed, Crawford appealed to the Tennessee Supreme Court.

---

**Anderson, Justice**    The determinative issue raised in this appeal is whether an exculpatory clause in a residential lease bars recovery against the landlord for negligence which caused the tenant injury. An exculpatory clause in the context of a landlord-tenant relationship refers to a clause which deprives the tenant of the right to recover damages . . . by releasing the landlord from liability for future acts of negligence. [T]he argument for enforceability of such clauses has often been based upon the doctrine of freedom of contract. Some cases, especially older ones, have reasoned that the relationship of landlord and tenant is in no event a matter of public interest, but is purely a private affair, so that such clauses cannot be held void on public policy grounds. However, because of the burden-shifting effect of such clauses, which [purport to] grant immunity from [liability], it is not surprising that their validity has been challenged and that courts have reached different conclusions as to their enforceability.

McKenzie and MDC contend that freedom to contract in the residential lease setting is the majority rule in the United States, and that holding exculpatory provisions in residential leases invalid on public policy grounds would require this court to adopt the minority rule. We find, as the Washington Supreme Court found in *McCutcheon v. United Homes Corp.* (1971), that there is no majority rule, "only numerous conflicting decisions . . . and a disposition of the courts to emasculate such exculpatory clauses by means of strict construction."

Tennessee courts have long recognized that, subject to certain exceptions, parties may contract that one shall not be liable for his negligence to another. We held in *Olson v. Molzen* (1977), however, that if an exculpatory provision [adversely affects] the public interest, it is void as against public policy, despite the general rule that parties may contract that one shall not be liable for his negligence to another. In *Olson,* we said that a exculpatory clause signed by a patient as a condition of receiving medical treatment is invalid as contrary to public policy and may not be pleaded as a bar to the patient's suit for negligence.

Crawford contends in this case that the exculpatory provision in her lease falls squarely within criteria set forth in *Olson* [and that] the exculpatory provision [should therefore be held] void as against public policy. In order to determine whether an exculpatory provision [adversely] affects the public interest, we adopted the following criteria in *Olson:*

1. It concerns a business of a type generally thought suitable for public regulation.

2. The party seeking exculpation is engaged in performing a service of great importance to the public (often a matter of practical necessity for some members of the public).

3. The party [seeking exculpation] holds himself out as willing to perform this service for any member of the public who seeks it, or at least for any member coming within certain established standards.

4. As a result of the essential nature of the service, in the economic setting of the transaction, the party invoking exculpation possesses a decisive advantage of bargaining strength against any member of the public who seeks his services.

5. In exercising a superior bargaining power, that party confronts the public with a standardized adhesion contract of exculpation, and makes no provision whereby a purchaser [or lessee] may pay additional reasonable fees and obtain protection against negligence.

6. As a result of the transaction, the person or property of the purchaser [or lessee] is placed under the control of the seller [or lessor], subject to the risk of carelessness by the seller [or lessor] or his agents.

In adopting these factors, we stated that "it is not necessary that all be present . . . , but generally a transaction that has some of these characteristics would be offensive."

[W]e conclude that a residential lease concerns a business of a type generally thought suitable for public regulation. Our conclusion is bolstered by the fact that the legislature of this state has seen fit to regulate [some aspects of the residential landlord-tenant relationship]. [W]e no longer live in a society where land, not housing, was the important part of a rental agreement. Residential landlords offer shelter, a basic necessity of life, to more than a million inhabitants of this state. Accordingly, it is self-evident that a residential landlord is engaged in performing a service of great importance to the public [and that this service] is often a matter of practical necessity for some members of the public. In addition, a residential landlord holds itself out as willing to perform a service for any member of the public who seeks it.

As a result of the essential nature of the service and the economic setting of the transaction, a residential landlord has a decisive advantage in bargaining strength against any member of the public who seeks its services. A potential tenant is usually confronted with a "take it or leave it" form contract, which the tenant is powerless to alter. Moreover, due to its superior bargaining position, a residential landlord confronts the public with a standardized adhesion contract of exculpation, which contains no provision whereby a tenant can pay additional reasonable fees to obtain protection from the landlord's negligence. Finally, we conclude that by definition, a residential lease places the person and the property of the tenant under the control of the landlord, subject to the risk of carelessness by the landlord and his agents. The allegations of this case [provide] common examples of landlord negligence [allegedly] causing injury to either the person or property of the tenant.

Accordingly, we find that the residential landlord-tenant relationship here satisfies all six of the public interest criteria adopted in *Olson v. Molzen.* However, McKenzie and MDC insist that a residential lease between a landlord and a tenant is a purely private affair. We disagree. We find persuasive the reasoning of the Washington Supreme Court, which, in response to the very same argument, stated:

[W]e are not faced merely with the theoretical duty of construing a provision in an isolated contract specifically bargained for by *one landlord and one tenant* as a purely private affair. Considered realistically, we are asked to construe an exculpatory clause, the generalized use of which may have an impact upon thousands of potential tenants.

*McCutcheon v. United Homes Corp.* (1971) (emphasis in original).

Based on the foregoing, we conclude that the exculpatory clause in the residential lease in this case is contrary to public policy. In reaching this conclusion, we join a growing number of states, [which either by statute or judicial decision] have declared exculpatory clauses [in residential leases] void as against public policy.

**Summary judgment for McKenzie and MDC reversed; case remanded to trial court for further proceedings.**

---

**Landlord's Liability for Injuries Resulting from Others' Criminal Conduct**   Another aspect of the trend toward increasing landlords' legal accountability is that many courts have imposed on landlords the duty to take reasonable steps to protect tenants and others on their property from foreseeable criminal conduct.[5] Although landlords are not insurers of the safety of persons on their property, an increasing number of courts have found them liable for injuries sustained by individuals who were criminally attacked on the landlord's property, if the attack was facilitated by the landlord's failure to comply with housing codes or maintain reasonable security. This liability has been imposed on residential and commercial landlords (such as shopping mall owners). Some courts have held that the implied warranty of habitability includes the obligation to provide reasonable security, but in most

---

[5]Chapter 16 contains a more extensive discussion of courts' recent inclination to impose this duty on owners and possessors of property.

states that have imposed this type of liability, principles of negligence furnish the controlling rationale.

*Muniz v. Lefran Realty Corp.* builds on these principles in holding that a pedestrian injured by criminal conduct on the landlord's property stated a cause of action against the landlord, when the criminal conduct was made more likely by a tenant's known and unlawful use of the leased property.

---

## MUNIZ V. LEFRAN REALTY CORP.
### 553 N.Y.S.2d 313 (Sup. Ct. of N.Y., App. Div. 1990)

Miguel Muniz, a nine-year-old boy, was permanently blinded when he was shot in the head while passing in front of a building owned by Lefran Realty. The bullet that struck Miguel was shot from inside Lefran Realty's building during a robbery of the allegedly known, illegal "drug supermarket" operated by the tenant of a store located in the building. The illegal use of the store was well known to many people prior to the day when Miguel was shot. Although it had been raided by police on five occasions, the store reopened with the sale of drugs and narcotics soon after each raid. The building superintendent stated that patrons of the store went there to buy drugs rather than clothing and that he had reported the misuse of the store to the landlord several times before the shooting. The executive director of the neighborhood association had received many complaints about the store from persons in the neighborhood.

Miguel and his mother brought suit against Lefran Realty. The trial court granted summary judgment in favor of Lefran Realty and dismissed the case. The Munizes appealed.

---

**Rosenberger, Justice**    The [lower court] concluded that even if the landlord had knowledge of the drug operation, it "stretches foreseeability much too far" to conclude the landlord should have foreseen an attempted robbery of the drug operation. We disagree.

While the intervening criminal act of a third person will generally be deemed a superseding cause which severs the liability of the original tort-feasor, this is not the case "when the intentional or criminal intervention of a third party is reasonably foreseeable." Thus, a landlord may be held liable for the personal injury inflicted upon a tenant or guest by a criminal intruder in a common area of the building if the landlord should have anticipated a risk of harm from criminal activity to persons on the premises.

In this case, however, neither the injured infant nor his mother had any relationship with Lefran Realty; they were merely passersby. Consequently, Lefran Realty argues, the Munizes were not within the orbit of duty imposed on the owner of the building, and a landlord has no duty to the public at large, with no connection to the premises, who might be victimized by street predators.

The Munizes contend that the crime which led to the infant's injury was directly related to the illegal drug operation which was openly and notoriously conducted on Lefran Realty's premises. Lefran Realty's building was not merely a fortuitous site randomly chosen by a malefactor, but was itself the scene of an unlawful activity which is known to attract violent crime.

It is the duty of the owner of a building, abutting upon a public street, to maintain it in such a condition that it shall not become dangerous to the traveling public. We need not look to the terms of the lease to determine whether the landlord retained the power to remedy a dangerous condition arising from unlawful activity on his premises. Under Real Property Law section 231, an owner of real property who knowingly allows that property to be used or occupied for any unlawful trade, manufacture, or business is liable for any damage resulting from such unlawful use. This statute expresses the clear public policy of the state which requires that owners of real property be vigilant in preventing their property from being used for unlawful purposes. To this end, [the law] provides that whenever a lessee uses any part of a building for an unlawful trade or business, the lease shall thereupon become void, and the landlord of such lessee may enter upon the premises so let. It is to be noted that the owner of these premises was not reluctant to enlist the aid of the courts when the tenant of the premises was late in rent payments, having twice commenced summary proceedings for non-payment. The common law also imposes a duty upon landlords to control the conduct of persons on their premises when they are reasonably aware of the necessity to do so. This duty extends to the protection of persons lawfully present in public places adjacent to the landlords' premises.

These compelling reasons of public policy lead us to conclude that the intervening criminal act of another is not a superseding cause which will relieve a landlord, who knows or has reason to know of illegal activities on his premises, of liability for injuries to innocent persons not in privity with the landlord where the intervening criminal act is a reasonably foreseeable sequela of such illegal use. Public policy is furthered by requiring that property owners not permit illegal enterprises which attract violent confrontations to flourish on their premises.

The plaintiffs' allegations are legally sufficient to state a cause of action against Lefran Realty.

**Summary judgment for Lefran Realty reversed.**

## RIGHTS, DUTIES, AND LIABILITIES OF THE TENANT

### Rights of the Tenant

The tenant has the right to *exclusive possession* and *quiet enjoyment* of the property during the term of the lease. The landlord is not entitled to enter the leased property without the tenant's consent, unless an emergency threatens the property or the landlord is acting under an express lease provision giving her the right to enter. The tenant may use the leased premises for any lawful purpose that is reasonable and appropriate, unless the purpose for which it may be used is expressly limited in the lease. Furthermore, the tenant has both the right to receive leased residential property in a habitable condition at the beginning of the lease and the right to have the property maintained in a habitable condition for the duration of the lease.

### Duty to Pay Rent

The tenant, of course, has the duty to pay rent in the agreed amount and at the agreed times. If two or more persons are cotenants, their liability under the lease is *joint and several*. This means that each cotenant has complete responsibility—not just partial responsibility—for performing the tenants' duties under the lease. For example, Alberts and Baker rent an apartment from Caldwell, with both Alberts and Baker signing a one-year lease. If Alberts moves out after three months, Caldwell may hold Baker responsible for the entire rent, not just half of it. (Naturally, Alberts remains liable on the lease—as well as to Baker under any rent-sharing agreement the two of them had—but Caldwell is free to proceed against Baker solely if Caldwell so chooses.)

### Duty Not to Commit Waste

The tenant also has the duty not to commit **waste** on the property. This means that the tenant is responsible for the routine care and upkeep of the property and that he has the duty not to commit any act that would harm the property. In the past, fulfillment of this duty required that the tenant perform necessary repairs. Today, the duty to make repairs has generally been shifted to the landlord by court ruling, statute, or lease provision. The tenant now has no duty to make major repairs unless the relevant damage was caused by his own negligence. When damage exists through no fault of the tenant and the tenant therefore is not obligated to make the actual repairs, the tenant nonetheless has the duty to take reasonable interim steps to prevent further damage from the elements. This duty would include, but not necessarily be limited to, informing the landlord of the problem. The duty would be triggered, for instance, when a window breaks or the roof leaks.

## Assignment and Subleasing

As with rights and duties under most other types of contracts, the rights and duties under a lease may generally be assigned and delegated to third parties. **Assignment** occurs when the landlord or the tenant transfers all of her remaining rights under the lease to another person. For example, a landlord may sell an apartment building and assign the relevant leases to the buyer, who will then become the new landlord. A tenant may assign the remainder of her lease to someone else, who then acquires whatever rights the original tenant had under the lease (including, of course, the right to exclusive possession of the leased premises).

**Subleasing** occurs when the tenant transfers to another person some, but not all, of his remaining right to possess the property. The relationship of tenant to sublessee then becomes one of landlord and tenant. For example, Dorfman, a college student whose 18-month lease on an apartment is to terminate on December 31, 1995, sublets his apartment to Wembley for the summer months of 1995. This is a sublease rather than an assignment, because Dorfman has not transferred all of his remaining rights under the lease.

The significance of the assignment-sublease distinction is that an assignee acquires rights and duties under the lease between the landlord and the original tenant, but a sublessee does not. An assignee steps into the shoes of the original tenant and acquires any rights she had under the lease.[6] For example, if the lease contained an option to renew, the assignee would have the right to exercise this option if he desired to do so. The assignee, of course, becomes personally liable to the landlord for the payment of rent.

Under both an assignment and a sublease, the original tenant remains liable to the landlord for the commitments made in the lease. If the assignee or sublessee fails to pay rent, for example, the tenant has the legal obligation to pay it. Figure 1 compares the characteristics of assignments and subleases.

### Lease Provisions Limiting Assignment

Leases commonly contain limitations on assignment and subleasing. This is especially true of commercial leases. Such provisions typically require the landlord's consent to any assignment or sublease, or purport to prohibit such a transfer of the tenant's interests. Provisions requiring the landlord's consent are upheld by the courts, although some courts hold

---

[6]Assignment is discussed in detail in Chapter 9.

**FIGURE 1**   Comparison of Assignment and Sublease

|  | Assignment | Sublease |
|---|---|---|
| Does the tenant transfer to the third party *all* his remaining rights under the lease? | Yes | No |
| Does the tenant remain liable on the lease? | Yes | Yes |
| Does the third party (assignee or sublessee) acquire rights and duties under the tenant's lease with the landlord? | Yes | No |

that the landlord cannot withhold consent unreasonably. Total prohibitions against assignment may be enforced as well, but they are disfavored in the law. Courts usually construe them narrowly, resolving ambiguities against the landlord.

## Tenant's Liability for Injuries to Third Persons

The tenant is normally liable to persons who suffer harm while on the portion of the property over which the tenant has control, *if the injuries resulted from the tenant's negligence.*

## TERMINATION OF THE LEASEHOLD

A leasehold typically terminates because the lease term has expired. Sometimes, however, the lease is terminated early because of a party's material breach of the lease or because of mutual agreement.

## Eviction

If a tenant breaches the lease (most commonly, by nonpayment of rent), the landlord may take action to **evict** the tenant. State statutes usually establish a relatively speedy eviction procedure. The landlord who desires to evict a tenant must be careful to comply with any applicable state or city regulations governing evictions. These regulations usually forbid self-help measures on the landlord's part, such as forcible entry to change locks. At common law, a landlord had a lien on the tenant's personal property. The landlord therefore could remove and hold such property as security for the rent obligation. This lien has been abolished in many states. Where the lien still exists, it is subject to constitutional limitations requiring that the tenant be given notice of the lien, as well as an opportunity to defend and protect his belongings before they can be sold to satisfy the rent obligation.

## Agreement to Surrender

A lease may terminate prematurely by mutual agreement between landlord and tenant to **surrender** the lease (i.e., return the property to the landlord prior to the end of the lease). A valid surrender discharges the tenant from further liability under the lease.

## Abandonment

Abandonment occurs when the tenant unjustifiably and permanently vacates the leased premises before the end of the lease term, and defaults in the payment of rent. If a tenant abandons the leased property, he is making an offer to surrender the leasehold. As shown in Figure 2, the landlord must make a decision at this point. If the landlord's conduct shows acceptance of the tenant's offer of surrender,

**FIGURE 2   Termination of a Leasehold by Abandonment**

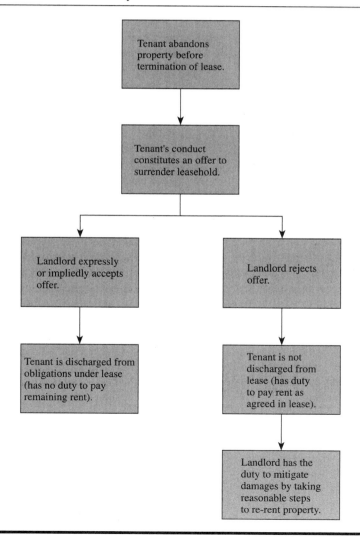

the tenant is relieved of the obligation to pay rent for the remaining period of the lease. If the landlord does not accept the surrender, she may sue the tenant for the rent due until such time as she (the landlord) rents the property to someone else, or, if she cannot find a new tenant, for the rent due for the remainder of the term.

At common law, the landlord had no obligation to mitigate (decrease) the damages caused by the abandonment by attempting to rent the leased property to a new tenant. In fact, taking possession of the property for the purpose of trying to rent it to someone else was a risky move for the landlord—her retaking of possession might be construed as acceptance of the surrender. Many states now place the duty on the landlord to attempt to mitigate damages by making a reasonable effort to rerent the property. These states also hold that the landlord's retaking of possession for the purpose of rerenting does not constitute a waiver of her right to pursue an action to collect unpaid rent.

## PROBLEMS AND PROBLEM CASES

**1.** Dr. Kaminsky performed elective abortions in his medical practice. He leased office space from Fidelity in the Red Oak Atrium Building for a two-year term, beginning June 1983. The written lease included an express covenant of quiet enjoyment. In June 1984, anti-abortion demonstrators began picketing at the building on Saturdays, when Dr. Kaminsky scheduled abortions. Singing and chanting demonstrators picketed in the building's parking lot, inner lobby, and atrium area. They approached patients to discourage them from entering the building, accused Dr. Kaminsky of killing babies, and distributed literature. The demonstrators frequently occupied the stairs leading to Dr. Kaminsky's office and prevented patients from entering the office by blocking the doorway. Occasionally, they gained access to the office waiting area. Dr. Kaminsky asked Fidelity for help in keeping the demonstrators away, but became frustrated by Fidelity's failures to respond. No security personnel were present on Saturdays, even though the lease obligated Fidelity to provide security service on Saturdays. Fidelity's attorneys prepared a notice to inform the demonstrators that they risked prosecution by not leaving when asked to do so, but Fidelity's agent did not distribute the notice. The Sheriff's office refused to ask the demonstrators to leave

without a directive from Fidelity, whose only response was to state that it was aware of Dr. Kaminsky's problems. In early December 1984, Dr. Kaminsky abandoned the property and ceased paying rent. Fidelity sued for the balance due under the lease. Dr. Kaminsky argued that Fidelity constructively evicted him by breaching the covenant of quiet enjoyment. Was Dr. Kaminsky correct?

**2.** Garwacki and Mastello shared a second-story apartment, which Garwacki rented from LaFraneire. Mastello invited Young to attend a dinner party at the apartment. Young went to the porch of the apartment to call down to Mastello, who was in the driveway below. As she placed her hands on the porch railing and leaned forward, the railing gave way. Young fell to the ground and was injured. The porch was accessible only from the living room of the apartment and was not a common area shared with other tenants. Should LaFraneire be liable for Young's injuries?

**3.** Skiver rented an apartment from Brighton for a 12-month period beginning May 1, 1990. His monthly rent was $430.83. Skiver paid Brighton a $350 security deposit. Skiver moved elsewhere in June 1990. He paid $100 toward the June rent, and nothing thereafter. A substitute tenant was not located until March 1991. Brighton retained Skiver's security deposit and sued him in small claims court for unpaid rent. State law allowed landlords to retain security deposits to satisfy all or part of a rent arrearage and to compensate for "actual damages to the rental unit." However, a state statute also provided that "[i]n the case of damage to the rental unit or other obligation against the security deposit, the landlord shall mail to the tenant, within 45 days after the termination of occupancy, an itemized list of damages claimed for which the security deposit may be used." Another statute stated that if the landlord failed to provide such a list within the 45-day period, the landlord was obligated to refund the full security deposit and was disqualified from recovering damages from the tenant. Brighton provided no itemized list to Skiver. The small claims court concluded that Skiver owed Brighton eight months' rent plus the unpaid portion of the June 1990 rent. It granted Brighton a judgment of $2,650 (the court's $3,000 jurisdictional limit minus the retained security deposit). The court determined that Brighton did not need to provide an itemized list because Brighton did not claim that Skiver had caused any physical damage to the premises.

Skiver appealed. Was Brighton entitled to retain the security deposit? Was Brighton entitled to judgment against Skiver for the rent arrearage exceeding the security deposit amount?

**4.** Kridel entered into a lease with Sommer, owner of the Pierre Apartments, to lease apartment 6-L for two years. Kridel, who was to be married in June, planned to move into the apartment in May. His parents and future parents-in-law had agreed to assume responsibility for the rent, because Kridel was a full-time student who had no funds of his own. Shortly before Kridel was to have moved in, his engagement was broken. He wrote Sommer a letter explaining his situation and stating that he could not take the apartment. Sommer did not answer the letter. When another party inquired about renting apartment 6-L, the person in charge told her that the apartment was already rented to Kridel. Sommer did not enter the apartment or show it to anyone until he rented apartment 6-L to someone else when there were approximately eight months left on Kridel's lease. He sued Kridel for the full rent for the period of approximately 16 months before the new tenant's lease took effect. Kridel argued that Sommer should not be able to collect rent for the first 16 months of the lease because he did not take reasonable steps to rerent the apartment. Was Sommer entitled to collect the rent he sought?

**5.** Brock, the administrator of Jackson's estate, sued Levie and Watts Realty in a wrongful death action. Prior to her death, Jackson lived in a Birmingham, Alabama, apartment building owned by Levie. Watts Realty had leased the apartment to Jackson. In her complaint, Brock alleged that Jackson had twice asked the defendants to repair the locks on the back door of Jackson's apartment, but that the defendants had failed to respond. After Jackson made these requests, she notified the police that a prowler was at the "back part" of the apartment. When the police came to the apartment to investigate, they discovered that Jackson had been fatally stabbed. Brock's complaint alleged that Jackson's murderer acquired access to the apartment because of the broken locks on the back door, and that Levie and Watts Realty should be held liable because they violated two Birmingham ordinances in failing to maintain the locks. These ordinances required locks on exterior doors and specified that the locks must be kept "in sound working condition and good repair." Apparently concluding as a matter

of law that Levie and Watts Realty could not be held liable for Jackson's death at the hand of a murderer, the trial judge granted summary judgment in favor of Levie and Watts Realty. Was the trial judge correct in doing so?

**6.** Kessler was employed as a part-time rental agent at White Oak Park Apartments. Her duties included showing and renting apartments, receiving rent money, arranging for repairs, and similar responsibilities. According to Kessler, her supervisor, Chase, instructed her to enter (while the tenants were not present) the apartments of tenants whose rent was overdue, to "snoop" around the apartments, and to look through private papers in order to obtain information regarding their places of employment, wage or salary information, and other information that might be helpful in collecting overdue rent. Kessler did so reluctantly a few times, but felt bad about having done so. She told Chase that she would not do this any more. Kessler was ultimately discharged. She alleged that she was discharged because of her refusal to carry out her supervisor's instructions regarding snooping into tenants' apartments. Is the type of entry that Kessler was allegedly instructed to conduct lawful?

**7.** From 1984 to 1986, Hardy occupied an apartment at 18 Arthur Street, which she leased from Griffin. Griffin had painted the apartment, but the previous coat of paint had not been scraped off. It was described as "thick, chipped, and peeling." Hardy saw her young son, Verron, eating paint chips in the apartment. This prompted her to have him tested for the presence of lead in his blood. She learned that Verron had abnormally high levels of lead in his blood and that this condition was due to his exposure to the lead-based paint present at 18 Arthur Street. Verron suffered severe brain damage as a result. Griffin admitted that in January 1987, he had received notice from the city about the presence of lead paint at 18 Arthur Street. On previous occasions, he had been put on notice that repairs to Hardy's unit were necessary. A state statute provided that "[t]he presence of paint which does not conform to federal standards as required in accordance with the Lead-Based Paint Poisoning Prevention Act . . . or of cracked, chipped, blistered, flaking, loose or peeling paint which constitutes a health hazard on accessible surfaces in any dwelling unit, tenement or any real property intended for human habitation shall be construed to render such dwelling unit . . . unfit for human habitation. . . ." A city ordinance imposed a duty on landlords to "make all repairs and do whatever is necessary to put and keep the premises in a fit and habitable condition." Hardy brought suit against Griffin for Verron's injuries. Should Griffin be liable?

**8.** In October 1981, Cook entered into an oral lease to rent a residence to Melson. Melson agreed to pay $400 per month, in advance, as rent. In November 1987, Cook sent Melson a letter advising that the rent would be increased to $525 per month, effective January 1, 1988, and asking whether Melson was going to pay. On December 10, 1987, Melson replied that he would not pay the increased rent. On January 2, 1988, Melson sent Cook a check for $400 as rent for January. Cook returned the check and stated that the rent was now $525. Melson did not vacate the premises until February 1, 1988. Cook brought a suit against Melson for $525, allegedly the unpaid rent for the month of January. Was Melson liable for the $525?

**9.** Sippin owned property on Main Street in Monroe, Connecticut. He rented this property to Longo and Ellam pursuant to a written lease, which stipulated that the premises was to be used exclusively for Longo's and Ellam's real estate business. Longo and Ellam did not know that the deed by which Sippin had acquired the property contained a restrictive covenant barring any commercial use of the property. After Longo and Ellam had been in possession of the property for a few months, the local zoning enforcement agency ordered them to remove a commercial real estate sign and to cease operating their business on the property because it was located in a residential zone. Although the residential zoning of the property was in effect at the time they entered into their lease with Sippin, Longo and Ellam had not previously known of this zoning designation. Further zoning enforcement action caused Longo and Ellam to wind up their real estate business and to vacate the property (without paying further rent) prior to the expiration of the term contemplated by their lease with Sippin. Sippin sued Longo and Ellam in an effort to recover the unpaid rent (as called for by the lease) for the remainder of the lease term, or, in the alternative, to recover the fair rental value of the premises pursuant to a line of Connecticut cases allowing landlords to collect the fair rental value of property from any tenant at sufferance. When the trial court ruled in

favor of Long and Ellam, Sippin appealed. Was Sippin entitled to a judgment for the unpaid rent contemplated by the lease? Alternatively, did the line of cases dealing with tenants at sufferance entitle Sippin to a judgment for the fair rental value of the premises?

**10.** Norman owned a three-bedroom duplex in Dane County, Wisconsin. He adopted a policy of renting to married persons (and their families) or to a divorced, widowed, separated, or single person. Norman would not, however, rent to any *group of unrelated* individuals. A Dane County ordinance prohibited landlords from discriminating against potential tenants on the basis of "marital status." When Norman refused to rent his duplex to a group of three single women and to a later group consisting of two women plus a child of one of the women, Dane County instituted legal proceedings against Norman. The county alleged that he violated the ordinance referred to above. Did Norman violate the ordinance?

## CAPSTONE QUESTIONS

Leaseco, Inc., owns an office building and several apartment complexes. The firm's business consists of leasing these commercial and residential properties to tenants. All of these properties are located in the City of Averageville, where South Northern State University (SNSU) is located. Leaseco is the lessor in each of the situations described below:

- Leaseco has leased an apartment to SNSU law student Prudence Juris for a one-year term beginning September 1. The parties have entered into a written lease.

- Leaseco has leased an apartment to SNSU offensive tackle Hugh Mongous, who pays his rent on the first day of each month. Although Leaseco usually insists on one-year leases of its apartments, Leaseco did not require a one-year lease in this instance because Leaseco's property manager and Mongous are friends. Leaseco and Mongous therefore have no explicit agreement regarding the duration of the lease. Mongous has decided to quit school and move out of the apartment. He intends to leave Averageville and begin playing professional football for the Boise Spuds (of the new Regional Football League).

Leaseco leased office space in one of its office buildings to accountant Delbert Dull. The parties' written lease established a two-year term and a monthly rent of $800. It did not contain a provision prohibiting assignments. After the first year and two months of the lease, Dull decided that he would prefer to have his office in a building not owned by Leaseco and located elsewhere in Averageville. Because he had eight months to go on his lease with Leaseco, Dull assigned the lease to accountant Gilbert Gaap. Gaap occupied the office space for two months and paid Leaseco the $800 per month rent for each of those two months. Gaap then disappeared and ceased paying rent. His whereabouts remain unknown. Despite its reasonable efforts to locate another tenant for the office space, Leaseco was unable to do so during the last six months of the lease. Leaseco made demand upon Dull for $4,800 in unpaid rent, but Dull refused to pay, asserting that "Gilbert Gaap stepped into my shoes under the lease, so you're sadly mistaken if you think you've got a good claim against me."

On February 1, Averageville experienced heavy snowfall. Leaseco cleared ice and snow off the sidewalks located in front of its apartment complexes but took no action to remove ice and snow from the parking lot of, and driveway leading to, its Roachmont Manor complex. On the evening of February 3, Elroy Hefty happened to visit his daughter, who lives in Roachmont Manor. As Hefty exited his car, which he had parked in the Roachmont Manor lot, he slipped on an icy patch that was hidden beneath the snow. Hefty fell to the pavement and fractured his hip. Hefty later filed a negligence suit against Leaseco, which argues that it cannot be liable to Hefty because he was not a tenant.

SNSU students Lucy Lucas and Wilma Wilmot are cotenants under a one-year written lease of an apartment in Leaseco's Roachmont Manor complex. The monthly rent set forth in the lease is $550. Both cotenants signed the lease, which has four more months to go. Lucas and Wilmot were each paying $275 per month in order to cover the rent. Leaseco was aware of their rent-sharing arrangement. Lucas, however, recently moved to Paris, Texas. She has informed Wilmot and Leaseco that she will no longer be sharing in the rent.

## Required:

Answer the following and give reasons for your conclusions.

1. In addition to whatever duties it owes Juris under the express language of the parties' lease, what three major implied warranties is Leaseco legally regarded as having made to Juris? Briefly describe these implied warranties.

2. What type of tenancy exists between Leaseco and Mongous? In view of his decision to move out, what must Mongous do in order to terminate the tenancy properly?

3. Was Dull correct in asserting that Leaseco did not have a valid claim against him?

4. Will Hefty's nontenant status prevent him from recovering in a negligence suit against Leaseco?

5. What amount of rent is Leaseco entitled to insist on collecting from Wilmot for the remaining months of its lease with Lucas and Wilmot?

# CHAPTER

## 19

# ESTATES

# AND TRUSTS

**INTRODUCTION**

*One of the basic features of the ownership of property is the right to dispose of the property during life and at death. You have already learned about the ways in which property is transferred during the owner's life. The owner's death is another major event for the transfer of property. Most people want to be able to choose who will get their property when they die. There are a variety of ways in which a person may control the ultimate disposition of his property. He may take title to the property in a form of joint ownership that gives his co-owner a right of survivorship. He may create a trust and transfer property to it to be used for the benefit of a spouse, child, elderly parent, or other beneficiary. He may execute a will in which he directs that his real and personal property be distributed to persons named in the will. If, however, a person makes no provision for the disposition of his property at his death, his property will be distributed to his heirs as defined by state law. This chapter focuses on the transfer of property at death and on the use of trusts for the transfer and management of property, both during life and at death.*

## THE LAW OF ESTATES AND TRUSTS

Each state has its own statutes and common law regulating the distribution of property upon death. Legal requirements and procedures may vary from state to state, but many general principles can be stated. The **Uniform Probate Code (UPC)** is a comprehensive, uniform law that has been enacted in 16 states. It is intended to update and unify state law concerning the disposition and administration of property at death. Several relevant UPC provisions will be discussed in this chapter.

### Estate Planning

A person's **estate** is all of the property owned by that person. **Estate planning** is the popular name for the complicated process of planning for the transfer of a person's estate in later life and at death. Estate planning also concerns planning for the possibility of prolonged illness or disability. An attorney who is creating an estate plan will take an inventory of the client's assets, learn the client's objectives, and draft the instruments necessary to carry out the plan. This plan is normally guided by the desire to reduce the amount of tax liability and to provide for the orderly disposition of the estate.

## WILLS

### Right of Disposition by Will

The right to control the disposition of property at death has not always existed. In the English feudal system, the king owned all land. The lords and knights had only the right to use land for their lifetime. A land-holder's rights in land terminated upon his death, and no rights descended to his heirs. In 1215, the king granted the nobility the right to pass their interest in the land they held to their heirs. Later, that right was extended to all property owners. In the United States, each state has enacted statutes that establish the requirements for a valid will, including the formalities that must be met to pass property by will.

### Nature of a Will

A **will** is a document executed with specific legal formalities by a **testator** (person making a will) that contains his instructions about the way his property will be disposed of at his death. A will can dispose only of property belonging to the testator at the time of his death. Furthermore, wills do not control property that goes to others through other planning devices (such as life insurance policies) or by operation of law (such as by right of survivorship). For example, property held in joint tenancy or tenancy by the entirety is not controlled by a will, because the property passes automatically to the surviving cotenant by right of survivorship. In addition, life insurance proceeds are controlled by the insured's designation of beneficiaries, not by any provision of a will. (Because joint tenancy and life insurance are ways of directing the disposition of property, they are sometimes referred to as "will substitutes.")

### Common Will Terminology

Some legal terms commonly used in wills include the following:

**1.** *Bequest.* A **bequest** (also called **legacy**) is a gift of personal property or money. For example, a

will might provide for a bequest of a family heirloom to the testator's daughter. Since a will can direct only property that is owned by the testator at the time of his death, a specific bequest of property that the testator has disposed of before his death is ineffective. This is called **ademption**. For example, Samuel's will states that Warren is to receive Samuel's collection of antique guns. If the guns are destroyed before Warren's death, however, the bequest is ineffective because of ademption.

**2.** *Devise.* A **devise** is a gift of real property. For example, the testator might devise his family farm to his grandson.

**3.** *Residuary.* The **residuary** is the balance of the estate that is left after specific devises and bequests are made by the will. After providing for the disposition of specific personal and real property, a testator might provide that the residuary of his estate is to go to his spouse or be divided among his descendants.

**4.** *Issue.* A person's **issue** are his lineal descendants (children, grandchildren, great-grandchildren, and so forth). This category of persons includes adopted children.

**5.** *Per capita.* This term and the next one, *per stirpes*, are used to describe the way in which a group of persons are to share a gift. **Per capita** means that each of that group of persons will share equally. For example, Grandfather dies, leaving a will that provides that the residuary of his estate is to go to his issue or descendants *per capita*. Grandfather had two children, Mary and Bill. Mary has two children, John and James. Bill has one child, Margaret. Mary and Bill die before Grandfather (in legal terms, *predecease* him), but all three of Grandfather's grandchildren are living at the time of his death. In this case, John, James, and Margaret would each take one third of the residuary of Grandfather's estate.

**6.** *Per stirpes.* When a gift is given to the testator's issue or descendants **per stirpes** (also called **by right of representation**), each surviving descendant divides the share that his or her parent would have taken if the parent had survived. In the preceding example, if Grandfather's will had stated that the residuary of his estate was to go to his issue or descendants *per stirpes*, Margaret would take one half and John and James would take one quarter each (that is, they would divide the share that would have gone to their mother).

## Testamentary Capacity

The capacity to make a valid will is called **testamentary capacity**. To have testamentary capacity, a person must be *of sound mind* and *of legal age*, which is 18 in most states. A person does not have to be in perfect mental health to have testamentary capacity. Because people often delay executing wills until they are weak and in ill health, the standard for mental capacity to make a will is fairly low. To be of "sound mind," a person need only be sufficiently rational to be capable of understanding the nature and character of his property, of realizing that he is making a will, and of knowing the persons who would normally be the beneficiaries of his affection. A person could move in and out of periods of lucidity and still have testamentary capacity if he executed his will during a lucid period.

Lack of testamentary capacity is a common ground upon which wills are challenged by persons who were excluded from a will. *Fraud* and *undue influence* are also common grounds for challenging the validity of a will.[1] Testamentary capacity and undue influence are discussed in the following case, *In the Matter of the Estate of Davidson.*

---

[1] Fraud and undue influence are discussed in Chapter 5.

---

## In the Matter of the Estate of Davidson
### 839 S.W.2d 214 (Sup. Ct. Ark. 1992)

Charlye Vera Forrester Davidson died in a nursing home at the age of 90, leaving an estate in excess of $2 million. For a number of years before Davidson's death, Donald Goodner had served as her lawyer. Goodner and his wife also ran personal errands for Davidson. In 1984, Goodner prepared a will for Davidson in which he was appointed her executor and was given, after other bequests, the residue and remainder of her property. Later, in 1985, Goodner prepared another will for Davidson in which he was named coexecutor and from which he was dropped as residual beneficiary in favor of Davidson's nephews, John and William Forrester. Over the next three years, Davidson gave Goodner and his wife gifts totaling $60,000.

Following Davidson's death in 1989, her 1984 will was admitted to probate. William Forrester challenged the will on the ground of undue influence and Davidson's allegedly unsound mind. After the will contest was filed, Goodner found Davidson's 1985 will behind a dishwasher in her house. A petition to admit the 1985 will to probate was filed, and that will was contested by Forrester on the same grounds—undue influence and unsound mind. The probate court decided that the 1985 will revoked the 1984 will and it admitted the 1985 will to probate and appointed Goodner as executor. The court also found that Davidson was "in all respects competent, and was not acting under restraint or undue influence." Forrester appealed, seeking to invalidate both the 1984 and the 1985 wills on the ground of lack of testamentary capacity and to have the estate pass by intestacy.

---

**Brown, Justice**    Once the proponent of a will shows that the will is rational on its face and has been executed and witnessed in accordance with testamentary formalities, the party challenging the will's validity is required to prove by a preponderance of the evidence that the testator lacked mental capacity or was unduly influenced at the time the will was executed.

Davidson's physician, Dr. Lambiotte, testified that between 1960 and 1985, Mrs. Davidson began suffering from diseases associated with aging. He further testified that she always recognized him and knew where she was. A psychiatrist who saw Davidson in 1985 diagnosed her primary problem as deteriorating memory caused by either Alzheimer's dementia or multi-infarct dementia. Other witnesses described Mrs. Davidson as strongwilled, eccentric, and "nutty." Toward the end of her life, and in 1985, she was obsessed by the fact that someone was trying to enter her house and take her things. This caused her to lock her house and nail her doors shut.

Our generally expressed rule for testamentary capacity is that the testatrix must be able to know the natural objects of her bounty and the extent of her property; to understand to whom the property is being given; and to realize those who are being excluded from the will. In the present case, nothing before us suggests the elements of mental competency were not present when Davidson executed her 1985 will. Three witnesses attested to her signature on the will, and none espoused the view that there was any unusual behavior on Davidson's part or any problem concerning soundness of mind. Two witnesses in fact recall Mrs. Davidson's specifically declaring that she was there to sign her will. Moreover, there was testimony that at the time Davidson was aware of the property she owned by Lake Waldron and of her properties in Colorado and Texas.

Our probate law does not require that a testatrix mete out exact justice in the devise of her property. So long as she has the capacity to make a will, she may be unfair, eccentric, injudicious, or capricious in making distribution. Moreover, the fact that Davidson was suffering ideation relative to her house and incipient dementia does not, in itself, establish an impairment of testamentary capacity. As Dr. Lambiotte testified, this could represent only "a slot of abnormality."

Any assertion that Davidson was unfair to her nephews is difficult to fathom in light of the fact that they received almost ninety percent of the estate's assets as residuary beneficiaries under the 1985 will. But, more importantly, the proposition that she did not know her property or who her heirs were and was unable to interrelate those factors was simply not proven. Because there was insufficient proof that the testatrix lacked the requisite mental

capacity to make a will in 1985, Forrester's contest must fail.

The additional assertion of undue influence really pertains more to the 1984 will where Goodner was a residuary beneficiary than to the 1985 will where he was not a recipient of the residuary estate. Forrester contends, however, that the circumstances surrounding the two wills taints the 1985 will. He further looks to Davidson's signature on the 1985 will which, he urges, indicates that she was assisted in her execution, the $60,000 in gifts to Goodner and his wife, and the line and different type for the residuary beneficiaries in the 1985 will as highly suspicious.

Undue influence sufficient to void a will must not spring from natural affection but must result from fear and coercion so as to deprive a testatrix of free will and direct the benefits of the will to particular parties. Undue influence is generally difficult of proof. Because of the allocation of the assets of her estate, it is difficult to discern a sinister or insidious effect from the 1985 will. It is true that Goodner had a confidential relationship with Davidson. Beyond that, we can only speculate about what her susceptibility to any testamentary suggestions by Goodner might have been. Our major problem with Forrester's argument is that neither Goodner nor any persons associated with him are distributees under the 1985 will. Without some assets flowing to particular parties sought to be benefitted by the supposed culprit, an undue influence claim is hard to sustain. Here, the proof was deficient and the claim of undue influence cannot prevail.

**Probate of the will affirmed.**

---

## Execution of a Will

Unless a will is executed with the formalities required by state law, it is *void*. The courts are strict in interpreting statutes concerning the execution of wills. If a will is declared void, the property of the deceased person will be distributed according to the provisions of state laws that will be discussed later.

The formalities required for a valid will differ from state to state. For that reason, an individual should consult the laws of his state before making a will. If he should move to another state after having executed a will, he should consult a lawyer in his

new state to determine whether a new will needs to be executed. All states require that a will be *in writing*. State law also requires that a formal will be *witnessed*, generally by two or three *disinterested* witnesses (persons who do not stand to inherit any property under the will), and that it be *signed* by the testator or by someone else at the testator's direction. Most states also require that the testator *publish* the will—that is, declare or indicate at the time of signing that the instrument is his will. Another formality required by most states is that the testator sign the will in the presence and the sight of the witnesses and that the witnesses sign in the presence and the sight of each other. As a general rule, an **attestation clause**, which states the formalities that have been followed in the execution of the will, is written following the testator's signature. These detailed formalities are designed to prevent fraud. Section 2–502 of the UPC requires that a will must be in writing, signed by the testator (or in the testator's name by some other individual in the testator's conscious presence and by the testator's direction), and signed by at least two individuals, each of whom signed within a reasonable time after he witnessed either the signing of the will or the testator's acknowledgment of that signature or will. Also, under the UPC, any individual who is generally competent to be a witness may witness a will, and the fact that the witness is an interested party does not invalidate the will [2–505]. When a testator has made a technical error in executing a will, however, the UPC permits the document to be treated as if it had been executed properly if it can be proven by clear and convincing evidence that the testator intended the document to constitute his will [2–503].

In some situations, a lawyer might arrange to have the execution of a will *videotaped* to provide evidence relating to the testator's capacity and the use of proper formalities. (Note that the will is executed in the normal way; the videotape merely records the execution of the will.) Some state probate codes specifically provide that videotapes of the executions of wills are admissible into evidence.

### Incorporation by Reference

In some situations, a testator might want his will to refer to and incorporate an existing writing. For example, the testator may have created a list of specific gifts of personal property that he wants to incorporate in the will. A writing such as this is called an **extrinsic document**—that is, a writing apart from the will. In most states, the contents of extrinsic documents can be essentially incorporated into the will when the circumstances satisfy rules that have been designed to ensure that the document is genuine and that it was intended by the testator to be incorporated in the will. This is called **incorporation by reference**. For an extrinsic document to be incorporated by reference, it must have been *in existence at the time the will was executed*. In addition, the writ-

ing and the will must refer to each other so that the extrinsic document can be identified and so that it is clear that the testator intended the extrinsic document to be incorporated in the will. Under the UPC, incorporation by reference is allowed when the extrinsic document was in existence when the will was executed, the language of the will manifests the intent to incorporate the writing, and the will describes the writing sufficiently to identify it [2–510].

### Informal Wills

Some states recognize certain types of wills that are not executed with these formalities. These are:

**1.** *Nuncupative wills.* A **nuncupative will** is an oral will. Such wills are recognized as valid in some states, but only under limited circumstances and to a limited extent. In a number of states, for example, nuncupative wills are valid only when made by soldiers in military service and sailors at sea, and even then they will be effective only to dispose of personal property that was in the actual possession of the person at the time the oral will was made. Other states place low dollar limits on the amount of property that can be passed by a nuncupative will.

**2.** *Holographic wills.* **Holographic wills** are wills that are written and signed in the testator's handwriting. The fact that holographic wills are not properly witnessed makes them suspect. They are recognized in about half of the states and by section 2–502(b) of the UPC, even though they are not executed with the formalities usually required of valid wills. For a holographic will to be valid in the states that recognize them, it must evidence testamentary intent and must actually be *handwritten* by the testator. A typed holographic will would be invalid. Some states require that the holographic will be *entirely* handwritten—although the UPC requires only that the signature and material portions of the will be handwritten by the testator [2–502(b)]—and some also require that the will be dated.

### Joint and Mutual Wills

In some circumstances, two or more people—a married couple, for example—decide together on a plan for the disposition of their property at death. To carry out this plan, they may execute a **joint will** (a single instrument that constitutes the will of both or all of the testators and is executed by both or all) or they may execute **mutual wills** (joint or separate, individual wills that reflect the common plan of distribution).

Underlying a joint or mutual will is an agreement on a common plan. This common plan often includes an express or implied contract (a contract to make a will or not to revoke the will). One issue that sometimes arises is whether a testator who has made a joint or mutual will can later change his will. Whether joint and mutual wills are revocable depends on the language of the will, on state law, and on the timing of the revocation. For example, a testator who made a joint will with his spouse may be able to revoke his will during the life of his spouse, because the spouse still has a chance to change her own will, but he may be unable to revoke or change

the will after the death of his spouse. The UPC provides that the mere fact that a joint or mutual will has been executed does *not* create the presumption of a contract not to revoke the will or wills [2–514].

## Construction of Wills

Even in carefully drafted wills, questions sometimes arise as to the meaning or legal effect of a term or provision. Disputes about the meaning of the will are even more likely to occur in wills drafted by the testator himself, such as holographic wills. To interpret a will, a court will examine the entire instrument in an attempt to determine the testator's intent. The following case, *Haag v. Stickley*, provides a good example of the methods and principles courts use to interpret wills.

---

### HAAG V. STICKLEY
#### 389 S.E.2d 691 (Va. Sup. Ct. 1990)

Kenneth Haag owned Front Royal Supply Company. Charles Smoot had worked for Haag as the manager of the Front Royal store for a number of years. John Stickley was the manager of the company's Winchester store, but had not worked for Haag as long as Smoot had. Wayne Blye was assistant manager of the Winchester store, and had worked for the company for a lesser amount of time than had Stickley. Melvin Printz was also an employee of Haag's, but was fired in 1984–85.

On January 20, 1983, Haag executed a holographic will. The will contained a specific bequest of stock to his employees who were still with Front Royal at the time of his death. It stated as follows:

In October 1985, Haag executed a holographic codicil. This codicil provided that "In case Chs. Smoot is deceased or any other receipient [sic] their stare [sic] will go back in the estate." Haag died in 1986. His will was admitted to probate, and his former wife, Helen, was named executor. At the time of Haag's death, he owned 689 shares of Front Royal stock, the value of which was at least $254,000. A dispute arose between Mrs. Haag, as executor, and Stickley and Blye about whether they were entitled to any shares. Mrs. Haag maintained that the will should be interpreted to give 500 shares of stock to Smoot, and none to Stickley and Blye, with the remaining 189 shares going into the residuary of the estate. Stickley and Blye filed this action asking the court to construe and interpret the will in order to determine their rights to the shares of stock. The court determined that Smoot should get the first 500 shares, and the remaining 189 shares should be divided equally between Stickley and Blye, with the odd share going to the person with longer service. Mrs. Haag appealed.

---

**Compton, Justice**    In construing a will, the testator's intention controls, unless contrary to an established rule of law. The whole will must be examined to determine the testator's intention and effect should be given to all parts of the document, as far as possible. Even though the language of the will may be obscure or uncertain, the testator's intention will prevail, if it can be ascertained.

Moreover, when the words of the will are capable of two different constructions, that should be adopted which is most consistent with the intention of the testator as ascertained by other provisions in the will; and when the intention of the testator is incorrectly expressed, the court will effectuate it by supplying the proper words.

It is true that in ascertaining the testator's intent we examine the words used in light of the circumstances surrounding the testator at the time of the will's execution. However, we cannot ignore subsequent changes to the will as we consider that intent. A will is an ambulatory instrument, not intended or allowed to take effect until the death of the maker. It may be changed during life as often as the mind and purposes of the testator change.

Against the background of the foregoing principles, we cannot say that the chancellor misinterpreted or misconstrued the testamentary documents. Insofar as the bequest of company stock is concerned, the testator's plan clearly appears from the will and from the circumstances prevailing at the time the will was drawn. The testator wished to reward company employees for their past and continued service by leaving all his stock in the company to such of those employees who were living and still working for the company at the time of his death.

Thus, he bequeathed "my shares of the stock" in the company, intending to give all the shares he owned. The quantity "500 shares" follows Smoot's name. No quantity is shown after Stickley's or Blye's names. Mrs. Haag contends the bequest is incomplete because it contains what she has labeled "blanks" or omissions. We perceive no blanks or omissions. Rather, we view the terms to state individual bequests.

Where a bequest is to several individuals, whatever may be their relationship to each other, equality is the rule, unless the testator has established a different one. Therefore, we conclude from the language and arrangement of the words that the testator intended to make a gift of all of his shares to three persons with one receiving 500 shares and the other two receiving the balance, which they divide equally, the longer in service to the company receiving the odd share.

The testator's intent is further indicated by the manner in which he made corrections on the holograph. He struck through the name of Melvin Printz, probably after Printz had been fired in 1984–85. He initialled the deletion writing "no" before "shares." This demonstrates the testator's method of deleting a beneficiary and canceling a bequest. He made other deletions in other portions of the will and codicil and initialled them also. In contrast, the names of Stickley and Blye remained in the will without being initialled but separately joined to the words "shares" by dashes or connecting lines, not blanks. The lines are undulating and not straight as a blank line usually appears. It cannot be successfully argued that these lines serve to negate the bequest to Stickley or Blye. There are at least two plausible reasons why the testator did not specify the number of shares allocated to Stickley or Blye. First, the testator was probably uncertain whether both would remain company employees until his death. Second, the testator was uncertain about the number of shares of company stock he would own when he died. For these reasons, the testator probably concluded that the exact number of shares passing to these two employees could be more accurately determined after his death.

For these reasons, we find no error in the decision of the trial court.

**Judgment for Stickley and Blye affirmed.**

## Limitations on Disposition by Will

A person who takes property by will takes it subject to all outstanding claims against the property. For example, if real property is subject to a mortgage or other lien, the beneficiary who takes the property gets it subject to the mortgage or lien. In addition, the rights of the testator's creditors are superior to the rights of beneficiaries under his will. Thus, if the testator was insolvent (his debts exceeded his assets), persons named as beneficiaries do not receive any property by virtue of the will.

Under the laws of most states, the surviving spouse of the testator has statutory rights in property owned solely by the testator that cannot be defeated by a contrary will provision. This means that a husband cannot effectively disinherit his wife, and vice versa. Even if the will provides for the surviving spouse, he or she can elect to take the share of the decedent's estate that would be provided by state law rather than the amount specified in the will. In some states, personal property, such as furniture, passes automatically to the surviving spouse.

At common law, a widow had the right to a life estate in one third of the lands owned by her husband during their marriage. This was known as a widow's **dower right**. A similar right for a widower was known as **curtesy**. A number of states have changed the right by statute to give a surviving spouse a one-third interest in fee simple in the real and personal property owned by the deceased spouse at the time of his or her death. (Naturally, a testator can leave his spouse more than this if he desires.) Under UPC 2–201, the surviving spouse's elective share varies depending on the length of the surviving spouse's marriage to the testator—the elective share increases with the length of marriage.

As a general rule, a surviving spouse is given the right to use the family home for a stated period as well as a portion of the deceased spouse's estate. In community property states, each spouse has a one-half interest in community property that cannot be defeated by a contrary will provision. (Note that the surviving spouse will obtain *full* ownership of any property owned by the testator and the surviving spouse as joint tenants or tenants by the entirety.)

Children of the testator who were born or adopted after the will was executed are called **pretermitted** children. There is a presumption that the testator intended to provide for such a child, unless there is evidence to the contrary. State law gives pretermitted children the right to a share of the testator's estate. For example, under section 2–302 of the Uniform Probate Code, a pretermitted child has the right to receive the share he would have received under the state intestacy statute unless it appears that the omission of this child was intentional, the testator gave substantially all of his estate to the child's other parent, or the testator provided for the child outside of the will.

## Revocation of Wills

One important feature of a will is that it is *revocable* until the moment of the testator's death. For this reason, a will confers *no present interest* in the testator's property. A person is free to revoke a prior will and, if she wishes, to make a new will. Wills can be revoked in a variety of ways. Physical destruction and mutilation done with intent to revoke a will constitute revocation, as do other acts such as crossing out the will or creating a writing that expressly cancels the will.

In addition, a will is revoked if the testator later executes a valid will that expressly revokes the earlier will. A later will that does not *expressly* revoke an earlier will operates to revoke only those portions of the earlier will that are inconsistent with the later will. Under the UPC, a later will that does not expressly revoke a prior will operates to revoke it by inconsistency if the testator intended the subsequent will to *replace* rather than *supplement* the prior will [2–507(b)]. Furthermore, the UPC presumes that the testator intended the subsequent will to replace rather than supplement the prior will if the subsequent one makes a complete disposition of her estate, but it presumes that the testator intended merely to supplement and not replace the prior will if the subsequent will disposes of only part of her estate [2–507(c), 2–507(d)]. In some states, a will is presumed to have been revoked if it cannot be located after the testator's death, although this presumption can be rebutted with contrary evidence.

Wills can also be revoked by operation of law without any act on the part of the testator signifying revocation. State statutes provide that certain changes in relationships operate as revocations of a will. In some states, marriage will operate to revoke a will that was made when the testator was single. Similarly, a divorce may revoke provisions in a will made during marriage that leave property to the divorced spouse. Under the laws of some states, the birth of a child after the execution of a will may operate as a partial revocation of the will.

## Codicils

A **codicil** is an amendment of a will. If a person wants to change a provision of a will without making an entirely new will, she may amend the will by executing a codicil. One may *not* amend a will by merely striking out objectionable provisions and inserting new provisions. The same formalities are required for the creation of a valid codicil as for the creation of a valid will.

## ADVANCE DIRECTIVES: PLANNING FOR DISABILITY

Advances in medical technology now permit a person to be kept alive by artificial means, even in many cases in which there is no hope of the person's being able to function without life support. Many people are opposed to having their lives prolonged with no chance of recovery. In response to these concerns, almost all states have enacted statutes permitting individuals to state their choices about the medical procedures that should be administered or withheld if they should become incapacitated in the future and cannot recover. Collectively, these devices are called **advance directives**. An advance directive is a written document (such as a living will or durable power of attorney) that directs others how future health care decisions should be made in the event that the individual becomes incapacitated.

## Living Wills

**Living wills** are documents in which a person states in advance his intention to forgo or obtain certain life prolonging medical procedures. Almost all states have enacted statutes recognizing living wills. These statutes also establish the elements and formalities required to create a valid living will and describe the legal effect of living wills. Currently, the law concerning living wills is primarily a matter of state law and differs from state to state. Living wills are typically included with a patient's medical records. Many states require physicians and other health care providers to follow the provisions of a valid living will. Because living wills are created by statute, it is important that all terms and conditions of the statute be followed. Figure 1 shows a living will form that is contained in Indiana's current living will statute.[2]

The importance of living wills and durable powers of attorney (which are discussed in the next section) was underscored in a 1990 U.S. Supreme Court case, *Cruzan v. Director, Missouri Department of Health. Cruzan,* which follows, held that it was constitutionally permissible for a state to refuse to permit the guardians of an incompetent person to terminate life support without clear and convincing evidence that the incompetent person would consent to such termination.

---

[2]Indiana Code 16-36-4-10 (1993).

**FIGURE 1    Living Will**

---

### LIVING WILL DECLARATION

Declaration made this _____ day of _____ , _____ . I, _____ , being at least eighteen (18) years of age and of sound mind, willfully and voluntarily make known my desires that my dying shall not be artificially prolonged under the circumstances set forth below, and I declare:

If at any time I have an incurable injury, disease, or illness certified in writing to be a terminal condition by my attending physician, and my attending physician has determined that my death will occur within a short time, and the use of life prolonging procedures would serve only to artificially prolong the dying process, I direct that such procedures be withheld or withdrawn and that I be permitted to die naturally with only the provision of appropriate nutrition and hydration and the administration of medication and the performance of any medical procedure necessary to provide me with comfort, care, or to alleviate pain.

In the absence of my ability to give directions regarding the use of life prolonging procedures, it is my intention that his declaration be honored by my family and physicians as the final expression of my legal right to refuse medical or surgical treatment and accept the consequences of the refusal.

I understand the full import of this declaration,

Signed: _____
City, County, and State of Residence

The declarant has been personally known to me, and I believe (him/her) to be of sound mind. I did not sign the declarant's signature above for or at the direction of the declarant. I am not a parent, spouse, or child of the declarant. I am not entitled to any part of the declarant's estate or directly financially responsible for the declarant's medical care. I am competent and at least eighteen (18) years of age.

Witness _____ Date _____
Witness _____ Date _____

---

## CRUZAN V. DIRECTOR, MISSOURI DEPARTMENT OF HEALTH
### 110 S. Ct. 2841 (U.S. S. Ct. 1990)

On the night of January 11, 1983, 25-year-old Nancy Cruzan lost control of her car while driving down Elm Road in Jasper County, Missouri. The vehicle overturned and Cruzan was discovered lying face down in a ditch without detectable respiratory or cardiac function. Paramedics were able to restore her breathing and heartbeat at the accident site and she was transported to a hospital. There she was diagnosed as having sustained probable cerebral contusions compounded by significant anoxia (lack of oxygen). She remained in a coma for three weeks and then progressed to an unconscious state in which she was able to orally ingest some nutrition. To ease feeding and further her recovery, surgeons implanted a gastrostomy feeding and hydration tube. She then remained in a Missouri state hospital in what is commonly referred to as a persistent vegetative state.

After it became apparent that Cruzan had virtually no chance of regaining her mental faculties, her parents (also her legal guardians) asked hospital employees to terminate the artificial nutrition and hydration procedures, which would cause her death. The employees refused to do so without court approval. The parents then sought authorization from the state trial court for termination. Cruzan had not executed a living will, but a former roommate of Cruzan's testified that Cruzan had told her that if she were sick or injured she would not wish to continue her life unless she could live at least halfway normally. The trial court granted authorization to terminate nutrition and hydration, holding that a person in Cruzan's position had a fundamental constitutional right to refuse or direct the withdrawal of "death prolonging procedures." It also found that Cruzan's conversation with her roommate indicated that she would not want to continue with life support. The Supreme Court of Missouri reversed on the ground that no one can assume the choice regarding termination of medical treatment for an incompetent person in the absence of the formalities required under the Living Will Statute or clear and convincing evidence, which evidence it found to be lacking in this case. The U.S. Supreme Court then granted certiorari to consider whether the U.S. Constitution would require the hospital to withdraw life-sustaining treatment from Cruzan under these circumstances.

---

**Rehnquist, Chief Justice**     Petitioners insist that the forced administration of life-sustaining medical treatment, and even of artificially-delivered food and water essential to life, would implicate a competent person's liberty interest. For purposes of this case, we assume that the United States Constitution would grant a competent person a constitutionally protected right to refuse lifesaving hydration and nutrition.

Petitioners go on to assert that an incompetent person should possess the same right in this respect as is possessed by a competent person. The difficulty with petitioner's claim is that an incompetent person is not able to make an informed and voluntary choice to exercise a hypothetical right to refuse treatment or any other right. Such a "right" must be exercised for her, if at all, by some sort of surrogate. Here, Missouri has in effect recognized that under certain circumstances a surrogate may act for the patient in electing to have hydration and nutrition withdrawn in such a way as to cause death, but it has established a procedural safeguard to assure that the action of the surrogate conforms as best it may to the wishes expressed by the patient while competent. Missouri requires that evidence of the incompetent's wishes as to the withdrawal of treatment be proved by clear and convincing evidence. The question, then, is whether the United States Constitution forbids the establishment of this procedural requirement by the State. We hold that it does not.

The choice between life and death is a deeply personal decision of obvious and overwhelming finality. We believe Missouri may legitimately seek to safeguard the personal element of this choice through the imposition of heightened evidentiary requirements. It cannot be disputed that the Due Process Clause protects an interest in life as well as an interest in refusing life-sustaining medical treatment. Not all incompetent patients will have loved ones available to serve as surrogate decisionmakers. And

even where family members are present, there will, of course, be some unfortunate situations in which family members will not act to protect a patient. A State is entitled to guard against potential abuses in such situations. Similarly, a State is entitled to consider that a judicial proceeding to make a determination regarding an incompetent's wishes may very well not be an adversarial one, with the added guarantee of accurate factfinding that the adversary process brings with it. Finally, we think a State may properly decline to make judgments about the "quality" of life that a particular individual may enjoy, and simply assert an unqualified interest in the preservation of human life to be weighed against the constitutionally protected interests of the individual.

It is also worth noting that most, if not all, States simply forbid oral testimony entirely in determining the wishes of parties in transactions which, while important, simply do not have the consequences that a decision to terminate a person's life does. In most states, the parol evidence rule prevents the variation of the terms of a written contract by oral testimony. The statute of frauds makes unenforceable oral contracts to leave property by will, and statutes regulating the making of wills universally require that those instruments be in writing. There is no doubt that [these statutes] on occasion frustrate effectuation of the intent of a particular decedent just as Missouri's requirement of proof in this case may have frustrated the effectuation of the not-fully-expressed desires of Nancy Cruzan. But the Constitution does not require general rules to work faultlessly; no general rule can.

In sum, we conclude that a State may apply a clear and convincing evidence standard in proceedings where a guardian seeks to discontinue nutrition and hydration of a person diagnosed to be in a persistent vegetative state. The Supreme Court of Missouri held that the testimony adduced at trial did not amount to clear and convincing proof of the patient's desire to have hydration and nutrition withdrawn. We cannot say that the Supreme Court of Missouri committed constitutional error in reaching the conclusion that it did.

**Judgment for the Missouri Department of Health affirmed.**

## Durable Power of Attorney

Another technique of planning for the eventuality that one may be unable to make decisions for oneself is to execute a document that gives another person the legal authority to act on one's behalf in the case of mental or physical incapacity. This document is called a **durable power of attorney**.

A *power of attorney* is an express statement in which one person (the **principal**) gives another person (the **attorney in fact**) the authority to do an act or series of acts on his behalf. For example, Andrews enters into a contract to sell his house to Willis, but he must be out of state on the date of the real estate closing. He gives Paulsen a power of attorney to attend the closing and execute the deed on his behalf. Ordinary powers of attorney terminate upon the principal's incapacity. By contrast, the *durable power of attorney* is not affected if the principal becomes incompetent.

A durable power of attorney permits a person to give someone else extremely broad powers to make decisions and enter transactions such as those involving real and personal property, bank accounts, and health care, and to specify that those powers will not terminate upon incapacity. The durable power of attorney is an extremely important planning device. For example, a durable power of attorney executed by an elderly parent to an adult child at a time in which the parent is competent would permit the child to take care of matters such as investments, property, bank accounts, and hospital admission. Without the durable power of attorney, the child would be forced to apply to a court for a guardianship, which is a more expensive, and often a less efficient, manner in which to handle personal and business affairs.

## Durable Power of Attorney for Health Care

The majority of states have enacted statutes specifically providing for **durable powers of attorney for health care** (sometimes called **health care representatives**). This is a type of durable power of attorney in which the principal specifically gives the attorney in fact the authority to make certain health care decisions for him if the principal should become incompetent. Depending on state law and the instructions given by the principal to the attorney in fact, this could include decisions such as consenting or withholding consent to surgery, admitting the principal to a nursing home, and possibly withdrawing or prolonging life support. Note that the durable power of attorney becomes relevant only in the event that the principal becomes incompetent. So long as the principal is competent, he retains the ability to make his own health care decisions. This power of attorney is also revocable at the will of the principal. The precise requirements for creation of the durable power of attorney differ from state to state, but all states require a written and signed document executed with specified formalities, such as witnessing by disinterested witnesses.

## Federal Law and Advance Directives

A new federal statute, The Patient Self-Determination Act,[3] requires health care providers to take active steps to educate people about the opportunity to make advance decisions about medical care and the prolonging of life and to record the choices that they make. This statute, which became effective in 1992, requires health care providers such as hospitals, nursing homes, hospices, and home health agencies, to provide written information to adults receiving medical care about their rights concerning the ability to accept or refuse medical or surgical treatment, the health care provider's policies concerning those rights, and their right to formulate advance directives. The act also requires the provider to document in the patient's medical record whether the patient has executed an advance directive, and it forbids discrimination against the patient based on the individual's choice regarding an advance directive. In addition, the provider is required to ensure compliance with the

---

[3]42 U.S.C. section 1395cc (1993).

**FIGURE 2**   Example of a Distribution Scheme under an Intestacy Statute

| Person Dying Intestate Is Survived by | Result |
| --- | --- |
| 1. Spouse* and child or issue of a deceased child | Spouse ½, Child ½ |
| 2. Spouse and parent(s) but no issue | Spouse ¾, Parent ¼ |
| 3. Spouse but no parent or issue | All of the estate to spouse |
| 4. Issue but no spouse | Estate is divided among issue |
| 5. Parent(s), brothers, sisters, and/or issue of deceased brothers and sisters but no spouse or issue | Estate is divided among parent(s), brothers, sisters, and issue of deceased brothers and sisters |
| 6. Issue of brothers and sisters but no spouse, issue, parents, brothers, and sisters | Estate is divided among issue of deceased brothers and sisters |
| 7. Grandparents, but no spouse, issue, parents, brothers, sisters, or issue of deceased brothers and sisters | All of the estate goes to grandparents |
| 8. None of the above | Estate goes to the state |

*Note, however, second and subsequent spouses who had no children by the decedent may be assigned a smaller share.

requirements of state law concerning advance directives and to educate its staff and the community on issues concerning advance directives.

## INTESTACY

If a person dies without making a will, or if he makes a will that is declared invalid, he is said to have died **intestate**. When that occurs, his property will be distributed to the persons designated as the intestate's heirs under the appropriate state's **intestacy** or **intestate succession** statute. The intestate's real property will be distributed according to the intestacy statute of the state in which the property is located. His personal property will be distributed according to the intestacy statute of the state in which he was **domiciled** at the time of his death. A domicile is a person's permanent home. A person can have only one domicile at a time. Determinations of a person's domicile turn on facts that tend to show that person's intent to make a specific state his permanent home.

### Characteristics of Intestacy Statutes

The provisions of intestacy statutes are not uniform. Their purpose, however, is to distribute property in a way that reflects the *presumed intent* of the

deceased—that is, to distribute it to the persons most closely related to him. In general, such statutes first provide for the distribution of most or all of a person's estate to his surviving spouse, children, or grandchildren. If no such survivors exist, the statutes typically provide for the distribution of the estate to parents, siblings, or nieces and nephews. If no relatives at this level are living, the property may be distributed to surviving grandparents, uncles, aunts, or cousins. Generally, persons with the same degree of relationship to the deceased person take equal shares. If the deceased had no surviving relatives, the property **escheats** (goes) to the state.

Figure 2 shows an example of a distribution scheme under an intestacy statute.

### Special Rules

Under intestacy statutes, a person must have a relationship to the deceased person through blood or marriage in order to inherit any part of his property. State law includes adopted children within the definition of "children," and treats adopted children in the same way as it treats biological children. (An adopted child would inherit from his adoptive parents, not from his biological parents.) Half brothers and half sisters are usually treated in the same way as brothers and sisters related by whole blood. An illegitimate child may inherit from his mother, but as a general rule, illegitimate children do not inherit from their fathers unless paternity has been either acknowledged or established in a legal proceeding.

A person must be alive at the time the decedent dies to claim a share of the decedent's estate. An exception may be made for pretermitted children or other descendants who are born *after* the decedent's death. If a person who is entitled to a share of the decedent's estate survives the decedent but dies before receiving his share, his share in the decedent's estate becomes part of his own estate.

## Simultaneous Death

A statute known as the Uniform Simultaneous Death Act provides that where two persons who would inherit from each other (such as husband and wife) die under circumstances that make it difficult or impossible to determine who died first, each person's property is to be distributed as though he or she survived. This means, for example, that the husband's property will go to his relatives and the wife's property to her relatives.

## ADMINISTRATION OF ESTATES

When a person dies, an orderly procedure is needed to collect his property, settle his debts, and distribute any remaining property to those who will inherit it under his will or by intestate succession. This process occurs under the supervision of a probate court and is known as the **administration process** or the **probate process**. Summary (simple) procedures are sometimes available when an estate is relatively small—for example, when it has assets of less than $7,500.

## The Probate Estate

The probate process operates only on the decedent's property that is considered to be part of his **probate estate**. The probate estate is that property belonging to the decedent at the time of his death other than property held in joint ownership with right of survivorship, proceeds of insurance policies payable to a trust or a third party, property held in a revocable trust during the decedent's lifetime in which a third party is the beneficiary, or retirement benefits, such as pensions, payable to a third party. Assets that pass by operation of law and assets that are transferred by other devices such as trusts or life insurance policies do not pass through probate.

Note that the decedent's probate estate and his *taxable estate* for purposes of federal estate tax are two different concepts. The taxable estate includes all property owned or controlled by the decedent at the time of his death. For example, if a person purchased a $1 million life insurance policy made payable to his spouse or children, the policy would be included in his taxable estate, but not in his probate estate.

## Determining the Existence of a Will

The first step in the probate process is to determine whether the deceased left a will. This may require a search of the deceased person's personal papers and safe-deposit box. If a will is found, it must be *proved* to be admitted to probate. This involves the testimony of the persons who witnessed the will, if they are still alive. If the witnesses are no longer alive, the signatures of the witnesses and the testator will have to be established in some other way. In many states and under UPC section 2–504, a will may be proved by an affidavit (declaration under oath) sworn to and signed by the testator and the witnesses at the time the will was executed. This is called a **self-proving affidavit**. If a will is located and proved, it will be admitted to probate and govern many of the decisions that must be made in the administration of the estate.

## Selecting a Personal Representative

Another early step in the administration of an estate is the selection of a personal representative to administer the estate. If the deceased left a will, it is likely that he designated his personal representative in the will. The personal representative under a will is also known as the **executor**. Almost anyone could serve as an executor. The testator may have chosen, for example, his spouse, a grown child, a close friend, an attorney, or the trust department of a bank.

If the decedent died intestate, or if the personal representative named in a will is unable to serve, the probate court will name a personal representative to administer the estate. In the case of an intestate estate, the personal representative is called an

**administrator**. A preference is usually accorded to a surviving spouse, child, or other close relative. If no relative is available and qualified to serve, a creditor, bank, or other person may be appointed by the court.

Most states require that the personal representative *post a bond* in an amount in excess of the estimated value of the estate to ensure that her duties will be properly and faithfully performed. A person making a will often directs that his executor may serve without posting a bond, and this exemption may be accepted by the court.

### Responsibilities of the Personal Representative

The personal representative has a number of important tasks in the administration of the estate. She must see that an inventory is taken of the estate's assets and that the assets are appraised. Notice must then be given to creditors or potential claimants against the estate so that they can file and prove their claims within a specified time, normally five months. As a general rule, the surviving spouse of the deceased person is entitled to be paid an allowance during the time the estate is being settled. This allowance has priority over other debts of the estate. The personal representative must see that any properly payable funeral or burial expenses are paid and that the creditors' claims are satisfied.

Both federal and state governments impose estate or inheritance taxes on estates of a certain size. The personal representative is responsible for filing estate tax returns. The federal tax is a tax on the deceased's estate, with provisions for deducting items such as debts, expenses of administration, and charitable gifts. In addition, an amount equal to the amount left to the surviving spouse may be deducted from the gross estate before the tax is computed. State inheritance taxes are imposed on the person who receives a gift or statutory share from an estate. It is common, however, for wills to provide that the estate will pay all taxes, including inheritance taxes, so that the beneficiaries will not have to do so. The personal representative must also make provisions for filing an income tax return and for paying any income tax due for the partial year prior to the decedent's death.

When the debts, expenses, and taxes have been taken care of, the remaining assets of the estate are distributed to the decedent's heirs (if there was no will) or to the beneficiaries of the decedent's will.

Special rules apply when the estate is too small to satisfy all of the bequests made in a will or when some or all of the designated beneficiaries are no longer living.

When the personal representative has completed all of these duties, the probate court will close the estate and discharge the personal representative.

## TRUSTS

### Nature of a Trust

A **trust** is a legal relationship in which a person who has legal title to property has the duty to hold it for the use or benefit of another person. The person benefited by a trust is considered to have **equitable title** to the property, because it is being maintained for his benefit. This means that he is the real owner even though the trustee has the legal title in his or her name. A trust can be created in a number of ways. An owner of property may *declare* that he is holding certain property in trust. For example, a mother might state that she is holding 100 shares of General Motors stock in trust for her daughter. A trust may also arise *by operation of law*. For example, when a lawyer representing a client injured in an automobile accident receives a settlement payment from an insurance company, the lawyer holds the settlement payment as trustee for the client. Most commonly, however, trusts are created through *express instruments* whereby an owner of property transfers title to the property to a trustee who is to hold, manage, and invest the property for the benefit of either the original owner or a third person. For example, Long transfers certain stock to First Trust Bank with instructions to pay the income to his daughter during her lifetime and to distribute the stock to her children after her death.

### Trust Terminology

A person who creates a trust is known as a **settlor** or **trustor**. The person who holds the property for the benefit of another person is called the **trustee**. The person for whose benefit the property is held in trust is the **beneficiary**. Figure 3 illustrates the relationship between these parties. A single person may occupy more than one of these positions; however, if there is only one beneficiary, he cannot be the sole trustee. The property held in trust is called the **corpus** or **res**. A distinction is made between the property in trust,

**FIGURE 3**   **Trust**

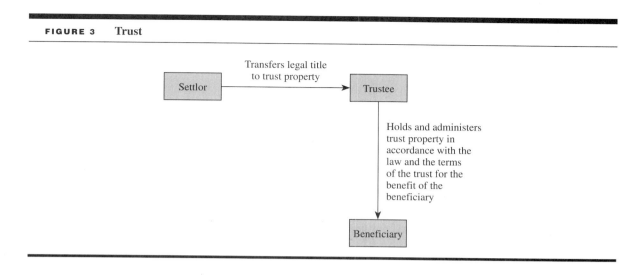

which is the principal, and the income that is produced by the principal.

A trust that is established and effective during the settlor's lifetime is known as an **inter vivos trust**. A trust can also be established in a person's will. Such trusts take effect only at the death of the settlor. They are called **testamentary trusts**.

## Why People Create Trusts

Bennett owns a portfolio of valuable stock. Her husband has predeceased her. She has two children and an elderly father for whom she would like to provide. Why might it be advantageous to Bennett to transfer the stock to a trust for the benefit of the members of her family?

First, there may be income tax or estate tax advantages in doing so, depending on the type of trust she establishes and the provisions of that trust. For example, she can establish an irrevocable trust for her children and remove the property transferred to her trust from her estate so that it is not taxable at her death. In addition, the trust property can be used for the benefit of others and may even pass to others after the settlor's death without the necessity of having a will. Many people prefer to pass their property by trust rather than by will because trusts afford more privacy: unlike a probated will, they do not become an item of public record. Trusts also afford greater opportunity for postgift management than do outright gifts and bequests. If Bennett wants her children to enjoy the

income of the trust property during their young adulthood without distributing unfettered ownership of the property to them before she considers them able to manage it properly, she can accomplish this through a trust provision. A trust can prevent the property from being squandered or spent too quickly. Trusts can be set up so that a beneficiary's interest cannot be reached by his creditors in many situations. Such trusts, called **spendthrift trusts**, will be discussed later.

Placing property in trust can operate to increase the amount of property held for the beneficiaries if the trustee makes good investment decisions. Another important consideration is that a trust can be used to provide for the needs of disabled beneficiaries who are not capable of managing funds.

## Creation of Express Trusts

There are five basic requirements for the creation of a valid express trust, although special and somewhat less restrictive rules govern the establishment of charitable trusts. The requirements for forming an express trust are:

1. *Capacity.* The settlor must have had the **legal capacity** to convey the property to the trust. This means that the settlor must have had the capacity needed to make a valid contract if the trust is an *inter vivos* trust or the capacity to make a will if the trust is a testamentary trust. For example, a trust would fail under this requirement if at the time the trust was created, the settlor had not attained the age

required by state law for the creation of valid wills and contracts (age 18 in most states).

**2.** *Intent and formalities.* The settlor must *intend* to create a trust at the present time. To impose enforceable duties on the trustee, the settlor must meet certain formalities. Under the laws of most states, for example, the trustee must accept the trust by signing the trust instrument. In the case of a trust of land, the trust must be in writing so as to meet the statute of frauds. If the trust is a testamentary trust, it must satisfy the formal requirements for wills.

**3.** *Conveyance of specific property.* The settlor must convey *specific property* to the trust. The property conveyed must be property that the settlor has the *right to convey*.

**4.** *Proper purpose.* The trust must be created for a *proper purpose*. It cannot be created for a reason that is contrary to public policy, such as the commission of a crime.

**5.** *Identity of the beneficiaries.* The *beneficiaries* of the trust must be described clearly enough so that their identities can be ascertained. Sometimes, beneficiaries may be members of a specific class, such as "my children."

## Charitable Trusts

A distinction is made between private trusts and trusts created for charitable purposes. In a private trust, property is devoted to the benefit of specific persons, whereas in a charitable trust, property is devoted to a charitable organization or to some other purposes beneficial to society. While some of the rules governing private and charitable trusts are the same, a number of these rules are different. For example, when a private trust is created, the beneficiary must be known at the time or ascertainable within a certain time (established by a legal rule known as the **rule against perpetuities**). However, a charitable trust is valid even though no definitely ascertainable beneficiary is named and even though it is to continue for an indefinite or unlimited period.

## Doctrine of Cy Pres

A doctrine known as **cy pres** is applicable to charitable trusts when property is given in trust to be applied to a particular charitable purpose that becomes impossible, impracticable, or illegal to carry out. Under the doctrine of *cy pres*, the trust will not fail if the settlor indicated a general intention to devote the property to charitable purposes. If the settlor has not specifically provided for a substitute beneficiary, the court will direct the application of the property to some charitable purpose that falls within the settlor's general charitable intention.

## Totten Trusts

A **Totten trust** is a deposit of money in a bank or other financial institution in the name of the depositor *as trustee* for a named beneficiary. For example, Bliss deposits money in First Bank in trust for his daughter, Bessie. The Totten trust creates a revocable living trust. At Bliss's death, if he has not revoked this trust, the money in the account will belong to Bessie.

## Powers and Duties of the Trustee

In most express trusts, the settlor names a specific person to act as trustee. If the settlor does not name a trustee, the court will appoint one. Similarly, a court will replace a trustee who resigns, is incompetent, or refuses to act.

The trust codes of most states contain provisions giving trustees broad management powers over trust property. These provisions can be limited or expanded by express provisions in the trust instrument. The trustee must use a *reasonable degree of skill, judgment, and care* in the exercise of his duties unless he holds himself out as having a greater degree of skill, in which case he will be held to a higher standard. Section 7–302 of the UPC provides that the trustee is held to the standard of a prudent person dealing with the property of another, and if he has special skills or is named trustee based on a representation of special skills, he is required to use those special skills. He *may not commingle* the property he holds in trust with his own property or with that of another trust.

A trustee owes a *duty of loyalty* (fiduciary duty) to the beneficiaries. This means that he must administer the trust for the benefit of the beneficiaries and avoid any conflict between his personal interests and the interest of the trust. For example, a trustee cannot do business with a trust that he administers without express permission in the trust agreement. He must not prefer one beneficiary's interest to another's, and he must account to the beneficiaries for all transactions. Unless the trust agreement provides otherwise, the trustee must make the trust productive. He may not delegate the performance of discretionary duties (such as the duty to select investments) to another, but he may delegate the performance of ministerial duties (such as the preparation of statements of account).

A trust may give the trustee discretion as to the amount of principal or income paid to a beneficiary. In such a case, the beneficiary cannot require the trustee to exercise his discretion in the manner desired by the beneficiary.

**Allocating between Principal and Income**
One of the duties of the trustee is to distribute the principal and income of the trust in accordance with the terms of the trust instrument. Suppose Wheeler's will created a testamentary trust providing that his wife was to receive the income from the trust for life, and at her death, the trust property was to be distributed to his children. During the duration of the trust, the trust earns profits, such as interest or rents, and has expenses, such as taxes or repairs. How should the trustee allocate these items as between Wheeler's surviving spouse, who is an **income beneficiary**, and his children, who are **remaindermen**?

The terms of the trust and state law bind the trustee in making this determination. As a general rule, ordinary profits received from the investment of trust property are allocated to income. For example, interest on trust property or assets and rents earned from leasing real property held in trust would be allocated to income. Ordinary expenses such as insurance premiums, the cost of ordinary maintenance and repairs of trust property, and property taxes, would be chargeable to income. The

principal of the trust includes the trust property itself and any extraordinary receipts, such as proceeds or gains derived from the sale of trust property or assets. Extraordinary expenses—for example, the cost of long-term permanent improvements to real property or expenses relating to the sale of property—would ordinarily be charged against principal.

**Liability of Trustee**

A trustee who breaches any of the duties of a trustee or whose conduct falls below the standard of care applicable to trustees may incur personal liability. For example, if the trustee invests unwisely and imprudently, the trustee may be personally liable to reimburse the trust estate for the shortfall. The language of the trust affects the trustee's liability and the level of care owed by the trustee. A settlor might, for example, include language lowering the trustee's duty of care or relieving the trustee of some liability that he might otherwise incur. The following *Neuhaus v. Richards* case discusses both trustee liability and the extent to which a trust instrument can limit the trustee's liability.

The trustee can also have liability to third persons who are injured by the operation of the trust. Because a trust is not in itself a legal entity that can be sued, a third party who has a claim (such as a tort claim or a claim for breach of contract) must file his claim against the trustee of the trust. The trustee's actual personal liability to a third party depends on the language of the trust and of any contracts he might enter on behalf of the trust as well as the extent to which the injury complained of by the third party was a result of the personal fault or omission of the trustee.

## Neuhaus v. Richards
### 846 S.W.2d 70 (Tex. Ct. App. 1992)

In 1976, V. F. and Gertrude Neuhaus executed a Trust Indenture Creating the Neuhaus Family Trusts, which established a number of separate individual trusts for the benefit of their children and grandchildren, Vernon and Lacey Neuhaus. The trusts were both managed by the same cotrustees, Grace Neuhaus Richards and Robert Schwarz. The initial corpus of both trusts consisted of stock in McAllen State Bank. However, in 1982, First City Bancorporation of Texas acquired all the stock of McAllen State Bank, and First City substituted its own stock for the McAllen State Bank Stock in the trusts. From 1985 through 1987, the First City stock declined in value, but the trustees refused to sell until the stock in Lacey Neuhaus's trust became virtually worthless, and they delayed selling the stock in Vernon Neuhaus's trust until significant losses had been sustained. The Neuhauses sued both trustees alleging a breach of fiduciary duties, including a failure to exercise judgment and care, willful misconduct, and conscious disregard for the rights and welfare of the beneficiaries, among other claims. The trial court granted a summary judgment against the Neuhauses, and the Neuhauses appealed.

---

**Hinojosa, Justice**   The fundamental duties of a trustee include the use of the skill and prudence that an ordinary, capable, and careful person would use in the conduct of his own affairs and loyalty to the beneficiaries of the trust. In particular, one of the basic duties of a trustee is to make the assets of the trust productive while at the same time preserving the assets. Under these principles, it would appear in the present case that the trustees could be held liable for failing to sell the First City stock if their decision not to sell was imprudent. However, the settlor may within the trust instrument relieve the trustee of certain duties, restrictions, responsibilities, and liabilities imposed by statute. However, exculpatory clauses are strictly construed, and the trustee is relieved of liability only to the extent that the trust instrument clearly provides that he shall be excused.

In the present case, the trustees point to two supposedly exculpatory provisions in the present trust indenture: section V(k) and section V(v). Section V(k) provides that:

All property transferred by gift to any trust and any property acquired by the Trustees . . . shall be deemed a proper investment, and the Trustees shall be under no obligation to dispose of or convert any such property.

The trustees suggest that section V(k) completely relieves them of any duty to sell the First City stock. However, we hold that this provision is ambiguous. Section V(k) leaves uncertain whether the trustees are still under a duty to prudently manage and, if need be, sell an investment that is otherwise deemed proper, and whether the obligation to dispose of assets includes the generalized duty to manage the trust prudently or merely relieves the trustees of any specific obligation to sell a particular kind or class of investments. Even if we were to accept the trustees' interpretation that this section generally

relieved them of a duty to sell or of liability for failing to sell the First City stock, nevertheless, it could not have validly relieved them of all liability for failing to sell the stock. Under Texas law, an exculpatory provision in the trust instrument is not effective to relieve the trustee of liability for action taken in bad faith or for acting intentionally adverse or with reckless indifference to the interests of the beneficiary. Courts have held that the trust instrument may relieve the trustee of the duty to act as a prudent man in determining to retain unproductive property, but not of the duty to do so honestly, in good faith, and without willful misconduct or reckless indifference to the interests of the beneficiaries. In other words, the trustee's determination to retain unproductive investments is generally protected as long as that determination was not made dishonestly, in bad faith, recklessly, or with the intent to harm the trust.

Turning to the second exculpatory provision relied upon by the trustees, section V(v) provides that "no Trustee shall be liable for negligence or error of judgment but shall be liable only for his willful misconduct or personal dishonesty." Thus, under this general exculpatory provision, the trustees are not held to the prudent person standard but may be liable only for willful misconduct or personal dishonesty. As we stated earlier, the Neuhauses alleged that in failing to sell the First City stock the trustees not only failed to act prudently but also that they acted out of willful misconduct. Because the trustees made no attempt by summary judgment evidence to negate these allegations of willful misconduct, summary judgment should not have been granted in their favor on the basis of exculpatory provisions of the trust indenture.

**Reversed in favor of the Neuhauses and remanded for trial.**

## Spendthrift Trusts

Generally, the beneficiary of a trust may voluntarily assign his rights to the principal or income of the trust to another person. In addition, any distributions to the beneficiary are subject to the claims of his creditors. Sometimes, however, trusts contain provisions known as **spendthrift clauses**, which restrict the voluntary or involuntary transfer of a beneficiary's interest. Such clauses are generally enforced, and they preclude assignees or creditors from compelling a trustee to recognize their claims to the trust. The enforceability of such clauses is subject to four exceptions, however:

1. A person cannot put his own property beyond the claims of his own creditors. Thus, a spendthrift clause is not effective in a trust when the settlor makes himself a beneficiary.
2. Divorced spouses and minor children of the beneficiary can compel payment for alimony and child support.
3. Creditors of the beneficiary who have furnished necessaries can compel payment.
4. Once the trustee distributes property to a beneficiary, it can be subject to valid claims of others.

## Termination and Modification of a Trust

Normally, a settlor cannot revoke or modify a trust unless he reserves the power to do so at the time he establishes the trust. However, a trust may be modified or terminated with the consent of the settlor and all of the beneficiaries. When the settlor is dead or otherwise unable to consent, a trust can be modified or terminated by consent of all the persons with a beneficial interest, but only when this would not frustrate a material purpose of the trust. Because trusts are under the supervisory jurisdiction of a court, the court can permit a deviation from the terms of a trust when unanticipated changes in circumstances threaten accomplishment of the settlor's purpose.

## Implied and Constructive Trusts

Under exceptional circumstances in which the creation of a trust is necessary to effectuate a settlor's intent or avoid unjust enrichment, the law *implies* or imposes a trust even though no express trust exists or an express trust exists but has failed. One trust of this type is a **resulting trust**, which arises when there has been an incomplete disposition of trust property. For example, if Hess transferred property to Wickes as trustee to provide for the needs of Hess's grandfather and the grandfather died before the trust funds were exhausted, Wickes will be deemed to hold the property in a resulting trust for Hess or Hess's heirs. Similarly, if Hess had transferred the property to Wickes as trustee and the trust had failed because Hess did not meet one of the requirements of a valid trust, Wickes would not be permitted to keep the trust property as his own. A resulting trust would be implied.

A **constructive trust** is a trust created by operation of law to avoid fraud, injustice, or unjust enrichment. This type of trust imposes on the constructive trustee a duty to convey property he holds to another person on the ground that the constructive trustee would be unjustly enriched if he were allowed to retain it. For example, when a person procures the transfer of property by means of fraud or duress, he becomes a constructive trustee and is under an obligation to return the property to its original owner.

### PROBLEMS AND PROBLEM CASES

1. Cunningham died in 1983, leaving a writing that purported to be his will. The writing was on a preprinted will form in which the first and last part of the will were printed and the rest of the will was handwritten by Cunningham. The first paragraph reads: "In the name of God, Amen. I," which is printed, followed by the handwriting: "Thomas John Cunningham—Social Security number 55–24–3083," which in turn is followed by printing: "being of sound mind, memory and understanding, do make and publish this my Last Will and Testament, in the manner following, that is to say: . . ." This is followed by the body of the will in Cunningham's handwriting, which gives instructions concerning the donation of bodily remains, specific bequests, and the distribution of the remainder of his estate. A printed clause appears after the body of the will, and immediately below this clause is a printed line upon which a testator normally signs his name,

at the end of which is printed "Seal." Cunningham did not sign his name on this line; instead, the line contains the signature of a Notary Public of New Jersey, together with his notarial seal impressed over the printed word "Seal." Two people, a realtor (who was also the notary) and the realtor's secretary, witnessed the writing. Cunningham came to the realtor's office with the proposed will fully completed except for the witnesses' signatures. The writing was offered for probate as a will. Is the will valid?

**2.** Prigge died in 1982, survived by two sisters, Marian and Jean; one brother, Louis; and some nephews and nieces. John had never married and had been a farmer all his life. In 1980, he sold his farm and moved in with his sister Marian. While John was living with her, Marian, at John's request, prepared a handwritten document expressing his testamentary intent. John took the document to a lawyer, who prepared a will based on the contents of the document. John executed the will in 1981. In the will, John devised his entire estate to Marian and her six children in equal shares and specifically excluded Louis and Jean. John died in 1982. Louis and Jean contested the will on grounds of lack of testamentary capacity and undue influence. Was the will valid?

**3.** Roy and Icie Johnson established two revocable *inter vivos* trusts in 1966. The trusts provided that upon Roy and Icie's deaths, income from the trusts was to be paid in equal shares to their two sons, James and Robert, for life. Upon the death of the survivor of the sons, the trust was to be *"divided equally between all of my grandchildren, per stirpes."* James had two daughters, Barbara and Elizabeth. Robert had four children, David, Rosalyn, Catherine, and Elizabeth. James and Robert disclaimed their interest in the trust in 1979, and a dispute arose about how the trust should be distributed to the grandchildren. The trustee filed an action seeking instructions on how the trusts should be distributed. What should the court hold?

**4.** Bruce Tidrow, a mentally retarded adult, was cared for at home until his mother became critically ill. When his mother died, his father applied for future residential services for him, which at that time cost $1,234 per month. Mr. Tidrow was aware that funds were generally available for financial assistance of residential-type programs and that his son would have to be institutionalized as long as he lived. A week after making this application, Mr. Tidrow

executed a will, leaving the bulk of his estate in a discretionary, spendthrift trust for the benefit of Bruce, and secondarily for the benefit of his other son, Kim, with the remainder to go to Kim outright upon Bruce's death. The assets of the trust, valued at approximately $175,000, consisted mainly of a residence and proceeds of life insurance policies. Mr. Tidrow died in July 1981, and Bruce was placed in a residential program. Medical assistance to pay the cost of this residential care was applied for. State law prohibits assistance payments to anyone who is the owner or beneficial owner of cash or securities in the amount of $1,000 or more or any kind of property of a value in excess of $20,500. The Division of Family Services imputed the $175,000 trust assets to Bruce and denied his application on the ground that he had "resources in excess of the maximum allowed," and was thus financially unqualified for public assistance. Was it correct to conclude that Bruce was the beneficial owner of the trust assets?

**5.** Crawshaw bequeathed the bulk of his estate to two residuary beneficiaries, the Salvation Army and Marymount College. Crawshaw's will provided for 15 percent of the residue to go to the Salvation Army outright and 85 percent to Marymount College in trust. The stated purpose of this trust was to provide loans to nursing and other students at Marymount. Marymount ceased operation on June 30, 1989. It sought to have the trust funds directed to Marymount Memorial Educational Trust Fund. The Salvation Army challenged this, arguing that Crawshaw did not intend to benefit students attending colleges other than Marymount. It asked that the court distribute the trust funds to the Salvation Army as the remaining beneficiary of Crawshaw's residuary estate. What should the court do?

**6.** Hotarek's parents were divorced when he was two. For about 13 years after that, Hotarek's mother, Benson, had no contact with him, did not provide financial support to him, and did not display interest in her son. In 1986, at the age of 15, Hotarek was killed in an automobile accident. After his death, his estate settled a claim against the other driver for $20,000 and was awarded uninsured motorist's benefits in the amount of $525,000. These proceeds made up Hotarek's estate. Following Hotarek's death, Benson could not be located. Once she was located, the probate court ordered half of Hotarek's estate distributed to her in accordance with Connecticut's intestacy statute. It provides that if a person dies intestate leaving no spouse or children, the residue of the state shall be distributed equally to the decedent's parent or parents. Hotarek's father objected to the distribution to Benson on the ground that she had abandoned her minor child during his life and should not be entitled to share in his estate after his death. Is Benson entitled to share in her intestate son's estate?

7. Fickes, a resident of Washington, died in December 1943, leaving a will dated November 19, 1940. The will provided for the creation of a trust upon his death. The will also provided that upon the death of Fickes's last surviving child, one half of the trust property was to be distributed to Renssalaer Polytechnic Institute and the other half of the trust property distributed "in equal portions" between Fickes's "grandchildren then living." At the time of death of Fickes's last surviving child, there were four biological grandchildren living. In addition, there were four adopted grandchildren living. Two of them, grandsons, had been adopted by Fickes's son while Fickes was still living. The other two, granddaughters, were adopted by Fickes's son in 1962 and 1965, long after Fickes's death. Were the granddaughters entitled to share in the trust distribution?

## CAPSTONE QUESTIONS

Sam Jackson created a valid testamentary spendthrift trust to provide for the welfare of his daughter Wanda. Jeff Leaper, an attorney and CPA, was named trustee. The trust property included $500,000 in stock, $500,000 in bonds, and $1 million in income-producing real estate. Wanda was to receive all income from the trust. Also, the trust agreement gave Jeff the authority to disburse up to $10,000 of principal to Wanda each year, at Jeff's option.

During 1994, Jeff made a $5,000 principal payment to Wanda to help pay her college tuition. Later that year, he refused Wanda's request to give her an additional $5,000 in principal so that she could speculate in the commodity futures markets. Still

later in 1994, Jeff borrowed $15,000 from the trust so that *he* could do some commodity futures trading. Jeff agreed in writing to repay the $15,000 plus 10 percent of his trading profits.

Meanwhile, the trust was making money and incurring expenses. Also, Jeff occasionally would sell trust property in an effort to make the trust more productive. All these activities required Jeff to allocate trust monies between principal and income. His 1994 decisions in this regard included the following:

- A sale of 1,000 shares of XYZ stock, for a capital gain of $5,000. Jeff allocated these proceeds to income.
- The trust's payment of $15,000 in insurance premiums to insure the trust's real property was also allocated to income.
- The trust's payment of $50,000 in real property taxes, however, was allocated to principal.
- The fund received $100,000 in rental receipts from trust property. These Jeff allocated to income.
- Jeff also allocated the trust's $50,000 in bond interest payments to income.
- Finally, the trust received $10,000 in dividends from its stock holdings. These Jeff allocated to principal.

### Required:

Answer the following and give reasons for your conclusions.

1. Did Jeff's $5,000 principal payment to Wanda violate any of his fiduciary duties?

2. Did Jeff's refusal to pay Wanda an additional $5,000 for futures trading violate any of his fiduciary duties?

3. Did Jeff violate any of his fiduciary duties when he borrowed $15,000 to speculate in the futures markets?

4. Were Jeff's allocations of trust monies to principal and income correct or incorrect?

# DEBTORS' AND CREDITORS' RIGHTS

# INTRODUCTION TO CREDIT AND SECURED TRANSACTIONS

*In the United States, a substantial portion of business transactions involves the extension of credit. The term* credit *has many meanings. In this chapter, it will be used to mean transactions in which goods are sold, services are rendered, or money is loaned in exchange for a promise to pay for them at some future date.*

*In some of these transactions, a creditor is willing to rely on the debtor's promise to pay at a later time; in others, the creditor wants some further assurance or security that the debtor will make good on his promise to pay. This chapter will discuss the differences between secured and unsecured credit and will detail various mechanisms that are available to the creditor who wants to obtain security. These mechanisms include obtaining liens or security interests in personal or real property, sureties, and guarantors. Security interests in real property, sureties and guarantors, and common law liens on personal property will be covered in this chapter, and the Uniform Commercial Code (UCC or Code) rules concerning security interests in personal property will be covered in Chapter 21, Security Interests in Personal Property. The last chapter in this part deals with bankruptcy law, which may come into play when a debtor is unable to fulfill his obligation to pay his debts when they are due.*

## CREDIT

### Unsecured Credit

Many common transactions are based on unsecured credit. For example, a person may have a charge account at a department store or a MasterCard account. If the person buys a sweater and charges it to his charge account or MasterCard account, unsecured credit has been extended to him. He has received goods in return for his promise to pay for them later. Similarly, if a person goes to a dentist to have a tooth filled and the dentist sends her a bill payable by the end of the month, services have been rendered on the basis of unsecured credit. Consumers are not the only people who use unsecured credit. Many transactions between businesspeople utilize it. For example, a retailer buys merchandise or a manufacturer buys raw materials, promising to pay for the merchandise or materials within 30 days after receipt.

The unsecured credit transaction involves a maximum of risk to the creditor—the person who extends the credit. When goods are delivered, services are rendered, or money is loaned on unsecured credit, the creditor gives up all rights in the goods, services, or money. In return, the creditor gets a promise by the debtor to pay or to perform the promised act. If the debtor does not pay or keep the promise, the creditor's options are more limited than if he had obtained security to ensure the debtor's performance. One course of action is to bring a lawsuit against the debtor and obtain a judgment. The creditor might then have the sheriff execute the judgment on any property owned by the debtor that is subject to execution. The creditor might also try to **garnish** the wages or other moneys to which the debtor is entitled. However, the debtor might be **judgment-proof;** that is, the debtor may not have any property subject to execution or may not have a steady job. Under these circumstances, execution or garnishment would be of little aid to the creditor in collecting the judgment.

A businessperson may obtain credit insurance to stabilize the credit risk of doing business on an unsecured credit basis. However, he passes the costs of the insurance to the business, or of the unsecured credit losses that the business sustains, on to the consumer. The consumer pays a higher price for goods or services purchased, or a higher interest rate on any money borrowed, from a business that has high credit losses.

## Secured Credit

To minimize his credit risk, a creditor may contract for security. The creditor may require the debtor to convey to the creditor a security interest or lien on the debtor's property. Suppose a person borrows $3,000 from a credit union. The credit union might require her to put up her car as security for the loan or might ask that some other person agree to be liable if she defaults. For example, if a student who does not have a regular job goes to a bank to borrow money, the bank might ask that the student's father or mother cosign the note for the loan.

When the creditor has security for the credit he extends and the debtor defaults, the creditor can go against the security to collect the obligation. Assume that a person borrows $18,000 from a bank to buy a new car and that the bank takes a security interest (lien) on the car. If the person fails to make his monthly payments, the bank has the right to repossess the car and have it sold so that it can recover its money. Similarly, if the borrower's father cosigned for the car loan and the borrower defaults, the bank can sue the father to collect the balance due on the loan.

## Development of Security

Various types of security devices have been developed as social and economic need for them arose. The rights and liabilities of the parties to a secured transaction depend on the nature of the security—that is, on whether (1) the security pledged is the promise of another person to pay if the debtor does not, or (2) a security interest in goods, intangibles, or real estate is conveyed as security for the payment of a debt or obligation.

If personal credit is pledged, the other person may guarantee the payment of the debt—that is, become a guarantor—or the other person may join the debtor in the debtor's promise to pay, in which case the other person would become surety for the debt.

The oldest and simplest security device was the pledge. To have a pledge valid against third persons with an interest in the goods, such as subsequent purchasers or creditors, it was necessary that the property used as security be delivered to the pledgee or a pledge holder. Upon default by the pledger, the pledgee had the right to sell the property and apply the proceeds to the payment of the debt.

Situations arose in which it was desirable to leave the property used as security in the possession of the debtor. To accomplish this objective, the debtor would give the creditor a bill of sale to the property, thus passing title to the creditor. The bill of sale would provide that if the debtor performed his promise, the bill of sale would become null and void, thus revesting title to the property in the debtor. A secret lien on the goods was created by this device, and the early courts held that such a transaction was a fraud on third-party claimants and void as to them. An undisclosed or secret lien is unfair to creditors who might extend credit to the debtor on the strength of property that they see in the debtor's possession but that in fact is subject to the prior claim of another creditor. Statutes were enacted providing for the recording or filing of the bill of sale, which was later designated as a chattel mortgage. These statutes were not uniform in their provisions. Most of them set up formal requirements for the execution of the chattel mortgage and also stated the effect of recording or filing on the rights of third-party claimants.

To avoid the requirements for the execution and filing of the chattel mortgage, sellers of goods would sell the goods on a "conditional sales contract" under which the seller retained title to the goods until their purchase price had been paid in full. Upon default by the buyer, the seller could (a) repossess the goods or (b) pass title and recover a judgment for the unpaid balance of the purchase price. Abuses of this security device gave rise to some regulatory statutes. About half of the states enacted statutes providing that the conditional sales contract was void as to third parties unless it was filed or recorded.

No satisfactory device was developed whereby inventory could be used as security. The inherent difficulty is that inventory is intended to be sold and turned into cash and the creditor is interested in protecting his interest in the cash rather than in maintaining a lien on the sold goods. Field warehousing was used under the pledge, and an after-acquired property clause in a chattel mortgage on a stock of goods held for resale partially fulfilled this need. One of the devices used was the trust receipt. This short-term marketing security arrangement had its origin in the export-import trade. It was later used extensively as a means of financing retailers of consumer goods having a high unit value.

## Security Interests in Personal Property

Chapter 21 will discuss how a creditor can obtain a security interest in the personal property or fixtures of a debtor. It will also explain the rights to the debtor's property of the creditor, the debtor, and other creditors of the debtor. These security interests are covered by Article 9 of the Uniform Commercial Code, which sets out a comprehensive scheme for regulating security interests in personal property and fixtures. The Code abolishes the old formal distinctions between different types of security devices used to create security interests in personal property.

## Security Interests in Real Property

Three types of contractual security devices have been developed by which real estate may be used as security: (1) the real estate mortgage, (2) the trust deed, and (3) the land contract. In addition to these contract security devices, all of the states have enacted statutes granting the right to mechanic's liens on real estate. Security interests in real property are covered later in this chapter.

## SURETYSHIP AND GUARANTY

### Sureties and Guarantors

As a condition of making a loan, granting credit, or employing someone (particularly as a fiduciary), a creditor may demand that the debtor, contractor, or employee provide as security for his performance the liability of a third person as surety or guarantor. The purpose of the contract of suretyship or guaranty is to provide the creditor with additional protection against loss in the event of default by the debtor, contractor, or employee.

A **surety** is a person who is *liable for the payment of another person's debt or for the performance of another person's duty.* The surety joins with the person primarily liable in promising to make the payment or to perform the duty. For example, Kathleen Kelly, who is 17 years old, buys a used car on credit from Harry's Used Cars. She signs a promissory note, agreeing to pay $75 a month on the note until the note is paid in full. Harry's has Kathleen's father cosign the note; thus, her father is a surety. Similarly, the city of Chicago hires the B&B Construction Company to build a new sewage treatment plant. The city will probably require B&B to have a surety agree to be liable for B&B's performance of its contract. There are insurance companies that, for a fee, will agree to be a surety on the contract of a company such as B&B.

If the person who is primarily liable (the principal) defaults, the surety is liable to pay or perform. Upon default, the creditor may ask the surety to pay even if he has not asked the principal debtor to pay. If the surety makes good on his contract of suretyship, he is entitled to be reimbursed by the principal. While a contract of surety does not have to be in writing to be enforceable, it normally is.

A guaranty contract is similar to a suretyship contract in that the promisor agrees to answer for the obligation of another. However, a guarantor does not join the principal in making a promise; rather, a guarantor makes a separate promise and agrees to be liable upon the happening of a certain event. For example, a father tells a merchant, "I will guarantee payment of my daughter Rachel's debt to you if she does not pay it," or "If Rachel becomes bankrupt, I will guarantee payment of her debt to you." While a surety is *primarily liable,* a guarantor is *secondarily* liable and can be held to his guarantee only after the principal defaults and cannot be held to his promise or payment. Generally, a guarantor's promise must be made in writing to be enforceable under the statute of frauds.

The rights and liabilities of the surety and the guarantor are substantially the same. No distinction will be made between them in this chapter except where the distinction is of basic importance. Moreover, most commercial contracts and promissory notes today that are to be signed by multiple parties provide for the parties to be "jointly and severally" liable, thus making the surety relationship the predominate one.

## Creation of Principal and Surety Relation

The relationship of principal and surety, or that of principal and guarantor, is created by contract. The basic rules of contract law apply in determining the existence and nature of the relationship as well as the rights and duties of the parties.

## Defenses of a Surety

Suppose Jeffrey's mother agrees to be a surety for Jeffrey on his purchase of a motorcycle. If the motorcycle was defectively made and Jeffrey refuses to make further payments on it, the dealer might try to collect the balance due from Jeffrey's mother. As a surety, Jeffrey's mother can use any defenses against the dealer that Jeffrey has if they go to the merits of the primary contract. Thus, if Jeffrey has a valid defense of breach of warranty against the dealer, his mother can use it as a basis for not paying the dealer.

Other defenses that go to the merits include (1) lack or failure of consideration, (2) inducement of the contract by fraud or duress, and (3) breach of contract by the other party. Certain defenses of the principal cannot be used by the surety. These defenses include lack of capacity, such as minority or insanity, and bankruptcy. Thus, if Jeffrey is only 17 years old, the fact that he is a minor cannot be used by Jeffrey's mother to defend against the dealer. This defense of Jeffrey's lack of capacity to contract does not go to the merits of the contract between Jeffrey and the dealer and cannot be used by Jeffrey's mother.

A surety contracts to be responsible for the performance of the principal's obligation. If the principal and the creditor change that obligation by agreement, the surety is relieved of responsibility unless the surety agrees to the change. This is because the surety's obligation cannot be changed without his consent.

For example, Fredericks cosigns a note for his friend Kato, which she has given to Credit Union to secure a loan. Suppose the note was originally for $2,500 and payable in 12 months with interest at 11 percent a year. Credit Union and Kato later agree that Kato will have 24 months to repay the note but that the interest will be 13 percent per year. Unless Fredericks consents to this change, he is discharged from his responsibility as surety. The obligation he agreed to assume was altered by the changes in the repayment period and the interest rate.

The most common kind of change affecting a surety is an extension of time to perform the contract. If the creditor merely allows the principal more time without the surety's consent, this does not relieve the surety of responsibility. The surety's consent is required only where there is an actual binding agreement between the creditor and the principal as to the extension of time.

In addition, the courts usually make a distinction between **accommodation sureties** and **compensated sureties.** An accommodation surety is a person who acts as a surety without compensation, such as a friend who cosigns a note as a favor. A compensated surety is a person, usually a professional such as a bonding company, who is paid for serving as a surety.

The courts are more protective of accommodation sureties than of compensated sureties. Accommodation sureties are relieved of liability unless they consent to an extension of time. Compensated sureties, on the other hand, must show that they will be harmed by an extension of time before they are relieved of responsibility because of a binding extension without their consent. A compensated surety must show that a change in the contract was both material and prejudicial to him if he is to be relieved of his obligation as surety. This principle is illustrated in the *United States v. Reliance Insurance Co.* case, which follows.

If the debtor's obligation to the creditor is paid or satisfied, the surety is discharged from her obligation.

---

## UNITED STATES V. RELIANCE INSURANCE CO.
### 799 F.2d 1382 (9th Cir. 1986)

On February 18, 1983, the Army-Navy Foundation, a nonprofit organization formed to facilitate preparations for the 1983 Army-Navy game, and the U.S. Military and Naval Academies entered into a contract to play the game at the Rose Bowl in Pasadena. Traditionally, the game was played in Philadelphia. The parties drew the contract to ensure that the Academies would receive approximately the same revenue from the 1983 game as they had received from the 1982 game and would not incur additional expenses as a result of the change in location.

The Foundation was entitled to "revenue generated from ticket sales and broadcast rights." The Foundation was required to pay each Academy $875,000—$550,000 from television revenues and $325,000 from ticket sales and concession proceeds. The Foundation agreed also to compensate each Academy up to $100,000 for additional costs that were "in excess of those expenses actually incurred by the Army and Navy in conjunction with the 1982 Army-Navy game." Finally, the Foundation agreed to provide funds to transport cadets, midshipmen, and support personnel to Pasadena and to provide housing and meals for them while there.

The contract required the Foundation to obtain two bonds. One bond guaranteed the Foundation's obligation of $650,000 for ticket sales and concession proceeds. The Academies released this bond when they collected the money. The second bond guaranteed the Foundation's obligation to pay up to $200,000 to cover additional expenses incurred by the Academies.

An insurance broker put the Foundation in touch with Reliance Insurance Company to obtain the bonds. Because the Foundation had no assets, Reliance required 100 percent collateral. The Foundation assured Reliance that it was entitled to the television proceeds from the game and by letter dated February 18 assured Reliance that it would assign the television proceeds to it up to the face amount of the bonds. Although initially estimated to be $1,100,000, after negotiation with ABC, the television contract amounted to $1,450,000. The Foundation never made the assignment and on their face the bonds did not mention an assignment of the television proceeds.

Subsequent to the issuance of the bonds, the Academies and the Foundation executed three modifications to the contract. The first modification changed the date of the game from December 3 to November 25; this change was required by ABC. The second modification was required by the National Collegiate Athletic Association and changed the contract to direct payment of the television proceeds to the Army as the host school, rather than to the Foundation. As a result of this modification, the Foundation was entitled to only $350,000 of the television proceeds; however, it was relieved of its $1,100,000 obligation to the Academies.

Finally, less than a week before the game, a third modification to the contract was executed. Because the air carriers hired to transport the cadets, midshipmen, and support personnel to Pasadena unexpectedly required payment prior to takeoff and the Foundation was unable to meet its contractual responsibility to make such payments because it had not yet received any ticket or television revenue, the Academies made the payments. In turn, the Foundation waived its rights to ticket revenue already retained by the Academies, which was payable to the Foundation, and to television revenues in excess of $1,100,000 (i.e., $350,000).

The only persons who had knowledge of both the Foundation's assurance that Reliance would receive an assignment of the television proceeds and the three subsequent modifications to the contract were the officers of the Foundation. Reliance knew nothing of the modifications to the contract and the Academies knew nothing of the agreement to assign the television proceeds to Reliance. When the Foundation failed to pay for the Academies' additional expenses, the Academies brought suit to recover on the bond provided by Reliance. The trial court held for Reliance and the Foundation (which was involved in the case as a third-party defendant) appealed.

---

**Jameson, District Judge** The primary issue is whether modifications of the bonded contract exonerate Reliance. As a general rule a surety will be discharged where a bonded contract is materially altered or changed without the surety's knowledge or consent. In addition, where, as here, a compensated surety seeks exoneration, it must show that the alteration caused prejudice or damage. Thus Reliance must demonstrate that the modifications were material and that some prejudices resulted.

The second modification had no net effect. The Foundation lost the rights to $1,100,000 in television revenues, but it was also relieved of its obligation to guarantee that amount. The third modification did not relieve the Foundation of its obligation to pay the airlines. The language of the third modification clearly indicates that the Foundation remained liable for the costs of transportation. The third modification merely shifted from the Foundation to the Academies the immediate burden of providing funds for transportation. In exchange, the Foundation relinquished its sole remaining right of any significance under the contract—the right to receive the excess television revenues.

The Academies argue that this court should view the modifications of the contract only to the extent they modify the Foundation's obligation which was the subject of the bond in question—the obligation to cover the Academies' additional expenses for the football team. Because the modifications did not affect this obligation, the Academies argue that there was no material alteration of the bonded contract. This view is much too narrow.

First, courts construe a bond and its underlying contract together. Second, the bond specifically incorporated the contract. Reliance guaranteed the Foundation's obligation on the basis of the entire contract, not just a single provision. When the bond and its underlying contract are viewed together, it is clear that the modifications were both material and prejudicial.

The contract funded the otherwise assetless Foundation with ticket, concession, and television proceeds. These funds provided the Foundation with a means to satisfy its obligations. As evidenced by the Foundation's February 18 letter promising to assign television proceeds, Reliance relied on the Foundation's funding as provided in the original contract. As the District Court concluded, "The impact of the third modification on the Foundation was that it was deprived of the excess television revenues on which it depended to meet its contractual obligations, including those secured by the bond in question." Absent the provision that the Foundation would receive the television proceeds, Reliance would likely have determined the risk was too great and declined to issue the bonds. Had there been no third modification, the Foundation may have had funds available to cover its obligations. The prejudice suffered by Reliance is the increased risk resulting from the modifications. As the Court of Appeals for the District of Columbia has stated:

A surety company is not a public utility. It may, for any or no reason conclude not to furnish its bond with respect to a particular contract. When it has committed itself with respect to one contract, amendments which convert that agreement into a significantly different one should be brought to the attention of the surety so that it may exercise its own business judgment as to whether it wishes to continue its commitment. It is not for the parties to the contract to decide among themselves that their amendments are of no interest to the surety, at least when, as here, those amendments go beyond mere matters of form.

The modifications of the contract between the Academies and the Foundation were material, at least one of which, the third, was prejudicial to the rights of Reliance as surety. Reliance had no knowledge of the modifications and did not consent to them.

**Judgment for Reliance affirmed.**

---

## Creditor's Duties to Surety

The creditor is required to disclose any material facts about the risk involved to the surety. If he does not do so, the surety is relieved of liability. For example, a bank (creditor) knows that an employee, Arthur, has been guilty of criminal conduct in the past. If the bank applies to a bonding company to obtain a bond on Arthur, the bank must disclose this information about Arthur. Similarly, suppose the bank has an employee, Alison, covered by a bond and discovers that Alison is embezzling money. If the bank agrees to give Alison another chance but does not report her actions to the bonding company, the bonding company is relieved of responsibility for further wrongful acts by Alison.

If the debtor posts security for the performance of an obligation, the creditor must not surrender the security without the consent of the surety. If the creditor does so, the surety is relieved of liability to the extent of the value surrendered.

## Subrogation, Reimbursement, and Contribution

If the surety has to perform or pay the principal's obligation, then the surety acquires all of the rights that the creditor had against the principal. This is known as the surety's **right of subrogation.** The rights acquired could include the right to any collateral in the possession of the creditor, any judgment right the creditor had against the principal on the obligation, and the rights of a creditor in bankruptcy proceedings.

If the surety performs or pays the principal's obligation, she is entitled to recover her costs from the principal; this is known as the surety's **right to reimbursement.** For example, Amado cosigns a promissory note for $250 at the credit union for her friend Anders. Anders defaults on the note, and the credit union collects $250 from Amado on her suretyship obligation. Amado then not only gets the credit union's rights against Anders, but also the right to collect $250 from Anders.

Suppose several persons (Tom, Dick, and Harry) are cosureties of their friend Sam. When Sam defaults, Tom pays the whole obligation. Tom is entitled to collect one third from both Dick and Harry since he paid more than his prorated share. This is known as the cosurety's **right to contribution.** The relative shares of cosureties, as well as any limitations on their liability, are normally set out in the contract of suretyship.

## LIENS ON PERSONAL PROPERTY

### Common Law Liens

Under the common—or judge-made—law, artisans, innkeepers, and common carriers (such as airlines and trucking companies) were entitled to liens to secure the reasonable value of the services they performed. An artisan such as a furniture upholsterer or an auto mechanic uses his labor or materials to improve personal property that belongs to someone else. The improvement becomes part of the property and belongs to the owner of the property. Therefore, the artisan who made the improvement is given a **lien** on the property until she is paid.

For example, the upholsterer who recovers a sofa for a customer is entitled to a lien on the sofa. The innkeeper and common carrier are in business to serve the public and are required by law to do so. Under the common law, the innkeeper, to secure payment for his reasonable charges for food and lodging, was allowed to claim a lien on the property that the guest brought to the hotel or inn. Similarly, the common carrier, such as a trucking company, was allowed to claim a lien on the goods carried for the reasonable charges for the service. The justification for such liens was that the innkeeper and common carrier were entitled to the protection of a lien because they were required by law to provide the service to anyone seeking it.

## Statutory Liens

While common law liens are still generally recognized today, many states have incorporated this concept into statutes. Some of the state statutes have created additional liens, while others have modified the common law liens to some extent. The statutes commonly provide a procedure for foreclosing the lien. **Foreclosure** is the method by which the rights of the property owner are cut off so that the lienholder can realize her security interest. Typically, the statutes provide for a court to authorize the sale of the personal property subject to the lien so that the creditor can obtain the money to which she is entitled.

Carriers' liens and warehousemen's liens are provided for in Article 7, Documents of Title, of the Uniform Commercial Code. They are covered in Chapter 26, Checks and Documents of Title.

## Characteristics of Liens

The common law lien and most of the statutory liens are known as **possessory liens.** They give the artisan or other lienholder the right to keep possession of the debtor's property until the reasonable charges for services have been paid. For the lien to come into play, possession of the goods must have been entrusted to the artisan. Suppose a person takes a chair to an upholsterer to have it repaired. The upholsterer can keep possession of the chair until the person pays the reasonable value of the repair work. However, if the upholsterer comes to the person's home to make the repair, the upholsterer would not have a lien on the chair as the person did not give up possession of it.

The two essential elements of the lien are: (1) possession by the improver or the provider of services and (2) a debt created by the improvement or the provision of services concerning the goods. If the artisan or other lienholder gives up the goods voluntarily, he loses the lien. For example, if a person has a new engine put in his car and the mechanic gives the car back to him before he pays for the engine, the mechanic loses the lien on the car to secure the person's payment for the work and materials. However, if the person uses a spare set of keys to regain possession, or does so by fraud or another illegal act, the lien is not lost. Once the debt has been paid, the lien is terminated and the artisan or other lienholder no longer has the right to retain the goods. If the artisan keeps the goods after the debt has been paid, or keeps the goods without the right to a lien, he is liable for conversion or unlawful detention of goods.

Another important aspect of common law liens is that the work or service must have been performed at the request of the owner of the property. If the work or service is performed without the consent of the owner, no lien is created. This is one of the issues raised in the *Navistar Financial Corporation v. Allen's Corner Garage and Towing Service, Inc.* case, which follows.

---

### NAVISTAR FINANCIAL CORPORATION v. ALLEN'S CORNER GARAGE AND TOWING SERVICE, INC.
#### 505 N.E.2d 1321 (Ill. App. Ct. 1987)

Wieslaw Wik was the owner of a truck tractor on which Navistar Financial Corporation held a lien to secure a purchase loan agreement. On February 21, 1986, Wik was driving his truck tractor and pulling a trailer owned by the V. Seng Teaming Company. The tractor/trailer unit overturned in a ditch. Allen's Corner Garage and Towing Service was called by the Illinois State Police. Its crew removed the cargo from the trailer and hoisted the tractor and trailer out of the ditch and onto the highway. They then took the truck, trailer, and cargo to Allen's garage for storage. The uprighting and towing of semitrailer trucks is an intricate process and involves a good deal of specialized equipment. Allen's was licensed by the Interstate Commerce Commission and the Illinois Commerce Commission as a common carrier and owned over 50 specialized trucks and trailers for such operations.

Wik defaulted on his loan agreement with Navistar, and the right to possession passed to Navistar. One of its employees contacted Allen's and offered to pay the towing plus storage charges on the truck in exchange for possession of it. Allen's refused, saying it would not release the truck unless the charges for the truck, trailer, and cargo were all paid. Navistar then brought suit against Allen's to recover possession of the truck. Subsequently, V. Seng Teaming Company paid $13,000 in towing and storage charges on the trailer and cargo and took possession of them. Navistar then reiterated its willingness to pay the towing charges but refused to pay any storage charges accruing after its initial offer.

The trial court held that Allen's had a common law artisan's lien against the tractor for towing charges but not for storage fees. It held that Navistar was entitled to possession of the tractor, subject to payment of $1,162 for towing. Allen's appealed and Navistar cross-appealed the portion of the order granting Allen's a common law lien for towing.

---

**Unverzagt, Judge**     Illinois recognizes the common law possessory lien. Such liens are fundamentally consensual in nature and can be created only by agreement, by some fixed rule of law, or by usage of trade or commerce. The common law lien has no provision for forfeiture and sale, but is limited to the right to possession of the chattel until all charges are paid. The lien applies to categories of persons: (1) those who impart added value to the property and (2) common carriers who are bound by law to accept and carry the goods. In Illinois, a common carrier has a lien on goods delivered to it for carriage; the carrier is not bound to part with the goods until the charges are paid.

Allen's argues that its services fall within both categories of common law liens. It claims that its towing and cargo salvaging operations are so specialized as to qualify it as an artisan, or alternatively, that it is a common carrier. Navistar responds that Allen's is not an artisan, citing a number of cases from Illinois and from foreign jurisdictions for the principle that mere towing of a vehicle, no matter how difficult or specialized, does not give rise to a common law lien. Most of these cases are distinguishable as they involve towing of a vehicle without the owner's consent. Nonetheless, we agree with Navistar that mere towing of a vehicle from one place to another does not add anything of value to the "intrinsic value" of the vehicle towed.

We agree with Allen's, however, that it is entitled to a lien as a common carrier. As a common carrier, it is entitled to a lien for carriage charges. Navistar does not directly challenge this conclusion, but argues that Allen's towed the tractor without its consent. As an agreement is a necessary element of a common law lien, Navistar's lack of consent would defeat Allen's lien. Although police have the power to remove disabled vehicles from highways, they may not create a lien upon a vehicle without the owner's consent. John Allen testified that a representative from Seng was at the scene when he arrived and that the entire unit was under Seng's control. Allen also testified that the driver came to Allen's place of business the following day. Testifying later, Allen stated unequivocally that Allen's Corner Garage was authorized to make the tow. The court could have concluded that the representative of Seng was authorized to and did give his consent to the towing, or that the driver subsequently ratified these actions.

Having decided that Allen's was entitled to a common law lien as a common carrier, we now turn to the question of whether it may also claim a lien for storage charges. The rule has been stated that when a common carrier hauls freight and then stores it at the destination until claimed by the receiver, the carrier becomes a warehouseman and obtains a lien for storage charges. [Citations omitted.] In those cases, the commodities involved, coal and grain, required special handling and storage. The carrier in each case sustained some inconvenience or expense by storing the property until the receiver was ready to remove it.

In the present case, Allen's did not keep the truck on the lot for the benefit of Navistar, but did so only to preserve its lien right. A garage owner is not entitled to a lien for storage in a garage. Since Allen's retained and stored the truck for no reason other than to be able to insist on its lien rights, the trial court was correct in denying it a lien for storage charges.

**Judgment affirmed.**

## Foreclosure of Lien

The right of a lienholder to possess goods does not automatically give the lienholder the right to sell the goods or to claim ownership if his charges are not paid. Commonly, there is a procedure provided by statute for selling property once it has been held for a certain period of time. The lienholder is required to give notice to the debtor and to advertise the proposed sale by posting or publishing notices. If there is no statutory procedure, the lienholder must first bring a lawsuit against the debtor. After obtaining a judgment for his charges, the lienholder can have the sheriff seize the property and have it sold at a judicial sale.

## SECURITY INTERESTS IN REAL PROPERTY

There are three basic contract devices for using real estate as security for an obligation: (1) the real estate mortgage, (2) the deed of trust, and (3) the land contract. In addition, the states have enacted statutes giving mechanics such as carpenters and plumbers, and materialmen such as lumberyards, a right to a lien on real property into which their labor or materials have been incorporated.

## Historical Developments of Mortgages

A **mortgage** is a security interest in real property or a deed to real property that is given by the owner (the **mortgagor**) as security for a debt owed to the creditor (the **mortgagee**). The real estate mortgage was used as a form of security in England as early as the middle of the 12th century, but our present-day mortgage law developed from the common law mortgage of the 15th century. The common law mortgage was a deed that conveyed the land to the mortgagee, with the title to the land to return to the mortgagor upon payment of the debt secured by the mortgage. The mortgagee was given possession of the land during the term of the mortgage. If the mortgagor defaulted on the debt, the mortgagee's title to the land became absolute. The land was forfeited as a penalty, but the forfeiture did not discharge the debt. In addition to keeping the land, the mortgagee could sue on the debt, recover a judgment, and seek to collect the debt.

The early equity courts did not favor the imposition of penalties and would relieve mortgagors from such forfeitures, provided that the mortgagor's default was minor and was due to causes beyond his control. Gradually, the courts became more lenient in permitting redemptions and allowed the mortgagor to **redeem** (reclaim his property) if he tendered performance without unreasonable delay. Finally, the courts of equity recognized the mortgagor's right to redeem as an absolute right that would continue until the mortgagee asked the court of equity to decree that the mortgagor's right to redeem be foreclosed and cut off. Our present law regarding the foreclosure of mortgages developed from this practice.

Today, the mortgage is generally viewed as a lien on land rather than a conveyance of title to the land. There are still some states where the mortgagor goes through the process of giving the mortgagee some sort of legal title to the property. Even in these states, however, the mortgagee's title is minimal and the real ownership of the property remains in the mortgagor.

## Form, Execution, and Recording

Because the real estate mortgage conveys an interest in real property, it must be executed with the same formality as a deed. Unless it is executed with the required formalities, it will not be eligible for recording in the local land records. Recordation of the mortgage does not affect its validity as between the mortgagor and the mortgagee. However, if it is not recorded, it will not be effective against subsequent purchasers of the property or creditors, including other mortgagees, who have no notice of the earlier mortgage. It is important to the mortgagee that the mortgage be recorded so that the world will be on notice of the mortgagee's interest in the property. See Figure 1 for an example of a mortgage.

## Rights and Liabilities

The owner (mortgagor) of property subject to a mortgage can sell the interest in the property without the consent of the mortgagee. However, the sale does not affect the mortgagee's interest in the property or the mortgagee's claim against the mortgagor. In some cases, the mortgage may provide that if the property is sold, then any remaining balance becomes immediately due and payable. This is known as a "due on sale" clause.

Suppose Erica Smith owns a lot on a lake. She wants to build a cottage on the land, so she borrows $55,000 from First National Bank. She signs a note

**FIGURE 1**   A Mortgage

---

### MORTGAGE

THIS INDENTURE, made this 18th day of October, A.D. 1995, BETWEEN Raymond A. Dole and Deborah H. Dole, hereinafter called the Mortgagor, and First Federal Savings and Loan Association, hereinafter called the Mortgagee,

WITNESSETH, That the said Mortgagor, for and in consideration of the sum of One Dollar, to us in hand paid by the said Mortgagee, the receipt whereof is hereby acknowledged, have granted, bargained, and sold to the said Mortgagee, its heirs and assigns forever, the following described land situate, lying and being in the County of Genesee, State of Michigan, to wit:

All that certain plot, piece, or parcel of land located in the County of Genesee, State of Michigan and known and described as Lot number Thirty-nine (39) in William D. Green's subdivision of part of Lot numbered Twenty-two (22) in Square numbered Twelve Hundred Nineteen (1219), as per plot recorded in the Office of the Surveyor for the County of Genesee in Liber 30 at folio 32, together with the buildings and improvements thereon, and the said Mortgagor do hereby fully warrant the title to said land, and will defend the same against the lawful claims of all persons whomsoever.

PROVIDED ALWAYS, That if said Mortgagor, their heirs, legal representatives, or assigns shall pay unto the said Mortgagee, its legal representatives or assigns, a certain promissory note dated the 18th day of October, A.D. 1995, for the sum of Thirty-eight Thousand Dollars ($38,000.00), payable in monthly installments of Three Hundred Fifteen Dollars ($315.00) with interest at ten percent (10%) beginning on November 18, 1995, and signed by Raymond A. Dole and Deborah H. Dole and shall perform, comply with, and abide by this mortgage, and shall pay all taxes which may accrue on said land and all costs and expenses said Mortgagee may be put to in collecting said promissory note by foreclosure of this mortgage or otherwise, including a reasonable attorney's fee, then this mortgage and the estate hereby created shall cease and be null and void.

IN WITNESS WHEREOF, the said Mortgagor hereunto set their hands and seals the day and year first above written. Signed, sealed, and delivered in presence of us:

*John R. Bacon* )  *Raymond A. Dole*
*James A. Brown* )  *Deborah H. Dole*

ACKNOWLEDGMENT OF MORTGAGE
State of Michigan )
County of Genesee) ss

I, an officer authorized to take acknowledgments according to the laws of the State of Michigan, duly qualified and acting, HEREBY CERTIFY that Raymond A. Dole and Deborah H. Dole to me personally known, this day personally appeared and acknowledged before me that they executed the foregoing Mortgage, and I further certify that I know the said persons making said acknowledgment to be the individuals described in and who executed the said Mortgage.
Susan B. Clark
Notary Public

*Susan B. Clark*
Susan B. Clark
Notary Public

---

for $55,000 and gives the bank a $55,000 mortgage on the land and cottage as security for her repayment of the loan. Several years later, Smith sells her land and cottage to Melinda Mason. The mortgage she gave First National might make the unpaid balance due on the mortgage payable on sale. If it does not, Smith can sell the property with the mortgage on it. If Mason defaults on making the mortgage payments, the bank can foreclose on the mortgage. If at the foreclosure sale the property does not bring enough money to cover the costs, interest, and balance due on the mortgage, First National is entitled to a deficiency judgment against Smith. However, some courts are reluctant to give deficiency judgments where real property is used as security for a debt. If on foreclosure the property sells for more than the debt, Mason is entitled to the surplus.

A purchaser of mortgaged property may buy it **subject to** the mortgage or may **assume** the mortgage. If she buys subject to the mortgage and there is a default and foreclosure, the purchaser is not personally liable for any deficiency. The property is liable for the mortgage debt and can be sold to satisfy it in case of default; in addition, the original mortgagor remains liable for its payment. If the buyer assumes the mortgage, then she becomes personally liable for the debt and for any deficiency on default and foreclosure.

The creditor (mortgagee) may assign his interest in the mortgaged property. To do this, the mortgagee must assign the mortgage as well as the debt for which the mortgage is security. In most jurisdictions, the negotiation of the note carries with it the right to the security and the holder of the note is entitled to the benefits of the mortgage.

## Foreclosure

Foreclosure is the process by which any rights of the mortgagor or the current property owner are cut off. Foreclosure proceedings are regulated by statute in the state in which the property is located. In many states, two or more alternative methods of foreclosure are available to the mortgagee or his assignee. The methods in common use today are (1) strict foreclosure, (2) action and sale, and (3) power of sale.

A small number of states permit what is called **strict foreclosure.** The creditor keeps the property in satisfaction of the debt, and the owner's rights are cut off. This means that the creditor has no right to a deficiency and the debtor has no right to any surplus. Strict foreclosure is normally limited to situations where the amount of the debt exceeds the value of the property.

Foreclosure by **action and sale** is permitted in all states, and it is the only method of foreclosure permitted in some states. Although the state statutes are not uniform, they are alike in their basic requirements. In a foreclosure by action and

sale, suit is brought in a court having jurisdiction. Any party having a property interest that would be cut off by the foreclosure must be made a defendant, and if any such party has a defense, he must enter his appearance and set up his defense. After the case is tried, a judgment is entered and a sale of the property ordered. The proceeds of the sale are applied to the payment of the mortgage debt, and any surplus is paid over to the mortgagor. If there is a deficiency, a deficiency judgment is, as a general rule, entered against the mortgagor and such other persons as are liable on the debt. Deficiency judgments are generally not permitted where the property sold is the residence of the debtor.

The right to foreclose under a **power of sale** must be expressly conferred on the mortgagee by the terms of the mortgage. If the procedure for the exercise of the power is set out in the mortgage, that procedure must be followed. Several states have enacted statutes that set out the procedure to be followed in the exercise of a power of sale. No court action is required. As a general rule, notice of the default and sale must be given to the mortgagor. After the statutory period, the sale may be held. The sale must be advertised, and it must be at auction. The sale must be conducted fairly, and an effort must be made to sell the property at the highest price obtainable. The proceeds of the sale are applied to the payment of costs, interest, and the principal of the debt. Any surplus must be paid to the mortgagor. If there is a deficiency and the mortgagee wishes to recover a judgment for the deficiency, she must bring suit on the debt.

## Right of Redemption

At common law and under existing statutes, the mortgagor or an assignee of the mortgagor has what is called an **equity of redemption** in the mortgaged real estate. This means that he has the absolute right to discharge the mortgage when due and to have title to the mortgaged property restored free and clear of the mortgage debt. Under the statutes of all states, the mortgagor or any party having an interest in the mortgaged property that will be cut off by the foreclosure may redeem the property after default and before the mortgagee forecloses the mortgage. In several states, the mortgagor or any other party in interest is given by statute what is known as a redemption period (usually six months or one year, beginning either after the foreclosure proceedings are started or after a foreclosure sale of the mortgaged property has been made) in which to pay the mortgaged debt, costs, and interest and to redeem the property.

As a general rule, if a party in interest wishes to redeem, he must, if the redemption period runs after the foreclosure sale, pay to the purchaser at the foreclosure sale the amount that the purchaser has paid plus interest up to the time of redemption. If the redemption period runs before the sale, the party in interest must pay the amount of the debt plus the costs and interest. The person who wishes to redeem from a mortgage foreclosure sale must redeem the entire mortgage interest; he cannot redeem a partial interest by paying a proportionate amount of the debt or by paying a proportionate amount of the price bid at the foreclosure sale.

## Deed of Trust

States typically use either the mortgage or the **deed of trust** as the primary mechanism for holding a security interest in real property. There are three parties to a deed of trust: (1) the owner of the property who borrows the money (the debtor), (2) the trustee who holds legal title to the property put up as security, and (3) the lender who is the beneficiary of the trust. The trustee serves as a fiduciary for both the creditor and the debtor. The purpose of the deed of trust is to make it easy for the security to be liquidated. However, most states treat the deed of trust like a mortgage in giving the borrower a relatively long period of time to redeem the property, thereby defeating this rationale for the arrangement.

In a deed of trust transaction, the borrower deeds to the trustee the property that is to be put up as security. See Figure 2 for an example of a deed of trust. The trust agreement usually gives the trustee the right to foreclose or sell the property if the debtor fails to make a required payment on the debt. Normally, the trustee does not sell the property until the lender notifies him that the borrower is in default and demands that the property be sold. The trustee must notify the debtor that he is in default and that the land will be sold. The trustee advertises

the property for sale. After the statutory period, the trustee will sell the property at a public or private sale. The proceeds are applied to the costs of the foreclosure, interest, and debt. If there is a surplus, it is paid to the borrower. If there is a deficiency, the lender has to sue the borrower on the debt and recover a judgment.

## Land Contracts

The **land contract** is a device for securing the balance due the seller on the purchase price of real estate. Essentially, it is an installment contract for the purchase of land. The buyer agrees to pay the purchase price over a period of time. The seller agrees to convey title to the property to the buyer when the full price is paid. Usually, the buyer takes possession of the property, pays the taxes, insures the property, and assumes the other obligations of an owner. However, the seller keeps legal title and does not turn over the deed until the purchase price is paid.

If the buyer defaults, the seller usually has the right to declare a forfeiture and take over possession of the property. The buyer's rights to the property are cut off at that point. Most states give the buyer on a land contract a limited period of time to redeem his interest. Moreover, some states require the seller to go through a foreclosure proceeding. Generally, the procedure for declaring a forfeiture and recovering property sold on a land contract is simpler and less time-consuming than foreclosure of a mortgage. In most states, the procedure in case of default is set out by statute. If the buyer, after default, voluntarily surrenders possession to the seller, no court procedure is necessary; the seller's title will become absolute, and the buyer's equity will be cut off.

Purchases of farm property are commonly financed through the use of land contracts. See Figure 3 for an example of a land contract. As an interest in real estate, a land contract should be in writing and recorded in the local land records so as to protect the interests of both parties.

As can be seen in the following case, *Looney v. Farmers Home Administration*, some courts have invoked the equitable doctrine against forfeitures and have required that the seller on a land contract must foreclose on the property in order to avoid injustice to a defaulting buyer.

**FIGURE 2**    **A Deed of Trust**

DEED OF TRUST

THIS DEED made this 14th day of August, 1995, by and between Harold R. Holmes, grantor, party of the first part, and Frederick B. Cannon, trustee, party of the second part, and Sarah A Miles, party of the third part,

WITNESSETH:

The party of the first part does hereby grant unto the party of the second part, the following described property located in the District of Columbia and known as Lot number One Hundred Fourteen (114) in James B. Nicholson's subdivision in Square numbered Twelve Hundred Forty-seven (1247), formerly Square numbered Seventy-seven (77), "Georgetown," as per plat recorded in the Office of the Surveyor for the District of Columbia in Liber Georgetown 2 at folio 34, in trust, however, to secure the balance only of the purchase price of the above described premises, evidenced by the following described obligation:

Promissory note executed by the party of the first part, payable to the party of the third part and dated August 14, 1995, in the principal sum of Sixty-four Thousand Dollars ($64,000.00) bearing interest at the rate of ten percent (10%) per annum until paid. Said principal and interest are payable in monthly installments of Seven Hundred Thirty-five Dollars ($735.00) on the 14th day of each and every month beginning September 14, 1995, and continuing every month thereafter, with the unpaid balance of said principal and interest due and payable in full on August 14, 2005.

IN WITNESS WHEREOF, the party of the first part has set his hand and seal this the day and year first above written.

*Harold R. Holmes*
(SEAL)

Acknowledgment
This Deed of Trust accepted this 14th day of August, 1995.

*Frederick B. Cannon*
Trustee

## LOONEY v. FARMERS HOME ADMINISTRATION
### 794 F.2d 310 (7th Cir. 1986)

On October 7, 1976, Lowry and Helen McCord entered into a land contract to purchase a 260-acre farm from John and Esther Looney for $250,000. The contract specified that this was to be amortized over a 20-year period at an annual interest rate of 7 percent. The McCords were to make annual payments of $23,280 on November 15 of each year until the purchase price and all accrued interest was paid. They also agreed to pay real estate taxes, insurance, and maintenance costs for the property.

Four years later, the McCords received an economic emergency loan of $183,000 from the Farmers Home Administration (FmHA). They signed a promissory note for the amount of the loan with interest at 11 percent and, as security, also granted the FmHA a second mortgage on the land subject to the land sales contract.

The McCords subsequently defaulted on their obligations to the Looneys. At the time of the default, the McCords had paid $123,280 to the Looneys but still owed $249,360.12 on the contract price. At the time, the property was worth $455,000. The Looneys brought suit against the McCords and the FmHA seeking to eject the McCords from the property and forfeiture of the contract. The FmHA objected to the proposed forfeiture and argued that the court should order foreclosure proceedings.

The district court denied the FmHA's motion for foreclosure. It held that the traditional presumption under Indiana law did not apply because the McCords had made only minimal payments on the contract and had not paid their fall taxes or insurance installments. Because $249,360.12 was still owed on an initial base price of $250,000, the court found the McCords's equity to be $639.88, only .26 percent of the principal. The court therefore found forfeiture appropriate, awarded the FmHA $639.88, and extinguished the FmHA's mortgage. The FmHA appealed.

---

**Cudahy, Circuit Judge**   Under Indiana law a conditional land sales contract is considered in the nature of a secured transaction, "the provisions of which are subject to all proper and just remedies at law and in equity." *Skendzel v. Marshall.* Recognizing the common law maxim that "equity abhors forfeitures," the *Skendzel* court concluded that "judicial foreclosure of a land sales contract is in consonance with the notions of equity developed in American jurisprudence." Foreclosure generally protects the rights of all parties to a contract. Upon judicial sale the proceeds are first applied to the balance of the contract principal and interest owed the seller. Then, any junior lienholders take their share. Any surplus goes to the buyer.

*Skendzel* recognized, however, two instances where forfeiture was the appropriate remedy:

In the case of an abandoning, absconding vendee, forfeiture is a logical and equitable remedy. Forfeiture would also be appropriate where the vendee has paid a minimal amount on the contract at the time of default and seeks to retain possession while the vendor is paying taxes, insurance, and other upkeep in order to preserve the premises.

The district court did not rely on the first *Skendzel* exception in finding forfeiture appropriate. No evidence in the record supports such a finding. If forfeiture is justified, then, it is only because the second *Skendzel* exception is met. This requires that the vendee have paid only a minimum amount on the contract at the time of default. In this case, the district court concluded that "this is patently a situation contemplated by the court in *Skendzel* in which forfeiture is the logical and equitable remedy."

However, the buyers in *Skendzel* had in fact paid more than a minimum amount on the contract and the court cited no examples of what would "patently" constitute a "minimum amount." Rather, later Indiana cases have interpreted *Skendzel* as requiring a case by case analysis that examines the totality of circumstances surrounding the contract and its performance. Here, while $123,280 was paid to the Looneys, the court considered all but $639.88 to be interest rather than a part of the contract price. The court equated contract price with what was paid to reduce principal. But nothing in Indiana law compels the district court's construction of payments on the contract. On the contrary, several Indiana courts have considered and given weight to both payments to reduce principal and those to reduce interest in determining whether a buyer falls within the second *Skendzel* exception.

Even where no principal is paid, a buyer's stake in the property may be sufficient to justify foreclosure. Here, two uncontested affidavits indicate the property to be worth over $200,000 more than the McCords owe the Looneys. With the evidence of appreciation, the court was incorrect to conclusively value the McCords' equity at only $639.88.

When the second *Skendzel* exception has been invoked it frequently has been because the vendee is contributing to a decline in the value of the security. There is no allegation or evidence of waste in this case. Even the Looneys admit that the buyers "had paid substantial monies pursuant to the terms of the contracts." The Looneys received $123,280 and the McCords paid the necessary real estate taxes, insurance premiums and upkeep expenses for over six years. The Looneys make no showing that foreclosure would not satisfy their interest and the court below made no such determination. While foreclosure would appear to satisfy all parties' needs, forfeiture leaves the FmHA with a $639.88 recovery on a $183,800 loan. In view of the "totality of circumstances" this result seems inequitable.

**Judgment reversed in favor of Farmers Home Administration.**

**FIGURE 3**   **A Land Contract**

## LAND CONTRACT

THIS AGREEMENT, made this 15th day of September, A.D. 1995, between Sarah A. Collins, a single woman, hereinafter designated "Vendor," and Robert H. Bowen, a single man, hereinafter designated "Vendee," in the manner following: The Vendor hereby agrees to sell and the Vendee agrees to buy all that certain piece or parcel of land being in the Township of Fenton, County of Genesee and State of Michigan, and more particularly described as follows:

Part of the Northeast ¼ of the Northwest ¼ of Section 20, Township 5 North, Range 5 East, described as follows: Beginning at a point on the North line of said Section 20, which is West along said North line, 797.72 feet from the North ¼ corner of said Section 20; thence continuing West along said North line, 522.72 feet; thence South 0 degrees, 18 minutes, 12 seconds East along the West ⅛ line of said Section, 1000.0 feet; thence East parallel to the North line of said Section, 522.72 feet; thence North 0 degrees, 18 minutes, 12 seconds West parallel to said West ⅛ line 1000.0 feet to the point of beginning, containing 12.0 acres of land, more or less, and known as 1135 Long Lake Road.

Subject to all easements, laws, ordinances, reservations, applying to this property.

For the sum of Sixty-four Thousand Nine Hundred Dollars ($64,900.00), payable as follows: Ten Thousand Dollars ($10,000.00), cash in hand, receipt of which is hereby acknowledged before the signing of this contract and the balance payable as follows: Three Hundred Dollars ($300.00) or more payable on the 1st day of November, 1995, and a like amount on the 1st day of each and every month thereafter until the full sum of both interest and principal has been paid in full. Interest at the rate of ten percent (10%) per annum, starting October 1, 1995, shall be deducted from each and every monthly payment and the balance applied on the principal. The entire balance, both principal and interest, to be paid in full on or before 5 years from date of closing. It is understood and agreed that the above monthly payment includes taxes and insurance that may become due and payable subsequent to the date of this contract; said amounts to be paid by Vendor and added to the principal balance.

Vendee also agrees to pay all taxes and assessments extraordinary as well as ordinary that may be levied thereon, including taxes for the year 1995, and also deferred payments on special assessments that shall become due and payable after the date thereof to be prorated to date.

The Vendee agrees to keep the buildings upon or to be placed upon the premises insured against damage by fire and wind, in such company and amount as is approved by the Vendor, for the benefit of all parties in interest; such policies shall be delivered to and held by the Vendor.

And Vendee agrees to keep the buildings and other improvements on the premises in good repair. In case the Vendee shall fail to pay taxes, effect insurance, or make necessary repairs, the Vendor may do any or all of these things and the amount paid therefore by the Vendor shall be deemed a part of the principal sum under this contract and become payable immediately with interest at the rate of ten percent (10%) per annum until paid.

The Vendor on receiving payment in full of the principal and interest, and of all other sums chargeable under the contract, agrees, at his own proper cost and expense, to execute and deliver to the Vendee, or to his assigns, upon surrender of this contract, a good and sufficient conveyance in fee simple of the above described premises, free and clear of all liens and encumbrances, except such as may have accrued thereon subsequent to the date of this contract by or through the acts or negligences of others than the Vendor, and at the option of the Vendor furnish the Vendee an abstract of title or a policy of title insurance in an amount equal to the purchase price under this contract. The Vendor hereby reserves the right to mortgage said premises at any time in an amount not in excess of the amount then due on this contract, and the Vendee agrees that the said mortgage shall be a first lien on the premises.

It is mutually agreed that the Vendee shall have possession of said premises from and after October 1, 1995.

If the Vendee shall fail to comply with the terms of this contract, the Vendor may take possession of the property and all the improvements on it and treat the Vendee as a tenant holding over without permission and remove him therefrom and retain any money paid hereon as stipulated damages for nonperformance of this contract. It is hereby expressly understood and declared that time is and shall be taken as of the very essence of this contract. Notice of said forfeiture may be given by depositing the notice in post office, addressed to Vendee at his last known address.

It is agreed that the stipulations contained in this contract are to apply to and bind the heirs, executors, administrators, and assigns of the respective parties to this contract.

In witness whereof, the said parties have set their hands and seals the day and year first above written. Signed, sealed and delivered in presence of:

*Harriet Greene* )                                   *Sarah A. Collins*
                                                      Sarah A. Collins

*Samuel A. Griggs* )                                  *Robert H. Bowen*
                                                      Robert H. Bowen

---

**CONCEPT REVIEW**

## SECURITY INTERESTS IN REAL PROPERTY

| Type of Security Instrument | Parties | Features |
|---|---|---|
| **Mortgage** | 1. Mortgagor (property owner/debtor)<br>2. Mortgagee (creditor) | 1. Mortgagee holds a security interest (and in some states, title) in real property as security for a debt.<br>2. If mortgagor defaults on her obligation, mortgagee must *foreclose* on property to realize on his security interest.<br>3. Mortgagor has a limited time after foreclosure to *redeem* her interest. |
| **Deed of Trust** | 1. Owner/debtor<br>2. Lender/creditor<br>3. Trustee | 1. Trustee holds legal title to the real property put up as security.<br>2. If debt is satisfied, the trustee conveys property back to owner/debtor.<br>3. If debt is not paid as agreed, creditor notifies trustee to sell the property.<br>4. While intended to make foreclosure easier, most states treat it like a mortgage for purposes of foreclosure. |
| **Land Contract** | 1. Buyer<br>2. Seller | 1. Seller agrees to convey title when full price is paid.<br>2. Buyer usually takes possession, pays property taxes and insurance, and maintains the property.<br>3. If buyer defaults, seller may declare a forfeiture and retake possession (most states) after buyer has limited time to redeem; some states require foreclosure. |

---

## MECHANIC'S AND MATERIALMAN'S LIENS

Each state has a statute that permits persons who contract to furnish labor or materials to improve real estate to claim a lien on the property until they are paid. There are many differences among states as to exactly who can claim such a lien and the requirements that must be met to do so.

### Rights of Subcontractors and Materialmen

A general contractor is a person who has contracted with the owner to build, remodel, or improve real property. A subcontractor is a person who has contracted with the general contractor to perform a stipulated portion of the general contract. A materialman is a person who has contracted to furnish certain materials needed to perform a designated general contract.

Two distinct systems—the New York system and the Pennsylvania system—are followed by the states in allowing mechanic's liens on real estate to subcontractors and materialmen. The New York system is based on the theory of subrogation, and the subcontractors or materialmen cannot recover more than is owed to the contractor at the time they file a lien or give notice of a lien to the owner. Under the Pennsylvania system, the subcontractors or materialmen have direct liens and are entitled to liens for the value of labor and materials furnished, irrespective of the amount due from the owner to the contractor. Under the New York system, the general contractor's failure to perform his contract or his abandonment of the work has a direct effect on the lien rights of subcontractors and materialmen, whereas under the Pennsylvania system, such breach or abandonment by the general contractor does not directly affect the lien rights of subcontractors and materialmen.

## Basis for Mechanic's or Materialman's Lien

Some state statutes provide that no lien shall be claimed unless the contract for the improvement is in writing and embodies a statement of the materials to be furnished and a description of the land on which the improvement is to take place and of the work to be done. Other states permit the contract to be oral, but in no state is a licensee or volunteer entitled to a lien. No lien can be claimed unless the work is done or the materials are furnished in the performance of a contract to improve specific real property. A sale of materials without reference to the improvement of specific real property does not entitle the person furnishing the materials to a lien on real property that is, in fact, improved by the use of the materials at some time after the sale.

Unless the state statute specifically includes submaterialmen, they are not entitled to a lien. For example, if a lumber dealer contracts to furnish the lumber for the erection of a specific building and orders from a sawmill a carload of lumber that is needed to fulfill the contract, the sawmill will not be entitled to a lien on the building in which the lumber is used unless the state statute expressly provides that submaterialmen are entitled to a lien.

At times, the question has arisen as to whether materials have been furnished. Some courts have held that the materialman must prove that the material furnished was actually incorporated into the structure. Under this ruling, if material delivered on the job is diverted by the general contractor or others and not incorporated into the structure, the materialman will not be entitled to a lien. Other courts have held that the materialman is entitled to a lien if he can provide proof that the material was delivered on the job under a contract to furnish the material.

## Requirements for Obtaining Lien

The requirements for obtaining a mechanic's or materialman's lien must be complied with strictly. Although there is no uniformity in the statutes as to the requirements for obtaining a lien, the statutes generally require the filing of a notice of lien with a county official such as the register of deeds or the county clerk, which notice sets forth the amount claimed, the name of the owner, the names of the contractor and the claimant, and a description of the property. Frequently, the notice of lien must be verified by an affidavit of the claimant. In some states, a copy of the notice must be served on the owner or be posted on the property.

The notice of lien must be filed within a stipulated time. The time varies from 30 to 90 days, but the favored time is 60 days after the last work performed or after the last materials furnished. Some statutes distinguish between labor claims, materialmen's claims, and claims of general contractors as to time of filing. The lien, when filed, must be foreclosed within a specified time, which generally varies from six months to two years.

## Priorities and Foreclosure

The provisions for priorities vary widely, but most of the statutes provide that a mechanic's lien has priority over all liens attaching after the first work is performed or after the first materials are furnished. This statutory provision creates a hidden lien on the property, in that a mechanic's lien, filed within the allotted period of time after completion of the work, attaches as of the time the first work is done or the first material is furnished, but no notice of lien need be filed during this period. And if no notice of lien is filed during this period, third persons would have no means of knowing of the existence of a lien. There are no priorities among lien claimants under the majority of the statutes.

The following case, *In Re Skyline Properties,* illustrates a number of issues that can arise when a mechanic's claim that he has a lien on certain property because of work he did concerning it is challenged by another party claiming a competing interest in the property.

# In Re Skyline Properties, Inc.
# Century National Bank and Trust Co. v. Skyline Properties, Inc.
### 134 B.R. 830 (Bankr. W.D.Pa. 1992)

In 1987, Skyline Properties commenced development of an integrated, multifaceted resort encompassing approximately 1,000 acres to be known as Hunter's Station. David Mealy was engaged to perform excavating and grading work on the project and commenced visible work on April 20, 1987. Mealy's work included bulldozing new roads, constructing parking areas, digging footers and drainage ditches, grading a basement for a new building used as a tack shop, excavation of crawl spaces for new additions to an existing building subsequently used as a sales office, grading an area for a new horse barn, and the installation of drains and fencing on the property. The sales office was substantially complete and opened for business on June 4, 1987, while work continued on construction of the tack shop.

On June 5, 1987, Century National Bank extended $150,000 credit to Skyline, took as collateral a mortgage on several of the parcels in the development, and recorded the mortgage on June 5, 1987. Mealy completed his work on August 3, 1987, and filed a notice of a mechanic's lien claim on September 23, 1987. Pennsylvania law requires that claims for such liens be filed within four months after the completion of the work.

In October 1988, the bank filed a mortgage foreclosure action against Skyline's property that it held as security for the loan. In September 1989, Mealy obtained a judgment on his claim and scheduled a sheriff's sale of the Skyline property. The sale was halted by the filing of an involuntary petition in bankruptcy. One of the issues in the bankruptcy proceeding was the relative priority of the claims of the bank and Mealy to the Skyline property.

---

**Bemtz, Bankruptcy Judge** A mechanic's lien for services which constitute alterations and repairs takes effect and has priority as of the date the mechanic's lien claim is filed. 49 Pa.Stat.Ann. Sec. 1508(b). In the case of services constituting erection and construction, the lien of a claim takes effect and has priority "as of the date of the visible commencement upon the ground of the work of erecting or constructing the improvement." 49 Pa.Stat. Ann. Sec. 1508(a).

This matter involves the following relevant dates:

| | |
|---|---|
| Visible commencement of construction: | April 20, 1987 |
| Bank's mortgage: | June 5, 1987 |
| Mealy Claim filed: | September 23, 1987 |

Thus, if Mealy's work is erection and construction, Mealy's Claim has priority over the Bank; if the work is alteration or repair, the Bank's mortgage takes priority.

Section 1201(10) of the Mechanic's Lien Law defines "erection and construction" as follows:

"Erection and construction" means the erection and construction of a new improvement or of a substantial addition to an existing improvement or any adaption of an existing improvement rendering the same fit for a new or distinct use and effecting a material change in the interior or exterior thereof.

The Bank asserts that no buildings were erected or constructed in conjunction with Mealy's work and Mealy's lien is for alterations and repairs. Thus the Bank asserts that Mealy's lien takes priority as of the date of filing of the Claim and not the date of visible commencement of the work.

The concern in determining whether the work is "erection and construction" or "alterations or repairs" is whether a substantial change to the existing structure has occurred such that any third party, such as the Bank, would be on notice that potential liens could exist. A change in the appearance or use of a building is sufficient to give such notice.

In the present case, the evidence reveals that a farmhouse on the property, formerly used as a residential dwelling, was converted into a sales office used to sell ownership interests in the development. Skyline converted an existing farmhouse into a sales office by essentially "gutting" the structure and constructing additions to the original dwelling. The appearance of the house was transformed into a commercial building and the use was altogether different. The addition to the building made it substantially larger than it had been as a private residence. The additions are substantial enough to be considered new construction. The work was substantially completed and the sales office open for business on June 4, 1987, one day *before* the Bank recorded its mortgage. Had the Bank, which was aware of the scope of the planned construction, viewed the property at the time it recorded its mortgage, it certainly would have known that potential liens could exist.

The tack shop was built on existing concrete blocks which had served as the foundation for a building that [had] previously fallen down or been removed. The tack shop has both a "new use" and a "new appearance" and constitutes erection and construction.

Grading and excavation is the type of work which is properly lienable as incident to the erection or construction of an improvement. Another way of stating the test utilized by the Pennsylvania courts in determining whether a certain type of work is lienable is whether the work is incident to the construction of an improvement. Mealy graded the area for four structures—the sales office, the tack shop, the horse barn and arena, and the guardhouse. Mealy dug footers and drainage ditches for the sales office and the guardhouse and installed drains for the tack shop. The work Mealy performed was incident to the construction of these improvements and also designed to enhance their value by building a resort around them.

Mealy's lienable work, incident to the erection and construction of four structures, as opposed to merely alteration and repair, entitles Mealy to a claim which relates back in time to the date upon which work was commenced and therefore, is prior to the Bank's mortgage interest.

**Order upholding Mealy's lien claim.**

---

The procedure followed in the foreclosure of a mechanic's lien on real estate follows closely the procedure followed in a court foreclosure of a real estate mortgage. The rights acquired by the filing of a lien and the extent of the property covered by the lien are set out in some of the mechanic's lien statutes. In general, the lien attaches only to the interest that the person has in the property that has been improved at the time the notice is filed. Some statutes provide that the lien attaches to the building and to the city lot on which the building stands, or if the improvement is to farm property, the lien attaches to a specified amount of land.

## Waiver of Lien

The question often arises as to the effect of an express provision in a contract for the improvement of real estate that no lien shall attach to the property for the cost of the improvement. In some states, there is a statute requiring the recording or filing of the contract and making such a provision ineffective if the statute is not complied with. In some states, courts have held that such a provision is effective against everyone; in other states, courts have held that the provision is ineffective against everyone except the contractor; and in still other states, courts have held that such a provision is ineffective as to subcontractors, materialmen, and laborers. Whether the parties to the contract have notice of the waiver of lien provision plays an important part in several states in determining their right to a lien.

It is common practice that before a person who is having improvements made to his property makes final payment, he requires the contractor to sign an affidavit that all materialmen and subcontractors have been paid and to supply him with a release of lien signed by the subcontractors and materialmen.

**1.** Bayer was the general contractor on a Massachusetts state highway contract. He hired Deschenes as a subcontractor to do certain excavation work. Deschenes was to start the job by November 24, 1988, and to complete it on or before March 1, 1989. Deschenes was required to furnish a bond of $91,000 to ensure his faithful performance of the subcontract, and he purchased such a bond from Aetna Insurance Company. Deschenes began the work on December 1, 1988, and quit on June 22, 1989, after completing only about half of the work. Bayer had made numerous efforts to get Deschenes to do the work and then completed the job himself when Deschenes walked off the job. Bayer brought a lawsuit against Aetna on the bond, and Aetna claimed that it was discharged by the extension of time given to Deschenes. Should Bayer recover on the bond?

**2.** Rusty Jones, a used car dealer, applied to First Financial Federal Savings and Loan Association for a $50,000 line of credit to purchase an inventory of used cars. First Financial refused to make the loan to Jones alone but agreed to do so if Worth Camp, an attorney and friend of Jones, would cosign the note. Camp agreed to cosign as an accommodation maker or surety. The expectation of the parties was that the loans cosigned by Camp would be repaid from the proceeds of the car inventory. The original note for $25,000 was signed on August 2, 1984, and renewals were executed on January 25, 1985, September 11, 1985, and March 15, 1986, and the amount was eventually increased to $50,000. In August 1985, as Camp was considering whether to sign the September renewal note, he was advised by First Financial's loan officer that the interest on the loan had not been paid. In fact, interest payments were four months delinquent. In addition, unknown to Camp, as the $50,000 credit limit was approached, First Financial began making side, or personal, loans to Jones totaling about $25,000, which were also payable out of the used car inventory. Camp knew nothing of these loans and thought that Jones's used car business was making payments only on the loans he had cosigned. Jones defaulted on the $50,000 note cosigned by Camp and First Financial brought suit against Camp on his obligation as surety on the note. Was Camp relieved of his obligation as surety by First Financial's failure to disclose material facts to him?

**3.** Maxwell owned the timber on a certain tract of land. He hired Fitzgerald to cut the timber into logs and to put the logs in Maxwell's mill pond. Fitzgerald did the work but was not paid for it as promised. He claims a common law lien on the logs for his work in cutting and hauling them. Is Fitzgerald entitled to a common law lien on the logs?

**4.** During May and June, John Shumate regularly parked his automobile on a vacant lot in downtown Philadelphia. At that time, no signs were posted prohibiting parking on the lot or indicating that vehicles parked there without authorization would be towed. On July 7, Shumate again left his car on the lot. When he returned two days later, the car was gone and the lot was posted with signs warning that parking was prohibited. Shumate learned that his car had been towed away by Ruffie's Towing Service and that the car was being held by Ruffie's at its place of business. Ruffie's refused to release the car until Shumate paid a towing fee of $44.50 plus storage charges of $4 per day. Shumate refused to pay the fee, and Ruffie's kept possession of the car. Did Ruffie's have a common law possessory lien on the car?

**5.** Betty Nelson signed a promissory note payable to Family Bank in return for a loan the bank had made to her. The note was secured by a deed of trust on a duplex owned by Nelson. When the note was signed, the duplex was rented to third parties. Nelson defaulted on the note and Family Bank filed a complaint to foreclose the trust deed. Nelson advised the bank that she and her son were occupying the duplex as their residence. Under Oregon law, a lender can obtain a deficiency judgment in connection with the foreclosure of a commercial deed of trust; however, a deficiency judgment is not available in connection with the foreclosure of a noncommercial (residential) deed of trust. If Family Bank went forward with foreclosure of the deed of trust, could it obtain a deficiency judgment against Nelson if the sale of the property produced less than the amount of the debt?

**6.** Philip and Edith Beh purchased some property from Alfred M. Gromer and his wife. Sometime earlier, the Gromers had borrowed money from City Mortgage. They had signed a note and had given City Mortgage a second deed of trust on the property. There was also a first deed of trust on the property at the time the Behs purchased it. In the contract of sale between the Behs and the Gromers, the Behs promised to "assume" the second deed of trust of approximately $5,000 at 6 percent interest. The Behs later defaulted on the first deed of trust. Foreclosure was held on the first deed of trust, but the proceeds of the sale left nothing for City Mortgage on its second deed of trust. City Mortgage then brought a lawsuit against the Behs to collect the balance due on the second deed of trust. When the Behs "assumed" the second deed of trust, did they become personally liable for it?

**7.** Pope agreed to sell certain land to Pelz and retained a mortgage on the property to secure payment of the purchase price. The mortgage contained a clause providing that if Pelz defaulted, Pope had the "right to enter upon the above-described premises and sell the same at public sale" to pay the balance of the purchase price, accounting to Pelz for any surplus realized on the sale. What type of foreclosure does this provision contemplate: (1) strict foreclosure, (2) action and sale, or (3) private power of sale?

**8.** In October 1972, Verda Miller sold her 107-acre farm for $30,000 to Donald Kimball, who was acting on behalf of his own closely held corporation, American Wonderlands. Under the agreement, Miller retained title and Kimball was given possession pending full payment of all installments of the purchase price. The contract provided that Kimball was to pay all real estate taxes. If he did not pay them, Miller could discharge them and either add the amounts to the unpaid principal or demand immediate payment of the delinquencies plus interest. Miller also had the right to declare a forfeiture of the contract and regain possession if the terms of the agreement were not met. In 1975, Miller had to pay the real estate taxes on the property in the amount of $672.78. She demanded payment of this amount plus interest from Kimball. She also served a notice of forfeiture on him that he had 30 days to pay. Kimball paid the taxes but refused to pay interest of $10.48. Miller made continued demands on Kimball for two months, then filed notice of forfeiture with the county recorder in August 1975. She also advised Kimball of this. Was Miller justified in declaring a forfeiture and taking back possession of the land?

**9.** Edwin Bull was the owner of an 80-foot fishing trawler named the *Bull Head* that had been leased for use in dismantling a bridge over the Illinois River at Pekin, Illinois. At the termination of the lease, the *Bull Head* was towed upriver to Morris, Illinois, not operating on its own power. At Morris, a tugboat owned by Iowa Marine Repair Corporation was used to remove the *Bull Head* from the tow and to move it to the south bank of the river where it was tied up. Several months later, the *Bull Head* was moved across the river by Iowa Marine and moored at a place on the north bank where it maintained its fleeting operations. The *Bull Head* remained there for several years and greatly deteriorated. Iowa Marine sent Bull a bill for switching, fleeting, and other services. Bull refused to pay and brought suit against Iowa Marine to recover possession of the boat. In turn, Iowa Marine claimed that it had a mechanic's lien on the *Bull Head* and that the boat should be sold to satisfy the lien. Illinois law provides that:

any architect, contractor, subcontractor, materialman, or other person furnishing services, labor, or material for the purpose of, or in constructing, building, altering, repairing or ornamenting a boat, barge, or watercraft shall have a lien on such boat for the value of such services, labor, or material in the same manner as in this act provided for the purpose of building, altering, repairing, or ornamenting a house or other building.

Does Iowa Marine have a valid mechanic's lien on the boat for its switching, fleeting, and storage services?

**10.** Albert Sharkey was the owner of a commercial building that was leased to Consolidated Freightways for more than 10 years before the lease was terminated by Consolidated on October 25, 1982. Consolidated's lease with Sharkey provided that Consolidated would leave the property in as good condition as received. Consolidated was responsible for damaging 10 overhead doors and contacted Dewco Building Systems to repair the damage. Dewco ordered new doors from Overhead. Overhead specially ordered the doors and paid for them on delivery from the manufacturer. On March 18, 1983, Overhead submitted its bill to Dewco. Overhead was unable to collect since Dewco had gone out of business and filed for bankruptcy. Dewco had already collected $10,397 from Consolidated and owed $6,685 to Overhead. On May 10, 1983, Overhead filed a mechanic's lien against Sharkey's property and brought a lawsuit to enforce the lien. Iowa Code Section 572.2 provides that:

Every person who shall furnish any material or labor for, or perform any labor, upon any building or land for improvement, alteration or repair thereof, including those engaged in the construction or repair of any work of internal or external improvement ... by virtue of any contract with the owner, his agent, trustee, contractor, or subcontractor shall have a lien upon such building or improvement, and land belonging to the owner on which the same is situated ..., to secure payment for material or labor furnished or labor performed.

Does Overhead have a valid claim for a mechanic's lien on Sharkey's property?

## CAPSTONE QUESTIONS

**1.** Dana Developer owns 50 acres of land located on the state highway on the outskirts of the City of Berkley Springs. Preparatory to developing the property as a subdivision, Dana borrowed $500,000 from First National Bank to finance the cost of installing water and sewer lines and grading roads. First National Bank holds a first mortgage on the property to secure the loan. Developer also agreed to pay Bob Builder $150,000 to construct a model home on the property. The home has essentially been completed, but to date Developer has paid Builder only $70,000 and Builder, in turn, has paid his subcontractors and materialmen only about 50 percent of what he owes them. Developer concludes that the development of the subdivision is beyond her resources and now plans to sell the property to a larger developer. She is considering selling the property to Advent Homes under one of the following conditions:

· Advent Homes would buy the property subject to the mortgage of First National Bank.

· Advent Homes would assume the First National Bank mortgage.

### Required:

Answer the following questions, and give reasons for your conclusions.

**1.** In separate paragraphs, discuss the potential liability of Dan Developer and Advent Homes to First National Bank under the following two scenarios:

*a.* Advent Homes buys the property "subject to the mortgage," Advent Homes subsequently

defaults on paying the mortgage note, the mortgage is foreclosed, and the property is sold at a foreclosure sale for less than the amount of the balance due on the mortgage, resulting in a deficiency.

*b.* Advent Homes "assumes the mortgage" in connection with its purchase of the property, Advent Homes subsequently defaults on paying the mortgage note, the mortgage is foreclosed, and the property is sold at a foreclosure sale for less than the amount of the balance due on the mortgage, resulting in a deficiency.

**2.** What actions can Builder and his subcontractors and materialmen take to secure the amounts owing to them for the construction of the model home? What rights, if any, would they obtain against Developer of Advent Homes? What would their rights be vis-à-vis First National Bank?

**2.** Franklin Construction Company was the low bidder for a contract to construct a new highway bridge and was awarded the contract by the State Highway Department. The bridge was to be completed by January 1, 1994, and Franklin was required to have its performance of the contract secured by a surety. In consideration for a fee, Aetna Insurance Company agreed to serve as surety for Franklin's performance of the contract. The state unilaterally (without discussing it with Aetna) extended the time for completing the work, first to June 1, 1994, and then to January 1, 1995. When Franklin stopped work on the job in December 1994 without completing the bridge, the state had the job completed by another contractor at an additional cost of $100,000. Aetna then sought to recover the $100,000 from Aetna; Aetna contends that it is excused from its obligations as surety because of the extension of time granted to Franklin.

### Required:

Answer the following questions and give reasons for your conclusions.

**1.** What rights does the state have against Aetna? Is Aetna relieved of its obligations because of the extension of time?

**2.** If Aetna was liable to the state, what rights would it, in turn, have against Franklin?

# CHAPTER

## 2 1

# SECURITY INTERESTS

# IN

# PERSONAL PROPERTY

### INTRODUCTION

*In many credit transactions the creditor, in order to protect his investment, takes a security interest, or lien, in personal property belonging to the debtor. The law covering security interests in personal property is set forth in Article 9 of the Uniform Commercial Code. Article 9, entitled Secured Transactions, applies to situations that consumers and businesspeople commonly face; for example, the financing of an automobile, the purchase of a refrigerator on a time-payment plan, or the financing of business inventory.*

## ARTICLE 9

If a creditor wants to obtain a security interest in the personal property of the debtor, he also wants to be sure that his interest is superior to the claims of other creditors. To do so, the creditor must carefully comply with Article 9. In Part II, Sales, we pointed out that businesspersons sometimes leave out important terms in a contract or insert vague terms to be worked out later. Such looseness is a luxury that is not permitted in secured transactions. If a debtor gets into financial difficulties and cannot meet her obligations, even a minor noncompliance with Article 9 may cause the creditor to lose his preferred claim to the personal property of the debtor. A creditor who loses his secured interest is only a general creditor if the debtor is declared bankrupt. As a general creditor in bankruptcy proceedings, he may have little chance of recovering the money owed by the debtor because of the relatively low priority of such claims. Chapter 22, Bankruptcy, covers this matter in detail.

Article 9 has not been adopted in exactly the same form in every state. The law of each state must be examined carefully to determine the procedure for obtaining a security interest and the rights of creditors and debtors in that state. The general concepts are the same in every state, however, and these concepts are the basis of our discussion in this chapter.

## SECURITY INTERESTS UNDER THE CODE

### Security Interests

Basic to a discussion of secured consumer and commercial transactions is the term **security interest**. A security interest is an interest in personal property or fixtures obtained by a creditor to secure payment or performance of an obligation [1–201(37)].[1] For example, when a person borrows money from a bank to buy a new car, the bank takes a security interest, or puts a lien, on the car until the loan is repaid. If the person defaults on the loan, the bank can repossess the car and have it sold to cover the unpaid balance. A security interest is a property interest in the collateral.

While one usually thinks of goods as being put up as collateral, the Code actually covers secured interests in a much broader grouping of personal property. The Code breaks down personal property into a number of different classifications that are important in determining how a creditor acquires an enforceable security interest in a particular collateral. The Code classifications are:

**1.** *Instruments.* This category includes checks, notes, drafts, stocks, bonds, and other investment securities [9–105(i)].

**2.** *Documents of title.* This category includes bills of lading, dock warrants, dock receipts, and warehouse receipts.

**3.** *Accounts.* This category includes rights to payment for goods sold or leased or for services rendered that are not evidenced by instruments or chattel paper but are carried on open account. The category includes such rights to payment whether or not they have been earned by performance [9–106].

**4.** *Chattel paper.* This category includes written documents that evidence both an obligation to pay money and a security interest in specific goods [9–105]. A typical example of chattel paper is what is commonly known as a conditional sales contract. This is the type of contract that a consumer might sign when she buys a large appliance, such as a refrigerator, on a time-payment plan.

**5.** *General intangibles.* Among the items in this catchall category are patents, copyrights, literary royalty rights, franchises, and money [9–106].

**6.** *Goods.* Goods are divided into several classes; the same item of collateral may fall into different classes at different times, depending on its use.

   *a.* *Consumer goods.* These goods are used or bought for use primarily for personal,

family, or household purposes. They include automobiles, furniture, and appliances.

   *b.* *Equipment.* This includes goods used or bought for use primarily in business, including farming and the professions.

   *c.* *Farm products.* These are crops, livestock, or supplies used or produced in farming operations as long as they are still in the possession of a debtor engaged in farming.

   *d.* *Inventory.* This includes goods held for sale or lease or for use under contracts of service as well as raw materials, work in process, and materials used or consumed in a business.

   *e.* *Fixtures.* These are goods so affixed to real property as to be considered a part of it [9–109].

In different situations, an item such as a stove could be classified as inventory, equipment, or consumer goods. In the hands of the manufacturer or an appliance store, the stove is "inventory" goods. If it is used in a restaurant, it is "equipment." If it was purchased by a consumer for use in her home, it is "consumer goods."

## Obtaining a Security Interest

The goal of a creditor is to obtain a security interest in certain personal property that will be good against: (1) the debtor, (2) other creditors of the debtor, and (3) a person who might purchase the property from the debtor. In case the debtor defaults on the debt, the creditor wants to have a better right to claim the property than anyone else. Furthering these goals involves a two-step process—attachment and perfection.

## ATTACHMENT OF THE SECURITY INTEREST

### Attachment

A security interest is not legally enforceable against a debtor until it is attached to one or more particular items of the debtor's property. The **attachment** of the security interest takes place in a legal sense rather than in a physical sense. There are three basic requirements for a security interest to be attached to the goods of a debtor [9–203]: First is an *agreement* in which the debtor grants the creditor a security interest in particular property (collateral) in which the

---

[1]The numbers in brackets refer to sections of the Uniform Commercial Code.

debtor has an interest. Second, the debtor must have *rights in the collateral.* Third, the creditor must give value to the debtor. The creditor must, for example, lend money or advance goods on credit to the debtor. Unless the debtor owes a debt to the creditor, there can be no security interest. The purpose of obtaining a security interest is to secure a debt.

## The Security Agreement

The agreement in which a debtor grants a creditor a security interest in the debtor's property must generally be in writing and signed by the debtor. A written agreement is required in all cases except where the creditor has possession of the collateral [9–203]. Suppose Cole borrows $50 from Fox and gives Fox her wristwatch as a security for the loan. The agreement whereby Cole put up her watch as collateral does not have to be in writing to be enforceable. Because the creditor (Fox) is in possession of the collateral, an oral agreement is sufficient.

The security agreement must reasonably describe the collateral so that it can readily be identified. For example, it should list the year, make, and serial number of an automobile. The security agreement usually spells out the terms of the arrangement between the creditor and the debtor. Also, it normally contains a promise by the debtor to pay certain amounts of money in a certain way. The agreement specifies which events, such as nonpayment by the buyer, constitute a default. In addition, it may contain provisions that the creditor feels are necessary to protect his security interest. For example, the debtor may be required to keep the collateral insured, not to move it without the creditor's consent, or to periodically report sales of secured inventory goods. See Figure 1 for an example of a security agreement.

In the case that follows, *In Re Hardage,* Sears was deemed to have obtained a valid security agreement from its debtor even though the document constituting it was missing certain critical terms.

## IN RE HARDAGE
### 99 BR 738 (Bankr. N.D. Tex. 1989)

On June 14, 1986, Jimmy Hardage purchased a videocassette recorder for $315.36 from Sears Roebuck & Co. (Sears), and on November 8, 1987, he purchased a guitar board from Sears for $181.89. In each case he used his Sears charge card to make the purchase and signed the sales slips at the time of purchase. The sales slips contained, among other things, this information:

1. Hardage's credit account number.
2. Hardage's name.
3. The date of purchase.
4. The amount of the purchase.
5. A brief description of the goods sold.
6. An invoice number.
7. Hardage's address.
8. Hardage's signatures immediately below the following legend:

This purchase is subject to the approval of the Sears Credit Sales Department and is made under my SearsCharge Account Security Agreement for my SearsCharge Modernizing Credit Plan Security Agreement which is incorporated herein by reference. I agree that Sears retains a security interest under the Uniform Commercial Code in the merchandise purchased until fully paid.

On December 17, 1987, Hardage and his wife, Danelle, filed for relief under Chapter 7 of the Bankruptcy Code. They listed Sears as an unsecured creditor to which they owed $1,453.07. Sears claimed that it had a security interest in the videocassette recorder and the guitar board for the amount of $402.64 (the balance remaining unpaid on the two items).

**Akard, Bankruptcy Judge** The issue before the court is: Do the sales slips denominated "credit billing copy," of Sears, Roebuck & Co. (Sears), constitute valid security agreements such that pursuant to Uniform Commercial Code (UCC) Article 9 Sears has perfected security interests in the consumer goods sold?

The Texas version of the UCC sets forth the formal requisites a party must follow to create an Article 9 security interest enforceable against the buyer or third parties with respect to the collateral. In pertinent part, these steps are: (1) the debtor signs a security agreement which contains a description of the collateral; (2) value has been given; and (3) the debtor has rights in the collateral. Section 9–203(a). A financing statement is not necessary to perfect a purchase money security interest in consumer goods.

The writing requirement may be simply expressed as follows; it must: (1) contain sufficient language to embody a "security agreement"; (2) include an adequate description of the collateral; and (3) be signed by the debtor. Since items 2 and 3 are not in dispute, we turn to item one, the sufficiency of the language to embody a security agreement.

Section 9–105(a)(12) states a security agreement means "an agreement which creates or provides for a security interest." Where the parties are in dispute on the issue, the court may have to resolve first, as a question of law, whether the language in the agreement objectively indicates the parties may have intended to create or provide for a security interest.

Although some courts read "may have intended" to require more, other courts rely on Comment 5 to section 9–203, which states that the writing requirement is more in the nature of satisfaction of the statute of frauds.

The UCC does not require special words or any special form to show a possible security interest. Further, the courts have recognized unorthodox documents containing certain words as adequate security agreements. Even when conventional words do not appear, some courts find security agreements. Or, where one document is not sufficient to create a valid security interest, creditors may show such creation by introducing multiple executed documents. Therefore, once the agreement meets the section 9–203 writing requirement, the court may or may not ask for other evidence of whether the parties actually intended to create a security interest, a question of fact.

The court concludes that as a matter of law the sales slips retained a security interest in the items purchased. Clearly Sears intended for the sales slips to be a security agreement and the intention of Mr. Hardage for the sales slips to be a security agreement must be found from the fact that he signed the sales slips immediately below the language creating the security interest.

**Judgment for Sears.**

## Future Advances

A security agreement may stipulate that it covers advances of credit to be made at some time in the future [9–204(3)]. Such later extensions of credit are known as **future advances.** Future advances would be involved where, for example, a bank grants a business a line of credit for $100,000 but initially advances only $20,000. When the business draws further against its line of credit, it has received a future advance and the bank is considered to have given additional "value" at that time. The security interest that the creditor obtained earlier also covers these later advances of money.

## After-Acquired Property

A security agreement may be drafted to grant a creditor a security interest in the **after-acquired property** of the debtor. After-acquired property is property that the debtor does not currently own or have rights in but that he may acquire in the future. However, the security interest does not attach until the debtor actually obtains some rights to the new property [9–204].[2] For

[2]The Code imposes an additional requirement as to security interests in after-acquired consumer goods. Security interests do not attach to consumer goods other than accessions unless the consumer acquires them within 10 days after the secured party gave value [9–204(2)].

**FIGURE 1**   A Security Agreement

| | |
|---|---|
| BUYER ~~Mr. and Mrs.~~ ~~Mrs.~~ Miss *Cheryl Cole* | Account No. |
| ADDRESS *542 Oakdale* | |
| CITY *Chicago, Il*          TEL. NO. *828-0290* | *C-1005* |
| DELIVER TO *542 Oakdale* | Date |

SECURITY AGREEMENT
ACE APPLIANCE

THIS AGREEMENT, executed between Ace Appliance, as Secured Party ("Seller"), and Buyer named above, as Debtor ("Buyer"): Seller agrees to sell and Buyer agrees to purchase, subject to the terms, conditions, and agreements stated in this agreement, the goods described below (the "Collateral"), Seller reserving and Buyer granting a purchase money security interest in the Collateral to secure the payment of the balance owed (Item 7) and all other present and future obligations of Buyer to Seller.

| | DESCRIPTION OF COLLATERAL | | | | TERMS | |
|---|---|---|---|---|---|---|
| Quan. | Article | Unit Price | Total | | | |
| *1* | *Refrig* | *545* | — *545* | | (1) Cash Price *104 00* | |
| *1* | *Stove* | *495* | — *495* | | (2) Down Payment *100 00* | |
| | | | | | Trade-in | |
| | | | | | | |
| | | | | | Unpaid Principal | |
| | | | | | (3) Balance Owed *94 00* | |
| | | | | | (4) Finance Charge *100 00* | |
| | | | | | Time Balance | |
| | | | | | (5) Owed *1040 00* | |
| | | | | | (6) Sales tax *40 00* | |
| | | | | | (7) Balance Owed *1080 00* | |

Buyer agrees to pay Seller, without relief from valuation and appraisement laws, the balance owed (Item 7) of $ *1080 00*

in *11* successive ~~weekly~~ installments of $ *90 00* each and a final installment of $ *90 00* , commencing on

monthly

*Jan. 1* , 19 *95* and continuing thereafter on the same day of each ~~week~~ until paid, together with all deliquent

month

charges, costs of repossession, collection, disposition, maintenance, and other like charges, allowed by law, and reasonable attorney's fees.

   This sale is made subject to the terms, conditions, and agreements stated above on the reverse side. Buyer represents that the correct name and address of Buyer is as stated above, and that all statements made by buyer as to financial condition and credit information are true.

   Buyer acknowledges delivery by Seller to Buyer of a copy of this agreement.

   Buyer warrants and represents that the Collateral will be kept at Buyer's address unless otherwise specified as follows: _____

and will be used or is purchased for use primarily for: (check one) family or household purposes ☒; business use ☐; farming operations ☐. The Collateral will not be affixed to real estate unless checked here ☐. If the Collateral is to be affixed to real estate, a description of the real estate is as follows: _____

and the name of the record owner is _____

**FIGURE 1**   *(concluded)*

IN WITNESS WHEREOF, the parties have executed this agreement on this *1st* day of *Dec*, 19 *94*.
BUYER'S SIGNATURE (Ace Appliance) Seller (as Secured party) *Cheryl Cole* By *Frank Singer*
(as debtor)

---

TERMS, CONDITIONS, AND AGREEMENTS
　1.  The security interest of Seller shall extend to all replacements, proceeds (including tort claims and insurance), and accessories, and shall continue until full performance by Buyer of all conditions and obligations under this agreement.
　2.  Buyer shall maintain the Collateral in good repair, pay all taxes and other charges levied upon the Collateral when due, and shall defend the Collateral against any claims. Buyer shall not permit the Collateral to be removed from the place where kept without the prior written consent of Seller. Buyer shall give prompt witten notice to Seller of any transfer, pledge, assignment, or any other process or action taken or pending, voluntary or involuntary, whereby a third party is to obtain or is attempting to obtain possession of or any interest in the Collateral. Seller shall have the right to inspect the Collateral at all reasonable times. At its option, but without obligation to Buyer and without relieving Buyer from any default, Seller may discharge any taxes, liens, or other encumbrances levied or placed upon the Collateral for which Buyer agrees to reimburse Seller upon demand.
　3.  If the Collateral is damaged or destroyed in any manner, the entire balance remaining unpaid under this agreement (the "Agreement Balance") shall immediately become due and payable and Buyer shall first apply any insurance or other receipts compensating for such loss to the Agreement Balance. Buyer shall fully insure the Collateral, for the benefit of both Seller and Buyer, against loss of fire, theft, and other casualties by comprehensive extended coverage insurance in an amount equal to the balance owed under this agreement.
　4.  Buyer shall pay all amounts payable when due at the store of Seller from which this sale is made or at Seller's principal office in *Gary*, Indiana, and upon default shall pay the maximum delinquent charges permitted by law. Upon prepayment of the Agreement Balance, Seller shall allow the minimum discount permitted by law.
　5.  Time is of the essence of this agreement. Buyer agrees that the following shall constitute an event of default under this Security Agreement: (*a*) the failure of Buyer to perform any condition or obligation contained in this agreement; (*b*) when any statement, representation, or warranty made by Buyer shall be found to have been untrue in any material respect when made; or (*c*) if Seller in good faith believes that the prospect of payment or performance is impaired. Upon a default, Seller, at its option and without notice or demand to Buyer, shall be entitled to declare the Agreement Balance immediately due and payable, take immediate possession of the Collateral and enter the premises at which the Collateral is located for such purpose or to render the Collateral unusable. Upon request, Buyer shall assemble and make the Collateral available to Seller at a place to be designated by Seller which is reasonably convenient to both parties. Upon repossession, Seller may retain or dispose of any or all of the collateral in the manner prescribed by the Indiana Uniform Commercial Code and the proceeds of any such disposition shall be first applied in the following order: (*a*) to the reasonable expenses of retaking, holding, preparing for sale, selling, and the like; (*b*) to the reasonable attorney's fees and legal expenses incurred by Seller; and (*c*) to the satisfaction of the indebtedness secured by this security interest. Buyer convenants to release and hold harmless Seller from any and all claims arising out of the repossession of the Collateral. No waiver of any default or any failure or delay to exercise any right or remedy by Seller shall operate as a waiver of any other default, or of the same default in the future or as a waiver of any right or remedy with respect to the same or any other occurrence.
　6.  All rights and remedies of seller specified in this agreement are cumulative and are in addition to, and shall not exclude, any rights and remedies Seller may have by law.
　7.  Seller shall not be liable for any damages, including special or consequential damages, for failure to deliver the Collateral or for any delay in delivery of the Collateral to Buyer.
　8.  Buyer agrees that Seller may carry this agreement, together with any other agreements and accounts, with Buyer in one account upon its records and unless otherwise instructed in writing by Buyer, any payment of less than all amounts then due on all agreements and accounts shall be applied to any accrued delinquent charges, costs of collection and maintenance, and to the balances owing under all agreements or accounts in such oder as Seller in its discretion shall determine.
　9.  Buyer authorizes Seller to execute and file financing statements signed only by Seller covering the Collateral described.
　10.  Any notice required by this agreement shall be deemed sufficient when mailed to Seller (state Seller's address), or to Buyer at the address at which the Collateral is kept.
　11.  Buyer shall have the benefit of manufacturers' warranties, if any; however, Seller makes no express warranties (except a warranty of title) and no implied warranties, including any warranty of MERCHANTABILITY or FITNESS. Buyer agrees that there are no promises or agreements between the parties not contained in this agreement. Any modification or rescission of this agreement shall be ineffective unless in writing and signed by both Seller and Buyer.
　12.  ANY HOLDER OF THIS CONSUMER CREDIT CONTRACT IS SUBJECT TO ALL CLAIMS AND DEFENSES WHICH THE DEBTOR COULD ASSERT AGAINST THE SELLER OF GOODS OR SERVICES OBTAINED WITH THE PROCEEDS HEREOF. RECOVERY HEREUNDER BY THE DEBTOR SHALL NOT EXCEED AMOUNTS PAID BY THE DEBTOR HEREUNDER.

example, Dan's Diner borrows $25,000 from the bank and gives it a security interest in all of its present restaurant equipment as well as all of the restaurant equipment that it may "hereafter acquire." If Dan's owns only a stove at the time, then the bank has a security interest only in the stove. However, if a month later Dan's buys a refrigerator, the bank's security interest would "attach" to the refrigerator when Dan's acquires some rights to it.

A security interest in after-acquired property may not have priority over certain other creditors if the debtor acquires his new property subject to what is known as a **purchase money security interest.** When the seller of goods retains a security interest in goods until they are paid for, or when money is loaned for the purpose of acquiring certain goods and the lender takes a security interest in those goods, the security interest is a purchase money security interest. Later in this chapter, the section entitled Priority Rules discusses the rights of the holder of a purchase money security interest versus the rights of another creditor who filed earlier on after-acquired property of the debtor.

## Proceeds

The creditor is commonly interested in having his security interest cover not only the collateral described in the agreement but also the **proceeds** on the disposal of the collateral by the debtor. For example, if a bank lends money to Dealer to enable Dealer to finance its inventory of new automobiles and the bank takes a security interest in the inventory, the bank wants its interest to continue in any cash proceeds obtained by Dealer when the automobiles are sold to customers. Under the 1972 amendments to Article 9, these proceeds are automatically covered unless the security agreement specifically excludes them [9–203(3)].

## Assignment

In the past, installment sales contracts and security agreements commonly included a provision that the buyer would not assert against the assignee of a sales contract any claims or defenses that the buyer had against the seller. Such clauses made it easier for a retailer to assign its installment sales contracts, or security agreements, to a financial institution

such as a bank. The bank knew that it could collect from the buyer without having to worry about any claims that the buyer had against the retailer, such as for breach of warranty. The waiver clauses were usually presented to the buyer on a take-it-or-leave-it basis.

Such clauses can operate to the disadvantage of the buyer. For example, Ellen Horn agrees to buy some storm windows from Ace Home Improvement Company. She signs an installment sales contract, or security agreement, promising to pay $50 a month for 24 months and giving the company a security interest in the windows. The contract contains a waiver of defenses clause. Ace assigns the contract to First Bank and goes out of business. If the storm windows were of a poorer quality than was called for by the contract, Horn would have a claim of breach of warranty against Ace. She would not have to pay Ace the full amount if it tried to collect from her. Under these circumstances, however, Horn has to pay the full amount to the bank; then she can try to collect from Ace for breach of warranty. Here, Horn might be out of luck.

Under the Uniform Commercial Code, an express or implied waiver of defenses is generally valid and enforceable by an assignee who takes his assignment for value, in good faith, and without notice of a claim or defense [9–206(1)]. The two exceptions to this rule are (1) the waiver is not effective as to any type of defense that could be asserted against a holder in due course of a negotiable instrument; (2) the waiver is not effective if a statute or court decision establishes a different rule for buyers of consumer goods [9–206(1)].

Some states have enacted comprehensive legislation to abolish waiver of defenses clauses in consumer contracts, and other states have limited their use. The Uniform Consumer Credit Code (UCCC), which has been adopted by a number of states, gives the adopting states two alternatives regarding waiver of defenses clauses: Alternative A provides that an assignee of a consumer sales contract takes subject to all of the defenses that the buyer has against the seller arising out of the sale, regardless of whether the contract contains a waiver of defenses clause. Alternative B permits the enforcement of such clauses only by an assignee who is not related to the seller and who acquires the assignment of the contract in good faith and for value, gives the buyer notice of the assignment, and is not advised by the buyer in writing within three months that the buyer has any claims or defenses against the seller.

In addition, the Federal Trade Commission has promulgated a regulation that applies to situations in which a buyer signs a waiver of defenses clause as part of an installment sales contract. For a detailed discussion of this regulation, see Chapter 24, Negotiation and Holder in Due Course. The FTC regulation requires that a seller or financing agency insert in all consumer contracts and direct loan agreements a clause putting any holder of the contract on notice that the holder is subject to all of the claims and defenses that the buyer-debtor could assert against the seller of the goods or services covered by the contract.

## PERFECTING THE SECURITY INTEREST

### Perfection

While attachment of a security interest to collateral owned by the debtor gives the creditor rights vis-à-vis the debtor, a creditor is also concerned about making sure that she has a better right to the collateral than any other creditor if the debtor defaults. In addition, a creditor may be concerned about protecting her interest in the collateral if the debtor sells it to someone else. The creditor gets considerable (but not complete) protection against other creditors or purchasers of the collateral by perfecting her security interest. Perfection is not effective without an attachment of the security interest [9–303].

Under the Code, there are three main ways of perfecting a security interest:

1. By filing a public notice of the security interest.
2. By the creditor's taking possession of the collateral.
3. In certain transactions, by mere attachment of the security interest; this is known as automatic perfection.

### Perfection by Public Filing

The most common way of perfecting a security interest is to file a **financing statement** in the appropriate public office. The financing statement serves as constructive notice to the world that the creditor claims an interest in collateral that belongs to a certain named debtor. The financing statement usually consists of a multicopy form that is available from the office of the secretary of state. (See Figure 2.) However, the security agreement can be filed as the financing statement if it contains the required information and has been signed by the debtor.

To be sufficient, the financing statement must (1) contain the names of the debtor and of the secured party, or creditor; (2) be signed by the debtor; (3) give an address of the secured party from which additional information about the security interest can be obtained; (4) give a mailing address for the debtor; and (5) contain a statement listing the collateral or a description of the collateral. If the financing statement covers goods that are to become fixtures, a description of the real estate must be included.

Each state specifies by statute where the financing statement has to be filed. In all states, a financing statement that covers fixtures must be filed in the office where a mortgage on real estate would be filed [9–401]. To obtain maximum security, the secured party acquiring a security interest in property that is a fixture or is to become a fixture should double file—that is, file the security interest as a fixture and as a nonfixture.

In regard to collateral other than fixtures, the state may require only central filing, usually in the office of the secretary of state. However, most states require the local filing of local transactions, such as transactions in which the collateral is equipment used in farming operations; farm products; accounts, contract rights, or general intangibles arising from or relating to the sale of farm products by a farmer; or consumer goods.

A financing statement is effective for a period of five years from the date of filing, and it lapses then unless a continuation statement has been filed before that time. An exception is made for real estate mortgages that are effective as fixture filings—they are effective until the mortgage is released or terminates [9–403].

A **continuation statement** may be filed within six months before the five-year expiration date. The continuation statement must be signed by the secured party, identify the original statement by file number, and state that the original statement is still effective. Successive continuation statements may be filed [9–403(3)].

**FIGURE 2    A Financing Statement**

UNIFORM COMMERCIAL CODE      STATE OF INDIANA      FORM UCC-1
FINANCING STATEMENT

INSTRUCTIONS

1. Please type this form. Fold only along perforation for mailing.
2. Remove Secured Party and Debtor copies and send other three copies with interleaved carbon paper to the filing officer. Enclose filing fee of $1.00. (plus $ .50 if collateral is or to become a fixture).
3. When filing is to be with more than one office, Form UCC-2 may be placed over this set to avoid double typing.
4. If the space provided for any item(s) is inadequate, the item(s) may be continued on additional sheets, preferably 5"x 8" or sizes convenient to secured party in case of long schedules, indentures, etc. Only one sheet is required. Extra names of debtors may be continued below box "1" in space for description of property.
5. If the collateral is crops or goods which are or are to become fixtures, describe the goods and also the real estate with the name of the record owner if he is other than the debtor.
6. Persons filing a security agreement (as distinguished from a financing statement) are urged to complete this form with or without signature and send with security agreement.
7. If collateral is goods which are or are to become fixtures, use Form UCC-1a over this Form to avoid double typing, and enclose regular fee plus $ .50
8. The filing officer will return the third page of this Form as an acknowledgment. Secured party at a later time may use third page as a Termination Statement by dating and signing the termination legend on that page.

This Financing Statement is presented to Filing Officer for filing pursuant to the UCC:    3. Maturity Date (if any):

1. Debtor(s) (Last Name First) and Address(es)    2. Secured Party(ies) and Address(es)    For Filing Officer (Date, Time, Number, and Filing Office)

4. This financing statement covers the following types (or items) of property (also describe realty where collateral is crops or fixtures):

Assignee of Secured Party

This statement is filed without the debtor's signature to perfect a security interest in collateral (check ☐ if so)

☐ under a security agreement signed by debtor authorizing secured party to file this statement, or
☐ already subject to a security interest in another jurisdiction when it was brought into this state, or
☐ which is proceeds of the following described original collateral which was perfected:

Check ☐ if covered:    ☐ Proceeds of Collateral are also covered.    ☐ Products of Collateral are also covered.   No. of additional Sheets presented:

Filed with:   ☐ Secretary of State    ☐ Recorder of _____ County

By: _____    By: _____
Signature(s) of Debtor(s)    Signature(s) of Secured Party(ies)

(1) Filing Officer Copy—Alphabetical    Approved by:
FORM UCC-1—INDIANA UNIFORM COMMERCIAL CODE    Secretary of State

When a consumer debtor completely fulfills all debts and obligations secured by a financing statement, she is entitled to a **termination statement** signed by the secured party or an assignee of record. Failure of the affected secured party to furnish a termination statement after proper demand subjects him to a fine of $100 plus damages for any loss caused to the debtor by such failure [9–404].

## Possession by Secured Party as Public Notice

Public filing of a security interest is intended to put any interested members of the public on notice of the security interest. A potential creditor of the debtor, or a potential buyer of the collateral, can check the records to see whether anyone else claims an interest in the debtor's collateral. The same objective can be reached if the debtor gives up possession of the collateral to the creditor or to a third person who holds the collateral for the creditor. If a debtor does not have possession of collateral that he claims to own, then a potential creditor or debtor is on notice that someone else may claim an interest in it. Thus, a security interest is perfected by change of possession of collateral from the debtor to the creditor/secured party or his agent [9–302(1)(a)]. For example, Simpson borrows $50 from a pawnbroker and leaves his guitar as collateral for the loan. The pawnbroker's security interest in the guitar is perfected by virtue of her possession of the guitar.

Generally, possession by the secured party is *the* means for perfecting a security interest in instruments such as checks or notes and in money.[3] Possession of the collateral by the secured party is an alternative means, and often the most satisfactory means, of perfecting a security interest in chattel paper and negotiable documents of title. Possession is also a possible means for perfecting a security interest in inventory. This is sometimes done through the **field warehousing** arrangement, whereby part of the debtor's inventory is fenced off and withdrawals from it are permitted only on the approval of the secured party or his on-the-scene representative.

Possession by the secured party is usually not a practical means for perfecting a security interest in equipment or consumer goods because the debtor normally wants to retain possession to make use of the equipment or goods. Of course, possession by the secured party is not possible at all with accounts or general intangibles. The person to whom the collateral is delivered holds it as bailee, and he owes the duties of a bailee to the parties in interest [9–207].

## Perfection by Attachment

Perfection by mere attachment of the security interest, sometimes known as automatic perfection, is the only form of perfection that occurs without the giving of public notice. It occurs automatically when all the requirements of attachment are complete. This form of perfection is limited to certain classes of collateral; in addition, it may be only a temporary perfection in some situations.[4]

A creditor who sells goods to a consumer on credit, or who lends money to enable a consumer to buy goods, can perfect a security interest merely by attaching the security interest to the goods. A creditor under these circumstances has what is called a **purchase money security interest in consumer goods.** For example, an appliance store sells a television set to Margaret Morse on a conditional sales contract, or time-payment plan. The store does not have to file its purchase money security interest in the set. The security interest is considered perfected just by virtue of its attachment to the set in the hands of the consumer.

In the case that follows, *In Re Phillips,* the court rejected a creditor's claims that its security interest was perfected by attachment, holding that the goods were equipment and not consumer goods.

---

[3]Sections 9–304(4) and (5) permit a 21-day temporary perfection.

[4] Temporary perfection without filing or possession is automatically obtained for 21 days after attachment of the security interest in instruments and negotiable documents [9–304]. To get protection beyond the 21-day period, the secured party must perfect by filing or possession. During the 21-day period of temporary perfection, however, any holder in due course of commercial paper or any bona fide purchaser of a security or a negotiated document will prevail over the secured party relying on temporary perfection [9–309].

---

## In Re Phillips
## Creditway of America v. Phillips
### 42 UCC Rep. 679 (Bankr. W.D. Va. 1985)

Jacob Phillips and his wife, Charlene, jointly owned the Village Variety 5&10 Store in Bluefield, Virginia. In addition, Mrs. Phillips was a computer science teacher at the Wytheville Community College. On December 1, 1984, Mrs. Phillips entered into a retail installment sales contract with Holdren's, Inc., for the purchase of a Leading Edge color computer and a Panasonic printer. The contract, which was also a security agreement, provided for a total payment of $3,175.68, with monthly payments of $132.32 to begin on March 5, 1985. On December 1, 1984, Holdren's assigned the contract to Creditway of America.

At the time of purchase, Mrs. Phillips advised Holdren's that she was purchasing the computer for professional use in her teaching assignments as well as for use in the variety store. One of the software programs purchased was a practical accounting program for business transactions. Mrs. Phillips also received a special discount price given by Holdren's to state instructors buying for their teaching use. She used the computer in the Village Variety 5&10 Store until it closed in April 1985. In June, the Phillipses filed a petition under Chapter 7 of the Bankruptcy Act. At the time, they owed $2,597.79 on the computer. No financing statement was ever filed.

Creditway filed a motion in the bankruptcy proceeding, claiming that it had a valid lien on the computer and seeking to be permitted to repossess it.

---

**Pearson, Bankruptcy Judge**     The key factor in determining whether to grant Creditway's motion for relief is the classification of the collateral. Virginia Code Section 9–302(1)(d) provides that "a financing statement shall be filed to perfect all security interests except a purchase money security interest in consumer goods." If the computer goods are classified as consumer goods, then Creditway, as assignee of Holdren's, would not need to file a financing statement to have a perfected security interest in the collateral. However, if the computer items are classified as equipment, then, pursuant to Section 9–401(1)(c), it would be necessary for Creditway to have a dual filing to perfect its security interest.

Virginia Code Section 9–109 outlines the classification of collateral. In pertinent part it provides that

Goods are
(1) "consumer goods" if they are used or bought for use primarily for personal, family, or household purposes;
(2) "equipment" if they are used or bought for use primarily in business (including farming or a profession).

The test for the classification of goods is the owner's use of the goods. The two classes of goods are mutually exclusive. The same property cannot be in two classes at the same time and as to the same person. Thus, an item cannot, for example, be classified as both consumer goods and equipment.

The evidence before this court indicates that the computer items were purchased for use primarily in business rather than for personal, family, or household purposes. Mrs. Phillips's uncontradicted testimony is that at the time of purchase she informed the salesperson at Holdren's that the computer would be used for her teaching assignments as well as in the variety store. She received a special discount as a state instructor for purchase of the items for use in teaching. Mrs. Phillips also indicated that she purchased this computer with its memory capability to handle business transactions, and that she purchased a software package on Practical Accounting for business billing. These facts and circumstances should have provided sufficient notice of the use of the items for classification purposes such that financing statements could have been filed properly to perfect the security interest.

Courts have held without exception that the Uniform Commercial Code filing requirements are mandatory and that the filing of a financing statement in an improper place or not in all the places required is ineffective to perfect a security interest. Although the application of rules in a given case may be harsh, any other result would invite inconsistency which the Uniform Commercial Code was enacted to avoid. On the evidence presented the collateral should be found to be classified as equipment and, having not filed in all places required, Creditway holds an unperfected security interest against the debtor.

**Motion of Creditway to repossess the collateral denied.**

---

Perfection by attachment is not effective if the consumer goods are motor vehicles for which the state issues certificates of title and has only limited effectiveness if the goods are fixtures [9–302]. A later section of this chapter discusses the special rules covering these kinds of collateral.

There are also major limitations to the perfection by attachment principle. As discussed in the Priority section of this chapter, relying on attachment for perfection does not, in some instances, provide as much protection to the creditor as does public filing.

One potential concern for a creditor is that the use of the collateral will change from that anticipated when the security interest was obtained. For example, in the *Phillips* case, assume that the computer was originally purchased to be used in the home and later converted to use in the business. It is important that the creditor properly perfect the security interest initially so that it will not be adversely affected by a subsequent change in use and will continue to have the benefit of its initial perfection.

## Motor Vehicles

If state law requires a certificate of title for motor vehicles, then a creditor who takes a security interest in a motor vehicle (other than a creditor holding a security interest in inventory held for sale by a person in the business of selling goods of that kind) must have the security interest noted on the title [9–302]. Suppose a credit union lends Carlson money to buy a new car in a state that requires certificates of title for cars. The credit union cannot rely on filing or on attachment of its security interest in the car to perfect that interest; rather, it must have its security interest noted on the certificate of title.

This requirement protects the would-be buyer of the car or another creditor who might extend credit based on Carlson's ownership of the car. By checking the certificate of title to Carlson's car, a potential buyer or creditor would learn about the credit union's security interest in the car. If no security interest is noted on the certificate of title, the buyer can buy—or the creditor can extend credit—with confidence that there are no undisclosed security interests that would be effective against him.

## Fixtures

The Code also provides special rules for perfecting security interests in consumer goods that become fixtures by virtue of their attachment to or use with real property. A creditor with a purchase money security interest in consumer goods (including consumer goods that will become fixtures) obtains perfection merely by attachment of her security interest. However, as discussed in the Priority section of this chapter, a creditor who relies on attachment for perfection will not, in some instances,

prevail against other creditors who hold an interest in the real estate to which the consumer good is attached unless a financing statement is filed with the real estate records to perfect the security interest [9–401(1)(a)].

## Removal of Collateral

Even where a creditor has a perfected security interest in the collateral of her debtor, she needs to be concerned about the possibility that the debtor can take the collateral from the state where the creditor has filed on it to another state where the creditor does not have her claim filed on the public record. Commonly, the security agreement between the creditor and the debtor provides where the collateral is to be kept and stipulates that it is not to be moved unless the debtor gives notice to and/or obtains the permission of the creditor. There is, however, no absolute assurance that the debtor will be faithful to such an agreement.

Under the Code, a secured creditor who has perfected his security interest generally has four months after the collateral is brought into the new state to perfect his security interest in that state. If the creditor does not reperfect within the four months, his security interest becomes unperfected and he could lose the collateral to a person who purchases it, or takes an interest in it, after it has been removed [9–103(1)]. If the creditor has not perfected his security interest by the time the collateral is removed, or within the time period that the creditor has to perfect his security interest in the former location of the collateral, then his interest is unperfected and he does not obtain the advantage of the four-month grace period.

The Code rules that govern the removal of collateral covered by a state certificate of title— such as an automobile—are more complicated. If an automobile covered by a certificate of title on which a security interest is noted is moved to another state, the perfected security interest is perfected for four months in the new state, or until the automobile is registered in the new state. If the original state did not require that security interests be noted on the title, and if a new title is used in the second state without notation of the security interest, then under certain circumstances a buyer of the automobile can take free of the original security interest. To qualify, the buyer must not be in the business of buying and selling automobiles and must (1) give value, (2) take delivery after issuance of the new title, and (3) buy without notice of the security interest [9–103(2)].[5]

[5]Other rules are set out in the Code for accounts, general intangibles, chattel paper, and mobile goods removed to other states [9–103(3) and (4)].

---

**CONCEPT REVIEW**

## OBTAINING AN ENFORCEABLE SECURITY INTEREST

| Step | Purpose | Necessary Action |
|---|---|---|
| **Attachment of Security Interest** | To secure a debt. The debtor gives the creditor rights in the debtor's property to secure the debt owed by the creditor to the debtor. | 1. Agreement by the debtor giving the creditor a security interest in specific property (collateral) in which the debtor has a legal interest. This can include after-acquired property and proceeds of the collateral.<br>2. The debtor must have a legal interest in the collateral.<br>3. The creditor must give value to the debtor (e.g., money or goods). Future advances are value when actually given to the debtor. |
| **Perfection** | To obtain protection against other creditors of the debtor and against purchasers of the collateral from the debtor. | 1. *Public filing.* Filing a financing statement with the appropriate state or local office to put the world on notice that the creditor claims an interest in specific collateral belonging to the debtor; or in the case of a motor vehicle, noting the security interest on the certificate of title; or<br>2. *Possession by creditor.* The creditor may take possession of the collateral, thus putting other creditors and potential purchasers on notice that the creditor has an interest in the collateral (this is not practical for all kinds of collateral); or<br>3. *Perfection by attachment.* Limited perfection merely by attachment of the security interest is obtained where (a) a creditor sells consumer goods to a consumer on credit or (b) a creditor loans money to a consumer to enable him to buy consumer goods. |

---

# PRIORITY RULES

## Importance of Determining Priority

Because several creditors may claim a security interest in the same collateral of a debtor, the Code establishes a set of rules for determining which of the conflicting security interests has priority. Determining which creditor has priority, or the best claim, takes on particular importance in bankruptcy situations, where unless a creditor has a perfected security interest in collateral that fully protects the obligation owed to him, the creditor may realize nothing or only a few cents on every dollar owed to him.

## General Priority Rules

The basic rule established by the Code is that when more than one security interest in the same collateral has been filed or otherwise perfected, the first security interest to be filed or perfected has priority over any that are filed or perfected later. If only one security interest has been perfected—for example, by filing—then that security interest has priority. However, if none of the conflicting security interests has been perfected, then the first security interest to be attached to the collateral has priority [9–312(5)].

Thus, if Bank A filed a financing statement covering a retailer's inventory on February 1, 1995, and Bank B filed a financing statement covering that same inventory on March 1, 1995, Bank A would have priority over Bank B even though Bank B might have made its loan and attached its security interest to the inventory before Bank A did so. However, if Bank A neglected to perfect its security interest by filing and Bank B did perfect, then Bank B, as the holder of the only perfected security interest in the inventory, would prevail.

If both of the creditors neglected to perfect their security interest, then the first security interest that attached would have priority. For example, if Bank Y has a security agreement covering a dealer's equipment on June 1, 1995, and advances money to the dealer on that date, whereas Bank Z does not obtain a security agreement covering that equipment or advance money to the dealer until July 1, 1995, then Bank Y would have priority over Bank Z. In connection with the last situation, unperfected secured creditors do not enjoy a preferred position in bankruptcy proceedings, thus giving additional impetus to the desirability of filing or otherwise perfecting a security interest.

## Purchase Money Security Interests in Inventory

There are several very important exceptions to the general priority rules. First, a *perfected purchase money security interest in inventory* has priority over a conflicting security interest in the same inventory *if the purchase money security interest is perfected at the time the debtor receives possession of the inventory* and if the purchase money secured party gives *notification in writing* to the prior secured creditor *before* the debtor receives the inventory [9–312(3)].

Assume that Bank A takes and perfects a security interest in all the present and after-acquired inventory of a debtor. Then, the debtor acquires some additional inventory from a wholesaler, who retains a security interest in the inventory until the debtor pays for it and perfects this security interest. The wholesaler has a purchase money security interest in inventory goods and has priority over the prior secured creditor (Bank A) if the wholesaler has perfected the security interest by the time the collateral reaches the debtor and if the wholesaler sends notice of her purchase money security interest to Bank A before shipping the goods. Thus, to protect itself, the wholesaler must check the public records to see whether any of the debtor's creditors are claiming an interest in the debtor's inventory. When the wholesaler discovers that some are claiming an interest, it should file its own security interest and give notice to the existing creditors.

As the following *Borg-Warner Acceptance Corp.* case illustrates, the subsequent seller of inventory can obtain a priority position if it files a financing statement and notifies the prior secured party in a timely fashion.

---

### BORG-WARNER ACCEPTANCE CORP. v. TASCOSA NATIONAL BANK
#### 784 S.W.2d 129 (Tex. Ct. App. 1990)

On March 1, 1982, the Tascosa National Bank of Amarillo (Bank) extended a loan to T & L Ventures, Inc., doing business as (d/b/a) The Video Connection (T & L) in the amount of $30,006. A financing statement was obtained and filed with the secretary of state on March 4, 1982. The Bank's financing statement described the collateral as:

Video software and hardware, computer games hardware and software, all inventory, furniture, fixtures of above located at Amarillo, Potter County, Texas.

From time to time, the indebtedness was renewed and extended and additional funds were provided T & L, with the last note dated April 18, 1986, in the principal amount of $153,613.84. All indebtedness was evidenced by notes and secured by the same collateral.

On March 7, 1982, Borg-Warner Acceptance Corporation (Borg-Warner) entered into an Inventory Security Agreement pursuant to which T & L granted to Borg-Warner a security interest in its inventory purchased with the proceeds of loans made by Borg-Warner. Borg-Warner perfected its security interest as a purchase money security interest (PMSI) under section 9–312(3) by: (1) filing on March 11, 1982, a financing statement describing the collateral with the secretary of state's office; and (2) notifying the Bank of Borg-Warner's interest in T & L's inventory.

Following the perfection of Borg-Warner's PMSI, Borg-Warner commenced financing the acquisition of inventory by T & L and continued such financing through May 22, 1986. Pursuant to a "floor-planning arrangement," Borg-Warner purchased from vendors and paid directly to vendors the invoice purchase price of inventory acquired by T & L for resale. Indebtedness to Borg-Warner was not incurred for any purpose other than the purchase of inventory.

T & L defaulted on its indebtedness. On May 11, 1986, the Bank repossessed T & L's inventory, removed it from T & L's premises, and placed it in a warehouse. Borg-Warner demanded that the Bank deliver the inventory to it on the grounds it had a superior claim to it. The Bank refused and Borg-Warner brought suit against the Bank. The trial court granted summary judgment in favor of the Bank, and Borg-Warner appealed.

---

**Dodson, Judge**    The determinative issue on Borg-Warner's appeal is the priority of liens question. If Borg-Warner's security interest qualifies as a PMSI under section 9–312(3), Borg-Warner prevails. However, if Borg-Warner's security interest does not so qualify, then the Bank prevails under the "first to file rule." Section 9–312(5)(1).

The Uniform Commercial Code defines two types of PMSIs, those claimed by sellers and those claimed by financing agencies:

A security interest is a "purchase money security interest" to the extent that it is

(1) taken or retained by the seller of the collateral to secure all or part of its price; or

(2) taken by a person who by making advances or incurring an obligation gives value to enable the debtor to acquire rights in or the use of collateral if such value is so used. Section 9–107.

We reiterate, the general rule of priority among conflicting security interests in the same collateral where both interests are perfected by filing, is that the secured party who first files a financing statement prevails. Section 9–312(5)(1). However, section 9–312(3) states a special rule for a PMSI in inventory. That subsection reads in full as follows:

(3) A perfected purchase money security interest in inventory has priority over a conflicting security interest in the same inventory and also has priority in identifiable cash proceeds received on or before the delivery of the inventory to a buyer if

(1) the purchase money security interest is perfected at the time the debtor receives possession of the inventory; and

(2) except where excused by section 9–319 (oil and gas production), the purchase money secured party gives notification in writing to the holder of the conflicting security interest if the holder had filed a financing statement covering the same types of inventory (i) before the date of the filing made by the purchase money secured party, or (ii) before the beginning of the 21-day period where the purchase money security interest is temporarily perfected without filing or possession (Subsection (e) of Section 9–304); and

(3) the holder of the conflicting security interest receives any required notification within five years before the debtor receives possession of the inventory; and

(4) the notification states that the person giving the notice has or expects to acquire a purchase money security interest in inventory of the debtor, describing such inventory by item or type. [Emphasis added.] Section 9–312(3).

Under the above provisions, Borg-Warner's security interest is a PMSI to the extent that it is taken by Borg-Warner who by incurring an obligation gave value to enable T & L to acquire rights in or the use of collateral if such value was in fact used.

In determining the priority between Borg-Warner and the Bank, we note that the legislature has provided that a PMSI in inventory such as Borg-Warner's has priority over a conflicting security interest in the same inventory if: (1) the PMSI was perfected at the time T & L received possession of the inventory; (2) Borg-Warner gave notice in writing to the Bank who had filed a financing statement covering the same type of inventory before the date of the filing by Borg-Warner; (3) the Bank received any required notification within five years before T & L received possession of the inventory; and (4) the notification stated that Borg-Warner expected to ac-

quire a PMSI in the inventory of T & L, describing such inventory by item or type. Section 9–312(3).

Our earlier explication of the undisputed facts reveals that Borg-Warner complied with the statutory code requirements.

**Judgment reversed in favor of Borg-Warner.**

## Purchase Money Security Interests in Noninventory Collateral

The second exception to the general priority rule is that a *purchase money security interest in collateral other than inventory* has priority over a conflicting security interest in the same collateral *if the purchase money security interest is perfected at the time the debtor receives the collateral* or *within 10 days afterward* [9–312(4)].

Assume that Bank B takes and perfects a security interest in all the present and after-acquired equipment belonging to a debtor. Then, a supplier sells some equipment to the debtor, reserving a security interest in the equipment until it is paid for. If the supplier perfects the purchase money security interest by filing at the time the debtor obtains the collateral or within 10 days thereafter, it has priority over Bank B. This is because its purchase money security interest in noninventory collateral prevails over a prior perfected security interest if the purchase money security interest is perfected at the time the debtor takes possession or within 10 days afterward.

## Rationale for Protecting Purchase Money Security Interests

The preference given to purchase money security interests, provided that their holders comply with the statutory procedure in a timely manner, serves several ends. First, it prevents a single creditor from closing off all other sources of credit to a particular debtor and thus possibly preventing the debtor from obtaining additional inventory or equipment needed to maintain his business. Second, the preference makes it possible for a supplier to have first claim on inventory or equipment until it is paid for, at which time it may become subject to the after-

acquired property clause of another creditor's security agreement. By requiring that the first perfected creditor be given notice of a purchase money security interest at the time the new inventory comes into the debtor's inventory, the Code serves to alert the first creditor to the fact that some of the inventory on which it may be relying for security is subject to a prior secured interest until it is paid for.

## Buyers in the Ordinary Course of Business

A third exception to the general priority rule is that a **buyer in the ordinary course of business** (other than a person buying farm products from a person engaged in farming operations) takes free from a security interest created by his seller even though the security interest is perfected and even though the buyer knows of its existence [9–307(1)]. For example, a bank loans money to a dealership to finance that dealership's inventory of new automobiles and takes a security interest in the inventory, which it perfects by filing. Then, the dealership sells an automobile out of inventory to a customer. The customer takes the automobile free of the bank's security interest even though the dealership may be in default on its loan agreement and even if the customer knows about the bank's interest. As long as the customer is a buyer in the ordinary course of business, she is protected. The reasons for this rule are that a bank really expects to be paid from the proceeds of the dealership's automobile sales and that the rule is necessary to the smooth conduct of commerce. Customers would be very reluctant to buy goods if they could not be sure they were getting clear title to them from the merchants from whom they buy.

In the following case, *DBC Capital Fund, Inc. v. Snodgrass,* a buyer of an automobile from a dealer obtained title free of a security interest previously given by the dealer to his creditor.

## DBC Capital Fund, Inc. v. Snodgrass

### 551 N.E.2d 475 (Ind. Ct. App. 1990)

On February 19, 1988, DBC Capital Fund, Inc. (DBC), entered into an agreement with the owner of Devers Auto Sales whereby DBC obtained a security interest in the automobile inventory maintained by Devers. This security interest was perfected by filing with the secretary of state on February 25, 1988.

On March 24, 1989, Cheryl Snodgrass purchased a 1984 Oldsmobile from Devers for $5,000 in cash. This automobile was taken from the inventory covered by DBC's security interest, although Snodgrass was not made aware of the financing agreement between Devers and DBC. When Snodgrass took possession of the Oldsmobile, Devers told her that the automobile's certificate of title would be mailed to her. In the meantime, she was issued a temporary registration.

On April 28, 1989, Snodgrass was informed by letter that DBC had physical possession of the certificate of title for the Oldsmobile and that DBC considered itself to have a valid lien on the automobile. In a later telephone conversation, DBC's attorney informed Snodgrass that DBC would not release the certificate of title to the 1984 Oldsmobile until Snodgrass paid DBC $4,200.

On April 25, 1989, the temporary registration issued to Snodgrass by Devers expired. Because Snodgrass was not in possession of the certificate of title for the Oldsmobile, she was unable to obtain proper licensing for the vehicle and, therefore, could not use the automobile. In an effort to obtain the certificate of title, Snodgrass then filed suit against DBC. The trial court entered judgment in her favor on June 28, 1989, awarding her $1,920 in triple damages and $1,748.45 in attorney's fees. DBC appealed.

------◼------

**Ratliff, Judge**   DBC first contends that the trial court erred in determining that Snodgrass was a buyer in the ordinary course of business, and that, therefore, the trial court failed to recognize that, as a holder of a valid secured interest, DBC was entitled to possession of the certificate of title to the 1984 Oldsmobile. We disagree.

At the hearing the parties stipulated to the fact that DBC had a valid security interest in the 1984 Oldsmobile. The main issue litigated at trial was whether Snodgrass was in a legal position which would make her claim to the automobile superior to that of DBC. Under the relevant provision of the Uniform Commercial Code (UCC) the interest of a "buyer in the ordinary course of business" is superior to that of a holder of valid secured interest. Section 9–307(1).

DBC claims that Snodgrass cannot be considered a buyer in the ordinary course of business "because she failed to require delivery of the title at the time of purchase." According to DBC Snodgrass was charged with knowledge of Indiana Code sections 9-1-2-2(a) and 9-1-2-3(b) which made it unlawful for Devers to fail to deliver a certificate of title at the time of purchase. Because Devers failed to deliver the certificate of title at the time of sale, Snodgrass knew or should have known that the sale of the 1984 Oldsmobile was in violation of the ownership rights of a third party. DBC concludes that because Snodgrass was not a buyer in the ordinary course of business, Snodgrass cannot defeat DBC's valid security interest.

It is true that if there are grounds for suspecting that a security interest is being imperiled by a mode of dealing, a transaction cannot be considered in the ordinary course of business. However, we conclude that DBC has failed to prove that the mode of dealing in the present case was grounds for such a suspicion. DBC's analysis is flawed in that it rests on the supposition that sections 9-1-2-2(a) and 9-1-2-3(b) were enacted to protect the interests of secured creditors. Such simply is not the case. The plain purpose for enacting these statutes was to impede the trade in stolen vehicles. As stated by Judge Posner of the United States Court of Appeals, "as the statute is intended to protect purchasers . . . rather than lenders, there would be a considerable paradox in interpreting the statute to defeat the purchaser's interest." Therefore, we reject DBC's contention that these statutes create a duty on behalf of a purchaser to demand delivery of the certificate of title to an automobile at the time of sale.

Absent such a duty, nothing in the evidence suggests that Snodgrass' purchase of the 1984 Oldsmobile was outside the ordinary course of business. Therefore, under the provisions of section 9–307(1), as a buyer in the ordinary course of business, Snodgrass took free of the security interest held by DBC.

**Judgment in favor of Snodgrass.**

## Artisan's and Mechanic's Liens

The Code also provides that certain liens arising by operation of law (such as an artisan's lien) have priority over a perfected security interest in the collateral [9–310]. For example, Marshall takes her automobile, on which a credit union has a perfected security interest, to Frank's Garage to have it repaired. Under common or statutory law, Frank's may have a lien on the car to secure payment for the repair work; such a lien permits Frank's to keep the car until it receives payment. If Marshall defaults on her loan to the credit union and refuses to pay Frank's for the repair work, and the car is sold to satisfy the liens, Frank's is entitled to its share of the proceeds before the credit union gets anything.

## Liens on Consumer Goods Perfected by Attachment

A retailer of consumer goods who relies on attachment of a security interest to perfect it prevails over other creditors of the debtor-buyer. However, the retailer does not prevail over someone who buys the collateral from the debtor if the buyer (1) has no knowledge of the security interest; (2) gives value for the goods; and (3) buys the goods for his personal, family, or household use [9–307(2)]. The retailer does not have priority over such a **bona fide consumer purchaser** unless it filed its security interest.

For example, an appliance store sells a television set to Arthur for $750 on a conditional sales contract, reserving a security interest in the set until Arthur has paid for it. The store does not file a financing statement but relies on attachment for perfection. Arthur later borrows money from a credit union and gives it a security interest in the television set. When Arthur defaults on his loans and the credit union tries to claim the set, the appliance store has a better claim to the set than does the credit union. The credit union then has the rights of an unsecured creditor against Arthur.

Now, suppose Arthur sells the television set for $500 to his neighbor Andrews. Andrews is not aware that Arthur still owes money on the set to the appliance store. Andrews buys it to use in her home. If Arthur defaults on his obligation to the store, it cannot recover the television set from Andrews. To be protected against such a purchaser from its debtor, the appliance store must file a financing statement rather than relying on attachment for perfection.

## Lien Creditors

A lien creditor is a creditor who acquires a lien on property by attachment, levy, or the like [9–301(3)]. Examples include the pre- or postjudgment liens a creditor might obtain against the debtor's property in a civil suit against the debtor. An unperfected security interest in such property is usually subordinate to the rights of a person who becomes a lien creditor before the security interest is perfected [9–301(1)(b)]. Thus, a lien creditor normally defeats a party with an unperfected security interest but loses to a party whose security interest is perfected before the creditor gets lien creditor status.

## Fixtures

A separate set of problems arise when the collateral is goods that become fixtures by being so related to particular real estate that an interest in them arises under real estate law. Determining the priorities among a secured party with an interest in the fixtures, subsequent purchasers of the real estate, and those persons who have a security interest—such as a mortgage—on the real property can involve both real estate law and the Code. However, the Code does set out rules for determining when the holder of a perfected security interest in fixtures has priority over an encumbrancer or owner of the real estate. Some of the Code priority rules are as follows:

First, the holder of the secured interest in a fixture has priority if: (1) her interest is a purchase money security interest obtained prior to the time the goods become fixtures; (2) the security interest is perfected by "fixture filing"—that is, by filing in the recording office where a mortgage on the real estate would be filed prior to, or within 10 days of, the time when the goods become fixtures; and (3) the debtor has a recorded interest in the real estate or is in possession of it [9–313(4)(a)].

For example, Restaurant Supply sells Arnold Schwab, the operator of Arnie's Diner, a new gas stove on a conditional sales contract, reserving a security interest until the purchase price of the stove is paid. The stove, a replacement for an existing stove, is to be installed in a building owned by Arnold Schwab on which First National Bank holds a real estate mortgage. Restaurant Supply can ensure that its security interest in the stove has priority over any claims to it by First National Bank. To do this, Restaurant Supply must (1) enter into a security agreement with Schwab before the stove is delivered to him; and (2) perfect its security interest by fixture filing before the stove is hooked up by a plumber or within 10 days of that time.

Second, the secured party whose interest in fixtures is perfected has priority where: (1) the fixtures are removable factory or office machines or readily removable replacements of domestic appliances that are consumer goods; and (2) the security interest was perfected before the goods became fixtures [9–313(4)(c)]. For example, Harriet Hurd's dishwasher breaks down and she contracts with The Appliance Store to buy a new one on a time-payment plan. The mortgage on Hurd's house provides that it covers the real property along with all kitchen appliances or their replacements. The Appliance Store's security interest in the dishwasher has priority over the interest of the holder of the mortgage if The Appliance Store perfects its security interest before the new dishwasher is installed in Hurd's home. Perfection in consumer goods can, of course, be obtained merely by attaching the security interest through the signing of a valid security agreement.

Note that a creditor holding a security interest in consumer goods that become fixtures who relies on attachment for perfection prevails over other creditors with an interest in the real property *only* where the consumer goods are "readily removable replacements for domestic appliances."

Suppose a hardware store takes a security interest in some storm windows. Because the storm windows are likely to become fixtures through their use with the homeowner's home, the hardware store cannot rely merely on attachment to protect its security interest. It should file a financing statement to protect that security interest against other creditors of the homeowner with an interest in his home. This rule helps protect a person interested in buying the real property or a person considering lending money based on the real property. By checking the real estate records, the potential buyer or creditor would learn of the hardware store's security interest in the storm windows.

Once a secured party has filed his security interest as a fixture filing, he has priority over purchasers or encumbrancers whose interests are filed after that of the secured party [9–313(4)(b) and (d)].

Where the secured party has priority over all owners and encumbrancers of the real estate, he generally has the right on default to remove the collateral from the real estate. However, he must make reimbursement for the cost of any physical injury caused to the property by the removal [9–313(8)].

---

**CONCEPT REVIEW**

# PRIORITY RULES

| Parties | Rule |
|---|---|
| **Buyer of Collateral from Debtor versus Creditor with a Security Interest in the Collateral** | 1. A *buyer in ordinary course of business* (other than a person buying farm products from a person engaged in farming operations) takes *free* of a security interest created by his seller even though the security interest is *perfected* and even though the buyer knows of its existence. |

| Parties | Rule |
|---|---|
| | 2. A *bona fide purchaser* of collateral that is *consumer goods* from a debtor has priority over a creditor who holds a purchase money security interest in the collateral but did not file its security interest if the buyer (a) has no knowledge of the security interest, (b) gives value for the goods, and (c) buys them for her own personal, family, or household use.<br>3. Otherwise, buyers take subject to perfected or known security interests but free of unperfected and unknown security interests. |
| **Secured Creditor versus Other Creditors** | 1. As to collateral *other than fixtures,* the general rule is that when more than one security interest in the same collateral has been filed (or otherwise perfected), the first security interest to be filed or perfected has priority over other security interests.<br>2. Exceptions to this general rule are:<br> *a. Inventory.* A perfected purchase money security interest in inventory has priority over a conflicting security interest in the same inventory *if* the purchase money security interest is perfected at the time the debtor receives possession of the inventory *and* if the purchase money secured party gives notification in writing to the prior secured creditor *before* the debtor receives the inventory.<br> *b. Noninventory.* A purchase money security interest in noninventory collateral prevails over a prior perfected security interest *if* the purchase money security interest is perfected at the time the debtor takes possession or within 10 days afterward.<br> *c. Liens by operation of law.* Liens that arise by operation of law—such as artisan's liens—have priority over even perfected security interests in collateral.<br>3. If none of the conflicting security interests has been perfected, then the *first* security interest to be *attached* to the collateral has priority. |
| **Secured Creditor versus Other Persons with an Interest in Real Property on which Fixture Is Located** | 1. As to collateral that will become a *fixture:*<br> *a.* A creditor with a secured interest in a fixture has priority if (1) the interest is a purchase money security interest that was obtained prior to the time the goods became fixtures; (2) the security interest was perfected by fixture filing prior to, or within 10 days of, the time when the goods became fixtures; and (3) the debtor has a recorded interest in the real estate or is in possession of it.<br> *b.* A creditor with a perfected secured interest in fixtures will have priority where: (1) the fixtures are removable factory or office machines or readily removable replacements of domestic appliances that are consumer goods; and (2) the security interest is perfected *prior* to the time the goods become fixtures. |

## DEFAULT AND FORECLOSURE

### Default

Usually, the creditor and debtor state in their agreement which events constitute a default by the buyer.

The Code does not define what constitutes default. Defining default is left to the parties' agreement, subject to the Code requirement that the parties act in good faith in doing so. If the debtor defaults, the secured creditor has several options:

1. Forget the collateral, and sue the debtor on his note or promise to pay.
2. Repossess the collateral, and use strict foreclosure to keep the collateral in satisfaction of the remaining debt.
3. Repossess and foreclose on the collateral, and then, depending on the circumstances, either sue for any deficiency or return the surplus to the debtor.

## Right to Possession

The agreement between the creditor and the debtor may authorize the creditor to repossess the collateral in case of default. If the debtor does default, the creditor is entitled under the Code to possession of the collateral. If through self-help the creditor can obtain possession peaceably, he may do so. However, if the collateral is in the possession of the debtor and cannot be obtained without disturbing the peace, then the creditor must take court action to repossess the collateral [9−503]. See the *Ivy v. General Motors Acceptance Corp.* case, which follows shortly, for a discussion of what constitutes repossession without breach of the peace.

If the collateral is intangible, such as accounts, chattel paper, instruments, or documents, and performance has been rendered to the debtor, the secured party may give notice and have payments made or performance rendered to her [9−502].

## Sale of the Collateral

The secured party may dispose of the collateral by sale or lease or in any manner calculated to produce the greatest benefit to all parties concerned. However, the method of disposal must be commercially reasonable. If the creditor decides to sell the collateral at a public sale such as an auction, then the creditor must give the debtor notice of the time and place of the public sale. Similarly, if the creditor proposes to make a private sale of the collateral, notice of the time after which the collateral will be available for sale must be given to the debtor. This gives the debtor a chance to object to the proposed private sale if she considers it not to be commercially reasonable or to otherwise protect her interests. The sale of

the collateral to a good faith purchaser for value discharges the security interest and any other interests that are subordinate to it, and such a purchaser takes the collateral free of all those interests.

Until the collateral is actually disposed of by the creditor, the buyer has the right to **redeem** it. This means that if the buyer tenders fulfillment of all obligations then due as well as of the expenses incurred by the secured party in retaking, holding, and preparing the collateral for disposition, she can recover the collateral from the creditor.

## Consumer Goods

If the creditor has a security interest in consumer goods and the debtor has paid 60 percent or more of the purchase price or debt (and has not agreed in writing to a strict foreclosure), the creditor must sell the repossessed collateral within 90 days after the repossession. If less than 60 percent of the purchase price or debt related to consumer goods has been paid, or if collateral other than consumer goods is involved, the creditor must sell the collateral within a reasonable time, but may propose to the debtor that the creditor keep the collateral in satisfaction of the debt. The consumer-debtor has 21 days to object in writing. If the consumer objects, the creditor must sell the collateral. Otherwise, the creditor may keep the collateral in satisfaction of the debt.

## Distribution of Proceeds

The Code sets out the order in which any proceeds are to be distributed after the sale of collateral by the creditor. First, any expenses of repossessing, storing, and selling the collateral, including reasonable attorney's fees, are paid. Second, the proceeds are used to satisfy the debt. Third, any junior liens are paid. Finally, if any proceeds remain, the debtor is entitled to them. If the proceeds are not sufficient to satisfy the debt, then the creditor is usually entitled to a **deficiency judgment.** This means that the debtor remains personally liable for any debt remaining after the sale of the collateral [9−504].

For example, suppose a loan company lends Christy $5,000 to purchase a car and takes a security interest. After making several payments and reducing the debt to $4,800, Christy defaults. The loan company pays $50 to have the car repossessed and then has it sold at an auction, where it brings $4,500, thus incurring a sales commission of 10 percent ($450) and attorney's fees of $150. The repossession charges, sales commission, and attorney's fees, totaling $650, are paid first from the $4,500 proceeds. The remaining $3,850 is applied to the $4,800 debt, leaving a balance due of $950. Christy remains liable to the loan company for the $950.

## Liability of Creditor

A creditor who holds a security interest in collateral must be careful to comply with the provisions of Article 9 of the Code. A creditor acting improperly in repossessing collateral or in its foreclosure and sale is liable to the parties injured. Thus, a creditor can be liable to a debtor if she acts improperly in repossessing or selling collateral [9–507]. This potential liability is illustrated in the case of *Ivy v. General Motors Acceptance Corp.*

---

## IVY V. GENERAL MOTORS ACCEPTANCE CORP.
### 612 So.2d 1108 (Sup. Ct. Miss. 1992)

Lester Ivy borrowed money from General Motors Acceptance Corp. (GMAC) to purchase a van, and GMAC acquired a security interest in the van. The security agreement contained a so-called insecurity clause that provided GMAC with the right to immediately repossess the van upon default; notice was not a prerequisite to repossession. Ivy defaulted on his obligation on the loan, and GMAC hired American Lenders Service of Jackson to repossess Ivy's van. About 6:30 A.M., Dax Freeman and Jonathan Baker of American Lenders Service drove to Ivy's home. They drove on Ivy's gravel driveway, which is about a quarter-mile long, past a chicken house and the van parked near Ivy's mobile home. They quietly attempted to start the van, but their attempt failed. They then hitched the van to their tow truck and towed it away.

When Freeman and Baker reached the end of Ivy's driveway, Freeman stopped the tow truck and checked the van. At that point, he saw someone running from the chicken house toward the mobile home. Ivy testified that prior to running toward the mobile home, he ran toward the tow truck "hollering and flagging for them to stop" but Freeman and Baker apparently did not see or hear Ivy at the time. Freeman jumped back into the tow truck, drove off Ivy's property, and onto an adjacent road. Ivy decided to chase after Freeman and Baker because he thought they were stealing his van. He jumped into a pickup truck, passed Freeman and Baker, and—according to them—pulled in front of the tow truck and slammed on his brakes. Freeman claimed he was forced to slam on his brakes but was unable to avoid a slight collision with the rear bumper of Ivy's truck. Ivy claimed that he stopped well ahead of the tow truck, affording Freeman plenty of time to stop, but that he reved the engine and "rammed him." Ivy claimed that his head hit the rear window of the truck as a result of the collision and that he sustained a "severe vertical sprain." However, Ivy's medical bill totaled only $20 and he did not miss any work.

When Ivy exited his truck, Freeman showed him some "official looking documents," advised him that he worked for American Lenders, and stated that they were repossessing his truck at GMAC's request. There was a dispute as to whether Ivy sought to have the sheriff called concerning the accident. Freeman allowed Ivy to retrieve some personal belongings from the van and gave Ivy a telephone number to call to get his van back; at that point, they all departed the scene.

Seven months later, on October 20, Ivy filed a complaint against GMAC and American Lenders contending that the repossession of his van was invalid because there was a breach of the peace and he had been caused "personal injuries." Ivy sought actual and punitive damages. At the conclusion of a jury trial, the jury awarded Ivy $5,000 in actual damages and $100,000 in punitive damages. The trial court judge set aside the punitive damage award and both parties appealed.

---

**Prather, Judge**    GMAC contends that its agents did not breach the peace and, therefore, it should not have been liable for actual damages. Ivy, of course, disagrees.

Mississippi law authorizes a creditor or secured party to repossess collateral without judicial process if he or she can do so without breaching the peace. The legislature did not define "breach of peace," but this Court has provided some indication. For example, this court has held that entering a private driveway to repossess collateral without use of force does not constitute a breach of peace. This Court has also held that a creditor, who repossesses collateral despite the fact that the debtor has withheld his or her consent or has strongly objected, did not breach the peace. And, courts in other jurisdictions have generally held that the use of trickery or deceit to peaceably repossess collateral does not constitute a breach of peace.

On the other hand, a Florida Court of Appeal opined that a debtor's "physical objection"—"even from a public street"—bars repossession. A Georgia Court of Appeal found a breach of peace in a case in which: (1) the creditor repossessed the debtor's automobile by blocking it with another automobile; (2) the creditor informed the debtor that he could just "walk his a-- home"; and (3) the debtor "unequivocally protested" the manner of repossession. The Ohio Supreme Court opined that the use of intimidation or acts "fraught with the likelihood of violence" constitutes a breach of peace.

In sum, much of the litigation involving self-help repossession statutes involves the issue of whether a breach of peace has occurred. Disposition of this issue is not a simple task: Since physical violence will ordinarily result in a breach of peace, the secured party's right to repossession will end if repossession evokes physical violence, either on the part of the debtor or the secured party. At the other end from physical violence, a secured party may peaceably persuade the debtor to give up the collateral so that no breach of peace occurs. Between those two extreme situations—one in which violence occurs and the other in which the debtor peaceably gives up the collateral—lies the line which divides those cases in which the secured party may exercise self-help repossession and those in which he must resort to the courts. As with most dividing lines, the line between the two extremes is sometimes hard to locate, and even if it is located, it sometimes moves.

Application of the foregoing principles to the evidence viewed in the light most favorable to the verdict leads this Court to conclude that a breach of peace did occur. This Court, therefore, affirms on this issue.

**Judgment affirmed awarding actual damages and denying punitive damages.**

---

**McRae, Justice (concurring in part and dissenting in part)**    The majority complains that Mississippi case law provides little guidance on determining whether a creditor or agent's conduct is so malicious, oppressive or fraudulent that an award of punitive damages is warranted. While it is true that this Court has not often confronted this issue, the principle is well settled throughout the jurisdictions that punitive damages are proper where creditors seize property in a manner that reflects malice, fraud, oppression, gross negligence, or reckless disregard of the rights of the chattel holder.

In *Kirkwood v. Hickman,* perhaps the only Mississippi case to directly address this question, the Court found that when a creditor commits a trespass to retrieve secured property in an "intentional and highhanded manner," punitive damages are in order even if the trespass involved no violence. What could possibly be more "highhanded" than going onto a debtor's property without permission, hooking the debtor's van to a tow truck, and hauling it away in plain view of the debtor with no explanation whatsoever? In such circumstances the debtor would naturally think his property was being stolen and would set about to recapture the property. If the conduct of GMAC and American Lenders does not qualify as "reckless disregard for the rights of the chattel holder," then I am at a loss to imagine what might fit the description.

Clearly, given Ivy's version of the events the jury was justified in concluding that the conduct of GMAC and American Lenders was oppressive, highhanded and recklessly unmindful of Ivy's rights.

This entire misadventure might have been avoided if the creditor had simply followed the replevin procedures set out in the Mississippi Code. While Mississippi still permits creditors to employ the remedy of self-help when retrieving their property from chattel holders, creditors follow that path at their peril. GMAC and American Lenders in this case took the law into their own hand, and so could be held fully responsible for the consequences. I would reverse the judgment not withstanding the verdict and reinstate the jury's award of punitive damages.

---

## Constitutional Requirements in Regard to Repossession

In 1972, in *Fuentes v. Shevin,* the U.S. Supreme Court held that state repossession statutes that authorize summary seizure of goods and chattels by state agents such as a sheriff, on an application by some private person who claims he is lawfully entitled to the property and posts a bond, are unconstitutional.[6] This is because these statutes deny the current possessor of the property an opportunity to be heard in court before the property is taken from him. The Court did not accept the argument that because the possessors of the property in question had signed conditional sales contracts authorizing the sellers to take back or repossess the property on default, they had waived their rights to a hearing. This decision raised some speculation that the provisions of the Code permitting secured parties to repossess collateral, in some cases without even judicial process, might be constitutionally defective.

Then, in 1974, in *Mitchell v. W. T. Grant,* the Supreme Court limited the *Fuentes* holding to a requirement that where only property rights are involved, there must be some opportunity for a judicial hearing prior to any final determination of the rights of the parties claiming an interest in the property in question.[7] This decision permits property to be seized by state officials, following the filing of an application and the posting of a bond, so long as the person from whom the property is seized has a later opportunity in court to assert his rights to the property.

The repossession provisions of the Code have been attacked in court as lacking in due process. However, the courts to date have upheld the Code repossession provisions as they relate to private repossession without judicial process.[8] Where judicial process is used, the procedures must conform to the standards laid down in *Fuentes* and *Mitchell.*

---

[6] 407 U.S. 67 (1972).

[7]407 U.S. 600 (1974).

[8]See, for example, *Gibbs v. Titleman,* 502 F.2d 1107 (3rd Cir. 1974) and cases cited therein.

---

**1.** Symons, a full-time insurance salesperson, bought a set of drums and cymbals from Grinnel Brothers. A security agreement was executed between them but was never filed. Symons purchased the drums to supplement his income by playing with a band. He had done this before, and his income from his two jobs was about equal. He also played several other instruments. Symons became bankrupt, and the trustee tried to acquire the drums and cymbals as part of his bankruptcy estate. Grinnel's claimed that the drums and cymbals were consumer goods and thus it had a perfected security interest merely by attachment of the security interest. Were the drums and cymbals consumer goods?

**2.** Robert and Billie Brown operated a paint and gift store. They borrowed $36,628.31 from the First National Bank of Dewey and gave the bank a security interest in "all goods, wares, merchandise, gifts, inventory, fixtures, and accounts receivable owned or thereafter acquired and used in the business." The security agreement also covered "all additions, accessions, and substitutions" to or for collateral and required the Browns to insure the collateral for the benefit of the bank. The bank perfected its security interest. The Browns obtained fire insurance but did not name the bank as a loss payee. The Browns' business was destroyed by fire, and the Browns received a $25,000 check from the insurance company for the loss of inventory. The bank then filed suit to obtain the check. Shortly thereafter, the Browns were adjudicated bankrupt. Does the bank have a perfected security interest in the insurance check?

**3.** Ronald Allegretti purchased a bedroom set valued at $900 and a television set valued at $350 from Goldblatt Brothers, a furniture and appliance store, on a revolving credit account. Under the terms of the revolving credit agreement and the credit slip that was signed at the time of each purchase, Goldblatt's reserved a security interest in all goods sold on credit to Allegretti. Goldblatt's then assigned its interest in the extended credit agreement to General Electric Credit Corporation. Neither filed a financing statement. Allegretti subsequently filed a voluntary petition in bankruptcy, and one of the questions in the bankruptcy action was whether Goldblatt's, and in turn General Electric Credit Corporation, held a perfected security interest in the bedroom set and the television. Did the creditors hold a perfected secured interest in the bedroom set and the television set even though they had not filed financing statements?

**4.** On October 28, 1983, Steve Gresham, doing business as Midway Cycle Sales, entered into a Wholesale Financing Agreement with ITT Commercial Finance Corporation. The agreement was to finance the purchase of new motorcycles from Suzuki Motor Corporation. ITT filed a financing statement with the Indiana secretary of state on December 16, 1983. The description of the collateral in which ITT asserted a security interest included "all inventory . . . replacements and proceeds." On January 9, 1984, Union Bank filed a financing statement with the Indiana secretary of state claiming it was engaged in "floor planning of new motorcycles" for Midway Cycle Sales. In August 1984, ITT began paying Suzuki invoices for Gresham. In July 1985, ITT sent a letter to Union Bank notifying it that it expected to acquire purchase money security interests in the inventory of Stephan Gresham d/b/a Midway Cycle Sales. In early 1986, Union Bank began loaning money to Gresham under its floor planning agreement with him. Actually, Gresham was "double floor planning"—that is, he was taking invoices for motorcycles that had been paid for by ITT to the Union Bank and claiming that he had paid for the motorcycles but had decided to floor plan them. When Union Bank advanced money to him, he used the money to make payments on the loans to ITT. He made no payments to Union Bank and did not pay off all of his loan to ITT. Midway Cycle Sales went bankrupt when Union Bank repossessed 22 new Suzuki motorcycles. ITT brought suit against Union Bank, claiming it had paid for the motorcycles and had a perfected security interest in the motorcycles that had priority over Union Bank's security interest in them. Did ITT's security interest have priority over Union Bank's security interest?

**5.** On November 18, Firestone & Company made a loan to Edmund Carroll, doing business as Kozy Kitchen. To secure the loan, a security agree-

ment was executed, which listed the items of property included, and concluded as follows: "together with all property and articles now, and which may hereafter be, used or mixed with, added or attached to, and/or substituted for any of the described property." A financing statement that included all the items listed in the security agreement was filed with the town clerk on November 18, and with the secretary of state on November 22. On November 25, National Cash Register Company delivered a cash register to Carroll on a conditional sales contract. National Cash Register filed a financing statement on the cash register with the town clerk on December 20, and with the secretary of state on December 21. Carroll defaulted in his payments to both Firestone and National Cash Register. Firestone repossessed all of Carroll's fixtures and equipment covered by its security agreement, including the cash register, and then sold the cash register. National Cash Register claimed that it was the title owner of the cash register and brought suit against Firestone for conversion. Did Firestone or National Cash Register have the better right to the cash register?

**6.** Glatfelter purchased a stereo set under a purchase money security agreement from Mahaley's Store. This agreement was not perfected by filing. She sold the set to Colonial Trading Company, which in turn resold it. When Glatfelter did not meet her obligations, Mahaley's sued Colonial Trading for conversion of the stereo set in which it claimed a security interest. Is Colonial Trading liable for selling the stereo set in which Mahaley has a security interest?

**7.** Grimes purchased a new Dodge car from Hornish, a franchised Dodge dealer. The sale was made in the ordinary course of Hornish's business. Grimes paid Hornish the purchase price of the car at the time of the sale. Hornish had borrowed money from Sterling Acceptance and had given it a perfected security interest in its inventory, including the car Grimes bought. Hornish defaulted on its loan to Sterling and Sterling then tried to recover the Dodge from Grimes. Was the car Grimes bought from Hornish still subject to Sterling Acceptance's security interest?

**8.** On April 10, Benson purchased a new Ford Thunderbird automobile. She traded in her old automobile and financed the balance of $4,325 through the Magnavox Employees Credit Union, which took a security interest in the Thunderbird. In July, the Thunderbird sustained major damage in two accidents. It was taken to ACM Garage for repairs that took seven months to make and resulted in charges of $2,139.54. Benson was unable to pay the charges, and ACM claimed a garageman's lien. Does Magnavox Credit Union's lien or ACM's lien have priority?

**9.** Kahn applied for a home improvement loan to construct an in-ground swimming pool. Union National Bank approved the loan, and construction began on Kahn's land. State Bank held a valid mortgage on this land. After the pool was completed, Union National gave Kahn the money with which he paid the contractor. Union National then perfected its interest by filing. State Bank later attempted to foreclose on its mortgage. Union National claimed the value of the pool. Is Union National entitled to recover the value of the pool?

**10.** In August 1979, Norma Wade purchased a Ford Thunderbird automobile and gave Ford Motor Credit a security interest in it to secure her payment of the $7,000 balance of the purchase price. When Wade fell behind on her monthly payments, Ford engaged the Kansas Recovery Bureau to repossess the car. On February 10, 1980, an employee of the Recovery Bureau located the car in Wade's driveway, unlocked the door, got in, and started it. He then noticed a discrepancy between the serial number of the car and the number listed in his papers. He shut off the engine, got out, and locked the car. When Wade appeared at the door to her house, he advised her that he had been sent by Ford to repossess the car but would not do so until he had straightened out the serial number. She said that she had been making payments, that he was not going to take the car, and that she had a gun, which she would use. He suggested that Wade contact Ford to straighten out the problem. She called Ford and advised its representative that if she caught anybody on her property again trying to take her car, she would use her gun to "leave him laying right where I saw him." Wade made several more payments, but Ford again contracted to have the car repossessed. At 2:00 A.M. on March 5, 1980, the employee of the Kansas Recovery Bureau successfully took the car from Wade's driveway. She said that she heard a car burning rubber, looked out of her window, and saw that her car was missing. There was no confrontation between Wade and the employee since he had

safely left the area before she discovered that the car had been taken. Wade then brought a lawsuit against Ford claiming that the car had been wrongfully repossessed. She sought actual and punitive damages, plus attorney's fees. Should Ford be held liable for wrongful repossession?

**11.** Gibson, a collector of rare old Indian jewelry, took two of his pieces to Hagberg, a pawnbroker. The two pieces, a silver belt and a silver necklace, were worth $500 each. Hagberg loaned only $45 on the belt and $50 on the necklace. Gibson defaulted on both loans, and immediately and without notice, the necklace was sold for $240. A short time later, the belt was sold for $80. At the time of their sale, Gibson owed interest on the loans of $22. Gibson sued Hagberg to recover damages for improperly disposing of the collateral. Is Gibson entitled to damages because of Hagberg's actions in disposing of the collateral?

**12.** [■■] *Video Case.* See "A Good Night's Sleep." Appliance Dealer needed additional working capital, so it obtained a loan from bank, which took—and perfected by filing—a security interest in all present and after-acquired inventory and equipment of Appliance Dealer. Subsequently, the Appliance Dealer obtained inventory on credit from a Wholesaler, who retained and perfected a security interest in the inventory until Appliance Dealer paid for it. Appliance Dealer also purchased from Computer Retailer a computer for use in the store; Computer Retailer took and perfected a security interest in the computer before it was delivered. Can the bank obtain a security interest in the inventory and computer even though Appliance Dealer did not own them at the time it borrowed the money from Bank and gave it a security interest?

Cook, a Customer, buys a microwave oven and built-in range/oven on credit from Appliance Dealer. Both items were among the inventory that Appliance Dealer had purchased from Wholesaler, but it has not yet paid Wholesaler for either item. Appliance Dealer retained a security interest in the items it sold to Cook but it did not file a financing statement. Cook sold the microwave to her neighbor for about 60 percent of the price she agreed to pay Appliance Dealer. If Cook subsequently defaulted on her obligation to Appliance Dealer, could it recover the stove from Cook? Would your answer be different if the oven had been installed in a building on which Mortgage Company held a mortgage? Who would have the better right to the oven, Appliance Dealer or Mortgage Company? Does Appliance Dealer have the right to recover the microwave from Cook's neighbor?

If Appliance Dealer subsequently defaulted on its obligations to Bank, to Wholesaler, and to Computer Retailer, who would have the priority security interest in the appliances that remain in Appliance Dealer's inventory, the bank or Wholesaler? Would either have the legal right to recover the microwave or the stove that were sold to Cook? Who would have the priority security interest in the computer, Bank or Computer Retailer?

**13.** ▣ *Video Case.* See "TV Repair." Appliance Store acquired inventory on credit from TV Manufacturer, which retained and perfected a security interest in the TV sets until they were paid for. Appliance Store subsequently experienced financial difficulties and held a going-out-of-business sale. If TV Manufacturer had not been paid for the TV sets, would it have the legal right to recover them from individual customers who purchased them at the going-out-of-business sale?

## CAPSTONE QUESTIONS

**1.** On July 1, Darr bought a $15,000 computer on credit from Caltex Electronics for use in his business. On that date, Darr completed a contract giving him title to the computer and obligating him to pay for it in monthly installments over two years; he also completed a written security agreement giving Caltex a security interest in the computer. The security agreement described the computer in considerable detail and was signed by Darr. However, Caltex never filed a financing statement.

Later, Darr borrowed $13,000 from Bank, using the computer as security. The security interest attached on August 1, and Bank filed a financing statement on August 8.

Still later, Darr defaulted on each obligation. Both Caltex and Bank want to use the computer to satisfy their respective claims against Darr. Caltex makes the following arguments:

· Its security interest has attached.
· Its interest has priority over Bank's competing interest because Caltex was the first secured party to attach.

## Required:

Answer the following and give reasons for your conclusions.

Is each claim correct?

**2.** On January 1, Davis bought a $5,000 home computer on credit from Caltex Electronics. Davis was to use the computer for personal, family, and household purposes. As part of the deal, Davis completed an installment contract for the balance of the purchase price and a valid security agreement giving Caltex a security interest in the computer. This security interest attached on January 1. Caltex never filed a financing statement.

On February 1, Davis sold the computer to his friend Dworkin for $4,300 in cash. Like Davis, Dworkin used the computer for personal, family, or household purposes. He had no knowledge of Caltex's security interest.

Later, Davis defaulted on his payment obligation to Caltex, which wants to repossess the computer from Dworkin to satisfy the debt. The following major arguments have emerged in the disputes between the parties:

· Dworkin argues that Caltex cannot possibly win because its security interest was unperfected.
· Caltex replies that its interest was perfected, and that for this reason it can repossess the computer.
· Dworkin's rejoinder is that even if Caltex did perfect, Dworkin still wins. Dworkin adds that in most cases of this kind, the interests of secured parties like Caltex will be protected.

## Required:

Answer the following and give reasons for your conclusions.

**1.** Which, if any, of these assertions is correct?
**2.** Who finally has the right to the computer, and why?
**3.** What does Dworkin mean when he says that Caltex's interests will probably be protected even if it cannot repossess the computer?

# BANKRUPTCY

*When an individual, a partnership, or a corporation is unable to pay its debts to creditors, problems can arise. Some creditors may demand security for past debts or start court actions on their claims in an effort to protect themselves. Such actions may adversely affect other creditors by depriving them of their fair share of the debtor's assets. Also, quick depletion of the debtor's assets may effectively prevent the debtor who needs additional time to pay off his debts from having an opportunity to do so.*

*At the same time, creditors need to be protected against the actions a debtor in financial difficulty might be tempted to take to their detriment. For example, the debtor might run off with his remaining assets or might use them to pay certain favored creditors, leaving nothing for the other creditors. Finally, a means is needed by which a debtor can get a fresh start financially and not continue to be saddled with debts beyond his ability to pay. This chapter focuses on the body of law and procedure that has developed to deal with the competing interests that arise when a debtor is unable to pay his debts in a timely manner.*

## THE BANKRUPTCY ACT

The Bankruptcy Act is a federal law that provides an organized procedure under the supervision of a federal court for dealing with insolvent debtors. Debtors are considered insolvent if they are unable or fail to pay their debts as they become due. The power of Congress to enact bankruptcy legislation is provided in the Constitution. Through the years, there have been many amendments to the Bankruptcy Act. Congress completely revised the act in 1978 and then passed significant amendments to it in 1984. In 1986, Congress added provisions dealing with family farms.

The Bankruptcy Act has several major purposes. One is to ensure that the debtor's property is fairly distributed to the creditors and that some creditors do not obtain unfair advantage over the others. At the same time, the act protects all of the creditors against actions by the debtor that would unreasonably diminish the debtor's assets to which they are entitled. The act also provides the honest debtor with a measure of protection against the demands for payment by his creditors. Under some circumstances, the debtor is given additional time to pay the creditors, freeing him of those pressures creditors might otherwise exert. If the debtor makes a full and honest accounting of his assets and liabilities and deals fairly with his creditors, the debtor may have most—if not all—of the debts discharged so as to have a fresh start.

At one time, bankruptcy carried a strong stigma for the debtors who became involved in it. Today, this is less true. It is still desirable that a person conduct her financial affairs in a responsible manner. However, there is a greater understanding that such events as accidents, natural disasters, illness, divorce, and severe economic dislocations are often beyond the ability of individuals to control and may lead to financial difficulty and bankruptcy.

## Bankruptcy Proceedings

The Bankruptcy Act covers a number of bankruptcy proceedings. In this chapter, our focus will be on:

1. Straight bankruptcy (liquidations).
2. Reorganizations.
3. Family farms.
4. Consumer debt adjustments.

The Bankruptcy Act also contains provisions regarding municipal bankruptcies, which are not covered in this chapter.

## Liquidations

A liquidation proceeding, traditionally called **straight bankruptcy,** is brought under Chapter 7 of the Bankruptcy Act. The debtor must disclose all of the property she owns and surrender this bankruptcy estate to the **bankruptcy trustee.** The trustee separates out certain property that the debtor is permitted to keep and then administers, liquidates, and distributes the remainder of the bankrupt debtor's estate. There is a mechanism for determining the relative rights of the creditors, for recovering any preferential payments made to creditors, and for disallowing any preferential security interests obtained by creditors. If the bankrupt person has been honest in his business transactions and in the bankruptcy proceedings, she is usually given a **discharge** (relieved) of her debts.

## Reorganizations

Chapter 11 of the Bankruptcy Act provides a proceeding whereby a debtor can work out a plan to solve its financial problems under the supervision of a federal court. A reorganization plan is essentially a contract between a debtor and its creditors. The proceeding is intended for debtors, particularly businesses, whose financial problems may be solvable if they are given some time and guidance and if they are relieved of some pressure from creditors.

## Family Farms

Historically, farmers have been accorded special attention in the Bankruptcy Code. Chapter 12 of the Bankruptcy Act provides a special proceeding whereby a debtor involved in a family farming operation can develop a plan to work out his financial difficulties. Generally, the debtor remains in possession of the farm and continues to operate it while the plan is developed and implemented.

## Consumer Debt Adjustments

Under Chapter 13 of the Bankruptcy Act, individuals with regular incomes who are in financial difficulty can develop plans under court supervision to satisfy their creditors. Chapter 13 permits compositions (reductions) of debts and/or extensions of time to pay debts out of the debtor's future earnings.

## The Bankruptcy Courts

Bankruptcy cases and proceedings are filed in federal district courts. The district courts have the authority to refer the cases and proceedings to bankruptcy judges, who are considered to be units of the district court. If a dispute falls within what is known as a **core proceeding,** the bankruptcy judge can hear and determine the controversy. Core proceedings include a broad list of matters related to the administration of a bankruptcy estate. However, if a dispute is not a core proceeding but rather involves a state law claim, then the bankruptcy judge can only hear the case and prepare draft findings and conclusions for review by the district court judge.

Certain proceedings affecting interstate commerce have to be heard by the district court judge if any party requests that this be done. Moreover, even the district courts are precluded from deciding certain state law claims that could not normally be brought in federal court, even if those claims are related to the bankruptcy matter. Bankruptcy judges are appointed by the president for terms of 14 years.

## Chapter 7: Liquidation Proceedings

### Petitions

All bankruptcy proceedings, including liquidation proceedings, are begun by the filing of a petition. The petition may be either a **voluntary petition** filed by the debtor or an **involuntary petition** filed by a creditor or creditors of the debtor. A voluntary petition in bankruptcy may be filed by an individual, a partnership, or a corporation. However, municipal, railroad, insurance, and banking corporations and savings or building and loan associations are not permitted to file for straight bankruptcy proceedings. A person filing a voluntary petition need not be insolvent—that is, her debts need not be greater than her assets. However, the person must be able to allege that she has debts. The primary purpose for filing a voluntary petition is to obtain a discharge from some or all of the debts.

### Involuntary Petitions

An involuntary petition is a petition filed by creditors of a debtor. By filing it, they seek to have the debtor declared bankrupt and his assets distributed to the creditors. Involuntary petitions may be filed against many debtors. However, involuntary petitions in straight bankruptcy cannot be filed against (1) farmers; (2) ranchers; (3) nonprofit organizations; (4) municipal, railroad, insurance, and banking corporations; (5) credit unions; and (6) savings or building and loan associations. If a debtor has 12 or more creditors, an involuntary petition to declare him bankrupt must be signed by at least 3 creditors. If there are fewer than 12 creditors, then an involuntary petition can be filed by a single creditor. The creditor or creditors must have valid claims against the debtor exceeding the value of any security they hold by $5,000 or more. To be forced into involuntary bankruptcy, the debtor must be unable to pay his debts as they become due—or have had a custodian for his property appointed within the previous 120 days.

If an involuntary petition is filed against a debtor engaged in business, the debtor may be permitted to continue to operate the business. However, the court may appoint an **interim trustee** if this is necessary to preserve the bankruptcy estate or to prevent loss of the estate. A creditor who suspects that a debtor may dismantle her business or dispose of its assets at less than fair value may apply to the court for protection.

### Automatic Stay Provisions

The filing of a bankruptcy petition operates as an automatic stay, holding in abeyance various forms of creditor action against a debtor or her property. These actions include: (1) beginning or continuing judicial proceedings against the debtor; (2) actions to obtain possession of the debtor's property; (3) actions to create, perfect, or enforce a lien against the debtor's property; and (4) setoff of indebtedness owed to the debtor before commencement of the bankruptcy proceeding. A court may give a creditor relief from the stay if the creditor can show that the stay does not give her "adequate protection" and jeopardizes her interest in certain property. The relief to the creditor might take the form of periodic cash payments or the granting of a replacement lien or an additional lien on property.

The case that follows, *In Re Ionosphere Clubs, Inc.,* is an example of creditors trying to proceed independent of a bankruptcy court and having their efforts blocked.[1]

---

[1]While this case involved a petition for relief under Chapter 11 (Reorganization), the automatic stay provisions of the bankruptcy title of the U.S. Code are applicable to both Chapter 7 and Chapter 11 proceedings.

## IN RE IONOSPHERE CLUBS, INC.
### 111 B.R. 423 (Bankr. S.D. N.Y. 1990)

On March 4, 1989, the International Association of Machinists and Aerospace Workers, AFL-CIO (IAM), initiated a strike against Eastern Air Lines, Inc. Thereafter, both the Airline Pilots Association (ALPA) and the Transport Workers Union of America (TWU) initiated a sympathy strike. As a result, on March 9, 1989, Eastern and its affiliate, Ionosphere Clubs, Inc., each filed a voluntary petition for relief under Chapter 11. After the bankruptcy filing, Eastern and Ionosphere continued to operate their businesses as debtors in possession.

During the strike, Eastern hired new pilots as permanent replacements for the striking pilots. On November 22, 1989, the ALPA notified Eastern that the sympathy strike had been concluded and that the approximately 2,000 striking pilots were willing to return to work. Eastern was not willing to displace the replacement pilots to make room for the returning strikers.

In February 1990, Morteson Rolleston and 17 formerly striking pilots filed a class action lawsuit in federal district court in Atlanta, claiming, among other things, that Eastern had failed to fund its pilot pension plan and to pay interest on certain pension benefits that had already been paid. The lawsuit sought to freeze the assets of Eastern until amounts allegedly due to certain benefit plans were paid. Eastern sought an injunction from the bankruptcy court enjoining the Rolleston lawsuit as a violation of the automatic stay provisions of the Bankruptcy Act.

---

**Lifland, Chief Judge** Section 362(a)(3) of the [Bankruptcy] Code provides in pertinent part as follows:

(a) . . . a petition filed under . . . this title . . . operates as a stay, applicable to all entities, of—

(1) the commencement or continuation . . . of a judicial, administrative or other proceeding against the debtor that was or could have been commenced before the commencement of the case under this title, or to recover a claim against the debtor that arose before the commencement of the case under this title;

\* \* \* \* \*

(3) an act to obtain possession of the property of the estate or of property from the estate or to exercise control over property of the estate;

\* \* \* \* \*

(6) any act to collect, assess or recover a claim against the debtor that arose before the commencement of the case under this title.

It is beyond dispute that the Rolleston Plaintiffs seek to exercise control of at least $281 million of the cash assets of Eastern's estate by seeking to secure a court order "freezing" Eastern's assets and directing Eastern to pay this amount to the pilot pension plans. Additionally, the Rolleston Plaintiffs appear to request a temporary restraining order that would prohibit distributions under a reorganization plan, because "if the assets are distributed to creditors, it will be impossible for Plaintiffs to recover those assets." This direct attempt to secure preferred status for a discrete group of creditors runs directly counter to the distribution and oversight scheme established by the Code.

The Rolleston Plaintiffs also allege that the funds they seek to recover from Eastern on behalf of the pension plans "are not Eastern's assets but . . . are assets of the [Rolleston] Plaintiffs." It would appear that the Rolleston Plaintiffs are merely asserting unliquidated, contingent pre-petition claims against the Eastern estate and have no specific interest (other than the interest that all of Eastern's creditors have in property of the estate) in the property which they are attempting to gain control over.

Any attempt to "freeze" Eastern's assets and obtain an order requiring Eastern to transfer cash from its estate to the pilot pension plans is a direct and blatant attempt to assert control over the assets of the estate for the benefit of the Rolleston Plaintiffs. Such a distribution will reduce the amount to be paid to creditors and have an adverse effect on the feasibility of any plan of reorganization.

Additionally, the Rolleston lawsuit interferes with this court's jurisdiction over essential core matters in the Eastern case, including claims issues and confirmation of a plan of reorganization.

**Judgment in favor of Eastern enjoining the Rolleston lawsuit.**

## Order of Relief

Once a bankruptcy petition has been filed, the first step is a court determination that relief should be ordered. If a voluntary petition is filed by the debtor, or if the debtor does not contest an involuntary petition, this step is automatic. If the debtor contests an involuntary petition, then a trial is held on the question of whether the court should order relief. The court orders relief only (1) if the debtor is generally not paying his debts as they become due, or (2) if within four months of the filing of the petition a custodian was appointed or took possession of the debtor's property. The court also appoints an interim trustee pending election of a trustee by the creditors.

## Meeting of Creditors and Election of Trustee

The bankrupt person is required to file a list of her assets, liabilities, and creditors and a statement of her financial affairs. Then, the court calls a meeting of the creditors. The creditors may elect a creditors' committee and a trustee who, if approved by the judge, takes over administration of the bankrupt's estate. The trustee represents the creditors in handling the estate. At the meeting, the creditors have a chance to ask the debtor questions about her assets, liabilities, and financial difficulties. These questions commonly focus on whether the debtor has concealed or improperly disposed of assets. See Figure 1.

## Duties of the Trustee

The trustee takes possession of the debtor's property and has it appraised. The debtor must also turn over her records to the trustee. For a time, the trustee may operate the debtor's business. The trustee sets aside the items of property that a debtor is permitted to keep under state exemption statutes or federal law.

The trustee examines the claims filed by various creditors and objects to those that are improper in any way. The trustee separates the unsecured property from the secured and otherwise exempt property. He also sells the bankrupt's nonexempt property as soon as possible, consistent with the best interests of the creditors.

The trustee is required to keep an accurate account of all the property and money he receives and to promptly deposit moneys into the estate's accounts. At the final meeting of the creditors, the trustee presents a detailed statement of the administration of the bankruptcy estate.

## Exemptions

Even in a liquidation proceeding, the bankrupt is generally not required to give up all of his property; he is permitted to **exempt** certain items of property. Under the new Bankruptcy Act, the debtor may choose to keep certain items or property either exempted by state law, or exempt under federal law—unless state law specifically forbids use of the federal exemptions. However, any such property concealed or fraudulently transferred by the debtor may not be retained.

The debtor must elect to use *either* the set of exemptions provided by the state or the set provided by the federal bankruptcy law; she may not pick and choose between them. A husband and wife involved in bankruptcy proceedings must both elect either the federal or the state exemptions; where they cannot agree, the federal exemptions are deemed elected.

The exemptions permit the bankrupt person to retain a minimum amount of the assets considered necessary to life and to his ability to continue to earn a living. They are part of the fresh start philosophy that is one of the purposes of the Bankruptcy Act. The general effect of the federal exemptions is to make a minimum exemption

**FIGURE 1**    Order and Notice of Chapter 7 Bankruptcy Filing

| B16A | United States Bankruptcy Court for the District of Maryland | ORDER AND NOTICE OF CHAPTER 7 BANKRUPTCY FILING, MEETING OF CREDITORS, AND FIXING OF DATES (Individual or Joint Debtor No Asset Case) |
|---|---|---|

### A. GENERAL INFORMATION

| Name of Debtor<br>John B. Jones<br>D/B/A THE BATH SHOP | Address of Debtor<br>195 MAIN STREET<br>ANNAPOLIS MD. 21401 | | |
|---|---|---|---|
| | Date Filed<br>01/24/95 | Case Number<br>9060300-SD | Soc. Sec. Nos./Tax ID Nos.<br>050-30-4701 |
| Addressee:<br>WICKER PRODUCTS, INC.<br>2000 SMITH PIKE<br>ALMA, MI 48030 | Address of the Clerk of the Bankruptcy Court<br>United States Bankruptcy Court<br>101 W. Lombard Street<br>Baltimore, MD 21201 | | |
| Name and Address of Attorney for Debtor<br>MARC A. BURNS<br>215 WATER STREET,<br>BALTIMORE MD 21202 | Name and Address of Trustee<br>BRUCE A. SMITH<br>136 S. CHARLES STREET,<br>BALTIMORE MD 21201 | | |

### B. DATE, TIME AND LOCATION OF MEETING OF CREDITORS

February 28, 1995, 09:15 A.M., U.S. Trustee, Fallon Federal Bldg., Rm. G-13, 31 Hopkins Plaza, Baltimore, MD 21201

### C. DISCHARGE OF DEBTS

Deadline to File a Complaint Objecting to the Discharge of the Debtor or Dischargeability of a Debt: April 30, 1995

### D. BANKRUPTCY INFORMATION

THERE APPEAR TO BE NO ASSETS AT THIS TIME FROM WHICH PAYMENT MAY BE MADE TO CREDITORS. DO NOT FILE A PROOF OF CLAIM UNTIL YOU RECEIVE NOTICE TO DO SO.

FILING OF A BANKRUPTCY CASE. A bankruptcy petition has been filed in this court for the person or persons named above as the debtor, and an order for relief has been entered. You will not receive notice of all documents filed in this case. All documents which are filed with the court, including lists of the debtor's property and debts, are available for inspection at the office of the clerk of the bankruptcy court.

CREDITORS MAY NOT TAKE CERTAIN ACTIONS. Anyone to whom the debtor owes money or property is a creditor. Under the bankruptcy law, the debtor is granted certain protection against creditors. Common examples of prohibited actions are contacting the debtor to demand re-payment, taking action against the debtor to collect money owed to creditors or to take property of the debtor, except as specifically permitted by the bankruptcy law, and starting or continuing foreclosure actions, repossessions, or wage deductions. If unauthorized actions are taken by a creditor against a debtor, the court may punish that creditor. A creditor who is considering taking action against the debtor or the property of the debtor should review 11 U.S.C. § 362 and may wish to seek legal advice. The staff of the clerk's office is not permitted to give legal advice to anyone.

MEETING OF CREDITORS. The debtor (both husband and wife in a joint case) shall appear at the meeting of creditors at the date and place set forth above in box 'B' for the purpose of being examined under oath. ATTENDANCE BY CREDITORS AT THE MEETING IS WELCOMED, BUT NOT REQUIRED. At the meeting the creditors may elect a trustee as permitted by law, elect a committee of creditors, examine the debt-or, and transact such other business as may properly come before the meeting. The meeting may be continued or adjourned from time to time without further written notice to the creditors.

LIQUIDATION OF THE DEBTOR'S PROPERTY. A trustee has been appointed in this case to collect the debtor's property, if any, and turn it into money. At this time, however, it appears from the schedules of the debtor that there are no assets from which any dividend can be paid to creditors. If at a later date it appears that there are assets from which a dividend may be paid, creditors will be notified and given an oppor-tunity to file claims.

EXEMPT PROPERTY. Under state and federal law, the debtor is permitted to keep certain money or property as exempt. If a creditor believes that an exemption of money or property is not authorized by law, the creditor may file an objection. Any objection must be filed no later than 30 days after the conclusion of the meeting of creditors.

DISCHARGE OF DEBTS. The debtor is seeking a discharge of debts. A discharge means that certain debts are made unenforceable. Credi-tors whose claims against the debtor are discharged may never take action to collect the discharged debts. If a creditor believes the debtor should not receive a discharge under 11 U.S.C. § 727 or a specific debt should not be discharged under 11 U.S.C. § 523(c) for some valid reason specified in the bankruptcy law, the creditor must take action to challenge the discharge. The deadline for challenging a discharge is set forth above in box 'C.' Creditors considering taking such action may wish to seek legal advice.

DO NOT FILE A PROOF OF CLAIM UNLESS YOU RECEIVE A COURT NOTICE TO DO SO

| For the Court: | |
|---|---|
| January 31, 1995 | Michael Kostishak |
| Date | Clerk of the Bankruptcy Court |

available to debtors in all states. States that wish to be more generous to debtors can provide more liberal exemptions.

The specific items that are exempt under state statutes vary from state to state. Some states provide fairly liberal exemptions and are considered "debtors havens." Items that are commonly made exempt from sale to pay debts owed creditors include the

family Bible; tools or books of the trade; life insurance policies; health aids such as wheelchairs and hearing aids; personal and household goods, and jewelry, furniture, and motor vehicles worth up to a certain amount.

The case that follows, *In re Griffin,* illustrates a claim by a debtor for an exemption under a state statute.

## In Re Griffin
### 139 B.R. 415 (Bankr. W.D. Tex. 1992)

Troy Griffin was a debtor in a Chapter 7 bankruptcy proceeding. He claimed that his 1985 Hobie Magnum sailboat was exempt from his creditors under a Texas statute that provided an exemption for "athletic and sporting" equipment. A creditor objected to the claim of exemption.

**King, Bankruptcy Judge**   The question in this case is whether a sailboat may be claimed as exempt under the "athletic and sporting equipment" category of section 42.002(a)(8) of the Texas Property Code. This Court holds that a sailboat is not included within the Texas exemption for athletic and sporting equipment, and, therefore, the objection to the claim of exemption is sustained and the exemption is denied.

The exemption statutes in Texas were amended in May, 1991. Prior to the amendments, certain items of personal property were not exempt unless the property was reasonably necessary for the family or single adult. After the amendments, however, athletic and sporting equipment were no longer required to be reasonably necessary for the family to qualify as exempt property.

The most extensive discussion of the athletic and sporting equipment exemption is found in an unreported opinion by Judge Clark, *In re Schwarzbach,* in which he determined that a sixteen foot bass boat was not exempt as athletic or sporting equipment. *Schwarzbach* agreed with the analysis of an earlier case that "athletic and sporting equipment" is limited to small items for personal use. *Schwarzbach* also compared the language of two different exemptions and concluded that the

Legislature contemplated an exemption for a boat only if the boat is used in a trade or profession. At the time *Schwarzbach* was decided, section 42.002(3)(B) allowed an exemption for "tools, equipment, books, and apparatus, including a boat, used in a trade or profession." Today, that section includes "boats and motor vehicles." In contrast, the current 42.002(a)(8) exemption for athletic and sporting equipment expressly includes bicycles, but not boats.

The purpose of exemption laws is to work a balance between protecting the debtor from destitution and allowing creditors to obtain payment on legitimate debts from the debtor's assets. This court agrees with *Schwarzbach* in holding that "athletic and sporting equipment" under the Texas exemption statute should be limited to small items for individual use. Allowing exemption of a sailboat or ski boat as "athletic and sporting equipment" would permit debtors to take undue advantage of the exemption laws and shield assets which are not necessary to a fresh start from the just claims of creditors. As so aptly stated by *In re Henricksen,* "Bankruptcy is intended to provide debtors with a fresh start, not with a fine finish."

**Claim of exemption denied.**

Eleven categories of property are exempt under the federal exemptions, which the debtor may elect in lieu of the state exemptions. The federal exemptions include:

1. The debtor's interest (not to exceed $7,500 in value) in real or personal property that the debtor or a dependent of the debtor uses as a residence.

2. The debtor's interest (not to exceed $1,200 in value) in one motor vehicle.

3. The debtor's interest (not to exceed $200 in value for any particular item) up to a total of $4,000 in household furnishings, household goods, wearing apparel, appliances, books, animals, crops, or musical instruments that are held primarily for the personal, family, or household use of the debtor or a dependent of the debtor.

4. The debtor's aggregate interest (not to exceed $500 in value) in jewelry held primarily for the personal, family, or household use of the debtor or a dependent of the debtor.

5. $400 in value of any other property of the debtor's choosing, plus up to $3,750 of any unused homestead exemption.

6. The debtor's aggregate interest (not to exceed $750 in value) in any implements, professional books, or tools of the trade.

7. Life insurance contracts.

8. Interest up to $4,000 in specified kinds of dividends or interest in certain kinds of life insurance policies.

9. Professionally prescribed health aids.

10. Social security, disability, alimony, and other benefits reasonably necessary for the support of the debtor or his dependents.

11. The debtor's right to receive certain insurance and liability payments.

The term *value* means "fair market value as of the date of the filing of the petition." In determining the debtor's interest in property, the amount of any liens against the property must be deducted. Note, also, that the amount of the exemptions is doubled where a husband and wife are jointly involved in a single bankruptcy proceeding.

## Avoidance of Liens

The debtor is also permitted to **void** certain liens against exempt properties that impair her exemptions. Liens that can be voided on this basis are judicial liens or nonpossessory, nonpurchase money security interests in: (1) household furnishings, household goods, wearing apparel, appliances, books, animals, crops, musical instruments, or jewelry that are held primarily for the personal, family, or household use of the debtor or a dependent of the debtor; (2) implements, professional books, or tools of the trade of the debtor or a dependent of the debtor; and (3) professionally prescribed health aids for the debtor or a dependent of the debtor. Debtors are also permitted to **redeem** exempt personal property from secured creditors by paying them the value of the collateral. Then, the creditor is an unsecured creditor as to any remaining debt owed by the debtor.

## Preferences

One of the Bankruptcy Act's major purposes is to ensure equal treatment for the creditors of an insolvent debtor. Thus, the act's **preference** provision prevents an insolvent debtor from distributing her assets to favored creditors shortly before bankruptcy, leaving few assets for other creditors. It does so by empowering the trustee to avoid any transfer of the debtor's property interests (1) to a creditor or for his benefit, (2) on account of a preexisting debt, (3) made while the debtor was insolvent, (4) made within 90 days of the bankruptcy petition, and (5) enabling the creditor to receive more than he would have received under Chapter 7 if the transfer had not been made. The 90-day period is extended to one year if the creditor is an insider. The act's elaborate definition of the term *insider* includes relatives of the debtor; business entities in which the debtor is a general officer, director, or general partner; and the creditor's directors, officers, or general partners (if the debtor is a business entity). Finally, the debtor is presumed to have been insolvent during the 90 days preceding the petition.

For example, suppose Fredericks, who is insolvent, has $1,000 in cash and no other assets. The creditors on his preexisting debts are his friend Roberts (for $650), a credit union (for $1,500), and a finance company (for $2,000). On June 1, Fredericks transfers $650 to Roberts. Two weeks later, he goes bankrupt. Because the transfer plainly gives Roberts more than he would have received under Chapter 7, and because the other elements of a preference are present, the trustee can avoid the transfer and get the $650 back from Roberts. If the trustee did not have this power, only $350 would remain to satisfy the other creditors' debts, which means that they would recover only 10 cents on each dollar owed them.

**Article 9 Secured Parties**   The Bankruptcy Act gives the trustee the rights possessed by a hypothetical lien creditor of the debtor on the day of bankruptcy. As discussed in Chapter 21, a lien creditor normally defeats a party with an unperfected security interest [UCC section 9–301(1)(b)]. Thus, the trustee generally defeats an Article 9 secured party who has not perfected by the date of bankruptcy. But a secured party who has perfected by that time defeats the trustee. Such a party normally can proceed directly against the collateral or the proceeds from its sale.

Even a perfected security interest, however, may be preferential. The taking of such an interest is a transfer of the debtor's property to a creditor, and if it is enforced, it would give the creditor more than he would receive under Chapter 7. If the debtor is insolvent when the security interest is taken, the interest was taken to secure a preexisting debt, and if this occurred within 90 days of the petition, the security interest is preferential. The clearest example is a case in which a creditor tries to get an advantage over other creditors by taking a security interest on the debtor's property to secure an already-existing debt. However, timing problems can arise when the security interest and the debt are created almost simultaneously or when the interest is created near the 90-day cutoff point. Here, the critical issue is the time the transfer is deemed to occur. In the case of Article 9 security interests, this time is usually (1) the time of attachment, if the interest is perfected within 10 days of attachment; or (2) the time of perfection, if the interest is perfected more than 10 days after attachment. The many timing problems created by this provision are beyond the scope of this text.

**Exceptions**   The Bankruptcy Act provides several exceptions to the trustee's avoiding power that are designed to allow a debtor and his creditors to engage in ordinary business transactions. The exceptions include (1) transfers that are intended by the debtor and creditor to be a contemporaneous exchange for new value or (2) the creation of a purchase money security interest in new property where new value was given by the secured party to enable the debtor to obtain the property, the new value was in fact used by the debtor to obtain the property, and the interest was perfected within 10 days after the debtor received the property.

For example, George Grocer is insolvent. He is permitted to purchase and pay cash for new inventory, such as produce or meat, without the payment being considered preferential. His assets have not been reduced. He has simply traded money for goods to be sold in his business. Similarly, he could buy a new display counter and give the seller a purchase money security interest in the counter until he has paid for it. This would not be considered a preference. The seller of the counter has not gained an unfair advantage over other creditors, and Grocer's assets have not been reduced by the transaction. The unfair advantage comes where an existing creditor tries to take a security interest or obtain a payment of more than his share of the debtor's assets. Then, the creditor has obtained a preference over other creditors, which is what the trustee is allowed to avoid.

The Bankruptcy Act also excepts transfers made in payment of a debt incurred in the ordinary course of the business or financial affairs of the debtor and the transferee and made according to ordinary business terms. Thus, for example, a consumer could pay her monthly utility bills in a timely fashion without the creditor/utility being vulnerable to having the transfer of funds avoided by a trustee. The purpose of this exception is to leave undisturbed normal financial relations, and it is consistent with the general policy of the preference section of the Act to discourage *unusual* action by either a debtor or her creditors when the debtor is moving toward bankruptcy.

Exceptions to the trustee's avoidance power are also made for certain statutory liens, certain other perfected security interests, and cases filed by individual debtors whose debts are primarily consumer debts and the aggregate value of all property affected by the transfer is less than $600.

## Fraudulent Transfers

If a debtor transfers property or incurs an obligation with *intent to hinder, delay, or defraud creditors,* the transfer is *voidable* by the trustee. Transfers of property for less than reasonable value are similarly voidable. Suppose Kasper is in financial difficulty. She "sells" her $15,000 car to her mother for $100 so that her creditors cannot claim it. Kasper did not receive fair consideration for this transfer. The transfer could be declared void by a trustee if it was made within a year before the filing of a bankruptcy petition against Kasper. The provisions of law concerning **fraudulent transfers** are designed to prevent a debtor from concealing or disposing of his property in fraud of creditors. Such transfers may also subject the debtor to criminal penalties and prevent discharge of the debtor's unpaid liabilities.

The *In Re Beckman* case, which follows, illustrates the attempt of some debtors in anticipation of bankruptcy to put some of their assets beyond the reach of their creditors and the response of the trustee who was able to avoid the transfers as fraudulent.

---

## In Re Beckman

### 104 B.R. 866 (Bankr. S.D. Ohio 1989)

In September 1985, Richard and Nancy Beckman believed they collectively owned assets in excess of $3 million and had a joint net worth in excess of $1.5 million. However, after consulting an attorney and having their assets appraised, it became apparent during October 1985 that they had a negative net worth, that they were insolvent, and that bankruptcy was inevitable.

In December, the Beckmans each signed applications to Bankers National Life Insurance Company to purchase $100,000 worth of additional life insurance. At the time, Richard Beckman already had $300,000 in term life insurance, $100,000 in accidental life insurance, $10,000 in whole life, and $14,000 in credit life insurance. On January 11, 1986, Richard Beckman delivered $15,000 in cash to Bankers Life as the initial premium on the two policies ($10,000 on his policy and $5,000 on her policy). The source of the funds was fees earned in his dentistry practice during the preceding October through December. The beneficiaries on all of the insurance policies (except the credit life policy) were either the Beckmans or their children.

On January 9, 1986, the Beckmans signed a Chapter 7 bankruptcy petition, and it was filed on January 14, 1986. The trustee sought to avoid the purchase of insurance from Bankers Life as a fraud on creditors.

---

**Cole, Bankruptcy Judge**    The Beckmans argue that it was perfectly proper and, hence, not fraudulent, to convert nonexempt cash to exempt property—the life insurance policies—on the eve of bankruptcy. Further, according to the Beckmans, the insurance purchase was made merely to "provide for each other and their children in the event that one or both of them died." For these reasons, the Beckmans submit that because the insurance purchase was not fraudulent under either federal or state law, the transfer of $15,000 is not avoidable.

The Trustee maintains the insurance purchase was undertaken with actual intent to hinder, delay and defraud the creditors of the estate, thereby rendering the transaction avoidable pursuant to Bankruptcy Code section 548(a)(1). This section states:

(a) The trustee may avoid any transfer of an interest of the debtor in property or any obligation incurred by the debtor that was made or incurred on or within one year before the date of the filing of the petition, if the debtor voluntarily or involuntarily

(1) made such transfer or incurred such obligation with actual intent to hinder, delay or defraud any entity to which the debtor was or became, on or after the date that such transfer was made or such obligation was incurred, indebted;

The issue for decision is whether the Beckmans' eve-of-bankruptcy conversion of non-exempt cash into exempt life insurance policies constitutes fraudulent conduct or merely prudent pre-bankruptcy planning.

Considerable debate in the case law has been engendered by pre-bankruptcy engineering—i.e., the practice of converting non-exempt property into exempt property in contemplation of filing a bankruptcy case. The general rule which has emerged from the decisional law is that mere conversion of property from non-exempt to exempt status on the eve of bankruptcy does not establish fraud. However, if extrinsic evidence of intent to defraud creditors is adduced, courts have: (1) disallowed the debtor's exemption claim and (2) held that the pre-bankruptcy transactions constitute avoidable fraudulent transfers.

Hence, the Court must determine here whether the Trustee has shown the existence of extrinsic evidence of fraud. Among the circumstances which courts focus upon in determining a debtor's intent in purchasing exempt life insurance on the eve of bankruptcy are the following:

1. Whether there was fair consideration paid for the life insurance policy;
2. Whether the debtor was solvent or insolvent as a result of the transfer or whether he was insolvent at the time of the transfer;
3. The amount of the policy;
4. Whether the debtor intended, in good faith, to provide by moderate premiums some protection to those whom he had a duty to support;
5. The length of time between the purchase of a life insurance policy and the filing of the bankruptcy;
6. The amount of non-exempt property which the debtor had after purchasing the life insurance policy; and

7. The debtor's failure to produce available evidence and to testify with significant preciseness as to the pertinent details of his activities shortly before filing the bankruptcy petition.

Utilizing the foregoing factors as a guide, the Court concludes that in carrying out the insurance purchase the Beckmans intended to defraud their creditors. The factors delineated in paragraphs (2), (5) and (6) of the above list are clearly present. Debtors converted all of their remaining non-exempt property (p6) two days before their bankruptcy petition was filed (p5) and while they were admittedly insolvent (p2).

The amount of insurance purchased by the Beckmans (p3) likewise evinces a fraudulent purpose on their part. Notwithstanding the substantial amount of life insurance they had, the Beckmans consummated the purchase of additional insurance a mere three days prior to their bankruptcy filing. The Beckmans maintain the additional coverage was necessary for the protection of their family. But, having considered the record as a whole, the Court concludes that this testimony is not credible. To purchase an additional $200,000 in life insurance on the eve of bankruptcy and pre-pay the premiums thereon so that the cash surrender value of the policies would be obtainable by the Beckmans upon the termination of their bankruptcy proceeding goes far beyond "providing in good faith by moderate premiums some protection to those to whom they had a duty to support."

Perhaps the most telling indicator of the Beckmans fraudulent intent is their attempted concealment or, at best, obfuscation of the insurance purchase in their bankruptcy schedule and the accompanying schedules.

**Judgment in favor of Trustee avoiding the insurance purchase as made in fraud of creditors.**

## Claims

If creditors wish to participate in the estate of a bankrupt debtor, they must file a **proof of claim** in the estate within a certain time—usually six months—after the first meeting of creditors. Only unsecured creditors are required to file proofs of claims. However, a secured creditor whose secured claim exceeds the value of the collateral is an unsecured creditor to the extent of the deficiency. That creditor must file a proof of claim to support the recovery of the deficiency.

## Allowable Claims

The fact that a proof of claim is filed does not ensure that a creditor can participate in the distribution of the assets of the bankruptcy estate. The claim must also be allowed. If the trustee has a valid defense to the claim, he can use the defense to disallow or reduce it. For example, if the claim is based on goods sold to the debtor and the seller breached a warranty, the trustee can assert the breach as a defense. All of the defenses available to the bankrupt person are available to the trustee.

## Secured Claims

The trustee must also determine whether a creditor has a security interest to secure an allowable claim. As discussed earlier, a party with a perfected Article 9 security interest normally defeats the trustee so long as the security interest is not preferential. This means that the perfected secured party can proceed directly against the collateral or its proceeds. However, the trustee defeats an *unperfected* Article 9 secured party. As described later, such a party is a general creditor. Also, a perfected secured party is a general creditor to the extent that the collateral does not satisfy his debt. A perfected secured party is a general creditor for the whole debt in cases where the perfected security interest is preferential.

## Priority Claims

The Bankruptcy Act declares certain claims to have **priority** over other claims. The six classes of priority claims are:

1. Expenses and fees incurred in administering the bankruptcy estate.
2. Unsecured claims in involuntary cases that arise in the ordinary course of the debtor's business after the filing of the petition but before the appointment of a trustee or the order of relief.

3. Unsecured claims of up to $2,000 per individual for employees' wages, salaries, or commissions earned within 90 days before the petition was filed.
4. Claims of up to $2,000 per person for contributions to an employee benefit plan. Such contributions must arise from services rendered within 180 days before the petition or the cessation of the debtor's business (whichever is earlier). *Note*: The total for this claim and the preceding claim for wages cannot exceed $2,000 per employee.
5. Claims of up to $900 each by individuals for deposits made on goods or services for personal use that were not delivered or provided.
6. Certain taxes owed to governmental units.

## Distribution of the Debtor's Estate

The priority claims are paid *after* protected secured creditors realize on their collateral but *before* general creditors are paid. Payments are made to the six priority classes, in order, to the extent there are funds available. Each class must be paid in full before the next class is entitled to receive anything. To the extent that there are insufficient funds to satisfy all the creditors within a class, each class member receives a pro rata share of his claim.

General creditors include (1) unsecured creditors whose claims are not priority claims; (2) secured Article 9 creditors who did not perfect by the date of bankruptcy; (3) perfected Article 9 secured parties whose security interest is preferential; (4) perfected Article 9 secured parties, to the extent that the collateral does not satisfy the debt they are owed; and (5) priority claimholders, to the extent that their claim exceeds the dollar limits set for the relevant priority. If any funds are available for them, general creditors share in proportion to the amount of their claims. Frequently, they receive little or nothing on those claims. Protected secured claims, trustee fees, and other priority claims often consume a large part of the bankruptcy estate.

Special rules are set out in the Bankruptcy Act for distribution of the property of a bankrupt stockbroker or commodities broker.

# DISTRIBUTION OF A DEBTOR'S ESTATE (CHAPTER 7)

Unless there is a preference, perfected secured creditors proceed directly against the collateral. If debt is fully satisfied, they have no further interest; if debt is only partially satisfied, they are treated as general creditors for the balance.

**Debtor's Estate Is Liquidated and Distributed**

## Priority Creditors (six classes)

1. Costs and expenses of administration.
2. If involuntary proceeding, expenses incurred in the ordinary course of business after petition filed but before appointment of trustee.
3. Claims for wages, salaries, and commissions earned within 90 days of petition; limited to $2,000 per person.
4. Contributions to employee benefit plans arising out of services performed within 180 days of petition; limit of $2,000 (including claims for wages, salaries, and commissions) per person.
5. Claims of individuals, up to $900 per person, for deposits made on consumer goods or services that were not received.
6. Government claims for certain taxes.

   a. Distribution is made to the six classes of priority claims in order.
   b. Each class must be fully paid before the next class receives anything.
   c. If funds available are not sufficient to satisfy everyone in a class, then each member of the class receives the same proportion of claim.

## General Creditors

1. General unsecured creditors and creditors with unperfected security interests.
2. Perfected secured creditors for the portion of their debt that was not satisfied by collateral, or for all the debt if there was a preference.
3. Priority creditors for amounts beyond priority limits.

If funds remaining are not sufficient to satisfy all general creditors, then they each receive the same proportion of their claims.

## Debtor

Debtor receives any remaining funds.

# DISCHARGE IN BANKRUPTCY

## Discharge

A bankrupt person who has not been guilty of certain dishonest acts and has fulfilled his duties as a bankrupt is entitled to a **discharge** in bankruptcy. A discharge relieves the bankrupt person of further responsibility for dischargeable debts and gives him a fresh start. A corporation or a partnership is not eligible for a discharge in bankruptcy. A bankrupt person may file a written waiver of his right to a discharge. An individual may not be granted a discharge if she obtained one within the previous six years.

## Objections to Discharge

After the bankrupt has paid all of the required fees, the court gives creditors and others a chance to file objections to the discharge of the bankrupt. Objections may be filed by the trustee, a creditor, or the U.S. attorney. If objections are filed, the court holds a hearing to listen to them. At the hearing, the court must determine whether the bankrupt person has committed any act that is a bar to discharge. If the bankrupt has not committed such an act, the court grants the discharge. If the bankrupt has committed an act that is a bar to discharge, the discharge is denied. The discharge is also denied if the bankrupt fails to appear at the hearing on objections or if he refused earlier to submit to the questioning of the creditors.

## Acts that Bar Discharge

Discharges in bankruptcy are intended for honest debtors. Therefore, the following acts bar a debtor from being discharged: (1) the unjustified falsifying, concealing, or destroying of records; (2) making false statements, presenting false claims, or withholding recorded information relating to the debtor's property or financial affairs; (3) transferring, removing, or concealing property in order to hinder, delay, or defraud creditors; (4) failing to account satisfactorily for any loss or deficiency of assets; and (5) failing to obey court orders or to answer questions approved by the court. Discharge is also denied where the debtor has previously been discharged in a case begun within six years before the petition in the present case.

## Nondischargeable Debts

Certain debts are not affected by the discharge of a bankrupt debtor. The Bankruptcy Act provides that a discharge in bankruptcy releases a debtor from all provable debts. Exceptions include debts that:

1. Are due as a tax or fine to the United States or any state or local unit of government.
2. Result from liabilities for obtaining money by false pretenses or false representations.
3. Are due for willful or malicious injury to a person or his property.
4. Are due for alimony or child support.
5. Were created by the debtor's larceny or embezzlement or by the debtor's fraud while acting in a fiduciary capacity.
6. Are certain kinds of educational loans that became due within five years prior to the filing of the petition.
7. Were not scheduled in time for proof and allowance because the creditor holding the debt did not have notification of the proceeding even though the debtor was aware that he owed money to that creditor.

The case that follows, *In Re Hott,* involves a denial of discharge of a debt on the grounds that the debtor obtained a loan using a materially false financial statement.

---

## IN RE HOTT

### 99 B.R. 664 (Bankr. W.D. Pa. 1989)

David Hott was a college graduate with a degree in business administration who was employed as an insurance agent. He and his wife graduated from college in 1986. At the time he graduated, Hott had outstanding student loans of $14,500 for which he was given a grace period before he had to repay them.

Hott became unemployed. Bills began to accumulate and a number of outstanding bills were near the credit limits on his accounts. About that time, he received a promotional brochure by mail from Signal Consumer

Discount Company, offering the opportunity to borrow several thousand dollars. The Hotts decided that it appeared to be an attractive vehicle for them to use to consolidate their debts. Hott went to the Signal office and filled out a credit application. He did not list the student loan as a current debt. He later claimed that someone in the office told him he didn't have to list it if he owned an automobile, but there was significant doubt about this claim. Had he listed it, he would not have met the debt/income ratio required by Signal and it would not have made the loan. As it was, Signal agreed to make the loan on the condition that Hott pay off a car debt in order to reduce his debt/income ratio and Hott agreed to do so. On March 30, 1987, Signal loaned the Hotts $3,458.01.

On June 24, 1988, the Hotts filed for bankruptcy. Signal objected to the discharge of the balance remaining on its loan on the grounds that it had been obtained through the use of a materially false financial statement.

---

**Markovitz, Bankruptcy Judge**   Section 523(a)(2)(B) provides that a discharge under section 727 . . . does not discharge an individual debtor from any debt—

(2) for money . . . to the extent obtained by—
(B) use of a statement in writing—
(i) that is materially false;
(ii) respecting the debtor's financial condition;
(iii) on which the creditor to whom the debtor is liable for such money . . . reasonably relied; and
(iv) that the debtor caused to be made with intent to deceive.

The parties agree that Hott did in fact obtain money as a result of his submission to Signal of a written statement of his financial condition. It appears that Hott does not contest Signal's reliance on the statement and it is clear that Signal's loss was proximately caused by Hott's financial statement. It is not clear if Hott concedes that the omission of the student loan caused the statement to be materially false. The major contested issue is whether Hott intentionally deceived Signal as to his true financial status in order to obtain the funds.

Material falsity has been defined as "an important or substantial untruth." It includes any omission, concealment or understatement of the Hotts' material liabilities. By omitting his single largest debt, a debt which by itself is as great as the remainder of his debt in combination, Hott created a material falsity in his financial statement.

Hott asserts that he fully intended to list his student loan debt on the application. He claims that said debt was in fact listed on the payment schedule his wife had prepared for him to take to Signal's office. That paper has admittedly long since been destroyed. Hott claims to have discussed the placement of the student loan with one of Signal's employees. Hott provided a physical description of the alleged employee. Signal's manager advised that the office had only three employees including himself. None of the three people even vaguely matched Hott's description.

Hott claims that the employee told him not to worry about the debt, so he did not. Given the size of the student loan in relation to the remainder of his debt, Hott's attitude certainly qualified as indifference and/or reckless disregard for accuracy.

We additionally reiterate Hott's education and qualifications in relation to his claim of innocence. Hott has a Bachelor's Degree in Business. He admits to having a knowledge of the concept called debt/income ratio and its purpose. Hott would easily have been able to determine that inclusion of his student loan on his application would cause his debt/income ratio to skyrocket. Hott asserts that he never stopped to perform any of the calculations. Hott may not assume the position of an ostrich with his head in the sand and ignore facts which were readily available.

This court finds that Hott's position lacks credibility and that Signal's witness was fully credible. We find at the very least Hott recklessly omitted the existence of his student loan when completing the credit application submitted for Signal's approval. Therefore, the debt must be found to be nondischargeable.

**Judgment in favor of Signal.**

The 1984 amendments established several additional grounds for nondischargeability relating to debts incurred in contemplation of bankruptcy. Congress was concerned about debtors who ran up large expenditures on credit cards shortly before filing for bankruptcy relief. Cash advances in excess of $1,000 obtained by use of a credit card and a revolving line of credit at a credit union obtained within 20 days of filing a bankruptcy petition are presumed to be nondischargeable. Similarly, a debtor's purchase of more than $500 in luxury goods or services on credit from a single creditor within 40 days of filing a petition is presumed to be nondischargeable.

There is also an exception from dischargeability for debts reflected in a judgment arising out of a debtor's operation of a motor vehicle while legally intoxicated.

All of these nondischargeable debts are provable debts. The creditor who owns these claims can participate in the distribution of the bankrupt's estate. However, the creditor has an additional advantage: His right to recover the unpaid balance is not cut off by the bankrupt's discharge. All other provable debts are dischargeable; that is, the right to recover them is cut off by the bankrupt's discharge.

## Reaffirmation Agreements

Sometimes, creditors put pressure on debtors to reaffirm, or to agree to pay, debts that have been discharged in bankruptcy. When the 1978 amendments to the Bankruptcy Act were under consideration, some individuals urged Congress to prohibit such agreements. They argued that reaffirmation agreements were inconsistent with the fresh start philosophy of the Bankruptcy Act. Congress did not agree to a total prohibition; instead, it set up a rather elaborate procedure for a creditor to go through to get a debt reaffirmed. Essentially, the creditor must do so before the discharge is granted, and the court must approve the reaffirmation. The debtor has 60 days after he agrees to a reaffirmation to rescind it. Court approval is not required for the reaffirmation of loans secured by real estate.

A debtor may voluntarily pay any dischargeable obligation without entering into a reaffirmation agreement.

## Dismissal for Substantial Abuse

As it considered the 1984 amendments to the Bankruptcy Act, Congress was concerned that too many individuals with an ability to pay their debts over time pursuant to a Chapter 13 plan (discussed later in this chapter) were filing petitions to obtain Chapter 7 discharges of liability. The consumer finance industry urged Congress to preclude Chapter 7 petitions where a debtor had the prospect of future disposable income to satisfy more than 50 percent of his prepetition unsecured debts. Although Congress rejected this approach, it did authorize Bankruptcy Courts to dismiss cases that they determined were a **substantial abuse** of the bankruptcy process. This provision appears to cover situations where a debtor has acted in bad faith or where she has the present or future ability to pay a significant portion of her current debts.

The case that follows, *In Re Newsom,* illustrates a situation where the court found the filing of a Chapter 7 petition by debtors with the ability to eventually pay off much of the unsecured debt they had accumulated to be a "substantial abuse" of the bankruptcy process.

---

## In Re Newsom

### 69 B.R. 801 (Bankr. D. N.D. 1987)

John and Christine Newsom were noncommissioned officers in the U.S. Air Force who each earned $1,408 net a month. In October 1986, they filed a voluntary petition in bankruptcy under Chapter 7. At the time, they had three secured debts totaling $21,956, $21,820 of which stemmed from the purchase of a 1986 Ford Bronco and a 1985 Pontiac Trans Am. They proposed to surrender the Bronco and a secured television set to the trustee, leaving $10,000 owing on the Pontiac as the only secured debt. Their unsecured debts totaled $20,911: $6,611 from bank card use, $12,764 from retail credit, and $1,350 from credit union loans. Of the unsecured debt, $11,563 was incurred in 1986.

The Newsoms filed an income and expense schedule showing that their monthly expenses totaled $2,232, including $100 per month for recreation and $150 for cigarettes and "walk around money." This left a surplus of $276 per month. The Bankruptcy Court, on its own motion, issued an order to the Newsoms to show why their petition should not be dismissed pursuant to the substantial abuse provision of the Bankruptcy Code.

───────────────◾───────────────

**Hill, Bankruptcy Judge**    Section 707(b) of the Bankruptcy Code, providing for the dismissal of Chapter 7 cases, provides as follows:

(b) After notice and a hearing, the court on its own motion or on a motion by the United States Trustee but not at the request or suggestion of any party in interest, may dismiss a case filed by an individual debtor under this chapter whose debts are primarily consumer debts if it finds that the granting of relief would be a substantial abuse of the provisions of this chapter. There shall be a presumption in favor of granting the relief requested by the debtor.

This section was enacted as part of the consumer credit amendments to the Bankruptcy Act in 1984 as a means of combating what Congress viewed as an abuse of Chapter 7 by consumer debtors who had the ability to pay.

From the developing case law, this court has adopted the following as criteria against which the facts of a particular case ought to be judged in determining whether substantial abuse exists sufficient to mandate dismissal under section 707(b):

1. Whether the debtors have a likelihood of sufficient future income to fund a Chapter 13 plan which would pay a substantial portion of the secured claims;

2. Whether the debtors' petition was filed as a consequence of illness, disability, unemployment or some other calamity;

3. Whether the schedules suggest the debtors incurred cash advances and consumer purchases in excess of their ability to repay them;

4. Whether the debtors' proposed family budget is excessive or extravagant;

5. Whether the debtors' statement of income and expenses is misrepresentative of their true financial condition.

The Newsoms' unsecured obligations are composed exclusively of consumer debt. Their schedule of unsecured debt is highly suggestive of individuals who, already aware of their financial limitations and already faced with financial difficulties, went ahead and rang up at least $11,500 of consumer debt in 1986—an amount equal to thirty percent of their combined annual net income and which was incurred when they already had unsecured obligations of over $9,000. Even worse, they apparently purchased a second vehicle during this time period. Such action can only be regarded by the court as a completely irresponsible use of credit for non-essential items.

The Newsoms' proposed family budget seems extravagant insofar as they profess to need $250 for entertainment and recreation, including $150 for cigarettes and "walk around money." The court finds this aspect of the budget unacceptable. It appears that the Newsoms are making no effort to tighten their belts or maintain a conservative life style. With a combined annual net income of nearly $34,000 and no dependents, the Newsoms are far better off than many and ought to be able to live quite comfortably while at the same time making an effort to pay back at least a portion of their unsecured creditors.

The ability to pay back a substantial portion of unsecured debt does not require an ability to pay back one hundred percent. All that is required is that the payback be significant and that there be a likelihood of sufficient future income to maintain such a payback. In the present case, assuming future income and expenses remain stable, the Newsoms would at a minimum, be able to contribute $276 per month or $3,312 per year toward a repayment plan. Over a three-year period, they would have contributed $9,936 resulting in a repayment of forty-seven percent of their unsecured claims. Contributions over a five-year period would result in an eighty-percent payback. None of these figures can be regarded as insignificant as far as creditors are concerned and strongly suggest that a meaningful payback could be accomplished. An even greater payback could be accomplished by honing the Newsoms' entertainment budget to a more realistic level. At any rate, this court believes that the Newsoms have the financial means at hand and will continue to have the means to fund a Chapter 13 plan which

would retire a substantial portion of the unsecured claims.

**Newsoms' petition for Chapter 7 relief dismissed.**

## CHAPTER 11: REORGANIZATIONS

### Reorganization Proceeding

Sometimes, creditors benefit more from the continuation of a bankrupt debtor's business than from the liquidation of the debtor's property. Chapter 11 of the Bankruptcy Act provides a proceeding whereby, under the supervision of the Bankruptcy Court, the debtor's financial affairs can be reorganized rather than liquidated. Chapter 11 proceedings are available to individuals and to virtually all business enterprises, including individual proprietorships, partnerships, and corporations (except banks, savings and loan associations, insurance companies, commodities brokers, and stockbrokers).

Petitions for reorganization proceedings can be filed voluntarily by the debtor or involuntarily by its creditors. Once a petition for a reorganization proceeding is filed and relief is ordered, the court usually appoints (1) a committee of creditors holding unsecured claims, (2) a committee of equity security holders (shareholders), and (3) a trustee. The trustee may be given the responsibility for running the debtor's business. He is also usually responsible for developing a plan for handling the various claims of creditors and the various interests of persons such as shareholders.

The reorganization plan is essentially a contract between a debtor and its creditors. This contract may involve recapitalizing a debtor corporation and/or giving creditors some equity, or shares, in the corporation in exchange for part or all of the debt owed to them. The plan must (1) divide the creditors into classes; (2) set forth how each creditor will be satisfied; (3) state which claims, or classes of claims, are impaired or adversely affected by the plan; and (4) provide the same treatment to each creditor in a particular class, unless the creditors in that class consent to different treatment.

The plan is then submitted to the creditors for approval. Approval generally requires that creditors holding two thirds in amount and one half in number of each class of claims impaired by the plan must accept it. Once approved, the plan goes before the court for confirmation. If the plan is confirmed, the debtor is responsible for carrying it out.

The case that follows, *Official Committee of Equity Security Holders v. Mabey,* shows that until a plan is confirmed, the bankruptcy court has no authority to distribute a portion of the bankruptcy assets to a portion of the unsecured creditors.

## OFFICIAL COMMITTEE OF EQUITY SECURITY HOLDERS V. MABEY
### 832 F.2d 299 (4th Cir. 1987)

The A. H. Robins Company is a publicly held company that filed a voluntary petition for relief under Chapter 11 of the Bankruptcy Code. Robins sought refuge in Chapter 11 because of a multitude of civil actions filed against it by women who alleged they were injured by use of the Dalkon Shield intrauterine device that it manufactured and sold as a birth control device. Approximately 325,000 notices of claim against Robins were received by the Bankruptcy Court.

In 1985, the court appointed the Official Committee of Equity Security Holders to represent the interest of Robins's public shareholders. In April 1987, Robins filed a proposed plan of reorganization, but no action was taken on the proposed plan because of a merger proposal submitted by Rorer Group, Inc. Under this plan, Dalkon Shield claimants would be compensated out of a $1.75 billion fund, all other creditors would be paid in full, and Robins's stockholders would receive stock of the merged corporation. However, at the time of other critical activity in the bankruptcy proceeding, no revised plan incorporating the merger proposal had been filed or approved.

Earlier, in August 1986, the court had appointed Ralph Mabey as an examiner to evaluate and suggest proposed elements of a plan of reorganization. On Mabey's suggestion, a proposed order was put before the district court supervising the proceeding that would require Robins to establish a $15 million emergency treatment fund "for the purpose of assisting in providing tubal reconstructive surgery or in-vitro fertilization to eligible Dalkon Shield claimants." The purpose of the emergency fund was to assist those claimants who asserted that they had become infertile as a consequence of their use of the product. A program was proposed for administering the fund and for making the medical decisions required.

On May 21, 1987, the district court ordered that the emergency treatment fund be created, and the action was challenged by the committee representing the equity security holders.

---

**Chapman, Circuit Judge**     The May 21, 1987, order of the district court approving the Emergency Treatment Fund makes no mention of its authority to establish such a fund prior to the allowance of the claims of the women who would benefit from the fund, and prior to the confirmation of a plan of reorganization of Robins. In its order denying the Equity Committee's Motion for a Stay Pending Appeal of the May 21 order, the district court relied on the "expansive equity power" of the court to justify its action.

While one may understand and sympathize with the district court's concern for the Dalkon Shield claimants who may desire reconstructive surgery or in-vitro fertilization, the creation of the Emergency Treatment Fund at this stage of the Chapter 11 bankruptcy proceedings violates the clear language and intent of the Bankruptcy Code, and such action may not be justified as an exercise of the court's equitable powers.

The Bankruptcy Code does not permit a distribution to unsecured creditors in a Chapter 11 proceeding except under and pursuant to a plan of reorganization that has been properly presented and approved. Sections 1122–1129 of the Bankruptcy Code set forth the required contents of the reorganization plan, the classification of claims, the requirements of disclosure of the contents of the plan, the method for accepting the plan, the hearing required on confirmation of the plan, and the requirements for confirmation. The clear language of these statutes does not authorize the payment in part or full, or the advance of monies to or for the benefit of unsecured claimants prior to the approval of the plan of reorganization. The creation of the Emergency Treatment Fund has no authority to support it in the Bankruptcy Code and violates the clear policy of Chapter 11 reorganizations by allowing piecemeal pre-confirmation payments to certain unsecured creditors. Such action also violates Bankruptcy Rule 3021 which allows distribution to creditors only after the allowance of claims and the confirmation of a plan.

**Judgment reversed in favor of Official Committee of Equity Security Holders.**

---

## Use of Chapter 11

During the 1980s, attempts by a number of corporations to seek refuge in Chapter 11 as a means of escaping problems they were facing received considerable public attention. Some of the most visible cases involved efforts to obtain some protection against massive product liability claims and judgments for damages for breach of contract and to escape from collective bargaining agreements. Thus, for example, Johns-Manville Corporation filed under Chapter 11 because of the claims against it arising out of its production and sale of asbestos years earlier, while A. H. Robins Company, as illustrated in the preceding case, was concerned about a surfeit of claims arising out of its sale of the Dalkon Shield, an intrauterine birth control device. And, in 1987, Texaco, Inc., faced with a $10.3 billion judgment in favor of Pennzoil, filed a petition for reorganizational relief under Chapter 11. Companies such as LTV and Allegheny Industries sought changes in retirement and pension plans, and other companies such as Eastern Airlines sought refuge in Chapter 11 while embroiled in labor disputes.

As the 1990s began, a number of companies that were the subject of highly leveraged buyouts (LBOs) financed with so-called junk bonds, including a number of retailers, resorted to Chapter 11 to seek restructuring and relief from their creditors. Similarly, companies such as Pan Am and TWA that were hurt by the economic slowdown and the increase in fuel prices filed Chapter 11 petitions.

In recent years, Chapter 11 has been the subject of significant criticism and calls for its revision. Critics point out that many of the Chapter 11 cases are permitted to drag on for years, thus depleting the assets of the debtor through payments to trustees and lawyers involved in administration and diminishing the assets available to creditors.

## Collective Bargaining Agreements

Collective bargaining contracts pose special problems. Prior to the 1984 amendments, there was concern that some companies would use Chapter 11 reorganizations as a vehicle to avoid executed collective bargaining agreements. The concern was heightened by the Supreme Court's 1984 decision in *NLRB v. Bildisco and Bildisco*. In that case, the Supreme Court held that a reorganizing debtor did not have to engage in collective bargaining before modifying or rejecting portions of a collective bargaining agreement and that such unilateral alterations by a debtor did not violate the National Labor Relations Act.

Congress then acted to try to prevent the misuse of bankruptcy proceedings for collective bargaining purposes. The act's 1984 amendments adopt a rigorous multistep process that must be complied with in determining whether a labor contract can be rejected or modified as part of a reorganization. Among other things that must be done before a debtor or trustee can seek to avoid a collective bargaining agreement are the submission of a proposal to the employees' representative that details the "necessary" modifications to the collective bargaining agreement and ensures that "all creditors, the debtor and all affected parties are fairly treated." Then, before the bankruptcy court can authorize a rejection of the original collective bargaining agreement, it must review the proposal and find that (1) the employees' representative refused to accept it without good cause, and (2) the balance of equities clearly favors the rejection of the original collective bargaining agreement.

The following case, *In Re Royal Composing Room, Inc.,* shows the scrutiny that the court gives the action of a debtor seeking to avoid a collective bargaining agreement.

---

## IN RE ROYAL COMPOSING ROOM, INC.
**78 B.R. 671 (S.D. N.Y. 1987)**

Royal Composing Room, Inc., is an advertising typography company, one of the last unionized shops in an industry that was subjected to considerable stress as computer technology replaced the linotype machine. Royal was a party to a collective bargaining agreement with Typographical Union No. 6. Royal was a profitable company until 1982, when its gross revenues declined by $2 million; over the next four years, it sustained operating losses. Confronted with these difficulties, in 1983 Royal began to cut expenses by sharply cutting the compensation of its principal executives, freezing the salaries of salespeople and middle management foremen, eliminating company automobiles, and moving to a smaller location to save rent. At the start of 1986, Royal lost its largest customer, Doyle Dane Bernbach, Inc., and sought to convince the union, which theretofore had not made any sacrifices or concessions, to forgo a 3 percent wage increase agreed to earlier. When the union refused, Royal filed a petition for reorganization under Chapter 11 and sought to reject its collective bargaining agreement.

Under section 1113(b) of the Bankruptcy Code, before it could reject the collective bargaining agreement, Royal was required to make a proposal to the union "which provides for those necessary modifications in the employees' benefits and protections that are necessary to permit the reorganization of the debtor and assures that all creditors, the debtor and all of the affected parties are treated fairly and equally." Royal held a meeting with officials of the union and offered a proposal that included a reduction of benefits, changes in work rules, the elimination of the scheduled wage increase, and the elimination of the union's right to arbitration as the way to change the contract. The union rejected the proposal and did not negotiate.

After a trial before the bankruptcy judge, Royal's motion to reject the existing collective bargaining contract was granted. The union then appealed to the District Court.

---

**Keenan, District Judge**     Local 6 raises two arguments on appeal: (1) the Bankruptcy Court did not apply the proper definition of "necessary" under section 1113, and (2) Royal's proposal did not treat all affected parties fairly and equitably. Both positions are unavailing.

The Second Circuit has indicated that the term "necessary" contained in section 1113 does not mean "essential" or "bare minimum." It has ruled that "the necessary requirement places on the debtor the burden of proving that its proposal is made in good faith, and that it contains necessary, but not absolutely minimal, changes that will enable the debtor to complete the reorganization process successfully."

Applying the standard of necessity endorsed by the Second Circuit, Bankruptcy Judge Abram found that Royal had, "established that it had in good faith attempted to negotiate for necessary changes but had been unsuccessful because of the union's unwillingness to engage in serious discussions." The record supports this finding. Local 6 was unresponsive and dilatory in the face of management's financial condition and resulting proposal. Likewise, Judge Abram was correct in her analysis of Royal's proposal. She found that Royal had cut nonunion management and executive salaries, eliminated trade association memberships, and even reused old doorknobs. During this time, union labor costs were the only expenses not cut.

The correctness of Judge Abram's legal conclusion is bolstered by the Second Circuit's statement in *Carey Transportation* that courts "must consider whether rejection of a collective bargaining agreement would increase the likelihood of successful reorganization." This court cannot envision Royal being able to successfully reorganize absent at least enforcement of its proposal under section 1113. Rejection clearly increases the likelihood of successful reorganization.

Local 6 further asserts that Royal did not satisfy the statutory requirement that under the proposal "all creditors, the debtor and all affected parties are treated fairly and equitably." Judge Abram correctly found that Royal "had spread the burden of financial sacrifice." As noted earlier, Royal cut costs in many ways, including a decrease in executive compensation, the rescinding of raises and freezing of salaries of salesmen and middle level management, the elimination of company cars, and the moving of its premises to smaller quarters. The union's wages were neither frozen nor cut. The Second Circuit observed that a debtor need not show that managers and nonunion employees have their benefits cut to the degree union benefits are cut. In this case, the union's benefits were the last to be cut, and it certainly was not the only constituency in Royal to feel the financial pinch. Royal's proposal satisfied the statute's requirement of fairness and equity.

**Judgment of the Bankruptcy Court rejecting the collective bargaining agreement affirmed.**

# CHAPTER 12: FAMILY FARMS

## Relief for Family Farmers

Historically, farmers have been accorded special treatment in the Bankruptcy Code. In the 1978 act, as in earlier versions, small farmers were exempted from involuntary proceedings. Thus, a small farmer who filed a voluntary Chapter 11 or 13 petition could not have the proceeding converted into a Chapter 7 liquidation over his objection so long as he complied with the act's requirements in a timely fashion. Additional protection was also accorded through the provision allowing states to opt out of the federal exemption scheme and to provide their own exemptions. A number of states used this flexibility to provide generous exemptions for farmers so they would be able to keep their tools and implements.

Despite these provisions, the serious stress on the agricultural sector in the mid-1980s led Congress in 1986 to further amend the Bankruptcy Act by adding a new Chapter 12 targeted to the financial problems of the family farm. During the 1970s and 1980s, farmland prices appreciated and many farmers borrowed heavily to expand their productive capacity, creating a large debt load in the agricultural sector. When land values subsequently dropped and excess production in the world kept farm product prices low, many farmers faced extreme financial difficulty.

Chapter 12 is modeled after Chapter 13, which is discussed next. It is available only for family farmers with regular income. To qualify, a farmer and spouse must have not less than 80 percent of their total noncontingent, liquidated debts arising out of their farming operations. The aggregate debt must be less than $1.5 million, and at least 50 percent of an individual's or couple's income during the year preceding the filing of the petition must have come from the farming operation. A corporation or partnership can also qualify, provided that more than 50 percent of the stock or equity is held by one family or its relatives and they conduct the farming operation. Again, 80 percent of the debt must arise from the farming operation; the aggregate debt ceiling is $1.5 million.

The debtor is usually permitted to remain in possession to operate the farm. Although the debtor in possession has many of the rights of a Chapter 11

trustee, a trustee is appointed under Chapter 12 and the debtor is subject to his supervision. The trustee is permitted to sell unnecessary assets, including farmland and equipment, without the consent of secured creditors and before a plan is approved. However, the secured creditor's interest attaches to the proceeds of the sale.

The debtor is required to file a plan within 90 days of the filing of the Chapter 12 petition—although the bankruptcy court has the discretion to extend the time. A hearing is held on the proposed plan, and it can be confirmed over the objection of creditors. The debtor may release to any secured party the collateral that secures the claim to obtain confirmation without the acceptance by that creditor.

Unsecured creditors are required to receive at least liquidation value under the Chapter 12 plan. If an unsecured creditor or the trustee objects to the plan, the court may still confirm the plan despite the objection so long as it calls for full payment of the unsecured creditor's claim or it provides that the debtor's disposable income for the duration of the plan is applied to making payments on it. A debtor who fulfills his plan, or is excused from full performance because of subsequent hardship, is entitled to a discharge.

# CHAPTER 13: CONSUMER DEBT ADJUSTMENTS

## Relief for Individuals

Chapter 13 of the Bankruptcy Act, entitled Adjustments of Debts for Individuals, gives individuals who do not want to be declared bankrupt an opportunity to pay their debts in installments under the protection of a federal court. Under Chapter 13, the debtor has this opportunity free of such problems as garnishments and attachments of her property by creditors. Only individuals with regular incomes (including sole proprietors of businesses) who owe individually (or with their spouse) liquidated, unsecured debts of less than $100,000 and secured debts of less than $350,000 are eligible to file under Chapter 13. Under the pre-1978 Bankruptcy Act, Chapter 13 proceedings were known as "wage earner plans." The 1978 amendments expanded the coverage of these proceedings.

## Procedure

Chapter 13 proceedings are initiated only by the voluntary petition of a debtor filed in the Bankruptcy Court. Creditors of the debtor may not file an involuntary petition for a Chapter 13 proceeding. The debtor in the petition states that he is insolvent or unable to pay his debts as they mature and that he desires to effect a composition or an extension, or both, out of future earnings or income. A **composition of debts** is an arrangement whereby the amount the person owes is reduced, whereas an **extension** provides the person a longer period of time in which to pay his debts. Commonly, the debtor files at the same time a list of his creditors as well as a list of his assets, liabilities, and executory contracts.

Following the filing of the petition, the court calls a meeting of creditors, at which time proofs of claims are received and allowed or disallowed. The debtor is examined, and she submits a plan of payment. The plan is submitted to the secured creditors for acceptance. If they accept the plan and if the court is satisfied that the plan is proposed in good faith, meets the legal requirements, and is in the interest of the creditors, the court approves the plan. The court then appoints a trustee to carry out the plan. The plan must provide for payments over three years or less, unless the court approves a longer period of up to five years.

No plan may be approved if the trustee or an unsecured creditor objects, unless the plan provides for the objecting creditor to be paid the present value of what he is owed or provides for the debtor to commit all of his projected disposable income for a three-year period to pay his creditors.

The case that follows, *In Re Tucker,* deals with the issue of whether a proposed plan that provided for the commitment of all disposable income for a four-year period should be rejected because it unfairly discriminated against a class of unsecured creditors.

---

## In Re Tucker

### 159 B.R. 325 (Bankr. D.Mont. 1993)

Daniel and Betty Tucker filed a voluntary Chapter 13 petition on March 10, 1993, listing personal property totaling $3,015. They claimed virtually all of the personal property as exempt, except for $180 worth of an automobile that exceeded the allowed exemption. Their real property was either encumbered or exempt, leaving little available for distribution to unsecured creditors in the event of liquidation. They also listed unsecured claims in the amount of $14,208, of which $4,183 were claims for student loans. The remainder of claims were for services and purchases, all of which would be dischargeable.

In August 1993, the Tuckers filed a Chapter 13 plan that provided for monthly payments in the amount of $115, which corresponded to the difference between their current income and expenditures as shown on the schedules they filed with their petition. The plan provided for payment in full of the student loan debts over a 48-month period and 29 percent of the claims to the other unsecured creditors. The Trustee, relying on objections from unsecured creditors, filed an objection to the plan on the grounds that it discriminated unfairly against a class of unsecured claims.

---

**Peterson, Bankruptcy Judge**    At issue is whether the Plan unfairly discriminates against the unsecured creditors in violation of Bankruptcy Code section 1322(b)(1) by paying nondischargeable student loan debts in full while only paying a 29% dividend on the other secured claims. The Tuckers argue that the discrimination in the Plan is fair because it allows them to pay the student loans in full, which fulfills the intent of Congress in making student loans nondischargeable; the Plan pays 29% to the unsecured creditors where they would receive virtually nothing if the case were in Chapter 7; and finally it gives the Tuckers a "fresh start."

In determining whether a Plan discriminates unfairly against a class of unsecured claims, courts have developed a four-part test: (1) whether the discrimination has a reasonable basis; (2) whether the Debtor can carry out a Plan without discrimination; (3) whether the discrimination is proposed in good faith; and (4) whether the degree of discrimination is directly related to the basis or rationale for the discrimination.

The court in *In re Smallberger* (Bankr. D.Or. 1993) found discrimination in favor of student loans unfair and refused to allow separate classification simply on the basis that they were nondischargeable or in the interests of the debtor's "fresh start." The court in *In re Tucker* (Bankr. N.D.Ohio 1992) likewise found unfair discrimination in a plan which proposed paying 100% of student loans over 48 months while paying the unsecured claims five percent. The court deemed repayment of nondischargeable student loans to be the debtor's problem "which he cannot foist off on his other unsecured creditors."

Even the court in *Smallberger* notes that a "debtor might accomplish the result sought here by filing a chapter 7 case and then a chapter 13 case to deal with the nondischargeable obligations." This focuses the inquiry on whether the discrimination is indeed "unfair." Debtors in Chapter 13 have the unwaivable right to convert to Chapter 7 at any time. The parties agree that if the Debtors converted this case to Chapter 7 all of the unsecured claims would get virtually nothing after administrative expenses and their claims would be discharged with the exception of the student loan debts. The student loan debts, while not discharged, would be paid voluntarily by the Debtors from post-petition income in Chapter 7 as they would be under the proposed Chapter 13 Plan. By preventing the discrimination in favor of nondischargeable student loans, the courts in *Smallberger* and *Tucker* encourage debtors to utilize Chapter 7 instead of Chapter 13, despite Congressional intent favoring Chapter 13.

This court, looking at the facts on a case-by-case basis, deems a liquidation analysis highly significant. If this case is converted to a Chapter 7 case, the unsecured creditors will receive nothing and have their claims discharged. If the Plan is confirmed, they will receive 29% of their claims. The fairer treatment for the creditors is clearly the 29% dividend in Chapter 13 which Congress encourages Debtors to use in lieu of Chapter 7. The creditors who filed the rejections of the proposed Plan cannot hope to thereby force a larger dividend upon these Debtors (the Tuckers), who have nothing to lose by converting to Chapter 7, except all the unsecured claims which are not student loan debts.

Turning to the four-part test, I first find that the discrimination has a reasonable basis, i.e. that it provides for the payment in full of nondischargeable student loans. Second, I find that the Debtor cannot carry out a Plan without the discrimination. The Debtors already have extended the Plan period to four years, longer than the three year period of Bankruptcy Code section 1322(c). If the discrimination is not allowed the Plan payments would be completed without the student loans paid in full, thereby leaving the Debtors saddled with debt after four years under a Plan and defeating their "fresh start."

Third, I find that the discrimination is proposed in good faith. There is nothing to suggest that these Debtors proposed the discrimination in bad faith. Fourth, I find the degree of discrimination is directly related to the basis or rationale for the discrimination. They commit their disposable income for four years to the Plan, thereby providing a 29% dividend for creditors who would otherwise be left out in the cold in Chapter 7. The Plan pays in full a nondischargeable student loan and provides the Debtors with a "fresh start" at the end of 48 months free from all debts.

**Objections to confirmation overruled.**

---

Under the 1984 amendments, a Chapter 13 debtor must begin making the installment payments proposed in her plan within 30 days after the plan is filed. The interim payments must continue to be made until the plan is confirmed or denied. If the plan is denied, the money, less any administrative expenses, is returned to the debtor by the trustee. The interim payments give the trustee an opportunity to observe the debtor's performance and thus to be in a better position to make a recommendation about whether the plan should be approved.

Once approved, a plan may be subsequently modified on petition of a debtor or a creditor where there is a material change in the debtor's circumstances.

Suppose Curtis Brown has a monthly take-home pay of $1,000 and a few assets. He owes $1,500 to the credit union, borrowed for the purchase of furniture; he is supposed to repay the credit union $75 per month. He owes $1,800 to the finance company on the purchase of a used car; he is supposed to repay the company $90 a month. He has also run up charges of $1,200 on a MasterCard account, primarily for emergency repairs to his car; he must pay $60 per month to MasterCard. His rent is $350 per month, and food and other living expenses run him another $425 per month. Curtis was laid off from his job for a month and fell behind on his payments to his creditors. He then filed a Chapter 13 petition. In his plan, he might, for example, offer to repay the credit union $50 a month, the finance company $60 a month, and MasterCard $40 a month—with the payments spread over three years rather than the shorter time for which they are currently scheduled.

## Discharge

When the debtor has completed her performance of the plan, the court issues an order that discharges her from the debts covered by the plan. The debtor may also be discharged even though she did not complete her payments within the three years if the court is satisfied that the failure is due to circumstances for which the debtor cannot justly be held accountable. An active Chapter 13 proceeding stays, or holds in abeyance, any straight bankruptcy proceedings and any actions by creditors to collect consumer debts. However, if the Chapter 13 proceeding is dismissed (for example, because the debtor fails to file an acceptable plan or defaults on an accepted plan), straight bankruptcy proceedings may begin.

## Advantages of Chapter 13

A debtor may choose to file under Chapter 13 to avoid the stigma of bankruptcy or to retain more of his property than is exempt from bankruptcy under state law. Chapter 13 can provide some financial discipline to a debtor as well as an opportunity to get his financial affairs back in good shape. It also gives him relief from the pressures of individual creditors so long as he makes the payments called for by the plan. The debtor's creditors may benefit by recovering a greater percentage of the debt owed to them than would be obtainable in straight bankruptcy.

**CONCEPT REVIEW**

## COMPARISON OF MAJOR FORMS OF BANKRUPTCY PROCEEDINGS

| Purpose | Chapter 7 Liquidation | Chapter 11 Reorganization | Chapter 12 Adjustments of Debts | Chapter 13 Adjustments of Debts |
|---|---|---|---|---|
| **Eligible Debtors** | Individuals, partnerships, and corporations *except* municipal corporations, railroads, insurance companies, banks, and savings and loan associations. Farmers and ranchers are eligible only if they petition voluntarily. | Generally same as Chapter 7 except a railroad may be a debtor, and a stockbroker and commodity broker may not be a debtor under Chapter 11. | Family farmer with regular income, at least 50 percent of which comes from farming, and less than $1.5 million in debts, at least 80 percent of which is farm related. | Individual with regular income with liquidated unsecured debts less than $100,000 and secured debts of less than $350,000. |

| Purpose | Chapter 7 Liquidation | Chapter 11 Reorganization | Chapter 12 Adjustments of Debts | Chapter 13 Adjustments of Debts |
|---|---|---|---|---|
| **Initiation of Proceeding** | Petition by debtor (voluntary). Petition by creditors (involuntary). | Petition by debtor (voluntary). Petition by creditors (involuntary). | Petition by debtor. | Petition by debtor. |
| **Basic Procedure** | 1. Appointment of trustee. 2. Debtor retains exempt property. 3. Nonexempt property is sold and proceeds distributed based on priority of claims. 4. Dischargeable debts are terminated. | 1. Appointment of trustee and committees of creditors and equity security holders. 2. Debtor submits reorganization plan. 3. If plan is approved and implemented, debts are discharged. | 1. Trustee is appointed but debtor usually remains in possession of farm. 2. Debtor submits a plan in which unsecured creditors must receive at least liquidation value. 3. If plan is approved and fulfilled, debtor is entitled to a discharge. | 1. Debtor indicates in petition that he is seeking a composition of debts or an extension. 2. If plan is approved after submitted to creditors, then trustee is appointed. 3. If plan is approved and fulfilled, debts covered by plan are discharged. |
| **Advantages** | After liquidation and distribution of assets, most or all of debts may be discharged and debtor gets a fresh start. | Debtor remains in business and debts are liquidated through implementation of approved reorganization plan. | Debtor generally remains in possession and has opportunity to work out of financial difficulty over period of time (usually three years) through implementation of approved plan. | Debtor has opportunity to work out of financial difficulty over period of time (usually three years) through implementation of approved plan. |

## PROBLEMS AND PROBLEM CASES

**1.** Gilbert and Kimberly Barnes filed a voluntary Chapter 7 petition in the U.S. Bankruptcy Court for the District of Maryland. Subsequently, they moved to avoid a nonpurchase money lien held by ITT Financial Services on their exempt "household goods." Among the goods that the Barneses were claiming as "household goods" were a videocassette recorder (VCR), a 12-gauge pump shotgun, a 20-gauge shotgun, a 30–06 rifle, and a .22 pistol. ITT contended that the VCR and the firearms were not household goods that they could exempt. Under Maryland law, household goods are items of personal property reasonably necessary for the day-to-day existence of people in the context of their homes. Should the court consider the VCR and firearms to be "household goods"?

**2.** On June 29, 1979, Gary Johnson filed a Chapter 13 bankruptcy petition. Acting on the advice of his lawyer shortly before filing the petition, Johnson sold an interest in real estate and used the proceeds to buy a life insurance policy with a face value of $31,460 and a cash value of $12,118. His wife was named as the beneficiary. Johnson claimed that the policy was exempt under South Dakota law, which provides for an exemption of up to $20,000 for the proceeds of a life insurance policy payable directly to the insured, his surviving spouse, or his family. A creditor objected to the exemption but made no showing of fraudulent intent on Johnson's part. Should the exemption be allowed?

**3.** On October 19, 1976, Wallace Tuttle, an attorney, and Peninsula Roofing entered into a retainer agreement for the performance of legal services at a stipulated hourly rate. In 1978 and 1979,

Peninsula became delinquent in its payments for attorney's fees. The delinquencies reflected overall corporate financial problems that resulted in the permanent closing of Peninsula on July 25, 1979. On August 6, 1979, Peninsula received a check for $3,250 representing an account receivable due it. Peninsula turned the check over to Tuttle, who deposited it to his trust account, credited $1,946.96 against the past-due account, and created a trust fund from which payments for current services and disbursements would be made. On October 18, 1979, an involuntary petition was filed against Peninsula. The bankruptcy trustee sought to require Tuttle to return the $3,250 to him as a preferential payment. Should Tuttle be required to return the money he received?

**4.** William Kranich, Jr., was the sole shareholder in the DuVal Financial Corporation (DFC). On November 10, 1981, Kranich filed a voluntary petition for relief under Chapter 7; on January 6, 1982, DFC also filed a voluntary petition under Chapter 7. Prior to the commencement of the Chapter 7 proceedings, Kranich conveyed his personal residence in Clearwater, Florida, to DFC. The transfer was wholly without consideration. Shortly thereafter, DFC transferred the property to William Kranich III and June Elizabeth Kranich, Kranich's son and daughter, as tenants in common. This transfer was also without consideration. The bankruptcy trustee brought suit to recover the property from the son and daughter on the grounds that the transfer was fraudulent. Could the trustee recover the property on the grounds that its transfer, without consideration, was fraudulent?

**5.** Barnhart had borrowed money from Credit Plan and was behind in her payments. She applied for a new loan with which she intended to pay the existing loan and the interest on it. At the time the new loan was granted, the agent of Credit Plan prepared a financial statement showing that Barnhart owed $837.50. In fact, she owed approximately $1,800. The agent was a schoolmate of Barnhart's and was familiar with her financial affairs. At the time the statement was prepared, Barnhart talked to the agent about her other debts. She signed the statement without reading it. Credit Plan filed objections to Barnhart's discharge on the ground that she had obtained credit on a materially false credit statement in writing. Should Barnhart be denied a discharge on this ground?

**6.** While attending college, Barbara Barrington obtained a student loan from the New York State Higher Education Services Corporation. Barrington had had depressive illnesses all her life, as had previous generations in her family: Her grandmother was institutionalized for depression, and her mother had been on medication to treat depression for a long time. Barrington was discharged by Eastman Kodak Company because she could not face the problems and stress of her job. Since that time, she had stayed at home, slept a lot, and played with her dog. She made little or no effort to find other employment because of her depressed condition. She also filed for bankruptcy. In the bankruptcy proceeding, one of the questions was whether payment of her student loan would impose an undue hardship on Barrington, and thus whether the loan was dischargeable. Should the student loan be discharged?

**7.** On December 19, 1986, Brian Scholz was involved in an automobile collision with a person insured by The Travelers Insurance Company. At the time, Scholz was cited for, and plead no contest to, a criminal charge of driving under the influence of alcohol arising out of the accident. The Travelers paid its insured $4,303.68 and was subrogated to the rights of its insured against Scholz. Subsequently, The Travelers filed a civil action against Scholz to recover the amount it had paid, and a default judgment was entered against Scholz. Eleven months later, Scholz sought relief from the bankruptcy court by filing a voluntary petition under Chapter 7. One of the questions in the bankruptcy proceeding was whether the debt owing to The Travelers was nondischargeable. Is the debt dischargeable?

**8.** Bryant filed a Chapter 7 petition on January 7, 1984. On March 8, she filed an application to reaffirm an indebtedness owed to General Motors Acceptance Corporation (GMAC) on her 1980 Cadillac automobile. Bryant was not married, and she supported two teenage daughters. She was not currently employed, and she collected $771 a month in unemployment benefits and $150 a month in rental income from her mother. Her monthly house payments were $259. The present value of the Cadillac was $9,175; she owed $7,956.37 on it, and her monthly payments were $345.93. Bryant indicated that she wanted to keep the vehicle because it was reliable. GMAC admitted that Bryant had been, and continued to be, current in her payments. GMAC said that the car was in no danger of being repossessed but that, absent reaffirmation, it might decide to repossess it. Should the court grant Bryant's application to reaffirm her indebtedness to GMAC?

**9.** Winifred Doersam was the borrower on three student loans made to her by First Federal Savings and Loan and guaranteed by the state of Ohio Student Loan Commission (OSLC) totaling $10,000 to finance her graduate education at the University of Dayton. Doersam also signed as the cosigner for a $5,000 student loan for her daughter, also made by First Federal and guaranteed by OSLC. With the use of the loans, she was able to obtain a position as a systems analyst with NCR Corporation, which required her to obtain a master's degree in order to retain her position at an annual salary of $24,000. Approximately six weeks before her graduation, and before the first payment on her student loans was due, Doersam filed a petition and plan under Chapter 13. In her plan, she proposed to pay $375 a month to her unsecured creditors over a 36-month period. Doersam's total unsecured debt was $18,418, 81 percent of which was composed of the outstanding student loans. Her schedules provided for payment of rent of $300 per month and food of $400 per month. Her listed dependents included her 23-year-old daughter and her 1-year-old granddaughter. At the time, her daughter was employed in the Ohio Work Program, a program designed to help welfare recipients, for which she was paid a small salary. The OLSC objected to the plan proposed by Doersam on the grounds that it was filed in bad faith. Should the bankruptcy court refuse to confirm the plan on the grounds it was not filed in good faith?

**10.** On December 8, 1981, Thomas Thompson filed a petition under Chapter 13 to pay his debts through a wage earner plan. After the notice to creditors, Ford Motor Credit Company, a secured creditor to which Thompson was indebted for payments on a 1980 Ford, filed a proof of claim and rejected the plan. The plan was confirmed over Ford's objections. It provided for payments to Ford of $22.90 a week, equivalent to the same rate and adding up to the same total as in the original sales contract, and enjoined Ford from foreclosing on the automobile. In 1982, Thompson was injured at work and able to work only part time. He then fell behind in his payments to Ford, even though he was

regularly submitting his disability checks to the trustee. Ford then filed a petition to reclaim the car, alleging that Thompson had failed to make the payments due on the car. Should Ford be permitted to have the plan disregarded so that it can foreclose its security interest on the car?

## CAPSTONE QUESTIONS

On March 1, 1994, the ABC Corporation was involuntarily petitioned into bankruptcy under Chapter 7. ABC's creditors included the following:

| | | Amount Owed |
|---|---|---|
| **Secured Creditors** | 1. First Bank—security interest in equipment created and perfected during 1992 | $50,000 |
| | 2. Second Bank—security interest in inventory created and perfected during 1992 | $30,000 |
| **Unsecured Creditors** | 1. IRS—for unpaid 1992 income taxes | $20,000 |
| | 2. Able Cleaners—for office cleaning during December 1993 and January and February 1994 | $ 750 |
| | 3. ABC employee Joe Jones—for January and February 1994 commissions | $ 1,200 |
| | 4. ABC employee Joe Jones—for February 1994 contributions to ABC's employee benefit plan | $ 1,500 |
| | 5. Public Service Corporation—for December 1993 and January and February 1994 electric bills | $ 600 |

Before the filing of the petition, ABC engaged in the following transactions:

- On October 1, 1993, ABC paid off a $5,000 loan made earlier to the firm by one of its directors.

- On February 1, 1994, ABC made a $10,000 charitable contribution to a legitimate charity.
- On January 2, 1994, ABC gave Fidelity Finance Company a security interest in certain ABC office equipment. This was done in order to secure a previously unsecured loan Fidelity had made to ABC on December 15, 1993. Fidelity perfected its security interest on January 3, 1994.
- On February 15, 1994, ABC purchased a new fire alarm system from Safety, Inc. for $5,000.

Eventually, all of ABC's assets were liquidated as part of the Chapter 7 proceedings. The equipment subject to First Bank's security interest was sold for $75,000, and the computers subject to Second Bank's security interest were sold for $25,000. After bankruptcy administration expenses were disbursed and all priority creditors were paid, enough money remained to give each general creditor 50 cents on the dollar.

**Required:**

Answer the following and give reasons for your conclusions.

1. Examine each of the four prebankruptcy transactions described above. Is each preferential? Assume that each is a transfer and that ABC was insolvent when each was made. Also assume that in each case, the beneficiary of the transfer would not have fared as well under Chapter 7.

2. How much money will each of the secured and unsecured creditors receive? Assume that if a perfected secured creditor is entitled to recover, it first does so from the funds realized by the sale of its collateral.

3. Now suppose that the equipment and the inventory sell off as before and that the same amount is spent on bankruptcy administration. After that, however, only $15,000 remains. In this case, how much will each of the secured and unsecured creditors receive?

# PART 5

# COMMERCIAL PAPER

# CHAPTER

**23**

# NEGOTIABLE

# INSTRUMENTS

### INTRODUCTION

*As commerce and trade developed, people moved beyond exclusive reliance on barter to the use of money and then to the use of substitutes for money. The term* commercial paper *encompasses such substitutes in common usage today as checks, promissory notes, and certificates of deposit.*

*History discloses that every civilization that engaged to an appreciable extent in commerce used some form of commercial paper. Probably the oldest commercial paper used in the carrying on of trade is the promissory note. Archaeologists found a promissory note made payable to bearer that dated from about 2100 B.C. The merchants of Europe used commercial paper—which, under the law merchant, was negotiable—in the 13th and 14th centuries. Commercial paper does not appear to have been used in England until about A.D. 1600.*

*This chapter and the three following chapters outline and discuss the body of law that governs commercial paper. Of particular interest are those kinds of commercial paper having the attribute of negotiability—that is, they can generally be transferred from party to party and accepted as a substitute for money. This chapter discusses the nature and benefits of negotiable instruments and then outlines the requirements an instrument must meet to qualify as a negotiable instrument. Subsequent chapters discuss transfer and negotiation of instruments, the rights and liabilities of parties to negotiable instruments, and the special rules applicable to checks.*

## NATURE OF NEGOTIABLE INSTRUMENTS

When a person buys a television set and gives the merchant a check drawn on his checking account, that person uses a form of negotiable commercial paper. Similarly, a person who goes to a bank or a credit union to borrow money might sign a promissory note agreeing to pay the money back in 90 days. Again, the bank and borrower use a form of negotiable commercial paper.

**Commercial paper** is basically a *contract for the payment of money.* It may serve as a substitute for money payable immediately, such as a check. Or, it can be used as a means of extending credit. When a television set is bought by giving the merchant a check, the check is a substitute for money. If a credit union loans a borrower money now in exchange for the borrower's promise to repay it later, the promissory note signed by the borrower is a means of extending credit.

## Uniform Commercial Code

The law of commercial paper is covered in Article 3 (Negotiable Instruments) and Article 4 (Bank Deposits and Collections) of the Uniform Commercial Code. Other negotiable documents, such as investment securities and documents of title, are treated in other articles of the Code. The original Code Articles 3 and 4, adopted initially in the 1960s, generally followed the basic, centuries-old rules governing the use of commercial paper; but at the same time they adopted modern terminology and coordinated, clarified, and simplified the law. However, business practices continued to evolve and new technological developments have changed the way that banks process checks. Accordingly, in 1990, a joint effort by the American Law Institute and the National Conference of Commissioners on Uniform State Laws produced a Revised Article 3 and related amendments to Articles 1 and 4. The purpose was to clarify Articles 3 and 4, to bring them into better harmony with current business practice, and to acknowledge recent technological developments.

Because a majority of the states have now adopted the 1990 revision to Article 3 and the related amendments, we use them as the basis for this edition of the textbook. The reader should ascertain whether the state in which she lives has adopted the revised article/amendments and also should keep in mind that instruments may be interpreted under the version of the Code that was in effect when the instruments were issued. Moreover, for the period between the first adoption of the revised article/amendments by a state (Arkansas) and the adoption by the last state or the District of Columbia, the "uniform law" concerning negotiable instruments will be anything but uniform.

For the student of negotiable instruments law, this is an interesting—but also a particularly difficult—time to study this area of the law. Revised Article 3 and the related amendments introduce new concepts, change definitions and the wording of key elements, and delete numerous provisions from the original version of Article 3. As a result, in drafting this chapter and the three chapters that follow, the authors have relied heavily on tracking the language of the revised article and on statements by the drafters as to their intent. Further complicating the picture is the fact that, in a number of respects, the revision is more complex than the original version. Moreover, while more than 30 years of case law had helped flesh out the meaning of the original Article 3, the revision has diminished much of the value of that case law. Virtually all of the cases to date arose under the original version of Article 3 and are of mixed—and sometimes very limited—value in trying to assess how courts will decide issues under the revision.

Just as these factors posed a challenge to the authors of this edition of the textbook, they will pose a challenge to you and your instructor as you work your way through the material on negotiable instruments. More questions are likely to be left up in the air than is true in other, more settled areas of the law. It will take a number of years, considerable experience, and new case law to flesh out the updated law of negotiable instruments.

## Negotiable Instruments

The two basic types of negotiable instruments are *promises to pay money* and *orders to pay money*. Promissory notes and certificates of deposit issued by banks are promises to pay someone money. Checks and drafts are orders to another person to pay money to a third person. A check, which is a type of draft, is an order directed to a certain kind of person, namely a bank, to pay money from a person's account to a third person.

## Negotiability

Negotiable instruments are a special kind of commercial paper that can pass readily through our financial system and is accepted in place of money. This gives negotiable instruments many advantages.

For example, Searle, the owner of a clothing store in New York, contracts with Amado, a swimsuit manufacturer in Los Angeles, for $10,000 worth of swimsuits. If negotiable instruments did not exist, Searle would have to send or carry $10,000 across the country, which would be both inconvenient and risky. If someone stole the money along the way, Searle would lose the $10,000 unless he could

**FIGURE 1**   Promissory Note

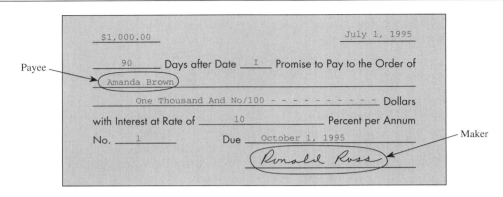

locate the thief. By using a check in which Searle orders his bank to pay $10,000 from his account to Amado, or to someone designated by Amado, Searle makes the payment in a far more convenient manner. He sends only a single piece of paper to Amado. If the check is properly prepared and sent, sending the check is less risky than sending money. Even if someone steals the check along the way, Searle's bank may not pay it to anyone but Amado or someone authorized by Amado. And, because the check gives Amado the right either to collect the $10,000 or to transfer the right to collect it to someone else, the check is a practical substitute for cash to Amado as well as Searle.

In this chapter and in the three following chapters, we discuss the requirements necessary for a contract for the payment of money to qualify as a negotiable instrument. We also explain the features that not only distinguish a negotiable instrument from a simple contract but also led to the widespread use of negotiable instruments as a substitute for money.

## KINDS OF NEGOTIABLE INSTRUMENTS

### Promissory Notes

The promissory note is the simplest form of commercial paper; it is simply a promise to pay money. A **promissory note** is a two-party instrument in which one person (known as the **maker**) makes an unconditional promise in writing to pay another person (the **payee**), a person specified by that person, or the bearer of the instrument, a fixed amount of money, with or without interest, either on demand or at a specified, future time [3–104].[1]

The promissory note, shown in Figures 1 and 2, is a credit instrument; it is used in a wide variety of transactions in which credit is extended. For example, if a person purchases an automobile using money borrowed from a bank, the bank has the person sign a promissory note for the unpaid balance of the purchase price. Similarly, if a person borrows money to purchase a house, the lender who makes the loan and takes a mortgage on the house has the person sign a promissory note for the amount due on the loan. The note probably states that it is secured by a mortgage. The terms of payment on the note should correspond with the terms of the sales contract for the purchase of the house.

### Certificates of Deposit

The certificate of deposit given by a bank or a savings and loan association when a deposit of money is made is a type of note—namely, a note of a bank. A **certificate of deposit** is an instrument containing (1) an acknowledgment by a bank that it has received a deposit of money and (2) a promise by the bank to repay the sum of money

---

[1]The numbers in brackets refer to the sections of the 1990 Revised Article 3 (and the conforming amendments to Articles 1 and 4) of the Uniform Commercial Code.

**FIGURE 2**   Promissory Note (Consumer Loan Note)

The National
**BANK OF
WASHINGTON**

**CONSUMER LOAN NOTE**

Date ___November 21,___ , 19_95_

The words I and me mean all borrowers who signed this note. The word bank means The National Bank of Washington.

**Promise to Pay**

___30___ months from today, I promise to pay to the order of The National Bank of Washington
Seventy-Eight Hundred Seventy Five and no/100 - - - - - - - - - - dollars ($ 7,875.00).

Payee

**Responsibility**

Although this note may be signed below by more than one person, I understand that we are each as individuals responsible for paying back the full amount.

**Breakdown of Loan**

This is what I will pay:

| | | |
|---|---|---|
| Amount of loan | 1. $ | 6,800.00 |
| Credit Life Insurance (optional) | 2. $ | 100.00 |
| Other (describe) | 3. $ | -0- |
| Amount Financed (Add 1 and 2 and 3) | 4. $ | 6,900 |
| FINANCE CHARGE | 5. $ | 975.00 |
| Total of Payments (Add 4 and 5) | $ | 7,875.00 |
| ANNUAL PERCENTAGE RATE | | 10.5 % |

**Repayment**

This is how I will repay:
I will repay the amount of this note in ___30___ equal uninterrupted monthly installments of $ 262.50 each on the _1st_ day of each month starting on the _1st_ day of _December_ , 19_95_ and ending on ___May 1,___ , 19_98_ .

**Prepayment**

I have the right to prepay the whole outstanding amount of this note at any time. If I do, or if this loan is refinanced—that is, replaced by a new note—you will refund the unearned finance charge, figured by the rule of 78—a commonly used formula for figuring rebates on installment loans.

**Late Charge**

Any installment not paid within ten days of its due date shall be subject to a late charge of 5% of the payment, not to exceed $5.00 for any such late installment.

**Security**

To protect the National Bank of Washington, I give what is known as a security interest in my auto and/or other: (Describe) _Ford Thunderbird_

_# Serial #115117-12-_

See the security agreement.

**Credit Life Insurance**

Credit life insurance is not required to obtain this loan. The bank need not provide it and I do not need to buy it unless I sign immediately below. The cost of credit life insurance is $___100.00___ for the term of the loan.

Signed: _A.J. Smith_

Date: ___November 21, 1995___

**Default**

If for any reason I fail to make any payment on time, I shall be in default. The bank can then demand immediate payment of the entire remaining unpaid balance of this loan, without giving anyone further notice. If I have not paid the full amount of the loan when the final payment is due, the bank will charge me interest on the unpaid balance at six percent (6%) per year.

**Right of Offset**

If this loan becomes past due, the bank will have the right to pay this loan from any deposit or security I have at this bank without telling me ahead of time. Even if the bank gives me an extension of time to pay this loan, I still must repay the entire loan.

**Collection Fees**

If this note is placed with an attorney for collection, then I agree to pay an attorney's fee of fifteen percent (15%) of the unpaid balance. This fee will be added to the unpaid balance of the loan.

**Co-borrowers**

If I am signing this note as a co-borrower, I agree to be equally responsible with the borrower for this loan. The bank does not have to notify me that this note has not been paid. The bank can change the terms of payment and release any security without notifying or releasing me from responsibility for this loan.

**Copy Received**

I received a completely filled in copy of this note. If I have signed for Credit Life Insurance, I received a copy of the Credit Life Insurance certificate.

Borrower: _A.J. Smith_ ◄—— Maker
A. J. Smith
3412 Brookdale, S. W. Washington D.C.
Address

Co-borrower: _Andrea H Smith_ ◄—— Comaker
Andrea H. Smith
3412 Brookdale, S. W. Washington D.C.
Address

Co-borrower: _____
Address

**CONSUMER CREDIT HOTLINE:** If you have any questions, please call us immediately at (202) 624-3450.
NBW 437 (Rev. 11-78)

1-Bank's copy   2-File copy   3-Customer's copy

[3–104(j)]. Figure 3 is an example of a certificate of deposit.

Many banks no longer issue certificates of deposit (CD) in paper form. Rather, the bank maintains an electronic deposit and provides the customer with a statement indicating the amount of principal held on a CD basis and the terms of the CD, such as the maturity and interest rate. In these instances, the certificate of deposit is not in negotiable instrument form.

**FIGURE 3**   **Certificate of Deposit**

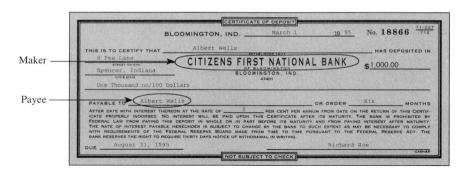

Maker

Payee

## Drafts

A **draft** is a form of commercial paper that involves an *order* to pay money rather than a promise to pay money [3–104(e)]. The most common example of a draft is a check. A draft has three parties to it: one person (known as the **drawer**) orders a second person (the **drawee**) to pay a certain sum of money to a third person (the **payee**), to a person specified by that person, or to bearer.

Drafts other than checks are used in a variety of commercial transactions. If Brown owes Ames money, Ames may draw a draft for the amount of the debt, naming Brown as drawee and herself or her bank as payee, and send the draft to Brown's bank for payment. Alternatively, Ames might send a draft providing for payment on a certain day in the future to Brown for "acceptance." Brown could "accept" the draft by signing his name to it, thereby obligating himself to pay the amount specified in the draft on that day in the future to Ames or to someone specified by Ames.

In freight shipments in which the terms are "cash on delivery," the seller commonly ships the goods to the buyer on an "order bill of lading" consigned to himself at the place of delivery. The seller then indorses the bill of lading and attaches a draft naming the buyer as drawee. He then sends the bill of lading and the draft through banking channels to the buyer's bank. A bank in the buyer's locale presents the draft to the buyer's bank for payment, and when the former bank receives payment, delivers the bill of lading to the buyer. Through this commercial transaction, the buyer gets the goods and the seller gets his money.

When credit is extended, the same procedure is followed, but the seller uses a time draft—a draft payable at some future time. See Figure 4. In such a transaction, the buyer "accepts" the draft (instead of paying it) and obligates herself to pay the amount of the draft when due. In these cases, the *drawee* (now called the **acceptor**) should date her signature so that the date at which payment is due is clear to all [3–409(c)].

## Checks

A **check** is a *draft payable on demand* and drawn on a bank (i.e., a bank is the drawee or person to whom the order to pay is addressed). Checks are the most widely used form of commercial paper. The issuer of a check orders the bank at which she maintains an account to pay a specified person, or someone designated by that person, a fixed amount of money from the account. For example, Elizabeth Brown has a checking account at the National Bank of Washington. She goes to Sears Roebuck & Co. and agrees to buy a washing machine priced at $459.95. If she writes a check to pay for it, she is the drawer of the check, the National Bank of Washington is the drawee, and Sears is the payee. By writing the check, Elizabeth is ordering her bank to pay $459.95 from her account to Sears or to Sears's order—that is, to whomever Sears asks the bank to pay the money. See Figure 5.

An instrument may qualify as a "check" and be governed by Article 3 even though it is described on its face by another term such as "money order." The Code definition of a "check" includes a "cashier's check" and a "teller's check." A **cashier's check** is a draft on which the drawer and drawee are the same

**FIGURE 4**   Draft

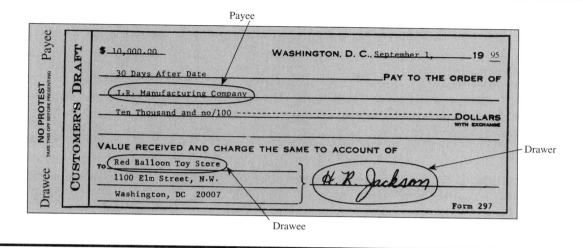

**FIGURE 5**   Check

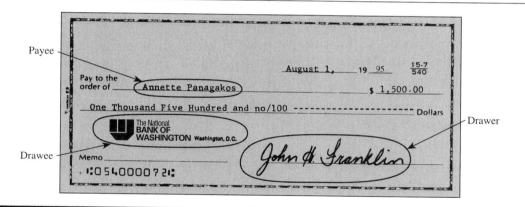

bank (or branches of the same bank); a **teller's check** is a draft drawn by a bank (as drawer) on another bank or payable at or through a bank [3–104(g) and (h)]. For example, a check drawn by a credit union on its account at a federally insured bank would be a teller's check.

## BENEFITS OF NEGOTIABLE INSTRUMENTS

### Rights of an Assignee of a Contract

As we noted in Chapter 9, Rights of Third Parties, the assignee of a contract can obtain no greater rights than the assignor had at the time of the

assignment. For example, Frank Farmer and Neam's Market enter into a contract providing that Farmer will sell Neam's a dozen crates of fresh eggs a week for a year and that Neam's will pay Farmer $4,000 at the end of the year. If at the end of the year Farmer assigns to Bill Sanders his rights under the contract—including the right to collect the money from Neam's—then Sanders has whatever rights Farmer had at that time. If Farmer has delivered all the eggs to Neam's as he promised, then Farmer would be entitled to $4,000 and Sanders would obtain that right from him. However, if Farmer has not delivered all the eggs that he had promised to deliver, or if the eggs he delivered were not fresh, then Neam's might have a valid defense or reason to refuse to pay the full $4,000. In that case, Sanders would have only what rights Farmer had and also would be subject to the defense Neam's has against full payment.

Taking an assignment of a contract involves assuming certain risks. The assignee (Sanders) may not be aware of the nature and extent of any defenses that the party liable on the contract (Neam's) might have against the assignor (Farmer). An assignee who does not know what rights he is getting, or which risks he is assuming, may be reluctant to take an assignment of the contract.

## Rights of a Holder of a Negotiable Instrument

The object of a negotiable instrument is to have it accepted readily as a substitute for money. In order to accept it readily, a person must be able to take it free of many of the risks assumed by the assignee of a regular contract. Under the law of negotiable instruments, this is possible if two conditions are met: (1) the contract for the payment of money must meet the formal requirements to qualify as a negotiable instrument; and (2) the person who acquires the instrument must qualify as a holder in due course. Basically, a *holder in due course* is a person who has good title to the instrument, paid value for it, acquired it in good faith, and had no notice of certain claims or defenses against payment. In addition, the instrument cannot bear facial irregularities (evidence of forgery or alteration or questions concerning its authenticity).

The next section of this chapter discusses the formal requirements for a negotiable instrument. Chapter 24, Negotiation and Holder in Due Course, outlines the requirements that a person must meet to qualify as a holder in due course.

A holder in due course of a negotiable instrument takes the instrument free of all defenses and claims to the instrument except those that concern its validity. For example, a holder in due course of a note given in payment for goods may enforce the obligation in spite of the buyer's claim that the seller breached a warranty. However, if the maker of a note wrote it under duress, such as a threat of force, or was a minor, then even a holder in due course is subject to the defenses of duress or infancy to the extent other law (1) would nullify the obliga-

tion for duress or (2) would permit infancy as a defense to a simple contract. In those instances, the person who holds the note could not obtain the payment from the maker but would have to recover from the person from whom he got the note.

The Federal Trade Commission (FTC) has adopted a regulation that alters the rights of a holder in due course in consumer purchase transactions. This regulation allows a consumer who gives a negotiable instrument to use additional defenses (such as breach of warranty or fraudulent inducement) against payment of the instrument against even a holder in due course. Similarly, some states have enacted the Uniform Consumer Credit Code (UCCC), which produces a similar result. Chapter 24 discusses the rights of a holder in due course, as well as the FTC rule.

## FORMAL REQUIREMENTS FOR NEGOTIABILITY

### Basic Requirements

An instrument such as a check or a note must meet certain formal requirements to be a negotiable instrument. If the instrument does not meet these requirements, it is non-negotiable; that is, it is treated as a simple contract and not as a negotiable instrument. A primary purpose for these formal requirements is to ensure the willingness of prospective purchasers of the instrument, particularly financial institutions such as banks, to accept it as a substitute for money.

For an instrument to be negotiable, it must:

1. Be in writing.
2. Be signed by the issuer (the *maker* in the case of a person undertaking to pay or the *drawer* in the case of a person giving an order or instruction to pay).
3. Contain an unconditional promise or order to pay a fixed amount of money, with or without interest or other charges described in the promise or order.
4. Be payable to order or to bearer at the time it is issued or first comes into possession of a holder.
5. Be payable on demand or at a definite time.
6. Not state any other undertaking or instruction by the person promising or ordering to do any

act in addition to the payment of money (but it may contain (*a*) an undertaking or promise relative to collateral to secure payment, (*b*) an authorization for confession of judgment, or (*c*) a waiver of benefit of any law intended for the advantage or protection of an obligor). [3–103; 3–104].

In addition, an instrument that otherwise qualifies as a check can be a negotiable even if it is not explicitly payable to order or to bearer [3–104(c)]. As explained later, this means that a check reading "pay John Doe" could be negotiable even though the normal form for a check is "pay to the order of _____ ."

A promise or order other than a check is not a negotiable instrument if at the time it is issued or first comes into the possession of a holder it contains a conspicious statement that the promise or order is not negotiable or is not an instrument governed by Article 3 [3–104(d)]. For example, if a promissory note contained the legend "NON–NEGOTIABLE," it would not qualify as a negotiable instrument even if it otherwise met the formal requirements for one.

## Importance of Form

Whether or not an instrument satisfies these formal requirements is important only for the purpose of determining whether an instrument is negotiable or nonnegotiable. Negotiability should not be confused with validity or collectibility. If an instrument is negotiable, the law of negotiable instruments in the Code controls in determining the rights and liabilities of the parties to the instrument. If an instrument is non-negotiable, the general rules of contract law control. The purpose of determining negotiability is to ascertain whether a possessor of the instrument can become a holder in due course.

An instrument that meets all of the formal requirements is a negotiable instrument even though it is void, voidable, unenforceable, or uncollectible for other reasons. Negotiability is a matter of form and nothing else. Suppose a person gives an instrument in payment of a gambling debt in a state that has a statute declaring that any instrument or promise given in payment of a gambling debt is void. The instrument is a negotiable instrument if it is negotiable in form even though it is absolutely void. Also, an instrument that is negotiable in form is a

negotiable instrument even though it is issued by a minor. The instrument is voidable at the option of the minor if state law makes infancy a defense to a simple contract, but it is negotiable.

## In Writing

To be negotiable, an instrument must be in writing. An instrument that is handwritten, typed, or printed is considered to be in writing [1–201(46)]. The writing does not have to be on any particular material; all that is required is that the instrument be in writing. A person could create a negotiable instrument in pencil on a piece of wrapping paper. It would be poor business practice to do so, but the instrument would meet the statutory requirement that it be in writing.

## Signed

To qualify as a negotiable instrument, an instrument in the form of a note must be signed by the person undertaking to pay (the maker) and an instrument in the form of a draft must be signed by the person giving the instruction to pay (the drawer) [3–103]. An instrument has been signed if the maker or drawer has put a name or other symbol on it with the intention of validating it [3–401(b)]. Normally, the maker or drawer signs an instrument by writing his name on it; however, this is not required. A person or company may authorize an agent to sign instruments for it. A typed or rubber-stamped signature is sufficient if it was put on the instrument to validate it. A person who cannot write her name might make an X and have it witnessed by someone else.

## Unconditional Promise or Order

### Requirement of a Promise or Order

If an instrument is promissory in nature, such as a note or a certificate of deposit, it must contain an unconditional promise to pay or it cannot be negotiable. Merely acknowledging a debt is not sufficient [3–103(9)]. For example, the statement "I owe you $100," does not constitute a promise to pay. An IOU in this form is not a negotiable instrument.

If an instrument is an order to pay, such as a check or a draft, it must contain an unconditional order. A simple request to pay as a favor is not sufficient; however, a politely phrased demand, such as "please pay," can meet the requirement. Checks commonly use the language "Pay to the order of." This satisfies the requirement that the check contain an order to pay. The order is the word "pay," not the word "order." The word "order" has another function—that of making the instrument payable "to order or to bearer."

## Promise or Order Must Be Unconditional

An instrument is not negotiable unless the promise or order is unconditional. For example, a note that provides, "I promise to pay to the order of Karl Adams $1,000 if he replaces the roof on my garage," is not negotiable because it is payable on a condition.

To be negotiable, an instrument must be written so that a person can tell from reading the instrument alone what the obligations of the parties are. If a note contains the statement, "Payment is subject to the terms of a mortgage dated November 20, 1995," it is not negotiable. To determine the rights of the parties on the note, one would have to examine another document—the mortgage.

However, a reference to another document for a statement of rights with respect to collateral, prepayment, or acceleration does not destroy the negotiability of a note [3–106(b)]. For example, a note could contain this statement: "This note is secured by a mortgage dated August 30, 1995" without affecting its negotiability. In this case, the mortgage does not affect rights and duties of the parties to the note. It would not be necessary to examine the mortgage document to determine the rights of the parties to the note; the parties only need examine the note.

The negotiability of an instrument is not affected by a statement of the consideration for which the instrument was given or by a statement of the transaction that gave rise to the instrument. For example, a negotiable instrument may state that it was given in payment of last month's rent or that it was given in payment of the purchase price of goods. The statement does not affect the negotiability of the instrument. The effect of a notation in the lower left corner of a check following the printed word *memo* is discussed in the *Western Bank v. RaDEC Construction Co., Inc.* case, which follows.

---

## WESTERN BANK V. RaDEC CONSTRUCTION CO., INC.
**42 UCC Rep. 1340 (S.D. Sup. Ct. 1986)**

RaDEC Construction Company was the general contractor in the construction of a medical center in Huron, South Dakota. One of RaDEC's subcontractors on this job was Carpet Center. RaDEC became aware that Carpet Center's financial problems were making it difficult for Carpet Center to furnish the necessary materials and labor for the medical center job. RaDEC's president, Clarence Hoesing, had a conversation with Carpet Center on December 13, 1982, in which he agreed to send a check for $8,743.52 to Carpet Center, provided that Carpet Center (1) furnish certain paid invoices for material delivered, (2) provide certain additional material, and (3) ensure the installation of the material on December 14. Hoesing then made out a handwritten check to Carpet Center. In the lower left corner of the check following the printed word *memo* Hoesing typed the phrase, "Payee must prove clear title to material." Hoesing considered the check to be conditioned on Carpet Center's performance of the three conditions. After the check was delivered on December 14, Carpet Center deposited the check in the Western Bank, which allowed it to make an immediate withdrawal of the money. Later that day, RaDEC learned that Carpet Center had not performed the three requirements and filed a stop payment order on the check.

Unable to recover the money from Carpet Center, which was insolvent, the bank brought suit against RaDEC, claiming to be a holder in due course of the check. The trial court held in favor of the bank and RaDEC appealed.

---

**Hertzel, Justice**   The trial court held as a matter of law that the phrase typed in at the lower left hand corner of the check, "Payee must prove clear title to material," did not have the effect of making the check conditional and that the bank was a bona fide holder in due course.

Section 3–104(1) sets forth four elements necessary to constitute a negotiable instrument: (a) It must be signed by the maker; (b) contain an unconditional promise or order to pay a sum certain in money and no other promise, order, obligation or power given by the maker or drawer except as authorized by this chapter; (c) be payable on demand or at a definite time; and (d) be payable to order or to bearer.

In this case there is no dispute that elements (a), (c) and (d) have been fulfilled. RaDEC claims, however, that element (b) has not been met because the check was a "conditional instrument" and therefore subject to its defenses.

RaDEC relies heavily on our decision in *Bank of America v. Butterfield.* In that case, the draft in question stated: "Subject to approval of title, pay to the order of Vernon H. Butterfield and Laura E. Butterfield." It is important to note that the phrase "subject to approval of title," immediately precedes the standard phrase, "Pay to the order of." In affirming the trial court we said: "The promise to pay money contained in the draft in question is clearly not unconditional. The payment ordered is subject to approval of title. Consequently, it is not a negotiable instrument."

Negotiability is determined from the face of the instrument without reference to extrinsic facts. The conditional or unconditional character is to be determined by what is expressed in the instrument itself.

RaDEC claims that the check was not a negotiable instrument because of the condition written on its face. Moreover, RaDEC argues that the location of the conditional language in the place usually reserved for "memo" is of little consequence, since the language itself was sufficient to give the bank notice that RaDEC's obligation to pay was conditioned upon Carpet Center's having proved clear title to the material. The bank, on the other hand, argues that the instant factual situation can be distinguished from that of *Bank of America* because in that case the conditional language, i.e., "subject to approval of title," preceded the words "Pay to the order of."

We conclude that the phrase "payee must prove clear title to material" written where it was, did not make the check conditional thereby depriving the bank of its status as a holder in due course. It appears that the notation in the "memo" area of the check is nothing more than a self-serving declaration by RaDEC for its own benefit and recordkeeping and for informational purposes only. An otherwise unconditional instrument cannot be rendered conditional by such a device.

### Judgment for Western Bank affirmed.

*Note:* Although this decision predates Revised Article 3, which modified the requirements for a negotiable instrument set out in original § 3–104, the result in this case would be the same under Revised Article 3.

---

A check may reference the account to be debited without making the check non-negotiable. For example, a check could contain the notation, "payroll account" or "petty cash." Similarly, the account number that appears on personal checks does not make the instrument payable only out of a specific fund. Under original Article 3, a check (other than a governmental check) that stated that it was payable only out of a specific fund or account was treated as a conditional order and thus was not negotiable. Revised Article 3 changed this rule so that limiting payment to a particular fund or source does not make the promise or order conditional [3–106(b)].

Revised Article 3 also addresses the negotiability of traveler's checks that commonly require, as a condition to payment, a countersignature of a person whose specimen signature appears on the draft. Under the revision, the condition does not prevent the instrument from meeting the "unconditional promise or order" requirement [3–106(c)]. However, if the person whose specimen signature appears on the instrument fails to countersign it, the failure to sign becomes a defense to the obligation of the issuer to pay. This concept will be discussed in the following chapter.

A conditional indorsement does not destroy the negotiability of an otherwise negotiable instrument and it is not affected by subsequent indorsement.

The Code determines negotiability at issuance, so that later indorsements do not affect the underlying negotiability of the instrument. We discuss conditional indorsements in Chapter 24, Negotiation and Holder in Due Course.

## FIXED AMOUNT OF MONEY

### Fixed Amount

The promise or order in an instrument must be to pay a fixed amount of money, with or without interest or other charges described in the promise or order. The requirement of a "fixed amount" applies only to principal, and the amount of any interest payable is that described in the instrument. If a variable rate of interest is prescribed, the amount of interest is calculated by reference to the formula or index referenced in the instrument. If the description of interest in the instrument does not allow the amount of interest to be ascertained, then interest is payable at the judgment rate in effect at the place of payment at the time interest first accrues [3–112].

The judgment rate is the rate of interest courts impose on losing parties until they pay the winning parties.

Under the original version of Article 3, a promise or order had to be to pay a "sum certain." Generally, to meet this requirement, a person had to be able to compute from the information in the instrument the amount required to discharge—or pay off—the instrument at any given time. Among other things, this caused problems when applied to variable rate instruments that came into common commercial usage in the United States after the original Article 3 was drafted. Some state courts held that instruments providing for variable interest rates ascertainable through reference to indexes outside the instrument were not negotiable; other courts sought to interpret the Code to accommodate this new commercial practice.

The case that follows, *Carnegie Bank v. Shalleck*, illustrates the challenge faced by a court presented with a variable rate note—drafted when the original Article 3 requirement for a sum certain was in effect—in a state that has now adopted Revised Article 3.

---

## CARNEGIE BANK V. SHALLECK
**17 UCC Rep.2d 799 (Sup. Ct. N.J. 1992)**

On July 11, 1988, Ann Anderson borrowed $150,000 from the Carnegie Bank and executed a note payable to the order of "Carnegie Bank." Her loan was secured by a mortgage and note also dated July 11, 1988 in favor of Anderson and signed by Alan B. Shalleck in his individual capacity and as president of two corporations. The note provided for interest at "two (2%) percent in excess of the Floating Base Rate at Carnegie Bank, as adjusted from time to time, provided, however, that at no time shall the rate be less than fifteen (15%) per annum." Anderson assigned the Shalleck mortgage and note to Carnegie Bank as security for her loan.

Shalleck defaulted on his note to Anderson and she, in turn, defaulted on her loan to Carnegie Bank. The Bank sued Shalleck to recover on the note that Anderson had assigned to it. One of the questions in the litigation was whether the note was a negotiable instrument. The trial court held that it was not negotiable.

---

**Coleman, Presiding Judge** We consider whether the Shalleck note was rendered non-negotiable because it provided for repayment at a variable interest rate rather than a rate fixed by the four corners of the note. If the note was not negotiable, Carnegie Bank could not become a holder in due course. The trial court found that the

"sum certain" requirement of section 104(1)(b) was not satisfied by the note.

The Code does not define "sum certain"; it only enumerates factors which do not destroy the "sum certain" requirement for negotiability. Sec. 106 (1). Official Comment 1 to sec. 3–106 of the Code states that the interest computation must be one which can be made from the instrument itself without reference to any outside source, and this section does not make negotiable a note payable with interest "at the current rate." The comment does not, however, cover a situation where the rate can be determined by reference to a generally accepted published index.

Whether a variable interest rate renders the instrument non-negotiable raises a question of first impression in this state. Some states have held generally that variable rate notes are not negotiable. Yet, some courts have held that certain variable rate provisions in notes do not affect negotiability.

Prior to the trial in this case, the National Conference of Commissioners on Uniform State Laws proposed an amendment to section 3–112 of the Uniform Commercial Code to permit the use of variable interest rates without affecting negotiability. The proposal was approved by the American Law Institute in 1990. The new revision with Comment is [in pertinent part] as follows:

Sec. 3–112. Interest
  (a)          *   *   *   *   *

(b) Interest may be stated in an instrument as a fixed or variable amount of money or it may be expressed as a fixed or variable rate or rates. The amount of interest may be stated or described in the instrument in any manner and may require reference to information not contained in the instrument. If an instrument provides for interest, but the amount of interest payable cannot be ascertained from the description, interest is payable at the judgment rate in effect at the place of payment of the instrument and at the time interest first accrues.

### OFFICIAL COMMENT

1. Under Section 3–104(a) the requirement of a "fixed amount" applies only to principal. The amount of interest payable is that described in the instrument. If the description of interest in the instrument does not allow for the amount of interest to be ascertained, interest is payable at the judgment rate. Hence, if an instrument calls for interest, the amount of interest will always be determinable. If a variable rate of interest is prescribed, the amount of interest is ascertainable by reference to the formula or index described or referred to in the instrument.

Two months before The American Law Institute was scheduled to discuss the proposed amendment in May 1990 and before the trial in this case, Senate

Bill No. 2431 was introduced in the New Jersey Senate essentially to adopt the proposal submitted to The American Law Institute. Senate Bill 2431 was enacted into law on January 9, 1992, effective immediately, and [among other things] adds Section 3–106(3) which reads:

A rate of interest that cannot be calculated by looking only to the instrument is a "stated rate of interest" in subsection (1) of this section if the rate is readily ascertainable by reference in the instrument to a published statute, regulation, rule of court, generally accepted commercial or financial index, compendium of interest rates, or announced or established rate of a named financial institution.

We recognize that as a general rule, New Jersey courts favor prospective application of new statutory amendments. The reason for this general rule is that retroactive application of new statutes carries a high risk of unfairness. However, there are three recognized exceptions to the general rule: (1) where the Legislature expressly or impliedly intends retroactive application; (2) where a statute is ameliorative or curative, and (3) where the expectations of the parties will be enhanced.

A statement attached to the legislation is a useful aid in ascertaining legislative intent. The sponsor's statement as well as the Senate Committee's statement to the legislation provide that:

This bill amends one of the provisions in the Uniform Commercial Code which establish the criteria for a negotiable instrument by providing that a variable rate of interest which requires reference to a source outside the instrument in order to ascertain the amount due would not make the instrument non-negotiable. Some courts in other states have ruled that instruments with variable interest rates tied to a market or other index are non-negotiable.

The clear implication is that, while no New Jersey decision has found that Section 106 rendered instruments with variable interest rates non-negotiable, other courts have and the Legislature wanted to clarify New Jersey's position on the issue before any decisions were rendered.

We believe the 1992 amendment is curative and it also enhances the expectations of the parties.

**Held that the sum certain requirement was satisfied by the variable rate note.**

## Payable in Money

The amount specified in the instrument must be payable in money, which is a medium of exchange authorized or adopted by a domestic or foreign government and includes a monetary unit of account established by an intergovernmental organization or by agreement between two or more nations [1−201(24)]. Unless the instrument otherwise provides, an instrument that states the amount payable in foreign money may be paid in the foreign money or in an equivalent dollar amount [3−107]. If the person obligated to pay off an instrument can do something other than pay money, the instrument is not negotiable. For example, if a note reads, "I promise to pay to the order of Sarah Smith, at my option, $40 or five bushels of apples, John Jones," the note is not negotiable.

## PAYABLE ON DEMAND OR AT A DEFINITE TIME

To be negotiable, the promise or order must be payable either on demand or at a specified time in the future. This is so that the time when the instrument is payable can be determined with some certainty. An instrument that is payable on the happening of some uncertain event is not negotiable. Thus, a note payable "when my son graduates from college" is not negotiable, even though the son does graduate subsequently.

## Payable on Demand

A promise or order is "payable on demand" if (1) it states that it is payable on "demand" or "sight" (or otherwise at the will of the holder of the instrument) or (2) does not state any time for payment [3−108(a)]. For example, if the maker forgets to state when a note is payable, it is payable immediately at the request of the holder of the note.

An instrument may be antedated or postdated, and normally an instrument payable on demand is not payable before the date of the instrument. [3−113(a)] Revised Article 3 makes an important exception for checks; a payor bank (a bank that is the drawee of a draft) may pay a postdated

check before the stated date *unless* the drawer has notified the bank of postdating pursuant to a procedure set out in the Code [3−113(a); 4−401(c)].

## Payable at a Definite Time

A promise or order is "payable at a definite time" if it is payable at a fixed date or dates or at a time or times readily ascertainable at the time the promise or order is issued [3−108(b)]. Thus, a note dated March 25, 1995, might be made payable at a fixed time after a stated date, such as "30 days after date."

Under the Code, an instrument that names a fixed date or time for payment—without losing its negotiable character—may also contain a clause permitting the time for payment to be accelerated at the option of the maker. Similarly, an instrument may allow an extension of time at the option of the holder or allow a maker or acceptor to extend payment to a further definite time. Or, the due date of a note might be triggered by the happening of an event, such as the filing of a petition in bankruptcy against the maker. The Code permits these clauses so long as one can determine the time for payment with certainty [3−108].

A promise or order is also "payable at a definite time" if it is payable on elapse of a definite period of time after "sight" or "acceptance." A draft payable at a specified time—such as "15 days after sight"—is, in effect, payable at a fixed time after the draft is presented to the drawee for acceptance.

If an instrument is undated, its "date" is the date it is issued by the maker or drawer [3−113(b)].

## PAYABLE TO ORDER OR BEARER

Except for checks, to be negotiable an instrument must be "payable to order or to bearer." A note that provides, "I promise to pay to the order of Sarah Smith" or "I promise to pay to Sarah Smith or bearer" is negotiable. However, one that provides "I promise to pay to Sarah Smith" is not. The words "to the order of" or "to bearer" show that the drawer of a draft, or the maker of a note, intends to issue a negotiable instrument. The drawer or maker is not restricting payment of the instrument to just Sarah Smith but is willing to pay someone else designated by Sarah Smith. This is the essence of negotiability.

In the original version of Article 3, an order in the form of a check also had to be "payable to order or bearer" to qualify as a negotiable instrument. However, the drafters of Revised Article 3 created an exception for instruments that otherwise meet the requirements for a negotiable instrument as well as the definition of a check [3–104(c)]. Under the revised article, a check that reads "Pay John Doe" could qualify as a negotiable instrument. As a result, the Code now treats checks, which are payment instruments, as negotiable instruments whether or not they contain the words "to the order of." The drafters explained that most checks are preprinted with these words but that occasionally the drawer may strike out the words before issuing the check and that a few check forms have been in use that do not contain these words. In these instances, the drafters preferred not to limit the rights of holders of such checks who may pay money or give credit for a check without being aware that it is not in the conventional form for a negotiable instrument.

The most common forms of a promise or order being payable to bearer use the words "payable to bearer," "payable to the order of bearer," "payable to cash," or "payable to the order of cash" [3–109(a)]. A promise or order is considered to be payable "to order" if it is payable (1) to the order of an identified person or (2) to an identified person or that person's order [3–109(b)]. Examples would include: "Pay to the order of Sandy Smith" and "Pay to Sandy Smith or order." A check sent with the payee line blank is payable to bearer. However, it is also considered an incomplete instrument, the rules concerning which will be discussed in the following two chapters.

The original payee of a check or a note can transfer the right to receive payment to someone else. By making the instrument payable "to the order of" or "to bearer," the drawer or maker is giving the payee the chance to negotiate the instrument to another person and to cut off certain defenses that the drawer or maker may have against payment of the instrument.

A check that is payable to the order of a specific person is known as "order paper." Order paper can be negotiated or transferred only by indorsement. A check payable "to bearer" or "to cash" is known as "bearer paper"; it can be negotiated or transferred without indorsement [3–201(b)]. The rules governing negotiation of instruments will be detailed in the next chapter.

An instrument can be made payable to two or more payees. For example, a check could be drawn payable "to the order of John Jones and Henry Smith." Then, both Jones and Smith have to be involved in negotiating it or enforcing its payment. An instrument also can be made payable to alternative persons—for example, "to the order of Susan Clark or Betsy Brown." In this case, either Clark or Brown could negotiate it or enforce its payment [3–110(d)].

## SPECIAL TERMS

### Additional Terms

Generally, if an instrument is to qualify as a negotiable instrument, the person promising or ordering payment may not state undertakings or instructions in additon to the payment of money [3–104(a)(3). However, the instrument may include clauses concerning (1) giving, maintaining, or protecting collateral to secure payment, (2) an authorization to confess judgment or to realize on or dispose of collateral, and (3) waiving the benefit of any law intended for the protection or benefit of any person obligated on the instrument.

Thus, a term authorizing the confession of judgment on an instrument when it is due does not affect the negotiability of the instrument. A confession of judgment clause authorizes the creditor to go into court if the debtor defaults and, with the debtor's acquiescence, to have a judgment entered against the debtor. However, some states prohibit confessions of judgment.

Banks and other businesses often use forms of commercial paper that meet their particular needs. These forms may include certain other terms that do not affect the negotiability of an instrument. For example, a note may designate a place of payment without affecting the instrument's negotiability. Where the instrument does not specify a place of payment, the Code sets out rules for ascertaining where payment is to be made [3–111].

**CONCEPT REVIEW**

## Requirements for Negotiability

| Requirement | Basic Rules |
|---|---|
| **Must Be in Writing** | 1. The instrument may be handwritten, typed, or printed. |
| **Must Be Signed by the Maker or Drawer** | 1. Person issuing the instrument must sign with intent of validating his or her obligation.<br>2. Person issuing may affix the signature in a variety of ways—for example, by word, mark, or rubber stamp.<br>3. Agent or authorized representative may supply the "signature." |
| **Must Contain a Promise or Order to Pay** | 1. Promise must be more than acknowledgment of a debt.<br>2. Order requirement is met if the drawer issues an instruction to "pay." |
| **Promise or Order Must Be Unconditional** | 1. Entire obligation must be found in the instrument itself and not in another document or documents.<br>2. Payment cannot be conditioned on the occurrence of an event. |
| **Must Call for Payment of a Fixed Amount of Money** | 1. Must be able to ascertain the principal from the face of the instrument.<br>2. May contain a clause providing for payment of interest or other charges such as collection or attorney's fees. |
| **Must Be Payable in Money** | 1. Obligation must be payable in a medium of exchange authorized or adopted by a government or by an international organization or agreement between two or more nations.<br>2. Maker or drawer cannot have the option to pay in something other than money. |
| **Must Be Payable on Demand or at a Definite Time** | 1. Requirement is met if instrument says it is payable on demand or if no time for payment is stated (then it is payable on demand).<br>2. Requirement is met if it is payable on a stated date, at a fixed time after a stated date, or a fixed time "after sight."<br>3. Instrument may contain an acceleration clause or a clause allowing maker or holder to extend the payment date. |
| **Generally Must Be Payable to Bearer or to Order** | 1. Bearer requirement is met if instrument is payable "to bearer" or "to cash."<br>2. Order requirement is met if instrument is payable "to the order of" a specified person or persons.<br>3. Exception from requirement is made for instruments meeting both the definition of a check and all the other requirements for a negotiable instrument. |
| **May Not State Any Other Undertaking or Instruction by the Person Promising or Ordering Payment to Do Any Act in Addition to the Payment of Money** | 1. However, it may contain (*a*) an undertaking or power to give, maintain, or protect collateral to secure payment, (*b*) an authorization or power to the holder to confess judgment or realize on or dispose of collateral, or (*c*) a waiver of the benefit of any law intended for the advantage or protection of an obligor on the instrument. |

## Ambiguous Terms

Occasionally, a person may write or receive a check on which the amount written in figures differs from the amount written in words. Or a note may have conflicting terms or an ambiguous term. Where a conflict or an ambiguous term exists, there are general rules of interpretation that are applied to resolve the conflict or ambiguity: Typewritten terms prevail over printed terms, handwritten terms prevail over printed and typewritten terms, and where words and numbers conflict, the words control the numbers [3–114].

The following *Galatia Community State Bank v. Kindy* case involves a check on which there was a difference between the numbers on a check placed there by a check-writing machine and those written by hand.

---

## GALATIA COMMUNITY STATE BANK V. KINDY
### 307 Ark. 467 (Ark. Sup. Ct. 1991)

Galatia Community State Bank honored a check it took for collection for $5,500, which was the amount imprinted by a check-writing machine in the center underline section of the check commonly used for stating the amount in words. The imprint looked like this:

RegistereD
No. 497345        **5550 DOL'S 00 CTS

The impression made by the check-writing machine could be felt on the front and back of the check, and "**5550 DOL'S 00 CTS" was imprinted in red ink. In the box on the right-hand side of the check commonly used for numbers, "6,550.00" appeared in handwriting. The check was in partial payment of the purchase price of two engines that Eugene Kindy was buying from the payee on the check, Tony Hicks. Kindy postdated the check by a month and deliberately placed two different amounts on the check because he thought the bank would check with him before paying it. Kindy wanted to be sure that the engines had been delivered to Canada before he paid the $6,550 balance of the purchase price.

After the check was deposited in the Galacia Bank and Hicks was given $5,550, an employee of the bank altered the "6" by hand to read "5." Because Kindy had stopped payment on the check, the drawee bank refused to pay it to Galatia Bank. Galatia Bank then brought suit against Kindy as the drawer of the check. One of the issues in the lawsuit was how the check should be constructed. The trial court found that the rules on construction provided in the Code were not helpful because they were contradictory.

---

**Newbern, Justice**    The trial court reviewed Code section 3–118(b) and (c) (1987) which has since been superceded by section 3–114 (1991) but which was in effect at the time in question in this case. The statute provided in relevant part:

3–118. Ambiguous terms and rules of construction.
   The following rules apply to every instrument:

                    *     *     *     *     *

(b) Handwritten terms control typewritten and printed terms, and typewritten control printed.

(c) Words control figures except that if the words are ambiguous figures control.

The frustration expressed by the trial court with respect to section 3–118 which stated the applicable rules of construction for negotiable instruments is understandable.

The 5550.00 amount imprinted by the checkwriting machine upon the line customarily used for words is expressed in figures and not in words. One question is whether imprinted numbers located where words are customarliy placed on a check control figures placed where figures are customarily placed. Another question is whether handwritten figures control printing.

We find both questions satisfactorily answered in *St. Paul Fire & Marine Ins. Co. v. Bank of Salem* [Ind. App. 1980]. In that case, there was a conflict between an amount imprinted by a check imprinting machine and numbers expressed in typewritten figures. The court recognized the imprinted amount was not expressed in words but held "the purposes of the UCC are best served by considering an amount imprinted by a checkwriting machine as 'words' for the purpose of resolving an ambiguity between an amount and an amount entered upon the line usually used to express the amount in figures." The court quoted from a pre-UCC case, *United States Fidelity and Guaranty Co. v. First National Bank of South Carolina* (1964), as follows:

A prime purpose, as we see it, of making a sum payable when expressed in words controlling over the sum payable expressed in figures is the very fact that words are much more difficult to alter. The perforated imprinting by a check-writing machine, while fully expressing the sum payable in figures, is even more difficult to successfully alter than a sum payable in written words.

Because a check imprinting machine's purpose is to protect against alterations, the amount shown on the imprint should control whether the number is in words or figures.

Turning to the question of whether typewriting controls printing, the Indiana court [in *St. Paul Fire & Marine Ins. Co. v. State Bank of Salem*] stated:

As the section makes clear, in the event of an ambiguity between printed terms and typewritten terms, the latter would control. We do not consider the impression made by the check imprinter to be 'printed terms' under this section.

A conflict between the two amounts on a check would be resolved by section 3–118(c) which states that words control figures. Arguably, the amount imprinted by the checkwriting machine upon the line customarily expressing the amount in words, is expressed in figures. . . . We think, however, that the purposes of the UCC are best served by considering an amount imprinted by a checkwriting machine as "words" for the purpose of resolving an ambiguity between that amount and an amount entered upon the line usually used to express the amount in figures.

Although the court did not say specifically that it regarded the portion written by the checkwriting machine was the equivalent of handwriting, that is the clear effect of the decision.

### Judgment for Kindy reversed on other grounds.

*Note:* The court here concluded that a conflict between the words and figures did not serve as "notice of a claim or defense" and thus did not prevent Galatia Bank from becoming a holder in due course who could recover from Kindy. The court's rationale was that section 3–118 treats the situation as a "mistake" which can be resolved through the rules of construction. Although, as the court notes, this case was decided under the original version of Article 3, the dilemma posed, and the statements made by the court concerning the construction of the check, would likely be the same if the dilemma came up under Revised Article 3.

---

#### PROBLEMS AND PROBLEM CASES

**1.** Is the following instrument a note, a check, or a draft? Why? If it is not a check, how would you have to change it to make it a check?

To: Arthur Adams January 1, 1995
TEN DAYS AFTER DATE PAY TO THE ORDER OF:
Bernie Brown
THE SUM OF: Ten and no/100 DOLLARS
SIGNED: Carl Clark

**2.** Wiley, Tate & Irby, buyers and sellers of used cars, sold several autos to Houston Auto Sales. Houston wrote out the order for payment on the outside of several envelopes. He signed them and they were drawn on his bank, Peoples Bank & Trust Co., to be paid on the demand of Wiley, Tate & Irby. Can the envelopes qualify as negotiable instruments?

**3.** Is the following a negotiable instrument?

IOU, A. Gay, the sum of seventeen and 5/100 dollars for value received.
John R. Rooke

**4.** Is the following a negotiable instrument?

Subject to Approval of Title
Pay to the Order of Vernon Butterfield
$1,997,90.

> The Culver Company
> By A. M. Culver

**5.** A promissory note provides as follows:

FOR VALUE RECEIVED, the undersigned promises to pay to the order of J. MONTE WILLIAMSON . . . the principal sum of Four Thousand Dollars ($4,000) payable as set forth in that certain agreement dated March 15, 1976, an executed copy of which is attached hereto and made a part thereof by this reference.
Is the note negotiable?

**6.** Strickland ordered a swimming pool from Kafko Manufacturing and gave it a check for the purchase price that included the following words in the space following the word memo: "for pool kit to be delivered." Is the check negotiable?

**7.** Olde Town Investment Corporation borrowed $18,000 from VMC Mortgage Company and signed a promissory note secured by a deed of trust on landit owned. The note provided for interest at "three percent (3.00%) over Chase Manhattan Prime to be adjusted monthly." Is a note providing for a variable amount of interest, not ascertainable from the face of the note, a negotiable instrument?

**8.** Nation-Wide Check Corporation sold money orders to drugstores. The money orders contained the words, "Payable to," followed by a blank. Can the money order qualify as a negotiable instrument?

**9.** Holliday made out a promissory note to Anderson, leaving the date of payment of the note blank. Anderson filled in the words "on demand" in the blank without Holliday's knowledge. Does this alter the rights or obligations of the parties?

**10.** Emmett McDonald, acting as the personal representative of the estate of Marion Cahill, wrote a check payable to himself, individually, on the estate checking account in the Commercial Bank & Trust Company. The instrument contained an obvious variance between the numbers and the written words that indicated the amount of the check. It said: "Pay to the order of Emmett E. McDonald $10075.00 Ten hundred seventy five . . . Dollars."

The bank paid the $10,075 sum stated by the numerals to McDonald, who absconded with the funds. Yates, the successor representative, sued the bank on behalf of the estate to recover the $9,000 difference between that amount and the $1,075 that was written out. Did the bank pay the correct amount on the check?

## CAPSTONE QUESTIONS

**1.** Which of the following would cause a promissory note to be non-negotiable?

*a.* The absence of a due date in the note.

*b.* The word non-negotiable printed in bold type on the face of the note.

*c.* The note reads "Pay to Sarah Jane Hughes."

*d.* An acceleration clause that allows the holder to demand immediate repayment in the event of a default.

*e.* A clause that allows the maker to satisfy the note by the performance of services or the payment of money.

*f.* A requirement that the maker provide additional collateral if the market value of the original collateral declines.

*g.* The promise to pay is conditional on receipt of 10,000 shares of Microsoft.

*h.* The note states that the terms of default and acceleration are "per" a real estate sales contract.

*i.* The absence of a date of issue.

*j.* The maker used a branding iron (one she specially designed and exclusively used for "signing" important documents) when supplying the signature.

### Required:

Answer the following and give reasons for your conclusions.

With respect to each of these items, state whether or not the instrument in question could be a negotiable instrument.

**2.** J. B. Sortware sells children's computer programs to Kid's Cargo. Seller sends to its bank for collection a document signed by its president, James R. Jones, that appears as follows:

$23,750        Bloomington, Indiana _____

15 days after sight

PAY TO THE ORDER OF J.B. Software Co.
Twenty-three thousand seven hundred fifty and no/100's dollars

VALUE RECEIVED AND CHARGE THE SAME TO ACCOUNT OF

To: Kid's Cargo
1300 Brooks Lane     *James R. Jones* _____
Vineyard Haven, Massachusetts

Reference: Our invoice # 12597

## Required:

Answer the following and give reasons for your conclusions.

1. Is this a negotiable instrument?
2. When can J. B. Software Co. expect to have payment of the sum mentioned?

# CHAPTER
## 24

# NEGOTIATION AND HOLDER IN DUE COURSE

## INTRODUCTION

*The preceding chapter discussed the nature and benefits of negotiable instruments. It also outlined the requirements an instrument must meet to qualify as a negotiable instrument and thus possess the qualities that allow it to be accepted as a substitute for money.*

*This chapter focuses on negotiation—the process by which rights to a negotiable instrument pass from one person to another. Commonly, this involves an indorsement and transfer of the instrument. This chapter also develops the requirements that a transferee of a negotiable instrument must meet to qualify as a holder in due course and to thus attain special rights under negotiable instruments law. These rights, which put a holder in due course in an enhanced position compared to an assignee of a contract, are discussed in some detail.*

## NEGOTIATION

### Nature of Negotiation

Under Revised Article 3, **negotiation** is the transfer of possession (whether voluntary or involuntary) of a negotiable instrument by a person (other than the issuer) to another person who becomes its *holder* [3–201]. A person is a **holder** if she is in possession of an instrument (1) that is payable to bearer or (2) made payable to an identified person and she is that identified person [1–201(20)].[1]

For example, when an employer gives an employee, Susan Adams, a paycheck payable "to the order of Susan Adams," she is the holder of the check because she is in possession of an instrument payable to an identified person (Susan Adams) and she is that person. When she indorses (writes her name) on the back of the check and exchanges it for cash and merchandise at Ace Grocery, she has negotiated the check to the grocery store and the store is now the holder because it is in possession by transfer of a check that now is payable to bearer. Similarly, if Susan Adams indorsed the check "Pay to the Order of Ace Grocery, Susan Adams" and transferred it to the grocery store, it would be a

---

[1] The numbers in parentheses refer to sections of the Uniform Commercial Code (UCC).

holder through the negotiation of the check to it. The grocery store would be in possession of an instrument payable to an identified person (Ace Grocery) and is the person identified in the check.

In certain circumstances, Revised Article 3 allows a person to become a holder by negotiation even though the transfer of possession is involuntary. For example, if a negotiable instrument is payable to bearer and is stolen by Tom Thief or found by Fred Finder, Thief or Finder becomes the holder when he obtains possession. The involuntary transfer of possession of a bearer instrument results in a negotiation to Thief or Finder.

## Formal Requirements for Negotiation

The formal requirements for negotiation are very simple. If an instrument is payable to the order of a specific payee, it is called **order paper** and it can be negotiated by transfer of possession of the instrument after indorsement by the person specified [3–201(b)].

For example, if Rachel's father gives her a check payable "to the order of Rachel Stern," then Rachel can negotiate the check by indorsing her name on the back of the check and giving it to the person to whom she wants to transfer it. Note that the check is order paper, not because the word *order* appears on the check but rather because it named a specific payee, Rachel Stern.

If an instrument is payable to bearer or to cash, it is called **bearer paper** and negotiating it is even simpler. An instrument payable to bearer may be negotiated by transfer of possession alone [3–201(b)]. Thus, if someone gives you a check that is made payable "to the order of cash," you can negotiate it simply by giving it to the person to whom you wish to transfer it. No indorsement is necessary to negotiate an instrument payable to bearer. However, the person who takes the instrument may ask for an indorsement for her protection. By indorsing the check, you agree to be liable for its payment to that person if it is not paid by the drawee bank when it is presented for payment. This liability will be discussed in Chapter 25, Liability of Parties.

## Nature of Indorsement

An indorsement is made by adding the signature of the holder of the instrument to the instrument, usually on the back of it, either alone or with other words. **Indorsement** is defined to mean "a signa-

ture (other than that of a maker, drawer or acceptor) that alone or accompanied by other words, is made on an instrument for purpose of (i) negotiating the instrument, (ii) restricting payment of the instrument, or (iii) incurring indorser's liability on the instrument" [3–204(a)]. The negotiation and restriction of payment aspects of indorsements will be discussed below; indorser's liability will be covered in the next chapter.

The signature constituting an indorsement can be put there either by the holder or by someone who is authorized to sign on behalf of the holder. For example, a check payable to "H&H Meat Market" might be indorsed "H&H Meat Market by Jane Frank, President," if Jane is authorized to do this on behalf of the market.

## Wrong or Misspelled Name

When indorsing an instrument, the holder should spell his name in the same way as it appears on the instrument. If the holder's name is misspelled or wrong, then legally the indorsement can be made either in his name or in the name that is on the instrument. However, any person who pays the instrument or otherwise gives value for it may require the indorser to sign both names [3–204(d)].

Suppose Joan Ash is issued a check payable to the order of "Joanne Ashe." She may indorse the check as either "Joan Ash" or "Joanne Ashe." However, if she takes the check to a bank to cash, the bank may require her to sign both "Joanne Ashe" and "Joan Ash."

## Checks Deposited without Indorsement

Occasionally, when a customer deposits a check to her account with a bank, she may forget to indorse the check; it is common practice for depositary banks to receive unindorsed checks under what are known as "lock-box" arrangements with customers who receive a high volume of checks. Normally, a check payable to the order of an identified person would require the indorsement of that person in order for a negotiation to the depositary bank to take place and for it to become a holder. Under the original Article 3, the depositary bank, in most cases, had the right to supply the customer's indorsement. Instead of actually signing the customer's name to the check as the indorsement, the bank might just stamp on it that it was deposited by the customer or credited to her account. Banks did not have the right to put the customer's indorsement on a check that the customer has deposited if the check specifically required the payee's signature. Insurance and government checks commonly require the payee's signature.

The revision to Article 3 and the conforming amendments to Articles 1 and 4 address the situation where a check is deposited in a depositary bank without indorsement differently. The depositary bank becomes a holder of a item delivered to it for collection, whether or not it is indorsed by the customer, if the customer at the time of delivery qualified as a holder [4−205]. Concomitantly, the depositary bank warrants to other collecting banks, the payor bank (drawee), and the drawer that it paid the amount of the item to the customer or deposited the amount to the customer's account.

## Transfer of Order Instrument

Except for the special provisions concerning depositary banks, if an order instrument is transferred without indorsement, the instrument has not been negotiated and the transferee cannot qualify as a holder. For example, Sue Brown gives a check payable "to the order of Susan Brown" to a drugstore in payment for some cosmetics. Until Sue indorses the check, she has not negotiated it and the druggist could not qualify as a holder of the check.

Transfer of an instrument, whether or not the transfer is a negotiation, vests in the transferee any right of the transferor to enforce the instrument. However, the transferee cannot obtain the rights of a holder in due course (discussed later in this chapter) if he is engaged in any fraud or illegality affecting the instrument. Unless otherwise agreed, if an instrument is transferred for value but without a required indorsement, the transferee has the right to the unqualified indorsement of the transferor; however, the negotiation only takes place when the transferor applies her indorsement [3−203(c)].

## INDORSEMENTS

### Effects of an Indorsement

There are three functions to an indorsement. First, an indorsement is necessary in order for the negotiation of an instrument that is payable to the order of a specified person. Thus, if a check is payable "to the order of James Lee," James must indorse the check before it can be negotiated. Second, the form of the indorsement that the indorser uses also affects future attempts to negotiate the instrument. For example, if James indorses it "Pay to the order of Sarah Hill," Sarah must indorse it before it can be negotiated further.

Third, an indorsement generally makes a person liable on the instrument. By indorsing an instrument, a person incurs an obligation to pay the instrument if the person primarily liable on it (for example, the maker of a note) does not pay it. We discuss the contractual liability of indorsers in Chapter 25. In this chapter, we discuss the effect of an indorsement on further negotiation of an instrument.

## Kinds of Indorsements

There are three basic kinds of indorsements: (1) special, (2) blank, and (3) restrictive. In addition, an indorsement may be "qualified."

**Special Indorsement**   A **special indorsement** contains the signature of the indorser along with words indicating to whom, or to whose order, the instrument is payable. For example, if a check is drawn "Pay to the Order of Marcia Morse" and Marcia indorses it "Pay to the Order of Sam Smith, Marcia Morse" or "Pay to Sam Smith, Marcia Morse," it has been indorsed with a special indorsement. An instrument that is indorsed with a special indorsement remains order paper. It can be negotiated only with the indorsement of the person specified [3−205(a)]. In this example, Sam Smith must indorse the check before he can negotiate it to someone else.

**Blank Indorsement**   If an indorser merely signs his name and does not specify to whom the instrument is payable, he has indorsed the instrument **in blank**. For example, if a check drawn "Pay to the Order of Natalie Owens" is indorsed "Natalie Owens" by Natalie, Natalie has indorsed it in blank. An instrument indorsed in blank is payable to the bearer (person in possession of it) and from that act is "bearer paper." As such, the bearer negotiates it by transfer alone and no further indorsement is necessary for negotiation [3−205(b)].

If Natalie indorsed the check in blank and gave it to Kevin Foley, Kevin would have the right to convert the blank indorsement into a special indorsement [3−205(c)]. He could do this by writing the words "Pay to the Order of Kevin Foley" above Natalie's indorsement. Then the check would have to be indorsed by Kevin before it could be negotiated further.

If Kevin took the check indorsed in blank to a bank and presented it for payment or for collection, the bank would normally ask him to indorse the check. It does this not because it needs his indorsement for the check to be negotiated to it; the check indorsed in blank can be negotiated merely by delivering it to the bank cashier. Rather, the bank asks for his indorsement because it wants to make him liable on the check if it is not paid when the bank sends it to the drawee bank for payment. Chapter 25 discusses the liability of indorsers.

**Restrictive Indorsement** A **restrictive indorsement** is one that specifies the purpose of the indorsement or specifies the use to be made of the instrument. Among the more common restrictive indorsements are:

1. Indorsements for deposit. For example, "For Deposit Only" or "For Deposit to My Account at First National Bank."

2. Indorsements for collection, which are commonly put on by banks involved in the collection process. For example, "Pay any bank, banker, or trust company" or "For collection only."

3. Indorsements indicating that the indorsement is for the benefit of someone other than the person to whom it is payable. For example, "Pay to Arthur Attorney in Trust for Mark Minor."

Generally, the person who takes an instrument with a restrictive indorsement must pay or apply any money or other value he gives for the instrument consistently with the indorsement. In the case of a check indorsed "for deposit" or "for collection," any person other than a bank who purchases the check is considered to have **converted** the check unless (1) the indorser received the amount paid for it or (2) the bank applied the amount of the check consistently with the indorsement (e.g., deposited it to the indorser's account). Similarly, a depositary bank (a bank that takes an item for collection) or payor bank (the drawee bank) that takes an instrument for deposit or for immediate payment over the counter that has been indorsed "for deposit" or "for collection" will be liable for conversion unless the indorser received the amount paid for the instrument or the proceeds or the bank applied the amount consistently with the indorsement [3−206(c)].[2]

By way of illustration, assume that Robert Franks has indorsed his paycheck "For Deposit to My Account No. 4068933 at Bank One." While on his way to the bank he loses the check, and Fred Finder finds it. If Finder tries to cash the check at a check-cashing service, the service must ensure that any value it gives for the check either is deposited to Franks's account at Bank One or is received by Franks. If it gives the money to Finder, it will be liable to Franks for converting his check. This principle is illustrated in the following case, *Lehigh Presbytery v. Merchants Bancorp, Inc.*, which involves a bank that failed to apply value given for checks consistently with restrictive indorsements on the checks.

---

[2] Otherwise, a payor bank as well as an intermediary bank may disregard the indorsement and is not liable if the proceeds of the instrument are not received by the indorser or applied consistently with the indorsement [3−206(c)(4)].

---

## LEHIGH PRESBYTERY v. MERCHANTS BANCORP, INC.
### 17 UCC Rep.2d 163 (Pa. Super. Ct. 1991)

Mary Ann Hunsberger was hired by the Lehigh Presbytery as a secretary/bookkeeper. In this capacity, she was responsible for opening the Presbytery's mail, affixing a rubber stamp indorsement to checks received by the Presbytery, and depositing the checks into the Presbytery's account at Merchants Bancorp, Inc. Over a period of more than five years, Hunsberger deposited into her own account 153 of these checks. Each check was indorsed: "For Deposit Only To The Credit of Presbytery of Lehigh, Ernest Hutcheson, Treas." The bank credited the checks to Hunsberger's account, despite the rubber stamp restrictive indorsement, because it relied solely on the account number handwritten on the deposit slips submitted by Hunsberger with the checks at the time of deposit. Hunsberger obtained the deposit slips in the lobby of the bank, wrote the proper account title, "Lehigh Presbytery," but inserted her own account number rather than the account number of her employer.

When Lehigh Presbytery discovered the diversionary scheme, it sued the bank to recover the funds credited to Hunsberger's account. The primary issue in the case was whether the bank was bound to follow the restrictive indorsements on the 153 checks that it instead had deposited to the personal account of Hunsberger. The trial court ruled in favor of the bank and Lehigh Presbytery appealed.

---

**McEwen, Judge**     UCC Section 3–205 provides:

An indorsement is restrictive which either:

\* \* \* \*

(3) includes the words "for collection," "for deposit," "pay any bank," or like terms signifying a purpose of deposit or collection; or

\* \* \* \*

It is undisputed that the indorsement stamped on each check by Ms. Hunsberger is a restrictive indorsement within the meaning of section 3–205.

Section 3–206 of the UCC addresses the effect of such an indorsement and provides, in pertinent part:

(c) Conditional or specified purpose indorsement.— Except for an intermediary bank, any transferee under an indorsement which is conditional or includes the words "for collection," "for deposit," "Pay any bank," or like terms (section 3–205(1) and (3) (relating to restrictive indorsements) must pay or apply any value given by him for or on the security of the instrument consistently with

the indorsement and to the extent he does he becomes a holder for value.

Thus, the UCC mandates application of the value of the checks consistently with the indorsement, i.e., for deposit to Lehigh Presbytery's account.

Courts considering the significance of a restrictive indorsement have consistently concluded that the UCC imposes an unwaivable obligation upon the bank to follow the indorsement. New York State's highest court has held that "[t]he presence of a restriction imposes upon the depositary bank an obligation not to accept that item other than in accord with the restriction. By disregarding the restriction, it not only subjects itself to liability for any losses resulting from its actions, but it also passes up what may be the best opportunity to prevent the fraud."

**Judgment reversed in favor of Lehigh Presbytery.**

*Note:* Although this case was decided under the original version of Article 3, the same result would be expected under Revised Article 3.

---

Some indorsements indicate payment to the indorsee as an agent, trustee, or fiduciary. A person who takes an instrument containing such an indorsement from the indorsee may pay the proceeds to the indorsee without regard to whether the indorsee violates a fiduciary duty to the indorser *unless* he is on *notice* of any breach of fiduciary duty that the indorser may be committing [3–206(d)]. A person would have such notice if he took the instrument in any transaction that benefited the indorsee personally [3–307]. Suppose a person takes a check indorsed to "Arthur Attorney in Trust for Mark Minor." The money given for the

check should be put in Mark Minor's trust account. A person would not be justified in taking the check in exchange for a television set that he knew Attorney was acquiring for his own—rather than Minor's—use.

There are two other kinds of indorsements that original Article 3 treated as restrictive indorsements but that Revised Article 3 no longer considers as restrictive indorsements. They are:

1. Indorsements purporting to prohibit further negotiation. For example, "Pay to Carl Clark Only."

2. Conditional indorsements, which indicate that they are effective only if the payee satisfies a certain condition For example, "Pay to Bernard Builder Only if He Completes Construction on My House by November 1, 1995."

Under Revised Article 3, any indorsement that purports to limit payment to a particular person, or to prohibit further transfer or negotiation of the instrument, is not effective to prevent further transfer or negotiation [3–206(a)]. Thus, if a note is indorsed "Pay to Carl Clark Only" and given to Clark, he may negotiate the note to subsequent holders who may ignore the restriction on the indorsement.

Indorsements that state a condition to the right of the indorsee to receive payment do not affect the right of the indorsee to enforce the instrument. Any person who pays the instrument or takes it for value or for collection may disregard the condition. Moreover, the rights and liabilities of the person are not affected by whether the condition has been fulfilled [3–206(b)].

**Qualified Indorsement**   A **qualified indorsement** is one where the indorser disclaims her liability to make the instrument good if the maker or drawer defaults on it. Words such as "Without Recourse" are used to qualify an indorsement. They can be used with either a blank indorsement or a special indorsement and thus make it a qualified blank indorsement or a qualified special indorsement. The use of a qualified indorsement does not change the negotiable nature of the instrument. Its effect is to eliminate the contractual liability of the indorser. Chapter 25 will discuss this liability in detail.

**CONCEPT REVIEW**

## INDORSEMENTS

(Assume a check is payable "To The Order of Mark Smith.")

| Type | Example | Consequences |
|---|---|---|
| Blank | Mark Smith | 1. Satisfies the indorsement requirement for the negotiation of order paper. 2. The instrument becomes bearer paper and can be negotiated by delivery alone. 3. The indorser becomes obligated on the instrument. (See Chapter 25, Liability of Parties.) |
| Special | Pay to the Order of Joan Brown, Mark Smith | 1. Satisfies the indorsement requirement for the negotiation of order paper. 2. The instrument remains order paper and Joan Brown's indorsement is required for further negotiation. 3. The indorser becomes obligated on the instrument. (See Chapter 25.) |
| Restrictive | For deposit only to my account in First American Bank Mark Smith | 1. Satisfies the indorsement requirement for the negotiation of order paper. 2. The person who pays value for the instrument is obligated to pay it consistent with the indorsement (i.e., to pay it into Mark Smith's account at First American Bank). 3. The indorser becomes obligated on the instrument. (See Chapter 25.) |
| Qualified | Mark Smith (without recourse) | 1. Satisfies the indorsement requirement for negotiation of order paper. 2. Eliminates the indorser's obligation. (See Chapter 25.) |

## Rescission of Indorsement

Negotiation is effective to transfer an instrument even if the negotiation is (1) made by a minor, a corporation exceeding its powers, or any other person without contractual capacity; (2) obtained by fraud, duress, or mistake of any kind; (3) made in breach of duty; or (4) part of an illegal transaction. A negotiation made under the preceding circumstances is subject to **rescission** before the instrument has been negotiated to a transferee who can qualify as a holder in due course [3–202]. The situation in such instances is analogous to a sale of goods where the sale has been induced by fraud or misrepresentation. In such a case, the seller may rescind the sale and recover the goods, provided that the seller acts before the goods are resold to a bona fide purchaser for value.

## HOLDER IN DUE COURSE

A person who qualifies as a holder in due course of a negotiable instrument gets special rights. Normally, the transferee of an instrument—like the assignee of a contract—gets only those rights in the instrument that are held by the person from whom he got the instrument. But a holder in due course can get better rights. A holder in due course takes a negotiable instrument free of all **personal defenses, claims to the instrument**, and **claims in recoupment** either of the obligor or of a third party. A holder in due course does not take free of the **real defenses**, which go to the validity of the instrument or of claims that develop after he becomes a holder. We develop the differences between personal and real defenses in more detail later in this chapter and also explain claims to the instrument and claims in recoupment. The following example illustrates the advantage that a holder in due course of a negotiable instrument may have.

Assume that Carl Carpenter contracts with Helen Homeowner to build her a garage for $9,500, payable on October 1 when he expects to complete the garage. Assume further that Carpenter assigns his right to the $9,500 to First National Bank in order to obtain money for materials. If the bank tries to collect the money from Homeowner on October 1 but Carpenter has not finished building the garage, then Homeowner may assert the fact that the garage is not complete as a defense to paying the bank. As

assignee of a simple contract, the bank has only those rights that its assignor, Carpenter, has and is subject to all claims and defenses that Homeowner has against Carpenter.

Now assume that instead of simply signing a contract with Homeowner, Carpenter had Homeowner give him a negotiable promissory note in the amount of $9,500 payable to the order of Carpenter on October 1 and that Carpenter then negotiated the note to the bank. If the bank is able to qualify as a holder in due course, it may collect the $9,500 from Homeowner on October 1 even though she might have a personal defense against payment of the note because Carpenter had not completed the work on the garage. Homeowner cannot assert that personal defense against a holder in due course. She would have to pay the note to the bank and then independently seek to recover from Carpenter for breach of their agreement. The bank's improved position is due to its status as a holder in due course of a negotiable instrument. If the instrument in question was not negotiable, or if the bank could not qualify as a holder in due course, then it would be in the same position as the assignee of a simple contract and would be subject to Homeowner's personal defense.

We turn now to a discussion of the requirements that must be met for the possessor of a negotiable instrument to qualify as a holder in due course.

## General Requirements

In order to become a **holder in due course**, a person who takes a negotiable instrument must be a *holder*, and take the instrument for *value*, in *good faith*, *without notice* that it is *overdue* or has been *dishonored* or that there is any uncured default with respect to payment of another instrument issued as part of the same series, *without notice that the instrument contains an unauthorized signature or has been altered, without notice of any claim of a property or possessory interest in it*, and *without notice* that any party has any *defense against it* or *claim in recoupment to it* [3–302(a)(2)].

In addition, the revision to Article 3 requires "that the instrument when issued or negotiated to the holder does not bear such *apparent evidence of forgery or alteration* or is not otherwise so *irregular* or *incomplete* as to call into question its authenticity" [3–302(a)(1)].

If a person who takes a negotiable instrument does not meet these requirements, he is not a holder in due course. Then the person is in the same position as an assignee of a contract.

## Holder

As noted earlier in this chapter, to be a **holder** of a negotiable instrument, a person must have possession of an instrument that is either payable to bearer or that is payable to him. For example, if Teresa Gonzales is given a check by her grandmother that is made payable "to the order of Teresa Gonzales," Teresa is a holder of the check because it is made out to her. If Teresa indorses the check "Pay to the order of Ames Hardware, Teresa Gonzales" and gives it to Ames Hardware in payment for some merchandise, then Ames Hardware is the holder of the check. Ames Hardware is a holder because it is in possession of a check that is indorsed to its order. If Ames Hardware indorses the check "Ames Hardware" and deposits it in its account at First National Bank, the bank becomes the holder. The bank is in possession of an instrument that is indorsed in blank and thus is payable to bearer.

It is important that all indorsements on the instrument at the time it is payable to the order of someone are *authorized indorsements*. With limited exceptions (discussed later), a forged indorsement is not an effective indorsement and prevents a person from becoming a holder.

To be a holder, a person must have a complete chain of authorized indorsements. Suppose the Internal Revenue Service mails to Robert Washington an income tax refund check payable to him. Tom Turner steals the check from Washington's mailbox, signs (indorses) "Robert Washington" on the back of the check, and cashes it at a shoe store. The shoe store is not a holder of the check because its transferor, Turner, was not a holder and because it needs Washington's signature to have a good chain of authorized indorsements. Robert Washington has to indorse the check in order for there to be a valid chain of indorsements. Turner's signature is not effective for this purpose because Washington did not authorize him to sign Washington's name to the check [1–201(20); 3–403(a); 3–416(a)(2)].

The case that follows, *LaJunta State Bank v. Travis*, illustrates that a party in possession of a check indorsed in blank is a holder of the instrument.

---

## La Junta State Bank v. Travis
### 727 P.2d 48 (Sup. Ct. Colo. 1986)

On November 15, 1979, Katherine Warnock purchased a cashier's check in the amount of $53,541.93 payable to her order and drawn on the Pueblo Bank and Trust Company. At some time between November 15 and November 30, Warnock indorsed "Katherine Warnock" on the reverse side of the check, and Warnock's attorney, Jerry Quick, wrote the words "deposit only" under Warnock's indorsement. On November 30, Quick deposited the check into a trust account he maintained at the La Junta State Bank. Warnock did not maintain any type of account with La Junta State Bank. La Junta collected the amount of the check from Pueblo Bank.

Warnock died on November 10, 1981. Robert Travis, Warnock's personal representative, was unable to find a receipt in her personal papers for the sum of $53,541.93. On June 24, Travis demanded that the La Junta Bank repay that sum to Warnock's estate. At the time, no funds remained in Quick's trust account at the bank. When the La Junta Bank refused the representative's demand, he brought suit against the bank claiming it had improperly paid the check by allowing it into any account other than one in Warnock's name. The trial court determined that Warnock had indorsed the check in blank and delivered it to Quick, that the check therefore became bearer paper upon Warnock's indorsement, and that the check was negotiable on delivery alone; it granted judgment to the bank. A divided court of appeals reversed in favor of the representative, holding that Quick's addition of the words "deposit only" below Warnock's signature created a restrictive indorsement and that because the bank failed to treat it as such, it was liable to the representative for the full amount of the check. The bank appealed.

---

**Kirshbaum, Justice**   It is undisputed that when Warnock indorsed the check in blank and delivered it to Quick, it was converted from order paper to bearer paper, negotiable by delivery alone until specially indorsed [3–204(2)]. The trial court also concluded that Quick's addition of "deposit only" below Warnock's signature did not convert Warnock's blank indorsement into a special indorsement.

Implicit in the trial court's conclusions is the assumption that Quick added the words "deposit only" to the check some time after Warnock's indorsement thereof. This implicit finding is supported by the stipulation of facts and the evidence disclosed by the record. Therefore, we also conclude that when Warnock indorsed the check in blank and delivered it to Quick, Quick became a holder of the instrument in bearer form with the right to transfer or negotiate it by delivery alone.

Warnock's representative argues that, assuming Quick was initially a holder of a check in bearer form, his act of affixing the words "deposit only" to the check deprived him of that status, destroyed the negotiability of the check, and converted Warnock's blank indorsement into a restrictive indorsement. This argument is untenable.

Quick, as holder of an instrument, was not authorized by any Code provision to convert this transferor's blank indorsement into a restrictive one (see section 3–204(3): "The holder may convert a blank indorsement by writing over the signature of the indorser in blank any contract consistent with the character of the indorsement."). Furthermore, the representative incorrectly assumes that a blank indorsement and a restrictive indorsement create mutually exclusive methods for negotiation. As UCC section 3–206 official comment 5 (1978) indicates, "indorsements 'for collection' or 'for deposit' may be either special or blank." A single indorsement, therefore, may be both in blank and restrictive. The nonrestrictive character of Warnock's indorsement was determined when she affixed her signature to the check.

The fact that Quick was a holder of bearer paper does not end the inquiry into the propriety of the bank's conduct. Section 3–206(3) of the Code requires a depository bank, upon being presented with a negotiable instrument containing an indorsement which includes the words "for deposit" or like terms, to "pay or apply any value given by him for or on the security of the instrument consistently with the indorsement. . . ." This obligation affords protection to payees or indorsers who indorse items "for deposit" in the belief that such indorsement will guard against further negotiation of the instrument to a holder in due course by a finder or a thief.

In this case the bank, as a depository bank, received a check containing what appeared to be a restrictive indorsement by Katherine Warnock. The record does not reveal who actually delivered the check and deposit slip to the bank. Thus, at the moment it received the restrictively indorsed check, the bank appeared to owe a duty to Warnock to either comply with the directions of the indorsement or to inquire further concerning the transaction because of the simultaneous receipt of a deposit slip into an account other than Warnock's. However, because the check was bearer paper when Quick received it, he was free to direct its deposit in any manner he elected. Any inquiry by the bank would have revealed that, although the language inscribed on the instrument appeared to constitute a restrictive indorsement by Katherine Warnock, the words "deposit only" had been added by Quick on his own behalf; and the bank owed a duty to Quick on November 30, 1979, to honor his restrictive indorsement. Under the circumstances of the case, the bank owed no duty to Warnock and Warnock's representative is entitled to no damages.

### Judgment for La Junta State Bank.

*Note:* Although this case was decided under the original version of Article 3, the same result would be anticipated under Revised Article 3.

---

## Value

To qualify as a holder in due course of a negotiable instrument, a person must give **value** for it. Value is not identical to simple consideration. Under the provisions of the Revised Article 3, a holder takes

for value if: (1) the agreed-on promise of performance has been performed—for example, if the instrument was given in exchange for a promise to deliver a refrigerator and the refrigerator has been delivered; (2) he acquires a security interest in, or a lien on, the instrument; (3) he takes the instrument in payment of, or as security for, an antecedent claim; (4) he gives a negotiable instrument for it; or (5) he makes an irrevocable commitment to a third person [3–303]. Thus, a person who gets a check as a gift or merely makes an executory promise in return for a check has not given value for it and cannot qualify as a holder in due course.

A bank or any person who discounts an instrument in the *regular course of trade* has given value for it. In this context, the discount is essentially a means for increasing the return or the rate of interest on the instrument. Likewise, if a loan is made and an instrument is pledged as security for the repayment of the loan, the secured party has given value for the instrument to the amount of the loan. If Axe, who owes Bell a past-due debt, indorses and delivers to Bell, in payment of the debt or as security for its repayment, an instrument issued to Axe, Bell has given value for the instrument. If a bank allows a customer to draw against a check deposited for collection, it has given value to the extent of the credit drawn against.

If the promise of performance that is the consideration for an instrument has been partially performed, the holder may assert rights as a holder in due course of the instrument only to the fraction of the amount payable under the instrument equal to the partial performance divided by the value of the promised performance [3–302(d)]. For example, Arthur Wells agrees to purchase a note payable to the order of Helda Parks. The note is for the sum of $5,000. Wells pays Parks $1,000 on the negotiation of the note to him and agrees to pay the balance of $4,000 in 10 days. Initially, Wells is a holder in due course for one fifth of the amount of the note. If he later pays the $4,000 due he may become a holder in due course for the full amount.

## Good Faith

To qualify as a holder in due course of a negotiable instrument, a person must take it in **good faith**, which means that the person obtained it honestly and in the observance of reasonable commercial standards of fair dealing [3–103(a)(4)]. If a person obtains a check by trickery or with knowledge that it has been stolen, the person has not obtained the check in good faith and cannot be a holder in due course. A person who pays too little for an instrument, perhaps because she suspects that something may be wrong with the way it was obtained, may

have trouble meeting the good faith test. Suppose a finance company works closely with a door-to-door sales company that engages in shoddy practices. If the finance company buys the consumers' notes from the sales company, it will not be able to meet the good faith test and qualify as a holder in due course of the notes.

## Overdue or Dishonored

In order to qualify as a holder in due course, a person must take a negotiable instrument before he has notice that it either is **overdue** or has been **dishonored**. The reason for this is that one should perform obligations when they are due. If a negotiable instrument is not paid when it is due, the Code considers the person taking it to be on notice that there may be defenses to the payment of it.

**Overdue Instruments**   If a negotiable instrument is payable on demand, it is overdue: (1) the day after demand for payment has been made in a proper manner and form; (2) 90 days after its date if it is a check; and (3) if it is an instrument other than a check, when it has been outstanding for an unreasonably long period of time in light of the nature of the instrument and trade practice [3–304(a)]. Thus, a check becomes stale after 90 days and, for other kinds of instruments, one must consider trade practices and the facts of the particular case. In a farming community, the normal period for loans to farmers may be six months. A demand note might be outstanding for six or seven months before it is considered overdue. On the other hand, a demand note issued in an industrial city where the normal period of such loans is 30 to 60 days would be considered overdue in a much shorter period of time.

If a negotiable instrument due on a certain date is not paid by that date, then normally it is overdue at the beginning of the next day after the due date. For example, if a promissory note dated January 1 is payable "30 days after date," it is due on January 31. If it is not paid by January 31, it is overdue beginning on February 1.

As to instruments payable at a definite time, Revised Article 3 sets out four rules: (1) if the principal is not payable in installments and the due date has not been accelerated, the instrument is overdue on the day after the due date; (2) if the principal is due in installments and a due date has not been accelerated, the instrument is overdue upon default for nonpayment of an installment and remains overdue until the default is cured; (3) if a due date for the principal has been accelerated, the instrument is overdue on the day after the accelerated due date; and (4) unless the due date of the principal has been accelerated, an instrument does not become overdue if there is a default in payment of interest but no default in payment of principal [3–304(b)].

**Dishonored Instruments**   To be a holder in due course, a person not only must take a negotiable instrument before he has notice that it is overdue but also must take it before it has been dishonored. A negotiable instrument has been *dishonored* when the holder has presented it for payment (or acceptance) and payment (or acceptance) has been refused.

For example, Susan writes a check on her account at First National Bank that is payable "to the order of Sven Sorensen." Sven takes the check to First National Bank to cash it but the bank refuses to pay it because Susan has insufficient funds in her account to cover it. The check has been dishonored. If Sven then takes Susan's check to Harry's Hardware and uses it to pay for some paint, Harry's cannot be a holder in due course of the check if it is on notice that the check has been dishonored. Harry's would have such notice if First National had stamped the check "Payment Refused NSF" (not sufficient funds).

Similarly, suppose Carol Carson signs a 30-day note payable to Ace Appliance for $500 and gives it to Ace as payment for a stereo set. When Ace asks Carol for payment, she refuses to pay because the stereo does not work properly. If Ace negotiates the note to First National Bank, First National cannot be a holder in due course if it knows about Carol's refusal to pay.

## Notice of Unauthorized Signature or Alteration

A holder who has notice that an instrument contains an unauthorized signature or has been altered cannot qualify as a holder in due course of the instrument. For example, Frank makes out a check in the amount of $5.00 payable to George Grocer and gives it to his daughter, Jane, to take to the grocery store to purchase some groceries. The groceries Frank wants cost $20.00 and Jane changes the check

to read $25.00, giving it to Grocer in exchange for the groceries and $5.00 in cash. Grocer cannot qualify as a holder in due course if he sees Jane make the alteration to the check or otherwise is on notice of it.

## Notice of Claims

If a person taking a negotiable instrument is *on notice of an adverse claim* to the instrument by someone else (for example, that she is the rightful owner of the instrument) or that someone is seeking to rescind a prior negotiation of the instrument, the current holder cannot qualify as a holder in due course. For example, a U.S. Treasury check is payable to Susan Samuels. Samuels loses the check and it is found by Robert Burns. Burns takes the check to a hardware store, signs "Susan Samuels" on the back of the check in the view of a clerk, and seeks to use it in payment of merchandise. The hardware store cannot be a holder in due course because it is on notice of a potential claim to the instrument by Susan Samuels.

**Notice of Breach of Fiduciary Duty**   One situation in which the Code considers a person to be on notice of a claim is if she is taking a negotiable instrument from a fiduciary, such as a trustee. If a negotiable instrument is payable to a person as a trustee or an attorney for someone, then any attempt by that person to negotiate it for his own behalf or for his use (or benefit) or to deposit it in an account other than that of the fiduciary puts the person on notice that the beneficiary of the trust may have a claim [3–307].

For example, a check is drawn "Pay to the order of Arthur Adams, Trustee for Mary Minor." Adams takes the check to Credit Union, indorses his name to it, and uses it to pay off the balance on a loan Adams had from Credit Union. Credit Union cannot be a holder in due course because it should know that the negotiation of the check is in violation of the fiduciary duty Adams owes to Mary Minor. Credit Union should know this because Adams is negotiating the check for his own benefit, not Mary's. The case that follows, *Smith v. Olympic Bank*, illustrates the consequences to a bank of not being careful in taking an instrument from a fiduciary.

## SMITH V. OLYMPIC BANK
### 693 P.2d 92 (Sup. Ct. Wash. 1985)

Charles Alcombrack was appointed guardian for his son, Chad Alcombrack, who was seven years old and the beneficiary of his grandfather's life insurance policy. The insurance company issued a check for $30,588.39 made payable to "Charles Alcombrack, Guardian of the Estate of Chad Stephen Alcombrack, a Minor." The attorney for the son's estate directed the father to take the check, along with the letters of guardianship issued to the father, to the bank and open a guardianship savings and checking account. Instead, the father took the check, without the letters of guardianship, to the Olympic Bank and opened a personal checking and a personal savings account.

Despite the fact that the check was payable to the father in his guardianship capacity, the bank allowed the father to place the entire amount in his newly opened personal accounts. The father used all but $320.60 of the trust money for his own benefit. A new guardian, J. David Smith, was appointed for Chad. Smith brought suit against the Olympic Bank, on Chad's behalf, to recover the amount of the check. The trial court granted judgment in favor of the bank and Smith appealed.

---

**Dore, Justice**     Olympic Bank claims that it is a holder in due course (HIDC) and, as such, is not subject to the claims of Smith. In order to qualify as a HIDC, the bank must meet five requirements. It must be (1) a holder (2) of a negotiable instrument, (3) that took the instrument for value (4) in good faith and (5) without notice that it was overdue, dishonored, or of any defense or claim to it on the part of any person. We need not decide whether the bank met the first four conditions as we hold that the bank took the check with notice of an adverse claim to the instrument and, therefore, is not a holder in due course. Consequently, the bank is liable to the son's estate.

A purchaser has notice of an adverse claim when "he has knowledge that a fiduciary has negotiated the instrument in payment of or as security for his own debt or in any transaction for his own benefit or otherwise in breach of duty." Section 3–304(2). Thus the issue raised by this case is whether the bank had knowledge that the guardian was breaching his fiduciary duty when it allowed him to deposit a check, made payable to him in his guardianship capacity, into his personal accounts.

The bank knew it was dealing with guardianship funds. The check was payable to the father as guardian and not to him personally. The father indorsed it in his guardianship capacity. The bank received a call from the guardian's attorney inquiring about the fee charged for guardianship accounts, and a trust officer for the bank replied in a letter referring to the "Estate of Chad Alcombrack."

Reasonable commercial practices dictate that when the bank knew that the funds were deposited in a personal account instead of a guardianship account, it knew that the father was breaching his fiduciary duty. The funds lost the protection they would have received in a guardianship account. If the funds had been placed in a guardianship account, the bank would not have been permitted to accept a check drawn on the guardianship account, from the father in satisfaction of the father's unsecured personal loan in the amount of approximately $3,000. Nor could the father, or bank, have authorized his new wife to write checks against the guardianship account without court approval. A fiduciary has a duty to ensure that trust funds are protected. Here, the father breached his duty.

The policy reasons for holding a bank liable are compelling—especially in the situation presented in this case. The ward has no control of his own estate. He must rely on his guardian and on the bank for the safekeeping of his money. In order to protect the ward, the guardian and bank must be held to a high standard of care. For the guardian, this means that he must deposit guardian funds in a guardianship account. For the bank, it means that when it receives a check made payable to an individual as a guardian, it must make sure that the check is placed in a guardianship account. This will not place an undue burden on either banks or guardians and will have the beneficial effect of protecting the ward.

**Judgment reversed in favor of son's guardian.**

*Note:* Although this case was decided under the original version of Article 3 and the applicable language has been changed, the decision is consistent with Revised Article 3's treatment of negotiations involving fiduciaries. See section 3–307.

---

## Notice of Defenses and Claims in Recoupment

To qualify as a holder in due course, a person must also acquire a negotiable instrument without notice that any party to it has any **defenses** or **claims in recoupment**. Potential defenses include infancy, duress, fraud, and failure of consideration. Thus, if a person knows that a signature on the instrument was obtained by fraud, misrepresentation, or duress, the person cannot be a holder in due course.

A *claim in recoupment* is a claim of the obligor against the original payee of the instrument. The claim must arise from the transaction that gave rise to the instrument. An example of a claim in recoupment would be as follows: Buyer purchases a used automobile from Dealer for $8,000, giving the dealer a note for $8,000 payable in one year. Because the automobile is not as warranted, Buyer has a breach of warranty claim that could be asserted against Dealer as counterclaim or "claim in recoupment" to offset the amount owing on the note.

The following case, *Parkhill v. Nusor*, illustrates the factors a court may consider in determining whether a person should be on notice of possible defenses or adverse claims by a party to a negotiable instrument and thus not able to claim the status of a holder in due course.

---

IN RE NUSOR

PARKHILL V. NUSOR

**13 UCC Rep.2d 773 (Bankr. App., 9th Cir. 1991)**

In the fall of 1987, Irene Nusor was behind in her mortgage payments. She received advertisements from Best Financial Consultants offering attractive refinancing opportunities. On October 14, 1987, she attended a meeting with Best representatives at a McDonald's restaurant who told her that Best would arrange for a complete refinancing of her home in the amount of $98,000, pay off the two existing lienholders, and provide Nusor with an additional $5,000 in spending money. In consideration for these services, Nusor was told that she would owe Best only $4,000.

Nusor agreed to the arrangement and proceeded to sign a fee agreement and a promissory note entitled "Installment Note" that was blank at the time and Best representatives later completed. As completed, it provided that Best would loan her a total sum of $14,986.61 payable in full in 60 days (on December 23, 1987) with an annual interest rate of 18 percent. Where the note provided for the name of the promissor to be filled in, the following words had been typed in: "I, the undersigned, Irene Vazquez Nusor, a married woman, as her sole and separate property." The note was payable to "Best Financial Consultants, a California Sole Proprietorship, or order." The note also contained the following statement: "This note is a [sic] junior to a first deed of trust of record." On November 13, 1987, Nusor went to a second meeting with Best representatives and signed a "short form deed of trust and assignment of rents." The deed indicated that it was secured by a promissory note in the amount of $14,986.61.

On December 2, 1987, Best assigned the note to Robin Parkhill for the discounted price of $13,812.19. Over the term of the note, Parkhill's total anticipated return was $1,624.02, representing the equivalent of an annual interest rate of over 203 percent. Parkhill, who responded to a newspaper ad placed by Best, bought the note without actual notice of the misrepresentations made to Nusor by Best. Nusor received only a single payment of $5,997.25 from Best to one of her lienholders; Best never refinanced Nusor's home or fulfilled its other promises. In June 1988, Nusor filed a Chapter 13 bankruptcy petition. One of the questions in the bankruptcy proceeding was the status of the promissory note that Parkhill claimed Nusor owed to her. A key issue was whether Parkhill was a holder in due course of a negotiable promissory note and thus not subject to the defenses of fraud in the inducement and failure of consideration that Nusor had against Best. The trial court held in favor of Nusor and Parkhill appealed.

---

**Volinn, Bankruptcy Judge**   Whether Parkhill is a holder in due course turns on Parkhill satisfying the requirements of Code Section 3–302. Nusor argues that Parkhill fails to meet this standard because of the note's clumsy draftsmanship and its exceptional rate of return (i.e., the maturation of the discounted note 21 days from the date of the assignment) gave Parkhill at least constructive notice of Nusor's defenses. Nusor states that these "irregularities ... would certainly cause a reasonably prudent person to question the note's validity and thereby be placed on notice." We agree and hold that Parkhill was not a holder in due course.

Code section 3–304(1) sets forth the conditions under which "irregularities" in the instrument puts the holder on notice:

(1) The purchaser has *notice of a claim or defense* if (a) the instrument is so incomplete, bears such visible evidence of forgery or alteration, or *is otherwise so irregular as to call into question its validity, terms or ownership* or to create an ambiguity as to the party to pay; [Emphasis added.]

The term "notice" is further defined in section 1–201(25)(c), which provides that one has notice of a fact when "[f]rom all the facts and circumstances known to him at the time in question he or she has *reason to know* that it exists." [Emphasis added.]

In this case, Parkhill did not seek interest income in the usual manner. She answered a newspaper advertisement. Presumably, after communicating with Best, she calculated the rate of return. The content of the Installment Note, particularly its extraordinarily favorable terms, clearly indicated that this was an unusual type of commercial trans-

action. For the discounted price of $13,812.19, Parkhill was assigned a note designed to provide her in 21 days (on December 23, 1987) the face value of the Installment Note ($14,986.61) plus 18% per annum interest that would accrue over the term of the note. Thus, Parkhill's total anticipated return was $1,624.02. This amount represents the equivalent of an annual rate of return of over 203%, a return far in excess of the reasonable expectations of any investor who in good faith seeks a favorable rate of return. In addition, we find it significant that Parkhill made no inquiry about the note's origins notwithstanding its manifestly unusual terms. See *Stewart v. Thornton* (holder in due course protection cannot be used to shield one who simply refuses to investigate when the facts known to him suggest an irregularity concerning the commercial paper he purchases).

The imprecise form of the Installment Note, combined with its exorbitant rate of return, were sufficient to divest Parkhill of holder in due course status and to subject her to Nusor's defenses against the note's enforceability. Accordingly, we hold that Parkhill is not a holder in due course and is therefore subject to Nusor's defenses of fraud in the inducement and failure of consideration.

**Judgment in favor of Nusor affirmed.**

*Note:* Although this case was decided under the original Article 3, the same result would be anticipated under Revised Article 3. And, as noted below, Revised Article 3 explicitly provides that a person cannot become a holder in due course of an instrument that is so irregular as to call into question its authenticity [3–302(a)(1)].

---

## Irregular and Incomplete Instruments

A person cannot be a holder in due course of a negotiable instrument if, when she takes it, it is irregular or some important or **material term** is blank.

If the negotiable instrument contains a facial irregularity, such as an obvious alteration in the amount, then it is considered to be **irregular paper**. If you take an irregular instrument, you are considered to be on notice of any possible defenses to it. For example, Kevin writes a check for "one dollar" payable to Karen. Karen inserts the word "hundred" in the amount, changes the figure "$1" to "$100," and gives the check to a druggist in exchange for a purchase of goods. If the alterations in the amount should be obvious to the druggist, perhaps because there are erasures, different handwritings, or different inks, then the druggist cannot be a holder in due course. She would have taken irregular paper and would be on notice that there might be defenses to it. These defenses include Kevin's defense that he is liable for only $1 because that is the amount for which he made the check.

Similarly, if someone receives a check that has been signed but the space where the amount of the check is to be written is blank, then the person cannot be a holder in due course of that check. The fact that a material term is blank means that the instrument is **incomplete** and should put the person on notice that the drawer may have a defense to payment of it. To be material, the omitted term must be one that affects the legal obligation of the parties to the negotiable instrument. Material terms include the amount of the instrument and the name of the payee. If a negotiable instrument is completed after the obligor signed it but before a person acquires it, the person can qualify as a holder in due course if she had no knowledge about the completion.

## Payee as Holder in Due Course

The original Article 3 provided explicitly that a *payee* could be a holder in due course if he complied with all the requirements for a holder in due course. Revised Article 3 drops the explicit statement; the drafters stated they intended no change in the law but that they were concerned that the explicit provision suggested that use of holder in due course status by payees was the normal situation. It is not the normal situation because a payee usually will have notice or knowledge of any defenses to the instrument and will know whether it is overdue or has been dishonored; consequently, the payee is unlikely to qualify as a holder in due course. For example, Drew draws a check on First Bank as drawee, payable to the order of Parks but leaves the amount blank. Drew delivers the check to Axe, his agent, and instructs Axe to fill in $300 as the amount. Axe, however, fills in $500 as the amount, and Parks gives Axe $500 for the check.

Axe then gives Drew $300 and absconds with the extra $200. In such a case, Parks, as payee, is a holder in due course of the check because he has taken it for value, in good faith, and without notice of defenses.

Similarly, assume that Jarvis owes Fields $200. Jarvis agrees to sell Kirk a used television set for $200; Jarvis assures Kirk that it is in working condition. In fact, the set is broken. Jarvis asks Kirk to make her check for $200 payable to Fields and then delivers the check to Fields in payment of the debt. Fields, as the payee, can be a holder in due course of the check if he is not aware of the misrepresentation that Jarvis made to Kirk in order to obtain the check.

## Shelter Rule

The transferee of an instrument—whether or not the transfer is a negotiation—obtains those rights that the transferor had, including (1) the transferor's right to enforce the instrument and (2) any right as a holder in due course [3–203(b)]. This means that any person who can trace his title to an instrument back to a holder in due course receives rights similar of a holder in due course even if he cannot meet the requirements himself. This is known as the **shelter rule** in Article 3. For example, Archer makes a note payable to Bryant. Bryant negotiates the note to Carlyle, who qualifies as a holder in due course. Carlyle then negotiates the note to Darby, who cannot qualify as a holder in due course because she knows the note is overdue. Because Darby can trace her title back to a holder in due course (Carlyle), Darby has rights like a holder in due course when she seeks payment of the note from Archer.

There is, however, a limitation on the shelter rule. A transferee who has himself been a party to any fraud or illegality affecting the instrument cannot improve his position by taking, directly or indirectly, from a later holder in due course [3–203(b)]. For example, Archer, through fraudulent representations, induced Bryant to execute a negotiable note payable to Archer and then negotiated the instrument to Carlyle, who took as a holder in due course. If Archer thereafter took the note for value from Carlyle, Archer could not acquire Carlyle's rights as a holder in due course. Archer was a party to the fraud that induced the note, and, accordingly, cannot improve his position by negotiating the instrument and then reacquiring it.

**CONCEPT REVIEW**

# REQUIREMENTS FOR A HOLDER IN DUE COURSE

| Requirement | Rule |
|---|---|
| **1. Must be a *holder*.** | A holder is a person in possession of an instrument payable to bearer or payable to an identified person and he is that person. |
| 2. Must take *for value*. | A holder has given value:<br>*a.* To the extent the agreed-on consideration has been paid or performed.<br>*b.* To the extent a security interest or lien has been obtained in the negotiable instrument.<br>*c.* By taking the negotiable instrument in payment of—or as security for—an antecedent claim.<br>*d.* By giving a negotiable instrument for it.<br>*e.* By making an irrevocable commitment to a third person. |
| 3. Must take in *good faith*. | Good faith means honesty in fact and the observance of reasonable commercial standards of fair dealing. |
| 4. Must take *without notice* that the instrument is *overdue*. | An instrument payable on demand is overdue the day after demand for payment has been duly made.<br>A check is overdue 90 days after its date.<br>If it is an instrument other than a check and payable on demand, when it has been outstanding for an unreasonably long period of time in light of nature of the instrument and trade practice.<br>If it is an instrument due on a certain date, then it is overdue at the beginning of the next day after the due date. |
| 5. Must take *without notice that the instrument has been dishonored.* | An instrument has been dishonored when the holder has presented it for payment (or acceptance) and payment (or acceptance) has been refused. |
| 6. Must take *without notice* of any *uncured default* with respect to payment of another instrument issued as part of the same series. | If there is a series of notes, holder must take without notice that there is an uncured default as to any other notes in the series. |
| 7. Must take *without notice* that the instrument contains an *unauthorized signature* or has been *altered*. | Notice of unauthorized signature or alteration—i.e., a change in a material term—prevents holder from obtaining HDC status. |
| 8. Must take *without notice* of any *claim of a property or possessory interest* in it. | Claims of property or possessory interest include:<br>*a.* Claim by someone that she is the rightful owner of the instrument.<br>*b.* Person seeking to rescind a prior negotiation of the instrument.<br>*c.* Claim by a beneficiary that a fiduciary negotiated the instrument for his own benefit. |
| 9. Must take *without notice* that any party has a *defense* against it. | Defenses include real defenses that go to the validity of the instrument and personal defenses that commonly are defenses to a simple contract. |
| 10. Must take *without notice* of a *claim in recoupment* to it. | A claim in recoupment is a claim of the obligor on the instrument against the original payee that arises from the transaction that gave rise to the instrument. |
| 11. The instrument must not bear *apparent evidence of forgery or alteration* or be *irregular* or *incomplete*. | The instrument must not contain obvious reasons to question its authenticity. |

# Rights of a Holder in Due Course

## Claims and Defenses Generally

Revised Article 3 establishes four categories of claims and defenses. They are:

1. Real defenses—which go to the validity of the instrument.
2. Personal defenses—which generally arise out of the transaction that gave rise to the instrument.
3. Claims to an instrument—which generally concern property or possessory rights in an instrument or its proceeds.
4. Claims in recoupment—which also arise out of the transaction that gave rise to the instrument.

These defenses and claims are discussed in some detail below.

## Importance of Being a Holder in Due Course

In the preceding chapter, we discussed that one advantage of negotiable instruments over other kinds of contracts is that they are accepted as substitutes for money. People are willing to accept them as substitutes for money because, generally, they can take them free of claims or defenses to payment between the original parties to the instrument. On the other hand, a person who takes an assignment of a simple contract gets only the same rights as the person had who assigned the contract.

There are two qualifications to the ability of a person who acquires a negotiable instrument to be free of claims or defenses between the original parties. First, the person in possession of a negotiable instrument must be a *person entitled to enforce the instrument* as well as a *holder in due course* (or must be a holder who has the rights of a holder in due course through the shelter rule). If the person is neither, then she is subject to all claims or defenses to payment that any party to it has. Second, the only claims or defenses that the holder in due course has to worry about are so-called real defenses—those that affect the validity of the instrument—or claims that arose after she became a holder. For example, if the maker or drawer did not have legal capacity because she was a minor, the maker or drawer has a real defense. The holder in due course does not have to worry about other defenses and claims that do not go to the validity of the instrument—the so-called personal defenses.

## Real Defenses

There are some claims and defenses to payment of an instrument that go to the validity of the instrument. These claims and defenses are known as **real defenses**. They can be used as reasons against payment of a negotiable instrument to any holder, including a holder in due course (or a person who has the rights of a holder in due course). Real defenses include:

1. Minority or infancy that under state law makes the instrument void or voidable; for example, if Mark Miller, age 17, signs a promissory note as maker, he can use his lack of capacity to contract as a defense against paying it even to a holder in due course.

2. Incapacity that under state law makes the instrument void; for example, if a person has been declared mentally incompetent by a court, then the person has a real defense if state law declares all contracts entered into by the person after the adjudication of incompetency to be void.

3. Duress that voids or nullifies the obligation of a party liable to pay the instrument; for example, if Harold points a gun at his grandmother and forces her to execute a promissory note, the grandmother can use duress as a defense against paying it even to a holder in due course.

4. Illegality that under state law renders the obligation void; for example, in some states, checks and notes given in payment of gambling debts are void.

5. Fraud in the execution (or fraud in the factum). This occurs where a person signs a negotiable instrument without knowing or having a reasonable opportunity to know that it is a negotiable instrument or of its essential terms. For example, Amy Jones is an illiterate person who lives alone. She signs a document that is actually a promissory note but she is told that it is a grant of permission for a television set to be left in her house on a trial basis. Amy has a real defense against payment of the note even to a holder in due course. Fraud in the execution is distinguished from fraud in the inducement, which is only a personal defense.

**6.** Discharge in bankruptcy; for example, if the maker of a promissory note has had the debt discharged in a bankruptcy proceeding, she no longer is liable on it and has a real defense against payment [3–305(a)(1)].

Real defenses can be asserted even against a holder in due course of a negotiable instrument because it is more desirable to protect people who have signed negotiable instruments in these situations than it is to protect persons who have taken negotiable instruments in the ordinary course of business.

In addition to the real defenses discussed above, there are several other reasons why a person otherwise liable to pay an instrument would have a defense against payment that would be effective, even against a holder in due course. They include:

**1.** Forgery; for example, if a maker's signature has been put on the instrument without his authorization and without his negligence, the maker has a defense against payment of the note.

**2.** Alteration of a completed instrument. This is a partial defense against a holder in due course (or a person having the rights of a holder in due course), and a complete defense against a nonholder in due course. A holder in due course can enforce an altered instrument against the maker or drawer according to its original tenor.

**3.** Discharge. If a person takes an instrument with knowledge that the obligation of any party obligated on the instrument has been discharged, the person takes subject to the discharge even if the person is a holder in due course.

## Personal Defenses

**Personal defenses** are legal reasons for avoiding or reducing liability of a person who is liable on a negotiable instrument. Generally, personal defenses arise out of the transaction in which the negotiable instrument was issued and are based on negotiable instruments law or contract law. A holder in due course of a negotiable instrument (or one who can claim the rights of one) is not subject to any personal defenses or claims that may exist between the original parties to the instrument. Personal defenses include:

**1.** Lack or failure of consideration; for example, a promissory note for $100 was given to someone without intent to make a gift and without receiving anything in return [3–303(b)].

**2.** Breach of contract, including breach of warranty; for example, a check was given in payment for repairs to an automobile but the repair work was defective.

**3.** Fraud in the inducement of any underlying contract; for example, an art dealer sells a lithograph to Cheryl, telling her that it is a Picasso, and takes Cheryl's check for $500 in payment. The art dealer knows that the lithograph is not a genuine Picasso but a forgery. Cheryl has been induced to make the purchase and to give her check by the art dealer's fraudulent representation. Because of this fraud, Cheryl has a personal defense against having to honor her check to the art dealer.

**4.** Incapacity to the extent that state law makes the obligation voidable, as opposed to void; for example, where state law makes the contract of a person of limited mental capacity but who has not been adjudicated incompetent voidable, the person has a personal defense to payment.

**5.** Illegality that makes a contract voidable, as opposed to void; for example, where the payee of a check given for certain professional services was required to have a license from the state but did not have one.

**6.** Duress, to the extent it is not so severe as to make the obligation void but rather only voidable; for example, if the instrument was signed under a threat to prosecute the maker's son if it was not signed, the maker might have a personal defense.

**7.** Unauthorized completion or material alteration of the instrument; for example, the instrument was completed in an unauthorized manner, or a material alteration was made to it, after it left the maker's or drawer's possession.

**8.** Nonissuance of the instrument, conditional issuance, and issuance for a special purpose; for example, the person in possession of the instrument obtained it by theft or by finding it, rather than through an intentional delivery of the instrument to him [3–105(b)].

**9.** Failure to countersign a traveler's check [3–106(c)].

**10.** Modification of the obligation by a separate agreement [3–117].

**11.** Payment that violates a restrictive indorsement [3–206(f)].

**12.** Breach of warranty when a draft is accepted (discussed in following chapter) [3–417(b)].

The following example illustrates the limited extent to which a maker or drawer can use personal defenses as a reason for not paying a negotiable instrument he signed. Suppose Trent Tucker bought a used truck from Honest Harry's and gave Harry a 60-day promissory note for $2,750 in payment for the truck. Honest Harry's "guaranteed" the truck to be in "good working condition," but in fact the truck had a cracked engine block. If Harry tries to collect the $2,750 from Trent, Trent could claim breach of warranty as a reason for not paying Harry the full $2,750 because Harry is not a holder in due course. However, if Harry negotiated the note to First National Bank and the bank was a holder in due course, the situation would be changed. If the bank tried to collect the $2,750 from Trent, Trent would have to pay the bank.

Trent cannot use his defense or claim of breach of warranty as a reason for not paying the bank, which qualified as a holder in due course. It is a personal defense. Trent must pay the bank the $2,750 and then pursue his breach of warranty claim against Harry.

The case below, *Standard Finance Co., Ltd. v. Ellis*, illustrates the distinction between fraud in the essence (a real defense) and fraud in the inducement (a personal defense) and discusses the real defense of duress and the personal defense of failure of consideration. In this case the court followed the Restatement (Second) of Contracts narrow interpretation of duress as excluding one spouse's alleged abuses of the other because the spouse claiming abuse did not prove that actual physical abuse compelled her to sign the instrument in question.

---

## STANDARD FINANCE CO., LTD. V. ELLIS
### 657 P.2d 1056 (Hawaii Ct. App. 1983)

On September 30, 1976, Betty Ellis and her then husband, W. G. Ellis, executed and delivered a promissory note for $2,800 payable to Standard Finance Company. They paid nothing on the note, and on May 15, 1980, Standard Finance brought a collection action against Betty Ellis, who was divorced from W. G. The trial court awarded a judgment of $5,413.35 against Ellis. She appealed, claiming that she had defenses against payment of misrepresentation, duress, and failure of consideration.

---

**Tanaka, Justice**   Betty Ellis indicates that "shortly before" W. G. Ellis executed the note, he gave her "constant assurance" that her "signature was a formality and that he alone was liable and that the debt would be repaid without any participation by her." Thereafter, Betty Ellis accompanied W. G. Ellis to Standard Finance's office and executed the note. Betty Ellis argues that W. G. Ellis's misrepresentation induced her to sign the note and since such misrepresentation dealt with its essential terms, her execution of the note was not a manifestation of her assent. Consequently, the note was *void ab initio* and unenforceable as to her.

The principles of law as to when misrepresentation prevents the formation of a contract and when it makes a contract voidable are set forth in Restatement (Second) of Contracts. Section 163 states:

Section 163. When a Misrepresentation Prevents Formation of a Contract.

If a misrepresentation as to the character or essential terms of a proposed contract induces conduct that appears to be a manifestation of assent by one who neither knows nor has reasonable opportunity to know of the character or essential terms of the proposed contract, his conduct is not effective as a manifestation of assent.

Comment a to Section 163 provides in part as follows:

This Section involves an application of that principle where a misrepresentation goes to what is sometimes called the "factum" or the "execution" rather than merely the "inducement." If, because of a misrepresentation as to the character or essential terms of a proposed contract, a party does not know or have reasonable opportunity to know of its character or essential terms, then he neither knows nor has reason to know that the other party may infer from his conduct that he assents to that contract. In such a case there is no effective manifestation of assent and no contract at all.

Based on the facts in the record, we hold as a matter of law that the misrepresentation by W. G. Ellis was not a "fraud in the factum" or a "fraud in the execution" to render the note void at its inception.

A common illustration of "fraud in the factum" is that of the "maker who is tricked into signing a note in the belief that it is merely a receipt or some other document."

In the instant case, no representation was made to Betty Ellis that the note was anything other than a note. In fact, as indicated above, it is uncontradicted that Standard Finance's representative explained the "terms and conditions of the note" to Betty and W. G. Ellis prior to their execution of the note. Comment 7 to Section 3–305 further states that the defense of "fraud in the factum" is that of "excusable ignorance of the contents of the writing signed" and the party claiming such fraud "must also have had no reasonable opportunity to obtain knowledge." *Page v. Krekey* and *First National Bank of Odessa v. Fazzari*, both cited by Betty Ellis, are examples in this category of "fraud in the factum." In *Page,* an intoxicated, illiterate defendant, who could not read or write, was induced to sign a guaranty on a false representation that it was an application for a license. In *Fazzari,* a defendant who was unable to read or write English was induced to sign a note upon the misrepresentation that it was a statement of wages earned.

The record in this case fails to show any fact constituting "excusable ignorance" of the contents of the paper signed or "no reasonable opportunity to obtain knowledge" on the part of Betty Ellis.

In her answers to interrogatories, Betty Ellis states that she was "forced" to sign the note under duress. "Physical beatings" and "psychological pressure" on her by Ellis for at least three years prior to signing the note constituted the duress. She argues that her execution of the note which was compelled by duress was not a manifestation of her assent. Thus, the note is void and unenforceable.

The law concerning duress resulting in void or voidable contracts is discussed in Restatement (Second) of Contracts.

Section 174 reads:

Section 174. When Duress by Physical Compulsion Prevents Formation of a Contract.

If conduct that appears to be a manifestation of assent by a party who does not intend to engage in that conduct is physically compelled by duress, the conduct is not effective as a manifestation of assent.

Comment a to Section 174 provides in part:

This Section involves an application of that principle to those relatively rare situations in which actual physical force has been used to compel a party to appear to assent to a contract. . . . The essence of this type of duress is that a party is compelled by physical force to do an act that he has no intention of doing.

We hold that as a matter of law the facts in the record do not constitute the type of duress which renders the note void under § 174. Such duress involves the use of actual physical force to compel a person to sign a document. It may include the example given in Comment 6 to Section 3–305 of an "instrument signed at the point of a gun" being void.

Here, the only evidence of duress is "physical beatings" and "psychological pressure" by W. G. Ellis on Betty Ellis over a course of three years prior to her signing of the note. Without more, such evidence does not constitute duress resulting in the voiding of the note. From such evidence it cannot reasonably be inferred that the physical beatings by W. G. Ellis directly resulted in Betty Ellis signing the note in question.

Finally, Betty Ellis claims that the entire amount of the loan of $2,800 went to Ellis and she received no part of it. Thus, there was lack or failure of consideration and summary judgment was improper. We cannot agree.

Standard Finance's check for $2,800 was made payable to "W. G. Ellis and Betty Ellis." The reverse side of the check bears the indorsement of "Betty Ellis." This was sufficient evidence of consideration for the transaction involved.

However, Betty Ellis states that she "never got the money or the use of it" and "it all went to my ex-husband and this was understood by Standard Finance." This fact does not constitute lack or failure of consideration. It is fundamental that consideration received by a co-maker on a note from the payee is sufficient consideration to bind the other co-maker.

**Judgment for Standard Finance affirmed.**

*Note:* Although this case was decided under the original version of Article 3, the same result would be anticipated under Revised Article 3.

The rule that a holder in due course takes a negotiable instrument free of any personal defenses or claims to it has been modified to some extent, particularly in relation to instruments given by consumers. These modifications will be discussed in the next section of this chapter.

## Claims to the Instrument

For purposes of Revised Article 3, the term *claims* to an instrument can include:

1. A claim to ownership of the instrument by one who asserts that he is the owner and was wrongfully deprived of possession.
2. A claim of a lien on the instrument.
3. A claim for rescission of an indorsement.

A holder in due course takes free of claims or defenses that arose before she became a holder, but is subject to those arising when or after she becomes a holder in due course. For example, if a holder impairs the collateral given for an obligation, he may be creating a defense for an obligor.

## Claims in Recoupment

A *claim in recoupment* is not actually a defense to an instrument but rather an *offset to liability*. For example, Ann Adams purchases a new automobile from Dealership, giving it a note for the balance of the purchase price beyond her down payment. After accepting delivery, she discovers a breach of warranty that the dealer fails to remedy. If Dealer has sold the note to a bank that subsequently seeks payment on the note from Adams, she has a claim in recoupment for breach of warranty. If the bank is a holder in due course, the claim in recoupment cannot be asserted against it. However, if the bank is a not a holder in due course, then Adams can assert the claim in recoupment to reduce the amount owing on the instrument at the time the action is brought against her on the note. Her claim could serve only to reduce the amount owing and not as a basis for a net recovery from the bank. However, if Dealer was the person bringing an action to collect the note Adams could assert the breach of warranty claim as a counterclaim and potentially might recover from Dealer any difference between the claim and the damages due for breach of warranty.

The obligor may assert a claim up to the amount of the instrument if the holder is the original payee, but cannot assert claims in recoupment against a holder in due course. In addition, the obligor may assert a claim against a transferee who does not qualify as a holder in due course, but only up to the amount owing on the instrument at the time it brought the claim in recoupment.

## CLAIMS AND DEFENSES AGAINST PAYMENT OF NEGOTIABLE INSTRUMENTS

| Claim or Defense | Examples |
| --- | --- |
| **Real Defense**<br>Valid against all holders, including holders in due course and holders who have the rights of holders in due course. | 1. Minority that under state law makes the contract void or voidable.<br>2. Other lack of capacity that makes the contract void.<br>3. Duress that makes the contract void.<br>4. Illegality that makes the contract void.<br>5. Fraud in the essence (fraud in the factum).<br>6. Discharge in bankruptcy. |
| **Personal Defense**<br>Valid against plain holders of instruments—but not against holders in due course or holders who have the rights of in due course holders through the shelter rule. | 1. Lack or failure of consideration.<br>2. Breach of contract (including breach of warranty).<br>3. Fraud in the inducement.<br>4. Lack of capacity that makes the contract voidable (except minority).<br>5. Illegality that makes the contract voidable.<br>6. Duress that makes the contract voidable. |

| Claim or Defense | Examples |
|---|---|
|  | 7. Unauthorized completion of an incomplete instrument, or material alteration of the instrument. |
|  | 8. Nonissuance of the instrument. |
|  | 9. Failure to countersign a traveler's check. |
|  | 10. Modification of the obligation by a separate agreement. |
|  | 11. Payment that violates a restrictive indorsement. |
|  | 12. Breach of warranty when a draft is accepted. |
| **Claim to an Instrument** | 1. Claim of ownership by someone who claims to be the owner and that he was wrongfully deprived of possession. |
|  | 2. Claim of a lien on the instrument. |
|  | 3. Claim for rescission of an indorsement. |
| **Claims in Recoupment** | 1. Breach of warranty in the sale of goods for which the instrument was issued. |

## CHANGES IN THE HOLDER IN DUE COURSE RULE

### Consumer Disadvantages

The rule that a holder in due course of a negotiable instrument is not subject to personal defenses between the original parties to it makes negotiable instruments a readily accepted substitute for money. This rule also can result in serious disadvantages to consumers. Consumers sometimes buy goods or services on credit and give the seller a negotiable instrument such as a promissory note. They often do this without knowing the consequences of their signing a negotiable instrument. If the goods or services are defective or not delivered, the consumer would like to withhold payment of the note until the seller corrects the problem or makes the delivery. Where the note is still held by the seller, the consumer can do this because any defenses of breach of warranty or nonperformance are good against the seller.

However, the seller may have negotiated the note at a discount to a third party such as a bank. If the bank qualifies as a holder in due course, the consumer must pay the note in full to the bank. The consumer's personal defenses are not valid against a holder in due course. The consumer must pay the holder in due course and then try to get her money back from the seller. This may be difficult if the seller cannot be found or will not accept responsibility. The consumer would be in a much stronger position if she could just withhold payment, even against the bank, until the goods or services are delivered or the performance is corrected.

### State Legislation

Some state legislatures and courts have limited the holder in due course doctrine, particularly as it affects consumers. State legislation limiting the doctrine typically amended state laws dealing with consumer credit transactions. For example, some state laws prohibit a seller from taking a negotiable instrument other than a check from a consumer in payment for consumer goods and services. Other state laws require promissory notes given by consumers in payment for goods and services to carry the words *consumer paper*; these state laws treat instruments with this legend as non-negotiable.[3] Thus, the rights of a consumer who has signed a negotiable instrument vary from state to state.

### Federal Trade Commission Rules

The Federal Trade Commission (FTC) has promulgated a regulation designed to protect consumers against operation of the holder in due course rule. The FTC rule applies to persons who sell to consumers on credit and have the consumer sign a note

[3] Revised Article 3 expressly deals with these state variations in Section 3-106(d) and Official Comments 3 to 3-106 and Comments 3 to 3-305. Section 3-106(d) permits instruments containing legends or statements required by statutory or administrative law that preserve the obligor's rights to assert claims or defenses against subsequent holders as within Article 3 except that no holder can be a holder in due course.

or an installment sale contract or arrange third-party financing of the purchase. The seller must ensure that the note or the contract contains the following clause:

NOTICE: ANY HOLDER OF THIS CONSUMER CREDIT CONTRACT IS SUBJECT TO ALL CLAIMS AND DEFENSES WHICH THE DEBTOR COULD ASSERT AGAINST THE SELLER OF THE GOODS OR SERVICES OBTAINED PURSUANT HERETO OR WITH THE PROCEEDS HEREOF. RECOVERY HEREUNDER BY THE DEBTOR SHALL NOT EXCEED AMOUNTS PAID BY THE DEBTOR HEREUNDER.

The effect of the notice is to make a potential holder of the note or contract subject to all claims and defenses of the consumer. This is illustrated in the *Ford Motor Credit Co. v. Morgan* case, which follows. If the note or contract does not include the clause required by the FTC rule, the consumer does not gain any rights that he would not otherwise have under state law, and a subsequent holder may qualify as a holder in due course. However, the FTC does have the right to seek a fine of as much as $10,000 against the seller who failed to include the notice.

---

## Ford Motor Credit Co. v. Morgan
### 536 N.E.2d 587 (Sup. Jud. Ct. Mass. 1989)

Rose and William Morgan purchased a new Mercury automobile from Neponset Lincoln Mercury, Inc. In order to finance their purchase through Ford Motor Credit Company, they signed a Note/Massachusetts Retail Installment Contract, a standard printed form contract prepared by Ford Credit. Printed in capital letters at the bottom of the first page of the form was the following statement:

NOTICE: ANY HOLDER OF THIS CONSUMER CREDIT CONTRACT IS SUBJECT TO ALL CLAIMS AND DEFENSES WHICH THE DEBTOR COULD ASSERT AGAINST THE SELLER OF GOODS OR SERVICES OBTAINED PURSUANT HERETO OR WITH THE PROCEEDS HEREOF. RECOVERY HEREUNDER BY THE DEBTOR SHALL NOT EXCEED AMOUNTS PAID BY THE DEBTOR HEREUNDER.

Ford Credit financed the car for $3,833, with payment to be made in 36 consecutive monthly installments of $137.13. During the first 18 months they owned the car, the Morgans experienced problems with it. These included water leaking into the trunk, a faulty head gasket, rust, hood misalignment, lack of shine, and, when left unattended, the car would shift from "park" to "reverse" and would have to be shifted back to "park" before it could be started. After making 15 payments totaling $2,056.95, the Morgans' defaulted on their remaining obligation to Ford Credit. Before the car could be resold by Ford Credit, it was extensively vandalized; the Morgans had not maintained insurance coverage on it and it was a total loss.

Ford Credit sued the Morgans on the note, seeking recovery of $2,628.87 plus attorney's fees. The Morgans counterclaimed, seeking recovery against Ford Credit of claims for fraud and deceit, unfair and deceptive practices, and breach of express and implied warranties. In a special verdict, a jury found that the dealer knowingly made false representations to the Morgans, on which the Morgans relied. In turn, the trial court judge determined that this gave the Morgans a valid defense that extinguished the claim of Ford Motor Credit for the balance due on the credit contract. He also denied the Morgans' claim for an affirmative recovery against Ford Motor Credit on their counterclaim. The Morgans appealed to the Appeals Court, which transferred the case to the Supreme Judicial Court.

---

**O'Connor, Justice**   The Morgans' first contention is that the explicit language of the notice provision contained in the contract, which subjects holder to all "claims and defenses which the debtor could assert against the seller" permits them to recover from Ford Credit for the dealer's wrongdoing. As the Morgans acknowledge, that notice provision is mandated by a Federal Trade Commission (FTC) rule that provides that it is an unfair or deceptive act or practice to take or receive a consumer credit contract which fails to include that provision. Therefore, we look to the FTC's purpose in enacting the rule as a guide to our interpretation of the contract provision.

The rule was designed to preserve the consumer's claims and defenses by cutting off the creditor's rights as a holder in due course. Under the holder in due course principle, which would apply were it not for the contract provision mandated by the FTC rule, the creditor could "assert his right to be paid by the consumer despite misrepresentation, breach of warranty or contract, or even fraud on the part of the seller, and despite the fact that the consumer's debt was generated by the sale. Thus, "being prevented from asserting the seller's breach of warranty or failure to perform against the assignee of the consumer's instrument, the consumer would be deprived of his most effective weapon—nonpayment." Eliminating holder in due course status prevents the assignee from demanding further payment when there has been assignor wrongdoing, and rearms the consumer with the "weapon" of nonpayment.

The FTC anticipated that in addition to nonpayment, affirmative recovery, a judgment for damages against the assignee-creditor, would be available in limited circumstances. Thus, in its statement of policy and purpose, the FTC spelled out the avenues of relief under the rule as follows: "A consumer can (1) defend a creditor suit for payment of an obligation by raising a valid claim against a seller as a setoff, and (2) maintain an affirmative action against a creditor who has received for a return of moneys paid on account."

However, the FTC made clear that "The latter alternative will only be available where a seller's breach is so substantial that a court is persuaded that rescission and restitution are justified. The most typical example of such a case would involve non-delivery, where delivery was scheduled after the date payments to a creditor commenced."

The FTC re-emphasized this point in stating, "consumers will not be in a position to obtain an affirmative recovery, unless they have actually commenced payments and received little or nothing of value from the seller. In the case of non-delivery, we believe the consumer is entitled to a refund of monies paid on account." Finally, the FTC anticipated that the rule would allow the courts to weigh the equities in the underlying sale, and "remain the final arbiters of equities between a seller and a consumer." Thus, the function of the rule is to allow consumers to stop payments, and, in limited circumstances not present here, where equity requires, to provide for a return of monies paid. The FTC did not intend that the rule would, as a matter of course, entitle a consumer to a full refund of monies paid on account. It follows, of course, that there is no merit to the Morgans' assertions that the contractual language allows them affirmative recovery even beyond the amount they paid in. To expose a creditor to further affirmative recovery would not only contravene the intention of the FTC, but "would place the creditor in the position of an absolute insurer or guarantor of the seller's performance." This we decline to do.

**Judgment affirmed.**

---

### PROBLEMS AND PROBLEM CASES

**1.** Stone & Webster drew three checks in the total amount of $64,755.44 payable to the order of Westinghouse Electric Corporation. An employee of Stone & Webster obtained possession of the checks, forged Westinghouse's indorsement to them, and cashed them at the First National Bank & Trust Company and put the proceeds to his own use. The first two checks were indorsed in typewriting, "For Deposit Only: Westinghouse Electric Corporation By: Mr. O. D. Costine, Treasury Representative," followed by the ink signature "O. D. Costine." The third check was indorsed in typewriting, "Westinghouse Electric Corporation by: [Sgd.] O. D. Costine, Treasury Representative." Were the checks negotiated to the bank?

**2.** Louis Agaliotis took out a policy of insurance on his son, Robert. Louis paid all of the premiums on the policy, and under the terms of the policy he was entitled to any refunds on the premiums. The insurance company sent a refund check for $1,852 to Louis. By mistake, the check was made payable to "Robert L. Agaliotis." Louis indorsed the check "Robert L. Agaliotis" and cashed it. Robert then sued Louis to get the $1,852. Was

Louis entitled to sign his son's name to the check and to keep the money when he cashed it?

**3.** Reliable Janitorial Service, Inc., maintained a bank account with AmSouth Bank. Rosa Pennington was employed by Reliable as a bookkeeper/office manager. She deposited checks made payable to Reliable but did not have authority to write checks on Reliable's account. Beginning in January 1985, Pennington obtained counter deposit slips from AmSouth. She wrote on the deposit slips that the depositor was "Reliable Janitorial Services, Inc.," but in the space for the account number, Pennington wrote the account number for her own personal account with AmSouth. She stamped the checks that were made payable to "Reliable Janitorial Service, Inc." with the indorsement "For Deposit Only, Reliable Carpet Cleaning, Inc." Over an 11-month period, Pennington was able to deposit 169 checks so indorsed. AmSouth credited the deposits to Pennington, not Reliable. Pennington spent all the funds that she diverted to her account. When Reliable discovered the fraud, it brought suit against AmSouth for conversion and sought to have its account credited with the improperly paid checks. Was AmSouth Bank liable to Reliable for the value of the restrictively indorsed checks that it paid inconsistently with the indorsement?

**4.** Reggie Bluiett worked at the Silver Slipper Gambling Hall and Saloon. She received her weekly paycheck made out to her from the Silver Slipper. She indorsed the check in blank and left it on her dresser at home. Fred Watkins broke into Bluiett's house and stole the check. Watkins took the check to the local auto store, where he bought two tires at a cost of $71.21. He obtained the balance of the check in cash. Could the auto store qualify as a holder in due course?

**5.** Horton wrote a check for $20,000 to Axe, who in turn indorsed it to Halbert. In return, Halbert advanced $8,000 in cash to Axe and promised to cancel a $12,000 debt owed him by Axe. The check, when presented by Halbert to the bank, was not paid due to insufficient funds. Halbert thus never regarded the debt as canceled. To what extent can Halbert be a holder in due course of the check?

**6.** In 1981, Anthony Maggio purchased a limited partnership interest in a new venture created by a former astronaut to develop an optoelectronic scanner designed to provide perimeter security for sprawling properties such as airfields, oil fields, and pipelines. As consideration for his partnership interest, Maggio gave the partnership a noninterest-bearing note for $55,000 maturing October 31, 1990. The partnership negotiated the note to a venture-capital company that in turn negotiated it to Goldman Sachs, which in turn negotiated it in 1988 to Northwestern National Insurance Company. Maggio's note was negotiated, along with a number of notes from other limited partners, at a 50 percent discount. On the due date, Northwestern demanded payment in full and Maggio refused, claiming that he was induced to enter the limited partnership by fraud. Could Northwestern be a holder in due course—and thus not subject to defense of fraud in the inducement—if it took the note at a 50 percent discount?

**7.** Eric Strober, the chairman of the board of Strober Bros., Inc., was approached by a business acquaintance, Sidney Pal, to make a short-term loan of $150,000 to a business venture operated by Pal. Pal indicated the loan would be collateralized by a negotiable certificate of deposit. Strober agreed to make the loan and made out a check for $150,000 drawn on the Strober Bros. account and made payable to the Tamara Trust, Pal's business venture. Pal urged the immediate delivery of the check to him and promised to deliver the negotiable certificate of deposit the next day. Strober agreed to deliver the check only on the condition that it be made non-negotiable, that a stop-payment order would be placed on it, and that a trust agreement and the certificate of deposit be delivered by 4 o'clock the following day, at which point the stop-payment order would be removed. Strober struck out the words "the order of" on the check so that it read "pay to Tamara Trust" and placed a stop-payment order on the check. Pal deposited the check in an account at the Key Bank and was allowed to draw out the funds in the account. When the check was sent to Strober's bank, payment was refused and it was returned marked "Payment Stopped." Pal never delivered a negotiable certificate of deposit. Key Bank brought suit against Strober Bros. on the check seeking to hold Strober Bros. liable on the basis of its drawer's liability on the check. Key Bank claimed to be a holder in due course of the check who held it free of any defenses Strober Bros. might have against Pal and the Tamara Trust. Was Key Bank a holder in due course of the check?

**8.** Two smooth-talking salesmen for Rich Plan of New Orleans called on Leona and George Henne at their home. They sold the Hennes a home food plan. One of the salesmen suggested that the Hennes sign a blank promissory note. The Hennes refused. The salesman then wrote in ink "$100" as the amount and "4" as the number of installments in which the note was to be paid, and the Hennes signed the note. Several days later, the Hennes received a payment book from Nationwide Acceptance. The payment book showed that a total of $843.38 was due, payable in 36 monthly installments. Rich Plan had erased the "$100" and "4" on the note and typed in the figures "$843.38" and "36." The erasures were cleverly done but were visible to the naked eye. Rich Plan then negotiated the Hennes' note to Nationwide Acceptance. The Hennes refused to pay the note. Nationwide claimed that it was a holder in due course and was entitled to receive payment. Was Nationwide Acceptance a holder in due course?

**9.** Culver, a farmer, entered into a business arrangement with Nasib Kalliel whereby Kalliel was to assume control over the financial aspects of Culver's farm while Culver was to manage the farming operation. Subsequently, Culver notified Kalliel that he urgently needed money to stave off foreclosure. One week later, $30,000 was wire-transferred from the Rexford State Bank in Rexford, Kansas, to Culver's bank account in King City, Missouri. Culver knew that the money had come from the Rexford State Bank but thought that Kalliel would be responsible for its repayment. A week later, Culver was approached by one of Kalliel's employees, Jerry Gilbert, who told him that "Rexford State Bank wanted to know where the $30,000 went . . . for their records." Gilbert presented Culver with a document and asked him to sign it. Gilbert led Culver to believe he was merely signing a receipt for the $30,000 he had received. In fact, Culver had signed a preprinted promissory note form that contained a number of blanks. The name of the payee, "The Rexford State Bank," was printed on the note along with a provision that principal and accrued interest were to be paid to the payee at its offices. While Culver assumed that the figure $30,000 would eventually be written on the document, someone completed the note showing the principal amount as $50,000, the execution date as

August 2, 1984, the maturity date as February 2, 1985, and that interest would be 14½ percent per annum until maturity and 18½ percent after that. Although Culver received only $30,000, Rexford State Bank deposited the full $50,000 in an account controlled by Kalliel. The Rexford Bank became insolvent and the Federal Deposit Insurance Corporation took over as its receiver and purchased a number of the bank's assets, including the note signed by Culver. At the time, the FDIC had no knowledge of the circumstances surrounding the signing and completion of the note. The FDIC brought suit against Culver to collect on the note. Culver sought to defend on the grounds he had been tricked into signing the note thinking it was only a receipt. He claimed he had a defense of "fraud in the factum" that was good even against a holder in due course (the FDIC). Did Culver have a real defense of fraud in the factum that could be asserted as a defense against payment of the promissory note to a holder in due course?

**10.** Ralph Herrmann wrote a check for $10,000 payable to Ormsby House, a hotel-casino in Carson City, Nevada, and exchanged it for three counter checks he had written earlier that evening to acquire gaming chips. Ormsby House was unable to collect the proceeds from the check because Herrmann had insufficient funds in his account. The debt evidenced by the check was assigned to Sea Air Support, Inc., d/b/a Automated Accounts Associates, for collection. Sea Air was also unsuccessful in its attempts to collect and filed a lawsuit against Herrmann to recover on the dishonored check. Nevada law then provided that all instruments drawn for the purpose of reimbursing or repaying any money knowingly lent or advanced for gaming are "utterly void, frustrate, and of none effect." Is Herrmann still liable to Sea Air?

**11.** Pedro and Paula de la Fuente were visited by a representative of Aluminum Industries, Inc., who was seeking to sell them aluminum siding for their home. They agreed to purchase the siding and signed a number of documents, including a retail installment contract and a promissory note for $9,138.24. The contract granted Aluminum Industries, Inc., a first lien on the de la Fuentes' residence; this was in violation of the Texas Civil Code, which prohibited such provisions. The promissory note contained a notice in bold type as required by the Federal Trade Commission. It read in part:

NOTICE: ANY HOLDER OF THIS CONSUMER CREDIT CONTRACT IS SUBJECT TO ALL CLAIMS AND DEFENSES WHICH THE DEBTOR COULD ASSERT AGAINST THE SELLER OF GOODS OR SERVICES OBTAINED PURSUANT HERETO WITH THE PROCEEDS THEREOF.

Aluminum Industries assigned the promissory note and first lien to Home Savings Association. Aluminum Industries subsequently went out of business. Home Savings brought suit against the de la Fuentes to collect the balance due on the note. Home Savings contended that it was a holder in due course and that the de la Fuentes could not assert any defenses against it that they had against Aluminum Industries. Can an assignee of a consumer promissory note that includes the notice required by the FTC qualify as a holder in due course?

**12.** ▣ *Video Case.* See "TV Repair." Arnold takes his old TV set to an appliance store for repair and purchases a new TV from the store. He signs a promissory note, which provides for installment payments, for the balance due on the new set. The note contains the notice that the FTC requires be included in consumer credit instruments. Arnold discovers that the TV is defective after making the first payment on the note to the appliance store. The appliance store assigns the promissory note to Acme Finance Company, which notifies Arnold of its interest in the note and that he should make his payments on the note to it. Arnold advises Acme Finance that he will not make any further payments on the promissory note until the TV is repaired. If Arnold has a valid claim for breach of warranty of merchantability of the TV set, can he assert this as a defense against paying the note to the appliance store and/or to Acme Finance?

## Capstone Questions

**1.** Richard had in his possession a negotiable instrument that he had received in payment of farm equipment he had sold to Roth's Farms, Inc. The instrument was payable to "the order of Mary Burns or bearer." Burns specially indorsed the instrument to Roth's, who in turn indorsed it in blank and delivered it to Richard. Thief stole the instrument, along with other property, from Richard on November 1, 1994. Thief then transferred the instrument to Appliance Store in payment for a large-screen TV.

**Required:**

Answer the following and give reasons for your conclusions.

1. Was the instrument negotiated from Burns to Roth, and did Roth become a holder of the instrument?
2. Was the instrument negotiated from Roth to Richard, and did Richard become a holder of the instrument? In Richard's hands, was the instrument a bearer or an order instrument?
3. Was Thief a holder of the instrument?
4. Did Appliance Store become a holder in due course of the instrument.

**2.** David induces Sarah to make a promissory note payable to David by a fraudulent promise to sell her his business. David negotiates the note at a discount to Barry, who was aware of the fraud. Barry indorses the note to Carrie, to whom he owed a debt that was due. Carrie was unaware of any of the prior events. After the due date of the note, Barry repurchased the note from Carrie.

**Required:**

Answer the following and give reasons for your conclusions.

1. Does Barry succeed to Carrie's rights as a holder in due course?
2. Was Barry a holder in due course upon taking the note from David?
3. Because of the fraud, does Sarah have a defense good as to all of the parties?
4. Is Barry's knowledge of David's fraud immaterial to his status as a holder in due course?

CHAPTER

25

# LIABILITY OF

# PARTIES

**INTRODUCTION**

*Thus far in Part 5, Commercial Paper, the focus has been on the nature of and requirements for negotiable instruments, as well as the rights that an owner of an instrument can obtain and how to obtain them. Another important aspect to negotiable instruments concerns how a person becomes liable on a negotiable instrument and the nature of the liability incurred.*

*When a person signs a promissory note, he expects to be liable for paying the note on the day it is due. Similarly, when a person signs a check and mails it off to pay a bill, she expects that the drawee bank will pay it from funds in her checking account and that if her account contains insufficient funds to cover it, she will have to make it good out of other funds she has. These liabilities concerning instruments are commonly understood.*

*However, there are a number of other ways in which a person can become liable on a negotiable instrument. For example, a person who indorses a paycheck assumes liability on it; and a bank that cashes a check with a forged indorsement on it is liable for conversion of the check. This chapter and the following chapter discuss the liabilities of the various parties to a negotiable instrument. These two chapters also explain what happens when an instrument is not paid when it is supposed to be paid. For example, a check usually should not be paid if the drawer's account contains insufficient funds or if the check has been forged. In addition, this chapter discusses the ways in which liability on an instrument can be discharged.*

## LIABILITY IN GENERAL

Liability on negotiable instruments flows from signatures on the instruments as well as actions taken concerning them. It can arise from the fact that a person has signed a negotiable instrument or has authorized someone else to sign it. The liability depends on the capacity in which the person signs the instrument. Liability also arises from (1) transfer or presentment of an instrument, (2) negligence relating to the issuance, alteration, or indorsement of the instrument, (3) improper payment, or (4) conversion.

# CONTRACTUAL LIABILITY

When a person signs a negotiable instrument, whether as maker, drawer, or indorser, or in some other capacity, she generally becomes contractually liable on the instrument. As mentioned above, this contractual liability depends on the capacity in which the person signed the instrument. The terms of the contract of the parties to a negotiable instrument are not set out in the text of the instrument. Rather, Article 3 of the Uniform Commercial Code supplies the terms, which are as much a part of the instrument as if they were part of its text.

## Primary and Secondary Liability

A party to a negotiable instrument may be either *primarily liable* or *secondarily liable* for payment of it. A person who is primarily liable has agreed to pay the negotiable instrument. For example, the maker of a promissory note is the person who is primarily liable on the note. A person who is secondarily liable is like a guarantor on a contract; Article 3 requires a secondary party to pay the negotiable instrument only if a person who is primarily liable defaults on that obligation. Chapter 20, Introduction to Credit and Secured Transactions, discusses guarantors.

## Obligation of a Maker

The **maker** of a promissory note is primarily liable for payment of it. The maker makes an unconditional promise to pay a fixed amount of money and is responsible for making good on that promise. The obligation of the maker is to pay the negotiable instrument according to its terms at the time he issues it or, if it is not issued, then according to its terms at the time it first came into possession of a holder [3–412].[1] If the material terms of the note are not complete when the maker signs it, then the maker's obligation is to pay the note as it is completed, provided that the terms filled in are as authorized. If the instrument is incomplete when the maker signs it and it is completed in an unauthorized manner, then the maker's liability will depend on whether the person seeking to enforce the instrument can qualify as a holder in due course.

The obligation of the maker is owed to (1) a *person entitled to enforce the instrument* or (2) any indorser who paid the instrument pursuant to her indorser's liability (discussed below). A person entitled to enforce an instrument includes: (1) the holder of the instrument, (2) a nonholder in possession of the instrument who has the rights of a holder, and (3) a person not in possession of the instrument who has the right to enforce the instrument under section 3–309 that deals with lost, destroyed, or stolen instruments.

Revised Article 3 provides that the *drawer of a cashier's check* has the same obligation as the maker or issuer of a note. Thus, it treats a draft drawn on a bank drawer the same as a note for purposes of the issuer's liability rather than treating the issuer as a drawer of a draft [3–412].

## Obligation of a Drawee or an Acceptor

The **acceptor** of a draft is obligated to pay the draft according to the terms at the time of its acceptance. As was discussed in Chapter 23, acceptance is the drawee's signed engagement to honor the draft as presented—and is commonly indicated by the signature of the acceptor on the instrument itself. The acceptor's obligation extends to (1) a person entitled to enforce the draft, (2) the drawer, and (3) an indorser who paid the instrument pursuant to her indorser's liability [3–413].

If the certification of a check or other acceptance of a draft states the amount certified or accepted, the obligation of the acceptor is that amount. If the certification or acceptance does not state an amount, or if the amount of the instrument is subsequently raised, and then the instrument is negotiated to a holder in due course, the obligation of the acceptor is the amount of the instrument at the time a holder in due course takes it [3–413(b)].

At the time a check or other draft issues, no party is primarily liable on it. Usually, the drawee bank pays a check when it is presented for payment and no person becomes primarily liable. However, the drawer or a holder of the check may ask the drawee bank to accept or certify the check. The drawee bank certifies the check by signing its name to the check and, with that act, accepts liability as acceptor. The drawee bank debits, or takes the money out of, the drawer's account and holds the money to pay the check. If the drawee bank certifies the check, it becomes primarily, or absolutely, liable for paying

---

[1] The numbers in brackets refer to sections of the Uniform Commercial Code (UCC).

the check as it reads at the time of its acceptance, [3–413]. Similarly, when a trade draft is presented for acceptance or payment, no party is liable on it. If the named drawee accepts it, perhaps by writing his name on the face of it, then he accepts the obligations set forth in the instrument.

A drawee has no liability on a check or other draft unless it certifies or accepts the check or draft—that is, agrees to be liable on it. However, a drawee bank that refuses to pay a check when it is presented for payment may be liable to the drawer for wrongfully refusing payment, assuming the drawer had sufficient funds in his checking account to cover it. The next chapter discusses this liability of a drawee bank.

## Obligation of a Drawer

The **drawer**'s obligation is that if the drawee dishonors an unaccepted check (or draft), the drawer will pay the check (or draft) according to its terms at the time he issued it or, if it was not issued, according to its terms at the time it first came into possession of a holder. If the draft was not complete when issued but was completed as authorized, then the obligation is to pay it as completed. If any completion is not authorized, then the obligation will depend on whether the person seeking to enforce the instrument can qualify as a holder in due course. A person entitled to enforce the draft or an indorser who paid the draft pursuant to his indorser's liability may enforce the drawer's obligation [3–414(b)].

For example, Janis draws a check on her account at First National Bank payable to the order of Collbert. If First National does not pay the check when Collbert presents it for payment, then Janis is liable to Collbert on the basis of her drawer's obligation.

If a draft is accepted by a bank—for example, if the drawee bank certifies a check—the drawer is discharged of her drawer's obligation. If someone other than a bank accepts a draft, then the obligation of the drawer to pay the draft, if the draft is dishonored, is the same as an indorser (discussed next) [3–414(c) and (d)].

The case that follows, *First American Bank of Virginia v. Litchfield Company of South Carolina, Inc.*, illustrates circumstances under which a drawer might be liable on its drawer's contractual obligation.

---

### FIRST AMERICAN BANK OF VIRGINIA V. LITCHFIELD COMPANY OF SOUTH CAROLINA, INC.
**353 S.E.2d 143 (S.C. Ct. App. 1987)**

On February 9, 1983, Litchfield Company drew a check payable to Jensen Farley Pictures, Inc., in the amount of $13,711.11, on its account with Bankers Trust of South Carolina. Litchfield sent the check to Jensen Farley, which negotiated the check on September 16 to First American Bank of Virginia with whom it had a checking account. First American gave Jensen Farley immediate credit on the check and forwarded it to Bankers Trust for payment. Unknown to First American, Litchfield had given Bankers Trust an oral stop-payment order on the check. On September 19, Jensen Farley withdrew most of the balance in its First American account; it subsequently filed for bankruptcy. On September 21, Bankers Trust returned the Litchfield check to First American marked "payment stopped."

First American then sued Litchfield, claiming that as drawer of the check, it was liable to First American, a holder in due course of the check. The trial court awarded First American Bank judgment for $9,369.37 (representing the amount it had been unable to recover from Jensen Farley), and Litchfield appealed.

---

**Bell, Judge**    The drawer of a check engages that upon dishonor he will pay the amount of the draft to a holder in due course. Section 3–413(2). The drawer has the right to stop payment, but remains liable on the instrument to a holder in due course.

Section 4–403 and comment 8; section 3–413(2). Since Litchfield has conceded First American was a holder in due course, Litchfield remains liable on the instrument unless it can establish a valid defense or set off.

Litchfield argues that its liability was discharged by First American's failure to give timely notice the check had been dishonored. This defense is unavailing for two reasons.

First, failure to give notice of dishonor discharges a drawer only to the extent he is deprived of funds maintained with the drawee bank to cover the check because the drawee bank became insolvent during the delay. Sections 3–501(2)(b) and 3–502(1)(b). A drawer is not otherwise discharged. In this case, Litchfield was not deprived of any funds in its account with Bankers Trust nor did Bankers Trust become insolvent during the delay.

Second, notice of dishonor is excused when the party to be charged has himself countermanded payment. Section 3–511(2)(b). Since Litchfield ordered payment stopped, it was not entitled to notice of dishonor.

Litchfield argues strenuously that it is unfair to apply section 3–511(2)(b) to the drawer of a check who has no means of knowing whether the check has been negotiated to a holder. This reasoning misses the mark. The maker of an outstanding negotiable instrument is presumed to know the instrument is subject to transfer to a holder in due course. The drawer is often without actual knowledge that his check has been negotiated, but that ignorance in no way diminishes the rights of a holder in due course. To hold otherwise would, as a practical matter, destroy the negotiability of a check.

**Judgment for First American affirmed.**

*Note:* Although this case was decided under the original Article 3 and Revised Article 3 restates the obligation of a drawer, the same result would be anticipated under Revised Article 3.

## Obligation of an Indorser

A person who indorses a negotiable instrument usually is secondarily liable. Unless the indorser qualifies or otherwise disclaims liability, the **indorser**'s obligation on dishonor of the instrument is to pay the amount due on the instrument according to its terms at the time he indorsed it or if he indorsed it when incomplete, then according to its terms when completed, provided that it is completed as authorized. The indorser owes the obligation to a person entitled to enforce the instrument or to any subsequent indorser who had to pay it [3–415].

The indorser can avoid this liability only by qualifying its indorsement, such as "without recourse," on the instrument when he indorses it [3–415(b)].

Indorsers are liable to each other in the chronological order in which they indorse, from the last indorser back to the first. For example, Mark Maker gives a promissory note to Paul Payee. Payee indorses it and negotiates it to Fred First, who indorses it and negotiates it to Shirley Second. If Maker does not pay the note when Second takes it to him for payment, then Second can require First to pay it to her. First is secondarily liable on the basis of his indorsement. First, in turn, can require Payee to pay him because Payee also became secondarily liable when he indorsed it. Then, Payee is left to try

to collect the note from Maker. Second also could have skipped over First and proceeded directly against Payee on his indorsement. First has no liability to Payee, however, because First indorsed after Payee indorsed the note.

If a bank accepted a draft (for example, by certifying a check) after an indorsement is made, the acceptance discharges the liability of the indorser [3–415(d)]. If notice of dishonor is required and proper notice is not given to the indorser, she is discharged of liability [3–415(c)]. And, where no one presents a check or gives it to a depositary bank for collection within 30 days after the date of an indorsement, the indorser's liability is discharged [3–415(e)].

## Obligation of an Accommodation Party

An **accommodation party** is a person who signs a negotiable instrument for the purpose of lending her credit to another party to the instrument but is not a direct beneficiary of the value given for the instrument. For example, a bank might be reluctant to lend money to—and take a note from—Payee because of his shaky financial condition. However, the bank may be willing to lend money to Payee if he signs the note and has a relative or a friend also sign the note as an accommodation maker.

The obligation of an accommodation party depends on the capacity in which the party signs the instrument [3–419]. If Payee has his brother Sam sign a note as an accommodation maker, then Sam has the same contractual liability as a maker. Sam is primarily liable on the note. The bank may ask Sam to pay the note before asking Payee to pay. However, if Sam pays the note to the bank, he has the right to recover his payment from Payee, the person on whose behalf he signed.

Similarly, if a person signs a check as an accommodation indorser, his contractual liability is that of an indorser. If the accommodation indorser has to make good on that liability, he can collect in turn from the person on whose behalf he signed.

## Signing an Instrument

No person is contractually liable on a negotiable instrument unless she or her authorized agent has signed it and the signature is binding on the represented person. A signature can be any name, word, or mark used in place of a written signature [3–401]. As discussed earlier, the capacity in which a person signs an instrument determines his liability on the instrument.

## Signature by an Authorized Agent

An authorized agent can sign a negotiable instrument. If Sandra Smith authorized her attorney to sign checks as her agent, then she is liable on any checks properly signed by the attorney as her agent. All negotiable instruments signed by corporations have to be signed by an agent of the corporation who is authorized to sign negotiable instruments.

If a person purporting to act as a representative signs an instrument by signing either the name of the represented person or the name of the signer, that signature binds the represented person to the same extent she would be bound if the signature were on a simple contract. If the represented person has authorized the signature of the representative, it is the "authorized signature of the represented person" and the represented person is liable on the instrument, whether or not identified in the instrument. This brings the Code in line with the general principle of agency law that binds an undisclosed principal on a simple contract. For example, if Principal authorizes Agent to borrow money on Principal's behalf and

Agent signs her name to a note without disclosing that the signature was on behalf of Principal, Agent is liable on the note. In addition, if the person entitled to enforce the note can show that Principal authorized Agent to sign on his behalf, then Principal is liable on the note as well.

When a representative signs an authorized signature to an instrument, then the representative is not bound provided the signature shows "unambiguously" that the signature was made on behalf of the represented person who is named in the instrument [3–402(b)(1)]. For example, if a note is signed "XYZ, Inc., by Flanigan, Treasurer," Flanigan is not liable on the instrument in his own right, but XYZ, Inc., is liable.

If an authorized representative signs his name as the representative of a drawer of a check without noting his representative status but the check is payable from an account of the represented person who is identified on the check, the signer is not liable on the check as long as his signature was authorized [3–402(c)]. The rationale for this provision is that because most checks today identify the person on whose account the check is drawn, no one is deceived into thinking that the person signing the check is meant to be liable.

Except for the check situation noted above, a representative is personally liable to a holder in due course that took the instrument without notice that the representative was not intended to be liable if (1) the form of the signature does not show unambiguously that the signature was made in a representative capacity or (2) the instrument does not identify the represented person. As to persons other than a holder in due course without notice of the representative nature of the signature, the representative is liable *unless* she can prove that the original parties did not intend her to be liable on the instrument [3–402(b)(2)].

Thus, if an agent or a representative signs a negotiable instrument on behalf of someone else, the agent should indicate clearly that he is signing as the representative of someone else. For example, Kim Darby, the president of Swimwear, Inc., is authorized to sign negotiable instruments for the company. If Swimwear borrows money from the bank and the bank asks her to sign a 90-day promissory note, Darby should sign it either "Swimwear, Inc. by Kim Darby, President" or "Kim Darby, President, for Swimwear, Inc." If Kim Darby signed the promissory note merely "Kim

Darby," she could be personally liable on the note. Similarly, if Clara Carson authorizes Arthur Anderson, an attorney, to sign checks for her, Anderson should make sure either that the checks identify Clara Carson as the account involved or should sign them "Clara Carson by Arthur Anderson, Agent." Otherwise, he risks being personally liable on them.

The liability of an authorized representative is discussed in the case that follows, *Mestco Distributors, Inc., v. Stamps.*

---

## MESTCO DISTRIBUTORS, INC. V. STAMPS
### 17 UCC Rep.2d 174 (Tex. Ct. App. 1992)

On seven separate occasions between May 1985 and December 1986, Mestco Distributors, Inc., loaned funds for business operations to Innovative Timber Specialties, Inc. (ITS), in which Mestco was a shareholder. The seven notes were signed as follows:

Promissory note 1, May 17, 1985, signed:

I.T.S. Inc.
by Ralph W. Stamps
Secty. Treas

Promissory note 2, June 25, 1985, signed:

Ralph W. Stamps

Promissory note 3, December 23, 1985, signed:

Innovative Timber Specialties
Inc.
by Secty-treas
Ralph W. Stamps

Promissory note 4, July 16, 1985, signed:

Ralph W. Stamps
Secty-Treas. I.T.S. Inc.

Promissory note 5, December 9, 1985, signed:

Ralph W. Stamps

Promissory note 6, August 6, 1986, signed:

Innovative Timber Specialties
Inc.
by Ralph W. Stamps

Promissory note 7, December 31, 1986, signed:

Ralph W. Stamps
Innovative Timber Specialties
Inc.
by: Secretary

The notes were not paid and Mestco sued Stamps, seeking to hold him personally liable for paying the seven notes. The trial court held in favor of Stamps, and Mestco appealed.

---

**Ellis, Judge** Mestco argues that none of the promissory notes meet the requirements of Section 3–403, and, therefore, Stamps was required to present evidence to overcome the presumption of individual liability as to all seven notes. We disagree.

Section 3–403(c) provides that a signature is established as being in a representative capacity *if it has the name of an organization preceded or followed by an authorized individual's name and office.* Four of the promissory notes meet these requirements (May 17, 1985; December 23, 1985; July 16, 1986; December 31, 1986). Clearly, these notes listed the names of the organization followed or preceded by Ralph Stamps' name and his office, designated as Secretary or Scty-Treas. Accordingly, there was evidence to support the trial court's finding that these four notes were executed in a representative capacity.

Three of the promissory notes clearly did not meet the requirements of Section 3–403. Two notes were signed solely with Ralph Stamps' name and one note was signed "Innovative Timber Specialties, Inc. by Ralph W. Stamps." As Mestco correctly points out, if a signature is not shown to be in a representative capacity pursuant to Section 3–403(c), the signer/maker, in a dispute between the immediate parties, has the burden to offer proof that he signed only in a representative capacity.

Although there is no evidence in the present case that Stamps actually told Mestco that he was signing the notes in a representative capacity, there was evidence of prior dealings between the parties as well as circumstances that communicated to Mestco that Stamps was executing the notes in a representative capacity.

The evidence before the court was as follows. Henry Mest was president and owner of Mestco Distributors, Inc. He was in business for 30 years in La Marque, Texas. Stamps and Mest knew each other for more than 30 years. Stamps approached Mest regarding investing in ITS after its original formation in 1982. They each became shareholders in ITS, neither being majority shareholders. Both became officers and Mest became a director. The chief operating officer and president resigned in 1985 and Mest took over. In 1985 Mest went to ITS's job site once or twice a week and was fully aware of what was going on with the business.

Stamps managed ITS from 1985 to 1986 per an agreement with Mest. Stamps would also let Mestco know of ITS's financial need. Mestco and Stamps both from time to time loaned money to ITS as needed. In 1986, both Mestco and Stamps repaid in equal amounts a loan made to ITS in the amount of $150,000. Mestco received at least seven notes in addition to the notes the subject of this suit. These notes were later written off by Mestco as bad debts. The seven promissory notes involved in the present suit were prepared at Mest's direction. The payment of each of the notes was a promise of ITS's named in the subject notes and there was no understanding that the loans represented loans to Stamps individually. The funding of the notes was to ITS directly and were often deposited to ITS's bank account by Mestco's accountant. Also the notes were carried on Mestco's books as notes receivable from ITS and not as notes receivable from Stamps. Further, the notes were charged-off by Mestco in 1986 and 1987.

Accordingly, there was sufficient evidence showing that Mestco knew the notes were executed in a representative capacity and not Stamps individually, and past dealings supported that Stamps executed in a representative capacity.

**Judgment for Stamps affirmed.**

*Note:* Although this case was decided under the original version of Article 3, the same result would likely be reached under Revised Article 3.

## Unauthorized Signature

If someone signs a person's name to a negotiable instrument without that person's authorization or approval, the signature does not bind the person whose name appears. However, the signature is effective as the signature of the unauthorized signer in favor of any person who in good faith pays the instrument or takes it for value [3–403(a)]. For example, if Tom Thorne steals Ben Brown's checkbook and signs Brown's name to a check, Brown is not liable on the check because Brown had not authorized Thorne to sign Brown's name. However,

Thorne can be liable on the check because he did sign it, even though he did not sign it in his own name. Thorne's forgery of Brown's signature operates as Thorne's signature. Thus, if Thorne cashed the check at the bank, Thorne would be liable to it; or if he negotiated it to a store for value, he would be liable to the store to make it good.

Even though a signature is not "authorized" when it is put on an instrument initially, it can be ratified later by the person represented [3–403(a)]. It should also be noted that if more than one person must sign to constitute the authorized signature of an organization, the signature of the organization is unauthorized if one of the required signatures is lacking [3–403(b)]. Corporate and other accounts sometimes require multiple signatures as a matter of maintaining sound financial control.

## CONTRACTUAL LIABILITY IN OPERATION

To bring the contractual liability of the various parties to a negotiable instrument into play, it is generally necessary that the instrument be *presented for payment*. In addition, to hold the parties that are secondarily liable on the instrument to their contractual liability, it is generally necessary that the instrument be *presented for payment* and *dishonored*.

### Presentment of a Note

The maker of a note is primarily liable to pay it when it is due. Normally, the holder takes the note to the maker at the time it is due and asks the maker to pay it. Sometimes, the note may provide for payment to be made at a bank, or the maker sends the payment to the holder at the due date. The party to whom the holder presents the instrument, without dishonoring the instrument, may (1) require the exhibition of the instrument, (2) ask for reasonable identification of the person making presentment, (3) ask for evidence of his authority to make it if he is making it for another person, or (4) return the instrument for lack of any necessary indorsement, (5) ask that a receipt be signed for any payment made, and (6) ask for surrender of the instrument if full payment is made [3–501].

Dishonor of a note occurs if the maker does not pay the amount due when: (1) it is presented in the case of (*a*) a demand note or (*b*) a note payable at or through a bank on a definite date that is presented

on or after that date, or (2) if it is not paid on the date payable in the case of a note payable on a definite date but not payable at or through a bank [3–502]. If the maker or payor dishonors the note, the holder can seek payment from any persons who indorsed the note before the holder took it. The basis for going after the indorsers is that they are secondarily liable. To hold the indorsers to their contractual obligation, the holder must give them notice of the dishonor. The notice can be either written or oral [3–503].

For example, Susan Strong borrows $1,000 from Jack Jones and gives him a promissory note for $1,000 at 9 percent annual interest payable in 90 days. Jones indorses the note "Pay to the order of Ralph Smith" and negotiates the note to Ralph Smith. At the end of the 90 days, Smith takes the note to Strong and presents it for payment. If Strong pays Smith the $1,000 and accrued interest, she can have Smith mark it "paid" and give it back to her. If Strong does not pay the note to Smith when he presents it for payment, then she has dishonored the note. Smith should give notice of the dishonor to Jones and advise him that he intends to hold Jones secondarily liable on his indorsement. Smith may collect payment of the note from Jones. Jones, after making the note good to Smith, can try to collect the note from Strong on the ground that she defaulted on the contract she made as maker of the note. Of course, Smith could also sue Strong on the basis of her maker's obligation.

### Presentment of a Check or a Draft

The holder should present a check or draft to the drawee. The presentment can be either for payment or for acceptance (certification) of the check or draft. Under Revised Article 3, the presentment may be made by any commercially reasonable means, including a written, oral, or electronic communication [3–501]. No one is primarily obligated on a check or draft, and the drawee is not obligated on a check or draft unless it accepts (certifies) it [3–408]. An acceptance of a draft is the drawee's signed commitment to honor the draft as presented. The acceptance must be written on the draft, and it may consist of the drawee's signature alone [3–409].

A drawer who writes a check issues an order to the drawee to pay a certain amount out of the drawer's account to the payee (or to someone authorized by the payee). This order is not an assignment of the funds in the drawer's account [3–408]. The drawee bank does not have an obligation to the payee to pay the check unless it certifies the check. However, the drawee bank usually does have a separate contractual obligation (apart from Article 3) to the drawer to pay any properly payable checks for which funds are available in the drawer's account.

For example, Janet Payne has $100 in a checking account at First National Bank and writes a check for $10 drawn on First National and payable to Ralph Smith. The writing of the check is the issuance of an order by Payne to First National to pay $10 from her account to Smith or to whomever Smith requests it to be paid. First National owes no obligation to Smith to pay the $10 unless it has certified the check. However, if Smith presents the check for payment and First National refuses to pay it even though there are sufficient funds in Payne's account, then First National is liable to Payne for breaching its contractual obligation to her to pay items properly payable from existing funds in her account. Chapter 26, Checks and Documents of Title, discusses the liability of a bank for wrongful dishonor of checks in more detail.

If the drawee bank does not pay or certify a check when it is properly presented for payment or acceptance (certification), the drawee bank has dishonored the check [3–502]. Similarly, if a draft is not paid on the date it is due (or accepted by the drawee on the due date for acceptance), it has been dishonored. The holder of the draft or check then can proceed against either the drawer or any indorsers on their secondary liability. To do so, the holder must give them notice of the dishonor [3–503]. Notice of dishonor, like presentment, can be by any commercially reasonable means, including oral, written, or electronic communication. Under certain circumstances, set out in section 3–504, presentment or notice of dishonor may be excused.

Suppose Matthews draws a check for $100 on her account at a bank payable to the order of Williams. Williams indorses the check "Pay to the order of Clark, Williams" and negotiates it to Clark. When Clark takes the check to the bank, it refuses to pay the check because there are insufficient funds in Matthews's account to cover the check. The check has been presented and dishonored. Clark has two options: He can proceed against Williams on Williams's secondary liability as an indorser (be-

cause by putting an unqualified indorsement on the check, Williams is obligated to make the check good if it was not honored by the drawee). Or, he can proceed against Matthews on Matthews's obligation as drawer because in drawing the check, Matthews must pay any person entitled to enforce the check if it is dishonored and he is given notice. Because Clark dealt with Williams, Clark is probably more likely to return the check to Williams for payment. Williams then has to go against Matthews on Matthews's liability as drawer.

## Time of Presentment

If an instrument is payable at a definite time, the holder should present it for payment on the due date. In the case of a demand instrument, the nature of the instrument, trade or bank usage, and the facts of the particular case determine a reasonable time for presentment for acceptance or payment. In a farming community, for example, a reasonable time to present a promissory note that is payable on demand may be six months or within a short time after the crops are ready for sale, because the holder commonly expects payment from the proceeds of the crops.

## WARRANTY LIABILITY

Whether or not a person signs a negotiable instrument, a person who transfers such an instrument or presents it for payment or acceptance may incur liability on the basis of certain implied warranties. These warranties are (1) **transfer warranties**, which persons who transfer negotiable instruments make to their transferees; and (2) **presentment warranties**, which persons who present negotiable instruments for payment or acceptance (certification) make to payors and drawees.

## Transfer Warranties

A person who transfers a negotiable instrument to someone else and for consideration makes five warranties to his immediate transferee. If the transfer is by indorsement, the transferor makes these warranties to all subsequent transferees. The five transfer warranties are:

**1.** The warrantor is a person entitled to enforce the instrument. In essence the transferor warrants that there are no unauthorized or missing indorsements that prevent the transferor from making the transferee a person entitled to enforce the instrument.

**2.** All signatures on the instrument are authentic or authorized.

**3.** The instrument has not been altered.

**4.** The instrument is not subject to a defense or a claim in recoupment that any party can assert against the warrantor.

**5.** The warrantor has no knowledge of any insolvency proceedings commenced with respect to the maker or acceptor or, in the case of an unaccepted draft, the drawer [3–416(a)]. Note that this is not a warranty against difficulty in collection or insolvency—the warranty stops with the warrantor's knowledge.

Revised Article 3 provides that in the event of a breach of a transfer warranty, a beneficiary of the transfer warranties who took the instrument in good faith may recover from the warrantor an amount equal to the loss suffered as a result of the breach. However, the damages recoverable may not be more than the amount of the instrument plus expenses and loss of interest incurred as a result of the breach [3–416(b)].

Transferors of instruments other than checks may disclaim the transfer warranties. Unless the warrantor receives notice of a claim for breach of warranty within 30 days after the claimant has reason to know of the breach and the identity of the warrantor, the delay in giving notice of the claim may discharge the warrantor's liability to the extent of any loss the warrantor suffers from the delay, such as the opportunity to proceed against the transferor [3–416(c)].

Although contractual liability often furnishes a sufficient basis for suing a transferor when the party primarily obligated does not pay, warranties are still important. First, they apply even when the transferor did not indorse. Second, unlike contractual liability, they do not depend on presentment, dishonor, and notice, but may be utilized before presentment has been made or after the time for giving notice has expired. Third, a holder may find it easier to return the instrument to a transferor on the ground of breach of warranty than to prove her status as a holder in due course against a maker or drawer.

---

**CONCEPT REVIEW**

## TRANSFER WARRANTIES

The five transfer warranties made by a person who transfers a negotiable instrument to someone else for consideration are:

1. The warrantor is entitled to enforce the instrument.
2. All signatures on the instrument are authentic or authorized.
3. The instrument has not been altered.
4. The instrument is not subject to a defense or a claim in recoupment that any party can assert against the warrantor.
5. The warrantor has no knowledge of any insolvency proceedings commenced with respect to the maker or acceptor or, in the case of an unaccepted draft, the drawer.

| Who | What Warranties | To Whom |
| --- | --- | --- |
| **Nonindorsing Transferor** | Makes all five transfer warranties | To his immediate transferor only |
| **Indorsing Transferor** | Makes all five transfer warranties | To all subsequent transferors |

## Presentment Warranties

Persons who present negotiable instruments for payment or drafts for acceptance also make warranties, but their warranties differ from those transferors make. If an unaccepted draft (such as a check) is presented to the drawee for payment or acceptance and the drawee pays or accepts the draft, then the person obtaining payment or acceptance warrants to the drawee making payment or accepting the draft in good faith that:

**1.** The warrantor is, or was, at the time the warrantor transferred the draft, a person entitled to enforce the draft or authorized to obtain payment or acceptance of the draft on behalf of a person entitled to enforce the draft.

**2.** The draft has not been altered.

**3.** The warrantor has no knowledge that the signature of the drawer of the draft has not been authorized [3–417(a)].

These warranties are also made by any prior transferor of the instrument at the time the person transfers the instrument; the warranties run to the drawee who makes payment or accepts the draft in good faith. Such a drawee would include a drawee bank paying a check presented to it for payment directly or through the bank collection process.

The effect of the third presentment warranty is to leave with the drawee the risk that the drawer's signature is unauthorized, unless the person presenting the draft for payment, or a prior transferor, had knowledge of any lack of authorization.

A drawee who makes payment may recover as damages for any breach of a presentment warranty an amount equal to the amount paid by the drawee less the amount the drawee received or is entitled to receive from the drawer because of the payment. In addition, the drawee is entitled to compensation for expenses and loss of interest resulting from the breach [3–417(b)]. The drawee's right to recover damages for breach of warranty is not affected by any failure on the part of the drawee to exercise ordinary care in making payment.

If a drawee asserts a claim for breach of a presentment warranty based on an unauthorized indorsement of the draft or an alteration of the draft, the warrantor may defend by showing that the indorsement is effective under the *impostor* or *fictitious payee* rules (discussed later in this chapter) or that the drawer's negligence precludes him from asserting against the drawee the unauthorized indorsement or alteration (also discussed below) [3–417(c)].

If (1) a *dishonored draft* is presented for payment to the drawer or an indorser or (2) any other instrument (such as a note) is presented for payment to a party obligated to pay the instrument and the presenter receives payment, the presenter makes the following presentment warranty:

The person obtaining payment is a person entitled to enforce the instrument or authorized to obtain payment on behalf of a person entitled to enforce the instrument [3–417(d)].

On breach of this warranty, the person making the payment may recover from the warrantor an amount equal to the amount paid plus expenses and loss of interest resulting from the breach.

With respect to checks, the party presenting the check for payment cannot disclaim the presentment warranties [3-417(e)]. Unless the payor or drawee provides notice of a claim for breach of a presentment warranty to the warrantor within 30 days after the claimant has reason to know of the breach and the identity of the warrantor, the warrantor is discharged to the extent of any loss caused by the delay in giving notice of the claim of breach.

## Payment or Acceptance by Mistake

A longstanding general rule of negotiable instruments law is that payment or acceptance is final in favor of a holder in due course or payee who changes his position in reliance on the payment or acceptance. Revised Article 3 retains this concept by making payment final in favor of a person who took the instrument in good faith and for value. However, payment is not final—and may be recovered from—a person who does not meet these criteria where the drawee acted on the mistaken belief that (1) payment of a draft or check has not been stopped, (2) the signature of the purported drawer of the draft was authorized, and (3) the balance in the drawer's account with the drawee represented available funds [3–418(a)].

As a result, this means that if the drawee bank mistakenly paid a check over a stop-payment order, paid a check with a forged or unauthorized drawer's signature on it, or paid despite the lack of sufficient funds in the drawer's account to cover the check, the bank cannot recover if it paid the check to a presenter who had taken the instrument in good faith and for value. In that case, the drawee bank would have to pursue someone else, such as the forger or unauthorized signer, or the drawer in the case of insufficient funds. On the other hand, if the presenter had not taken in good faith or for value, the bank could, in these enumerated instances, recover from the presenter the payment it made by mistake.

The *Garnac Grain Co. Inc. v. Boatmen's Bank & Trust Co. of Kansas City* case, which follows, illustrates the operation of presentment and transfer warranties.

---

## GARNAC GRAIN CO., INC. v. BOATMEN'S BANK & TRUST CO. OF KANSAS CITY

### 694 F. Supp 1389 (W.D. Mo. 1988)

Katherine Millison was employed by the Garnac Grain Company as a bookkeeper. She developed a scheme to embezzle money from Garnac whereby she would take home fully executed and valid checks payable to freight vendors and type "or L. R. Millison" (her husband's name) under the named payee with her manual typewriter. She would then indorse the check "L. R. Millison" on the back and deposit the check in a joint account she and her husband maintained at the State Bank of Oskaloosa. The bank forwarded the altered checks through the Federal Reserve System (through First National Bank of Kansas City), which presented them for payment to the drawee bank, Boatmen's Bank & Trust Company of Kansas City. Boatmen's paid the checks. Millison then would intercept the monthly bank statements from Boatmen's Bank & Trust, remove the altered checks, and obliterate the "or L. R. Millison" on the face of the checks and the indorsement on the back.

The scheme was discovered and Millison was convicted of embezzlement. Garnac brought suit against Boatmen's Bank & Trust, alleging that it wrongfully paid the altered checks. It settled with Garnac and then sued the State Bank of Oskaloosa, contending that it breached the UCC transfer warranties when it forwarded the altered checks for payment.

---

**Hunter, Senior District Judge**     Boatmen's and First National contend that Oskaloosa is liable for the amount of their settlement with Garnac because it breached the UCC transfer warranties it made to them when it sent the checks altered by Millison to First National for payment by Boatmen's. Specifically it alleges that Oskaloosa breached the good title, material alterations, and genuine signature warranties.

Section 4–207 provides in pertinent part:

**(1)** Each customer or collecting bank who obtains payment or acceptance of an item and each prior customer and collecting bank warrants to the payor bank or other payor who in good faith pays or accepts the item that

**(a)** he has good title to the item or is authorized to obtain payment or acceptance on behalf of one who has a good title; and

**(b)** he has no knowledge that the signature of the maker or drawer is unauthorized . . .; and

**(c)** the item has not been materially altered . . .

**(2)** Each customer and collecting bank who transfers an item and receives a settlement or other consideration for it warrants to his transferee and to any subsequent collecting bank who takes the item in good faith that

**(a)** he has a good title to the item or is authorized to obtain payment or acceptance on behalf of one who has a good title and the transfer is otherwise rightful; and

**(b)** all signatures are genuine and authorized; and

**(c)** the item has not been materially altered;

Under this system, a payor bank in possession of a check containing, for example, a material alteration has the choice of bringing a warranty claim against the bank that transferred the check to it, or any other intermediate collecting bank or the depositary bank. If the payor bank brings the action against a bank other than the depositary bank, that bank can bring a claim against its transferor bank or any other previous collecting bank. As between the banks involved in the collection process, the liability for a materially altered check falls on the depositary bank. This is in accord with the loss allocation framework of Articles 3 and 4 of the UCC which generally places the loss of a forged or altered item on the person or bank who dealt with the wrongdoer if the wrongdoer cannot be found or is judgment proof. Since there is no knowledge or notice requirement with respect to the material alteration warranties, the question of whether or not a party breached these warranties is simply a question of whether or not the checks were materially altered.

There seems to be no serious dispute among the parties but that the alterations made by Millison were material. Each check was drawn on Garnac's account at Boatmen's, was properly made out to barge freight vendors, and was properly signed by authorized representatives of Garnac. Millison altered the checks by typing "or L. R. Millison" underneath the payee's name. The court finds that, as a matter of law, an alteration which adds an alternative payee is a material alteration as that term is used in the UCC. See section 3–407. Thus, both Oskaloosa and First National breached their 3–207(1) warranties of no material alteration to Boatmen's; Oskaloosa breached its 4–207(2) warranty of no material alterations.

There is also no question that Oskaloosa breached its warranty of good title. Without the indorsement of the intended payees on the checks (i.e., the barge freight vendors) Oskaloosa could not obtain good title to the checks. The only indorsement on the back of the checks was "L. R. Millison." Neither Millison nor her husband was authorized to indorse the checks on behalf of the barge freight vendors shown as payees on the altered checks. Since Oskaloosa did not have good title when it transferred the checks to First National, it breached its section 4–207(1)(a) warranty to Boatmen's and its 4–207(2)(a) warranty to First National.

**Summary judgment in favor of Boatmen's on its claims that the State Bank of Oskaloosa breached its warranties of good title and no material alterations.**

*Note:* The court found that there were issues of material fact as to whether Garnac had exercised reasonable care and promptness in examining its bank statement to discover unauthorized signatures and alterations and whether Boatmen's had exercised ordinary care in paying the checks in question. It should also be noted that this case was decided under the original version of Articles 3 and 4. Revised Article 3 and the conforming amendments to Articles 1 and 4 change the wording of the transfer and presentment warranties and the warranties appear under different section numbers. However, the result reached in this case would be the same under the revisions to the Code.

---

**CONCEPT REVIEW**

**PRESENTMENT WARRANTIES**

If an unaccepted draft (such as a check) is presented for payment or acceptance and the drawee pays or accepts the draft, then the person obtaining payment or acceptance warrants to the drawee:

1. The warrantor is a person entitled to enforce payment or authorized to obtain payment or acceptance on behalf of a person entitled to enforce the draft.
2. The draft has not been altered.
3. The warrantor has no knowledge that the signature of the drawer of the draft has not been authorized.

If (*a*) a dishonored draft is presented for payment to the drawer or indorser or (*b*) any other instrument (such as a note) is presented for payment to a party obligated to pay the instrument and the presenter receives payment, the presenter (as well as a prior transferor of the instrument) makes the following warranty to the person making payment in good faith:

The person obtaining payment is a person entitled to enforce the instrument or authorized to obtain payment on behalf of a person entitled to enforce the instrument.

---

## Operation of Warranties

The following are three scenarios that show how the transfer and presentment warranties shift the liability back to a wrongdoer or to the person who dealt immediately with a wrongdoer and thus was in the best position to avert the wrongdoing.

**Scenario 1**    Arthur makes a promissory note for $200 payable to the order of Betts. Carlson steals the note from Betts, indorses her name on the back, and gives it to Davidson in exchange for a television set. Davidson negotiates the note for value to Earle, who presents the note to Arthur for payment. Assume that Arthur refuses to pay the note because Betts has advised him that it has been stolen and that he is the person entitled to enforce the instrument. Earle then can proceed to recover the face amount of the note from Davidson on the grounds that as a transferor Davidson has warranted that he is a person entitled to enforce the note and that all signatures were authentic. Davidson, in turn, can proceed against Carlson on the same basis—if he can find Carlson. If he cannot, then Davidson must bear the loss caused by Carlson's wrongdoing. Davidson was in the best position to ascertain whether Carlson was the owner of the note and whether the indorsement of Betts was genuine. Of course, even though Arthur does not have to pay the note to Earle, Arthur remains liable for his underlying obligation to Betts.

**Scenario 2**    Anderson draws a check for $10 on her checking account at First Bank payable to the order of Brown. Brown cleverly raises the check to $110, indorses it, and negotiates it to Carroll. Carroll then presents the check for payment to First Bank, which pays her $110 and charges Anderson's account for $110. Anderson then asks the bank to recredit her account for the altered check, and it does so. The bank can proceed against Carroll for breach of the presentment warranty that the instrument had not been altered, which she made to the bank when she presented the check for payment. Carroll in turn can proceed against Brown for breach of her transfer warranty that the check had not been altered—if she can find her. Unless she was negligent in drawing the check, Article 3 limits Anderson's liability to $10 because her obligation is to pay the amount in the instrument at the time she issued it.

**Scenario 3**    Bates steals Albers's checkbook and forges Albers's signature to a check for $100 payable to "cash," which he uses to buy $100 worth of groceries from a grocer. The grocer presents the check to Albers's bank. The bank pays the amount of the check to the grocer and charges Albers's account. Albers then demands that the bank recredit his account. The bank can recover against the grocer only if the grocer knew that Albers's signature had been forged. Otherwise, the bank must look for Bates. The bank had the responsibility to recognize the true signature of its drawer, Albers, and not to pay the check that contained an unauthorized signature. The bank may be able to resist recrediting Albers's account if it can show he was negligent. The next section of this chapter discusses negligence.

## OTHER LIABILITY RULES

Normally, a bank may not charge against (debit from) the drawer's account a check that has a forged payee's indorsement. Similarly, a maker does not have to pay a note to the person who currently possesses the note if the payee's signature has been forged. If a check or note has been altered—for example, by raising the amount—the drawer or maker is usually liable only for the instrument in the amount for which he originally issued it. However, there are a number of exceptions to these usual rules. These exceptions, as well as liability based on conversion of an instrument, are discussed below.

### Negligence

A person can be so negligent in writing or signing a negotiable instrument that she in effect invites an alteration or an unauthorized signature on it. If a person has been negligent, Article 3 precludes her from using the alteration or lack of authorization as a reason for not paying a person that in good faith pays the instrument or takes it for value [3–406]. For example, Mary Maker makes out a note for $10 in such a way that someone could alter it to read $10,000. Someone alters the note and negotiates it to Katherine Smith, who can qualify as a holder in due course. Smith can collect $10,000 from Maker. Maker's negligence precludes her from claiming alteration as a defense to paying it. Maker then has to find the person who "raised" her note and try to collect the $9,990 from him.

Where the person asserting the preclusion failed to exercise ordinary care in taking or paying the instrument and that failure substantially contributed to the loss, Article 3 allocates the loss between the two parties based on their comparative negligence [3–406(b)]. Thus, if a drawer was so negligent in drafting a check that he made it possible for the check to be altered and the bank that paid the check, in the exercise of ordinary care, should have noticed the alteration, then any loss occasioned by the fact that the person who made the alteration could not be found would be split by the drawer and the bank based on their comparative fault.

## Impostor Rule

Article 3 establishes special rules for negotiable instruments made payable to impostors and fictitious persons. An **impostor** is a person who poses as someone else and convinces a drawer to make a check payable to the person being impersonated— or to an organization the person purports to be authorized to represent. When this happens, the Code makes any indorsement "substantially similar" to that of the named payee effective [3–404(a)]. Where the impostor has impersonated a person authorized to act for a payee, such as claiming to be Jack Jones, the president of Jones Enterprises, the impostor has the power to negotiate a check to Jones Enterprises.

An example of a situation involving the impostor rule would be the following: Arthur steals Paulsen's automobile and finds the certificate of title in the automobile. Then, representing himself as Paulsen, he sells the automobile to Berger Used Car Company. The car dealership draws its check payable to Paulsen for the agreed purchase price of the automobile and delivers the check to Arthur. Any person can negotiate the check by indorsing it in the name of Paulsen.

The rationale for the impostor rule is to put the responsibility for determining the true identity of the payee on the drawer or maker of a negotiable instrument. The drawer is in a better position to do this than some later holder of the check who may be entirely innocent. The impostor rule allows that later holder to have good title to the check by making the payee's signature valid although it is not the signature of the person with whom the drawer or maker thought he was dealing. It forces the drawer or maker to find the wrongdoer who tricked him into signing the negotiable instrument or to bear the loss himself.

## Fictitious Payee Rule

A **fictitious payee** commonly arises in the following situation: A dishonest employee draws a check payable to someone who does not exist—or to a real person who does business with the employer but to whom the dishonest employee does not intend to send the check. If the employee has the authority to do so, he may sign the check himself. If he does not have such authority, he gives the check to his employer for signature and represents that the employer owes money to the person named as the payee of the check. The dishonest employee then takes the check, indorses it in the name of the payee, presents it for payment, and pockets the money. The employee may be in a position to cover up the wrongdoing by intercepting the canceled checks or juggling the company's books.

The Code allows any indorsement in the name of the fictitious payee to be effective as the payee's indorsement in favor of any person that pays the instrument in good faith or takes it for value or for collection [3–404(b) and (c)]. For example, Anderson, an accountant in charge of accounts payable at Moore Corporation, prepares a false invoice naming Parks, Inc., a supplier of Moore Corporation, as having supplied Moore Corporation with goods, and draws a check payable to Parks, Inc., for the amount of the invoice. Anderson then presents the check to Temple, Treasurer of Moore Corporation, together with other checks with invoices attached. Temple signs all of these checks and returns them to Anderson for mailing. Anderson then withdraws the check payable to Parks, Inc. Anyone, including Anderson, can negotiate the check by indorsing it in the name of Parks, Inc.

The rationale for the fictitious payee rule is similar to that for the impostor rule. If someone has a dishonest employee or agent who is responsible for the forgery of some checks, the employer of the wrongdoer should bear the immediate loss of those checks rather than some other innocent party. In turn, the employer must locate the un-faithful employee or agent and try to recover from him.

The *City of Phoenix v. Great Western Bank & Trust* case, which follows, illustrates the operation of the fictitious payee rule. As you read the case, determine what the City should have done to prevent the loss it suffered.

## CITY OF PHOENIX v. GREAT WESTERN BANK & TRUST
### 42 UCC Rep. 1364 (Ariz. Ct. App. 1985)

Gary Hann opened a checking account at the Tucson branch of Great Western Bank & Trust in the name of Duncan Industries with a cash deposit of $200. He told the bank that Duncan Industries was a sole proprietorship involved in investments. Hann listed the mailing address of the business as a post office box and designated himself as the authorized signature on the account. Hann's confederate, Jay Maisel, worked for the City of Phoenix in a government-funded program to assist ex-convicts. Maisel had served nine years in prison for theft. City officials were aware of his background and initially placed him in a nonsensitive position. However, the City promoted Maisel to a position in which he was responsible for preparing the documentation to pay the City's vendors. Six months after his promotion, Maisel prepared two claims packages for one vendor, Duncan Industries, causing the City to issue duplicate checks to the order of Duncan Industries, each in the amount of $514,320.40. The legitimate check was mailed to the vendor in Chicago; the fraudulent check was mailed to Hann in Tucson.

Hann deposited the check in the Duncan Industries account he had established, where it was subjected to a four-day hold. Once the hold expired, Hann withdrew over $441,000 from the account, much of it in cashier's checks made payable to coin, stamp, diamond, or bullion dealers. The City, on its own behalf and as assignee of the rights of the drawee bank, brought suit against the Great Western Bank to recover the amount of the check taken for deposit by it, contending, among other things, that the check contained a forged payee's indorsement. The trial court ruled in favor of the bank and the City appealed.

---

**Corcoran, Judge**   Section 3–405 provides an exception to the general rule that forged indorsements are ineffective to pass title or to authorize a drawee to pay. Under section 4–401, a drawer can usually require the drawee bank to recredit the drawer account when the drawee pays a check on which a necessary indorsement is forged. The drawee bank can then shift the loss to previous indorsers on the ground of breach of warranty. The loss under the general rule will ultimately rest with the person who forged the instrument or the bank which took the instrument from the forger.

Section 3–405(1)(c), often referred to as the "fictitious payee rule," provides in pertinent part:

A.   An indorsement by any person in the name of a named payee is effective if: . . . 3. An agent or employee of the maker or drawer has supplied him with the name of the payee intending the latter to have no such interest.

The exception places the loss from the activities of a faithless employee upon the employer rather than on the drawee bank. The loss is shifted by making the indorsement "effective" although it is unauthorized. Since the indorsement is "effective," the instrument passes as though there had been no forgery and as between a collecting bank and the drawer of the check, the loss must fall on the drawer employer. The rule, as applied, also eliminates any liability of a collecting bank for breach of warranty of the genuineness of the signatures because a signature that is "effective" is to be regarded as "genuine" for the purpose of warranty liability. Thus, in this case, the City, as assignee of its drawee bank, has no recourse against Great Western Bank based on the warranties contained in sections 3–417 and 4–207 owed by Great Western Bank to the drawee.

The basis of the fictitious payee rule is explained in section 3–405, Official Comment 4: The principle followed is that the loss should fall upon the employer as a risk of his business enterprise rather than upon the subsequent holder or drawee. The reasons are that the employer is normally in a better position to prevent such forgeries by reasonable care in the selection or supervision of his employees, or, if he is not, is at least in a better position to cover the loss by fidelity insurance: and that the cost of such insurance is properly an expense of his business rather than of the business of the holder or drawee.

The factual circumstances for application of the fictitious payee rule are met in this case. Maisel, an "employee" of the drawer, the City of Phoenix, supplied the City, as to the duplicate check, with the name of a "payee," Duncan Industries, with the intent of creating no interest in Duncan Industries.

**Judgment for Great Western Bank affirmed.**

*Note:* This case was decided under the original version of Article 3. Although Revised Article 3 changes the wording of the "fictitious payee rule" and sets it out in section 3–404 of Revised Article 3, the result would be the same under the revision.

## Comparative Negligence Rule Concerning Impostors and Fictitious Payees

Revised Article 3 also establishes a comparative negligence rule if (1) the person, in a situation covered by the impostor or fictitious payee rule, pays the instrument or takes it for value or collection without exercising ordinary care in paying or taking the instrument, and (2) that failure substantially contributes to the loss resulting from payment of the instrument. In these instances, the person bearing the loss may recover an allocable share of the loss from the person who did not exercise ordinary care [3–404(d)].

## Fraudulent Indorsements by Employees

Revised Article 3 specifically addresses employer responsibility for fraudulent indorsements by employees and adopts the principle that the risk of loss for such indorsements by employees who are entrusted with responsibilities for instruments (primarily checks) should fall on the employer rather than on the bank that takes the check or pays it [3–405]. As to any person who in good faith pays an instrument or takes it for value, a fraudulent indorsement by a responsible employee is effective as the indorsement of the payee if it is made in the name of the payee or in a substantially similar name [3–405(b)]. If the person taking or paying the instrument failed to exercise ordinary care and that failure substantially contributed to loss resulting from the fraud, the comparative negligence doctrine guides the allocation of the loss.

A fraudulent indorsement includes a forged indorsement purporting to be that of the employer on an instrument payable to the employer; it also includes a forged indorsement purporting to be that of the payee of an instrument on which the employer is drawer or maker [3–405(a)(2)]. "Responsibility" with respect to instruments means the authority (1) to sign or indorse instruments on behalf of the employer, (2) to process instruments received by the employer, (3) to prepare or process instruments for issue in the name of the employer, (4) to control the disposition of instruments to be issued in the name of the employer, or (5) to otherwise act with respect to instruments in a responsible capacity. "Responsibility" does not cover those who simply have access to instruments as they are stored, transported, or that are in incoming or outgoing mail [3–405(a)(3)].

## Conversion

Conversion of an instrument is an unauthorized assumption and exercise of ownership over it. A negotiable instrument can be converted in a number of ways. For example, it might be presented for payment or acceptance, and the person to whom it is presented might refuse to pay or accept and refuse to return it. An instrument is also converted if a person pays an instrument to a person not entitled to payment—for example, if it contains a forged indorsement.

Revised Article 3 modifies and expands the previous treatment of conversion and provides that the law applicable to conversion of personal property applies to instruments. It also specifically provides that conversion occurs if (1) an instrument lacks an indorsement necessary for negotiation and (2) it is (*a*) purchased, (*b*) taken for collection, or (*c*) paid by a drawee to a person not entitled to payment. An action for conversion may not be brought by (1) the maker, drawer, or acceptor of the instrument or (2) a payee or an indorsee who did not receive delivery of the instrument either directly or through delivery to an agent or copayee [3–420].

Thus, if a bank pays a check that contains a forged indorsement, the bank has converted the check by wrongfully paying it. The bank then becomes liable for the face amount of the check to the person whose indorsement was forged [3–420]. For example, Arthur Able draws a check for $50 on his account at First Bank, payable to the order of Bernard Barker. Carol Collins steals the check from Barker, forges Barker's indorsement on it, and cashes it at First Bank. First Bank has converted Barker's property, because it had no right to pay the check without Barker's valid indorsement. First Bank must pay Barker $50, and then it can try to locate Collins to get the $50 back from her.

As is true under the original version of Article 3, if a check contains a restrictive indorsement (such as "for deposit" or "for collection") that shows a purpose of having the check collected for the benefit of a particular account, then any person who purchases the check or any depositary bank or payor bank that takes it for immediate payment converts the check unless the indorser receives the proceeds or the bank applies them consistent with the indorsement [3–206]. This principle is illustrated in the case that follows, *Kelly v. Central Bank & Trust Co. of Denver.*

---

## KELLY V. CENTRAL BANK & TRUST CO. OF DENVER
### 794 P.2d 1037 (Colo. Ct. App. 1990)

A number of investors, including Kelly, invested in a Cayman Islands entity, Tradecom, Ltd., a business involved in precious metals arbitrage. Their investments, in the form of cashier's checks, were payable to Tradecom and delivered to Arvey Down, Tradecom's agent. Down indorsed the checks and deposited them at the Central Bank & Trust Company of Denver into a checking account.

Most of the 934 checks, which were worth $11,227,473, were indorsed:

Tradecom Limited For deposit only 072 575

Other checks, totaling $576,850, were indorsed:

For deposit only 072 575

This included one check for $57,000, which apparently was deposited without indorsement and was indorsed by Central Bank's officer:

For deposit only 072 575 Tradecom by Mark E. Thompson Commercial Loan officer

The referenced account, No. 072 575, was not that of Tradecom (which had no accounts at Central Bank) but rather was that of Equity Trading Corporation, a company owned and managed by Down, also purportedly an agent of Tradecom.

The investors subsequently lost most of their investments in Tradecom, and they sued Central Bank for, among other things, conversion. They alleged that: (1) neither Down nor Equity Trading was an agent of Tradecom and that the check indorsements were unauthorized and ineffective; (2) over the course of 13 months, the bank negligently or recklessly permitted Down to divert the checks payable to Tradecom into Equity Trading's checking account; and (3) Central Bank did not follow reasonable commercial standards. Central Bank moved for summary judgment and in support of its motion submitted an executed power of attorney that indicated Down had the authority to indorse checks on behalf of Tradecom. The trial court awarded summary judgment to the Central Bank and the investors appealed.

---

**Tursi, Judge**    Because there was no triable issue of fact concerning Down's agency and authority to indorse and deposit the cashier's checks, and because proof of a forged or unauthorized indorsement is a necessary predicate to Central Bank's liability, the investors could not prevail as to the 11 million dollars of checks that contained an indorsement which included the "Tradecom Limited" name. Consequently, with respect to the checks indorsed with Tradecom's name, we conclude that the trial court properly granted summary judgment for Central Bank.

The trial court erred, however, in granting Central Bank summary judgment on the $57,000 check indorsed by Central Bank's commercial loan officer. In order for Central Bank to have become a holder under this indorsement, and thus have obtained title, Central Bank would have had to have been authorized to provide Tradecom's indorsement under section 4–205(1). This, however, was impossible since Tradecom was not Central Bank's "customer." Consequently, this indorsement is unauthorized as a matter of law, and summary judgment should not have been ordered for Central Bank on this check.

The investors also contend that the trial court erred in granting summary judgment for Central Bank on the remaining $519,850 of cashier's checks lacking any signature and merely indorsed "For deposit only 072 575." We agree.

Under section 3–419(1)(c), a check is converted when it is paid on a forged indorsement. In this context, a collecting or paying bank "pays" a check when it credits its customer's account with the proceeds of a check collected from the drawee bank. If such a payment occurs on a check with no indorsement or a missing indorsement, it is the legal equivalent of payment on a forged indorsement.

The term "indorsement" is generally understood to mean the indorser's writing of his or her signature on the instrument or the affixing of the indorser's name or some designation identifying the indorser on the instrument. A check simply inscribed "For deposit only" to an account other than payee's account and without the payee's signature is not an effective "indorsement." If the instrument is order paper and the depository bank does not, or cannot, supply the missing indorsement of its customer, the absence of the indorsement can be fatal to negotiation and transfer of title. One such situation is when the depository bank's customer and the payee are not the same person. In this case, the depository bank is unauthorized to, and cannot, supply the missing indorsement of the payee since the payee is not the bank's "customer" under section 4–205. In this situation, the depository bank does not become a holder of the checks and does not obtain good title to them. Payment of such proceeds to its depositor subjects the depository bank to liability for conversion.

In this case it was undisputed that Down, or someone in his employ, deposited $519,850 worth of cashier's checks at Central Bank bearing the simple inscription "For Deposit only 072 575." These checks, which bore no signature indorsement of the payee, Tradecom, or anyone else, were paid and credited to account 072 575. This was not an account of Tradecom, which was not a customer of Central Bank. Under these circumstances, Central Bank was not a holder of these checks by negotiation. It obtained no title to these checks. It is, consequently, subject to conversion liability under section 3–419(1)(c) for making payment on the equivalent of a forged indorsement.

**Judgment for Central Bank reversed in part.**

*Note:* Although this case was decided under original Article 3, the same result would be expected under Revised Article 3.

# DISCHARGE OF NEGOTIABLE INSTRUMENTS

## Discharge of Liability

The obligation of a party to pay an instrument is discharged (1) if he meets the requirements set out in Revised Article 3 or (2) by any act or agreement that would discharge an obligation to pay money on a simple contract. Discharge of an obligation is not effective against a person who has the rights of a holder in due course of the instrument and took the instrument without notice of the discharge [3–601].

The most common ways that an obligor on an instrument is discharged from her liability are:

1. Payment of the instrument.
2. Cancellation of the instrument.
3. Alteration of the instrument.
4. Modification of the principal's obligation that causes loss to a surety or impairs the collateral.
5. Unexcused delay in presentment or notice of dishonor with respect to a check (discussed earlier in this chapter).
6. Acceptance of a draft but varying the terms from the draft as presented (this entitles the holder to treat the draft as dishonored and the drawee, in turn, to cancel the acceptance). [3–410]

In addition, as noted earlier in the chapter, a drawer is discharged of liability of a draft that is accepted by a bank (e.g., if a check is certified by a bank) because at that point, the holder is looking to the bank to make the instrument good.

## Discharge by Payment

Generally, payment in full discharges liability on an instrument to the extent payment is (1) by or on behalf of a party obligated to pay the instrument and (2) to a person entitled to enforce the instrument. To the extent of payment, the obligation of a party to pay the instrument is discharged even though payment is made with knowledge of a claim to the instrument by some other person. However, the obligation is not discharged if: (1) there is a claim enforceable against the person making payment and payment is made with knowledge of the fact that payment is prohibited by an injunction or similar legal process, or (2) in the case of an instrument other than a cashier's, certified, or teller's check, the person making the payment had accepted from the person making the claim indemnity against loss for refusing to make payment to the person entitled to enforce payment. It is also not discharged if he knows the instrument is a stolen instrument and pays someone he knows is in wrongful possession of the instrument [3–602].

Also, if the holder has indorsed a negotiable instrument restrictively, the person who pays must comply with the restrictive indorsement to be discharged [3–603(1)(b)]. For example, Arthur makes a note of $100 payable to the order of Bryan. Bryan indorses the note "Pay to the order of my account no. 16154 at First Bank, Bryan." Bryan then gives the note to his employee, Clark, to take to the bank. Clark takes the note to Arthur, who pays Clark the $100. Clark then runs off with the money. Arthur is not discharged of his primary liability on the note because he did not make his payment consistent with the restrictive indorsement. To be discharged, Arthur has to pay the $100 into Bryan's account at First Bank.

## Discharge by Cancellation

A person entitled to enforce a negotiable instrument may discharge the liability of the parties to the instrument by canceling or renouncing it. If the holder mutilates or destroys a negotiable instrument with the intent that it no longer evidences an obligation to pay money, the holder has canceled that obligation [3–604]. For example, a grandfather lends $1,000 to his grandson for college expenses. The grandson gives his grandfather a promissory note for $1,000. If the grandfather later tears up the note with the intent that the grandson no longer owes him $1,000, the grandfather has canceled the note.

An accidental destruction or mutilation of a negotiable instrument is not a cancellation and does not discharge the parties to it. If an instrument is lost, mutilated accidentally, or destroyed, the person entitled to enforce it can still enforce the instrument. In such a case, the person must prove that the instrument existed and that she was its holder when it was lost, mutilated, or destroyed.

## Altered Instruments; Discharge by Alteration

A person paying a fraudulently altered instrument, or taking it for value, in good faith, and without notice of the alteration, may enforce the instrument (1) according to its original terms or (2) in the case of an incomplete instrument later completed in an unauthorized manner, according to its terms as completed [3–407(c)]. An alteration occurs if there is (1) an unauthorized change that modifies the obligation of a party to the instrument or (2) an unauthorized addition of words or numbers or other change to an incomplete instrument that changes the obligation of any party [3–407(a)]. A change that does not affect the obligation of one of the parties, such as dotting an *i* or correcting the grammar, is not considered to be an alteration.

Two examples illustrate the situations where Revised Article 3 allows fraudulently altered instruments to be enforced. First, assume the amount due on a note is fraudulently raised from $100 to $10,000 without any negligence on the maker's part. The contract of the maker has been changed: The maker promised to pay $100, but after the change has been made, he would be promising to pay much more. If the note is negotiated to a person who can qualify as a holder in due course who was without notice of the alteration, that person can enforce the note against the maker for its original terms, i.e., $100.

Second, assume Swanson draws a check payable to Frank's Nursery, leaving the amount blank. He gives it to his gardener with instructions to purchase some fertilizer at Frank's and to fill in the purchase price of the fertilizer when it is known. The gardener fills in the check for $100 and gives it to Frank's in exchange for the fertilizer ($7.25) and the difference in cash ($92.75). The gardener then leaves town with the cash. If Frank's had no knowledge of the unauthorized completion, it could enforce the check for $100 against Swanson. A similar situation is illustrated in the case that follows, *American Federal Bank, FSB v. Parker.*

---

## AMERICAN FEDERAL BANK, FSB v. PARKER
### 392 SE2d 798 (Ct. App. S.C. 1990)

Thomas Kirkman was involved in the horse business and was a friend of John Roundtree, a loan officer for American Federal Bank. Kirkman and Roundtree conceived a business arrangement in which Kirkman would locate buyers for horses and the buyers could seek financing from American Federal. Roundtree gave Kirkman blank promissory notes and security agreements from American Federal. Kirkman was to locate the potential purchaser, take care of the paperwork, and bring the documents to the bank for approval of the purchaser's loan.

Kirkman entered into a purchase agreement with Gene Parker, a horse dealer, to copurchase for $35,000 a horse named Wills Hightime that Kirkman represented he owned. Parker signed the American Federal promissory note in blank and also executed in blank a security agreement that authorized the bank to disburse the funds to the seller of the collateral. Kirkman told Parker he would cosign the note and fill in the details of the transaction with the bank. While Kirkman did not cosign the note, he did complete it for $85,000 as opposed to $35,000. Kirkman took the note with Parker's signature to Roundtree at American Federal and received two checks from the bank payable to him in the amounts of $35,000 and $50,000. Kirkman took the $35,000 and gave it to the real owner of the horse. Parker then received the horse.

Parker began making payments to the bank and called on Kirkman to assist in making the payments pursuant to their agreement. However, Kirkman skipped town, taking the additional $50,000 with him. Parker repaid the $35,000 but refused to pay any more. He argued that he only agreed to borrow $35,000 and the other $50,000 was unauthorized by him. American Federal Bank filed suit to recover the balance due on the note. The trial court held in favor of the bank, and Parker appealed.

---

**Cureton, Judge**    Parker executed a promissory note in blank. Under the Uniform Commercial Code, the maker of a note agrees to pay the instrument according to its tenor at the time of engagement "or as completed pursuant to Section 3–115 on incomplete instruments." Under Section 3–115(2) if the completion of an instrument is unauthorized the rules as to material alteration apply. Under Section 3–407(1)(b) the completion of an incomplete instrument otherwise than as authorized is considered an alteration. However, under Section 3–407(3) a subsequent holder in due course may enforce an incomplete instrument as completed. Official Comment 4 indicates that where blanks are filled or an incomplete instrument is otherwise completed, the loss is placed upon the party who left the instrument incomplete and the holder is permitted to enforce it according to its completed form.

We agree with the trial court that the bank was entitled to the directed verdicts. The responsibility for the situation rests with Parker. He and Kirkman negotiated their deal. Parker signed a blank promissory note. He relied upon Kirkman to cosign the note and fill it in for $35,000. Parker's negligence substantially contributed to the material alteration as a matter of law.

Parker argues that its was not reasonable commercial practice for American Federal to give Kirkman possession of blank promissory notes. After the fact, Parker argues the bank should have contacted him or checked to be sure everything was correct before disbursing the proceeds of the loan to Kirkman. There is no evidence in the record to establish the bank had any reason to inquire into the facial validity of the note. The note was complete when presented to the bank and there were no obvious alterations on it.

The record establishes American Federal took the note in good faith and without notice of any defense to it by Parker. American Federal gave value for the note when it disbursed the funds to Kirkman. As a holder in due course, American Federal may enforce the note against Parker as completed. Sections 3–302; 3–407(3).

**Judgment for American Federal affirmed.**

*Note:* Although this case was decided under the original version of Article 3, the same result would be reached under Revised Article 3 so long as the court found Kirkman's completion (alteration) to be fraudulent.

---

In any other case, a fraudulent alteration **discharges** any party whose obligation is affected by the alteration *unless* (1) the party assents or (2) is precluded from asserting the alteration (e.g., because of the party's contributory negligence). Assume that Anderson signs a promissory note for $100 payable to Bond. Bond indorses the note "Pay to the order of Connolly, Bond" and negotiates it to Connolly. Connolly changes the $100 to read $100,000. Connolly's change is unauthorized and fraudulent. As a result, Anderson is discharged from her primary liability as maker of the note and Bond is discharged from her secondary liability as indorser. Neither of them has to pay Connolly. The obligations of both Anderson and Bond were changed because the amount for which they are liable was altered.

No other alteration—that is, one that is not fraudulent—discharges any party, and a holder may enforce the instrument according to its *original* terms [3–407(b)]. Thus, there would no discharge if a blank is filled in the honest belief that it is authorized or if a change is made, without any fraudulent intent, to give the maker on a note the benefit of a lower interest rate.

## Discharge of Indorsers and Accommodation Parties

If a person entitled to enforce an instrument agrees, with or without consideration, to a material modification of the obligation of a party to the instrument, including an extension of the due date, then any accommodation party or indorser who has a right of recourse against the person whose obligation is modified is discharged *to the extent the modification causes a loss to the indorser or accommodation party*. Similarly, if collateral secures the obligation of a party to an instrument and a person entitled to enforce the instrument impairs the value of the collateral, the obligation of the indorser or accommodation party having the right of recourse against the obligor is discharged to the extent of the impairment. These discharges are not effective unless the person agreeing to the modification or causing the impairment knows of the accommodation or has notice of it. Also, no discharge occurs if the obligor assented to the event or conduct, or if the obligor has waived the discharge [3–605].

For example, Frank goes to Credit Union to borrow $4,000 to purchase a used automobile. The credit union has Frank sign a promissory note and takes a security interest in the automobile (i.e., takes it as collateral for the loan). It also asks Frank's brother Bob to sign the note as an accommodation maker. Subsequently, Frank tells the credit union he wants to sell the automobile and it releases its security interest. Because release of the collateral adversely affects Bob's obligation as accommodation maker, he is discharged from his obligation as accommodation maker in the amount of the value of the automobile.

**1.** American Music Industries, Inc., and Disneyland Vista Records had ongoing business dealings during 1975 and 1976. As of May 21, 1976, American owed Disneyland over $93,000. As evidence of that indebtedness, American issued 10 promissory notes, payable to Disneyland and signed by Irv Schwartz, the president of American Music. The notes contained no reference to American Music Industries, Inc., nor was there any indication that Schwartz signed in a representative capacity. American paid four of the notes, then defaulted on the rest. Disneyland brought suit against Schwartz to recover on the remaining six promissory notes. Schwartz claimed that the notes had been prepared by Disneyland; that they did not reflect correctly the intent of the parties, because they did not name American as the maker; and that he signed the notes individually by mistake. Is Schwartz individually liable on the notes?

**2.** Frederick Dowie was the president and sole stockholder of Fred Dowie Enterprises, Inc., a catering company. He obtained the opportunity to operate the concession stands at the Living History Farms during the pope's visit to Des Moines, Iowa. With high expectations, Dowie ordered 325,000 hot dog buns from Colonial Baking Company. Before the buns were delivered, he presented to Colonial Baking a postdated check in the amount of $28,640. The check showed the name of the corporation and its address in the upper left-hand corner. The signature on the check read "Frederick J. Dowie," and there were no other words of explanation. Unfortunately, only 300 buns were sold. Following a dispute over the ownership and responsibility for the remaining buns, Dowie stopped payment on the check. Colonial Baking then sued Dowie in his personal capacity as signer of the check. Is Dowie personally liable for the check?

**3.** Clay Haynes was the bookkeeper for Johnstown Manufacturing, Inc. He had express check-signing authority, and his signature was on the signature card for the account that Johnstown maintained at BancOhio National Bank. Haynes was also the bookkeeper of another corporation, Lynn Polymers, Inc., which was operated by the same individuals that operated Johnstown. Over a period of a year, Haynes engaged in a check-cashing scheme from which he pocketed approximately $70,000. Haynes wrote 35 corporate checks to the order of BancOhio National Bank, and the bank, in return, gave the cash to Haynes. Johnstown brought suit against BancOhio to recover $300 for the one check written on the Johnstown account that the bank paid to Haynes. (The other checks were written on the Polymers's account.) Johnstown claimed that the check was written without the express authority of the corporation, and thus it contained an "unauthorized" signature. Was Haynes's signature on the check unauthorized as that term is used in the Uniform Commercial Code?

**4.** Gish operated a retail business under the name of Gish's General Store. He agreed to sell his business to Kenneth Smith and Barry Gill in exchange for two houses to be built for Gish by Smith and Gill. The transaction was to be consummated on completion of the houses. In the interim, Smith and Gill were to familiarize themselves with the business by assisting in its operation. However, without Gish's knowledge, Smith and Gill opened a checking account at Springhill Bank in the name of Gish's General Store. They then stole a number of checks from Gish's cash register, indorsed them with Gish's signature stamped "For deposit only, Gish's General Store," and deposited them to the account at Springfield Bank. Subsequently, Smith and Gill withdrew the money from the account and disappeared. Several of the checks were returned to Springfield Bank because the drawers had stopped payment on them. Springfield Bank then brought suit against Gish to recover the amount of the dishonored checks, claiming that he was liable as indorser of the checks because of the stamped indorsement. Was Gish liable as indorser of the dishonored checks?

**5.** Willard Cobb operated an insurance agency in Brattleboro, Vermont. Cobb received a check in the amount of $13,750 issued by the Hartford Insurance Company and payable to R. A. McQuaide Milk Transport. The check was issued in payment of a property loss incurred by McQuaide under a policy issued by Hartford Insurance through Cobb's agency. Willard Cobb, without authorization from McQuaide, fraudulently indorsed McQuaide's name to the check. He then added his own indorsement: "For Deposit Only— Franklin County Trust Co., Willard D. Cobb." He gave the check to his brother Leon to deposit at Franklin County Trust in a new partnership account they had opened in the name of "Econo Car Rental Center." The bank credited the partnership account with the money. Willard took the money from the account and left town. The bank had to pay back Hartford Insurance for the check it had wrongfully paid to Willard and Leon rather than to McQuaide. Then it sued Willard and Leon Cobb to recover the money from them. Were Leon and Willard liable to the bank on the ground that they breached transfer warranties?

**6.** Mrs. Gordon Neely hired Louise Bradshaw as the bookkeeper for a Midas Muffler shop she and her husband owned and operated as a corporation, J. Gordon Neely Enterprises, Inc. (Neely). Bradshaw's duties included preparing company checks for Mrs. Neely's signature and reconciling the checking account when the company received bank statement and canceled checks each month. Bradshaw prepared several checks payable to herself and containing a large space to the left of the amount written on the designated line. When Mrs. Neely signed the checks, she was aware of the large gaps. Subsequently, Bradshaw altered the checks by adding a digit or two to the left of the original amount and then cashed them at American National Bank, the drawee bank. Several months later, the Neelys hired a new accountant, who discovered the altered checks. Neely brought suit against American National Bank to have its account recredited for the altered checks, claiming that American was liable for paying out on altered instruments. The bank contended that Neely's negligence substantially contributed to a material alteration of the instrument and thus Neely was precluded from asserting the alteration against the bank. Between Neely and American National Bank, who should bear the loss caused by Bradshaw's fraud?

**7.** Mrs. Johnson mailed a loan application to First National Bank in her husband's name and without his knowledge. Having dealt with her husband before, the bank approved the application and mailed a check in the amount requested to Mr. Johnson. Mrs. Johnson then indorsed the check in her husband's name and cashed it at Merchant's Bank. Merchant's Bank indorsed the check and presented it for payment. First National, having discovered the deception, refused to pay. Is First National liable on the check?

**8.** Clarice Rich was employed by the New York City Board of Education as a clerk. It was her duty to prepare requisitions for checks to be issued by the board, to prepare the checks, to have them signed by the authorized personnel, and to send the checks to the recipients. In some instances, however, she retained them. Also, on a number of occasions, she prepared duplicate requisitions and checks that, when signed, she likewise retained. She then forged the indorsement of the named payees on the checks she had retained and cashed the checks at Chemical Bank, where the Board of Education maintained its account. After the board discovered the forgeries, it demanded that Chemical Bank credit its account for the amount of the forged checks. Is Chemical Bank required to credit the board's account as requested?

**9.** Wilson was presented with a check payable to Jones and Brown and drawn on Merchant's Bank. The check was indorsed by Brown alone. Wilson accepted the check, indorsed it, and submitted it to Merchant's Bank for payment. Merchant's Bank paid Wilson. Does Merchant's Bank have any liability to Jones?

**10.** Charles Peterson, a farmer and rancher, was indebted to Crown Financial Corporation on a $4,450,000 promissory note that was due on December 29, 1972. Shortly before the note was due, Crown sent Peterson a statement of interest due on the note ($499,658.85). Peterson paid the interest and executed a new note in the amount of $4,450,000 that was to mature in December 1975. The old note was then marked "canceled" and returned to Peterson. In 1975, Crown billed Peterson for $363,800 in interest that had been due on the first note but apparently not included in the statement. Peterson claimed that the interest had been forgiven and that he was not obligated to pay it. Was Peterson still obligated to pay interest on the note that had been returned to him marked "canceled"?

**11.** 🎞 *Video Case.* See "Cafeteria Conversion." Steve, an individual with a gambling and substance abuse problem, works in the accounts payable department of a company. He issues checks drawn on his employer's account that are made payable to suppliers who do business with his employer but who are not currently owed money. Then he forges the signature of the named payees, obtains payment of the checks from the drawee bank, and uses the funds to support his habits. Because Steve's responsibilities include reconciling the bank statements, his forgery scheme is not discovered for a considerable period of time. When it is discovered, is the drawee bank required to recredit the employer's account for the forged checks that were paid from it?

## CAPSTONE QUESTIONS

**1.** Jinxed Corporation retained Halefellow & Serious, PC, a public accounting firm, to examine its financial circumstances. Jinxed's president told the Halefellow account manager that he suspected embezzlement was occurring because the corporation's cash position was less than in previous fiscal years. During its investigation, Halefellow uncovered probable collusion between Jinxed's head of payroll and its assistant comptroller, as follows:

· The head of payroll supplied the assistant comptroller with punched time cards for fictitious employees. The assistant comptroller also prepared invoices, receiving reports, and purchase orders for fictitious suppliers. The assistant comptroller then prepared checks for the fictitious employees and suppliers, which the comptroller signed. Then, either the assistant comptroller or the head of payroll indorsed the checks and deposited them in the names of the fictitious payees. All checks cleared Omnibus Bank, the drawee, and were charged against the Jinxed account.

· The assistant comptroller had indorsed checks totaling more than $200,000 that were payable to the corporation with an indorsement that provided "For deposit only" and had deposited them to an account in his own name at Omnibus.

· The defalcations included several checks payable directly to the head of payroll and the assistant comptroller for "bonuses due." These checks bore very skillful forgeries of the comptroller's signature that were almost impossible to detect. These occurred while the comptroller was in the hospital and the assistant comptroller was in charge and authorized to

sign checks on behalf of the corporation. These checks were also paid by Omnibus.

## Required:

Answer the following and give reasons for your conclusions.

1. Which individuals and entities are obligated as indorsers? What is their obligation as indorser?
2. With respect to the checks made out to fictitious employees or to fictitious suppliers, would Jinxed be entitled to have its account recredited on the grounds that the named individuals and entities had not, in fact, indorsed the checks and thus the bank had paid the checks without authorized indorsements?
3. With respect to the checks payable to Jinxed that were indorsed by the assistant comptroller for deposit and credited by the bank to the assistant comptroller's personal account, does the bank have any liability to Jinxed?
4. With respect to the checks payable to Jinxed that were indorsed by the assistant comptroller for deposit and credited by the bank to his account, were any presentment warranties breached?
5. With respect to the checks signed by the assistant comptroller while the comptroller was in the hospital, would Jinxed be legally entitled to have its account recredited for the checks on the grounds that while the assistant comptroller was authorized to sign checks generally in the comptroller's absence, he was not authorized to sign these specific checks?

# CHAPTER

## 26

# CHECKS AND DOCUMENTS OF TITLE

## INTRODUCTION

*For most people, a checking account provides the majority of their contact with negotiable instruments. This chapter focuses on the relationship between the drawer with a checking account and the drawer's bank, known as the drawee bank. It addresses such common questions as: What happens when a bank refuses to pay a check even though the depositor has sufficient funds in her account? Does the bank have the right to create an overdraft in a depositor's account by paying an otherwise properly payable check? What are the depositor's rights and the bank's obligation when the depositor stops payment on a check? What is the difference between a certified check and a cashier's check? What are the depositor's responsibilities when she receives her monthly statement and canceled checks? The second half of the chapter discusses the Code rules that apply to negotiable documents of title such as warehouse receipts and bills of lading.*

---

## THE DRAWER-DRAWEE RELATIONSHIP

There are two sources that govern the relationship between the depositor and the drawee bank: the deposit agreement and Articles 3 and 4 of the Code. Article 4, which governs Bank Deposits and Collections, allows the depositor and drawee bank (which Article 4 calls the "payor bank") to vary Article 4's provisions with a few important exceptions. The deposit agreement cannot disclaim the bank's responsibility for its own lack of good faith or failure to exercise ordinary care or limit the measure of damages for the lack or failure; however, the parties may determine by agreement the standards by which to measure the bank's responsibility so long as the standards are not manifestly unreasonable [4–103].

The deposit agreement establishes many important relationships between the depositor and drawee/payor bank. The first of these is their relationship as creditor and debtor, respectively, so that when a person deposits money in an account at the bank, the law no longer considers him the owner of the money. Instead, he is a creditor of the bank to the extent of his deposits and the bank becomes his debtor. Also, when the depositor deposits a check to a checking account, the bank also becomes his agent for collection of the check. The bank as the person's agent owes a duty to him to follow his reasonable instructions concerning payment of checks and other items from his account and a duty of ordinary care in collecting checks and other items deposited to the account.

## Bank's Duty to Pay

When a bank receives a properly drawn and payable check on a person's account and there are sufficient funds to cover the check, the bank is under a duty to pay it. If the person has sufficient funds in the account and the bank refuses to pay, or dishonors, the check, the bank is liable for the actual damages proximately caused by its wrongful dishonor as well as consequential damages [4–402]. Actual damages may include charges imposed by retailers for returned checks as well as damages for arrest or prosecution of the customer. Consequential damages include injury to the depositor's credit rating that results from the dishonor.

For example, Donald Dodson writes a check for $1,500 to Ames Auto Sales in payment for a used car. At the time that Ames Auto presents the check for payment at Dodson's bank, First National Bank, Dodson has $1,800 in his account. However, a teller mistakenly refuses to pay the check and stamps it NSF (not sufficient funds). Ames Auto then goes to the local prosecutor and signs a complaint against Dodson for writing a bad check. As a result, Dodson is arrested. Dodson can recover from First National the damages that he sustained because the bank wrongfully dishonored his check, including the damages involved in his arrest, such as his attorney's fees.

In the case that follows, *Buckley v. Trenton Savings Fund Society,* the bank is potentially liable for consequential damages sustained by the drawer because it wrongfully dishonored a customer's check. In reading the case, you should keep in mind that Revised Article 3 deletes any reference to "mistake" by the bank; thus, the proof and measure of damages no longer turns on whether the bank can establish that it dishonored a check by mistake.

---

### BUCKLEY v. TRENTON SAVINGS FUND SOCIETY
#### 524 A.2d 886 (N.J. Super. Ct. 1987)

Buckley maintained a checking account at the Trenton Savings Fund Society. In 1981, he separated from his wife, Linda, and entered into a consent agreement with her in which he agreed to pay her $150 per week for food and support for herself and their children. On January 13, 1984, Buckley wrote a check for $150 and gave it to his wife. The next Saturday, she presented it for payment at one of Trenton Savings' branches but payment was refused even though Buckley had $900 in the account at the time. The following Monday, she took it to another branch where payment was refused again. The bank told Linda that it would not cash the check for her because Linda did not have an account at the bank. Subsequently, the bank agreed to cash checks for Linda, but on March 4, 1984, the bank again refused to pay one of Buckley's checks that she presented for payment. Linda was known to the bank because it held a mortgage on the home that she and Buckley jointly owned.

Shortly after Trenton Bank's failure to cash the two checks, Buckley received an irate call from Linda. He also received calls from his parents, his sister, and his best friend inquiring as to why he was not making the support payments. In addition, his children inquired "why daddy wouldn't give them food money." Buckley incurred severe emotional distress over the matter. He brought suit against Trenton Savings for wrongful dishonor and sought compensatory damages, as well as punitive damages, for the mental anguish he sustained. The trial court entered judgment for Buckley based on a jury verdict for $25,000, and the bank appealed.

---

**Stern, Judge**    The bank contends that the jury should not have been permitted to award damages for emotional distress under the facts of this case.

A bank's liability for wrongful dishonor of a customer's check is defined in section 4–402 of the Uniform Commercial Code:

A payor bank is liable to its customer for damages proximately caused by the wrongful dishonor of an item. When the dishonor occurs through mistake, liability is limited to actual damages proved. If so proximately caused and proved, damages may include damages for an arrest or prosecution of the customer or other consequential damages. Whether any consequential damages are proximately caused by the wrongful dishonor is a question of fact to be determined in each case.

The UCC does not indicate the theory or basis for a bank's liability for wrongful dishonor. As explained in the UCC official comment to section 4–402, "The liability of the drawee for dishonor has sometimes been stated as one for breach of contract, sometimes as for negligence or other breach of a tort duty, and sometimes as for defamation." The drafters of the UCC did not intend to exclude the possibility of mental distress damages upon a wrongful dishonor by a bank. Since section 4–402 is silent on any restriction of damages when the dishonor is grounded on an action other than mistake, it implies that these damages are not precluded by the Code. Thus, out-of-state courts interpreting section 4–402 have concluded that mental suffering is compensable under this section.

The Legislature adopted section 4–402 as promulgated in the Uniform Commercial Code without substantive change. The section expressly limits recovery for "actual damages" when the dishonor results from "mistake" but otherwise expressly permits recovery of "consequential damages" proximately caused. As White and Summer explains:

When wrongful dishonors occur not "through mistake" but willfully, the court may impose damages greater than "actual damages."

\* \* \* \* \*

Might one argue that "actual damages" excludes recovery for mental distress? We think not. In the first place, the drafters went to great efforts to assure that customers can recover for arrest and prosecution. It is inconsistent to allow recovery for embarrassment and mental distress deriving from arrest and prosecution and to deny similar recovery in other cases. Moreover, cases under the predecessor to 4–402, the American Association Statute, held that "actual damages" includes damages for mental distress. Thus we believe . . . that the Code drafters intended to allow recovery for mental distress and other intangible injury.

In this case the judge's instructions failed to delineate the distinction between mistake and intentional mistake and an intentional breach or wilful, wanton or reckless conduct. As a result, the matter must be remanded for a new trial and for a determination of damages based on appropriate instructions.

We preclude an award of punitive damages. Punitive damages are not generally recoverable for breach of contract, at least when the breach of contract does not also constitute a tort for which punitive damages are recoverable.

**Reversed and remanded for new trial.**

*Note:* This case was decided under the original version of Article 3 under which courts found that the Code appeared to allow a different measure of damages if the dishonor was other than by mistake. Revised Article 3 eliminates any distinction turning on mistake and provides that the depositor may recover actual damages, including consequential damages, proximately caused by a dishonor.

## Bank's Right to Charge to Customer's Account

The drawee bank has the right to charge any properly payable check to the account of the customer or drawer. The bank has this right even though payment of the check creates an overdraft in the account [4–401]. If an account is overdrawn, the customer owes the bank the amount of the overdraft and the bank may take that amount out of the next deposit that the customer makes or from another account that the depositor maintains with the bank. Alternatively, the bank might seek to collect the amount directly from the customer. If there is more than one customer who can draw from an account, only that customer—or those customers—who sign the items or who benefit from the proceeds of an overdraft are liable for the overdraft.

**Stale Checks** The bank does not owe a duty to its customer to pay any checks out of the account that are more than six months old. Such checks are called **stale checks.** However, the bank acting in good faith may pay a check that is more than six months old and charge it to the drawer-depositor's account [4–404].

**Altered and Incomplete Items** If the bank in good faith pays a check drawn by the drawer-depositor but subsequently altered, it may charge the customer's account with the amount of the check as originally drawn. Also, if an incomplete check of a customer gets into circulation, is completed, and is presented to the drawee bank for payment, and the bank pays the check, the bank can charge the amount as completed to the customer's account even though it knows that the check has been completed, unless it has notice that the completion was improper [4–401(d)]. The respective rights, obligations, and liabilities of drawee banks and their drawer-customers concerning forged and altered checks are discussed in more detail later in this chapter.

**Limitations on Bank's Right or Duty** Article 4 recognizes that the bank's right or duty to pay a check or to charge the depositor's account for the check (including exercising its right to set off an amount due to it by the depositor) may be terminated, suspended, or modified by the depositor's order to stop payment (which is discussed in the next section of this chapter). In addition, it may be stopped by events external to the relationship between the depositor and the bank. These external events include the filing of a bankruptcy petition by the depositor or by the depositor's creditors, and the garnishment of the account by a creditor of the depositor. The bank must receive the stop-payment order from its depositor or the notice of the bankruptcy filing or garnishment before the bank has certified the check, paid it in cash, settled with another bank for the amount of the item without a right to revoke the settlement, completed the process necessary to its decision to pay the check, or otherwise become accountable for the amount of the check under Article 4 [4–303]. These restrictions on the bank's right or duty to pay are discussed in later sections of this chapter.

**Postdated Checks** Under original Articles 3 and 4, a postdated check was not properly payable by the drawee bank until the date on the check. The recent amendments to Article 4 change this. Under the revision, an otherwise properly payable postdated check that is presented for payment before the date on the check may be paid and charged to the customer's account *unless* the customer has given notice of it to the bank. The customer must give notice of the postdating in a way that describes the check with reasonable certainty. It is effective for the same time periods as Article 4 provides for stop-payment orders (discussed below). The customer must give notice to the bank at such time and in such manner as to give the bank an opportunity to act on it before the bank takes any action with respect to paying the check. If the bank charges the customer's account for a postdated check before the date stated in the notice given to the bank, the bank is liable for damages for any loss that results. Such damages might include that associated with the bank's dishonor of subsequent items [3–113(a); 4–401(c)].

There are a variety of reasons why a person might want to postdate a check. For example, a person might have a mortgage payment due on the first of the month at a bank located in another state. To make sure that the check arrives on time, the customer may send the payment by mail several days before the due date. However, if the person is depending on a deposit of her next monthly paycheck on the first of the month to cover the mortgage payment, she might postdate the check to the first of the following month. Under the original version of Articles 3 and 4, the bank could not properly pay the check until the first of the month. However, under the revisions it could be properly paid by the bank before that date if presented earlier. To avoid the risk that the bank would dishonor the check for insufficient funds if presented before the first, the customer should notify the drawee bank in a manner similar to that required for stop payment of checks.

## Stop-Payment Order

A **stop-payment order** is a request made by a customer of a drawee bank instructing it not to pay or certify a specified check. As the drawer's agent in the payment of checks, the drawee bank must

**FIGURE 1    Stop-Payment Order**

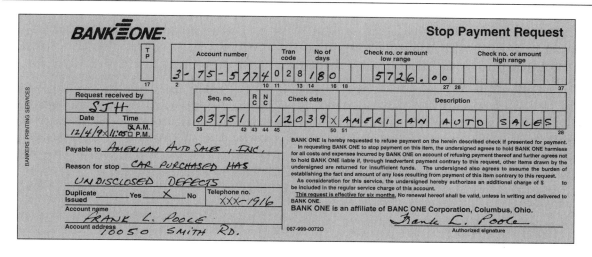

follow the reasonable orders of the customer/drawer about payments made on the drawer's behalf. Any person authorized to draw a check may stop payment of it. Thus, any person authorized to sign a check on the account may stop payment even if she did not sign the check in question [4–403(a)].

To be effective, the payor bank must receive the stop-payment order in time to give the bank a reasonable opportunity to act on the order. This means that the bank must receive the stop-payment order before it has paid or certified the check. In addition, the stop-payment order must come soon enough to give the bank time to instruct its tellers and other employees that they should not pay or certify the check [4–403(a)]. The stop-payment order must also describe the check with "reasonable certainty" so as to provide the bank's employees the ability to recognize it as the check corresponding to the stop-payment order.

The customer may give an oral stop-payment order to the bank, but it is valid for only 14 days unless the customer confirms it in writing during that time. A written stop-payment order is valid for six months and the customer can extend it for an additional six months by giving the bank instructions in writing to continue the order [4–403(b)]. See Figure 1.

Sometimes the information given the bank by the customer concerning the check on which payment is to be stopped is incorrect. For example, there may be an error in the payee's name, the amount of the check, or the number of the check. The question then arises whether the customer has accorded the bank a reasonable opportunity to act on his request. A common issue is whether the stop-payment order must have the dollar amount correct to the penny. Banks usually take the position that the stop-payment order must be correct to the penny because they program and rely on computers to focus on the customer's account number and the amount of the check in question to avoid paying an item subject to a stop-payment order.

The amendments to Article 4 do not resolve this question. In the Official Comments, the drafters indicate that "in describing an item, the customer, in the absence of a contrary agreement, must meet the standard of what information allows the bank under the technology then existing to identify the check with reasonable certainty." The following *FJS Electronics v. Fidelity Bank* case involves a situation in which the amount set out in a stop-payment order differed by $.50 from the amount actually on the check.

---

## FJS ELECTRONICS, INC. V. FIDELITY BANK

### 28 UCC Rep. 1462 (Pa. Ct. C.P. 1980)

On February 27, 1976, Multi-Tek issued check number 896 in the face amount of $1,844.98, drawn on Multi-Tek's account at Fidelity and made payable to Multilayer Computer Circuits. However, on March 9, 1976, Frank J. Suttill, Multi-Tek's president, telephoned Fidelity and placed a stop-payment order on the check. Rosana M. Sanders, Fidelity's employee, received and simultaneously recorded the order. This recordation contained the following information: the name of the account, the account number, the check number, the date of the check, the date and hour the stop-payment order was received, and the amount of the check as $1,844.48. This recordation was correct in most respects, except for a 50-cent difference between the face amount ($1,844.98) and the amount listed in the stop-payment order ($1,844.48).

Subsequently, Fidelity mailed a confirmation notice bearing the date "03/ 76" to Multi-Tek. It contained, among other things, the following information:

PAYEE: MULTILAYER COMPUTER CIRCUITS AMOUNT: $1,844.48
CK: NO.: 896
DATE: 02/ 27/76

The instructions in this confirmation notice concluded with: PLEASE ENSURE AMOUNT IS CORRECT. Suttill signed this confirmation notice and returned it to Fidelity.

Fidelity programmed its computer to pull checks only if all of the digits on the stop-payment order agreed with those on the check. As a result, Fidelity honored check number 896 and charged it to Multi-Tek's account. Multi-Tek then brought suit against Fidelity to recover $1,844.98 because the check was paid over the stop-payment order.

---

**Marutani, Judge** The Uniform Commercial Code, Section 4–403(1), provides in pertinent part that: "A customer may by order to his bank stop payment of any item payable for his account but the order must be received at such time and in such manner as to afford the bank a reasonable opportunity to act on it prior to any action by the bank with respect to the item." In this case, there is no question that the transmittal of the stop-payment order was made timely; this leaves for resolution only whether such order was given "in such *manner* as to afford the bank a reasonable opportunity to act on it": UCC Section 4–403(1); emphasis added. While the parties "may by agreement determine the standards by which [the bank's] responsibility is to be measured if such standards are not manifestly unreasonable," at the same time "no agreement can disclaim a bank's responsibility for its failure to exercise ordinary care": UCC Section 4–103(1).

The decisional law construing Section 4–403(1) appears to vary. Thus, in a recent decision of a trial court wherein the customer identified the check correctly as to the payee, the check number, and the

date of issuance, but erred by 10 cents as to the amount of the check—$1,804.00 instead of the correct amount of $1,804.10—it was held that "the check was described with sufficient particularity and accuracy so that the bank should have known to give effect to the stop-payment order." However, where the customer provided the correct amount of the check but erred as to the date and name of the payee—one-day error in date, "Walter Morris Buick" instead of the correct name "Frank Morris Buick"—the Alabama Supreme Court held such to be insufficient notice.

In this case, as the parties by the stipulation agreed, "the Bank did not tell Mr. Suttill, nor did he request, information as to the procedure whereby the computer pulls checks on which stop payments have been issued." Under such circumstances, where the customer (Mr. Suttill) was called upon by the bank (Fidelity) to provide numerous data relating to the check in question, but the bank failed to emphasize to him that all such information may well be ineffective unless the amount of the check were absolutely accurate, we are constrained to be guided by the official comment to Section 4–403 under "Purposes," which reads:

2. The position taken by this section is that stopping payment is a service which depositors expect and are entitled to receive from banks notwithstanding its difficulty, inconvenience and expense. The inevitable occasional losses through failure to stop should be borne by the banks as a cost of the business of banking.

**Judgment for Multi-Tek.**

*Note:* As noted above, the recent revisions of Articles 3 and 4 require the item to be described "with reasonable certainty" and do not explicitly address the question of whether the amount of the item has to be correct to the penny. It is not clear whether another court now faced with this same set of facts would find that the description of the item here would "meet the standard of what information allows the bank under the technology then existing to identify the item with reasonable certainty," as the drafters amplify the test in the Official Comments.

## Bank's Liability for Payment after Stop-Payment Order

While a stop-payment order is in effect, the drawee bank is liable to the drawer of a check that it pays for any loss that the drawer suffers by reason of such payment. However, the drawer-customer has the burden of establishing the fact and amount of the loss. To show a loss, the drawer must establish that the drawee bank paid a person against whom the drawer had a valid defense to payment. To the extent that the drawer has such a defense, he has suffered a loss due to the drawee's failure to honor the stop-payment order.

For example, Brown buys what is represented to be a new car from Foster Ford and gives Foster Ford his check for $12,280 drawn on First Bank. Brown then discovers that the car is in fact a used demonstrator model and calls First Bank, ordering it to stop payment on the check. If Foster Ford presents the check for payment the following day and First Bank pays the check despite the stop-payment order, Brown can require the bank to recredit his account. (The depositor-drawee bases her claim to recredit on the fact that the bank did not follow her final instruction—the instruction not to pay the check.) Brown had a valid defense of misrepresentation that she could have asserted against Foster Ford if it had sued her on the check. Foster Ford would have been required to sue on the check or on Brown's contractual obligation to pay for the car.

Assume, instead, that Foster Ford negotiated the check to Smith and that Smith qualified as a holder in due course. Then, if the bank paid the check to Smith over the stop-payment order, Brown would not be able to have his account recredited, because Brown would not be able to show that he sustained any loss. If the bank had refused to pay the check, so that Smith came against Brown on his drawer's liability, Brown cannot use his personal defense of misrepresentation of the proper use of the car as a reason for not paying Smith. Brown's only recourse would be to pursue Foster Ford on his misrepresentation claim.

The bank may ask the customer to sign a form in which the bank tries to disclaim or limit its liability for the stop-payment order. As explained at the beginning of this chapter, the bank cannot disclaim its responsibility for its failure to act in good faith or to exercise ordinary care in paying a check over a stop-payment order [4–103].

If a bank pays a check after it has received a stop-payment order and has to reimburse its customer for the improperly paid check, it acquires all the rights of its customer against the person to whom it originally made payment, including rights arising from the transaction on which the check was based [4–407]. In the previous example involving Brown and Foster Ford, assume that Brown was able to have his account recredited because First Bank had paid the check to Foster Ford over his stop-payment order. Then, the bank would have any rights that Brown had against Foster Ford for the misrepresentation.

If a person stops payment on a check and the bank honors the stop-payment order, the person may still be liable to the holder of the check. Suppose Peters writes a check for $450 to Ace Auto Repair in payment for repairs to her automobile. While driving the car home, she concludes that the car was not repaired properly. She calls her bank and stops payment on the check. Ace Auto negotiated the check to Sam's Auto Parts, which took the check as

**FIGURE 2**  **Certified Check**

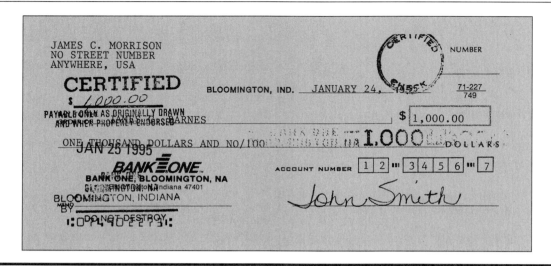

a holder in due course. When Sam's takes the check to Peters's bank, the bank refuses to pay because of the stop-payment order. Sam's then comes after Peters on her drawer's liability. All Peters has is a personal defense against payment, which is not good against a holder in due course. So, Peters must pay Sam's the $450 and pursue her claim separately against Ace. If Ace were still the holder of the check, however, the situation would be different. Peters could use her personal defense concerning the faulty work against Ace to reduce or possibly to cancel her obligation to pay the check.

## Certified Check

Normally, a drawee bank is not obligated to certify a check. When a drawee bank does certify a check, it substitutes its undertaking (promise) to pay the check for the drawer's undertaking and becomes obligated to pay the check. At the time the bank certifies a check, the bank usually debits the customer's account for the amount of the certified check and shifts the money to a special account at the bank. It also adds its signature to the check to show that it has accepted primary liability for paying it. The bank's signature is an essential part of the certification—the bank's signature must appear on the check [3−409]. If the holder of a check chooses to have it certified, rather than seeking

to have it paid at that time, the holder has made a conscious decision to look to the certifying bank for payment and no longer may rely on the drawer or the endorsers to pay it. See Figure 2 for an example of a certified check.

If the drawee bank certifies a check, then the drawer and any persons who previously indorsed the check are discharged of their liability on the check [3−414(c); 3−415(d)].

## Cashier's Check

A cashier's check differs from a certified check. A check on which a bank is both the drawer and the drawee is a cashier's check. The bank is primarily liable on the cashier's check. See Figure 3 for an example of a cashier's check. A teller's check is similar to a cashier's check in that it is a check on which one bank is the drawer and another bank is the drawee. An example of a teller's check is a check drawn by a credit union on its account at a bank.

## Death or Incompetence of Customer

Under the general principles of agency law, the death or incompetence of the principal terminates the agent's authority to act for the principal. How-

**FIGURE 3**  Cashier's Check

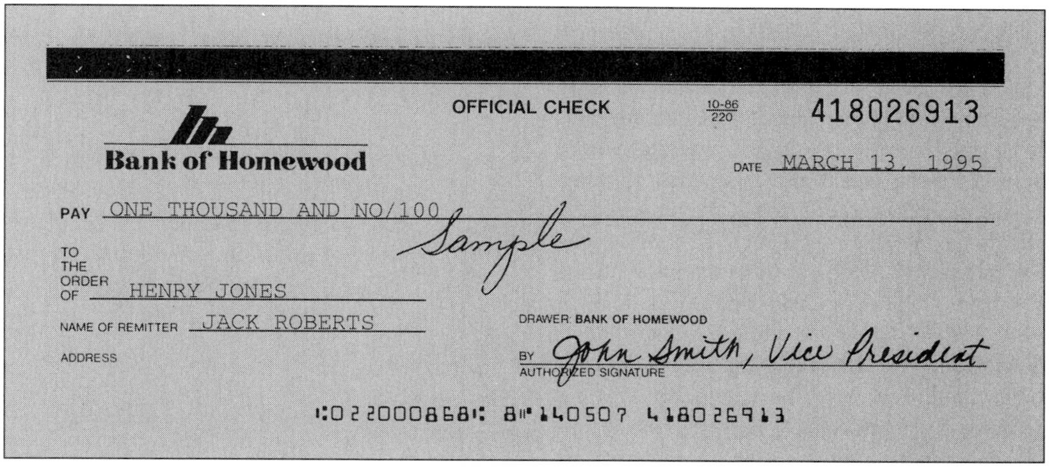

ever, slightly different rules apply to the authority of a bank to pay checks out of the account of a deceased or incompetent person. The bank has the right to pay the checks of an incompetent person until it has notice that a court has determined that the person is incompetent. Once the bank learns of this fact, it loses its authority to pay that person's checks—because the depositor is not competent to issue instructions to pay.

Similarly, a bank has the right to pay the checks of a deceased customer until it has notice of the customer's death. Even if a bank knows of a customer's death, for a period of 10 days after the customer's death, it can pay checks written by the customer prior to his death. However, the deceased person's heirs or other persons claiming an interest in the account can order the bank to stop payment [4–405].

## FORGED AND ALTERED CHECKS

### Bank's Right to Charge Account

A check that bears a forged signature of the drawer or payee is generally not properly payable from the customer's account because the bank is not following the instructions of the depositor precisely as he gave them. The bank is expected to be familiar with the authorized signature of its depositor. If it pays such a check, Article 4 will treat the transaction as one in which the bank paid out its own funds, rather than the depositor's funds.

Similarly, a check that was altered after the drawer made it out—for example, by increasing the amount of the check—is generally not properly payable from the customer's account. However, as noted earlier, if the drawer is negligent and contributes to the forgery or alteration, he may be barred from claiming it as the reason that a particular check should not be charged to his account.

For example, Barton makes a check for $1 in a way that makes it possible for someone to easily alter it to read $101, and it is so altered. If the drawee bank pays the check to a holder in good faith, it can charge the $101 to Barton's account if Barton's negligence contributed to the alteration. Similarly, if a company uses a mechanical checkwriter to write checks, it must use reasonable care to see that unauthorized persons do not have access to blank checks and to the checkwriter.

If the alteration is obvious, the bank should note that fact and refuse to pay the check when it is presented for payment. Occasionally, the alteration is so skillful that the bank cannot detect it. In that case, the bank is allowed to charge to the account the amount for which the check originally was written.

The bank has a duty to exercise "ordinary care" in the processing of negotiable instruments; it must observe the reasonable commercial standards prevailing among other banks in the area in which it does business. In the case of banks that take checks for collection or payment using automated means, it is important to note that reasonable commercial standards do not require the bank to examine every item *if* the failure to examine does not violate the bank's prescribed procedures and those procedures do not vary unreasonably from general banking practice or are not disapproved by the Code [3–103(a)(7); 4–103(c)]. For example, the bank's practice may be to examine those checks for more than $1,000 and a sample of smaller checks. Thus, if it did not examine a particular check in the amount of $250 for evidence of alteration or forgery, its actions would be commercially reasonable so long as (1) it followed its own protocol, (2) that protocol was not a great variance from general banking usage, and (3) the procedure followed was not specifically disallowed in the Code.

In a case where both a bank and its customer fail to use ordinary care, a comparative negligence standard is used [4–406(e)].

## Customer's Duty to Report Forgeries and Alterations

A bank must send a monthly (or quarterly) statement listing the transactions in an account and commonly returns the cancelled checks to the customer. Revised Article 3 recognizes the modern bank practice of truncating (or retaining) checks and permits the bank to supply only a statement showing the item number, amount, and date of payment [4–406(a)]. When the bank does not return the paid items to the customer, the bank must either retain the items or maintain the capacity to furnish legible copies of the items for seven years after their receipt. The customer may request an item and the bank has a reasonable time to provide either the item or a legible copy of it [4–406(b)].

If the bank sends or makes available a statement of account or items, the customer must exercise reasonable promptness to examine the statement or items to determine whether payment was not authorized because of an alteration of any item or because a signature of the customer was not authorized. If, based on the statement or items provided, the customer should discover the unauthorized pay-

ment, the customer must notify the bank of the relevant facts promptly [4–406(c)].

**Multiple Forgeries or Alterations**   Revised Article 3 provides a special rule to govern the situation in which the same wrongdoer makes a series of unauthorized drawer's signatures or alterations. The customer generally cannot hold the bank responsible for paying, in good faith, any such checks after the statement of account or item that contained the first unauthorized customer's signature or an alteration was available to the customer for a reasonable period, not exceeding 30 calendar days. This rule holds (1) if the customer did not notify the bank of the unauthorized signature or alteration and (2) the bank proves it suffered a loss because of the customer's failure to examine his statement and notify the bank [4–406(d)]. Unless the customer has notified the bank about the forgeries or alterations that he should have discovered by reviewing the statement or item, the customer generally bears responsibility for any subsequent forgeries or alterations by the same wrongdoer.

Suppose that Allen employs Farnum as an accountant and that over a period of three months, Farnum forges Allen's signature to 10 checks and cashes them. One of the forged checks is included in the checks returned to Allen at the end of the first month. Within 30 calendar days after the return of these checks, Farnum forges two more checks and cashes them. Allen does not examine the returned checks until three months after the checks that included the first forged check were returned to her. The bank would be responsible for the first forged check and for the two checks forged and cashed within the 30-day period after it sent the first statement and the canceled checks (unless the bank proves that it suffered a loss because of the customer's failure to examine the checks and notify it more promptly). It would not be liable for the seven forged checks cashed after the expiration of the 30-day period.

The case that follows, *Rhode Island Hospital Trust National Bank v. Zapata,* illustrates how the UCC applies to a series of forgeries. It was decided under the original version of Article 3, which provided a 14-day period for a customer to review a statement and notify the bank of any alterations or unauthorized signatures of the customer.

## RHODE ISLAND HOSPITAL TRUST NATIONAL BANK V. ZAPATA CORP.

**6 UCC Rep.2d 1 (1st Cir. 1988)**

In early 1985, an employee of the Zapata Corporation stole some blank checks from the company. She wrote a large number of forged checks, almost all in amounts of $150 to $800 each, on Zapata's account at Rhode Island Hospital Trust National Bank. The bank, from March through July 1985, received and paid them. Bank statements that the bank regularly sent Zapata first began to reflect the forged checks in early 1985. Zapata failed to examine its statements closely until July 1985, when it found the forgeries. It immediately notified the bank, which then stopped clearing the checks. The bank already had processed and paid checks containing forged drawer's signatures totaling $109,247.16. Zapata then brought suit against the bank to have its account recredited for the checks.

The district court held that the bank was liable to reimburse Zapata for the checks that it paid before April 25, 1985 (two weeks after Zapata received the first statement containing the forged checks), but held in favor of the bank as to the remaining checks. Zapata appealed.

---

**Breyer, Circuit Judge**   The issue that this appeal presents is whether Zapata Corporation has shown that the system used by Rhode Island Hospital Trust National Bank for detecting forged checks—a system used by a majority of American banks—lacks the "ordinary care" that a bank must exercise under the Uniform Commercial Code section 4–406(3). The question arises out of the following district court determinations, all of which are adequately supported by the record and by Rhode Island law.

The Bank will (and legally must) reimburse Zapata in respect to all checks it cleared before April 25 (or for at least two weeks after Zapata received the statement that reflected the forgeries). See sections 3–401(1), 4–406(2). In respect to checks cleared on and after April 25, the Bank need not reimburse Zapata because Zapata failed to "exercise reasonable care and promptness to examine the [bank] statements." Section 4–406(1).

The question before us is whether this last-mentioned conclusion is correct or whether Zapata can recover for the post–April 24 checks on the theory that, even if it was negligent, so was the Bank.

To understand this question, one must examine UCC section 4–406. Ordinarily a bank must reimburse an innocent customer for forgeries that it honors, section 3–401(1), but section 4–406 makes an important exception to the liability rule. The exception operates in respect to a series of forged checks, and it applies once a customer has had a chance to catch the forgeries by examining his bank statements and notifying the bank but has failed to do so.

The statute, in relevant part, reads as follows:

(1) When a bank sends to its customer a statement of account accompanied by items paid in good faith in support of the debit entries or holds the statement and items pursuant to a request or instructions of its customer or otherwise in a reasonable manner makes the statement and items available to the customer, the customer must exercise reasonable care and promptness to examine the statement and items to discover his unauthorized signature or any alteration on an item and must notify the bank promptly after discovery thereof.

(2) If the bank establishes that the customer failed with respect to an item to comply with the duties imposed on the customer by subsection (1) the customer is precluded from asserting against the bank (a) His unauthorized signature or any alteration on the item if the bank also establishes that it suffered a loss by reason of such failure; and (b) An unauthorized signature or alteration by the same wrongdoer on any other item paid in good faith by the bank after the first item and statement was available to the customer for a reasonable period not exceeding fourteen (14) calendar days and before the bank receives notification from the customer of any such unauthorized signature or alteration. Section 4–406(1) and (2). (Emphasis added.)

The statute goes on to specify an important exception. It says:

(3) The preclusion under subsection (2) does not apply if the customer establishes lack of ordinary care on the part of the bank in paying the item(s). Section 4–406(3).

Zapata's specific claim on this appeal is that it falls within this "exception to the exception"—that the bank's treatment of the post–April 24 checks lacked "ordinary care." The statute places the burden of proof on Zapata. It says that strict bank liability terminates fourteen days after the customer receives the bank's statement unless "the customer establishes lack of ordinary care." The record convinces us that Zapata failed to carry its burden of establishing "lack of ordinary care" on the part of the Bank.

First the Bank described its ordinary practices as follows: The Bank examines all signatures on checks for more than $1,000. It examines signatures on checks between $100 and $1,000 (those at issue here) if it has reason to suspect a problem, e.g., if a customer has warned it of a possible forgery or if the check was drawn on an account with insufficient funds. It examines the signatures of a randomly chosen one percent of all other checks between $100 and $1,000. But it does not examine the signatures on other checks between $100 and $1,000. Through expert testimony, the Bank also established that most other banks in the nation follow this practice and that banking industry experts recommend it. Indeed, the Bank's practices are conservative in this regard, as most banks set $2,500 or more, not $1,000, as the limit beneath which they will not examine each signature. This testimony made out a prima facie case of "ordinary care."

Second, both bank and industry experts pointed out that this industry practice, in general and in the particular case of the Bank, saved considerable expense, compared with the Bank's pre-1981 practice of examining each check by hand. To be specific, the change saved the bank about $125,000 annually.

Third, both a Bank official and an industry expert testified that changing from an "individual signature examination" system to the new "bulk-filing" system led to no significant increase in the number of forgeries that were detected. Under the Bank's prior "individual signature examination" some forgeries still slipped through.

Fourth, even if one assumes, contrary to this uncontradicted evidence, that the new system meant some increase in the number of undetected forged checks, Zapata still could not prevail, for it presented no evidence tending to show any such increased loss unreasonable in light of the costs that the new practice would save.

**Judgment for Rhode Island Hospital Trust National Bank affirmed.**

---

Regardless of which party may have been negligent, a customer must discover and report to the bank any unauthorized customer's signature or any alteration within one year from the time after the statement or items are made available to him. If the customer does not do so, he cannot require the bank to recredit his account for such items. Similarly, a customer has three years from the time his statement or item is made available to discover and report any unauthorized indorsement on the item. The customer's failure to discover and report these irregularities within the one- or three-year periods specified ends his right to have his account recredited for the amount of the checks [4–406(f)].

**CONCEPT REVIEW**

## LIABILITY FOR MULTIPLE FORGERIES OR ALTERATIONS BY THE SAME PERSON

| Date First Statement Disclosing an Altered or Forged Check Is Available to Customer | Date 30 Days Later | Date Customer Gives Notice of Alteration or Forgery |
|---|---|---|
| Customer is not liable for forged/altered checks paid during this period unless bank suffers a loss from customer's unreasonable delay in notifying bank of forgery or alteration. | Customer is liable for forged or altered checks paid during this period unless customer gives bank notice of forgery or alteration within a reasonable time after date the first statement containing a forged or altered check was available to customer. | Customer is not liable for forged or altered checks paid during this period. |

## CHECK COLLECTION AND FUNDS AVAILABILITY

### Check Collection

As Chapter 23, Negotiable Instruments, describes, checks and other drafts collected through the banking system usually have at least three parties—the drawer, the drawee bank, and the payee. If the payee deposits the check at the same bank as the drawee bank, the latter will take a series of steps necessary to reflect the deposit as a credit to the payee's account and to decide whether to pay the check from the drawer's account. In connection with its handling of the deposit for the payee's benefit, it will make one ledger entry showing the deposit as a credit to the payee's account. In connection with its decision to pay, the bank's employees and computers will perform several steps commonly referred to as the process of posting.

Original Article 4 contained special rules describing the process of posting and the legal effect. The amendments to Article 4 deleted these special rules because automated check processing limited the legal significance of particular acts in posting [4–109 and 4–213(a)]. These steps need not be taken in any particular order, but they customarily include determining whether there are sufficient funds to pay, debiting the drawer's account for the amount of the check, and placing the check into a folder for later return to the drawer (to satisfy its obligations under the "bank statement" rule [4–406]. Banks in those states that have not enacted the amendments to Article 4 also will compare the drawer's signature on the check with that on the deposit agreement as part of this process.

If the payee deposits the check at a bank other than the drawee bank, the depositary bank, acting as the agent of the payee, will make the ledger entry showing the deposit as a credit to the payee's account. The next step of the collection process depends on where the depositary bank is located. If the drawee and depositary banks are in the same town or county, the depositary bank will indorse the check and deliver (present) it to the drawee bank for payment. It may deliver it by courier or through a local association of banks known as a *"clearinghouse"* [4–104(1)(d)]. The drawee-payor bank must settle for the check before midnight of the banking day of its receipt of the check, which means that it must give the depositary bank funds

or a credit equal to the amount of the check. Once it settles for the check, the drawee-payor bank has until midnight of the banking day after the banking day of receipt to pay the check or to return the check or send notice of dishonor. This deadline for the drawee-payor bank's action on the check is known as the bank's "midnight deadline" [4–104(1)(h)]. The drawee-payor bank's failure to settle by midnight of the banking day of receipt, or its failure to pay or return the check, or send notice of dishonor, results in the drawee-payor bank becoming "accountable" for the amount of the check, which means it must pay the amount of the check [4–302(a)].

If the drawee and depositary banks are located in different counties, or in different states, the depositary bank will use an additional commercial bank, and one or more of the regional Federal Reserve Banks, in the collection of the check. In these cases, the depositary bank will send the check on to the drawee-payor bank through these "collecting banks." Each bank in the sequence must use ordinary care in presenting the check or sending it for presentment, and in sending notice of dishonor or returning the check after learning that the check has not been paid [4–202(a)]. The depositary and collecting banks have until their respective midnight deadlines—or, in some cases, a further reasonable time—to take the action required of them in the sequence of collection steps.

If the drawee-payor bank dishonors the check prior to its midnight deadline or shortly after the midnight deadline under circumstances specified in "Regulation CC" of the Federal Reserve Board (described in the next section of this chapter), it will send the check back to the depositary bank. Until September 1, 1988, the drawee-payor bank customarily sent the dishonored check back to the collecting bank from which it received the check, and the collecting bank sent it back to the bank from which it had received it, and through any other bank that handled the check in the "forward collection" process until the check again reached the depositary bank. The provisions of Article 4 still describe this sequence as the "return collection" process, although Regulation CC imposes new responsibilities on the payor bank and on any other returning bank. Each bank in the return sequence adjusts its accounts to reflect the return and has until its midnight deadline to send the check back to the bank from which it originally had received the check. After

September 1, 1988 (or in states that previously had adopted "direct return" [4–212(b)], the drawee-payor bank may return the check directly to the depositary bank—skipping all of the collecting banks and the delay represented by the midnight deadlines that each bank otherwise would have had.

Direct return also increases the likelihood that the depositary bank will know whether the check has been dishonored by the day on which Regulation CC requires the depositary bank to allow the payee to write checks or otherwise make withdrawals against the deposit. The next section of this chapter discusses this aspect of Regulation CC in more detail.

On receipt of the dishonored check, the depositary bank will return the check or otherwise notify its depositor (the payee) of the dishonor and will debit or charge back her account for the check it did not collect. The depositary bank may charge back the deposit even if it previously had allowed the payee-depositor to withdraw against the credit given for the deposit.

When the depositor receives the notice of dishonor and returned check, it will take one of several steps, depending on whether it received the check directly from the drawer or took it by indorsement from another person. If the depositor was not the original payee of the check, it usually will prefer to return the check—giving notice of dishonor unless already given by the drawee bank or another collecting bank—to the person who negotiated the check to her, the prior indorser. Recall that an indorser is obligated to pay the check following dishonor and notice of dishonor [3–415].

If the depositor received the check directly from the drawer, for example as payee, the depositor will normally demand payment from the drawer. Recall that the drawer is obligated to pay the check upon dishonor and notice of dishonor [3–414]; alternatively, the payee may seek to enforce the underlying obligation for which the drawer originally issued the check, such as the purchase of groceries or an automobile.

## Funds Availability

When a bank taxes a check for deposit to a customer's account, it typically places a hold on the funds represented by the deposited check because it runs a number of risks in allowing a customer to withdraw deposits that it has not collected from the drawee bank. The risks that the check may be returned include: (1) there may be insufficient funds in the drawer's account or the account may have been closed; (2) the check may contain a forged drawer's or indorser's signature, or there may have been a material alteration of the check; (3) the possibility that the drawer is kiting checks or playing two accounts against each other; or (4) a stop-payment order may have been placed against the check. These are real concerns to a depositary bank, and it has a significant interest in protecting itself against these possibilities.

Until recently, the risks run by a depositary bank were complicated by a very slow process used by drawee-payor banks in returning a dishonored check or notifying the bank of the dishonor. Moreover, depositary banks do not get direct notice from drawee-payor banks when they pay checks. Accordingly, banks often restricted the depositor's use of the deposit by placing relatively long holds on checks deposited with them for collection; these sometimes ran 15 to 20 days for items drawn on other than local banks.

The extensive use of holds, and a growing public sentiment that they were excessive and often unfair, led to the passage by Congress in 1987 of the Expedited Funds Availability Act. In the act, Congress set out mandatory schedules limiting check holds and specifying when funds are to be made available to customers by depositary institutions. The act also delegated to the Federal Reserve Board the authority to speed up the check-processing system. The regulations adopted by the Board to speed up check processing supersede the provisions of Article 4 of the UCC (Bank Deposits and Collections) in a number of respects but will not be covered in this text.

The key elements of the mandatory funds availability schedules, which are set out in Federal Reserve Board Regulation CC, are:

**1.** Local checks (those drawn on banks in the same Federal Reserve check-processing region as the depositary bank) must be made available for the depositor to draw against by the second business day following deposit.

**2.** Nonlocal checks (those drawn on banks located in the United States but outside the Federal Reserve check-processing region in which the depositary bank is located) must be made available by the fifth business day following deposit.

**3.** Certain items must be made available by the next day after the day of deposit. These include:

*a.* Cash deposits where the deposit is banked in person to an employee of the depositary bank (i.e., not at an ATM).

*b.* Electronic payments.

*c.* Checks drawn on the U.S. Treasury.

*d.* U.S. Postal Service money orders.

*e.* Checks drawn on a Federal Reserve Bank or Federal Home Loan Bank.

*f.* Checks drawn by a state or a unit of local government (under certain conditions).

*g.* Cashier's, certified, or teller's checks.

*h.* Checks drawn on the depositary bank.

*i.* The lesser of $100 or the aggregate deposit on any one banking day.

**4.** If the next-day items are not deposited in person with an employee of the depositary institution but rather are deposited in an ATM machine or by mail, then the deposit does not have to be made available for withdrawal until the second business day after deposit.

**5.** Generally, the depository bank must begin accruing interest to a depositor's interest-bearing account from the day it receives credit for cash and check deposits to an interest-bearing account.

There are six major exceptions to the mandatory availability schedules set out above that are designed to safeguard depositary banks against higher risk situations. The exceptions are:

**1.** *New account exception.* The depositary bank may suspend the availability rules for new accounts and can limit the next-day and second-day availability to the first $5,000 deposited.

**2.** *Large deposit exception.* The hold periods can be extended to the extent the aggregate deposit on any banking day exceeds $5,000.

**3.** *Redeposited check exception.* The hold period can be extended where a check has been returned one or more times.

**4.** *Repeated overdraft exception.* A longer hold period may be required for deposits to accounts that have been overdrawn repeatedly.

**5.** *Reasonable cause exception.* The scheduled availability may be extended where the bank has reasonable cause to believe the check is uncollectible.

**6.** *Emergency conditions exception.* The scheduled availability may be extended under certain emergency conditions such as a communications interruption or a computer failure.

Banks are required to disclose their funds availability policy to all of their customers; they may provide different policies to different classes or categories of customers.

## ELECTRONIC BANKING

With the development of computer technology, many banks encourage their customers to transfer funds electronically by using computers rather than paper drafts and checks. A bank customer may use a specially coded card at terminals provided by the bank to make deposits to an account, to transfer money from one checking or savings account to another, to pay bills, or to withdraw cash from an account. These new forms of transferring money have raised questions about the legal rules that apply to them, and the questions are only beginning to be resolved.

### Electronic Funds Transfer Act

The consumer who used electronic funds transfer systems (EFTs), the so-called cash machines or electronic tellers, in the early years often experienced problems in identifying and resolving mechanical errors resulting from malfunctioning EFTs. In response to these problems, Congress passed the Electronic Funds Transfer Act in 1978 to provide "a basic framework, establishing the rights, liabilities, and responsibilities of participants in electronic funds transfer systems" and especially to provide "individual consumer rights."

The four basic EFT systems are automated teller machines; point-of-sale terminals, which allow consumers to use their EFT cards like checks at retail establishments; preauthorized payments, such as automatic paycheck deposits or mortgage or utility payments; and telephone transfers between accounts or to pay specific bills by phone.

Similar to the Truth in Lending Act and the Fair Credit Billing Act (FCBA) discussed in Chapter 39, The Federal Trade Commission Act and Consumer Protection Laws, the EFT Act requires disclosure of the terms and conditions of electronic fund transfers at the time the consumer contracts for the EFT service. Among the nine disclosures required are the following: the consumer's liability for unauthorized electronic fund transfers (those resulting from loss or theft), the nature of the EFT services under the consumer's account, any pertinent dollar or frequency limitations, any charges for the right to make EFTs, the consumer's right to stop payment of a preauthorized transfer, the financial institution's liability to the consumer for failure to make or stop payments, and the consumer's right to receive documentation of transfers both at the point or time of transfer and periodically. The act also requires 21 days' notice prior to the effective date of any change in the terms or conditions of the consumer's account that pertains to the required disclosures.

The EFT Act does differ from the Fair Credit Billing Act in a number of important respects. For example, under the EFT Act, the operators of EFT systems are given a maximum of 10 working days to investigate errors or provisionally recredit the consumer's account, whereas issuers of credit cards are given a maximum of 60 days under the FCBA. The liability of the consumer is also different if an EFT card is lost or stolen than it is if a credit card is lost or stolen.

The case that follows, *Kruser v. Bank of America NT & SA,* illustrates the application of the EFT Act's provisions that require a customer to provide timely notification of any unauthorized use of his card in order to limit his liability for the unauthorized use of the card.

---

## KRUSER V. BANK OF AMERICA NT & SA
### 281 Cal.Rptr. 463 (Cal. Ct. App. 1991)

Lawrence and Georgene Kruser maintained a joint checking account with the Bank of America, and the bank issued each of them a "Versatel" card and separate personal identification numbers that would allow access to funds in their account from automatic teller machines. The Krusers also received with their cards a "Disclosure Booklet" that provided to the Krusers a summary of consumer liability, the bank's business hours, and the address and telephone number by which they could notify the bank in the event they believed an unauthorized transfer had been made.

The Krusers believed Mr. Kruser's card had been destroyed in September 1986. The December 1986 account statement mailed to the Krusers by the bank reflected a $20 unauthorized withdrawal of funds by someone using Mr. Kruser's card at an automatic teller machine. The Krusers reported this unauthorized transaction to the bank when they discovered it in August or September 1987.

Mrs. Kruser underwent surgery in late 1986 or early 1987 and remained hospitalized for 11 days. She then spent a period of six or seven months recuperating at home. During this time, she reviewed the statements the Krusers received from the bank.

In September 1987, the Krusers received bank statements for July and August 1987 that reflected 47 unauthorized withdrawals totaling $9,020 made from an automatic teller machine, again by someone using Mr. Kruser's card. They notified the bank of these withdrawals within a few days of receiving the statements. The bank refused to credit the Kruser's account with the amount of the unauthorized withdrawals. The Krusers sued the bank, claiming damages for the unauthorized withdrawals from their account. The trial court ruled in favor of the bank on the grounds that the Krusers had failed to comply with the note and reporting requirements of the Electronic Funds Transfer Act (EFTA). The Krusers appealed.

---

**Stone, Associate Justice** The ultimate issue we address is whether, as a matter of law, the unauthorized $20 withdrawal which appeared on the December 1986 statement barred the Krusers from recovery for the losses incurred in July and August 1987. Resolution of the issue requires the interpretation of the EFTA and section 205.6 of Regulation E, one of the regulations prescribed by the Board of Governors of the Federal Reserve System in order to carry out the EFTA.

Section 205.6 of Regulation E mirrors [the EFTA] and in particular provides:

(b) Limitations on amount of liability. The amount of a consumer's liability for an unauthorized electronic fund transfer or a series of related unauthorized transfers shall not exceed $50 or the amount of unauthorized transfers that occur before notice to the financial institution . . ., whichever is less, unless one of the following exceptions apply:

\*     \*     \*     \*     \*

(2) If the consumer fails to report within 60 days of transmittal of the periodic statement any unauthorized electronic fund transfer that appears on the statement, the consumer's liability shall not exceed the sum of (i) The lesser of $50 or the amount of unauthorized electronic fund transfers that appear on the periodic statement during the 60-day period and (ii) The amount of unauthorized electronic fund transfers that occur after the close of the 60 days and before notice to the financial institution and that the financial institution establishes would not have occurred but for the failure of the consumer to notify the financial institution within that time.

\*     \*     \*     \*     \*

(4) If a delay in notifying the financial statements was due to extenuating circumstances, such as extended travel or hospitalization, the time periods specified above shall be extended to a reasonable time.

The trial court concluded the Bank was entitled to judgment as a matter of law because the unauthorized withdrawals of July and August 1987 occurred more than 60 days after the Krusers received a statement which reflected an unauthorized transfer in December 1986. The court relied upon section 205.6(b)(2) of Regulation E.

The Krusers contend the December withdrawal of $20 was so isolated in time and minimal in amount that it cannot be considered in connection with the July and August withdrawals. They assert the court's interpretation of section 205.6(b)(2) of Regulation E would have absurd results which would be inconsistent with the primary objective of the EFTA—to protect the consumer. They argue that if a consumer receives a bank statement which reflects an unauthorized minimal electronic transfer and fails to report the transaction to the bank within 60 days of transmission of the bank statement, unauthorized transfers many years later, perhaps totalling thousands of dollars, would remain the responsibility of the consumer.

The result the Krusers fear is avoided by the requirement that the bank establish the subsequent unauthorized transfers could have been prevented had the consumer notified the bank of the first unauthorized transfer. Here, although the unauthorized transfer of $20 occurred approximately seven months before the unauthorized transfers totalling $9,020, it is undisputed that all transfers were made by using Mr. Kruser's card which the Krusers believed had been destroyed prior to December 1986. According to the declaration of Yvonne Maloon, the Bank's Versatel risk manager, the Bank could have and would have cancelled Mr. Kruser's card had it been timely notified of the December unauthorized transfer. In that event Mr. Kruser's card could not have been used to accomplish the unauthorized transactions in July and August 1987.

In the alternative, the Krusers contend the facts establish that Mrs. Kruser, who was solely responsible for reconciling the bank statements, was severely ill and was also caring for a terminally ill relative when the December withdrawal occurred. Therefore they claim they were entitled to an extension of time within which to notify the bank.

The evidence the Krusers rely upon indicates in late 1986 or early 1987 Mrs. Kruser underwent surgery and remained in the hospital for 11 days. She left her house infrequently during the first six or seven months of 1987 during which she was recuperating. Mrs. Kruser admits, however, she received and reviewed bank statements during her recuperation. Therefore, we need not consider whether Mrs. Kruser's illness created circumstances which might have excused her failure to notice the unauthorized withdrawal pursuant to the applicable sections. She in fact did review the statements in question.

**Judgment for Bank of America affirmed.**

## Documents of Title

### Introduction

Storing or shipping goods, giving a warehouse receipt or bill of lading representing the goods, and transferring such a receipt or bill of lading as representing the goods are practices of ancient origin. The warehouseman or the common carrier is a bailee of the goods who contracts to store or transport the goods and to deliver them to the owner or to act otherwise in accordance with the lawful directions of the owner. The **warehouse receipt** or the **bill of lading** may be either negotiable or non-negotiable. To be negotiable, a warehouse receipt, bill of lading, or other document of title must provide that the goods are to be delivered to the bearer or to the order of a named person [7–104(1)]. The primary differences between the law of negotiable instruments and the law of negotiable documents of title are based on the differences between the obligation to pay money and the obligation to deliver specific goods.

### Warehouse Receipts

A warehouse receipt, to be valid, need not be in any particular form, but if it does not embody within its written or printed form each of the following, the warehouseman is liable for damages caused by the omission to a person injured as a result of it: (1) the location of the warehouse where the goods are stored; (2) the date of issue; (3) the consecutive number of the receipt; (4) whether the goods are to be delivered to the bearer or to the order of a named person; (5) the rate of storage and handling charges; (6) a description of the goods or of the packages containing them; (7) the signature of the warehouseman or his agent; (8) whether the warehouseman is the owner of the goods, solely, jointly, or in common with others; and (9) a statement of the amount of the advances made and of the liabilities incurred for which the warehouseman claims a lien or security interest. Other terms may be inserted [7–202].

A warehouseman is liable to a purchaser for value in good faith of a warehouse receipt for nonreceipt or misdescription of goods. The receipt may conspicuously qualify the description by a statement such as "contents, condition, and quantity unknown" [7–203].

Because a warehouseman is a bailee of the goods, he owes to the holder of the warehouse receipt the duties of a mutual benefit bailee and must exercise reasonable care [7–204]. Chapter 15, Personal Property and Bailments, discusses the duties of a bailee in detail. The warehouseman may terminate the relation by notification where, for example, the goods are about to deteriorate or where they constitute a threat to other goods in the warehouse [7–206]. Unless the warehouse receipt provides otherwise, the warehouseman must keep separate the goods covered by each receipt; however, different lots of fungible goods such as grain may be mingled [7–207].

A warehouseman has a lien against the bailor on the goods covered by his receipt for his storage and other charges incurred in handling the goods [7–209]. The Code sets out a detailed procedure for enforcing this lien [7–210].

### Bills of Lading

In many respects, the rights and liabilities of the parties to a negotiable bill of lading are the same as the rights and liabilities of the parties to a negotiable warehouse receipt. The contract of the issuer of a bill of lading is to transport goods, whereas the contract of the issuer of a warehouse receipt is to store goods. Like the issuer of a warehouse receipt, the issuer of a bill of lading is liable for nonreceipt or misdescription of the goods, but he may protect himself from liability where he does not know the contents of packages by marking the bill of lading "contents or condition of packages unknown" or similar language. Such terms are ineffective when the goods are loaded by an issuer who is a common carrier unless the goods are concealed by packages [7–301].

### Duty of Care

A carrier who issues a bill of lading, or a warehouse operator who issues a warehouse receipt, must exercise the same degree of care in relation to the goods as a reasonably careful person would exercise under similar circumstances. Liability for damages not caused by the negligence of the carrier may be imposed on him by a special law or rule of law. Under tariff rules, a common carrier may limit her liability to a shipper's declaration of value, provided that the rates are dependent on value [7–309]. In the case that follows, *Calvin Klein Ltd. v. Trylon Trucking Corp.*, a court enforced a $50 per shipment limitation that had been part of a long series of shipping contracts where the customer had the opportunity to declare a higher value and failed to do so.

## CALVIN KLEIN LTD. v. TRYLON TRUCKING CORP.
### 892 F.2d 191 (2d Cir. 1989)

Trylon Trucking Corporation is a New Jersey trucking firm that engaged in the business of transporting goods from New York City's airports for delivery to its customers' facilities. For three years prior to 1986, Calvin Klein, a New York clothing company, used the services of Trylon involving hundreds of shipments. Calvin Klein, through its customs broker, would contact Trylon to pick up the shipment from the airport for delivery to Calvin Klein's facility. After completing the delivery carriage, Trylon would forward to Calvin Klein an invoice, which contained a limitation of liability provision as follows:

In consideration of the rate charged, the shipper agrees that the carrier shall not be liable for more than $50.00 on any shipment accepted for delivery to one consignee unless a greater value is declared, in writing, upon receipt at time of shipment and charge for such greater value paid, or agreed to be paid, by the shipper.

A shipment of 2,833 blouses from Hong Kong arrived at John F. Kennedy International Airport for Calvin Klein on March 27, 1986. Calvin Klein arranged for Trylon to pick up the shipment and deliver it to Calvin Klein's New Jersey warehouse. On April 2, Trylon dispatched its driver, J. Jefferson, to pick up this shipment. Jefferson signed a receipt for the shipment from Calvin Klein's broker. Later, on April 2, the parties discovered that Jefferson had stolen Trylon's truck and its shipment. The shipment was never recovered.

Calvin Klein sent a claim letter to Trylon for the full value of the lost blouses. When it did not receive a response from Trylon, Calvin Klein filed suit against Trylon, seeking to recover $150,000, the alleged value of the blouses. In the pleadings before the court, the parties agreed that Trylon was liable to Calvin Klein for the loss of the shipment and that it had been grossly negligent in the hiring and supervision of Jefferson. They also agreed that "the terms and conditions of Trylon's carriage were that liability for loss or damage to cargo is limited to $50 in accordance with the provision in Trylon's invoice forms." Calvin Klein conceded that it was aware of the limitation of liability and that it did not declare a value on the blouses at the time of shipment.

Trylon contended that its liability was limited to $50 in accordance with the provision in its invoice forms. Calvin Klein argued that the limitation clause was not enforceable for two reasons: (1) no agreement existed between it and Trylon as to the limitation of liability; and (2) even if an agreement existed, public policy would prevent its enforcement because of Trylon's gross negligence. The district court held that Calvin Klein had not assented to the limitation clause for this shipment and awarded damages to Calvin Klein of $101,542.62. Trylon appealed.

**Miner, Circuit Judge**  A common carrier is strictly liable for the loss of goods in its custody. Where the loss is not due to excepted causes [that is, act of God or public enemy, inherent nature of goods, or shipper's fault], it is immaterial whether the carrier was negligent or not. Even in the case of loss from theft by third parties, liability may be imposed upon a negligent common carrier.

A shipper and a common carrier may contract to limit the carrier's liability in cases of loss to an amount agreed to by the parties, so long as the language of the limitation is clear, the shipper is aware of the terms of the limitation, and the shipper can change the terms by indicating the true value of the goods being shipped. Section 7–309(2). Such a limitation agreement is generally valid and enforceable despite carrier negligence. The limitation of liability provision involved here clearly provides that, at the time of delivery, the shipper may increase the limitation by written notice of the value of the goods to be delivered and by payment of a commensurately higher fee.

The parties stipulated to this fact that the $50 limitation of liability was a term and condition of carriage and that Calvin Klein was aware of that limitation. This stipulated fact removes the first issue, namely whether an agreement existed as to a liability limitation between the parties. Calvin Klein's argument that it never previously acknowledged this limitation by accepting only $50 in settlement of a larger loss does not alter this explicit stipulation. The district court erred in not accepting the limitation of liability as stipulated.

The remaining issue concerns the enforceability of the limitation clause in the light of Trylon's conceded gross negligence.

Since carriers are strictly liable for loss of shipments in their custody and are insurers of those goods, the degree of carrier negligence is immaterial. The common carrier must exercise reasonable care in relation to the shipment in its custody. Section 7–309(2). Carriers can contract with their shipping customers on the amount of liability each party will bear for the loss of a shipment, regardless of the amount of carrier negligence. Unlike a merchant acquiring a burglar alarm, the shipper can calculate the specific amount of its potential damages in advance, declare the value of the shipment based on that calculation, can pay a commensurately higher rate to carry the goods, in effect buying additional insurance from the common carrier.

In this case Calvin Klein and Trylon were business entities with an ongoing commercial relationship involving numerous carriages of Calvin Klein goods by Trylon. Where such entities deal with each other in a commercial setting, and no special relationship exists between the parties, clear limitations between them will be enforced. Here, each carriage was under the same terms and conditions as the last, including a limitation of Trylon's liability. This is not a case in which the shipper was dealing with the common carrier for the first time or contracting under new or changed conditions. Calvin Klein was aware of the terms and was free to adjust the limitation upon a written declaration of the value of a given shipment, but failed to do so with the shipment at issue here. Since Calvin Klein failed to adjust the limitation, the limitation applies here, and no public policy that dictates otherwise can be identified.

Calvin Klein also argues that the limitation is so low as to be void. The amount is immaterial because Calvin Klein had the opportunity to negotiate the amount of coverage by declaring the value of the shipment. Commercial entities can easily negotiate the degree of risk each party will bear and which party will bear the cost of insurance. Calvin Klein had the opportunity to declare a higher value and we find all of its arguments relating to the unreasonableness of the limitation to be without merit.

**District court judgment reversed with instructions to enter judgment for Calvin Klein for $50.**

## Negotiation of Document of Title

A negotiable document of title and a negotiable instrument are negotiated in substantially the same manner. If the document of title provides for the delivery of the goods to bearer, it may be negotiated by delivery. If it provides for delivery of the goods to the order of a named person, it must be indorsed by that person and delivered. If an order document of title is indorsed in blank, it may be negotiated by delivery unless it

bears a special indorsement following the blank indorsement, in which event it must be indorsed by the special indorsee and delivered [7–501].

A person taking a negotiable document of title takes as a bona fide holder if she takes in good faith and in the regular course of business. The bona fide holder of a negotiable document of title has substantially the same advantages over a holder who is not a bona fide holder or over a holder of a non-negotiable document of title as does a holder in due course of a negotiable instrument over a holder who is not a holder in due course or over a holder of a non-negotiable instrument.

## Rights Acquired by Negotiation

A person who acquires a negotiable document of title by due negotiation acquires (1) title to the document, (2) title to the goods, (3) the right to the goods delivered to the bailee after the issuance of the document, and (4) the direct obligation of the issuer to hold or deliver the goods according to the terms of the document [7–502(1)].

Under the broad general principle that a person cannot transfer title to goods he does not own, a thief—or the owner of goods subject to a perfected security interest—cannot, by warehousing or shipping the goods on a negotiable document of title and then negotiating the document of title, transfer to the purchaser of the document of title a better title than he has [7–503].

## Warranties of Transferor of Document of Title

The transferor of a negotiable document of title warrants to his immediate transferee, in addition to any warranty of goods, only that the document is genuine, that he has no knowledge of any facts that would impair its validity or worth, and that his negotiation or transfer is rightful and fully effective with respect to the title to the document and the goods it represents [7–507].

### PROBLEMS AND PROBLEM CASES

**1.** J. E. B. Stewart received a check in the amount of $185.48 in payment of a fee from a client. Stewart presented the check, properly indorsed, to the Citizen's & Southern Bank. The bank refused to cash the check even though there were sufficient funds in the drawer's account. Stewart then sued the bank for actual damages of $185.48 and for punitive damages of $50,000 for its failure to cash a valid check drawn against a solvent account in the bank. Does Stewart have a good cause of action against the bank?

**2.** Louise Kalbe signed a check drawn on her account at the Pulaski State Bank; later, that check was lost or stolen. The check was drafted for $7,260 payable to cash. The bank paid the check, which created an overdraft of $6,542.12 in Kalbe's account. The bank brought a lawsuit against Kalbe to recover the overdraft. Kalbe asserted that the check was not properly payable from her account. Was the bank legally entitled to pay a check that exceeded the balance in her account and to recover the overdraft from her?

**3.** On November 15, Midgen, the drawer of a check, issued a written stop-payment order to Chase Manhattan Bank, the drawee on the check. Midgen provided the correct payee, check date, and account and check number. However, he incorrectly stated the amount of the check to be $759.92. In fact, the amount was $754.92. Chase Manhattan paid the check on December 7. Should the $5 difference in the amount relieve Chase Manhattan of liability for paying the check over the stop-payment order?

**4.** In November 1981, Marc Gardner, the president of M. G. Sales, Inc., made out two checks on the account of M. G. Sales at Chemical Bank. The checks were both in the amount of $6,000 and were payable to, signed, and indorsed by Gardner. Apparently, he lost both checks. Consequently, on November 16, 1981, he went to Chemical Bank and obtained two stop-payment orders that, by their terms, were valid for six months. In January and February 1983, the checks were deposited into an account at another branch of Chemical Bank and the proceeds were credited to that account. M. G. Sales then brought an action against Chemical Bank for paying the checks despite the earlier stop-payment order and the fact the check was more than six months old and thus "stale." Is M. G. Sales entitled to have its account recredited?

**5.** In December, Whalley Company hired Nancy Cherauka as its bookkeeper. Her duties included preparing checks, taking deposits to the bank, and reconciling the monthly checking account statements. She was not authorized to sign or cash checks. Between the following January 24 and May 31, Cherauka forged 49 checks on the Whalley account at National City Bank. Each month, National City Bank sent Whalley a statement and the canceled checks (including the forgeries) it had paid the previous month. The president of Whalley looked at the statement to see the balance in the account but he did not look at the individual checks. Then he gave the statement and checks to the bookkeeper. The January 24 forged check was sent to Whalley on February 3. In June, Whalley discovered that Cherauka was forging checks and fired her. It then brought a lawsuit against National City Bank to force it to recredit Whalley's account with the total amount of the 49 checks. Whalley claimed that the checks were not properly payable from the account. Is National City required to recredit Whalley's account?

**6.** Two couples, Edna and Larry Brown and Mary and James Knight, formed a cable television construction business known as Knight Communications, Inc., with the four principals as directors. The Browns provided about $50,000 in capital and the Knights operated the company. According to the deposit/account agreement for the corporate checking account opened in January 1986 at the Boatmen's National Bank of St. Louis and the understanding of the parties, each check required the signature of one of the Knights and one of the Browns. Beginning February 21, 1986, the bank began honoring checks with the signature of only one or both Knights. Between February and May 1986, 105 checks lacking a Brown signature (out of over 500 checks issued by the corporation during this time) were paid by the bank. The total of the improperly payable checks payable to the Knights was $7,696.94. One of the bank officers asserted that he had oral permission of Mr. Brown to pay the checks but Mr. Brown later denied that he ever gave oral or written permission to the bank to honor checks without a Brown signature. The bank regularly returned the cancelled checks to the corporation along with a periodic statement of account, but the corporation made no contemporaneous objection to the lack of signatures by a Brown. The Brown-Knight joint enterprise effectively ended in August 1986. At that time, Mr. Brown delivered some of the improperly paid checks to his attorney and other cancelled checks were delivered to that attorney by the Knights. In September 1988, a lawsuit was filed in the name of Knight Communications against the bank for breach of contract for unauthorized payment of the checks without the required Brown signature. This was the first time that the lack of authorization

issue was raised with the bank. Is the drawee bank liable to the drawer for the amount of checks it paid containing unauthorized drawer's signatures when it is notified of that fact two years after the checks were made available to the drawer?

**7.** On August 16, 1981, Frederick Ognibene went to the ATM area at a Citibank branch and activated one of the machines with his Citibank card, pressed in his personal identification code, and withdrew $20. When he approached the machine a person was using the customer service telephone located between two ATM machines and appeared to be telling customer service that one of the machines was malfunctioning. As Ognibene was making his withdrawal, the person said into the telephone, "I'll see if his card works in my machine." He then asked Ognibene if he could use his card to see if the other machine was working. Ognibene handed his card to him and saw him insert it into the adjoining machine at least two times while saying into the telephone, "Yes, it seems to be working." When Ognibene received his Citibank statement, it showed that two withdrawals of $200 each from his account were made at 5:42 P.M. and 5:43 P.M., respectively, on August 16. His own $20 withdrawal was made at 5:41 P.M.. At that time, Ognibene was unaware that any withdrawals from his account were being made from the adjoining machine. Ognibene sought to have his account recredited for $400, claiming that the withdrawals had been unauthorized. Citibank had been aware for some time of a scam being perpetrated against its customers by persons who observed the customer inserting his personal identification number into an ATM and then obtained access to the customer's ATM card in the same manner as Ognibene's card was obtained. After learning about the scam, Citibank posted signs in ATM areas containing a red circle approximately 2 ½ inches in diameter in which was written "Do Not Let Your Citicard Be Used For Any Transaction But Your Own." Was Citibank required under the Electronic Fund Transfer Act to recredit Ognibene's account on the grounds that the withdrawal of the $400 was unauthorized?

**8.** Griswold and Bateman Warehouse Company stored 337 cases of Chivas Regal Scotch Whiskey for Joseph H. Reinfeld, Inc., in its bonded warehouse. The warehouse receipt issued to Reinfeld limited Griswold and Bateman's liability for negligence to 250 times the monthly storage rate, a total of $1,925. When Reinfeld sent its truck to pick up the whiskey, 40 cases were missing. Reinfeld then brought suit seeking the wholesale market value of the whiskey, $6,417.60. Reinfeld presented evidence of the delivery of the whiskey, the demand for its return, and the failure of Griswold and Bateman to return it. Reinfeld claimed that the burden was on Griswold and Bateman to explain the disappearance of the whiskey. Griswold and Bateman admitted that it had been negligent, but sought to limit its liability to $1,925. Is Griswold and Bateman's liability limited to $1,925?

**9.** Everlens Mitchell entered into a written contract with All American Van & Storage to transport and store her household goods. She was to pay the storage charges on a monthly basis. As security, she granted All American a warehouseman's lien. All American had the right to sell the property if the charges remained unpaid for three months and if, in the opinion of the company, such action was necessary to protect the accrued charges. Mitchell fell eight months behind on her payments. On October 20, 1985, she received notice that if the unpaid charges, totaling $804.30, were not paid by October 31, her goods would be sold on November 7. Mitchell advised All American that she had a claim pending with the Social Security Administration and would soon receive a large sum of money. This was confirmed to All American by several government officials. However, All American sold Mitchell's property on November 7 for $925.50. At the end of the month, Mitchell received a $5,500 disability payment. She sued All American for improperly selling her goods. The trial court awarded judgment to All American. Should the decision be reversed on appeal?

**10.** On October 15, Young delivered 207 bags of rice to Atteberry's warehouse and received a non-negotiable receipt. Young then transferred the receipt to Brock for a valuable consideration, and Brock notified Atteberry of the transfer on November 3. Prior to November 3, however, Young had procured a negotiable receipt for the rice along with some other rice he had deposited with Atteberry. Brock presented his non-negotiable receipt to Atteberry and demanded delivery of the rice. Atteberry contended that no rice was being held at the warehouse on Brock's account. Who is correct?

**11.** [▶] *Video Case.* See "Sour Grapes." Jelly Manufacturer orders some grapes by phone from Grape Grower in California on a COD basis. When the grapes arrive, Jelly Manufacturer pays for them by check before discovering that they had spoiled enroute because they had been shipped in a nonrefrigerated truck. After calling Grape Grower to complain, Jelly Manufacturer calls its bank and places a stop-payment order on the check. The bank's computer fails to catch the check and the check is paid to Grape Grower. Does Jelly Manufacturer have any recourse against the bank for paying the check over the stop-payment order?

## CAPSTONE QUESTIONS

**1.** Bob Brown purchased a 1990 Ford Bronco from Honest Harry, a used car dealer, and gave Honest Harry a personal check in the amount of $5,575.35 in full payment of the purchase price (including sales tax). Honest Harry guaranteed the vehicle to be in good working order. While driving the car the following morning, Bob experienced some difficulty and discovered that it had a cracked engine block. When he reported this to Harry, Harry's response was "the truck was working fine when you got it yesterday." Bob immediately called his bank to place an oral stop-payment order on the check. He gave the bank the correct name of the payee, account number, and check number but made an error as to the amount, telling the bank the check was made out for $5,555.35. When the check was presented for payment by Harry several hours later, the drawee bank paid it despite the oral stop-payment that had been placed on it. Payment of the check also created an overdraft in Harry's account because a $2,000 check he had deposited earlier had been returned marked "Insufficient Funds"; thus, the balance in his account had not been sufficient to cover the check to Honest Harry.

### Required:

Answer the following and give reasons for your conclusion.

1. Can Bob require the bank to recredit his account for $5,575.35 on the grounds the bank had no authorization to pay it because of the stop-payment order?

2. Can Bob require the bank to recredit his account because the bank paid a check that exceeded the balance in his account?

3. If the bank had to recredit Bob's account because it improperly paid the check over the stop-payment order, what rights would the bank have against Honest Harry?

   **2.** Madelyn Murray stored some household furniture with Sam's Storage and was given a negotiable warehouse receipt acknowledging the receipt of the furniture. Sometime later, she sold the furniture to her brother, Mike, and gave him the warehouse receipt after signing it on the back with a blank indorsement. When Mike went to claim the furniture, the attendant refused to release it to Mike, saying that Madelyn had been the one who had placed it for storage and he could release it only to her. The attendant also indicated that several items had been stolen when the warehouse was broken into by some juveniles, and to date, the missing items had not been recovered.

### Required

Answer the following and give reasons for your conclusions:

1. Is the attendant correct in contending that he can release the furniture only to Madelyn?

2. Do Madelyn or Mike have any rights against the warehouse for the missing items?

PART

6

# AGENCY

# CHAPTER

**27**

# THE AGENCY
# RELATIONSHIP

**INTRODUCTION**

*Frequently, businesses are legally bound by the actions of their employees or other representatives. For example, corporations frequently are liable on contracts their employees make or for torts those employees commit. We take such liability for granted, but it is not immediately obvious why we should. A corporation is an artificial legal person distinct from the officers, employees, and other representatives who contract on its behalf and who may commit torts while performing their duties. Similarly, a sole proprietor is distinct from the people he may employ. How can these and other business actors be bound on contracts they did not make or for torts they did not commit? The reason is the law of agency.*

## DEFINITION OF AGENCY

**Agency** is a two-party relationship in which one party (the **agent**) is authorized to act on behalf of, and under the control of, the other party (the **principal**). Simple examples include hiring a salesperson to sell goods, retaining an attorney, and engaging a real estate broker to sell a house. Agency law's most important social function is to stimulate business and commercial activity. It does so by enabling businesses to increase the number of transactions they can complete within a given time. Without agency, for instance, a sole proprietor's ability to engage in trade would be limited by the need to make each of her purchase or sale contracts in person. As artificial persons, moreover, corporations can only act through their agents.

Agency law divides into two rough categories. The first involves legal relations *between the principal and the agent.* These include the rules governing formation of an agency, the duties the principal and the agent owe each other, and the ways an agency can be terminated. These topics are the main concern of this chapter. Chapter 28 discusses the principal's and the agent's relations with *third parties.* There, our main concerns are the principal's and the agent's liability on contracts the agent makes and for torts the agent commits.

# CREATION OF AN AGENCY AND RELATED MATTERS

## Formation

An agency is created by the manifested agreement of two parties that one party (the agent) will act for the benefit of the other (the principal) under the principal's direction.[1] As the term *manifested* suggests, the test for an agency's existence is *objective*. If the parties' behavior and the surrounding facts and circumstances indicate an agreement that one person is to act for the benefit and under the control of another, courts hold that the relationship exists. If the facts establish an agency, it is immaterial whether either party knows about the agency's existence or subjectively desires that it exist. In fact, an agency may be present even where the parties expressly state that they do not intend to create it or intend to create some other legal relationship instead.

Often, parties create an agency by a written contract. But an agency contract may be oral unless state law provides otherwise.[2] Some states, for example, require written evidence of contracts to pay an agent a commission for the sale of real estate. More importantly, the agency relation need not be contractual at all. Thus, consideration is not necessary to form an agency. As the *Warren* case (which follows shortly) illustrates, courts sometimes imply an agency from the parties' behavior and the surrounding circumstances without discussing the need for a contract or for consideration.

## Capacity

A principal or agent who lacks the necessary mental capacity when the agency is formed ordinarily can release himself from the agency at his option. Examples include those who are minors or are mentally incapacitated when the agency is created. Of course, incapacity may occur at other times as well; we discuss such situations at various points in this chapter and Chapter 28.

As you have seen, corporations can and must appoint agents. In a partnership, each partner normally acts as the agent of the partnership in transacting partnership business,[3] and partnerships can appoint nonpartner agents as well. In addition, corporations, partnerships, and other business organizations themselves can act as agents.

## Nondelegable Obligations

Certain duties or acts must be performed personally and cannot be delegated to an agent. Examples include making statements under oath, voting in public elections, and signing a will. The same is true for service contracts in which the principal's personal performance is crucial—for example, certain contracts by lawyers, doctors, artists, and entertainers.

---

[1]Sometimes it is said that an agency may also be created by *ratification, estoppel,* or *operation of law.* Usually, however, ratification and estoppel are regarded as ways of binding the principal to an agent's actions, not as ways of forming an agency in the first place. Ratification is discussed in Chapter 28, and estoppel resembles the concept of apparent authority discussed later in this chapter and in Chapter 28. It is unusual for an agency to be created by operation of law. An example might be a statute designating a state's secretary of state as an out-of-state motorist's "agent" for purposes of receiving a summons and a complaint in a lawsuit against the motorist.

[2]Usually, the state law in question is the statute of frauds, which is discussed in Chapter 8. Also, it sometimes is said that if the contract the agent is to form must be in writing, the agency agreement likewise must be written. However, it is doubtful whether this "equal dignity rule" enjoys widespread acceptance.

[3]Chapter 30 discusses how agency law operates in the partnership context.

---

# WARREN v. UNITED STATES
### 613 F.2d 591 (5th Cir. 1980)

For two years, Bobby and Modell Warren took their cotton crops to certain cotton gins that ginned and baled the cotton. After being so instructed by the Warrens, the gins obtained bids for the cotton from prospective buyers and the Warrens told the gins which bids to accept. Then the gins sold the cotton to the designated buyers, collecting the proceeds. At the Warrens' instruction, the gins deferred payment of the proceeds to the Warrens until the year after the one in which each sale was made.

The Warrens did not report the proceeds as taxable income for the year when the gins received the proceeds, instead including the proceeds in their return for the following year. After an IRS audit, the Warrens were compelled to treat the proceeds as taxable income for the year when the proceeds were received, and to pay accordingly. The Warrens eventually won a refund action in federal district court. The government appealed, arguing that the gins were agents of the Warrens. Because receipt of proceeds by an agent is receipt by the principal, this would mean that the proceeds were taxable income for the year when they were received by the gins.

---

**Johnson, Circuit Judge** The relationship between the Warrens and the gins for the purpose of selling the cotton was indisputably that of principal and agent. The Warrens instructed the gins to solicit bids, the Warrens decided whether to accept the highest price offered, and the Warrens determined whether or not to instruct the gins to hold the proceeds from the sale until the following year. The gins' role in the sale of the cotton was to adhere to the Warrens' instructions. The Warrens were the owners of the cotton held for sale; the Warrens were in complete control of its disposition.

This case is distinguishable from those cases where it was recognized that proceeds from the sale of a crop by a farmer, pursuant to a bona fide arm's-length contract between the buyer and seller calling for payment in the taxable year following delivery, are includable in gross income for the taxable year in which payment is received. In the case at bar the bona fide arm's-length agreement was not between the buyer and seller but rather between the seller and his agent. The income was received by the Warrens' agents in the year of the sale. The fact that the Warrens restricted their access to the sales proceeds does not change the tax status of the money received.

**Judgment reversed in favor of the government.**

## AGENCY CONCEPTS, DEFINITIONS, AND TYPES

Agency law includes various concepts, definitions, and distinctions. These matters often determine the rights, duties, and liabilities of the principal, the agent, and third parties. In addition, they sometimes are important outside agency law. Because these basic topics are so crucial in so many different contexts, we outline them together here.

### Authority

Although agency law lets people multiply their dealings by employing agents, a principal should not be liable for *any* deal his agent concludes. Thus, agency law normally lets an agent bind his principal only when the agent has **authority** to do so. Authority is an agent's ability to affect his principal's legal relations. Authority comes in two main forms: **actual authority** and **apparent authority.** Each is based on the principal's manifested consent that the agent may act for and bind the principal. For actual authority, this consent is communicated to the *agent;* for apparent authority, it is communicated to the *third party.*

Actual authority comes in two forms: **express authority** and **implied authority.** Express authority is created by the principal's actual words (whether written or oral). Thus, an agent has express authority to bind her principal in a certain fashion only when the principal has made a fairly precise statement to that effect. Often, however, it is impractical for a principal to specify the agent's authority fully and exactly. Thus, to avoid unnecessarily restricting an agent's ability to represent her principal, agency law also gives agents *implied authority* to bind their principals. An agent generally has implied authority to do whatever it is reasonable to assume that the principal wanted him to do, given the principal's express statements and the surrounding circumstances. Relevant factors include the principal's express statements, the nature of the agency, the acts reasonably necessary to carry on the agency business, and the acts customarily done when conducting that business.

Sometimes, an agent who lacks actual authority may still *appear* to have such authority, and third parties may reasonably rely on this appearance of authority. To protect third parties in such situations, agency law lets agents bind the principal on the basis of their *apparent authority*. Apparent authority arises when the principal's behavior causes a third party to form a reasonable belief that the agent is authorized to act in a certain way. Apparent authority depends on what the principal communicates to the third party—either directly or through the agent. A principal might clothe an agent with apparent authority by making direct statements to the third party, telling an agent to do so, or allowing an agent to behave in a way that creates an appearance of authority. Communica-

tions to the agent are irrelevant unless they become known to the third party or affect the agent's behavior. Also, agents cannot give themselves apparent authority, and apparent authority does not exist where the agent creates an appearance of authority without the principal's consent. Finally, the third party must *reasonably* believe in the agent's authority. Trade customs and business practices can help courts determine whether such a belief was reasonable.

Authority is important in a number of agency contexts. Chapter 28 examines its most important application—determining a principal's liability on contracts made by his agent. As the following *Towers* case illustrates, moreover, authority finds application outside agency law as well.

---

## Towers World Airways v. PHH Aviation Systems
### 933 F.2d 174 (2d Cir. 1991)

PHH Aviation Systems leased a corporate jet to Towers World Airways. PHH also issued a credit card to Towers to buy fuel for the jet from sellers of airplane fuel. The contract between PHH and Towers made Towers liable to PHH for fuel purchases Towers made with the card. A Towers officer allowed Fred Jay Schley, the jet's chief pilot, to use the card to make fuel purchases for *noncharter* flights. However, there was conflicting testimony regarding Schley's authorization to use the card for *chartered* flights. Nonetheless, Schley charged over $89,000 to Towers in connection with fuel purchases for chartered flights.

Claiming that it was not liable to PHH for the $89,000 because the Truth-in-Lending Act limited its liability to $50, Towers sued for a declaratory judgment to that effect. PHH counterclaimed for the $89,000 and then successfully moved for summary judgment. Towers appealed.

---

**Newman, Circuit Judge**    Congress enacted the 1970 amendments to the Truth-in-Lending Act to protect credit cardholders from unauthorized use by those able to obtain possession of a card from its original owner. The amendments enacted a scheme for limiting the liability of cardholders for all charges by third parties made without "actual [express], implied, or apparent authority." Where an unauthorized use has occurred, the cardholder can be held liable only up to a limit of $50, if certain conditions are satisfied.

Congress apparently contemplated reliance on background principles of agency law in determining the liability of cardholders for charges incurred by third-party card bearers. A cardholder, as principal, can create express and implied authority only

through manifestations to the user of consent to the particular transactions into which the user has entered. There remains an unresolved issue of fact as to whether the Towers officer who dealt with Schley expressly or impliedly authorized Schley to purchase fuel on chartered flights. Accordingly, we cannot affirm the grant of summary judgment on the theory that Schley possessed express or implied authority.

Unlike express or implied authority, apparent authority exists apart from the principal's manifestations of consent to the agent. Rather, the cardholder, as principal, creates apparent authority through words or conduct that, reasonably interpreted by a third party from whom the card bearer makes purchases, indicate that the card user acts with the cardholder's consent. Though a cardholder's relinquishment of possession may create in another the appearance of authority to use the card, the statute clearly precludes a finding of apparent authority where the transfer of the card was without the cardholder's consent, as in cases involving theft, loss, or fraud. Because the statute provides no guidance as to uses arising from the *voluntary* transfer of credit cards, the general principles of agency law govern disputes over whether a resulting use was unauthorized. These disputes frequently involve, as in this case, a cardholder's claim that the card bearer was given permission to use a card for only a limited purpose and that subsequent charges exceeded the consent originally given by the cardholder. Several state courts have declined to apply the Truth-in-Lending Act to limit the cardholder's liability [in such situations], reasoning that the cardholder's voluntary relinquishment of the card for one purpose gives the bearer apparent authority to make additional charges.

We need not decide whether voluntary relinquishment for one purpose creates in every case apparent authority to incur other charges. The appearance of authority for Schley to purchase fuel on chartered flights was established not only by Towers's consent to Schley's unrestricted access to the PHH card but by other conduct and circumstances as well. Nothing about the PHH card or the circumstances surrounding the purchases gave fuel sellers reason to distinguish the clearly authorized fuel purchases made in connection with non-charter flights from the purchases for chartered flights. It was the industry custom to entrust credit cards used to make airplane-related purchases to the pilot of the plane. By designating Schley as the pilot and subsequently giving him the card, Towers thereby imbued him with more apparent authority than might arise from voluntary relinquishment of a credit card in other contexts. In addition, with Towers's blessing Schley had used the card to purchase fuel on non-charter flights for the same plane. The only difference between those uses expressly authorized and those now claimed to be unauthorized—the identity of the passengers—was insufficient to provide notice to those who sold the fuel that Schley lacked authority for the charter flight purchases.

**Summary judgment for PHH affirmed.**

## General and Special Agents

Although it may be falling out of favor with courts, the blurred distinction between general agents and special agents still has some importance. A **general agent** is *continuously* employed to conduct a series of transactions, while a **special agent** is employed to conduct a single transaction or a small, simple group of transactions. Thus, a continuously employed general manager, construction project supervisor, or purchasing agent is normally a general agent; and a person employed to buy or sell a few objects on a one-shot basis is usually a special agent. In addition to being employed on a continuous basis, general agents often serve for longer periods, perform more acts, and deal with more parties than do special agents.

## Gratuitous Agents

An agent who receives no compensation for his services is called a **gratuitous agent.** Gratuitous agents have the same power to bind their principals as do paid agents with the same authority. As you will see, however, the fact that an agent is gratuitous sometimes lowers the duties principal and agent owe each other and may also increase the parties' ability to terminate the agency without incurring liability.

## Subagents

A **subagent** is basically an agent of an agent. More precisely, a subagent is a person appointed by an agent to perform functions that the agent has undertaken to perform for his principal. For example, if you retain an accounting firm as your agent, the accountant actually handling your affairs is the firm's agent and your subagent. For a subagency to exist, the agent must have the authority to make the subagent *his agent* for conducting the principal's business. Sometimes, however, a party appointed by an agent is not a subagent because the appointing agent only had authority to appoint agents *for the*

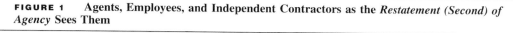

**FIGURE 1**   Agents, Employees, and Independent Contractors as the *Restatement (Second) of Agency* Sees Them

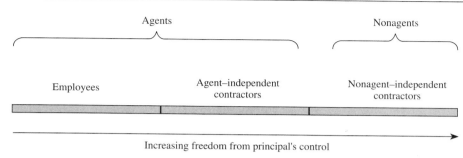

*principal.* For instance, sales agents appointed by a corporation's sales manager probably are agents of the corporation, not agents of the sales manager.

When an agent appoints a true subagent, the agent becomes a principal with respect to the subagent, his agent. Thus, the legal relations between agent and subagent closely parallel the legal relations between principal and agent. But a subagent is also the *original principal's* agent. Here, though, the normal rules governing principals and agents do not always apply. We occasionally refer to such situations in the pages ahead.

## Employees and Independent Contractors

Many important legal questions hinge on a distinction between two relationships that overlap with the principal-agent relationship. These are an employer's (or master's) relationship with his **employee** (or servant), and a principal's relationship with an **independent contractor.** No sharp line separates these two relationships; the following *VIP Tours* case lists some factors considered in making such determinations. The most important of these factors is the principal's *right to control the physical details of the work.* Employees are typically subject to such control. Independent contractors, on the other hand, generally contract with the principal to produce some result, and determine for themselves how that result will be accomplished.

Although many employees perform physical labor or are paid on an hourly basis, corporate officers are usually employees as well. Profession-als such as brokers, accountants, and attorneys are often independent contractors, although they are sometimes employees. Consider the difference between a corporation represented by an attorney engaged in her own practice and a corporation that maintains a staff of salaried in-house counsel. Finally, franchisees are usually independent contractors.

When are employees and independent contractors agents? Although there is little consensus on this question, this text follows the *Restatement* position. According to the *Restatement,* employees are *always* agents, while independent contractors *may or may not* be agents.[4] An independent contractor is an agent when the tests for the existence of an agency—most importantly, sufficient control by the principal—are met. Figure 1 sketches the *Restatement* position on the relationships among agents, employees, and independent contractors.

As Chapter 28 makes clear, the employee–independent contractor distinction is often crucial in determining the principal's liability for an agent's torts. The distinction also helps define the coverage of some employment regulations discussed in Chapter 40. Unemployment compensation (the subject of *VIP Tours*) and workers' compensation are two clear examples.

---

[4]*Restatement (Second) of Agency* §§ 2, 14N, 25, and the Introductory Note following § 218 (1959).

## VIP TOURS, INC. V. FLORIDA
### 449 So. 2d 1307 (Fla. Ct. App. 1984)

VIP Tours, Inc. arranged tours of central Florida's attractions. Cynthia Hoogland conducted 29 such tours for VIP between July 1980 and March 1981. Both Hoogland and VIP considered Hoogland an independent contractor. She worked for VIP only when it needed her services and she could reject particular assignments. She was also free to work for other tour services, and she did so.

Once Hoogland accepted a job from VIP, she was told where to report and was given instructions about the job. She also had to use a VIP-furnished vehicle and wear a uniform with the VIP logo when conducting tours. Aside from ensuring that she departed on time, however, VIP did not tell her how long to stay or what kind of tour to conduct at each tourist attraction. Finally, Hoogland was paid on a per tour basis.

Hoogland later filed a claim for unemployment compensation benefits with the Florida Division of Labor and Employment Security. The Division concluded that she was entitled to these benefits because she was VIP Tours' employee. VIP appealed the Division's order to an intermediate appellate court.

---

**Upchurch, Judge**   The [Florida] Supreme Court has approved the test set out in *Restatement (Second) of Agency* section 220 for determining whether one is an employee or an independent contractor:

In determining whether one acting for another is a servant or an independent contractor, the following matters of fact, among others, are considered:

(a) the extent of control which, by the agreement, the master may exercise over the details of the work;

(b) whether or not the one employed is engaged in a distinct occupation or business;

(c) the kind of occupation, with reference to whether, in the locality, the work is usually done under the direction of the employer or by a specialist without supervision;

(d) the skill required in the particular occupation;

(e) whether the employer or the workman supplies the instrumentalities, tools, and the place of work for the person doing the work;

(f) the length of time for which the person is employed;

(g) the method of payment, whether by the time or by the job;

(h) whether or not the work is part of the regular business of the employer;

(i) whether or not the parties believe that they are creating the relationship of master and servant; and

(j) whether the principal is or is not in business.

It has been said repeatedly that of all the factors, the right of control as to the mode of doing the work is the principal consideration.

VIP had no right of control over the tour guides other than to require them to show up at a particular place at a particular time wearing the VIP uniform and to travel in VIP transportation. VIP had little interest in the details of the guides' work, as is illustrated by the fact that the guides controlled the number of hours spent at a particular attraction and the nature of the tour at each exhibit. In addition, the guides were free to contract with other tour companies, as Hoogland did, and could accept or reject any assignment, factors further indicating a lack of control by VIP.

Other factors in the *Restatement* also point toward independent contractor status. The tour guides were engaged in a distinct occupation. They worked and were paid on a per-job basis. Both VIP and Hoogland considered the guides to be independent contractors.

**Division order reversed.**

## DUTIES OF AGENT TO PRINCIPAL

If an agency is created by contract, the agent must perform according to its terms. Regardless of whether the relationship is contractual, agency law also establishes certain *fiduciary duties* that the agent owes the principal. These duties supplement the duties created by an agency contract. They exist because agency is a relationship of trust and confidence. Often, however, the parties may eliminate or modify fiduciary duties by agreement.

Despite certain exceptions noted later, a *gratuitous agent* usually has the same fiduciary duties as a paid agent. But this is true only so long as a gratuitous agent continues to act as an agent. In other words, a gratuitous agent need not perform as promised, he normally can terminate the agency without incurring liability, and his fiduciary duties cease once the agency ends. However, a gratuitous agent *is* liable for failing to perform as promised when his promise causes the principal to rely on him to undertake certain acts, and the principal suffers losses because she refrained from performing those acts herself. For example, suppose the principal refrains from bidding at an auction because her agent has gratuitously promised to bid for her, the agent attends the auction but fails to make the bid, and the bid would have succeeded had it been made.

A *subagent* owes the agent (his principal) all the duties agents owe their principals. A subagent who knows of the original principal's existence also owes that principal all the duties agents owe their principals, except for duties arising solely from the original principal's contract with the agent. Finally, the agent who appointed the subagent is generally liable to the original principal when the principal is harmed by the subagent's conduct.

## Agent's Duty of Loyalty

Because agency is a relationship of trust and confidence, an agent has a **duty of loyalty** to his principal. Thus, an agent must subordinate personal concerns by: (1) avoiding conflicts of interest with the principal, and (2) not disclosing confidential information received from the principal.

**Conflicts of Interest**   An agent whose interests conflict with the principal's interests may be unable to represent his principal effectively. When conducting the principal's business, therefore, an agent is forbidden to *deal with himself.* For example, an agent authorized to sell property cannot sell that property to himself. This rule often includes an agent's transactions with his relatives or business associates, or with business organizations in which he has an interest. However, an agent may engage in self-dealing transactions if the principal consents. For this consent to be effective, the agent must disclose all relevant facts to the principal before dealing with the principal on his own behalf.

Unless the principal agrees otherwise, an agent is also forbidden to *compete with the principal* regarding the agency business so long as he remains an agent. Thus, an agent employed to purchase specific property may not buy it himself if the principal still desires it. As the following *Chernow* case states, moreover, an agent ordinarily may not solicit customers for a planned competing business while still employed by the principal.

Finally, an agent who is authorized to make a certain transaction cannot *act on behalf of the other party* to the transaction unless the principal knowingly consents. Thus, one ordinarily cannot act as agent for both parties to a transaction without first disclosing the double role to, and obtaining the consent of, both principals. Here, the agent must disclose to each principal all the factors reasonably affecting each principal's decision. Occasionally, though, an agent who acts as a middleman may serve both parties to a transaction without notifying either. For instance, an agent may simultaneously be employed as a "finder" by a firm seeking suitable businesses to acquire and a firm looking for prospective buyers, so long as neither principal expects the agent to advise it or negotiate for it.

## CHERNOW V. REYES
### 570 A.2d 1282 (N.J. Ct. App. 1990)

Ronald Chernow is in the business of auditing telephone bills for customers. Typically, he determines whether the customers' phone equipment is in place, properly billed, and in working order; checks for overcharges; and receives half of any overcharge refund the customer receives from the telephone company. In October 1982, Chernow hired Angelo Reyes as an auditor. The employment lasted until July 1983, when Reyes either quit or was fired.

Prior to leaving Chernow's employ and without his knowledge, Reyes took various steps to form and operate a business that competed with Chernow's business. Most importantly, he obtained three auditing contracts and performed work under those contracts during that period. He also solicited a fourth account, but did no work for that firm until after ceasing to work for Chernow. None of these businesses was an existing customer of Chernow. Reyes's soliciting and auditing activities did not take place during his regular working hours, which he devoted to Chernow's business.

Chernow sued Reyes for breach of his agent's duty of loyalty. The trial court held for Reyes. Its main reason was that Reyes's customers were neither clients of Chernow nor within the pool of businesses Chernow was soliciting. Chernow appealed.

---

**Stein, Judge**    An employee owes a duty of loyalty to the employer and must not, while employed, act contrary to the employer's interest. "Unless otherwise agreed, an agent is subject to a duty not to compete with the principal concerning the subject matter of his agency." *Restatement (Second) of Agency* section 393. Comment e to section 393 states:

. . . [B]efore the end of his employment, [the agent] can properly purchase a rival business and upon termination of employment immediately compete. *He is not, however, entitled to solicit customers for such rival business before the end of his employment nor can he properly do other similar acts in direct competition with the employer's business* [emphasis added].

By engaging in a competitive enterprise, Reyes crossed the line between permissible preparation to change jobs and actionable conduct. Chernow was entitled to expect that a person on his payroll would not undertake to pursue competitive commercial opportunities. The protection accorded is not limited to the diversion of an employer's customers. It extends to pursuing and transacting business within the larger pool of potential customers who might have been solicited by the employer.

**Judgment reversed in favor of Chernow.**

---

**Confidentiality**    Unless otherwise agreed, an agent may not *use or disclose confidential information* acquired through the agency. Confidential information means facts that are valuable to the principal because they are not widely known, or that would harm the principal's business if they became widely known. Examples include the principal's business plans, financial condition, contract bids, technological discoveries, manufacturing methods, customer files, and other trade secrets. In the absence of an agreement to the contrary,[5] an agent may compete with her principal after termination of the agency. But as the following *ABKCO* case illustrates, the duty not to use or disclose confidential information continues. The former agent may, however, utilize general knowledge and skills acquired during the agency.

---

[5]Agreements not to compete are discussed in Chapter 7.

## ABKCO Music, Inc. v. Harrisongs Music, Ltd.
### 722 F.2d 988 (2d Cir. 1983)

In 1963, a song called "He's So Fine" was a huge hit in the United States and Great Britain. In February 1971, Bright Tunes Music Corporation, the copyright holder of "He's So Fine," sued ex-Beatle George Harrison and Harrisongs, Music, Ltd. in federal district court. Bright Tunes claimed that the Harrison composition "My Sweet Lord" infringed its copyright to "He's So Fine." At this time, Harrison's business affairs were handled by ABKCO Music, Inc. and Allen B. Klein, its president. Shortly after the suit began, Klein unsuccessfully tried to settle it by having ABKCO purchase Bright Tunes.

Shortly thereafter, Bright Tunes went into receivership, and it did not resume the suit until 1973. At this time, coincidentally, ABKCO's management contract with Harrison expired. In late 1975 and early 1976, however, Klein continued his efforts to have ABKCO purchase Bright Tunes. As part of these efforts, he gave Bright Tunes three schedules summarizing Harrison's royalty income from "My Sweet Lord," information he possessed because of his previous service to Harrison. Throughout the 1973–76 period, Harrison's attorneys had been trying to settle the copyright infringement suit with Bright Tunes. Because Klein's activities not only gave Bright Tunes information about the economic potential of its suit but also gave it an economic alternative to settling with Harrison, Klein may have impeded Harrison's efforts to settle.

When the copyright infringement suit finally came to trial in 1976, the court found that Harrison had infringed Bright Tunes' copyright. The issue of damages was scheduled for trial at a later date, and this trial was delayed for some time. In 1978, ABKCO purchased the "He's So Fine" copyright and all rights to the infringement suit from Bright Tunes. This made ABKCO the plaintiff in the 1979 trial for damages on the infringement suit. At trial, Harrison counterclaimed for damages resulting from Klein's and ABKCO's alleged breaches of the duty of loyalty. Finding a breach of duty, the district judge issued a complex order reducing ABKCO's recovery. ABKCO appealed.

---

**Pierce, Circuit Judge**   The relationship between Harrison and ABKCO prior to termination of the management agreement in 1973 was that of principal and agent. An agent has a duty not to use confidential knowledge acquired in his employment in competition with his principal. This duty exists as well after the employment as during its continuance. On the other hand, use of information based on general business knowledge is not covered by the rule, and the former agent is permitted to compete with his former principal in reliance on such publicly available information. The principal issue before us, then, is whether Klein (hence, ABKCO) improperly used confidential information, gained as Harrison's former agent, in negotiating for the purchase of Bright Tunes' stock in 1975–76.

One aspect of this inquiry concerns the nature of the schedules of "My Sweet Lord" earnings which Klein furnished to Bright Tunes in connection with the 1975–76 negotiations. It appears that at least some of [this] information was confidential. The evidence is not at all convincing that the information was publicly available.

Another aspect of the breach of duty issue concerns the timing and nature of Klein's entry into the negotiation picture and the manner in which he became a plaintiff in this action. We find this case analogous to those where an employee, with the use of information acquired through his former employment, completes for his own benefit a transaction originally undertaken on the former employer's behalf. Klein had commenced a purchase transaction with Bright Tunes in 1971 on behalf of Harrison, which he pursued on his own account after termination of his fiduciary relationship with Harrison. Klein pursued the later discussions armed with the intimate knowledge not only of Harrison's business affairs, but of the value of this lawsuit. Taking all of these circumstances together, we agree that Klein's conduct during the period 1975–78 did not meet the standard required of him as a former fiduciary.

**District court decision in Harrison's favor on the breach of duty issue affirmed.**

## Agent's Duty to Obey Instructions

Because an agent acts under the principal's control and for the principal's benefit, she has a duty to *obey the principal's reasonable instructions* for carrying out the agency business. However, a gratuitous agent need not obey his principal's order to continue to act as an agent. Also, agents generally have no duty to obey orders to behave illegally or unethically. Thus, a sales agent need not follow directions to misrepresent the quality of the principal's goods, and professionals such as attorneys and accountants are not obligated to obey directions that conflict with the ethical rules of their professions.

## Agent's Duty to Act with Care and Skill

A paid agent must *possess and exercise the degree of care and skill* that is standard in the locality for the kind of work the agent performs. A gratuitous agent need only exercise the care and skill required of nonagents who perform similar gratuitous undertakings. Paid agents who represent that they possess a higher than customary level of skill may be held to a correspondingly higher standard of performance.

Similarly, an agent's duty may change if the principal and the agent agree that the agent must possess and exercise greater or lesser than customary care and skill.

## Agent's Duty to Notify the Principal

An agent must promptly communicate to the principal matters within his knowledge that are reasonably relevant to the agency business and that he knows or should know are of concern to the principal. As the following *Levin* case suggests, this *duty to notify* is sometimes treated as one facet of the duty to act with care and skill. The basis for the duty to notify is the principal's interest in being informed of matters that are important to the agency business.

However, there is no duty to notify where the agent receives privileged or confidential information. For example, an attorney may acquire confidential information from a client and thus be obligated not to disclose it to a second client. If the attorney cannot properly represent the second client without revealing this information, he should refuse to represent that client.

### LEVIN V. KASMIR WORLD TRAVEL
**540 N.Y.S.2d 639 (N.Y. Civ. Ct. 1989)**

In July 1987, Marsha Levin bought her daughter a round-trip plane ticket from New York City to Paris from Kasmir World Travel, Inc. Upon arriving in Paris, Mrs. Levin's daughter was denied entry and was placed on the next return flight to the United States because she did not have a visa. The apparent reason for the visa requirement was the French government's effort to deal with terrorist activities directed at Americans abroad. Neither Mrs. Levin nor her daughter was aware of the requirement; indeed, a few years earlier Mrs. Levin had traveled to France without being required to present a visa.

Levin sued Kasmir for failing to notify her about the visa requirement. Kasmir moved to dismiss her complaint.

**Saxe, Judge**     The duty of a travel agent includes such responsibilities as verifying or confirming reservations. Travel agents are required to have the degree of skill and knowledge requisite to the calling; to exercise good faith and reasonable skill, care, and diligence; and to possess reasonable knowledge of the types of carriers, lines, and accommodations that they select for their principals, and all significant attendant matters. Beyond the duty to confirm travel reservations, travel agents should provide information which is necessary and of importance to the traveler.

Kasmir had a duty to notify the traveler about the need for a visa before entering France. This is in accord with the expanding role of the travel agent to provide all relevant and necessary information to the consumer who reasonably relies on the agent's expertise. Here, it was reasonable to expect Kasmir to alert its [principal] to important changes in the visa requirements of foreign nations. It was also reasonable for Mrs. Levin to rely on Kasmir to supply this information. The travel agency was clearly in a position to assemble and disseminate this basic and significant type of travel information.

I am aware of Kasmir's contention that its relationship to the claimant was merely that of a ticketing agent, and that consequently duties beyond the actual sale of the ticket could not implicate such an agent. [But] information concerning entry or visa requirements into foreign lands is so basic to the purchase or sale of the ticket that the seller must be obliged to furnish it to all affected consumers.

**Kasmir's motion to dismiss denied.**

## Agent's Duties to Account

An agent's duties of loyalty and care require that she give the principal any money or property received in the course of the agency business. This includes profits resulting from the agent's breach of the duty of loyalty, or other duties. It also includes incidental benefits received through the agency business. Examples include bribes, kickbacks, and gifts from parties with whom the agent deals on the principal's behalf. However, the principal and the agent may agree that the agent can retain certain benefits received during the agency. Courts may imply such an agreement when it is customary for agents to retain tips or accept entertainment while doing the principal's business.

Another type of *duty to account* concerns agents whose business involves collections, receipts, or expenditures. Such agents must keep accurate records and accounts of all transactions, and disclose these to the principal once the principal makes a reasonable demand for them. Also, an agent who obtains or holds property for the principal usually may not commingle that property with her own property. For example, an agent ordinarily cannot deposit the principal's funds in her own name or in her own bank account.

## Remedies of the Principal

Many claims and remedies are possible when an agent breaches a duty to her principal. If the agency was created by contract, for example, the agent's wrongdoing may breach that contract and may enable the principal to obtain the various kinds of contract damages. Also, a principal may obtain injunctive relief where, for instance, an agent discloses or threatens to disclose confidential information, or misappropriates or threatens to misappropriate the principal's property. In addition, a principal may rescind contracts made by an agent who has represented two principals without the knowledge of one or both, has dealt with himself, or has failed to disclose relevant facts. Finally, agents who retain money or property due the principal (including bribes or gifts), or who profit from the breach of duty, may be liable for the amount of their unjust enrichment.

Tort claims are possible when the agent has misbehaved. A principal may recover for losses caused by his agent's negligent failure to follow instructions, to notify, or to perform with appropriate skill and care. The tort of conversion is available where an agent has unjustifiably retained, stolen, transferred, destroyed, failed to separate, or otherwise misappropriated the principal's property.

## DUTIES OF PRINCIPAL TO AGENT

If an agency is formed by contract, the contract normally states the duties the principal owes the agent. In addition, the law implies certain duties from the existence of an agency relationship, however formed. The most important of these duties are the principal's obligations to **compensate** the agent, to **reimburse** the agent for money spent in the principal's service, and to **indemnify** the agent for losses suffered in conducting the principal's business.[6] These duties can generally be eliminated or modified by agreement between the parties. Although there is no duty to compensate a gratuitous agent, the principal still owes such an agent the other two duties unless there is an agreement to the contrary.

An agent's duties to a subagent are the same as a principal's duties to an agent. If there is no agreement to the contrary, however, the original principal has no contractual liability to a subagent. For example, such a principal is normally not obligated to compensate a subagent. But a principal must reimburse and indemnify subagents as he would agents.

### Duty to Compensate Agent

Where an agency contract states the agent's compensation, the contract generally controls questions on that issue. In other cases, the relationship of the parties and the surrounding circumstances determine whether and in what amount the agent is to be compensated. If there is no contract provision on compensation, for example, a principal generally is not required to pay for undertakings that she did not request, services to which she did not consent, and tasks that typically are undertaken without pay. Also, a principal usually need not compensate an agent who has materially breached the agency contract or has committed a serious breach of a fiduciary duty. Where compensation is due but its amount is not expressly stated, the amount is the market price or the customary price for the agent's services, or, if neither is available, their reasonable value.

Sometimes an agent's compensation depends on the accomplishment of a specific result. For instance, a plaintiff's attorney may be retained on a contingent fee basis (being paid a certain percentage of the recovery if the suit succeeds or is settled), or a real estate broker may be entitled to a fee only if a suitable buyer is found. In such cases, the agent is not entitled to compensation unless he achieves the result within the time stated or, if no time is stated, within a reasonable time. This is true no matter how much effort or money the agent expends. However, the principal must cooperate with the agent in achieving the result and must not do anything to frustrate the agent's efforts. Otherwise, the agent is entitled to compensation despite the failure to perform as specified.

### Duties of Reimbursement and Indemnity

If, while acting on the principal's behalf, an agent makes expressly or impliedly authorized expenditures, the agent is entitled to **reimbursement** for those expenditures if there is no agreement to the contrary. Unless otherwise agreed, for example, an agent requested to make overnight trips as part of his agency duties can recover reasonable transportation and hotel expenses.

A principal's duty of reimbursement overlaps with her duty of **indemnity.** Agency law implies a promise by the principal to indemnify an agent for losses that result from the agent's authorized activities. These include authorized payments made on the principal's behalf and payments on contracts on which the agent was authorized to become liable. A principal may also have to indemnify an agent if the agent's authorized acts constitute a breach of contract or a tort for which the agent is required to pay damages to a third party.

So long as the principal did not benefit from such behavior, however, he is *not* required to indemnify an agent for losses resulting: (1) from unauthorized acts, or (2) solely from the agent's negligence or other fault. Even where the principal directed the agent to commit a tortious act, moreover, there is no duty to indemnify if the agent knew the act was tortious. But the principal must indemnify the agent for tort damages resulting from authorized conduct that the agent did not believe was tortious. For

---

[6]A principal may also have other duties, including the duties to: provide the agent with an opportunity for service, not interfere with the agent's work, keep accounts, act in a manner not harmful to the agent's reputation or self-esteem, and (in the case of employees) maintain a safe workplace. The last duty has been greatly affected, if not superseded, by workers' compensation systems and the Occupational Safety and Health Act, which are discussed in Chapter 40.

example, if a principal directs his agent to repossess goods located on another's property and the agent, believing her acts legal, becomes liable for conversion or trespass, the principal must indemnify the agent for the damages the agent pays.

## Remedies of the Agent

An agent's claim for breach of the duties just discussed is often contractual, and normal contract remedies—except specific performance—are available. In some cases, a principal's failure to pay, indemnify, or reimburse an agent enables the agent to acquire a lien on property or funds of the principal that are in the agent's possession. This usually allows the agent to hold the property or funds until the principal pays his obligation. Also, an agent whose principal violates the duties to pay, indemnify, or reimburse can refuse to render further services to the principal.

Of course, an agent's *own* breach of duty— especially the duties of loyalty and obedience—may defeat his claim against the principal. Where the breach is not serious enough to give the principal a complete defense, the principal may still set off losses caused by the breach against the agent's recovery.

## TERMINATION OF THE AGENCY RELATIONSHIP

An agency can terminate in many ways.[7] Such terminations fall under two general headings: (1) termination by act of the parties, and (2) termination by operation of law.

## Termination by Act of the Parties

Termination by act of the parties occurs:

**1.** *At a time or upon the happening of an event stated in the agreement.* If no such time or event is stated, the agency terminates after a reasonable time.

**2.** *When a specified result has been accomplished, if the agency was created to accomplish a specified result.* For example, if an agency's only

objective is to sell certain property, the agency terminates when the property is sold.

**3.** *By mutual agreement of the parties,* at any time.

**4.** *At the option of either party.* This is called **revocation** when done by the principal and **renunciation** when done by the agent. Revocation or renunciation occurs when either party manifests to the other that he does not wish the agency to continue. This includes conduct inconsistent with the agency's continuance. For example, an agent may learn that his principal has hired another agent to perform the same job.

A party can revoke or renounce even if this violates the agency agreement. However, although either party has the *power* to terminate in such cases, there is no *right* to do so. This means that where one party terminates in violation of the agreement, she need not perform any further, but she may be liable for damages to the other party. However, a gratuitous agency is normally terminable by either party without liability. Also, the terminating party is not liable where the revocation or renunciation is justified by the other party's serious breach of a fiduciary duty.

## Termination by Operation of Law

Termination by operation of law normally involves situations where it is reasonable to believe that the principal would not wish the agent to act further, or where accomplishment of the agency objectives has become impossible or illegal. Although courts may recognize exceptions in certain cases, an agency relationship is usually terminated by:

**1.** *The death of the principal.* This normally is true even where the agent has no notice of the principal's death.

**2.** *The death of the agent.*

**3.** *The principal's permanent loss of capacity.* This is a *permanent* loss of capacity occurring *after* creation of the agency—most likely due to the principal's insanity. The principal's permanent incapacity ends the agency even without notice to the agent. But a brief period of insanity may only temporarily suspend the agency for the time the principal is insane.

**4.** *The agent's loss of capacity to perform the agency business.* The scope of this basis for

---

[7]The rules stated below generally apply to the termination of a subagent's authority as well. In general, a subagency terminates when relations between either the principal and the agent or the agent and the subagent are terminated in any of the ways to be described.

termination is unclear. As Chapter 28 relates, an agent who becomes insane or otherwise incapacitated after the agency is formed still can bind his principal to contracts with third parties. Thus, it probably makes little sense to treat the agency relationship as terminated in such cases. As a result, termination under this heading may be limited to such situations as the loss of a license needed to perform agency duties.

**5.** *Changes in the value of the agency property or subject matter* (e.g., a significant decline in the value of land to be sold by an agent).

**6.** *Changes in business conditions* (e.g., a much lower supply and a much increased price for goods to be purchased by an agent).

**7.** *The loss or destruction of the agency property or subject matter or the termination of the principal's interest therein* (e.g., where a house to be sold by a real estate broker burns down or is taken by a mortgage holder to satisfy a debt owed by the principal).

**8.** *Changes in the law that make the agency business illegal* (e.g., where drugs to be sold by an agent are banned by the government).

**9.** *The principal's bankruptcy*—as to transactions the agent should realize the principal no longer desires. For example, consider the likely effect of the principal's bankruptcy on an agency to purchase antiques for the principal's home versus its likely effect on an agency to purchase necessities of life for the principal.

**10.** *The agent's bankruptcy*—where the agent's financial condition affects his ability to serve the principal. This could occur where an agent is employed to purchase goods on his own credit for the principal.

**11.** *Impossibility of performance by the agent.* This covers various events, some of which fall within the categories just stated. The *Restatement*'s definition of impossibility, for example, includes: (*a*) destruction of the agency subject matter, (*b*) termination of the principal's interest in the agency subject matter (as, for example, by the principal's bankruptcy), and (*c*) changes in the law or in other circumstances that make it impossible for the agent to accomplish the agency's aims.

**12.** *A serious breach of the agent's duty of loyalty.*

**13.** *The outbreak of war*—where this leads the agent to the reasonable belief that his services are no longer desired. An example might be the outbreak of war between the principal's country and the agent's country.

## Termination of Agency Powers Given as Security

An agency power given as security for a duty owed by the principal, sometimes called an *agency coupled with an interest,* is an exception to some of the termination rules just discussed. Here, the agent has an interest in the subject matter of the agency that is distinct from the principal's interest and that is not exercised for the principal's benefit. This interest exists to benefit the agent or a third person by securing performance of an obligation owed by the principal. A common example is a secured loan agreement authorizing a lender (the agent) to sell property used as security if the debtor (the principal) defaults. For instance, suppose that Allen lends Peters $100,000 and Peters gives Allen a lien or security interest on Peters's land to secure the loan. The agreement might authorize Allen to act as Peters's "agent" to sell the land if Peters fails to repay the loan.

Because the power given the "agent" in such cases is not for the principal's benefit, it is sometimes said that an agency coupled with an interest is not truly an agency. In any event, courts distinguish it from genuine agency relations in which the agent is compensated from the profits or proceeds of property held for the principal's benefit. For example, if an agent is promised a commission for selling the principal's property, the relationship is not an agency coupled with an interest. Here, the power exercised by the agent (selling the principal's property) benefits the principal. The following *Smith* case provides another example.

Why is the agency coupled with an interest important? The main reason is that it is *not terminated* by: (1) the principal's revocation, (2) the principal's or the agent's loss of capacity, (3) the agent's death, and (4) (usually) the principal's death. However, unless an agency coupled with an interest is held for the benefit of a third party, the agent can voluntarily surrender it. Of course, an agency

---

**FIGURE 2**   Termination of an Agent's Authority after Termination of the Agency

| Type of Termination | Actual Authority | Apparent Authority |
|---|---|---|
| **By Acts of the Parties** | Ceases | Persists unless appropriate notice or notification to third party |
| **By Operation of Law** | Ceases | Ceases if termination by principal's death or loss of capacity, or by impossibility; persists in other cases unless appropriate notice or notification to third party |

---

coupled with an interest terminates when the principal performs her obligation.

## Effect of Termination on Agent's Authority

Sometimes, former agents continue to act on their ex-principals' behalf even though the agency has ended. Do such "agents" still have authority to bind their former principals? As Figure 2 states, once an agency terminates by any of the means just described, the agent's *express* and *implied* authority end as well.

Third parties who are unaware of the termination, however, may reasonably believe that an ex-agent still has authority. To protect third parties who rely on such a reasonable appearance of authority, an agent's *apparent authority* often persists after termination. Thus, a former agent may be able to bind the principal under his apparent authority even though the agency has ended. But as Figure 2 also states, apparent authority ends where the termination was caused by: (1) the *principal's death*, (2) the *principal's loss of capacity,* or (3) *impossibility.*[8] Note from the previous discussion that certain other bases for termination may also end the agent's apparent authority because they fit within the broad category of impossibility.

---

[8]*Restatement (Second) of Agency* § 124A, comment *a*; and § 133 (1959). Subject to certain exceptions; moreover, § 132 of the *Restatement (Second)* says that the apparent authority of a *special agent* terminates along with termination of the agency.

**Notice to Third Parties**   Apparent authority ends when the third party receives appropriate *notice* of the termination. In general, any facts known to the third party that reasonably indicate the agency's termination constitute suitable notice. Some bases for termination by operation of law (e.g., changed business conditions) may provide such notice.

To protect themselves against unwanted liability, however, prudent principals may want to notify third parties themselves. The required type of notification varies with the third party in question.

**1.** *For third parties who have previously dealt with the agent or who have begun to deal with the agent,* **actual notification** *is necessary.* This can be accomplished by: (*a*) a direct personal statement to the third party; or (*b*) a writing delivered to the third party personally, to his place of business, or to some other place reasonably believed to be appropriate.

**2.** *For all other parties,* **constructive notification** *suffices.* Usually, these other parties are aware of the agency but did no business with the agent. Constructive notification can normally be accomplished by advertising the agency's termination in a newspaper of general circulation in the place where the agency business is regularly carried on. If no suitable publication exists, notification by other means reasonably likely to inform third parties—for example, posting a notice in public places—may suffice.

## SMITH V. CYNFAX CORPORATION
### 618 A.2d 937 (N.J. Super. Ct. 1992)

Brenda Smith was injured by a falling ceiling in a building owned by the Cynfax Corporation. She retained Floyd Goldsman as her attorney, and Goldsman sued Cynfax on her behalf. On February 4, 1992, Cynfax's insurer, the Cumberland Mutual Fire Insurance Company, made Smith a $7,000 settlement offer through Goldsman. Goldsman immediately tried to inform Smith of the offer, but learned that she had died on February 2.

Goldsman later accepted Cumberland's offer to Smith. Still later, Cumberland refused to pay Smith's estate the $7,000. Smith's estate then moved to enforce the alleged settlement agreement. One issue before the court was whether Goldsman had authority to accept Cumberland's offer on Smith's behalf.

---

**Yanoff, Judge**    As Mrs. Smith's attorney, Goldsman was an agent of his client. For Goldsman to have accepted the settlement offer, his agency must have survived the death of his client. Goldsman's agency immediately ceased when his client died. It makes no difference that the settlement negotiations were undertaken in good faith and in ignorance of Smith's death. A general principle of agency is that the death of the principal terminates the authority of the agent. Knowledge of the principal's death only becomes an issue where the agency is derived from a written power of attorney [citing a New Jersey statute].

An agency coupled with an interest survives the principal, even after notice of his death. This requires that the agent have some interest, such as a security interest, in the subject-matter of the agency independent of the power conferred upon him by the principal. An interest merely in the proceeds which will arise from the exercise of the power of the agency is not sufficient for this purpose. Goldsman's agency was controlled by an agreement which provided that "the law firm will protect your legal rights and do all necessary legal work to represent you in this matter" in exchange for a percentage contingency fee. This created an interest in the proceeds of a successful exercise of the powers of the agency, not in its subject-matter. An attorney's contingent fee contract creates an agency which is not coupled with an interest and which terminates upon the death of the principal.

**Motion of Smith's estate denied; Cumberland wins.**

---

### PROBLEMS AND PROBLEM CASES

**1.** Joan Marie Ottensmeyer was a contestant for the title of Miss Hawaii-USA 1974. The pageant was run by Richard You as a franchisee of Miss Universe, Inc. After finishing as first runner-up, Ottensmeyer sued Miss Universe, arguing that as its agent You had prevented her from winning a title to which she was rightfully entitled and from obtaining the benefits thereof. The franchise agreement between Miss Universe and You explicitly stated that You was not Miss Universe's agent. By itself, is this statement sufficient to prevent the formation of an agency relationship between Miss Universe and You?

**2.** Norman Finnegan purchased a 1986 Lincoln town car from Tri-County Auto Group, Inc., for $8,093. The purchase agreement provided "30-day interest-free finance." At the time of the sale, Finnegan also completed an installment payment finance agreement with General Motors Acceptance Corporation (GMAC). Later, within the 30-day period, Finnegan paid Tri-County the entire balance due on the car. Previously, GMAC had allowed customers to pay off its installment contracts through dealerships in this fashion. Generally, the dealership would then send a check to GMAC to complete the payment.

Rather than forwarding Finnegan's lump-sum payment to GMAC, however, Tri-County began to pay GMAC Finnegan's monthly installments under the contract. After making four such payments, Tri-County became insolvent. GMAC then sued Finnegan for the balance due on the contract. Finnegan argued that Tri-County was GMAC's agent for the purpose of collecting payment, that Tri-County had authority to collect his payment, and that payment to Tri-County therefore was payment to GMAC. Did Tri-County have apparent authority to receive Finnegan's payment for GMAC? Assume that at the time he paid Tri-County, Finnegan was aware of GMAC's practice of letting installment contract customers pay the balance through the dealership.

**3.** 🎞 *Video Case.* See "In the Cards." Jack runs a video card shop. Linda, who knows little or nothing about baseball or baseball cards, agreed to run the shop for Jack while he went out for dinner. Jack told Linda that she could sell any card for the price marked on the card. Then, he pointed to a case containing the more expensive cards, and said that he might negotiate the price on those cards if customers would wait until he returned. Shortly after Jack left, Linda sold a small boy an Ernie Banks rookie card for $12. The card bore a price sticker that stated: "1200." The boy apparently was unaware of the card's true value and did not try to negotiate its price. Did Linda have express, implied, or apparent authority to sell the card for $12? In any event, on what bases might Jack sue her for his losses?

**4.** 🎞 *Video Case.* "See Martin Manufacturing." Mr. Martin, the president of Martin Manufacturing, fires a purchasing agent named Mitch. The reason is that Mitch has been taking kickbacks from suppliers. Martin also withholds Mitch's last paycheck until Martin can determine how much Mitch's misbehavior has cost him.

Has Mitch breached any fiduciary duty or duties to Martin? If so, which ones? Will Mitch be required to give Martin the amount of any kickbacks he has received? Can Martin fire Mitch without incurring liability under these circumstances? Finally, is Martin justified in withholding Mitch's paycheck?

**5.** Mark and Roberta Murray purchased a single-family home. Some time after they moved in, cracks appeared at various places in the house, and the Murrays eventually discovered that its foundation was defective. They sued the real estate broker who had represented them in the purchase, arguing that he breached his duty of care and skill by failing to conduct a reasonable investigation of the house. Did their broker owe the Murrays such a duty? Assume that the *seller's* broker had a duty to make such an inspection and to disclose to the purchaser all facts materially affecting the value or desirability of the house.

**6.** Ted and Sharon Markland arranged for a trip to the Virgin Islands with Travel Travel Southland, Inc. Travel Travel made the necessary arrangements with Eastern Airlines, which was having financial problems. The Marklands then paid Travel Travel $6,548 for the trip. There was conflicting testimony as to whether Travel Travel warned the Marklands about Eastern's difficulties, and for purposes of this question assume that it did not. It is also unclear how much the Marklands knew about Eastern's troubles, but assume that they had at least a general knowledge of them.

Ten days after the Marklands reached the Virgin Islands, their hotel informed them that their reservations were no longer valid because Eastern had not paid for them and (due to its declaring bankruptcy) most likely would not. The Marklands wound up having to pay the hotel an additional $4,900, and also had to expend another $1,756 for a return flight to the United States. Afterwards, they sued Travel Travel for failing to advise them about Eastern's precarious position. Did Travel Travel breach either its duty of care and skill or its duty to notify?

**7.** In February 1989, Thomas Fix arranged for a Florida vacation package for himself and his sister with Travel Help, a travel agency. The travel agent selected an Eastern Airlines package that included Eastern vouchers for a rental car, Howard Johnson's Fountain Park, and Sea World. Aware of the labor and other problems Eastern was experiencing at that time, Fix's sister contacted the agent several times requesting that all the arrangements be made with another airline. The agent assured her that the flights could be changed and that the vouchers would be honored. After Eastern went into bankruptcy on March 9, 1989, the agent arranged for Fix and his sister to be transported to Florida on a different airline.

After they arrived, however, the providers of the voucher bookings refused to honor Eastern's vouchers. Did the agent breach a duty to Fix (and his sister)? If so, which one? You can assume that the travel agent was acting for both Fix and his sister, and that the communications to the agent by Fix's sister were communications to an agent by his principal.

**8.** Southeastern Agri-Systems, Inc., was an agent for Otto Niederer. James Stanford was Agri-Systems' president and sole employee. Niederer instructed Stanford to accept payment for the sale of some equipment owned by Niederer, to deduct his commission from the payment, and to wire the remainder to Niederer. Instead, Stanford diverted the funds to his own purposes and refused to pay Niederer the amount due. When sued individually for breach of the agent's duty to obey, Stanford argued that Niederer had employed Agri-Systems as its agent, that he was merely an employee of Agri-Systems, and that he thus owed no duty to Niederer. Is Stanford correct?

**9.** Stanley Mazur owned an Oldsmobile Cutlass and a small Subaru pickup truck. He asked his insurance agent, Ken Curtis, to arrange "full coverage" on the truck similar to the coverage on his Cutlass. Although the policy on the Cutlass included personal injury protection, Curtis negligently failed to include such protection in the policy he obtained for the Subaru. Later, Mazur suffered personal injury from an accident in which he was involved while driving the Subaru. Because the policy did not cover such injury, he was unable to recover for it from the insurer, the Selected Risks Insurance Company.

Mazur recovered against Curtis for Curtis's failure to procure the requested coverage. Curtis then sued to have Selected indemnify him for this loss. Is Selected required to indemnify Curtis? Why or why not? Assume that Curtis was acting as an agent for Selected as well as for Mazur.

**10.** 📼 *Video Case.* See "Martin Manufacturing." Immediately after being fired by Martin Manufacturing in Problem Case 4 above, Mitch decides to squeeze one last bit of profit from his relationship with Martin. Thus, he calls a customer with whom he has dealt on many occasions, and orders several cases of fasteners on Martin's behalf. Later, he resells the fasteners himself, pocketing the money. Is Martin liable to the supplier for the fasteners? In any event, what should Martin do to protect itself in cases like this one?

## CAPSTONE QUESTIONS

Biggers, a wealthy investor, had been aggressively acquiring land for investment purposes in the southeast corner of state X. He hired Jim Bales, a local broker, as his agent to make the land purchases. Jim was well known throughout the area, and both Biggers's activities and Jim's role in advancing them attracted considerable local attention.

One of Jim's duties was to recommend suitable properties to Biggers. Unknown to Biggers, one of the properties recommended and ultimately purchased by Jim for Biggers was owned by Jim himself. This deal, which occurred on June 1, 1994, was for the price of $1 million. Assume that Jim had express authority to make the purchase.

Soon thereafter, Biggers discovered what Jim had done. Thus, on June 5, he unilaterally told Jim that he was terminating the agency. Then Biggers immediately gave written notification of this action to every third party with whom Jim had had any business contacts on his behalf. However, he did nothing else to announce the agency's termination. On June 9, Jim contracted for Biggers to buy 100 acres of land from Thompson for $750,000. Like everyone else in the area, Thompson knew that Jim had been buying land on Biggers's behalf. However, he knew nothing about Biggers's attempt to terminate the agency, and reasonably believed that Jim still had authority to buy land for Biggers. Biggers, on the other hand, did not know that Thompson existed.

### Required:

Answer the following and give reasons for your conclusion.

1. Jim argues that even though he may have behaved unethically when he convinced Biggers to buy land Jim owned, Biggers still is bound to the contract. Is he right? Again, assume that Jim had express authority to make the contract.
2. Did the agency really terminate by June 5?
3. Assuming for the sake of argument that the agency had terminated by June 5, is Biggers still bound to the June 9 contract with Thompson?

# CHAPTER

**28**

# THIRD-PARTY RELATIONS OF THE PRINCIPAL AND THE AGENT

## INTRODUCTION

*By letting principals contract through their agents and thereby multiply their dealings, agency law stimulates business activity. For this process to succeed, there must be rules for determining when the principal and the agent are liable on the agent's contracts. Principals need to predict and control their liability on agreements their agents make. Also, third parties need assurance that such agreements really bind the principal. Furthermore, both agents and third parties have an interest in knowing when an agent is bound on these contracts. The first half of this chapter discusses the principal's and the agent's contract liability.*

*While acting on the principal's behalf, agents sometimes harm third parties in various ways. Normally, this makes the agent liable to the injured party in tort. Sometimes, moreover, a principal is liable for his agent's torts. Because tort judgments can be expensive, the rules for determining the principal's and the agent's tort liability are of great concern to principals, their agents, and third parties. Thus, we examine these subjects in this chapter's second half.*

## CONTRACT LIABILITY OF THE PRINCIPAL

A principal is normally liable on a contract made by his agent if the agent had **express, implied, or apparent authority** to make the contract. Occasionally, however, a principal's contract liability may be affected by other factors. Even where the agent lacked authority to contract, moreover, a principal may bind herself by later **ratifying** the agent's contract.

### Express Authority

As discussed in Chapter 27, **express authority** is created by a principal's *words* to his agent, whether written or oral. Thus, an agent has express authority to bind her principal to a particular contract if the principal clearly told the agent that she could make that contract on the principal's behalf. For example, suppose that Payne instructs his agent Andrews to contract to sell a specific antique chair for $400 or more. If Andrews contracts to sell the chair to

Tucker for $425, Payne is liable to Tucker on the basis of Andrews's express authority. However, Andrews would not have express authority to sell the chair for $375, or to sell a different chair.

## Implied Authority

Often, it is difficult or impossible for a principal to specify his agent's authority completely and precisely. Thus, agents also can bind their principals on the basis of the agent's **implied authority.** As Chapter 27 states, an agent generally has implied authority to do whatever it is reasonable to assume that his principal wanted him to do, in light of the principal's express statements and the surrounding circumstances. Relevant factors include the principal's express statements, the nature of the agency, the acts reasonably necessary to carry on the agency business, the acts customarily done when conducting that business, and the relations between principal and agent.

Implied authority often derives from a grant of express authority or some other express statement by the principal. Ordinarily, an agent has implied authority to make those contracts that are reasonably necessary for conducting the business he has been expressly authorized to perform, or that are customarily made in conducting that business. Implied authority, however, cannot conflict with the principal's express statements. Thus, there is no implied authority to contract where a principal has limited her agent's authority by express statement or clear implication and the contract would conflict with that limitation.

On occasion, implied authority may exist even though there is no relevant grant of express authority. Here, courts generally derive implied authority from the nature of the agency business, the relations between principal and agent, customs in the trade, and other facts and circumstances. For example, there may be implied authority to make a certain contract if the agent has made similar past contracts with the principal's knowledge and without his objection.

**Examples of Implied Authority**    Courts have created general rules or presumptions for determining the implied authority of certain agents in certain situations. For example:

**1.** An agent hired to *manage a business* normally has implied authority to make those contracts that are reasonably necessary for conducting the business or that are customary in the business. These include contracts for obtaining equipment and supplies, making repairs, employing employees, and selling goods or services. However, a manager has no power to borrow money or issue negotiable instruments in the principal's name unless the principal is a banking or financial concern regularly performing such activities.

**2.** An agent given *full control over real property* has implied authority to contract for repairs and insurance, and may rent the property if this is customary. But such an agent may not sell the property or allow any third-party liens or other interests to be taken on it.

**3.** Agents appointed to *sell the principal's goods* may have implied authority to make customary warranties on those goods. In states that still recognize the distinction, the *general agent* described in Chapter 27 is more likely to have such authority than a *special agent*.

## Apparent Authority

As discussed in Chapter 27, **apparent authority** arises when the *principal's behavior* causes a third party to form a *reasonable belief* that the agent is authorized to act in a certain way. Principals can give their agents apparent authority through the statements they make, or tell their agents to make, to third parties, and through the actions they knowingly allow their agents to take. Background factors such as trade customs and established business practices often determine whether it is reasonable for the third party to believe such manifestations of authority. For instance, if a principal appoints his agent to a position such as general manager that customarily involves the power to make certain contracts, the agent normally has apparent authority to make those contracts. Here, the principal's behavior in appointing the agent to the position, as reasonably interpreted in light of business customs, creates apparent authority in the agent. This is true even if the principal expressly told the agent not to make such contracts, so long as this limitation remains unknown to the third party. Because agents cannot give themselves apparent authority, however, there would be no such authority if an agent falsely told third parties that he had been promoted to general manager without the principal's knowledge or permission.

Established business customs can help create apparent authority in other ways as well. For example, an agent can often bind his principal to forbidden promises that customarily accompany contracts the agent actually is authorized to complete, if the third party is unaware that the promises were forbidden. In states that still recognize the distinction, general agents are more likely to have this kind of apparent authority than are special agents. Suppose that Perry employs Arthur as general sales agent for his manufacturing business. Certain warranties customarily accompany the products Perry sells, and agents like Arthur are ordinarily empowered to give these warranties. But Perry tells Arthur not to make any such warranties to buyers, thus cutting off Arthur's express and implied authority. Despite Perry's orders, however, Arthur makes the usual warranties in a sale to Thomas, who is familiar with customs in the trade. If Thomas did not know about the limitation on Arthur's authority, Perry is bound by Arthur's warranties.

Finally, apparent authority may exist where a principal has, to the knowledge of a third person, permitted his agent to make contracts that the agent was expressly forbidden to make. Suppose Potter has told Abram, the manager of his business, to hire loaders for his trucks for no more than one day at a time. No one else knows about this limitation on Abram's actual authority. With Potter's knowledge and without his objection, however, Abram frequently has employed loaders by the week. Then Abram agrees to employ Trapp as a loader for a week. If Trapp knew about the earlier employment by the week, Potter would be bound to the one-week employment contract on the basis of Abram's apparent authority.

## Other Factors Affecting a Principal's Contract Liability

**Agent's Notification and Knowledge**  Sometimes the general agency rules regarding *notification* and *knowledge* affect a principal's contract liability. If a third party gives proper notification to an agent with actual or apparent authority to receive it, the principal is bound as if the notification had been given directly to him. For example, where a contract between Phillips and Thomas made by Phillips's agent Anderson contains a clause allowing Thomas to cancel if she notifies Phillips, she can cancel by notifying Anderson if Anderson has actual or apparent authority to receive the notification. Similarly, notification *to* a third party *by* an agent with the necessary authority is considered notification by the principal.

In certain circumstances, an agent's knowledge of certain facts is imputed to the principal. This means

that the principal's rights and liabilities are what they would have been if the principal had known what the agent knew. Generally, an agent's knowledge is imputed to a principal when it is relevant to activities that the agent is authorized to undertake, or when the agent is under a duty to disclose the knowledge to the principal. Suppose that Ames contracts with Timmons on Pike's behalf, knowing that Timmons is completely mistaken about a matter material to the contract. Even though Pike knew nothing about Timmons's unilateral mistake, Timmons probably can avoid his contract with Pike.[1]

**Incapacity of Principal or Agent**  As discussed in Chapter 27, a principal who lacks capacity at the time an agency is formed may usually avoid the agency, and a principal's permanent loss of capacity after the agency's formation terminates the agency. Where the agency continues to exist, is a minor or a person of limited mental capacity bound on contracts made by his agent? Subject to the exceptions discussed in Chapter 6, such contracts are voidable at the principal's option. These contracts would normally be voidable if made by the principal himself, and it is difficult to see why acting through an agent should increase the principal's capacity.

Like the principal, an agent can avoid the agency agreement if she lacks capacity at the time it is formed. Where the agency survives, however, the agent's incapacity usually does *not* affect the contract liability of a principal who has capacity. Just as an agent cannot increase the principal's capacity, neither can she diminish it. However, the principal may sometimes escape liability where an agent's incapacity is so extreme that the agent cannot receive or convey ideas, or cannot follow the principal's instructions.

## Ratification

Ratification is a process whereby a principal binds himself to an unauthorized act done by an agent or by a person purporting to act as an agent. Ratification relates back to the time when the act was performed. For contracts, its effect is to bind the principal as if the agent had possessed authority at the time the contract was made.

**Conduct Amounting to Ratification**  Ratification can be express or implied. An *express ratification*

---

[1]Unilateral mistake is discussed in Chapter 5.

occurs when the principal communicates an intent to ratify by written or oral words to that effect. *Implied ratification* arises when the principal's behavior evidences an intent to ratify. Part performance of the agent's contract by a principal or a principal's acceptance of benefits under the contract may work an implied ratification. Sometimes even a principal's silence, acquiescence, or failure to repudiate the transaction may constitute ratification. This can occur where the principal would be expected to object if he did not consent to the contract, the principal's silence leads the third party to believe that he does consent, and the principal is aware of all relevant facts.

**Additional Requirements**   Even if a principal's words or behavior indicate an intent to ratify, other requirements must be met before ratification occurs. These requirements have been variously stated; the following list is typical.

1. The act ratified must be one that was *valid* at the time it was performed. For example, an agent's illegal contract cannot be made binding by the principal's subsequent ratification. However, a contract that was voidable when made due to the principal's incapacity may be ratified by a principal who has later attained or regained capacity.

2. The principal must have been *in existence* at the time the agent acted. However, as discussed in Chapter 34, corporations may bind themselves to their promoters' preincorporation contracts by adopting such contracts.

3. When the act to be ratified occurred, the agent must have indicated to the third party that she was acting for *a* principal and not for herself. But the agent need not have disclosed the principal's identity.

4. The principal must be *legally competent* at the time of ratification. For instance, an insane principal cannot ratify.

5. The principal must have *knowledge* of all material facts regarding the prior act or contract at the time it is ratified. Here, an agent's knowledge is not imputed to the principal. In the following *Adams* case, the principal did not ratify because it lacked sufficient knowledge.

6. The principal must ratify the *entire* act or contract. He cannot ratify the beneficial parts of a contract and reject those that are detrimental.

7. In ratifying, the principal must use the *same formalities* required to give the agent authority to execute the transaction. As Chapter 27 related, few formalities are normally needed to give an agent authority. But where the original agency contract requires a writing, ratification likewise must be written.

**Intervening Events**   Certain events occurring after an agent's contract but before the principal's ratification may cut off the principal's power to ratify. These include: (1) the third party's *withdrawal* from the contract; (2) the third party's *death* or *loss of capacity*; (3) the principal's *failure to ratify within a reasonable time* (assuming that the principal's silence did not already work a ratification); and (4) *changed circumstances* (especially where the change places a greater burden on the third party than he assumed when the contract was made).

---

### ADAMS V. LOUISIANA COCA-COLA BOTTLING CO.
#### 531 So. 2d 501 (La. Ct. App. 1988).

Rosia Adams, an employee at a Jefferson Parish School Board warehouse, was injured when she slipped on a wet floor at the warehouse. The floor was wet because it had been mopped to clean a spill from a malfunctioning Coca-Cola vending machine leased to the school board by the Louisiana Coca-Cola Bottling Company (Coca-Cola). A warehouse inventory clerk signed the lease on behalf of the school board.

Adams sued Coca-Cola for her injuries. Coca-Cola then filed a third-party action against the school board, alleging that under the terms of the lease the school board was required to indemnify and insure Coca-Cola against injuries to employees like Adams. After trial, Adams obtained a jury verdict against Coca-Cola, and the trial judge dismissed Coca-Cola's claim against the school board. Coca-Cola then appealed the trial judge's decision dismissing its claim against the school board.

---

**Ciaccio, Judge**   The question is whether the school board is obligated under the lease. The clerk who signed the lease did not have express authority to do so. Whether he had implied authority, the other component of actual authority, is determined by inference from the circumstances, purposes, and nature of the agency. An agent is invested with the implied authority to do all those things necessary or incidental to the accomplishment of the purpose of the agency. Coca-Cola argues that the clerk was empowered with general authority to operate the warehouse. Such a mandate confers only a power of administration. The proof does not establish any particular circumstances, purposes, or nature of the agency beyond receiving and inventorying goods delivered to the warehouse. We do not find therein any implied authority to agree to indemnify and insure the lessor of a vending machine placed on the premises.

For apparent authority to apply, the principal must first act to manifest the agent's authority to [a] third party. Second, the third party must rely reasonably on the manifested authority of the agent. In support of its argument for the clerk's apparent authority to execute this lease on behalf of the board, Coca-Cola relies on the following facts. The clerk has worked for the school board for twenty years. During this time he has always handled soft drink vending machines on the premises. Either he or another school board employee initially contacted Coca-Cola to have a machine installed at the warehouse. The school board's representative admitted that employees all over the school board system were signing similar leases. He also admitted that some of the seven thousand school board employees have previously bound the school board without formal authorization.

There is no indication that the school board acted to manifest authority for the clerk to execute this lease. There is no evidence that the school board knew of the lease, much less its provisions. The board's role was passive; it apparently paid no attention to the vending machines on its premises. We do not find that this passiveness manifested authority in its employees to agree to indemnify and insure the lessor of these machines.

Further, we find unreasonable any reliance by Coca-Cola upon any perception of authority in the clerk. Coca-Cola did not inquire into the nature and extent of the clerk's authority. Agreeing to indemnify and insure Coca-Cola as lessor requires greater authority than one would reasonably perceive to be vested in an inventory clerk.

Coca-Cola finally argues that the school board ratified the lease by permitting the machine to remain at the warehouse, permitting another machine to be placed there, and [later] permitting over one hundred other machines to be placed at various other school board locations under similar lease conditions. There is no indication that the school board was aware that the machines were being leased, that the leases were being executed in its name, or that the leases contained onerous provisions that the board indemnify and insure Coca-Cola as lessor. We do not find the board's permitting the presence of the machines to be a ratification of the lease provisions confected by Coca-Cola.

**Judgment in favor of the school board on Coca-Cola's third-party claim affirmed.**

## Contracts Made by Subagents

The rules governing a principal's liability for her agent's contracts generally apply to contracts made by her subagents. If an agent has authorized his subagent to make a certain contract and this authorization is within the authority granted the agent by his principal, the principal is bound to the subagent's contract. Suppose that Peters employs the Ajax Company to sell certain personal property while she is out of the country, with the understanding that one of Ajax's agents will handle the sale from start to finish. If Ajax authorizes its agent Sampson (Peters's subagent) to contract to sell the property and Sampson does so, Peters is bound to the contract.

Because the relationship between agent and subagent closely resembles the relationship between principal and agent, a subagent acting within the authority conferred by her principal (the agent) can bind the *agent* in contract. Finally, although the authorities do not clearly address the subject, both the principal and the agent can probably ratify the contracts of subagents.

## Contract Liability of the Agent

An *agent's* liability on contracts he makes for the principal usually depends on a different set of factors than the factors determining the principal's liability.[2] The most important of these variables is the *nature of the principal*. Thus, this section first examines the liability of agents who contract for several distinct kinds of principals. Then it discusses two ways that an agent can be bound after contracting for almost any type of principal—by agreeing to be liable, or by contracting without the necessary authority.

### The Nature of the Principal

**Disclosed Principal**     A principal is **disclosed** if a third party knows or has reason to know: (1) that the agent is acting for a principal, and (2) the principal's identity. Unless he agrees otherwise, an agent who represents a disclosed principal is *not liable* on authorized contracts made for such a principal. Suppose that Adkins, a sales agent for Parker, calls on Thompson and presents a business card clearly identifying her as Parker's agent. If Adkins contracts to sell Parker's goods to Thompson with authority to do so, Adkins is not bound because Parker is a disclosed principal. This rule is usually consistent with the third party's intentions; for example, Thompson probably intended to contract only with Parker. In the following *Cahn* case, the agents were bound even though they

contracted for a disclosed principal, because they had impliedly agreed to be bound.

**Partially Disclosed Principal**     A principal is **partially disclosed** if the third party: (1) knows or has reason to know that the agent is acting for *a* principal, but (2) lacks knowledge or reason to know the principal's *identity*. This can occur where an agent simply neglects to disclose his principal's identity. Also, a principal may tell her agent to keep her (the principal's) identity secret to preserve her bargaining position.

Among the factors affecting anyone's decision to contract are the integrity, reliability, and creditworthiness of the other party to the contract. Where the principal is partially disclosed, the third party ordinarily cannot judge these matters. As a result, he usually depends on the agent's reliability to some degree. For this reason, and to give the third party additional protection, an agent is liable on contracts made for a partially disclosed principal unless the parties agree otherwise.

**Undisclosed Principal**     A principal is **undisclosed** where the third party lacks knowledge or reason to know *both* the principal's existence and the principal's identity. This can occur where a principal judges that he will get a better deal if his existence and identity remain secret, or where the agent simply neglects to make adequate disclosure.

A third party who deals with an agent for an undisclosed principal obviously cannot assess the principal's reliability, integrity, and creditworthiness. Indeed, here the third party reasonably believes that the *agent* is the other party to the contract. Thus, an agent is liable on contracts made for an undisclosed principal.

---

[2]The rules stated here should generally govern the contract liability of subagents as well as agents. See *Restatement (Second) of Agency* § 361 (1959).

---

## Cahn v. Fisher
### 805 P.2d 1040 (Ariz. Ct. App. 1991)

H. Richmond Fisher and Francis Smith, two attorneys, ordered three deposition transcripts from Harry Cahn and Conrad Blain, two court reporters. The attorneys did so as part of some litigation work they were performing for two clients. Fisher and Smith did not tell Cahn and Blain that they were acting on their clients' behalf when ordering the transcripts; nor did they specifically identify their clients to the court reporters. Presumably, however, the depositions contained a caption identifying those clients and suggesting that Fisher and Smith were acting in a representative capacity.

After the lawyers placed their order with Cahn and Blain, their clients went bankrupt. Thus, they did not pay the reporters' $579.95 bill for the transcripts. Cahn and Blain then sued Fisher and Smith for this amount.

Later, they moved for summary judgment. Included in their summary judgment motion was another court reporter's affidavit stating that it was the "custom and usage" of local court reporters to bill and extend credit to lawyers rather than their clients. The trial court granted the reporters' summary judgment motion, and the lawyers appealed.

---

**Lankford, Judge**    The lawyers argue that agency law protects an agent from liability on a contract entered into on behalf of a disclosed principal. Unless otherwise agreed, a person making or purporting to make a contract with another as agent for a disclosed principal does not become a party to the contract. Disclosure of the principal requires that the agent give the other party both notice that the agent is acting for a principal and the principal's identity. Reasonable inferences can be drawn that the court reporters were aware that the lawyers were ordering the transcripts not for themselves but on behalf of their clients, and that the reporters were aware of the clients' identities. Under these circumstances, agency law precludes a judgment resting on the theory that lawyers are generally liable on a contract with court reporters.

While the lawyers ordinarily would not be bound under agency law to a contract entered into on behalf of their disclosed principals, the parties were certainly free to agree otherwise. In this case, the court reporters attempted to show that "custom and usage" between court reporters and lawyers is that the lawyers are directly liable for the reporters' fees. Court reporters might also be able to establish such liability by proof of a course of dealing between the parties. The lawyers argued below that the affidavit offered by the reporters was insufficient to show custom and usage. However, they abandoned that argument on appeal and we therefore decline to consider the sufficiency of the affidavit. [This] evidence of custom and usage was uncontroverted. It showed that the parties' understanding was that the lawyers would be responsible for paying the reporters. This evidence fully sustains the [trial] court's entry of summary judgment against the lawyers.

**Judgment for Cahn and Blain affirmed.**

---

**Nonexistent Principal**    In the absence of an agreement to the contrary, an agent who purports to act for a **legally nonexistent** principal such as an unincorporated association is personally liable. This is true even where the third party knows that the principal is nonexistent.[3]

**Principal Lacking Capacity**    As stated earlier, a principal who lacks contractual capacity due to insanity or infancy can avoid contracts made by his agent. In this case, the *agent* also escapes liability unless: (1) she misrepresents the capacity of her principal, or (2) she has reason to believe that the third party is unaware of the principal's incapacity and she fails to disclose this. Also, unless the parties agree otherwise, an agent is liable on contracts made for a *wholly incompetent* principal such as a person who has been adjudicated insane.

## Liability of Agent by Agreement

An agent may bind herself on contracts she makes for a principal by *expressly or impliedly agreeing* to be liable. This is true regardless of the principal's nature. An agent may expressly bind herself by: (1) making the contract in her own name rather than in the principal's name, (2) joining the principal as an obligor on the contract, or (3) acting as surety or guarantor for the principal.

Problems of contract interpretation can arise when it is claimed that an agent has expressly promised to be bound. The two most important factors affecting the agent's liability are the wording of the contract and the way the agent has signed it. An agent who wishes to avoid liability should make

---

[3]For a closely analogous situation, see Chapter 34's discussion of a promoter's liability on contracts made for a corporation before it comes into existence.

no express promises in her own name and should try to ensure that the agreement only obligates the principal. In addition, the agent should use a signature form that clearly identifies the principal and indicates the agent's representative capacity—for example, "Parker, by Adkins," or "Adkins, for Parker." Simply adding the word "agent" when signing her name (Adkins, Agent) or signing without any indication of her status (Adkins) could subject the agent to liability. Sometimes, as in the following *Wired Music* case, the body of the agreement suggests one result and the signature form another. Here, and generally, oral evidence or other extrinsic evidence of the parties' understanding may help resolve the uncertainty.[4]

---

[4]However, the introduction of such evidence may be blocked by the parol evidence rule. See Chapter 8.

---

## WIRED MUSIC, INC. v. GREAT RIVER STEAMBOAT CO.
### 554 S.W.2d 466 (Mo. Ct. App. 1977)

A sales representative of Wired Music, Inc., sold Frank Pierson, president of the Great River Steamboat Company, a five-year Muzak Program Service for a riverboat and restaurant owned by Great River. Pierson signed a form contract drafted by Wired Music in the following manner:

By /s/ Frank C. Pierson, Pres.

    Title

The Great River Steamboat Co.

~~Port of St. Louis Investments, Inc.~~

For the Corporation

In signing, Pierson crossed out "Port of St. Louis Investments, Inc.," which had been incorrectly listed as the name of the corporation, and inserted the proper name. The contract included the following clause arguably making Pierson a surety or guarantor for Great River: "The individual signing this agreement for the subscriber guarantees that all of the above provisions shall be complied with."

Great River made approximately four payments under the contract and then ceased to pay. Wired Music brought an action for contract damages against Pierson personally. The trial court ruled in Pierson's favor, and Wired Music appealed.

---

**Gunn, Judge**   The general rule regarding liability incurred by an individual who signs an instrument on behalf of another party is: where the principal is disclosed and the capacity in which the individual signs is evident, e.g., president, secretary, agent, the liability is the principal's and not that of the individual signing for the principal. Of course, where the circumstances surrounding the transaction disclose a mutual intention to impose personal responsibility on the individual executing the agreement, the individual may be personally liable even though the form of the signature is that of the agent.

The determinative issue here is whether, in view of the form of the signature to the agreement, the language of the so-called guaranty clause is sufficient to manifest a clear and explicit intent by Pierson to assume a personal guaranty contract. We hold that standing alone it does not. The contract language imposing a personal obligation is inconsistent with the form of execution, which positively limited Pierson's participation to his official corporate capacity and not as an individual. Such inconsistency creates at least a latent ambiguity which permits the admission of parol evidence to explain the true intent of the parties.

Pierson has stressed that he neglected to read the contract prior to its signing. One who signs a contract is presumed to have known its contents and accepted its terms. Thus, Pierson's failure to examine the terms of the instrument would afford no defense to the corporation regarding its obligations under the contract, as his signature was sufficient to bind the corporation. Such neglect *is* a relevant circumstance, however, in ascertaining Pierson's intent to assume personal liability, as his personal signature appeared nowhere on the instrument. Without knowledge of the guaranty clause he could not have possessed the requisite intent to assume

obligations under it. The record is destitute of any indication that Pierson was ever made aware of potential personal liability under the guaranty clause, and he steadfastly denied any such knowledge. Wired Music drafted the contract, and its agents procured Pierson's corporate signature without explanation of or bargaining over its terms. Under these circumstances we find that there was an absence of the meeting of the minds as to the nature and the extent of the personal obligations imposed, essential to the formation of a binding guaranty.

**Judgment for Pierson affirmed.**

## Agent's Liability on Unauthorized Contracts

An agent may also become liable to a third party if he contracts for the principal while *lacking authority* to do so. Here, the principal is not bound, and it is arguably unfair to leave the third party without any recovery. Thus, an agent is normally bound on the theory that he made an implied warranty of his authority to contract.[5] This liability exists regardless of whether the agent is otherwise bound to the third party.

To illustrate, suppose that Allen is a salesperson for Prine, a seller of furs. Allen has actual authority to receive offers for the sale of Prine's furs, but not to make contracts of sale, which must be approved by Prine himself. Prine has long followed this practice, and it is customary in the markets where his agents work. Representing himself as Prine's agent but saying nothing about his authority, Allen contracts to sell Prine's furs to Thatcher on Prine's behalf. Thatcher, who should have known better, honestly believes that Allen has authority to contract to sell Prine's furs. Prine is not liable on Allen's contract because Allen lacked actual or apparent authority to bind him. But Allen is liable

to Thatcher for breaching his implied warranty of authority.

However, an agent is *not* liable for making an unauthorized contract if:

**1.** The third party *actually knows* that the agent lacks authority. However, note from the Allen-Prine example that the agent is still liable where the third party only had *reason to know* that authority was lacking.

**2.** The principal subsequently *ratifies* the contract. Here, the principal is bound and the agent is discharged. Because ratification relates back to the time the contract was made, the relation of the parties is the same as if the agent had possessed authority in the first place.

**3.** The agent adequately *notifies* the third party that he does not warrant his authority to contract.

## CONTRACT SUITS AGAINST PRINCIPAL AND AGENT

Figure 1 sketches the most important situations where the principal, the agent, or both are liable due to the agent's contracts. As it suggests, a third party usually has *someone* to sue if neither the principal nor the agent performs.

Without ratification, a principal is not liable on contracts made by an agent who lacks authority. Here, though, the agent is usually bound under an implied warranty of authority. In addition, the agent is bound on the contract where the principal was partially disclosed, undisclosed, or legally nonexis-

---

[5]An agent who intentionally misrepresents his authority also may be liable to the third party in tort. In addition, some states may allow tort liability for negligent misrepresentations. Where the third party has a tort suit, he may often elect to recover damages or to rescind the contract.

---

**FIGURE 1**    Contract Liability of Principal and Agent: The Major Possibilities

| Principal | Agent's Authority | | |
|---|---|---|---|
| | **Actual** | **Apparent** | **None** |
| **Disclosed** | P liable; A not liable unless agreement | P liable; A not liable unless agreement | P not liable; A usually liable |
| **Partially Disclosed** | P liable; A liable | P liable; A liable | P not liable; A liable |
| **Undisclosed** | P liable; A liable | Impossible | P not liable; A liable |

---

tent.[6] Authorized contracts for a disclosed principal do not bind an agent unless he has agreed to be bound. But here the agent's actual or apparent authority binds the principal.

As Figure 1 further illustrates, in certain situations both the principal and the agent are liable on a contract made by the agent. This can occur where an agent with appropriate authority contracts on behalf of a partially disclosed or undisclosed principal. Also, an agent can bind himself by express or implied agreement in situations where the principal is also bound. In such cases, which party is ultimately responsible to the third person? The complicated rules governing this question vary from situation to situation. Due to their complexity and variety, they are beyond the scope of this text.

## TORT LIABILITY OF THE PRINCIPAL

A principal's liability for her agent's torts involves four distinct subjects, which we consider in turn.[7]

### Respondeat Superior Liability

Under the doctrine of *respondeat superior* (let the master answer), a principal who is an **employer** is liable for torts committed by agents who are **employees** and who commit the tort while acting within the **scope of their employment.** This doctrine applies to an employee's negligence, recklessness, or intentional torts. Chapter 27 outlined the main factors courts consider when determining whether an agent is an employee.[8] The most important of these factors is a principal's right to control the physical details of an agent's work.

*Respondeat superior* is a rule of *imputed* or *vicarious* liability because it bases an employer's liability on his relationship with the employee rather than his own fault. This imputation of liability reflects the following beliefs: (1) that the economic burdens of employee torts can best be borne by employers; (2) that employers can often protect themselves against such burdens by self-insuring or purchasing insurance; and (3) that the resulting costs can frequently be passed on to consumers, thus "socializing" the economic risk posed by employee torts. *Respondeat superior* also motivates employers to ensure that their employees avoid tortious behavior. Because they typically control the physical details of the work, employers are fairly well positioned to do so.

---

[6]Note, however, that it is impossible for an agent for an undisclosed principal to have apparent authority. Apparent authority exists when the principal's communications to the third party cause that party to reasonably believe that the agent has authority to contract for another. How can this occur when the principal is undisclosed?

[7]In addition to the various forms of tort liability discussed in this section, a principal can also *ratify* an agent's torts. Furthermore, the *Restatement* says that the rules governing a principal's liability for an agent's torts generally control a principal's liability for the torts of *subagents*. *Restatement (Second) of Agency* § 255 (1959).

[8]Recall from Chapter 27 that this text follows the *Restatement (Second) of Agency* by treating all employees as agents. Independent contractors, on the other hand, may or may not be agents.

**Scope of Employment**   *Respondeat superior*'s scope-of-employment requirement has been stated in many ways and is notoriously ambiguous. In the past, for example, some courts considering this question asked whether the employee was on a "frolic" of his own, or merely made a "detour" from his assigned activity. According to the *Restatement*,[9] an employee's conduct is within the scope of his employment if it meets *each* of the following four tests:

**1.** It was of the *kind* that the employee was employed to perform. To meet this test, an employee's conduct need only be of the same general nature as work expressly authorized, or be incidental to its performance. For instance, the following *Gatzke* case treats on-the-job smoking as an act incidental to an employee's authorized work. But an employee hired only to care for his employer's horses is probably not within the scope of employment if he paints the employer's house without the employer's authorization.

Even criminal conduct may occasionally be within the scope of employment. Here, the test seems to be whether the employer could reasonably anticipate the criminal behavior in question. Thus, a delivery driver who exceeds the speed limit while on a rush job is probably covered, but a driver who shoots another driver after a traffic altercation almost certainly is not.

**2.** It occurred substantially within the authorized *time* period. This is simply the employee's assigned time of work. Beyond this, there is an extra period of time during which the employment may con-

tinue. For instance, a security guard whose regular quitting time is 5:00 probably meets the time test if he unjustifiably injures an intruder at 5:15. Doing the same thing three hours later, however, would put the guard outside the scope of employment.

**3.** It occurred substantially within the *location* authorized by the employer. This includes locations not unreasonably distant from the authorized location. For example, a salesperson told to limit her activities to New York City probably would satisfy the location requirement while pursuing the employer's business in suburbs just outside the city limits but not while pursuing the same business in Philadelphia. Generally, the smaller the authorized area of activity, the smaller the departure from that area needed to put the employee outside the scope of employment. For example, consider the different physical distance limitations that should apply to a factory worker and a traveling salesperson.

**4.** It was motivated *at least in part* by the *purpose* of serving the employer. This test is met where the employee's conduct was motivated *to any appreciable extent* by the desire to serve the employer. Thus, an employee's tort may be within the scope of employment even if the motives for committing it were partly personal. For example, suppose that a delivery employee is behind schedule and for that reason has an accident while speeding to make a delivery in his employer's truck. The employee would be within the scope of employment even if another reason for his speeding was to impress a friend who was riding with him.

In the following *Gatzke* case, all four *Restatement* tests were met and the employer was liable. In applying those tests, was the court influenced by a desire to see the plaintiff recover?

[9]*Restatement (Second) of Agency* § 228(1) (1959). This section adds that if an employee intentionally uses force on another, this must have been "not unexpectable" by the employer to be within the scope of employment.

---

# Edgewater Motels, Inc. v. Gatzke
**277 N.W.2d 11 (Minn. Sup. Ct. 1979)**

A. J. Gatzke, a district manager for the Walgreen Company, spent several weeks in Duluth, Minnesota, supervising the opening of a new Walgreen restaurant there. He remained at the restaurant approximately 17 hours a day, and he was on call 24 hours a day to handle problems arising in other Walgreen restaurants in the district. While in Duluth, he lived at the Edgewater Motel at Walgreen's expense. After some heavy drinking late one night, Gatzke returned to his motel room and spent some time at a desk filling out an expense account required by his employer. Gatzke was a heavy smoker, and he testified that he probably smoked a cigarette while completing the expense account. Shortly after Gatzke went to bed, a fire broke out in his motel room. Gatzke escaped, but fire damage to the motel totaled over $330,000. An expert witness testified that the fire was caused by a burning cigarette or a match and that it started in or near a wastebasket located beside the desk at which Gatzke worked.

Edgewater sued Walgreen for Gatzke's negligence. The jury found for Edgewater, in the process concluding that Gatzke acted within the scope of his employment when he filled out the form and disposed of the cigarette. The trial court, however, granted Walgreen's motion for judgment notwithstanding the verdict. Edgewater appealed. The question for the appellate court was whether Gatzke's negligent conduct occurred within the scope of his employment.

---

**Scott, Justice**   Gatzke's negligent smoking of a cigarette was a direct cause of the damages sustained by Edgewater. The question is whether the facts reasonably support the imposition of vicarious liability on Walgreen's for the conceded negligent act of its employee.

For an employer to be held vicariously liable for an employee's negligent conduct, the employee's wrongful act must be committed within the scope of his employment. To support [such] a finding, it must be shown that his conduct was, to some degree, in furtherance of the interests of his employer. This principle is recognized by *Restatement (Second) of Agency* section 235, which states: "An act of a servant is not within the scope of employment if it is done with no intention to perform it as a part of or incident to a service on account of which he is employed." Other factors to be considered in the scope-of-employment determination are whether the conduct is of the kind that the employee is authorized to perform and whether the act occurs substantially within authorized time and space restrictions.

The question is whether an employee's smoking of a cigarette can constitute conduct within his scope of employment. The courts which have considered the question have not agreed on its resolution. A number of courts have ruled that the act of smoking, even when done simultaneously with work-related activity, is not within the employee's scope of employment because it is a matter personal to the employee which is not done in furtherance of the employer's interest. Other courts have reasoned that the smoking of a cigarette, if done while engaged in the business of the employer, is within an employee's scope of employment because it is a minor deviation from the employee's work-related activities, and thus merely in-

cidental to employment. We agree with this analysis and hold that an employer can be vicariously liable for an employee's negligent smoking of a cigarette if he was otherwise acting in the scope of his employment at the time of the negligent act.

Thus, we must next determine whether Gatzke was otherwise in the scope of his employment at the time of his negligent act. Even assuming that Gatzke was outside the scope of his employment while he was at the bar, Gatzke resumed his employment activities after he returned to his motel room and filled out his expense account. The expense account was completed so that Gatzke could be reimbursed by Walgreen's for his work-related expenses. In this sense, Gatzke is performing an act for his own personal benefit. However, the completion of the expense account also furthers the employer's business in that it provides detailed documentation of business expenses so that they are properly deductible for tax purposes. In this light, the filling out of the expense form can be viewed as serving a dual purpose: that of furthering Gatzke's personal interests and promoting his employer's business purposes. Accordingly, the completion of the expense account is an act done in furtherance of the employer's business purposes.

Additionally, the record indicates that Gatzke was an executive type of employee who had no set working hours. He considered himself a 24-hour-a-day man; his room at the Edgewater Motel was his "office away from home." It [is] therefore reasonable to determine that the filling out of his expense account was done within authorized time and space limits of his employment.

**Judgment reversed in favor of Edgewater.**

## Direct Liability

As the following *Victory Tabernacle* case makes clear, a principal's **direct liability** for an agent's torts differs considerably from *respondeat superior* liability. Here, the principal *himself* is at fault, and there is no need to impute liability to him. Also, no scope-of-employment requirement exists in direct liability cases, and the agent need not be an employee. Of course, a principal might incur both direct liability and *respondeat superior* liability in cases where due to the principal's fault, an employee commits a tort within the scope of her employment.

A principal is directly liable for an agent's tortious conduct if the principal *directs* that conduct and *intends* that it occur. In such cases, the *agent's* behavior might be intentional, reckless, or negli-gent. For instance, if Petty tells his agent Able to beat up Tabler and Able does so, Petty is directly liable to Tabler. Petty also would be liable for harm to third parties that results from his telling Able to do construction work in a negligent, substandard fashion.

The typical direct liability case, however, involves harm caused by the principal's *negligence* regarding the agent. Examples of direct liability for negligence include: (1) giving the agent improper or unclear instructions; (2) failing to make and enforce appropriate regulations to govern the agent's conduct; (3) hiring an unsuitable agent; (4) failing to discharge an unsuitable agent; (5) furnishing an agent with improper tools, instruments, or materials; and (6) carelessly supervising an agent.

---

## J. v. VICTORY TABERNACLE BAPTIST CHURCH
### 372 S.E.2d 391 (Va. Sup. Ct. 1988)

A woman sued the Victory Tabernacle Baptist Church, alleging that due to its negligence her 10-year-old daughter had been repeatedly raped and sexually assaulted by a church employee. The plaintiff's complaint claimed that when the church hired the employee, it knew or should have known that he had recently been convicted of aggravated sexual assault on a young girl, that he was on probation for this offense, and that a condition of his probation was that he not be involved with children. Despite all this, the complaint continued, the employee's duties allowed him to freely come into contact with children, including the plaintiff's daughter, and he was given keys enabling him to lock and unlock all the church's doors.

The complaint alleged (among other things) negligent hiring on the church's part. The church filed a demurrer to the complaint, and the trial court sustained the demurrer. The plaintiff appealed this decision, and the case reached the Virginia Supreme Court.

---

**Thomas, Justice**  We decide only whether the allegations of negligent hiring state a cause of action in Virginia. Victory Baptist argues that the trial court properly sustained the demurrer on [this] question because plaintiff failed to allege that the harm to the victim was caused by negligence on the part of the employee. According to this argument, the negligent hiring cause of action requires that the negligently hired individual negligently injured the plaintiff. We disagree. The very thing that allegedly should have been foreseen in this case is that the employee would commit a violent act upon a child. To say that a negligently hired employee who acts willfully or criminally thus relieves his employer of liability for negligent hiring when willful or criminal conduct is precisely what the employer should have foreseen would rob the tort of vitality.

Victory Baptist also argues that the [plaintiff's] allegations do not establish a sufficient nexus among the employer's breach of duty, the employee's conduct, and the employee's employment. In oral argument, counsel explained that there were no allegations that the employee was engaged in the church's business when the child was injured—no allegation, for example, that the employee was on duty for the church at the time the girl was raped.

Counsel then made clear that what he was complaining about was that there were no allegations to bring the employee's conduct within the scope of his employment.

This argument demonstrates that Victory Baptist is confusing the doctrine of *respondeat superior* with the tort of negligent hiring. This distinction was succinctly stated in a recent law review article:

Under *respondeat superior,* an employer is vicariously liable for an employee's tortious acts committed within the scope of employment. In contrast, negligent hiring is a doctrine of primary liability; the employer is principally liable for negligently placing an unfit person in an employment situation involving an unreasonable risk of harm to others. Negligent hiring, therefore, enables plaintiffs to recover in situations where *respondeat superior's* scope of employment limitation previously protected employers from liability.

Thus, Victory Baptist's contention is misplaced.

In our opinion, the [complaint] was fully sufficient to state a claim of negligent hiring, and thus it was error for the trial court to sustain the demurrer on that issue.

**Judgment for the church on the negligent hiring claim reversed. Case remanded for trial consistent with the Supreme Court's opinion.**

## Liability for Torts of Independent Contractors

A principal ordinarily is *not* liable for torts committed by **independent contractors.** As compared with employees, independent contractors are more likely to have the size and resources to insure against tort liability and to pass on the resulting costs themselves. Sometimes, therefore, the risk can still be socialized if only the independent contractor is held responsible. Because the principal does not control the manner in which an independent contractor's work is performed, moreover, he has less ability to prevent a contractor's torts than an employer has to prevent an employee's torts. Thus, imposing liability on principals for the torts of independent contractors may do little to eliminate the contractor's torts.

However, the rule that principals are not liable for torts committed by independent contractors has exceptions. For example:

**1.** A principal can be *directly* liable for tortious behavior connected with the retention of an independent contractor. One example is the hiring of a dangerously incompetent independent contractor.

**2.** A principal is liable for harm resulting from the independent contractor's failure to perform a *nondelegable duty.* A nondelegable duty is a duty whose proper performance is so important that a principal cannot avoid liability by contracting it away. Examples include a carrier's duty to transport its passengers safely, a municipality's duty to keep its streets in repair, a railroad's duty to maintain safe crossings, and a landlord's duties to make repairs and to use care in doing so. Thus, a landlord who retains an independent contractor to repair the stairs in an apartment building is liable for injuries caused by the contractor's failure to repair the stairs properly.

**3.** A principal is liable for an independent contractor's negligent failure to take the special precautions needed to conduct certain *highly dangerous* or *inherently dangerous* activities.[10] Examples of such activities include excavations in publicly traveled areas, the clearing of land by fire, the construction of a dam, and the demolition of a building. For example, a contractor engaged in demolishing a building presumably has duties to warn pedestrians and to keep them at a safe distance. If injury results from the independent contractor's failure to meet these duties, the principal is liable.

## Liability for Agent's Misrepresentations

A principal's liability for misrepresentations made by agents to third parties involves both contract and tort principles.[11] A principal is *directly* liable for

---

[10]The range of activities considered "highly dangerous" or "inherently dangerous" is probably greater than the range of activities considered "ultrahazardous" or "abnormally dangerous" for strict liability purposes.

[11]On fraud and misrepresentation in the contract context, see Chapter 5.

misrepresentations made by her agent during authorized transactions if she *intended* that the agent make the misrepresentations. In some states, a principal may also be directly liable if she *negligently* allows the agent to make misrepresentations.

Even where a principal is not directly at fault, she may be liable for an agent's misrepresentations if the agent had *actual or apparent authority to make true statements on the subject.* Suppose that an agent to sell farmland falsely states that a stream on the land has never flooded the property when in fact it does so almost every year, and that this statement induces a third party to buy the land. The principal is directly liable if she intended that the agent make this false statement. Even if the principal is personally blameless, she is liable if the agent had actual or apparent authority to make true statements about the spring.

If the agent intended to make the misrepresentation, or if the principal intended that the agent make it, the third party can recover in tort for the losses

that result. In some states, a third party may also recover in tort for misrepresentations resulting from the principal's or the agent's negligence. In either case, the third party can elect to rescind the transaction instead of pursuing a tort suit.

**Exculpatory Clauses**  Both honest and dishonest principals may try to escape liability for an agent's misrepresentations by including an exculpatory clause in contracts the agent makes with third parties. Such clauses typically state that the agent only has authority to make the representations contained in the contract and that only those representations bind the principal. Exculpatory clauses do not protect a principal who intends or expects that an agent will make false statements. Otherwise, though, they insulate the principal from *tort* liability if the agent misrepresents. But the third party still may *rescind* the transaction, because it would be unjust to let the principal benefit from the transaction while disclaiming responsibility for it.

### CONCEPT REVIEW
## AN OUTLINE OF THE PRINCIPAL'S TORT LIABILITY

| | |
|---|---|
| *Respondeat Superior* | 1. Agent must be an employee, *and* <br> 2. Employee must act within scope of employment while committing tort |
| **Direct Liability** | 1. Principal intends and directs agent's intentional tort, recklessness, or negligence, *or* <br> 2. Principal is negligent regarding agent |
| **Torts of Independent Contractors** | 1. Principal generally is *not* liable <br> 2. Exceptions for direct liability, highly dangerous activities, and nondelegable duties |
| **Misrepresentation** | 1. Direct liability <br> 2. Vicarious liability where agent had authority to make true statements on the subject of the misrepresentation <br> 3. An exculpatory clause may eliminate the principal's tort liability, but the third party still can rescind |
| **Torts of Subagents** | The preceding rules govern the principal's liability, but their application varies |

## TORT LIABILITY OF THE AGENT

Agents are usually liable for their own torts.[12] Normally, they are not absolved from liability just

because they acted at the principal's command. However, there are exceptions to this generalization.

**1.** An agent can escape liability if she is *exercising a privilege of the principal.* Suppose that Tingle grants Parkham a right-of-way to transport his farm products over a private road crossing Tingle's land. Parkham's agent Adams would not be liable in

---

[12]The rules stated in the previous section generally govern an agent's liability for torts committed by his subagents. *Restatement (Second) of Agency* § 362 (1959).

trespass for driving across Tingle's land to transport farm products if she did so at Parkam's command. However, an agent must not exceed the scope of the privilege and must act for the purpose for which the privilege was given. Thus, Adams would not be protected if she took her Jeep on a midnight joyride across Tingle's land. Also, the privilege given the agent must be delegable in the first place. If Tingle had given the easement to Parkham exclusively, Adams would not be privileged to drive across Tingle's land.

**2.** A principal who is *privileged to take certain actions in defense of his person or property* may often authorize an agent to do the same. In such cases, the agent escapes liability if the principal could have done so. For example, a properly authorized agent may use force to protect the life or property of his principal if the principal could have done the same.

**3.** An agent who makes *misrepresentations* while conducting the principal's business is not liable in tort unless he either *knew or had reason to know* their falsity. Suppose Parker authorizes Arnold to sell his house, falsely telling Arnold that the house is fully insulated. Arnold does not know that the statement is false, and could not discover its falsity through a reasonable inspection. If Arnold tells Thomas that the house is fully insulated and Thomas relies on this statement in purchasing the house, Parker is directly liable to Thomas, but Arnold is not liable.

**4.** An agent is not liable for injuries to third persons caused by *defective tools or instrumentalities* furnished by the principal unless the agent had actual knowledge or reason to know of the defect.

## TORT SUITS AGAINST PRINCIPAL AND AGENT

Both principal and agent are sometimes liable for an agent's torts. Here, the parties are *jointly and severally* liable. This means that a third party may join the principal and the agent in one suit and get a judgment against each, or may sue either or both individually and get a judgment against either or both. However, once a third party actually collects in full from either the principal or the agent, no further recovery is possible.

In some cases, therefore, either the principal or the agent has to satisfy the judgment alone despite the other party's liability. Here, the other party is sometimes required to *indemnify* the party who has satisfied

the judgment. As discussed in Chapter 27, for example, sometimes a principal is required to indemnify an agent for tort liability the agent incurs. On the other hand, some torts committed by agents may involve a breach of duty to their principal, and the principal may be able to recover from an agent on this basis.

**PROBLEMS AND PROBLEM CASES**

**1.** The Capital Dredge and Dock Corporation sued the city of Detroit for damages associated with certain construction work it had been performing for the city. One of the city's defenses was that Capital had released the city from liability on some of Capital's present claims during earlier, related litigation between Capital and the city. The releases were part of a settlement document signed by Capital Dredge's attorney, Alteri. Capital Dredge had held Alteri out as having authority to represent it in the relevant litigation, and this included authority to negotiate a settlement. However, unknown to the city, Capital Dredge had also specifically told Alteri not to compromise some of the claims he later settled. Under these circumstances, could Alteri have had implied authority to settle the claims in question? Could he have had apparent authority to do so?

**2.** Jeff Hartman, a hauler of hay, contracted to purchase Larry Draper's entire 1988 alfalfa hay crop. According to that contract, Hartman had to pay in advance for any hay taken from Draper's farm. Later, Hartman approached Cecil Hilt about buying some of the hay crop Hartman had purchased. Hartman told Hilt that the hay was from Draper's farm, but he did not say that he was acting as Draper's agent. Nonetheless, Hilt believed that Hartman was acting on Draper's behalf. On July 5, 1988, Hilt agreed to buy 400 tons of hay at $60 per ton. As part of the deal, he wrote a $3,000 check payable to Draper as a deposit. Hartman then gave the check to Draper, who indorsed and cashed it.

Much later, Hartman found himself unable to produce the money needed to get Hilt's hay from Draper. Draper eventually sold the hay to another party, and Hilt sued Draper for breach of contract. Assuming for the sake of argument that Hartman was Draper's agent, did Hartman have apparent authority to bind Draper to the deal with Hilt?

**3.** Roma Funk, who co-owned a piece of land along with her seven brothers and sisters, contracted to sell the land to her neighbors. It was unclear whether Funk had authority to sell the land on behalf of her siblings. For certain, there was no writing giving her such authority. Funk's siblings eventually backed out of the deal, and the buyers sued for specific performance. They argued that Funk's siblings had ratified her contract by failing to come forward and repudiate it. Can a contract ever be ratified in this way? Regardless of your answer to this question, there is another reason why Funk's siblings could not have ratified this particular contract. What is it? Assume that in this state an agent who executes an agreement conveying an interest in land on behalf of his principal must be authorized in writing.

**4.** Seascape Restaurants, Inc., operated a restaurant called The Magic Moment. Jeff Rosenberg was one-third owner and president of Seascape. Van D. Costas, the president of Van D. Costas, Inc., contracted to construct a "magical entrance" to the Magic Moment. Jeff Rosenberg signed the contract on a line under which appeared the words "Jeff Rosenberg, the Magic Moment." The contract did not refer to Seascape, and Costas knew nothing of Seascape's existence. After a dispute over performance of the contract, Costas sued Rosenberg for breach of contract. Is Rosenberg personally liable to Costas?

**5.** Dale F. Everett did business as the Dale F. Everett Company, Inc. (the Company). He also formed a retail business known as The Clubhouse, which had no legal status aside from its registration as a trade name for the Company. Everett contracted with James Smith for $8,424 of advertising time. Everett signed his contract with Smith as follows: "THE CLUBHOUSE, Client, By Dale F. Everett." Smith later sent billing statements for the ads to "The Clubhouse, Inc." Everett never paid Smith the $8,424, and Smith sued Everett personally. Is Everett personally liable on the contract with Smith?

**6.** ▶️  *Video Case.*  See "Martin Manufacturing." Mr. Martin, the president of Martin Manufacturing, was talking with Arnold, a new traveling salesman, about Arnold's first week on the road. Arnold told Martin that he hit one of Martin's customers in the customer's store, causing the customer some physical harm. The blow came after Arnold and the customer got into an argument, during which the customer ordered Arnold out of his store. In striking the customer, Arnold was motivated at least in part by a feeling that no Martin employee should have to endure such disrespect.

Shortly after this, Martin also learned from Arnold that Arnold had gotten into an accident while driving a company van. The accident came after Arnold negligently ran a stop sign while thinking about the fight. The driver of the other car was seriously injured in the accident.

Assuming that Arnold is an employee, is Martin liable to the customer for any battery Arnold committed, and to the driver of the car for Arnold's negligence?

**7.** Redford had been a backhoe operator for five years. Although he had worked for other sign companies, he had spent 90 percent of his time during the past three years working for Tube Art Display, Inc. Redford generally dug holes exactly as directed by the sign company employing him. He did, however, pay his own business taxes, and he did not participate in any of the fringe benefits available to Tube Art employees.

Tube Art obtained a permit to install a sign in the parking lot of a combination commercial and apartment building. Telling Redford how to proceed, Tube Art's service manager laid out the exact location of a 4 × 4-foot square on the asphalt surface with yellow paint and directed that the hole be 6 feet deep. After Redford began the job, he struck a small natural gas pipeline with the backhoe. He examined the pipe, and, finding no indication of a leak or break, concluded that the line was not in use and left the worksite. Later, an explosion and fire occurred in the building serviced by the line. As a result, a business owned by Massey was destroyed. Massey sued Tube Art for Redford's negligence under the doctrine of *respondeat superior.* Will Massey recover? Assume that Redford was negligent.

**8.** John Hondzinski delivered newspapers in his own car for a newspaper called the *News Herald.* Under the contract between Hondzinski and the *News Herald,* Hondzinski was obligated to pick up and promptly deliver newspapers provided by the *News Herald,* but the means and the routes for doing so were within Hondzinski's control. While making deliveries for the *News Herald* one day, Hondzinski negligently allowed his car to collide with a car driven by Peter Janice. Janice sued the *News Herald* for Hondzinski's negligence. Can Janice recover against the *News Herald* under the doctrine of *respondeat superior*? Why or why not?

**9.** William Smith was employed by P&M Heating and Air Conditioning, Inc., as a service technician. Smith normally worked a 40-hour week. P&M

provided Smith with a service van containing the tools he used in his work. P&M allowed Smith to drive his van home after work, keep it there overnight, call in to P&M to receive his first job assignment each morning, and travel to that assignment in the van.

On July 23, 1986, Smith worked a normal eight-hour day, finishing at 4:00 P.M. After Smith drove the van home and had dinner, his stepdaughter called to tell him that she was having problems with her home air-conditioning unit. As a favor to his stepdaughter, Smith, accompanied by his wife, drove the van to the stepdaughter's home to check out the unit. He did not tell P&M about this work, he did not fill out a customer receipt or any other paperwork for it, and P&M apparently never billed his stepdaughter for it. Smith finished working on his stepdaughter's unit about 10:45 P.M. After that, he took a swim in her pool. About midnight, Smith and his wife left for home. At about 1:00 A.M., the P&M van driven by Smith collided with a vehicle driven by Anthony S. Giannoble, killing Giannoble.

Assuming that the collision was due to Smith's negligence, is P&M liable to Giannoble's estate for that negligence? Assume that Smith was an employee of P&M.

**10.** Susie Mae Woodson's husband was killed due to a cave-in at a construction site where he was laying sewer pipe in a trench dug by an independent contractor of Davidson & Jones, Inc. (D&J). The trench in which Mr. Woodson was working had not been braced or shored to prevent a cave-in, and this was a violation of federal occupational safety regulations. Mrs. Woodson sued D&J for the independent contractor's negligence. Will she recover? Assume that D&J was not in any way *directly* liable regarding the independent contractor.

**11.** Edward J. Opatz maintained an investment account with John G. Kinnard and Company. Byron Jensen, a Kinnard broker, handled Opatz's account. In January 1985, Jensen told Opatz that he would buy three fourths of a $24,000 investment unit if Opatz would buy the remaining fourth. Relying on this statement and believing that the transaction was within Jensen's authority, Opatz gave Jensen a $6,000 check payable to Jensen. One week later, Jensen admitted to Opatz that he had never purchased the unit, and gave Opatz a personal check for $6,000. Still later, the check bounced and Jensen disappeared. Is Kinnard liable to Opatz for the $6,000? Assume that: (1) Jensen's statement that he

would invest the $6,000 was actionable fraud, (2) Kinnard was not directly liable for Jensen's behavior, and (3) Kinnard did not expressly or impliedly authorize Jensen's statements to Opatz.

## CAPSTONE QUESTIONS

Phillips hired Anderson to run his pet store. Phillips gave Anderson detailed instructions for the conduct of his responsibilities and expected him to follow them. Because Anderson was experienced in the business, however, Phillips gave him broad authority to buy animals for the store. Soon enough, though, Anderson began to abuse his authority, buying all kinds of weird and expensive animals for the store. Finally, Phillips told Anderson: "Don't buy anything Ozzie and Harriet wouldn't want, and don't pay more than $1,000 for it."

Anderson restrained himself for a while, but his will finally failed when he saw a beautiful rattlesnake offered for sale by Thomas for $1,500. To get Thomas to lower his price, Anderson pretended to be buying the snake for himself. Thomas knew Anderson only casually, and he was unaware of Phillips's existence or of the agency relationship between Phillips and Anderson. Eventually, Anderson bought the snake on credit from Thomas for $1,150 and brought it back to Phillips's store, where he put it in a cage. A few minutes later, while following Phillips's previous instructions to clean up the store, Anderson inadvertently opened the door to the snake's cage. A few minutes after that, the snake bit Calbert Customer, who had come on the premises to buy some goldfish. Customer nearly died as a result of the bite. All relevant events occurred during regular store hours.

### Required:

Answer the following and give reasons for your conclusions. If it matters, assume that the price for the snake was reasonable. Also, assume that Anderson would be liable in negligence to Calbert.

1. Is Phillips contractually liable to Thomas on the snake-purchase agreement?

2. Is Anderson contractually liable to Thomas on the snake-purchase agreement?

3. Is Phillips liable to Calbert for Anderson's negligence?

# PARTNERSHIPS

# CHAPTER

## 29

# INTRODUCTION TO FORMS OF BUSINESS AND FORMATION OF PARTNERSHIPS

**INTRODUCTION**

*In this chapter, you begin your study of business organizations. Early in this chapter, you will preview the basic characteristics of the most important forms of business and learn how to select an appropriate form for a business venture. Following that introduction, you will begin your in-depth study of partnerships, learning their characteristics and the formalities for their creation.*

## CHOOSING A FORM OF BUSINESS

One of the most important decisions made by a person beginning a business is choosing a **form of business**. This decision is important because the business owner's liability and control of the business vary greatly among the many forms of business. In addition, some business forms offer significant tax advantages to their owners.

Although other forms of business exist, usually a person starting a business will wish to organize the business as a sole proprietorship, partnership, limited liability partnership, limited partnership, corporation, or limited liability company.

### Sole Proprietorship

A **sole proprietorship** has only one owner. The sole proprietorship is merely an extension of its only owner, the **sole proprietor**.

As the only owner, the sole proprietor has the right to make all the management decisions of the business. In addition, all the profits of the business are his. A sole proprietor assumes great liability: He is personally liable for all the obligations of the business. All the debts of the business, including debts on contracts signed only in the name of the business, are his debts. If the assets of the business are insufficient to pay the claims of its creditors, the creditors may require the sole proprietor to pay the claims using his individual, nonbusiness assets such as money from his bank account and the proceeds from the sale of his house. A sole proprietor may lose everything if his business becomes insolvent. Hence, the sole proprietorship is a risky form of business for its owner.

Despite this risk, there are two reasons why a person may organize a business as a sole proprietorship. First, the sole proprietorship is formed very easily and inexpensively. No formalities are necessary. Second, few people consider the business form decision. They merely begin their businesses. Thus, by default, a person going into business by herself automatically creates a sole proprietorship when she fails to choose another business form. These two reasons explain why the sole proprietorship is the most common form of business in the United States.

Because the sole proprietorship is merely an extension of its owner, it has no life apart from its owner. Therefore, while the business of a sole proprietorship may be freely sold to someone else, legally the sole proprietorship as a form of business cannot be transferred to another person. The buyer of the business must create his own form of business to continue the business.

A sole proprietorship is not a legal entity. It cannot sue or be sued. Instead, creditors must sue the owner. The sole proprietor—in his own name—must sue those who harm the business.

A sole proprietor may hire employees for the business, but they are employees of the sole proprietor. Under the law of agency, the sole proprietor is responsible for her employees' authorized contracts and for the torts they commit in the course of their employment. Also, a sole proprietorship is not a tax-paying entity for federal income tax purposes. All of the income of a sole proprietorship is income to its owner and must be reported on the sole proprietor's individual federal income tax return. Likewise, any business losses are deductible without limit on the sole proprietor's individual tax return. This loss-deduction advantage explains why some wealthier taxpayers use the sole proprietorship for selected business investments—when losses are expected in the early years of the business, yet the risk of liability is low. Such an investor may form a sole proprietorship and hire a professional manager to operate the business.

Many sole proprietorships have trade names. For example, Caryl Stanley may operate her bagel shop under the name Caryl's Bagel Shop. Caryl would be required to file the trade name under a state statute requiring the registration of fictitious business names. If she were sued by a creditor, the creditor would address his complaint to "Caryl Stanley, doing business as Caryl's Bagel Shop."

## Partnership

A **partnership** has two or more owners, called **partners.** The partners have the right to make all the management decisions for the business. In addition, all the profits of the business are shared by the partners.

The partners assume personal liability for all the obligations of the business. All the debts of the business are the debts of all the partners. Likewise, partners are liable for the torts committed in the course of business by their partners or by partnership employees. If the assets of the business are insufficient to pay the claims of its creditors, the creditors may require one or more of the partners to pay the claims using their individual, nonbusiness assets. Thus, a partner may have to pay more than his share of partnership liabilities.

Like the sole proprietorship, the partnership is not a tax-paying entity for federal income tax purposes. All of the income of the partnership is income to its partners and must be reported on the individual partner's federal income tax return. Likewise, any business losses are deductible without limit on the partner's individual tax return.

The partnership has no life apart from its owners. When a partner dies or otherwise leaves the business, the partnership is dissolved. A partner's ownership interest in a partnership is not freely transferable: A purchaser of the partner's interest is not a partner of the partnership, unless the other partners agree to admit the purchaser as a partner.

Why would persons organize a business as a partnership? Formation of a partnership requires no formalities and may be formed by default. A partnership is created automatically when two or more persons own a business together without selecting another form. Also, each partner's right to manage the business and the deductibility of partnership losses on individual tax returns are attractive features.

## Limited Liability Partnership

Reacting to the large personal liability sometimes imposed on lawyers and accountants for the professional malpractice of their partners, Texas enacted in 1991 the first statute permitting the formation of **limited liability partnerships (LLP).** An LLP is similar to a partnership, except that a partner's liability for his partners' professional malpractice is limited to the partnership's assets; a partner retains unlimited liability for his *own* malpractice and for all *non*professional obligations of the partnership.

An LLP is managed by its partners, who have equal say in the business of the partnership, unless they agree otherwise. An LLP has no life apart from its partners, and a partner's ownership interest in an LLP is not freely transferable: The purchaser will not be a partner of the partnership, unless the other partners agree that the purchaser may join the LLP.

The Internal Revenue Service has privately indicated that LLPs will be taxed like partnerships: the partnership pays no federal income tax; instead each partner reports his share of the LLP's profits and losses on his individual federal income tax return.

The formation of an LLP requires filing a form with the secretary of state and maintaining adequate professional liability insurance for the firm.

The LLP is an especially good form of business for professionals such as accountants, allowing them flexibility of management, while insulating them in part from personal liability. As more states adopt LLP statutes, the LLP will become the preferred form of business for professionals who do not incorporate. As of February 1994, four states and the District of Columbia had passed LLP statutes.

## Limited Partnership

A **limited partnership** has one or more general partners and one or more limited partners. General partners have rights and liabilities similar to partners in a partnership. They manage the business of the limited partnership and have unlimited liability for the obligations of the limited partnership. Typically, however, the only general partner is a corporation, thereby protecting the human managers from unlimited liability.

Because the limited partnership is not a taxpaying entity for federal income tax purposes, general partners report their shares of the limited partnership's income and losses on their individual federal income tax returns. For general partners, losses of the business are deductible without limit.

Limited partners usually have no liability for the obligations of the limited partnership once they have paid their capital contributions to the limited partnership. Limited partners have no right to manage the business and may lose their limited liability for the business's obligations if they do manage the business.

A limited partner must pay federal income tax on his share of the profits of the business, but he may deduct his share of losses only to the extent of his investment in the business. As a passive investor, a limited partner may use the losses only to offset income from other passive investments.

A limited partnership may have a life apart from its owners. When a limited partner dies or otherwise leaves the business, the limited partnership is not dissolved. When a general partner dies or withdraws, however, the limited partnership is dissolved in the absence of a contrary agreement. A general or limited partner's rights may not be wholly transferred to another person unless the other partners agree to admit the new person as a partner.

Unlike a sole proprietorship or partnership, a limited partnership may be created only by complying with a state statute permitting limited partnerships. Thus, no limited partnership may be created by default.

There are three main reasons why persons organize a business as a limited partnership. First, by using a corporate general partner, no human will have unlimited liability for the debts of the business. Second, losses of the business are deductible on the owners' federal income tax returns. Third, investors may contribute capital to the business yet avoid unlimited liability and the obligation to manage the business. Thus, the limited partnership has the ability to attract large amounts of capital, much more than the sole proprietorship, which has only one owner, or the partnership, whose partners' fear of unlimited liability restricts the size of the business. Hence, for a business needing millions of dollars of capital and expecting to lose money in its early years, the limited partnership is a particularly good form of business.

## Corporation

A **corporation** is owned by shareholders who elect a board of directors to manage the business. The board of directors often selects officers to run the day-to-day affairs of the business. Consequently, ownership and management of a corporation may be completely separate: No shareholder has the right to manage, and no officer or director needs to be a shareholder.

Shareholders have limited liability for the obligations of the corporation, even if a shareholder is elected as a director or selected as an officer. Directors and officers have no liability for the contracts they or the corporation's employees negotiate in the name of the corporation. While managers have liability for their own misconduct, they have no liability for corporate torts committed by other corporate managers or employees. Therefore, shareholders, officers, and directors have limited liability for the obligations of the business.

The usual corporation is a tax-paying entity for federal income tax purposes. The corporation pays taxes on its profits. Shareholders do not report their shares of corporation profits on their individual federal income tax returns. Instead, only when the corporation distributes its profits to the shareholders in the form of dividends or the shareholders sell their investments at a profit do the shareholders report income on their individual returns. This creates a double-tax possibility, as profits are taxed once at the corporation level and again at the shareholder level when dividends are paid.

Also, shareholders do not deduct corporate losses on their individual returns. They may, however, deduct their investment losses after they have sold their shares of the corporation.

There is one important exception to these corporate tax rules. The shareholders may elect to have the corporation and its shareholders taxed under Subchapter S of the Internal Revenue Code. By electing **S Corporation** status, the corporation and its shareholders are taxed nearly entirely like a partnership: Income and losses of the business are reported on the shareholders' individual federal income tax returns. A corporation electing S Corporation status may have no more than 35 shareholders.

A corporation has a life separate from its owners and its managers. When a shareholder or manager dies or otherwise leaves the business, the corporation is not dissolved. A shareholder may sell his shares of the corporation to other persons without limitation unless there is a contrary agreement. The purchaser becomes a shareholder with all the rights of the selling shareholder.

There are several reasons why persons organize a business as a corporation. First, no human has unlimited liability for the debts of the business. As a result, businesses in the riskiest industries—such as manufacturing—incorporate. Second, because investors may contribute capital to the business, avoid unlimited liability, escape the obligation to manage the business, and easily liquidate their investments by selling their shares, the corporation has the ability to attract large amounts of capital, even more than the limited partnership, whose partnership interests are not as freely transferable. Thus, the corporation has the capacity to raise the largest amount of capital.

The S Corporation has an additional advantage: Losses of the business are deductible on individual federal income tax returns. However, because the S Corporation is limited to 35 shareholders—who must be individuals or estates of individuals—its ability to raise capital is severely limited. Also, while legally permitted to sell their shares, S Corporation shareholders may be unable to find investors willing to buy their shares or may be restricted from selling their shares pursuant to an agreement between the shareholders.

## Limited Liability Company

A **limited liability company (LLC)** is a new business form intended to combine the nontax advantages of corporations with the favorable tax treatment of partnerships. An LLC is owned by members, who may manage the LLC themselves or elect the manager or managers who will operate the business. Members have limited liability for the obligations of the LLC.

The LLC has the purported federal taxation advantage of the partnership—no federal income taxation at the firm level. Instead, LLC owners pay taxes on their shares of the firm's profits. However, partnership treatment appears to require a lack of free transferability of the members' ownership interests: Transfer of membership interests is prohibited without the consent of all the members. In addition, the death, retirement, or bankruptcy of any member dissolves and forces the liquidation of the LLC, unless all the remaining members vote to continue the business.

What are the advantages of the LLC? The LLC has the limited liability advantage and the management advantage of the corporation. The LLC and its members receive the same federal tax treatment as the S Corporation and its shareholders, yet the LLC has no limit on the number or type of owners, as does an S Corporation. The major disadvantage of the LLC, however, is that the death of a member requires a vote by the remaining members to continue the business. This requirement practically limits the number of members of an LLC.

See Figure 1 for a summary of the general characteristics of business forms.

## Franchising

Franchising is an agreement by which a **franchisee** has the right to sell goods or services under a marketing plan prescribed in substantial part by a **franchisor**. Thus, when a franchisee purchases a franchise, the franchisee buys a *business opportunity*, which the franchisee may choose to operate as any form of business. For example, if you obtain a McDonald's restaurant franchise for the south side of Santa Fe, you will probably choose to operate the business as a corporation.

Franchising has advantages for both the franchisee and the franchisor. The franchisee receives the franchisor's assistance in setting up the business and training employees. In addition, the franchisee may benefit from the franchisor's national advertising and strong trademark and goodwill. For example, a McDonald's franchisee obtains instant visibility and credibility from displaying the McDonald's golden arches. In return for this assistance, the franchisee usually pays a substantial purchase price plus a fee based on income, sales, or the purchase price of specified supplies. For example, an ice-cream restaurant franchise may pay its franchisor 15 percent of the price it pays for its ice-cream mix. The fee is collected for the franchisor by an authorized supplier of the mix.

The franchisor also benefits. Instead of making a high investment in several business locations, the franchisor shifts most of the investment risk to the franchisees. Yet the franchisor receives income from the franchisees' operation of their businesses. And while the franchisor's profits are tied to the franchisees' success, the franchisees typically have a sizable investment in the franchises and have a strong incentive to succeed. Also, the franchisor can adopt standards to ensure it selects high-quality franchisees with superior financial strength. Using franchising allows a franchisor to exploit its trademark and goodwill yet also protect itself by requiring franchisees to adopt uniform image and marketing practices.

**Nature of Franchisor/Franchisee Relationship**
Because a franchisor may exercise some control over parts of a franchisee's business, there is a risk that the franchisor may be liable for the torts and contracts of the franchisee. Most franchising agreements provide that the franchisee is not an agent or partner of the franchisor. Some courts refuse to accept this characterization of the relationship, especially when the degree and type of control by the franchisor suggest an agency relationship. For example, when a franchisor has the right to control a franchisee's prices, the franchisor may be responsible for any resulting antitrust violation resulting from the franchisee's pricing decisions.

**Franchisee Protection**   In response to abuses by franchisors, the courts, the Federal Trade Commission, and the state legislatures have created rules that protect franchisees. The typical franchising agreement gives a franchisor wide latitude to terminate a franchisee. Some courts have invalidated such termination power or required that terminations be made in good faith. The Federal Trade Commission has issued a franchise disclosure rule and guidelines requiring franchisors to disclose their financial fees and charges, the franchisees' obligations to purchase supplies, and territorial restrictions on the franchisees. In addition, most of the states require disclosure and termination protection for franchisees.

## PARTNERSHIPS

The basic concept of partnership is as ancient as the history of collective human activity. Partnerships were known in ancient Babylonia, ancient Greece, and the Roman Empire. Hammurabi's Code of 2300 B.C. regulated partnerships. The definition of a partnership in the 6th-century Justinian Code of the Roman Empire does not differ materially from that in our laws today. The partnership was likewise known in Asian countries, including China. During the Middle Ages, much trade between nations was carried on by partnerships.

By the close of the 17th century, the partnership was recognized in the English common law. When the United States became an independent nation and adopted the English common law in 1776, the English law of partnerships became a part of American

**FIGURE 1**    General Characteristics of Forms of Business

| | Sole Proprietorship | Partnership | Limited Liability Partnership | Limited Partnership | Corporation | S Corporation | Limited Liability Company |
|---|---|---|---|---|---|---|---|
| **Formation** | When one person conducts business without forming a corporation | By agreement of owners *or* by default when two or more owners conduct business together without forming a limited partnership or a corporation | By agreement of owners: must comply with limited liability partnership statute | By agreement of owners; must comply with limited partnership statute | By agreement of owners; must comply with corporation statute | By agreement of owners; must comply with corporation statute; must elect S Corporation status under Subchapter S of Internal Revenue Code | By agreement of owners; must comply with limited liability company statute |
| **Duration** | Terminates on death or withdrawal of sole proprietor | Dissolves on death or withdrawal of partner | Dissolves on death or withdrawal of partner | Dissolves on death or withdrawal of general partner | Unaffected by death or withdrawal of shareholder | Unaffected by death or withdrawal of shareholder | Dissolves on death or withdrawal of member |
| **Management** | By sole proprietor | By partners | By partners | By general partners | By board of directors | By board of directors | By managers or members |
| **Owner Liability** | Unlimited | Unlimited | Unlimited for general obligations of partnership; limited to capital contribution for professional malpractice of a fellow partner | Unlimited for general partners; limited to capital contribution for limited partners | Limited to capital contribution | Limited to capital contribution | Limited to capital contribution |
| **Transferability of Owners' Interest** | None | None | None | None | Freely transferable | Freely transferable unless shareholders agree otherwise | None |
| **Federal Income Taxation** | Only sole proprietor taxed | Only partners taxed | Only partners taxed | Only partners taxed | Corporation taxed; shareholders taxed on dividends (double tax) | Only shareholders taxed | Only members taxed |

---

**FIGURE 2**   **Principal Characteristics of Partnerships under the UPA**

1. A partnership may be created with no formalities. Two or more people merely need to agree to own and conduct a business together in order to create a partnership (aggregate theory).
2. Partners have unlimited liability for the obligations of the business (aggregate theory). However, a partner's personal creditors have first priority to that partner's assets, while partnership creditors have first priority to partnership assets (entity theory).
3. Each partner, merely by being an owner of the business, has a right to manage the business of the partnership (aggregate theory). He is an agent of the partnership and may make the partnership liable for contracts, torts, and crimes (entity theory). Because partners are liable for all obligations of the partnership, in effect each partner is an agent of the other partners. Each partner may hire agents, and every partner is liable for the agents' authorized contracts and for torts that the agents commit in the course of their employments (aggregate theory).
4. A partnership is not an employer of the partners, for most purposes. As a result, for example, a partner who leaves a partnership is not entitled to unemployment benefits (aggregate theory).
5. Partners are fiduciaries of the partnership. They must act in the best interests of the partnership, not in their individual best interests (entity theory).
6. The profits or losses of the business are shared by the partners, who report their shares of the profits or losses on their individual federal income tax returns, because the partnership does not pay federal income taxes (aggregate theory). Nonetheless, a partnership does keep its own financial records and must file an information return with the Internal Revenue Service (entity theory).*
7. A partnership may own property in its own name (entity theory).
8. A partnership may not sue or be sued in its own name. The partners must sue or be sued (aggregate theory).
9. A partner may not sue her partners. Her sole remedy is to seek an accounting between the partners (aggregate theory).
10. A partner's ownership interest in a partnership is not freely transferable. A purchaser of a partner's interest does not become a partner, but is entitled to receive only the partner's share of the partnership's profits (aggregate theory).
11. Generally, a partnership has no life apart from its owners. If a partner dies, the partnership dissolves and may be terminated (aggregate theory). Under certain circumstances, however, the partnership may continue after the death of a partner (entity theory).

---

*The federal income tax return filed by a partnership is merely an information return in which the partnership indicates its gross income and deductions and the names and addresses of its partners (IRC Sec. 6031). The information return allows the Internal Revenue Service to determine whether the partners accurately report partnership income on their individual returns.

law. In the early part of the 19th century, the partnership became the most important form of association in the United States.

Today, the American common law of partnership has been largely replaced by statutory law. Every state has a statute on partnership law. The Uniform Partnership Act (UPA) of 1914 has been adopted in 49 states (Louisiana is the exception) and the District of Columbia. The UPA is a model partnership statute that is the product of the National Conference of Commissioners on Uniform State Laws, a group of practicing lawyers, judges, and law professors. The aims of the UPA are to codify partnership law in one document, to make that law more nearly consistent with itself, and to attain uniformity throughout the country.

A Revised Uniform Partnership Act (RUPA) was proposed in 1992. As of February 1994, only Wyoming and Montana had adopted the RUPA. The

RUPA has been heavily criticized for changing partnership rules protecting creditors of partnerships and, therefore, is not likely to become law in a majority of states without some major changes. Because the UPA of 1914 has been adopted by nearly every state in the United States, the UPA is the framework of your study of partnerships.

### Entity and Aggregate Theories

Studying the list of partnership characteristics in Figure 2, you may perceive that in some respects the partnership is treated as an **entity**—that is, as a person separate and distinct from its partners. In other respects, the partnership is viewed as an **aggregate** of the partners, with no life or powers apart from them. The UPA recognizes the partnership primarily as an aggregate of the partners. In a few situations, however, the UPA confers entity status on a partnership.

## CREATION OF PARTNERSHIP

No formalities are necessary to create a partnership. Two or more persons may become partners in accordance with a written partnership contract (articles of partnership), they may agree orally to be partners, or they may become partners merely by arranging their affairs as if they were partners. If partners conduct business under a trade name, they must file the name with the secretary of state in compliance with state statutes requiring the registration of fictitious business names.

When people decide to become partners, they should employ a lawyer to prepare a written partnership agreement. Although such **articles of partnership** are not required to form a partnership, they are highly desirable for the same reasons that written contracts are generally preferred. In addition, the statute of frauds requires a writing for a partnership having a term exceeding one year.

When there is no written partnership agreement, a dispute may arise over whether persons who are associated in some enterprise are partners. For example, someone may assert that she is a partner and, therefore, claim a share of the value of a successful enterprise. More frequently, an unpaid creditor may seek to hold a person liable for a debt incurred by another person in the same enterprise. To determine whether there is a partnership in the absence of an express agreement, the courts use the definition of partnership in the UPA.

### UPA Definition of Partnership

The UPA defines a partnership as an "association of two or more persons to carry on as co-owners a business for profit." If the definition is satisfied, then the courts will treat those involved as partners. A relationship may meet the UPA definition of partnership even when a person does not believe he is a partner, and occasionally, even if the parties agree that they are not partners.

**Association of Two or More Persons**  As an association, a partnership is a *voluntary and consensual relationship*. It cannot be imposed on a person; a person must agree expressly or impliedly to have a person associate with her. For example, a partner cannot force her partners to accept her daughter into the partnership.

No person can be a partner with herself—a partnership must have *at least two partners*. A person may be a partner with her spouse.

Not everyone or everything may be a partner. An individual, partnership, limited partnership, corporation, or other association may be a partner. Most states do not permit a trust to be a partner, but they allow the trustee of the trust to be a partner for the benefit of the trust.

**Carrying On a Business**  Any trade, occupation, or profession may qualify as a business. Carrying on a business usually requires a series of transactions conducted over a period of time. For example, a group of farmers that buys supplies in quantity to get lower prices is not carrying on a business but only part of one. If the group buys harvesting equipment with which it intends to harvest crops for others for a fee for many years, it is carrying on a business.

**Co-Ownership**  Partners must *co-own the business* in which they associate. There is no requirement that the capital contributions or the assets of the business be co-owned.

Also, by itself, co-ownership of assets does not establish a partnership. For example, two persons who own a building as joint tenants are not necessarily partners. To be partners, they must co-own a business.

The two most important factors in establishing co-ownership of the business are the sharing of profits and the sharing of management of the business. The UPA declares that a person's **sharing the profits** of a business is *prima facie* evidence that she is a partner in the business. This means that persons sharing profits are partners, unless other evidence exists to disprove they are partners. The rationale for this rule is that a person ordinarily would not be sharing the profits of a business unless she were a co-owner. This rule brings under partnership law many persons who fail to realize that they are partners. For example, two college students who purchase college basketball tickets, resell them, and split the profits are partners.

Sharing the gross revenues of a business does not create a presumption of partnership. The profits, not the gross receipts, must be shared. For example, a broker who receives a commission on a sale of land is not a partner of the seller of that land.

Although sharing profits usually is prima facie proof of partnership, the UPA provides that **no** presumption of partnership may be made when a share of profits is received:

1. By a creditor as payment on a debt.
2. By a creditor as interest on a loan.
3. By an employee as wages.
4. By a landlord as rent.
5. By a widow, widower, or representative of a deceased partner for the value of that partner's share of the partnership.
6. As consideration to the transferor of a business or other property for his sale of the goodwill of the business or other property.

These exceptions reflect the normal expectations of the parties that no partnership exists in such situations.

**Sharing management** of a business is additional evidence tending to prove the existence of a partnership. However, by itself, participation in management is not conclusive proof of the existence of a partnership. For example, a creditor may be granted considerable control in a business, such as a veto power over partnership decisions and the right of consultation, without becoming a partner. Also, a sole proprietor may hire someone to manage his business, yet the manager will not be a partner of the sole proprietor.

However, when the parties claim that they share profits for one of the six reasons above, the sharing of management may overcome the presumption that they are not partners. When the parties arrange their affairs in a manner that otherwise establishes an objective intent to create a partnership, the courts find that a partnership exists. For example, when a nonmanagerial employee initially shares profits as a form of employment compensation, the employee is not a partner of his employer. But when the employer and employee modify their relationship by having the employee exercise the managerial control of a partner and fail to reaffirm that the manager is merely an employee, a partnership may exist.

Creditors occupy a privileged position. Many cases have permitted creditors to share profits and to exercise considerable control over a business without becoming partners. Creditor control is often justified on the grounds that it is merely reasonable protection for the creditor's risk.

---

**FIGURE 3   Important Consequences of Being a Partner**

1. You share ownership of the business. For example, you want to bring an employee into your business, which is worth $250,000. If you and the employee conduct your affairs like partners, your employee will own half of your business.
2. You share the profits of the business.
3. You share management of the business. Your partner must be allowed to participate in management decisions.
4. Your partner is your agent. You are liable for your partner's torts and contracts made in the ordinary course of business.
5. You owe fiduciary duties to your partnership and your partner, such as the duties to devote full time to the business, not to compete with the business, not to self-deal, and not to disclose confidential matters.
6. Your have unlimited personal liability for all the obligations of the partnership.

---

**For Profit**     The owners of an enterprise must *intend to make a profit* to create a partnership. If the enterprise suffers losses, yet the owners intend to make a profit, a partnership may result. When an endeavor is carried on by several people for charitable or other nonprofit objectives, it is not a partnership. For example, Alex and Geri operate a restaurant booth at a county fair each year to raise money for a Boy Scout troop. Their relationship is not a partnership, but merely an association. (Nonetheless, like partners, they may be individually liable for the debts of the enterprise.)

**Intent**     Frequently, courts say that there must be intent to form a partnership. This rule is more correctly stated as follows: The *parties must intend to create a relationship that the law recognizes as a partnership.* A partnership may exist even if the parties entered it inadvertently, without considering whether they had created a partnership. A written agreement to the effect that the parties do not intend to form a partnership is not conclusive if their actions provide evidence of their intent to form a relationship that meets the UPA partnership test.

There are several important consequences of being a partner. See Figure 3 for a summary of the most important consequences.

## Creation of Joint Ventures

Courts frequently distinguish **joint ventures** from partnerships. A joint venture may be found when a court is reluctant to call an arrangement a partnership because the purpose of the arrangement is not to establish an ongoing business involving many transactions; instead, it is limited to a single project. For example, an agreement to buy, develop, and resell for profit a particular piece of real estate is likely to be viewed as a joint venture rather than a partnership. In all other respects, joint ventures are created just as partnerships are created. The joint venturers may have a formal written agreement. In its absence, a court applies the UPA definition of partnership—modified so as not to require the carrying on of a business—to determine whether a joint venture has been created.

The legal implications of the distinction between a partnership and a joint venture are not entirely clear. Generally, partnership law applies to joint ventures. For example, all of the participants in a joint venture are personally liable for its debts, and joint venturers owe each other the fiduciary duties imposed on partners. Joint ventures are treated as partnerships for federal income tax purposes. The most significant difference between joint venturers and partners is that joint venturers are usually held to have *less implied and apparent authority* than partners, due to the limited scope of the enterprise.

The following case applies partnership law to the question of whether a joint venture has been created by players of the Illinois state lottery.

---

## FITCHIE v. YURKO
### 570 N.E.2d 892 (Ill. App. Ct. 1991)

Phyllis Huisel operated a coffee shop called the Hitching-A-Ride, from which she sold tickets for the Illinois state lottery. A regular customer, Rick Yurko, frequently purchased lottery tickets from Phyllis. In mid-February 1990, Yurko purchased $100 dollars worth of $1 Fortune Hunt lottery tickets. The lottery tickets were the scratch-off variety, which revealed instant winners when the lottery player scratched off a film covering the tickets. Yurko asked Phyllis to help him scratch off the tickets, but she suggested that Judy Fitchie, one of her employees, should scratch off the tickets because Judy was luckier than Phyllis. Yurko placed several tickets in front of Judy and Frances Vincent, another customer at the coffee shop, and invited them to help him scratch them off. Yurko stated that if they would help him scratch off the lottery tickets, they would be his partners and would share in any winnings.

After playing for some time, Judy uncovered three television sets and announced that she had a winner. The ticket scratched by Judy gave the owner a chance to compete for a $100,000 prize. The owner of the ticket was required to complete the back of ticket, indicating the name, address, and phone number of the owner. Completed tickets were to be mailed to the Illinois Department of the Lottery; six tickets would be drawn and their owners would appear on the lottery television show.

Judy placed the ticket near Phyllis, and Yurko urged Phyllis to fill it out. Phyllis did not want to appear on television. Yurko indicated he would appear on television, and after discussion, Phyllis, Judy, Frances, and Yurko agreed that Yurko would be their representative and go on television. Yurko then printed on the back of the ticket "F.J.P. Rick Yurko." F.J.P. represented the first initials of Frances, Judy, and Phyllis. When Yurko started filling out the ticket, he told Phyllis that he was going to put all their initials and his name on the ticket and that they would be partners no matter what they might win.

The ticket was mailed to the Lottery and was one of six drawn for the lottery television show. Yurko appeared on the show and won the $100,000 prize. Thereafter, Yurko claimed all the $100,000 for himself. Phyllis, Judy, and Frances sued Yurko to recover shares of the winnings. The trial court held that they were partners or joint venturers entitled to an equal share of the winnings. Yurko appealed to the Appellate Court of Illinois.

---

**Bowman, Justice** The evidence indicates that the arrangement between Yurko, Phyllis, Judy, and Frances constituted a joint venture. A joint venture is essentially a partnership carried on for a single enterprise.

A joint venture is an association of two or more persons to carry out a single enterprise for profit. Whether a joint venture exists is a question of the intent of the parties. The elements to be considered in determining the parties' intent are: an agreement to carry on an enterprise; a demonstration of intent by the parties to be joint venturers; a joint interest, as reflected in the contribution of property, finances, effort, skill, or knowledge by each party; a measure of proprietorship or joint control over the enterprise; and a provision for sharing of profits and losses. A formal agreement is not essential to establish a joint venture. Rather, the existence of a joint venture may be inferred from facts and circumstances demonstrating that the parties, in fact, undertook a joint enterprise.

The parties entered into an agreement and showed their intent to be joint venturers when they started playing the lottery together. Yurko invited the women, both verbally and by placing tickets in front of them, to play the lottery with him. Yurko told them that if they would help him scratch tickets they would be his partners and would share in any prize winnings. They expressed agreement with Yurko's proposal when they began scratching off the tickets.

Both Judy and Frances uncovered tickets that were good for small cash prizes or more tickets. None of the players tried to claim any of those prizes as their own. Rather, the tickets were turned in for more tickets, and the players kept on scratching. After the winning ticket was revealed, there was discussion amongst all the parties as to who would appear on the television show. Together, not individually, they decided that Yurko would be the one to go. Yurko impliedly acknowledged a joint effort when he printed the women's initials right alongside his own name on the back of the winning ticket, again amidst talk that he and the women were partners.

A joint interest in the effort to win the lottery is also found in the evidence. It is undisputed that Yurko paid for the tickets. Frances and Judy expended their time and energy and put forth effort to scratch the tickets. While Phyllis's part in this is not altogether clear, Phyllis scratched off a couple of tickets, and it is evident the other parties considered her part of the enterprise.

Finally, with regard to provision for sharing of profits, Yurko told the women they would share in anything that was won if they helped scratch the tickets. Yurko also wrote the women's initials next to his own on the line provided on the lottery ticket for the ticket holder's name. This evidence proves that the joint venturers planned to share equally in any lottery prize ultimately won.

We acknowledge the informality of the arrangement between Yurko and the women. Nonetheless, the parties should be bound by the terms of their agreement to jointly carry out an enterprise for profit.

**Judgment for Fitchie, Huisel, and Vincent affirmed.**

## Creation of Mining Partnerships

Although similar to an ordinary partnership or a joint venture, a mining partnership is recognized as a distinct relationship in a number of states. Persons who cooperate in the working of either a mine or an oil or gas well are treated as mining partners if there is (1) joint ownership of a mineral interest, (2) joint operation of the property, and (3) sharing of profits and losses. Joint operation requires more than merely financing the development of a mineral interest, but it does not require active physical participation in operations; it may be proved by furnishing labor, supplies, services, or advice. The delegation of sole operating responsibility to one of the participants does not bar treatment as a mining partnership.

## Creation of Limited Liability Partnerships

Unlike an ordinary partnership, a limited liability partnership (LLP) may not be created merely by partners conducting a business together. The partners must expressly agree to create an LLP by complying with a limited liability partnership statute. In Texas—the first state to permit the formation of an LLP—the formation of an LLP requires filing a form with the secretary of state, paying an annual fee ($200 per partner), adding the words "Registered Limited Liability Partnership" or the acronym "LLP" to the partnership's name, and maintaining at least $100,000 of professional liability insurance for the firm.

## PARTNERSHIP BY ESTOPPEL

Two persons may not be partners, yet in the eyes of a third person they may **appear** to be partners. If the third person deals with one of the apparent partners, he may be harmed and seek to recover damages from both of the apparent partners. The question, then, is whether the third person may collect damages from both of the apparent partners.

For example, Thomas thinks that Wilson, a wealthy person, is a partner of Porter, a poor person. Thomas decides to do business with Porter on the grounds that if Porter does not perform as agreed, he can recover damages from Wilson. If Thomas is wrong and Wilson is not Porter's partner, Thomas ordinarily has no recourse against Wilson. UPA Section 7(1) states that "persons who are not partners as to each other are not partners as to third persons." However, if Thomas can prove that Wilson misled him to believe that Wilson and Porter were partners, he may sue Wilson for damages suffered when Porter failed to perform as agreed. This is an application of the doctrine of **partnership by estoppel**.

Partnership by estoppel is based on substantial, detrimental reliance on the appearance of partnership. Partnership by estoppel has three elements:

1. A person holds herself out or consents to being held out as a partner of another person.
2. A third party justifiably relies on the holding out.
3. The third person is injured as a result of the reliance.

The third party who is damaged may recover his loss from the person who held herself out or consented to being held out as the partner of the other person.

### Holding Out

A person might hold himself out as a partner by referring to himself as another person's partner. Or he might appear frequently in the office of a purported partner and confer with him. Perhaps he and another person share office space, have one door to an office with both of their names on it, have one telephone number, and share a secretary who answers the phone giving the names of both persons.

More difficult is determining when a person *consents* to being held out as another's partner. Mere knowledge that one is being held out as a partner is not consent. But a person's silence in response to a statement that the person is another's partner is consent. For example, suppose Chavez tells Eaton that Gold is a partner in Birt's new retail shoe business. In fact, Gold is not Birt's partner. Later, Gold learns of the conversation between Chavez and Eaton. Gold does not have to seek out Chavez and Eaton to tell them that he is not Birt's partner in order to avoid being held liable as a partner for Birt's business debts. Had Chavez made the statement to Eaton in Gold's presence, however, Gold must deny the partnership relation or he will be held liable for Eaton's subsequent reliance on Gold's silence.

### Reasonable Reliance and Injury

A partner by estoppel is liable only to those persons who reasonably rely on the holding out and suffer injury thereby. This means that partnership by estoppel is determined on a case-by-case basis.

A third person's reliance on the appearance of a partnership must be reasonable. When a person has information that would prevent a reasonable person from relying on the holding out, no partnership by estoppel may result. For example, Litz knows that Frank and Stump are employer and employee. Frank calls Stump "my partner" in the presence of Stump and Litz. Frank and Stump are not partners by estoppel. Because Litz knows that Frank and Stump are employer and employee, she may not reasonably rely on Frank's calling Stump "my partner."

The injury suffered by the third person must be the result of her reliance. If the third person would have done business with another person whether or not that person was a partner of someone held out as a partner, there is no injury as a result of reliance. Hence, there is no partnership by estoppel.

## Effect of Partnership by Estoppel

Once partnership by estoppel has been proved, the person who held himself out or who consented to being held out is liable as though he were a partner. He is liable on contracts entered into by third persons on their belief that he was a partner. He is liable for torts committed during the course of relationships entered by third persons who believed he was a partner.

Although two parties are partners by estoppel to a person who knows of the holding out and who justifiably relies on it to his injury, the partners by estoppel are *not partners in fact* and do not share the profits, management, or value of the business of the purported partnership. Partnership by estoppel is merely a device to allow creditors to sue parties who mislead them into believing that a partnership exists.

In the following case, the appearance of partnership led the court to a finding of partnership by estoppel.

---

## VOLKMAN V. DP ASSOCIATES
### 268 S.E.2d 265 (N.C. Ct. App. 1980)

Alvin and Carol Volkman decided to build a house. They contacted David McNamee for construction advice. McNamee informed the Volkmans that he was doing business with Phillip Carroll. Subsequently, the Volkmans received a letter from McNamee on DP Associates stationery. They assumed that the DP was derived from the first names of McNamee and Carroll: David and Phillip. Prior to the signing of the contract, McNamee introduced Carroll to Mr. Volkman at the DP Associates office, where Carroll said, "I hope we'll be working together." Carroll stated that McNamee would be the person at DP Associates primarily doing business with the Volkmans, but indicated that he also would be available for consultation.

The Volkmans reviewed the written contract in the DP Associates office with McNamee. McNamee suggested that they use a form to identify DP Associates as acting as a general contractor. He then left the room saying, "I will ask Phil." When he returned, he said that they would use the form.

After the contract was signed but before construction of the house began, Mr. Volkman visited the office of DP Associates. He again saw and spoke with Carroll, who said to him, "I am happy that we will be working with you." During construction, Mr. Volkman visited the office of DP Associates several times and saw Carroll there. During one visit, he expressed to Carroll his concern about construction delays, but Carroll told him not to worry because McNamee would take care of it.

When DP Associates failed to perform the contract, the Volkmans sued DP Associates, McNamee, and Carroll. Carroll argued that he could not be liable to the Volkmans because he and McNamee were not partners. The trial court agreed and refused to let the jury decide the case. The Volkmans appealed to the North Carolina Court of Appeals.

---

**Vaughn, Judge**    If the Volkmans are unable to prove a partnership in fact, they may be able to show that Carroll should be held as a partner by estoppel.

Liability by estoppel may result either from Carroll's representation of himself as a partner "by words spoken or written" or "by conduct" or Carroll's "consent" to such a representation by another. The Volkmans indicated they may be able to show that Carroll by his oral statements to them and conduct in their presence and by his consent to the representations of McNamee to the Volkmans, some of which were in the presence of Carroll, represented himself as a partner and should be estopped to deny such association. They may be able to show further they relied upon these representations not knowing them to be false and that based upon the representations of Carroll and McNamee, the Volkmans changed their position and were thereby damaged.

The liability of the person seeking to deny partner status is based on the objective theory of contract law, i.e., a person should be bound by his words and conduct. Thus, when Carroll told Mr. Volkman, "I am happy that we will be working with you," and conducted himself as he did in the DP

Associates office in the presence of Mr. Volkman, the jury may find that Carroll was indicating a willingness to be bound by the statements and acts of McNamee, that Carroll held himself out as a partner of McNamee in DP Associates, that McNamee had apparent authority to act for Carroll, and that the Volkmans reasonably relied upon this holding out. If so, Carroll is bound as if he directly dealt with the Volkmans.

**Judgment reversed in favor of the Volkmans. Remanded to the trial court for jury trial.**

## PARTNERSHIP CAPITAL

When a partnership or limited liability partnership is formed, partners contribute cash or other property to the partnership. The partners' contribution is called **partnership capital.** To supplement beginning capital, other property may be contributed to the partnership as needed, such as by the partners permitting the partnership to retain some of its profits. Partnership capital is the equity of the business.

Loans made by partners to a partnership are not partnership capital but instead are liabilities of the business. Partners who make loans to a partnership are both owners and creditors.

## PARTNERSHIP PROPERTY

A partnership or limited liability partnership may own all or only a part of the property it uses. For example, it may own the business and perhaps a small amount of working capital in the form of cash or a checking account, yet own no other assets. All other tangible and intangible property used by the partnership may be individually or jointly owned by one or more of the partners or rented by the partnership from third parties. A determination of what is partnership property becomes essential when the partnership is dissolved and the assets are being distributed and when creditors of either the partnership or one of the partners is seeking assets to satisfy a debt.

The UPA provides that (1) all property originally brought into the partnership or subsequently acquired by purchase or otherwise, on account of the partnership, is partnership property, and (2) unless the contrary intention appears, property acquired with partnership funds is partnership property.

The intent of the partners controls whether the partnership or an individual partner owns the property. It is best to have a written record of the partners' intent as to ownership of all property used by the partnership, such as in the articles of partnership. Other writings—such as accounting records—show the partnership assets; assets appearing in the partnership's books are presumed to belong to the partnership. Also, the partnership's paying rent on property provides strong evidence that the property belongs to the partner receiving the rent.

The presumption is very strong that property purchased with partnership funds and used in the partnership is partnership property. No such presumption is accorded to a partner who purchases property with her own funds and then allows the partnership to use the property; other factors besides the partner's funding the purchase determine who owns the property.

If title is taken in the partnership name, it is presumed that the property is partnership property. However, the presumption is not as strong that real property held in the name of a partner is individual property. Other indicia may prove that property held in a partner's name belongs to the partnership. For example, the partnership's payment of property taxes or insurance premiums, the maintainance, repair, and improvement of property by the partnership, and the deduction of these expenses on the partnership income tax return are indications of the intent of the partners that property belongs to the partnership, despite title being held in the name of a partner.

## Examples

A tax accountant discovers that a partnership is using a building to which a partner, Jacob Smith, holds title. The partnership pays rent monthly to Smith, but the partnership pays for all maintenance and repairs on the building. The accountant wants to know whether the partnership or Smith should be paying real property taxes on the building. Smith is the owner and should be paying taxes on it because his partners' intent to allow Smith to retain ownership is evidenced by the partnership paying rent to Smith.

Changing the facts, suppose the partnership pays no rent to Smith, the partnership maintains and repairs the building, and the partnership pays real property taxes on the building, but the title is in Smith's name. Who owns the building? The property belongs to the partnership, because all the objective criteria of ownership point toward partnership ownership, especially the payment of taxes. Therefore, when the partnership is liquidated, the building will be sold along with other partnership assets, and the proceeds of its sale will be distributed to partnership creditors and to all of the partners.

In the following case, the court held that a truck trailer held in the partnership's name was partnership property.

---

## In Re Fulton
### 43 B.R. 273 (M.D. Tenn. 1984)

Padgett Carroll and Walter Fulton operated as a partnership a trucking business under the name of C & F Trucking. Carroll contributed a semi truck, which Fulton drove for the business. Carroll used $4,600 of his personal funds to purchase a used 42-foot trailer for C & F Trucking. The seller's invoice listed C & F Trucking as the purchaser of the trailer. The trailer's certificate of title listed C & F Trucking as the owner.

Fulton's personal financial problems forced him to file for bankruptcy. Fulton claimed ownership of the trailer among his assets. Carroll claimed that the trailer was his individual asset.

---

**Paine, Bankruptcy Judge** In determining whether property is partnership property or property owned by an individual, the court must focus primarily on the intentions of the partners at the time the property was acquired. Such intention of the partners must be determined from their apparent intention at the time the property was acquired and the conduct of the partners toward the property after the purchase.

Viewing evidence surrounding the purpose and use of the property, Tennessee courts have held that when property is titled in the name of the partnership, the party asserting that the property is not partnership property has the burden of proof.

The evidence establishes that the trailer is partnership property. Both a sales invoice and a certificate of title list the owner of the trailer as C & F Trucking. The trailer was purchased by Carroll for use in the C & F Trucking business and Fulton actually used the trailer in the business.

The claims of individual ownership asserted by both Fulton and Carroll lack substance. The property was indeed partnership property.

**Judgment for Carroll.**

## PARTNERS' PROPERTY RIGHTS

In a partnership or limited liability partnership, a partner has three property rights:

1. Her rights in specific partnership property.
2. Her partnership interest.
3. Her right to participate in the management of the business.

The first two rights are discussed here. The management right is discussed in Chapter 30, Operation of Partnership and Related Forms.

### Rights in Partnership Property

Partnership property is owned by partners as **tenants in partnership.** This means that the partners as a group own partnership property as a whole; the partners as individuals do not own proportionate interests in separate items of partnership property.

As a tenant in partnership, each partner has the right to possess partnership property for partnership purposes. A partner has no individual right to use or possess partnership property for her own purposes, such as paying a personal debt, unless she has the consent of the other partners. Likewise, a partner's personal creditor may not make a claim against partnership assets.

On the death or other withdrawal of a partner, his rights in partnership property pass to the surviving partners. This is called the **right of survivorship.**

### Partnership Interest

As a co-owner of a partnership, a partner has an ownership interest in the partnership. A partner's ownership interest is called a **partnership interest** and is part of his personal property. Although a partner may not give his personal creditors any interest in separate items of partnership property, a partner may sell or **assign his partnership interest** to a creditor. And although a partner's personal creditor has no right to seize separate items of partnership property, a creditor may obtain rights in a partner's partnership interest by obtaining a **charging order** against that interest.

**Assignment**    The sale or **assignment of a partnership interest** is a voluntary act of a partner. It entitles the buyer or assignee to receive the assigning partner's share of the partnership's profits, but it does not make the assignee a partner of the partnership: The assignee has no right to inspect the partnership's books and records or to manage the partnership. The assignee's only other right beyond receiving a share of the profits is to ask a court to dissolve the partnership, but only if the partnership is at will. (A partnership at will has no term and may rightfully be dissolved by a partner at any time.) An assignee who obtains a judicial dissolution may obtain liquidation of the partnership's assets and obtain payment from the proceeds of the sale of the partnership's assets.

By itself a partner's assignment of his partnership interest does not dissolve the partnership; the assigning partner remains a partner and can continue to manage the partnership.

The nonassigning partners may not exclude the assigning partner from the partnership. They may, however, rightfully dissolve the partnership by their *unanimous* agreement, even if the term or objective of the partnership has not been met.

The following case illustrates that an assignee of a partnership interest has the right to receive profits but has no liability to partnership creditors due to the assignment.

---

## CONNORS v. MIDDLE FORK CORP.
### 790 F.Supp. 6 (D.D.C. 1992)

In 1983, Odell Rogers, John Lockhart, and Caleb Cooley formed MFC Partnership, a partnership formed under the laws of Kentucky. In 1984, Odell Rogers made a gift of his 41 percent interest in MFC to his three sons: 4-year-old Shannon Rogers, 19-year-old James Rogers, and 20-year-old Arthur Rogers. Odell made the gift for the purpose of providing income to his sons to pay their college expenses. The Rogers sons received income from MFC, which was reported on both the partnership's and the sons' individual federal income tax returns. The sons were identified as partners on MFC's unaudited balance sheet of December 31, 1985. In addition, MFC's 1986 income statement listed the sons as partners.

In 1987, MFC incurred liability to an employee pension fund under the federal Employee Retirement Income Security Act (ERISA). Joseph Connors, a trustee for the fund, contended that the Rogers sons were partners of MFC and therefore were personally liable to the fund on MFC's ERISA liability. The Rogers sons asked the trial court to grant a summary judgment for the sons on the grounds that they were merely assignees of their father's partnership interest and had no liability for MFC's obligations.

---

**Revercomb, District Judge**    Under the Uniform Partnership Act, the receipt of profits from a business is *prima facie* evidence that one is a partner in the business. One may rebut this presumption by showing that one falls within a statutorily protected relationship. The Rogers sons argue that the 1984 transfer to them was no more than an assignment of Odell Rogers's partnership interest. An assignment of a partnership interest merely entitles the assignee to receive the assignor's profits from the firm, but does not entitle the assignee to interfere otherwise in the management of the firm. Assignees are not partners, and cannot be held personally liable for the firm's obligations.

Although the sharing of profits and losses is prima facie evidence of a partnership, the issue of control is the more important criterion in determining the existence of a partnership. Both Arthur and James Rogers did none of the acts which usually denote management or control of a partnership: request information about the firm's finances, attend its meetings or vote, attempt to withdraw its money, represent the firm to third parties, or even speak with the other partners about the firm. Neither James nor Arthur knew where the offices of MFC Partnership were located. Neither Arthur nor James was employed by MFC.

Connors notes that the Rogers sons on one occasion received "management fees" totalling $3,000, without any further showing of what these "fees" were paid for. The Court regards such evidence as no more than a mere scintilla upon which a jury could not reasonably find for Connors.

Thus, there can be *no* doubt that the transfer conveyed *less* than full partnership status. Connors has failed to carry his burden of proof of showing sufficient indicia of partnership. It follows that the Rogers sons are not jointly or severally liable to the pension fund as partners.

**Motion for summary judgment granted in favor of the Rogers sons.**

---

**Charging Order**    A partner's personal creditor with a judgment against the partner may ask a court to issue a **charging order**—that is, an order charging the partner's partnership interest with payment of the unsatisfied amount of the judgment. Unlike assignment, a charging order is obtained without the partner's consent. As with assignment, however, the partner remains a partner and may manage the partnership, and the creditor is entitled to receive only the partner's share of the profits. If the profits are insufficient to pay the debt, the creditor may ask the court to order foreclosure and to sell the partner's interest to satisfy the charging order.

Neither the issuance of a charging order nor the purchase of a partnership interest at a foreclosure sale causes a dissolution. But the purchaser of a partnership interest at the foreclosure sale may ask a court to dissolve a partnership at will. The other partners may eliminate this potential threat to the continuation of the partnership by **redeeming the charging order.** To redeem a charging order, the other partners must pay the creditor the amount due on the judgment against the partner. If the other partners so choose, however, they may dissolve the partnership by their unanimous agreement, even if the term or objective of the partnership has not been met.

**Joint Venturers and Mining Partners**    Transfers of interests in joint ventures are treated in the same way as transfers of partnership interests. However, a mining partner's interest is *freely transferable*. The transferee becomes a partner with all the rights of ownership and management, and the transferor loses all of his partnership rights. The other mining partners cannot object to the transfer, and their consent to a transfer is not required.

**PROBLEMS AND PROBLEM CASES**

**1.** 📹 *Video Case.* See "The Reunion." When friends reunite at a wedding, they reveal their plans for future business ventures. Al and Amy, an unmarried couple, propose opening a Thai restaurant. Al is a dentist, and Amy is director of public relations for a publishing company. Amy will quit her job eventually to manage the restaurant. They will hire a chef whose restaurant is about to close.

Carl is a successful real estate agent who wants to open his own real estate firm.

Bob has tried several business ventures, but all have failed, including a venture to manufacture ski racks for motorcycles.

Dave and Donna, the newly married couple, plan to quit their jobs, move to Wyoming, and open a software development business. They want the business to have few investors. They have lined up potential clients who will finance their initial efforts in return for software customization.

What business forms should they use for their business ventures? What additional questions do you want to ask to help you determine the best business forms for their ventures?

**2.** Daon Corporation developed a housing subdivision, improving the building lots for resale. To promote the sales of lots, Daon created a marketing scheme, named Showcase of Homes, that involved area builders. The builders, including Raymond Driesel, purchased lots from Daon and built custom homes on the homesites. Daon advertised the Showcase of Homes, decorated and furnished model homes, and provided a landscaping plan to the builders. Both Driesel and Daon benefited from the Showcase program. Driesel benefited from Daon's advertising and the chance to show his home, leading to future home-building jobs. Daon benefited from having homes constructed in the subdivision, proving to prospective lot buyers the feasibility and desirability of buying a lot from Daon, leading to further lot sales. Theo Dority purchased the home built by Driesel. All negotiations and

documents for the sale were between Dority and Driesel. The home was defective. Driesel promised to correct the defects, but he failed to do so. Dority corrected the defects at a cost of $20,000. Will Dority successfully sue Daon for $20,000 on the grounds that Daon and Driesel were partners?

**3.** OWLP, a Hawaii limited partnership, owned the Outrigger West Hotel. OWLP and Hawaii Hotels Operating Company (HHOC) agreed that OWLP and HHOC would jointly operate the hotel and share its revenues, allocating 73 percent to OWLP and 27 percent to HHOC. The agreement provided that revenues would be collected from the hotel and allocated daily according to the percentages above. However, the allocation percentages were changed six times during a four-year period to permit each party to recover out-of-pocket expenses and to provide a return of 98 percent of the net income to OWLP and of 2 percent of the net income to HHOC. Thus, any amount recovered by each party according to the predetermined percentage in excess of its expenses would be its profit. Losses were shared pro rata like the profits. Are OWLP and HHOC partners?

**4.** Vearle Edwards owned and operated Edwards IGA grocery. Vearle advertised his grocery in the South Sioux City *Star* but failed to pay for the advertising. When Vearle filed for bankruptcy, the *Star* sued Vearle's wife, Ila. The *Star*'s managing editor believed that the grocery was a family-owned business, but he said that he spoke very few times with Ila about advertising since "she was not around." At one time, Ila had done some bookkeeping at the store, but for the last seven years she had no dealings with the grocery. She at no time dealt directly with any suppliers, made any management decisions, ordered any food or supplies, supervised any employees, or placed any advertisements. She contributed no resources to the store. She did not share in the profits or losses of the store, except as the wife of Vearle. Is Ila obligated to pay for the advertising in the *Star?*

**5.** 📹 *Video Case.* See "The Partnership." Art, Ben, and Diedre are partners of Alphabet Builders, a partnership in the construction business. They meet at a restaurant with a prospective new partner, Don, who says he will decide whether to enter the partnership after discussing the matter with his wife. During the meeting, they are approached by John, with whom the partnership has been attempting to do business. Art introduces Don to John, stating, "We're celebrating Don's joining Alphabet Builders." Don and John shake hands, and John says, "Congratulations! Alphabet Builders has a very good reputation. In fact, I'm about to become one of your new clients. I signed the contract this morning." Don says nothing in response to John's statement. Subsequently, however, Don decides not to join Alphabet Builders. Nonetheless, when Alphabet Builders breaches its contract with John, John sues Don on the contract. Is Don liable to John?

**6.** Coy Stephens did business as Audio Works. When he needed a bank loan for the business, Coy and his father, Vastine Stephens, executed a document stating that they were partners in the business and that Coy had the authority to sign for the business in all respects. In fact, Coy and Vastine were not partners, but they executed the document solely to induce a bank to loan the necessary funds to Coy. Relying on the document, Angelina National Bank loaned $33,000 to Audio Works. Angelina would not have loaned the money to Audio Works had it not believed that Vastine was Coy's partner. When Coy failed to repay the loan, Angelina sued Vastine. Was Vastine liable to Angelina?

**7.** Barry Wilen owned a one-third interest in Bay Country Investments, a partnership. During the term of Barry's marriage to Loveta Wilen, Bay Country sold real property for $126,500. The partnership reinvested the proceeds in other real property. Subsequently, Loveta and Barry had marital problems. During a divorce proceeding, Loveta claimed that she was entitled to receive half of Barry's one-third share of the $126,500 proceeds. Was she correct?

**8.** Richard DeLong and Ken Birch formed a partnership to build houses. They agreed that all sales proceeds would be deposited in a partnership bank checking account and that both of them must sign all checks. For two years, Birch and DeLong signed all checks, but then DeLong agreed that Birch could sign partnership checks by himself. Six years later, DeLong discovered that Birch paid some of his personal expenses with partnership checks. DeLong reported his discovery to the Washington state prosecuting attorney, who prosecuted Birch for the crime of embezzlement. Embezzlement was defined in the Washington statute as exerting unauthorized control over the property of another. Has Birch committed embezzlement?

**9.** Claude Gauldin and Joe Corn formed a partnership to raise cattle and hogs on land owned by Corn. Partnership funds were used to build two buildings on the land for use by the partnership. Gauldin and Corn did not discuss who owned the buildings. Gauldin knew when the buildings were constructed that they would be permanent improvements to the land and would become part of it. The partnership paid no rent for the land, and there was no agreement to consider the use of the land as a contribution by Corn. The taxes on the land were paid by Corn, as was the cost of upkeep. When Corn left the partnership, Gauldin claimed that the buildings were partnership assets and that he was entitled to half of their fair market value. Was Gauldin correct?

## CAPSTONE QUESTIONS

Duane Dullard and Debbie Denson are partners in Double D Partnership, whose business is the retail sale of clothing, hats, posters, and other items bearing Easy State University (ESU) trademarks. Dullard considered, but rejected, other possible forms of business organizations before approaching Denson about such a business venture, forming the partnership, and launching the business with her under the partnership form. The other forms considered by Dullard, and the reasons he rejected them, were as follows:

- *Sole proprietorship*—rejected by Dullard because of his understanding that sole proprietors face unlimited personal liability for debts of the business. Dullard found this prospect unsettling.

- *Corporation*—rejected by Dullard because of his understanding that corporate shareholders are legally barred from engaging in management of the corporate business. Dullard wanted to manage the business in addition to having an ownership interest in it.

- *Subchapter S Corporation*—rejected by Dullard because of his understanding that S Corporation status is unavailable unless the firm has at least 35 shareholders. Dullard knew that having such a number of shareholders would be neither feasible nor desirable.

- *Limited liability company (LLC)*—though allowed by applicable state law, rejected by Dullard for these reasons: (*a*) his understanding that LLC members are legally barred from engaging in management of the firm's business; and (*b*) his understanding that a firm cannot utilize the LLC form unless it meets the requirements for S Corporation status. Dullard wanted to manage the business in addition to having an ownership interest in it. He also concluded that the S Corporation requirements could not be met.

ESU has notified Dullard and Denson of its position that Double D's sales of items bearing ESU trademarks constitute trademark infringement because Double D did not obtain ESU's consent to use the trademarks. While Dullard and Denson were discussing the likelihood that ESU would soon file a trademark infringement suit, Dullard said he was "glad that if there's some liability to ESU, our exposure will be limited to the value of the partnership's assets. It's good we can't be held personally liable." Denson responded this way: "This is a partnership, pal. You and I can be held personally liable for the partnership obligations, including what might be owed to ESU. If you think our exposure is limited to the value of the partnership's assets, I'd advise you not to consider going to law school or sitting for the CPA exam."

When Dullard and Denson formed Double D, they entered into a written partnership agreement. The agreement made no mention of whether either partner could assign his or her partnership interest. Denson has numerous personal debts of a past-due nature. The most significant of these is a large debt owed by Denson to Derek Domino. Denson has been considering assigning her partnership interest to Domino as a means of taking care of her debt to him. When Denson mentioned this possibility to Dullard, Dullard responded this way: "No can do. You can't assign your partnership interest without my consent, and I refuse to consent. I don't want Derek Domino or anyone else coming into this business as a partner and deciding how the business is going to be run."

While at the Double D place of business, Denson met with a sales representative for Perfect Posters, Inc. Denson wished to order from Perfect Posters a large quantity of posters that Denson and Dullard would then sell to Double D customers. Although Perfect Posters normally refuses to extend credit when a retailer makes an order of the size Denson

wished to make, the sales representative decided to waive the company's usual cash-only requirement and make a credit sale after Denson pointed to a man standing near a rack of ESU sweatshirts and said: "My partner and I are good for it. I think you'll agree that you're dealing with a safe credit risk." The man to whom Denson pointed and referred was none other than legendary former ESU basketball coach Lou Doo, who won five national championships before retiring from coaching and launching a lucrative career as a movie actor and sports commentator on national television. The sales representative's decision to make a credit sale was based on his assumptions that Doo was Denson's partner and that Doo's financial resources were considerable. Doo saw and heard what Denson had done and said but made no comments in the presence of the sales representative. He merely smiled politely. After the sales representative left the premises, Doo informed Denson that he had no intention of assuming liability for any of Denson's or Double D's debts. Double D later failed to pay for the posters when payment was due. After various efforts to collect payment from Double D proved unsuccessful, Perfect Posters sued Denson, Dullard, and Doo in an effort to collect the debt.

## Required:

Answer the following and give reasons for your conclusions.

1. Consider each of the identified understandings that led Dullard to reject the sole proprietorship, corporation, S Corporation, and LLC forms of business organization. State whether those understandings were legally accurate or inaccurate.

2. Evaluate, for legal accuracy or inaccuracy, the respective statements made by Dullard and Denson during their discussion of the potential liability to ESU.

3. Evaluate, for legal accuracy or inaccuracy, Dullard's comments in response to Denson's statement that she was considering assigning her partnership interest to Domino.

4. Discuss the claim of Perfect Posters against Doo, noting whether he is or is not liable.

# CHAPTER

## 3 0

# OPERATION OF PARTNERSHIP AND RELATED FORMS

**INTRODUCTION**

*Two relationships are important during the operation of a partnership business: (1) the relation of the partners to each other and the partnership; and (2) the relation of the partners to third parties who are affected by the business of the partnership.*

## DUTIES OF PARTNERS TO THE PARTNERSHIP AND EACH OTHER

The relation between partners and the partnership is a fiduciary relation of the highest order. It is one of mutual trust, confidence, and honesty. Therefore, partners owe to the partnership and each other the highest degree of *loyalty and good faith* in all partnership matters. The duties partners owe each other are the same in ordinary partnerships and in limited liability partnerships.

### Profiting Secretly

Unless there is a contrary agreement, a partner's sole compensation from partnership affairs is a share of partnership profits. Therefore, a partner may not make a secret profit out of the transaction of partnership business. For example, a partner may not profit personally by receiving an undisclosed kickback from a partnership supplier. In addition, a partner may not profit secretly when she makes a contract with her partnership, such as selling a building she owns to her partnership without disclosing her ownership or her profit to her partners.

When a partner receives a secret profit, she has a conflict of interests, and there is a risk that she may prefer her own interests over those of the partnership. Therefore, the law permits a partner to profit personally from partnership transactions only if she deals in good faith, makes a full disclosure of all material facts affecting the transaction, and obtains approval from her partners. The remedy for a breach of this duty not to make a secret profit is a return of the profit that she made in the transaction with the partnership.

The following case imposed liability on a partner who profited secretly from the sale of a jet plane to the partnership.

---

## LEVY V. DISHAROON
### 749 P.2d 84 (N. Mex. Sup. Ct. 1988)

Walter Levy and Henry Disharoon formed a partnership to purchase a jet airplane and to operate a charter airline business. Disharoon located a jet and informed Levy that the price was $963,000. After Levy approved the purchase, Disharoon contracted to buy the jet for $860,000. The partnership borrowed $975,000 to pay for the jet. Disharoon paid the seller $860,000 and deposited in Disharoon's personal bank account the $103,000 difference between the actual purchase price and the purchase price represented to Levy.

Levy asked a trial court for a formal accounting of the partnership affairs. The trial court found that Disharoon misrepresented the purchase price of the jet with the intention of deceiving Levy. The trial court awarded Levy actual damages of $70,000 and punitive damages of $100,000. Disharoon appealed to the Supreme Court of New Mexico.

---

**Sosa, Senior Justice**    Each partner has the right to have his co-partner exercise good faith in partnership matters. A partner is not allowed to gain any advantage over a co-partner by fraud, misrepresentation, or concealment. For any advantage so obtained he must account to the co-partner. The jet was actually purchased for $860,000, but Disharoon told Levy the sale price was $963,000. The difference was wired to Disharoon's personal banking account in Chicago. Thus, Disharoon defrauded the partnership in the amount of $103,000.

We conclude the trial court was correct in holding Disharoon accountable, but erred in awarding Levy $70,000 in actual damages. Levy's compensatory damages were one-half of the misappropriated funds or $51,500.

The trial court also awarded Levy $100,000 in punitive damages. The amount of punitive damages is left to the discretion of the fact finder and will not be disturbed on appeal unless it is so unrelated to the injury and actual damages proven as to plainly manifest passion and prejudice rather than reason and justice. The $100,000 punitive damage award is not so unrelated to the actual damages to be clearly erroneous. Disharoon's conduct in misrepresenting the jet's actual sale price and misappropriating the partnership's funds deserves punishment.

**Judgment for Levy affirmed as modified.**

---

## Competing against the Partnership

A partner may not compete against his partnership unless he obtains consent from the other partners. For example, a partner of a retail clothing store may not open a clothing store nearby. However, he may open a grocery store and not breach his fiduciary duty. The partnership has the remedy of recovering the profits of the partner's competing venture.

In the following case, a partner in an accounting partnership breached the duty not to compete by providing his own clients with the same types of accounting services that his accounting partnership could have provided.

## VEALE V. ROSE

**657 S.W.2d 834 (Tex. Ct. App. 1983)**

Larry Rose, Paul G. Veale, Sr., Paul G. Veale, Jr., Gary Gibson, and James Parker offered professional accounting services as partners under the firm name Paul G. Veale and Co. Their written partnership agreement expressed the general duties of the partners, but it recognized that Veale, Sr., and Rose had outside investments and a number of other business commitments. All of the partners were allowed to pursue other business activities so long as the activities did not conflict with the partnership practice of public accounting or materially interfere with the partners' duties to the partnership.

While a partner of Paul G. Veale and Co., Larry Rose performed accounting services for Right Away Foods and Ed Payne. He was paid personally by those clients. Rose was an officer and shareholder of Right Away. When the other partners discovered these actions, they claimed Rose owed them a share of his profits from the actions, which competed with the partnership. The jury found that Rose had not competed with the partnership. Rose's partners appealed.

---

**Nye, Chief Justice** Partners may be said to occupy a fiduciary relationship toward one another which requires of them the utmost degree of good faith and honesty in dealing with one another. Breaches of a partner's duty not to compete with the partnership are compensable at law by awarding to the injured partners their proportionate shares of the profits wrongfully acquired by the offending partner.

While a partner of Veale and Co., Rose rendered accounting services for Right Away Foods for which he billed and received payment personally. Rose admitted that he billed Right Away Foods for the services of a CPA. He also admitted that there was no reason why he could not have rendered the same services to Right Away Foods as a partner in the accounting firm. The preponderance of all of the evidence clearly establishes that Rose performed accounting services for Right Away Foods while a partner of Paul G. Veale and Co., in competition with the partnership.

Rose also admitted that he performed accounting services for various enterprises owned by Payne during his tenure as a partner at Veale, for which he billed and received payment personally. His later testimony that he performed these services, in effect, after hours, or in addition to his duties to the partnership, is of no value in light of the obligations imposed by the partnership agreement and by the common understanding of the term "competition."

**Judgment reversed in favor of Rose's partners. Remanded for a new trial.**

---

## Duty to Serve

The duty to serve requires a partner to undertake his share of responsibility for running the day-to-day operations of the partnership business. The basis of this duty is the expectation that all partners will work. Sometimes, this duty is termed the duty to devote full time to the partnership.

Partners may agree to relieve a partner of the duty to serve. So-called *silent partners* merely contribute capital to the partnership. Silent partners do not have the duty to serve, but they have the same liability for partnership debts as any other partner.

The remedies for breach of the duty to serve include assessing the partner for the cost of hiring a person to do his work and paying the other partners additional compensation.

## Duty of Care

In transacting partnership business, each partner owes a duty to use **reasonable skill and care.** A partner is not liable to her partnership for losses resulting from honest errors in judgment, but a partner is liable for losses resulting from her negligence or lack of skill and care. She must make a **reasonable investigation** before making a decision, so that she has an adequate basis for making the decision. The decision she makes must be that of an **ordinarily prudent business manager** in her position.

For example, a grocery store has stocked avocados for three years and has always sold them. If one of the partners buys the same amount of avocados as usual but they do not sell, the partner is not liable for the loss to the partnership. Her decision appears reasonable as of the time she made it. If prior to the time she made the decision, however, sales of avocados have fallen and trade magazines that she should have read published customer surveys showing lower expected sales of avocados, she would be liable.

## Duty to Act within Actual Authority

A partner has the duty not to exceed the authority granted him by the partnership agreement or, if there is no agreement, the authority normally held by partners in his position. He is responsible to the partnership for losses resulting from unauthorized transactions negotiated in the name of the partnership. For example, suppose partners agree that no partner shall purchase supplies from Jasper Supply Company, which is unaware of the limitation on the partners' authority. When one partner purchases supplies from Jasper and the partnership suffers a loss because the supplies are of low quality, the wrongdoing partner must bear the loss due to her breach of the partnership agreement.

## Duty to Account

Partners have a duty to account for their use or disposal of partnership funds and partnership property, as well as their receipt of any benefit or profit without the consent of the other partners. Partnership property should be used for partnership purposes, not for a partner's personal use.

For example, when a partner of a firm that leases residential property to college students allows his daughter to live in a partnership-owned apartment, the partner must collect rent for the partnership from his daughter or risk breaching the duty to account.

Each partner owes a duty to keep a reasonable record of all business transacted by him for the partnership and to make such records available to the person keeping the partnership books. The books must be kept at the partnership's principal place of business. Every partner must at all times have access to them and may inspect and copy them.

In addition to a right to inspect the books of the partnership, a partner has a right to a formal **accounting** of the partnership affairs. It is generally by an accounting that a partner can recover from his partners for their breaches of their fiduciary duties.

An accounting is not merely a presentation of financial statements. It is a judicial review of all partnership and partners' transactions to determine whether partners have properly used partnership assets and to award each partner his rightful share of partnership assets. The court takes into consideration breaches of fiduciary duties and adjusts appropriately the amounts payable to the partners.

An accounting is an extreme action and is ordinarily taken only after dissolution of a partnership. The Uniform Partnership Act (UPA), however, specifically permits an accounting prior to dissolution.

Closely related to the duty to account is the right of a partner to be **indemnified** for expenditures made from personal funds and for personal liabilities incurred during the ordinary conduct of the business. For example, a partner uses her own truck to pick up some partnership supplies, which she pays for with her personal check. The partner is entitled to be reimbursed for the cost of the supplies and for her cost of picking up the supplies, including fuel.

## Other Duties

A partner must maintain the **confidentiality** of partnership information such as a trade secret or a customer list. This means a partner should not disclose to third parties confidential information of the partnership unless disclosure benefits the partnership.

On the other hand, each partner owes a duty to disclose to the other partners all information that is material to the partnership business. She also owes a duty to inform the partners of notices she has received that affect the rights of the partnership. For example, Gordon Gekko, a partner of a stock brokerage firm, learns that National Motors Corporation is projecting a loss for the current year. The projection reduces the value of National stock, which the firm has been recommending that its customers buy. Gekko has a duty to disclose the projection to his partners to allow them to advise customers of the brokerage.

---

**CONCEPT REVIEW**

## PARTNER'S DUTIES

1.  Duty not to make a secret profit while transacting for the partnership.

2.  Duty not to compete with the partnership.

3.  Duty to serve the partnership.

4.  Duty to exercise the skill and care of the ordinarily prudent business manager.

5.  Duty to act within the actual authority possessed by the partner.

6.  Duty to account for the use and disposal of partnership funds and property.

7.  Duty to indemnify other partners for expenditures they made from their personal funds and for liabilities they incurred on behalf of the partnership.

8.  Duty to maintain the confidentiality of partnership information.

9.  Duty to disclose to the other partners information material to the partnership business.

10. Duty to inform partners of notices he has received.

---

### Joint Ventures and Mining Partnerships

The fiduciary duties of partners also exist in joint ventures and mining partnerships, although there are a few special rules regarding their enforcement. For example, a joint venturer may seek an accounting to settle claims between the joint venturers, or he may sue his joint venturers to recover joint property or to be indemnified for expenditures that he has made on behalf of the joint venture. A mining partner's remedy against his partners is an accounting; however, a mining partner has a lien against his partners' shares in the mining partnership for his expenditures on behalf of the mining partnership. The lien can be enforced against purchasers of his partners' shares.

### COMPENSATION OF PARTNERS

A partner's compensation for working for a partnership or limited liability partnership is a share of the profits of the business. Ordinarily, a partner is not entitled to a salary or wages, even if he spends a disproportionate amount of time conducting the business of the partnership.

### Profits and Losses

Unless there is an agreement to the contrary, partners share partnership profits equally, according to the number of partners, and not according to their capital contributions or the amount of time that each devotes to the partnership. For example, a partnership has two partners, Juarez, who contributes $85,000 of capital to the partnership and does 35 percent of the work, and Easton, who contributes $15,000 and does 65 percent of the work. If they have made no agreement how to share profits, when the partnership makes a $50,000 profit in the first year, each partner receives $25,000, half of the profits.

**Losses**    When the partnership agreement is silent on how to share losses, losses are shared in the same proportion that profits are shared. The basis of this rule is the presumption that partners want to share benefits and detriments in the same proportions. Nonetheless, the presumption does not work in reverse. If a partnership agreement specifies how losses are shared but does not specify how profits are shared, profits are shared equally by the partners, not as losses are shared.

**Examples**     For example, when there is no agreement regarding how profits or losses are shared, profits are shared equally, and because losses are shared like profits, losses are shared equally as well. When two partners agree to share profits 70–30 and make no agreement on losses, both profits and losses are shared 70–30.

However, when two partners make no agreement how to share profits but agree to share losses 60–40, losses are shared in that proportion but profits are shared equally.

Partners may agree to split profits on one basis and losses on another basis for many reasons, including their making different capital and personal service contributions or a partner's having higher outside income than the other partners, which better enables him to use a partnership loss as a tax deduction.

**Effect of Agreement on Creditors' Rights**     Each partner has unlimited personal liability to partnership creditors. Loss-sharing agreements between partners do not bind partnership creditors unless the creditors agree to be bound. For example, two partners agree to share losses 60–40, the same proportion in which they contributed capital to the partnership. After the partnership assets have been distributed to the creditors, $50,000 is still owed to them. The creditors may collect the entire $50,000 from the partner who agreed to assume only 60 percent of the losses. That partner may, however, collect $20,000—40 percent of the amount from the other partner.

In the following case, the court held that the partners' oral agreement regarding partners' compensation bound the partners.

---

## Warren v. Warren
### 784 S.W.2d 247 (Mo. App. 1989)

In 1969, brothers Harold and Ray Warren formed a partnership to operate a funeral home in Columbia, Missouri. In 1970, they created a second partnership, The Warren Yard and Tree Service. The brothers based their partnerships solely on oral agreements, never putting them in writing. They adopted a system under which each partner drew from the partnerships' funds a reasonable compensation for his actual services rendered to the two businesses.

After a few years, Harold—a licensed embalmer and funeral director—spent an increasing amount of his time in the funeral home, performing all the lab work and specialized mortuary services. By 1978, Harold spent nearly all his time at the funeral home. Ray—licensed only as a funeral director—devoted most of his time to the tree service partnership, spending only a few hours each week assisting with funerals. Consequently, during the term of their partnership, Harold drew large sums of compensation from the funeral home partnership and only about $400 from the tree service partnership. Ray drew his primary compensation from the tree service partnership and a smaller compensation from the funeral home partnership. Because the funeral home was the more profitable business, Harold's total compensation exceeded Ray's by a considerable amount.

In 1983, Ray sued Harold, claiming that he was entitled to receive compensation equal to Harold for the entire 14-year term of the funeral home partnership. Ray asked the trial court to order Harold to pay Ray an amount that would equalize their 14-year compensation. The trial court held that Ray was not entitled to additional compensation, and Ray appealed.

---

**Nugent, Chief Judge**     Ray Warren first asserts that the trial court erred in finding that an oral agreement bound each partner to draw compensa-

tion commensurate with his services. The Warren brothers adopted a compensation system abstruse as to a method of payment but clear as to intent and business customs. There was an agreement between Ray and Harold under which Ray would run the tree service, Harold the funeral home, and each would draw compensation commensurate with his input of services. For nearly fifteen years, Ray knew of and did not protest the perquisites afforded his brother by the funeral home partnership, such as use of an apartment above the funeral home and of a car.

Section 18 of the Uniform Partnership Act enunciates the rules determining the rights and duties of a partner: "The rights and duties of the partners in relation to the partnership shall be determined, subject to any agreement between them, by the following rules: . . . (f) No partner is entitled to remuneration for acting in the partnership business." The oral agreement between the brothers negates the statute's proscription of compensation to partners. Missouri law recognizes the validity of oral and implied agreements between partners. Indeed, for more than a century, Missouri has recognized that, in the presence of an agreement linking compensation to a part-

ner's efforts, partners providing services vital to the enterprise, or those devoting much of their time to the partnership's commonweal, deserve compensation often far in excess of that owed partners providing less importance services or those giving only a little time to the business.

Harold provided the expert services vital to the partnership. His skills in the mortuary business far exceeded Ray's. The brothers agreed that Harold would run the funeral home and Ray, the tree service. Thus, implicitly if not expressly, they acknowledged each other's expertise, and, accordingly, each concentrated his efforts in the area of his own ability.

Moreover, Ray derived substantial financial benefit from the funeral home, to which he contributed but minimal efforts. Concomitantly, Harold succeeded in continuing to operate the business despite the effective withdrawal of Ray. Thus, Harold became entitled to suitable compensation for his efforts.

**Judgment for Harold Warren affirmed.**

---

**CONCEPT REVIEW**

**PARTNERS' SHARE OF PROFITS AND LOSSES**

| | |
|---|---|
| **Profits** | Partners share profits equally, unless the partners agree otherwise. |
| **Losses** | Partners share losses in the same way they share profits, unless the partners agree to share losses in a different manner. |
| **Tax Effect** | A partner's share of partnership profits is income to the partner, on which the partner pays federal income tax. <br> A partner's share of partnership losses may be deducted on the partner's individual federal income tax return. |
| **Right of Contribution** | A partner who pays more than his share of a partnership loss may collect the excess paid from those partners whose shares he paid. |

## MANAGEMENT POWERS OF PARTNERS

### Individual Authority of Partners

In a partnership or limited liability partnership, every partner is a general manager of the business. This power is expressed in the UPA, which states

that a partnership is bound by the act of every partner for apparently carrying on in the usual way the business of the partnership. Such authority is implied from the nature of the business. It permits a partner to bind the partnership and his partners for acts within the ordinary affairs of the business. The scope of this **implied authority** is determined with reference to what is usual business for partnerships of the same general type in the locality.

Implied authority of a partner may not contradict a partner's **express authority**, which is created by agreement of the partners. An agreement among the partners can expand, restrict, or even completely eliminate the implied authority of a partner. For example, the partners in a newspaper publishing business may agree that one partner shall have the authority to purchase a magazine business for the partnership and that another partner shall not have the authority to sell advertising space in the newspaper. The partners may agree also that all partners must consent to borrow money for the partnership. The partners' implied authority to be general managers is modified in accordance with these express agreements.

Express authority may be stated orally or in writing, or it may be obtained by acquiescence. Regardless of the method of agreement, all of the partners must agree to the modification of implied authority. Together, a partner's express and implied authority constitute her **actual authority.**

**Apparent Authority**    When implied authority is restricted or eliminated, the partnership risks the possibility that **apparent authority** to do a denied act will remain. Apparent authority exists because it reasonably appears a partner has authority to do an act. To prevent apparent authority from continuing when there is a limitation of a partner's actual authority, third persons with whom the partner deals must have knowledge of the limitation of his actual authority. Just as a principal must notify third persons of limitations of an agent's authority, so must a partnership notify its customers, suppliers, and others of express limitations of the actual authority of partners.

Suppose that Carroll, Melton, and Ramirez are partners and that they agree that Carroll will be the only purchasing agent for the partnership. This agreement must be communicated to third parties selling goods to the partnership, or Melton and Ramirez will have apparent authority to bind the partnership on purchase contracts. Melton and Ramirez do not have express authority to purchase goods, because they have agreed to such a restriction on their authority. They do not have implied authority to purchase, because implied authority may not contradict express authority.

**Ratification**    A partnership may ratify the unauthorized acts of partners. Essentially, **ratification** occurs when the partners accept an act of a partner who had no actual or apparent authority to do the act when it was done.

For example, suppose Cabrillo and Boeglin are partners in an accounting firm. They agree that only Cabrillo has authority to make contracts to perform audits of clients, an agreement known by Mantron Company. Nonetheless, Boeglin and Mantron contract for the partnership to audit Mantron's financial statements. At this point, the partnership is not liable on the contract, because Boeglin has no express, implied, or apparent authority to make the contract. But suppose Boeglin takes the contract to Cabrillo, who reads it and says, "OK, we'll do this audit." Cabrillo, as the partner with express authority to make audit contracts, has ratified the contract and thereby bound the partnership to the contract.

## Special Transactions

The validity of some partner's actions is affected by special partnership rules that reflect a concern for protecting important property and the credit standing of partners. This concern is especially evident in the rules for conveying the partnership's real property and for borrowing money in the name of the partnership.

**Power to Convey Partnership Real Property**
To bind the partnership, an individual partner's conveyance of a partnership's real property must be expressly, impliedly, or apparently authorized or be ratified by the partnership. For example, the partners may expressly agree that a partner may sell the partnership's real property.

The more difficult determination is whether a partner has *implied* and *apparent* authority to convey real property. A partner has implied and apparent authority to sell real property if a partnership sells real property in the usual course of the partnership business. Such would be the case with the partner of a real estate investment partnership that buys and sells land as its regular business. By contrast, a partner has no implied or apparent authority to sell the building in which the partnership's retail business is conducted. Here, unanimous agreement of the partners is required, since the sale of the building may affect the ability of the firm to continue. In addition, a partner has no implied or apparent authority to sell land held for investment not in the usual course of business. A sale of such land would be authorized only if the partners concurred.

When title to partnership real property is recorded in the name of the partners and not the partnership, those partners in whose name title is recorded have apparent authority to convey title to a bona fide purchaser unaware of the partnership's interest in the real property.

**Borrowing Money**    Partnership law restricts the ability of a partner to borrow money in the name of a partnership. Essentially, a partner must possess express, implied, or apparent authority to borrow. Express authority presents few problems. Finding implied and apparent authority to borrow is more difficult.

Although the UPA does not explicitly recognize the distinction, a number of courts have distinguished between trading and nontrading partnerships for purposes of determining whether a partner has implied or apparent authority to borrow money on behalf of the partnership. A **trading partnership** has an inventory; that is, its regular business is buying and selling merchandise, such as retailing, wholesaling, importing, or exporting. For example, a toy store and a clothing store are trading partnerships. Since there is a time lag between the date they pay for their inventory and the date they sell inventory to their customers, these firms ordinarily need to borrow to avoid cash flow problems. Therefore, a partner of a trading partnership has implied and apparent authority to borrow money for the partnership.

A **nontrading partnership** has no substantial inventory and is usually engaged in providing services—for example, accounting services or real estate brokerage. Such partnerships have no normal borrowing needs. Therefore, a partner of a nontrading partnership has no implied or apparent authority to borrow money for the partnership.

The distinction between trading and nontrading partnerships is not always clear. Businesses such as general contracting, manufacturing, and dairy farming, although not exclusively devoted to buying and selling inventory, have been held to be trading partnerships. The rationale for their inclusion in this category is that borrowing is necessary in the ordinary course of business to augment their working capital.

This suggests why the distinction between trading partnerships and nontrading partnerships is useless or misleading. There is no necessary connection between borrowing money and buying and selling. The more important inquiry should be whether a partner's borrowing is in the ordinary course of business. When borrowing is in the ordinary course of business, a partner has implied and apparent authority to borrow money. If borrowing is not in the ordinary course of business, then no individual partner has implied or apparent authority to borrow money.

If a court finds that a partner has authority to borrow money, the partnership is liable for his borrowings on behalf of the partnership. There is a limit, however, to a partner's capacity to borrow. A partner may have authority to borrow, yet borrow beyond the ordinary needs of the business. A partnership will not be liable for any loan whose amount exceeds the ordinary needs of the business, unless otherwise agreed by the partners.

The power to borrow money on the firm's credit will ordinarily carry with it the power to grant the lender a lien or security interest in firm assets to secure the repayment of the borrowed money. Security interests are a normal part of business loan transactions.

**Issuing Negotiable Instruments**    A partner who has the authority to borrow money also has authority to issue negotiable instruments such as promissory notes for that purpose. When a partnership has a checking account and a partner's name appears on the signature card filed with the bank, the partner has express authority to draw checks. A partner whose name is not on the signature card filed with the bank has apparent authority to issue checks, but only in respect to a third person who has no knowledge of the limitation on the partner's authority.

**Negotiating Instruments**    A partnership receives many negotiable instruments during the course of its business. For example, an accounting firm's clients often pay fees by check. Even though borrowing money and issuing negotiable instruments may be beyond a partner's implied and apparent authority, a partner usually has implied and apparent authority to transfer or negotiate instruments on behalf of the partnership.

For example, when a partnership has a bank account, a partner has implied and apparent authority to indorse and deposit in the account checks drawn payable to the partnership. As a general rule, a partner also has implied and apparent authority to indorse and cash checks drawn payable to the order of the partnership.

Likewise, partners have implied authority to indorse drafts and notes payable to the order of the partnership and to sell them at a discount.

In the following case, the court found that a partner had implied authority to indorse and deposit checks payable to the partnership.

---

## GROSBERG V. MICHIGAN NATIONAL BANK
### 62 N.W.2d 715 (Mich. Sup. Ct. 1984)

---

Mervin Grosberg and Sheldon Goldman, as partners, constructed and operated the Chatham Fox Hills Shopping Center. Grosberg and Goldman had agreed that Goldman would receive rental checks from the shopping center's tenants and deposit them in an account in Grosberg's name at Manufacturers National Bank.

Without Grosberg's knowledge or permission, Goldman opened an account in both their names at Michigan National Bank. Goldman deposited in that account checks relating to the partnership business that were payable to the partnership or its partners. Goldman indorsed each check by signing the name of the partnership or the partners. Later, Goldman embezzled $112,000 of the deposited funds. At no time was Michigan National Bank aware that Grosberg and Goldman were partners.

When Grosberg discovered Goldman's embezzlement, Grosberg sued Michigan National Bank for conversion for accepting checks on which Grosberg's or the partnership's indorsement was forged. The trial court found that Goldman had authority to indorse and to deposit partnership checks in the account. The court of appeals affirmed the trial court's decision, and Grosberg appealed.

---

**Boyle, Justice**    Goldman had *express* authority to indorse and deposit checks only in the account maintained by Grosberg at Manufacturers National Bank. We find, however, that Goldman's partner status invested him with *implied* authority to indorse and deposit each of the incoming checks in the account at Michigan National Bank.

Section 9 of the Uniform Partnership Act states:

The act of every partner, including the execution in the partnership name of any instrument, for apparently carrying in the usual way the business of the partnership of which he is a member binds the partnership, unless the partner so acting has in fact no authority to act for the partnership in the particular matter, and the person with whom he is dealing has knowledge of the fact that he has no such authority.

The UPA phrase "for apparently carrying on in the usual way the business of the partnership," although it contains the word "apparent," need not be read to exclude the implied-authority notion of powers *that naturally flow from the partnership relationship*. Accordingly, we find that section 9 of the UPA applies regardless of the bank's lack of knowledge of the partnership relationship.

Grosberg entrusted Goldman with responsibility to receive and deposit incoming partnership checks. In light of the partnership relationship, we easily conclude that Goldman had *implied* authority to indorse all incoming checks on behalf of the partnership and the partners. The possibility that Goldman may have secretly intended at the time of indorsement to embezzle the funds cannot detract from his authority to affix indorsements, since at that time he was "apparently carrying on in the usual way the business of the partnership."

The question remains whether Goldman's subsequent conduct in depositing the checks in the account at Michigan National Bank invalidates that authority. This case involves a partner with general authority to indorse, a diversion to a joint account in which Grosberg had an equal ownership interest, and diverted checks in which Goldman had a partial ownership interest. The present circumstances are not so inconsistent with "carrying on in the usual way the business of the partnership" that Goldman's authority to make the deposits at issue cannot be implied.

Goldman's inherent authority as a partner extended by implication to the deposit of partnership checks in an account ostensibly maintained in both partners' names.

Because of Goldman's implied authority both to indorse incoming checks and to deposit them in an account created in a manner consistent with "apparent partnership purposes," we conclude that no forgery occurred. Therefore, Michigan National Bank is free from liability in conversion.

**Judgment for Michigan National Bank affirmed.**

---

**Admissions and Notice**   A partnership is bound by admissions or representations made by a partner concerning partnership affairs that are within her express, implied, or apparent authority. Likewise, notice to a partner is considered to be received by the partnership. Also, a partner's knowledge of material information relating to partnership affairs is **imputed** to the partnership. These rules reflect the reality that a partnership speaks, sees, and hears through its partners.

## Disagreement among Partners

Usually, partners will discuss management decisions among themselves before taking action, even when doing so is not required by a partnership agreement and even when a partner has the implied authority to take the action by herself. When partners discuss a prospective action, they will usually vote on what action to take. Each partner has one vote, regardless of the relative sizes of their partnership interests or their shares of the profits. The vote of a majority of the partners controls ordinary business decisions and, thereby, limits the actual authority of the partners. Nonetheless, the apparent authority of the partners to bind the partnership on contracts in the ordinary course of business is unaffected by the majority vote of partners, unless the limitation on the partners' actual authority is communicated to third parties.

## Effect of Partnership Agreement

The partners may modify the rules of management by their unanimous agreement. They may agree that a partner will relinquish his management right, thus removing the partner's express and implied author-

ity to manage the partnership. They may grant sole authority to manage the business to one or more partners. Such removals or delegations of management powers will not, however, eliminate a partner's apparent authority to bind the partnership for his acts within the usual course of business.

A partnership agreement may create classes of partners, some of which will have the power to veto certain actions. Some classes of partners may be given greater voting rights. Unequal voting rights are often found in very large partnerships, such as an accounting firm with several hundred partners.

## Unanimous Partners' Agreement Required

Some partnership actions are so important that one partner should not be able to do them by himself. To make clear that no single partner has implied or apparent authority to do certain acts, in the absence of a contrary agreement, the UPA requires unanimity for several actions. These actions are:

1. Assignment of partnership property for the benefit of creditors.
2. Disposal of the goodwill of the business (such as selling the right to do business with a firm's customers to another business).
3. Action making it impossible to carry on the ordinary business of the partnership (such as the distress sale of the entire inventory of a retailing partnership).
4. Confession of judgment against the partnership.
5. Submission of a partnership claim or liability to arbitration.
6. An agreement for the partnership to pay or assume an individual debt of a partner.

7. An agreement for the partnership to serve as a surety or guarantor of the debt of another (unless the partnership's ordinary business is suretyship and guaranty).

8. Any act not apparently for the carrying on of business of the partnership in the usual way.

Essentially, this list contains acts that are not in the usual course of business of the partnership. Such actions must be approved by all partners, unless there is a contrary agreement. For example, a decision to merge one accounting partnership with another partnership must be approved by all partners. Similarly, the decision of a grocery store partnership to move the business to another city requires unanimous partner approval.

In the following case, the court required unanimous partners' agreement for the sale of a motel building that housed the partnership's only business.

## PATEL V. PATEL
### 260 Cal. Rptr. 255 (Cal. Ct. App. 1989)

L. G. and S. L. Patel, husband and wife, owned the City Center Motel in Eureka, California. On April 16, 1986, the Patels formed a partnership with their son, Raj. The purpose of the partnership was to own and operate the motel. The partnership agreement required Raj's approval of any sale of the motel building. Real estate records were not changed, however, and the motel remained recorded only in the names of L. G. and S. L. Patel.

On May 2, 1986, L. G. and S. L. contracted to sell the motel to P. V. and Kirit Patel, who were unaware of Raj's interest as a partner in the motel. When Raj was informed of the contract to sell the motel, he refused to give his approval. Three weeks later, P. V. and Kirit sued L. G., S. L., and Raj for specific performance to compel them to sell the motel. The trial court held the contract unenforceable; P. V. and Kirit appealed.

**Channel, Associate Justice**   Generally, every partner is an agent of the partnership for the purpose of its business, and the act of every partner to carry on the business of the partnership binds the partnership. UPA Section 9(1). However, partners acting without the approval of the remaining partners may not do any act that would make it impossible to carry on the ordinary business of the partnership. UPA Section 9(3)(c).

Historically, partnerships were divided into two types: commercial or trading partnerships and noncommercial or nontrading partnerships. Although this distinction has been rejected in California, it remains a valuable tool in considering whether L. G. and S. L. exceeded their statutory authority by entering into the real estate contract, thus making it impossible to carry on the ordinary business of the partnership. In the case of a commercial or trading partnership in which the usual partnership business is to hold and sell real property, a contract such as that involved in this case—to sell the sole partnership asset—would be enforceable. By contrast, when—as in the present case—the usual partnership business is to run a business, rather than to hold it in anticipation of its eventual sale, the partnership is not bound by a contract selling that business without the approval of all the partners. Under these circumstances, the trial court properly denied specific performance of the unauthorized contract in order to prevent destruction of the partnership.

Nevertheless, P. V. and Kirit contend that the trial court should have applied UPA Section 10(3). It states:

Where title to real property is in the name of one or more of the partners, whether or not the record discloses the right of the partnership, the partners in whose name the title stands may convey title to such property, but the partnership may recover such property unless the property has been conveyed to a bona fide purchaser for value without knowledge that the partner executing the conveyance has exceeded his authority.

P. V. and Kirit contend that they are bona fide purchasers for value because they had no knowledge of Raj's unrecorded interest in the motel.

To enforce the contract of sale without Raj's approval would frustrate the purpose of UPA Section 9(3)(c) by making it impossible for the partnership to continue. As the purpose of the partnership is to operate a motel, rather than to hold it for eventual sale, we believe that the better result would be to preserve the partnership and hold the contract unenforceable.

**Judgment for L. G., S. L., and Raj Patel affirmed.**

---

## Joint Ventures and Mining Partnerships

Most of the authority rules of partnerships apply to joint ventures and mining partnerships. These business organizations are in essence partnerships with limited purposes. Therefore, their members have less implied and apparent authority than do partners. Joint venturers have considerable apparent authority if third persons are unaware of the limited scope of the joint venture. A mining partner has no implied authority to borrow money or issue negotiable instruments. As with partners, joint venturers and mining partners may by agreement expand or restrict each other's agency powers.

## LIABILITY FOR TORTS AND CRIMES

### Torts

The standards and principles of agency law's respondeat superior are applied in determining the liability of the partnership and of the other partners for the torts of a partner and other partnership employees. In addition, the partnership and the other partners are liable for the torts of a partner committed within the ordinary course of partnership business or within the ordinary authority of that partner. Finally, when a partner commits a breach of trust, the partnership and all of the partners are liable. For example, all of the partners in a stock brokerage firm are liable for a partner's embezzlement of a customer's securities and funds.

**Intentional Torts**   While the doctrine of respondeat superior usually imposes liability on a partnership and its partners for a partner's negligence, the doctrine does not usually impose liability for a partner's intentional torts. The reason for this rule is that intentional torts are not usually within the ordinary scope of business or within the ordinary authority of a partner.

A few intentional torts impose liability on a partnership and its partners. For example, a partner who repossesses consumer goods from debtors of the partnership may trespass on consumer property or batter a consumer. Such activities have been held to be in the ordinary course of business. Also, a partner who authorizes a partner to commit an intentional tort is liable for such torts.

In the following case, a partner was not held liable for the intentional tort of her partner.

---

## VRABEL V. ACRI
### 103 N.E.2d 564 (Ohio Sup. Ct. 1952)

On February 17, 1947, Stephen Vrabel and a companion went into the Acri Cafe in Youngstown, Ohio, to drink a few beers. While Vrabel and his companion were sitting at the bar drinking, a partner of the bar, Michael Acri, without provocation drew a .38-caliber handgun, shot and killed Vrabel's companion, and shot and seriously injured Vrabel. Michael Acri was convicted of murder and sentenced to a life term in the state prison.

Since 1933, Florence and Michael Acri, as partners, had owned and operated the Acri Cafe. From the time of his marriage to Florence in 1931 until 1946, Michael had been in and out of hospitals, clinics, and sanitaria for the treatment of mental disorders and nervousness. Although Michael beat Florence when they had marital difficulties, he had not attacked, abused, or mistreated anyone else. Florence and Michael separated in September 1946, and Florence sued Michael for divorce soon afterward. Before their separation, Florence had operated and managed the cafe primarily only when Michael was ill. Following the marital separation and up until the time he shot Vrabel, Michael was in exclusive control of the management of the cafe.

Vrabel brought suit against Florence to recover damages for his injuries on the ground that, as Michael's partner, she was liable for Michael's tort of battery of Vrabel. The trial court ordered Florence to pay Vrabel damages of $7,500. Florence appealed.

---

**Zimmerman, Judge**   When a partnership is shown to exist, each member of the partnership project acts both as principal and agent of the others as to those things done within the apparent scope of the business of the project and for its benefit.

However, it is equally true that where one member of a partnership commits a wrongful and malicious tort not within the actual or apparent scope of the agency or the common business of the particular venture, to which the other members have not assented and which has not been concurred in or ratified by them, they are not liable for the harm thereby caused.

Because at the time of Vrabel's injuries and for a long time prior thereto Florence had been excluded from the Acri Cafe and had no voice or control in its management, and because Florence did not know or have good reason to know that Michael was a dangerous individual prone to assault cafe patrons, the theory of negligence urged by Vrabel is hardly tenable. The willful and malicious attack by Michael Acri upon Vrabel in the Acri Cafe cannot reasonably be said to have come within the scope of the business of operating the cafe, so as to have rendered the absent Florence accountable.

Since the liability of a partner for the acts of his associates is founded upon the principles of agency, the statement is in point that an intentional and willful attack committed by an agent or employee, to vent his own spleen or malevolence against the injured person, is a clear departure from his employment, and his principal or employer is not responsible therefor.

**Judgment reversed in favor of Florence Acri.**

---

**Partners' Remedies**   When a partnership and the other partners are held liable for a partner's tort, they may, during an accounting, recover the amount of their vicarious liability from the wrongdoing partner. This rule places ultimate liability on the wrongdoing partner without affecting the ability of tort victims to obtain recovery from the partnership or the other partners.

## Tort Liability and Limited Liability Partnerships

State legislatures created the limited liability partnership (LLP) as a means of reducing the personal liability of professional partners, such as accountants. Consequently, an innocent partner of an LLP has no liability for the professional malpractice of his partners. Arguably, LLP statutes grant partners broad protection, eliminating an innocent partner's liability for errors, omissions, negligence, incompetence, or malfeasance of his partners or employees.

That is the limit of protection, however. The LLP itself is liable for the tort of a wrongdoing partner or employee under the doctrine of respondeat superior. In addition, a wrongdoing partner is liable for his own malpractice or negligence. Also, the partner supervising the work of the wrongdoing partner has unlimited liability for the wrongdoing partner's tort. Thus, the LLP's assets, the wrongdoing partner's personal assets, and the supervising partners' personal assets are at risk. Finally, the LLP and its partners have unlimited liability for other debts of the business, such as a supplier's bill, lease obligations, and bank loans.

## Crimes

When a partner commits a crime in the course and scope of transacting partnership business, rarely are his partners criminally liable. But when the partners have participated in the criminal act or authorized its commission, they are liable. They may also be liable when they know of a partner's criminal tendencies yet place him in a position in which he may commit a crime.

Until recent times, a partnership could not be held liable for a crime in most states because it was not viewed as a legal entity. However, modern criminal codes usually define a partnership as a "person" that may commit a crime when a partner, acting within the scope of his authority, engages in a criminal act.

## LAWSUITS BY AND AGAINST PARTNERSHIPS AND PARTNERS

Under the UPA, a partnership may not sue in its own name; instead, all of the partners must join in the suit. This means that if the partnership wants to sue someone for breaching a contract or defaming the partnership business, all of the partners must agree to bring the suit. Especially for large partnerships, this requirement is cumbersome. Today, many state statutes differ from the UPA by permitting a partnership to sue in its own name.

Because the UPA imposes on partners a different type of liability for torts than it does for contracts, different rules apply to tort actions than apply to contract actions against the partnership and its partners. Partners are **jointly and severally** liable for partnership **torts.** This means that a tort victim may sue all of the partners (jointly) or sue fewer than all of the partners (severally). If a tort victim sues all of the partners jointly, the judgment may be satisfied against assets of the partnership and assets of the individual partners. If fewer than all of the partners are sued severally, the judgment may generally be satisfied from only the individual assets of the partners sued.

If fewer than all of the partners are sued and made to pay the entire amount of the tort victim's damages, those partners may seek **indemnification** or **contribution** from the other partners for their shares of the liability.

Partners are **jointly liable** for **contractual** obligations of the partnership. This means that all of the partners must be sued if the partnership has breached a contract. Otherwise, no individual partner may be required to pay a judgment and the assets of the partnership cannot be used to satisfy the contract creditor's judgment.

Courts and legislatures have fashioned many modifications to this requirement of joining all the partners in contract actions. Some states make partners jointly and severally liable for contracts. Others have joint debtor statutes that permit creditors—both contract and tort claimants—to sue fewer than all of the partners and yet collect from partnership property. Some courts refuse to permit partners to be sued on contract actions until partnership assets have been exhausted.

The UPA does not permit a partnership to be sued in its own name. This prohibition is especially cumbersome for a party suing for breach of contract because the UPA imposes joint liability on partners for partnership contracts. Thus, it is necessary to sue each of the partners, which is especially difficult when the partners live in a number of states.

Many states have responded to this difficulty by enacting statutes that make all joint obligations joint and several. In addition, *common-name statutes* permit suits against the partnership even if fewer than all of the partners are notified of the suit. Pursuant to such statutes, a judgment against the partnership is enforceable against the assets of the partnership and against the individual assets of those partners who have been served with process.

### PROBLEMS AND PROBLEM CASES

**1.** Saul Birnbaum, Jay Birnbaum, and Ilene Flaum owned a partnership that developed and operated a shopping center. Due to a conflict between the partners, Saul was the sole manager of the partnership. Rather than develop the shopping center himself, Saul hired Victoria Tree, who later became his wife, to develop the shopping center for the partnership. Saul paid Victoria from partnership funds. Saul did not disclose his hiring of Victoria to Jay and Ilene. Did Saul violate a fiduciary duty?

**2.** Larry Rose, a partner of an accounting firm, used the firm's employees and computers to render services to his personal clients. The partnership received no compensation from Rose for the use of its employees and computers. Has Rose breached a fiduciary duty?

**3.** Holiday Inns, Inc., and L & M Enterprises, Inc. (L & M), were 50–50 partners of Marina Associates, a partnership formed to develop a gambling casino in Atlantic City. Holiday Inns conducted the day-to-day operation of Marina. The partnership was unprofitable during its early years, and rather than contribute more capital to the partnership, L & M agreed to sell most of its 50 percent interest to Holiday Inns. Subsequently, the casino became profitable, a fact that was a matter of public record. Also, L & M was aware that Marina had become highly profitable. Nonetheless, L & M sold its remaining 1 percent interest to Holiday Inns. After a newspaper article suggested that Holiday Inns had taken advantage of L & M, L & M sued Holiday Inns. L & M argued that Holiday Inns breached a fiduciary duty by failing to provide to L & M a 35-year financial forecast prepared by Holiday Inns, which projected large cash flows and high profits for the casino. Was Holiday Inns held liable to L & M?

**4.** Russel Daub, Daniel Smith, and Frederick Stehlik formed a partnership. No formal partnership agreement was executed. During 1980, profits were distributed monthly, with Daub receiving $3,000 per month, Smith $1,500, and Stehlik $1,500. In the latter months of 1980, Stehlik received $1,700 per month, but the 1980 partnership tax return indicated that profits were divided 50 percent to Daub and 25 percent each to Smith and Stehlik. During 1981, profits were distributed 50 percent to Daub and 25 percent each to Smith and Stehlik. The 1981 partnership tax return showed the 50–25–25 profit ratio at the beginning of the year, but it showed a year-end ratio of one third to each partner. In 1982, profits were distributed 50–25–25. When the partnership was dissolved and liquidated, Smith and Stehlik argued that each was entitled to one third of the profits and one third of the value of the partnership. Are they correct?

**5.** Two brothers, Sydney and Ashley Altman, operated several partnerships in Pennsylvania. They shared equally in the management of the partnerships. They agreed that each would receive identical salaries and that each was permitted to charge an equal amount of personal expenses to the partnerships. After Sydney moved to Florida, Sydney commuted to Pennsylvania every week to work for two to three days. After a year passed, Sydney told Ashley that he was considering retiring and remaining in Florida permanently. They tried to reach an agreement on Ashley's purchase of Sydney's partnership interests but were unable to do so. Ashley continued to manage the businesses by himself for nearly four years. During that time, Ashley paid himself salaries in excess of what the brothers had agreed. Has Ashley received excessive compensation as a partner?

**6.** Roy Moyle and Kenneth McCue were the general partners of McCue-Moyle Development Company, a real estate investment partnership that bought, developed, and sold real estate. Robert Baker offered $1.1 million for one piece of partnership property. On behalf of the partnership, Moyle signed the offer. Subsequently, McCue objected to the sale price and argued that the contract was not binding on the partnership because McCue had not signed it. Was the partnership bound on the contract?

**7.** ▣ *Video Case.* See "The Partnership." Art is a partner of Alphabet Builders, a partnership in the construction business. The three partners of Alphabet Builders have agreed that the partnership may not borrow money unless all the partners approve the borrowing. In the name of the partnership but without the consent of his partners, Art borrows money from a bank. Art tells the bank that the partnership will use the money for general purposes. Art indorses the loan check in the name of the partnership but deposits the money in his personal account. Art uses the money to purchase commodities futures. Art loses money on the futures and is unable to repay the loan. The bank sues Alphabet Builders and its partners. Are Alphabet Builders and its partners liable to the bank on the loan? Does Art have any liability to his partners?

**8.** Harold Schwartz, Gerald Dowell, and Lester Dowell formed a partnership to develop residential real estate. The Dowells gave Schwartz complete responsibility to sell the land. Although Schwartz and the Dowells knew that the land had not been surveyed, they conducted no survey because of the high cost of surveying. Instead, Schwartz relied on boundary information from a survey map, from land to the east that had been surveyed, and from boundary stakes placed by previous owners. In preparation for sale, Schwartz marked the boundaries with stakes and surveyor's ribbons. A prospective purchaser, Charles Nuttall, saw the stakes and flags placed by Schwartz and was told that they were "accurate within a couple of feet at the most." Nuttall bought land from the partnership relying on the representations made by Schwartz. Subsequent survey proved the boundaries to be off by 130 feet, resulting in damages of $1,900 to Nuttall. Nuttall sued the Dowells. Are they liable for Schwartz's misrepresentations?

**9.** Ramada Inn West was a partnership operating a motel in Asheville, North Carolina. The partners were James Brandis, Ann Brandis, and Wallace Hyde. One evening, a Ramada Inn West waitress served four double shots of Tequila and four bottles of beer to Wayne Jordan, an underage drinker. Driving a car on his way home, Jordan died in a one-car automobile accident allegedly caused by his intoxication. When Jordan's estate sued the partnership for causing his death by serving him alcoholic beverages when he was too young, to whom did it address the complaint?

**10.** Alvin Meyer was a resident of 100 Central Park South, an apartment building in Manhattan, New York, owned by a partnership, Park South Associates. Meyer sued the partnership and one of its partners, Donald Trump, on three grounds: for violation of the lease between Meyer and the partnership, for breach of the warranty of habitability, and for the tort of intentional infliction of emotional distress due to the partnership's harassment of Meyer. Meyer did not allege in his complaint that Park South Associates was insolvent or otherwise unable to pay its obligations. Trump asked the trial court to dismiss the suit against him on the grounds that he personally could not be sued on partnership obligations unless it was insolvent or otherwise unable to pay its obligations. Did the court agree with Trump?

## CAPSTONE QUESTIONS

Amy, Joey, Lorena, and John formed a partnership known as AJLJ Enterprises. The partnership's business is the sale of new and used guns, knives, and other weapons. Questions have arisen in the minds of the partners as a result of these facts:

- When AJLJ Enterprises was formed, the partners made no express agreement on how profits were to be divided or on how losses were to be apportioned. Of the $100,000 initial capital of the firm, Amy and Joey each contributed $40,000. Lorena and John each contributed $10,000. The partnership made a profit of $150,000 during the first year its business was in operation. Amy asserts that she and Joey are each entitled to $60,000 of the firm's $150,000 profit. Joey agrees with Amy on this point, but Lorena and John do not.

- The four partners agree that because AJLJ's business has grown so rapidly, the firm needs to find a place of business that is considerably larger than the building the firm is currently leasing. In addition, the partners agree that purchasing a new business site would be preferable to continuing to lease. John, who is independently wealthy, owns a building that, in his estimation, would be ideal as a place of business for the partnership. Although he would be interested in selling the property to the partnership, he has not mentioned this interest to his partners because his understanding is that any sale by him to the partnership would amount to unlawful self-dealing.

- Joey owes a substantial personal debt (i.e., a debt unrelated to the partnership business) to Earl Sleazeman, owner of Sleazeman's Pawn Shop. In recognition of the substantial contributions Joey has made to the success of the partnership business, he, Amy, and Lorena would like to have the partnership assume liability for Joey's debt to Sleazeman. John, however, is adamantly opposed to the idea.

- In order to have used guns and knives to sell to customers, AJLJ Enterprises buys them from various sources, including persons who come in off the street and wish to sell their weapons to AJLJ. The four partners have agreed among themselves, however, that only Amy, Lorena, and John will have authority to purchase weapons for resale. The partners have agreed that Joey will have no such authority. On a recent afternoon, while Joey was the only partner present at the AJLJ place of business, a customer who wanted to sell several used handguns and shotguns came to the place of business. Joey ended up purchasing the guns, ostensibly on behalf of the partnership, for $500. (Joey used $500 from the firm's cash register for this purpose.) When the other partners learned what Joey had done, they disapproved. Amy contacted the person from whom Joey had bought the guns, explained that Joey exceeded his authority in making the purchase, and proposed to return the guns to the seller in exchange for a refund of the firm's $500. The seller declined, noting that "a deal's a deal."

· Recently, while Lorena was showing a prospective customer a knife in which he was interested, Lorena negligently let the knife slip from her hand. The knife came in contact with the customer, who was badly injured. The customer will be filing suit shortly. When he learned of the incident, John said this to Joey: "I know how the dude feels. And I've got another reason to feel bad over this deal: the injured dude probably knows I've got substantial assets, so he'll be looking to me for payment. Maybe he'll even go after you and Amy, in addition to Lorena." Joey responded by urging John to "hold your horses. Lorena's the only one liable to the guy she slashed. The rest of us ain't got a thing to worry about."

· The four AJLJ partners recently had a discussion about how losses would be apportioned among themselves if the firm's business took a severe downturn and losses became so extensive that the firm's liabilities exceeded its assets. Lorena asserted that in view of the amount of Amy's capital

contribution, Amy would bear 40 percent of the firm's losses. Amy disagreed with this conclusion, though she admitted that she did not know exactly what her share of the losses should be. Joey and John confessed that they, too, were totally in the dark on the loss apportionment issue.

## Required:

Answer the following and give reasons for your conclusions.

1. Is Amy's assertion about her share of the firm's profits correct?
2. Is John's understanding regarding self-dealing transactions legally accurate?
3. Because Joey, Amy, and Lorena form a majority, may they override John's objection and cause the firm to assume Joey's personal debt to Sleazeman?
4. Is Joey's purchase of the handguns and shotguns binding on the partnership?
5. With regard to the incident in which Lorena negligently injured a customer, whose analysis—John's or Joey's—is closer to the mark in a legal sense?
6. Is Lorena's assertion about Amy's share of losses legally accurate?

CHAPTER

31

# DISSOLUTION, WINDING UP, AND TERMINATION OF PARTNERSHIPS

**INTRODUCTION**

*This chapter is about the death of partnerships. Three terms are important in this connection: dissolution, winding up, and termination. Dissolution is a change in the relation of the partners, as when a partner dies. Winding up, which may follow dissolution, is the orderly liquidation of the partnership assets and the distribution of the proceeds to those having claims against the partnership. Termination, the end of the partnership's existence, automatically follows winding up. A limited liability partnership is dissolved, wound up, and terminated in the same manner as an ordinary partnership.*

## DISSOLUTION

**Dissolution** is defined in the Uniform Partnership Act (UPA) as "the change in the relation of the partners caused by any partner ceasing to be associated in the carrying on as distinguished from the winding up of the business." A dissolution may be caused by a partner's retirement, death, or bankruptcy, among other things. Whatever the cause of dissolution, however, it is characterized by a partner's *ceasing to take part in the carrying on of the partnership's business.*

Dissolution is the starting place for the winding up (liquidation) and termination of a partnership. Although winding up does not always follow dissolution, it often does. Winding up usually has a severe effect on a business: It usually ends the business, because the assets of the business are sold and the proceeds of the sale are distributed to creditors and partners.

A partner has the *power* to dissolve the partnership *at any time*, such as by withdrawing from the partnership. A partner does not, however, always have the *right* to dissolve a partnership. A partner has the right to dissolve a partnership only when a dissolution does not violate the partnership agreement. For example, a partner has the power to withdraw from a partnership with a 20-year term before the term expires, but has no right to do so.

When a partner's dissolution does not violate the partnership agreement, the partner has the right to dissolve the partnership: Such a dissolution is **nonwrongful.** When a partner's dissolution violates the partnership agreement, the partner has the power—

but not the right—to dissolve the partnership: Such a dissolution is **wrongful.** The consequences that follow a nonwrongful dissolution may differ from those that follow a wrongful dissolution.

## Nonwrongful Dissolution

A dissolution is nonwrongful when the dissolution does not violate the partnership agreement. The following actions are nonwrongful dissolutions:

**1.** Automatic dissolution at the end of the term stated in the partnership agreement. For example, a partnership with a 20-year term is automatically dissolved at the expiration of that term.

**2.** Automatic dissolution on the partnership's accomplishment of its objective. For example, a partnership organized to build 15 condominiums dissolves when it completes their construction.

**3.** Withdrawal of a partner at any time from a partnership at will. A partnership at will is a partnership whose partnership agreement does not specify any specific term or objective.

**4.** Unanimous agreement of the partners who have not assigned their partnership interests or suffered charging orders against their partnership interests.

**5.** Expulsion of a partner in accordance with the partnership agreement. For example, the removal of a partner who has stolen partnership property dissolves the partnership if the partnership agreement allows removal on such grounds.

**6.** The illegality of the partnership business.

**7.** The death of a partner.

**8.** The bankruptcy of a partner. The partner must be adjudicated a bankrupt. Mere insolvency does not effect a dissolution.

In addition, a partner or other may go to court to request that a judge order a judicial dissolution in several situations. The following grounds for **judicial dissolution** are nonwrongful:

**9.** The adjudicated insanity of a partner.

**10.** The inability of a partner to perform the partnership contract. For example, a two-person partnership that remodels kitchens may be dissolved by a court when one of the partners becomes paralyzed in an automobile accident.

**11.** The inability of the partnership to conduct business except at a loss. Often, a partnership is not making a profit because of irreconcilable differences among the partners that prevent the business from being conducted beneficially.

**12.** At the request of a purchaser of a partnership interest in a partnership at will. This allows the creditor to whom a partner has assigned his partnership interest to obtain a dissolution and then to seek a winding up. During winding up, the creditor is paid from the debtor/partner's share of the proceeds of the sale of partnership assets.

**Consequences of Nonwrongful Dissolution** When a dissolution is nonwrongful, each partner, including the dissolving partner, may demand that the business of the partnership be wound up; also, each partner—unless deceased or bankrupt—may participate in the winding-up process. In addition, by their unanimous agreement, the partners—including the nonwrongfully dissolving partner—may decide to allow one or more of the partners to continue the business using the partnership's name. If unanimity to continue the business cannot be obtained, any partner may force the business to wind up.

## Wrongful Dissolution

A partner wrongfully dissolves a partnership when she dissolves her partnership in violation of the partnership agreement. For example, a partner wrongfully dissolves a partnership by retiring before the partnership accomplishes its stated objective of building vacation homes in Aspen, Colorado.

In addition, some judicial dissolutions on the following grounds are wrongful dissolutions for the wrongdoing partner: (1) when a partner's conduct prejudicially affects the business, or (2) when a partner willfully and persistently breaches the partnership agreement or her fiduciary duties. For example, a partner may continually insult customers, causing a loss of business; or a partner may persistently and substantially use partnership property for his own benefit; or three partners may refuse to allow a fourth partner to manage the partnership's business. In all of these situations, the harmed partners may seek judicial dissolution. As to the harmed partners, the dissolution would be nonwrongful. As to the wrongdoing partners, the dissolution would be wrongful.

**Consequences of Wrongful Dissolution** A partner who wrongfully dissolves a partnership (1) has no right to demand that the business be wound up; (2) has no right to participate in the winding up if the business is wound up; (3) has no right to have the goodwill of the business taken into account in valuing his partnership interest; (4) may not use the firm's name in connection with any business he conducts after dissolution; and (5) is liable for damages for breach of the partnership agreement, such as loss of profits. Nonetheless, a wrongfully dissolving partner is entitled to his share of the value of the partnership, minus his share of the partnership goodwill and the damages he caused the partnership.

**Right to Continue**   In the event of a wrongful dissolution, the innocent partners may continue the business themselves or with new partners. They may continue to use the partnership's name. This right to continue the business prevents a wrongfully dissolving partner from forcing a liquidation of the partnership. In addition, each of the innocent partners has all of the rights that are possessed by partners when there is a nonwrongful dissolution. This means that if there is a wrongful dissolution, any innocent partner may force a winding up. Usually, innocent partners choose to continue the business.

## Acts Not Causing Dissolution

A partner's assignment of his partnership interest does not dissolve a partnership, and neither does a creditor's obtaining a charging order. Also, the addition of a partner to a partnership does not dissolve the partnership, because no one disassociates from the partnership.

Mere disagreements, even irreconcilable differences, between the partners are expectable, but they are not grounds for dissolution. If the disagreements threaten partnership assets or profitability, then a court may order dissolution.

The partnership agreement may state that death or withdrawal shall not cause a dissolution. Although death or withdrawal clearly disassociates a partner from the carrying on of the business, several states permit the partners to vary the definition of dissolution by their agreement. Other states permit the partners to eliminate the right to demand a winding up after the death or withdrawal of a partner.

## Joint Ventures and Mining Partnerships

Essentially, the partnership rules of dissolution apply to joint ventures. It is more likely in a joint venture than in a partnership that a member's death will not dissolve the joint venture or not permit a demand to wind up; courts often find that joint venturers made an implied agreement that the limited objective of the joint venture be completed, as in *Rhue v. Dawson*, which follows.

Mining partnerships are more difficult to dissolve than general partnerships due to the free transferability of mining partnership interests. The death or bankruptcy of a mining partner does not effect a dissolution. In addition, a mining partner may sell his interest to another person and disassociate himself from the carrying on of the mining partnership's business without causing a dissolution. The other rules of partnership dissolution apply to mining partnerships.

---

## RHUE V. DAWSON
**841 P.2d 215 (Ariz. App. Div. 1992)**

James Rhue and John Dawson formed a partnership or joint venture to acquire and develop a shopping center. They named the enterprise Shopping Center Enterprises of Arizona (SCEA). Rhue had shopping center expertise and handled day-to-day details. Dawson contributed most of the capital and promised to seek bank financing for the project. They agreed to share profits and equity equally. They did not immediately put their agreement in writing, although drafts of an agreement were circulated.

Rhue located two adjacent shopping centers that the partnership purchased for $7.2 million. The estimated cost of renovating the combined shopping centers was $4.6 million. To obtain bank financing of the purchase and development of the combined shopping centers, Dawson obtained an appraisal of the projected value of the combined shopping center assuming redevelopment according to the plans prepared by SCEA. The appraisal projected the value at $15.6 million, indicating a projected profit of $3.8 for the venture. Rhue's one-half share of the projected profits would have been $1.9 million.

Seven days after receiving the appraisal, Dawson asked Rhue to sign a form entitled "Joint Venture Agreement." Dawson pressured Rhue to sign the agreement before Rhue could read it. Rhue specifically asked whether certain changes that they had discussed and agreed on were in the written agreement. Dawson replied that they were included; however, Dawson failed to tell Rhue that the agreement contained an "Option to Purchase" clause. Previous drafts lacked this clause. The clause allowed Dawson to buy Rhue's interest in the partnership merely by returning Rhue's capital contribution. Because Rhue contributed mostly expertise, not capital, this clause was highly favorable to Dawson. Rhue signed the agreement without reading it.

Two months later, Rhue learned about the "Option to Purchase" clause and indicated to Dawson that he did not intend to be bound by it. Dawson answered by notifying Rhue of his intent to exercise the buyout provision. Dawson then locked Rhue out of the partnership's offices. Rhue sued Dawson, claiming wrongful dissolution by Dawson and asking for lost profits. The trial judge held that Dawson had wrongfully dissolved the partnership and ordered Dawson to pay Rhue $8.4 million, which included Rhue's attorney's fees, punitive damages of $2 million, and the profits Rhue would have made on the venture, which were tripled under Arizona's racketeering statute. Dawson appealed.

---

**Lankford, Judge**    Arizona law recognizes three types of partnerships differentiated by term: a partnership at will, a partnership for a particular undertaking, and a partnership for a definite term. A partnership for a definite term or for a particular undertaking may be dissolved without violating the partnership agreement only at the end of the term or on completion of the undertaking. Only a partnership having no specified definite term or particular undertaking is a partnership at will. Such a partnership is subject to dissolution by express will of a partner without violating the partnership agreement.

Evidence supports a finding of a partnership other than one at will. Rhue and Dawson contemplated purchase of a single shopping center. They anticipated no other undertakings. This suggests a partnership for a particular undertaking.

Dawson could dissolve the partnership only in accordance with the terms of the agreement. Dawson delivered a letter notifying Rhue of the buyout and dissolving the partnership. Dawson locked Rhue out of the partnership offices. These actions effectively ousted Rhue as a partner. Dawson's conduct wrongfully dissolved the partnership in contravention of the parties' agreement.

A partner who has been wrongfully excluded from the partnership has the right, as against the partner who wrongfully excluded him, to damages for breach of the agreement, including loss of probable profits. To prove lost profits, Rhue must establish a reasonably certain factual basis for computation of lost profits. Dawson objects to the lost profits as too uncertain because SCEA was a new business.

While SCEA was a new business association, the two pieces of property held by SCEA had been operated in the commercial real estate market for many years. The appraiser estimated the value of the property based on the assumption that the property was to be developed in accordance with SCEA's plans and specifications. Dawson himself had utilized the same appraisal after the dissolution in various financial statements to a lending institution. Valuation methods utilized by the appraiser included comparable sales, net income, discounted cash flows, and replacement costs. The evidence was sufficient to support an award of lost profits.

Dawson next argues that his conduct was not sufficiently outrageous to justify an award of punitive damages. Rhue's claim for punitive damages is proper. Both fraud and deliberate, overt, dishonest dealings will suffice to sustain punitive damages. Dawson deliberately misled Rhue and intended to injure Rhue. Moreover, the relationship between the parties affects whether punitive damages can be awarded. Rhue and Dawson were partners. Dawson failed to discharge his fiduciary duty and his duty to exercise the utmost good faith and to discharge the obligation of loyalty, fairness, and honesty in his dealings with Rhue.

Dawson acted with an evil mind. Dawson deliberately failed to disclose to Rhue that the agreement signed by the parties contained a buyout provision. Dawson locked Rhue out of the partnership offices. Dawson's actions were consciously malicious.

Dawson also questions whether punitive damages may be imposed in addition to civil racketeering treble damages. Appellate courts will not interfere with the trial court's verdict on damages unless the verdict is not supported by the evidence or unless it is so outrageously excessive as to suggest passion or prejudice. We remand for the trial court to review the amount of punitive damages in light of the trebled compensatory damages to ensure that the former are not excessive.

**Judgment for Rhue affirmed; remanded to trial court for review of the punitive damage award.**

---

### CONCEPT REVIEW
## CAUSES OF DISSOLUTION AND ACTS NOT CAUSING DISSOLUTION

| | |
|---|---|
| **Causes of Dissolution** | **Wrongful Dissolutions**<br>1. Any dissolution that violates the partnership agreement.<br>2. Judicial dissolution due to a partner's conduct prejudicially affecting the business.<br>3. Judicial dissolution due to a partner's willful and persistent breach of the partnership agreement or her fiduciary duties.<br><br>**Nonwrongful Dissolutions**<br>1. End of the term stated in the partnership agreement.<br>2. The partnership's accomplishment of its objective.<br>3. Withdrawal of a partner at any time from a partnership at will.<br>4. Withdrawal of a partner in accordance with the partnership agreement.<br>5. Expulsion of a partner in accordance with the partnership agreement.<br>6. Unanimous agreement of the partners who have not assigned their partnership interests or suffered charging orders against their partnership interests.<br>7. Illegality of the partnership business.<br>8. Death of a partner.<br>9. Bankruptcy of a partner.<br>10. Judicial dissolution due to the adjudicated insanity of a partner.<br>11. Judicial dissolution due to the inability of a partner to perform the partnership contract.<br>12. Judicial dissolution due to the inability of the partnership to conduct business except at a loss.<br>13. Judicial dissolution at the request of a purchaser of a partnership interest in a partnership at will. |
| **Acts Not Causing Dissolution** | 1. A partner's assignment of a partnership interest.<br>2. A creditor's obtaining a charging order against a partnership interest.<br>3. Addition of a partner to a partnership.<br>4. Disagreement among the partners that does not threaten partnership assets or profitability.<br>5. Death or withdrawal of a partner, when the partnership agreement states that death or withdrawal shall not cause a dissolution. |

---

## WINDING UP THE PARTNERSHIP BUSINESS

When a partnership is to be terminated, the next step after dissolution is **winding up** the partnership's affairs. This involves the orderly liquidation—or sale—of the assets of the business. Liquidation may be accomplished asset by asset; that is, each asset may be sold separately. It may also be accomplished by a sale of the business as a whole. Or it may be accomplished by a means somewhere between these two extremes.

Winding up does not always require the sale of the assets or the business. When a partnership has valuable assets, the partners may wish to receive the assets rather than the proceeds from their sale. Such *distributions-in-kind* are rarely permitted. They are allowed when there are no creditors' claims against the partnership, the value of the assets can be ascertained, and the assets can be distributed in a manner that is fair to each partner.

During winding up, the partners continue as fiduciaries to each other, especially in negotiating sales or making distributions of partnership assets to members of the partnership. Nonetheless, there is a termination of the fiduciary duties unrelated to winding up. For example, a partner who is not winding up the business may compete with his partnership during winding up.

## Demanding and Performing Winding Up

A partner who has not wrongfully dissolved the partnership may demand winding up. Thus, when a partnership has been dissolved nonwrongfully, any partner, even the dissolving partner, may demand winding up. If the partnership has been wrongfully dissolved, only the innocent partners may demand winding up.

Any surviving, nonbankrupt partner who has not wrongfully dissolved the partnership may perform the winding up. A partner who has wrongfully dissolved the partnership has no right to wind up the business. When a dissolution is caused by the death or bankruptcy of a partner, the surviving partners and the nonbankrupt partners have the right to wind up the business.

If the dissolution is by court decree, usually no partner winds up. Instead, a *receiver* is appointed by the court to wind up the business.

✳ The compensation to a winding up partner is only his share of the profits, unless the partners agree to give special compensation to the winding up partner. In addition, when the winding up partner provides extraordinary services or is the sole surviving partner after dissolution by death, he is entitled to the reasonable value of his winding up services.

## Partner's Authority during Winding Up

**Express and Implied Authority**     During winding up, a partner has the express authority to act as the partners have agreed. The implied authority of a winding up partner is the power to do those acts *reasonably necessary to the winding up* of the partnership affairs. That is, he has the power to bind the partnership in any transaction necessary to the liquidation of the assets. He may collect money due, sue to enforce partnership rights, prepare assets for sale, sell partnership assets, pay partnership creditors, and do whatever else is appropriate to wind up the business. He may maintain and preserve assets or enhance them for sale, for example, by painting a building or by paying a debt to prevent foreclosure on partnership land. A winding up partner may temporarily continue the business when the effect is to preserve the value of the partnership.

**Performing Executory Contracts**     The implied authority of a winding up partner includes the power to perform contracts made before dissolution. A partner may not enter into *new* contracts unless the contracts aid the liquidation of the partnership's assets. For example, a partner may fulfill a contract to deliver coal if the contract was made before dissolution. She may not make a new contract to deliver coal unless doing so disposes of coal that the partnership owns or has contracted to purchase.

**Borrowing Money**     Usually, the implied authority of a winding up partner includes no power to borrow money in the name of the partnership. Nonetheless, when a partner can preserve the assets of the partnership or enhance them for sale by borrowing money, he has implied authority to engage in new borrowing. For example, a partnership may have a valuable machine repossessed and sold far below its value at a foreclosure sale unless it can refinance a loan. A partner may borrow the money needed to refinance the loan, thereby preserving the asset. A partner may also borrow money to perform executory contracts.

**Apparent Authority**     Winding up partners have apparent authority to conduct business as they did before dissolution, when notice of dissolution is not given to those persons who knew of the partnership prior to its dissolution. For example, a construction partnership dissolves and begins winding up but does not notify anyone of its dissolution. After dissolution, a partner makes a contract with a customer to remodel the customer's building. The partner would have no implied authority to make the contract, because the contract is new business and does not help liquidate assets. Nonetheless, the contract may be within the partner's apparent authority, because to persons unaware of the dissolution, it appears that a partner may continue to make contracts that have been in the usual course of business.

To eliminate this apparent authority to conduct business in the normal way, the partnership must do both of the following:

1. Give **actual**—or personal—**notice** of the dissolution to persons who extended credit to the partnership prior to dissolution, and
2. Give either actual notice or **constructive notice** of the dissolution to persons who were not creditors but had merely done business with the partnership without extending credit or had merely been aware of the existence of the partnership.

Actual notice may be given by telephone or by a letter mailed or faxed to the creditor's place of business. Creditors may also receive actual notice by hearing of the dissolution by word of mouth or reading of it in a newspaper.

Constructive notice is notice published in a newspaper of general circulation in the places where the partnership did business. Constructive notice eliminates apparent authority of the partners as to noncreditors even if the notice is not read by the noncreditors.

For persons who were previously unaware of the partnership's existence, no notice of any type need be given to eliminate apparent authority.

**Disputes among Winding Up Partners**  When more than one partner has the right to wind up the partnership, the partners may disagree concerning which steps should be taken during winding up. For decisions in the ordinary course of winding up, the decision of a majority of the partners controls. When the decision is an extraordinary one, such as continuing the business for an extended period of time, unanimous partner approval is required.

In the following case, the court found that the business of the partnership to train and race a horse should continue during winding up.

## PACIARONI V. CRANE
### 408 A.2d 946 (Del. Ct. Ch. 1979)

Black Ace, a harness racehorse of exceptional speed, was the fourth best pacer in the United States in 1979. He was owned by a partnership: Richard Paciaroni owned 50 percent; James Cassidy, 25 percent; and James Crane, 25 percent. Crane, a professional trainer, was in charge of the daily supervision of Black Ace, including training. It was understood that all of the partners would be consulted on the races in which Black Ace would be entered, the selection of drivers, and other major decisions; however, the recommendations of Crane were always followed by the other partners because of his superior knowledge of harness racing.

In 1979, Black Ace won $96,969 through mid-August. Seven other races remained in 1979, including the prestigious Little Brown Jug and the Messenger at Roosevelt Raceway. The purse for these races was $600,000.

A disagreement among the partners arose when Black Ace developed a ringbone condition and Crane followed the advice of a veterinarian not selected by Paciaroni and Cassidy. The ringbone condition disappeared, but later Black Ace became uncontrollable by his driver, and in a subsequent race he fell and failed to finish the race. Soon thereafter, Paciaroni and Cassidy sent a telegram to Crane rightfully dissolving the partnership and directing him to deliver Black Ace to another trainer they had selected. Crane refused to relinquish control of Black Ace, so Paciaroni and Cassidy sued him in August 1979, asking the court to appoint a receiver who would race Black Ace in the remaining 1979 stakes races and then sell the horse. Crane objected to allowing anyone other than himself to enter the horse in races. Before the trial court issued the following decision, Black Ace had entered three additional races and won $40,000.

**Brown, Vice Chancellor**   It is generally accepted that once dissolution occurs, the partnership continues only to the extent necessary to close out affairs and complete transactions begun but not then finished. It is not generally contemplated that new business will be generated or that new contractual commitments will be made. This, in principle, would work against permitting Black Ace to participate in the remaining few races for which he is eligible.

However, in Delaware, there have been exceptions to this. Where, because of the nature of the partnership business, a better price upon final liquidation is likely to be obtained by the temporary continuation of the business, it is permissible, during the winding up process, to have the business continue to the degree necessary to preserve or enhance its value upon liquidation, provided that such continuation is done in good faith with the intent to bring affairs to a conclusion as soon as reasonably possible. And one way to accomplish this is through an application to the Court for a winding up under UPA Section 37, which carries with it the power of the Court to appoint a receiver for that purpose.

The business purpose of the partnership was to own and race Black Ace for profit. The horse was bred to race. He has the ability to be competitive with the top pacers in the country. He is currently "racing fit" according to the evidence. He has at best only seven more races to go over a period of the next six weeks, after which time there are established horse sales at which he can be disposed of to the highest bidder. The purse for these remaining stake races is substantial. The fact that he could possibly sustain a disabling injury during this six-week period appears to be no greater than it was when the season commenced. Admittedly, an injury could occur at any time. But this is a fact of racing life which all owners and trainers are forced to accept. And the remaining stake races are races in which all three partners originally intended that he would compete, if able.

Under these circumstances, I conclude that the winding up of the partnership affairs should include the right to race Black Ace in some or all of the remaining 1979 stakes races for which he is now eligible. The final question, then, is who shall be in charge of racing him.

On this point, I rule in favor of Paciaroni and Cassidy. They may, on behalf of the partnership, continue to race the horse through their new trainer, subject, however, to the conditions hereafter set forth. Crane does have a monetary interest in the partnership assets that must be protected if Paciaroni and Cassidy are to be permitted to test the whims of providence in the name of the partnership during the next six weeks. Accordingly, I make the following ruling:

**1.** Paciaroni and Cassidy shall first post security in the sum of $100,000 so as to secure to Crane his share of the value of Black Ace.

**2.** If Paciaroni and Cassidy are unable or unwilling to meet this condition, then they shall forgo the right to act as liquidating partners. In that event, each party, within seven days, shall submit to the Court the names of two persons who they believe to be qualified, and who they know to be willing, to act as receiver for the winding up of partnership affairs.

**3.** In the event that no suitable person can be found to act as receiver, or in the event that the Court should deem it unwise to appoint any person from the names so submitted, then the Court reserves the power to terminate any further racing by Black Ace and to require that he simply be maintained and cared for until such time as he can be sold as a part of the final liquidation of the partnership.

**Judgment for Paciaroni and Cassidy.**

---

**CONCEPT REVIEW**

## Partner's Authority during Winding Up

| | |
|---|---|
| **Express Authority** | · To do anything the partners agree a partner may perform. |
| **Implied Authority** | · To do those acts reasonably necessary to winding up.<br>· Preserve and enhance assets<br>· Sell assets<br>· Complete executory contracts |

| Apparent Authority | · To conduct business in the usual way, unless proper notice of dissolution has been given.<br>  · Actual notice—must be given to prior creditors of the partnership.<br>  · Constructive notice (or actual notice)—must be given to noncreditors who conducted business with the partnership.<br>  · Constructive notice (or actual notice)—must be given to persons who did not conduct business with the partnership but knew of its existence.<br>  · No notice—to persons who previously were unaware of the partnership's existence. |
|---|---|

## WHEN THE BUSINESS IS CONTINUED

Cessation of business need not follow dissolution of a partnership. The remaining partners could purchase the business during winding up, someone else could purchase the business, or the partnership agreement could provide that there will be no winding up and that the business may be carried on by the remaining partners.

When there is no winding up and the business is continued, the claims of creditors against the partnership and the partners may be affected, because old partners are no longer with the business and new partners may enter the business.

### Successor's Liability for Predecessor's Obligations

When the business of a partnership is continued after dissolution, creditors of the old partnership are creditors of the person or partnership continuing the business. In addition, the original partners remain liable for obligations incurred prior to dissolution unless there is agreement with the creditors to the contrary. Thus, partners may not usually escape liability by forming a new partnership or a corporation to carry on the old business of the partnership.

### Outgoing Partner's Liability for Obligations Incurred While a Partner

Outgoing partners remain liable to partnership creditors for partnership liabilities incurred while they were partners; however, an outgoing partner's liability may be eliminated by the process of **novation.** Novation occurs when the following two conditions are met:

1. The continuing partners release an outgoing partner from liability on a partnership debt, and
2. A partnership creditor releases the outgoing partner from liability on the same obligation.

Partners usually expressly release an outgoing partner from liability, but the release may be implied as well. To complete the requirements for novation, an outgoing partner must also secure his release by the partnership's creditors. A creditor's agreement to release an outgoing partner from liability may be express, but usually it is implied. *Implied* novation may be proved by a creditor's knowledge of a partner's withdrawal and his continued extension of credit to the partnership. In addition, a *material modification* of an obligation operates as a novation for an outgoing partner, when the creditor has knowledge that the continuing partners have released the outgoing partner from liability.

When former partners release an outgoing partner from liability but creditors do not, there is not a novation. As a result, creditors may enforce a partnership liability against an outgoing partner. However, the outgoing partner may recover from his former partners who have agreed to release him from liability.

Nonetheless, an outgoing partner may not enforce a release-of-liability agreement when he obtains the release by failing to disclose material facts to the partners or creditors. For example, an outgoing partner who obtains release from the partners without disclosing that he has bound the partnership on a contract retains his liability to the other partners.

In the following case, the court found both an implied novation and a material alteration operating as a novation. Consequently, the court relieved an outgoing partner from liability to a landlord.

## WESTER & CO. V. NESTLE
### 669 P.2d 1046 (Colo. Ct. App. 1983)

Junior Nestle and Eric Ellis were the owners of Red Rocks Meat and Deli, a partnership. They had no partnership agreement and no specified term for the partnership. They operated the partnership in a building that they leased from Wester & Company. In October 1978, Nestle left the business. John Herline purchased Nestle's partnership interest, including Nestle's entire interest in partnership equipment, leases, and other assets. In return, a new partnership of Ellis and Herline agreed to assume all the liabilities of the former partnership and to release Nestle from liability. A copy of the purchase and release agreement was mailed to Wester & Co., giving notice to Wester & Co. that Nestle was no longer a partner. Ellis introduced Herline to Wester & Co. as his new partner. Wester & Co. did not object to a change in partners or request that Nestle remain liable.

Soon after, Herline left the partnership, and Ellis operated the business as a sole proprietorship. In January 1980, Wester & Co. and Ellis modified the original lease to include adjacent space and to increase the rent. When the lease was modified, it was clear to Wester & Co. that Ellis was then operating the business as a sole proprietor. The president of Wester & Co. was told when the lease was modified that Nestle was no longer a partner.

In May 1980, when Ellis failed to pay the rent, Wester & Co. sued Nestle for the rent. The court found that due to Wester & Company's knowledge of the situation and the parties' course of dealings, it had consented to Nestle's release from liability. The court also concluded that the modified lease materially altered Nestle's liability on the underlying lease, thereby discharging Nestle from liability. Wester & Co. appealed.

---

**Steinberg, Judge**    The dissolution of a partnership does not of itself discharge the existing liability of any partner. A partner is discharged from existing liability by an agreement to that effect between the withdrawing partner, the remaining partners, and the partnership creditor, and "such agreement may be inferred from the course of dealing between the creditor and the person or partnership continuing the business." A material alteration in an existing liability will discharge from liability a partner whose obligations have been assumed.

The trial court found that the conditions for discharge from liability under both of these subsections existed, and such factual findings, supported by the evidence, may not be disturbed upon appeal.

**Judgment for Nestle affirmed.**

---

## Outgoing Partner's Liability for Obligations Incurred after Leaving the Partnership

Ordinarily, an outgoing partner has no liability on partnership obligations incurred after he leaves the partnership because he no longer controls the partnership or shares as a co-owner in its profits. Nonetheless, outgoing partners may be liable for obligations incurred by a person or partnership continuing the business after their departure, under the theory of *partnership by estoppel*. There is no such liability to creditors who are aware of the change in partners. Also, the risk of estoppel liability can be eliminated by giving the appropriate notice that the partner has left the partnership.

Actual—or personal—notice must be given to those persons who extended credit to the partnership prior to dissolution. Such notice may be either oral or written and must be actually delivered or received. Constructive notice—notice published several times in a newspaper of general circulation—is sufficient for those who knew of the partnership but were not prior creditors. No notice need be given to persons who were not previously aware of the partnership's existence or who knew of the dissolution.

## Liability of Incoming Partners

A person joining an existing partnership has unlimited liability for all partnership obligations incurred *after* she becomes a partner. For partnership obligations incurred *before* she became a partner, she is liable as if she had been a partner when the obligations were incurred; however, her liability is limited to the partnership's assets. Once partnership assets are exhausted, she has no further liability for partnership obligations that were incurred prior to her affiliation with the partnership. Nonetheless, if she has expressly or impliedly agreed to undertake unlimited liability for prior obligations, her liability will be unlimited. For example, she may agree with an outgoing partner to assume the outgoing partner's partnership obligations.

In the following case, incoming partners had no liability beyond the assets of the partnership on a debt that arose prior to their joining the partnership.

---

### KALICHMAN V. BEVERLY HOLDING CO.
#### 520 N.Y.S.2d 255 (N.Y. App. Div. 1987)

---

Joseph Kalichman and Joseph Klein formed a partnership that owned and managed an apartment building in the Bronx, New York. The partnership borrowed $189,000 from National Savings Bank of Albany. Before the loan was repaid, Joseph Klein died, and his interest in the partnership passed to his sons, Jack and Frank, who received Joseph Klein's share of the partnership income. Jack and Frank did not, however, engage in management of the partnership business. When the partnership defaulted on the loans, National Savings Bank sued Kalichman. Kalichman settled the lawsuit by paying $100,000 to National Savings Bank and then sued Jack and Frank Klein to require them to pay their share of the liability. The trial court found Jack and Frank liable to Kalichman; Jack and Frank appealed.

---

**Casey, Justice**    Jack and Frank assert that the existence of a partnership arrangement does not demonstrate or indicate their assumption of a preexisting obligation on the bonds, rendering them personally liable for such debt. We agree. UPA section 41(7) provides:

The liability of a third person becoming a partner in the partnership continuing the business under this section to the creditors of the dissolved partnership shall be satisfied out of partnership property only.

Although the primary purpose of UPA section 41 is the protection of creditors, it also limits incoming partners' liability to the partnership property unless personal liability is expressly assumed through the partnership agreement or otherwise. Here, Joseph Klein's death dissolved his partnership with Kalichman. Kalichman then had the right to possess the property for a partnership purpose, as well as the duty to wind up the affairs of the partnership and to pay to Joseph Klein's legal representative Klein's proportionate share in partnership surplus. These events did not occur here, however, since Kalichman continued the partnership business with Jack and Frank's consent. Having continued to carry on the partnership business after Joseph Klein's death, Kalichman must bear all of the losses, while UPA section 41(7) limits Jack and Frank's liability to their interest in the Bronx property. Jack and Frank's only association with the partnership was to receive income from the same. While this fact might evidence the formation of a partnership between Jack, Frank, and Kalichman, it does not evidence that Jack and Frank ever assumed personal liability for preexisting loans incurred by Joseph Klein.

**Judgment reversed in favor of Jack and Frank Klein.**

## Rights of Outgoing Partners

An outgoing partner is entitled to receive the value of his partnership interest. He becomes a creditor of the new partnership for the value of his partnership interest, but his claim is subordinate to the claims of other creditors of the partnership.

### Valuation of the Outgoing Partner's Interest

The value of an outgoing partner's interest in the partnership is determined at the time of the dissolution. Often, the partnership agreement includes a method for calculating the value of a partnership interest.

The value of a partnership includes its goodwill. **Goodwill** is the well-founded expectation of continued public patronage of a business. It represents the difference between the going-concern value of a business and the liquidation value of its assets.

When a partnership business is continued after dissolution, it is frequently difficult to determine the value of the goodwill that is transferred to the continuing partners. In service partnerships, the goodwill may be so closely tied to the individual partners that no goodwill remains with the business when valuable partners withdraw from the partnership. These difficulties and uncertainties also make it advisable to have a partnership agreement on valuing the partnership, including the value of its goodwill.

**Payment Options**     In the absence of a contrary agreement, when dissolution results from death or retirement, the outgoing partner may choose one of the following payment options:

1. Taking the value of his partnership interest at the time of dissolution plus interest, or
2. Taking the value of his partnership interest at the time of dissolution plus a pro rata share of subsequent profits.

These options provide incentive for the continuing partners to settle promptly with an outgoing partner.

When there is no agreement and dissolution results from a cause other than death or retirement—as with dissolutions caused by bankruptcy or by willful, persistent breaches of the partnership agreement—the partner is entitled to receive the value of her interest at the time of dissolution. The outgoing partner may insist on immediate payment and receive interest for late payment.

**Valuation of Interest of Wrongfully Dissolving Partner**     A wrongfully dissolving partner must be paid the value of his partnership interest in cash by the continuing partners, or the partners must post a bond to have the privilege of continuing the business. In addition, they must agree to release him from all present and future partnership liabilities. However, goodwill is excluded from the valuation of the partnership interest of a partner who has wrongfully caused dissolution, and the valuation of that interest is further reduced by the damages that he has caused his partners due to his dissolution.

## DISTRIBUTION OF ASSETS

After the partnership's assets have been sold during winding up, the proceeds are distributed to those persons who have claims against the partnership. Not only creditors but also partners have claims against the proceeds. As you might expect, the claims of creditors must be satisfied before the claims of partners may be paid. The UPA states the order of distribution of the partnership assets:

1. Those owing to creditors other than partners.
2. Those owing to partners other than for capital and profits.
3. Those owing to partners in respect of capital.
4. Those owing to partners in respect of profits.

Note that item 2 places partners who are also creditors of the partnership subordinate to other creditors. This is done to prevent partners from underfunding a partnership to the detriment of creditors. The subordination of partner-creditors also emphasizes that the partners are liable for all the partnership's liabilities.

A partner who is also a creditor of the partnership, however, is paid his claim as a creditor before any partner receives any return of his capital contribution. Thus, for example, a partner's loan to the partnership is repaid before any partner has his capital returned.

If a partnership has not suffered losses that impair its capital, few problems are presented in the distribution of its assets. Everyone having an interest in the partnership is paid in full. If there is a disagreement about the amount due to a claimant, the dispute is usually resolved by an accounting ordered by the court. In the following case, the court calculated each partner's share of the assets of a solvent partnership.

## LANGNESS v. O STREET CARPET SHOP
### 353 N.W.2d 709 (Neb. Sup. Ct. 1984)

NFL Associates was a partnership of three partners: Herbert Friedman, Strelsa Lee Langness, and The O Street Carpet Shop, Inc. At the partnership's creation in 1973, O Street Carpet contributed a contract worth $9,000, Langness contributed $14,000 in cash, and Friedman contributed his legal services, which were not valued. The partners used part of Langness's contribution to make an $8,000 payment to O Street Carpet. They used the remaining $6,000 to purchase investment property and for working capital. Later, O Street Carpet contributed an additional $4,005 in capital. The partners agreed that Friedman would receive 10 percent of the profits and that each of the other two partners would receive 45 percent of the profits. The partners also agreed that Langness would receive payments of $116.66 each month.

During the five-year term of the partnership, Langness received checks totaling $6,300.30. Langness did not pay income tax on these monthly payments. The partnership did not take expense deductions for those payments on its information return filed with the Internal Revenue Service. In 1978, the partnership dissolved and wound up its business, selling its investment property for $52,001.20. After paying partnership liabilities of $3,176.79, Friedman distributed the remaining $48,824.41 to the partners. Langness received $16,792.01, O Street Carpet received $26,808.58, and Friedman received $5,223.82. Langness was unhappy with the distribution and sued Friedman and O Street Carpet for a larger share. The trial court held that Langness was entitled to receive $24,082.43. The court imposed liability on Friedman and O Street Carpet for $7,290.42, the additional amount Langness should have received. Friedman appealed.

---

**Per Curiam**   Friedman's appeal is best analyzed by reviewing the capital contributions made by the partners, the nature of the payments made to Langness, and the distributions made to each of the three partners upon the winding up of the partnership. O Street Carpet made a contribution of property worth $9,000. However, $8,000 of the $14,000 contributed by Langness went to O Street Carpet, thereby reducing its capital contribution at that time to $1,000. O Street Carpet contributed an additional $4,005 in capital. Thus, O Street Carpet's total capital contribution is $5,005.

Friedman contributed no money or property. It is the general rule that a partner who contributes only services to a partnership is not deemed to have made a capital contribution to the partnership, unless the partners have agreed to the contrary. Friedman argues that since, by agreement, he was given 10 percent of the partnership, he was entitled to be credited with a like amount of the partnership capital upon dissolution. While the agreement specifically states that Friedman is entitled to 10 percent of the partnership profits, it mentions nothing concerning his rights to partnership capital upon dissolution. Therefore, Friedman made no capital contribution to the venture.

We next address the nature of the payments made to Langness. The partnership agreement called for the partnership to pay to Langness $116.66 per month for the life of the partnership. While this provision of the articles is found under a section labeled "Distribution of Profits and Losses," the agreement does not state whether it is to be treated as an advance on profits or a capital withdrawal. Both accountants who testified at the trial stated that the payments were treated as capital withdrawals. Langness treated the payments as such when preparing her tax returns. The tax returns of the partnership did not treat them as expenses. We calculate her total capital withdrawals as $6,300.30, which reduced her capital in the partnership to $7,699.70.

We now reach the question of the appropriate amounts of the distribution to each of the partners. The partnership agreement provides: "Upon the dissolution of the partnership after settlement of all of its liabilities, the partners are entitled to all remaining assets of the partnership in equal proportions in liquidation of all of their respective interests in the partnership." Amounts owing to partners to reimburse them for capital contributions take priority over amounts owing to partners in respect to profits.

Of the $48,824.41 in assets remaining after payment of the partnership's debts, $7,699.70 is to be paid to Langness for her capital contribution and $5,005 to O Street Carpet for its capital contribution. The remaining $36,119.71 is to be divided according to the partners' share in the profits, which is on a 45–45–10 basis. This action requires $16,253.87 to be paid to Langness for profit, the same amount to O Street Carpet, and $3,611.97 to Friedman.

Therefore, Langness was entitled to a total distribution of $23,953.57. Since Langness was paid only $16,792.01, she is entitled to an additional $7,161.56.

**Judgment for Langness affirmed as modified.**

---

## Distribution of Assets of Insolvent Partnership

When a partnership has suffered losses, distribution of the assets may be troublesome. For example, partnership creditors may compete with the creditors of individual partners to obtain payment from partnership assets and the assets of individual partners. Also, the partnership losses must be allocated among partners. In adjusting the rights of partnership creditors and the creditors of individual partners, the rule is usually that partnership creditors have first claim on partnership assets and that individual creditors have first claim on individual assets. This is called **marshaling of assets**.

**Example**   The distribution of assets and allocation of losses of an insolvent partnership can best be explained with an example. Suppose that Alden, Bass, and Casey form a partnership and that Alden contributes $25,000, Bass contributes $15,000, and Casey contributes $10,000. After operating for several years, the firm suffers losses and becomes insolvent. When the partnership is liquidated, its assets total $30,000 in cash. It owes $40,000 to partnership creditors. Therefore, the capital balance (net worth) of the partnership is a negative $10,000. This means that partnership losses totaled $60,000 ($50,000 of capital already contributed and lost plus the $10,000 negative net worth). The situation could be represented by the following equation:

Profit = Ending owner's capital − Beginning owner's capital

−$60,000 =       −$10,000        −        $50,000

Because the profit is negative, this is a loss of $60,000.

In the absence of a provision in the partnership agreement concerning the partners' shares of profits and losses, they are shared equally. Therefore, each partner's **share of the loss** is one third of the loss, $20,000. Their shares of the loss reduce the partners' capital claims against partnership assets, as shown in the following table.

|  | Capital at Beginning | | Share of Loss | | Capital at Liquidation |
|---|---|---|---|---|---|
| Alden | $25,000 | − | $20,000 | = | $ 5,000 |
| Bass | 15,000 | − | 20,000 | = | (5,000) |
| Casey | 10,000 | − | 20,000 | = | (10,000) |
| Totals | $50,000 | − | $60,000 | = | $(10,000) |

The table shows that while each partner should have assumed $20,000 of the loss, Alden has taken $25,000 of the loss due to her $25,000 capital contribution. Therefore, unless she has $5,000 of her capital returned, she has assumed $5,000 of the loss she should not have assumed. Bass and Casey, on the other hand, have assumed too little of the loss, because their capital contributions were less than $20,000. Bass should undertake $5,000 more of the loss, and Casey should assume $10,000 more, amounts reflected in the last column of the table.

Now we shall distribute partnership assets and pay the claims against the partnership. Following the order of distribution in the UPA, the $30,000 in cash from the liquidation is distributed pro rata to pay the nonpartner creditors of the partnership. Because the creditors are owed $40,000, the $30,000 payment leaves $10,000 of partnership debts to outsiders unpaid. The partners are liable for the remaining $10,000. Because the partnership assets are gone, the partners must pay the debt from their individual assets.

To undertake their **shares of the partnership liabilities**, Bass is legally liable to contribute $5,000 and Casey $10,000 to the partnership, the negative amounts in the Capital at Liquidation column in the table. This permits completion of the payment of the partnership creditors ($10,000) and the return of Alden's capital to the extent that it exceeded her share of the partnership loss—the $5,000 figure in the Capital at Liquidation column.

Unpaid partnership creditors have a right to collect from any solvent partner. Had they chosen to collect the entire amount from Alden, she would then have had to proceed against Bass and Casey for the amount she paid that Bass and Casey should have paid.

## Termination

After the assets of a partnership have been distributed, **termination** of the partnership occurs automatically.

### PROBLEMS AND PROBLEM CASES

**1.** Jackson Wanlass and D. W. Ogden operated a title search business as partners at will. After Ogden and Wanlass died, the Ogden children excluded Mrs. Wanlass from the business and converted partnership funds. Mrs. Wanlass claimed that these actions amounted to a wrongful dissolution by the Ogden children. Was she correct?

**2.** Hilolani Acres Joint Venture was a partnership of 42 partners, including Benjamin Aiu. Four of the partners were designated managing partners. The partnership agreement stated that the purpose of the partnership was "dealing with" the Hilolani Acres, a housing development in Hawaii. The partnership agreement also provided for continuation of the business of the partnership in the event of a withdrawal of partners from the partnership. In 1971, three of the managing partners withdrew from the partnership; in addition, title to Hilolani Acres was transferred to Great Hawaiian Mortgage Corporation, which would manage the development of Hilolani Acres for the partnership; Great Hawaiian received 35 percent of the profits from Hilolani Acres, the remainder going to the partnership. The nonmanaging partners claimed that these acts dissolved the partnership, and they sought to wind it up. Were they right?

**3.** Robert Cowan was a partner in a six-person law firm. The partnership agreement provided that the firm would not dissolve upon the withdrawal of a partner. Cowan initially indicated that he would withdraw from the partnership but later changed his mind. By that time, however, the other partners had resolved to force Cowan from the partnership. The other partners transferred all partnership funds to accounts in their names only. However, a few days later, they set up an escrow account to protect the value of Cowan's partnership interest. Did the other partners' actions entitle Cowan to obtain a judicial dissolution of the partnership?

**4.** Kenneth Flynn and Rick Haddad were partners owning a beachfront lot with a small inn on it. Title to the lot was in both partners' names. Flynn gave Haddad a deed to Flynn's interest in the property, which was effective only upon Flynn's nonpayment of a loan. When the inn was destroyed by fire, the partners began construction of a new inn, but construction was stopped because it violated local zoning laws. The effect of halting construction was also to eliminate the market of potential buyers of the property. Haddad decided to sever his relationship with Flynn and, consequently, filed the deed to the property that had earlier been executed by Flynn, although Flynn had already repaid the loan. Has the partnership been dissolved? Should the property be sold during winding up, or should Haddad receive title to it and be required to pay Flynn his share of the value of the property?

**5.** Roger Steeby and Charles Fial were the only partners of an auditing firm. They contracted to provide audit services for their clients, but instead of performing the audits themselves, they hired independent contractors to do the audits. Because Fial generated about 80 percent of the business of the firm, he became unhappy with their profit-sharing agreement and dissolved the partnership. Fial terminated the contracts with the firm's clients and signed the clients to contracts with Fial's corporation, Audit Consultants of Colorado, Inc. Fial's corporation used the same independent contractors to perform audits for the clients. Has Fial acted properly?

**6.** Brothers Eugene and Marlowe Mehl operated a family farm as a partnership. Each partner was active in the partnership until Marlowe suffered a stroke. Eleven years later, the partnership was dissolved, and Eugene by himself wound up the partnership's affairs. Was Eugene entitled to wages as compensation for winding up the partnership?

**7.** Ralph Neitzert and his brother were the only partners of Jolly Jug Liquors, a retail liquor store. The partners signed a contract to lease refrigeration equipment from Colo-Tex Leasing, Inc. A month later, Ralph sold his interest in the partnership to his sister. Ralph did not notify Colo-Tex that he sold his interest to his sister. A year later, when the partnership breached the lease, Colo-Tex sued Ralph, his brother, and his sister. Is Ralph liable to Colo-Tex?

**8.** Weintraub, Gold & Alper, a law firm partnership, was dissolved. The firm's partners continued to occupy the same office space and to use the firm's name and letterhead as an aid in the partners' transition to individual law practices. Roger Allen sought a $60,000 loan from Royal Bank. Allen told Royal Bank that the $60,000 would be kept in an escrow account of his lawyers, the firm of Weintraub, Gold & Alper. Allen gave Royal Bank a letter on the law firm's stationery addressed to Allen and signed by Weintraub acknowledging that the money would be placed in a firm escrow account. Royal Bank discovered that Weintraub, Gold, and Alper were listed separately in a lawyer directory as practicing law at the address given on the firm stationery. Royal Bank also found the firm listing in the current New York phone book at the address and phone number on the letterhead. When Royal Bank dialed the number, the receptionist answered, "Weintraub, Gold and Alper." Royal Bank spoke with Weintraub, who confirmed the escrow arrangement. That same day, Royal Bank made the loan to Allen, giving him a check payable to the law firm. The check was deposited in the escrow account. When the loan was due, the escrowed check was not returned and the loan was not repaid. Royal Bank sued Gold and Alper to recover the $60,000. Were Gold and Alper liable to Royal Bank?

**9.** In 1980, Southern Distilleries, a partnership, executed two promissory notes totaling $140,000 payable to Commercial State Bank. In 1981, the partnership admitted Julius Moselely as a partner. He contributed $100,000 to the partnership. Two months later, Southern Distilleries executed a new promissory note to replace the old notes. The old notes were marked paid. The new note was in the amount of $140,000 payable to Commercial State Bank. The note was not paid when it was due, and the bank sued Southern Distilleries and its partners.

What is the amount of Moselely's liability to the bank on the $140,000 note?

**10.** 📢  *Video Case.* See "The Partnership." Art retires from Alphabet Builders, a partnership with Ben and Diedre. Zack agrees to replace Art in the partnership. Zack signs an agreement with Art assuming Art's liability for all partnership obligations. After Art leaves the partnership, Alphabet Builders falls behind in payments to its creditors, including the following:

**a.** The bank from which Art obtained a loan in the name of the partnership prior to his leaving the partnership. Art pocketed the bank loan and used it for his personal investment in commodities futures. Art did not disclose the loan to his partners or to Zack.

**b.** The creditor who leases office equipment to Alphabet Builders. The lease agreement predates the time Art left the partnership.

**c.** Subcontractors owed money on contracts entered into after Art left and Zack entered the partnership.

What is Art's liability on these obligations? What is Zack's liability on these obligations? What other facts do you need to help you answer these questions?

**11.** Thomas Bernabei, James Serra, and Howard Wenger formed a partnership, Fairway Development I. In 1981, Bernabei and Serra ceased their involvement with Fairway Development I and transferred all their rights in the partnership to Wenger and James Valentine. Wenger and Valentine continued the business as partners, using the name Fairway Development II. Subsequently, Fairway II sought to enforce Fairway I's contract with Title Insurance Company of Minnesota (TICOM). TICOM argued that it was liable to Fairway I only and that Fairway I had been dissolved and terminated. Therefore, TICOM argued that Fairway II was a new partnership, was not a party to the contract, and could not sue TICOM. Was TICOM correct?

## CAPSTONE QUESTIONS

Joe Varset, Gina Corfus, and Wendi Parker are the only partners of Klamath Associates, a partnership. In 1990, the partners sign a partnership agreementment stating that the partnership will expire on

December 31, 2022. The agreement also states that any partner has the right to retire from Klamath upon reaching the age of 60.

The partners enjoy good relations until 1994. During and after that year, Varset and Corfus commonly take positions opposite Parker on matters in the ordinary course of business. Consequently, Varset and Corfus cause Klamath to engage in business that Parker opposes.

Parker informs her partners that she does not want to continue the business with them. Varset and Corfus indicate that they would be willing to let Parker leave Klamath if she finds someone acceptable to them who can take her place in the business. Parker, who is 35 years old, would like to continue the business herself, but she would be willing to allow Varset, Corfus, and a new partner to continue the business if she has no liability for partnership obligations after she leaves Klamath.

Parker is considering the following options:

- Forcing Varset and Corfus from the partnership by obtaining a judicial dissolution of Klamath on the grounds that Varset and Corfus are dominating Klamath by outvoting Parker.
- Retiring from Klamath and then liquidating the assets of Klamath. Under this option, Parker proposes to sell all the partnership's assets to herself and continue the business using her own name.
- Selling her partnership interest to Bart Needham. Needham is willing to assume all of Parker's liabilities on Klamath's obligations. Varset and Corfus are willing to accept Needham as a replacement partner, to release Parker from liability for Klamath's obligations, and to continue Klamath's business.
- Obtaining Varset's and Corfus's agreement to dissolve the partnership. Under this option, Parker wants to wind up the business and sell the partnership assets individually, including the building in which Klamath has its principal place of business.

## Required:

Answer the following and give reasons for your conclusions.

1. Can Parker accomplish the first and second options?
2. What effect would the third option have on the liability of Parker and Needham?
3. Under the fourth option, does Parker have the power to sell the partnership building?
4. Indicate what steps Parker should take to ensure that during winding up, Varset and Corfus have authority only to wind up the business of Klamath?

# LIMITED PARTNERSHIPS AND LIMITED LIABILITY COMPANIES

## INTRODUCTION

*While the taxation advantages of the partnership form of business may attract investors to a partnership, the partners' unlimited liability for partnership debts scares away some investors. State legislatures and the Internal Revenue Service have cooperated to permit the creation of two business forms that offer taxation advantages similar to the partnership, yet extend limited liability to the owners of the business. These forms are the limited partnership and the limited liability company.*

## LIMITED PARTNERSHIPS

The partnership form—with managerial control and unlimited liability for all partners—is not acceptable for all business arrangements. Often, business managers want an infusion of capital into a business yet are reluctant to surrender managerial control to those contributing capital. Investors wish to contribute capital to a business and share in its profits yet limit their liability to the amount of their investment and be relieved of the obligation to manage the business.

The **limited partnership** serves these needs. The limited partnership has two classes of owners: **general partners**, who contribute capital to the business, manage it, share in its profits, and possess unlimited liability for its obligations; and **limited partners**, who contribute capital and share profits, but possess no management powers and have liability limited to their investments in the business.

In 1822, New York and Connecticut were the first states to recognize the limited partnership. Today, every state has a statute permitting the creation of limited partnerships, although Louisiana calls them partnerships *in commendam.*

### The Uniform Limited Partnership Acts

The National Conference of Commissioners on Uniform State Laws—a body of lawyers, judges, and legal scholars—drafted the Uniform Limited Partnership Act (ULPA) in 1916. In 1976, the commissioners drafted the Revised Uniform Limited Partnership Act (RULPA), which more clearly and

---

**FIGURE 1** **Principal Characteristics of Limited Partnerships**

1. A limited partnership may be *created only in accordance with a statute.*
2. A limited partnership has two types of partners: *general partners* and *limited partners.* It must have one or more of each type.
3. All partners, limited and general, *share the profits* of the business.
4. Each general partner has *unlimited liability* for the obligations of the business. Each limited partner has liability *limited to his capital contribution* to the business.
5. Each general partner has a *right to manage* the business, and she is an agent of the limited partnership. A limited partner has *no right to manage* the business or to act as its agent, but he does have the right to vote on fundamental matters. If a limited partner does manage the business, he may incur unlimited liability for partnership obligations.
6. General partners, as agents, are *fiduciaries* of the business. Limited partners are not fiduciaries.
7. A partner's interest in a limited partnership *is not freely transferable.* An assignee of a general or limited partnership interest is not a partner, but is entitled only to the assigning partner's share of capital and profits, absent a contrary agreement.
8. Withdrawal of a general partner *dissolves* a limited partnership absent a contrary agreement of the partners. The withdrawal of a limited partner does not automatically dissolve a limited partnership.
9. A limited partnership *pays no federal income taxes.* Its partners report their shares of the profits and losses on their individual federal income tax returns. A limited partnership files an *information return* with the Internal Revenue Service, notifying the IRS of each partner's share of the year's profit or loss.

---

comprehensively states the law of limited partnership. The RULPA was amended in several significant ways in 1985. Forty-eight states have adopted the RULPA, Vermont follows the ULPA, and Louisiana follows neither. The RULPA as amended in 1985 forms the foundation of the discussion in this chapter. References are made to the Uniform Partnership Act (UPA), which applies to limited partnerships in the absence of an applicable provision in the RULPA. As shown in Figure 1, many characteristics of a limited partnership under the RULPA are similar to those of a partnership under the UPA.

## Use of Limited Partnerships

The limited partnership form is used primarily in tax shelter ventures and activities such as real estate investment, oil and gas drilling, and professional sports. Limited partnerships operate as tax shelters by allowing partners to reduce their personal federal income tax liability by deducting limited partnership losses on their individual income tax returns. General partners, however, receive a greater tax shelter advantage than do limited partners. Losses of the business allocated to a general partner offset his income from any other sources. Losses of the business allocated to

limited partners may be used to offset only income from other *passive* investments. If a limited partner has sold her limited partnership interest or the limited partnership has terminated, her loss offsets any income.

## CREATION OF LIMITED PARTNERSHIPS

A limited partnership may be created only by complying with the applicable state statute. Yet the statutory requirements of the RULPA are minimal. A **certificate of limited partnership** must be executed and filed with the secretary of state. The certificate must be signed by all general partners. A limited partnership begins its existence at the time the certificate is filed with the office of the secretary of state or at any later time specified in the certificate. Figure 2 lists the contents of the certificate of limited partnership.

The certificate is not required to state the names of the limited partners, the partners' capital contributions, the partners' shares of profits and other distributions, or the acts that cause a dissolution of the limited partnership. Nonetheless, the partners will usually include those and other matters in the certificate or in a separate **limited partnership agreement.**

**FIGURE 2    Contents of Certificate of Limited Partnership**

The following must be in the certificate:

1. The name of the limited partnership, which must contain the words *limited partnership*. The name may not include the surname of a limited partner, unless it is the same as the surname of a general partner or unless the business of the limited partnership has been carried on under that name prior to the admission of the limited partner.
2. The name and address of each general partner. Each general partner must sign the certificate.
3. The latest date the limited partnership will dissolve.
4. The name and address of an agent for service of process. Designating an agent for service of process in the certificate eases a creditor's obligation to notify a limited partnership that it is being sued by the creditor.

Any *person* may be a general or limited partner. Persons include a natural person, partnership, limited partnership, trust, estate, association, or corporation. Hence, as commonly occurs, a corporation may be the sole general partner of a limited partnership.

The RULPA permits partners to make capital contributions of cash, property, services rendered, a promissory note, or a binding promise to contribute cash, property, or services.

## Defective Compliance with Limited Partnership Statute

The RULPA requires at least *substantial compliance* with the previously listed requirements to create a limited partnership. If the persons attempting to create a limited partnership do not substantially comply with the RULPA, a limited partnership does not exist; therefore, a limited partner may lose her limited liability and become liable as a general partner. A lack of substantial compliance might result from failing to file a certificate of limited partnership or from filing a defective certificate. A defective certificate might, for example, misstate the name of the limited partnership.

Infrequently, a person will believe that she is a limited partner but discover later that she has been designated a general partner or that the general partners have not filed a certificate of limited partnership. In such circumstances and others, she will be liable as a general partner unless she in good faith believes she is a limited partner and upon discovering she is not a limited partner she either:

1. Causes a proper certificate of limited partnership (or an amendment thereto) to be filed with the secretary of state, or
2. Withdraws from future equity participation in the firm by filing a certificate declaring such withdrawal with the secretary of state.

However, such a person remains liable as a general partner to third parties who previously believed in good faith that the person was a general partner.

A limited partnership must keep its filed certificate current. Current filings allow creditors to discover current facts, not merely those facts that existed when the original certificate was filed. For example, a certificate amendment must be filed when a new general partner is admitted or withdraws.

In the following case, the court considered the liability of new investors who believed they were limited partners although a limited partnership certificate had not been filed.

## BRIARGATE CONDOMINIUM ASSOC. V. CARPENTER
### 976 F.2d 868 (4th Cir. 1992)

In 1984, Judith Carpenter invested in Briargate Homes, a business that purchased several condominium units in the Briargate Condominium complex. Although Carpenter believed that Briargate was a limited partnership and that she was a limited partner, in fact Briargate Homes was a partnership and she was a general partner. No attempt had been made to achieve actual or substantial compliance with the North Carolina limited partnership statute.

Carpenter never signed the partnership agreement or saw copies of the partnership's K-1 tax returns, which clearly identified her as a general partner. However, deductions for partnership losses that Carpenter claimed on her individual income tax returns were allowable only if she was a general partner. In early 1987, Carpenter or her attorneys had possession of documents explicitly stating that Briargate Homes was a general partnership and that her interest was one of a general partner. In June and December 1987, Carpenter received additional documents identifying Briargate Homes as a general partnership. Carpenter was an experienced business-woman, served on the board of directors of a bank, and had ready access to legal and other professional advice.

As an owner of condominiums, the partnership was liable to the Briargate Condominium Association for assessments for maintenance, repair, and replacement of common areas in the complex. In late 1987 and early 1988, the partnership failed to pay the Association assessed fees of $85,106. The Association sued the partnership and its partners.

On February 5, 1988, Carpenter notified the other partners and the Association that she was withdrawing from any equity participation and renouncing any interest in the profits of the partnership.

At the trial, Carpenter contended that because she believed she was a limited partner, she should not be liable to the Association for the fees. The district court found that because Carpenter had not promptly withdrawn from the partnership upon discovering she was a general partner, she was liable for the full amount of the debt. Carpenter appealed.

---

**Hamilton, Circuit Judge**    Carpenter's defense is grounded in the Revised Uniform Partnership Act sec. 304, which provides:

(a) Except as provided in subsection (b), a person who makes a contribution to a business enterprise and errone-ously but in good faith believes that he has become a limited partner in the enterprise is not a general partner in the enterprise and is not bound by its obligations, . . . if, on ascertaining the mistake, he:
> (1) Causes an appropriate certificate of limited part-nership to be executed and filed; or
> (2) Withdraws from future equity participation in the enterprise.

(b) A person who makes a contribution of the kind described in subsection (a) is liable as a general partner to any third party who transacts business with the enterprise (i) before the person withdraws from the enterprise, or (ii) before the person gives notice to the partnership of his withdrawal from future equity participation, but only if the third party actually believed in good faith that the person was a general partner at the time of the transaction.

First, the person must have a good faith belief that he has become a limited partner. Second, the person must on ascertaining the mistake take one of two courses of action. He may file an appropriate certificate of limited partnership. Under this option, the person may continue in the business with limited liability. In the alternative, the person may give notice and withdraw completely from future equity participation in the business. If the two elements are met, then the person is liable *only* as a limited partner, effectively cutting off all personal liability of a general partner, unless subsection (b) applies.

Subsection (b) sets forth the *only* circumstances under which a person who meets the requirements of subsection (a) may incur liability like a general partner. Personal liability to third parties arises when the third party transacts business with the enterprise before the person files a proper certificate or withdraws. Imposition of liability is limited, however, by the requirement that at the time he transacts business, the third party actually believed in good faith that the person was a general partner at the time of the transaction. Reliance of the third party in the resources of the general partner is absolutely essential before liability may be imposed for transactions occurring before withdrawal.

Unlike its predecessor statute, RULPA sec. 304 does not specify how quickly a proper certificate or notice of withdrawal must be filed after a person ascertains he is not a limited partner. The current statute deletes the word "promptly" contained in the prior statute. The present statute also added the language in subsection (b) regarding reliance. This difference between the old and new statutes reflects a shift in emphasis away from the speed with which withdrawal is effected to an emphasis on protection of reliance by third parties. The key to liability is reliance by the third party on a person's apparent status as a general partner.

Given this interpretation of the statute, we believe the judgment of the district must be vacated, and the case remanded to the district court for additional findings. First, the district court must determine whether or not Carpenter held a good faith belief that she was a limited partner at the time she initially joined and contributed to the partnership. The district court did conclude that by at least mid-1986, Carpenter could not have held a good faith belief she was a limited partner, but the key date is the date of the contribution to the enterprise. Should the district court conclude that Carpenter did not have a good faith belief that she was a limited partner at the time of the initial contribution, then the statute affords her no relief.

Second, assuming Carpenter demonstrates a good faith belief at the time she invested, then her notice of withdrawal effectively cut off liability for any fees accrued after such notice. To hold Carpenter liable for fees accrued prior to the notice, the district court must determine if and when the Association actually believed in good faith that Carpenter was a general partner. Carpenter may be held liable only for those assessments made in reliance on the belief that the Association could look to assets of Carpenter as a general partner to satisfy the debt.

Carpenter points to statements indicating that agents of the Association apparently believed they were dealing with a limited partnership and were totally unaware of Carpenter's interest in the partnership until the time of her notice withdrawing from any equity participation and renouncing any interest in the profits of the partnership. We decline, however, to rule on the issue. It does not appear that this issue received much attention at trial. The district court should, on remand, review the record and may take additional evidence if necessary to aid its fact-finding on this issue.

**Judgment for the Association vacated; remanded to the district court.**

## Foreign Limited Partnerships

A limited partnership is **domestic** in the state in which it is organized; it is **foreign** in every other state. The RULPA makes it clear that the laws of the domestic state apply to the internal affairs of the limited partnership, allowing a limited partner protection regardless of where business is conducted.

Nonetheless, to be privileged to do business in a foreign state, a limited partnership must *register* to do business in that state. To register, a limited partnership must file an **application for registration** with the secretary of state of the foreign state. The application must include the name and address of the limited partnership, the names and addresses of the general partners, the name and address of an agent for service of process, and the address of the office where the names, addresses, and capital contributions of the limited partners are kept. The application must be accompanied by the payment of a fee. The secretary of state reviews the application and, if all requirements are met, issues a **certificate of registration.**

There are few penalties for failing to register as a foreign limited partnership. Although the RULPA does not impose fines for a failure to register, a few states have amended it to do so. In addition, an unregistered foreign limited partnership may not use the foreign state's courts to sue to enforce any right or contract. Once it registers, a limited partnership may use the state's courts, even when it sues to enforce a contract that was made before it registered.

Failure to register does not invalidate any contracts made in the foreign state or prevent a limited partnership from defending itself in a suit brought in the state's courts. The failure to register, by itself, does not make a limited partner liable as a general partner.

## RIGHTS AND LIABILITIES OF PARTNERS IN LIMITED PARTNERSHIPS

The partners of a limited partnership have many rights and liabilities. Some are identical to those of partners in an ordinary partnership, but others are special to limited partnerships. Some are common to both general and limited partners, while others are not shared.

## Rights and Liabilities Shared by General and Limited Partners

**Capital Contributions** A partner is obligated to contribute as capital the cash, property, or other services that he promised to contribute. This obligation may be enforced by the limited partnership or by any of its creditors.

**Share of Profits and Losses** Under the RULPA, profits and losses are shared on the basis of the value of each partner's capital contribution unless there is a written agreement to the contrary. For example, if 2 general partners contribute $1,000 each and 20 limited partners contribute $20,000 each, and the profit is $40,200, each general partner's share of the profits is $100 and each limited partner's share is $2,000.

Because most limited partnerships are tax shelters, partnership agreements often provide for limited partners to take all the losses of the business, up to the limit of their capital contributions.

**Voting Rights** The partnership agreement may require that certain transactions be approved by general partners, by limited partners, or by all the partners. The agreement may give each general partner more votes than it grants limited partners, or vice versa. The RULPA makes it clear that limited partners have no inherent right to vote on any matter as a class. They may receive such a right only by agreement of the partners.

**Admission of New Partners** No new partner may be admitted unless each partner has consented to the admission. New partners may be admitted by unanimous written consent of the partners or in accordance with the limited partnership agreement.

**Partnership Interest** Each partner in a limited partnership owns a partnership interest. It is his personal property. He may sell or assign it to others, such as his personal creditors. Or his personal creditor may obtain a charging order against it. Generally, a buyer or assignee—or a creditor with a charging order—is entitled to receive only the partner's share of distributions.

Nonetheless, when the limited partnership agreement so provides or all the partners consent, a buyer or assignee of a limited or a general partnership interest may become a limited partner. The new limited partner then assumes all the rights and liabilities of a limited partner, except for liabilities unknown to her at the time she became a partner.

A partner's assignment of his partnership interest terminates his status as a partner. The assignment does not, however, relieve him of liability for illegal distributions or for false filings with the secretary of state. When a court grants a charging order to a creditor, however, the partner remains a partner.

**Right to Withdraw** Partners in a limited partnership have the power to withdraw from the partnership and receive the fair value of their partnership interests. Fair value includes the going concern value of the partnership business, that is, its goodwill.

A general partner may withdraw from a limited partnership at any time; if a general partner's withdrawal breaches the limited partnership agreement, the value of her interest is reduced by the damages suffered by the limited partnership. A limited partner may withdraw after giving six months' prior notice to each general partner.

When a partner withdraws from a limited partnership, the partner may receive a return of his capital contribution. However, the return of capital may not impair the limited partnership's ability to pay its creditors. After the withdrawal of capital, the fair value of partnership assets must at least equal the limited partnership's liabilities to creditors.

## Other Rights of General Partners

A general partner has the same right to manage and the same agency powers as a partner in an ordinary partnership. He has the express authority to act as the partners have agreed he should and the implied authority to do what is in the usual course of business. In addition, he may have apparent authority to bind the partnership to contracts when his implied authority is limited yet no notice of the limitation has been given to third parties.

A general partner has no right to compensation beyond his share of the profits, absent an agreement to the contrary. Since most limited partnerships are tax shelters that are designed to lose money during their early years of operation, most limited partnership agreements provide for the payment of salaries to general partners.

## Other Liabilities of General Partners

A general partner has unlimited liability to creditors of his limited partnership. In addition, a general partner is in a position of trust when he manages the business, and therefore owes fiduciary duties to the limited partnership and the limited partners (e.g., he may not profit secretly from limited partnership transactions or compete with the limited partnership). The following case imposed fiduciary liability on a general partner for misusing partnership property.

---

### IN RE THE MONETARY GROUP
#### 2 F.3d 1098 (11th Cir. 1993)

The Securities Group (TSG), The Monetary Group (TMG), and The Securities Group 1980 (TSG80) were New York limited partnerships. The Securities Groups (Groups) was a New York *general* partnership whose general partners included TSG, TMG, and TSG80. Charles Barnett and Randall Atkins were general partners of TSG; they were limited partners of TMG. Barnett was also a limited partner of TSG80.

In need of office space, TSG entered negotiations to purchase the Hotel Nassau and the adjacent Olivetti Building at 500 Park Avenue in New York City from Olivetti Properties. Eventually, it was decided that a Kentucky limited partnership—500 Park Avenue Associates (Associates)—would purchase the buildings for $22 million and lease three floors of the Olivetti Building to Groups. Atkins was a limited partner in Associates, which Atkins helped form for the express purpose of buying the buildings.

Under the lease agreement, Associates received a $1 million cash rent security deposit and a $4 million damage deposit from Groups. The $4 million damage deposit comprised marketable securities. Associates immediately gave the $1 million cash to Olivetti as a down payment on the buildings. Associates financed the remainder of the purchase price with a mortgage loan from Manufacturers Hanover Trust Company. Security for the loan was the buildings and the $4 million in marketable securities that Associates received from Groups. When Manufacturers Hanover required an additional $2.8 million collateral, Groups gave Associates another $2.8 million in marketable securities, which Associates transferred to Manufacturers Hanover.

Immediately after completing its purchase of the buildings, Associates placed the buildings on the market. A year and a half later, Associates sold the buildings to Equitable Life Assurance Company for $54.5 million plus a share of Equitable's future profits from developments on the Hotel Nassau site. As part of the sale, Associates assigned its lease with Groups to Equitable.

After six years, TMS, TMG, TMS80, and Groups sought Chapter 11 bankruptcy protection. The court-appointed administrator for the partnerships sued Barnett and Atkins on behalf of the partnership, alleging that they had breached their fiduciary duty to the partnership. The bankruptcy court found Barnett and Atkins liable for all gains received by them from the sale of the property, almost $32 million. Barnett and Atkins appealed to the district court, which affirmed the bankruptcy court's decision. Barnett and Atkins then appealed to the court of appeals.

---

**Per Curiam**   A general partner in a limited partnership stands in a fiduciary relationship with the limited partners of that limited partnership. Atkins was general partner of TSG. Thus, Atkins owed a fiduciary duty to TSG's limited partners. Additionally, TSG was a general partner of Groups. Therefore, Atkins' fiduciary duty extended to Groups.

A limited partner is liable to the other limited partners of a partnership where that limited partner acts in concert with a general partner of that partnership in derogation of that general partner's fiduciary duty. Atkins was a limited partner of TMG. TSG and TMG were partners operating as Groups. Thus, if Atkins violated his duty to TSG as general partner by participating in diverting partnership assets, then Atkins can be said to have joined in the wrong against TMG thereby necessitating the finding that Atkins is liable to the other limited partners of TMG.

A partner breaches his fiduciary where that partner diverts for non-partnership purposes monies belonging to the partnership. Partners are liable to each other for such wrongfully appropriated partnership property.

Funds and other assets of TSG, TMG, TSG80, and Groups were misused, thus enabling Associates to purchase the buildings. Negotiations were initiated on TSG's behalf. Even after Associates assumed the role of purchaser, the deal depended on the use of Groups' assets. The security deposits were obviously tailored to meet Associates' needs.

Atkins contends that such a transaction constitutes a valid lease agreement and should not be characterized as a misappropriation of partnership property. This court, however, need not determine whether the dubious lease agreement is an indirect misappropriation of partnership property, because there is ample evidence of a direct misappropriation of partnership property. When Associates' lender required an additional $2.8 million in security, the malefactors simply transferred an additional $2.8 million from Groups to Associates as an additional security. The additional $2.8 million was not transferred pursuant to an agreement. Groups was under no contractual obligation to pay Associates an additional security. The transfer of an extra $2.8 million represented nothing more than a naked misuse of the partnerships' property for Associates' benefit. Thus,

Associates directly misappropriated at least $2.8 million worth of the partnerships' securities.

We must next consider whether Atkins was guilty of any wrongdoing. Atkins actively participated in the purchase of the property and facilitated the transfer of the security deposit from Groups to Associates. Moreover, Atkins enjoyed a personal windfall from the transactions through his limited partnership interest in Associates. Atkins' conduct directly violated his fiduciary duty as a partner of TSG and TMG to refrain from personally profiting from the misuse of partnership assets.

The bankruptcy court found that Barnett was liable by virtue of his position as a general partner of TSG. An innocent general partner may be held liable to third parties for the wrongful conduct of a fellow partner even though that partner had no knowledge of the offending partners' action. No cases have applied this principle of partnership liability in other than the third-party context. At least one state court has held that an innocent general partner does not bear agency liability to limited partners for another general partner's misuse of partnership funds. We decline to extend this principle of agency liability to the interpartnership suit context. Potentially, such an extension would make all innocent general partners in a partnership liable to each other for the secret misappropriation of partnership funds by one general partner. The bankruptcy court erred by imposing such liability on Barnett.

**Judgment affirmed in favor of TMG against Atkins; judgment reversed in favor of Barnett.**

---

## Other Rights of Limited Partners

Limited partners have the right to be informed about partnership affairs. The RULPA obligates the general partners to provide financial information and tax returns to the limited partners on demand. In addition, a limited partner may inspect and copy a list of the partners, information concerning contributions by partners, the certificate of limited partnership, tax returns, and partnership agreements.

A limited partner may sue to enforce a limited partnership right of action against a person who has harmed the limited partnership. This right of action is called a **derivative suit** or a derivative action because it derives from the limited partnership. Any recovery obtained by the limited partner goes to the limited partnership, since it is the entity that was harmed. In addition, when a limited partnership is sued and the general partners fail to assert a defense, a limited partner may appear on behalf of the limited partnership and assert the defense.

## Other Liabilities of Limited Partners

Once a limited partner has contributed all of his promised capital contribution, generally he has no further liability for partnership losses or obligations. In return for limited liability, however, a limited partner gives up the right to participate in the management of a limited partnership. When a limited partner engages in management activities, he may lose his limited liability.

**Limited Partner Engaged in Management**   A limited partner who participates in the control of the business may be liable to creditors of the limited partnership. Under the RULPA, a limited partner who participates in control is liable only to those persons who transact with the limited partnership reasonably believing, based on the limited partner's conduct, that the limited partner is a general partner. Thus, three elements must be met in order for a limited partner to be liable as a general partner due to his participation in management:

1. The limited partner must participate in the control of the limited partnership.
2. That participation must lead a person to believe reasonably that the limited partner is a general partner.
3. That person must transact with the limited partnership while holding that belief.

For example, Larry Link is a limited partner whom the general partners have allowed to make management decisions. A creditor of the partnership observes Link's management of the partnership, with the result that the creditor extends $10,000 credit to the limited partnership believing that Link is a general partner. Link is liable on the $10,000 debt to the creditor.

It is sometimes difficult to determine whether a limited partner's acts amount to control of the limited partnership. Control is best defined as participation in the firm's day-to-day management decisions as contrasted with isolated involvement with major decisions. For example, a limited partner of a real estate investment partnership

---

**FIGURE 3   Activities Not Constituting Control by a Limited Partner**

1. Being *an agent, an employee,* or *a contractor* for the limited partnership or a general partner; or being an officer, director, or shareholder of a general partner that is a corporation.
2. Being a *consultant* or *adviser* to a general partner.
3. Acting as a *surety* for the limited partnership or guaranteeing or assuming specific obligations of the limited partnership. However, a limited partner who specifically assumes liability on a partnership obligation is liable on that obligation.
4. Pursuing a derivative suit on behalf of the limited partnership.
5. Requesting or attending a meeting of partners.
6. Proposing or voting on such partnership matters as dissolution, sale of substantially all the assets, changes in the nature of the business, admissions and removals of general or limited partners, and amendments to the partnership agreement.
7. Winding up the limited partnership as permitted by the RULPA.

---

participates in control if she regularly decides which real estate the limited partnership should purchase. A limited partner who only once vetoed a loan agreement with a bank is not participating in control.

The RULPA lists the kinds of management activities that limited partners may perform without becoming personally liable for partnership debts. Therefore, a limited partner may perform these acts and still retain his limited liability. The list of such activities appears in Figure 3.

For most well-planned limited partnerships, the general partner is a corporation. Usually, the only shareholders, directors, and officers of the corporate general partner are the individuals who manage the limited partnership. Sometimes, these individuals are limited partners as well. These individuals will not have the liability of a general partner, because the RULPA permits limited partners to be officers, directors, or shareholders of a general partner (see item 1 of Figure 3).

In the following case, the court held that a limited partner had not exercised sufficient control over the limited partnership to render the limited partner liable as a general partner.

## ALZADO V. BLINDER, ROBINSON & CO.
### 752 P.2d 544 (Colo. Sup. Ct. 1988)

In 1979, Blinder, Robinson & Co. as limited partner and Combat Promotions, Inc., as general partner created Combat Associates to promote an eight-round exhibition boxing match between Muhammad Ali and Lyle Alzado, the pro football player. Combat Promotions was owned entirely by Alzado, his accountant, and his professional agent. Alzado was also vice president of Combat Promotions. Combat Associates agreed to pay Alzado $100,000 for his participation in the match.

Few tickets were sold, and the match proved to be a financial debacle. Alzado received no payments for participating in the boxing match. Alzado sued Blinder, Robinson, claiming that because of its conduct, Blinder, Robinson must be deemed a general partner of Combat Associates and, therefore, liable to Alzado under the agreement between Alzado and the limited partnership for Alzado's participation in the match. The trial court agreed with Alzado, but Blinder, Robinson appealed to the court of appeals, which held that Blinder, Robinson had no liability to Alzado. Alzado appealed to the Supreme Court of Colorado.

---

**Kirshbaum, Justice**    A limited partner may become liable to partnership creditors as a general partner if the limited partner assumes control of partnership business. RULPA Section 303 provides that a limited partner does not participate in the control of partnership business solely by doing one or more of the following:

(a) Being a contractor for or an agent or employee of the limited partnership or of a general partner;
(b) Being an officer, director, or shareholder of a corporate general partner;
(c) Consulting with and advising a general partner with respect to the business of the limited partnership . . . .

Any determination of whether a limited partner's conduct amounts to control over the business affairs of the partnership must be determined by consideration of several factors, including the purpose of the partnership, the administrative activities undertaken, the manner in which the entity actually functioned, and the nature and frequency of the limited partner's purported activities.

The record here reflects that Blinder, Robinson used its Denver office as a ticket outlet, gave two parties to promote the exhibition match, and provided a meeting room for many of Combat Associates' meetings. Meyer Blinder, president of Blinder, Robinson, personally appeared on a television talk show and gave television interviews to promote the match. Blinder, Robinson made no investment, accounting or other financial decisions for the partnership; all such fiscal decisions were made by officers or employees of Combat Promotions, the general partner. The evidence established at most that Blinder, Robinson engaged in a few promotional activities. It does not establish that it took part in the management or control of the business affairs of the partnership.

Alzado finally asserts that Blinder, Robinson fostered the appearance of being in control of Combat Associates, that such actions rendered Blinder, Robinson liable as a general partner and that this conduct allowed third parties to believe that Blinder, Robinson was in fact a general partner. The evidence does not support this argument. Certainly, as Vice President of Combat Promotions, Alzado had no misconception concerning the function and role of Blinder, Robinson as a limited partner only.

**Judgment for Blinder, Robinson affirmed.**

---

**Limited Partner's Name in Firm Name**    Including a limited partner's *surname* in the name of a limited partnership may mislead a creditor to believe that a limited partner is a general partner. Under the RULPA, a limited partner who *knowingly* permits her name to be included in the firm name is liable to creditors who have *no actual knowledge* that she is a limited partner, unless a general partner has the same surname as that of the limited partner or the business of the limited partnership was conducted under that name prior to the limited partner's admission to the limited partnership.

## DISSOLUTION AND WINDING UP OF A LIMITED PARTNERSHIP

### Dissolution

A limited partnership may be dissolved and its affairs wound up. There are five causes of dissolution:

**1.** Expiration of the term specified in the certificate of limited partnership. For example, the certificate may provide that a limited partnership has a 20-year term.

**2.** Upon the happening of events specified in writing in the partnership agreement. For example, a written partnership agreement may provide for dissolution of a limited partnership after it has accomplished its objective of building a shopping mall.

**3.** By the written consent of all the partners.

**4.** Upon the withdrawal of a *general* partner, with few exceptions. Such a withdrawal includes retirement, death, bankruptcy, assignment of a general partnership interest, removal by the other partners, and adjudicated insanity. For a general partner that is not a natural person, such as a partnership or a corporation, its own dissolution is a withdrawal causing a dissolution of the limited partnership. The RULPA specifically permits a limited partnership to avoid dissolution after the withdrawal of a general partner if a written partnership agreement permits the business to be conducted by the remaining general partners or if all of the partners agree in writing to continue the business.

**5.** By court order, when it is *not reasonably practicable* to carry on the business in conformity with the limited partnership agreement. Judicial dissolution has frequently been granted when general partners continually violate their fiduciary duties, such as by secretly profiting from self-dealing with the limited partnership.

The RULPA requires a limited partnership to file a **certificate of cancellation** upon its dissolution and the commencement of winding up. The certificate of cancellation cancels the certificate of limited partnership. However, the failure to file a certificate of cancellation does not prevent a dissolution.

### Winding Up

Winding up is the orderly liquidation of the limited partnership's assets and payment of the proceeds to creditors and other claimants. Dissolution requires the winding up of a limited partnership's affairs. The only way to prevent winding up is to prevent dissolution, such as by an agreement of the partners that an event shall not cause a dissolution.

General partners who have *not wrongfully dissolved* a limited partnership may perform the winding up. Wrongful dissolution includes a dissolution in violation of the limited partnership agreement or wrongful conduct that leads to a judicial dissolution, such as a general partner's breach of his fiduciary duties. Limited partners may wind up if there are no surviving general partners. In addition, any partner may *ask a court* to perform a winding up.

The winding up partner has express authority to act as the partners have agreed he should act. More importantly, he has the implied authority to do those acts that are reasonably necessary to liquidate the assets. He possesses the apparent authority to do all of the acts that he was able to do before dissolution, unless appropriate notice is given to persons who dealt with the partnership or knew of its existence.

**Distribution of Assets**   After the assets have been sold during winding up, the proceeds of the sale of assets are distributed to those persons having claims against the limited partnership. Figure 4 states the RULPA rule for distribution of limited partnership assets.

**Continuation of the Business**   Usually, the assets of a limited partnership are sold individually during winding up. However, all the assets of the business of the limited partnership could be sold to someone who desires to continue the business. For example, some of the partners may wish to continue the business despite dissolution. The continuing partners are required to pay the outgoing partners the fair value of their partnership interests, including goodwill.

**Events Not Causing Dissolution**   The death, bankruptcy, insanity, or withdrawal of a *limited* partner does not result in dissolution unless the certificate of limited partnership compels dissolution. Also, the *addition* of a partner—general or limited—does not cause a dissolution.

**FIGURE 4    Order of Distribution of Limited Partnership Assets during Winding Up**

1. To firm *creditors,* including partners who are creditors, except for unpaid distributions to partners.
2. To partners for *unpaid distributions,* including the return of capital to previously withdrawn partners.
3. To partners to the extent of their *capital contributions.*
4. To partners in the proportion in which they share distributions. Hence, the partners share the proceeds that remain after all other claimants have been paid.

Between partners, the order of distribution may be changed by a partnership agreement. For example, a limited partnership agreement may combine priorities (2) and (3) to provide that unpaid distributions to partners shall be paid at the same time capital contributions are returned. However, the priority of creditors may not be harmed by a partner's agreement, such as an agreement to pay creditors *after* partners have received the return of their capital.

## LIMITED LIABILITY COMPANIES

The limited liability company (LLC) is the product of attempts by state legislators to create a new business organization that combines the nontax advantages of the corporation and the favorable tax status of the partnership. Wyoming, in 1977, passed the first LLC statute. Florida followed in 1982. In 1988, the Internal Revenue Service ruled that a Wyoming LLC would be recognized as a partnership for federal income tax purposes. As a result, the LLC pays no federal income tax. Instead, all income and losses of the LLC are reported by the LLC's owners on their individual income tax returns. Typically, the LLC is a tax shelter for wealthy investors, allowing such investors to reduce their taxable income by deducting LLC losses on their federal income tax returns. Thirty-six states have adopted LLC laws, and it is expected that by 1995 nearly every state will have such a law.

### Formation of LLCs

To create an LLC, two or more persons must file **articles of organization** with the secretary of state. The articles must include the name of the LLC, its duration, and the name and address of its registered agent. The name of the LLC must include the words "limited liability company" or some other words indicating that the liability of its owners is limited.

Although not required, an LLC will typically have an **operating agreement**, which is an agreement of the owners as to how the LLC will be operated.

Many states also require an LLC to file an annual report with the secretary of state. The annual report may include financial information such as the capital accounts of the owners and the LLC's balance sheet.

### Owners of LLCs

Owners of LLCs are called **members.** Most statutes require an LLC to have at least two members at all times, although there is no maximum limit on members. An individual, partnership, corporation, and even another LLC may be a member of an LLC.

A member has no personal liability for LLC obligations. A member must, however, make capital contributions to the LLC as she has agreed.

LLC statutes restrict the members' ability to sell their interests in the LLC. An LLC interest is the personal property of the member and may be transferred as stated in the operating agreement; however, the transferee has no right to become a member or participate in management unless the other members consent to the transfer. The transferee who does not become a member is entitled only to the transferring member's share of profits.

A member is entitled to withdraw from the LLC and receive either the value of his interest or a return of his capital contribution. Such a distribution of assets to a member may be executed only if the LLC's assets exceed its liabilities after the distribution.

### LLC as an Entity

The LLC is technically a corporation. Like any corporation, it is an entity separate from its owners. It may sue and be sued in its own name. It can buy, hold, and sell property. It can make contracts and incur liabilities.

Because the LLC is an entity liable for its own obligations, the members have no individual liability on LLC obligations. However, a court will pierce the veil between the LLC and its members and impose personal liability on the members when the LLC is used to defraud creditors. For example, suppose the members provide very little capital to an LLC that is engaging in a highly risky business. As a result, the business is unsuccessful and unable to pay its creditors. A court will likely require the members to pay the obligations of the business.

## Management of LLCs

Members of an LLC share management power in proportion to their capital contributions to the LLC. If there is no member vote restricting the actual authority of a member, however, members have considerable implied and apparent authority to bind the LLC on transactions in the ordinary course of business.

The members may agree to entrust management to managers selected by the members. Managers of an LLC are comparable to directors of a corporation.

The members or managers who manage the LLC are fiduciaries of the LLC. They must manage the LLC in the best interest of the LLC and not prefer their individual interests over the interests of the LLC.

## Dissolution of LLCs

An LLC must be easily dissolved to obtain partnership tax treatment under the Internal Revenue Code. Dissolution is caused by the death, retirement, bankruptcy, or dissolution of any member. However, the remaining members may avoid liquidation by *unanimously* agreeing to continue the business. Under most statutes, an LLC's term cannot exceed 30 years.

### PROBLEMS AND PROBLEM CASES

**1.** In 1979, Jeffrey Shaughnessy organized a limited partnership, Capital City Investments. The partnership agreement listed Shaughnessy as the sole general partner. Shaughnessy signed the agreement. The limited partners were listed in the agreement but none signed it. No certificate of limited partnership was filed in the county recorder's office, where recording was required. Has a limited partnership been created?

**2.** Brookwood Fund was a limited partnership formed to trade investment securities. The original certificate of limited partnership filed in April 1987 listed Kenneth Stein as the "General Partner" and Barbara Stein as the "Original Limited Partner." Between May and August 1987, additional limited partners were added to Brookwood. The new limited partners did not participate in the management of Brookwood. However, an amended certificate of limited partnership reflecting the new limited partners was not filed. What should the new limited partners do to protect themselves from having the liability of general partners?

**3.** Virginia Partners, Ltd., a limited partnership organized in Florida, was in the business of drilling oil wells. When Virginia Partners injected acid into an oil well in Kentucky, a bystander, Robert Day, was injured by acid that sprayed on him from a ruptured hose. Virginia Partners had failed to register as a foreign limited partnership in Kentucky. Are the limited partners of Virginia Partners liable to Day for his injuries?

**4.** Palmetto Federal Savings & Loan Association made real estate loans to Beacon Reef Limited Partnership. When Beacon Reef defaulted on the loans, Palmetto Federal sued Beacon Reef. Beacon Reef's general partners decided not to raise the defense that Palmetto Federal charged a usurious rate on the loan. May Howard Wulsin, the only limited partner, on behalf of Beacon Reef, assert the defense of usury against Palmetto Federal?

**5.** Cornel Peleo was a general partner of Livonia Associates, a limited partnership. On December 3, 1971, Peleo and his wife purchased land for $9,000. On April 15, 1972, they sold the land to Livonia Associates for $18,000. Peleo told one limited partner that he had an interest in the property, but he did not tell him the amount. Has Peleo breached a fiduciary duty?

**6.** Paul Linnane was the sole general partner and Richard Stover was the sole limited partner of Linnane Magnavox Home Entertainment Center, a limited partnership. Stover possessed no power to manage daily partnership affairs and took no part in any partnership business. Linnane negotiated with General Electric Credit Corporation (GE Credit) to obtain financing for Linnane Magnavox. Two written contracts were executed and signed by GE Credit, Linnane, and Stover. Stover signed one contract, "by Richard Stover (Officer, Partner, Owner)." He signed the other contract, "by Richard Stover (V. Pres., Secy., Treas., Partner)." GE Credit would not have extended financing to Linnane Magnavox had Stover not signed the contracts. GE Credit was not aware of the limited partnership agreement between Linnane and Stover, although it was aware that Stover was a silent partner of Linnane. Stover signed the contracts at the request of Linnane, intended the signatures to be only in the capacity of limited partner, but did not communicate that intention to GE Credit. Is Stover liable on the contracts with GE Credit?

**7.** The Securities Group 1980, a limited partnership, was created to provide tax deferral advantages for its limited partners. To offset a potential adverse tax consequence when the tax laws changed, the general partners arranged a sale of the limited partnership interests to a new partnership owned by the Securities Group's general partners. The limited partners received cash and promissory notes worth 105 percent of the net asset value of Securities Group. At that time, Securities Group was indebted to various creditors. The new partnership subsequently became insolvent, with the result that the Securities Group creditors were unpaid. Are the Securities Group creditors able to collect from the former limited partners of Securities Group?

**8.** OKC Corporation adopted a plan to become a limited partnership. Under the plan, the shareholders became limited partners in OKC Limited Partnership. They did not receive actual possession of their limited partnership interests. Instead, the limited partnership interests were deposited in MBank of Dallas, which then issued depositary receipts to the limited partners. The depositary receipts were traded on the Pacific Stock Exchange. Some of the limited partners sold their depositary receipts to other investors. In 1987, a committee of receipt holders attempted to replace the general partners, an action within the powers of the limited partners under the limited partnership agreement. The general partners opposed the action and claimed that only the original limited partners who were still receipt holders could vote to replace the general partners. Were the general partners correct?

**9.** Excel Associates was a New York limited partnership. Lipkin was Excel's only individual general partner. Tribute Music Inc. was the only other general partner. Chalpin, the only limited partner, was also the president and sole shareholder and director of Tribute Music. Chalpin hired Bernabe Gonzales to be the superintendent of Excel's apartment building in Long Beach, Long Island, New York. Later, Chalpin hired Gonzales to renovate the building. Chalpin signed all Excel's checks paying Gonzalez. Chalpin did not name Tribute Music on the checks or indicate that he was signing in a representative capacity. Chalpin terminated Gonzales's employment with Excel. Gonzales sued

Excel for breach of an employment contract. Gonzales also claimed that Chalpin was liable on the breached contract. On what grounds did Gonzales base his argument for Chalpin's liability?

**10.** Canal East Company was a limited partnership formed to operate a commercial real estate project known as Packett's Landing. John Flowers was the sole general partner. Scott Arrington, William May, and Robert Klimasewski were the only limited partners. Fishers Development Company was another partnership in which Arrington, May, and Klimasewski were the only limited partners. Fishers Development bought restaurant equipment and leased it to a restaurant-tenant at Packett's Landing. Flowers and Arrington were guarantors of the lease obligation to Fishers Development. When the restaurant-tenant became bankrupt, Flowers and Arrington obtained possession of the equipment pursuant to an assignment from the restaurant-tenant. They assigned the equipment lease to Canal East, which agreed to assume Flowers and Arrington's guaranty of the lease and to indemnify them from their liabilities under the lease or guaranty. Flowers and Arrington signed the agreement as assignors. In addition, Flowers signed the agreement as the general partner of Canal East, the assignee. May and Klimasewski sought judicial dissolution of the limited partnership, claiming that Flowers and Arrington breached fiduciary duties. Will the court order dissolution?

## CAPSTONE QUESTIONS

Patricia Knight, a wealthy investor, purchases limited partnership interests in two limited partnerships. Knight buys a $300,000 limited partnership interest in Lukasfilms Limited Partnership, a motion picture production company. Knight also buys an $800,000 limited partnership interest in Memphis Sound Professional Soccer Team Limited Partnership. Neither business is profitable, but Knight deducts her share of losses on her tax returns.

After a few years, Knight becomes concerned that neither limited partnership will become profitable. She investigates Lukasfilms and discovers that the general partners never filed its certificate of limited partnership with the secretary of state.

Knight has expertise in sports management. After speaking with Memphis Sound's general partners, she believes that the general partners are mismanaging the business. Knight is considering four options:

·   Suing Memphis Sound's general managers for mismanaging the business.

·   Selling her limited partnership interest to Art Finkel. Finkel is willing to purchase Knight's limited partnership interest only if he becomes a limited partner of Memphis Sound.

·   Withdrawing her capital contribution from Memphis Sound.

·   Becoming involved in the management of Memphis Sound as a limited partner. Knight wants to be involved in all personnel decisions, especially negotiating contracts with the athletes who sign contracts to play soccer for the Memphis Sound.

### Required:

Answer the following and give reasons for your conclusions.

1.   What is the legal effect of Lukasfilms not filing its certificate of limited partnership? What should Knight do to reduce her risk of liability?

2.   Assess each of Knight's options regarding Memphis Sound.

# CORPORATIONS

CHAPTER

**3 3**

# History

# and Nature

# of Corporations

**INTRODUCTION**

*The modern corporation has facilitated the rapid economic development of the last 150 years by permitting businesses to attain economies of scale. Businesses organized as corporations can attain such economies because they have a greater capacity to raise capital than do other business forms. This capital-raising advantage is ensured by corporation law, which allows persons to invest their money in a corporation and become owners without imposing unlimited liability or management responsibilities on themselves. Many people are willing to invest their savings in a large, risky business if they have limited liability and no management responsibilities. Far fewer are willing to invest in a partnership or other business form in which owners have unlimited liability and management duties.*

## History of Corporations

Although modern corporation law emerged only in the last 150 years, ancestors of the modern corporation existed in the times of Hammurabi, ancient Greece, and the Roman Empire. As early as 1248 in France, privileges of incorporation were given to mercantile ventures to encourage investment for the benefit of society. In England, the corporate form was used extensively before the 16th century.

The famous British trading companies—such as the Massachusetts Bay Company—were the forerunners of the modern corporation. The British government gave these companies monopolies in trade and granted them powers to govern in the areas they colonized. They were permitted to operate as corporations due to the benefits they would confer on the British empire, such as the development of natural resources. Although these trading companies were among the few corporations of the time whose owners were granted limited liability, they sought corporate status primarily because the government granted them monopolies and governmental powers.

### American Corporation Law

Beginning in 1776, corporation law in the United States evolved independently of English corporation

---

**FIGURE 1**   **Principal Characteristics of Corporations**

1. **Creation.** A corporation may be created only by **permission of a government.**

2. **Legal status.** A corporation is a legal person and a legal entity independent of its owners (**shareholders**) and its managers (officers and the **board of directors**). Its life is unaffected by the retirement or death of its shareholders, officers, and directors. A corporation is a person under the Constitution of the United States.

3. **Powers.** A corporation may **acquire, hold, and convey property** in its own name. A corporation may **sue and be sued** in its own name. Harm to a corporation is not harm to the shareholders; therefore, with few exceptions, a shareholder may not sue to enforce a claim of the corporation.

4. **Management.** Shareholders elect a board of directors, which manages the corporation. The board of directors may delegate management duties to officers. A shareholder has **no right or duty to manage** the business of a corporation, unless he is elected to the board of directors or is appointed an officer. The directors and officers need not be shareholders.

5. **Owners' liability.** The shareholders have **limited liability.** With few exceptions, they are not liable for the debts of a corporation after they have paid their promised capital contributions to the corporation.

6. **Transferability of owner's interest.** Generally, the ownership interest in a corporation is **freely transferable.** A shareholder may sell her shares to whomever she wants whenever she wants. The purchaser becomes a shareholder with the same rights that the seller had.

7. **Taxation.** A corporation pays **federal income taxes** on its income. Shareholders have personal income from the corporation only when the corporation makes a distribution of its income to them. For example, a shareholder would have personal income from the corporation when the corporation pays him a dividend. This creates a **double-taxation** possibility: The corporation pays income tax on its profits, and when the corporation distributes the after-tax profits as dividends, the shareholders pay tax on the dividends.

---

law. Early American corporations received **special charters** from state legislatures. These charters were granted one at a time by special action of the legislatures; few special charters were granted.

In the late 18th century, general incorporation statutes emerged in the United States. Initially, these statutes permitted incorporation only for limited purposes beneficial to the public, such as operating toll bridges and water systems. Incorporation was still viewed as a privilege, and many restrictions were placed on corporations: incorporation was permitted for only short periods of time; maximum limits on capitalization were low; ownership of real and personal property was often restricted.

During the last 150 years, such restrictive provisions have disappeared in most states. Today, modern incorporation statutes are mostly enabling, granting the persons who control a corporation great flexibility in establishing, financing, and operating it.

See Figure 1 for a statement of the characteristics of corporations.

## CLASSIFICATIONS OF CORPORATIONS

Corporations may be divided into three classes: (1) corporations **for profit,** (2) corporations **not for profit,** and (3) **government-owned** corporations. State corporation statutes establish procedures for the incorporation of each of these classes and for their operation. In addition, a large body of common law applies to all corporations.

Most business corporations are **for-profit corporations.** For-profit corporations issue stock to their shareholders, who invest in the corporation with the expectation that they will earn a profit on their investment. That profit may take the form of dividends paid by the corporation or increased market value of their shares.

Nearly all for-profit corporations are incorporated under the **general incorporation law** of a state. All of the states require professionals who wish to incorporate, such as physicians, dentists, lawyers, and accountants, to incorporate under **professional corporation acts.** In addition, for-profit corporations that especially affect the public interest, such as banks, insurance companies, and savings and loan associations, are usually required to incorporate under special statutes.

For-profit corporations range from huge international organizations such as General Motors Corporation to small, one-owner businesses. GM is an example of a **publicly held corporation** because its shares are generally available to public investors. The publicly held corporation tends to be managed by professional managers who own small percentages of the corporation. Nearly all the shareholders of the typical publicly held corporation are merely investors who are not concerned in the management of the corporation.

Corporations with very few shareholders whose shares are not available to the general public are called **close corporations.** In the typical close corporation, the controlling shareholders are the only managers of the business.

Usually, close corporations and publicly held corporations are subject to the same rules under state corporation law. Many states, however, allow close corporations greater latitude in the operation of their internal affairs than is granted to public corporations. For example, the shareholders of a close corporation may be permitted to dispense with the board of directors and manage the close corporation as if it were a partnership.

A Subchapter S corporation, or **S Corporation,** is a special type of close corporation. It is treated nearly like a partnership for federal tax purposes. Its shareholders report the earnings or losses of the business on their individual federal income tax returns. This means that an S Corporation's profits are taxed only once—at the shareholder level, eliminating the double-taxation penalty of incorporation. All shareholders must consent to an S Corporation election. The Internal Revenue Code requires an S corporation to have only one class of shares and 35 or fewer shareholders. Shareholders may be only individuals or trusts.

**Not-for-profit corporations** do not issue stock and do not expect to make a profit. Instead, they provide services to their members under a plan that eliminates any profit motive. These corporations have **members** rather than shareholders, and none of the surplus revenue from their operations may be distributed to their members. Since they generally pay no income tax, nonprofit corporations can reinvest a larger share of their incomes in the business

than can for-profit corporations. Examples of nonprofit corporations are charities, churches, fraternal organizations, community arts councils, cooperative grocery stores, and cooperative farmers' feed and supplies stores.

Some corporations are owned by governments and perform governmental and business functions. A municipality (city) is one type of **government-owned corporation.** Other types are created to furnish more specific services—for example, school corporations and water companies. Others—such as the Tennessee Valley Authority and the Federal Deposit Insurance Corporation—operate much like for-profit corporations except that at least some of their directors are appointed by governmental officials, and some or all of their financing frequently comes from government. The TVA and the FDIC are chartered by Congress, but government-owned corporations may also be authorized by states. Government-operated businesses seek corporate status to free themselves from governmental operating procedures, which are more cumbersome than business operating procedures.

## REGULATION OF FOR-PROFIT CORPORATIONS

To become a corporation, a business must **incorporate** by complying with an incorporation statute. Incorporation is a fairly simple process usually requiring little more than paying a fee and filing a document with a designated government official—usually the secretary of state of the state of incorporation. Incorporation of for-profit businesses has been entrusted primarily to the governments of the 50 states.

### State Incorporation Statutes

State incorporation statutes set out the basic rules regarding the relationship between the corporation, its shareholders, and its managers. For example, an incorporation statute sets the requirements for a business to incorporate, the procedures for shareholders' election of directors, and the duties directors and officers owe to the corporation. Although a corporation may do business in several states, usually the relationship between the corporation, its shareholders, and its managers is regulated only by the state of incorporation.

The American Bar Association's Committee on Corporate Laws has prepared a *model* statute for adoption by state legislatures. The purpose of the model statute is to improve the rationality of corporation law. It is called the **Model Business Corporation Act (MBCA).** The MBCA has been amended many times, and it was completely revised in 1984.

The revised MBCA is the basis of corporation law in most states. Your study of statutory corporation law in this book concentrates on the revised MBCA. Delaware and several other major commercial and industrial states such as New York and California do not follow the MBCA. Therefore, selected provisions of the Delaware and other acts will be addressed.

Several states have special provisions or statutes that are applicable only to close corporations. The ABA's Committee on Corporate Laws has adopted the *Statutory Close Corporation Supplement to the Model Business Corporation Act.* The Supplement is designed to provide a rational, statutory solution to the special problems facing close corporations.

## State Common Law of Corporations

Although nearly all of corporation law is statutory law, including the courts' interpretation of the statutes, there is a substantial body of common law of corporations (judge-made law). Most of this common law deals with creditor and shareholder rights. For example, the law of piercing the corporate veil, which you will study later in this chapter, is common law protecting creditors of corporations.

## REGULATION OF NONPROFIT CORPORATIONS

Nonprofit corporations are regulated primarily by the states. Nonprofit corporations may be created only by complying with a nonprofit incorporation statute. Incorporation under state law requires delivering articles of incorporation to the secretary of state. The existence of a nonprofit corporation begins when the secretary of state files the articles. Most states have statutes based on the revised **Model Nonprofit Corporation Act (MNCA).** Because of constitutional protection of freedom of religion, many states have special statutes regulating nonprofit religious organizations.

The law applied to nonprofit corporations is substantially similar to for-profit corporation law. At various points in the corporations chapters of this book, you will study the law of nonprofit corporations and examine how this form of business and its laws differ from the for-profit corporation and its laws. The Model Nonprofit Corporation Act will be the basis of your study of nonprofit corporation law.

## REGULATION OF FOREIGN CORPORATIONS

A corporation may be incorporated in one state yet do business in many other states in which it is not incorporated. The corporation's contacts with other persons in those states may permit the states to regulate the corporation's transactions with their citizens, to subject the corporation to suits in their courts, or to tax the corporation. The circumstances under which states may impose their laws on a business incorporated in another state is determined by the law of foreign corporations.

A corporation is a **domestic corporation** in the state that has granted its charter; it is a **foreign corporation** in all the other states in which it does business. For example, a corporation organized in Delaware and doing business in Florida is domestic in Delaware and foreign in Florida. Note that a corporation domiciled in one country is an **alien corporation** in other countries in which it does business. Many of the rules that apply to foreign corporations apply as well to alien corporations.

Generally, a state may impose its laws on a foreign corporation if such imposition does not violate the Constitution of the United States, notably the Due Process Clause of the Fourteenth Amendment and the Commerce Clause.

### Due Process Clause

The Due Process Clause requires that a foreign corporation have sufficient contacts with a state before a state may exercise jurisdiction over the corporation. The leading case in this area is the *International Shoe* case.[1] In that case, the Supreme Court ruled that a foreign corporation must have "certain minimum contacts" with the state such that

---

[1] *International Shoe Co. v. State of Washington,* 326 U.S. 310 (1945).

asserting jurisdiction over the corporation does not offend "traditional notions of fair play and substantial justice." The Supreme Court justified its holding with a **benefit theory**: When a foreign corporation avails itself of the protection of a state's laws, it should suffer any reasonable burden that the state imposes as a consequence of such benefit. In other words, a foreign corporation should be required to pay for the benefits that it receives from the state.

## Commerce Clause

Under the Commerce Clause, the power to regulate interstate commerce is given to the federal government. The states have no power to exclude or to discriminate against foreign corporations that are engaged solely in *interstate* commerce. Nevertheless, a state may require a foreign corporation doing interstate business in the state to comply with its laws if the application of these laws does not unduly burden interstate commerce. When a foreign corporation enters interstate commerce to do *intrastate* business in a state, the state may regulate the corporation's activities, provided again that the regulation does not unduly burden interstate commerce.

A state statute does not unduly burden interstate commerce if (1) the statute serves a legitimate state interest, (2) the state has chosen the least burdensome means of promoting that interest, and (3) that legitimate state interest outweighs the statute's burden on interstate commerce. Because conducting intrastate business increases a corporation's contact with a state, it is easier to prove that the state has a legitimate interest and that there is no undue burden on interstate commerce when the corporation is conducting intrastate business.

**Doing Business**    To aid their determination of whether a state may constitutionally impose its laws on a foreign corporation, courts have traditionally used the concept of **doing business.** Courts have generally held that a foreign corporation is subject to the laws of a state when it is doing business in the state. The activities that constitute doing business differ, however, depending on the purpose of the determination. There are four such purposes: (1) to determine whether a corporation is subject to a lawsuit in a state's courts, (2) to determine whether the corporation's activities are subject to taxation, (3) to determine whether the corporation must qualify to carry on its activities in the state, and (4) to determine whether the state may regulate the internal affairs of the corporation.

## Subjecting Foreign Corporations to Suit

The Supreme Court of the United States has held that a foreign corporation may be brought into a state's court in connection with its activities within the state, provided that the state does not violate the corporation's due process rights under the Fourteenth Amendment of the Constitution and its rights under the Commerce Clause.

The *International Shoe* minimum contacts test must be met. Subjecting the corporation to suit cannot offend "traditional notions of fair play and substantial justice." A court must weigh the corporation's contacts within the state against the inconvenience to the corporation of requiring it to defend a suit within the state. The burden on the corporation must be reasonable in relation to the benefit that it receives from conducting activities in the state.

Under the minimum contacts test, even an isolated event may be sufficient to confer jurisdiction on a state's courts. For example, driving a truck from Arizona through New Mexico toward a final destination in Florida provides sufficient contacts with New Mexico to permit a suit in New Mexico's courts against the foreign corporation for its driver's negligently causing an accident within New Mexico.

Most of the states have passed **long-arm statutes** to permit their courts to exercise jurisdiction under the decision of the *International Shoe* case. These statutes frequently specify several kinds of corporate activities that make foreign corporations subject to suit within the state, such as the commission of a tort, the making of a contract, or the ownership of property. Most of the long-arm statutes grant jurisdiction over causes of action growing out of any transaction within the state.

In the following case, the court applied the Louisiana long-arm statute.

## HERVISH v. GROWABLES, INC.
### 449 So.2d 684 (La. Ct. App. 1984)

Growables, Inc., a manufacturer of furniture, was incorporated in St. Petersburg, Florida. In July 1982, Debra Hervish, a resident of Florida, obtained a brochure about Growables' line of children's furniture. She went to Growables' offices in Florida to place an order for 14 pieces of furniture. While at Growables' office, she deposited $2,000 toward the total purchase price of $2,662. She told Growables that she would soon be moving to Louisiana, and she asked that the furniture be shipped there. Growables agreed to do so.

In early August 1982, Mrs. Hervish moved to Kenner, Louisiana, and informed Growables of her new address. Thereafter, she contacted Growables three or four times to find out why shipment of the furniture had been delayed beyond the eight weeks estimated by Growables.

On November 2, 1982, the furniture was delivered to Mrs. Hervish by Ryder Truck Lines. At the time of delivery, she paid the Ryder driver the balance of the purchase price plus the shipping charges, a total of $877. Upon opening the cardboard cartons in which the furniture had been shipped, Mrs. Hervish discovered that every piece of furniture was damaged. After making futile demands for recovery from Ryder and Growables, she sued Growables in a Louisiana trial court.

Growables asked the trial court to dismiss the suit on the grounds that the Louisiana courts could not take long-arm jurisdiction over Growables. The trial court agreed with Growables and dismissed Hervish's suit. Hervish appealed.

---

**Chehardy, Judge**     The Louisiana long-arm statute provides, in pertinent part,

A court may exercise personal jurisdiction over a nonresident, who acts directly or by an agent, as to a cause of action arising from the nonresident's:

(a) transacting any business in this state;
(b) contracting to supply services or things in this state;
(c) causing injury or damage by an offense or quasi-offense committed through an act or omission in this state;
(d) causing injury or damage in this state by an offense or quasi-offense committed through an act or omission outside of this state, if he regularly does or solicits business, or engages in any other persistent course of conduct, or derives substantial revenue from goods used or consumed or services rendered, in this state.

This statute was intended by the Legislature to extend the personal jurisdiction of Louisiana courts over nonresidents to the full limits of due process under the Fourteenth Amendment.

In order for the proper exercise of jurisdiction over a nonresident, there must be sufficient minimum contacts between the nonresident defendant and the forum state to satisfy due process and traditional notions of fair play and substantial justice. Whether or not a particular defendant has sufficient minimum contracts with a state is to be determined from the facts and circumstances peculiar to each case.

It is essential in each case that there be some act by which the defendant purposefully avails itself of the privilege of conducting activities within the state, thus invoking the benefits and protections of its law. It appears that knowledge alone or foreseeability that property will come to rest in a particular state is insufficient to subject a defendant to jurisdiction, unless the facts and circumstances lead to a conclusion that the defendant purposefully availed itself of the privilege of conducting activities within the forum state in such a manner that the defendant has clear notice that it would be subject to suit there.

Applying these standards to the case before us, we must examine the contacts between Growables, Inc., and Louisiana to determine whether the relationship is sufficient to satisfy due process requirements. At the time Mrs. Hervish ordered the furniture, she was a Florida resident. She obtained the brochure advertising the furniture in Florida; she went personally to the Growables office in Florida to place the order. The only incidents that took place in Louisiana are Mrs. Hervish's calls to Growables to question the delay in shipment, the delivery—through a third-party truck—of the furniture into this state, and Mrs. Hervish's payment of the balance of the purchase price to the truck driver upon delivery.

There is no evidence that Growables transacts any business in Louisiana, that its representatives or agents travel to Louisiana for business purposes, or that it advertises or otherwise solicits business in Louisiana or from Louisiana residents, either directly or by mail. There is no evidence that Growables derives any substantial revenue from business in Louisiana, or "engages in any persistent course of conduct" in this state.

In fact, the only classification of the long-arm statute Growables will fit into is subparagraph (b),

"contracting to supply services or things in this state." We can, however, find no other case in which a Louisiana court has found an isolated incident of delivery, without other affiliating circumstances, sufficient to apply long-arm jurisdiction to a foreign corporation. This single transaction would not justify our concluding that Growables purposefully availed itself of the privilege of conducting activities within Louisiana in such a manner that it had clear notice it would be subject to suit here.

Accordingly, we conclude the district court properly found a lack of personal jurisdiction over Growables.

**Judgment for Growables affirmed.**

## Taxation

A state may tax a foreign corporation if such taxation does not violate the Due Process Clause or the Commerce Clause. Generally, a state's imposition of a tax must serve a legitimate state interest and be reasonable in relation to a foreign corporation's contacts with the state. For example, a North Carolina corporation's property located in Pennsylvania is subject to property tax in Pennsylvania. The corporation enjoys Pennsylvania's protection of private property. It may be required to pay its share of the cost of such protection.

Greater contacts are needed to subject a corporation to state income and sales taxation in a state than are needed to subject it to property taxation. A state tax does not violate the Commerce Clause when the tax (1) is applied to an activity with a substantial connection with the taxing state, (2) is fairly apportioned, (3) does not discriminate against interstate commerce, and (4) is fairly related to the services provided by the state.

For example, New Jersey has been permitted to tax a portion of the entire net income of a corporation for the privilege of doing business, employing or owning capital or property, or maintaining an office in New Jersey when the portion of entire net income taxed is determined by an average of three ratios: in-state property to

total property, in-state to total receipts, and in-state to total wages, salaries, and other employee compensation.[2] However, Pennsylvania could not assess a flat tax on the operation of all trucks on Pennsylvania highways. The flat tax imposed a disproportionate burden on interstate trucks as compared with intrastate trucks because interstate trucks traveled fewer miles per year on Pennsylvania highways.[3]

## Qualifying to Do Business

A state may require that foreign corporations **qualify** to conduct **intrastate** business in the state. The level of doing business that constitutes intrastate business for qualification purposes has been difficult to define. To help clarify the confusion in this area, the MBCA lists several activities that do *not* require qualification. For example, soliciting—by mail or through employees—orders that require acceptance outside the state is not doing intrastate business requiring qualification. Selling through independent contractors

---

[2]*Amerada Hess Corp. v. Director of Taxation,* 490 U.S. 66 (1989).

[3]*American Trucking Assns., Inc. v. Scheiner,* 483 U.S. 266 (1987).

or owning real or personal property does not require qualification.

Also classified as not doing business for qualification purposes is conducting an **isolated transaction** that is completed within 30 days and is not one in the course of repeated transactions of a like nature. This isolated transaction safe harbor allows a tree grower to bring Christmas trees into a state in order to sell them to one retailer. However, a Christmas tree retailer who comes into a state for 29 days before Christmas and sells to consumers from a street corner is required to qualify. Although both merchants have consummated their transactions within 30 days, the grower has engaged in only one transaction, but the retailer has engaged in a series of transactions.

Maintaining an office to conduct intrastate business, selling personal property not in interstate commerce, entering into contracts relating to local business or sales, or owning or using real estate for general corporate purposes does constitute doing intrastate business. Passive ownership of real estate for investment, however, is not doing intrastate business.

Maintaining a stock of goods within a state from which to fill orders, even if the orders are taken or accepted outside the state, is doing intrastate business requiring qualification. Performing service activities such as machinery repair and construction work may be doing intrastate business.

In the next case, the court applied the isolated transaction safe harbor and held that providing services for four days annually to an independent in-state business was not doing intrastate business requiring qualification.

---

## COMMONWEALTH OF KENTUCKY v. NATIONAL STEEPLECHASE AND HUNT ASS'N.
### 612 S.W.2d 347 (Ky. Ct. App. 1981)

The National Steeplechase and Hunt Association (NSHA) is a New York corporation that sanctions, regulates, and supervises steeplechase races. Its first sanctioned race was the Oxmoor Steeplechase, near Louisville, Kentucky, in 1948. It has supervised the High Hope Steeplechase in Fayette County, Kentucky, since 1967 and the Hard Scuffle Steeplechase in Oldham County, near Louisville, since 1975. Each of the sanctioned events lasts no more than three to four days every year.

The NSHA has never obtained from the Kentucky secretary of state a certificate to do business in Kentucky as a foreign corporation. No annual reports have been filed, and no registration fees have been paid. The NSHA does not maintain a registered office or a registered agent in the state.

In 1975, the Commonwealth of Kentucky sued the NSHA to collect all of the fees and penalties due to the Commonwealth as a result of the failure of the NSHA to qualify to do business in Kentucky. The trial court held that the NSHA was not doing business in Kentucky and therefore did not need to qualify. The Commonwealth appealed.

---

**Wintersheimer, Judge**   The sanctioning of steeplechase meetings does not constitute the transaction of business in Kentucky. The NSHA promulgates rules; approves the racecourses, race officials, and the financial responsibility of the sponsoring organization; receives entries for each meeting by telephone or mail; assembles the information on the meetings; and prepares a booklet and identification badges for each meet. All of these functions are performed in the New York office. The NSHA maintains no offices or employees in Kentucky. All communications are conducted by mail or telephone. The NSHA provides a service and information to the local sponsoring organization. The attendance by NSHA employees at the meetings does not constitute the transaction of business in Kentucky.

The leasing of fences and jumps by the NSHA to the local organizations in Kentucky is within the exception provided for interstate commerce in the Kentucky statute. The NSHA driver transporting the jumps to Kentucky does not assist the local organization in setting up the equipment. The NSHA employee does not deal with the equipment after it is delivered.

The isolated transaction section applies to the activities of the NSHA employees in Kentucky. The statute makes an exception for isolated transactions completed within 30 days and not in the course of a number of repeated transactions of a like nature. Here, the meetings generally last no more than three

to four days. Three different locations are now used annually. The presence of the NSHA's employees at these meetings and the occasional utilization of them as stewards falls within the isolated transaction section.

**Judgment for the NSHA affirmed.**

**Qualification Requirements**    To qualify to do intrastate business in a state, a foreign corporation must apply for a **certificate of authority** from the secretary of state, pay an application fee, maintain a registered office and a registered agent in the state, file an annual report with the secretary of state, and pay an annual fee.

Doing intrastate business without qualifying usually subjects a foreign corporation to a fine, in some states as much as $10,000. The MBCA disables the corporation to use the state's courts to bring a lawsuit until it obtains a certificate of authority. The corporation may defend itself in the state's courts, however, even if it has no certificate of authority.

## Regulation of a Corporation's Internal Affairs

Regulation of the internal affairs of a corporation—that is, the relation between the corporation and its directors, officers, and shareholders—is usually only exercised by the state of incorporation. Nonetheless, a foreign corporation may conduct most of its business in a state other than the one in which it is incorporated. Such a corporation is called a **pseudo-foreign corporation** in the state in which it conducts most of its business.

A few states subject pseudo-foreign corporations to extensive regulation of their internal affairs, regulation similar to that imposed on their domestic corporations. California's statute requires corporations that have more than 50 percent of their business and ownership in California to elect directors by cumulative voting, to hold annual directors' elections, and to comply with California's dividend payment restrictions. Foreign corporations raise many constitutional objections to the California statute, including violations of the Commerce Clause and the Due Process Clause.

## Regulation of Foreign Nonprofit Corporations

The Model Nonprofit Corporation Act and other laws impose the same requirements and penalties on nonprofit corporations as are imposed on for-profit corporations. For example, the MNCA requires a foreign nonprofit corporation to qualify to do intrastate business in a state. The failure to qualify prevents the foreign nonprofit corporation from using the state's courts to bring lawsuits and subjects it to fines for each day it transacts intrastate business without a certificate of authority.

## Piercing the Corporate Veil

A corporation is a legal entity separate from its shareholders. Corporation law erects an imaginary wall between a corporation and its shareholders that protects shareholders from liability for a corporation's actions. Once shareholders have made their promised capital contributions to the corporation, they have no further financial liability. This means that contracts of a corporation are not contracts of its shareholders, and debts of a corporation are not debts of its shareholders.

Nonetheless, in order *to promote justice and to prevent inequity*, courts will sometimes ignore the separateness of a corporation and its shareholders by **piercing the corporate veil.** The primary consequence of piercing the corporate veil is that a corporation's shareholders may lose their limited liability.

Two requirements must exist for a court to pierce the corporate veil: (1) **domination** of a corporation by its shareholders; and (2) use of that domination for an **improper purpose.**

As an entity separate from its shareholders, a corporation should act for itself, not for its shareholders. If the shareholders cause the corporation to act to its detriment and to the personal benefit of shareholders, *domination*—the first requirement for piercing the corporate veil—is proved. For example, shareholders' directing a corporation to pay a shareholder's personal expenses is domination. Domination is also proved if the shareholders cause the corporation to fail to observe corporate formalities (such as failing to hold shareholder and director meetings or to maintain separate accounting records). Some courts say that shareholder domination makes the corporation the *alter ego* (other self) of the shareholders. Other courts say that domination makes the corporation an *instrumentality* of the shareholders.

To prove domination, it is not sufficient, or even necessary, to show that there is only one shareholder. Many one-shareholder corporations will never have their veils pierced. However, nearly all corporations whose veils are pierced are close corporations, since domination is more easily accomplished in a close corporation than in a publicly held one.

In addition to domination, there must be an *improper use* of the corporation. The improper use may be any of three types: defrauding creditors, circumventing a statute, or evading an existing obligation.

Shareholders must organize a corporation with sufficient capital to meet the initial capital needs of the business. Inadequate capitalization, called **thin capitalization**, is proved when capitalization is very small in relation to the nature of the business of the corporation and the risks the business necessarily entails.

Thin capitalization defrauds creditors of a corporation. An example of thin capitalization is forming a business with a high debt-to-equity ratio, such as a $10-million-asset business with only $1,000 of equity capital, with the shareholders sometimes contributing the remainder of the needed capital as secured creditors. By doing so, the shareholders elevate a portion of their bankruptcy repayment priority to a level above that of general creditors, thereby reducing the shareholders' risk. The high debt-to-equity ratio harms nonshareholder-creditors by failing to provide an equity cushion sufficient to protect their claims. In such a situation, either the shareholders will be liable for the corporation's debts or the shareholders' loans to the corporation will be subordinated to the claims of other creditors. As a result, the nonshareholder-creditors are repaid all of their claims prior to the shareholder-creditors receiving payment from the corporation.

In the next case, the court held that $3,000 was inadequate initial capital for a business with assets of $430,000.

---

## J. L. BROCK BUILDERS, INC. v. DAHLBECK
### 391 N.W.2d 110 (Neb. Sup. Ct. 1986)

In 1971, Eric Dahlbeck incorporated Viking Construction, Inc. Its initial capital was $3,000. In addition, Dahlbeck made a $7,000 loan to Viking. It had as assets 65 lots of land for development, which cost $430,000. For its entire existence, Viking's liabilities exceeded the book value of its assets. From 1972 through 1974, Dahlbeck and another officer received salaries totaling $53,750. Beginning in 1975, Viking's business steadily declined and creditors' claims became overdue. No salaries were paid thereafter. In 1978, Viking began liquidation and transferred assets to Dahlbeck to repay loans that Dahlbeck had made to Viking. Viking dissolved in 1980, having not paid several creditors, including J. L. Brock Builders, which was owed about $16,000. Brock sued Dahlbeck personally, claiming that Viking's corporate veil should be pierced. The trial court refused to pierce Viking's veil. Brock appealed to the Supreme Court of Nebraska.

---

**Shanahan, Justice**  A creditor seeking to pierce the corporate veil and impose on a shareholder liability for a corporate debt has the burden to show that the corporate entity must be disregarded to prevent fraud or injustice to the creditor. One of the factors that is relevant in determining whether to disregard the corporate entity on the basis of fraud is grossly inadequate capitalization.

Viking was grossly inadequately capitalized at the time of its formation. Viking's capital was $3,000 at formation and it had as an asset 65 lots, 25 at $10,000 each and the remaining at $4,500 an acre. The scale of operations anticipated by both the number of lots and their value cannot be adequately capitalized by $3,000. The risk to creditors must be balanced by the availability of more capital should the corporation fail. In reaching our conclusion that Viking was inadequately capitalized, we note Dahlberg could have provided more capital to Viking at its formation, but chose instead to loan Viking $7,000.

Shareholders of an insolvent corporation cannot participate in the distribution of its assets until claims of creditors are paid. If the shareholders are allowed to withdraw assets leaving creditors unpaid, they may be compelled to repay what they have received.

Although he was aware of $78,000 in debts to Viking creditors, Dahlbeck, as Viking's sole shareholder, transferred all Viking's assets to himself. Dahlbeck's action constitutes an improper use of corporate funds, an injustice perpetrated by a shareholder.

Viking's corporate existence was used to commit a fraud upon Brock. Viking's corporate entity should be disregarded and liability imposed on Dahlbeck for the debt incurred by Viking.

**Judgment reversed in favor of Brock.**

Transfers of corporate assets to shareholders for less than fair market value (called **looting**) also defraud creditors. For example, shareholder-managers loot a corporation by paying themselves excessively high salaries or by having the corporation pay their personal credit card bills. When such payments leave insufficient assets in the corporation to pay creditors' claims, a court will hold the shareholders liable to the creditors.

Frequently, the same shareholders may own two corporations that transact with each other. The shareholders may cause one corporation to loot the other. When such looting occurs between corporations of common ownership, courts pierce the veils of these corporations. This makes each corporation liable to the creditors of the other corporation. For example, a shareholder-manager operates two corporations from the same office. Corporation 1 transfers inventory to Corporation 2, but it receives less than fair market value for the inventory. Also, both corporations employ the same workers, but all of the wages are paid by Corporation 1. In such a situation, the veils of the corporations will be pierced, allowing the creditors of Corporation 1 to satisfy their claims against the assets of Corporation 2.

In the next case, the shareholders' looting of a corporation was grounds to pierce the corporate veil.

### CASTLEBERRY V. BRANSCUM
**721 S.W.2d 270 (Tex. Sup. Ct. 1986)**

In September 1980, Joe Castleberry, Byron Branscum, and Michael Byboth incorporated their furniture-moving business as Texan Transfer, Inc. Each owned one third of the shares of Texan Transfer. Byboth was president, Castleberry was vice president, and Branscum was secretary-treasurer. Soon thereafter, Branscum formed Elite Moving Company, a business that competed with Texan Transfer. Castleberry discovered the existence of Elite Moving and sued to claim that Texan Transfer owned the assets and revenues of Elite Moving. As a result, Branscum became very upset and threatened that Castleberry would not receive any return on his investment in Texan Transfer unless Castleberry abandoned his attempts to claim ownership of Elite Moving.

In July 1981, Castleberry sold his Texan Transfer shares back to Texan Transfer in exchange for a $42,000 promissory note payable by Texan Transfer. After the sale, Elite Moving took over more and more of Texan

Transfer's business. Controlled by Branscum and Byboth, Texan Transfer allowed Elite Moving to use its employees and trucks. Elite Moving advertised for furniture moving, but Texan Transfer did not. While Texan Transfer's business declined, Elite Moving's prospered. For the 18 months prior to Castleberry's sale of his shares, Texan Transfer had a net income of $65,479. After the sale, its net income fell to $2,814 for the second half of 1981. In 1982, it lost more than $16,000. By contrast, Elite Moving had income in 1982 of $195,765.

In 1982, Branscum told his wife that Castleberry "would never get a dime, that he would file bankruptcy before Castleberry got any money out of the company and that he would open the company in another name so that Joe wouldn't get paid." In September 1982, Byboth and Branscum started Custom Carriers, Inc. At that time, Byboth and Branscum terminated Texan Transfer's contract with Freed Furniture, which contract comprised the majority of Texan Transfer's business. Byboth and Branscum obtained for Custom Carriers an identical contract with Freed Furniture, doing the same deliveries at the same rate. Byboth and Branscum then sold Texan Transfer's trucks to drivers hired to make deliveries for Custom Carriers. With the proceeds of the sales, Byboth and Branscum paid themselves back salaries.

Castleberry was paid only $1,000 of the $42,000 promissory note. He sued Branscum and Byboth, claiming that the corporate veil of Texan Transfer should be pierced to make them personally liable on the promissory note. The trial court found Branscum and Byboth liable to Castleberry. Branscum and Byboth appealed. The court of appeals reversed and held for Branscum and Byboth. Castleberry appealed to the Supreme Court of Texas.

---

**Spears, Justice** The corporate form normally insulates shareholders, officers, and directors from liability for corporate obligations; but when these individuals abuse the corporate privilege, courts will disregard the corporate fiction and hold them individually liable.

We disregard the corporate fiction when the corporate form has been used as part of a basically unfair device to achieve an inequitable result. Specifically, we disregard the corporate fiction:

1. When the fiction is used as a means of perpetrating fraud;

2. When the corporate fiction is resorted to as a means of evading an existing legal obligation;

3. When the corporate fiction is used to circumvent a statute.

We hold that there is some evidence of a sham to perpetrate a fraud. A jury could find that both Byboth and Branscum manipulated a closely held corporation—Texan Transfer—and formed competing businesses to ensure that Castleberry did not get paid.

The variety of shams is infinite, but many fit this case's pattern: a closely held corporation owes unwanted obligations; it siphons off corporate revenues, sells off much of the corporate assets, or does other acts to hinder the on-going business and its ability to pay off its debts; a new business then starts up that is basically a continuation of the old business with many of the same shareholders, officers, and directors.

**Judgment reversed in favor of Castleberry.**

---

Looting may occur also when one corporation (called the **parent corporation**) owns at least a majority of the shares of another corporation (called the **subsidiary corporation**). Ordinarily, the parent is liable for its own obligations and the subsidiary is liable for its own obligations, but the parent is not liable for its subsidiary's debts and the subsidiary is not liable for the parent's debts. Nonetheless, because a parent corporation is able to elect the directors of its subsidiary and therefore can control the management of the subsidiary, the parent may cause its subsidiary to transact with the parent in a manner that benefits the parent but harms the subsidiary.

For example, a parent corporation may direct its subsidiary to sell its assets to the parent for less than fair market value. Because the subsidiary has given more assets to the parent than it has received from the parent, creditors of the subsidiary have been defrauded. Consequently, a court will pierce the veil between the parent and its subsidiary and hold the parent liable to the creditors of the subsidiary.

**FIGURE 2**    Examples of Piercing the Corporate Veil

| Event | Proof of Domination | Proof of Improper Purpose | Result |
|---|---|---|---|
| Sole shareholder/ director causes corporation to pay shareholder's personal debt. | Sole shareholder/ director controls corporation's use of assets. | Creditors defrauded when corporate assets used to pay shareholder's debt, not corporation's debt. | Shareholder liable to creditors of corporation. |
| Shareholders/ directors fail to hold annual shareholders' and directors' meetings. | Shareholders and directors control corporation's decision to hold meetings. | Circumvention of incorporation statute requiring annual meetings. | Shareholders liable to creditors of corporation. |
| To avoid union contract, shareholders vote to transfer business of corporation to new corporation owned by the same shareholders. | Shareholders' vote controlled corporation's decision to transfer business to new corporation. | Obligation to employees evaded by the business. | New corporation liable to employees under union contract. |
| Parent of wholly owned subsidiary causes subsidiary to buy asset from parent at price higher than fair market value. | Parent owns 100% of subsidiary, elects its directors, and thereby controls subsidiary. | Creditors of subsidiary defrauded when parent gives fewer assets to subsidiary than subsidiary gives to parent. | Parent liable to creditors of subsidiary. |
| Shareholders organize corporation by contributing $1,000 of capital and by loaning $99,000 to corporation. The loan is secured by all the corporation's assets. | Shareholders control organization of corporation. | Nonshareholder creditors defrauded by thin capitalization. | Part or all of loans treated as capital, thereby subordinating shareholders' loans to claims of nonshareholders. |

A corporation should not engage in a course of conduct that is prohibited by a statute. For example, a city ordinance prohibits retail businesses from being open on consecutive Sundays. To avoid the statute, a retail corporation forms a subsidiary owned entirely by the retail corporation; on alternate weeks, it leases its building and inventory to the subsidiary. A court will pierce the veil because the purpose of creating the subsidiary corporation is to circumvent the statutory prohibition. Consequently, both the parent and the subsidiary will be liable for violating the statute.

Sometimes, a corporation will attempt to escape liability on a contract by reincorporating or by forming a subsidiary corporation. The new corporation will claim that it is not bound by the contract, even though it is doing the same business as was done by the old corporation. In such a situation, courts pierce the corporate veil and hold the new corporation liable on the contract.

For example, to avoid an onerous labor union contract, a corporation creates a wholly owned subsidiary and sells its entire business to the subsidiary. The subsidiary will claim that it is not a party to the labor contract and may hire nonunion labor. A court will pierce the veil between the two corporations because the subsidiary was created only to avoid the union contract.

For a summary of the law of piercing the corporate veil, see Figure 2.

## Nonprofit Corporations

Like a for-profit corporation, a nonprofit corporation is an entity separate and distinct from its members. A member is not personally liable for a nonprofit corporation's acts or liabilities merely by being a member. However, a court may pierce the veil of a nonprofit corporation if it is used to defraud creditors, circumvent a statute, or evade an existing obligation, the same grounds on which a for-profit corporation's veil may be pierced.

### PROBLEMS AND PROBLEM CASES

**1.** Nippon Electric Co., Ltd., a Japanese corporation with its principal place of business in Tokyo, manufactured telephone and computer equipment in Japan, which it sold to its wholly owned subsidiary, NEC America, a New York corporation authorized to do business in New Jersey. NEC America distributed Nippon equipment to its wholly owned subsidiary, NEC Telephone. NEC Telephone sold Nippon telephone equipment to Telecom Equipment Corporation, a New Jersey corporation. Telecom sold a portion of the equipment to Charles Gendler & Co. for installation at Gendler's place of business in New Jersey. The equipment failed to perform as promised, and Gendler sued Nippon in a New Jersey court. Nippon claimed that it could not be sued in a New Jersey court because it had not conducted any business in New Jersey, had no agents located there, had not advertised for or solicited business in New Jersey, did not have a telephone listing in the state, had not contracted with Gendler for the sale of the equipment, and had not received any direct income from Gendler or any other New Jersey resident. Nonetheless, Nippon acknowledged that the sale to Gendler was not an isolated transaction and that other Nippon equipment may have been sold in New Jersey. May Gendler sue Nippon in a New Jersey court?

**2.** A Hawaiian statute imposed a 20 percent wholesale excise tax on liquor sold in Hawaii. To encourage the development of Hawaiian liquor, the statute exempted from taxation Okolehao, a brandy distilled from the root of the ti plant, a native Hawaiian shrub. Bacchus Imports, a liquor wholesaler, claimed that the excise tax violated the Commerce Clause. Was Bacchus correct?

**3.** Campaign Works, Ltd., a business incorporated in Florida, was a consultant to candidates for political office. Campaign Works had offices in Florida and Washington, D.C. It had no office and no employees in Missouri and had not qualified to do business in Missouri. Campaign Works contracted to provide political consulting services to Doug Hughes, a candidate to the U.S. Congress for Missouri. The contract was negotiated by telephone and concluded by mail between Campaign Works in Florida or Washington and Hughes in Missouri. The contract called for consultations with Hughes in Missouri and political research appropriate to his election campaign. Campaign Works actually performed election research for Hughes from its offices in Florida and Washington, and its president traveled to Missouri twice to consult with Hughes and his staff. The parties terminated the contract, with Hughes owing Campaign Works nearly $9,000. Hughes failed to pay this amount, and Campaign

Works sued Hughes in a Missouri trial court. Does Campaign Works's failure to qualify to do business in Missouri prevent it from suing Hughes in a Missouri court?

**4.** Section 2115 of the California General Corporation Law requires that a foreign corporation doing a majority of its business in California (on the basis of its property, payroll, and sales) and having a majority of its outstanding voting securities owned by persons with addresses in California comply with certain internal governance provisions of the California corporation law, including section 708, which provides for the cumulative voting of shares for the election of directors. Louisiana-Pacific Resources, Inc., was a Utah corporation. The average of its property, payroll, and sales in California exceeded 50 percent, and more than 50 percent of its shareholders entitled to vote resided in California. Except for being domiciled in Utah and having a transfer agent there, Louisiana-Pacific had virtually no business connections with Utah. Its principal place of business was in California; its meetings of shareholders and directors were held in California; and all of its employees and bank accounts were in California. Louisiana-Pacific argued that application of section 2115 to Louisiana-Pacific violated the Constitution of the United States. Is it correct?

**5.** Pacific Development, Inc., was incorporated in the District of Columbia in 1968 to engage in the business of international brokerage and consulting. Tongsun Park was Pacific's founder, president, and sole shareholder. It was doubtful whether Pacific had a board of directors prior to December 1974. The directors met infrequently after 1974. When they did meet, they approved without discussion or question corporate decisions made by Park. Park wrote checks on Pacific's bank accounts to cover his unrelated personal and business expenses. Pacific employees served as Park's household servants. Park made loans with Pacific funds to politically influential people and then forgave the loans. Pacific personnel provided administrative and managerial services for Park's other business ventures, and Pacific's profits were assigned to Park or to his other companies. In 1977, the Internal Revenue Service assessed $4.5 million in back income taxes against Park. To collect the taxes, the IRS seized some of Pacific's assets, claiming that the company was a mere alter ego of Park. Was the IRS correct?

**6.** Sea Pines Company owned 90 percent of the shares of Point South, Inc. The directors and officers of Point South were under the control of Sea Pines. Point South was organized with initial capital of $1,000. In February 1973, Point South had assets of $2.5 million and total net worth of $65,000, of which only $1,000 was capital contributions. By February 1974, Point South had become so unprofitable that it had a negative net worth of $177,000. During the period of unprofitability, Sea Pines paid the salary and expenses of Point South with the expectation that it would be reimbursed. In February 1974, when Point South was insolvent, its directors mortgaged a piece of property (worth $350,000) to secure a debt of Sea Pines. In exchange for the mortgage, Sea Pines reduced by $8,000 the amount it was owed by Point South. When Point South failed to repay a construction loan to American Bank & Trust Company, American sued Sea Pines. Was Sea Pines liable to American?

**7.** Vassilis Morfopolous was the sole shareholder of American Standards Testing Bureau (ASTB). ASTB was the sole shareholder of Architectural Research Corporation (ARC) and Ar-Lite Panelcraft, Inc. (API). ASTB, ARC, and API had the same officers, and Morfopolous ran all three businesses. ASTB made periodic loans to ARC that were secured by all of ARC's assets. When ARC defaulted on an obligation to Bodenhamer Building Corporation, Bodenhamer sued ARC and obtained a judgment for $50,000. To prevent Bodenhamer from collecting his judgment, ASTB foreclosed on its loan to ARC and obtained the auction sale of ARC's assets. At the auction, ASTB submitted the only bid, $115,000, which was considerably less than previous purchase offers ranging from $1 million to $2.2 million and earlier estimates that ARC's assets were worth from $345,000 to $600,000. ASTB took possession of the assets, leaving Bodenhamer and other ARC creditors unpaid. ARC ceased operations, and ASTB leased the purchased assets to API, which had been incorporated solely to continue ARC's business had Bodenhamer been successful in obtaining a judgment against ARC. Bodenhamer sued ASTB and API to obtain payment of the judgment. Are they liable to Bodenhamer?

**8.** New York law required that every taxicab company carry $10,000 of accident liability insurance for each cab in its fleet. The purpose of the law was to ensure that passengers and pedestrians injured by cabs operated by these companies would be adequately compensated for their injuries. Carlton organized 10 corporations, each owning and operating two taxicabs in New York City. Each of these corporations carried $20,000 of liability insurance. Carlton was the principal shareholder of each corporation. The vehicles, the only freely transferable assets of these corporations, were collateral for claims of secured creditors. The 10 corporations were operated more or less as a unit with respect to supplies, repairs, and employees. Walkovszky was severely injured when he was run down by one of the taxicabs. He sued Carlton personally, alleging that the multiple corporate structure amounted to fraud upon those who might be injured by the taxicabs. Should the court pierce the corporate veil to reach Carlton individually?

**9.** Denzil and Stephanie Cooper obtained a court judgment for $31,800 against Seaside Pools, Inc. (SPI), a wholly owned subsidiary of Seaside Industries, Inc. (SI). SPI had sufficient funds to pay the judgment. Two weeks later, Bernard Leff, the sole owner of SI, incorporated Seaside Pools of Texas, Inc. (SPOT), and Seaside Enterprises, Inc. (SE). Leff transferred all his SI shares to SE, which as a result owned all the shares of SI, which still owned SPI. In addition, SE was the only shareholder of SPOT. Leff was president of all the corporations. Two months later, SPI ceased business, but SPOT began business using the same location, personnel, telephone, trade name, and advertising as SPI. When SPI failed to pay the Coopers, they sued Leff, SPOT, SE, and SI. Did the Coopers succeed?

**10.** Maintenance Contractors, Inc., owed $13,600 to Westinghouse Electric Supply Co. Robert Pilkerton, the majority shareholder of Maintenance Contractors, caused Maintenance Contractors to cease operations. Twelve days later, Robert Pilkerton incorporated R.E. Pilkerton, Inc, which carried on the same business as Maintenance Contractors. Are Pilkerton and R.E. Pilkerton, Inc., liable to Westinghouse on the $13,600 debt?

## Capstone Questions

Hannah Clintrock has been an executive for a leading company in the book-publishing field. Frustrated by senior executives, she decides to open her own book-publishing business, specializing in self-help manuals. Concerned about her personal liability and taxation issues, Clintrock incorporates the business in Maryland and names it Morningstar Publishing Company. Clintrock is the only shareholder, director, and officer of Morningstar. Needing $300,000 to get started, Clintrock contributes $5,000 of equity capital to Morningstar and lends the corporation another $255,000 secured by a claim against all of Morningstar's assets. Clintrock obtains the remaining $40,000 of funding from a trust she manages for her children.

During the next 13 months, the following occur:

- Morningstar opens a retail bookstore in Richmond, Virginia, from which Morningstar sells its own books and books published by other publishers. Annual sales reach $350,000 in the Richmond location. Morningstar does not apply for a certificate of authority to do business in Virginia. Morningstar contracts to purchase $20,000 of books from R.E.L. Publishing, a publisher based in Richmond. Although Morningstar pays for the books, R.E.L. Publishing never delivers the books to Morningstar. Morningstar sues R.E.L. Publishing in a Virginia state court. R.E.L. Publishing claims that Morningstar may not sue in a Virginia court and that the contract is void due to Morningstar's failure to apply for a certificate of authority in Virginia.

- During its first month of operation, Morningstar signs a contract with Shelby Eineman, who has authored a medical self-help manual. The contract provides that Morningstar will pay Eineman a royalty of 25 percent of book sales; it guarantees Eineman royalties of at least $100,000 for the first year the book is offered for sale. Eineman's book sells only 6,000 copies during its first year of sale, generating sales of $120,000. Morningstar pays Eineman $30,000 royalties, but it refuses to pay the remainder of the guaranteed royalty. Morningstar is insolvent, having assets of $20,000 and liabilities of $480,000. Because Clintrock's loan to Morningstar is secured by all of Morningstar's assets, Morningstar distributes the remainder of its assets to Clintrock. Eineman discovers that during Morningstar's 13 months of operation, Morningstar's board of directors never held a meeting. In addition, Morningstar never had a shareholders' meeting. Moreover, Clintrock caused Morningstar to hire her 6-year-old daughter at a salary of $3,000 per month. The daughter filed documents for Morningstar on Saturday mornings when her mother worked at the corporate office. Finally, Eineman discovers that Clintrock caused Morningstar to pay for an $8,000 vacation that Clintrock and her family took to Alaska.

**Required:**

Answer the following and give reasons for your conclusions.

1. Is Morningstar or R.E.L. Publishing correct concerning the lawsuit in Virginia?
2. Does Eineman have grounds to hold Clintrock personally liable on the royalty contract?

# CHAPTER

## 3 4

# ORGANIZATION AND FINANCIAL STRUCTURE OF CORPORATIONS

**INTRODUCTION**

*A person desiring to incorporate a business must comply with the applicable corporation law. Failing to comply can create various problems. For example, a person may make a contract on behalf of the corporation before it is incorporated. Is the corporation liable on this contract? Is the person who made the contract on behalf of the prospective corporation liable on the contract? Do the people who thought that they were shareholders of a corporation have limited liability, or do they have unlimited liability as partners of a partnership?*

## PROMOTERS AND PREINCORPORATION TRANSACTIONS

A **promoter** of a corporation incorporates a business, organizes its initial management, and raises its initial capital. Typically, a promoter discovers a business or an idea to be developed, finds people who are willing to invest in the business, negotiates the contracts necessary for the initial operation of the proposed venture, incorporates the business, and helps management start the operation of the business. Consequently, a promoter may engage in many acts prior to the incorporation of the business. As a result, the promoter may have liability on the contracts he negotiates on behalf of the prospective corporation. In addition, the corporation may *not* be liable on the contracts the promoter makes on its behalf.

### Corporation's Liability on Preincorporation Contracts

A nonexistent corporation has no liability on contracts made by a promoter prior to its incorporation. This is because the corporation does not exist.

Even when the corporation comes into existence, it does not automatically become liable on a preincorporation contract made by a promoter on its behalf. It cannot be held liable as a principal whose agent made the contracts because the promoter was not its agent and the corporation was not in existence when the contracts were made.

The only way a corporation may become bound on a promoter's preincorporation contracts is by the corporation's **adoption** of the promoter's contracts. For a corporation to adopt a promoter's contract, the corporation must accept the contract with knowledge of all its material facts.

Acceptance may be express or implied. The corporation's knowing receipt of the benefits of the contract is sufficient for acceptance. For example, a promoter makes a preincorporation contract with a genetic engineer, requiring the engineer to work for a prospective corporation for 10 years. After incorporation, the promoter presents the contract to the board of directors. Although the board takes no formal action to accept the contract, the board allows the engineer to work for the corporation for one year as the contract provides and pays him the salary required by the contract. The board's actions constitute an acceptance of the contract, binding the corporation to the contract for its 10-year term.

## Promoter's Liability on Preincorporation Contracts

A promoter and her copromoters are jointly and severally liable on preincorporation contracts the promoter negotiates in the name of the nonexistent corporation. This liability exists even when the promoters' names do not appear on the contract. Promoters are also jointly and severally liable for torts committed by their copromoters prior to incorporation.

A promoter retains liability on a preincorporation contract until **novation** occurs. For novation to occur, the corporation and the third party must agree to release the promoter from liability and to substitute the corporation for the promoter as the party liable on the contract. Usually, novation will occur by express or implied agreement of all the parties.

If the corporation is not formed, a promoter remains liable on a preincorporation contract unless the third party releases the promoter from liability. In addition, the mere formation of the corporation does not release a promoter from liability. A promoter remains liable on a preincorporation contract even after the corporation's adoption of the contract, since adoption does not automatically release the promoter. The corporation cannot by itself relieve the promoter of liability to the third party; the third party must also agree, expressly or impliedly, to release the promoter from liability.

A few courts have held that a promoter is not liable on preincorporation contracts if the third party *knew of the nonexistence* of the corporation yet insisted that the promoter sign the contract on behalf of the nonexistent corporation. Other courts have found that the promoter is not liable if the third party clearly stated that he would *look only to the prospective corporation* for performance.

In the next case, the court held that a promoter failed to prove that the third party agreed to look only to the corporation for performance.

---

## COOPERS & LYBRAND V. FOX
### 758 P.2d 683 (Colo. Ct. App. 1988)

On November 3, 1981, Garry Fox met with Coopers & Lybrand, a national accounting firm, to request a tax opinion and other accounting services. Fox told Coopers that he was acting on behalf of a corporation that he was in the process of forming, to be named G. Fox and Partners, Inc. Coopers accepted its engagement to provide services with the knowledge that the corporation was not yet in existence. Fox and Coopers had no agreement regarding Fox's personal liability for payment of the fee for the services.

G. Fox and Partners, Inc., was incorporated on December 4, 1981. Coopers completed its work on the contract by mid-December and billed "Mr. Garry Fox, Fox and Partners, Inc." in the amount of $10,827. When neither Fox nor the corporation paid the bill, Coopers sued Garry Fox individually based on the theory of promoter liability. The trial court held that Fox had no personal liability to Coopers. Coopers appealed to the Colorado Court of Appeals.

**Kelly, Chief Judge**   As a preliminary matter, we reject Fox's argument that he was acting only as an agent for the future corporation. One cannot act as the agent of a nonexistent principal.

On the contrary, the uncontroverted facts place Fox squarely within the definition of a promoter. A promoter is one who, alone or with others, undertakes to form a corporation and to procure for it the rights, instrumentalities, and capital to enable it to conduct business.

As a general rule, promoters are personally liable for the contracts they make, though made on behalf of a corporation to be formed. A well-recognized exception to the general rule of promoter liability is that if the contracting party knows the corporation is not in existence but nevertheless agrees to look solely to the corporation and not to the promoter for payment, then the promoter incurs no personal liability. In the absence of an express agreement, the existence of an agreement to release the promoter from liability may be shown by circumstances making it reasonably certain that the parties intended to and did enter into the agreement. Release of the promoter depends on the intent of the parties. The promoter has the burden of proving an alleged agreement to release the promoter from liability.

Fox seeks to bring himself within the exception to the general rule of promoter liability. However, as the proponent of the exception, he must bear the burden of proving the existence of the alleged agreement releasing him from liability. There was no agreement regarding Fox's liability. Thus, Fox failed to sustain his burden of proof, and the trial court erred in granting judgment in his favor.

**Judgment reversed in favor of Coopers.**

## Obtaining a Binding Preincorporation Contract

While it may be desirable for the promoter to escape liability on a preincorporation contract, there is one disadvantage: Only when the promoter is liable on the preincorporation contract is the other party liable on the contract. This means that when the promoter is not liable on the contract, the other party to the contract may rescind the contract at any time prior to adoption by the corporation. Once the corporation has adopted the contract, the corporation and the third party are liable on it, and the contract cannot be rescinded without the consent of both parties.

To maintain the enforceability of a preincorporation contract prior to adoption, a promoter may want to be liable on a preincorporation contract at least until the corporation comes into existence and adopts the contract. To limit his liability, however, the promoter may wish to have his liability cease automatically upon adoption. The promoter should ensure that the contract has an **automatic novation clause**. For example, a preincorporation contract may read that "the promoter's liability on this contract shall terminate upon the corporation's adoption of this contract."

Instead of using automatic novation clauses, today most well-advised promoters incorporate the business prior to making any contracts for the corporation. By doing so, only the corporation and the third party—and not the promoter—have liability on the contract.

## Preincorporation Share Subscriptions

Promoters sometimes use **preincorporation share subscriptions** to ensure that the corporation will have adequate capital when it begins its business. Under the terms of a share subscription, a prospective shareholder offers to buy a specific number of the corporation's shares at a stated price. Under the Model Business Corporation Act (MBCA), a prospective shareholder may not revoke a preincorporation subscription for a six-month period, in the absence of a contrary provision in the subscription. Generally, corporate acceptance of preincorporation subscriptions occurs by action of the board of directors after incorporation.

Promoters have no liability on preincorporation share subscriptions. They have a duty, however, to make a good faith effort to bring the corporation into existence. When a corporation fails to accept a preincorporation subscription or becomes insolvent, the promoter is not liable to the disappointed subscriber, in the absence of fraud or other wrongdoing by the promoter.

Today, most promoters incorporate the business and obtain promises to buy shares from prospective shareholders. These promises, which may take the form of postincorporation subscriptions, are discussed later in this chapter.

## Relation of Promoter and Prospective Corporation

A promoter of a nonexistent corporation is not an agent of the prospective corporation but nonetheless owes fiduciary duties to it. A promoter is not an agent of prospective investors in the business because they did not appoint him and they have no power to control him.

Although not an agent of the proposed corporation or its investors, a promoter owes a **fiduciary duty** to the corporation and to its prospective investors. A promoter owes such parties a duty of full disclosure and honesty. For example, a promoter

breaches this duty when she diverts money received from prospective shareholders to pay her expenses, unless the shareholders agree to such payment. The fiduciary duty also prevents a promoter from diverting a business opportunity from the corporation and giving it to himself instead. In addition, the promoter may not purchase shares of the corporation at a price lower than that paid by the public shareholders.

A promoter may not profit personally by transacting secretly with the corporation in his personal capacity. The promoter's failure to disclose her interest in the transaction and the material facts permits the corporation to rescind the transaction or to recover the promoter's secret profit. On the other hand, the promoter's full disclosure of her interest and the material facts of the transaction to an independent board of directors that approves the transaction prevents the corporation from recovering the promoter's profit. Note, however, that when a promoter is a director, approval of the transaction by the board of directors is not sufficient; the transaction must be intrinsically fair to the corporation.

In the following case, the court held that promoters are fiduciaries of the corporation they organize.

---

### SMITH v. BITTER
**319 N.W.2d 196 (Iowa Sup. Ct. 1982)**

Joseph J. Smith, Steve J. Smith, and Joseph Bitter planned to open a tavern in the college town of Dubuque, Iowa. In the name of Gomer's, Inc., a corporation not yet formed, all three signed an offer to purchase a building in which to operate the tavern. After Gomer's, Inc., had been incorporated, the Smiths as corporate officers signed a contract to purchase the building in the name of the corporation. Soon after business began, differences arose between the Smiths and Bitter. Despite Bitter's protests, the Smiths assumed control of the corporation, including the building. Bitter sued the Smiths, asking the court to declare that Bitter and the Smiths as individuals owned the building and that Gomer's, Inc., had no interest in the building. The trial court held that Gomer's, Inc., owned the building. Bitter appealed to the Supreme Court of Iowa.

---

**LeGrand, Justice**   This litigation culminates what started as a business venture among friends and terminated in acrimony and distrust.

In negotiating for the purchase of the real estate, Bitter and the Smiths were promoters acting for the corporation they were then in the process of organizing. A promoter stands in a fiduciary position toward

both the corporation and its stockholders and is prohibited from acquiring a secret personal advantage from any action taken on behalf of the corporation.

The Smiths and Bitter owed a fiduciary duty to the corporation for which they were acting and to its shareholders. The fact that the promoters themselves were the stockholders does not alter that obligation. The record is clear that all negotiations for purchase of the real estate were made on behalf of Gomer's, Inc., which the Smiths and Bitter were then organizing. Bitter cannot profit personally from this transaction nor can he assert personal ownership of the real estate against those toward whom he was bound to exercise the utmost good faith.

**Judgment for the Smiths affirmed.**

## Liability of Corporation to Promoter

Valuable as the services of a promoter may be to a prospective corporation and to society, a corporation is generally not required to compensate a promoter for her promotional services, or even her expenses, unless the corporation has agreed expressly to compensate the promoter. The justification for this rule is that the promoter is self-appointed and acts for a corporation that is not in existence.

Nonetheless, a corporation may choose to reimburse the promoter for her reasonable expenses and to pay her the value of her services to the corporation. Corporations often compensate their promoters with shares. The MBCA permits the issuance of shares for a promoter's preincorporation services.

To ensure that she is compensated for her services, a promoter may tie herself to a person or property that the corporation needs to succeed. For example, a promoter may purchase the invention that the corporation was formed to exploit. Another way to ensure compensation is by the promoter dominating the board of directors during the early months of its life. By doing so, the promoter may direct the corporation to compensate her.

---

**CONCEPT REVIEW**

### PREINCORPORATION CONTRACTS

| | |
|---|---|
| **Promoter Liability** | A promoter is liable on a preincorporation contract unless either: |
| | 1. The third party knows of the nonexistence of the corporation and insists that the promoter sign in the name of the corporation, or |
| | 2. The third party knows of the nonexistence of corporation and agrees only to look to prospective corporation for performance, or |
| | 3. Novation occurs either: |
| |    *a.* By agreement of the corporation and the third party, or |
| |    *b.* By use of an automatic novation clause. |
| **Corporation Liability** | A corporation is *not* liable on a preincorporation contract until the board of directors adopts the contract. |
| **Third-Party Liability** | A third party is liable on a preincorporation contract if either the promoter or the corporation is liable on the contract. |

---

## INCORPORATION

Anyone seeking to incorporate a business must decide where to do so. If the business of a proposed corporation is to be primarily *intrastate*, it is usually cheaper to incorporate in the state where the corporation's business is to be conducted. For the business that is primarily *interstate*, however, the business may benefit by incorporating in a state different from the state in which it has its principal place of business.

Incorporation fees and taxes, annual fees, and other fees such as those on the transfer of shares or the dissolution of the corporation vary considerably from state to state. Delaware has been a popular state in which to incorporate because its fees tend to be low.

Promoters frequently choose to incorporate in a state whose corporation statute and court decisions grant managers broad management discretion. For example, it is easier to pay a large dividend and to effect a merger in Delaware than in many other states.

## Steps in Incorporation

There are only a few requirements for incorporation. It is a fairly simple process and can be accomplished inexpensively in most cases. The steps prescribed by the incorporation statutes of the different states vary, but they generally include the following, which appear in the MBCA:

1. Preparation of articles of incorporation.
2. Signing and authenticating the articles by one or more incorporators.
3. Filing the articles with the secretary of state, accompanied by the payment of specified fees.
4. Receipt of a copy of the articles of incorporation stamped "Filed" by the secretary of state, accompanied by a fee receipt. (Some states retain the old MBCA rule requiring receipt of a certificate of incorporation issued by the secretary of state.)
5. Holding an organization meeting for the purpose of adopting bylaws, electing officers, and transacting other business.

**Articles of Incorporation**     The basic governing document of the corporation is the **articles of incorporation** (sometimes called the charter). The articles are similar to a constitution. They state many of the rights and responsibilities of the corporation, its management, and its shareholders. Figure 1 lists the contents of the articles.

The corporation must have a name that is distinguishable from the name of any other corporation incorporated or qualified to do business in the state. The name must include the word *corporation, incorporated, company,* or *limited,* or the abbreviation *corp., inc., co.,* or *ltd.*

The MBCA does not require the inclusion of a statement of purpose in the articles. When a purpose

---

**FIGURE 1     Contents of Articles of Incorporation (pursuant to MBCA)**

The following *must* be in the articles:

1. The name of the corporation.
2. The number of shares that the corporation has authority to issue.
3. The address of the initial registered office of the corporation and the name of its registered agent.
4. The name and address of each incorporator.

The following *may* be included in the articles:

1. The names and addresses of the individuals who are to serve as the initial directors.
2. The purpose of the corporation.
3. The duration of the corporation.
4. The par value of shares of the corporation.
5. Additional provisions not inconsistent with law for managing the corporation, regulating the internal affairs of the corporation, and establishing the powers of the corporation and its directors and shareholders.

---

is stated, it is sufficient to state, alone or together with specific purposes, that the corporation may engage in "any lawful activity."

The MBCA permits a corporation to have perpetual existence. If desired, the articles of incorporation may provide for a shorter duration.

Most of the state corporation statutes require the articles to recite the initial capitalization of the business. Usually, the statutes require that there be a minimum amount of initial capital, such as $1,000. Since such a small amount of capital is rarely enough to protect creditors adequately, the MBCA dispenses with the need to recite a minimum amount of capital.

The articles may contain additional provisions not inconsistent with law for managing the corporation, regulating the internal affairs of the corporation, and establishing the powers of the corporation and its directors and shareholders. For example, these additional provisions may contain the procedures for electing directors, the quorum requirements for shareholders' and directors' meetings, and the dividend rights of shareholders.

The MBCA specifies that one or more persons, including corporations, partnerships, and unincorporated associations, may serve as the **incorporators**.

Incorporators have no function beyond lending their names and signatures to the process of bringing the corporation into existence. No special liability attaches to a person merely because she serves as an incorporator.

**Filing Articles of Incorporation**   The articles of incorporation must be delivered to the office of the secretary of state, and a filing fee must be paid. The office of the secretary of state reviews the articles of incorporation that are delivered to it. If the articles contain everything that is required, the secretary of state stamps the articles "Filed" and returns a copy of the stamped articles to the corporation along with a receipt for payment of incorporation fees. Some states require a duplicate filing of the articles with an office—usually the county recorder's office—in the county in which the corporation has its principal place of business.

The existence of the corporation begins when the articles are filed by the secretary of state. Filing of the articles is conclusive proof of the existence of the corporation.

Because the articles of incorporation embody the basic contract between a corporation and its shareholders, shareholders must approve most changes in the articles. For example, when the articles are amended to increase the number of authorized shares, shareholder approval is required.

**The Organization Meeting**   After the articles of incorporation have been filed by the secretary of state, an organization meeting is held. Usually, it is the first formal meeting of the directors. Frequently, only bylaws are adopted and officers elected. The function of the bylaws is to supplement the articles of incorporation by defining more precisely the powers, rights, and responsibilities of the corporation, its managers, and its shareholders and by stating other rules under which the corporation and its activities will be governed. Its common contents are listed in Figure 2.

The MBCA gives the incorporators or the initial directors the power to adopt the initial bylaws. The board of directors holds the power to repeal and to amend the bylaws, unless the articles reserve this power to the shareholders. Under the MBCA, the shareholders, as the ultimate owners of the corporation, always retain the power to amend the bylaws,

---

**FIGURE 2   Contents of the Bylaws**

1. The authority of the officers and the directors, specifying what they may or may not do.
2. The time and place at which the annual shareholders' meetings will be held.
3. The procedure for calling special meetings of shareholders.
4. The procedures for shareholders' and directors' meetings, including whether more than a majority is required for approval of specified actions.
5. Provisions for special committees of the board, defining their membership and the scope of their activities.
6. The procedures for the maintenance of share records.
7. The machinery for the transfer of shares.
8. The procedures and standards for the declaration and payment of dividends.

---

even if the directors also have such power. To be valid, bylaws must be consistent with the law and with the articles of incorporation.

If the organization meeting is the first meeting of the board of directors, the board may adopt a corporate seal for use on corporate documents, approve the form of share certificates, accept share subscriptions, authorize the issuance of shares, adopt preincorporation contracts, authorize reimbursement for promoters' expenses, and fix the salaries of officers.

**Filing Annual Report**   To retain its status as a corporation in good standing, a corporation must file an annual report with the secretary of state of the state of incorporation and pay an annual franchise fee or tax. The amount of annual franchise tax varies greatly from state to state. While the annual report includes very little information and repeats information already filed in the articles of incorporation, failure to file an annual report or pay the annual fee or tax may result in a dissolution of the corporation and an imposition of monetary penalties.

## Close Corporation Elections

Close corporations face problems that normally do not affect publicly held corporations. In recognition of these problems, nearly half of the states have statutes that attend to the special needs of close corporations. For example, some corporation statutes allow a close corporation to be managed by its shareholders.

To take advantage of these close corporation statutes, most statutes require that a corporation make an *election* to be treated as a close corporation. The Statutory Close Corporation Supplement to the MBCA permits a corporation with *fewer than 50 shareholders* to elect to become a close corporation. The Close Corporation Supplement requires the articles of incorporation to state that the corporation is a statutory close corporation.

There is no penalty for a corporation's failure to make a close corporation election. The only consequence of a failure to meet the requirements is that the close corporation statutory provisions are inapplicable. Instead, statutory corporation law will treat the corporation as it treats any other general corporation.

Note, however, that even when a corporation fails to meet the statutory requirements for treatment as a close corporation, a court may decide to apply special *common law* rules applicable only to close corporations.

## DEFECTIVE ATTEMPTS TO INCORPORATE

When business managers attempt to incorporate a business, sometimes they fail to comply with all the conditions for incorporation. For example, the incorporators may not have filed articles of incorporation or the directors may not have held an organization meeting. These are examples of **defective attempts to incorporate,** which may result in the business managers and investors having personal liability for the obligations of the defectively formed corporation.

One possible consequence of defective incorporation is to make the managers and the purported shareholders *personally liable* for the obligations of the defectively formed corporation. For example, an employee of an insolvent corporation drives the corporation's truck over a pedestrian. If the pedestrian proves that the corporation was defectively formed, he may be able to recover damages for his injuries from the managers and the shareholders.

A second possible consequence of defective incorporation is that a party to a contract involving the purported corporation may claim nonexistence of the corporation in order to avoid a contract made in the name of the corporation. For example, a person makes an ill-advised contract with a corporation. If the person proves that the corporation was defectively formed, he may escape liability on the contract because he made a contract with a nonexistent person, the defectively formed corporation. As an alternative, the defectively formed corporation may escape liability on the contract on the grounds that its nonexistence makes it impossible for it to have liability.

The courts have tried to determine when these two consequences should arise by making a distinction between de jure corporations, de facto corporations, corporations by estoppel, and corporations so defectively formed that they are treated as being nonexistent.

## De Jure Corporation

A de jure corporation is formed when the promoters substantially comply with each of the **mandatory conditions precedent** to the incorporation of the business. Mandatory provisions are distinguished from directory provisions by statutory language and the purpose of the provision. Mandatory provisions are those that the corporation statute states "shall" or "must" be done or those that are necessary to protect the public interest. Directory provisions are those that "may" be done and that are unnecessary to protect the public interest.

For example, statutes provide that the incorporators shall file the articles of incorporation with the secretary of state. This is a mandatory provision, due not only to the use of the word *shall* but also to the importance of the filing in protecting the public interest. Other mandatory provisions include conducting an organization meeting. Directory provisions include minor matters such as the inclusion of the incorporators' addresses in the articles of incorporation.

If a corporation has complied with each mandatory provision, it is a de jure corporation and is treated as a corporation for all purposes. The validity of a de jure corporation cannot be attacked, except in a few states in which the state, in a *quo warranto* proceeding, may attack the corporation for noncompliance with a condition subsequent to incorporation, such as a failure to file an annual report with the secretary of state.

## De Facto Corporation

A de facto corporation exists when the incorporators fail in some material respect to comply with all of the mandatory provisions of the incorporation statute yet comply with most mandatory provisions. There are three requirements for a de facto corporation:

1. There is a valid statute under which the corporation could be organized.
2. The promoters or managers make an honest attempt to organize under the statute. This requires substantial compliance with the mandatory provisions taken as a whole.
3. The promoters or managers exercise corporate powers. That is, they act as if they were acting for a corporation.

Generally, failing to file the articles of incorporation with the secretary of state will prevent the creation of a de facto corporation. However, a de facto corporation will exist despite the lack of an organization meeting or the failure to make a duplicate filing of the articles with a county recorder.

A de facto corporation is treated as a corporation against either an attack by a third party or an attempt of the business itself to deny that it is a corporation. The state, however, may attack the claimed corporate status of the business in a *quo warranto* action.

## Corporation by Estoppel

When people hold themselves out as representing a corporation or believe themselves to be dealing with a corporation, a court will estop those people from denying the existence of a corporation. This is called **corporation by estoppel**. For example, a manager states that a business has been incorporated and induces a third person to contract with the purported corporation. The manager will not be permitted to use a failure to incorporate as a defense to the contract because he has misled others to believe reasonably that a corporation exists.

Under the doctrine of estoppel, each contract must be considered individually to determine whether either party to the contract is estopped from denying the corporation's existence.

## Liability for Defective Incorporation

If people attempt to organize a corporation but their efforts are so defective that not even a corporation by estoppel is found to exist, the courts have generally held such persons to be partners with unlimited liability for the contracts and torts of the business. However, most courts impose the unlimited *contractual* liability of a partner only on those who are *actively engaged in the management* of the business or who are responsible for the defects in its organization. *Tort* liability, however, is generally imposed on everyone—the managers and the purported shareholders of the defectively formed corporation.

## Modern Approaches to the Defective Incorporation Problem

As you can see, the law of defective incorporation is confusing. It becomes even more confusing when you consider that many of the defective incorporation cases look like promoter liability cases, and vice versa. A court may have difficulty deciding whether to apply the law of promoter liability or the law of defective incorporation to preincorporation contracts. It is not surprising, therefore, that modern corporation statutes have attempted to eliminate this confusion by adopting simple rules for determining the existence of a corporation and the liability of its promoters, managers, and shareholders.

The MBCA states that incorporation occurs when the articles are filed by the secretary of state. The **filing** of the articles is **conclusive proof** of the existence of the corporation, except in a proceeding brought by the state. Consequently, the incorporators may omit even a mandatory provision, yet create a corporation, provided that the secretary of state has filed the articles of incorporation. Conversely, courts have held that a failure to obtain a filing of the articles is conclusive proof of the nonexistence of the corporation, on the grounds that the MBCA eliminates the concepts of de facto corporation and corporation by estoppel.

Figure 3 summarizes the preceding discussion.

**Liability for Defective Incorporation under the MBCA**    The MBCA imposes joint and several liability on those persons who purport to act on behalf of a corporation and know that there has been

**FIGURE 3**   Defective Attempts to Incorporate

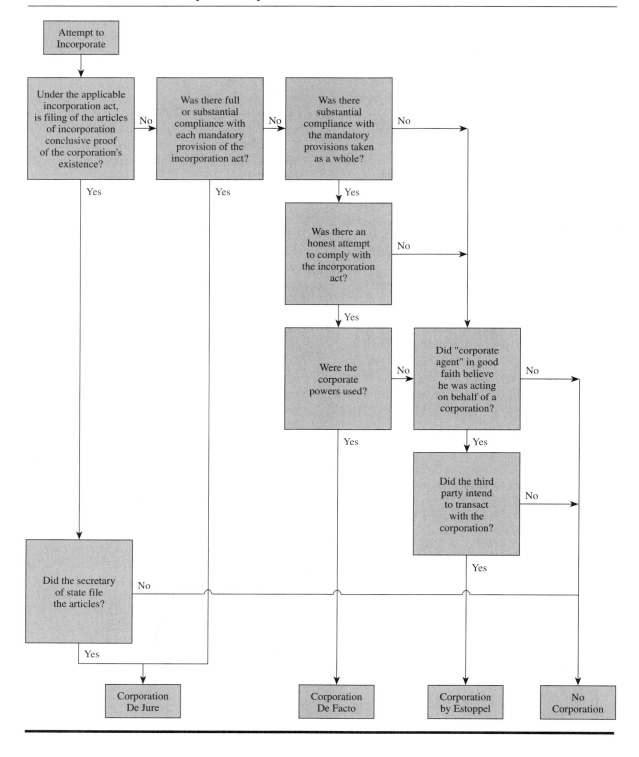

no incorporation. Managers and shareholders who both (1) *participate* in the operational decisions of the business and (2) *know* that the corporation does not exist are liable for the purported corporation's contracts and torts.

The MBCA releases from liability shareholders and others who either (1) take no part in the management of the defectively formed corporation *or* (2) mistakenly believe that the corporation is in existence.

Consequently, *passive* shareholders have no liability for the obligations of a defectively formed corporation even when they know that the corporation has not been formed. Likewise, managers of a defectively formed corporation have no liability when they believe that the corporation exists.

In the following case, the court held that filing the articles of incorporation conclusively established the existence of a closely held corporation.

---

## WARTHAN V. MIDWEST CONSOLIDATED INSURANCE AGENCIES, INC.
### 450 N.W.2d 145 (Minn. Ct. App. 1990)

David Warthan and Mary Knettel owned an insurance agency in St. Cloud, Minnesota. Clifford Koltes, James McMahill, and Thomas Kellin owned an insurance agency in Minnetonka, Minnesota. The two groups agreed to combine their insurance agencies into one agency. They agreed that each group would own 50 percent of the new agency. They agreed to transfer their existing insurance policy business to a new corporation, to be named Midwest Consolidated Insurance Agencies, Inc. (MCIA), to renew insurance policies in the name of MCIA, and to seek new insurance business for MCIA. Articles of incorporation for MCIA were filed by the secretary of state of Minnesota.

Several contracts were made in the name of MCIA to purchase the businesses of three additional insurance agencies. However, the two groups had difficulty combining their operations. No shares of stock were issued. No formal shareholder or directors meetings were held. Although bylaws were drafted, they were never approved. Eventually, the groups agreed to separate their operations as they had existed prior to their combination. However, the Minnetonka group continued to operate the three agencies purchased in the name of MCIA, eventually transferring the agencies to MCI, Inc., a corporation owned by the Minnetonka group. The St. Cloud group filed for a judicial dissolution of MCIA on the grounds that the Minnetonka group had breached a fiduciary duty. The trial court held that MCIA never came into existence and that, therefore, no fiduciary duties existed and MCIA could not be dissolved. The St. Cloud group appealed.

---

**Parker, Judge**     The trial court concluded that MCIA was not a closely held corporation in law or fact because it did not conform with the Minnesota Business Corporation Act (MBCA).

The corporate existence begins when the articles of incorporation are filed with the secretary of state accompanied by a payment of the incorporation and filing fees. The filing creates an irrefutable presumption that the corporation is and has been incorporated in this state.

Articles of incorporation were filed and the required fee paid on behalf of MCIA; as a matter of law, MCIA is a corporation and the trial court erred in concluding otherwise.

The trial court determined that because MCIA failed to follow certain organizational formalities in the Minnesota Business Corporation Act (MBCA), it was a defectively formed corporation. The MBCA provides that a closely held corporation may, but need not, have bylaws. Annual or otherwise regular meetings of the shareholders need only be held if required by the articles or bylaws or by demand. Unless provided for in the articles or bylaws, meetings of the board are not required unless called by a board member.

MCIA's articles do not require regular meetings. There is no evidence that any shareholder or director demanded or called a meeting. Therefore, the trial court erred in finding a deficiency in MCIA's failure to follow these particular organization guidelines. Further, the facts demonstrate that MCIA was more than a corporation in name only. Among other things, it entered into contracts to purchase the business of three insurance agencies, paid salaries, and maintained an office in Minnetonka.

The trial court's second conclusion of law is expressly based on its determination that MCIA is not a corporation; because erroneous, it must fail. This second conclusion concerns the fiduciary duties owed by the Minnetonka group to the St. Cloud group. As these parties were partners in a closely held corporation, they had a fiduciary duty to deal openly, honestly, and fairly with each other.

In determining whether to order dissolution involving a closely held corporation, the court shall take into consideration the duty which all shareholders in a closely held corporation owe one another to act in an honest, fair, and reasonable manner. The Minnetonka group controlled the operation of the newly acquired insurance agencies, eventually transferring them from MCIA to another corporation without consent of the St. Cloud group. The Minnetonka group therefore acted illegally and prejudicially toward the St. Cloud group.

**Judgment reversed in favor of Warthan and Knettel; remanded to the trial court.**

# INCORPORATION OF NONPROFIT CORPORATIONS

Nonprofit corporations are incorporated in substantially the same manner as for-profit corporations. One or more persons serve as incorporators and deliver articles of incorporation to the secretary of state for filing. A nonprofit corporation's articles must include the name and address of the corporation and state its registered agent. Unlike a for-profit corporation, a nonprofit corporation must state that it is either a public benefit corporation, a mutual benefit corporation, or a religious corporation. A public benefit corporation is incorporated primarily for the benefit of the public—for example, a community arts council that promotes the arts. A mutual benefit corporation is designed to benefit its members—for example, a golf country club. An example of a religious corporation is a church.

A nonprofit corporation's articles must also state whether it will have members. While it is typical for nonprofit corporations to have members, the Model Nonprofit Corporation Act (MNCA) does not require a nonprofit corporation to have members. An example of a nonprofit corporation having no members is a public benefit corporation established to promote business development in a city, whose directors are appointed by the city's mayor.

A nonprofit corporation's articles may include the purpose of the corporation, its initial directors,

and any matter regarding the rights and duties of the corporation and its directors and members. Each incorporator and director named in the articles must sign the articles.

A nonprofit corporation's existence begins when the secretary of state files the articles. After incorporation, the initial directors or incorporators hold an organization meeting to adopt bylaws and conduct other business.

## Liability for Preincorporation Transactions

Nonprofit corporation status normally protects the members and managers from personal liability. However, when a nonprofit corporation is not formed or is defectively formed, promoters and others who transact for the nonexistent nonprofit corporation have the same liability as promoters and others who transact for a nonexistent for-profit corporation. The MNCA states the same rule as the MBCA: Persons who act on behalf of a corporation knowing there is no corporation are jointly and severally liable for all liabilities created while so acting.

Similarly, promoters have no authority to make contracts for a nonexistent nonprofit corporation. The corporation becomes liable on preincorporation contracts when its board of directors adopts the contracts.

# FINANCING FOR–PROFIT CORPORATIONS

Any business needs money to operate and to grow. One advantage of incorporation is the large number of sources of funds that are available to businesses that incorporate. One such source is the sale of corporate **securities**, including shares, debentures, bonds, and long-term notes payable.

In addition to obtaining funds from the sale of securities, a corporation may be financed by other sources. A bank may lend money to the corporation in exchange for the corporation's short-term promissory notes, called commercial paper. Earnings provide a source of funds once the corporation is operating profitably. In addition, the corporation may use normal short-term financing, such as accounts receivable financing and inventory financing.

In this section, you will study only one source of corporate funds—a corporation's sale of securities. A corporate security may be either (1) a share in the corporation or (2) an obligation of the corporation. These two kinds of securities are called equity securities and debt securities.

## Equity Securities

Every business corporation issues equity securities, which are commonly called stock or **shares.** The issuance of shares creates an ownership relationship: the holders of the shares—called stockholders or **shareholders**—are the owners of the corporation.

Modern statutes permit corporations to issue several classes of shares and to determine the rights of the various classes. Subject to minimum guarantees contained in the state business corporation law, the shareholders' rights are a matter of contract and appear in the articles of incorporation, in the bylaws, in a shareholder agreement, and on the share certificates.

**Common Shares**    Common shares (or common stock) are a type of equity security. Ordinarily, the owners of common shares—called **common shareholders**—have the exclusive right to elect the directors, who manage the corporation.

The common shareholders often occupy a position inferior to that of other investors, notably creditors and preferred shareholders. The claims of common shareholders are subordinate to the claims of creditors and other classes of shareholders when liabilities and dividends are paid and when assets are distributed upon liquidation.

In return for this subordination, however, the common shareholders have an exclusive claim to the corporate earnings and assets that exceed the claims of creditors and other shareholders. Therefore, the common shareholders bear the major risks of the corporate venture, yet stand to profit the most if it is successful.

**Preferred Shares**    Shares that have preferences with regard to assets or dividends over other classes of shares are called preferred shares (or preferred stock). **Preferred shareholders** are customarily given liquidation and dividend preferences over common shareholders. A corporation may have several classes of preferred shares. In such a situation, one class of preferred shares may be given preferences over another class of preferred shares. Under the MBCA, the preferences of preferred shareholders must be set out in the articles of incorporation.

The **liquidation preference** of preferred shares is usually a stated dollar amount. During a liquidation, this amount must be paid to each preferred shareholder before any common shareholder or other shareholder subordinated to the preferred class may receive his share of the corporation's assets.

**Dividend preferences** may vary greatly. For example, the dividends may be cumulative or noncumulative. Dividends on **cumulative** preferred shares, if not paid in any year, accumulate until paid. The entire accumulation must be paid before any dividends may be paid to common shareholders. Dividends on **noncumulative** preferred shares do not accumulate if unpaid. For such shares, only the current year's dividends must be paid to preferred shareholders prior to the payment of dividends to common shareholders.

**Participating** preferred shares have priority up to a stated amount or percentage of the dividends to be paid by the corporation. Then, the preferred shareholders participate with the common shareholders in additional dividends paid.

Some close corporations attempt to create preferred shares with a **mandatory dividend** right. These mandatory dividend provisions have generally been held illegal as unduly restricting the powers of the board of directors. Today, a few courts and some special close corporation statutes permit mandatory dividends.

A **redemption** provision in the articles allows a corporation at its option to repurchase preferred shareholders' shares at a price stated in the articles, despite the shareholders' unwillingness to sell. Some statutes permit the articles to give the shareholders the right to force the corporation to redeem preferred shares.

Preferred shares may be **convertible** into another class of shares, usually common shares. A **conversion** right allows a preferred shareholder to exchange her preferred shares for another class of shares, usually common shares. The conversion rate or price is stated in the articles.

Preferred shares have **voting rights** unless the articles provide otherwise. Usually, most voting rights are taken from preferred shares, except for important matters such as voting for a merger or a change in preferred shareholders' dividend rights. Rarely are preferred shareholders given the right to vote for directors, except in the event of a corporation's default in the payment of dividends.

## Authorized, Issued, and Outstanding Shares

**Authorized** shares are shares that a corporation is permitted to issue by its articles of incorporation. A corporation may not issue more shares than are authorized. **Issued** shares are shares that have been sold to shareholders. **Outstanding** shares are shares that are currently held by shareholders. The distinctions between these terms are important. For example, a corporation pays cash, property, and share dividends only on outstanding shares. Only outstanding shares may be voted at a shareholders' meeting.

**Canceled Shares**     Sometimes, a corporation will purchase its own shares. A corporation may cancel repurchased shares. Canceled shares do not exist: they are neither authorized, issued, nor outstanding. Since canceled shares do not exist, they cannot be reissued.

**Shares Restored to Unissued Status**     Repurchased shares may be restored to unissued status instead of being canceled. If this is done, the shares are merely authorized and they may be reissued at a later time.

**Treasury Shares**     If repurchased shares are neither canceled nor restored to unissued status, they are called **treasury shares**. Such shares are authorized and issued, but not outstanding. They may be sold by the corporation at a later time. The corporation may not vote them at shareholders' meetings, and it may not pay a cash or property dividend on them.

The MBCA abolishes the concept of treasury shares. It provides that repurchased shares are restored to unissued status and may be reissued, unless the articles of incorporation require cancellation.

## Options, Warrants, and Rights

Equity securities include options to purchase common shares and preferred shares. The MBCA expressly permits the board of directors to issue **options** for the purchase of the corporation's shares. Share options are often issued to top-level managers as an incentive to increase the profitability of the corporation. An increase in profitability should increase the market value of the corporation's shares, resulting in increased compensation to the employees who own and exercise share options.

**Warrants** are options evidenced by certificates. They are sometimes part of a package of securities sold as a unit. For example, they may be sold along with notes, bonds, or even shares. Underwriters may receive warrants as part of their compensation for aiding a corporation in selling its shares to the public.

**Rights** are short-term certificated options that are usually transferable. Rights are used to give present security holders an option to subscribe to a proportional quantity of the same or a different security of the corporation. They are most often issued in connection with a **preemptive right** requirement, which obligates a corporation to offer each existing shareholder the opportunity to buy the corporation's newly issued shares in the same proportion as the shareholder's current ownership of the corporation's shares.

## Debt Securities

Corporations have inherent power to borrow money necessary for their operations by issuing debt securities. Debt securities create a debtor-creditor relationship between the corporation and the security holder. With the typical debt security, the corporation is obligated to pay interest periodically and to pay the amount of the debt (the principal) on the maturity date. Debt securities include debentures, bonds, and notes payable.

**Debentures** are long-term, unsecured debt securities. Typically, a debenture has a term of 10 to 30 years. Debentures usually have indentures. An indenture is a contract that states the rights of the debenture holders. For example, an indenture defines what acts constitute default by the corporation and what rights the debenture holders have upon default. It may place restrictions on the corporation's right to issue other debt securities.

**Bonds** are long-term, secured debt securities that usually have indentures. They are identical to debentures except that bonds are secured by collateral. The collateral for bonds may be real property such as a building, or personal property such as a commercial airplane. If the debt is not paid, the bondholders may force the sale of the collateral and take the proceeds of the sale.

Generally, **notes** have a shorter duration than debentures or bonds. They seldom have terms exceeding five years. Notes may be secured or unsecured.

It is not uncommon for notes or debentures to be **convertible** into other securities, usually preferred or common shares. The right to convert belongs to the holder of the convertible note or debenture. This conversion right permits an investor to receive interest as a debt holder and, after conversion, to share in the increased value of the corporation as a shareholder.

## CONSIDERATION FOR SHARES

The board of directors has the power to issue shares on behalf of the corporation. The board must decide at what *price* and for what *type of consideration* it will issue the shares. Corporation statutes restrict the discretion of the board in accepting specified kinds of consideration and in determining the value of the shares it issues.

### Quality of Consideration for Shares

Not all kinds of consideration in contract law are acceptable as legal consideration for shares in corporation law. To protect creditors and other shareholders, the statutes require legal consideration to have *real value*. Modern statutes, however, place few limits on the type of consideration that may be received for shares. The MBCA permits shares to be issued in return for any tangible or intangible *property* or *benefit to the corporation,* including cash, promissory notes, services performed for the corporation, contracts for services *to be performed* for the corporation, and securities of the corporation or another corporation. The rationale for the MBCA rule is a recognition that future services and promises of future services have value that is as real as that of tangible property. Consequently, for example, a corporation may issue common shares to its president in exchange for the president's commitment to work for the corporation for three years or in exchange for bonds of the corporation or debentures issued by another corporation. In addition, the MBCA permits corporations to issue shares to their promoters in consideration for their promoters' preincorporation services. This rule acknowledges that a corporation benefits from a promoter's preincorporation services.

Several states' constitutions place stricter limits on permissible consideration for shares. They provide that shares may be issued only for money paid to the corporation, labor done for the corporation, or property actually received by the corporation. Such a rule prohibits a corporation from issuing its shares for a promise to pay money or a promise to provide services to the corporation in the future.

### Quantity of Consideration for Shares

The board is required to issue shares for an adequate dollar amount of consideration. Whether shares have been issued for an adequate amount of consideration depends in part on the *par value* of the shares. The more important concern, however, is whether the shares have been issued for *fair value*.

**Par Value**    Par value is an arbitrary dollar amount that may be assigned to the shares by the articles of incorporation. Par value does not reflect the fair market value of the shares, but par value is the minimum amount of consideration for which the shares may be issued.

Shares issued for less than par value are called **discount shares**. The board of directors is liable to the corporation for issuing shares for less than par value. A shareholder who purchases shares from the corporation for less than par value is liable to the corporation for the difference between the par value and the amount she paid.

**Fair Value**    It is not always enough, however, for the board to issue shares for their par value. Many times, shares are worth more than their par value. In addition, many shares today do not have a par value. In fact, the MBCA purports to eliminate the concept of par value as it affects the issuance of shares. In such cases, the board must exercise care to ensure that the corporation receives the *fair value* of the shares it issues. If there are no par value problems, the board's judgment as to the amount of consideration that is received for the shares is *conclusive* when the board acts in good faith, exercises the care of ordinarily prudent directors, and acts in the best interests of the corporation.

Disputes may arise concerning the *value* of property that the corporation receives for its shares. The board's valuation of the consideration is conclusive if it acts in good faith with the care of prudent directors and in a manner it reasonably believes to be in the best interests of the corporation. When the board impermissibly overvalues the consideration for shares, the shareholder receives **watered shares**. Both the board and the shareholder are liable to the corporation when there is a watered shares problem.

When a shareholder pays less than the amount of consideration determined by the board of directors, the corporation or its creditors may sue the shareholder to recover the deficit. When a shareholder has paid the proper amount of consideration, the shares are said to be *fully paid and nonassessable*.

In the following case, the court considered whether a promissory note was legal and valuable consideration to be received for shares.

### KIRK V. KIRK'S AUTO ELECTRIC, INC.
#### 728 S.W.2d 529 (Ky. Sup. Ct. 1987)

Kirk's Auto Electric, Inc., issued 11 shares of common stock to Billy H. Bone, 10 shares to Andre Bone, and 5 shares to Joe T. Bone. In exchange for each issuance of shares, the Bones gave the corporation unsecured interest-bearing promissory notes payable on demand. The Bones were issued share certificates, which were signed on behalf of the corporation by Billy H. Bone, who was a director and president of the corporation, and by Clarence Kirk, who was a director and secretary of the corporation. No payments were made on the notes. Later, Kirk contested the issuance on the grounds that the Bones had not paid proper or sufficient consideration for the shares. The trial court and the court of appeals held that Kirk could not contest the issuance of the shares because he had participated in the issuance. Kirk appealed to the Kentucky Supreme Court.

**Lambert, Justice**    Section 193 of the Constitution of Kentucky states:

No corporation shall issue stock, except for an equivalent in money paid or labor done, or property actually received and applied to the purposes for which such corporation was created, and neither labor nor property shall be received in payment of stock at a greater value than the market price at the time such labor was done or property delivered.

The constitutional provisions quoted herein evince a strong policy in this Commonwealth toward protecting corporations, shareholders, and corporate creditors from the dissipation of corporate assets. The issuance of shares must be attended by good faith and the corporation must receive value not disproportionate to the value of the shares issued.

The promissory notes received by Kirk's Auto Electric were unsecured and were payable only upon demand. The only persons eligible to demand payment from the makers of the notes were the members of the board of directors, Kirk and Billy H. Bone, the same persons who authorized issuance of the shares and acceptance of the unsecured notes. Billy H. Bone was himself maker of one of the notes. Therefore, appropriate vigilance would be less than assured. This transaction well illustrates the need for strict enforcement of the constitutional requirements.

Our holding in this case may appear to be too restrictive and represent an interference with the power of a corporation to conduct its business affairs. In ordinary commercial transactions, unsecured promissory notes are essential and undoubtedly constitute valuable consideration. Nevertheless, the constitutional provisions are impressed with a public interest and their primary purpose is to prevent fraud and to protect creditors or purchasers of stock of corporations. If the public interest is to be protected, strict adherence to the law must be required.

**Judgment reversed in favor of Kirk; remanded to the trial court.**

---

**Accounting for Consideration Received**   The consideration received by a corporation for its equity securities appears in the equity or capital accounts in the shareholders' equity section of the corporation's balance sheet. The **stated capital** account records the product of the number of shares outstanding multiplied by the par value of each share. When the shares are sold for more than par value, the excess or surplus consideration received by the corporation is **capital surplus**.

Under the MBCA, the terms *stated capital* and *capital surplus* have been eliminated. All consideration received for shares is lumped under one accounting entry for that class of shares, such as common equity.

**Resales of Shares**   The par value of shares is important *only when the shares are issued* by the corporation. Since treasury shares are issued but not outstanding, the corporation does not issue treasury shares when it resells them. Therefore, the board may sell treasury shares for less than par, provided that it sells the shares for an amount equal to their fair value.

Because par value and fair value are designed to ensure only that the corporation receives adequate consideration for its shares, a shareholder may buy shares from another shareholder for less than par value or fair value and incur no liability. However, if the purchasing shareholder *knows* that the selling shareholder bought the shares from the corporation for less than par value, the purchasing shareholder is liable to the corporation for the difference between the par value and the amount paid by the selling shareholder.

## SHARE SUBSCRIPTIONS

Under the terms of a **share subscription**, a prospective shareholder promises to buy a specific number of shares of a corporation at a stated price. If the subscription is accepted by the corporation and the subscriber has paid for the shares, the subscriber is a shareholder of the corporation, even if the shares have not been issued. Under the MBCA, subscriptions need not be in writing to be enforceable. Usually, however, subscriptions are written.

Promoters use written share subscriptions in the course of selling shares of a proposed corporation to ensure that equity capital will be provided once the corporation comes into existence. These are called **preincorporation subscriptions**, which were covered in this chapter's discussion of promoters. Preincorporation subscriptions are not contracts binding on the corporation and the shareholders until the corporation comes into existence and its board of directors accepts the share subscriptions.

Close corporations may use share subscriptions when they seek to sell additional shares after incorporation. These are examples of **postincorporation subscriptions**, subscription agreements made *after* incorporation. A postincorporation subscription is a contract between the corporation and the subscriber at the time the subscription agreement is made.

A subscription may provide for payment of the price of the shares on a specified day, in installments, or upon the demand of the board of directors. The board may not discriminate when it demands payment: It must demand payment from all the subscribers of a class of shares or from none of them.

A share certificate may not be issued to a share subscriber until the price of the shares has been fully paid. If the subscriber fails to pay as agreed, the corporation may sue the subscriber for the amount owed.

## ISSUANCE OF SHARES

Uniform Commercial Code (UCC) Article 8 regulates the issuance of securities. Under Article 8, a corporation has a duty to issue only the number of shares authorized by its articles. Overissued shares are void.

When a person is entitled to overissued shares, the corporation may not issue the shares. However, the person has two remedies. The corporation must obtain identical shares and deliver them to the person entitled to issuance, or the corporation must reimburse the person for the value paid for the shares plus interest.

The directors may incur liability, including criminal liability, for an overissuance of shares. To prevent overissuance through error in the issuance or transfer of their shares, corporations often employ a bank or a trust company as a registrar.

A share certificate is evidence that a person has been issued shares, owns the shares, and is a shareholder. The certificate states the corporation's name, the shareholder's name, and the number and class of shares. A person can be a shareholder without receiving a share certificate, such as a holder of a share subscription. Under the MBCA, a corporation is not required to issue share certificates.

## TRANSFER OF SHARES

Because share certificates are evidence of the ownership of shares, their transfer is evidence of the transfer of the ownership of shares. UCC Article 8 covers the registration and transfer of shares, as represented by certificates.

Share certificates are issued in *registered* form; that is, they are registered with the corporation in the name of a specific person. The indorsement of a share certificate on its back by its registered owner and the delivery of the certificate to another person transfers ownership of the shares to the other person. The transfer of a share certificate without naming a transferee creates a *street certificate*. The transfer of a street certificate may be made by delivery without indorsement. Any holder of a street certificate is presumed to be the owner of the shares it represents. Therefore, a transferee should ask the corporation to reregister the shares in his name.

Under the UCC, a corporation owes a duty to register the transfer of any registered shares presented to it for registration, provided that the shares have been properly indorsed. If the corporation refuses to make the transfer, it is liable to the transferee for either conversion or specific performance.

When an owner of shares claims that his certificate has been lost, destroyed, or stolen, the corporation must issue a new certificate to the owner if the corporation has not received notice that the shares have been acquired by a bona fide purchaser, the owner files with the corporation a sufficient indemnity bond, and the owner meets any other reasonable requirements of the corporation. A **bona fide purchaser** is a purchaser of the shares for value in good faith with no notice of any adverse claim against the shares.

If, after the issuance of the new certificated shares, a bona fide purchaser of the original shares presents them for registration, the corporation must register the transfer, unless overissuance would result. In addition, the corporation may recover the new certificated shares from the original owner.

## Restrictions on Transferability of Shares

Historically, a shareholder has been free to sell her shares to whomever she wants whenever she wants. The courts have been reluctant to allow restrictions on the free transferability of shares, even if the shareholder agreed to a restriction on the transfer of her shares. Gradually, the courts and the legislatures have recognized that there are good reasons to permit the use of some restrictions on the transfer of shares. Today, modern corporation statutes allow most transfer restrictions, especially for close corporations.

**Types of Restrictions on Transfer**    There are four categories of transfer restrictions that may be used to accomplish the objectives addressed above: (1) rights of first refusal and option agreements, (2) buy-and-sell agreements, (3) consent restraints, and (4) provisions disqualifying purchasers.

A **right of first refusal** grants to the corporation or the other shareholders the right to match the offer that a selling shareholder receives for her shares. An **option agreement** grants the corporation or the other shareholders an option to buy the selling shareholder's shares at a price determined by the agreement. An option agreement will usually state a formula used to calculate the price of the shares.

A **buy-and-sell agreement** compels a shareholder to sell his shares to the corporation or to the other shareholders at the price stated in the agreement. It also obligates the corporation or the other shareholders to buy the selling shareholder's shares at that price. The agreement is called a cross-purchase agreement when the shareholders are obligated to buy and sell. It is called a redemption agreement when the corporation is the person that is obligated to buy. The price of the shares is usually determined by a stated formula.

A **consent restraint** requires a selling shareholder to obtain the consent of the corporation or the other shareholders before she may sell her shares. A **provision disqualifying purchasers** may be used in rare situations to exclude unwanted persons from the corporation. For example, a transfer restriction may prohibit the shareholders from selling to a competitor of the business.

**Uses of Transfer Restrictions**   A corporation and its shareholders may use transfer restrictions to maintain the balance of shareholder power in the corporation. For example, four persons may own 25 shares each in a corporation. No single person can control such a corporation. If one of the four can buy 26 additional shares from the other shareholders, he will acquire control. The shareholders may therefore agree that each shareholder is entitled or required to buy an equal amount of any shares sold by any selling shareholder. The right of first refusal, option agreement, or buy-and-sell agreement may serve this purpose.

A buy-and-sell agreement may be used to guarantee a shareholder a market for his shares. For example, in a close corporation, there may be no ready market for the shares of the corporation. To ensure that a shareholder can obtain the value of her investment upon her retirement or death, the shareholders or the corporation may be required to buy a shareholder's shares upon the occurrence of a specific event such as death or retirement.

A buy-and-sell agreement may also be used to determine who should be required to sell and who should be required to buy shares when there is a severe disagreement between shareholders that threatens the profitability of the corporation.

In a close corporation, the shareholders may want only themselves or other approved persons as shareholders. A buy-and-sell agreement or right of first refusal may be used to prevent unwanted persons from becoming shareholders.

A provision disqualifying purchasers may be used in limited situations, such as when the purchaser is a competitor of the business or has a criminal background.

A consent restraint is used to preserve a close corporation or Subchapter S taxation election. Close corporation statutes and Subchapter S of the Internal Revenue Code limit the number of shareholders that a close corporation or S Corporation may have. A transfer restriction may prohibit the shareholders from selling shares if, as a result of the sale, there would be too many shareholders to preserve a close corporation or S Corporation election. A consent restraint is also used to preserve an exemption from registration of a securities offering. Under the Securities Act of 1933 and the state securities acts, an offering of securities is exempt from registration if the offering is to a limited number of investors, usually 35. A transfer restriction may require a selling shareholder to obtain permission from the corporation's legal counsel, which permission will be granted upon proof that the shareholder's sale of the shares does not cause the corporation to lose its registration exemption.

**Legality of Transfer Restrictions**   Corporation statutes permit the use of option agreements, rights of first refusal, and buy-and-sell agreements with virtually no restrictions. The MBCA authorizes transfer restrictions for any reasonable purpose. The reasonableness of a restraint is judged in light of the character and needs of the corporation.

Consent restraints and provisions disqualifying purchasers may be used if they are not *manifestly unreasonable*. The MBCA makes per se reasonable any consent restraint that maintains a corporation's status when that status is dependent on the number or identity of shareholders, as with close corporation or S Corporation status. The MBCA also makes per se reasonable any restriction that preserves registration exemptions under the Securities Act of 1933 and state securities laws.

**Enforceability**   To be enforceable against a shareholder, a transfer restriction must be contained in the articles of incorporation, the bylaws, an agreement among the shareholders, or an agreement between the corporation and the shareholders. In addition, the shareholder must either agree to the restriction or purchase the shares with notice of the restriction. Under the MBCA, a purchaser of the shares has notice of a restriction if it is noted conspicuously on the face or the back of a share certificate or if it is a restriction of which he has knowledge.

The next case addresses the issue of whether a restriction is reasonable and whether it is conspicuously noted on the certificate.

---

# LING AND CO. V. TRINITY SAVINGS AND LOAN ASS'N.
## 482 S.W.2d 841 (Tex. Sup. Ct. 1972)

When Bruce Bowman borrowed some money from Trinity Savings and Loan Association, he pledged 1,500 shares of Ling and Company Class A common stock as collateral for the loan. Bowman failed to repay Trinity. Trinity sued Bowman on the loan and asked the court to order the sale of the shares pledged as collateral. Ling and Company objected to the sale of the shares on the grounds that Ling's articles of incorporation restricted transfer of its shares. Trinity asked the court to invalidate the transfer restrictions. The restrictions appeared in Article 4 of Ling's articles of incorporation. One restriction was an option agreement that granted to the corporation and the other shareholders a 10-day option to buy the shares before the shares could be sold to any other person.

On the front side of the share certificate, in small print, it was stated that the shares were subject to the provisions of the articles of incorporation, that a copy of the articles could be obtained from the secretary of the corporation or the secretary of state, and that specific references to provisions setting forth restrictions were on the back of the certificate. On the back side, also in small type, the reference to the articles was repeated and specific mention was made of Article 4. Here, the option agreement was referred to but not stated fully.

The trial court held that the restrictions were invalid and ordered the sale of the shares. After the court of appeals affirmed the trial court's decision, Ling appealed to the Supreme Court of Texas.

---

**Reavley, Justice**    The court of civil appeals struck down the restrictions for the lack of conspicuous notice on the share certificate and the unreasonableness of the restrictions.

The Texas Business Corporation Act provides that a corporation may impose restrictions on the transfer of its shares, if they are "expressly set forth in the articles of incorporation and copied at length or in summary form on the face or so copied on the back and referred to on the face of each certificate." The Legislature, at the same time, permitted an incorporation by reference on the face or back of a certificate of a provision in the articles of incorporation that restricts the transfer of the shares. In the present case, reference is made on the face of the certificate to the restrictions described on the reverse side; the notice on the reverse side refers to the particular article of the articles of incorporation as restricting the transfer or encumbrance of the shares and requiring "the holder thereof to grant options to purchase the shares represented hereby first to the Corporation and then pro rata to the other holders of the Class A

Common Stock." We hold that the content of the certificate complies with the requirements of the Texas Business Corporation Act.

There remains the requirement that the restriction or reference on transferability be "noted conspicuously on the security." The UCC provides that a conspicuous term is so written as to be noticed by a reasonable person. Examples of conspicuous matter are given there as a "printed heading in capitals or larger or other contrasting type or color." This means that something must appear on the face of the certificate to attract the attention of a reasonable person when he looks at it. The line of print on the face of the Ling certificate does not stand out and cannot be considered conspicuous.

Our holding that the restriction is not noted conspicuously on the certificate does not entitle Trinity to a judgment under this record. The restriction is effective against a person with actual knowledge of it. The record does not establish conclusively that Trinity lacked knowledge of the restriction when Bowman executed an assignment of these shares to Trinity Savings and Loan.

A corporation may impose restrictions on the disposition of its shares, if the restrictions "do not unreasonably restrain or prohibit transferability." The court of appeals held that it is unreasonable to require a shareholder to notify all other record holders of Class A Common Stock of his intent to sell and give the other holders a 10-day option to buy. The record does not reveal the number of holders of this class of shares; we know only that there are more than 20. We find nothing unusual or oppressive in these first option provisions. Conceiv-ably the number of shareholders might be so great as to make the burden too heavy upon the shareholder who wishes to sell and, at the same time, dispel any justification for contending that there exists a reasonable corporate purpose in restricting the ownership. There is, however, no proof of that.

**Judgment reversed in favor of Ling. Case remanded to the trial court.**

---

Although transfer restrictions are important to close corporations, many close corporation shareholders fail to address the share transferability problem. Therefore, a few states provide statutory resolution of the close corporation transferability problem. In these states, statutes offer solutions to the transferability problem that are similar to the solutions that the shareholders would have provided had they thought about the problem. Not all transferability problems are settled by the Close Corporation Supplement, however. For example, there is no statutory buy-and-sell provision.

## Financing Nonprofit Corporations

Nonprofit corporations are financed differently from for-profit corporations. This is especially true of a public benefit corporation such as a public television station, which obtains annual financing from government sources, private foundations, members, and public contributors. A religious corporation such as a church receives weekly offerings from its congregation and may occasionally conduct capital drives to obtain additional funding from its members. A mutual benefit corporation, such as a fraternal or social organization like an Elks Club or golf country club, obtains initial funding from its original members to build facilities and assesses its members annually and monthly to pay operating expenses. In addition, nonprofit corporations have the power to obtain debt financing, such as borrowing from a bank or issuing notes and debentures.

A nonprofit corporation may admit members whether or not they pay consideration for their membership. There is no statutory limit on the number of members a nonprofit corporation may admit, although the articles may place a limit on the number of members. Social clubs typically limit the number of members. Members must be admitted in compliance with procedures stated in the articles or the bylaws.

Generally, memberships in a nonpublic corporation are not freely transferable. No member of a public benefit corporation or religious corporation may transfer her membership or any rights she possesses as a member. A member of a mutual benefit corporation may transfer her membership and rights only if the articles or bylaws permit. When transfer rights are permitted, restrictions on transfer are valid only if approved by the members, including the affected member.

### PROBLEMS AND PROBLEM CASES

**1.** RKO-Stanley Warner Theatres, Inc., contracted to sell a theater to Jack Jenofsky and Ralph Graziano, who were in the process of forming a corporation to be known as Kent Enterprises, Inc. The contract included the following, added by Jenofsky and Graziano's lawyer:

It is understood by the parties hereto that it is the intention of the Purchaser to incorporate. Upon condition that such incorporation be completed by the closing date, all agreements contained herein shall be construed to have been made between Seller and the resultant corporation.

Subsequently, Kent Enterprises, Inc., was incorporated. A final closing date was set, but the sale was never completed. RKO sued Jenofsky and Graziano on the contract. Jenofsky claimed that the quoted provision in the contract released him from any personal liability. Was he correct?

**2.** Max and Edward Gurwicz developed the Regency Towers Condominium (Towers), which sold condominium units to residents. The Gurwiczes also formed the Regency Towers Condominium Association (Association), which was to serve as an association of the condominium owners. Prior to the drafting of the Association's articles of incorporation, the Gurwiczes signed a lease in the name of the Association obligating the Association to make rental payment to Towers. Three weeks later, the articles were filed by the secretary of state. After the filing, the Association's board of directors took no action in respect to the lease and made no rental payments to Towers. The condominium owners, who indirectly would be liable on the lease if the Association was bound by it, believed that the lease unreasonably burdened the Association. The condominium owners asked a court to rule that the Association was not liable on the lease. What did the court hold?

**3.** Stuart Lakes Club, Inc., a New York corporation, was a private game club owning 75 acres of land, two lakes, and a clubhouse. The board of directors adopted a bylaw provision that stated, "When any member ceases to be a member of the Club, either by death, resignation, or otherwise, his share shall be considered void and the certificate returned to the Treasurer for cancellation." The purpose of the bylaw provision was to make the last surviving member of the club its sole owner and therefore the beneficial owner of the club's valuable land and clubhouse. Has the board of directors adopted an enforceable bylaw?

**4.** On April 9, 1980, Bowers Building Co. and Division 8, Inc., entered a contract for Division 8 to provide labor and materials to Bowers for a construction project. Division 8 was unable to complete the contract, which it assigned to Altura Glass Co., Inc., on January 9, 1981. On that date, Altura's president, Jack Crownover, wrote Bowers a letter requesting that Bowers issue future checks to "Altura Glass Co." Crownover signed the letter "Pres. Jack Crownover." On that same date, Crownover delivered to Altura's lawyer its articles of incorporation, which the lawyer mailed to the secretary of

state of Colorado. The secretary of state issued a certificate of incorporation to Altura on January 12, 1981. The next day, Bowers issued a check payable to Altura Glass Company, which Altura accepted. When Altura breached the contract, Bowers sued Altura and its president, Crownover. Are Altura and Crownover liable to Bowers?

**5.** Eugene Levy agreed to buy a retail record business from Martin Robertson. Levy submitted for filing the articles of incorporation for Record Shack, Inc., but they were rejected by the secretary of state. Six days later, Robertson sold the assets of the business to the Record Shack and received a promissory note for the purchase price signed "Penn Ave. Record Shack, Inc., by Eugene M. Levy, President." Subsequently, Levy resubmitted the articles, and a certificate of incorporation of Penn Ave. Record Shack, Inc., was issued. Robertson accepted one payment on the promissory note from the corporation, but within six months, Record Shack ceased doing business; no assets remained. Robertson sued Levy for the balance of the promissory note. Was Levy liable on the promissory note?

**6.** Arthur Kaiser and Jerry Kaiser incorporated Jerry Kaiser & Associates, Inc., a real estate development company. Arthur told Jerry about the availability of some unimproved land. The land was subsequently acquired by Jerry Kaiser & Associates and developed as Sherwood Manor Apartments. At a meeting of the directors, Jerry, as the chairman of the board, announced that Arthur had rendered services to the corporation. The board then approved the issuance to Arthur of 25 shares of $10 par value Class A common stock. The corporation issued to Arthur share certificate number 1 for 25 shares "of the $10 par value Class A nonvoting stock of Jerry Kaiser & Associates, Inc., fully paid and non-assessable." Has Arthur paid for the stock with a proper type of consideration?

**7.** Dale Frey intended to develop a 33-acre apartment complex, to be operated by Mt. Carmel Apartments, Inc., a corporation not yet formed. To promote and develop the complex, Frey contracted with Jess Burge. Their agreement provided that Burge would receive $70,000 payable in 12.5 percent of the shares of the corporation. Subsequently, Burge consulted with architects, calculated construction costs, executed a loan application, and consulted with prospective contractors on behalf of the complex. After incorporation of Mt. Carmel

Apartments, Inc., the board of directors accepted the agreement between Frey and Burge, placed a $70,000 value on his services performed prior to incorporation, and issued 12.5 percent of the corporation's shares to Burge. After a dispute arose between Burge and the corporation, Frey claimed that the corporation acted wrongly by issuing the shares to Burge. Was Frey correct?

**8.** John Gazda, Anthony Kolinski, and John Giamartino formed a corporation to operate Big Boy restaurants, with each owning one third of the shares. After a dispute resulted in the removal of Gazda as an officer, Kolinski and Giamartino as controlling directors voted to issue shares of the corporation for $100 per share. At the time, the book value of the corporation was $266 per share and the fair market value was between $497 and $572 per share. Gazda opposed the issuance of the shares. Was he successful with stopping the issuance?

**9.** The shareholders of KBM, Inc., a close corporation, executed a shareholders' agreement that required a shareholder who resigned his employment with the corporation to first offer to sell all his shares to the corporation at book value. If the corporation did not buy all the shares, the shareholder was required to offer the unpurchased shares to the other shareholders. If there were any remaining unsold shares, the shareholder and the corporation were required to attempt to negotiate a "sale mutually satisfactory to all parties." If no mutually satisfactory agreement could be reached, the corporation was to be dissolved and liquidated, and its assets distributed to shareholders. Is this agreement legal?

**10.** 📷 *Video Case.* See "The Stock Option." An employee of FAMCO purchases common shares of FAMCO through its fringe benefit plan. Transfer of the shares purchased under the plan is restricted in two ways. First, when employment terminates for any reason, FAMCO has an option to purchase the shares at book value. Second, if an employee attempts to sell the shares while employed, FAMCO has a right of first refusal to purchase the shares at the sale price. FAMCO informs an employee that for the good of the company, she must sell her shares to FAMCO. She believes that she will be terminated unless she sells the shares to FAMCO, but nonetheless she sells the shares on the open market at a price much greater

than book value. Can FAMCO invalidate the employee's sale of the shares?

**11.** Alice Marr owned 800 of the 11,340 shares outstanding of Gloucester Ice & Storage Co., a closely held corporation with no ready market for its shares. When Marr died, Thomas Goode, the administrator of her will, demanded that Gloucester or its majority shareholder purchase Marr's shares. No provision restricting the transfer of shares or requiring the corporation or remaining shareholders to purchase shares on the death of a shareholder appeared in the corporation's articles of incorporation, bylaws, or agreement among shareholders. Is Gloucester or its majority shareholder required to purchase Marr's shares at fair market value?

## CAPSTONE QUESTIONS

Ann Romano and Rob Kardesh want to enter the software-manufacturing business. They decide to incorporate the business, to be named CompTech Corporation, and they hire a lawyer to incorporate the business for them. The lawyer drafts articles of incorporation for the business and asks Romano and Kardesh to examine the articles and suggest changes. During the three-week period when Romano, Kardesh, and the lawyer are drafting and revising the articles, Romano and Kardesh line up 15 investors for the business. Each investor contributes $10,000 to the business and receives 1,000 common shares of CompTech, which will be issued after the business is incorporated. The investors are informed that CompTech has not yet been incorporated. The investors are passive shareholders not involved in the management of the business.

Romano and Kardesh also enter negotiations to lease office space from Crocker Financial Corporation (CFC). In the name of CompTech Corporation, Romano and Kardesh sign a lease with CFC obligating CompTech to lease 3,000 square feet of office space for $750 per month. Romano and Kardesh sign the lease in the name of CompTech only.

In their own names, Romano and Kardesh purchase all rights to a spreadsheet software program, agreeing to pay $100,000 to the author over a five-year period.

Romano, Kardesh, and the lawyer draft the final version of the articles, and the lawyer submits the articles to the secretary of state. A week later, the secretary of state files the articles, returning a copy of the articles to the lawyer, along with a receipt for payment of the incorporation fees. At the organization meeting, the five initial directors, including Romano and Kardesh, conduct the following business:

- The board of directors refuses to lease space from CFC, deciding instead to lease a larger, less expensive building from Talbott Properties, Inc.
- The board purchases all rights to the spreadsheet software program from Romano and Kardesh for $125,000, payable immediately.
- The board issues 5,000 common shares each to Romano and Kardesh in return for their efforts of promoting the business. The board values the promotional efforts of each promoter at $25,000 apiece.
- The board issues 1,000 common shares to an investor who has given CompTech a promissory note to pay $10,000 to CompTech exactly six months after the issuance.
- The board issues the remaining 14,000 common shares to the investors. Each share certificate states on its back in small print that resale of the shares is subject to conditions contained in an agreement signed by all the shareholders. The shareholder agreement states that a shareholder may not sell his shares until the shareholder gives the corporation 30 days' notice of his intent to sell, he offers the shares to the corporation at book value, and the corporation refuses to buy the shares. The shareholder agreement also prohibits the

shareholder from selling his shares without the consent of the corporation, which consent will be given if the sale does not cause the corporation to lose its S Corporation election under the Internal Revenue Code.

CFC is upset that CompTech is not leasing space from CFC. In addition, several CompTech shareholders have expressed concern about the purchase of the software rights and the issuance of shares. Shareholders are also concerned about the share transfer restrictions.

## Required:

Answer the following and give reasons for your conclusions.

1. Is CompTech liable to CFC on the lease?
2. Are Romano, Kardesh, and the other CompTech shareholders liable on the CFC lease?
3. Was Romano and Kardesh's purchase and sale of the software rights proper?
4. Did the board act properly by issuing common shares to Romano and Kardesh in exchange for their promoters' services?
5. Did the board act properly by issuing common shares to the investor who gave the corporation a promissory note?
6. Are the resale restrictions on the common shares valid? Against whom are they enforceable?

CHAPTER

35

# Management of

# Corporations

**INTRODUCTION**

*Although shareholders own a corporation, they traditionally have possessed no right to manage the business of the corporation. Instead, shareholders elect individuals to a* board of directors, *to which management is entrusted. Often, the board delegates much of its management responsibilities to* officers.

*This chapter explains the legal aspects of the board's and officers' management of the corporation. Their management of the corporation must be consistent with the objectives and powers of the corporation, and they owe duties to the corporation to manage it prudently and in the best interests of the corporation and the shareholders as a whole.*

## Corporate Objectives

The traditional objective of the business corporation has been to *enhance corporate profits and shareholder gain.* According to this objective, the managers of a corporation must seek the accomplishment of the profit objective to the exclusion of all inconsistent goals. Interests other than profit maximization may be considered, provided that they do not hinder the ultimate profit objective.

Nonetheless, some courts have permitted corporations to take *socially responsible actions* that are *beyond the profit maximization requirement.* In addition, every state recognizes corporate powers that are not economically inspired. For example, corporations may make contributions to colleges, political campaigns, child abuse prevention centers, literary associations, and employee benefit plans, regardless of economic benefit to the corporations. Also, every state expressly recognizes the right of shareholders to choose freely the extent to which profit maximization captures all of their interests and all of their sense of responsibility.

In the following case, the court held that the board of directors acted improperly by failing to maximize shareholder profit.

## REVLON, INC. V. MACANDREWS & FORBES HOLDINGS, INC.
### 506 A.2d 173 (Del. Sup. Ct. 1986)

In 1985, Pantry Pride, Inc., informed Revlon, Inc., of its intent to acquire Revlon. Pantry Pride planned to "bust up" Revlon after the acquisition by selling its various lines of businesses individually. Revlon's board of directors rejected Pantry Pride's plan. Nonetheless, Pantry Pride made a hostile takeover bid for Revlon's shares at $47.50 per share.

In response to Pantry Pride's bid, Revlon's board sought to reduce the number of shares Pantry Pride could acquire by repurchasing some of it shares in exchange for new Senior Notes. The contract with the new Senior Noteholders protected the noteholders with covenants limiting Revlon's ability to incur more debt, sell assets, or pay dividends. The covenants, however, could be waived by the board's independent directors.

When this defense failed to deter Pantry Pride, the board recognized that a takeover was inevitable. Consequently, the board agreed to a friendly acquisition by Forstmann Little & Co. for $56 per share. Realizing the inevitability of a bust-up, Revlon's board agreed to break up its assets by selling its cosmetic division; Forstmann planned to sell two other divisions after the purchase.

In addition, Revlon's independent directors agreed to waive the Senior Note covenants. As a result, the value of the Senior Notes dropped 12 percent. Angry Senior Noteholders threatened to sue Revlon's directors. Concerned about their personal liability to the Senior Noteholders, the Revlon directors amended their agreement with Forstmann. Forstmann increased its offer to $57.25 per share and agreed to support the value of the Senior Notes. In return, Revlon gave Forstmann a lock-up option, promising to sell two valuable divisions to Forstmann at nearly $200 million below their market value if Pantry Pride was successful in taking over Revlon.

Pantry Pride sued Revlon to invalidate the lock-up option as beyond the objectives of the corporation. The trial court enjoined Revlon's directors from making concessions to Forstmann. Revlon appealed to the Supreme Court of Delaware.

---

**Moore, Justice**    The lock-up with Forstmann had as its emphasis shoring up the market value of the Senior Notes. The directors made support of the Senior Notes an integral part of the company's dealings with Forstmann, even though their primary responsibility at this stage was to the shareholders.

The original threat posed by Pantry Pride—the break-up of the company—had become a reality that even the directors embraced. Selective dealing to fend off a hostile bidder was no longer a proper objective. Instead, obtaining the highest price for the benefit of the shareholders should have been the central theme guiding director action.

The Revlon board argued that it acted in good faith in protecting the Senior Noteholders because Delaware law permits consideration of other corporate constituencies. Although such considerations may be permissible, there are fundamental limitations upon that prerogative. A board may have regard for various constituencies, provided there are rationally related benefits accruing to the shareholders. However, such concern for non-shareholder interests is inappropriate when an auction among active bidders is in progress, and the object no longer is to protect or maintain the corporate enterprise but to sell it to the highest bidder.

Revlon also contended that it had contractual obligations to the Senior Noteholders. However, any such duties are limited to the principle that one may not interfere with contractual relationships by improper actions. Here the rights of the Senior Noteholders were fixed by agreement, and there is nothing to suggest that any of those terms were violated. The Senior Notes covenants specifically contemplated a waiver.

In granting an asset option lock-up to Forstmann, the directors allowed considerations other than the maximization of shareholder profit to affect their judgment to the ultimate detriment of shareholders. No such defensive measure can be sustained.

**Judgment for Pantry Pride affirmed.**

**FIGURE 1    Indiana Code 23-1-35-1**

(d) A director may, in considering the best interests of a corporation, consider the effects of any action on shareholders, employees, suppliers, and customers of the corporation, and the communities in which the offices or other facilities of the corporation are located, and any other factors the director considers pertinent

(f) [D]irectors are not required to consider the effects of a proposed corporate action of any particular corporate constituent group or interest as a dominant or controlling factor.

The decision in *Revlon* prodded most of the states to enact **corporate constituency statutes,** which broaden the legal objectives of corporations. Such statutes permit or require directors to take into account the interests of constituencies other than shareholders. These statutes direct the board to act in the best interests of the corporation, not just the interests of the shareholders, and to maximize corporate profits *over the long term.* The new laws promote the view that a corporation is a collection of interests working together for the purpose of producing goods and services at a profit, and that the goal of corporate profit maximization over the long term is not necessarily the same as the goal of stock price maximization over the short term. For an example of the new statutes, see the excerpt from the Indiana statute in Figure 1.

## CORPORATE POWERS

The actions of management are limited not only by the objectives of business corporations but also by the *powers* granted to business corporations. Such limitations may appear in the state statute, the articles of incorporation, and the bylaws.

The primary source of a corporation's powers is the corporation statute of the state in which it is incorporated. Some state corporation statutes expressly specify the powers of corporations. These powers include making gifts for charitable and educational purposes, lending money to corporate officers and directors, and purchasing and disposing of the corporation's shares. Other state corporation

statutes limit the powers of corporations, such as prohibiting the acquisition of agricultural land by corporations.

Modern statutes attempt to authorize corporations to engage in any activity. The Model Business Corporation Act (MBCA) states that a corporation has the power to do *anything that an individual may do.*

## Purpose Clauses in Articles of Incorporation

Most corporations state their purposes in the articles of incorporation. The purpose is usually phrased in broad terms, even if the corporation has been formed with only one type of business in mind. Most corporations have purpose clauses stating that they may engage in any lawful business.

Under the MBCA, the inclusion of a purpose clause in the articles is optional. Any corporation incorporated under the MBCA has the purpose of engaging in any lawful business, unless the articles state a narrower purpose.

**The Ultra Vires Doctrine**    Historically, an act of a corporation beyond its powers was a nullity, as it was *ultra vires,* which is Latin for "beyond the powers." Therefore, any act not permitted by the corporation statute or by the corporation's articles of incorporation was void due to lack of capacity.

This lack of capacity or power of the corporation was a defense to a contract assertable either by the corporation or by the other party that dealt with the corporation. Often, *ultra vires* was merely a convenient justification for reneging on an agreement that was no longer considered desirable. This misuse of the doctrine has led to its near abandonment.

Today, the *ultra vires* doctrine is of small importance for two reasons. First, nearly all corporations have broad purpose clauses, thereby preventing any *ultra vires* problem. Second, the MBCA and most other statutes do not permit a corporation or the other party to an agreement to avoid an obligation on the ground that the corporate action is *ultra vires.*

Under the MBCA, *ultra vires* may be asserted by only three types of persons: (1) by a shareholder seeking to enjoin a corporation from executing a proposed action that is *ultra vires,* (2) by the corporation suing its management for damages caused by exceeding the corporation's powers, and

(3) by the state's attorney general, who may have the power to enjoin an *ultra vires* act or to dissolve a corporation that exceeds its powers.

## POWERS OF NONPROFIT CORPORATIONS

Nonprofit corporations, like for-profit corporations, have the power to transact business granted by the incorporation statute, the articles, and the bylaws. The Model Nonprofit Corporation Act (MNCA), like the MBCA, grants nonprofit corporations the power to engage in any lawful activity and to do anything an individual may do. Thus, a nonprofit corporation may sue and be sued, purchase, hold, and sell real property, lend and borrow money, and make charitable and other donations, among its many powers.

Commonly, a nonprofit corporation's articles will limit its powers pursuant to a purpose clause. For example, a nonprofit corporation established to operate a junior baseball league may limit its powers to that business and matters reasonably connected to it. When a nonprofit corporation limits its powers, a risk arises that the corporation may commit an *ultra vires* act. The MNCA adopts the same rules for *ultra vires* contracts as does the MBCA: Generally, neither the corporation nor the other party may use *ultra vires* as a defense to a contract.

## THE BOARD OF DIRECTORS

Traditionally, the **board of directors** has had the authority and the duty to manage the corporation. Yet in a large publicly held corporation, it is impossible for the board to manage the corporation on a day-to-day basis, because many of the directors are high-level executives in other corporations and devote most of their time to their other business interests. Therefore, the MBCA permits a corporation to be managed *under the direction of* the board of directors. Consequently, the board of directors delegates major responsibility for management to committees of the board such as an executive committee, to individual board members such as the chairman of the board, and to the officers of the corporation, especially the chief executive officer (CEO). In theory, the board supervises the actions of its committees, the chairman, and the officers to ensure that the board's

**FIGURE 2    Primary Responsibilities of Directors**

| | Percent* |
|---|---|
| 1. Ensure integrity of corporation's operations | 60% |
| 2. Counsel top management | 58 |
| 3. Ensure strategic plan for the future | 55 |
| 4. Monitor performance of the CEO | 47 |
| 5. Ensure management succession | 43 |
| 6. Serve the public interest | 15 |
| 7. Monitor financial reporting | 9 |

*Percent of directors surveyed citing each responsibility. Source: Survey of directors, published by Arthur Young Executive Resource Consultants in *The New Director: Changing Views of the Board's Role* (1989).

policies are being carried out and that the delegatees are managing the corporation prudently. Figure 2 lists the results of a survey of directors concerning their primary responsibilities.

## Board Authority under Corporation Statutes

A corporation's board of directors has the authority to do almost everything within the powers of the corporation. The board's authority includes not only the general power to manage or direct the corporation in the ordinary course of its business but also the power to issue shares of stock and to set the price of shares. Among its other powers, the board may repurchase shares, declare dividends, adopt and amend bylaws, elect and remove officers, and fill vacancies on the board.

Some corporate actions require *board initiative* and shareholder approval. That is, board approval is necessary to *propose such actions to the shareholders,* who then must approve the action. Board initiative is required for important changes in the corporation, such as amendment of the articles of incorporation, merger of the corporation, the sale of all or substantially all of the corporation's assets, and voluntary dissolution.

## Committees of the Board

Most publicly held corporations have committees of the board of directors. These committees, which have fewer members than the board has, can more efficiently handle management decisions and exercise board powers than can a large board. Only directors may serve on board committees.

Although many board powers may be delegated to committees of the board, some decisions are so important that corporation statutes require their *approval by the board as a whole.* Under the MBCA, the powers that may not be delegated concern important corporate actions such as declaring dividends, filling vacancies on the board or its committees, adopting and amending bylaws, approving issuances of shares, and approving repurchases of the corporation's shares.

The most common board committee is the **executive committee.** It is usually given authority to act for the board on most matters when the board is not in session. Generally, it consists of the inside directors and perhaps one or two outside directors who can attend a meeting on short notice. An inside director is an officer of the corporation who devotes substantially full time to the corporation. Outside directors have no such affiliation with the corporation.

**Audit committees** recommend independent public accountants and supervise the public accountants' audit of the corporate financial records. Nearly all publicly held firms have audit committees comprising independent directors.

**Nominating committees** choose management's slate of directors that is to be submitted to shareholders at the annual election of directors. Nominating committees also often plan generally for management succession. Nominating committees wholly or largely comprise outside directors.

**Compensation committees** review and approve the salaries, bonuses, stock options, and other benefits of high-level corporate executives. Although compensation committees usually comprise directors who have no affiliation with the executives or directors whose compensation is being approved, compensation committees may also set the compensation of their members. Directors of a typical corporation receive annual compensation between $30,000 to $60,000.

A **shareholder litigation committee** is given the task of determining whether a corporation should sue someone who has allegedly harmed the corporation. Usually, the committee of disinterested directors is formed when a shareholder asks the board of directors to cause the corporation to sue some or all of the directors for mismanaging the corporation.

## Powers, Rights, and Liabilities of Directors as Individuals

A director is not an agent of the corporation *merely* by being a director. The directors may manage the corporation only when they act as a board, unless the board of directors grants agency powers to the directors individually.

A director has the *right to inspect* corporate books and records that contain corporate information essential to the director's performance of her duties. The director's right of inspection is denied when the director has an interest adverse to the corporation, as in the case of a director who plans to sell a corporation's trade secrets to a competitor.

Normally, a director does not have any personal liability for the contracts and torts of the corporation.

## Election of Directors

Generally, any individual may serve as a director of a corporation. A director need not even be a shareholder. Nonetheless, a corporation is permitted to specify qualifications for directors in the articles of incorporation.

A corporation must have the number of directors required by the state corporation law. The MBCA and several state corporation statutes require a minimum of one director, recognizing that in close corporations with a single shareholder-manager, additional board members are superfluous. Several statutes, including the New York statute, require at least three directors, unless there are fewer than three shareholders, in which case the corporation may have no fewer directors than it has shareholders.

A corporation may have more than the minimum number of directors required by the corporation statute. The articles of incorporation or bylaws will state the number of directors of the corporation. Most large publicly held corporations have boards with more than 10 members.

Directors are elected by the shareholders at the annual shareholder meeting. Usually, each shareholder is permitted to vote for as many nominees as there are directors to be elected. The shareholder may cast as many votes for each nominee as he has shares. The top votegetters among the nominees are elected as directors. This voting process, called **straight voting,** permits a holder of more than 50 percent of the shares of a corporation to dominate the corporation by electing a board of directors that will manage the corporation as he wants it to be managed.

To avoid domination by a large shareholder, some corporations allow class voting or cumulative voting. **Class voting** may give certain classes of shareholders the right to elect a specified number of directors. **Cumulative voting** permits shareholders to multiply the number of their shares by the number of directors to be elected and to cast the resulting total of votes for one or more directors. As a result, cumulative voting may permit minority shareholders to obtain representation on the board of directors.

Directors usually hold office for only one year, but they may have longer terms. The MBCA permits *staggered terms* for directors. A corporation having a board of nine or more members may establish either two or three approximately equal classes of directors, with only one class of directors coming up for election at each annual shareholders' meeting. If there are two classes of directors, the directors serve two-year terms; if there are three classes, they serve three-year terms.

The original purpose of staggered terms was to permit continuity of management. Staggered terms also frustrate the ability of minority shareholders to use cumulative voting to elect their representatives to the board of directors.

**The Proxy Solicitation Process**   Most individual investors purchase corporate shares in the public market to increase their wealth, not to elect or to influence the directors of corporations. Nearly all institutional investors—such as pension funds, mutual funds, and bank trust departments—have the same profit motive. Generally, they are passive investors with little interest in exercising their shareholder right to elect directors by attending shareholder meetings.

Once public ownership of the corporation's shares exceeds 50 percent, the corporation cannot conduct any business at its shareholder meetings unless some of the shares of these passive investors are voted. This is because the corporation will have a shareholder quorum requirement, which usually requires that 50 percent or more of the shares be voted for a shareholder vote to be valid. Since passive investors rarely attend shareholder meetings, the management of the corporation must solicit **proxies** if it wishes to have a valid shareholder vote. Shareholders who will not attend a shareholder meeting must be asked to appoint someone else to vote their shares for them. This is done by furnishing each such shareholder with a proxy form to sign. The proxy designates a person who may vote the shares for the shareholder.

**Management Solicitation of Proxies**   To ensure its perpetuation in office and the approval of other matters submitted for a shareholder vote, the corporation's management solicits proxies from shareholders for directors' elections and other important matters on which shareholders vote, such as mergers. The management designates an officer, a director, or some other person to vote the proxies received. The person who is designated to vote for the shareholder is also called a proxy. Typically, the chief executive officer (CEO) of the corporation, the president, or the chairman of the board of directors names the person who serves as the proxy.

Usually, the proxies are merely signed and returned by the public shareholders, including the institutional shareholders. Passive investors follow the **Wall Street rule:** Either support management or sell the shares. As a result, management almost always receives enough votes from its proxy solicitation to ensure the reelection of directors and the approval of other matters submitted to the shareholders, even when other parties solicit proxies in opposition to management.

Management's solicitation of proxies produces a result that is quite different from the theory of corporate management that directors serve as representatives of the shareholders. The CEO usually nominates directors of his choice, and they are almost always elected. The directors appoint officers chosen by the CEO. The CEO's nominees for director are not unduly critical of his programs or of his methods for carrying them out. This is particularly true if a large proportion of the directors are officers of the company and thus are more likely to be dominated by the CEO. In such situations, the board of directors does not even function effectively as a representative of the shareholders in supervis-

**FIGURE 3    Influence of Board on Key Management Decisions**

|  | Strong | Moderate | None or Unknown |
|---|---|---|---|
| Compensation of top management | 71% | 27% | 2% |
| Mergers and acquisitions | 62 | 33 | 5 |
| Capital expenditures | 32 | 60 | 8 |
| Selection of senior executives | 22 | 64 | 14 |
| Long-range planning | 21 | 70 | 9 |

Note: Figures are percentages of directors surveyed citing the board's influence as strong, moderate, none, or unknown.
Source: Survey of directors, published by Arthur Young Executive Resource Consultants in *The New Director: Changing Views of the Board's Role* (1989).

ing and evaluating the CEO and the other officers of the corporation. The board members and the other officers are subordinates of the CEO, even though the CEO is not a major shareholder of the corporation.

Proposals for improving corporate governance in public-issue corporations seek to develop a board that is capable of functioning independently of the CEO by changing the composition or operation of the board of directors. Some corporate governance critics propose that a federal agency such as the Securities and Exchange Commission (SEC) appoint one or more directors to serve as watchdogs of the public interest. Other critics would require that shareholders elect at least a majority of directors without prior ties to the corporation, thus excluding shareholders, suppliers, and customers from the board. The New York Stock Exchange requires a minimum of two directors independent of management for its listed companies.

Other proposals recommend changing the method by which directors are nominated for election. One proposal would encourage shareholders to make nominations for directors. Supporters of this proposal argue that in addition to reducing the influence of the CEO, it would also broaden the range of backgrounds represented on the board. The SEC recommends that publicly held corporations establish a nominating committee composed of outside directors. Many publicly held corporations have nomination committees.

Mostly due to SEC and public pressures for changes in corporate governance, current boards of directors operate significantly differently from the boards of the 1960s and the early 1970s. Boards supervise officers more closely. More directors are outside rather than inside directors. Boards meet more frequently, and more important, they have working committees that assume specific responsibilities. In addition, today's directors *perceive* themselves as being more nearly independent of the CEO. As a consequence, they *are* more nearly independent of the CEO. See Figure 3.

## Vacancies on the Board

The MBCA permits the directors to fill vacancies on the board. A majority vote of the remaining directors is sufficient to select persons to serve out unexpired terms, even though the remaining directors are less than a quorum.

## Removal of Directors

Modern corporation statutes permit shareholders to remove directors *with or without cause*. The rationale for the modern rule is that the shareholders should have the power to judge the fitness of directors at any time.

However, most corporations have provisions in their articles authorizing the shareholders to remove directors *only for cause*. Cause for removal would include mismanagement or conflicts of interest. Before removal for cause, the director must be given notice and an opportunity for a hearing.

A director elected by a class of shareholders may be removed only by that class of shareholders, thereby protecting the voting rights of the class. A director elected by cumulative voting may not be removed if the votes cast against her removal would have been sufficient to elect her to the board, thereby protecting the voting rights of minority shareholders.

In the following case, a director—a minority shareholder—would not have been removed as a director had there been cumulative voting of shares.

---

## LEHMAN V. PIONTKOWSKI
### 460 N.Y.S.2d 817 (N.Y. App. Div. 1983)

Jacob Lehman and Shlomo Piontkowski were surgeons who practiced together in a professional corporation. They were the directors and only shareholders, Lehman owning six shares and Piontkowski owning four shares. Each was an employee of the corporation. Piontkowski's employment contract granted to the board of directors of the corporation the power to terminate his employment for "personal misconduct of such a material nature as to be professionally detrimental to the corporation."

From 1977 to 1979, Lehman and Piontkowski disagreed on the distribution of the corporation's income. Dissatisfied with his share of the income, Piontkowski canceled surgery, informed his patients that he was on vacation, and planned to open his own office nearby.

Acting as president of the corporation, Lehman sent Piontkowski a letter stating that Piontkowski's actions violated his employment contract. As president, Lehman stated that he deemed these actions to be personal misconduct so material as to be professionally detrimental to the corporation.

At a special shareholder meeting, Lehman proposed that Piontkowski be removed as a director and voted his six shares to oust Piontkowski. Piontkowski did not vote his four shares. Lehman then nominated himself as sole director, voted his shares to elect himself sole director, and adjourned the shareholder meeting. Lehman then called the special directors' meeting to order and, as the sole director, dismissed Piontkowski as an employee.

Afterward, Lehman and the corporation sued Piontkowski, seeking to recover damages of $500,000 for Piontkowski's breach of contract by opening a competing medical practice. Piontkowski argued that his expulsion from the corporation was illegal and that therefore the corporation was not entitled to enforce the contract. The trial court denied Piontkowski's motion for summary judgment, and Piontkowski appealed.

---

**Memorandum by the Court**   Piontkowski's expulsion as director and the termination of his employment were improper.

By letter, Piontkowski was informed that Lehman, as president, deemed Piontkowski's actions to be personal misconduct that was so material as to be professionally detrimental to the corporation. This opinion was not that of the board of directors, as was required by the employment contract, but rather was that of Lehman individually and as president of the corporation. The board had not formally met to make a determination that Piontkowski had committed detrimental misconduct as a material breach of the contract. Therefore, the letter was of no legal effect.

At the special shareholder meeting, Lehman's first order of business was to vote his majority of the shares to dismiss Piontkowski as a director. Such an act was of no effect in the present matter. The New York Business Corporation Law provides that "the number of directors . . . shall not be less than three, except that where all the shares of a corporation are owned . . . by less than three shareholders, the number of directors may be less than three but not less than the number of shareholders."

Here there were two shareholders at the commencement of the special shareholder meeting. Piontkowski's expulsion as a director and the election of Lehman as the sole director were therefore improper. The removal of Piontkowski as a director left the corporation with only one director and without a validly constituted board of directors. The New York statute prohibits such an occurrence. The subsequent act of an illegally constituted one-man board of directors in terminating Piontkowski's employment was invalid.

As Piontkowski's unilateral expulsion from the corporation was illegal, the corporation is not entitled to enforce Piontkowski's employment contract.

**Judgment reversed in favor of Piontkowski.**

## Directors' Meetings

Traditionally, directors could act only when they were properly convened as a board. They could not vote by proxy or informally, as by telephone. This rule was based on a belief in the value of consultation and collective judgment.

Today, the corporation laws of a majority of the states and the MBCA specifically permit action by the directors without a meeting if all of the directors consent in writing to the action taken. Such authorization is useful for dealing with routine matters or for formally approving an action based on an earlier policy decision made after full discussion.

The MBCA also permits a board to meet by telephone or television hookup. This section permits a meeting of directors who may otherwise be unable to convene. The only requirement is that the directors be able to hear one another simultaneously.

Directors are entitled to reasonable notice of all *special meetings,* but not of regularly scheduled meetings. The MBCA does not require the notice for a special meeting to state the purpose of the meeting. A director's attendance at a meeting waives any required notice, unless at the beginning of the meeting the director objects to the lack of notice.

For the directors to act, a *quorum* of the directors must be present. The quorum requirement ensures that the decision of the board will represent the views of a substantial portion of the directors. A quorum is usually a *majority* of the number of directors.

Each director has *one vote*. If a quorum is present, a vote of a majority of the directors present is an act of the board, unless the articles or the bylaws require the vote of a greater number of directors. Such *supermajority voting provisions* are common in close corporations but not in publicly held corporations. The use of supermajority voting provisions by close corporations is covered later in this chapter.

## Officers of the Corporation

The board of directors has the authority to appoint the officers of the corporation. Many corporation statutes provide that the officers of a corporation shall be the *president,* one or more *vice presidents,* a *secretary,* and a *treasurer.* Usually, any two or more offices may be held by the same person, except for the offices of president and secretary.

The MBCA requires only that there be an officer performing the duties normally granted to a corporate secretary. Under the MBCA, one person may hold several offices, including the offices of president and secretary.

The officers are agents of the corporation. As agents, officers have *express authority* conferred on them by the bylaws or the board of directors. In addition, officers have *implied authority* to do the things that are reasonably necessary to accomplish their express duties. Also, officers have *apparent authority* when the corporation leads third parties to believe reasonably that the officers have authority to act for the corporation. Like any principal, the corporation may *ratify* the unauthorized acts of its officers. This may be done expressly by a resolution of the board of directors or impliedly by the board's acceptance of the benefits of the officer's acts.

The most perplexing issue with regard to the authority of officers is whether an officer has *inherent authority* merely by virtue of the title of his office. Courts have held that certain official titles confer authority on officers, but such powers are much more restricted than you might expect.

Traditionally, a *president* possesses no power to bind the corporation by virtue of the office. Instead, she serves merely as the presiding officer at shareholder meetings and directors' meetings. A president with an additional title such as *general manager* or *chief executive officer* has broad implied authority to make contracts and to do other acts in the ordinary business of the corporation.

A *vice president* has no authority by virtue of that office. An executive who is vice president of a specified department, however, such as a vice president of marketing, will have the authority to transact the normal corporate business falling within the function of the department.

The *secretary* usually keeps the minutes of directors' and shareholder meetings, maintains other corporate records, retains custody of the corporate seal, and certifies corporate records as being authentic. Although the secretary has no authority to make contracts for the corporation by virtue of that office, the corporation is bound by documents certified by the secretary.

The *treasurer* has custody of the corporation's funds. He is the proper officer to receive payments to the corporation and to disburse corporate funds for authorized purposes. The treasurer binds the corporation by his receipts, checks, and indorsements, but he does not by virtue of that office alone have authority to borrow money, to issue negotiable instruments, or to make other contracts on behalf of the corporation.

Like any agent, a corporate officer ordinarily has *no liability on contracts* that he makes on behalf of his principal, the corporation, if he signs for the corporation and not in his personal capacity.

Officers serve the corporation at the pleasure of the board of directors, which may remove an officer at any time with or without cause. An officer who has been removed without cause has no recourse against the corporation, unless the removal violates an employment contract between the officer and the corporation.

## MANAGING CLOSE CORPORATIONS

Many of the management formalities that you have studied in this chapter are appropriate for publicly held corporations yet inappropriate for close corporations. Close corporations tend to be more loosely managed than public corporations. For example, they may have few board meetings. Each shareholder may want to be *involved in management* of the close corporation. If a shareholder is not involved in management, he may want to protect his interest by placing *restrictions on the managerial discretion* of those who do manage the corporation.

Modern close corporation statutes permit close corporations to dispense with most, if not all, management formalities. The Statutory Close Corporation Supplement to the MBCA permits a close corporation to *dispense with a board of directors* and to be *managed by the shareholders*. The California General Corporation Law permits the close corporation to be managed *as if it were a partnership*.

Because a minority shareholder of a close corporation may be dominated by the shareholders who control the board of directors, close corporation shareholders have resorted to two devices: **supermajority voting** requirements for board actions and **restrictions on the managerial discretion** of the board of directors.

Any corporation may require that board action be possible only with the approval of more than a majority of the directors, such as three fourths or unanimous approval. A supermajority vote is often required to terminate the employment contract of an employee-shareholder, to reduce the level of dividends, and to change the corporation's line of business. Supermajority votes are rarely required for ordinary business matters, such as deciding with which suppliers the corporation should deal.

Traditionally, shareholders could not restrict the managerial discretion of directors. This rule recognized the traditional roles of the board as manager and of the shareholders as passive owners. Modern close corporation statutes permit shareholders to intrude into the sanctity of the boardroom. The Statutory Close Corporation Supplement grants the shareholders *unlimited* power to restrict the discretion of the board of directors. For example, the shareholders may agree that the directors may not terminate or reduce the salaries of employee-shareholders and may not lower or eliminate dividends. And, as was stated above, close corporation statutes even permit the shareholders to dispense with a board of directors altogether and to manage the close corporation as if it were a partnership.

## MANAGING NONPROFIT CORPORATIONS

A nonprofit corporation is managed under the direction of a board of directors. The board of directors must have at least three directors. All corporate powers are exercised by or under the authority of the board of directors. Any person may serve as a director; however, the Model Nonprofit Corporation Act has an optional provision stating that no more than 49 percent of directors of a public service corporation may be financially interested in the business of the public service corporation. An interested person is, for example, the musical director of a city's symphony orchestra who receives a salary from the nonprofit corporation operating the orchestra.

If a nonprofit corporation has members, typically the members elect the directors. However, the articles may provide for the directors to be appointed or elected by other persons. Directors serve for one year, unless the articles or bylaws provide otherwise. Directors who are elected may not serve terms longer than five years, but appointed directors may serve longer terms.

Directors may be elected by straight or cumulative voting and by class voting. Members may elect directors in person or by proxy. Directors may be removed at any time with or without cause by the members or other persons who elected or appointed the directors. When a director engages in fraudulent or dishonest conduct or breaches a fiduciary duty, members holding at least 10 percent of the voting power may petition a court to remove the wrongdoing director. Generally, a vacancy may be filled by the members or the board of directors; however, if a removed director was elected by a class of members or appointed by another person, only the class or person electing or appointing the director may fill the vacancy.

The board is permitted to set directors' compensation. Typically, directors of public benefit corporations and religious corporations are volunteers and receive no compensation.

Directors of a nonprofit corporation usually act at a meeting at which all directors may simultaneously hear each other, such as a meeting in person or by telephone conference call. The board may also act without a meeting if all directors consent in writing to the action. The board has the power to do most actions that are within the powers of the corporation, although some actions, such as mergers and amendments of the articles, require member action also. Ordinarily, an individual director has no authority to transact for a nonprofit corporation.

The board of directors of a nonprofit corporation may delegate some of its authority to committees of the board and to officers. A nonprofit corporation is not required to have officers, except for an officer performing the duties of corporate secretary. If a corporation chooses to have more officers, one person may hold more than one office. The board may remove an officer at any time with or without cause.

Officers have the authority granted them by the bylaws or by board resolution. However, a nonprofit corporation is bound by a contract signed by both the presiding officer of the board and the president, when the other party had no knowledge that the signing officers had no authority. The corporation is also bound to a contract signed by either the presiding officer or the president which is also signed by either a vice president, the secretary, the treasurer, or the executive director.

## DIRECTORS' AND OFFICERS' DUTIES TO THE CORPORATION

Directors and officers are in positions of trust; they are entrusted with property belonging to the corporation and with power to act for the corporation. Therefore, directors and officers owe **fiduciary duties** to the corporation. They are the duties to act within the authority of the position and within the objectives and powers of the corporation, to act with due care in conducting the affairs of the corporation, and to act with loyalty to the corporation.

### Acting within Authority

An officer or director has a duty to **act within the authority** conferred on her by the articles of incorporation, the bylaws, and the board of directors. The directors and officers must act within the scope of the powers of the corporation. An officer or a director may be liable to the corporation if it is damaged by an act exceeding that person's or the corporation's authority.

## Duty of Care

Directors and officers are liable for losses to the corporation resulting from their lack of *care or diligence*. The MBCA expressly states the standard of care that must be exercised by directors and officers. MBCA Section 8.30 states:

(a) A director shall discharge his duties as a director, including his duties as a member of a committee:

(1) in good faith;

(2) with the care an ordinarily prudent person in a like position would exercise under similar circumstances; and

(3) in a manner he reasonably believes to be in the best interests of the corporation.

Managers need merely meet the standard of the **ordinarily prudent person in the same circumstances,** a standard focusing on the basic manager attributes of common sense, practical wisdom, and informed judgment. The duty of care does not hold directors and officers to the standard of a prudent businessperson, a person of some undefined level of business skill. A director or officer's performance is evaluated at the time of the decision, thereby preventing the application of hindsight in judging her performance.

The MBCA duty of care test requires that a director or officer make a **reasonable investigation** and **honestly believe** that her decision is in the **best interests of the corporation.** For example, the board of directors decides to purchase an existing manufacturing business for $15 million without inquiring into the value of the business or examining its past financial performance. Although the directors may believe that they made a prudent decision, they have no reasonable basis for that belief. Therefore, if the plant is worth only $5 million, the directors will be liable to the corporation for its damages—$10 million—for breaching the duty of care.

**The Business Judgment Rule**    The directors' and officers' duty of care is sometimes expressed as the **business judgment rule:** absent bad faith, fraud, or breach of fiduciary duty, the judgment of the board of directors is conclusive. When directors and officers have complied with the business judgment rule, they are protected from liability to the corporation for their unwise decisions. The business judgment rule precludes the courts from substituting their business judgment for that of the corporation's

managers. The business judgment rule recognizes that the directors and officers—not the shareholders and the courts—are best able to make business judgments and should not ordinarily be vulnerable to second-guessing. Shareholders and the courts are ill-equipped to make better business decisions than those made by the officers and directors of a corporation, who have more business experience and are more familiar with the needs, strengths, and limitations of the corporation.

Three requirements must be met for the business judgment rule to protect managers from liability:

**1.** The managers must make an **informed decision.** They must take the steps necessary to become informed about the relevant facts before making a decision. These steps may include merely listening to a proposal, reviewing written materials, or making inquiries. Managers may rely on information collected and presented by other persons. In essence, the informed-decision component means that managers should do their homework if they want the protection of the business judgment rule.

**2.** The managers may have **no conflicts of interest.** The managers may not benefit personally—other than as shareholders—when they transact on behalf of the corporation.

**3.** The managers must have a **rational basis** for believing that the decision is in the best interests of the corporation. The rational basis element requires only that the managers' decision have a *logical connection to the facts* revealed by a reasonable investigation or that the decision *not be manifestly unreasonable.* Some courts have held that the managers' wrongdoing must amount to *gross negligence* for the directors to lose the protection of the business judgment rule.

If the business judgment rule does not apply because one or more of its elements are missing, a court may *substitute its judgment* for that of the managers.

Nonetheless, courts rarely refuse to apply the business judgment rule. As a result, the rule has been criticized frequently as providing too much protection for the managers of corporations. In one famous case, the court applied the business judgment rule to protect a 1965 decision made by the board of directors of the Chicago Cubs not to install lights and not to hold night baseball games at

Wrigley Field.[1] Yet the business judgment rule is so flexible that it protected the decision of the Cubs' board of directors to install lights in 1988.

The *Trans Union* case[2] is one of the few cases that have held directors liable for failing to comply with the business judgment rule. The Supreme Court of Delaware found that the business judgment rule was not satisfied by the board's approval of an acquisition of the corporation for $55 per share. The board approved the acquisition after only two hours' consideration. The board received no documentation to support the adequacy of the $55 price. Instead, it relied entirely on a 20-minute *oral*

report of the chairman of the board. No written summary of the acquisition was presented to the board. The directors failed to obtain an investment banker's report, prepared after careful consideration, that the acquisition price was fair.

In addition, the court held that the mere fact that the acquisition price exceeded the market price by $17 per share did not legitimize the board's decision. The board had frequently made statements prior to the acquisition that the market had undervalued the shares, yet the board took no steps to determine the intrinsic value of the shares. Consequently, the court found that at a minimum, the directors had been grossly negligent.

In the following case, the court considered whether a bank loan officer complied with the business judgment rule.

---

[1]*Shlensky v. Wrigley*, 237 N.E.2d 776 (Ill. Ct. App. 1968).
[2]*Smith v. Van Gorkom*, 488 A.2d 858 (Del. Sup. Ct. 1985).

---

## OMNIBANK OF MANTEE V. UNITED SOUTHERN BANK
### 607 So.2d 76 (Miss. Sup. Ct. 1992)

James R. Gray was president and managing officer of the Peoples Bank and Trust Company in Olive Branch, Mississippi, a branch bank owned by United Southern Bank (USB). Gray had complete charge of the day-to-day banking business of Peoples Bank. He had discretionary loan authority, subject to USB's limits for all senior loan officers: $75,000 for unsecured loans and $150,000 for secured loans.

Frank Piecara was an established customer of Peoples Bank. Piecara was president of Mirage Construction, Inc., which was obligated on a subcontract to provide earthwork and roadwork for Rogers Construction Company at the Pacacho Pumping Plant in Arizona. Gray directed Peoples Bank to make loans in the amount of $536,000 to a trust managed by Piecara. The loan proceeds were used to provide working capital for Mirage. In addition, Gray directed Peoples Bank to issue a $300,000 irrevocable letter of credit to Rogers Construction for the purpose of securing Mirage's performance as Rogers's subcontractor. Gray called USB's senior vice president, Edward P. Peacock III, to request authorization of the letter of credit. Gray and Peacock each had $150,000 authority to make secured loans, which they combined to issue the letter of credit. As security for the loans and letter of credit, Gray obtained a security interest in Mirage's accounts receivable and contract rights, in particular the payments Rogers might make to Mirage under the subcontract. Gray did not perfect the security interest in the subcontract. Gray did not notify Rogers or the owner of the Pacacho Pumping Plant of the security interest or require Rogers or the owner to remit subcontract payments directly to Peoples Bank.

Piecara and Mirage defaulted on the loans and letter of credit, with USB suffering a loss of almost $600,000. USB sued Gray alleging his breach of a fiduciary duty. The trial court found Gray liable to USB. Gray appealed to the Mississippi Supreme Court.

---

**Robertson, Justice** The law devolves upon those in the upper echelons of a corporate entity certain duties owing to the entity, over and above those of an ordinary agent or employee. The question is whether Gray is one of those so burdened. We doubt a definitional line may be drawn with precision or permanence. For the moment, we are prepared to accept that

"Officer" means (a) the chief executive, operating, financial, legal and accounting officers of a corporation; (b) to the extent not encompassed by the foregoing, the chairman of the board of directors . . ., president, treasurer, and secretary, and a *vice-president or vice-chairman who is in charge of a principal business unit, division,* or function . . . and (c) any other individual designated by the corporation as an officer.
American Law Institute, *Principles of Corporate Governance: Analysis and Recommendations,* section 1.27.

His title aside, Gray served USB as the chief operating official at Peoples Bank where he had substantial discretionary authority. We think a banking office such as the Peoples Bank branch is one of USB's principal business units. Gray was the man in charge. He presided over a branch worth over twenty million dollars, had substantial loan authority, and had considerable autonomy in directing the day-to-day operations of the branch. The trial court was correct in treating Gray as an officer of USB.

By law, officer Gray owed USB two principal duties: a duty of care and a duty of loyalty and fair dealing. These duties differ in nature and content, though they doubtless intersect and overlap. There is a bit of lore born no doubt of thought of failed banks and helpless widows that we ought demand more of bank officers than one who runs a foundry or a pest control company.

We begin with the duty of care. A director or officer has a duty to the corporation to perform the director's or officer's functions in good faith, in a manner he or she reasonably believes to be in the best interests of the corporation, and with the care that an ordinarily prudent person would reasonably be expected to exercise in a like position and under similar circumstances. The duty includes the obligation to make, or cause to make, an inquiry when, but only when, the circumstances would alert a reasonable director or officer to the need therefor. The extent of such inquiry shall be such as the director or officer reasonably believes to be necessary.

We long ago recognized this duty in a banking setting and said an officer who "very negligently" makes unreasonably risky loans may on his borrowers' default be held personally to make good the bank's loss.

The duty of care is subject to a well-settled common law, known as the business judgment rule. That rule has recently been stated with care:

A director or officer who makes a business judgment in good faith fulfills the duty . . . [of care] if the director or officer:
(1) is not interested . . . in the subject of the business judgment;
(2) is informed with respect to the subject of the business judgment to the extent the director or officer reasonably believes to be appropriate under the circumstances; and
(3) rationally believes that the business judgment is in the best interests of the corporation.
*Principles of Corporate Governance,* section 4.01. *See* MBCA section 8.42.

Gray's defaults in the Piecara loans are apparent. To be sure, there is nothing improper about a banker securing a credit by taking a security interest in contract rights or assignment of accounts. On the other hand, there are risks associated with the receivables form of collateral not associated with more tangible security, and a prudent loan officer must reasonably assess and control these risks. These risks are exacerbated where, as here, the subcontract is to be performed some 1500 miles away.

Gray made no inquiry of the financial responsibility of Rogers or the owner of the Picacho Pumping Plant. A prudent loan officer taking such collateral will give notice of his bank's interest to the prime contractor and the owner and demand that all payments due under the subcontract be routed through the bank. Gray did none of this, nor did he monitor performance of the subcontract and have Piecara remit as his company was paid. Gray failed to perfect the security interest. Moreover, it appears clear the value of the collateral was far below what prudently should have been required for credit of this size. We accept the trial court's holding that Gray breached his duty of care to USB in handling the Piecara loans.

Gray's argument in reply is laced with implied references to the business judgment rule. He insists he acted in subjective good faith at all times, and of this there is little doubt. The trial court found Gray had no "interest" in any of the credits at issue. Gray insists he reasonably believed the debtors would respond to their obligations in a reasonably timely fashion. Gray insists he thought the risks reasonable and, where unsecured, backed by adequate financial statements. Reports of these loans, their terms, and periodic status were routinely available to USB, which offered nothing but praise until a state bank examiner's probe in January, 1985.

These are not irrelevancies. They are evidence that Gray may have acted with reasonable business judgment. Most assuredly, the duty of care holds no truck with Monday morning quarterbacking, and the business judgment rule stands to prevent this. A loan officer is no guarantor of the success of each credit extension. The prudence of the practice is judged objectively in the circumstances then existing and reasonably knowable by the officer.

The defense ultimately founders. The trial court impliedly found unreasonable Gray's belief regarding the extent to which he should have informed himself at the time regarding these debtors. Further, the court impliedly found there was no rational basis for a belief that his handling of these matters was in USB's best interest.

**Judgment for United Southern Bank affirmed.**

## Recent Changes in the Duty of Care

In response to the *Trans Union* case and insurance companies' increasing unwillingness to insure directors and officers for breaches of their duty of care (and the resulting exodus of outside directors from corporate boards of directors), many state legislatures changed the wording of the duty of care, typically imposing liability only for willful or wanton misconduct or for gross negligence.

For example, Ohio protects directors from monetary liability except when clear and convincing evidence demonstrates the directors' deliberate intent to injure the corporation or the directors' reckless disregard for its welfare. Delaware corporation law and the MBCA allow corporations to amend their articles to reduce or eliminate directors' liability for monetary damages for breaches of the duty of care. Figure 4 contains the MBCA provision.

## Board Opposition to Acquisition of Control of a Corporation

In the last 30 years, many outsiders have attempted to acquire control of publicly held corporations. Typically, these outsiders (called **raiders**) will make a **tender offer** for the shares of a corporation (called the **target**). A tender offer is an offer to the shareholders to buy their shares at a price above the current market price. The raider hopes to acquire a majority of the shares, which will give it control of the target corporation.

---

**FIGURE 4     MBCA Section 2.02**

(b) The articles of incorporation may set forth:

(4) a provision eliminating or limiting the liability of a director to the corporation or its shareholders for money damages for any action taken or any failure to take any action, as a director, except liability for

(A) the amount of financial benefit received by a director to which he is not entitled;

(B) an intentional infliction of harm on the corporation or the shareholders;

(C) a violation of Section 8.33 [illegal payment of dividends]; or

(D) an intentional violation of criminal law.

---

Most tender offers are opposed by the target corporation's management. The defenses to tender offers are many and varied, and they carry interesting names, such as the Pac-Man defense, the white knight, greenmail, the poison pill, and the lock-up option. See Figure 5 for definitions of these defenses.

When takeover defenses are successful, shareholders of the target may lose the opportunity to sell their shares at a price up to twice the market price of the shares prior to the announcement of the hostile bid. Frequently, the loss of this opportunity upsets shareholders, who then decide to sue the directors

---

**FIGURE 5**    Tender Offer Defenses

---

**Pac-Man**

The target corporation turns the tables on the tender offeror or raider (which is often another publicly held corporation) by making a tender offer for the raider's shares. As a result, two tender offerors are trying to buy each other's shares. This is similar to the Pac-Man video game, in which Pac-Man and his enemies chase each other.

**Greenmail**

The target's repurchase of its shares from the raider at a substantial profit to the raider, upon the condition that the raider sign a standstill agreement in which it promises not to buy additional shares of the target for a stated period of time.

**White Knight**

A friendly tender offeror whom management prefers over the original tender offeror–called a black knight. The white knight rescues the corporation from the black knight (the raider) by offering more money for the corporation's shares. In the *Revlon* case that appeared earlier in the chapter, Forstmann was a white knight for Revlon.

**Lock-Up Option**

Used in conjunction with a white knight to ensure the success of the white knight's bid. The target and the white knight agree that the white knight will buy a highly valuable asset of the target at a very attractive price for the white knight (usually a below-market price) if the raider succeeds in taking over the target. For example, in the *Revlon* case, Revlon gave a lock-up option to Forstmann to reduce the amount of profit that Pantry Pride would make had it completed its takeover of Revlon.

**Poison Pill**

Also called a shareholders' rights plan. There are many types, but the typical poison pill involves the target's issuance of a new class of preferred shares to its common shareholders. The preferred shares have rights (share options) attached to them. These rights allow the target's shareholders to purchase shares of the raider or shares of the target at less than fair market value. The poison pill deters hostile takeover attempts by threatening the raider and its shareholders with severe dilutions in the value of the shares they hold.

---

who have opposed the tender offer. Shareholders contend that the directors have opposed the tender offer only to preserve their corporate jobs. Shareholders also argue that the target corporation's interests would have been better served if the tender offer had succeeded.

Generally, courts have refused to find directors liable for opposing a tender offer because the business judgment rule applies to a board's decision to oppose a tender offer.

Nonetheless, the business judgment rule will not apply when the directors make a decision to oppose the tender offer before they have carefully studied it. In addition, if the directors' actions indicate that they opposed the tender offer in order to preserve their jobs, they will be liable to the corporation.

Court decisions have seemingly modified the business judgment rule as it is applied in the tender offer context. For example, in *Unocal Corp. v. Mesa Petroleum Co.,*[3] the Supreme Court of Delaware upheld the application of the business judgment rule to a board's decision to block a hostile tender offer

by making a tender offer for its own shares that excluded the raider.[4] But in so ruling, the court held that the board may use only those defense tactics that are *reasonable* compared to the takeover threat. The board may consider a variety of concerns, including the inadequacy of the price offered, nature and timing of the offer, questions of illegality, the impact on constituencies other than shareholders (i.e., creditors, customers, employees, and perhaps even the community generally), the risk of nonconsummation, and the quality of securities being offered in the exchange.

In *Unocal,* the threat was a two-tier, highly coercive tender offer. In the typical two-tier offer, the raider first offers cash for a majority of the shares. After acquiring a majority of the shares, the offeror initiates the second tier, in which the remaining shareholders are forced to sell their shares for a package of securities less attractive than the first tier. Because shareholders fear that they will be forced to take the less attractive second-tier securities

---

[3]493 A.2d 946 (Del. Sup. Ct. 1985).

[4]Discriminatory tender offers are now illegal pursuant to Securities Act Rule 13e-4.

if they fail to tender during the first tier, shareholders—including those who oppose the offer—are coerced into tendering during the first tier. *Unocal* and later cases specifically authorize the use of defenses to defeat a coercive two-tier tender offer.

Since its decision in *Unocal,* the Supreme Court of Delaware has applied this modified business judgment rule to validate a poison pill tender offer defense tactic in *Moran v. Household Int'l, Inc.*[5] and to invalidate a lock-up option tender offer defense in the *Revlon* case, which appears earlier in this chapter. These cases confirmed the *Unocal* holding that the board of directors must show that:

1. It had reasonable grounds to believe that a danger to corporate policy and effectiveness was posed by the takeover attempt.

2. It acted primarily to protect the corporation and its shareholders from that danger.

---

[5] 500 A.2d 346 (Del. Sup. Ct. 1985).

3. The defense tactic was reasonable in relation to the threat posed to the corporation.

Such a standard appeared to impose a higher standard on directors than the rational basis requirement of the business judgment rule, which historically has been interpreted to require only that a decision of a board not be manifestly unreasonable. In addition, the *Revlon* case required the board to establish an auction market for the company and to sell it to the highest bidder when the directors have abandoned the long-term business objectives of the company by embracing a bust-up of the company.

In the following case, the Supreme Court of Delaware expanded board discretion in fighting hostile takeovers, holding that a board may oppose a hostile takeover provided the board had a *preexisting, deliberately conceived corporate plan* justifying its opposition. The existence of such a plan enabled Time's board to meet the reasonable-tactic element of the *Unocal* test.

---

## PARAMOUNT COMMUNICATIONS, INC. v. TIME, INC.
### 571 A.2d 1140 (Del. Sup. Ct. 1989)

Since 1983, Time, Inc., had considered expanding its business beyond publishing magazines and books, owning Home Box Office and Cinemax, and operating television stations. In 1988, Time's board approved in principle a strategic plan for Time's acquisition of an entertainment company. The board gave management permission to negotiate a merger with Warner Communications, Inc. The board's consensus was that a merger of Time and Warner was feasible, but only if Time controlled the resulting corporation, preserving the editorial integrity of Time's magazines. The board concluded that Warner was the superior candidate because Warner could make movies and TV shows for HBO, Warner had an international distribution system, Warner was a giant in the music business, Time and Warner would control half of New York City's cable TV system, and the Time network could promote Warner's movies.

Negotiations with Warner broke down when Warner refused to agree to Time dominating the combined companies. Time continued to seek expansion, but informal discussions with other companies terminated when it was suggested the other companies purchase Time or control the resulting board. In January 1989, Warner and Time resumed negotiations, and on March 4, 1989, they agreed to a combination by which Warner shareholders would own 62 percent of the resulting corporation, to be named Time-Warner. To retain the editorial integrity of Time, the merger agreement provided for a board committee dominated by Time representatives.

On June 7, 1989, Paramount Communications, Inc., announced a cash tender offer for all of Time's shares at $175 per share. (The day before, Time shares traded at $126 per share.) Time's financial advisers informed the outside directors that Time's auction value was materially higher than $175 per share. The board concluded that Paramount's $175 offer was inadequate. Also, the board viewed the Paramount offer as a threat to Time's control of its own destiny and retention of the Time editorial policy; the board found that a combination with Warner offered greater potential for Time.

In addition, concerned that shareholders would not comprehend the long-term benefits of the merger with Warner, on June 16, 1989, Time's board recast its acquisition with Warner into a two-tier acquisition, in which it would make a tender offer to buy 51 percent of Warner's shares for cash immediately and later buy the remaining 49 percent for cash and securities. The tender offer would eliminate the need for Time to obtain shareholder approval of the transaction.

On June 23, 1989, Paramount raised its offer to $200 per Time share. Three days later, Time's board rejected the offer as a threat to Time's survival and its editorial integrity; the board viewed the Warner acquisition as offering greater long-term value for the shareholders. Time shareholders and Paramount then sued Time and its board to enjoin Time's acquisition of Warner. The trial court held for Time. Paramount and Time shareholders appealed to the Supreme Court of Delaware.

**Horsey, Justice** Our decision does not require us to pass on the wisdom of the board's decision. That is not a court's task. Our task is simply to determine whether there is sufficient evidence to support the initial Time-Warner agreement as the product of a proper exercise of business judgment.

We have purposely detailed the evidence of the Time board's deliberative approach, beginning in 1983–84, to expand itself. Time's decision in 1988 to combine with Warner was made only after what could be fairly characterized as an exhaustive appraisal of Time's future as a corporation. Time's board was convinced that Warner would provide the best fit for Time to achieve its strategic objectives. The record attests to the zealousness of Time's executives, fully supported by their directors, in seeing to the preservation of Time's perceived editorial integrity in journalism. The Time board's decision to expand the business of the company through its March 4 merger with Warner was entitled to the protection of the business judgment rule.

The revised June 16 agreement was defense-motivated and designed to avoid the potentially disruptive effect that Paramount's offer would have had on consummation of the proposed merger were it put to a shareholder vote. Thus, we decline to apply the traditional business judgment rule to the revised transaction and instead analyze the Time board's June 16 decision under *Unocal.*

In *Unocal,* we held that before the business judgment rule is applied to a board's adoption of a defensive measure, the burden will lie with the board to prove (a) reasonable grounds for believing that a danger to corporate policy and effectiveness existed; and (b) that the defensive measure adopted was reasonable in relation to the threat posed.

Paramount argues a hostile tender offer can pose only two types of threats: the threat of coercion that results from a two-tier offer promising unequal treatment for nontendering shareholders; and the threat of inadequate value from an all-shares, all-cash offer at a price below what a target board in good faith deems to be the present value of its shares.

Paramount would have us hold that only if the value of Paramount's offer were determined to be clearly inferior to the value created by management's plan to merge with Warner could the offer be viewed—objectively—as a threat.

Paramount's position represents a fundamental misconception of our standard of review under *Unocal* principally because it would involve the court in substituting its judgment as to what is a "better" deal for that of a corporation's board of directors. The usefulness of *Unocal* as an analytical tool is precisely its flexibility in the face of a variety of fact scenarios. Thus, directors may consider, when evaluating the threat posed by a takeover bid, the inadequacy of the price offered, nature and timing of the offer, questions of illegality, the impact on constituencies other than shareholders, the risk of nonconsummation, and the quality of securities being offered in the exchange.

The Time board reasonably determined that inadequate value was not the only threat that Paramount's all-cash, all-shares offer could present. Time's board concluded that Paramount's offer posed other threats. One concern was that Time shareholders might elect to tender into Paramount's cash offer in ignorance or a mistaken belief of the strategic benefit which a business combination with Warner might produce.

Paramount also contends that Time's board had not duly investigated Paramount's offer. We find that Time explored the available entertainment companies, including Paramount, before determining that Warner provided the best strategic "fit." In addition, Time's board rejected Paramount's offer because Paramount did not serve Time's objectives or meet Time's needs. Time's board was adequately informed of the potential benefits of a transaction with Paramount. Time's failure to negotiate cannot be fairly found to have been uninformed. The evidence supporting this finding is materially enhanced by the fact that twelve of Time's sixteen board members were outside independent directors.

We turn to the second part of the *Unocal* analysis. The obvious requisite to determining the reasonableness of a defensive action is a clear identification of the nature of the threat. This requires an evaluation of the importance of the corporate objective threatened; alternative methods of protecting that objective; impacts of the defensive action, and other relevant factors.

The fiduciary duty to manage a corporate enterprise includes the selection of a time frame for achievement of corporate goals. Directors are not obliged to abandon a deliberately conceived corporate plan for a short-term shareholder profit unless there is clearly no basis to sustain the corporate strategy. Time's responsive action to Paramount's tender offer was not aimed at "cramming down" on its shareholders a management-sponsored alternative, but rather had as its goal the carrying forward of a pre-existing transaction in an altered form. Thus, the response was reasonably related to the threat. The revised agreement did not preclude Paramount from making an offer for the combined Time-Warner company or from changing the conditions of its offer so as not to make the offer dependent upon the nullification of the Time-Warner agreement. Thus, the response was proportionate.

**Judgment for Time affirmed.**

**The *QVC* Decision**   In February 1994, the Delaware Supreme Court confirmed its holdings in *Unocal* and *Revlon*. Some commentators have expressed that the decision also casts doubt on the future of the *Time* decision. In *Paramount Communications Inc. v. QVC Network Inc.,*[6] the Delaware Supreme Court enjoined defensive measures taken by Paramount's board of directors. The defensive tactics were designed to facilitate a friendly takeover of Paramount by Viacom Inc. (at $85 per share) and to thwart a more valuable unsolicited takeover bid by QVC (at $90 per share). The Paramount-Viacom agreement provided that Paramount's board would make Paramount's poison pill rights agreement inapplicable to Viacom's bid and grant Viacom a lock-up option to purchase almost 20 percent of Paramount's shares at a bargain price. In addition, Paramount promised to pay Viacom a termination fee of $100 million if Paramount's directors terminated the merger because of a competing transaction, if the directors recommended a competing merger, or if the shareholders failed to approve the merger. When Para-

mount's board rejected QVC's $90 offer, QVC sued Paramount to enjoin enforcement of the defense tactics preferring Viacom.

The Delaware Supreme Court pointed out that the Paramount-Viacom merger would result in a transfer of control of Paramount from public shareholders to a single shareholder, with the public shareholders receiving a minority voting position in the surviving company. Once control shifted, the public shareholders would have no leverage to demand another premium for transferring control to the majority shareholder. As a result, the Delaware court held that the public shareholders of Paramount were entitled to receive "a control premium and/or protective devices of significant value." The court held that when a corporation undertakes a transaction that will cause a change in corporate control, the directors have an obligation "to seek the best value reasonably available to the shareholders." Having decided to sell control of Paramount, the directors were obligated "to evaluate critically whether or not all material aspects of the Paramount-Viacom merger (separately and in the aggregate) were reasonable and in the best interests of the public stockholders."

[6] 637 A.2d 34 (Del. Sup. Ct. 1994).

Applying the standard above, the Delaware Supreme Court found that the Paramount directors' process was not reasonable and the result achieved for the shareholders was not reasonable. The court ruled that the Paramount directors had the opportunity to improve the economic terms of the Paramount-Viacom transaction, but failed to do so, ultimately squandering their "final opportunity to negotiate on the stockholders' behalf and to fulfill their obligation to seek the best value reasonably available." Rather than taking advantage of the opportunity, the Paramount directors "chose to wall themselves off from material information that was reasonably available and to hide behind defensive measures as a rationalization for refusing to negotiate with QVC or seeking other alternatives." Consequently, the Delaware Supreme Court affirmed the lower court's grant of a preliminary injunction.

It is difficult at this time to assess the importance of the *QVC* decision. The ruling may signal a retreat from the Delaware court's decision in *Time,* which emphasized the need to defer to directors' judgments regarding long-term strategy and granted boards wide latitude to ignore unsolicited bids after a friendly merger was announced. The *QVC* decision may indicate that when there are two bids for a company, the board should not stand in the way of only one of them.

## Duties of Loyalty

Directors and officers owe a duty of **utmost loyalty and fidelity** to the corporation. Judge Benjamin Cardozo stated this duty of trust. He declared that a director:

owes loyalty and allegiance to the corporation—a loyalty that is undivided and an allegiance that is influenced by no consideration other than the welfare of the corporation. Any adverse interest of a director will be subjected to a scrutiny rigid and uncompromising. He may not profit at the expense of his corporation and in conflict with its rights; he may not for personal gain divert unto himself the opportunities which in equity and fairness belong to his corporation.[7]

Directors and officers owe the corporation the same duties of loyalty that agents owe their principals, though many of these duties have special names in

corporation law. The most important of these duties of loyalty are the duties not to *self-deal,* not to *usurp a corporate opportunity,* not to *oppress minority shareholders,* and not to *trade on inside information.*

## Self-Dealing with the Corporation

When a director or officer *self-deals* with his corporation, the director or officer has a **conflict of interest** and may prefer his own interests over those of the corporation. The director's or officer's interest may be *direct,* such as his interest in selling his land to the corporation, or it may be *indirect,* such as his interest in having another business of which he is an owner, director, or officer supply goods to the corporation. When a director has a conflict of interest, the director's transaction with the corporation may be voided or rescinded.

Under the MBCA, a self-dealing transaction will not be voided merely on the grounds of a director's conflict of interest when *any one* of the following is true:

1. The transaction has been approved by a majority of informed, disinterested directors,
2. The transaction has been approved by a majority of the shares held by informed, disinterested shareholders, or
3. The transaction is fair to the corporation.

Nonetheless, even when disinterested directors' or shareholders' approval has been obtained, courts will void a conflict-of-interest transaction that is unfair to the corporation. Therefore, every corporate transaction in which a director has a conflict of interest must be fair to the corporation. If the transaction is fair, the self-dealing (interested) director is excused from liability to the corporation. A transaction is fair if reasonable persons in an *arm's-length bargain* would have bound the corporation to it. This standard is often called the **intrinsic fairness standard.**

The function of disinterested director or disinterested shareholder approval of a conflict-of-interest transaction is merely to shift the burden of proving unfairness. Under the MBCA, the burden of proving fairness lies initially on the interested director. The burden of proof shifts to the corporation that is suing the officer or director for self-dealing if the transaction was approved by the board of directors or the shareholders. Nonetheless, when disinterested directors approve a self-dealing transaction, substantial

---

[7]*Meinhard v. Salmon,* 164 N.E.2d 545, 546 (N.Y. Ct. App. 1928).

deference is given to the decision in accordance with the business judgment rule, especially when the disinterested directors compose a majority of the board.

Generally, *unanimous* approval of a self-dealing transaction by informed shareholders *conclusively* releases an interested director or officer from liability for self-dealing even if the transaction is unfair to the corporation. The rationale for this rule is that fully informed shareholders should know what is best for themselves and their corporation.

**Loans to Directors**  Under early corporation law, *loans* by the corporation *to directors* or *officers* were illegal, on the grounds that such loans might result in the looting of corporate assets. The MBCA allows loans to directors only after certain procedures have been followed. Either the shareholders must approve the loan, or the directors, after finding that the loan benefits the corporation, must approve it.

**Parent-Subsidiary Transactions**  Self-dealing is a concern when a parent corporation *dominates* a subsidiary corporation. Often, the subsidiary's directors will be directors or officers of the parent also. When persons with dual directorships approve transactions between the parent and the subsidiary, the opportunity for *overreaching* arises. There may be *no arm's-length bargaining* between the two corporations. Hence, such transactions must meet the *intrinsic fairness* test.

## Usurpation of a Corporate Opportunity

Directors and officers may steal not only assets of their corporations (such as computer hardware and software) but also *opportunities* that their corporations could have exploited. Both types of theft are equally wrongful. As fiduciaries, directors and officers are liable to their corporation for **usurping corporate opportunities.**

The opportunity must come to the director or officer *in her corporate capacity.* Clearly, opportunities received at the corporate offices are received by the manager in her corporate capacity. In addition, courts hold that CEOs and other high-level officers are nearly always acting in their corporate capacities, even when they are away from their corporate offices.

The opportunity must have a *relation or connection* to an *existing or prospective* corporate activity. Some courts apply the *line of business test*, considering how closely related the opportunity is to the lines of business in which the corporation is engaged. Other courts use the *interest or expectancy test*, requiring the opportunity to relate to property in which the corporation has an existing interest or in which it has an expectancy growing out of an existing right.

The corporation must be *able financially* to take advantage of the opportunity. Managers are required to make a good faith effort to obtain external financing for the corporation, but they are not required to use their personal funds to enable the corporation to take advantage of the opportunity.

A director or officer is free to exploit an opportunity that has been rejected by the corporation.

In the following case, the court found that an opportunity to become the manufacturer of Pepsi-Cola syrup was usurped by the president of a corporation that manufactured beverage syrups and operated soda fountains.

### GUTH V. LOFT, INC.
**5 A.2d 503 (Del. Sup. Ct. 1939)**

Loft, Inc., manufactured and sold candies, syrups, and beverages and operated 115 retail candy and soda fountain stores. Loft sold Coca-Cola at all of its stores, but it did not manufacture Coca-Cola syrup. Instead, it purchased its 30,000-gallon annual requirement of syrup and mixed it with carbonated water at its various soda fountains.

In May 1931, Charles Guth, the president and general manager of Loft, became dissatisfied with the price of Coca-Cola syrup and suggested to Loft's vice president that Loft buy Pepsi-Cola syrup from National

Pepsi-Cola Company, the owner of the secret formula and trademark for Pepsi-Cola. The vice president said he was investigating the purchase of Pepsi syrup.

Before being employed by Loft, Guth had been asked by the controlling shareholder of National Pepsi, Megargel, to acquire the assets of National Pepsi. Guth refused at that time. However, a few months after Guth had suggested that Loft purchase Pepsi syrup, Megargel again contacted Guth about buying National Pepsi's secret formula and trademark for only $10,000. This time, Guth agreed to the purchase, and Guth and Megargel organized a new corporation, Pepsi-Cola Company, to acquire the Pepsi-Cola secret formula and trademark from National Pepsi. Eventually, Guth and his family's corporation owned a majority of the shares of Pepsi-Cola Company.

Very little of Megargel's or Guth's funds were used to develop the business of Pepsi-Cola. Instead, without the knowledge or consent of Loft's board of directors, Guth used Loft's working capital, its credit, its plant and equipment, and its executives and employees to produce Pepsi-Cola syrup. In addition, Guth's domination of Loft's board of directors ensured that Loft would become Pepsi-Cola's chief customer.

By 1935, the value of Pepsi-Cola's business was several million dollars. Loft sued Guth, asking the court to order Guth to transfer to Loft his shares of Pepsi-Cola Company and to pay Loft the dividends he had received from Pepsi-Cola Company. The trial court found that Guth had usurped a corporate opportunity and ordered Guth to transfer the shares and to pay Loft the dividends. Guth appealed.

---

**Layton, Chief Justice**    Public policy demands of a corporate officer or director the most scrupulous observance of his duty to refrain from doing anything that would deprive the corporation of profit or advantage. The rule that requires an undivided and unselfish loyalty to the corporation demands that there shall be no conflict between duty and self-interest.

The real issue is whether the opportunity to secure a very substantial stock interest in a corporation to be formed for the purpose of exploiting a cola beverage on a wholesale scale was so closely associated with the existing business activities of Loft, and so essential thereto, as to bring the transaction within that class of cases where the acquisition of the property would throw the corporate officer purchasing it into competition with his company.

Guth suggests a doubt whether Loft would have been able to finance the project. The answer to this suggestion is two-fold. Loft's net asset position was amply sufficient to finance the enterprise, and its plant, equipment, executives, personnel and facilities were adequate. The second answer is that Loft's resources were found to be sufficient, for Guth made use of no other resources to any important extent.

Guth asserts that Loft's primary business was the manufacturing and selling of candy in its own chain of retail stores, and that it never had the idea of turning a subsidiary product into a highly advertised, nation-wide specialty. It is contended that the Pepsi-Cola opportunity was not in the line of Loft's activities, which essentially were of a retail nature.

Loft, however, had many wholesale activities. Its wholesale business in 1931 amounted to over $800,000. It was a large company by any standard, with assets exceeding $9 million, excluding goodwill. It had an enormous plant. It paid enormous rentals. Guth, himself, said that Loft's success depended upon the fullest utilization of its large plant facilities. Moreover, it was a manufacturer of syrups and, with the exception of cola syrup, it supplied its own extensive needs. Guth, president of Loft, was an able and experienced man in that field. Loft, then, through its own personnel, possessed the technical knowledge, the practical business experience, and the resources necessary for the development of the Pepsi-Cola enterprise. Conceding that the essential of an opportunity is reasonably within the scope of a corporation's activities, latitude should be allowed for development and expansion. To deny this would be to deny the history of industrial development.

We cannot agree that Loft had no concern or expectancy in the opportunity. Loft had a practical and essential concern with respect to some cola syrup with an established formula and trademark. A cola beverage has come to be a business necessity for soft drink establishments; and it was essential to the success of Loft to serve at its soda fountains an acceptable five-cent cola drink in order to attract into its stores the great multitude of people who have formed the habit of drinking cola beverages.

When Guth determined to discontinue the sale of Coca-Cola in the Loft stores, it became, by his own act, a matter of urgent necessity for Loft to acquire a constant supply of some satisfactory cola syrup, secure against probable attack, as a replacement; and when the Pepsi-Cola opportunity presented itself, Guth having already considered the availability of the syrup, it became impressed with a Loft interest and expectancy arising out of the circumstances and the urgent and practical need created by him as the directing head of Loft.

The fiduciary relation demands something more than the morals of the marketplace. Guth did not offer the Pepsi-Cola opportunity to Loft, but captured it for himself. He invested little or no money of his own in the venture, but commandeered for his own benefit and advantage the money, resources, and facilities of his corporation and the services of his officials. He thrust upon Loft the hazard, while he reaped the benefit. In such a manner he acquired for himself 91 percent of the capital stock of Pepsi-Cola, now worth many millions. A genius in his line he may be, but the law makes no distinction between the wrongdoing genius and the one less endowed.

**Judgment for Loft affirmed.**

## Oppression of Minority Shareholders

Directors and officers owe a duty to manage a corporation in the best interests of the corporation and the shareholders as a whole. When, however, a group of shareholders has been isolated for beneficial treatment to the detriment of another isolated group of shareholders, the disadvantaged group may complain of **oppression.**

For example, oppression may occur when directors of a close corporation who are also the majority shareholders pay themselves high salaries yet refuse to pay dividends or to hire minority shareholders as employees of the corporation. Since there is no market for the shares of a close corporation (apart from selling to the other shareholders), these oppressed minority shareholders have investments that provide them no return. They receive no dividends or salaries, and they can sell their shares only to the other shareholders, who are usually unwilling to pay the true value of the shares.

Generally, courts treat oppression of minority shareholders the same way courts treat director self-dealing: The transaction must be intrinsically fair to the corporation and the minority shareholders.

A special form of oppression is the **freeze-out.** A freeze-out is usually accomplished by merging a corporation with a newly formed corporation under terms by which the minority shareholders do not receive shares of the new corporation but instead receive only cash or other securities. The minority shareholders are thereby *frozen out as shareholders.*

**Going private** is a special term for a freeze-out of shareholders of *publicly owned corporations.* Some public corporations discover that the burdens of public ownership—such as the periodic disclosure requirements of the SEC—exceed the benefits of being public. Many of these publicly owned companies choose to freeze out their minority shareholders to avoid such burdens. Often, going private transactions appear abusive because the corporation goes public at a high price and goes private at a much lower price.

Some courts have adopted a fairness test and a business purpose test for freeze-outs. Most states apply the **total fairness test** to freeze-outs. In the freeze-out context, total fairness has two basic aspects: *fair dealing* and *fair price.* Fair dealing requires disclosing material information to directors and shareholders and providing an opportunity for negotiation. A determination of fair value requires the consideration of all the factors relevant to the value of the shares, except speculative projections.

Some states apply the **business purpose test** to freeze-outs. This test requires that the freeze-out accomplish some legitimate business purpose and not serve the special interests of the majority shareholders or the managers.

Other states place no restrictions on freeze-outs provided a shareholder has a **right of appraisal,** which permits a shareholder to require the corporation to purchase his shares at a fair price.

In addition, the SEC requires a *publicly held* company to make a statement on the fairness of its proposed going private transaction and to discuss in detail the material facts on which the statement is based.

In the next case, the court required that a freeze-out of minority shareholders of the New England Patriots football team meet both the business purpose and intrinsic fairness tests. The court held that freezing out the minority shareholders merely to allow the corporation to repay the majority shareholder's personal debts was not a proper business purpose.

---

## COGGINS V. NEW ENGLAND PATRIOTS FOOTBALL CLUB, INC.
### 492 N.E.2d 1112 (Mass. Sup. Jud. Ct. 1986)

In 1959, the New England Patriots Football Club, Inc. (Old Patriots), was formed with one class of voting shares and one class of nonvoting shares. Each of the original 10 voting shareholders, including William H. Sullivan, purchased 10,000 voting shares for $2.50 per share. The 120,000 nonvoting shares were sold for $5 per share to the general public in order to generate loyalty to the Patriots football team. In 1974, Sullivan was ousted as president of Old Patriots. In November 1975, Sullivan succeeded in regaining control of Old Patriots by purchasing all 100,000 voting shares for $102 per share. He again became a director and president of Old Patriots.

To finance his purchase of the voting shares, Sullivan borrowed $5,350,000 from two banks. The banks insisted that Sullivan reorganize Old Patriots so that its income could be used to repay the loans made to Sullivan and its assets used to secure the loans. To make the use of Old Patriots' income and assets legal, it was necessary to freeze out the nonvoting shareholders. In November 1976, Sullivan organized a new corporation called the New Patriots Football Club, Inc. (New Patriots). Sullivan was the sole shareholder of New Patriots. In December 1976, the shareholders of Old Patriots approved a merger of Old Patriots and New Patriots. Under the terms of the merger, Old Patriots went out of business, New Patriots assumed the business of Old Patriots, Sullivan became the only owner of New Patriots, and the nonvoting shareholders of Old Patriots received $15 for each share they owned.

David A. Coggins, a Patriots fan from the time of its formation and owner of 10 Old Patriots nonvoting shares, objected to the merger and refused to accept the $15 per share payment for his shares. Coggins sued Sullivan and Old Patriots to obtain rescission of the merger. The trial judge found the merger to be illegal and ordered the payment of damages to Coggins and all other Old Patriots shareholders who voted against the merger and had not accepted the $15 per share merger payment. Sullivan and Old Patriots appealed to the Massachusetts Supreme Judicial Court.

---

**Liacos, Justice** When the director's duty of loyalty to the corporation is in conflict with his self-interest, the court will vigorously scrutinize the situation. The dangers of self-dealing and abuse of fiduciary duty are greatest in freeze-out situations like the Patriots merger, when a controlling shareholder and corporate director chooses to eliminate public ownership. Because the danger of abuse of fiduciary duty is especially great in a freeze-out merger, the court must be satisfied that the freeze-out was for the advancement of a legitimate corporate purpose. If satisfied that elimination of public ownership is in furtherance of a business purpose, the court should then proceed to determine if the transaction was fair by examining the totality of the circumstances. Consequently, Sullivan and Old Patriots bear the burden of proving, first, that the merger was for a legitimate business purpose, and second, that, considering the totality of circumstances, it was fair to the minority.

Sullivan and Old Patriots have failed to demonstrate that the merger served any valid corporate objective unrelated to the personal interests of Sullivan, the majority shareholder. The sole reason for the merger was to effectuate a restructuring of Old Patriots that would enable the repayment of the personal indebtedness incurred by Sullivan. Under the approach we set forth above, there is no need to consider further the elements of fairness of a transaction that is not related to a valid corporate purpose.

**Judgment for Coggins affirmed as modified.**

## Trading on Inside Information

Officers and directors have *confidential access* to nonpublic information about the corporation. Sometimes, directors and officers purchase their corporation's securities with knowledge of confidential information. Often, disclosure of previously nonpublic, **inside information** affects the value of the corporation's securities. Therefore, directors and officers may make a profit when the prices of the securities increase after the inside information has been disclosed publicly. Shareholders of the corporation claim that they have been harmed by such activity, either because the directors and officers misused confidential information that should have been used only for corporate purposes or because the directors and officers had an unfair informational advantage over the shareholders.

In this century, there has been a judicial trend toward finding a duty of directors and officers to disclose information that they have received confidentially from the corporation before they buy or sell the corporation's securities. As will be discussed fully in Chapter 37, Securities Regulation, the illegality of insider trading is already federal law under the Securities Exchange Act; however, it remains only a minority rule under state corporation law.

## Director's Right to Dissent

A director who assents to an action of the board of directors may be held liable for the board's exceeding its authority or its failing to meet its duty of due care or loyalty. A director who attends a board meeting is deemed to have assented to any action taken at the meeting, unless he dissents.

Under the MBCA, to register his **dissent** to a board action, and thereby to protect himself from liability, the director must **not vote in favor** of the action and **must make his position clear** to the other board members. His position is made clear either by requesting that his dissent appear in the minutes or by giving written notice of his dissent to the chairman of the board at the meeting or to the secretary immediately after the meeting. These procedures ensure that the dissenting director will attempt to dissuade the board from approving an imprudent action.

Generally, directors are not liable for failing to attend meetings. However, a director is liable for *continually failing* to attend meetings, with the result that the director is unable to prevent the board from harming the corporation by its self-dealing.

## DUTIES OF DIRECTORS AND OFFICERS OF NONPROFIT CORPORATIONS

Directors and officers of nonprofit corporations owe fiduciary duties to their corporations that are similar to the duties owed by managers of for-profit corporations. Directors and officers owe a duty of care and duties of loyalty to the nonprofit corporation. They must act in good faith, with the care of an ordinarily prudent person, and with a reasonable belief that they are acting in the best interests of the corporation. In addition, a director should not have a conflict of interest in any transaction of the nonprofit corporation. As with for-profit corporations, conflict-of-interest transactions must meet the intrinsic fairness standard. Finally, a nonprofit corporation may not lend money to a director.

Liability concerns of directors of nonprofit corporations, especially public benefit corporations in which directors typically receive no compensation, have made it difficult for some nonprofit corporations to find and retain directors. Therefore, the Model Nonprofit Corporation Act permits nonprofit corporations to limit or eliminate the liability of directors for breach of the duty of care. The articles may not limit or eliminate a director's liability for failing to act in good faith, engaging in intentional misconduct, breaching the duty of loyalty, or having a conflict of interest.

## CORPORATE AND MANAGEMENT LIABILITY FOR TORTS AND CRIMES

When directors, officers, and other employees of the corporation commit torts and crimes while conducting corporate affairs, the issue arises concerning who has liability. Should the individuals committing the torts and crimes be held liable, the corporation, or both?

### Liability of the Corporation

For torts, the vicarious liability rule of *respondeat superior* applies to corporations. The only issue is whether an employee acted within the scope of her employment, which encompasses not only acts the employee is authorized to commit but may also include acts that the employee is expressly instructed to avoid.

The traditional view was that a corporation could not be guilty of a crime because criminal guilt required intent. A corporation, not having a mind, could form no intent. Other courts held that a corporation was not a person for purposes of criminal liability.

Today, few courts have difficulty holding corporations liable for crimes. Modern criminal statutes either expressly provide that corporations may commit crimes or define the term *person* to include corporations. In addition, some criminal statutes designed to protect the public welfare do not require intent as an element of some crimes, thereby removing the grounds used by early courts to justify relieving corporations of criminal liability.

Courts are especially likely to impose criminal liability on a corporation when the criminal act is requested, authorized, or performed by:

1. The board of directors.
2. An officer.
3. Another person having responsibility for formulating company policy.
4. A high-level administrator having supervisory responsibility over the subject matter of the offense and acting within the scope of his employment.

In addition, courts hold a corporation liable for crimes of its agent or employee committed within the scope of his authority, even if a higher corporate official has no knowledge of the act and has not ratified it.

## DIRECTORS' AND OFFICERS' LIABILITY FOR TORTS AND CRIMES

A person is always *liable for his own torts and crimes,* even when committed on behalf of his principal. Every person in our society is expected to exercise independent judgment and not merely to follow orders. Therefore, directors and officers are personally liable when they commit torts or crimes during the performance of their corporate duties.

A director or officer is usually not liable for the torts of employees of the corporation, since the corporation, not the director or the officer, is the principal. He will have **tort** liability, however, if he *authorizes* the tort or *participates* in its commission. A director or officer has **criminal** liability if she *requests, authorizes, conspires,* or *aids and abets* the commission of a crime by an employee.

In the next case, the court considered the criminal liability of a corporation and its officers.

---

## UNITED STATES V. CATTLE KING PACKING CO., INC.
**793 F.2d 232 (10th Cir. 1986)**

On June 1, 1981, Butch Stanko started a meatpacking plant in Adams County, Colorado, under the name of Cattle King Packing Company, Inc. Stanko was an officer and shareholder of Cattle King. Gary Waderich was a general sales manager primarily responsible for commercial sales of meat food products and for the daily operation of Cattle King. Stanko set company policies and practices to circumvent the Federal Meat Inspection Act (FMIA), which policies and practices he instructed Waderich and other employees to follow. When Stanko returned to his home in Scottsbluff, Nebraska, he monitored operations by phone and visits to the plant to make certain that the policies and practices that he had established were being followed.

Among the violations of the Federal Meat Inspection Act were the following:

1. Stanko gave a Cattle King employee directions on how, when the government inspector was not around, to mix inedible scrap with edible meat and thereby increase the poundage of the meat.
2. When a shipment of meat was rejected by a grocer and returned to Cattle King, Waderich instructed an employee to rebox the meat and resell it, without government inspection. (The FMIA required all returned meat to be government inspected.) When a government veterinarian came on the reboxing scene and demanded to know what was going on, Waderich denied he knew of the reboxing. Later, Waderich told another employee, "Well, we tried, but we got caught."
3. Cattle King employees dated meat the date it was shipped rather than the date it was produced, as required by the FMIA.
4. Spoiled meat rejected by a buyer and returned to Cattle King was in bags that were puffy with gas caused by the spoilage. On instructions by Waderich, an employee reworked the meat by poking the bags to release the gas, and the meat was reshipped to the same buyer.

The U.S. Attorney General prosecuted Waderich, Stanko, and Cattle King for criminal violations of the FMIA. The jury convicted them, and all three defendants appealed.

---

**McWilliams, Circuit Judge** There is little doubt that Cattle King's operation violated federal meat inspection law at about every turn. Cattle King employees adulterated the meat, misdated the meat, and evaded federal inspection when rejected meat was returned to the plant. Cattle King employees also reworked the returned meat and resold it. Because this activity directly involved Gary Waderich, his challenge of the sufficiency of the evidence must clearly fail.

Stanko would make much of the fact that he returned to Scottsbluff, Nebraska in February 1982, and points out that all of the crimes occurred after that date. He would have us believe that he was somehow insulated from transactions occurring in Colorado when he was in Nebraska. This is an overly simplistic view of the matter. The fact that Stanko was in Scottsbluff does not absolve him of the criminal acts, for example of Waderich, which were committed pursuant to instructions from Stanko himself.

As a variation on his "I-was-in-Scottsbluff" defense, Stanko charges that the trial court's reliance on *United States v. Park* (1975) was error. The rationale of the Supreme Court's decision in *Park* is based upon this premise: Companies that engage in the food business, and the people who manage them, have an affirmative duty to insure that the food they sell to the public is safe. Accordingly, a corporate officer, who is in a "responsible relationship" to

some activity within a company that violates federal food laws, can be held criminally responsible even though that officer did not personally engage in that activity. The trial court gave the jury the opportunity to decide whether Butch Stanko was responsible for Cattle King's violations of federal meat inspection laws. The jury found that he was.

In any event, this is not an instance where Stanko was in Scottsbluff, Nebraska, *not* knowing what his employees were doing in Colorado. Rather, Stanko set in motion the very acts which were carried out, pursuant to his direction, by his employees. Scottsbluff is not a shield for Stanko.

The trial court instructed the jury that Cattle King could be found guilty only if one of its agents committed the crimes, and the other three elements were met:

1. The agent was acting within the scope of his or her employment.
2. The agent was authorized to do the act.
3. The agent was motivated, at least in part, to benefit the corporation.

Gary Waderich, an officer of Cattle King, was personally responsible for the commission of all the crimes. Given Waderich's position within Cattle King, there is no doubt that elements 1 and 2 are met. As for element 3, there is also no doubt that Cattle King benefited by the commission of these crimes. The principal effect of all the crimes committed was that Cattle King reaped great economic rewards. Selling meat which should be condemned, misdating boxes so that meat could be stockpiled and thus produced more cheaply, all directly benefited Cattle King economically. There is, therefore, sufficient evidence that Cattle King, as a company, is also guilty of all the crimes.

**Judgment convicting Waderich, Stanko, and Cattle King affirmed.**

## INSURANCE AND INDEMNIFICATION

The extensive potential liability of directors deters many persons from becoming directors. They fear that their liability for their actions as directors may far exceed their fees as directors. To encourage persons to become directors, corporations **indemnify** them for their outlays associated with defending lawsuits brought against them and paying judgments and settlement amounts. In addition, or as an alternative, corporations purchase **insurance** that will make such payments for the directors. Indemnification and insurance are provided for officers, also.

### Mandatory Indemnification of Directors

Under the MBCA, a director is entitled to *mandatory indemnification* of her reasonable litigation expenses when she is sued and *wins completely* (is *wholly successful*). The greatest part of such expenses is attorney's fees. Because indemnification is mandatory in this context, when the corporation refuses to indemnify a director who has won completely, she may ask a court to order the corporation to indemnify her.

### Permissible Indemnification of Directors

Under the MBCA, a director who loses a lawsuit *may* be indemnified by the corporation. This is called *permissible indemnification,* because the corporation is permitted to indemnify the director but is not required to do so.

The corporation must establish that the director acted in *good faith* and reasonably believed that she acted in the *best interests* of the corporation. When a director seeks indemnification for a *criminal* fine, the corporation must establish a third requirement—that the director had no reasonable cause to believe that her conduct was unlawful. Finally, any permissible indemnification must be approved by someone independent of the director receiving indemnification—a disinterested board of directors, disinterested shareholders, or independent legal counsel. Permissible indemnification may cover not only the director's reasonable expenses but also fines and damages that the director has been ordered to pay.

A corporation may not elect to indemnify a director who was found to have received a *financial benefit* to which he was not entitled. Such a rule tends to prevent indemnification of directors who acted from self-interest. If a director received no financial benefit but was held liable to his corporation or paid an amount to the corporation as part of a *settlement,* the director may be indemnified only for his reasonable expenses, not for the amount that he paid to the corporation. The purpose of these rules is to avoid the circularity of having the director pay damages to the corporation and then having the corporation indemnify the director for the same amount of money.

**Advances**    A director may not be able to afford to make payments to her lawyer prior to the end of a lawsuit. More important, a lawyer may refuse to defend a director who cannot pay legal fees. Therefore, the MBCA permits a corporation to make advances to a director to allow the director to afford a lawyer, if the director affirms that she meets the requirements for permissible indemnification and she promises to repay the advances if she is found not entitled to indemnification.

**Court-Ordered Indemnification**    A court may order a corporation to indemnify a director if it determines that the director meets the standard for *mandatory* indemnification or if the director is *fairly and reasonably* entitled to indemnification in view of all the relevant circumstances.

**Indemnification of Nondirectors** Under the MBCA, officers and employees who are not directors are entitled to the same mandatory indemnification rights as directors.

## Insurance

The MBCA does not limit the ability of a corporation to purchase insurance on behalf of its directors, officers, and employees. Insurance companies, however, are unwilling to insure all risks. In addition, some risks are *legally uninsurable as against public policy*. Therefore, liability for misconduct such as self-dealing, usurpation, and securities fraud is uninsurable.

## Nonprofit Corporations

A nonprofit corporation may obtain insurance and indemnify its officers and directors for liabilities incurred in the course of their performance of their official duties. The MNCA requires indemnification when the director or officer wins the lawsuit completely. A corporation is permitted to indemnify an officer or director who is found liable if he acted in good faith and reasonably believed he acted in the best interests of the corporation.

### PROBLEMS AND PROBLEM CASES

1. A ballot in the San Francisco city election included Proposition T, which would prohibit the construction of any building more than 72 feet high unless plans for the proposed building were approved in advance by the voters. Pacific Gas & Electric Company's (PG&E) management concluded that the proposition would raise its property taxes by an estimated $380,000 in the first year and by as much as $1,135,000 per year in 10 years and that the proposition would also require redesigning and obtaining additional land for an already planned electric power substation. Consequently, the executive committee approved a $10,000 political contribution to a group opposing Proposition T. Neither PG&E's articles of incorporation nor the laws of California expressly permitted PG&E to make political donations. Is the contribution *ultra vires*?

2. Pilot House Motor Inns, Inc., issued demand promissory notes for $540,000 to Marvin Herko-

witz. No meeting of the directors was held to approve the issuance of the notes, but minutes of a supposed meeting at which the corporation resolved to issue the notes was signed by all the directors. The minutes stated, "We, the undersigned directors, hereby ratify and confirm the actions reflected in the foregoing minutes." Has the board officially acted to authorize the issuance of the notes?

3. Lillian Pritchard was a director of Pritchard & Baird Corporation, a business founded by her husband. After the death of her husband, her sons took control of the corporation. For two years, they looted the assets of the corporation through theft and improper payments. The corporation's financial statements revealed the improper payments to the sons, but Mrs. Pritchard did not read the financial statements. She did not know what her sons were doing to the corporation or that what they were doing was unlawful. When Mrs. Pritchard was sued for failing to protect the assets of the corporation, she argued that she was a figurehead director, a simple housewife who served as a director as an accommodation to her husband and sons. Was Mrs. Pritchard held liable?

4. The Chicago National League Ball Club, Inc. (Chicago Cubs), operated Wrigley Field, the Cubs' home park. Through the 1965 baseball season, the Cubs were the only major league baseball team that played no home games at night because Wrigley Field had no lights for nighttime baseball. Philip K. Wrigley, director and president of the corporation, refused to install lights because of his personal opinion that baseball was a daytime sport and that installing lights and scheduling night baseball games would result in the deterioration of the surrounding neighborhood. The other directors assented to this policy. From 1961 to 1965, the Cubs suffered losses from their baseball operations. The Chicago White Sox, whose weekday games were generally played at night, drew many more fans than did the Cubs. A shareholder sued the board of directors to force them to install lights at Wrigley Field and to schedule night games. What did the court rule?

5. Paul Brane, Kenneth Richison, Ralph Dawes, and John Thompson were directors of LaFontaine Grain Co-op, a grain elevator cooperative. Co-op hired Eldon Richison as its manager with authority to buy and sell grain, which accounted for 90 percent of its business. After Co-op

suffered a substantial loss in 1979, its independent accountant recommended to the directors that Co-op hedge its grain positions to protect itself from future losses. The directors authorized Eldon Richison to hedge for Co-op, but he was inexperienced in hedging. Moreover, the board failed to attain knowledge of the basic fundamentals of hedging to be able to direct hedging activities and supervise Eldon Richison. He hedged only $20,050 in 1980, whereas Co-op had $7,300,000 in grain sales. Co-op lost over $400,000 in 1980, due primarily to the failure to hedge. Did the directors have liability to Co-op?

**6.** The management of MacMillan Corporation recognized that it would not be able to prevent a takeover of the corporation. Therefore, management convinced the directors to authorize an auction of the company. Only two bidders emerged: Kohlberg Kravis Roberts & Co. (KKR) and Robert Maxwell. Management preferred KKR and took steps to ensure that KKR would win the auction. Only hours before the deadline for bids, MacMillan's chairman and CEO tipped KKR that Maxwell's bid was lower than KKR's. MacMillan's auctioneer understood that Maxwell would top any KKR bid yet allowed Maxwell to believe that he had made the higher bid. The board granted KKR a lock-up option of MacMillan's crown jewels—its most valuable assets. Has MacMillan's board acted properly?

**7.** CSX Corp. owned 100 percent of the stock of Chesapeake & Ohio Railway (C&O). C&O owned 98 percent of the stock of Baltimore & Ohio Railroad (B&O). B&O owed 66 percent of the stock of Western Maryland Railway Company; C&O owned 20 percent of Western Maryland. C&O also owned 100 percent of the stock of Peakbay Corporation. The directors of B&O were also the directors of C&O and Western Maryland. First Boston, an investment banking firm, prepared a study for CSX in which financial data for Western Maryland was compared with that of other railroad companies. Paul Goodwin, the senior vice president for finance for B&O and C&O, and his staff formulated a value of $55 per share for Western Maryland's stock. CSX proposed a merger of Western Maryland and Peakbay, by which each share of Western Maryland would be converted into the right to receive $55 cash or CSX common shares of equivalent value. The book value of Western Maryland shares was $63.43 per share; the market price of the shares, which were traded over-the-counter, was $31.50.

The merger was approved by the appropriate boards of directors and shareholders. B&O elected to receive cash of $64 million for its Western Maryland shares. A minority B&O shareholder sued the B&O directors, alleging that the sale price was less than B&O would have received had it solicited bids from outside parties for the controlling interest in Western Maryland. What standard did the court apply in determining whether the B&O directors acted properly? Did the directors sell the shares for insufficient consideration?

**8.** Lindenhurst Drugs, Inc., was owned equally by Allen Becker, Burton Steinberg, and Marvin Steinberg. Each was also an officer and director. The corporation operated a drugstore in leased space in the Linden Plaza Shopping Center. Burton was the manager of the drugstore. In 1979, wanting more retail space to expand their product lines, Becker and the Steinbergs offered to purchase the Ben Franklin store franchise in the Linden Plaza Shopping Center. Their offer was rejected, but the corporation still had an interest in buying the Ben Franklin store. In 1981, the Linden Plaza Shopping Center notified the corporation that its lease would not be renewed at the end of the year. Becker did not immediately inform the Steinbergs of the termination notice. He did nothing to find a new space for the store. Instead, Becker purchased the Ben Franklin store in the name of his own corporation and leased space for the Ben Franklin store from Linden Plaza Shopping Center. Has Becker done anything wrong?

**9.** Brothers Theodore and Lawrence Lerner were the only shareholders of Lerner Corporation, a real estate development and management company in Washington, D.C. Theodore owned 70 shares and Lawrence 25 shares of the corporation. Each was an officer and director. In April 1983, Lawrence discovered that Theodore was excluding Lawrence from the benefit of investment opportunities that had been developed through Lawrence's efforts and the use of the corporation's resources. Lawrence sued for judicial dissolution of the corporation. The suit was publicized in a Washington newspaper. Theodore believed that Lawrence would challenge future salary decisions and otherwise engage in behavior that would adversely affect the morale and productivity of key employees. He also believed that word of mouth and the newspaper notoriety about dissension in the corporation would cause prospective customers to prefer other real estate management companies. Theodore removed Lawrence as an officer and director and removed him from the payroll. Theodore also proposed to amend the articles to effect a 1-for-35 reverse stock split, by which Theodore's 70 shares would become 2 shares and Lawrence's 25 shares would become a fractional share. Corporation law allowed the corporation to purchase Lawrence's fractional share, which would result in Lawrence being forced to sell his interest in the corporation for $241,000. The articles amendment was approved by a majority of the outstanding shares. Lawrence sued to enjoin the reverse stock split. Should he be successful?

**10.** A school bus was returning children to their homes in Livingston County, Kentucky. Phillip Kirkham, age 10, and his sister, Windy Kirkham, age 6, left the bus and attempted to cross the highway when a truck came on the scene. The truck was owned by Fortner LP Gas Company, Inc. The driver of the truck saw the bus, geared down, applied the brakes, but failed to stop the truck. The truck struck both children, injuring Phillip and killing Windy instantly. A subsequent inspection of the truck revealed grossly defective brakes. The Commonwealth of Kentucky prosecuted the corporation for manslaughter in the second degree for causing Windy's death. The corporation claimed that it could not commit the crime of manslaughter. Was it correct?

**11.** Shareholders collectively owning 80 percent of the shares of the Bank of New Mexico Holding Company made a shareholder's buy-sell agreement. Those shareholders included directors of the corporation. One of the agreeing shareholders sued the other shareholders, including the directors, to obtain a determination of the price of the shares under the agreement. The corporation reimbursed the legal expenses of the directors who, as shareholders, were defendants in the litigation. Did the corporation act properly in indemnifying the directors?

## Capstone Questions

Weger Corporation is in the business of producing paper products, including cardboard and newsprint. It owns 800,000 acres of hardwood and evergreen forests in the Pacific northwest and has seven paper mills in that area.

Caitlin Demetz is one of 12 directors of Weger. Demetz is also the majority shareholder, chairman of the board, and chief executive officer of Hardin Forestry Company. Hardin's articles of incorporation state that its business is "to plant, cultivate, harvest, and sell trees and logs and to engage in any other business necessary to the forestry business." Hardin owns 25,000 acres of forests in Oregon and California. It sells harvested logs to paper mills throughout the world, but it does not operate its own paper mills.

During the next year, several events occur.

· Demetz negotiates a contract for Hardin to sell 12,000 pine logs to Weger.

· Demetz receives a phone call from the chairman of the board of Greenbow Corporation. The chairman states that Greenbow is willing to sell its two paper mills in Oregon to any acceptable buyer. Demetz tells Greenbow that Hardin is interested in buying the mills. A week later, Hardin's board agrees to purchase the mills for $6 million, the fair market value. Hardin's minority shareholders are examining the purchase of the mills. In addition, Weger's shareholders are concerned about the purchase.

· KRR Corporation privately informs Weger's board of directors that KRR offers to acquire 55 percent of Weger's outstanding common shares in exchange for a package of cash and KRR securities worth a total of $52 per share. The current market price of Weger common shares is $44 per share. For some time, Weger has been considering merging with a compatible business, but it has not found an acceptable partner that would allow Weger to remain an independent business that efficiently combines forestry and paper-producing activities. KRR is a conglomerate whose management has no expertise in the forestry or paper products field. KRR plans to divide Weger into two companies, one that manages forests and one that exclusively produces paper products. KRR has informed Weger's board that KRR will announce a public tender offer for Weger's common shares if Weger's board does not approve KRR's acquisition of Weger. Weger's board believes that Weger and its shareholders will be harmed if KRR acquires Weger.

· Concerned about falling lumber prices, Hardin's board of directors authorizes Demetz to meet with executives of Hardin's competitors to discuss industry pricing policy. Demetz meets secretly with the chief executive officers of five other forestry companies. The executives discuss and exchange price information. The shared pricing information is used by each of the companies to set prices. As a result, all the companies have substantially similar prices. The U.S. Department of Justice prosecutes Hardin for price-fixing under the federal antitrust laws.

· Due to exchanging Hardin's price data with the executives of Hardin's competitors, Demetz is found guilty of the crime of price-fixing under the antitrust laws and is sentenced to pay a fine of $750,000 and to serve one year in prison. Demetz seeks from Hardin permissible indemnification of the criminal fine and her legal fees of $35,000.

· If Demetz fails in her efforts to obtain permissible indemnification from Hardin, Demetz wants Hardin's board wants to freeze out Hardin's minority shareholders, leaving Demetz as the only Hardin shareholder. Demetz then plans to use Hardin's assets to pay the criminal fine.

**Required:**

Answer the following and give reasons for your conclusions.

1. To reduce the risk of Demetz being liable for breaching a fiduciary duty to Hardin or Weger from the sale of the logs, what procedures should the Weger and Hardin boards of directors follow?

2. May Hardin's shareholders prove that the purchase of the paper mills is an *ultra vires* act?

3. Does Hardin's purchase of the mills cause Demetz to breach a fiduciary duty owed to Weger?

4. What tactics are available to the Weger board to defeat KRR's takeover attempt? What rule judges the legality of the Weger board's efforts to defeat KRR's takeover?

5. Is Hardin guilty of the crime of price-fixing?

6. What are the standards for Hardin to indemnify Demetz? Is Demetz able to meet those standards?

7. By what procedure can Hardin's board freeze out the minority shareholders? What standards determine whether the freeze-out is legal?

CHAPTER

3 6

# SHAREHOLDERS' RIGHTS
# AND LIABILITIES

## INTRODUCTION

*The* shareholders *are the ultimate owners of a corporation, but a shareholder has* no right to manage *the corporation. Instead, a corporation is managed by its board of directors and its officers for the benefit of its shareholders.*

*The shareholders' role in a corporation is limited to electing and removing directors, approving certain important matters, and ensuring that the actions of the corporation's managers are consistent with the applicable state corporation statute, the articles of incorporation, and the bylaws.*

*Shareholders also assume a few responsibilities. For example, all shareholders are required to pay the promised consideration for shares. Shareholders are liable for receiving dividends beyond the lawful amount. In addition, controlling shareholders may owe special duties to minority shareholders.*

*Close corporation shareholders enjoy rights and owe duties beyond the rights and duties of shareholders of publicly owned corporations. In addition, some courts have found close corporation shareholders to be fiduciaries of each other.*

*This chapter's study of the rights and responsibilities of shareholders begins with an examination of shareholders' meetings and voting rights.*

## SHAREHOLDERS' MEETINGS

The general corporation statutes of most states and the Model Business Corporation Act (MBCA) provide that an **annual meeting of shareholders** shall be held. The purpose of an annual shareholders' meeting is to elect new directors and to conduct other necessary business. Often, the shareholders are asked to approve the corporation's independent auditors and to vote on shareholders' proposals.

**Special meetings of shareholders** may be held whenever a corporate matter arises that requires immediate shareholders' action, such as the approval of a merger that cannot wait until the next annual shareholders' meeting. Under the MBCA, a special shareholders' meeting may be called by the board of directors or by a person authorized to do so by the bylaws, usually the president or the chairman of the board. In addition, the holders of at least 10 percent of the shares entitled to vote at the meeting may call a special meeting.

## Notice of Meetings

To permit shareholders to arrange their schedules for attendance at shareholders' meetings, the MBCA requires the corporation to give shareholders **notice** of annual and special meetings of shareholders. Notice of a *special meeting* must list the purpose of the meeting. Under the MBCA, notice of an *annual meeting* need not include the purpose of the meeting unless shareholders will be asked to approve extraordinary corporate changes—for example, amendments to the articles of incorporation and mergers.

Notice need be given only to shareholders entitled to vote who are **shareholders of record** on a date fixed by the board of directors. Shareholders of record are those whose names appear on the share-transfer book of the corporation. Usually, only shareholders of record are entitled to vote at shareholders' meetings.

## Conduct of Meetings

To conduct business at a shareholders' meeting, a **quorum** of the outstanding shares must be represented at the meeting. If the approval of more than one class of shares is required, a quorum of each class of shares must be present. A quorum is a majority of shares outstanding, unless a greater percentage is established in the articles. The president or the chairman of the board usually presides at shareholders' meetings. Minutes of shareholders' meetings are usually kept by the secretary.

A majority of the votes cast at the shareholders' meeting will decide issues that are put to a vote. If the approval of more than one class of shares is required, a majority of the votes cast by each class must favor the issue. The articles may require a greater than majority vote. Ordinarily, a shareholder is entitled to cast as many votes as he has shares.

Shareholders have a right of *full participation* in shareholders' meetings. This includes the right to offer resolutions, to speak for and against proposed resolutions, and to ask questions of the officers of the corporation.

Typical shareholder resolutions are aimed at protecting or enhancing the interests of minority shareholders and promoting current social issues. Proposals have included limiting corporate charitable contributions, restricting the production of nuclear power, banning the manufacture of weapons, and requiring the protection of the environment.

## Shareholder Action without a Meeting

Generally, shareholders can act only at a properly called meeting. However, the MBCA permits shareholders to act without a meeting if *all of the shareholders entitled to vote consent in writing* to the action.

## SHAREHOLDERS' ELECTION OF DIRECTORS

The most important shareholder voting right exercised at a shareholder meeting is the right to elect the directors. Normally, directors are elected by a single class of shareholders in **straight voting**, in which each share has one vote for each new director to be elected. With straight voting, a shareholder may vote for as many nominees as there are directors to be elected; a shareholder may cast for each such nominee as many votes as she has shares. For example, in a director election in which 15 people have been nominated for 5 director positions, a shareholder with 100 shares can vote for up to 5 nominees and can cast up to 100 votes for each of those 5 nominees.

Under straight voting, the nominees with the most votes are elected. Consequently, straight voting allows a majority shareholder to elect the entire board of directors. Thus, minority shareholders are unable to elect any representatives to the board without the cooperation of the majority shareholder.

Straight voting is also a problem in close corporations in which a few shareholders own equal numbers of shares. In such corporations, no shareholder individually controls the corporation, yet if the holders of a majority of the shares act together, those holders will elect all of the directors and control the corporation. Such control may be exercised to the detriment of the other shareholders.

Two alternatives to straight voting aid minority shareholders' attempts to gain representation on the board and prevent harmful coalitions in close corporations: cumulative voting and class voting.

**Cumulative Voting**   With cumulative voting, a corporation allows a shareholder to cumulate her votes by multiplying the number of directors to be elected by the shareholder's number of shares. A shareholder may then allocate her votes among the nominees as she chooses. She may vote only for as many nominees as there are directors to be elected,

**FIGURE 1    Cumulative Voting Formula**

The formula for determining the minimum number of shares required to elect a desired number of directors under cumulative voting is:

$$X = \frac{S \times R}{D + 1} + 1$$

$X$ = Number of shares needed to elect the desired number of directors

$S$ = Total number of shares voting at the shareholders' meeting

$R$ = Number of director representatives desired

$D$ = Total number of directors to be elected at the meeting

Example: Sarah Smiles wants to elect two of the five directors of Oates Corporation. One thousand shares will be voted. In this case:

$$S = 1,000$$

$$R = 2$$

$$D = 5$$

Therefore:

$$X = 334.33$$

Fractions are ignored; thus, Sarah will need to hold at least 334 shares to be able to elect two directors.

but she may vote for fewer nominees. For example, she may choose to cast all of her votes for only one nominee.

See Figure 1 for a further explanation of the mechanics of cumulative voting.

**Classes of Shares**    A corporation may have several classes of shares. The two most common classes are *common shares* and *preferred shares*, but a corporation may have several classes of common shares and several classes of preferred shares. Many close corporations have two or more classes of common shares with different voting rights. Each class may be entitled to elect one or more directors, in order to balance power in a corporation.

For example, suppose a corporation has four directors and 100 shares held by four shareholders—each of whom owns 25 shares. With straight voting and no classes of shares, no shareholder owns enough shares to elect himself as a director, because 51 shares are necessary to elect a director. Suppose, however, that the corporation has four classes of shares, each with the right to elect one of the directors. Each class of shares is issued to only one shareholder. Now, as the sole owner of a class of shares entitling the class to elect one director, each shareholder can elect himself to the board.

## Shareholder Control Devices

While cumulative voting and class voting are two useful methods by which shareholders can allocate or acquire voting control of a corporation, there are other devices that may also be used for these purposes: voting trusts; shareholder voting agreements; and proxies, especially irrevocable proxies.

**Voting Trusts**    With a **voting trust**, shareholders transfer their shares to one or more voting trustees and receive voting trust certificates in exchange. The shareholders retain many of their rights, including the right to receive dividends, but the voting trustees vote for directors and other matters submitted to shareholders.

The purpose of a voting trust is to control the corporation through the concentration of shareholder voting power in the voting trustees, who often are participating shareholders. If several minority shareholders collectively own a majority of the shares of a corporation, they may create a voting trust and thereby control the corporation. You may ask why shareholders need a voting trust when they are in apparent agreement on how to vote their shares. The reason is that they may have disputes in the future that could prevent the shareholders from agreeing on how to vote. The voting trust ensures that the shareholder group will control the corporation despite the emergence of differences.

The MBCA limits the duration of voting trusts to 10 years, though the participating shareholders may agree to extend the term for another 10 years. Also, a voting trust must be made public, with copies of the voting trust document available for inspection at the corporation's offices.

**Shareholder Voting Agreements**   As an alternative to a voting trust, shareholders may merely agree how they will vote their shares. For example, shareholders collectively owning a majority of the shares may agree to vote for each other as directors, resulting in each being elected to the board of directors.

A shareholder voting agreement must be written; only shareholders signing the agreement are bound by it. When a shareholder refuses to vote as agreed, courts specifically enforce the agreement.

Shareholder voting agreements have two advantages over voting trusts. First, their duration may be *perpetual*. Second, they may be kept secret from the other shareholders; they usually do not have to be filed in the corporation's offices.

**Proxies**   A shareholder may appoint a **proxy** to vote his shares. If several minority shareholders collectively own a majority of the shares of a corporation, they may appoint a proxy to vote their shares and thereby control the corporation. The ordinary proxy has only a limited duration—11 months under the MBCA—unless a longer term is specified. Also, the ordinary proxy is *revocable* at any time. As a result, there is no guarantee that control agreements accomplished through the use of revocable proxies will survive future shareholder disputes.

However, a proxy is *irrevocable* if it is coupled with an interest. A proxy is coupled with an interest when, among other things, the person holding the proxy is a party to a shareholder voting agreement or a buy-and-sell agreement. The principal use of irrevocable proxies is in conjunction with shareholder voting agreements.

In the next case, the court considered the legality of a shareholder voting agreement.

SCHREIBER V. CARNEY
**447 A.2d 17 (Del. Ch. Ct. 1982)**

Texas International Airlines, Inc. (TIA), proposed a new corporate structure in order to strengthen its financial position. To effect the restructuring, TIA would merge with Texas Air Company. The merger required approval of each of the four classes of TIA shareholders. Jet Capital Corporation owned all of the shares of Class C stock. Although Jet Capital believed that the merger would benefit TIA and the other shareholders, Jet Capital would suffer adverse tax consequences if the merger was effected. Thus, Jet Capital decided to vote against the merger. Jet Capital's adverse tax burden was due to its ownership of warrants to purchase TIA shares. Jet Capital could eliminate the merger's adverse tax impact by exercising the warrants prior to the merger, an alternative that Jet Capital was unwilling to choose since it would require a cash payment of over $3 million. Beyond its shares of TIA, Jet Capital had assets of only $200,000. To borrow the $3 million at market interest rates was too expensive.

Therefore, TIA and Jet Capital agreed that TIA would loan Jet Capital $3 million at a below-market interest rate. Since Jet Capital would give the cash from the loan immediately back to TIA when it exercised the warrants, the loan had virtually no impact on TIA's cash position. As a condition of the loan, Jet Capital agreed to vote in favor of the merger. The loan agreement was approved by a majority of the shares held by shareholders other than Jet Capital. Subsequently, the merger was approved by the TIA shareholders.

Leonard Schreiber, a TIA shareholder, brought a derivative suit on behalf of TIA against TIA's directors, including Robert Carney. Schreiber argued that the loan transaction constituted vote-buying and, therefore, was an illegal voting agreement.

**Hartnett, Vice Chancellor**   There are essentially two principles regarding vote-buying that appear in the Delaware caselaw. The first is that vote-buying is illegal *per se* if its object or purpose is to defraud or disenfranchise the other shareholders.

The second principle is that vote-buying is illegal *per se* as a matter of public policy, the reason being that each shareholder should be entitled to rely upon the independent judgment of his fellow shareholders.

The agreement in question was entered into primarily to further the interests of TIA's other shareholders. Indeed, the shareholders voted overwhelmingly in favor of the loan agreement. Thus, the underlying rationale for the argument that vote-buying is illegal *per se*, as a matter of public policy, ceases to exist when measured against the undisputed reason for the transaction.

Moreover, the rationale that vote-buying is, as a matter of public policy, illegal *per se* is founded upon considerations of policy that are now outmoded as a necessary result of an evolving corporate environment. According to 5 Fletcher *Cyclopedia Corporation* (Perm.Ed.) section 2066:

The theory that each shareholder is entitled to the personal judgment of each other shareholder expressed in his vote, and that any agreement among shareholders frustrating it was invalid, is obsolete because it is both impracticable and impossible of application to modern corporations with many widely scattered shareholders.

In *Ringling Bros.-Barnum & Bailey Combined Shows v. Ringling* (1947), the Delaware Supreme Court adopted a liberal approach to voting agreements. The court stated:

Generally speaking, a shareholder may exercise wide liberality of judgment in the matter of voting, and it is not objectionable that his motives may be for personal profit, or determined by whims or caprice, so long as he violates no duty owed his fellow shareholders.

It is clear that Delaware has discarded the presumption against voting agreements. Thus, an agreement involving the transfer of share voting rights without the transfer of ownership is not necessarily illegal and each arrangement must be examined in light of its object or purpose. To hold otherwise would be to exalt form over substance. Voting agreements in whatever form, therefore, should not be considered to be illegal *per se* unless the object or purpose is to defraud or in some way disenfranchise the other shareholders. This is not to say, however, that vote-buying accomplished for some laudable purpose is automatically free from challenge. Because vote-buying is so easily susceptible of abuse, it must be viewed as a voidable transaction subject to a test for intrinsic fairness.

**Schreiber's motion for summary judgment is denied.**

## FUNDAMENTAL CORPORATE CHANGES

Other matters besides the election of directors require shareholder action, some because they make fundamental changes in the structure or business of the corporation.

Because the articles of incorporation embody the basic contract between a corporation and its shareholders, shareholders must approve most **amendments of the articles of incorporation**. For example, when the articles are amended to increase the number of authorized shares or reduce the dividend rights of preferred shareholders, shareholder approval is needed.

A **merger** is a transaction in which one corporation merges into a second corporation. Usually, the first corporation dissolves; the second corporation takes all the business and assets of both corporations and becomes liable for the debts of both corporations. Usually, the shareholders of the dissolved corporation become shareholders of the surviving corporation. Ordinarily, both corporations' shareholders must approve a merger.

A **consolidation** is similar to a merger except that both old corporations go out of existence and a new corporation takes the business, assets, and liabilities of the old corporations. Both corporations' shareholders must approve the consolidation. Modern corporate practice makes consolidations obsolete, since it is usually desirable to have one of the old corporations survive. The MBCA does not recognize consolidations. However, the effect of a consolidation can be achieved by creating a new corporation and merging the two old corporations into it.

A **share exchange** is a transaction by which one corporation becomes the owner of all of the outstanding shares of a second corporation through a *compulsory* exchange of shares: The shareholders of the second corporation are compelled to exchange their shares for shares of the first corporation. The second corporation remains in existence and becomes a wholly owned subsidiary of the first corporation. Only the selling shareholders must approve the share exchange.

A **sale of all or substantially all of the assets** of the business other than in the regular course of business must be approved by the shareholders of the selling corporation, since it drastically changes the shareholders' investment. Thus, a corporation's sale of all its real property and equipment is a sale of substantially all its assets, even though the corporation continues its business by leasing the assets back from the purchaser. However, a corporation that sells its building, but retains its machinery with the intent of continuing operations at another location, has not sold all or substantially all of its assets.

A **dissolution** is the first step in the termination of the corporation's business. The typical dissolution requires shareholder approval. Dissolution of corporations is covered more fully at the end of this chapter.

The articles of incorporation and the bylaws may require or permit other matters to be submitted for shareholder approval. For example, loans to officers, self-dealing transactions, and indemnifications of managers for litigation expenses may be approved by shareholders. Also, many of the states require shareholder approval of share option plans for high-level executive officers, but the MBCA does not.

## Procedures Required

Similar procedures must be met to effect each of the above fundamental changes. The procedures include approval of the board of directors, notice to all of the shareholders whether or not they are entitled to vote, and majority approval of the votes held by shareholders entitled to vote under the statute, articles, or bylaws. Majority approval will be insufficient if a corporation has a supermajority shareholder voting requirement, such as one requiring two-thirds approval.

If there are two or more classes of shares, the articles may provide that matters voted on by shareholders must be approved by each class substantially affected by the proposed transaction. For example, a merger may have to be approved by a

majority of the preferred shareholders and a majority of the common shareholders. As an alternative, the articles may require only the approval of the shareholders as a whole.

Under the MBCA, voting by classes is required for mergers, share exchanges, and amendments of the articles if these would substantially affect the rights of the classes. For example, the approval of preferred shareholders is required if a merger would change the dividend rights of preferred shareholders.

In many states, no approval of shareholders of the *surviving corporation* is required for a merger *if* the merger does not fundamentally alter the character of the business or substantially reduce the shareholders' voting or dividend rights.

Also, many statutes, including the MBCA, permit a merger between a parent corporation and its subsidiary without the approval of the shareholders of either corporation. Instead, the board of directors of the parent approves the merger and sends a copy of the merger plan to the subsidiary's shareholders. This simplified merger is called a **short-form merger**. It is available only if the parent owns a high percentage of the subsidiary's shares—90 percent under the MBCA and the Delaware statute.

## DISSENTERS' RIGHTS

Many times, shareholders approve a corporate action by less than a unanimous vote, indicating that some shareholders oppose the action. For the most part, the dissenting shareholders have little recourse. Their choice is to remain shareholders or to sell their shares. For close corporation shareholders, there is no choice—the dissenting close corporation shareholder has no ready market for her shares, so she will remain a shareholder.

Some corporate transactions, however, so materially change a shareholder's investment in the corporation or have such an adverse effect on the value of a shareholder's shares that it has been deemed unfair to require the dissenting shareholder either to remain a shareholder (because there is no fair market for the shares) or to suffer a loss in value when he sells his shares on a market that has been adversely affected by the news of the corporate action. Corporate law has therefore responded by creating **dissenters' rights** (a right of appraisal) for shareholders who disagree with specified fundamental corporate transactions. Dissenters' rights require the corporation to pay dissenting shareholders the *fair value* of their shares.

Under the MBCA, the dissenters' rights cover mergers, short-form mergers, share exchanges, significant amendments of the articles of incorporation, and sales of all or substantially all the assets other than in the ordinary course of business. Some statutes cover consolidations also.

A dissenting shareholder seeking payment of the fair value of his shares must have the *right to vote* on the action to which he objects; however, a shareholder of a subsidiary in a short-form merger has dissenters' rights despite his lack of voting power. In addition, the shareholder must *not vote in favor* of the transaction. The shareholder may either vote against the action or abstain from voting.

Most states' statutes exclude from dissenters' rights shares that are traded on a recognized securities exchange such as the New York Stock Exchange. Instead, these statutes expect a shareholder to sell his shares on the stock exchange if he dissents to the corporate action. The MBCA has no such exclusion, on the grounds that the market price may be adversely affected by the news of the proposed or consummated corporate action to which the shareholder objects.

Generally, a shareholder must notify the corporation of his intent to seek payment before the shareholders have voted on the action. Next, the corporation informs a dissenting shareholder how to demand payment. After the dissenting shareholder demands payment, the corporation and the shareholder negotiate a mutually acceptable price. If they cannot agree, a court will determine the fair value of the shares and order the corporation to pay that amount.

To determine fair value, most judges use the **Delaware Block Method**, a weighted average of several valuation techniques—such as market value, comparisons with other similar companies, capitalization of earnings, and book value.

In the following case, the court granted dissenters' rights to a shareholder of a corporation that sold substantially all its assets.

---

## Waters v. Double L, Inc.
### 755 P.2d 1294 (Idaho Ct. App. 1987)

Dale Waters was a minority shareholder of Double L, Inc., a business engaged in manufacturing agricultural machinery and related products. When Double L became financially distressed, the directors agreed to sell to Pioneer Astro all of Double L's real property and equipment and to issue sufficient shares to make Pioneer Astro an 80 percent shareholder of Double L. To improve Double L's financial position, Pioneer Astro agreed to pay cash for the assets and shares and to loan money to Double L. To allow Double L to continue its business, Pioneer Astro agreed to lease the purchased assets back to Double L.

At a shareholder meeting, shareholders approved the transaction with Pioneer Astro. Waters, however, abstained from voting and demanded that Double L pay him the fair value of his shares pursuant to dissenters' rights under Idaho law. When Double L refused to buy Waters's shares, Waters sued. The trial court ordered Double L to buy Waters's shares. Double L appealed.

---

**Burnett, Judge** Idaho Code section 30-1-80 lists the categories of corporate actions that trigger the right to dissent:

(a) Any shareholder of a corporation shall have the right to dissent from, and to obtain payment for his shares in the event of any of the following corporate actions:

\* \* \* \* \*

(2) Any sale, lease, exchange, or other disposition of all or substantially all of the property and assets of the corporation not made in the usual or regular course of its business.

Double L points to the fact that it retained certain assets in the form of inventory, accounts receivable, and goodwill. However, in the deposition of Lynn

Johnson, Double L's president, Johnson testified as follows:

Q: You made an agreement whereby Pioneer Astro invested heavily in Double L; is that right?
A: Yes.
Q: Pioneer Astro bought your land, your machinery, and the buildings owned by Double L?
A: Yes.
Q: Was that substantially all of your assets?
A: Yes.

Moreover, the corporation's own conduct—seeking and obtaining shareholder approval of the Pioneer Astro transaction—implicitly indicated that the transaction comprised a sale of substantially all of the corporation's assets. Had the transaction not embraced substantially all of the assets, or the transaction been in the ordinary course of business, it would not have required shareholder approval.

The corporation would have us hold that because its business continued to operate after the transaction was consummated, the transaction could not be regarded as a sale of all or substantially all of the corporation's assets. However, the mere fact that the corporation remained in business under the same name is not the critical criterion. The nature of the transaction takes precedence over its form. Our focus is upon the relationship between the assets transferred and those remaining. Here, the corporation sold all of its hard assets, retaining intangible assets of admittedly dubious value. Only by renting the hard assets back from Pioneer Astro was the corporation able to continue its operations. This is a classic "sale of assets" transaction. The corporation after the Pioneer Astro transaction was not, in any real sense, the same entity that existed before the transaction.

**Judgment for Waters affirmed.**

## SHAREHOLDERS' INSPECTION AND INFORMATION RIGHTS

Inspecting a corporation's books and records is sometimes essential to the exercise of a shareholder's rights. For example, a shareholder may be able to decide how to vote in a director election only after examining corporate financial records that reveal whether the present directors are managing the corporation profitably. Also, a close corporation shareholder may need to look at the books to determine the value of his shares.

Many corporate managers are resistant to shareholders inspecting the corporation's books and records, charging that shareholders are nuisances or that shareholders often have improper purposes for making such an inspection. Sometimes, management objects solely on the ground that it desires secrecy.

Most of the state corporation statutes specifically grant shareholders inspection rights. The purpose of these statutes is to facilitate the shareholder's inspection of the books and records of corporations whose managements resist or delay proper requests by shareholders. A shareholder's lawyer or accountant may assist the shareholder's exercise of his inspection rights.

The MBCA grants shareholders an **absolute right of inspection** of an alphabetical listing of the shareholders entitled to notice of a meeting, including the number of shares owned. Access to a shareholder list allows a shareholder to contact other shareholders about important matters such as shareholder proposals.

The MBCA also grants an absolute right of inspection of, among other things, the articles, bylaws, and minutes of shareholder meetings within the past three years.

Shareholders have a **qualified right to inspect** other records, however. To inspect accounting records, board and committee minutes, and shareholder minutes more than three years old, a shareholder must make the demand in *good faith* and have a *proper purpose*. Proper purposes include inspecting the books of account to determine the value of shares or the propriety of dividends. On the other hand, learning business secrets and aiding a competitor are clearly improper purposes.

In the next case, the court found that valuing shares and checking on allegations of corporate mismanagement were proper purposes.

## CARTER V. WILSON CONSTRUCTION CO.
### 348 S.E.2d 830 (N.C. Ct. App. 1986)

William Carter owned 317 shares of Wilson Construction Company. He also owned 20 percent of the shares of Wilson Equipment Leasing, Inc., a company that leased equipment to and engaged in other transactions with Wilson Construction. Carter worked for Wilson Construction until he resigned his position in November 1983. Immediately, he organized and became a part owner and employee of C & L Contracting, Inc., a competitor of Wilson Construction. Carter offered to sell his shares to Wilson Construction, but his offer was rejected. In 1984, Carter demanded that Wilson Construction make available to him its books, records of account, minutes, and record of shareholders, on the grounds that he had been told and believed that the financial condition of Wilson Construction had deteriorated due to improper management. In addition, he requested the information to determine the value of his shares, the financial condition of the corporation, and whether it was efficiently managed in the best interests of the corporation. Wilson Construction refused the request. Carter sued Wilson Construction and its president, Ray Wilson. The trial court ordered the corporation to make the records available to Carter and allowed Carter to recover $500 in penalties from Wilson Construction and $500 in penalties from Ray Wilson. Wilson Construction and Ray Wilson appealed.

**Johnson, Judge**    North Carolina law does not give a shareholder an absolute right of inspection and examination for a mere fishing expedition, or for a purpose not germane to the protection of his economic interest as a shareholder of the corporation. For a shareholder to have the right to visit a corporation's office and possibly disrupt its normal operation in order to inspect corporate books and records of account, his motives must be "proper." Purposes that previously have been deemed proper are the shareholder's good faith desire to (1) determine the value of his shares; (2) investigate the conduct of management; and (3) determine the financial condition of the corporation. The burden of proof rests upon Wilson Construction, if it wishes to defeat Carter's demand, to show that Carter is motivated by some improper purpose.

Here, Carter stated a proper purpose. Carter tried to sell his shares in Wilson Construction back to Wilson Construction, which declined his offer to sell. Carter had personally guaranteed the debts of Wilson Equipment Leasing, a corporation that conducted related transactions with Wilson Construction, including indemnifying its debts and extending loans. Carter had reason to believe, based upon information from Wilson Construction's management consultant, that certain purchases had not been put on the corporate books and that funds were shuffled between Wilson Equipment Leasing and Wilson Construction, and that the net worth of Wilson Construction decreased from August 1983 to August 1984. This evidence supports Carter's allegation of a proper purpose.

The evidence produced by Wilson Construction showed that Carter is currently part owner and employee of C & L Contracting. According to Ray Wilson, "We are in direct competition on all work in the Piedmont, North Carolina, that is bridge work" and to allow Carter access to the books and records of Wilson Construction "would put us at a disadvantage."

This evidence is insufficient to override the presumption that Carter is acting in good faith. The mere possibility that a shareholder may abuse his right to gain access to corporate information will not be held to justify a denial of a legal right, if such right exists in the shareholder.

**Judgment for Carter affirmed.**

Shareholders also have the right to receive from the corporation **information** that is important to their voting and investing decisions. The MBCA requires a corporation to furnish its shareholders *financial statements*, including a balance sheet, an income statement, and a statement of changes in shareholders' equity. The Securities Exchange Act of 1934 also requires publicly held companies to furnish such statements, as well as other information that is important to a shareholders' voting and investing decisions.

## PREEMPTIVE RIGHT

The market price of a shareholder's shares will be reduced if a corporation issues additional shares at a price less than the market price. In addition, a shareholder's proportionate voting, dividend, and liquidation rights may be adversely affected by the issuance of additional shares. For example, if a corporation's only four shareholders each own 100 shares worth $10 per share, then each shareholder has shares worth $1,000, a 25 percent interest in any dividends declared, 25 percent of the voting power, and a claim against 25 percent of the corporation's assets after creditors' claims have been satisfied. If the corporation subsequently issues 100 shares to another person for only $5 per share, the value of each shareholder's shares falls to $900 and his dividend, voting, and liquidation rights are reduced to 20 percent. In a worse scenario, the corporation issues 201 shares to one of the existing shareholders, giving that shareholder majority control of the corporation and reducing the other shareholders' interests to less than 17 percent each. As a result, the minority shareholders will be dominated by the majority shareholder and will receive a greatly reduced share of the corporation's dividends.

Such harmful effects of an issuance could have been prevented if the corporation had been required to offer each existing shareholder a percentage of the new shares equal to her current proportionate ownership. If, for example, in the situation described above, the corporation had offered 50 shares to each shareholder, each shareholder could have remained a 25 percent owner of the corporation; her interests in the corporation would not have been reduced, and her total wealth would not have been decreased.

Corporation law recognizes the importance of giving a shareholder the option of maintaining the value of his shares and retaining his proportionate interest in the corporation. This is the shareholder's **preemptive right**, an option to subscribe to a new issuance of shares in proportion to the shareholder's current interest in the corporation.

The MBCA adopts a comprehensive scheme for determining preemptive rights. It provides that the preemptive right does not exist except to the extent provided by the articles. The MBCA permits the corporation to state expressly when the preemptive right arises.

When the preemptive right exists, the corporation must notify a shareholder of her option to buy shares, the number of shares that she is entitled to buy, the price of the shares, and when the option must be exercised. Usually, the shareholder is issued a **right**, a written option that she may exercise herself or sell to a person who wishes to buy the shares.

## DISTRIBUTIONS TO SHAREHOLDERS

During the life of a corporation, shareholders may receive distributions of the corporation's assets. Most people are familiar with one type of distribution—dividends—but there are other important types of distributions to shareholders, including payments to shareholders upon the corporation's repurchase of its shares.

There is one crucial similarity among all the types of distributions to shareholders: Corporate assets are transferred to shareholders. Consequently, an asset transfer to shareholders may harm the corporation's creditors and others with claims against the corporation's assets. For example, a distribution of assets may impair a corporation's ability to pay its creditors. In addition, a distribution to one class of shareholders may harm another class of shareholders that has a liquidation priority over the class of shareholders receiving the distribution. The existence of these potential harms compels corporation law to restrict the ability of corporations to make distributions to shareholders.

### Dividends

One important objective of a business corporation is to make a profit. Shareholders invest in a corporation primarily to share in the expected profit either through appreciation of the value of their shares or through dividends. There are two types of dividends: *cash or property dividends* and *share dividends*. Only cash or property dividends are distributions of the corporation's assets. Share dividends are *not* distributions.

**Cash or Property Dividends**   Dividends are usually paid in cash. However, other assets of the corporation—such as airline discount coupons or shares of another corporation—may also be distributed as dividends. Cash or property dividends are declared by the board of directors and paid by the corporation on the date stated by the directors. Once declared, dividends are *debts* of the corporation and shareholders may sue to force payment of the dividends. The board's dividend declaration, including the amount of dividend and whether to

declare a dividend, is protected by the business judgment rule.

Preferred shares nearly always have a set dividend rate stated in the articles of incorporation. Even so, unless the preferred dividend is mandatory, the board has discretion to determine whether to pay a preferred dividend and what amount to pay. Most preferred shares are *cumulative preferred shares*, on which unpaid dividends cumulate. The entire accumulation must be paid before common shareholders may receive any dividend. Even when preferred shares are noncumulative, the current dividend must be paid to preferred shareholders before any dividend may be paid to common shareholders.

The following, is one of the few cases in which a court ordered the payment of a dividend to common shareholders. The court found that Henry Ford had the wrong motives for causing Ford Motor Company to refuse to pay a dividend.

---

## DODGE V. FORD MOTOR CO.
### 170 N.W. 668 (Mich. Sup. Ct. 1919)

In 1916, brothers John and Horace Dodge owned 10 percent of the common shares of the Ford Motor Company. Henry Ford owned 58 percent of the outstanding common shares and controlled the corporation and its board of directors. Starting in 1911, the corporation paid a regular annual dividend of $1.2 million, which was 60 percent of its capital stock of $2 million but only about 1 percent of its total equity of $114 million. In addition, from 1911 to 1915, the corporation paid special dividends totaling $41 million.

The policy of the corporation was to reduce the selling price of its cars each year. In June 1915, the board and officers agreed to increase production by constructing new plants for $10 million, acquiring land for $3 million, and erecting an $11 million smelter. To finance the planned expansion, the board decided not to reduce the selling price of cars beginning in August 1915 and to accumulate a large surplus.

A year later, the board reduced the selling price of cars by $80 per car. The corporation was able to produce 600,000 cars annually, all of which, and more, could have been sold for $440 instead of the new $360 price, a forgone revenue of $48 million. At the same time, the corporation announced a new dividend policy of paying no special dividend. Instead, it would reinvest all earnings except the regular dividend of $1.2 million.

Henry Ford announced his justification for the new dividend policy in a press release: "My ambition is to employ still more men, to spread the benefits of this industrial system to the greatest possible number, to help them build up their lives and their homes." The corporation had a $112 million surplus, expected profits of $60 million, total liabilities of $18 million, $52.5 million in cash on hand, and municipal bonds worth $1.3 million.

The Dodge brothers sued the corporation and the directors to force them to declare a special dividend. The trial court ordered the board to declare a dividend of $19.3 million. Ford Motor Company appealed.

---

**Ostrander, Chief Justice**   It is a well-recognized principle of law that the directors of a corporation, and they alone, have the power to declare a dividend of the

earnings of the corporation, and to determine its amount. Courts will not interfere in the management of the directors unless it is clearly made to appear that they are guilty of fraud or misappropriation of the corporate funds, or they refuse to declare a dividend when the corporation has a surplus of net profits which it can, without detriment to the business, divide among its stockholders, and when a refusal to do so would amount to such an abuse of discretion as would constitute a fraud, or breach of that good faith that they are bound to exercise towards the shareholders.

The testimony of Mr. Ford convinces this court that he has to some extent the attitude towards shareholders of one who has dispensed and distributed to them large gains and that they should be content to take what he chooses to give. His testimony creates the impression that he thinks the Ford Motor Company has made too much money, has had too large profits, and that, although large profits might be still earned, a sharing of them with the public, by reducing the price of the output of the company, ought to be undertaken. We have no doubt that certain sentiments, philanthropic and altruistic, creditable to Mr. Ford, had large influence in determining the policy to be pursued by the Ford Motor Company.

There should be no confusion of the duties that Mr. Ford conceives that he and the shareholders owe to the general public and the duties that in law he and his co-directors owe to protesting, minority shareholders. A business corporation is organized and carried on primarily for the profit of the shareholders. The powers of the directors are to be employed for that end.

We are not, however, persuaded that we should interfere with the proposed expansion of the Ford Motor Company. In view of the fact that the selling price of products may be increased at any time, the ultimate results of the larger business cannot be certainly estimated. The judges are not business experts. It is recognized that plans must often be made for a long future, for expected competition, for a continuing as well as an immediately profitable venture. We are not satisfied that the alleged motives of the directors, in so far as they are reflected in the conduct of the business, menace the interests of shareholders.

Assuming the general plan and policy of expansion were for the best ultimate interest of the company and therefore of its shareholders, what does it amount to in justification of a refusal to declare and pay a special dividend? The Ford Motor Company was able to estimate with nicety its income and profit. It could sell more cars than it could make. The profit upon each car depended upon the selling price. That being fixed, the yearly income and profit was determinable, and, within slight variations, was certain.

There was appropriated for the smelter $11 million. Assuming that the plans required an expenditure sooner or later of $10 million for duplication of the plant, and for land $3 million, the total is $24 million. The company was a cash business. If the total cost of proposed expenditures had been withdrawn in cash from the cash surplus on hand August 1, 1916, there would have remained $30 million.

The directors of Ford Motor Company say, and it is true, that a considerable cash balance must be at all times carried by such a concern. But there was a large daily, weekly, monthly receipt of cash. The output was practically continuous and was continuously, and within a few days, turned into cash. Moreover, the contemplated expenditures were not to be immediately made. The large sum appropriated for the smelter plant was payable over a considerable period of time. So that, without going further, it would appear that, accepting and approving the plan of the directors, it was their duty to distribute on and near the 1st of August 1916, a very large sum of money to stockholders.

**Judgment for the Dodge brothers affirmed.**

---

To protect the claims of the corporation's creditors, all of the corporation statutes limit the extent to which dividends may be paid. The MBCA imposes two limits: (1) the *solvency test* and (2) the *balance sheet test*.

**Solvency Test**    A dividend may not make a corporation insolvent; that is, unable to pay its debts as they come due in the usual course of business. This means that a corporation may pay a dividend to the extent it has *excess solvency*—that is, liquidity that it does not need to pay its currently maturing obligations. This requirement protects creditors, who are concerned primarily with the corporation's ability to pay debts as they mature.

**Balance Sheet Test**   After the dividend has been paid, the corporation's assets must be sufficient to cover its liabilities and the liquidation preference of shareholders having a priority in liquidation over the shareholders receiving the dividend. This means that a corporation may pay a dividend to the extent it has *excess assets*—that is, assets it does not need to cover its liabilities and the liquidation preferences of shareholders having a priority in liquidation over the shareholders receiving the dividends. This requirement protects not only creditors but also preferred shareholders. It prevents a corporation from paying to common shareholders a dividend that will impair the liquidation rights of preferred shareholders.

**Example**   Batt Company has $27,000 in excess liquidity that it does not need to pay its currently maturing obligations. It has assets of $200,000 and liabilities of $160,000. It has one class of common shareholders. Its one class of preferred shareholders has a liquidation preference of $15,000. Examining these facts, we find that Batt's excess solvency is $27,000, but its excess assets are only $25,000 ($200,000 − 160,000 − 15,000). Therefore, Batt's shareholders may receive a maximum cash or property dividend of $25,000, which will eliminate all of Batt's excess assets and leave Batt with $2,000 of excess solvency.

**Share Dividends and Share Splits**   Corporations sometimes distribute additional shares of the corporation to their shareholders. Often, this is done in order to give shareholders something instead of a cash dividend so that the cash can be retained and reinvested in the business. Such an action may be called either a **share dividend** or a **share split**.

A **share dividend** of a *specified percentage of outstanding shares* is declared by the board of directors. For example, the board may declare a 10 percent share dividend. As a result, each shareholder will receive 10 percent more shares than she currently owns. A share dividend is paid on outstanding shares only. Unlike a cash or property dividend, a share dividend may be revoked by the board after it has been declared.

A **share split** results in shareholders receiving a specified number of shares in exchange for each share that they currently own. For example, shares may be split two for one. Each shareholder will now have two shares for each share that he previously owned. A holder of 50 shares will now have 100 shares instead of 50.

The MBCA recognizes that a share split or a share dividend in the same class of shares does not affect the value of the corporation or the shareholders' wealth, because no assets have been transferred from the corporation to the shareholders. The effect is like that produced by taking a pie with four pieces and dividing each piece in half. Each person may receive twice as many pieces of the pie, but each piece is worth only half as much. The total amount received by each person is unchanged.

Therefore, the MBCA permits share splits and share dividends of the same class of shares to be made merely by action of the directors. The directors merely have the corporation issue to the shareholders the number of shares needed to effect the share dividend or split. The corporation must have a sufficient number of authorized, unissued shares to effect the share split or dividend; when it does not, its articles must be amended to create the required number of additional authorized shares.

**Reverse Share Split**   A *reverse share split* is a decrease in the number of shares of a class such that, for example, two shares become one share. Most of the state corporation statutes require shareholder action to amend the articles to effect a reverse share split because the number of authorized shares is reduced. The purpose of a reverse share split is usually to increase the market price of the shares.

## Share Repurchases

Declaring a cash or property dividend is only one of the ways in which a corporation may distribute its assets. A corporation may also distribute its assets by repurchasing its shares from its shareholders. Such a repurchase may be either a *redemption* or an *open-market repurchase*.

The right of **redemption** (or a call) is usually a right of the corporation to force an *involuntary* sale by a shareholder at a fixed price. The shareholder must sell the shares to the corporation at the corporation's request; in most states, the shareholder cannot force the corporation to redeem the shares.

Under the MBCA, the right of redemption must appear in the articles of incorporation. It is common for a corporation to issue preferred shares subject to redemption at the corporation's option. Usually, common shares are not redeemable.

In addition, a corporation may repurchase its shares **on the open market**. A corporation is empowered to purchase its shares from any shareholder who is willing to sell them. Such repurchases are *voluntary* on the shareholder's part, requiring the corporation to pay a current market price to entice the shareholder to sell.

A corporation's repurchase of its shares may harm creditors and other shareholders. The MBCA requires a corporation repurchasing shares to meet tests that are the same as its cash and property dividend rules, recognizing that financially, a repurchase of shares is no different from a dividend or any other distribution of assets to shareholders.

1. **Solvency Test:** The repurchase may not make the corporation insolvent, that is, unable to pay its debts as they come due in the usual course of business. This means that a corporation may repurchase shares to the extent it has *excess solvency*.
2. **Balance Sheet Test:** After the repurchase of shares, the corporation's assets must be sufficient to cover its liabilities and the liquidation preference of shareholders having a priority in liquidation over the shareholders whose shares were repurchased. This means that a corporation may repurchase shares to the extent that it has *excess assets*.

## SHAREHOLDERS' LAWSUITS

### Shareholders' Individual Lawsuits

A shareholder has the right to sue in his own name to prevent or redress a breach of the shareholder's contract. For example, a shareholder may sue to recover dividends declared but not paid or dividends that should have been declared, to enjoin the corporation from committing an *ultra vires* act, to enforce the shareholder's right of inspection, and to enforce preemptive rights.

### Shareholder Class Action Suits

When several people have been injured similarly by the same persons in similar situations, one of the injured people may sue for the benefit of all the people injured. Likewise, if several shareholders have been similarly affected by a wrongful act of another, one of these shareholders may bring a **class action** on behalf of all the affected shareholders.

An appropriate class action under state corporation law would be an action seeking a dividend payment that has been brought by a preferred shareholder for all of the preferred shareholders. Any recovery is prorated to all members of the class.

A shareholder who successfully brings a class action is entitled to be reimbursed from the award amount for his *reasonable expenses*, including attorney's fees. If the class action suit is unsuccessful and has no reasonable foundation, the court may order the suing shareholder to pay the defendants' reasonable litigation expenses, including attorney's fees.

### Shareholders' Derivative Actions

When a corporation has been harmed by the actions of another person, the right to sue belongs to the corporation and any damages awarded by a court belong to the corporation. Hence, as a general rule, a shareholder has no right to sue in his own name when someone has harmed the corporation, and he may not recover for himself damages from that person. This is the rule even when the value of the shareholder's investment in the corporation has been impaired.

Nonetheless, one or more shareholders are permitted under certain circumstances to bring an action for the benefit of the corporation when the directors have failed to pursue a corporate cause of action. For example, if the corporation has a claim against its chief executive for wrongfully diverting corporate assets to her personal use, the corporation is unlikely to sue the chief executive because she controls the board of directors. Clearly, the CEO should not go unpunished. Consequently, corporation law authorizes a shareholder to bring a **derivative action** (or derivative suit) against the CEO on behalf of the corporation and for its benefit. Such a suit may also be used to bring a corporate claim against an outsider.

If the derivative action succeeds and damages are awarded, the damages ordinarily go to the corporate treasury for the benefit of the corporation. The suing shareholder is entitled only to reimbursement of his reasonable attorney's fees that he incurred in bringing the action.

**Eligible Shareholders**    Although allowing shareholders to bring derivative suits creates a viable procedure for suing wrongdoing officers and directors, this procedure is also susceptible to abuse. **Strike suits** (lawsuits brought to gain out-of-court settlements for the complaining shareholders personally or to earn large attorney's fees, rather than to obtain a recovery for the corporation) have not been uncommon. To discourage strike suits, the person bringing the action must be a current shareholder who also held his shares at the time the alleged wrong occurred. In addition, the shareholder must fairly and adequately represent the interests of shareholders similarly situated in enforcing the right of the corporation.

One exception to these rules is the **double derivative suit**, a suit brought by a shareholder of a parent corporation on behalf of a subsidiary corporation owned by the parent. Courts regularly permit double derivative suits.

**Demand on Directors**    Since a decision to sue someone is ordinarily made by corporate managers, a shareholder must first **demand** that the board of directors bring the suit. A demand informs the board that the corporation may have a right of action against a person that the board, in its business judgment, may decide to pursue. Therefore, if a demand is made and the board decides to bring the suit, the shareholder may not institute a derivative suit.

Ordinarily, a shareholder's failure to make a demand on the board prevents her from bringing a derivative suit. Nonetheless, the shareholder may initiate the suit if she proves that a demand on the board would have been useless or **futile**. Demand is futile, and therefore **excused**, if the board is unable to make a disinterested decision regarding whether to sue. Futility may be proved when all or a majority of the directors are interested in the challenged transaction, such as in a suit alleging that the directors issued shares to themselves at below-market prices.

If a shareholder makes a demand on the board and it **refuses** the shareholder's demand to bring a suit, ordinarily the shareholder is not permitted to continue the derivative action. The decision to bring a lawsuit is an ordinary business decision appropriate for a board of directors to make. The business judgment rule, therefore, is available to insulate from court review a board's decision not to bring a suit.

Of course, if a shareholder derivative suit accuses the board of harming the corporation, such as by misappropriating the corporation's assets, the board's refusal will not be protected by the business judgment rule because the board has a conflict of interest in its decision to sue. In such a situation, the shareholder may sue the directors despite the board's refusal.

**Shareholder Litigation Committees**    In an attempt to ensure the application of the business judgment rule in demand refusal and demand futility situations, interested directors have tried to isolate themselves from the decision whether to sue by creating a special committee of the board, called a *shareholder litigation committee* (SLC) (or independent investigation committee) whose purpose is to decide whether to sue. The SLC should consist of directors who are not defendants in the derivative suit, who are not interested in the challenged action, are independent of the defendant directors, and if possible, were not directors at the time the wrong occurred. Usually, the SLC has independent legal counsel that assists its determination whether to sue. Because the SLC is a committee of the board, its decision may be protected by the business judgment rule. Therefore, an SLC's decision not to sue may prevent a shareholder from suing.

Shareholders have challenged the application of the business judgment rule to an SLC's decision to dismiss a shareholder derivative suit against some of the directors. The suing shareholders argue that it is improper for an SLC to dismiss a shareholder derivative suit because there is a *structural bias*. That is, the SLC members are motivated by a desire to avoid hurting their fellow directors and adversely affecting future working relationships within the board.

When demand is **not futile**, most of the courts that have been faced with this question have upheld the decisions of special litigation committees that comply with the business judgment rule. The courts require that the SLC members be *independent* of the defendant directors, be *disinterested* with regard to the subject matter of the suit, make a *reasonable investigation* into whether to dismiss the suit, and act in *good faith.*

When demand is **futile or excused**, most courts faced with the decision of an SLC have applied the rule of the *Zapata* case, which follows.

---

## Zapata Corp. v. Maldonado
### 430 A.2d 779 (Del. Sup. Ct. 1981)

Zapata Corporation had a share option plan that permitted its executives to purchase Zapata shares at a below-market price. Most of the directors participated in the share option plan. In 1974, the directors voted to advance the share option exercise date in order to reduce the federal income tax liability of the executives who exercised the share options, including the directors. An additional effect, however, was to increase the corporation's federal tax liability.

William Maldonado, a Zapata shareholder, believed that the board action was a breach of a fiduciary duty and that it harmed the corporation. In 1975, he instituted a derivative suit in a Delaware court on behalf of Zapata against all of the directors. He failed to make a demand on the directors to sue themselves, alleging that this would be futile since they were all defendants.

The derivative suit was still pending in 1979, when four of the defendants were no longer directors. The remaining directors then appointed two new outside directors to the board and created an Independent Investigation Committee consisting solely of the two new directors. The board authorized the committee to make a final and binding decision regarding whether the derivative suit should be brought on behalf of the corporation. Following a three-month investigation, the committee concluded that Maldonado's derivative suit should be dismissed as against Zapata's best interests.

Zapata asked the Delaware court to dismiss the derivative suit. The court refused, holding that Maldonado possessed an individual right to maintain the derivative action and that the business judgment rule did not apply. Zapata appealed to the Supreme Court of Delaware.

---

**Quillen, Justice**   We find that the trial court's determination that a shareholder, once demand is made and refused, possesses an independent, individual right to continue a derivative suit for breaches of fiduciary duty over objection by the corporation, as an absolute rule, is erroneous.

Derivative suits enforce corporate rights, and any recovery obtained goes to the corporation. We see no inherent reason why a derivative suit should automatically place in the hands of the litigating shareholder sole control of the corporate right throughout the litigation. Such an inflexible rule would recognize the interest of one person or group to the exclusion of all others within the corporate entity.

When, if at all, should an authorized board committee be permitted to cause litigation, properly initiated by a derivative stockholder in his own right, to be dismissed? The problem is relatively simple. If, on the one hand, corporations can con-sistently wrest bona fide derivative actions away from well-meaning derivative plaintiffs through the use of the committee mechanism, the derivative suit will lose much, if not all, of its effectiveness as an intracorporate means of policing boards of directors. If, on the other hand, corporations are unable to rid themselves of meritless or harmful litigation and strike suits, the derivative action, created to benefit the corporation, will produce the opposite, unintended result. It thus appears desirable to us to find a balancing point where bona fide shareholder power to bring corporate causes of action cannot be unfairly trampled on by the board of directors, but the corporation can rid itself of detrimental litigation.

We are not satisfied that acceptance of the business judgment rationale at this stage of derivative litigation is a proper balancing point. We must be mindful that directors are passing judgment on fellow directors in the same corporation and fellow directors, in this instance, who designated them to serve both as directors and committee members. The question naturally arises whether a "there but for the grace of God go I" empathy might not play a role. And the further question arises whether inquiry as to independence, good faith and reasonable investigation is sufficient safeguard against abuse, perhaps subconscious abuse.

We thus steer a middle course between those cases that yield to the independent business judgment of a board committee and this case as determined below, which would yield to unbridled shareholder control.

We recognize that the final substantive judgment whether a particular lawsuit should be maintained requires a balance of many factors—ethical, commercial, promotional, public relations, employee relations, fiscal, as well as legal. We recognize the danger of judicial overreaching but the alternatives seem to us to be outweighed by the fresh view of a judicial outsider.

After an objective and thorough investigation of a derivative suit, an independent committee may cause its corporation to file a motion to dismiss the derivative suit. The Court should apply a two-step test to the motion. First, the Court should inquire into the independence and good faith of the committee and the bases supporting its conclusions. The corporation should have the burden of proving independence, good faith, and reasonable investigation, rather than presuming independence, good faith, and reasonableness. If the Court determines either that the committee is not independent or has

not shown reasonable bases for its conclusions, or if the Court is not satisfied for other reasons relating to the process, including but not limited to the good faith of the committee, the Court shall deny the corporation's motion to dismiss the derivative suit.

The second step provides the essential key in striking the balance between legitimate corporate claims as expressed in a derivative stockholder suit and a corporation's best interests as expressed by an independent investigating committee. The Court should determine, applying its own independent business judgment, whether the motion should be granted. The second step is intended to thwart instances where corporate actions meet the criteria of step one, but the result does not appear to satisfy its spirit, or where corporate actions would simply prematurely terminate a stockholder grievance deserving of further consideration in the corporation's interest. The Court of course must carefully consider and weigh how compelling the corporate interest in dismissal is when faced with a non-frivolous lawsuit. The Court should, when appropriate, give special consideration to matters of law and public policy in addition to the corporation's best interests.

The second step shares some of the same spirit and philosophy of the statement of the trial court: "Under our system of law, courts and not litigants should decide the merits of litigation."

**Judgment reversed in favor of Zapata. Case remanded to the trial court.**

**Litigation Expenses**    If a shareholder is successful in a derivative suit, she is entitled to a reimbursement of her reasonable litigation expenses out of the corporation's damage award. On the other hand, if the suit is unsuccessful and has been brought without reasonable cause, the shareholder must pay the defendants' expenses, including attorney's fees. The purpose of this rule is to deter strike suits by punishing shareholders who litigate in bad faith.

## Defense of Corporation by Shareholder

Occasionally, the officers or managers will refuse to defend a suit brought against a corporation. If a shareholder shows that the corporation has a valid

defense to the suit and that the refusal or failure of the directors to defend is a breach of their fiduciary duty to the corporation, the courts will permit the shareholder to defend for the benefit of the corporation, its shareholders, and its creditors.

## SHAREHOLDER LIABILITY

Shareholders have many responsibilities and liabilities in addition to their many rights. You have already studied shareholder liability when a shareholder pays too little consideration for shares, when a corporation is defectively formed, and when a corporation's veil is pierced. In this section, four other grounds for shareholder liability are discussed.

## Shareholder Liability for Illegal Distributions

Dividends and other distributions of a corporation's assets received by a shareholder with *knowledge of their illegality* may be recovered on behalf of the corporation. Under the MBCA, primary liability is placed on the directors who, failing to comply with the business judgment rule, authorized the unlawful distribution. However, the directors are entitled to contribution from shareholders who received an asset distribution knowing that it was illegally made. These liability rules enforce the limits on asset distributions that were discussed earlier in this chapter.

## Shareholder Liability for Corporate Debts

One of the chief attributes of a shareholder is his *limited liability*: Ordinarily, he has no liability for corporate obligations beyond his capital contribution. Defective attempts to incorporate and piercing the corporate veil are grounds on which a shareholder may be held liable for corporate debts beyond his capital contribution. In addition, a few states impose personal liability on shareholders for *wages owed to corporate employees*, even if the shareholders have fully paid for their shares.

## Sale of a Control Block of Shares

The per share value of the shares of a majority shareholder of a corporation is greater than the per share value of the shares of a minority shareholder. This difference in value is due to the majority shareholder's ability to control the corporation and to cause it to hire her as an employee at a high salary. Therefore, a majority shareholder can sell her shares for a *premium* over the fair market value of minority shares.

Majority ownership is not always required for control of a corporation. In a close corporation it is required, but in a publicly held corporation with a widely dispersed, hard-to-mobilize shareholder group, minority ownership of from 5 to 30 percent may be enough to obtain control. Therefore, a holder of minority control in such a corporation will also be able to receive a premium.

Current corporation law imposes no liability on any shareholder, whether or not the shareholder is a controlling shareholder, *merely* because she is able to sell her shares for a premium. Nonetheless, if the premium is accompanied by wrongdoing, controlling shareholders have been held liable either for the amount of the premium or for the damages suffered by the corporation.

For example, a seller of control shares is liable for selling to a purchaser who harms the corporation if the seller had or should have had a *reasonable suspicion* that the purchaser would mismanage or loot the corporation. A seller may be placed on notice of a purchaser's bad motives by facts indicating the purchasers' history of *mismanagement and personal use of corporate assets*, by the purchaser's *lack of interest in the physical facilities* of the corporation, or the purchaser's great *interest in the liquid assets* of the corporation. These factors tend to indicate that the purchaser has a short-term interest in the corporation.

The mere payment of a premium is not enough to put the seller on notice. If the *premium is unduly high*, however, such as a $50 offer for shares traded for $10, a seller must doubt whether the purchaser will be able to recoup his investment without looting the corporation.

When a seller has, or should have, a reasonable suspicion that a purchaser will mismanage or loot the corporation, he must not sell to the purchaser unless a *reasonable investigation* shows there is no reasonable risk of wrongdoing.

A few courts find liability when a selling shareholder takes or sells a *corporate asset*. For example, if a purchaser wants to buy the corporation's assets and the controlling shareholder proposes that the purchaser buy her shares instead, the controlling shareholder is liable for usurping a corporate opportunity.

A more unusual situation existed in *Perlman v. Feldman*.[1] In that case, Newport Steel Corporation had excess demand for its steel production, due to the Korean War. Another corporation, in order to guarantee a steady supply of steel, bought at a premium a minority yet controlling block of shares of Newport from Feldman, its chairman and president. The court ruled that Feldman was required to share the premium with the other shareholders because he had sold a corporate asset—the ability to exploit an excess demand for steel. The court reasoned that Newport could have exploited that asset to its advantage.

---

[1]219 F.2d 173 (2d Cir. 1955).

## Oppression of Minority Shareholders

A few courts have recognized a fiduciary duty of controlling shareholders to use their ability to control the corporation in a fair, just, and equitable manner that benefits all of the shareholders proportionately. This is in part a duty to be impartial—that is, not to prefer themselves over the minority shareholders. For example, controlling shareholders have a fiduciary duty not to cause the corporation to repurchase their own shares or to pay themselves a dividend unless the same offer is made to the minority shareholder.

One of the most common examples of oppression is the **freeze-out** of minority shareholders. It occurs in close corporations when controlling shareholders pay themselves high salaries while not employing or paying dividends to noncontrolling shareholders. Since there is usually no liquid market for the shares of the noncontrolling shareholders, they have an investment that provides them no return, while the controlling shareholders reap large gains. Such actions by the majority are especially wrongful when the controlling shareholders follow with an offer to buy the minority's shares at an unreasonably low price.

In the following case, the court held that a majority shareholder violated a duty not to freeze out minority shareholders.

---

### Sugarman v. Sugarman
#### 797 F.2d 3 (1st Cir. 1986)

Three brothers—Joseph, Myer, and Samuel Sugarman—owned equal amounts of the shares of Statler Tissue Corporation. Although ownership was initially balanced, a series of stock transactions resulted in Myer's son Leonard becoming the majority shareholder of the corporation. Samuel gave some of his shares to his son Hyman and to Hyman's children, James, Marjorie, and Jon Sugarman. Hyman sold his shares to Leonard. Joseph Sugarman's shares were repurchased by the corporation. By 1974, Leonard owned 61 percent of the shares and was president and chairman of the board. James, Marjorie, and Jon Sugarman owned 22 percent of the shares.

Marjorie had sought employment with the corporation but was not hired. Jon was employed from 1974 until his discharge in 1978. James never sought employment with the company. After 1975, Myer's value to the corporation was near zero because he had Alzheimer's disease; nonetheless, Myer was employed by the corporation and received a salary equal to Hyman's salary. In 1980, Leonard caused the company to double Myer's salary to $85,000 for 1980 and 1981, when Myer was 87 and 88 years of age. Hyman received no such increase. When Myer retired in 1982, Leonard caused the corporation to pay Myer a yearly pension of $75,000. When Hyman retired in 1980, he received no pension.

The corporation paid no dividends. In 1980, Leonard offered to buy Jon's and Marjorie's shares for $3.33 per share. At that time, Price Waterhouse had advised Leonard that the book value of the corporation's shares was $16.30 per share. Jon and Marjorie refused to sell their shares and instead sued Leonard, alleging he had frozen them out of the corporation by depriving them of employment, paying himself and Myer excessive salaries, and refusing to pay dividends. The district court found Leonard liable to Jon and Marjorie for $538,000. Leonard appealed.

---

**Coffin, Circuit Judge**    We first examine the legal standard that must be met to establish a freeze-out of minority shareholders. In *Donahue v. Rodd Electrotype Co.* (1975), the Massachusetts Supreme Judicial Court held that shareholders in a close corporation owe one another a fiduciary duty of "utmost good faith and loyalty." Stockholders in a close corporation "may not act out of avarice, expediency or self-interest in derogation of their duty of loyalty to the other stockholders and the corporation."

The court's decision in *Donahue* was premised on the rationale that the corporate form of a close corporation "supplies an opportunity for the majority stockholders to oppress or disadvantage minority stockholders."

Those who employ the freeze-out technique may refuse to declare dividends; they may drain off the corporation's earnings in the form of exorbitant salaries and bonuses to the majority shareholder-officers and perhaps their relatives; they may deprive minority shareholders of corporate offices and of employment by the company; they may cause the corporation to sell its assets at an inadequate price to the majority shareholders. All of these devices are designed to ensure that the minority shareholders do not receive any financial benefits from the corporation. The minority stockholders must either suffer their losses or seek a buyer for their shares. This is often the capstone of the majority plan. Because minority shareholders cannot sell their stock on the open market, as can shareholders in public corporations, the minority shareholders may be compelled to deal with the majority and be vulnerable to low offers for their stock. When the minority stockholder agrees to sell out at less than fair value, the majority has won.

It is not sufficient to allege that the majority shareholder has offered to buy the stock of a minority shareholder at an inadequate price. In a close corporation, a minority shareholder who merely receives an offer from a majority shareholder to sell stock at an inadequate price, but does not accept that offer, can seek damages if the shareholder can prove that the offer was part of a plan to freeze the minority shareholder out of the corporation. That is, the minority shareholder must first establish that the majority shareholder employed various devices to ensure that the minority shareholder is frozen out of any financial benefits from the corporation through such means as the receipt of dividends or employment, and that the offer to buy stock at a low price is the capstone of the majority plan to freeze out the minority.

The necessary ingredients of a freeze-out of minority shareholders are present in this case. Leonard Sugarman took actions to ensure that Jon and Marjorie would not receive any financial benefits from the corporation. Leonard's overcompensation was designed to freeze out Jon and Marjorie from the company's benefits. Dividends had never been paid by the company. Marjorie had sought and been denied employment and Jon was improperly discharged from employment.

Leonard's offer to buy Jon and Marjorie's stock at an inadequate price was the capstone of a plan to freeze out Jon and Marjorie.

**Judgment for Jon and Marjorie affirmed.**

---

## LIABILITY OF SHAREHOLDERS OF STATUTORY CLOSE CORPORATIONS

Some statutes, such as the Statutory Close Corporation Supplement to the MBCA, permit close corporation shareholders to dispense with a board of directors or to arrange corporate affairs as if the corporation were a partnership. The effect of these statutes is to impose management responsibilities, including the fiduciary duties of directors, on the shareholders. In essence, the shareholders are partners and owe each other fiduciary duties similar to those owed between partners of a partnership.

## MEMBERS' RIGHTS AND DUTIES IN NONPROFIT CORPORATIONS

In a for-profit corporation, the shareholders' rights to elect directors and to receive dividends are their most important rights. The shareholders' duty to contribute capital as promised is the most important responsibility. By contrast, in a nonprofit corporation, the members' rights and duties—especially in a mutual benefit corporation—are defined by the ability of the members to use the facilities of the corporation (as in a social club) or to consume its output (as in a cooperative grocery store) and by their obligations to support the enterprise periodically with their money (such as dues paid to a social club) or with their labor (such as the duty to work a specified number of hours in a cooperative grocery store).

Nonprofit corporation law grants a corporation and its members considerable flexibility in determining the rights and liabilities of its members. The Model Nonprofit Corporation Act (MNCA) provides that all members of a nonprofit corporation have equal rights and obligations with respect to voting, dissolution, redemption of membership, and transfer of membership, unless the articles or bylaws establish classes of membership with different rights and obligations. For other rights and obligations, the MNCA provides that all members have the same rights and obligations, unless the articles or bylaws provide otherwise.

For example, a mutual benefit corporation that operates a golf country club may have two classes of membership. A full membership may entitle a full member to use all the club's facilities (including the swimming pool and tennis courts), grant the full member two votes on all matters submitted to members, and require the full member to pay monthly dues of $500. A limited membership may give a limited member the right to play the golf course only, grant the limited member one vote on all matters submitted to members, and require the limited member to pay monthly dues of $300 per month.

While members are primarily concerned about their consumption rights and financial obligations—such as those addressed above—that are embodied in the articles and the bylaws, they have other rights and obligations as well, including voting, inspection, and information rights similar to those held by shareholders of for-profit corporations.

## Members' Meeting and Voting Rights

A nonprofit corporation must hold an annual meeting of its members and may hold meetings at other times as well. Members holding at least 5 percent of the voting power may call for a special meeting of members at any time.

All members of record have one vote on all matters submitted to members, unless the articles or bylaws grant lesser or greater voting power. The articles or bylaws may provide for different classes of members. Members of one class may be given greater voting rights than the members of another class. The articles or bylaws may provide that a class has no voting power.

Members may not act at a meeting unless a quorum is present. Under the MNCA, a quorum is 10 percent of the votes entitled to be cast on a matter. However, unless at least one third of the voting power is present at the meeting, the only matters that may be voted on are matters listed in the meeting notice sent to members. The articles or bylaws may require higher percentages.

Members may elect directors by straight or cumulative voting and by class voting. The articles or bylaws may also permit members to elect directors on the basis of chapter or other organizational unit,

by region or other geographical unit, or by any other reasonable method. For example, a national humanitarian fraternity such as Lions Club may divide the United States into seven regions whose members are entitled to elect one director. Members also have the right to remove directors they have elected with or without cause.

In addition to the rights to elect and to remove directors, members have the right to vote on most amendments of the articles and bylaws, merger of the corporation with another corporation, sale of substantially all the corporation's assets, and dissolution of the corporation. Ordinarily, members must approve such matters by two thirds of the votes cast or a majority of the voting power, whichever is less. This requirement is more lenient than the rule applied to for-profit corporations. Combined with the 10 percent quorum requirement, members with less than 7 percent of the voting power may approve matters submitted to members.

However, the unfairness of such voting rules is offset by the MNCA's notice requirement. A members' meeting may not consider important matters such as mergers and articles amendments unless the corporation gave members fair and reasonable notice that such matters were to be submitted to the members for a vote.

In addition, the MNCA requires approval of each class of members whose rights are substantially affected by the matter. This requirement may increase the difficulty of obtaining member approval. For example, full members of a golf country club may not change the rights of limited members without the approval of the limited members. In addition, the articles or bylaws may require third person approval as well. For example, a city industrial development board may not be permitted to amend its articles without the consent of the mayor.

Members may vote in person or by proxy. They may also have written voting agreements. However, member voting agreements may not have a term exceeding 10 years. Members may act without a meeting if the action is approved in writing by at least 80 percent of the voting power.

## Member Inspection and Information Rights

A member may not be able to exercise his voting and other rights unless he is informed. Moreover, a member must be able to communicate with other members to be able to influence the way they vote on matters submitted to members. Consequently, the MNCA grants members inspection and information rights.

Members have an absolute right to inspect and copy the articles, bylaws, board resolutions, and minutes of members' meetings. Members have a qualified right to inspect and copy a list of the members. The members' demand to inspect the members' list must be in good faith and for a proper purpose—that is, a purpose related to the member's interest as a member. Improper purposes include selling the list or using the list to solicit money. Members also have a qualified right to inspect minutes of board meetings and records of actions taken by committees of the board.

A nonprofit corporation is required to maintain appropriate accounting records, and members have a qualified right to inspect them. Upon demand, the corporation must provide to a member its latest annual financial statements, including a balance sheet and statement of operations. However, the MNCA permits a religious corporation to abolish or limit the right of a member to inspect any corporate record.

## Distributions of Assets

Because it is not intended to make a profit, a nonprofit corporation does not pay dividends to its members. In fact, a nonprofit corporation is generally prohibited from making any distribution of its assets to its members.

Nonetheless, a mutual benefit corporation may purchase a membership and thereby distribute its assets to the selling member, but only if the corporation is able to pay its currently maturing obligations and has assets at least equal to its liabilities. For example, when a farmer joins a farmers' purchasing cooperative, he purchases a membership interest having economic value—it entitles him to purchase supplies from the cooperative at a bargain price. The mutual benefit corporation may repurchase the farmer's membership when he retires from farming. Religious and public benefit corporations may not repurchase their memberships.

## Resignation and Expulsion of Members

A member may resign at any time from a nonprofit corporation. When a member resigns, generally a member may not sell or transfer her membership to

any other person. A member of a mutual benefit corporation may transfer her interest to a buyer if the articles or bylaws permit.

It is fairly easy for a nonprofit corporation to expel a member or terminate her membership. The corporation must follow procedures that are fair and reasonable and carried out in good faith. The MNCA does not require the corporation to have a proper purpose to expel or terminate a member but only to follow proper procedures. The MNCA places no limits on a religious corporation's expulsion of its members.

The MNCA does not require a nonprofit corporation to purchase the membership of an expelled member, and—as explained above—permits only a mutual benefit corporation to purchase a membership. Members of mutual benefit corporations who fear expulsion should provide for repurchase rights in the articles or bylaws.

## Derivative Suits

Members of a nonprofit corporation have a limited right to bring derivative actions on behalf of the corporation. A derivative action may be brought by members having at least 5 percent of the voting power or by 50 members, whichever is less. Members must first demand that the directors bring the suit or establish that demand is futile. If the action is successful, a court may require the corporation to pay the suing members' reasonable expenses. When the action is unsuccessful and has been commenced frivolously or in bad faith, a court may require the suing members to pay the other party's expenses.

## DISSOLUTION AND TERMINATION OF CORPORATIONS

The MBCA provides that a corporation doing business may be dissolved by action of its directors and shareholders. The directors must adopt a dissolution resolution, and a majority of the shares outstanding must be cast in favor of dissolution at a shareholders' meeting. For a **voluntary dissolution** to be effective, the corporation must file articles of dissolution with the secretary of state. The dissolution is effective when the articles are filed.

A corporation may be also dissolved **without its consent** by administrative action of the secretary of state or by judicial action of a court. The secretary of state may commence an administrative proceeding to dissolve a corporation that has not filed its annual report, paid its annual franchise tax, appointed or maintained a registered office or agent in the state, or whose period of duration has expired. **Administrative dissolution** requires that the secretary of state give written notice to the corporation of the grounds for dissolution. If, within 60 days, the corporation has not corrected the default or demonstrated that the default does not exist, the secretary dissolves the corporation by signing a certificate of dissolution.

The shareholders, secretary of state, or the creditors of a corporation may ask a court to order the involuntary dissolution of a corporation. Any **shareholder** may obtain judicial dissolution when there is a deadlock of the directors that is harmful to the corporation, when the shareholders are deadlocked and cannot elect directors for two years, or when the directors are acting contrary to the best interests of the corporation. The **secretary of state** may obtain judicial dissolution if it is proved that a corporation obtained its articles of incorporation by fraud or exceeded or abused its legal authority. **Creditors** may request dissolution if the corporation is insolvent.

Under the MBCA, a corporation that has not issued shares or commenced business may be dissolved by the vote of a majority of its incorporators or initial directors.

Many close corporations are nothing more than incorporated partnerships, in which all the shareholders are managers and friends or relatives. Recently, corporation law has reflected the special needs of those shareholders of close corporations who want to arrange their affairs to make the close corporation more like a partnership. The Close Corporation Supplement to the MBCA recognizes that a **close corporation shareholder** should have the same dissolution power as a partner. This section, like similar provisions in many states, permits the articles of incorporation to empower any shareholder to dissolve the corporation at will or upon the occurrence of a specified event such as the death of a shareholder.

## Winding Up and Termination

A dissolved corporation continues its corporate existence but may not carry on any business except that appropriate to winding up its affairs. Therefore, winding up (liquidation) must follow dissolution. Winding up is the orderly collection and disposal of the corporation's assets and the distribution of the proceeds of the sale of assets. From these proceeds, the claims of creditors will be paid first. Next, the liquidation preferences of preferred shareholders will be paid. Then, common shareholders receive any proceeds that remain.

After winding up has been completed, the corporation's existence terminates. A person who purports to act on behalf of a terminated corporation has the liability of a person acting for a corporation prior to its incorporation. Some courts, like the court in the next case, impose similar liability on a person acting on behalf of a dissolved corporation, especially when dissolution is obtained by the secretary of state such as for the failure to file an annual report or to pay franchise taxes.

---

### BODINE ALUMINUM CO., INC. v. MITAUER
**776 S.W.2d 485 (Mo. Ct. App. 1989)**

East Side Metals, Inc., a Missouri corporation, failed to file an annual registration statement required by the Missouri corporation statute. Consequently, in November 1984, its corporate charter was forfeited. On East Side's last annual registration statement, Harlin, Louis, and Bernice Mitauer were listed as its officers and directors. Although East Side's charter was forfeited, the Mitauers continued to operate the business. In 1985, the business purchased scrap aluminum from Bodine Aluminum Co., Inc. When the business failed to pay $17,064 of the purchase price, Bodine sued the Mitauers to recover the remainder. The trial court held that the Mitauers individually owed Bodine $17,064. The Mitauers appealed to the Missouri Court of Appeals.

---

**Grimm, Judge**   The Missouri corporation statute provides:

If any corporation: (1) Fails to comply with the provisions of this chapter with respect to its annual registration the corporate rights and privileges of the corporation shall be forfeited, and the secretary of state shall notify the corporation that its corporate existence and rights in this state have been forfeited and canceled, and the corporation dissolved; and the directors and officers in office when the forfeiture occurs shall be the trustees of the corporation, who shall have full authority to wind up its business and affairs; and the trustees shall be jointly and severally responsible to the creditors and shareholders of the corporation to the extent of its property and effects that shall have come into their hands.

This statute places a limit on the liability of officers and directors as they wind up the affairs of a corporation after its corporate rights and privileges have been forfeited. When, however, the officers and directors continue to operate the business after forfeiture, individual liability may be imposed on them.

East Side's charter was forfeited on November 1, 1984. The Mitauers then became statutory trustees for the purpose of winding up the affairs of the corporation. When no effort was made to wind up, all post-forfeiture debts became the personal liability of the Mitauers.

**Judgment affirmed for Bodine.**

## Dissolution of Nonprofit Corporations

A nonprofit corporation may be dissolved voluntarily, administratively, or judicially. Voluntary dissolution will usually require approval of both the directors and the members. However, a nonprofit corporation may include a provision in its articles requiring the approval of a third person also. For example, such a third person might be a state governor who appointed some of the directors to the board of a nonprofit corporation organized to encourage industrial development in the state. The dissolution is effective when the corporation delivers articles of dissolution to the secretary of state and the secretary of state files them. The dissolved corporation continues its existence, but only for the purpose of liquidating its assets and winding up its affairs.

The secretary of state may administratively dissolve a nonprofit corporation that fails to pay incorporation taxes or to deliver its annual report to the secretary of state, among other things. Minority members or directors may obtain judicial dissolution by a court if the directors are deadlocked, the directors in control are acting illegally or fraudulently, or the members are deadlocked and cannot elect directors for two successive elections, among other reasons.

**CONCEPT REVIEW**
## ROLES OF SHAREHOLDERS AND THE BOARD OF DIRECTORS

| Corporate Action | Board's Role | Shareholders' Role |
| --- | --- | --- |
| **Day-to-Day Management** | Selects officers; supervises management | Elect and remove directors |
| **Issuance of Shares** | Issues shares | Protected by preemptive right |
| **Merger and Share Exchange** | Adopts articles of merger or share exchange | Vote to approve merger or share exchange; protected by dissenters' rights |
| **Amendment of Articles of Incorporation** | Proposes amendment | Vote to approve amendment |

| Corporate Action | Board's Role | Shareholders' Role |
|---|---|---|
| **Dissolution** | Proposes dissolution | Vote to approve dissolution |
| **Dividends** | Declares dividends | Receive dividends |
| **Board of Directors Harms Individual Shareholder Rights** | Has harmed shareholders | Bring individual or class action against directors or the corporation |
| **Directors Harm Corporation** | Sues wrongdoing directors | Bring derivative action against wrongdoing directors |

## PROBLEMS AND PROBLEM CASES

**1.** Facing billions of dollars of creditors' claims, Manville Corporation sought a bankruptcy reorganization. In 1985, Manville's management and its creditors agreed to a reorganization plan, but a group of Manville shareholders objected to the plan's intent to eliminate 90 percent of the shareholders' equity in Manville. The shareholders sued to force Manville to have a shareholders' meeting at which shareholders would remove the current directors and replace them with directors who would negotiate a reorganization plan that would better preserve the shareholders' equity. Manville had not held a shareholders' meeting since 1982. Manville claimed that holding a shareholders' meeting would obstruct its reorganization. Should the court grant the shareholders' request for a meeting?

**2.** Edward Carey owned 109,000 of the 2,700,341 outstanding shares of Pennsylvania Enterprises, Inc. (PEI). Concerned that Carey would attempt to take over PEI, its board of directors announced a proposal to widen the distribution of PEI shares. The proposal required shareholder approval. PEI announced that a special meeting of shareholders would be held on October 12, and its board of directors set the record date as September 2, 1988. Needing 1,350,171 votes to pass, the proposal received 1,373,968 votes in favor, passing with a margin of almost 24,000 votes. However, 79,118 of the shares voted in favor of the proposal were recorded in the names of Loriot & Co. and Cede & Co. but voted by other persons. Loriot and Cede were nominees for Manufacturer's Hanover Trust, which administered PEI's Dividend Reinvestment Plan (DRIP). Under the DRIP, PEI shareholders could opt to reinvest their cash dividends with PEI, which would issue new shares to the shareholders. Instead of registering the new shares in the names of the individual shareholders, however, PEI registered new shares to Loriot or Cede. A provision of the DRIP provided that the individual shareholders (beneficial shareholders), not Loriot and Cede, were able to vote the shares. At the special shareholders' meeting, the election judges permitted the DRIP beneficial shareholders to vote the DRIP shares in favor of the proposal. Did the election judges act properly?

**3.** Don Sanders owned 2 percent of the shares of Houston Sports Association (HSA). A group of minority shareholders, including Sanders, tried to enter a voting agreement with 51 percent of HSA shares. The purpose of the agreement was to oust from management John McMullen, the largest shareholder (34 percent) of HSA. However, McMullen promised Sanders that McMullen would vote his shares annually to elect Sanders to the HSA board of directors if Sanders agreed to withdraw his support from the minority shareholder group and to vote his shares to retain McMullen in management. Sanders agreed. Their agreement was only oral. Subsequently, McMullen was able to acquire 63 percent ownership of HSA, and Sanders—at McMullen's request—increased his holdings to 13 percent. Two years later, Sanders was not reelected to the board despite McMullen's majority ownership of shares. Sanders sued McMullen for violating their voting agreement. Was McMullen held liable?

**4.** In July 1981, Amplica, Inc., made a public offering of its shares. David Steinberg bought 75 shares for $10 each. Three months later, Amplica announced that it planned to merge with another company. Under the terms of the merger, Amplica shareholders would receive $13.50 per share, which was $.50 more than the market price of Amplica shares on the day prior to the announcement of the merger. Amplica's shareholders approved the merger. Steinberg did not vote for or against the merger, but he turned in his shares and received $13.50 for each share. One month later, Steinberg discovered facts that he believed proved that Amplica's directors acted improperly in approving the merger. He also believed that the price he and other shareholders received was grossly inadequate. Is Steinberg able to enforce his dissenter's rights or to bring a derivative suit on behalf of Amplica against the directors?

**5.** In July 1969, Charles Pillsbury discovered that Honeywell, Inc., manufactured munitions used in the Vietnam war. Pillsbury had long opposed the Vietnam war, and he was upset to learn that bombs were produced in his own community. On July 14, Pillsbury's agent purchased 100 Honeywell shares in the name of a Pillsbury family nominee. The sole purpose of Pillsbury's purchase was to permit him to communicate with other Honeywell shareholders in the hope of persuading Honeywell's board of directors to cease producing munitions. Later in July, he learned that he was a contingent beneficiary of 242 shares of Honeywell under the terms of a trust formed for his benefit by his grandmother. On August 11, Pillsbury purchased one share of Honeywell in his own name. Pillsbury demanded to inspect Honeywell's shareholder list and all corporate records dealing with munitions manufacture. Must Honeywell make these records available to Pillsbury?

**6.** Historically, Liggett Group, Inc., had paid quarterly dividends to its shareholders in March, June, September, and December of each year. On May 14, 1980, the Liggett board of directors recommended that shareholders accept a tender offer by GM Sub Corporation at $69 per share. The tender offer provided that if GM Sub acquired more than 50 percent of the Liggett shares, GM Sub and Liggett would merge; the Liggett shareholders who did not tender during the tender offer would receive $69 per share under the merger. Subsequently, 87.4 percent of Liggett shareholders tendered their shares. The cash-out merger was effected on August 7. Because the Liggett board believed that it would have been unfair to the shareholders who accepted the tender offer, the board skipped the June 1980 dividend. The board believed that the shareholders who did not tender should not be rewarded for

refusing to tender their shares to GM Sub knowing that they would receive the same price per share in the merger. Also, the board believed that $69 was a fair price for the shares. Gabelli & Co. surrendered its Liggett shares pursuant to the merger agreement but then sued Liggett to force payment of the June 1980 dividend. Did Gabelli succeed?

**7.** Fred and Maxine Brandon and their four children owned all the shares of Brandon Construction Co., a family corporation. Fred and Maxine owned a majority of the shares. In 1987, the shareholders agreed that Fred and Maxine each would receive a monthly salary of $12,500. Two months later, daughter Betty Brandon alleged that the salaries were excessive, and that Fred and Maxine were dismantling the corporation and distributing its assets to themselves, without regard for the children's rights as minority shareholders. She initiated a derivative action against her parents, but her siblings responded that Betty did not represent their interests as minority shareholders and that they were content with the salaries paid to their parents. Is Betty a proper person to bring a derivative suit?

**8.** Robert Orchard and Albert Covelli owned a majority of the shares of six corporations and all the shares of one corporation that operated McDonald's restaurant franchises. Covelli purchased the shares of the minority shareholders of the six corporations, making him the owner of 73 percent of the shares of the corporations and Orchard owner of 27 percent. Covelli owned 85 percent and Orchard 15 percent of the seventh corporation. Since Orchard and Covelli were by then dissatisfied with their relationship, Orchard asked Covelli to repurchase his shares at the same price Covelli paid for the minority shareholders' shares. Covelli agreed to pay Orchard for his shares of the six corporations, but wanted Orchard to give him the shares of the seventh corporation for no consideration. When Orchard refused to do so, Covelli made known his intent to force Orchard into bankruptcy and to remove him from any responsible positions in the corporations. Covelli terminated Orchard's employment with the corporations, removed him as a director, and replaced him with Covelli's son. Orchard remained a minority shareholder of the seven corporations, but the corporations paid no dividends. Does Orchard have any grounds upon which to sue Covelli?

**9.** H. F. Ahmanson & Co. was the controlling shareholder of United Savings and Loan Association.

There was very little trading in the Association's shares, however. To create a public market for their shares, Ahmanson and a few other shareholders of the Association incorporated United Financial Corporation and exchanged each of their Association shares for United shares. United then owned more than 85 percent of the shares of the Association. The minority shareholders of the Association were not given an opportunity to exchange their shares. United made two public offerings of its shares. As a result, trading in United shares was very active, while sales of Association shares decreased to half of the formerly low level, with United as virtually the only purchaser. United offered to purchase Association shares from the minority shareholders for $1,100 per share. Some of the minority shareholders accepted this offer. At that time, the shares held by the majority shareholders were worth $3,700. United also caused the Association to decrease its dividend payments. Has Ahmanson done anything wrong?

**10.** Albert Martin and Raymond Martin were brothers, each owning 50 percent of Martin's News Service, Inc., a retail store selling newspapers, lottery tickets, and cigarettes. Beginning in 1973, they had difficulty working together, eventually communicating only through their accountant. Directors' and shareholders' meetings ceased. In 1983, Albert fell ill and was unable to work in the store. In December 1983, Albert sued for a judicial dissolution of the corporation. Will the court order dissolution?

## Capstone Questions

**1.** Patton Corporation is a close corporation in the business of publishing trade magazines such as *CPA World, OptiWorld,* and *Global Dental Management.* Patton has four directors who collectively own a majority of Patton's common shares: Of Patton's 10,000 outstanding common shares, Andrew Bowers owns 1,400, Betsy Kelley owns 1,300, Julie Reed owns 1,250, and Mitch Parry owns 1,200. The remaining 4,850 common shares are owned by 22 minority shareholders.

- Bowers, Kelley, Reed, and Parry are good friends and have for the life of the corporation always voted their shares to elect each other to the board of directors. Nonetheless, they are concerned that one of them may join with the minority shareholders to elect other persons to the board.

**Required:**

Answer the following and give reasons for your conclusions.

What shareholder control devices may they use to ensure that they will continue to be elected to Patton's board of directors for as long as they own their shares?

- Times-Tribune Company, a publisher of newspapers, magazines, and books, approaches Patton's directors, offering to acquire Patton through a merger of Times-Tribune and Patton. Times-Tribune will be the surviving company, and each Patton shareholder will receive for each Patton share a Times-Tribune preferred share worth $400. The directors and majority shareholders—Bowers, Kelley, Reed, and Parry—ask Times-Tribune whether it would be willing to buy only the majority shareholders' shares in exchange for common shares of Times-Tribune. Times-Tribune replies that it is willing to exchange 15 Times-Tribune common shares worth a total of $750 for each Patton share held by the majority shareholders. Times-Tribune's purchase of the majority shares will make Times-Tribune the majority shareholder of Patton. The Patton majority shareholders will receive Times-Tribune shares, which are traded on the New York Stock Exchange. The Patton minority shareholders will remain shareholders of Patton, a corporation that would be dominated by Times-Tribune and whose shares will not be publicly traded.

**Required:**

Answer the following and give reasons for your conclusions.

**a.** If Times-Tribune buys only the shares held by Patton's majority shareholders, will the majority shareholders breach a duty to the minority shareholders?

**b.** Patton's directors decide informally that they will accept Times-Tribune's offer to acquire all of Patton's shares through a merger. What procedures must be followed to effect the merger between Patton and Times-Tribune?

**c.** Bill Walters, one of Patton's minority shareholders, expresses his need for information to be able to evaluate the merger. Walters requests access to Patton's financial records and a copy of Patton's shareholder list to allow him to communicate with other minority shareholders regarding the merger. Must Patton give Walters access to its financial records and shareholder list? What type of legal action may Walters bring against Patton if it refuses his request for access?

**d.** Walters believes that the board of directors has breached its fiduciary duty to the corporation by negotiating unfavorable merger terms. Walters want to stop the merger from being effected. What type of legal action must Walters bring against the board of directors if he wants to stop the merger? What procedures must he follow to bring that action? What type of board committee should the board establish to reduce the probability that Walters's suit will be successful?

**e.** Walters decides that he will not vote in favor of the merger, yet he knows that he cannot stop the merger. What right does Walters have if he wishes not to participate in the merger? What procedures must he follow to elect that right?

**2.** Argos Corporation has the following balance sheet:

**Assets**

| | | |
|---|---|---|
| Current assets | $ 500,000 | |
| Long-term assets | 4,310,000 | |
| Total assets | | $4,810,000 |

**Liabilities and Equity**

Liabilities:

| | | |
|---|---|---|
| Current liabilities | $ 400,000 | |
| Long-term liabilities | 3,600,000 | |
| Total liabilities | | $4,000,000 |

Equity:

| | | |
|---|---|---|
| Preferred Class A, 2,000 shares, $100 par value | $200,000 | |
| Preferred Class B, 5,000 shares, $100 par value | 500,000 | |
| Common shares, 100,000 shares, stated value | 10,000 | |
| Additional paid-in capital | 90,000 | |
| Retained earnings | 10,000 | |
| Total equity | | 810,000 |
| Total assets and equity | | $4,810,000 |

Argos has another 200,000 common shares that are authorized but have not been issued. Preferred Class A shares are preferred over Preferred Class B shares and common shares in regard to dividends and liquidation. Preferred Class B shares are preferred over common shares in regard to dividends and liquidation. The liquidation preference of the preferred shares is the same as their par value. The preferred shares are redeemable at the option of Argos at any time at a price of $110 per share. The preferred shares carry a cumulative annual dividend of $5 per share. Preferred dividends are paid semi-annually, and there is no unpaid accumulation. Argos has excess liquidity of $121,000 that it does not need to pay its currently maturing obligations.

**Required:**

Answer the following and give reasons for your conclusions.

**a.** What is the maximum cash dividend that Argos may pay to its common shareholders?

**b.** What is the maximum number of Class B Preferred Shares that Argos may redeem at the $110 redemption price?

**c.** What is the maximum common share dividend that may be issued to common shareholders?

**d.** What procedures must the Argos board of directors follow to effect a 3-for-1 share split of its common shares?

PART

9

# SPECIAL

# TOPICS

# CHAPTER

**3 7**

# SECURITIES

# REGULATION

## INTRODUCTION

*Modern securities regulation arose from the rubble of the great stock market crash of October 1929. After the crash, Congress studied its causes and discovered several common problems in securities transactions, the most important ones being:*

1. *Investors lacked the necessary information to make intelligent decisions whether to buy, sell, or hold securities.*
2. *Disreputable sellers of securities made outlandish claims about the expected performance of securities and sold securities in nonexistent companies.*

*Faced with these perceived problems, Congress chose to require securities sellers to disclose the information that investors need to make intelligent investment decisions. Congress found that investors are able to make intelligent investment decisions if they are given sufficient information about the company whose securities they are to buy. This* disclosure scheme *assumes that investors need assistance from government in acquiring information but that they need no help in evaluating information.*

---

## PURPOSES OF SECURITIES REGULATION

To implement its disclosure scheme, in the early 1930s Congress passed two major statutes, which are the hub of federal securities regulation in the United States today. These two statutes, the **Securities Act of 1933** and the **Securities Exchange Act of 1934**, have three basic purposes:

1. To require the disclosure of meaningful information about a security and its issuer to allow investors to make intelligent investment decisions.
2. To impose liability on those persons who make inadequate and erroneous disclosures of information.
3. To require the registration of issuers, insiders, professional sellers of securities, securities exchanges, and other self-regulatory securities organizations.

The crux of the securities acts is to impose on issuers of securities, other sellers of securities, and selected buyers of securities the affirmative duty to disclose important information, even if they are not asked by investors to make the disclosures. By requiring disclosure, Congress hoped to restore investor confidence in the securities markets. Congress wanted to bolster investor confidence in the honesty of the stock market and thus encourage more investors to invest in securities. Building investor confidence would increase capital formation and, it was hoped, help the American economy emerge from the Great Depression of the 1930s.

## SECURITIES AND EXCHANGE COMMISSION

The Securities and Exchange Commission (SEC) was created by the 1934 Act. Its responsibility is to administer the 1933 Act, 1934 Act, and other securities statutes. Like other federal administrative agencies, the SEC has legislative, executive, and judicial functions. Its legislative branch promulgates rules and regulations; its executive branch brings enforcement actions against alleged violators of the securities statutes and their rules and regulations; its judicial branch decides whether a person has violated the securities laws.

### SEC Actions

The SEC is empowered to investigate violations of the 1933 Act and 1934 Act and to hold hearings to determine whether the acts have been violated. Such hearings are held before an administrative law judge (ALJ), who is an employee of the SEC. The administrative law judge is a finder of both fact and law. Decisions of the ALJ are reviewed by the commissioners of the SEC. Decisions of the commissioners are appealed to the U.S. courts of appeals. Most SEC actions are not litigated. Instead, the SEC issues consent orders, by which the defendant promises not to violate the securities laws in the future but does not admit to having violated them in the past.

The SEC has the power to impose civil penalties (fines) up to $500,000 and to issue **cease and desist orders**. A cease and desist order directs a defendant to stop violating the securities laws and to desist from future violations. Nonetheless, the SEC does not have the power to issue injunctions; only courts may issue injunctions. The 1933 Act and the 1934 Act empower the SEC only to ask federal district courts for injunctions against persons who have violated or are about to violate either act. The SEC may also ask the courts to grant ancillary relief, a remedy in addition to an injunction. Ancillary relief may include, for example, the disgorgement of profits that a defendant has made in a fraudulent sale or in an illegal insider trading transaction.

## WHAT IS A SECURITY?

The first issue in securities regulation is the definition of a security. If a transaction involves no security, then the law of securities regulation does not apply. The 1933 Act defines the term **security** broadly:

Unless the context otherwise requires the term "security" means any note, stock, bond, debenture, evidence of indebtedness, certificate of interest of participation in any profit-sharing agreement, . . . preorganization certificate or subscription, . . . investment contract, voting trust certificate, . . . fractional undivided interest in oil, gas, or mineral rights, . . . or, in general, any interest or instrument commonly known as a "security."

The 1934 Act definition of security is similar, but excludes notes and drafts that mature not more than nine months from the date of issuance.

While typical securities like common shares, preferred shares, bonds, and debentures are defined as securities, the definition of a security also includes many contracts that the general public may believe are not securities. This is because the term **investment contract** is broadly defined by the courts. The Supreme Court's three-part test for an investment contract, called the *Howey* test, has been the guiding beacon in the area for the past 45 years.[1] The *Howey* test states that an investment contract is an investment of money in a common enterprise with an expectation of profits solely from the efforts of others.

In the *Howey* case, the sales of plots in an orange grove along with a management contract were held to be sales of securities. The purchasers had investment motives (they intended to make a profit from, not to consume the oranges produced by the trees). There was a common enterprise, because the investors were similarly affected by the efforts of the sellers who grew and sold the oranges for all investors. The sellers, not the buyers, did all of the work needed to make the plots profitable.

---

[1]*SEC v. W. J. Howey Co.,* 328 U.S. 293 (U.S. Sup. Ct. 1946).

In other cases, sales of limited partnership interests, Scotch whisky receipts, and restaurant franchises have been held to constitute investment contracts and, therefore, securities. In the following case, the court applied the *Howey* test to cattle-feeding consulting agreements.

---

## LONG V. SHULTZ CATTLE CO., INC.
**881 F.2d 129 (5th Cir. 1989)**

Jim Long, Jerome Atchley, and Jon and Linda Coleman invested in a cattle-feeding program offered by Shultz Cattle Company, Inc. (SCCI). They participated in SCCI's individual feeding program, under which investors would purchase and raise their own cattle. Each investor was required to sign a consulting agreement by which SCCI agreed to provide advice regarding the purchase, feeding, and sale of the investor's cattle. SCCI received only a flat-rate consulting fee of $20 per head of cattle for these services and received no share of the investors' profits.

To receive tax benefits from the investment, the tax laws required investors to participate actively in farming. Therefore, SCCI required each investor to represent that "he will exert substantial and significant control over, and will, exercising independent judgment, make all principal and significant management decisions concerning his cattle feeding operations."

Investors could limit any real risk of loss of investment by hedging their cattle: By buying or selling commodities futures they could lock in a price and minimize their potential losses. SCCI arranged for hedging transactions to be conducted through financial institutions, feedyards, and a brokerage firm of which SCCI was a branch office.

Long's, Atchley's, and the Colemans' cattle were fed, along with those of many other SCCI clients, in a feedyard in which the cattle were commingled. The cattle were tagged by pen number and not by individual investor. Each investor therefore owned a percentage of the total pounds of cattle in the pen. If any cattle died, the loss was not attributed to a single investor but was distributed pro rata among the investors.

During the first year, Long, Atchley, and the Colemans hedged all their cattle and lost half of the money they had invested. In the second year, they decided to hedge only half of their 1,450 head of cattle. When beef prices declined drastically, they lost over $100,000. They sued SCCI for selling unregistered securities. The jury found that the consulting agreements were not investment contracts or otherwise securities. Long, Atchley, and the Colemans appealed.

---

**King, Circuit Judge**   In *S.E.C. v. W. J. Howey Co.* (1946), the Supreme Court held that to determine whether a scheme is an investment contract, the test is whether the scheme involves (1) an investment of money (2) in a common enterprise (3) with profits to come solely from the efforts of others. The parties do not dispute that the first prong of the *Howey* test is satisfied in this case. Only the latter two elements are contested. Because the controversy centers primarily on the third prong, we will discuss that issue first.

To ensure that the securities laws are not easily circumvented by agreements requiring a "modicum of effort" by investors, the word "solely" in the third prong of the *Howey* test has not been construed literally. The critical inquiry is instead whether the efforts made by those other than the investor are the undeniably significant ones, those essential managerial efforts which affect the failure or success of the enterprise. Even where an investor formally possesses substantial powers, the third prong of the *Howey* test may be met if the investor demonstrates that he is so inexperienced and unknowledgeable in the field of business at issue that he is incapable of intelligently exercising the rights he formally possesses.

Long, Atchley, and the Colemans had a substantial degree of theoretical control over their investments. They could, theoretically, move their cattle to a different feedyard, decide what to feed them, provide their own veterinary care, or seek buyers on their own. Moreover, the investors were *required* to authorize every management decision involving their cattle. However, at each juncture, the investors relied solely on the advice of SCCI: they followed SCCI's recommendations regarding the purchase of cattle, the choice of a feedyard, the choice of financial institution to provide financing, the choice of commodities brokers, the decision when to sell, and the decision to whom to sell.

Long, Atchley, and the Colemans, who lived in places far removed from their cattle, lacked the experience necessary to care for, feed, and market their cattle. They acquired *from* SCCI all of the knowledge necessary to "actively manage" their "individual" cattle-feeding businesses. We do not believe that the securities laws may be avoided so easily.

SCCI hopes to avoid the securities laws by simply attaching the label "consulting agreement" to a package of services which otherwise would clearly be an investment contract. The label "consulting agreement" cannot bear the meaning SCCI has given it.

Although Long, Atchley, and the Colemans' decision to hedge only half of their cattle was "undeniably significant" in terms of the risks to which the investors were exposed, it does not alter the essential character of the SCCI scheme. An investor may authorize the assumption of particular risks that would create the possibility of greater profits or losses but still depend on a third party for all of the essential managerial efforts without which the risk could not pay off. The fact that Long, Atchley, and the Colemans chose the riskier course cannot, by itself, transform the essential nature of the underlying contract any more than the fact that an individual investor chooses to buy high-risk junk bonds rather than low-risk AAA bonds causes one bond and not the other to be a security.

We conclude that the third prong of the *Howey* test was established as a matter of law. The jury's verdict would nevertheless stand if the evidence could support the conclusion that the second prong of the *Howey* test—the existence of a common enterprise—was not met. The Third, Sixth, and Seventh Circuits hold that a showing of "horizontal commonality"—a pooling of investors—is necessary to meet the common enterprise requirement. Under this standard, investors' fortunes must be tied to one another in order to constitute a common enterprise.

This court, together with the Ninth and Eleventh Circuits, has explicitly rejected the view that horizontal commonality is a prerequisite to establishing a common enterprise and has focused instead on the "vertical commonality" between the investors and the promoter. The critical factor is not the similitude or coincidence of investor input, but rather the uniformity of impact of the promoter's decisions.

While our standard requires interdependence between the investors and the promoter, it does not define that interdependence narrowly in terms of shared profits and losses. Rather, the necessary interdependence may be demonstrated by the investors' collective reliance on the promoter's expertise even where the promoter receives only a flat fee or commission rather than a share in the profits of the venture.

We recognize that under our standard the second and third prongs of the *Howey* test may in some cases overlap and that our standard has been criticized for that reason. We are not convinced that it would be desirable to adopt a rigid requirement that profits and losses be shared on a *pro rata* basis among investors, or that the promoter's fortunes correlate directly to the profits and losses of investors.

Here, all of SCCI's clients were dependent on SCCI's expertise to manage their investments. Moreover, SCCI's fortunes clearly were interwoven with those of their clients. SCCI received substantial "consulting fees" from its clients in exchange for its services in constructing and administering effective tax shelters through the cattle-feeding business. Through the inexorable force of the market, SCCI's success would correspond to that of its clients.

**Judgment reversed in favor of Long, Atchley, and the Colemans.**

Courts have used the *Howey* test to hold that some contracts with typical security names are not securities. Using an **economic realities test**, the courts point out that some of these contracts possess few of the typical characteristics of a security. For example, in *United Housing Foundation, Inc. v. Forman*,[2] the Supreme Court held that although tenants in a cooperative apartment building purchased contracts labeled as stock, the contracts were not securities. The "stock" possessed few of the typical characteristics of stock and the economic realities of the transaction bore few similarities to those of the typical stock sale: The stock gave tenants no dividend rights or voting rights in proportion to the number of shares owned, it was not negotiable, and it could not appreciate in value. More important, tenants bought the stock not for the purpose of investment but to acquire suitable living space.

However, when investors are misled to believe that the securities laws apply because a seller sold a contract bearing both the name of a typical security and significant characteristics of that security, the securities laws do apply to the sale of the security.

In 1990, the Supreme Court further extended this rationale in *Reves v. Ernst & Young*,[3] adopting the **family resemblance test** to determine whether promissory notes were securities. The Supreme Court held that it is inappropriate to apply the *Howey* test to notes. Instead, applying the family resemblance test, the Court held that notes are presumed to be securities unless they bear a "strong family resemblance" to a type of note that is not a security. Types of notes that are not securities include consumer notes, mortgage notes, short-term notes secured by a lien on a small business, short-term notes secured by accounts receivable, and notes evidencing loans by commercial banks for current operations.

## SECURITIES ACT OF 1933

The Securities Act of 1933 (1933 Act) is concerned primarily with public distributions of securities. That is, the 1933 Act regulates the sale of securities

while they are passing from the hands of the issuer into the hands of public investors. An issuer selling securities publicly must make necessary disclosures at the time the issuer sells the securities to the public.

The 1933 Act has two principal regulatory components: (1) registration provisions and (2) liability provisions. The registration requirements of the 1933 Act are designed to give investors the information they need to make intelligent decisions whether to purchase securities when an issuer sells its securities to the public. The various liability provisions in the 1933 Act impose liability on sellers of securities for misstating or omitting facts of material significance to investors.

## REGISTRATION OF SECURITIES UNDER THE 1933 ACT

The 1933 Act requires that *every* offering of securities be registered with the SEC prior to any offer or sale of the securities, unless the offering or the securities are exempt from registration. That is, an issuer and its underwriters may not offer or sell securities unless the securities are registered with the SEC or exempt from registration. Over the next few pages, we will cover the registration process. Then the exemptions from registration will be addressed.

### Mechanics of a Registered Offering

When an issuer makes a decision to raise money by a public offering of securities, the issuer needs to obtain the assistance of securities market professionals. The issuer will contact a managing underwriter, the primary person assisting the issuer in selling the securities. The managing underwriter will review the issuer's operations and financial statements and reach an agreement with the issuer regarding the type of securities to sell, the offering price, and the compensation to be paid to the underwriters. The issuer and the managing underwriter will determine what type of underwriting to use.

In a **stand-by underwriting,** the underwriters obtain subscriptions from prospective investors, but the issuer sells the securities only if there is sufficient investor interest in the securities. The underwriters receive warrants—options to purchase

---

[2]*United Housing Foundation, Inc. v. Forman*, 421 U.S. 837 (U.S. Sup. Ct. 1975).
[3]494 U.S. 56 (U.S. Sup. Ct. 1990).

the issuer's securities at a bargain price as compensation for their efforts. The stand-by underwriting is typically used only to sell common shares to existing shareholders pursuant to a preemptive rights offering.

With a **best efforts underwriting,** the underwriters are merely agents making their best efforts to sell the issuer's securities. The underwriters receive a commission for their selling efforts. The best efforts underwriting is used when an issuer is not well established and the underwriter is unwilling to risk being unable to sell the securities.

The classic underwriting arrangement is a **firm commitment underwriting.** Here the managing underwriter forms an underwriting group and a selling group. The underwriting group agrees to purchase the securities from the issuer at a discount from the public offering price, for example 25 cents per share below the offering price. The selling group agrees to buy the securities from the underwriters also at a discount, for example 12½ cents per share below the offering price. Consequently, the underwriters and selling group bear much of the risk with a firm commitment underwriting, but they also stand to make the most profit under such an arrangement.

## Registration Statement and Prospectus

The 1933 Act requires the issuer of securities to register the securities with the SEC before the issuer or underwriters may offer or sell the securities. Registration requires filing a **registration statement** with the SEC. Historical and current data about the issuer and its business, full details about the securities to be offered, and the use of the proceeds of the issuance, among other information, must be included in the registration statement prepared by the issuer of the securities with the assistance of the managing underwriter, securities lawyers, and independent accountants. Generally, the registration statement must include audited balance sheets as of the end of each of the two most recent fiscal years, in addition to audited income statements and audited statements of changes in financial position for each of the last three fiscal years.

The registration statement becomes effective after it has been reviewed by the SEC. The 1933 Act provides that the registration statement becomes

effective automatically on the 20th day after its filing, unless the SEC delays or advances the effective date.

The **prospectus** is the basic selling document of an offering registered under the 1933 Act. Most of the information in the registration statement must be included in the prospectus. It must be furnished to every purchaser of the registered security prior to or concurrently with the sale of the security to the purchaser. The prospectus enables an investor to base his investment decision on all of the relevant data concerning the issuer, not merely on the favorable information that the issuer may be inclined to disclose voluntarily.

## Section 5: Timing, Manner, and Content of Offers and Sales

The 1933 Act restricts the issuer's and underwriter's ability to communicate with prospective purchasers of the securities. Section 5 of the 1933 Act states the basic rules regarding the timing, manner, and content of offers and sales. It creates three important periods of time in the life of a securities offering: (1) the pre-filing period, (2) the waiting period, and (3) the post-effective period.

**The Pre-Filing Period**  Prior to the filing of the registration statement (the pre-filing period), the issuer and any other person may **not offer or sell** the securities to be registered. A prospective issuer, its directors and officers, and its underwriters must avoid publicity about the issuer and the prospective issuance of securities during the prefiling period. Press releases, advertisements, speeches, and press conferences may be deemed offers if their intent or effect is to condition the market to receive the securities.

SEC Rule 135 permits the issuer to publish a notice about a prospective offering during the pre-filing period. The notice may contain only the name of the issuer and a basic description of the securities and the offering. It may not name the underwriters or state the price at which the securities will be offered.

**The Waiting Period**  The waiting period is the time between the filing date and the effective date of the registration statement, when the issuer is waiting for the SEC to declare the registration statement effective. During the waiting period, Section 5 permits the securities to be **offered but not sold.** However, not all kinds of offers are permitted. Face-to-face oral offers (including personal phone calls) are allowed during the waiting period. However, written offers may be made only by a statutory prospectus, usually a **preliminary prospectus** that often omits the price of the securities. (A final prospectus will be available after the registration statement becomes effective. It will contain the price of the securities.)

General publicity during the waiting period may be construed as an illegal offer because it conditions the market to receive the securities. One type of general advertisement, called the **tombstone ad**, is permitted during the waiting period and thereafter. The tombstone ad, which appears in financial pub-

---

### CONCEPT REVIEW

### COMMUNICATIONS WITH INVESTORS BY OR ON BEHALF OF ISSUER PERMITTED BY SECTION 5 DURING A 1933 ACT REGISTRATION

| Type of Communication | Filing Date of Registration Statement | | Effective Date of Registration Statement |
| --- | --- | --- | --- |
| | **Pre-Filing Period** | **Waiting Period** | **Post-Effective Period** |
| **Annual Reports, Press Releases, and Quarterly Reports** | Permitted; unless designed to assist the placement of securities or arouse interest in a prospective sale of securities | Permitted; unless designed to assist the placement of securities or arouse interest in a prospective sale of securities | Permitted; without restriction if used contemporaneously with or after delivery of final prospectus |
| **Notice of Proposed Offering (Rule 135)** | Permitted | Permitted | Permitted |
| **Tombstone Ad (Rule 134)** | Not permitted | Permitted | Permitted |
| **Offer by Preliminary Prospectus** | Not permitted | Permitted | Not permitted |
| **Offer by Final Prospectus** | Not permitted | Not permitted | Permitted |
| **Oral Face-to-Face Offers (including telephone calls)** | Not permitted | Permitted | Permitted |
| **Oral Offers at Sales Meeting** | Not permitted | Permitted; if each investor has an opportunity to ask unlimited questions | Permitted; if each investor has an opportunity to ask unlimited questions, or if each investor has received a final prospectus |
| **Written Offers Other than a Prospectus** | Not permitted | Not permitted | Permitted; contemporaneously with or after delivery of final prospectus |
| **Sales** | Not permitted | Not permitted | Permitted; contemporaneously with or after delivery of final prospectus |

lications, is permitted by SEC Rule 134, which allows disclosure of the same information as is allowed by Rule 135 plus the general business of the issuer, the price of the securities, and the names of the underwriters who are helping the issuer to sell the securities. In addition, Rule 134 requires the tombstone ad to state that it is not an offer.

The waiting period is an important part of the regulatory scheme of the 1933 Act. It provides an investor with adequate time (at least 20 days) to judge the wisdom of buying the security during a period when he cannot be pressured to buy it. Not even a contract to buy the security may be made during the waiting period.

**The Post-Effective Period**    After the effective date (the date on which the SEC declares the registration effective), Section 5 permits the security to be **offered and also to be sold,** provided that the buyer has received a **final prospectus** (a preliminary prospectus is not acceptable for this purpose). Written offers not previously allowed are permitted during the post-effective period, but only if the offeree has received a final prospectus.

**Liability for Violating Section 5**    Section 12(1) of the 1933 Act imposes liability on any person who violates the provisions of Section 5. Liability extends to any *purchaser* to whom an illegal offer or sale was made. The purchaser's remedy is *rescission* or damages.

## EXEMPTIONS FROM THE REGISTRATION REQUIREMENTS OF THE 1933 ACT

Complying with the registration requirements of the 1933 Act, including the restrictions of Section 5, is a burdensome, time-consuming, and expensive process. Planning and executing an issuer's first public offering may consume six months and cost in excess of $1 million. Consequently, some issuers prefer to avoid registration when they sell securities. There are two types of exemptions from the registration requirements of the 1933 Act: securities exemptions and transaction exemptions.

### Securities Exemptions

Exempt securities never need to be registered, regardless who sells the securities, how they are sold,

or to whom they are sold. The following are the most important securities exemptions.[4]

1. Securities issued or guaranteed by any government in the United States and its territories.
2. A note or draft that has a maturity date not more than nine months after its date of issuance.
3. A security issued by a nonprofit religious, charitable, educational, benevolent, or fraternal organization.
4. Securities issued by banks and by savings and loan associations.
5. Securities issued by railroads and trucking companies regulated by the Interstate Commerce Commission.
6. An insurance policy or an annuity contract.

Although the types of securities listed above are exempt from the registration provisions of the 1933 Act, they are not exempt from the liability provisions of the act. For example, any fraud committed in the course of selling such securities can be attacked by the SEC and by the persons who were defrauded.

### Transaction Exemptions

The most important 1933 Act registration exemptions are the transaction exemptions. If a security is sold pursuant to a transaction exemption, that sale is exempt from registration. Subsequent sales, however, are not automatically exempt. Future sales must be made pursuant to a registration or another exemption.

The transaction exemptions are exemptions from the registration provisions only. The antifraud provisions of the 1933 Act apply equally to exempted and nonexempted transactions.

---

[4]Excluded from the list of securities exemptions are the intrastate offering and small offering exemptions. Although the 1933 Act denotes them (except for the section 4(6) exemption) as securities exemptions, they are in practice transaction exemptions. An exempt security is exempt from registration forever. But when securities originally sold pursuant to an intrastate or small offering exemption are resold at a later date, the subsequent sales may have to be registered. The exemption of the earlier offering does not exempt a future offering. The SEC treats these two exemptions as transaction exemptions. Consequently, this chapter also treats them as transaction exemptions.

The most important transaction exemptions are those available to issuers of securities. These exemptions are the intrastate offering exemption, the private offering exemption, and the small offering exemptions.

## Intrastate Offering Exemption

Under section 3(a)(11), an offering of securities solely to investors in one state by an issuer resident and doing business in that state is exempt from the 1933 Act's registration requirements. The reason for the exemption is that there is little federal government interest in an offering that occurs in only one state. Although the offering may be exempt from SEC regulation, state securities law may require a registration. The expectation is that state securities regulation will adequately protect investors.

The SEC has defined the intrastate offering exemption more precisely in Rule 147. An issuer must have at least 80 percent of its gross revenues and 80 percent of its assets in the state and use at least 80 percent of the proceeds of the offering in the state. Resale of the securities is limited to persons within the state for nine months.

Rule 147, however, is not an exclusive rule. In the following case, the court applied only the statutory standard of section 3(a)(11).

---

### BUSCH V. CARPENTER
**827 F.2d 653 (10th Cir. 1987)**

Sonic Petroleum, Inc., was incorporated in Utah for the purpose of acquiring, extracting, and marketing natural resources such as oil, gas, and coal. Its corporate office, books, and records were in Utah. During October and November 1980, Sonic publicly offered and sold 25 million shares entirely to residents of Utah. The proceeds were $500,000. Sonic did not file a Securities Act registration statement with the SEC, instead relying on the exemption from registration for intrastate offerings. At the time of the offering, Sonic had not undertaken any business activities in Utah or anywhere else.

Craig Carpenter, Sonic's president, negotiated Sonic's acquisition of an Illinois drilling corporation owned by William Mason. On May 25, 1981, Sonic issued a controlling block of its shares to Mason in exchange for Mason's corporation. Shortly thereafter, Sonic deposited in Illinois $350,000 of the proceeds from the sale of shares to Utah residents. At about the same time, Mason and Carpenter helped create a public market for Sonic shares. As a result, Paul and Linda Busch, who were California residents, purchased Sonic shares from Utah residents who had purchased shares in October and November 1980. When the shares' value dropped, the Busches sued Carpenter for selling unregistered securities. The trial court held that Sonic sold the shares pursuant to the intrastate offering exemption and, therefore, did not need to register the shares. The Busches appealed.

---

**Seymour, Circuit Judge** Section 5 of the Securities Act of 1933 prohibits the offer or sale of any security unless a proper registration statement has first been filed with the SEC. However, Congress also recognized that the protections of the 1933 Act were not essential for those securities that could be supervised effectively by the states. Section 3(a)(11) therefore exempts from the Act's registration requirements

Any security which is part of an issue offered and sold only to persons resident within a single State or Territory, where the issuer of such security is a person resident and doing business within or, if a corporation, incorporated by and doing business within, such State or Territory.

In order to fall within the intrastate exemption, initial sales to state residents must be bona fide. The intrastate exemption becomes unavailable whenever sales or purchases by a subsequent purchaser circumvent the federal securities laws. The SEC has consistently maintained that a distribution of securities must have actually come to rest in the hands of the resident investors—persons purchasing for investment intent and not for purpose of resale.

The Busches contend that Sonic had the burden to prove that the original buyers bought with investment intent. We reject this argument. The intrastate offering exemption requires that the issue be "offered and sold only to persons resident within a single state." In face of Sonic's undisputed showing that all of the original buyers were Utah residents, the Busches were therefore required to produce evidence that the stock had not come to rest but had been sold to people who intended to resell it out of state. The interstate purchases of freely trading shares several months after the completion of the intrastate offering do not, without more, impugn the investment intent of the original buyers.

The Busches alternatively contend that Sonic was not entitled to the intrastate exemption because the corporate issuer was not doing business in Utah as required by section 3(a)(11). An issuer cannot claim the exemption simply by opening an office in a particular state. Conducting substantially all income-producing operations elsewhere defeats the exemption, as do the plans of recently organized companies to invest the net proceeds of initial public offerings only in other states.

Here Sonic never did more than maintain its office, books, and records in Utah. Sonic transferred essentially all of its assets to Illinois and made no prior efforts whatever at locating investment opportunities within Utah. Sonic may have been intending all along to invest its assets outside the state. A newly formed company may not claim the exemption while planning covertly to invest the proceeds of a local offering in other states.

**Judgment reversed in favor of the Busches; remanded for trial.**

## Private Offering Exemption

Section 4(2) of the 1933 Act provides that the registration requirements of the 1933 Act "shall not apply to transactions by an issuer not involving any public offering." A private offering is an offering to a small number of purchasers who can protect themselves because they are wealthy or because they are sophisticated in investment matters and have access to the information that they need to make intelligent investment decisions.

To create greater certainty about what a private offering is, the SEC adopted Rule 506. Although an issuer may exempt a private offering under either the courts' interpretation of section 4(2) or Rule 506, the SEC tends to treat Rule 506 as the exclusive way to obtain the exemption.

**Rule 506** Under Rule 506, which is part of Securities Act Regulation D, the issuer must reasonably believe that each purchaser is either (a) an accredited investor or (b) an unaccredited investor who "has such knowledge and experience in financial and business matters that he is capable of evaluating the merits and risks of the prospective investment." Accredited investors include institutional investors (such as banks and mutual funds), wealthy investors, and high-level insiders of the issuer (such as executive officers, directors, and partners).

An issuer may sell to no more than 35 unaccredited purchasers who have sufficient investment knowledge and experience; it may sell to an unlimited number of accredited purchasers, regardless of their investment sophistication.

Each purchaser must be given or have access to the information she needs to make an informed investment decision. For a public company making a nonpublic offering under Rule 506, purchasers must receive information in a form required by the 1934 Act, such as a 10-K or annual report. The issuer must provide the following audited financial statements: two years' balance sheets, three years' income statements, and three years' statements of changes in financial position.

For a nonpublic company making a nonpublic offering under Rule 506, the issuer must provide much of the same nonfinancial information required in a registered offering. A nonpublic company may, however, obtain some relief from the burden of providing audited financial statements to investors. When the amount of the issuance is $2 million or less, only one year's balance sheet need be audited. If the amount issued exceeds $2 million but not $7.5 million, only one year's balance sheet, one year's income statement, and one year's statement of changes in financial position need be audited. When the amount issued exceeds $7.5 million, the issuer must provide two years' balance sheets, three years' income statements, and three years' statements of changes in financial position. In any offering of any amount by a nonpublic issuer, when auditing would involve unreasonable effort or expense, only an audited balance sheet is needed. When a limited partnership issuer finds that auditing involves unreasonable effort or expense, the limited partnership may use financial statements prepared by an independent accountant in conformance with the requirements of federal tax law.

Rule 506 prohibits the issuer from making any general public selling effort. This prevents the issuer from using the radio, newspapers, and television. However, offers to an individual one-on-one are permitted.

In addition, the issuer must take reasonable steps to ensure that the purchasers do not resell the securities in a manner that makes the issuance a public distribution rather than a private one. Usually, the investor must hold the security for a minimum of two years.

In the following case, the issuer failed to prove it was entitled to a private offering exemption under Rule 506.

---

## MARK V. FSC SECURITIES CORP.
### 870 F.2d 331 (6th Cir. 1989)

FSC Securities Corp., a securities brokerage, sold limited partnership interests in Malaga Arabian Limited Partnership to Mr. and Mrs. Mark. A total of 28 investors purchased limited partnership interests in Malaga. All investors were asked to execute subscription documents, including a suitability letter in which the purchaser stated his income level, that he had an opportunity to obtain relevant information, and that he had sufficient knowledge and experience in business affairs to evaluate the risks of the investment.

When the value of the limited partnership interests fell, the Marks sued FSC to rescind their purchase on the grounds that FSC sold unregistered securities in violation of the Securities Act of 1933. The jury held that the offering was exempt as an offering not involving a public offering. The Marks appealed.

---

**Simpson, Judge**    Section 4(2) of the Securities Act exempts from registration with the SEC "transactions by an issuer not involving any public offering." There are no hard and fast rules for determining whether a securities offering is exempt from registration under the general language of section 4(2).

However, the "safe harbor" provision of Regulation D, Rule 506, deems certain transactions to be not involving any public offering within the meaning of section 4(2). FSC had to prove that certain objective tests were met. These conditions include the general conditions not in dispute here, and the following specific conditions:

(i) Limitation on number of purchasers. The issuer shall reasonably believe that there are no more than thirty-five purchasers of securities in any offering under this Section.

(ii) Nature of purchasers. The issuer shall reasonably believe immediately prior to making any sale that each purchaser who is not an accredited investor either alone or with his purchaser representative(s) has such knowledge and experience in financial and business matters that he is capable of evaluating the merits and risks of the prospective investment.

In this case, we take the issuer to be the general partners of Malaga. FSC is required to offer evidence of the issuer's reasonable belief as to the nature of each purchaser. The only testimony at trial competent to establish the issuer's belief as to the nature of the purchasers was that of Laurence Leafer, a general partner in Malaga. By his own admission, he had no knowledge about any purchaser, much less any belief, reasonable or not, as to the purchasers' knowledge and experience in financial and business matters.

Q: What was done to determine if investors were, in fact, reasonably sophisticated?

A: Well, there were two things. Number one, we had investor suitability standards that had to be met. You had to have a certain income, be in a certain tax bracket, this kind of thing. Then in the subscription documents themselves, they, when they sign it, supposedly represented that they had received information necessary to make an informed investment decision, and that they were sophisticated. And if they were not, they relied on an offering representative who was.

Q: Did you review the subscription documents that came in for the Malaga offering?

A: No.

Q: So do you know whether all of the investors in the Malaga offering met the suitability and sophistication requirements?

A: I don't.

FSC also offered as evidence the Marks' executed subscription documents, as well as a set of documents in blank, to establish the procedure it followed in the Malaga sales offering. Although the Marks' executed documents may have been sufficient to establish the reasonableness of any belief the issuer may have had as to the Marks' particular qualifications, that does not satisfy Rule 506. The documents offered no evidence from which a jury could conclude the issuer reasonably believed each purchaser was suitable. Instead, all that was proved was the sale of 28 limited partnership interests, and the circumstances under which those sales were intended to have been made. The blank subscriptions documents simply do not amount to probative evidence, when it is the answers and information received from purchasers that determine whether the conditions of Rule 506 have been met.

Having concluded that the Malaga limited-partnership offering did not meet the registration exemption requirement of Rule 506 of Regulation D, we conclude that the Marks are entitled to the remedy of rescission.

**Judgment reversed in favor of the Marks; remanded to the trial court.**

## Small Offering Exemptions

Sections 3(b) and 4(6) of the 1933 Act permit the SEC to exempt from registration any offering by an issuer not exceeding $5 million. Several SEC rules and regulations permit an issuer to sell small amounts of securities and avoid registration. The rationale for these exemptions is that the dollar amount of the securities offered or the number of purchasers is too small for the federal government to be concerned with registration. State securities law may require registration, however.

**Rule 504**    SEC Rule 504 of Regulation D allows the issuer to sell up to $1 million of securities in a 12-month period and avoid registration. Rule 504 sets no limits on the number of offerees or purchasers. The purchasers need not be sophisticated in investment matters, and the issuer need disclose information only as required by state securities law. Rule 504 permits general selling efforts, and purchasers are free to resell the securities at any time.

**Rule 505**    Rule 505 of Regulation D allows the issuer to sell up to $5 million of securities in a 12-month period and avoid registration. No general selling efforts are allowed, and purchasers may not resell the securities for at least two years. The issuer may sell to no more than 35 unaccredited purchasers, but there is no limit on the number of accredited purchasers. The purchasers need not be sophisticated in investment matters. Rule 505 has the same disclosure requirements as Rule 506.

**Regulation A**    Regulation A permits an issuer to sell up to $5 million of securities in a one-year period. There is no limit on the number of purchasers, no purchaser sophistication requirement, and no purchaser resale restriction.

The Regulation A disclosure document is the offering circular, which must be filed with the SEC. Usually, financial statements in the offering circular need not be audited. The offering circular is required to contain a balance sheet dated within 90 days before the filing date of the offering circular. It

**CONCEPT REVIEW**

## COMPARISON OF 1933 ACT REGISTRATION EXEMPTIONS

| | Type of Issuer that May Use the Rule | Limit of Amount Sold | Limit of Number of Purchasers |
|---|---|---|---|
| **Rule 504** | Only an issuer that is not a public company | $1 million | No limit |
| **Rule 505** | All issuers | $5 million | 35 unaccredited purchasers; unlimited number of accredited purchasers |
| **Rule 506** | All issuers | No limit | 35 unaccredited purchasers; unlimited number of accredited purchasers |
| **Regulation A** | Only an issuer that is not a public company | $5 million | No limit |
| **Rule 147** | Only an issuer organized and doing business in the same state as the offerees and purchasers (80% of assets, 80% of sales, 80% of proceeds used in that state) | No limit | No limit |

must also contain two years' income statements, cash flow statements, and statements of shareholder equity. Ordinarily, the financial statements need not be audited unless the issuer is otherwise required to have audited financial statements.

There is a 20-day waiting period after the filing of the offering circular, during which offers may be made. Oral offers are permitted, as are brief advertisements and written offers by an offering circular. Sales are permitted after the waiting period.

Regulation A also permits issuers to determine investors' interest in a planned offering prior to undertaking the expense of preparing an offering circular.

## Sale of Restricted Securities

Restricted securities are securities issued pursuant to Rules 505 and 506. Restricted securities are supposed to be held by the purchaser for at least two years. If they are sold earlier, the investor may be deemed an underwriter who has assisted the issuer in selling the securities to the general public. Consequently, both the issuer and the investor may have violated Section 5 of the 1933 Act by selling non-exempted securities prior to a registration of the securities with the SEC. As a result, all investors who purchased securities from the issuer in the Rule 506

| Must Purchasers Meet Any Requirements? | Is Disclosure Required? | Are General Solicitations Permitted? | Is Resale Restricted? | Is a Filing with the SEC Required? |
|---|---|---|---|---|
| No | No | Yes | No | Yes; Form D must be filed not later than 15 days after the first sale. |
| No | Yes, unless selling to accredited purchasers only | No | Yes; for at least 2 years | Yes; Form D must be filed not later than 15 days after the first sale. |
| Yes; each purchaser must either be accredited or have such knowledge and experience in business and financial matters as to be capable of evaluating the merits and risks of the investment. | Yes; unless selling to accredited purchasers only | No | Yes; for at least 2 years | Yes, Form D must be filed not later than 15 days after the first sale. |
| No | Yes; an offering circular must be given to investors | Yes | No | The offering circular and other offering material must be filed. |
| Yes; all offerees and purchasers must reside in the issuer's state | No | Yes | Yes; for 9 months sales may not be made outside the state of the issuance | No |

offering may have the remedy of rescission under Section 12(1), resulting in the issuer being required to return to investors all the proceeds of the issuance.

For example, an investor buys 10,000 common shares issued by Arcom Corporation pursuant to a Rule 506 private offering exemption. One month later, the investor sells the securities to 40 other investors. The original investor has acted as an underwriter because he has helped Arcom distribute the shares to the public. The original investor may not use the issuer's private offering exemption because it exempted only the issuer's sale to him. As a result, both the original investor and Arcom have violated Section 5. The 40 investors who purchased the securities from the original investor—and all other investors who purchased common shares from the issuer in the Rule 506 offering—may rescind their purchases under Section 12(1) of the 1933 Act, receiving from their seller the return of their investment.

SEC Rule 144 allows purchasers of restricted securities to resell the securities and not be deemed underwriters. The resellers must hold the securities for at least two years. Investment information concerning the issuer of the securities must be publicly available. In any three-month period, the reseller may sell only a limited amount of securities—the greater of 1 percent of the outstanding securities or the average weekly volume of trading. The reseller must file a notice (Form 144) with the SEC.

If a purchaser who is not an insider of the issuer has held the restricted securities for at least three years, Rule 144 permits her to sell unlimited amounts of the securities. In addition, investment information concerning the issuer need not be publicly available.

## Consequence of Obtaining a Securities or Transaction Exemption

When an issuer has obtained an exemption from the registration provisions of the 1933 Act, the Section 5 limits on when and how offers and sales may be made do not apply. Consequently, Section 12(1)'s remedy of rescission is unavailable to an investor who has purchased securities in an exempt offering.

When an issuer has attempted to comply with a registration exemption and has failed to do so, any offer or sale of securities by the issuer may violate Section 5. Because, the issuer has offered or sold nonexempted securities prior to filing a registration statement with the SEC, any purchaser may sue the issuer under Section 12(1) of the 1933 Act.

Although the registration provisions of the 1933 Act do not apply to an exempt offering, the antifraud provisions of the 1933 Act and 1934 Act, which are discussed later, are applicable. For example, when an issuer gives false information to a purchaser in a Rule 504 offering, the issuer may have violated the antifraud provisions of the two acts. The purchaser may obtain damages from the issuer.

## LIABILITY PROVISIONS OF THE 1933 ACT

To deter fraud, deception, and manipulation and to provide remedies to the victims of such practices, Congress included a number of liability provisions in the Securities Act of 1933.

## Liability for Defective Registration Statements

Section 11 of the 1933 Act provides civil liabilities for damages when a 1933 Act registration statement on its effective date misstates or omits a material fact. A purchaser of securities issued pursuant to the defective registration statement may sue certain classes of persons that are listed in Section 11—the issuer, its chief executive officer, its chief accounting officer, its chief financial officer, the directors, other signers of the registration statement, the underwriter, and experts who contributed to the registration statement (such as auditors who certified the financial statements or lawyers who issued an opinion concerning the tax aspects of a limited partnership). The purchaser's remedy under Section 11 is for damages caused by the misstatement or omission. Damages are presumed to be equal to the difference between the purchase price of the securities less the price of the securities at the time of the lawsuit.

Section 11 is a radical liability section for three reasons. First, reliance is usually not required; that is, the purchaser need not show that she relied on the misstatement or omission in the registration statement. In fact, the purchaser need not have read the registration statement or have seen it. Second, privity is not required; that is, the purchaser need not prove that she purchased the securities from the defendant. All she has to prove is that the defendant is in one of the classes of persons liable under Section 11. Third, the purchaser need not prove that the defendant negligently or intentionally misstated or omitted a material fact. Instead, a defendant who otherwise would be liable under Section 11 may escape liability by proving that he exercised due diligence.

**Section 11 Defenses**   A defendant can escape liability under Section 11 by proving that the purchaser knew of the misstatement or omission when she purchased the security. In addition, a defendant may raise the **due diligence defense**. It is the more important of the two defenses.

Any defendant except the issuer may escape liability under Section 11 by proving that he acted with due diligence in determining the accuracy of the registration statement. The due diligence defense basically requires the defendant to prove that he was not negligent. The exact defense varies, however, according to the class of defendant and the portion of the registration statement that is defective. Most defendants must prove that after a **reasonable investigation** they had **reasonable grounds to believe** and **did believe** that the registration statement was true and contained no omission of material fact.

Experts need to prove due diligence only in respect to the parts that they have contributed. For example, independent auditors must prove due diligence in ascertaining the accuracy of financial statements they certify. Due diligence requires that an auditor at least comply with generally accepted auditing standards (GAAS).

Nonexperts meet their due diligence defense for parts contributed by experts if they had no reason to believe and did not believe that the expertised parts misstated or omitted any material fact. This defense does not require the nonexpert to investigate the accuracy of expertised portions, unless something alerted the nonexpert to problems with the expertised portions.

The following is the most famous case construing the due diligence defense of Section 11.

## Escott v. BarChris Construction Corp.
### 283 F.Supp. 643 (S.D.N.Y. 1968)

BarChris Construction Corporation was in the business of constructing bowling centers. With the introduction of automatic pinsetters in 1952, there was a rapid growth in the popularity of bowling, and BarChris's sales increased from $800,000 in 1956 to over $9 million in 1960. By 1960, it was building about 3 percent of the lanes constructed, while Brunswick Corporation and AMF were building 97 percent. BarChris contracted with its customers to construct and equip bowling alleys for them. Under the contracts, a customer was required to make a small down payment in cash. After the alleys were constructed, customers gave BarChris promissory notes for the balance of the purchase price. BarChris discounted the notes with a factor. The factor kept part of the face value of the notes as a reserve until the customer paid the notes. BarChris was obligated to repurchase the notes if the customer defaulted.

In 1960, BarChris offered its customers an alternative financing method in which BarChris sold the interior of a bowling alley to a factor, James Talcott, Inc. Talcott then leased the alley either to a BarChris customer (Type A financing) or to a BarChris subsidiary that then subleased to the customer (Type B financing). Under Type A financing, BarChris guaranteed 25 percent of the customer's obligation under the lease. With Type B financing, BarChris was liable for 100 percent of its subsidiaries' lease obligations. Under either financing method, BarChris made substantial expenditures before receiving payment from customers and, therefore, experienced a constant need of cash.

In early 1961, BarChris decided to issue debentures and to use part of the proceeds to help its cash position. In March 1961, BarChris filed with the SEC a registration statement covering the debentures. The statement became effective on May 16. The proceeds of the offering were received by BarChris on May 24, 1961. By that time, BarChris had difficulty collecting from some of its customers, and other customers were in arrears on their payments to the factors of the discounted notes. Due to overexpansion in the bowling alley industry, many BarChris customers failed. On October 29, 1962, BarChris filed a petition for bankruptcy. On November 1, it defaulted on the payment of interest on the debentures.

Escott and other purchasers of the debentures sued BarChris and its officers, directors, and auditors, among others, under Section 11 of the Securities Act of 1933. BarChris's registration statement contained material misstatements and omitted material facts. It overstated current assets by $609,689 (15.6 percent), sales by $653,900 (7.7 percent), and earnings per share by 10 cents (15.4 percent) in the 1960 balance sheet and income statement certified by its auditors, Peat, Marwick, Mitchell & Co. The registration statement also understated BarChris's contingent liabilities by $618,853 (42.8 percent) as of April 30, 1961. It overstated gross profit for the first quarter of 1961 by $230,755 (92 percent) and sales for the first quarter of 1961 by $519,810 (32.1 percent). The March 31, 1961, backlog was overstated by $4,490,000 (186 percent). The 1961 figures were not audited by Peat, Marwick.

In addition, the registration statement reported that prior loans from officers had been repaid, but failed to disclose that officers had made new loans to BarChris totaling $386,615. BarChris had used $1,160,000 of the proceeds of the debentures to pay old debts, a use not disclosed in the registration statement. BarChris's potential liability of $1,350,000 to factors due to customer delinquencies on factored notes was not disclosed. The registration statement represented BarChris's contingent liability on Type B financings as 25 percent instead of 100 percent. It misrepresented the nature of BarChris's business by failing to disclose that BarChris was already engaged and was about to become more heavily engaged in the operation of bowling alleys, including one called Capitol Lanes, as a way of minimizing its losses from customer defaults.

Trilling, BarChris's comptroller, signed the registration statement. Auslander, a director, signed the registration statement. Peat, Marwick consented to being named as an expert in the registration statement. All three would be liable to Escott unless they could meet the due diligence defense of Section 11.

---

**McLean, District Judge**    The question is whether Trilling, Auslander, and Peat, Marwick have proved their due diligence defenses. The position of each defendant will be separately considered.

### Trilling

Trilling was BarChris's controller. He signed the registration statement in that capacity. Trilling entered BarChris's employ in October 1960. He was Kircher's [BarChris's treasurer] subordinate. When Kircher asked him for information, he furnished it.

Trilling was not a member of the executive committee. He was a comparatively minor figure in BarChris. The description of BarChris's management in the prospectus does not mention him. He was not considered to be an executive officer.

Trilling may well have been unaware of several of the inaccuracies in the prospectus. But he must have known of some of them. As a financial officer, he was familiar with BarChris's finances and with its books of account. He knew that part of the cash on deposit on December 31, 1960, had been procured temporarily by Russo [BarChris's executive vice president] for window-dressing purposes. He knew that BarChris was operating Capitol Lanes in 1960. He should have known, although perhaps through carelessness he did not know at the time, that BarChris's contingent liability on Type B lease transactions was greater than the prospectus stated. In the light of these facts, I cannot find that Trilling believed the entire prospectus to be true.

But even if he did, he still did not establish his due diligence defenses. He did not prove that as to the parts of the prospectus expertised by Peat, Marwick he had no reasonable ground to believe that it was untrue. He also failed to prove, as to the parts of the prospectus not expertised by Peat, Marwick, that he made a reasonable investigation which afforded him a reasonable ground to believe that it was true. As far as appears, he made no investigation. He did what was asked of him and assumed that others would properly take care of supplying accurate data as to the other aspects of the company's business. This would have been well enough but for the fact that he signed the registration statement. As a signer, he could not avoid responsibility by leaving it up to others to make it accurate. Trilling did not sustain the burden of proving his due diligence defenses.

### Auslander

Auslander was an outside director, i.e., one who was not an officer of BarChris. He was chairman of the board of Valley Stream National Bank in Valley Stream, Long Island. In February 1961, Vitolo [BarChris's president] asked him to become a director of BarChris. In February and early March 1961, before accepting Vitolo's invitation, Auslander made some investigation of BarChris. He obtained Dun & Bradstreet reports that contained sales and earnings figures for periods earlier than December 31, 1960. He caused inquiry to be made of certain of BarChris's banks and was advised that they regarded BarChris favorably. He was informed that inquiry of Talcott had also produced a favorable response.

On March 3, 1961, Auslander indicated his willingness to accept a place on the board. Shortly thereafter, on March 14, Kircher sent him a copy of BarChris's annual report for 1960. Auslander observed that BarChris's auditors were Peat, Marwick. They were also the auditors for the Valley Stream National Bank. He thought well of them.

Auslander was elected a director on April 17, 1961. The registration statement in its original form had already been filed, of course without his signature. On May 10, 1961, he signed a signature page for the first amendment to the registration statement which was filed on May 11, 1961. This was a separate sheet without any document attached. Auslander did not know that it was a signature page for a registration statement. He vaguely understood that it was something "for the SEC."

At the May 15 directors' meeting, however, Auslander did realize that what he was signing was a signature sheet to a registration statement. This was the first time that he had appreciated the fact. A copy of the registration statement in its earlier form as amended on May 11, 1961, was passed around at the meeting. Auslander glanced at it briefly. He did not read it thoroughly. At the May 15 meeting, Russo and Vitolo stated that everything was in order and that the prospectus was correct. Auslander believed this statement.

In considering Auslander's due diligence defenses, a distinction must be drawn between the expertised and nonexpertised portions of the prospectus. As to the former, Auslander knew that Peat, Marwick had audited the 1960 figures. He believed them to be correct because he had confidence in Peat, Marwick. He had no reasonable ground to believe otherwise.

As to the nonexpertised portions, however, Auslander is in a different position. He seems to have been under the impression that Peat, Marwick was responsible for all the figures. This impression was not correct, as he would have realized if he had read the prospectus carefully. Auslander made no investigation of the accuracy of the prospectus. He relied on the assurance of Vitolo and Russo, and upon the information he had received in answer to his inquiries back in February and early March. These inquiries were general ones, in the nature of a credit check. The information which he received in answer to them was also general, without specific reference to the statements in the prospectus, which was not prepared until some time thereafter.

It is true that Auslander became a director on the eve of the financing. He had little opportunity to familiarize himself with the company's affairs. The question is whether, under such circumstances, Auslander did enough to establish his due diligence.

Section 11 imposes liability upon a director, no matter how new he is. He is presumed to know his responsibility when he becomes a director. He can

escape liability only by using that reasonable care to investigate the facts that a prudent man would employ in the management of his own property. In my opinion, a prudent man would not act in an important matter without any knowledge of the relevant facts, in sole reliance upon general information which does not purport to cover the particular case. To say that such minimal conduct measures up to the statutory standard would, to all intents and purposes, absolve new directors from responsibility merely because they are new. This is not a sensible construction of Section 11, when one bears in mind its fundamental purpose of requiring full and truthful disclosure for the protection of investors.

Auslander has not established his due diligence defense with respect to the misstatements and omissions in those portions of the prospectus other than the audited 1960 figures.

### Peat, Marwick

The part of the registration statement purporting to be made upon the authority of Peat, Marwick as an expert was the 1960 figures. But because the statute requires the court to determine Peat, Marwick's belief, and the grounds thereof, "at the time such part of the registration statement became effective," for the purposes of this affirmative defense, the matter must be viewed as of May 16, 1961, and the question is whether at that time Peat, Marwick, after reasonable investigation, had reasonable ground to believe and did believe that the 1960 figures were true and that no material fact had been omitted from the registration statement which should have been included in order to make the 1960 figures not misleading. In deciding this issue, the court must consider not only what Peat, Marwick did in its 1960 audit, but also what it did in its subsequent S–1 review. The proper scope of that review must also be determined.

#### The 1960 Audit

Peat, Marwick's work was in general charge of a member of the firm, Cummings, and more immediately in charge of Peat, Marwick's manager, Logan. Most of the actual work was performed by a senior accountant, Berardi, who had junior assistants, one of whom was Kennedy.

Berardi was then about 30 years old. He was not yet a CPA. He had had no previous experience with the bowling industry. This was his first job as a senior accountant. He could hardly have been given a more difficult assignment.

It is unnecessary to recount everything that Berardi did in the course of the audit. We are concerned only with the evidence relating to what Berardi did or did not do with respect to those items which I have found to have been incorrectly reported in the 1960 figures in the prospectus. More narrowly, we are directly concerned only with such of those items as I have found to be material.

First and foremost is Berardi's failure to discover that Capitol Lanes had not been sold. This error affected both the sales figure and the liability side of the balance sheet. Fundamentally, the error stemmed from the fact that Berardi never realized that Heavenly Lanes and Capitol were two different names for the same alley. Berardi assumed that Heavenly was to be treated like any other completed job.

Berardi read the minutes of the board of directors meeting of November 22, 1960, which recited that "the Chairman recommended that the Corporation operate Capitol Lanes." Berardi knew from various BarChris records that Capitol Lanes, Inc., was paying rentals to Talcott. Also, a Peat, Marwick work paper bearing Kennedy's initials recorded that Capitol Lanes, Inc., held certain insurance policies.

Berardi testified that he inquired of Russo about Capitol Lanes and that Russo told him that Capitol Lanes, Inc., was going to operate an alley someday but as yet it had no alley. Berardi testified that he understood that the alley had not been built and that he believed that the rental payments were on vacant land.

I am not satisfied with this testimony. If Berardi did hold this belief, he should not have held it. The entries as to insurance and as to "operation of alley" should have alerted him to the fact that an alley existed. He should have made further inquiry on the subject. It is apparent that Berardi did not understand this transaction.

He never identified this mysterious Capitol with the Heavenly Lanes which he had included in his sales and profit figures. The vital question is whether he failed to make a reasonable investigation which, if he had made it, would have revealed the truth.

Certain accounting records of BarChris, which Berardi testified he did not see, would have put him on inquiry. One was a job cost ledger card for job no. 6036, the job number which Berardi put on his own sheet for Heavenly Lanes. This card read

"Capitol Theatre (Heavenly)." In addition, two accounts receivable cards each showed both names on the same card, Capitol and Heavenly. Berardi testified that he looked at the accounts receivable records but that he did not see these particular cards. He testified that he did not look on the job cost ledger cards because he took the costs from another record, the costs register.

The burden of proof on this issue is on Peat, Marwick. Although the question is a rather close one, I find that Peat, Marwick has not sustained that burden. Peat, Marwick has not proved that Berardi made a reasonable investigation as far as Capitol Lanes was concerned and that his ignorance of the true facts was justified.

I turn now to the errors in the current assets. As to cash, Berardi properly obtained a confirmation from the bank as to BarChris's cash balance on December 31, 1960. He did not know that part of this balance had been temporarily increased by the deposit of reserves returned by Talcott to BarChris conditionally for a limited time. I do not believe that Berardi reasonably should have known this. It would not be reasonable to require Berardi to examine all of BarChris's correspondence files [which contained correspondence indicating that BarChris was to return the cash to Talcott] when he had no reason to suspect any irregularity.

### The S-1 Review

The purpose of reviewing events subsequent to the date of a certified balance sheet (referred to as an S-1 review when made with reference to a registration statement) is to ascertain whether any material change has occurred in the company's financial position which should be disclosed in order to prevent the balance sheet figures from being misleading. The scope of such a review, under generally accepted auditing standards, is limited. It does not amount to a complete audit.

Berardi made the S-1 review in May 1961. He devoted a little over two days to it, a total of 20½ hours. He did not discover any of the errors or omissions pertaining to the state of affairs in 1961, all of which were material. The question is whether, despite his failure to find out anything, his investigation was reasonable within the meaning of the statute.

What Berardi did was to look at a consolidating trial balance as of March 31, 1961, which had been prepared by BarChris, compare it with the audited

December 31, 1960 figures, discuss with Trilling certain unfavorable developments which the comparison disclosed, and read certain minutes. He did not examine any important financial records other than the trial balance.

In substance, Berardi asked questions, he got answers which he considered satisfactory, and he did nothing to verify them. Since he never read the prospectus, he was not even aware that there had ever been any problem about loans from officers. He made no inquiry of factors about delinquent notes in his S–1 review. Since he knew nothing about Kircher's notes of the executive committee meetings, he did not learn that the delinquency situation had grown worse. He was content with Trilling's assurance that no liability theretofore contingent had become direct. Apparently the only BarChris officer with whom Berardi communicated was Trilling. He could not recall making any inquiries of Russo, Vitolo, or Pugliese [a BarChris vice president].

There had been a material change for the worse in BarChris's financial position. That change was sufficiently serious so that the failure to disclose it made the 1960 figures misleading. Berardi did not discover it. As far as results were concerned, his S–1 review was useless.

Accountants should not be held to a standard higher than that recognized in their profession. I do not do so here. Berardi's review did not come up to that standard. He did not take some of the steps which Peat, Marwick's written program prescribed. He did not spend an adequate amount of time on a task of this magnitude. Most important of all, he was too easily satisfied with glib answers to his inquiries.

This is not to say that he should have made a complete audit. But there were enough danger signals in the materials which he did examine to require some further investigation on his part. Generally accepted auditing standards require such further investigation under these circumstances. It is not always sufficient merely to ask questions.

Here again, the burden of proof is on Peat, Marwick. I find that burden has not been satisfied. I conclude that Peat, Marwick has not established its due diligence defense.

**Judgment for Escott and the other purchasers.**

**Due Diligence Meeting**   Officers, directors, underwriters, accountants, and other experts attempt to reduce their Section 11 liability by holding a due diligence meeting just prior to the effective date of a registration statement. At the due diligence meeting, the participants obtain assurances and demand proof from each other that the registration statement contains no misstatements or omissions of material fact. If it appears from the meeting that there are inadequacies in the investigation of the information in the registration statement, the issuer will delay the effective date until an appropriate investigation is undertaken.

## Other Liability Provisions

Section 12(2) of the 1933 Act prohibits misstatements or omissions of material fact in any written or oral communication in connection with the offer or sale of any security (except government-issued or government-guaranteed securities). Section 17(a) prohibits the use of any device or artifice to defraud, or the use of any untrue or misleading statement, in connection with the offer or sale of any security. Two of the subsections of Section 17(a) require that the defendant merely act negligently, while the third subsection requires proof of scienter. Scienter is the intent to deceive, manipulate, or defraud the purchaser. Some courts have held that scienter also includes recklessness.

Since these liability sections are part of federal law, there must be some connection between the illegal activity and interstate commerce for liability to exist. Section 11 merely requires the filing of a registration statement with the SEC. Sections 12(1), 12(2), and 17(a) require the use of the mails or other instrumentality or means of interstate communication or transportation.

## Criminal Liability

Section 24 of the 1933 Act provides for criminal liability for any person who willfully violates the Act or its rules and regulations. The maximum penalty is a $10,000 fine and five years' imprisonment. Criminal actions under the 1933 Act are brought by the attorney general of the United States, not by the SEC.

## SECURITIES EXCHANGE ACT OF 1934

The Securities Exchange Act of 1934 is chiefly concerned with requiring the disclosure of material information to investors. Unlike the 1933 Act, which is primarily a one-time disclosure statute, the 1934 Act requires **periodic disclosure** by issuers with publicly held equity securities. An issuer with publicly traded equity securities must report annually and quarterly to its shareholders. Also, any material information about the issuer must be disclosed as the issuer obtains it, unless the issuer has a valid business purpose for withholding disclosure.

In addition, the 1934 Act regulates insiders' transactions in securities, proxy solicitations, tender offers, brokers and dealers, and securities exchanges. The 1934 Act also has several sections prohibiting fraud and manipulation in securities transactions. The ultimate purpose of the 1934 Act is to keep investors fully informed to allow them to make intelligent investment decisions at any time.

### Registration of Securities under the 1934 Act

Under the 1934 Act, issuers must **register classes of securities**. This is different from the 1933 Act, which requires issuers to register issuances of securities. Under the 1933 Act, securities are registered only for the term of an issuance. Under the 1934 Act, registered classes of securities remain registered until the issuer takes steps to deregister the securities. The chief consequence of having securities registered under the 1934 Act is that the issuer is required to disclose information about itself to its owners and the SEC.

**Registration Requirement**    Two types of issuers must register securities with the SEC under the 1934 Act.

1. An issuer whose total assets exceed $5 million must register a class of equity securities held by at least 500 shareholders if the securities are traded in interstate commerce.

2. An issuer must register any security traded on a national security exchange, such as common shares traded on the American Stock Exchange.

To register the securities, the issuer must file a 1934 Act **registration statement** with the SEC. The information required in the 1934 Act registration statement is similar to that required in the 1933 Act registration statement, except that offering information is omitted.

**Termination of Registration**    An issuer may avoid the expense and burden of complying with the periodic disclosure and other requirements of the 1934 Act if the issuer terminates its registration. A 1934 Act registration may be terminated if the issuer has fewer than 300 shareholders. In addition, a registration may be terminated if the issuer has fewer than 500 shareholders of any class of equity securities and assets of no more than $5 million. However, an issuer with securities listed on a national securities exchange would not be able to terminate a registration of the listed securities.

**Periodic Reporting Requirement**    To maintain a steady flow of material information to investors, the 1934 Act requires public issuers to file periodic reports with the SEC. Three types of issuers must file such reports:

1. An issuer whose total assets exceed $5 million and who has a class of equity securities held by at least 500 shareholders, if the securities are traded in interstate commerce.

2. An issuer whose equity securities are traded on a national securities exchange.

3. An issuer who has made a registered offering under the 1933 Act.

The first two types of issuers—which are issuers that must also register securities under the 1934 Act—must file several periodic reports, including an annual report (Form 10-K) and a quarterly report (Form 10-Q). They must file a monthly report (Form 8-K) when material events occur. Comparable reports must also be sent to their shareholders. The third type of issuer—an issuer who must disclose under the 1934 Act only because it has made a registered offering under the 1933 Act—must file the same reports as the other issuers, except that it need not provide an annual report to its shareholders.

1934 Act disclosure required of the third type of issuer is in addition to the disclosure required by the 1933 Act.

The 10-K annual report must include audited financial statements plus current information about the conduct of the business, its management, and the status of its securities. The 10-K auditing requirements are the same as for a 1933 Act registration statement—two years' audited balance sheets, three years' audited income statements, and three years' audited statements of changes in financial position.

The quarterly report, the 10-Q, requires only a summarized, unaudited operating statement and un-audited figures on capitalization and shareholders' equity. The 8-K monthly report must be filed within 10 days of the end of any month in which any specified event occurs, such as a change in the amount of securities, an acquisition or disposition of assets, a change in control of the company, a revaluation of assets, or "any materially important event."

The SEC permits issuers to file reports electronically, transmitting them by telephone or by sending computer tapes or disks to the SEC. These electronic filings are made with the SEC's Electronic Data Gathering, Analysis, and Retrieval system: EDGAR.

**Suspension of Duty to File Reports**   An issuer's duty to file periodic reports is suspended if the issuer has fewer than 300 shareholders. In addition, a suspension occurs if the issuer has fewer than 500 shareholders of any class of equity securities and assets of no more than $5 million. However, an issuer with securities traded on a national securities exchange would remain obligated to file periodic reports.

## Holdings and Trading by Insiders

Section 16 of the 1934 Act is designed to promote investor confidence in the integrity of the securities markets by limiting the ability of insiders to profit from trading in the shares of their issuers. Section 16(a) requires statutory insiders to disclose their ownership of their company's securities. In addition, statutory insiders must report any transaction in such securities within 10 days following the end of the month in which the transaction occurs. They

must also report purchases and sales made up to six months before and up to six months after becoming an officer, director, or a 10 percent holder.

A statutory insider is a person who falls into any of the following categories:

1. An officer of a corporation having equity securities registered under the 1934 Act.
2. A director of such a corporation.
3. An owner of more than 10 percent of a class of equity securities registered under the 1934 Act.

Section 16(b) prevents an insider from profiting from short-swing trading in his company's shares. Any profit made by a statutory insider is recoverable by the issuer if the profit resulted from the purchase and sale (or the sale and purchase) of any class of the issuer's equity securities within less than a six-month period. This provision was designed to stop speculative insider trading on the basis of information that "may have been obtained by such owner, director, or officer by reason of his relationship to the issuer." The application of the provision is without regard to intent to use or actual use of inside information. However, a few cases have held that sales made by a statutory insider without actual access to inside information do not violate Section 16(b).

## Proxy Solicitation Regulation

In a public corporation, shareholders rarely attend and vote at shareholder meetings. Many shareholders are able to vote at shareholder meetings only by **proxy**, a document by which shareholders direct other persons to vote their shares. Just as investors need information to be able to make intelligent investment decisions, shareholders need information to make intelligent voting and proxy decisions.

The 1934 Act regulates the solicitation of proxies. SEC Regulation 14A requires any person soliciting proxies from holders of securities registered under the 1934 Act to furnish each holder with a **proxy statement** containing voting information. Usually, the only party soliciting proxies is the corporation's management, which is seeking proxies from common shareholders to enable it to reelect itself to the board of directors.

If the management of the corporation does not solicit proxies, it must nevertheless inform the shareholders of material information affecting matters that are to be put to a vote of the shareholders. This **information statement**, which contains about the same information as a proxy statement, must be sent to all shareholders that are entitled to vote at the meeting.

The primary purpose of the SEC rules concerning information that must be included in the proxy or information statement is to permit shareholders to make informed decisions while voting for directors and considering any resolutions proposed by the management or shareholders. Information on each director nominee must include the candidate's principal occupation, his shareholdings in the corporation, his previous service as a director of the corporation, his material transactions with the corporation (such as goods or services provided), and his directorships in other corporations. The total remuneration of the five directors or officers who are highest paid, including bonuses, grants under stock option plans, fringe benefits, and other perquisites, must also be included in the proxy statement.

SEC rules regarding the content of proxies ensure that the shareholder understands how his proxy will be voted. The proxy form must indicate in boldface type on whose behalf it is being solicited—for example, the corporation's management. Generally, the proxy must permit the shareholder to vote for or against the proposal or to abstain from voting on any resolutions on the meeting's agenda. The proxy form may ask for discretionary voting authority if the proxy indicates in bold print how the shares will be voted. For directors' elections, the shareholders must be provided with a means for withholding approval for each nominee.

SEC Rule 14a-9 prohibits misstatements or omissions of material fact in the course of a proxy solicitation. If a violation is proved, a court may enjoin the holding of the shareholders' meeting, void the proxies that were illegally obtained, or rescind the action taken at the shareholders' meeting.

**Proxy Contests**   A shareholder may decide to solicit proxies in competition with management. Such a competition is called a proxy contest, and a solicitation of this kind is also subject to SEC rules. To facilitate proxy contests, the SEC requires the corporation either to furnish a shareholder list to shareholders who desire to wage a proxy contest or to mail the competing proxy material for them.

**Shareholder Proposals**   In a large public corporation, it is very expensive for a shareholder to solicit proxies in support of a proposal for corporate action that she will offer at a shareholders' meeting. Therefore, she usually asks the management to include her proposal in its proxy statement. SEC Rule 14a-8 covers proposals by shareholders.

Under SEC Rule 14a-8, the corporation must include a shareholder's proposal in its proxy statement if, among other things, the shareholder owns at least 1 percent or $1,000 of the securities to be voted at the shareholders' meeting. A shareholder may submit only one proposal per meeting. The proposal and its supporting statement may not exceed 500 words.

Under Rule 14a-8, a corporation's management may exclude many types of shareholder proposals from its proxy statement. For example, a proposal is excludable if:

**1.** The proposal deals with the ordinary business operations of the corporation. For example, Pacific Telesis Group was permitted on this ground to omit a proposal that the board consider adding an environmentalist director and designate a vice president for environmental matters for each subsidiary. However, TRW, Inc., was required to include in its proxy statement a proposal that it establish a shareholder advisory committee that would advise the board of directors on the interests of shareholders.

**2.** The proposal relates to operations that account for less than 5 percent of a corporation's total assets and is not otherwise significantly related to the company's business. For example, Harsco Corp. could not omit a proposal that it sell its 50 percent interest in a South African firm even though the investment was arguably economically insignificant—only 4.5 percent of net earnings—because the issues raised by the proposal were significantly related to Harsco's business.

**3.** The proposal requires the issuer to violate a state or federal law. For example, one shareholder asked North American Bank to put a lesbian on the board of directors. The proposal was excludable because it may have required the bank to violate antidiscrimination laws.

**4.** The proposal relates to a personal claim or grievance. A proposal that the corporation pay the shareholder $1 million for damages that she suffered from using one of the corporation's products would be excludable.

In addition, Rule 14a-8 prevents a shareholder from submitting a proposal similar to recent proposals that have been overwhelmingly rejected by shareholders in recent years.

## LIABILITY PROVISIONS OF THE 1934 ACT

To prevent fraud, deception, or manipulation and to provide remedies to the victims of such practices, Congress included provisions in the 1934 Act that impose liability on persons who engage in wrongful conduct.

### Liability for False Statements in Filed Documents

Section 18 is the 1934 Act counterpart to Section 11 of the 1933 Act. Section 18 imposes liability on any person responsible for a false or misleading statement of material fact in any document filed with the SEC under the 1934 Act. (Filed documents include the 10-K report, 8-K report, and proxy statements, but not the 10-Q report.) Any person who relies on a false or misleading statement in such a filed document may sue for damages. The purchaser need not prove that the defendant was at fault. Instead, the defendant has a defense that he acted in good faith and had no knowledge that the statement was false or misleading. This defense requires only that the defendant prove that he did not act with scienter.

### Section 10(b) and Rule 10b-5

The most important liability section in the 1934 Act is Section 10(b), an extremely broad provision prohibiting the use of any manipulative or deceptive device in contravention of any rules that the SEC prescribes as "necessary or appropriate in the public interest or for the protection of investors." Rule 10b-5 was adopted by the SEC under Section 10(b). The rule states:

It shall be unlawful for any person, directly or indirectly, by use of any means or instrumentality of interstate commerce or of the mails, or of any facility of any national securities exchange,

(a) to employ any device, scheme, or artifice to defraud,

(b) to make any untrue statement of a material fact or to omit to state a material fact necessary in order to make the statements made, in the light of the circumstances under which they were made, not misleading, or

(c) to engage in any act, practice, or course of business which operates or would operate as a fraud or deceit upon any person,

in connection with the purchase or sale of any security.

Rule 10b-5 applies to all transactions in all securities, whether or not registered under the 1933 Act or the 1934 Act.

Rule 10b-5 prohibits only *misstatements or omissions of material fact*. A person **misstates** material facts, for example, when a manager of an unprofitable business induces shareholders to sell their stock to him by stating that the business will fail, although he knows that the business has become potentially profitable.

Liability for an **omission of a material fact** arises when a person fails to disclose material facts when he has a duty to disclose. For example, a securities broker is liable to his customer for not disclosing that he owns the shares that he recommends to the customer. As an agent of the customer, he owes a fiduciary duty to his customer to disclose his conflict of interest. In addition, a person is liable for omitting to tell all of the material facts after he has chosen to disclose some of them. His incomplete disclosure creates the duty to disclose all of the material facts.

Under Rule 10b-5, the misstated or omitted fact must be **material**. In essence, material information is any information that is likely to have an impact on the price of a security in the market. A fact is material if there is a substantial likelihood that a reasonable investor would consider it important to his decision, that the fact would have assumed actual significance in the deliberations of the reasonable investor, and that the disclosure of the fact would have been viewed by the reasonable investor as having significantly altered the total mix of information made available.

Under Rule 10b-5, the defendant is not liable unless he acted with **scienter**. Scienter is an intent to deceive, manipulate, or defraud. Scienter probably includes gross recklessness of the defendant in ascertaining the truth of his statements. Mere negligence is not scienter.

Rule 10b-5 requires that private plaintiffs seeking damages be **actual purchasers or sellers** of securities. Persons who were deterred from purchasing securities by fraudulent statements may not recover lost profits under Rule 10b-5.

Under Rule 10b-5, private plaintiffs alleging damages due to misstatements by the defendant must prove that they **relied** on the misstatement of material fact. The SEC as plaintiff need not prove reliance. For private plaintiffs, reliance is not usually required in omission cases; the investor need merely prove that the omitted fact was material. In addition, the misstatement or omission must **cause the investor's loss.**

Several courts have held that an investor's reliance on the availability of the securities on the market satisfies the reliance requirement of Rule 10b-5 because the securities market is defrauded as to the value of the securities. This **fraud-on-the-market theory** is based on the hypothesis that, in an open and developed securities market, the price of a company's stock is determined by the available material information regarding the company and its business. With the presence of a market, the market is interposed between seller and buyer and, ideally, transmits information to the investor in the processed form of a market price. Thus, the market is performing a substantial part of the valuation process performed by the investor in a face-to-face transaction. The market is acting as the unpaid agent of the investor, informing him that given all the information available to it, the value of the stock is the same as the market price. Misleading statements will therefore defraud purchasers of stock even if the purchasers do not directly rely on the misstatements and even if the defendants never communicated with the plaintiffs.

In *Levinson v. Basic, Inc.*, which follows this section, the Supreme Court held that the fraud-on-the-market theory permits a court to presume an investor's reliance merely from the public availability of material misrepresentations. That presumption, however, is rebuttable, such as by evidence that an investor knew the market price was incorrect.

For Rule 10b-5 to apply, the wrongful action must be accomplished *by the mails, with any means or instrumentality of interstate commerce,* or *on a national securities exchange*. This element satisfies the federal jurisdiction requirement. Use of the mails or a telephone within one state has been held to meet this element.

The scope of activities proscribed by Rule 10b-5 is not immediately obvious. While it is easy to understand that actual fraud and price manipulation are covered by the rule, two other areas are less easily mastered—the corporation's continuous disclosure obligation and insider trading.

**Continuous Disclosure Obligation**   The purpose of the 1934 Act is to ensure that investors have the information they need in order to make intelligent investment decisions at all times. The periodic reporting requirements of the 1934 Act are especially designed to accomplish this result. If important developments arise between the disclosure dates of reports, however, investors will not have all of the information they need to make intelligent decisions unless the corporation discloses the material information immediately. Rule 10b-5 requires a corporation to disclose material information immediately, unless the corporation has a valid business purpose for withholding disclosure. When a corporation chooses to disclose information or to comment on information that it has no duty to disclose, it must do so accurately.

Until 1988, courts had disagreed on whether Rule 10b-5 requires disclosure of merger and other acquisition negotiations prior to an agreement in principle. In the following case, the Supreme Court of the United States held that materiality of merger negotiations is to be determined on a case-by-case basis. The Court held that materiality depends on the probability that the transaction will be consummated and its significance to the issuer of the securities. In addition, the Court stated that a corporation that chooses to comment on acquisition negotiations must do so truthfully.

---

## LEVINSON V. BASIC, INC.
### 485 U.S. 224 (U.S. Sup. Ct. 1988)

For over a decade, Combustion Engineering, Inc. (CEI), had been interested in acquiring Basic, Inc. When antitrust barriers to such an acquisition were eliminated in 1976, CEI's secret strategic plan listed the acquisition of Basic as an objective. Between September 1976 and October 1977, the managements of Basic and CEI privately discussed several times a possible acquisition of Basic by CEI. Throughout 1977 and

1978, despite the secrecy of merger negotiations, there were repeated instances of abnormal trading in Basic's shares on the New York Stock Exchange. On October 19 and 20, 1977, the trading volume in Basic's shares rose from an average of 7,000 shares per day to 29,000 shares. On October 21, 1977, Max Muller, the president of Basic, made a public announcement, reported in a major newspaper, that "the company knew no reason for the stock's activity and that no negotiations were under way with any company for a merger."

Secret contacts between Basic and CEI continued, however. On June 7, 1978, CEI offered $28 per share for Basic, which Basic rejected as too low. CEI stated it would make a better offer, but Muller told CEI to "hold off until we tell you," because Muller wanted to see an investment banker's valuation of Basic before evaluating any CEI offer. Muller and other Basic officials decided to ask CEI for its best offer. On July 10, 1978, Muller and CEI agreed that CEI would make an informal offer to Basic. CEI advised Muller to make no public disclosures about the negotiations.

On July 14, 1978, the price of Basic shares rose more than 12 percent to $27 per share on trading of 18,200 shares. The New York Stock Exchange called Basic and asked it to explain the trading in its shares. Basic denied that any undisclosed merger or acquisition plans or any other significant corporate development existed. On September 24, 1978, the price of Basic shares rose more than 2 points to $30 per share on volume of 31,900 shares. The next day, the price rose almost 3 points to $33 per share on volume of 28,500 shares, even though the Dow Jones Industrial Average fell more than 3 points. Again the Exchange asked Basic whether there were any undisclosed acquisition plans or any other significant corporate developments. Basic flatly denied that there were any corporate developments and issued a press release that stated:

management is unaware of any present or pending corporate development that would result in the abnormally heavy trading activity and price fluctuation in company shares that have been experienced in the past few days.

Secret contacts between Basic and CEI continued. In early November, Basic sent a quarterly report to its shareholders in which it stated:

With regard to the stock market activity in the Company's shares we remain unaware of any present or pending developments that would account for the high volume of trading and price fluctuations in recent months.

On November 27, 1978, CEI secretly offered to buy Basic's outstanding shares for $35 per share. Basic rejected the offer. On December 14, 1978, CEI offered $46 per share. The next day, Friday, December 15, the price of Basic's shares soared. Again Basic answered the Exchange's inquiry with a denial of corporate developments. On Monday, December 18, 1978, Basic asked the Exchange to suspend trading in Basic shares, because it had been "approached" concerning a possible merger. The next day, Basic accepted CEI's offer. On the following day, December 19, Basic announced its acceptance of CEI's offer to buy Basic's outstanding shares for $46 per share.

Max Levinson and several other Basic shareholders sold their Basic shares between October 21, 1977 and December 15, 1978, at a price lower than CEI's offer. They claimed that Basic's statements denying that any merger discussions were occurring violated Section 10(b) and Rule 10b-5 of the Securities Exchange Act of 1934. The district court held that the statements were not material. Levinson appealed to the Sixth Circuit Court of Appeals, which held that Basic possessed no general duty to disclose the merger negotiations. However, the court found that Basic released statements that were so incomplete as to be misleading. Basic appealed to the Supreme Court.

---

**Blackmun, Justice**   Underlying the adoption of extensive disclosure requirements of the 1934 Act was a legislative philosophy: There cannot be honest markets without honest publicity. Manipulation and dishonest practices of the market place thrive upon mystery and secrecy.

The Court previously has explicitly defined a standard of materiality under the securities laws, concluding in the proxy-solicitation context that "[a]n omitted fact is material if there is a substantial likelihood that a reasonable shareholder would consider it important in deciding how to vote." *TSC*

*Industries, Inc. v. Northway, Inc.* (1976). The Court was careful not to set too low a standard of materiality; it was concerned that a minimal standard might bring an overabundance of information within its reach, and lead management "simply to bury the shareholders in an avalanche of trivial information—a result that is hardly conducive to informed decisionmaking." To fulfill the materiality requirement "there must be a substantial likelihood that the disclosure of the omitted fact would have been viewed by the reasonable investor as having significantly altered the "total mix" of information made available." We now expressly adopt the *TSC Industries* standard of materiality for the Section 10(b) and Rule 10b-5 context.

The application of this materiality standard to preliminary merger discussions is not self-evident. Where the event is contingent or speculative in nature, it is difficult to ascertain whether the "reasonable investor" would have considered the omitted information significant at the time. Merger negotiations, because of the ever-present possibility that the contemplated transaction will not be effectuated, fall into this category.

Basic urges upon us the Third Circuit test for resolving this difficulty. Under this approach, preliminary merger discussions do not become material until "agreement-in-principle" as to the price and structure of the transaction has been reached between the would-be merger partners. See *Greenfield v. Heublein, Inc.* (3d Cir. 1984). By definition, then, information concerning any negotiations not yet at the agreement-in-principle stage could be withheld or even misrepresented without a violation of Rule 10b-5.

Three rationales have been offered in support of the "agreement-in-principle" test. The first derives from the concern that an investor not be overwhelmed by excessively detailed and trivial information and focuses on the substantial risk that preliminary merger discussions may collapse: because such discussions are inherently tentative, disclosure of their existence itself could mislead investors and foster false optimism. The other two justifications for the agreement-in-principle standard are based on management concerns: because the requirement of "agreement-in-principle" limits the scope of disclosure obligations, it helps preserve the confidentiality of merger discussions where earlier disclosure might prejudice the negotiations; and

the test also provides a usable, bright-line rule for determining when disclosure must be made.

None of these policy-based rationales, however, purports to explain why drawing the line at agreement-in-principle reflects the significance of the information upon the investor's decision. The first rationale "assumes that investors are nitwits, unable to appreciate—even when told—that mergers are risky propositions up until the closing." *Flamm v. Eberstadt* (7th Cir. 1987).

The second rationale, the importance of secrecy during the early stages of merger discussions, also seems irrelevant to an assessment whether their existence is significant to the trading decision of a reasonable investor. To avoid a "bidding war" over its target, an acquiring firm often will insist that negotiations remain confidential and at least one Court of Appeals has stated that "silence pending settlement of the price and structure of a deal is beneficial to most investors, most of the time." *Flamm v. Eberstadt.*

We need not ascertain, however, whether secrecy necessarily maximizes shareholder wealth—although we note that the proposition is at least disputed as a matter of theory and empirical research—for this case does not concern the timing of a disclosure; it concerns only its accuracy and completeness. We face here the narrow question whether information concerning the existence and status of preliminary merger discussions is significant to the reasonable investor's trading decision. Arguments based on the premise that some disclosure would be "premature" in a sense are more properly considered under the rubric of an issuer's duty to disclose. The "secrecy" rationale is simply inapposite to the definition of materiality.

The final justification offered in support of the agreement-in-principle test seems to be directed solely at the comfort of corporate managers. A bright-line rule indeed is easier to follow than a standard that requires the exercise of judgment in light of all the circumstances. But ease of application alone is not an excuse for ignoring the purposes of the securities acts and Congress' policy decisions.

We therefore find no valid justification for artificially excluding from the definition of materiality information concerning merger discussions, which would otherwise be considered significant to the trading decision of a reasonable investor, merely because agreement-in-principle as to price and structure has not yet been reached by the parties or their representatives.

Even before this Court's decision in *TSC Industries*, the Second Circuit had explained the role of the materiality requirement of Rule 10b-5, with respect to contingent or speculative information or events. Under such circumstances, materiality "will depend at any given time upon a balancing of both the indicated probability that the event will occur and the anticipated magnitude of the event in light of the totality of the company activity." *SEC v. Texas Gulf Sulphur Co.* (2d Cir. 1968).

The late Judge Friendly applied the Texas Gulf Sulphur probability/magnitude approach in the specific context of preliminary merger negotiations. He stated:

Since a merger in which it is bought out is the most important event that can occur in a small corporation's life, to wit, its death, we think that inside information, as regards a merger of this sort, can become material at an earlier stage than would be the case as regards lesser transactions—and this even though the mortality rate of mergers in such formative stages is doubtless high. *SEC v. Geon Industries, Inc.* (2d Cir. 1976).

We agree with that analysis.

In response to the *Basic* decision, in 1989 the SEC released guidelines to help public companies decide whether they must disclose merger negotiations. A company is not required to disclose merger negotiations if all three of the following requirements are met:

1. The company did not make any prior disclosures about the merger negotiations,
2. Disclosure is not compelled by other SEC rules, and
3. Management determines that disclosure would jeopardize completion of the merger transaction.

**Trading on Inside Information**   One of the greatest destroyers of public confidence in the integrity of the securities market is the belief that insiders can trade securities while possessing corporate information that is not available to the general public.

Whether merger discussions in any particular case are material therefore depends on the facts. Generally, in order to assess the probability that the event will occur, a factfinder will need to look to indicia of interest in the transaction at the highest corporate levels. Board resolutions, instructions to investment bankers, and actual negotiations between principals or their intermediaries may serve as indicia of interest. To assess the magnitude of the transaction to the issuer of the securities allegedly manipulated, a factfinder will need to consider such facts as the size of the two corporate entities and of the potential premiums over market value. No particular event or factor short of closing the transaction need be either necessary or sufficient by itself to render merger discussions material.

As we clarify today, materiality depends on the significance the reasonable investor would place on the withheld or misrepresented information. Because the standard of materiality we have adopted differs from that used by both courts below, we remand the case for reconsideration.

**Judgment vacated and remanded to the Court of Appeals.**

Rule 10b-5 prohibits **insider trading** on nonpublic corporate information. A person with nonpublic, confidential, inside information may not use that information when trading with a person who does not possess that information. He must either disclose the information before trading or refrain from trading. The difficult task in the insider trading area is determining when a person is subject to this **disclose-or-refrain** rule.

In *United States v. Chiarella*,[5] the Supreme Court laid down the test for determining an insider's liability for trading on nonpublic, corporate information:

The duty to disclose arises when one party has information that the other party is entitled to know because of a fiduciary or similar relation of trust and confidence between them. A relationship of trust and confidence exists between the shareholders of a corporation and those

[5]445 U.S. 222 (U.S. Sup. Ct. 1980).

insiders who have obtained confidential information by reason of their position with that corporation. This relationship gives rise to a duty to disclose because of the necessity of preventing a corporate insider from taking unfair advantage of the uninformed stockholders.

Under this test, **insiders** include not only officers and directors of the corporation, but also anyone who is *entrusted with corporate information for a corporate purpose*. Insiders include outside consultants, lawyers, independent auditors, engineers, investment bankers, public relations advisers, news reporters, and personnel of government agencies who are given confidential corporate information for a corporate purpose.

**Tippees** are recipients of inside information (tips) from insiders. Tippees of insiders—such as relatives and friends of insiders, stockbrokers, and security analysts—are forbidden to trade on inside information and are subject to recovery of their profits if they do.

In the following case, the Supreme Court stated the applicability of Rule 10b-5 to tippees. The Court held that a tippee has liability if (1) an insider has breached a fiduciary duty of trust and confidence to the shareholders by disclosing to the tippee and (2) the tippee knows or should know of the insider's breach. In addition, the court held that an insider has not breached her fiduciary duty to the shareholders unless she has received a personal benefit by disclosing to the tippee.

---

## SEC v. DIRKS
### 463 U.S. 646 (U.S. Sup. Ct. 1983)

On March 6, 1973, Raymond Dirks, a security analyst in a New York brokerage firm, received nonpublic information from Ronald Secrist, a former officer of Equity Funding of America, a seller of life insurance and mutual funds. Secrist alleged that the assets of Equity Funding were vastly overstated as the result of fraudulent corporate practices. He also stated that the SEC and state insurance departments had failed to act on similar charges of fraud made by Equity Funding employees. Secrist urged Dirks to verify the fraud and to disclose it publicly.

Dirks visited Equity Funding's headquarters in Los Angeles and interviewed several officers and employees of the corporation. The senior management denied any wrongdoing, but certain employees corroborated the charges of fraud. Dirks openly discussed the information he had obtained with a number of his clients and investors. Some of these persons sold their holdings of Equity Funding securities.

Dirks urged a *Wall Street Journal* reporter to write a story on the fraud allegations. The reporter, fearing libel, declined to write the story.

During the two-week period in which Dirks investigated the fraud and spread the word of Secrist's charges, the price of Equity Funding stock fell from $26 per share to less than $15 per share. The New York Stock Exchange halted trading in Equity Funding stock on March 27. On that date, Dirks voluntarily presented his information on the fraud to the SEC. Only then did the SEC bring an action for fraud against Equity Funding. Shortly thereafter, California insurance authorities impounded Equity Funding's records and uncovered evidence of the fraud. On April 2, *The Wall Street Journal* published a front-page story based largely on information assembled by Dirks. Equity Funding immediately went into receivership.

The SEC brought an administrative proceeding against Dirks for violating Rule 10b-5 by passing along confidential inside information to his clients. The SEC found that he had violated Rule 10b-5, but it merely censured him, since he had played an important role in bringing the fraud to light. Dirks appealed to the Court of Appeals, which affirmed the judgment. Dirks then appealed to the Supreme Court.

---

**Powell, Justice**   In *U.S. v. Chiarella* (1980), we accepted the two elements set out in *In re Cady, Roberts* (1961) for establishing a Rule 10b-5 violation: (i) the existence of a relationship affording access to inside information intended to be available only for a corporate purpose, and (ii) the unfairness of allowing a corporate insider to take advantage of that information by trading without disclosure. The

Court found that a duty to disclose under Section 10(b) does not arise from the mere possession of nonpublic market information. Such a duty arises from the existence of a fiduciary relationship.

There can be no duty to disclose when the person who has traded on inside information was not the corporation's agent, was not a fiduciary, or was not a person in whom the sellers of the securities had placed their trust and confidence.

This requirement of a specific relationship between the shareholders and the individual trading on inside information has created analytical difficulties for the SEC and courts in policing tippees who trade on inside information. Unlike insiders who have independent fiduciary duties to both the corporation and its shareholders, the typical tippee has no such relationship. In view of this absence, it has been unclear how a tippee acquires the duty to refrain from trading on inside information.

Not only are insiders forbidden by their fiduciary relationship from personally using undisclosed corporate information to their advantage, but also they may not give such information to an outsider for the same improper purpose of exploiting the information for their personal gain. The transactions of those who knowingly participate with the fiduciary in such a breach are as forbidden as transactions on behalf on the trustee himself. Thus, the tippee's duty to disclose or abstain is derivative from that of the insider's duty. The tippee's obligation has been viewed as arising from his role as a participant after the fact in the insider's breach of a fiduciary duty.

A tippee assumes a fiduciary duty to the shareholders of a corporation not to trade on material nonpublic information only when the insider has breached his fiduciary duty to the shareholders by disclosing the information to the tippee and the tippee knows or should know that there has been a breach.

In determining whether a tippee is under an obligation to disclose or abstain, it thus is necessary to determine whether the insider's tip constituted a breach of the insider's fiduciary duty. Whether disclosure is a breach of duty therefore depends in large part on the purpose of the disclosure. Thus, the test is whether the insider personally will benefit, directly or indirectly, from his disclosure. Absent some personal gain, there has been no breach of

duty to stockholders. And absent a breach by the insider, there is no derivative breach.

This requires courts to focus on objective criteria, *i.e.*, whether the insider receives a direct or indirect personal benefit from the disclosure, such as a pecuniary gain or a reputational benefit that will translate into future earnings. For example, there may be a relationship between the insider and the recipient that suggests a *quid pro quo* from the latter, or an intention to benefit the particular recipient. The elements of fiduciary duty and exploitation of nonpublic information also exist when an insider makes a gift of confidential information to a relative or friend who trades. The tip and trade resemble trading by the insider himself followed by a gift of the profits to the recipient.

Under the inside-trading and tipping rules set forth above, we find that there was no violation by Dirks. Dirks was a stranger to Equity Funding, with no pre-existing fiduciary duty to its shareholders. He took no action, directly or indirectly, that induced the shareholders or officers of Equity Funding to repose trust or confidence in him. There was no expectation by Dirks' sources that he would keep their information in confidence. Nor did Dirks misappropriate or illegally obtain the information about Equity Funding. Unless the insiders breached their *Cady, Roberts* duty to shareholders in disclosing the nonpublic information to Dirks, he breached no duty when he passed it on to investors as well as to *The Wall Street Journal*.

It is clear that neither Secrist nor the other Equity Funding employees violated their *Cady, Roberts* duty to the corporation's shareholders by providing information to Dirks. Secrist intended to convey relevant information that management was unlawfully concealing, and he believed that persuading Dirks to investigate was the best way to disclose the fraud. The tippers received no monetary or personal benefit for revealing Equity Funding's secrets, nor was their purpose to make a gift of valuable information to Dirks. The tippers were motivated by a desire to expose the fraud. In the absence of a breach of duty to shareholders by the insiders, there was no derivative breach by Dirks. Dirks therefore could not have been a participant after the fact in an insider's breach of a fiduciary duty.

**Judgment reversed in favor of Dirks.**

**Extent of Liability for Insider Trading** Section 20A of the 1934 Act allows persons who traded in the securities at about the same time as the insider or tippee to recover damages from the insider or tippee. Although there may be several persons trading at about the same time, the insider or tippee's total liability cannot exceed the profit she has made or the loss she has avoided by trading on inside information.

This limitation, which merely requires disgorgement of profits, has been assailed as not adequately deterring insider trading, because the defendant may realize an enormous profit if her trading is not discovered, but lose nothing beyond her profits if it is. In response to this issue of liability, Congress passed an amendment to the 1934 Act permitting the SEC to seek a civil penalty of three times the profit gained or the loss avoided by trading on inside information. This treble penalty is paid to the Treasury of the United States. The penalty applies only to SEC actions; it does not affect the amount of damages that may be recovered by private plaintiffs. The 1934 Act also grants the SEC power to award up to 10 percent of any triple-damage penalty as a bounty to informants who helped the SEC uncover insider trading.

## Criminal Liability

Like the 1933 Act, the 1934 Act provides for liability for criminal violations of the Act. Section 32 provides that individuals may be fined up to $1 million and imprisoned up to 10 years for willful violations of the 1934 Act or the related SEC rules. Businesses may be fined up to $2.5 million.

## TENDER OFFER REGULATION

Historically, the predominant procedure by which one corporation acquired another was the merger, a transaction requiring the cooperation of the acquired corporation's management. Since the early 1970s, the **tender offer** has become an often used acquisition device. A tender offer is a public offer by a **bidder** to purchase a **subject company's** equity securities directly from its shareholders at a specified price for a fixed period of time. The offering price is usually well above the market price of the shares. Such offers are often made even though there is opposition from the subject company's

management. Opposed offers are called hostile tender offers. The legality of efforts opposing a tender offer is covered in Chapter 35.

The Williams Act amendments to the 1934 Act require bidders and subject companies to provide a shareholder with information on which to base his decision whether to sell his shares to a bidder. The aim of the Williams Act is to protect investors and to give the bidder and the subject company equal opportunities to present their cases to the shareholder. The intent is to encourage an auction of the shares with the highest bidder purchasing the shares. The Williams Act applies only when the subject company's equity securities are registered under the 1934 Act.

The Williams Act does not define a tender offer, but the courts have compiled a list of factors to determine whether a person has made a tender offer. The greater the number of people solicited and the lower their investment sophistication, the more likely it is that the bidder will be held to have made a tender offer. Also, the shorter the offering period, the more rigid the price, and the greater the publicity concerning the offer, the more likely it is that the purchase efforts of the bidder will be treated as a tender offer. Given these factors, a person who offers to purchase shares directly from several shareholders at a set price for only a few days risks having a court treat the offer like a tender offer. The Williams Act clearly states, however, that there is no tender offer unless the bidder intends to become a holder of at least 5 percent of the subject company's shares.

A bidder making a tender offer must file a tender offer statement (Schedule 14D-1) with the SEC when the offer commences. The information in this schedule includes the terms of the offer (for example, the price), the background of the bidder, and the purpose of the tender offer (including whether the bidder intends to control the subject company).

The SEC requires the bidder to keep the tender offer open for at least 20 business days and prohibits any purchase of shares during that time. This rule is to give shareholders adequate time to make informed decisions regarding whether to tender their shares. Tendering shareholders may withdraw their tendered shares during the entire term of the offer. This rules allow the highest bidder to buy the shares, as in an auction.

All tender offers, whether made by the issuer or by a third-party bidder, must be made to all holders of the targeted class of shares. When a bidder increases the offering price during the term of the tender offer, all of the shareholders must be paid the higher price even if they tendered their shares at a lower price. If more shares are tendered than the bidder offered to buy, the bidder must prorate its purchases among all of the shares tendered. This proration rule is designed to foster careful shareholder decisions about whether to sell shares. Shareholders might rush to tender their shares if the bidder could accept shares on a first-come, first-served basis.

The management of the subject company is required to inform the shareholders of its position on the tender offer, with its reasons, within 10 days after the offer has been made. It must also provide the bidder with a list of the holders of the equity securities that the bidder seeks to acquire.

SEC Rule 14e-3 prohibits persons who have knowledge of an impending tender offer from using such information prior to its public disclosure. The rule limits insider trading in the tender offer context.

### Private Acquisitions of Shares

The Williams Act regulates private acquisitions of shares differently from tender offers. When the bidder privately seeks a controlling block of the subject company's shares on a stock exchange or in face-to-face negotiations with only a few shareholders, no advance notice to the SEC or disclosure to shareholders is required. However, a person making a private acquisition is required to file a Schedule 13D with the SEC and to send a copy to the subject company within 10 days after he becomes a holder of 5 percent of its shares. A Schedule 13G (which requires less disclosure than a 13D) must be filed when a 5 percent holder has purchased no more than 2 percent of the shares within the past 12 months.

### State Regulation of Tender Offers

Statutes that apply to tender offers have been enacted by about two thirds of the states. State statutes have become highly protective of subject companies. For example, the Indiana statute gives shareholders other than the bidder the right to determine whether the shares acquired by the bidder may be voted in directors' elections and other matters. The statute, which essentially gives a subject company the power to require shareholder approval of a hostile tender offer, has been copied by several states.

Other states, such as Delaware, have adopted business combination moratorium statutes. These statutes delay the effectuation of a merger of the corporation with a shareholder owning a large percentage of shares (such as 15 percent) unless the board of director's approval is obtained. Because the typical large shareholder in a public company is a bidder who has made a tender offer, these state statutes primarily affect the ability of a bidder to effectuate a merger after a tender offer and, therefore, may have the effect of deterring hostile acquisitions.

## THE FOREIGN CORRUPT PRACTICES ACT

The Foreign Corrupt Practices Act (FCPA) was passed by Congress in 1977 as an amendment to the Securities Exchange Act of 1934. Its passage followed discoveries that more than 400 American corporations had given bribes or made other improper or questionable payments in connection with business abroad and within the United States. Many of these payments were bribes to high-level officials of foreign governments for the purpose of obtaining contracts for the sale of goods or services. Officers of the companies that had made the payments argued that such payments were customary and necessary in business transactions in many countries. This argument was pressed forcefully with regard to facilitating payments. Such payments were said to be essential to get lower-level government officials in a number of countries to perform their nondiscretionary or ministerial tasks, such as preparing or approving necessary import or export documents.

In a significant number of cases, bribes had been accounted for as commission payments, as normal transactions with foreign subsidiaries, or as payments for services rendered by professionals or other firms, or had in other ways been made to appear as normal business expenses. These bribes were then illegally deducted as normal business expenses in income tax returns filed with the Internal Revenue Service.

### The Payments Prohibition

The FCPA makes it a crime for any American firm—whether or not it has securities registered under the 1934 Act—to offer, promise, or make payments or gifts of anything of value to foreign officials and certain others. Payments are prohibited if the person making the payment knows or should know that some or all of it will be used for the purpose of influencing a governmental decision, even if the offer is not accepted or the promise is not carried out. The FCPA prohibits offers or payments to foreign political parties and candidates for office as well as offers and payments to government officials. Payments of kickbacks to foreign businesses and their officials are not prohibited unless it is known or should be known that these payments will be passed on to government officials or other illegal recipients.

Facilitating or grease payments are not prohibited by the FCPA. For example, suppose a corporation applies for a radio license in Italy and makes a payment to the government official who issues the licenses. If the official grants licenses to every applicant and the payment merely speeds up the processing of the application, the FCPA is not violated.

Substantial penalties for violations may be imposed. A company may be fined up to $2 million. Directors, officers, employees, or agents participating in violations are liable for fines of up to $100,000 and prison terms of up to five years.

## Record-Keeping and Internal Controls Requirements

The FCPA also establishes record-keeping and internal control requirements for firms subject to the periodic disclosure provisions of the Securities Exchange Act of 1934. The purpose of such controls is to prevent unauthorized payments and transactions and unauthorized access to company assets that may result in illegal payments.

The FCPA requires the making and keeping of records and accounts "which, in reasonable detail, accurately, and fairly reflect the transactions and dispositions of the assets of the issuer" of securities. It also requires the establishment and maintenance of a system of internal accounting controls that provides "reasonable assurances" that the firm's transactions are executed in accordance with management's authorization and that the firm's assets are used or disposed of only as authorized by management.

## STATE SECURITIES LAW

State securities laws are frequently referred to as blue-sky laws, since the early state securities statutes were designed to protect investors from promoters and security salespersons who would "sell

building lots in the blue sky." The first state to enact a securities law was Kansas, in 1911. All of the states now have such legislation.

The National Conference of Commissioners on Uniform State Laws has adopted the Uniform Securities Act of 1956. The Act contains antifraud provisions, requires the registration of securities, and demands broker-dealer registration. About two thirds of the states have adopted the Act, but many states have made significant changes in it.

All of the state securities statutes provide penalties for fraudulent sales and permit the issuance of injunctions to protect investors from additional or anticipated fraudulent acts. Most of the statutes grant broad power to investigate fraud to some state official—usually the attorney general or his appointee as securities administrator. All of the statutes provide criminal penalties for selling fraudulent securities and conducting fraudulent transactions.

## Registration of Securities

Most of the state securities statutes adopt the philosophy of the 1933 Act that informed investors can make intelligent investment decisions. The states with such statutes have a registration scheme much like the 1933 Act, with required disclosures for public offerings and exemptions from registration for small and private offerings. Other states reject the contention that investors with full information can make intelligent investment decisions. The securities statutes in these states have a **merit registration** requirement, giving a securities administrator power to deny registration on the merits of the security and its issuer. Only securities that are not unduly risky and promise an adequate return to investors may receive administrator approval.

All state statutes have a limited number of exemptions from registration. Most statutes have private offering exemptions that are similar to Securities Act Rule 506 of Regulation D. In addition, a person may avoid the registration requirements of state securities laws by not offering or selling securities. However, as illustrated by the *Capital General* case, which follows, state courts broadly define the term *sale* in order to prevent abusive attempts to circumvent the registration requirements.

**Registration by Coordination** The Uniform Securities Act permits an issuer to register its securities by coordination. Instead of filing a registration statement under the Securities Act of 1933 and a different one as required by state law, registration by coordination allows an issuer to file the 1933 Act registration statement with the state securities administrator. Registration by coordination decreases an issuer's expense of complying with state law when making an interstate offering of its securities.

---

## CAPITAL GENERAL CORP. v. UTAH DEPARTMENT OF BUSINESS REGULATION, SECURITIES DIVISION
**777 P. 2d 494 (Utah Ct. App. 1989)**

On January 7, 1986, Amenity, Inc., was incorporated with capitalization of 100 million shares. On January 8, 1986, 1 million shares of Amenity, Inc., stock were issued to Capital General Corporation (CGC), a financial consulting firm, for $2,000. CGC distributed a total of 90,000 of those shares to approximately 900 of its clients, business associates, and other contacts to create and maintain goodwill among its clients and contacts. CGC did not receive any monetary or other direct financial consideration from those receiving the stock.

Amenity, Inc., had no actual business function at this time, and its sole asset was the $2,000 CGC had paid for the 1 million shares. Through CGC's efforts, Amenity, Inc., was acquired by another company, which paid CGC $25,000 for its efforts.

On June 5, 1986, the Utah Securities Division sought to suspend trading in Amenity, Inc., stock on the grounds that CGC distributed the Amenity, Inc., stock in violation of the Utah Securities Act.

A hearing was held before an administrative law judge, who held that the Act's registration requirements did not apply to CGC's distribution of the Amenity, Inc., stock. The Securities Division obtained a hearing by the Utah Securities Advisory Board. The Board concluded that CGC's distribution of the 90,000 shares was covered by the Act. The Board issued an order of suspension. CGC filed a petition in the district court seeking reversal of the Board's order. The district court affirmed the Board's decision, and CGC appealed.

---

**Orme, Judge**   The Utah Securities Act provides, "It is unlawful for any person to offer or sell any security in this state unless it is registered . . . or the security or transaction is exempted." Thus, we must determine if CGC's disposition of the 90,000 shares was an "offer or sale" of Amenity, Inc., securities.

The Act provides that an "offer or sale" includes the "disposition of . . . a security for value."

The Board's determination that CGC's disposition of the Amenity, Inc. stock was "for value" is reasonable and rational. By "giving away" 90,000 shares (or 9 percent of its total holdings), CGC essentially transformed Amenity, Inc., into a publicly held company, ripe for acquisition, in which it held most of the stock. "Value" can include enhanced abilities to borrow, raise capital, and other general benefits associated with publicly held companies, all of which CGC received through the disposition. These economic benefits render the disposition "for value" even though those benefits flowed indirectly from the marketplace rather than directly from the transferees.

CGC additionally argues the disposition was a "good faith gift" under the Act. CGC bears the burden to prove its entitlement to the "good faith gift" exception to the definition of "offer or sale." CGC fails to meet this burden. CGC's veiled but fairly obvious purpose was to advance its own economic objectives rather than to make a gift for reasons of simple generosity.

CGC's actual purpose in making the distribution included an intent to convert a private company into a public company without registration. CGC similarly converted at least thirty other private companies into public companies using the same method employed here. At least three of these companies were then acquired by other companies, resulting in substantial profits for CGC.

**Judgment for the Securities Division affirmed.**

**1.** Beverly Chew and other promoters created 35 general partnerships, each of which purchased 80 acres of land for the purpose of farming jojoba, "the super bean of the future." Each general partner had one operating general partner and several other general partners. The general partners had full and exclusive control of the business of each partnership; however, none of the general partners had any experience in jojoba farming. Most were doctors, dentists, and their relatives. Even the operating general partners made decisions as directed by the promoters. Actual farming was under the control of the promoters. One person farmed all the acreage, because it was not feasible to farm jojoba in 80-acre parcels. The same business plan was followed for all the general partnerships. All the partnerships shared the same field office. When the general partnerships failed, the investors sued the promoters for selling unregistered securities. Were the general partnership interests securities?

**2.** Attempting to reach as wide an audience as possible, a mutual fund company inserts prospectuses for the issuance of its shares in local newspapers and magazines. In subsequent editions of the newspapers and issues of the magazines, the company distributes additional sales materials. Has the company violated Section 5 of the Securities Act of 1933?

**3.** King's College is a private college organized under the not-for-profit corporation law of New York. The Internal Revenue Service has issued King's College an exemption from federal income taxation. The college proposes to sell $500,000 of bonds to raise funds for equipment purchases and other capital improvements. The college will sell the bonds in the minimum amount of $500 and will offer them to no more than 1,000 individuals. Only individuals having shown a prior interest in King's College will be solicited. Is the bond offering exempt from the registration requirements of the 1933 Act?

**4.** Western-Realco Limited Partnership sold $800,000 of its limited partnership interests through the services of securities brokers. Western-Realco did not supervise the brokers and was unaware of whether the brokers solicited their clients in a newsletter or to the public in general. Will Western-Realco be able to use the private offering exemption or Rule 504 to avoid a 1933 Act registration?

**5.** Capital Sunbelt Securities, Inc. (Sunbelt), and Phoenix Financial Corp. were two brokerages that sold limited partnership interests in Capital: Maple Leaf Estates, Ltd. (Capital) and Maple Leaf Estates, Ltd. (Maple Leaf). Capital was to purchase a mobile home park that would be operated by Maple Leaf. Sunbelt and Phoenix kept logs reflecting the persons to whom they distributed copies of the limited offering circulars for Capital and Maple Leaf. Ninety-six persons received copies of the Capital offering circular and 34 received the Maple Leaf circular. The circulars contained the same information as a 1933 Act registration statement. In addition, Capital and Maple Leaf promised to make available any additional information requested by investors. All offerees had a prior relationship with Phoenix or Sunbelt, and there were no seminars or meetings attended by the general public. There was no advertising, and each offering circular was addressed to a specific person. All investors were required to state that they were acquiring the limited partnership interests for investment. Proceeds of the offerings were $2,677,000 for Capital and $950,000 for Maple Leaf. Phoenix offered to sell Capital limited partnership interests to 228 persons and sold to 33 investors, 16 of which had a net worth in excess of $1 million. There were 187 offerees of the Maple Leaf limited partnership interests and 13 purchasers, 9 of whom had a net worth over $1 million. At the conclusion of the offerings, no Form D was filed with the SEC. Were the offerings exempt from registration under Section 4(2) or Rule 506 of the Securities Act?

**6.** Commonwealth Edison Co. registered 3 million common shares with the SEC and sold the shares for about $28 per share. The price of the purchasers' stock dropped to $21 when the Atomic Safety and Licensing Board denied ComEd's application to license one of its reactors. It was the first and only time the Board had denied a license application. ComEd assumed that the license would be granted; therefore, its registration statement failed to disclose the pendency of the license application. Did ComEd violate Section 11 of the Securities Act?

**7.** Joseph Crotty was a vice president of United Artists Communications, Inc. (UA), a corporation with equity securities registered under the Securities Exchange Act of 1934. Crotty was the head film buyer of UA's western division. He had virtually complete and autonomous control of film buying for the 351 UA theaters in the western United States, including negotiating and signing movie acquisition agreements, supervising movie distribution, and settling contracts after the movies had been shown. Crotty knew how many contracts were being negotiated at any one time and the price UA was paying for the rental of each movie. Crotty was required to consult with higher officers only if he wanted to exceed a certain limit on the amount of the cash advance paid to a distributor for a movie. This occurred no more than two or three times a year. The gross revenue from Crotty's division was about 35 percent of UA's gross revenue from movie exhibitions and around 17 percent of its total gross revenue. During a six-month period, Crotty purchased 7,500 shares of UA and sold 3,500 shares, realizing a large profit. Has Crotty violated Section 16(b) of the 1934 Act?

**8.** Potlatch Corporation was in the forests products industry, an industry that had experienced a wave of takeovers. The Potlatch board of directors approved a voting rights amendment to the articles of incorporation that granted four votes per share to current shareholders and other specified shareholders. New shareholders would have only one vote per share until they held the shares for four years. The effect of the amendment would be to deter and frustrate a hostile takeover of Potlatch. The board issued a proxy statement in connection with its solicitation of proxies from the shareholders. A letter issued with the proxy statement stated that the intent of the voting rights amendment was to give long-term shareholders a greater voice in the affairs of Potlatch. The voting rights amendment was approved by shareholders. Potlatch shareholders sued the company under Section 14(a) of the 1934 Act, seeking to void the shareholders' approval of the voting rights amendment. They alleged that the shareholders' votes were procured by fraud because the board failed to disclose the real purpose of the voting rights amendment—entrenchment of current management. Should the shareholders succeed?

**9.** J. C. Harrelson, the president and chief shareholder of Alabama Supply and Equipment Company (ASECo), and Clarence Hamilton conspired to defraud investors. They induced Frisco City, Alabama, to create the Industrial Development Board of Frisco City to issue tax-exempt bonds to investors. The Board offered and sold bonds pursu-

ant to an offering circular, which misstated or omitted several material facts, due to misrepresentations made by Harrelson and Hamilton. The Board used the proceeds of the bond issuance to build a manufacturing plant for ASECo. After the ASECo plant was constructed, ASECo ceased all operations and defaulted on its rental payments to the Board, causing the value of the bonds to drop precipitously. The bondholders received only $373.33 for each $1,000 bond. Clarence Bishop had purchased four of the bonds for $4,096. He never saw the offering circular or knew that one existed. He bought the bonds solely on his broker's oral representations that they were a good investment and that others in the community had purchased them. Can Bishop sue Harrelson and Hamilton under Rule 10b-5 even though he failed to read or even to seek to read the offering circular?

**10.** James Jordan was a shareholder of Duff & Phelps, Inc., a closely held corporation, and one of its employees in its Chicago office. The transferability of his shares was restricted: If he terminated his employment with Duff & Phelps, he was required to resell his shares to the corporation. Between May and August 1983, Duff & Phelps and Security Pacific Corporation negotiated a merger of the two corporations. The negotiators reached an agreement, but it was vetoed by a high official within Security Pacific on August 11, 1983. During this same time, Jordan was looking for a new job. On November 16, 1983, Jordan told Duff & Phelps that he was going to resign effective at the end of the year in order to accept a job in Houston. Jordan did not ask about any potential merger. Duff & Phelps did not volunteer any information, even though two days earlier its board of directors had decided to seek offers to acquire the company. In December 1983, Duff & Phelps and Security Pacific had serious merger discussions after the high official who vetoed the deal on August 11 changed his mind. On December 30, 1983, Jordan delivered his shares to Duff & Phelps and received a check for $23,225. On January 10, 1984, Duff & Phelps and Security announced their agreement to merge. Jordan would have received at least $452,000 for his shares had he not resigned from Duff & Phelps. Does Jordan have any recourse against Duff & Phelps under Rule 10b-5?

**11.** In May 1983, Phil Gutter read a report in *The Wall Street Journal* that listed certain corporate bonds as trading with interest. Relying on the report,

Gutter purchased $36,000 of the bonds. In reality, the bonds were trading without interest. When *The Wall Street Journal* corrected its error, the price of the bonds fell, resulting in Gutter suffering a loss of $1,692. Is *The Wall Street Journal* liable to Gutter for his loss under Rule 10b-5?

**12.** When he was the Oklahoma Sooner football coach, Barry Switzer attended a track meet, where he spoke with friends and acquaintances, including G. Platt, a director of Phoenix Corporation and chief executive officer of Texas International Company (TIC), a business that sponsored Switzer's coach's television show. TIC owned more than 50 percent of Phoenix's shares. Switzer moved around the bleachers at the track meet in order to talk to various people. After speaking with Platt and his wife Linda for the last of five times, Switzer lay down to sunbathe on a row of bleachers behind the Platts. G. Platt, unaware that Switzer was behind him, carelessly spoke too loud while talking with his wife about his desire to sell or liquidate Phoenix. He also talked about several companies making bids to buy Phoenix. Switzer also overheard that an announcement of a possible liquidation of Phoenix might be made within a week. Switzer used the information he obtained in deciding to purchase Phoenix shares. Did Switzer trade illegally on inside information?

**13.** Edper, Inc., identified Brascan, Inc., as a potential takeover target. On behalf of Edper, a securities broker contacted 40 institutional investors and 12 substantial individual holders of Brascan shares who were his clients. The broker told the investors that Edper was interested in buying 3 to 4 million shares. Eventually, Edper bought 6.3 million shares—nearly 25 percent of Brascan's outstanding shares—from these investors at a price that the broker and each individual investor agreed on. Did Edper make a tender offer for Brascan's shares that required it to file a Schedule 14D-1 prior to the making the offers to the investors?

**14.** First City Financial Corp., a Canadian company controlled by the Belzberg family, was engaged in the business of investing in publicly held American corporations. Marc Belzberg identified Ashland Oil Company as a potential target, and on February 11, 1986, he secretly purchased 61,000 shares of Ashland stock for First City. By February 26, additional secret purchases of Ashland shares pushed First City's holdings to just over 4.9 percent of Ashland's stock. These last two purchases were

effected for First City by Alan "Ace" Greenberg, the chief executive officer of Bear Stearns, a large Wall Street brokerage. On March 4, Belzberg called Greenberg and told him, "It wouldn't be a bad idea if you bought Ashland Oil here." Immediately after the phone call, Greenberg purchased 20,500 Ashland shares for about $44 per share. If purchased for First City, those shares would have increased First City's Ashland holdings above 5 percent. Greenberg believed he was buying the shares for First City under a put and call agreement, under which First City had the right to buy the shares from Bear Stearns and Bear Stearns had the right to require First City to buy the shares from it. Between March 4 and 14, Greenberg purchased an additional 330,700 shares. On March 17, First City and Bear Stearns signed a formal put and call agreement covering all the shares Greenberg purchased. On March 25, First City announced publicly for the first time that it intended to make a tender offer for all of Ashland's shares. First City filed a Schedule 13D on March 26. Has First City violated the Williams Act?

**15.** ▮▮▮ *Video Case.* See "Cafeteria Conversation." Steve has authority to write checks on the account of his employer, a public company under the Securities Exchange Act of 1934. Because Steve is a compulsive gambler and substance abuser, he needs a constant supply of cash to finance his habits. Steve regularly issues checks payable to actual suppliers not currently owed money, steals the checks, signs the names of the payees, and cashes the checks. Because Steve is also in charge of reconciling his employer's bank statements, his embezzlement scheme is not discovered by the employer's independent auditor during a routine audit. Is the independent auditor liable to its client for its losses resulting from Steve's embezzlement?

## CAPSTONE QUESTIONS

**1.** Daggett Development Corporation is in the business of constructing condominium complexes. It is incorporated in Utah but does business throughout the midwestern and western United States. It is a nonpublic company not required to file periodic reports with the Securities and Exchange Commission.

To finance the construction of 50 condominiums in Fort Collins, Colorado, near the campus of Colorado State University, Daggett offers to sell 50 ownership rights to interested persons. Each ownership right is offered for $85,000 and grants the owner title to a specific condominium unit upon its completion. Each owner has legal possession of the unit but may not physically possess or use the unit. By purchasing an ownership right, each owner grants Daggett full authority to lease the unit. It is expected that Daggett will lease units to Colorado State students. Daggett promises to pool the rental income from all units, to deduct the combined expense of leasing the units and managing the complex, and to allocate an equal share of the resulting net income to each unit owner.

*a.* Daggett is concerned that it may be selling securities under the federal securities laws.

## Required:

Answer the following and give reasons for your conclusion.

Are the ownership rights securities?

*b.* Daggett concludes that the ownership rights are securities. Daggett proposes to sell the rights only to investors who reside or work in Colorado. Daggett wishes to sell the ownership rights pursuant to the Rule 147 intrastate offering exemption of the Securities Act of 1933.

## Required:

Answer the following and give reasons for your conclusions.

What are the requirements of Rule 147? Can Daggett comply with Rule 147?

*c.* Daggett decides to exempt the offering from the Securities Act registration provisions by complying with Regulation D or Regulation A of the Securities Act. Daggett identifies 42 potential buyers of the ownership rights (Daggett expects some investors to buy more than one ownership right), including a bank trust department, an insurance company, and a lawyer taking care of the legal aspects of the construction of the condominiums. Daggett wants to advertise the offering in *The Wall Street Journal* and other investor-oriented newspapers.

## Required:

Answer the following and give reasons for your conclusions.

What are the requirements of Rules 504, 505, and 506 of Regulation D? What are the requirements of Regulation A? Will Daggett be able to comply with any of those rules? What audited financial statements must Daggett provide to prospective investors to be able to comply with each of those rules?

*d.* Daggett sells the securities in compliance with Rule 506 of Regulation D. During the course of the offering, Daggett tells David McKinney, a wealthy investor from Indiana who purchased two of the ownership interests, that studies indicate demand for condominiums in Fort Collins has increased 10 percent each year for the past 10 years. McKinney relies on Daggett's statements in deciding to purchase his two ownership interests. Two years after his purchases, McKinney is receiving less than a 2 percent return on his investment. McKinney discovers that condominium demand in Fort Collins has been declining for the last five years, a fact Daggett knew at the time McKinney purchased his ownership rights. As a result of low demand, the ownership rights have a fair market value of $53,000. McKinney sues Daggett under Section 10(b) and Rule 10b-5 of the Securities Exchange Act of 1934.

## Required:

Answer the following and give reasons for your conclusion.

Will McKinney be successful in his suit against Daggett.?

**2.** Needing $50 million of capital, Plexor Corporation plans to make a registered offering of its common shares under the Securities Act of 1933. Plexor hires Silverman, Baggs & Company as its managing underwriter for the offering.

*a.* Plexor has not yet filed a registration statement with the Securities and Exchange Commission. Plexor and Silverman Baggs have the following communications with prospective investors.

- Plexor's officers conduct a press conference announcing their expectation that earnings will be 50 percent higher in the next fiscal year. The announcement is reasonably based and is made at the same time of year that such projections have been made in previous years.

- Plexor publishes a notice in *The Wall Street Journal* stating that Plexor plans to issue common shares in one month. The notice includes the price of the shares and names Silverman Baggs as underwriter of the shares.
- Silverman Baggs telephones several investors to ask whether they are interested in purchasing the shares. Silverman Baggs warns the investors, however, that the shares cannot be purchased yet.

*b.* Plexor files a registration statement with the SEC, but the registration statement is not yet effective. Plexor and Silverman Baggs have the following communications with prospective investors.

- During a telephone call, Silverman Baggs offers to sell 500 common shares to an investor.
- Plexor holds a one-hour information meeting to which 500 prospective investors are invited. All investors receive a preliminary prospectus when they enter the meeting.
- Silverman Baggs sells 100 common shares to a wealthy investor.
- Silverman Baggs sends a fax to an investor emphasizing Plexor's earnings prospects and asking the investor to consider purchasing Plexor's common shares.
- Silverman Baggs sends a preliminary prospectus through the mail to an investor. A letter summarizing Plexor's financial performance for the previous year is attached to the prospectus.

*c.* The SEC declares Plexor's registration statement effective. Plexor and Silverman Baggs have the following communications with prospective investors.

- Plexor holds a one-hour information meeting to which 500 prospective investors are invited. All investors receive a final prospectus when they enter the meeting.
- Silverman Baggs sends a final prospectus through the mail to an investor. A letter summarizing Plexor's financial performance for the previous year is attached to the prospectus.
- Silverman Baggs sends a confirmation of sale to an investor accompanied by a preliminary prospectus.

**Required:**

Answer the following and give reasons for your conclusions.

Do any of the above communications violate Section 5 of the Securities Act of 1933?

**3.** Justin Park purchases 1,500 Plexor common shares issued pursuant to Plexor's 1933 Act registration statement filed with the SEC. Park purchases the shares for $12,000 from Merritt Securities Corporation, a member of the offering's selling group. A year after purchasing the shares, Plexor announces that the registration statement failed to state that Plexor's future earnings were primarily dependent on the renewal of a contract with the U.S. Department of the Navy and that the Navy was likely to cancel that contract. As of the effective date, Plexor knew the Navy was likely to cancel the contract. Plexor had hoped that it could obtain other contracts and did not disclose the Navy's likely nonrenewal in order to maintain demand for the common shares. Silverman Baggs knew of the Navy contract and its importance to Plexor's earnings but was unaware of the Navy's impending cancellation because it had not read Plexor's correspondence file with the Navy. Consequently, Silverman Baggs did not insist that Plexor's registration statement include the Navy contract's effect on Plexor's earnings.

Now Plexor announces that the Navy has refused to renew the contract. Immediately and due only to the nonrenewal of the Navy contract, the price of Plexor's shares falls 60 percent, resulting in the value of Park's shares declining to $4,800. Park did not read the registration statement or a copy of the prospectus. Until Plexor's announcement, Park was not aware that Plexor's earnings were heavily dependent on the Navy contract or that the Navy planned to cancel the contract. Park bought the shares merely because he thought the shares were a good investment. Park sues Plexor and Silverman Baggs under Section 11 of the Securities Act.

**Required:**

Answer the following and give reasons for your conclusion.

Will Park's suit be successful?

**4.** Kolpar Corporation is a consumer products manufacturer doing business in all 50 states. Kolpar has 720 holders of its only class of common shares, which are traded interstate in the over-the-counter market. Kolpar has annual sales of $24 million, annual profits of $1.2 million, and total assets of $7 million. Kolpar has never made a public offering of its shares under the Securities Act of 1933.

*a.* Kolpar is concerned about the registration and reporting requirements of the Securities Exchange Act of 1934.

## Required:

Answer the following and give reasons for your conclusion.

Does the Securities Exchange Act of 1934 require Kolpar to register its common shares with the Securities and Exchange Commission? What periodic reports must Kolpar file with the SEC under the Securities Exchange Act? What audited financial statements are required in reports filed with the SEC?

*b.* Kolpar registers its common shares with the SEC under the Securities Exchange Act of 1934. Rene Raplok, the retired founder of Kolpar, owns 80,000 of the 500,000 shares of Kolpar. Raplok sells 20,000 Kolpar shares for $10 per share. Four months later, Raplok purchases 15,000 Kolpar shares for $8 per share. At no time does Raplok use nonpublic, inside information.

## Required:

Answer the following and give reasons for your conclusion.

Has Raplok violated the Securities Exchange Act of 1934?

*c.* Nancy Gore, Kolpar's vice president of innovation, knows that Kolpar is about to begin manufacturing a new consumer product that will increase Kolpar's profits by 18 percent. The new product has been secretly developed by Kolpar and has not yet been announced publicly. Gore tells her cousin, Leslie Sinatra, about the new product, and says, "You can make a lot of money buying Kolpar shares, because this information hasn't been re-

leased publicly yet. In fact, I shouldn't be telling you this."

Sinatra immediately buys 11,000 Kolpar common shares for $8 per share. A week later, the new product is announced, and Sinatra sells the 11,000 shares for $11 per share. The Securities and Exchange Commission is examining Sinatra's and Gore's actions.

## Required:

Answer the following and give reasons for your conclusions.

Have Gore and Sinatra violated the Securities Exchange Act of 1934?

*d.* Kolpar announces that its annual meeting of shareholders will be held on May 15. Jimmy Falgood, the owner of 100 Kolpar common shares worth $1,100, asks Kolpar to include the following shareholder proposal in Kolpar's proxy statement:

Kolpar's board of directors shall adopt employment and other policies that respect and promote the traditional roles of men and women in American society.

Falgood's proposal is followed by a 1,000-word supporting statement.

## Required:

Answer the following and give reasons for your conclusion.

Must Kolpar include Falgood's proposal and its supporting statement in its proxy statement?

*e.* Kolpar enters merger negotiations with Smead Industries, Inc. Although the merger terms have not been firmly established, it is clear that the merger will be approved by directors of both corporations within a month, with Kolpar shareholders receiving a package of Smead securities and cash worth between $18 and $21 per share. Kolpar common shares are currently trading at $13 per share, but the price has been climbing due to abnormally high demand for the shares. Smead is willing to negotiate a merger with Kolpar only if negotiations are kept secret because Smead does not want another company to outbid it for the Kolpar shares. Kolpar issues a press release stating that it "cannot explain why demand for Kolpar has been abnormally high. There are no corporate developments that can explain the increase in share volume and price."

After reading Kolpar's press release, Kyle Lovett sells 100 Kolpar shares for $13 per share. Three weeks later, Kolpar and Smead announce that Smead is merging with Kolpar and that Kolpar shareholders will receive a package of Smead securities worth $20 per share. Lovett sues Kolpar under Section 10(b) and Rule 10b-5 of the Securities Exchange Act of 1934.

**Required:**

Answer the following and give reasons for your conclusion.

Is Kolpar liable to Lovett under Section 10(b) and Rule 10b-5 of the Securities Exchange Act of 1934?

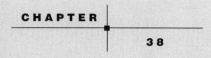

CHAPTER

38

# LEGAL

# RESPONSIBILITIES OF

# ACCOUNTANTS

**INTRODUCTION**

*This chapter covers the legal responsibilities of accountants. It considers the professional relationships of accountants with their clients and others who rely on their work. This chapter also covers the criminal and administrative sanctions for wrongful professional conduct by accountants.*

## GENERAL STANDARD OF PERFORMANCE

The general duty that accountants owe to their clients and to other persons who are affected by their actions is to exercise the skill and care of the ordinarily prudent accountant in the same circumstances. Hence, accountants must act carefully and diligently; they are *not* guarantors of the accuracy of their work. The accountant's duty to exercise reasonable care is a subset of the negligence standard of tort law. Two elements compose the general duty of performance: skill and care.

An accountant must have the **skill of the ordinarily prudent accountant**. This element focuses on the education or knowledge of the accountant, whether acquired formally at school or by self-instruction. For example, to prepare tax returns, an accountant must know the tax laws as well as the ordinarily prudent accountant does. To audit financial records, an accountant must know generally accepted auditing standards (GAAS) and generally accepted accounting principles (GAAP). GAAS and GAAP are standards and principles embodied in the rules, releases, and pronouncements of the Securities and Exchange Commission, the American Institute of Certified Public Accountants (AICPA), and the Financial Accounting Standards Board (FASB).

The care element requires an accountant to act **as carefully as the ordinarily prudent accountant**. For example, in preparing a tax return, he must discover the income exclusions, the deductions, and the tax credits that the reasonably careful accountant would find are available to the client. When auditing financial statements, he must follow the rules of GAAS and GAAP.

Courts and legislatures usually defer to the members of the accounting profession in determining what the ordinarily prudent accountant would do. Such deference recognizes the lawmakers' lack of understanding of the nuances of accounting practice. However, the accounting profession will not be permitted to establish a standard of conduct that is harmful to the interests of clients or other members of society.

Originally, accountants were held to the standard of the ordinarily prudent accountant in his locality. This local standard has given way to a national standard in recent years. Due to improved means of communication in the modern world and the widespread availability of continuing accounting education courses, few accountants today can argue that they are unaware of modern accounting techniques.

## ACCOUNTANTS' LIABILITY TO CLIENTS

Accountants are frequently sued by their clients. For example, an accountant may wrongfully claim deductions on a client's tax return. When the IRS discovers the wrongful deduction, the individual will have to pay the extra tax, interest, and perhaps a penalty. The individual may sue his accountant to recover the amount of the penalty. For another example, consider an accountant who prepares an income statement that understates a client's income. The client uses the income statement to apply for a loan, but is denied the loan because her stated net income is inadequate. The client may sue her accountant for damages caused by the erroneous income statement.

There are three principal bases of liability of an accountant to his client: contract, tort, and trust.

## Contractual Liability

As a party to a contract with her client, an accountant owes a duty to the client to perform as she has agreed to perform. This includes an implied duty to perform the contract as the ordinarily prudent accountant would perform it. If the accountant fails to perform as agreed, ordinarily an accountant is liable only for those damages that are reasonably contemplated by the client and the accountant.

An accountant is not liable for breach of contract if the client obstructs the accountant's performance of the contract. For example, an accounting firm is not liable for failing to complete an audit on time when the client refuses to give the firm access to needed records and property.

An accountant may not delegate his duty to perform a contract without the consent of the client. Delegation is not permitted because the performance of a contract for accounting services depends on the skill, training, and character of the accountant. As a result, for example, Price Waterhouse & Co., a public accounting firm, may not delegate to Ernst & Young, another public accounting firm, the contractual duty to audit the financial statements of GM, even though both firms are nearly equally skillful and careful.

## Tort Liability

Accountants' tort liability to their clients may be based on the common law concepts of negligence and fraud or on the violation of a statute, principally the federal and state securities laws.

**Negligence**    The essence of negligence is the failure of an accountant to exercise the skill and care of the ordinarily prudent accountant. An accountant is negligent when the accountant breaches the duty to act skillfully and carefully and proximately causes damages to the client. For example, a client may recover the interest on excess taxes that he paid as a result of his accountant's lack of due care in claiming allowable deductions on a tax return.

Sometimes, an accountant will audit a company, yet fail to uncover fraud, embezzlement, or other intentional wrongdoing by an employee of the company. Ordinarily, an accountant has no specific duty to uncover employee fraud or embezzlement. Nonetheless, an accountant must uncover employee fraud or embezzlement if an ordinarily prudent accountant would have discovered it. The accountant who fails to uncover such fraud or embezzlement is negligent and liable to his client. In addition, an accountant owes a duty to investigate suspicious circumstances that tend to indicate fraud, regardless of how he became aware of those circumstances. Also, an accountant has a duty to inform a proper party of his suspicions. It is not enough to inform or confront the person suspected of fraud.

When an accountant is hired to perform a fraud audit to investigate suspected fraud or embezzlement, she has a greater duty to investigate. She must be as skillful and careful as the ordinarily prudent auditor performing a fraud audit.

When an accountant negligently fails to discover embezzlement, generally he is liable to his client only for an amount equal to the embezzlement that occurred after he should have discovered the embezzlement. The accountant is usually not liable for any part of the embezzlement that occurred prior to the time he should have uncovered the embezzlement unless his tardy discovery prevented the client from recovering embezzled funds.

In the following case, an accounting firm was held liable to its client for failing to meet the standard of the profession.

---

## DIVERSIFIED GRAPHICS, LTD. v. GROVES

### 868 F.2d 293 (8th Cir. 1989)

Diversified Graphics, Ltd. (D.G.), hired Ernst & Whinney (E & W) to assist it in obtaining a computer system to fit its data processing needs. D.G. had a longstanding relationship with E & W during which D.G. developed great trust and reliance on E & W's services. Because D.G. lacked computer expertise, it decided to entrust E & W with the selection and implementation of an in-house computer data processing system. E & W had promised to locate a "turnkey" system, which would be fully operational without the need for extensive employee training. D.G. instead received a system that was difficult to operate and failed to meet its needs. D.G. sued E & W and its partners, including Ray Groves, for negligence. The jury found in favor of D.G.; E & W and its partners appealed.

---

**Lay, Chief Judge**    D.G.'s theory for recovery based on negligence encompasses the notion of a consultant-client relationship and therefore the existence of a professional standard of care.

The degree of skill and care that may be required of a professional is a question of fact for the jury. We find that there was substantial evidence regarding the applicable standard of a professional consultant.

E & W's Guidelines to Practice incorporates the Management Advisory Services Practice Standards which were adopted by the American Institute of Certified Public Accountants, Inc. (AICPA Standards). The AICPA Standards require that "due professional care" is to be exercised in providing management advisory services. These standards in part generally provide:

In performing management advisory services, a practitioner must act with integrity and objectivity and be independent in mental attitude.

Engagements are to be performed by practitioners having competence in the analytical approach and process, and in the technical subject matter under consideration.

Due professional care is to be exercised in the performance of a management advisory services engagement.

Before accepting an engagement, a practitioner is to notify the client of any reservations he has regarding anticipated benefits.

Before undertaking an engagement, a practitioner is to inform his client of all significant matters related to the engagement.

Engagements are to be adequately planned, supervised, and controlled.

Sufficient relevant data is to be obtained, documented, and evaluated in developing conclusions and recommendations.

All significant matters relating to the results of the engagement are to be communicated to the client.

AICPA Standards Nos. 1–8.

D.G. had determined that it required a "turnkey" computer system that would fully perform all of its data processing in-house. The term "turnkey" is intended to describe a self-sufficient system which the purchaser need only "turn the key" to commence operation. The purchaser should not have to hire programmers, and current employees should not have to undergo extensive training to be able to operate the system. To procure this type of customized and fully operational system, great care must be taken to carefully detail a business's needs and to properly develop specifications for the computer system. Potential vendors must be carefully scrutinized to discover all of the inadequacies of their data processing systems. Once a vendor is chosen, proper implementation is imperative to ensure that the purchaser truly need only "turn the key" to commence full operation of the system. A fundamental part of implementation involves testing the system through parallel data processing operation. Finally, the existence of adequate documentation regarding the operation of the system is crucial once the system is up and running. As previously stated,

employees will have had only minimal training and will depend heavily on the instructions for operation. Moreover, documentation is particularly important because this type of system is highly customized and standard instruction sources will have only limited value.

Thus, the jury could conclude that E & W's conduct fell short of adhering to the applicable professional standard of care.

**Judgment for Diversified Graphics affirmed.**

---

**Contributory Negligence of Client**   Courts are reluctant to permit an accountant to escape liability to a client merely because the client was **contributorily negligent**. Since the accountant has skills superior to those of the client, courts generally allow clients to rely on the accountant's duty to discover employee fraud, available tax deductions, and other matters for which the accountant is hired. The client is not required to exercise reasonable care to discover these things himself.

Nonetheless, some courts allow the defense of contributory negligence or the defense of comparative negligence, such as when clients negligently fail to follow an accountant's advice or when clients possess information that makes their reliance on the accountant unwarranted.

**Fraud**   An accountant is liable to his client for fraud when he misstates or omits facts in communications with his client and acts with **scienter**. An accountant acts with scienter when he knows of the falsity of a statement or he recklessly disregards the truth. Thus, accountants are liable in fraud for their intentional or reckless disregard for accuracy in their work.

For example, an accountant chooses not to examine the current figures in a client's books of account, but relies on last year's figures because he is behind in his work for other clients. As a result, the accountant understates the client's income on an income statement that the client uses to apply for a loan. The client obtains a loan, but he has to pay a higher interest rate because his low stated income

makes the loan a higher risk for the bank. Such misconduct by the accountant proves scienter and, therefore, amounts to fraud.

Scienter also includes recklessly ignoring facts, such as an auditor's finding obvious evidence of embezzlement yet failing to notify a client of the embezzlement.

The chief advantage of establishing fraud is that the client may get a higher damage award than when the accountant is merely negligent. Usually, a client may receive only compensatory damages for a breach of contract or negligence. By proving fraud, a client may be awarded punitive damages as well.

### Breach of Trust

An accountant owes a duty of trust to his client. Information and assets that are entrusted to an accountant may be used only to benefit the client. Therefore, an accountant may not disclose sensitive matters such as a client's income and wealth. In addition, an accountant may not use the assets of his client for his own benefit. The duty of trust also requires the accountant to maintain the confidentiality of the client's information entrusted to the accounting firm.

### Securities Law

Federal and state securities law creates several rights of action for persons harmed in connection with the purchase or sale of securities. These rights of action are based in tort. Although available to clients of an accountant, they are rarely used for that purpose. Usually, only third parties (nonclients) sue under the securities law. The securities law sections that apply to accountants are discussed later in this chapter.

## ACCOUNTANTS' LIABILITY TO THIRD PERSONS: COMMON LAW

Other persons besides an accountant's clients may use her work product. Banks may use financial statements prepared by a loan applicant's accountant in deciding whether to make a loan to the applicant. Investors may use financial statements certified by a company's auditors in deciding whether to buy or sell the company's securities. These documents prepared by an accountant may prove incorrect, resulting in damages to the nonclients who relied on them. For example, banks may lend money to a corporation only because an income statement prepared by an accountant overstated the corporation's income. When the corporation fails to repay the loan, the bank may sue the accountant to recover the damages it suffered.

Nonclients may sue accountants for common law negligence, common law fraud, and violations of the securities laws. In this section, common law negligence and fraud are discussed.

### Negligence and Negligent Misrepresentation

When an accountant fails to perform as the ordinarily prudent accountant would perform, she risks having liability for negligence. Many courts have restricted the ability of nonclients to sue an accountant for damages proximately caused by the accountant's negligent conduct. These courts limit nonclient suits on the grounds that nonclient users of an accountant's work product have not contracted with the accountant and, therefore, are not in **privity of contract** with the accountant. Essentially, these courts hold that an accountant owes no duty to nonclients to exercise ordinary skill and care.

This judicial stance conflicts with the usual principles of negligence law under which a negligent person is liable to all persons who are reasonably foreseeably damaged by his negligence. The rationale for the restrictive judicial stance was expressed

in the *Ultramares* case,[1] a decision of the highest court in New York. In that case, Judge Benjamin Cardozo refused to hold an auditor liable to third parties for mere negligence. His rationale was stated as follows:

If liability for negligence exists, a thoughtless slip or blunder, the failure to detect a theft or forgery beneath the cover of deceptive entries, may expose accountants to a liability in an indeterminate amount for an indeterminate time to an indeterminate class.

*Ultramares* dominated the thinking of judges for many years, and its impact is still felt today. However, many courts understand that many nonclients use and reasonably rely on the work product of accountants. To varying degrees, these courts have relaxed the privity requirement and expanded the class of persons who may sue an accountant for negligence conduct. Today, most courts adopt one of the following three tests to determine whether a nonclient may sue an accountant for negligence.

**Primary Benefit Test**    The *Ultramares* court adopted a primary benefit test for imposing liability for negligence. Under this test, an accountant's duty of care extends only to those persons for whose primary benefit the accountant prepares financial reports and other documents. The accountant must actually foresee the nonclient's use and prepare the document primarily for use by a specified nonclient. That is, the nonclient must be a **foreseen user** of the accountant's work product. The accountant must know two things: (1) the name of the person who will use the accountant's work product and (2) the particular purpose for which that person will use the work product.

**Foreseen Users and Foreseen Class of Users Test**    By 1965, a draft of the *Restatement (Second) of Torts* proposed that the law of professional negligence expand the class of protected persons to **foreseen users** and **users within a foreseen class of users** of reports. Under this test, the accountant must know either the user of the work product or the use to be made of the work product. The protected

---

[1] *Ultramares Corp. v. Touche*, 174 N.E. 441 (N.Y. Ct. App. 1931).

persons are (1) those persons who an accountant knows will use the accountant's work product and (2) those persons who use an accountant's work product in a way the accountant knew the work product would be used.

For example, an accountant prepares an income statement that he knows his client will use to obtain a loan at Bank X. Any bank to which the client supplies the statement to obtain a loan, including Bank Y, may sue the accountant for damages caused by a negligently prepared income statement. Bank X is a foreseen user, and Bank Y is in a foreseen class of users. On the other hand, if an accountant prepares an income statement for a tax return and the client, without the accountant's knowledge, uses the income statement to apply for a loan from a bank, the bank is not among the protected class of persons—the accountant did not

know that the tax return would be used for that purpose.

**Foreseeable Users Test**     A few courts have applied traditional negligence causation principles to accountants' negligence. They have extended liability to **foreseeable users** of an accountant's reports who suffered damages that were proximately caused by the accountant's negligence. To be liable to a nonclient under this test, an accountant need merely be able to expect or foresee the nonclient's use of the accountant's work product. It is not necessary for the nonclient to prove that the accountant actually expected or foresaw the nonclient's use.

In the following case, the court rejected the foreseeable users test as too broad and instead adopted the *Restatement*'s foreseen class of users test in the negligent misrepresentation context.

---

## BILY v. ARTHUR YOUNG & CO.
### 834 P.2d 745 (Cal. Sup. Ct. 1992)

Founded in 1980 by enterpreneur Adam Osborne, Osborne Computer Company manufactured the first personal computer for the mass market. By fall 1982, sales of the Osborne I computer reached $10 million per month, making Osborne Computer one of the fastest growing businesses in American history.

The company proposed an early 1983 public offering of its common shares. To obtain temporary financing until the company went public, Osborne Computer issued warrants to investors in exchange for the investors making or securing loans to Osborne Computer. The warrants entitled the investors to purchase Osborne Computer shares at a favorable price. It was expected that once the public offering was made, the investors holding warrants would make a substantial profit. The investors were individuals, pension funds, and capital investment firms. Other investors purchased common shares of Osborne Computer. Robert Bily, a director of the company, was one of the investors; he purchased 37,500 shares for $1.5 million from Adam Osborne.

The investors were given and relied on an unqualified audit opinion of Osborne Computer's 1982 financial statements. The audit opinion, issued by Arthur Young & Co., stated that Arthur Young had examined the financial statements in compliance with GAAS, that the statements had been prepared in compliance with GAAP, and that the statements presented fairly Osborne Computer's financial position. The 1982 financial statements revealed that Osborne Computer had a net operating profit of $69,000 on sales of $68 million. Arthur Young delivered 100 sets of the opinion to Osborne Computer.

In the first half of 1983, Osborne Computer's sales declined sharply because of manufacturing problems with its new Executive model computer. In June 1983, the IBM personal computer became a major factor in the small-computer market. Osborne never made a public offering of its shares, and on September 13, 1983, filed for bankruptcy. The investors lost their investments.

The investors sued Arthur Young, alleging professional negligence and negligent misrepresentation. At trial, evidence showed that Arthur Young did not comply with GAAS, resulting in its failure to find that Osborne Computer's liabilities were understated by $3 million. As a result, the supposed operating profit of $69,000 was actually a loss of $3 million. Also, Arthur Young had failed to detect weaknesses in Osborne

Computer's accounting procedures and systems. The jury was instructed that liability for professional negligence extended to those third parties who reasonably and foreseeably relied on the audited financial statements. The court also instructed the jury that for Arthur Young to have liability for negligent misrepresentation, Arthur Young must have intended to induce the plaintiff or a particular class of persons to which the plaintiff belongs to rely on the audit opinion. The jury found Arthur Young liable for professional negligence but not negligent misrepresentation, and it awarded the investors damages of $4.3 million. The California Court of Appeals affirmed, and Arthur Young appealed to the Supreme Court of California.

---

**Lucas, Chief Justice**    We decline to permit all merely foreseeable third party users of audit reports to sue the auditor on a theory of professional negligence.

An auditor is a watchdog, not a bloodhound. Audits are performed in a client-controlled environment. The client typically prepares its own financial statements. Because, the auditor cannot in the time available become an expert in the client's business and record-keeping systems, the client necessarily furnishes the information base for the audit. Moreover, an audit report is not a simple statement of verifiable fact that, like the weight of a load of beans, can be easily checked against uniform standards of indisputable accuracy. Rather, an audit report is a professional opinion based on numerous and complex factors, involving discretion and judgment on the part of the auditor at every stage.

Although the auditor's role in the financial reporting process is secondary, the liability it faces is primary and personal and can be massive. The client, its promoters, and its managers have generally left the scene, headed in most cases for bankruptcy. The auditor has now assumed center stage as the remaining solvent defendant and is faced with a claim for all sums of money ever loaned to or invested in the client. Such disproportionate liability cannot fairly be justified on moral, ethical, or economic grounds.

Investors, creditors, and others who read and rely on audit reports and financial statements possess considerable sophistication in analyzing financial information and are aware from training and experience of the limits of an audit report. The third party in an audit negligence case can "privately order" the risk of inaccurate financial reporting by contractual arrangements with the client. For example, a third party might expend its own resources to verify the client's financial statements. It might commission its own audit or investigation, thus establishing privity between itself and an auditor. In

addition, it might bargain with the client for special security or improved terms in a credit or investment transaction. Finally, the third party could insist that an audit be conducted on its behalf or establish direct communications with the auditor.

As a matter of economic and social policy, third parties should be encouraged to rely on their own prudence, diligence, and contracting power. This kind of self-reliance promotes sound investment and credit practices and discourages the careless use of monetary resources. If, instead, third parties are simply permitted to recover from the auditor for mistakes in the client's financial statements, the auditor becomes an insurer of not only the financial statements, but also of bad loans and investments in general.

We doubt that a significant and desirable improvement in audit care would result from an expanded rule of liability. In view of the inherent dependence of the auditor on the client and the labor-intensive nature of auditing, we doubt whether audits can be done in ways that would yield significantly greater accuracy without disadvantages. Auditors may rationally respond to increased liability by simply reducing audit services in fledgling industries where the business failure rate is high, reasoning that they will inevitably be singled out and sued when their client goes into bankruptcy regardless of the care or detail of their audits. It might also be doubted whether auditors are the most efficient absorbers of the losses from inaccuracies in financial information. Investors and creditors can limit the impact of losses by diversifying investments and loan portfolios.

A foreseeability rule applied in this context inevitably produces large numbers of expensive and complex lawsuits of questionable merit as scores of investors and lenders seek to recoup business losses. We hold that an auditor's liability for general negligence in the conduct of an audit of its client's financial statements is confined to the client, i.e., the person who contracts for or engages the audit services.

There is, however, a further narrow class of persons who, although not clients, may reasonably come to receive and rely on an audit report and whose existence constitutes a risk of auditing reporting that may fairly be imposed on the auditor. Such persons are specifically intended beneficiaries of the audited report who are known to the auditor and for whose benefit it renders the report. While such persons may not recover on a general negligence theory, we hold they may recover on a theory of negligent misrepresentation. Negligent misrepresentation is a separate and distinct tort. Where the defendant makes false statements, honestly believing that they are true, but without reasonable ground for such belief, he may be liable for negligent misrepresentation, a form of deceit.

Under certain circumstances, expressions of professional opinion are treated as representations of fact. When a party possesses superior knowledge or expertise regarding the subject matter and a plaintiff is so situated that it may reasonably rely on such supposed knowledge or expertise, the defendant's representation may be treated as one of material fact. There is no dispute that Arthur Young's statements in audit opinions fall within these principles.

But the person or class of persons entitled to rely upon the representations is restricted to those to whom or for whom the misrepresentations were made. Restatement Second of Tort section 552 is most consistent with the elements and policy foundations of the tort of negligent misrepresentation. By confining liability to those persons whom the engagement is designed to benefit, the Restatement rule requires that the supplier of information receive notice of potential third party claims, thereby allowing it to ascertain the potential scope of its liability and make rational decisions regarding the undertaking. Liability should be confined to cases in which the supplier *manifests* an intent to supply the information for the *sort of use* in which the plaintiff's loss occurs.

Having determined that intended beneficiaries of an audit report are entitled to recovery on a theory of negligent misrepresentation, we must consider whether they may also recover on a general negligence theory. We conclude they may not. Because the audit report, not the audit itself, is the foundation of the third person's claim, negligent misrepresentation more precisely captures the gravamen of the cause of action and more clearly conveys the elements essential to a recovery.

Based on our decision, the California standard jury instructions concerning negligent misrepresentation should be amended in future auditor liability cases to permit the jury to determine whether plaintiff belongs to the class of persons to whom or for whom the representations in the audit report were made. The representation must have been made with the intent to induce plaintiff, or a particular class of persons to which plaintiff belongs, to act in reliance upon the representation in a specific transaction, or a specific type of transaction, that defendant intended to influence. Defendant is deemed to have intended to influence its client's transaction with plaintiff whenever defendant knows with substantial certainty that plaintiff, or the particular class of persons to which plaintiff belongs, will rely on the representation in the course of the transaction. If others become aware of the representation and act upon it, there is no liability even though defendant should reasonably have foreseen such a possibility.

**Judgment reversed in favor of Arthur Young.**

---

## Fraud

Fraud is such reprehensible conduct that all courts have extended an accountant's liability for fraud to all foreseeable users of his work product who suffered damages that were proximately caused by the accountant's fraud. Privity of contract, therefore, is not required when a person sues an accountant for fraud, even in a state that has adopted the *Ultramares* test for negligence actions. To prove fraud, a nonclient must establish that an accountant acted with scienter.

Some courts recognize a tort called constructive fraud that applies when an accountant misstates a material fact. For a misstatement to amount to constructive fraud, the accountant must have recklessly or grossly negligently failed to ascertain the truth of the statement. As with actual fraud, an accountant's liability for constructive fraud extends to all persons who justifiably rely on the misstatement.

---

**CONCEPT REVIEW**

## COMMON LAW BASES OF LIABILITY OF ACCOUNTANT TO NONCLIENTS

| Privity Test Adopted by State | Basis of Liability | |
|---|---|---|
| | Negligence | Fraud |
| **Primary Benefit Test** (*Ultramares*) | Accountant liable only to foreseen users (accountant knew name of user and purpose of the user's use) | Regardless of test adopted, accountant liable to all persons whose damages were caused by their reliance on accountant's fraud |
| *Restatement (Second) of Torts* **Test** | Accountant liable to foreseen users and users in a foreseen class of users (accountant knew at least the purpose of the user's use) | |
| **Foreseeable Users Test** | Accountant liable to all foreseeable users (accountant can expect or foresee the purpose of the user's use) | |

## ACCOUNTANT'S LIABILITY TO THIRD PARTIES: SECURITIES LAW

The slow reaction of the common law in creating a negligence remedy for third parties has led to an increased use of securities law by nonclients—that is, persons not in privity with an accountant. Many liability sections in these statutes either eliminate the privity requirement or expansively define privity.

### Securities Act of 1933

There are several liability sections under the Securities Act of 1933 (1933 Act). The most important liability section of the Securities Act of 1933 is Section 11, but Sections 12(2) and 17(a) are also important.

**Section 11 Liability**  Section 11 imposes on auditors liability for misstatements or omissions of material fact in certified financial statements that they provide for Securities Act registration statements. The 1933 Act registration statement must be filed with the Securities and Exchange Commission by an issuer making a public distribution of securities. An auditor is liable to any purchaser of securities issued pursuant to a defective registration statement. The purchaser need not establish privity of contract with the auditor; he need merely prove that the auditor is a person who furnished the certified financial statements for inclusion in the registration statement. Usually, the purchaser need not prove he relied on the misstated or omitted material fact; he need not even have read or seen the defective financial statement.

For example, an auditor certifies a client's income statement that overstates net income by 85 percent. The defective income statement is included in the client's registration statement pursuant to which the client sells its preferred shares. Without reading the registration statement or the income statement, a person buys from the client 100 preferred shares for $105 per share. After the correct income figure is released, the price of the shares drops to $25 per share. The auditor will most likely be liable to the purchaser for $8,000.

Under Section 11, auditors may escape liability by proving that they exercised due diligence. This **due diligence defense** requires that an auditor of certified financial statements prove that she made a reasonable investigation and that she reasonably believed that there were no misstatements or omissions of material fact in the certified financial statements at time the registration statement became effective. Because the effective date is often several

**CONCEPT REVIEW**

## LIABILITY SECTIONS OF THE 1933 ACT AND 1934 ACT

| | Wrongful Conduct | Covered Communications | Who May Sue? | Must the Plaintiff Prove Reliance on the Wrongful Conduct? |
|---|---|---|---|---|
| **Securities Act of 1933 Section 11** | Misstatement or omission of material fact | 1933 Act registration statement only | Any purchaser of securities issued pursuant to the registration statement | No |
| **Securities Act of 1933 Section 12(2)** | Misstatement or omission of material fact | Any communication in connection with any offer to sell or a sale of any security (except government issued or guaranteed securities) | Any purchaser of the securities offered or sold | No |
| **Securities Act of 1933 Section 17(a)** | Misstatement or omission of material fact | Any communication in connection with any offer to sell or sale of any security | Any purchaser of the securities offered or sold | Yes |
| **Securities Exchange Act of 1934 Section 10(b) and Rule 10b-5** | Misstatement or omission of material fact | Any communication in connection with a purchase or sale of any security | Any purchaser or seller of the securities | Yes |
| **Securities Exchange Act of 1934 Section 18** | False or misleading statement of material fact | Any document filed with the SEC under the 1934 Act (includes the 1934 Act registration statement, 10-K, 8-K, and proxy statements) | Any purchaser or seller of a security whose price was affected by the statement | Yes |

| Who May Be Sued? | Must the Plaintiff and Defendant Be in Privity of Contract? | Defendant's Level of Fault | Who Has the Burden of Proving or Disproving Defendant's Level of Fault? | Amount of Defendant's Liability to Plaintiff |
|---|---|---|---|---|
| Issuer, underwriters, directors, selected officers, and experts who contribute to the registration statement | No | Negligence | Defendant may escape liability by proving he made a reasonable investigation and had reason to believe and did believe there were no misstatements or omissions of material fact | The price the purchaser paid for the securities less the market price of the securities at the time of the suit |
| Any person who sells a security or actively solicits a sale of a security | Yes (although met by a defendant who has a financial interest in a sale of securities) | Negligence | Defendant may escape liability by proving he did not know and could not reasonably have known of the misstatement or omission of material fact | The price the purchaser paid for the securities (upon the purchaser's return of the securities) |
| Any person responsible for the misstatement or omission | No | Negligence for some parts of Section 17(a); scienter for one part | Plaintiff must prove the defendant acted negligently or with scienter | Plaintiff's damages caused by his reliance on the misstatement or omission |
| Any person responsible for the misstatement or omission | No | Scienter | Plaintiff must prove the defendant acted with scienter | Plaintiff's damages caused by his reliance on the misstatement or omission |
| Any person who made or caused the statement to be made | No | Scienter | Defendant may escape liability by proving he acted in good faith with no knowledge that the statement was false or misleading | Plaintiff's damages caused by his reliance on the false or misleading statement |

months after an audit has been completed, an auditor must perform an additional review of the audited statements to ensure that the statements are accurate as of the effective date. In essence, due diligence means that an auditor was not negligent, which is usually proved by showing that she complied with GAAS and GAAP. The due diligence defense is explained more fully in *Escott v. BarChris Construction Corp.*, which appears in Chapter 37, Securities Regulation, at page 809.

Under Section 11, an auditor has liability for only a limited period of time, pursuant to a **statute of limitations.** A purchaser must sue the auditor within one year after the misstatement or omission was or should have been discovered. In addition, a purchaser may sue the auditor no more than three years after the securities were offered to the public.

**Section 12(2)**   Section 12(2) imposes liability on any person who misstates or omits a material fact in connection with an offer or sale of a security. Privity of contract between the plaintiff and the defendant apparently is required, because Section 12(2) states that the defendant is liable to the person *purchasing* the security *from him.*

Until recently, Section 12(2) had been interpreted broadly to impose liability on auditors of financial statements that misstate or omit material facts. Recent decisions of the Supreme Court, including the *Central Bank* case that appears below, suggest that auditors are unlikely to be held liable under Section 12(2) in the future. An accountant must have direct contact with a buyer of a security to be liable. Merely performing professional services, such as drafting or certifying financial statements, is not enough for Section 12(2) liability. The accountant must actively solicit the sale, motivated at least by a desire to serve his own financial interest. Such a financial interest is unlikely to be met by an accountant whose compensation is a fee unconnected to the proceeds of the securities sale. In addition, the *Central Bank* case makes it fairly clear that auditors who merely *aid and abet* a client's Section 12(2) violation will not have liability under Section 12(2).

In the event that an accountant has sufficient contact with a purchaser to incur Section 12(2) liability, the accountant may escape liability by proving that she did not know and could not reasonably have known of the untruth or omission; that is, she must prove that she was not negligent.

**Section 17(a)**   Under Section 17(a), a purchaser of a security must prove his reliance on a misstatement or omission of material fact for which an accountant is responsible. Under two of the subsections of Section 17(a), the investor need prove only negligence by the accountant. Under the third, the investor must prove the accountant acted with scienter.

## Securities Exchange Act of 1934

Two sections of the 1934 Act—Section 18 and Section 10(b)—especially affect the liability of accountants to nonclients.

**Section 18**   Section 18 of the 1934 Act imposes liability on accountants who furnish misleading and false statements of material fact in any report or document filed with the Securities and Exchange Commission under the 1934 Act. Such reports or documents include the annual 10-K report, which includes certified financial statements, the monthly 8-K report, and proxy statements.

Under Section 18, a purchaser or seller of a security may sue the accountant if he relied on the defective statement in the filed document and it caused his damages. Usually, this means that a plaintiff must have *read and relied* on the defective statement in the filed document. The purchaser or seller may sue the accountant even if they are not in privity of contract.

An accountant may escape Section 18 liability by proving that she acted in *good faith* and had *no knowledge* that the information was misleading. That is, she must show that she acted *without scienter.*

**Section 10(b) and Rule 10b-5**   Securities Exchange Act Rule 10b-5, pursuant to Section 10(b), has been the basis for most of the recent suits investors have brought against accountants. Rule 10b-5 prohibits any person from making a misstatement or omission of material fact in connection with the purchase or sale of any security. Rule 10b-5 applies to misstatements or omissions in any communications with investors, covering any use of financial statements certified by accountants resulting in a purchase or sale of a security. The wrongful act must have a connection with interstate commerce, the mails, or a national securities exchange.

A purchaser or seller of a security may sue an accountant who has misstated or omitted a material fact. Privity is not required. The purchaser or seller must rely on the misstatement or omission. In omission cases, reliance may be inferred from materiality.

In addition, the accountant must act with scienter. In this context, scienter is an intent to deceive, manipulate, or defraud. Negligence is not enough.

**Aiding and Abetting** Until recently, a common way investors held an accountant liable under Rule 10b-5 was to prove that the accountant aided and abetted a client's fraud. Most courts had recognized accountants' aiding and abetting liability under Rule 10b-5 by requiring (1) a primary violation by another person (such as a client fraudulently overstating its earnings), (2) the accountant's knowledge of the primary violation, and (3) the accountant's substantial assistance in the achievement of the primary violation (such as an accountant's failure to disclose a client's fraud known to the accountant).

In April 1994 in the *Central Bank* case that follows, the Supreme Court of the United States by a 5–4 decision held that those who merely aid and abet Rule 10b-5 violations have no liability to those injured by the fraud. The court drew a distinction between those **primarily** responsible for the fraud—

who retain Rule 10b-5 liability—and those **secondarily** responsible—who no longer have liability under Rule 10b-5. The distinction between primary and secondary responsibility is unclear. Intentionally certifying false financial statements is primary fault and would impose Rule 10b-5 liability on the auditor. However, an independent accountant's work in connection with false unaudited statements or other financial information released by a client may be only secondary and may not impose Rule 10b-5 liability on the accountant.

While the defendants in the *Central Bank* case were not accountants, the issue decided is of crucial importance to accountants and other professionals who are not directly involved in a client's fraudulent conduct but either have knowledge of the fraud or recklessly disregard facts indicating fraud. It appears that *Central Bank* substantially reduces an accountant's risk of liability. However, injured parties may attempt to circumvent the limits of *Central Bank* by recharacterizing an accountant as a primary wrongdoer. In addition, the issue is certain to be considered by Congress, which may decide to reinstate aiding and abetting liability under Rule 10b-5.

## CENTRAL BANK OF DENVER V. FIRST INTERSTATE BANK OF DENVER
**114 S. Ct. 1439 (U.S. Sup. Ct. 1994)**

In 1986 and 1988, the Colorado Springs-Stetson Hills Public Building Authority (Authority) issued $26 million in bonds to finance public improvements at Stetson Hills, a planned residential and commercial development in Colorado Springs. Central Bank served as the trustee for the bondholders, undertaking a fiduciary duty to the bondholders to ensure that the Authority complied with indenture provisions protecting bondholders. The bonds were secured by liens against 522 acres of land. The indenture required that the land be worth at least 160 percent of the bonds' outstanding principal and interest.

In January 1988, AmWest Development—the developer of Stetson Hills—gave Central Bank an appraisal of the land. The appraisal showed land values almost unchanged from a 1986 appraisal, even though property values were declining in Colorado Springs. Central Bank's in-house appraiser reviewed the 1988 appraisal and decided that it was optimistic. He suggested that Central Bank use an independent outside appraiser to review the 1988 appraisal. After an exchange of letters between Central Bank and AmWest in early 1988, Central Bank agreed to delay independent review of the appraisal until the end of 1988, six months after the 1988 bonds had been issued to investors. Before the independent review was complete, the Authority defaulted on the 1988 bonds.

First Interstate Bank and others purchased $2.1 million of the 1988 bonds relying on the 1988 appraisal. They sued the Authority, the bond's underwriters, an AmWest director, and Central Bank for violations of section 10(b) of the Securities Exchange Act of 1934. They alleged that Central Bank was secondarily liable under section 19 (b) for aiding and abetting the Authority's fraudulent sale of the bonds by failing to act on its knowledge that the 1988 appraisal may have been wrong. The district court granted judgment in favor of Central Bank. The 10th Circuit Court of Appeals reversed, holding that Central Bank could be liable as an aider and abetter. Central Bank asked the Supreme Court of the United States to review the decision.

———————————— ■ ————————————

**Kennedy, Justice**   In the wake of the 1929 stock market crash and in response to reports of widespread abuses in the securities industry, Congress enacted two landmark pieces of securities legislation: the Securities Act of 1933 and the Securities Exchange Act of 1934. The 1933 Act regulates initial distributions of securities, and the 1934 Act for the most part regulates post-distribution trading. Together, the Acts embrace a fundamental purpose to substitute a philosophy of full disclosure for the philosophy of *caveat emptor*

The 1933 and 1934 Acts create an extensive scheme of civil liability. The Securities and Exchange Commission (SEC) may bring administrative actions and injunctive proceedings to enforce a variety of statutory prohibitions. Private plaintiffs may sue under the express private rights of action contained in the Acts. They may also sue under private rights of action we have found to be implied by the terms of section 10(b) and section 14(a) of the 1934 Act. This case concerns the most familiar private cause of action: the one we have found to be implied by section 10(b), the general antifraud provision of the 1934 Act. Section 10(b) states:

It shall be unlawful for any person, directly or indirectly, by the use of any means or instrumentality of interstate commerce or of the mails, or of any facility of any national securities exchange—

\*   \*   \*   \*   \*

(b) To use or employ, in connection with the purchase or sale of any security registered on a national securities exchange or any security not so registered, any manipulative or deceptive device or contrivance in contravention of such rules and regulations as the [SEC] may prescribe.

Rule 10b-5, adopted by the SEC in 1942, casts the proscription in similar terms.

With respect to the scope of conduct prohibited by section 10(b), the text of the statute controls our decision. The private plaintiff may not bring a 10b-5 suit against a defendant for acts not prohibited by the text of section 10(b). That bodes ill for First Interstate, for the language of section 10(b) does not in terms mention aiding and abetting. To overcome this problem, First Interstate and the SEC suggest (or hint at) the novel argument that the use of the phrases "directly or indirectly" in the text of section 10(b) covers aiding and abetting.

There is a basic flaw with the interpretation. The problem, of course, is that aiding and abetting liability extends beyond persons who engage, even indirectly, in a proscribed activity; aiding and abetting liability reaches persons who do not engage in the proscribed activities at all, but who give a degree of aid to those who do. A further problem with First Interstate's interpretation of the "directly or indirectly" language is posed by the numerous provisions of the 1934 Act that use the term in a way that does not impose aiding and abetting liability.

Congress knew how to impose aiding and abetting liability when it chose to do so. If Congress intended to impose aiding and abetting liability, we presume it would have used the words "aid" and "abet" in the statutory text. But it did not.

We reach the uncontroversial conclusion that the text of the 1934 Act does not itself reach those who aid and abet a section 10(b) violation. We think that conclusion resolves the case. We cannot amend the statute to create liability for acts that are not themselves manipulative or deceptive within the meaning of the statute.

The absence of section 10(b) aiding and abetting liability does not mean that secondary actors in the securities markets are always free from liability under the securities Acts. Any person or entity, including a lawyer, accountant, or bank, who employs a manipulative device or makes a material misstatement (or omission) on which a purchaser or seller of securities relies may be liable as a primary violator under 10b-5.

**Judgment reversed in favor of Central Bank.**

## State Securities Law

All states have securities statutes with liability sections. Most of the states have a liability section similar to Section 12(2) of the Securities Act.

## LIMITING ACCOUNTANTS' LIABILITY: PROFESSIONAL CORPORATIONS AND LIMITED LIABILITY PARTNERSHIPS

Every state permits professionals to incorporate their business under a professional incorporation statute. Most statutes permit a professional accounting corporation to be owned only by accountants.

While there are significant taxation advantages to incorporation, the principal advantage of incorporation—*limited liability of the shareholders*—does not isolate accountants from liability for professional misconduct. For example, an accountant who injures his client by failing to act as the ordinarily prudent accountant would act has liability to his client, despite the incorporation of the accountant's business.

When two or more accountants conduct an accounting business as co-owners, incorporation may offer them limited liability. While partners in a partnership are jointly and severally liable for each other's negligence, some states permit incorporated accountants to escape liability for their associate's torts, unless the accountant actually supervised the wrongdoing associate or participated in the tort. Other states do not allow incorporated accountants to limit their liability for their associates' torts, making all the shareholder/accountants jointly and severally liable for the professional misconduct of any of its accountants.

Reacting to the large personal liability sometimes imposed on lawyers and accountants for the professional malpractice of their partners, Texas enacted in 1991 the first statute permitting the formation of limited liability partnerships (LLP). An LLP is similar to a partnership, except that a partner's liability for his partners' professional malpractice is limited to the partnership's assets, unless the partner supervised the work of the wrongdoing partner. In addition, a partner retains unlimited liability for his *own* malpractice and for all *non*professional obligations of the partnership.

As of October 1994, 17 states and the District of Columbia have passed LLP statutes. Several other states are considering such laws. As more states adopt LLP statutes, the LLP will become the preferred form of business for accountants who do not incorporate.

For more information on the limited liability partnership, see Chapter 29.

## QUALIFIED OPINIONS, DISCLAIMERS OF OPINION, ADVERSE OPINIONS, AND UNAUDITED STATEMENTS

After performing an audit of financial statements, an independent auditor **certifies** the financial statements by issuing an opinion letter. The **opinion letter** expresses whether the audit has been performed in compliance with GAAS and whether, in the auditor's opinion, the financial statements fairly present the client's financial position and results of operations in conformity with GAAP. Usually, an auditor issues an **unqualified opinion**—that is, an opinion that there has been compliance with GAAS and GAAP. Sometimes, an auditor issues a qualified opinion, a disclaimer of opinion, or an adverse opinion. Up to this point, you have studied the liability of an auditor who has issued unqualified opinions yet has not complied with GAAS and GAAP.

What liability should be imposed on an auditor who discloses that he has not complied with GAAS and GAAP? An auditor is relieved of responsibility only to the extent that a qualification or disclaimer is specifically expressed in the opinion letter. Therefore, letters that purport to totally disclaim liability for false and misleading financial statements are too general to excuse an accountant from exercising ordinary skill and care.

For example, an auditor qualifies his opinion of the ability of financial statements to present the financial position of a company by indicating that there is uncertainty about how an antitrust suit against the company may be decided. He would not be held liable for damages resulting from an unfavorable verdict in the antitrust suit. He would remain liable, however, for failing to make an examination in compliance with GAAS that would have revealed other serious problems.

For another example, consider an auditor who, due to the limited scope of the audit, disclaims any opinion on the ability of the financial statements to present the financial position of the company. She would nonetheless be liable for the nondiscovery of problems that the limited audit should have revealed.

Likewise, an accountant who issued an adverse opinion that depreciation had not been calculated according to GAAP would not be liable for damages resulting from the wrongful accounting treatment of depreciation, but he would be liable for damages resulting from the wrongful treatment of receivables.

Merely preparing unaudited statements does not create a disclaimer as to their accuracy. The mere fact that the statements are unaudited only permits an accountant to exercise a lower level of inquiry. Even so, an accountant must act as the ordinarily prudent accountant would act under the same circumstances in preparing unaudited financial statements.

## CRIMINAL, INJUNCTIVE, AND ADMINISTRATIVE PROCEEDINGS

In addition to being held liable for damages to clients and third parties, an accountant may be found criminally liable for his violations of securities, tax, and other laws. For criminal violations, he may be fined and imprisoned. His wrongful conduct may also result in the issuance of an injunction, which bars him from doing the same acts in the future. In addition, his wrongful conduct may be the subject of administrative proceedings by the Securities and Exchange Commission and state licensing boards. An administrative proceeding may result in the revocation of an accountant's license to practice or the suspension from practice. Finally, disciplinary proceedings may be brought against an accountant by professional societies such as the AICPA.

## Criminal Liability under the Securities Laws

Both the Securities Act of 1933 and the Securities Exchange Act of 1934 have criminal provisions that can be applied to accountants. The 1933 Act imposes criminal liability for willful violations of any section of the 1933 Act, including Sections 11, 12(2), and 17(a), or any 1933 Act rule or regulation. For example, willfully making an untrue statement or omitting any material fact in a 1933 Act registration statement imposes criminal liability on an accountant. The maximum penalty for a criminal violation of the 1933 Act is a $10,000 fine and five years' imprisonment.

The 1934 Act imposes criminal penalties for willful violations of any section of the 1934 Act, such as Sections 10(b) and 18, and any 1934 Act rule or regulation, such as Rule 10b-5. For example, willfully making false or misleading statements in reports that are required to be filed under the 1934 Act incurs criminal liability. Such filings include 10-Ks, 8-Ks, and proxy statements. An individual accountant may be fined up to $1 million and imprisoned for up to 10 years for a criminal violation of the 1934 Act; however, an individual accountant who proves that he had no knowledge of an SEC rule or regulation may not be imprisoned for violating that rule or regulation. An accounting firm may be fined up to $2.5 million.

Most of the states have statutes imposing criminal penalties on accountants who willfully falsify financial statements or other reports in filings under the state securities laws and who willfully violate the state securities laws or aid and abet criminal violations of these laws by others.

In the following case, accountants permitting a client to book unbilled sales after the close of the fiscal period subjected the accountants to the criminal penalties of the 1934 Act.

---

## UNITED STATES V. NATELLI
### 527 F.2d 311 (2d Cir. 1975)

Anthony Natelli was the partner in charge of the Washington, D.C., office of Peat, Marwick, Mitchell & Co., a large CPA firm. In August 1968, Peat, Marwick became the independent public auditor of National Student Marketing Corporation. Natelli was the engagement partner for the audit of Student Marketing. Joseph Scansaroli was Peat, Marwick's audit supervisor on that engagement.

Student Marketing provided its corporate clients with a wide range of marketing services to help them reach the lucrative youth market. In its financial statements for the nine months ended May 31, 1968, Student Marketing had counted as income the entire amount of oral customer commitments to pay fees in Student Marketing's "fixed-fee marketing programs," even though those fees had not yet been paid. They were to be paid for services that Student Marketing would provide over a period of several years. Standard accounting practice required that part of the unpaid fees be considered income in the present year but that part be deferred as income until the years when Student Marketing actually performed the services for which the fees were paid. Therefore, in making the year-end audit, Natelli concluded that he would use a percentage-of-completion approach on these commitments, taking as income in the present year only those fees that were to be paid for services in that year.

The customer fee commitments were oral only, making it difficult to verify whether they really existed. Natelli directed Scansaroli to try to verify the fee commitments by telephoning the customers but not by seeking written verification. However, Scansaroli never called Student Marketing's clients. Instead, Scansaroli accepted a schedule prepared by Student Marketing showing estimates of the percentage of completion of services for each corporate client and the amount of the fee commitment from each client. This resulted in an adjustment of $1.7 million for "unbilled accounts receivable." The adjustment turned a loss for the year into a profit twice that of the year before.

By May 1969, a total of $1 million of the customer fee commitments had been written off as uncollectible. The effect of the write-off was to reduce 1968 income by $209,750. However, Scansaroli, with Natelli's approval, offset this by reversing a deferred tax item of approximately the same amount.

Student Marketing issued a proxy statement in September 1969 in connection with a shareholders' meeting to consider merging six companies into Student Marketing. The proxy statement was filed with the Securities and Exchange Commission. It contained several financial statements, some of which had been audited by Peat, Marwick. Others had not been audited, but Peat, Marwick had aided in their preparation. In the proxy statement, a footnote to the financial statements failed to show that the write-off of customer fee commitments had affected Student Marketing's fiscal 1968 income.

The proxy statement required an unaudited statement of nine months' earnings through May 31, 1969. This statement was prepared by Student Marketing with Peat, Marwick's assistance. Student Marketing produced a $1.2 million commitment from the Pontiac Division of General Motors Corporation two months after the end of May, but it was dated April 28, 1969. At 3 A.M. on the day the proxy statement was to be printed, Natelli informed Randall, the chief executive officer and founder of Student Marketing, that this commitment could not be included because it was not a legally binding contract. Randall responded at once that he had "a commitment from Eastern Airlines" for a somewhat comparable amount attributable to the same period. Such a letter was produced at the printing plant a few hours later, and the Eastern commitment was substituted for the Pontiac sale in the proxy. Shortly thereafter, another Peat, Marwick accountant, Oberlander, discovered $177,547 in "bad" commitments from 1968. These were known to Scansaroli in May 1969 as being doubtful, but they had not been written off. Oberlander suggested to the company that these commitments plus others, for a total of $320,000, be written off, but Scansaroli, after consulting with Natelli, decided against the suggested write-off.

There was no disclosure in the proxy statement that Student Marketing had written off $1 million (20 percent) of its 1968 sales and over $2 million of the $3.3 million of unbilled sales booked in 1968 and 1969. A true disclosure would have shown that Student Marketing had made no profit for the first nine months of 1969.

Subsequently, it was revealed that many of Student Marketing's fee commitments were fictitious. The attorney general of the United States brought a criminal action against Natelli and Scansaroli for violating the Securities Exchange Act of 1934 by willfully and knowingly making false and misleading statements in a proxy statement. The district court jury convicted both Natelli and Scansaroli, and they appealed.

---

**Gurfein, Circuit Judge** The original action of Natelli in permitting the booking of unbilled sales after the close of the fiscal period in an amount sufficient to convert a loss into a profit was contrary to sound accounting practice. When the uncollectibility, and indeed, the nonexistence of these large receivables was established in 1969, the revelation stood to cause Natelli severe criticism and possible liability. He had a motive, therefore, intentionally to conceal the write-offs that had to be made.

Honesty should have impelled Natelli and Scansaroli to disclose in the footnote that annotated their own audited statement for fiscal 1968 that substantial write-offs had been taken, after year-end, to reflect a loss for the year. A simple desire to right the wrong that had been perpetrated on the stockholders and others by the false audited financial statement should have dictated that course.

The accountant owes a duty to the public not to assert a privilege of silence until the next audited annual statement comes around in due time. Since companies were being acquired by Student Marketing for its shares in this period, Natelli had to know that the 1968 audited statement was being used continuously.

Natelli contends that he had no duty to verify the Eastern commitment because the earnings statement within which it was included was unaudited. This raises the issue of the duty of the CPA in relation to an unaudited financial statement contained within a proxy statement where the figures are reviewed and to some extent supplied by the auditors. The auditors were associated with the statement and were required to object to anything they actually knew to be materially false. In the ordinary case involving an unaudited statement, the auditor would not be chargeable simply because he failed to discover the invalidity of booked accounts receivable, inasmuch as he had not undertaken an audit with verification. In this case, however, Natelli knew the history of post-period bookings and the dismal consequences later discovered.

In terms of professional standards, the accountant may not shut his eyes in reckless disregard of his knowledge that highly suspicious figures, known to him to be suspicious, were being included in the unaudited earnings figures in the proxy statement with which he was associated.

There is some merit to Scansaroli's point that he was simply carrying out the judgments of his superior, Natelli. The defense of obedience to higher authority has always been troublesome. There is no sure yardstick to measure criminal responsibility except by measurement of the degree of awareness on the part of a defendant that he is participating in a criminal act, in the absence of physical coercion such as a soldier might face. Here the motivation to conceal undermines Scansaroli's argument that he was merely implementing Natelli's instructions, at least with respect to concealment of matters that were within his own ken. The jury could properly have found him guilty on the specification relating to the footnote.

With respect to the Eastern commitment, Scansaroli stands in a position different from that of Natelli. Natelli was his superior. He was the man to make the judgment whether or not to object to the last-minute inclusion of a new commitment in the nine-months statement. There is insufficient evidence that Scansaroli engaged in any conversations about the Eastern commitment or that he was a participant with Natelli in any check on its authenticity. Since in the hierarchy of the accounting firm it was not his responsibility to decide whether to book the Eastern contract, his mere adjustment of the figures to reflect it under orders was not a matter for his discretion.

**Conviction of Natelli affirmed. Conviction of Scansaroli affirmed in part and reversed in part.**

## Other Criminal Law Violations

Federal tax law imposes on accountants a wide range of penalties for a wide variety of wrongful conduct. At one end of the penalty spectrum is a $25 fine for failing to furnish a client with a copy of his income tax return or failing to sign a client's return. At the other end is a fine of $100,000 and imprisonment of three years for tax fraud. In between is the penalty for promoting abusive tax shelters. The fine is $1,000, or 20 percent of the accountant's income from her partici-

pation in the tax shelter, whichever is greater. In addition, all of the states impose criminal penalties for specified violations of their tax laws.

Several other federal statutes also impose criminal liability on accountants. The most notable of these statutes is the general mail fraud statute, which prohibits the use of the mails to commit fraud. To be held liable, an accountant must know or foresee that the mails will be used to transmit materials containing fraudulent statements provided by her.

In addition, the general false-statement-to-government-personnel statute prohibits fraudulent statements to government personnel. The false-statement-to-bank statute proscribes fraudulent statements on a loan application to a bank or other financial institution.

**RICO**  The Racketeer Influenced and Corrupt Organizations Act (RICO) makes it a federal crime to engage in a pattern of racketeering activity. Although RICO was designed to attack the activities of organized crime enterprises, it applies to accountants who conduct or participate in the affairs of an enterprise in almost any pattern of business fraud. A pattern of fraud is proved by the commission of two predicate offenses within a 10-year period. Predicate offenses include securities law violations, mail fraud, and bribery. Individuals convicted of a RICO violation may be fined up to $25,000 and imprisoned up to 20 years.

A person who is injured in his business or property by reason of an accountant's conduct or participation, directly or indirectly, in an enterprise's affairs through a pattern of racketeering activity may recover treble damages (three times his actual damages) from the accountant. In *Reves v. Ernst & Young*,[2] the Supreme Court held that merely by auditing financial statements that substantially overvalued a client's assets, an accounting firm was not conducting or participating in the affairs of the client's business. The Court held that the accounting firm must participate in the "operation or management" of the enterprise itself to be liable under RICO.

### Injunctions

Administrative agencies such as the SEC and the Internal Revenue Service may bring injunctive actions against an accountant in a federal district court. The purpose of such an injunction is to prevent an accountant from committing a future violation of the securities or tax laws.

After an injunction has been issued by a court, violating the injunction may result in serious sanctions. Not only may penalties be imposed for contempt, but a criminal violation may also be more easily proven.

---

[2]113 S. Ct. 1163 (1993).

### Administrative Proceedings

The SEC has the authority to bring administrative proceedings against persons who violate the provisions of the federal securities acts. In recent years, the SEC has stepped up enforcement of SEC Rule of Practice 2(e). Rule 2(e) permits the SEC to bar temporarily or permanently from practicing before the SEC an accountant who has demonstrated a lack of the qualifications required to practice before it, such as an accountant who has prepared financial statements not complying with GAAP. Rule 2(e) also permits the SEC to take action against an accountant who has willfully violated or aided and abetted another's violation of the securities acts. An SEC administrative law judge hears the case and makes an initial determination. The SEC commissioners then issue a final order, which may be appealed to a federal court of appeals.

Rule 2(e) administrative proceedings can impose severe penalties on an accountant. By suspending an accountant from practicing before it, the SEC may take away a substantial part of an accountant's practice. Also, the SEC may impose civil penalties up to $500,000.

In addition, state licensing boards may suspend or revoke an accountant's license to practice if she engages in illegal or unethical conduct. If such action is taken, an accountant may lose her entire ability to practice accounting.

### OWNERSHIP OF WORKING PAPERS

The personal records that a client entrusts to an accountant remain the property of the client. An accountant must return these records to his client. Nonetheless, the working papers produced by independent auditors belong to the accountant, not the client.

Working papers are the records made during an audit. They include such items as work programs or plans for the audit, evidence of the testing of accounts, explanations of the handling of unusual matters, data reconciling the accountant's report with the client's records, and comments about the client's internal controls. The client has a right of access to the working papers. The accountant must obtain the client's permission before the working papers can be transferred to another accountant.

## ACCOUNTANT–CLIENT PRIVILEGE

An accountant-client privilege of confidentiality protects many of the communications between accountants and their clients from the prying eyes of courts and other government agencies. In addition, it protects an accountant's working papers from the discovery procedures available in a lawsuit.

Although the common law does not recognize an accountant-client privilege, a large number of states have granted such a privilege by statute. The provisions of the statutes vary, but usually the privilege belongs to the client, and an accountant may not refuse to disclose the privileged material in a courtroom if the client consents to its disclosure.

Generally, the state-granted privileges are recognized in both state and federal courts deciding questions of state law. Nonetheless, federal courts do not recognize the privilege in matters involving federal questions, including antitrust and criminal matters.

In federal tax matters, for example, no privilege of confidentiality is recognized on the grounds that an accountant has a duty as a public watchdog to ensure that his client correctly reports his income tax liability. Consequently, an accountant can be required to bring his working papers into court and to testify as to matters involving the client's tax records and discussions with the client regarding tax matters. In addition, an accountant may be required by subpoena to make available his working papers involving a client who is being investigated by the IRS or who has been charged with tax irregularities. The same holds true for SEC investigations.

In the next case, the court held that Pennsylvania's accountant-client privilege did not cover a business appraisal or the communications concerning the appraisal.

---

### GATEWOOD V. U.S. CELLULAR CORP.
**124 F.R.D. 504 (D.D.C. 1989)**

Robert Gatewood and two other limited partners entered a limited partnership agreement with United States Cellular Corporation (USCC), the sole general partner. The agreement provided that in the event the partners were unable to agree on the value of a cellular phone system in which they had an interest, each would select an appraiser, and the two appraisers would select a third. An impasse arose concerning the selection of this third appraiser, and a federal district court was asked to resolve the dispute.

During litigation, USCC took the deposition of Terry Korn, a Pennsylvania certified public accountant and appraiser selected by the limited partners. USCC sought to inquire about the conduct and results of Korn's appraisal as well as any communications between Korn and the limited partners. The limited partners directed Korn not to respond to any of these questions, asserting that the communications were covered by the Pennsylvania statutory accountant-client privilege.

---

**Attridge, Magistrate**    The Pennsylvania accountant-client privilege protects from disclosure ". . . information of which he may have come possessed relative to and in connection with any professional services as a certified public accountant, (or) public accountant. . . ." This statute being in derogation of common law is to be strictly construed. Thus, in order for the statute to be at least prima facially applicable, there must be a showing that an accountant's services were sought in an accounting capacity. In these proceedings, there is nothing to show that Korn was acting in his capacity as an accountant in making his appraisal. Appraisals may be rendered by experts with varying backgrounds who may be otherwise qualified. The appraisal process is not unique to the accounting field. Moreover, the records used to evaluate the financial value of the cellular phone system were not private documents of the limited partners, but rather, records of the system to be evaluated. The purpose of the statute, to foster the free flow of financial data to an accountant by a client in order to obtain financial advice, would not be advanced nor promoted by applying the statute to the events that took place in these proceedings.

The appraisal performed by Korn was not an accounting function and the communications he had with the limited partners were not communications protected by the accountant-client privilege. The fact that Korn is an accountant is merely an accidental circumstance rather than a controlling event.

**Judgment for United States Cellular Corporation.**

---

**PROBLEMS AND PROBLEM CASES**

**1.** The 1136 Tenants' Corporation, a cooperative apartment house, hired Max Rothenberg & Co., a firm of certified public accountants, to perform accounting services for it. Rothenberg discovered that several invoices were missing from the financial records of the apartment house. These invoices were needed to prove that payments of $44,000 had been made to creditors of the apartment house and were not embezzled by someone with authority to make payments for the apartment house. Rothenberg noted the missing invoices on his worksheet, but failed to notify the apartment house that there were missing invoices. In fact, there were no invoices. Jerome Riker, the apartment house manager, had embezzled the $44,000 from the apartment house by ordering it to make unauthorized payments to him. Riker embezzled more money after the audit was completed. Is Rothenberg liable to its client for failing to inform it of Riker's embezzlement?

**2.** O'Connor, Brooks & Co., an accounting firm, negligently failed to discover embezzlements by an officer of its client, American Trust & Savings Bank. O'Connor, Brooks claimed that certain bank directors breached their duty of care to the bank, thereby permitting the embezzlement to occur. Does O'Connor, Brooks have a defense to liability?

**3.** From 1983 to 1985, Baumann-Furrie & Co. provided accounting services to Halla Nursery, Inc. During this time, Halla's bookkeeper embezzled $135,000. In 1986, Halla sued Baumann-Furrie alleging it negligently failed to detect the embezzlement. Baumann-Furrie claimed that Halla negligently failed to put in place internal financial controls to protect the company from embezzlement. The jury found Halla 80 percent at fault and Baumann-Furrie 20 percent at fault. Is Baumann-Furrie nonetheless liable to Halla?

**4.** *Video Case.* See "Cafeteria Conversation." Steve has authority to write checks on the account of his employer, a public company under the Securities Exchange Act of 1934. Because Steve is a compulsive gambler and substance abuser, he needs a constant supply of cash to finance his habits. Steve regularly issues checks payable to actual suppliers not currently owed money, steals the checks, signs the names of the payees, and cashes the checks. Because Steve is also in charge of reconciling his employer's bank statements, his embezzlement scheme is not discovered by the employer's independent auditor during a routine audit. Is the independent auditor liable to its client for damages resulting from Steve's embezzlement?

**5.** When Robert Hicks offered to sell his shares in Intermountain Merchandising, Inc. (IMI), to Montana Merchandising (MM), IMI hired Alan Bloomgren, a CPA, to audit IMI. Based on Bloomgren's clean opinion on IMI's balance sheet, MM purchased Hicks's shares, advanced funds to IMI, and signed financial guaranties for IMI. Bloomgren knew that MM would rely on the audit and that the audit would be used to aid MM in buying out IMI, including making loans and guaranties. Bloomgren's audit was materially defective, failing to discover that IMI had a negative net worth. MM sued Bloomgren for negligence. Is Bloomgren liable to MM?

**6.** Max Mitchell & Co., a public accounting firm, performed an audit of the financial statements of C.M. Systems, Inc. At the time Mitchell performed the audit, it was not known that the audited financial statements would be used to obtain a loan from First Florida Bank. However, subsequent to preparing the audited financial statements, Mitchell negotiated a loan with First Florida Bank on behalf of C.M. and personally delivered the financial statements to the bank. Relying on the financial statements, First Florida loaned $500,000 to C.M. After C.M. defaulted on the loan, First Florida discovered that the financial statements materially understated C.M.'s liabilities and materially overstated its assets and net income. Is Mitchell liable to First Florida under the theory of negligence?

**7.** For the years 1973 to 1976, Timm, Schmidt & Co., an accounting firm, prepared financial statements for Clintonville Fire Apparatus, Inc. (CFA). For every year except 1973, Timm sent an opinion letter to CFA stating that the financial statements fairly presented the financial condition of CFA and that the statements were prepared in accordance with generally accepted accounting principles. In November 1975, CFA obtained a $300,000 loan from Citizens State Bank. Citizens made the loan to CFA after reviewing the financial statements that Timm had prepared. Citizens made additional loans to CFA in 1976. By the end of 1976, CFA owed Citizens $380,000. In early 1977, Timm employees discovered that the 1974 and 1975 financial statements contained a number of material errors totaling over $400,000. When Timm informed Citizens of the errors, Citizens called all of CFA's loans due. As a result, CFA was liquidated. CFA's assets were insufficient to pay the loans from Citizens. Citizens sued Timm, seeking to recover $152,000, the amount due on its loans to CFA. If Timm failed to comply with generally accepted auditing standards (GAAS) when it first audited the 1974 and 1975 financial statements, is Timm liable to Citizens for negligence?

**8.** To aid its decision whether to purchase all the shares of Gillespie Furniture Company, DMI Furniture, Inc., hired Arthur Young & Co. to review an audit of Gillespie's financial statements that had been performed by Brown, Kraft & Company. Arthur Young wrote a letter stating that Brown, Kraft had "performed a quality audit." Based on this letter, DMI decided to buy all of Gillespie's shares. When Gillespie became less profitable than DMI expected, DMI sued Arthur Young under Securities Exchange Act Rule 10b-5. DMI alleged that Arthur Young acted recklessly in failing to detect and to disclose that Brown, Kraft's audit report was inaccurate and misleading because it grossly overstated inventory and showed a profit when there was a loss. Do DMI's allegations establish that Arthur Young has violated Rule 10b-5?

**9.** In early 1984, Arthur Andersen & Co. advised Financial Corporation of America (FCA) that FCA could account for Government National Mortgage Association (Ginny Mae) repurchase transac-

tions as it accounted for financing transactions, thereby recording the purchase liability without recognizing any loss or gain. Following this advice, FCA bought $2 billion of Ginny Maes and resold them to the original holders subject to reverse repurchase agreements. In mid-1984, the Securities and Exchange Commission announced that repurchase transactions must be accounted for as forward commitments with profits or losses recognized as they accrue. As a result, FCA was obliged to report a net loss of $107 million for the quarter ended June 30, 1984, resulting in a drop in the price of FCA's shares. FCA alleged that it would not have purchased the Ginny Maes had not Arthur Andersen knowingly or recklessly disregarded the fact that accounting for the repurchases as financing transactions was wholly inappropriate. Do FCA's allegations establish a Rule 10b-5 violation?

**10.** John Schulzetenberg was the engagement partner for Touche Ross & Co.'s audit of the financial statements of Inter-Regional Financial Group, Inc. (IRF). The audited financial statements were filed with the Securities and Exchange Commission. From 1981 through 1983, IRF's management misrepresented the delinquency status of its receivables, which accounted for more than 90 percent of its assets. Schulzetenberg's 1981 audit of the receivables was insufficiently planned, supervised, and executed, and did not meet the requirements of GAAS. As a result, he failed to detect that IRF's allowance for uncollectible receivables was materially understated. In 1982, Schulzetenberg failed to correct the 1981 errors, even though it should have been clear to him that the 1981 allowance was materially understated. Is Schulzetenberg subject to penalties under SEC Rule of Practice 2(e)?

**11.** Bill Thomas, a CPA, was a member of Lawhon, Thomas, Holmes & Co. (LTH), a public accounting firm. When LTH performed accounting services for Xenerex Corp., LTH received 144,000 Xenerex shares instead of cash. LTH continued to hold the Xenerex shares when the three LTH members joined the accounting firm of Oppenheim, Appel, Dixon & Co. (OAD). LTH ceased operations and sold all its assets except the Xenerex shares to OAD. The three former LTH members, including Thomas, retained ownership of LTH. After he joined OAD, Thomas immediately solicited Xenerex as a client for OAD. Thomas, on behalf of OAD, signed a new client acceptance form for Xenerex, giving a negative response to the question, "Are there any known independence problems?" Thomas prepared and signed OAD's report on Xenerex's financial statements and annual report filed on Form 10-K with the SEC. Has Thomas violated SEC Rule of Practice 2(e)?

**12.** While performing a routine audit of the tax returns of Amerada Hess Corporation, the Internal Revenue Service discovered questionable payments of $7,830. The IRS issued a summons to Arthur Young & Co., the accounting firm that had prepared the tax accrual working papers that might reveal the nature of the payments. The working papers had been prepared in the process of Arthur Young's review of Amerada Hess's financial statements, as required by federal securities law. In the summons, the IRS ordered Arthur Young to make available to the IRS all of its Amerada Hess files, including its tax accrual working papers. Amerada Hess directed Arthur Young not to comply with the summons on the grounds that they were protected by an accountant-client privilege. Is Amerada Hess correct?

---

## CAPSTONE QUESTIONS

**1.** Griswold Corporation retains Barton, Martin & Fargo Company (BMF), CPAs, to audit Griswold's financial records and to prepare financial statements that Griswold will present to Commercial Equities Insurance Company (CEI) for purposes of obtaining a loan from CEI. The contract between Griswold and BMF provides that BMF will complete the audit and prepare financial statements no later than June 15. That date is of the essence because Griswold needs the infusion of cash that the CEI loan will provide.

BMF carelessly fails to assign a sufficient number of staff auditors to the Griswold audit. In addition, BMF's staff auditors carelessly examine Griswold's accounts. As a result, BMF does not complete the audit and prepare financial statements until July 24. In addition, Griswold's financial statements prepared by BMF materially understate BMF's earnings and assets. Consequently, CEI refuses to make a loan to Griswold. No other financial institution is willing to make a loan to Griswold based on the financial statements prepared by BMF. Griswold suffers large losses due to its inability to obtain a loan. Subsequent examinations by another CPA firm reveal Griswold's true financial position and indicate that Griswold

would have been able to obtain a loan from CEI and would have been highly profitable had BMF performed its audit carefully and timely.

*a.* Griswold is considering legal action against BMF under state contract and tort law.

## Required:

Answer the following and give reasons for your conclusion.

Does BMF have potential liability to Griswold under the state law of contract and tort?

*b.* Biff Tanner, one of BMF's staff auditors assigned to the Griswold audit, is informed by Griswold's management during the course of the audit that Griswold is secretly negotiating a merger with Metcalf Corporation. The preliminary merger terms are favorable to Griswold. Tanner buys 1,000 Griswold shares for $10 per share. As news of the prospective merger is leaked, the price of Griswold shares increases to $15 per share, at which point Tanner sells the 1,000 shares. The merger deal is abandoned when BMF's audit erroneously reports Griswold's earnings and assets. Griswold is examining Tanner's purchase of its shares.

## Required:

Answer the following and give reasons for your conclusion.

Does Tanner have liability to Griswold for using the prospective merger information?

*c.* The Internal Revenue Service serves a subpoena on BMF, asking BMF to produce and disclose all its workpapers prepared during BMF's audit of Griswold. The IRS believes that Griswold underreported its income in reliance on the financial statements prepared by BMF and seeks to recover additional taxes and penalties from Griswold. Griswold informs BMF that it is invoking the client-accountant privilege and orders BMF to make no disclosures to the IRS regarding Griswold's financial position. Griswold requests that BMF turn over possession of the workpapers to Griswold.

## Required:

Answer the following and give reasons for your conclusions.

Should BMF obey the IRS subpoena? Should BMF turn over possession of the workpapers to Griswold?

**2.** Astra Corporation retains Angst & Whimsey Company (A&W), CPAs, to certify its financial statements. Astra informs A&W that the certified financial statements will be included in a Securities Act registration statement that Astra will file with the Securities and Exchange Commission. Astra plans to sell 10 million common shares pursuant to the registration statement.

A&W certifies that Astra's financial statements fairly present the financial position of Astra. Astra's financial statements show that Astra earned a 22 percent return on equity in its most recent fiscal year. Astra includes the certified financial statements in its Securities Act registration statement. Rochelle Dixson purchases 200 Astra common shares for $20 per share pursuant to the registration statement. Dixson does not read the financial statements in the registration statement or in the prospectus. She did, however, buy the shares while relying on her broker's statement that Astra's certified financial statements indicated Astra earned a 22 percent return on equity in its most recent fiscal year.

Nine months after purchasing the shares, Astra discovers that the financial statements certified by A&W materially overstated Astra's earnings. A&W's audit failed to discover that Astra's financial statements overstated earnings because A&W did not comply with generally accepted auditing standards. Astra immediately issues amended financial statements. As a result, Astra's common shares' price falls to $15 per share.

Eight months later, Dixson sues A&W under the common law of negligence, Section 11 of the Securities Act of 1933, and Section 10(b) and Rule 10b-5 of the Securities Exchange Act of 1934. The market value of the shares is $15 per share. A&W raises the following issues:

· While A&W knew that Astra was using the certified financial statements to sell its common shares, A&W did not know that Dixson would be a purchaser of the shares. A&W believes that Dixson may not sue A&W under the state common law of negligence.

· A&W believes it has no liability to Dixson under Section 11 or Rule 10b-5 because Dixson did not read the materially erroneous financial statements.

· A&W believes it has no liability to Dixson under Section 11 or Rule 10b-5 because Dixson did not buy the shares from A&W.

· A&W believes it has no liability to Dixson under Section 11 or Rule 10b-5 because A&W's noncompliance with GAAS is not sufficient misconduct to incur liability under those laws.

· A&W believes it has no liability to Dixson under Section 11 because Dixson waited too long to bring an action against A&W.

## Required:

Answer the following and give reasons for your conclusions.

Evaluate the issues raised by A&W.

# The Federal Trade Commission Act and Consumer Protection Laws

**INTRODUCTION**

*As Chapter 12 demonstrates, consumers' ability to recover civil damages for defective products increased dramatically during the 1960s and 1970s. But direct government regulation of consumer matters also grew tremendously during those decades. This chapter examines the many kinds of federal consumer protection regulation. It begins with a general discussion of America's main consumer watchdog: the Federal Trade Commission (FTC). After describing how the FTC operates, the chapter examines its regulation of anticompetitive, deceptive, and unfair business practices. Then we examine the many other federal laws that regulate consumer matters, many of which involve consumer credit.*

## The Federal Trade Commission

The Federal Trade Commission was formed shortly after passage of the Federal Trade Commission Act (FTC Act) in 1914. The FTC is an independent federal agency, which means that it is outside the executive branch of the federal government and is less subject to political control than agencies that are executive departments. The FTC is headed by five commissioners appointed by the president and confirmed by the Senate for staggered seven-year terms. The president also designates one of the commissioners as chairman of the FTC. The FTC has a Washington headquarters and several regional offices located throughout the United States.

### The FTC's Powers

The FTC's principal missions are to keep the U.S. economy both *free* and *fair.* As Figure 1 suggests, Congress has given the Commission many tools for accomplishing these missions. By far the most important is section 5 of the FTC Act, which empowers the Commission to prevent: (1) unfair methods of competition, and (2) unfair or deceptive acts or practices. We examine each of these bases of FTC authority later in this chapter. The Commission also enforces the consumer protection and

---

**FIGURE 1**   Some of the Major Acts Enforced by the FTC

---

**Regulation of Economic Competition**

FTC Act Section 5 (including Sherman Act standards)

Clayton Act

Robinson-Patman Act

Hart-Scott-Rodino Antitrust Improvements Act of 1976—requires that certain companies planning mergers notify and provide information to the FTC and the Justice Department

---

**Consumer Protection Measures Discussed in This Chapter**

FTC Act Section 5

Magnuson-Moss Warranty Act

Truth in Lending Act (including 1988 Fair Credit and Charge Card Disclosure Act and Home Equity Loan Consumer Protection Act)

Consumer Leasing Act

Fair Credit Reporting Act

Equal Credit Opportunity Act

Fair Credit Billing Act

Fair Debt Collection Practices Act

---

**Other Measures**

Export Trade Act—empowers FTC to supervise registration and operation of associations of American exporters engaged in export trade

Fair Packaging and Labeling Act—regulates packaging and labeling of consumer products to ensure accurate quality and value comparisons

Flammable Fabrics Act—FTC has some enforcement powers under act regulating manufacture, sale, and importation of flammable fabrics

Fur Products Labeling Act—regulates labeling, other identification, and advertising of fur products

Hobby Protection Act—regulates certain imitations of political campaign materials and certain imitation coins and paper money

Lanham Act—empowers FTC to petition for the cancellation of certain trademarks

Smokeless Tobacco Act—empowers FTC to approve manufacturers' plans for rotation and display of statements on smokeless tobacco packages and ads

Textile Fiber Products Identification Act—regulates labeling and other identification of textile fiber products

Wool Products Labeling Act—regulates labeling and other identification of wool products

---

Sources: *1993 United States Government Manual* and various statutes.

---

consumer credit measures discussed in the last half of the chapter. Finally, the FTC enforces various other federal acts, some of which are listed in Figure 1.

## FTC Enforcement Procedures

The FTC has many legal tools for ensuring compliance with the statutes it administers. The three most important FTC enforcement devices are its procedures for facilitating voluntary compliance, its issuance of trade regulation rules, and its adjudicative proceedings.

**Voluntary Compliance**   The FTC promotes voluntary, cooperative business behavior by giving advisory opinions and issuing industry guides. An **advisory opinion** is the Commission's response to a private party's query about the legality of proposed business conduct. The FTC is not obligated to furnish advisory opinions. Even where it does furnish such an opinion, the Commission may rescind it when the public interest requires. But when the FTC does so, it cannot proceed against the opinion's recipient for actions taken in good faith reliance on the opinion without giving the recipient notice of the rescission and an opportunity to discontinue those actions.

**Industry guides** are FTC interpretations of the laws it administers. Their purpose is to encourage businesses to voluntarily abandon certain unlawful practices. To further this end, industry guides are written in lay language. Industry guides lack the force of law. Often, however, behavior that violates an industry guide also violates one of the statutes or other rules the Commission enforces.

**Trade Regulation Rules**   Unlike industry guides, FTC **trade regulation rules** are written in legalistic language and have the force of law. Thus, the FTC can proceed directly against practices forbidden by a trade regulation rule. This can occur through the *adjudicative proceedings* discussed immediately below. The Commission can also obtain a federal district court *civil penalty* of up to $10,000 for each knowing violation of a rule. Furthermore, it may institute court proceedings to obtain various forms of *consumer redress,* including the payment of damages, the refund of money, the return of property, and the reformation or rescission of contracts.

**FTC Adjudicative Proceedings**   Often, the FTC proceeds against violations of its statutes or trade regulation rules by administrative action within the Commission itself. The FTC gets evidence of possible violations from private parties, government bodies, and its own investigations. If, after further investigation and discussion, it decides to proceed against the alleged offender (the *respondent*), it enters a formal complaint. The case itself is heard in a public administrative hearing called an *adjudicative proceeding* before an FTC administrative law judge. The judge's decision can be appealed to the FTC's five commissioners and then to the federal courts of appeals and the U.S. Supreme Court.

The usual penalty resulting from a final decision against the respondent is an FTC **cease-and-desist order.** This is basically a command to the respondent ordering it to stop its illegal behavior. As you will see later in the chapter, however, courts have upheld FTC orders going beyond the command to cease and desist. The civil penalty for noncompliance with a cease-and-desist order is up to $10,000 per violation. Where there is a continuing failure to obey a final order, each day that the violation continues is considered a separate violation.

Many alleged violations are never adjudicated by the FTC but instead are settled through a **consent order.** This is an order approving a negotiated agreement in which the respondent promises to cease certain activities. Consent orders normally provide that the respondent does not admit any violation of the law. The failure to observe a consent order is punishable by civil penalties.

## ANTICOMPETITIVE BEHAVIOR

Section 5 of the FTC Act empowers the Commission to prevent "unfair methods of competition." This language allows the FTC to regulate anticompetitive practices made illegal by the Sherman Act. The Commission also has specific statutory authority to enforce the Clayton and Robinson-Patman acts.

For the most part, section 5's application to anticompetitive behavior involves the orthodox antitrust violations discussed in the following two chapters. But section 5 also reaches anticompetitive behavior not covered by other antitrust statutes. Section 5 also enables the FTC to proceed against *potential* or *incipient* antitrust violations.

## DECEPTION AND UNFAIRNESS

Section 5 of the FTC Act also prohibits "unfair or deceptive acts or practices." This language enables the FTC to regulate a wide range of activities that disadvantage consumers. In doing so, the Commission may proceed under the theory that the activity is *deceptive,* or that it is *unfair.* Here, we set out the general standards that the FTC now uses to define each of these section 5 violations. Much of this discussion involves FTC regulation of advertising, but the standards we outline apply to many other misrepresentations, omissions, and practices. Although their details are beyond the scope of this text, the Commission also has enacted numerous trade regulation rules defining specific deceptive and unfair practices.

### Deception

The FTC determines the deceptiveness of advertising and other business practices on a case-by-case basis. Courts usually defer to the Commission's determinations. To be considered deceptive under the FTC's 1983 Policy Statement on Deception, an activity must: (1) involve a *material* misrepresentation, omission, or practice; (2) that is *likely to mislead* a consumer; (3) who acts *reasonably* under the circumstances.

**Representation, Omission, or Practice Likely to Mislead**    Often, sellers expressly make false or misleading claims in their advertisements or other representations. But as stated in the *International Harvester* case (which follows shortly), false or misleading statements can also be implied from the surrounding circumstances. As that case also states, a seller's *omissions* may be deceptive. Finally, certain deceptive *marketing practices* can violate section 5. In one such case, encyclopedia salespeople gained entry to the homes of potential customers by posing as surveyors engaged in advertising research.

In all of these situations, the statement, omission, or practice must be *likely to mislead* a consumer. Actual deception is not required. Determining whether an ad or practice is likely to mislead requires that the FTC evaluate the accuracy of the seller's claims. In some cases, moreover, the Commission requires that sellers *substantiate* objective claims about their products by showing that they have a reasonable basis for making such claims.

**The "Reasonable Consumer" Test**    To be deceptive, the representation, omission, or practice must also be likely to mislead *reasonable consumers under the circumstances.* This requirement aims to protect sellers from liability for foolish, ignorant, or outlandish misconceptions that some consumers might entertain. As the Commission noted some years ago, advertising an American-made pastry as "Danish Pastry" does not violate section 5 just because "a few misguided souls believe . . . that all Danish Pastry is made in Denmark."[1] Also, section 5 is usually not violated by statements of opinion, sales talk, or "puffing"; statements about matters that consumers can easily evaluate for themselves; and statements regarding subjective matters such as taste or smell. Such statements are unlikely to deceive reasonable consumers.

---

[1]*Heinz v. W. Kirchner,* 63 F.T.C. 1282, 1290 (1963).

**Materiality**    Finally, the representation, omission, or practice must be *material.* Material information is important to reasonable consumers and is likely to affect their choice of a product or service. Examples include statements or omissions regarding a product's cost, safety, effectiveness, performance, durability, quality, and warranty protection. In addition, the Commission presumes that express statements are material.

## Unfairness

Section 5's prohibition of *unfair* acts or practices enables the FTC to attack behavior that, while not necessarily deceptive, is objectionable for other reasons. As *International Harvester* demonstrates, the FTC now focuses on *consumer injury* when it attacks unfair acts or practices in its own adjudicative proceedings. To violate section 5, this injury must be:

1. *Substantial.* Monetary loss and unwarranted health and safety risks usually constitute substantial harm, but emotional distress or the perceived offensiveness of certain advertisements generally do not.

2. *Not outweighed by any offsetting consumer or competitive benefits produced by the challenged practice.* This element requires the Commission to balance the harm caused by the act or practice against its benefits to consumers and to competition generally. A seller's failure to give a consumer complex technical data about a product, for example, may disadvantage the consumer, but it may also reduce the product's price. Only when an act or practice is injurious in its *net effects* can it be unfair under section 5.

3. *One that consumers could not reasonably have avoided.* An injury is considered reasonably unavoidable when a seller's actions significantly interfere with a consumer's ability to make informed decisions that would have prevented the injury. For example, a seller may withhold otherwise-unavailable information about important product features, or use high-pressure sales tactics on vulnerable consumers.

## Remedies

Several types of orders can result from a successful FTC adjudicative proceeding attacking deceptive or unfair behavior.[2] One possibility is an order telling the respondent to *cease* engaging in the deceptive or unfair conduct. Another is the *affirmative disclosure* of information whose absence made the advertise-

ment deceptive or unfair. Yet another is *corrective advertising*. This requires the seller's future advertisements to correct false impressions created by its past advertisements. In certain cases, moreover, the FTC may issue an *all-products order* extending beyond the product or service whose advertisements violated section 5, and including future advertisements for other products or services marketed by the seller. Finally, the FTC may sometimes go to court to seek the civil penalties or consumer redress noted earlier or to seek injunctive relief.

---

[2]Such orders, and FTC regulation of deceptive and unfair advertising generally, may collide with the First Amendment protection of commercial speech. For the most part, however, the First Amendment has not been a major obstacle to the Commission. One reason is that the constitutional protection given commercial speech does not extend to false or misleading statements and thus does not protect most deceptive advertising.

---

## In the Matter of International Harvester Company
### 104 F.T.C. 949 (1984)

Since at least the early 1950s, the International Harvester Company's gasoline-powered tractors had been subject to "fuel geysering." This was a phenomenon in which hot liquid gasoline would shoot from the tractor's gas tank when the filler cap was opened. The hot gasoline could cause severe burns and could ignite and cause a fire. Over the years, at least 90 fuel geysering incidents involving International Harvester tractors occurred, at least 12 of these involved significant burn injuries, and at least one caused a death.

International Harvester first discovered the full dimensions of the fuel geysering problem in 1963. In that year, it revised its owner's manuals to warn buyers of new gas-powered tractors not to remove the gas cap from a hot or running tractor. In 1976, it produced a new fuel tank decal with a similar warning. Due to an industrywide shift to diesel-powered tractors, however, this warning had a very limited distribution to buyers of new tractors, and it rarely reached former buyers. International Harvester never specifically warned either new or old buyers about the geysering problem until 1980, when it voluntarily made a mass mailing to 630,000 customers.

In 1980, the FTC issued a complaint against International Harvester, alleging that its failure to warn buyers of the fuel geysering problem for 17 years was both deceptive and unfair under FTC Act section 5. The administrative law judge agreed with the Commission on each charge. Due to International Harvester's notification program, however, he concluded that a cease-and-desist order was unnecessary. Both International Harvester and the FTC's complaint counsel appealed to the full Commission.

---

**Douglas, Commissioner**    The basic law of this case is section 5 of the FTC Act. That section states that "unfair or deceptive acts or practices . . . are declared unlawful."

### Deception
A deception case requires a showing of three elements: (1) there must be a representation, practice, or omission likely to mislead consumers; (2) consumers must be interpreting the message reasonably under the circumstances; and (3) the misleading effects must be material. Our deception analysis focuses on risk of consumer harm, and actual injury

need not be shown. Deception is harmful to consumers, undermines the rational functioning of the marketplace, and never offers increased efficiency or other countervailing benefits.

Deception theory is not limited to false or misleading statements. Under two general circumstances it can also reach omissions. First, it can be deceptive to tell only half the truth, and to omit the rest. This may occur where a seller fails to disclose qualifying information necessary to prevent his affirmative statements from creating a misleading impression. The Commission has challenged the advertising of baldness cures for failing to disclose that most baldness results from male heredity and cannot be treated. It can also be deceptive for a seller to simply remain silent, if he does so under circumstances that constitute an implied but false representation. Such implied representations may arise from the physical appearance of the product, or from the circumstances of a transaction, or they may be based on ordinary consumer expectations. The Commission has upheld charges against sellers who failed to disclose that an apparently new product was actually used, that land sold for investment purposes was poorly suited to that use due to its remote location, and that a book was an abridged rather than a complete edition. One generalization that emerges from these cases is that by offering goods for sale, the seller impliedly represents that they are reasonably fit for their intended uses. The concept of reasonable fitness includes a further implied representation that the products are free of gross safety hazards.

However, the implied warranty of fitness is not violated by all undisclosed safety problems. Where the risk of mishap is very small, it cannot be said that the product is unfit for normal use. Such a case could therefore not satisfy the first element of the deception test, a misleading representation. Harvester manufactured approximately 1.3 million gasoline-powered tractors in the period after 1939. Of this number, twelve are known to have been involved in geysering incidents involving bodily injury. This is an accident rate of less than .001 percent, over a period of more than 40 years.

**Unfairness**

Unfairness analysis focuses on three criteria: (1) whether the practice creates a serious consumer injury; (2) whether this injury exceeds any offsetting consumer benefits; and (3) whether the injury was one that consumers could not reasonably have avoided. We find that all three criteria are satisfied in the present case.

There clearly has been serious consumer injury. At least one person has been killed and eleven others burned. Many of the burn injuries have been major ones. It is true that [these injuries] involve only limited numbers of people, but conduct causing a very severe harm to a small number will be covered.

The second criterion states that the consumer injury must not be outweighed by any countervailing benefits to consumers or to competition that the practice also brings about. The principal tradeoff to be considered in this analysis is that involving compliance costs. More information may be helpful to consumers, but such information can be produced only by incurring costs that are ultimately borne as higher prices by those same consumers. Harvester's program which finally led to an effective warning cost the company approximately $2.8 million. Here, however, Harvester's expenses were not large in relation to the injuries that could have been avoided. We therefore conclude that the costs and benefits in this case satisfy the second unfairness criterion.

Finally, the injury must be one that consumers could not reasonably have avoided. Here, tractor operators could have avoided their injuries if they had refrained from removing the cap from a hot or running tractor—something that both the owner's manuals and common knowledge suggested was a dangerous practice. However, whether some consequence is reasonably avoidable depends, not just on whether people know the steps to take to prevent it, but also on whether they understand the necessity of taking those steps. Farmers may have known that loosening the fuel cap was generally a poor practice, but they did not know the full consequences that might follow. Since fuel geysering was a risk that they were not aware of, they could not reasonably have avoided it. This is so even though they had been informed of measures to prevent it. Such information was not the same thing as an effective warning.

**Remedy**

Having found that Harvester was engaged in unfair practices, we must now determine what corrective measures the public interest will require. Under the particular circumstances of this case, we will issue no order at all. First, Harvester's voluntary notification program has already provided all the relief that could be expected from a Commission order. Second, Harvester has not made a gasoline tractor since 1978 and does not appear likely to do so again in the future.

**Decision of the administrative law judge affirmed in part and reversed in part.**

## CONSUMER PROTECTION LAWS

The term *consumer protection* can include everything from Chapter 12's product liability law to the packaging and labeling regulations listed earlier in Figure 1. Here, we examine federal regulation of product warranties, consumer credit, and product safety. Our main concern is the collection of federal laws governing consumer credit sales.

### The Magnuson-Moss Warranty Act

The Magnuson-Moss Warranty Act of 1975 mainly applies to *written warranties* for *consumer products.* Nothing in the act makes sellers give a written warranty, and sellers who decline to give such a warranty generally escape coverage. A consumer product is personal property that is ordinarily used for personal, family, or household purposes. In addition, many Magnuson-Moss provisions apply only when a written warranty is given in connection with the sale of a consumer product to a *consumer.* A consumer is a buyer or transferee of a consumer product who does not use it either for resale or in his own business.

Chapter 12 discusses Magnuson-Moss's provisions giving consumers minimum warranty protection. Here, we examine its rules requiring that consumer warranties contain certain information and that this information be made available to buyers before the sale. Any failure to comply with these rules violates section 5 of the FTC Act and can trigger Commission action. Also, either the FTC or the attorney general may sue to obtain injunctive relief against such violations.

**Required Warranty Information**  The Magnuson-Moss Act and its regulations require the simple, clear, and conspicuous presentation of certain information in written warranties to consumers for consumer products costing more than $15.[3] That information includes: (1) the persons protected by the warranty when coverage is limited to the original purchaser or is otherwise limited; (2) the products, parts, characteristics, components, or properties covered by the warranty; (3) what the warrantor will do in case of a product defect or other failure to

conform to the warranty; (4) the time the warranty begins (if different from the purchase date) and its duration; and (5) the procedure the consumer should follow to obtain the performance of warranty obligations. The act also requires that a warrantor disclose: (1) any limitations on the duration of implied warranties and (2) any attempt to limit consequential damages or other consumer remedies.[4]

**Presale Availability of Warranty Information**  The regulations accompanying Magnuson-Moss also contain detailed rules requiring that warranty terms be made available to a buyer before the sale. These rules generally govern sales of consumer products costing more than $15 to consumers. They set out certain duties that must be met by sellers (usually retailers) and by warrantors (usually manufacturers) of such products. For example:

**1.** *Sellers* must make the text of the warranty available for the prospective buyer's review before the sale, either by displaying the warranty in close proximity to the product or by furnishing the warranty upon request after posting signs informing buyers of its availability.

**2.** *Catalog or mail-order sellers* must clearly and conspicuously disclose in their catalog or solicitation either the full text of the warranty or the address from which a free copy can be obtained.

**3.** *Door-to-door sales.* To give you a concrete illustration of an FTC trade regulation rule, we include the full text of its door-to-door sales rule in Figure 2. As FTC rules go, this one is fairly short and straightforward.

**4.** *Warrantors* must give sellers the warranty materials necessary for them to comply with the duties stated in paragraph 1; and must give catalog, mail-order, and door-to-door sellers copies of the warranties they need to meet their duties.

### Truth in Lending Act

When Congress passed the Truth in Lending Act (TILA) in 1968, its main aims were to increase consumer knowledge and understanding of credit terms by compelling their *disclosure*, and to help

---

[3]Actually, the act states a $5 figure, while the regulations accompanying it state a $15 figure.

[4]Chapter 12 discusses limitations on an implied warranty's duration and on a consumer's remedies.

**FIGURE 2**   The FTC's Door-to-Door Sales Rule: 16 C.F.R. section 702.3(d) (1993)

(d) *Door-to-door sales.* (1) For purposes of this paragraph:

(i) "Door-to-Door sale" means a sale of consumer products in which the seller or his representative personally solicits the sale, including those in response to or following an invitation by a buyer, and the buyer's agreement to offer to purchase is made at a place other than the place of business of the seller.

(ii) "Prospective buyer" means an individual solicited by a door-to-door seller to buy a consumer product who indicates sufficient interest in that consumer product or maintains sufficient contact with the seller for the seller reasonably to conclude that the person solicited is considering purchasing the product.

(2) Any seller who offers for sale to consumers consumer products with written warranties by means of door-to-door sales shall, prior to the consummation of the sale, disclose the fact that the sales representative has copies of the warranties for the warranted products being offered for sale, which may be inspected by the prospective buyer at any time during the sales presentation. Such disclosure shall be made orally and shall be included in any written materials shown to prospective buyers.

consumers better shop for credit by commanding *uniform* disclosures. By now, however, the act protects consumers in other ways as well.

**Coverage**   The TILA generally applies to creditors who extend consumer credit to a debtor in an amount not exceeding $25,000.[5] A *creditor* is a party who regularly extends consumer credit; examples include banks, credit card issuers, and savings and loan associations. Extending credit need not be a creditor's primary business; for instance, auto dealers and retail stores can be creditors so long as they regularly extend credit. To qualify as a creditor, the party in question must also either impose a finance charge or by agreement require payment in more than four installments. *Consumer credit* is credit enabling the purchase of goods, services, or real estate used primarily for personal, family, or household purposes—not business or agricultural purposes. The TILA *debtor* must be a natural person; the act does not protect business organizations.

**Disclosure Provisions**   The TILA's detailed disclosure provisions break down into three categories.

---

[5]The $25,000 maximum does not apply where a creditor takes a security interest in a debtor's real property or in personal property, such as a mobile home, used as the debtor's principal dwelling. Here, the disclosure rules differ slightly from the rules for closed-end credit discussed shortly. In certain transactions of this kind, moreover, the debtor has a three-day rescission right whose details are beyond the scope of this text.

**1.** *Open-end credit.* The TILA defines an open-end credit plan as one that contemplates repeated transactions and that involves a finance charge which may be computed from time to time on the unpaid balance. Examples include credit card plans and revolving charge accounts offered by retail stores. Open-end credit plans require two forms of disclosure: (1) an *initial statement* made before the first transaction under the plan, and (2) a series of *periodic statements* (usually, one for each billing cycle). In each case, the required disclosures must be made clearly, conspicuously, and in meaningful sequence.

Among the disclosures required in the initial statement are: (1) when a finance charge is imposed and how it is determined, (2) the amount of any additional charges and the method for computing them, (3) the fact that the creditor has taken or will acquire a security interest in the debtor's property, and (4) the debtor's billing rights. Periodic statements require an even lengthier set of disclosures. Much of the information contained in a monthly credit card statement, for example, is compelled by the TILA.

**2.** *Closed-end credit.* The TILA requires a different set of disclosures for other credit plans, which generally involve closed-end credit. Closed-end credit such as a car loan or a consumer loan from a finance company is extended for a specific time period; the total amount financed, number of payments, and due dates are all agreed on at the time of the transaction. Examples of the disclosures necessary before the completion of closed-end credit transaction include: (1) the total finance charge; (2) the annual percentage rate (APR); (3) the amount financed; (4) the total number of payments, their due dates, and the amount of each payment; (5) the total dollar value of all payments; (6) any late charges imposed for past-due payments; and (7) any security interest taken by the creditor and the property that it covers.

**3.** *Credit card applications and solicitations.* In 1988, Congress amended the TILA to impose disclosure requirements on credit card applications and solicitations. These elaborate requirements differ depending on whether the application or solicitation is made by direct mail, telephone, or other means such as catalogs and magazines. To take just one example, direct mail applications and solicitations must include information about matters such as the APR, annual fees, the grace period for paying without incurring a finance charge, and the method for computing the balance on which the finance charge is based.

**Other TILA Provisions**   The TILA has provisions dealing with *consumer credit advertising*. For example, the act prevents a creditor from "baiting" customers by advertising loan or down payment amounts that it does not usually make available. To help consumers put advertised terms in perspective, ads for open-end consumer credit plans that state any of the plan's specific terms must state various other terms as well. For instance, an advertisement using such terms as "$100 down payment," "8 percent interest," or "$99 per month" must also state other relevant terms such as the APR.

Due to a 1988 amendment, the TILA now regulates open-end consumer credit plans involving an extension of credit secured by a consumer's principal dwelling—basically, the popular home equity loans. The act controls *advertisements* for such plans, requiring certain information such as the APR if the ad states any specific terms and forbidding misleading terms such as "free money." It also imposes elaborate disclosure requirements on *applications* for such plans. These include matters such as interest rates, fees, repayment options, minimum payments, and repayment periods. Finally, the act also controls the *terms* of such a plan and the *actions* a creditor can take under it.

For example: (1) if the plan involves a variable interest rate, the "index rate" to which changes in the APR are pegged must be based on some publicly available rate and must not be under the creditor's control; (2) a creditor cannot unilaterally terminate the plan and require immediate repayment of the outstanding balance unless a consumer has made material misrepresentations, has failed to repay the balance, or has adversely affected the creditor's security; and (3) the plan cannot allow a creditor to unilaterally alter its important terms.

Finally, the TILA has a few rules concerning *credit cards*. The most important such rule limits a cardholder's liability for unauthorized use of the card to a maximum of $50. Unauthorized use is use by a person other than the cardholder, where this person lacks express, implied, or apparent authority for such use.[6]

**Enforcement**   Various federal agencies enforce the TILA. Except in areas committed to a particular agency, overall enforcement authority rests in the FTC. In addition, those who willfully and knowingly violate the act may face criminal prosecution. Civil actions by private parties, including class actions, are also possible.

## Consumer Leasing Act

The Consumer Leasing Act, which was passed in 1976, covers leases of personal property: (1) to natural persons (not organizations), (2) for consumer purposes, (3) for an amount not exceeding $25,000, and (4) for a period exceeding four months.

The act requires that a lessor make numerous written *disclosures* to a lessee before the consummation of the lease transaction. Examples include: a description or identification of the leased property; the number, amount, and due dates of the lease payments; their total amount; any express warranties made by the lessor; and any security interest taken by the lessor. The act also requires that lease *advertisements* include certain additional information if they

---

[6]Express, implied, and apparent authority are discussed in Chapter 27. The *Towers* case in that chapter applies this provision of the TILA.

already state: the amount of any payment, the number of required payments, the amount of the down payment, or that no down payment is required.

The Consumer Leasing Act subjects creditors violating its disclosure requirements to the same civil suits that are permitted under the TILA. Also, the FTC enforces the act.

## Fair Credit Reporting Act

The reports credit bureaus provide to various users can significantly affect one's ability to obtain credit, insurance, employment, and many of life's other goods. Often, affected individuals are unaware of the influence that credit reports had on such decisions. The Fair Credit Reporting Act (FCRA) was enacted in 1970 to give people some protection against abuses in the process of disseminating information about their creditworthiness.

**Duties of Consumer Reporting Agencies**  The FCRA imposes certain duties on consumer reporting agencies—agencies that regularly compile credit-related information on individuals for the purpose of furnishing consumer credit reports to users. A consumer reporting agency must adopt *reasonable procedures* to:

**1.** Ensure that *users employ* the information only for the following purposes: consumer credit sales, employment evaluations, the underwriting of insurance, the granting of a government license or other benefit, or any other business transaction where the user has a legitimate business need for the information.

**2.** Avoid including in a report *obsolete information* predating the report by more than a stated period. This period usually is 7 years; for a prior bankruptcy, it is 10 years. This duty does not apply to credit reports used in connection with certain life insurance policies, large credit transactions, and applications for employment.

**3.** Assure *maximum possible accuracy* regarding the personal information in credit reports. The *Grant* case (which follows shortly) discusses this duty. However, the act does little to limit the *types* of data included in credit reports. In fact, all kinds of information about a person's character, reputation, personal traits, and mode of life seemingly are permitted.

**Disclosure Duties on Users**  The FCRA also imposes disclosure duties on *users* of credit reports—mainly, credit sellers, lenders, employers, and insurers.[7] One of these duties applies to users who order an *investigative consumer report*. This is a credit report that includes information on a person's character, reputation, personal traits, or mode of living and that is based on interviews with neighbors, friends, associates, and the like. If a user procures such a report on a person, it must inform him that the report has been requested, that the report may contain sensitive information, and that he has a right to obtain further disclosures about the user's investigation. If the person requests such disclosures within a reasonable time, the user must reveal the nature and scope of the investigation.

Another disclosure duty arises when, because of information contained in any credit report, a user: (1) rejects an applicant for consumer credit, insurance, or employment; or (2) charges a higher rate for credit or insurance. Here, the user must maintain *reasonable procedures* for advising the affected individual that it relied on the credit report in making its decision, and for stating the name and address of the consumer reporting agency that supplied the report.

**Disclosure and Correction of Credit Report Information**  After a request from a properly identified individual, a *consumer reporting agency* must normally disclose to that individual: (1) the nature and substance of all its information about the individual, (2) the sources of this information, and (3) the recipients of any credit reports that it has furnished within certain time periods. Then, a person disputing the completeness or accuracy of the agency's information can compel it to reinvestigate. As *Grant* makes clear, the credit bureau must delete the information from the person's file if it finds the information to be inaccurate or unverifiable. An individual who is not satisfied with the agency's investigation may file a brief statement setting forth the nature of her dispute with the agency. If so, any subsequent credit report containing the disputed information must note that it is disputed and must

---

[7]In addition to the duties stated here, the FCRA also imposes disclosure duties on users who deny consumer credit, or increase the charge for such credit, because of information obtained from *someone other than a consumer reporting agency.*

provide either the individual's statement or a clear and accurate summary of it. Also, an agency may be required to notify certain prior recipients of deleted, unverifiable, or disputed information if the individual requests this. However, there is no duty to investigate or to include the consumer's version of the facts if the credit bureau has reason to believe that the individual's request is frivolous or irrelevant.

**Enforcement**    Violations of the FCRA are violations of FTC Act section 5, and the Commission

may use its normal enforcement procedures in such cases. Other federal agencies may also enforce the FCRA in certain situations. The FCRA establishes criminal penalties for: (1) persons who knowingly and willfully obtain consumer information from a credit bureau under false pretenses and (2) credit bureau officers or employees who knowingly or willfully provide information to unauthorized persons. Violations of the FCRA may also trigger private civil suits against consumer reporting agencies and users.

## GRANT v. TRW, INC.
### 789 F. Supp. 690 (D. Md. 1992)

In 1989, Samuel Grant sued, and was sued by, his landlord in a Maryland trial court. Grant recovered $608 against the landlord, and the landlord recovered $476.10 against Grant, leaving Grant with a net recovery of $131.90. In 1990, Texaco denied Grant's application for a Texaco credit card because a TRW, Inc., credit report obtained by Texaco stated that a judgment of $400 had been entered against Grant. After obtaining a credit report from TRW, Grant informed the credit bureau that the litigation between him and his landlord had resulted in a net judgment in his favor. Eventually, TRW sent Grant an "Updated Credit Profile" showing that the $400 judgment had been deleted from Grant's file.

In May 1991, Grant again applied for a Texaco credit card. His application again was denied because the $400 debt appeared on his credit report. Grant then sued TRW under the FCRA in a Maryland trial court. After the case was removed to federal district court, TRW moved to dismiss Grant's claim.

**Motz, District Judge**    Grant first alleges that TRW violated the FCRA by failing to follow reasonable procedures assuring "maximum possible accuracy of the information concerning the individual about whom the report relates." In order to make out a prima facie violation of [this provision], a consumer must present evidence that a credit reporting agency prepared a report containing inaccurate information. Here, plaintiff concedes that the notation in the credit report that a judgment had been entered against him was accurate insofar as it went. There may be extreme instances in which a technically accurate statement is so inherently misleading that it would run afoul of the "maximum possible accuracy" requirement. For example, if a consumer were a victim of a credit card scam, it would hardly seem accurate for a consumer reporting agency to report that the person was "involved" in the scam. How-

ever, the possibility that such extreme cases might be presented does not justify rewriting the FCRA to render actionable the initial reporting of information which, although accurate, is deemed to be misleading because it is incomplete. "Accuracy" can be tested by verification, whereas a determination of "completeness" requires the exercise of judgment on potentially difficult questions concerning the meaning and effect of contextual information. Adding a "completeness" element substantially expands the duties imposed upon consumer reporting agencies and exposes them to dramatically increased litigation.

That is not the end of the matter, however. [The FCRA also] provides: "If the completeness or accuracy of any item of information contained in his file is disputed by a consumer, . . . the consumer reporting agency shall within a reasonable period of time reinvestigate and record the current status of that information unless it has reasonable grounds to believe that the dispute by the consumer is frivolous or irrelevant.'' This provision . . . places the burden upon the consumer to challenge incomplete information, but, once the challenge is made, it requires reinvestigation and recording of the information provided by the consumer. Here, Grant did notify TRW of the full circumstances surrounding the

Maryland trial court judgment, but, inexplicably, after advising Grant that it would delete the challenged notation from his report, TRW neither effected the deletion nor recorded the information which Grant had provided. This dereliction is actionable under [the FCRA].

**TRW's motion to dismiss denied.**

## Equal Credit Opportunity Act

The Equal Credit Opportunity Act (ECOA), originally passed in 1974, prohibits credit discrimination on the bases of sex, marital status, age, race, color, national origin, religion, and the obtaining of income from public assistance. The ECOA covers all entities that regularly arrange, extend, renew, or continue credit. Examples include banks; savings and loan associations; credit card issuers; and many retailers, auto dealers, and realtors. The act is not limited to consumer credit, and also covers business and commercial loans.

The ECOA governs all phases of a credit transaction. As authorized by the act, the Federal Reserve Board has promulgated regulations detailing permissible and impermissible creditor behavior at each stage. Even where the regulations do not specifically prohibit certain creditor behavior, that behavior may still violate the act itself. Even credit practices that are perfectly neutral on their face may result in ECOA violations if the practice has an adverse statistical impact on one of the ECOA's protected classes.[8]

The ECOA also requires that creditors notify applicants of the action taken on a credit application within 30 days of its receipt or any longer reasonable time stated in the regulations. If the action is unfavorable, an applicant is entitled to a statement of reasons from the creditor.

The ECOA is enforced by several federal agencies, with overall enforcement resting in the hands of the FTC. Which agency enforces the act depends on the type of creditor or credit involved. Civil

actions by aggrieved private parties, including class actions, also are possible.

## Fair Credit Billing Act

The Fair Credit Billing Act, effective in 1975, is mainly aimed at credit card issuers. Although the act regulates the credit card business in other ways, its most important provisions involve billing disputes.[9] To trigger these provisions, a cardholder must give the issuer written notice of an alleged error in a billing statement within 60 days of the time that the statement is sent to the cardholder. Then, within two complete billing cycles or 90 days (whichever is less), the issuer must either: (1) correct the cardholder's account, or (2) send the cardholder a written statement justifying the statement's accuracy. Until the issuer takes either of these steps, it may not: (1) restrict or close the cardholder's account because of her failure to pay the disputed amount, (2) try to collect the disputed amount, or (3) report or threaten to report the cardholder's failure to pay the disputed amount to a third party such as a consumer reporting agency.

Once an issuer has met the act's requirements, it must also give a cardholder at least 10 days to pay the disputed amount before making an unfavorable report to a third party. If the cardholder disputes the issuer's justification within the 10-day period allowed for payment, the issuer can make such a report only if it also tells the third party that the debt is disputed and gives the cardholder the third party's name and address. In addition, the issuer must report the final resolution of the dispute to the third party.

---

[8]This resembles the adverse impact or disparate impact method of proof used in employment discrimination cases under Title VII of the 1964 Civil Rights Act. See Chapter 40.

[9]The Federal Reserve Board has promulgated regulations regarding the resolution of billing errors, and the FTC has some enforcement authority under the act as well.

An issuer that fails to comply with any of these rules forfeits its right to collect $50 of the disputed amount from the cardholder. Because the issuer may still be able to collect the balance on large disputed debts, it is doubtful whether this provision does much to deter violations of the act.

## Fair Debt Collection Practices Act

Concern over abusive, deceptive, and unfair practices by debt collectors led Congress to pass the Fair Debt Collection Practices Act (FDCPA) in 1977. The act applies to debts that involve money, property, insurance, or services obtained by a *consumer* for *consumer purposes*. Normally, the act only covers those who are in the business of collecting debts owed to *others*. However, creditors who collect their own debts are covered when by using a name other than their own name they indicate that a third party is collecting the debt.

**Communication Rules**    Except where necessary to locate a debtor, the FDCPA generally prevents debt collectors from contacting third parties such as the debtor's employer, relatives, or friends. The act also limits a collector's contacts with the debtor himself. Unless the debtor consents, for instance, a collector cannot contact him at unusual or inconvenient times or places, or at his place of employment if the employer forbids such contacts. Also, a collector cannot contact a debtor if it knows that the debtor is represented by an attorney, unless the attorney consents to such contact or fails to respond to the collector's communications. In addition, a collector must cease most communications with a debtor if the debtor gives the creditor written notification that he refuses to pay the debt or that he does not desire further communications from the collector.

The FDCPA also requires a collector to give a debtor certain information about the debt within five days of the collector's first communication with the debtor. If the debtor disputes the debt in writing within 30 days after receiving this information, the collector must cease its collection efforts until it sends verification of the debt to the debtor. The *Miller* case (which follows shortly) applies this provision of the FDCPA.

**Specific Forbidden Practices**    The FDCPA sets out categories of forbidden collector practices and lists specific examples of each category. The listed examples, however, do not exhaust the ways that debt collectors can violate the act. The categories are:

1. *Harassment, oppression, or abuse.* Examples include threats of violence, obscene or abusive language, and repeated phone calls.

2. *False or misleading misrepresentations.* Among the FDCPA's listed examples are statements that a debtor will be imprisoned for failure to pay, that a collector will take an action it is not legally entitled to take, that a collector is affiliated with the government, or that misstate the amount of the debt.

3. *Unfair practices.* These include: collecting from a debtor an amount not authorized by the agreement creating the debt, getting a debtor to accept a collect call before revealing the call's true purpose, and falsely or unjustifiably threatening to take a debtor's property.

**Enforcement**    The FTC is the main enforcement agency for the FDCPA, although other agencies enforce it in certain cases. The FDCPA also permits individual civil actions and class actions by the affected debtor or debtors.[10]

---

[10]Also, some debt collection practices might lead to tort liability for invasion of privacy or perhaps even for intentional infliction of emotional distress.

---

## MILLER V. PAYCO-GENERAL AMERICAN CREDITS, INC.
### 943 F.2d 482 (4th Cir. 1991)

Lenvil Miller owed $2,501.61 to the Star Bank of Cincinnati. The bank referred the collection of Miller's account to Payco-General American Credits, Inc., a debt collection agency. Payco sent Miller a one-page collection form whose front side provided information about the creditor, the amount of the debt, and Payco's address. In the middle of the page, in large, red, boldfaced type, was the statement: THIS IS A DEMAND FOR

IMMEDIATE FULL PAYMENT OF YOUR DEBT. After that came the following sentences: YOUR SERIOUSLY PAST DUE ACCOUNT HAS BEEN GIVEN TO US FOR IMMEDIATE ACTION. YOU HAVE HAD AMPLE TIME TO PAY YOUR DEBT, BUT YOU HAVE NOT. IF THERE IS A VALID REASON, PHONE US AT [telephone number] TODAY. IF NOT, PAY US—NOW. The bottom third of the form was almost completely filled by the single word NOW in white letters nearly two inches tall against a red background.

At the very bottom of the page in the smallest type appearing on the form was the statement: NOTICE: SEE REVERSE SIDE FOR IMPORTANT INFORMATION. The reverse side of the form contained the "validation notice" required by the FDCPA—statements informing a consumer how to obtain verification of the debt.

Miller sued in federal district court, alleging that the form did not comply with the FDCPA. After the court granted Payco's motion for summary judgment, Miller appealed.

———————————————————■———————————————————

**Wilkinson, Circuit Judge**    The FDCPA requires a debt collector to send a consumer, either in its initial communication or within five days of its initial communication, a written notice containing: (1) the debt amount; (2) the name of the current creditor; (3) a statement that if the consumer disputes the debt in writing within thirty days, the collector will send verification of the debt to the consumer; (4) a statement that if the consumer does not dispute the debt within thirty days, the collector will assume the debt to be valid; and (5) a statement that the collector will send the name of the original creditor, upon written request within thirty days. If the consumer, in writing, disputes the debt or requests the name of the original creditor, then the collector must halt all collection efforts until it mails verification of the debt or the creditor's name to the consumer.

In interpreting the FDCPA, we bear in mind that the statute was enacted to eliminate abusive debt collection practices. Congress included the debt validation provisions to guarantee that consumers would receive adequate notice of their legal rights. Thus, a debt collector does not comply with the act merely by inclusion of the required debt validation notice; the notice must be conveyed effectively to the debtor. For example, a validation notice printed on the back of a form letter where the front of the letter contains no reference to the notice does not comply with the act. Furthermore, the notice must not be overshadowed or contradicted by other messages or notices appearing in the initial communication.

We agree with Miller that the form both contradicted and overshadowed the validation notice, preventing the notice's effective communication. The front of the form demands IMMEDIATE FULL PAYMENT, and commands the consumer to PHONE US TODAY, emphasized by the word NOW in white letters nearly two inches tall against a red background. The message conveyed by those statements on the face of the form flatly contradicts the information contained on the back.

A consumer who wished to obtain validation of his debt could lose his rights under the statute if he followed the commands to telephone. The FDCPA guarantees that validation will be sent and collection activities will cease only when the consumer disputes the debt in writing. If a consumer attempted to exercise his statutory rights by making the requested telephone call, Payco would be under no obligation to comply with the act's directives to verify the debt and to cease collection efforts.

The emphasis on immediate action also stands in contradiction to the FDCPA [provision] which provides consumers a thirty-day period to decide to request validation. A consumer who received Payco's form could easily be confused between the commands to respond "immediately," "now," and "today," and the thirty-day response time required by the statute.

Payco responds that [the FDCPA] does not mandate a particular format, type size, location, or conspicuous position for the validation notice, but rather looks entirely to its content. We agree that to prescribe the exact size, color, or method of presentation for the validation notice would be judicial rule-writing in which we shall not indulge. Our role instead is the essentially negative one of examining whether a given notice comports with the statute. There are numerous and ingenious ways of circumventing the act under cover of a technical compliance. Payco has devised one such way, and we think that to uphold it would strip the statute of its meaning.

**Judgment reversed in favor of Miller. Case remanded to the district court for further proceedings.**

## Product Safety Regulation

Yet another facet of consumer protection law is federal regulation of product safety. As discussed in Chapter 12, sellers and manufacturers of dangerously defective products often are civilly liable to those injured by such products. Damage recoveries, however, are at best an after-the-fact remedy for injuries caused by such products. Thus, federal law also seeks to promote product safety by *direct regulation* of consumer products.

**The Consumer Product Safety Act**    The most important federal product safety measure is the Consumer Product Safety Act of 1972 (CPSA). The CPSA established the Consumer Product Safety Commission (CPSC), an independent regulatory agency that is the main federal body concerned with the safety of consumer products. Among the CPSC's activities are the following: (1) issuing *consumer product safety standards* (which normally involve the performance of consumer products or require product warnings or instructions); (2) issuing rules *banning* certain *hazardous products*; (3) bringing suit in federal district court to eliminate the dangers presented by *imminently hazardous* consumer products (products that pose an immediate and unreasonable risk of death, serious illness, or severe personal injury); and (4) *ordering private parties to address "substantial product hazards"* after receiving notice of such hazards. The CPSA's remedies and enforcement devices include injunctions, the seizure of products, civil penalties, criminal penalties, and private damage suits.

**Other Federal Product Safety Regulations**    Other federal statutes besides the CPSA regulate various specific consumer products. Among the subjects so regulated are toys, cigarette labeling and advertising, eggs, meat, poultry, smokeless tobacco,

flammable fabrics, drugs, cosmetics, pesticides, and motor vehicles. Some of these laws are enforced by the CPSC and some by other bodies.

### PROBLEMS AND PROBLEM CASES

**1.** For a long time, advertisements for Listerine Antiseptic Mouthwash had claimed that Listerine was beneficial in the treatment of colds, cold symptoms, and sore throats. An FTC adjudicative proceeding concluded that these claims were false. Thus, the Commission ordered Warner-Lambert Company, the manufacturer of Listerine, to include the following statement in future Listerine advertisements: "Contrary to prior advertising, Listerine will not help prevent colds or sore throats or lessen their severity." Warner-Lambert argued that this order was invalid because it went beyond a command to simply cease and desist from illegal behavior. Is Warner-Lambert correct?

**2.** Patriot Alcohol Testers, Inc. marketed a coin-operated blood alcohol measuring device that could be placed in bars and restaurants for use by patrons. Patriot falsely represented that distributors' annual income from the device would be $130 per week per device installed. Make *two* arguments that this representation is material under the deception standard the FTC uses under FTC Act section 5.

**3.** World Travel Vacation Brokers, Inc., advertised Hawaii vacations by offering $29 certificates that could be redeemed for roundtrip airfare to Hawaii. To get these certificates, consumers had to book hotel reservations through World Travel for a minimum of eight days and seven nights at World Travel's "hotel cost." The ads stated that World Travel could offer this $29 price because it had purchased excess frequent flyer coupons, its huge purchasing volume had enabled it to obtain big discounts from airlines, and the package was part of a promotional "deregulation special" offered by the airlines.

World Travel sold between 600,000 and 700,000 of the $29 Hawaii vacation certificates. Unfortunately for their purchasers, World Travel had effectively charged them full airfare by jacking up the "hotel cost." Language on the certificates, however, stated that "prices do not reflect actual hotel rates." Under the FTC's section 5 policy statement on deceptive advertising, did the consumers who purchased the certificates act reasonably under the circumstances?

**4.** Between 1966 and 1975, the Orkin Exterminating Company, the world's largest termite and pest control firm, offered its customers a "lifetime" guarantee that could be renewed each year by paying a definite amount specified in its contracts with the customers. The contracts gave no indication that the fees could be raised for any but narrowly specified reasons. Beginning in 1980, Orkin unilaterally breached these contracts by imposing higher-than-agreed-upon annual renewal fees. About 200,000 contracts were breached in this way, and Orkin realized about $7 million in additional revenues from customers who renewed at the higher fees. The additional fees did not purchase a higher level of service than that originally provided for in the contracts. Also, while some of Orkin's competitors may have been willing to assume Orkin's pre-1975 contracts at the fees stated therein, they would not have offered a fixed, locked-in "lifetime" renewal fee like that Orkin originally provided. Under the three-part test stated in the text, did Orkin's behavior violate FTC Act section 5's prohibition against *unfair* acts or practices?

**5.** Patron Aviation, Inc., an aviation company, bought an airplane engine from L&M Aircraft. The engine was assembled and shipped to L&M by Teledyne Industries, Inc. L&M installed the engine in one of Patron's airplanes. The engine turned out to be defective, and Patron sued L&M and Teledyne. One of the issues presented by the case was whether the Magnuson-Moss Act was applicable. Does the Magnuson-Moss Act apply to this transaction?

**6.** John and Marilyn Olson ran their farming business through a corporation. They obtained a number of loans from a local bank. Give *two* reasons why the Truth in Lending Act does *not* apply to these loans.

**7.** Smith rented a television set from ABC Rental Systems. The rental agreement stated that the lease was a week-to-week arrangement and that it was terminable by either party at any time. The agreement stated the figures "$16.00/55.00" in a space provided for the rental rate. The $16 figure was the weekly rate, and the $55 figure was a reduced monthly rate available to a consumer who wished to pay monthly. Smith was never provided with any of the disclosures required by the Consumer Leasing Act. Does the Consumer Leasing Act apply to this transaction?

**8.** In 1988, Vincent Mone quit his job at Sawyer of Napa, Inc., a California corporation whose president and CEO was Milton Dranow. When Mone established a competing firm, Dranow sued him for $5 million, alleging unfair competition. Three days before filing suit, Dranow had obtained a credit report on Mone from TRW, Inc., a credit reporting agency. Under the Fair Credit Reporting Act, did TRW act properly in giving Dranow the credit report on Mone?

**9.** The Credit Bureau, Inc. (CBI), maintains credit records on consumers, among them a Mr. and Mrs. Rush. The Rushes obtained a CBI report on themselves, and found an "R-9" credit rating (the lowest possible) next to the entry for their Macy's account. This poor credit rating caused the Rushes to be denied credit on several occasions. The Rushes sued Macy's under the Fair Credit Reporting Act. Will they win under the FCRA? Assume for purposes of argument that the entry was erroneous and was the fault of Macy's.

**10.** Sylvia Miller, a married woman, wanted to buy a pair of loveseats from a retail furniture store. The store offered to arrange financing for her through the Public Industrial Loan Company. Public later refused to extend credit to Miller unless her husband cosigned the debt obligation. The reason was a consumer reporting agency's unfavorable credit report on Miller. Was Public's action forbidden sex discrimination under the Equal Credit Opportunity Act? In any event, what other legal remedy might Miller have here?

**11.** John E. Koerner & Co., Inc. applied for a credit card account with the American Express Company. The application was for a company account designed for business customers. Koerner asked American Express to issue cards bearing the company's name to Louis Koerner and four other officers of the corporation. Koerner was required to sign a company account form, agreeing that he would be jointly and severally liable with the company for all charges incurred through use of the company card. American Express issued the cards requested by the company. Thereafter, the cards were used almost totally for business purposes, although Koerner occasionally used his card for personal expenses. Later, a dispute regarding charges appearing on the company account arose. Does the Fair Credit Billing Act apply to this dispute?

**12.** In connection with its attempt to collect a debt, Collection Accounts Terminal, Inc., sent Josephine Rutyna a letter stating: "Our field investigator has . . . been instructed to make an investigation in your neighborhood and to personally call on your employer." Does this statement violate the Fair Debt Collection Practices Act? Why or why not?

**13.** ▮▮▮ *Video Case.* See "Henry and Wanda." Henry and Wanda, a married couple, had a joint charge account. After Henry left Wanda following an argument over money, he made many purchases on the account, eventually overdrawing it. As a result, Wanda received numerous phone calls at all hours of the day and night. In one of these calls, the caller referred to Wanda as a "deadbeat" because she would not pay her husband's debts. In another, the caller threatened to contact Wanda's employer. Eventually, one of the callers located Henry by contacting his mother, telling her that Henry's father had been involved in a serious accident, and asserting that it was necessary to contact Henry so that he could donate blood to his father. Assuming that all these actions were taken by a covered debt collector and that Henry and Wanda both are protected debtors, explain how these various practices *may* have violated the Fair Debt Collection Practices Act.

## CAPSTONE QUESTIONS

EcoGenics, Inc., has been making money marketing a cancer cure to certain terminally ill patients. The alleged cure is the firm's "Logan Pass Spring Water," which allegedly comes from a small stream deep in the wilds of Glacier Park. This spring, EcoGenics's advertisements claim, is free from any industrial pollutants whatever. For this reason, the ads continue, the body responds to the spring water's natural purity by pumping out millions of cancer cell–killing immune system cells. The premise of the ads is that all or most cancer is caused by environmental pollution. They claim that Logan Pass Spring Water has completely cured thousands of people of their otherwise terminal disease.

A bottle of Logan Pass Spring Water costs $400. Each bottle represents approximately a one-week treatment. Because the ads claim that a six-month course of treatment is required, one patient's maximum total outlay would be approximately $10,000. EcoGenics's total revenues last year were $10 million.

So far as can be discerned, EcoGenics's claim that Logan Pass Spring Water has caused thousands of cancer cures is simply false. Assume for purposes of this question that its assertions about the genesis of cancer are unproven. You are an FTC staff attorney contemplating proceedings against EcoGenics under FTC Act section 5. You are considering the following questions.

## Required:

Answer the following and give reasons for your conclusions.

**1.** Are the ads deceptive under section 5?

**2.** Are the ads unfair under section 5?

CHAPTER

40

# EMPLOYMENT LAW

**INTRODUCTION**

*Years ago, it was unusual to see a separate employment law chapter in a business law text. At that time, the rights, duties, and liabilities accompanying employment were usually determined by basic legal institutions such as contract, tort, and agency. These common law principles continue to control employer-employee relations unless displaced by government regulations or by new judge-made rules applying specifically to employment. Today, however, such rules and regulations are so numerous that they touch almost every facet of employment. This chapter discusses the most important of these modern legal controls on employment.*

## SOME BASIC EMPLOYMENT STATUTES

Modern American employment law is so vast and complex a subject that texts designed for lawyers seldom address it in its entirety. Indeed, specialized subjects like labor law and employment discrimination often get book-length treatment in their own right. This chapter's overview of employment law focuses mainly on three topics that have attracted much recent attention—employment discrimination, employee privacy, and common law claims for wrongful discharge. But no discussion of employment law is complete without outlining certain basic regulations that significantly affect the conditions of employment for most Americans. Figure 1 outlines these regulations and the functions they perform.

### Workers' Compensation

Nineteenth-century law made it difficult for employees to recover when they sued their employer in negligence for on-the-job injuries.[1] At that time, employers had an *implied assumption of risk* defense under which an employee was said to assume all the normal and customary risks of his employment simply by taking the job. If an employee's own carelessness played some role in his injury, employers could often avoid negligence liability under the traditional rule that even a slight degree of

---

[1] This chapter assumes some familiarity with negligence law and most of the negligence defenses noted in this section—as well as with tort law in general.

**FIGURE 1**   The Ends and Means of Modern Employment Law

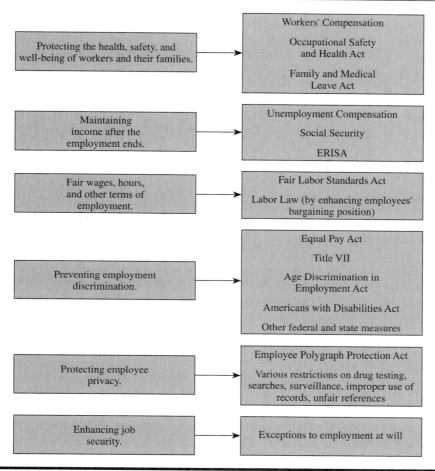

contributory negligence is a complete defense. Another employer defense, the *fellow-servant rule,* said that where an employee's injury resulted from the negligence of a coemployee (or fellow servant), the employer would not be liable. Finally, employees routinely had problems *proving* the employer's negligence. State workers' compensation statutes, which first appeared early in the 20th century, were a response to this situation. Today, all 50 states have such systems.[2]

**Basic Features**   Workers' compensation only protects *employees*, and not independent contractors.[3] However, many states exempt casual, agricultural, and domestic employees, among others. State and local government employees may be covered by workers' compensation or by some alternative state system. Also, states usually exempt certain *employers*—for example, firms employing fewer than a stated number of employees (often three).

---

[2]In addition, various federal statutes regulate on-the-job injuries suffered by employees of the federal government and other employees such as railroad workers, seamen, longshoremen, and harbor workers.

[3]Chapter 27 discusses the employee–independent contractor distinction.

Where they apply, however, all workers' compensation systems share certain basic features. They allow injured employees to recover under *strict liability,* thus removing any need to prove employer negligence. They also *eliminate the employer's traditional defenses* of contributory negligence, assumption of risk, and the fellow-servant rule. In addition, they make workers' compensation an employee's *exclusive remedy* against her employer for covered injuries. Usually, however, employees injured by their employer's *intentional torts* sue the employer outside workers' compensation.

Workers' compensation is basically a social compromise. Because it involves strict liability and eliminates the three traditional employer defenses, workers' compensation greatly increases the *probability* that an injured employee will recover. Such recoveries usually include: (1) hospital and medical expenses (including vocational rehabilitation), (2) disability benefits, (3) specified recoveries for the loss of certain body parts, and (4) death benefits to survivors and/or dependents. But the *amount* recoverable under each category of damages is usually less than would be obtained in a negligence suit. Thus, as the *Tolbert* case (which follows shortly) illustrates, injured employees sometimes deny that they are covered by workers' compensation so that they can pursue a tort suit against their employer instead.

Although workers' compensation is an injured employee's sole remedy against her employer, she may be able to sue *other parties* whose behavior helped cause her injury. One example is a product liability suit against a manufacturer who supplies an employer with defective machinery or raw materials that cause an on-the-job injury. However, many states immunize coemployees from ordinary tort liability for injuries they inflict on other employees. Complicated questions of contribution, indemnity, and subrogation can arise where an injured employee is able to recover against both an employer and a third party.

**The Work-Related Injury Requirement**   Another basic feature of workers' compensation is that employees recover only for *work-related* injuries. To be work-related, the injury must: (1) arise out of the employment, and (2) happen in the course of the employment. These tests have been variously interpreted.

The arising-out-of-the-employment requirement usually requires a sufficiently close relationship between the injury and the *nature* of the employment. As *Tolbert* illustrates, courts use different tests to define this requirement. A factory worker assaulted by a trespasser, for example, would probably be denied workers' compensation recovery under the "increased risk" test discussed in *Tolbert* but probably would recover under the "positional risk" test described there. If the same trespasser assaulted an on-duty security guard, however, the guard should recover under either test.

The in-the-course-of-the-employment requirement inquires whether the injury occurred within the *time, place,* and *circumstances* of the employment. Employees injured off the employer's premises are generally outside the course of the employment. For example, injuries suffered while traveling to or from work are usually not compensable. But an employee may be covered where the off-the-premises injury occurred while she was performing employment-related duties such as going on a business trip or running an employment-related errand.

Other work-related injury problems on which courts have disagreed include mental injuries allegedly arising from the employment and injuries resulting from employee horseplay. Virtually all states, however, regard intentionally self-inflicted injuries as outside workers' compensation. Recovery for occupational diseases, on the other hand, is usually allowed today. An employee whose preexisting diseased condition is aggravated by her employment sometimes recovers as well.

**Administration and Funding**   Workers' compensation systems are usually administered by a state agency that adjudicates workers' claims and administers the system. Its decisions on such claims are normally appealable to the state courts. The states fund workers' compensation by compelling covered employers to: (1) purchase private insurance, (2) self-insure (e.g., by maintaining a contingency fund), or (3) make payments into a state insurance fund. Because employers generally pass on the costs of insurance to their customers, workers' compensation tends to spread the economic risk of workplace injuries throughout society.

## TOLBERT V. MARTIN MARIETTA CORPORATION
### 621 F. Supp. 1099 (D. Colo. 1985)

Deborah Tolbert, a secretary employed by the Martin Marietta Corporation, was raped by a Martin Marietta janitor while on her way to lunch within the secured defense facility where she worked. She sued Martin Marietta, alleging that it had negligently hired the janitor and had negligently failed to make its premises safe for employees. Martin Marietta moved for summary judgment, claiming that Tolbert could not sue in negligence because workers' compensation was her sole remedy.

■

**Carrigan, District Judge**   The sole issue is whether the Colorado Workmen's Compensation Act covers Tolbert's injury. If it does, workers' compensation is her exclusive remedy and this tort action is barred. Tolbert asserts that her injury is not covered by workers' compensation, presumably because she expects that a tort action would yield a larger recovery. Martin Marietta, on the other hand, apparently is willing to pay the workers' compensation award to avoid risking a large tort verdict.

Workers' compensation applies where the injury or death is proximately caused by an injury or occupational disease arising out of and in the course of the employee's employment and is not intentionally self-inflicted. Although her injury did arise in the course of her employment, Tolbert contends that it did not "arise out of" the employment. The "arising out of" condition [requires] that there be some causal relationship between the employment and the injury. Courts have interpreted the "arising out of" language in different ways. Unfortunately, Colorado courts have not consistently applied any single test. Martin Marietta argues that positional-risk analysis applies to categorize the case as one [making workers' compensation applicable]. The positional-risk doctrine has been defined thus:

An injury arises out of the employment if it would not have occurred but for the fact that the conditions and obligations of the employment placed claimant in the position where he was injured. . . . This theory supports compensation in cases of stray bullets, roving lunatics and other situations in which the only connection of the employment with the injury is that its obligations placed the employee in the particular place at the particular time when he was injured by some neutral force, meaning by "neutral" neither personal to the claimant nor distinctly associated with the employment.

Invoking this rule, Martin Marietta asserts that Tolbert's injury is covered by workers' compensation because: (1) her employment placed her within the building where she was injured, and (2) the assault was a neutral force.

[However, a 1923 Colorado case] . . . applied the "increased-risk" test of causality. Under the increased-risk test, compensation is awarded only if the employment increases the worker's risk of injury above that to which the general public is exposed. If Colorado presently applies the increased-risk analysis, Tolbert would not be covered by workers' compensation. Certainly her employment as a secretary within a secured defense facility would not be expected to increase her risk of sexual assault above that to which women in the general public are exposed.

Colorado first applied positional risk analysis four years after [the 1923 case] was decided. [In this later positional-risk case,] the court upheld an award to a farmhand who was struck by lightning. It can readily be seen that the positional-risk test provides substantially broader coverage than does the increased-risk test. Unfortunately, the Colorado courts on several more recent occasions have departed from the positional-risk test to impose a higher standard of causal relationship to the employment.

The rape was a nonemployment-motivated act directed at the plaintiff because she was a woman. There is nothing to indicate that any other woman—whether or not a Martin employee—who happened to be in the same area at the time of the attack would not have become the victim. Tolbert was not raped because of the nature of her duties or the nature of her workplace environment, or because of any incident or quarrel growing out of the work.

Both applicable Colorado precedent and sound rationale support holding that the workers' compensation statute has not abolished Tolbert's tort claim. Adopting this position has the additional advantage of providing employers an incentive to make reasonable efforts to screen prospective employees so as to avoid hiring rapists or those having the identifiable characteristics of potential rapists. Tort law does not impose strict liability; Tolbert still has the burden of showing negligence, causation, and damages.

**Martin Marietta's motion for summary judgment denied; case proceeds to trial on Tolbert's negligence theories.**

## The Occupational Safety and Health Act

Although it may stimulate employers to remedy hazardous working conditions, workers' compensation does not directly forbid such conditions. The most important measure directly regulating workplace safety is the federal Occupational Safety and Health Act of 1970. The Occupational Safety and Health Act applies to all employers engaged in a business affecting interstate commerce. Exempted, however, are the U.S. government, the states and their political subdivisions, and certain industries regulated by other federal safety legislation. The Occupational Safety and Health Act is mainly administered by the Occupational Safety and Health Administration (OSHA) of the Labor Department. It does not preempt state workplace safety regulation, and the states can regulate matters subject to federal standards, albeit under federal supervision and control.

The Occupational Safety and Health Act requires employers to provide their employees with employment and a place of employment free from recognized hazards that are likely to cause death or serious physical harm. It also requires employers to comply with the many detailed regulations promulgated by OSHA. OSHA can inspect places of employment for violations of the act and its regulations. However, employers can require the agency to obtain a search warrant first. If an employer is found to violate the act's general duty provision or any specific standard, OSHA issues a written citation. It must do so with reasonable promptness, and in no event more than six months after the violation. The citation becomes final after 15 workdays following its service on the employer, unless it is contested. Contested citations are reviewed by the Occupational Safety and Health Review Commission, a three-member body composed of presidential appointees. Further review by the federal courts of appeals is possible.

The main sanctions for violations of the act and the regulations are the various civil penalties imposed by OSHA. In addition, any employer who commits a willful violation resulting in death to an employee may suffer a fine, imprisonment, or both. Also, the secretary of labor may seek injunctive relief when an employment hazard presents an imminent danger of death or physical harm that cannot be promptly eliminated by normal citation procedures. In addition, the act imposes various record-keeping and reporting requirements on employers. Finally, the act protects workers who notify the agency of possible violations from employer retaliation.

## Social Security

Today, the law requires that employers help ensure their employees' financial security after the employment ends. One example is the federal social security system, which began in 1935. Social security is mainly financed by the Federal Insurance Contributions Act (FICA). FICA imposes a flat percentage tax on all employee income below a certain base figure and requires employers to pay a matching amount. Self-employed people pay a different rate on a different wage base. FICA revenues finance various forms of financial assistance in addition to the old-age benefits that people usually call social security. These include survivors' benefits to family members of deceased workers, disability benefits, and medical and hospitalization benefits for the elderly (the medicare system).

## Unemployment Compensation

Another way that the law protects employees after their employment ends is by providing unemployment compensation for discharged workers. Since

1935, federal law has authorized joint federal-state efforts in this area. Today, each state administers its own unemployment compensation system under federal guidelines. The system's costs are met by subjecting covered employers to federal and state unemployment compensation taxes. The tax imposed by the Federal Unemployment Tax Act (FUTA) does not apply to all of an employee's compensation. Unlike FICA, only employers pay the tax.

Unemployment insurance plans vary from state to state but usually share certain features. States often condition the receipt of benefits on the recipient's having worked for a covered employer for a specified time period, and/or having earned a certain minimum income over such a period. Generally, those who voluntarily quit work without good cause, are fired for bad conduct, fail to actively seek suitable new work, or refuse such work are ineligible for benefits. Benefit levels vary from state to state, as do the time periods during which benefits can be received.

## ERISA

Many employers voluntarily contribute to their employees' postemployment income by maintaining pension plans. For years, pension plan abuses such as arbitrary termination of participation in the plan, arbitrary benefit reduction, and mismanagement of fund assets were not uncommon. The Employee Retirement Income Security Act of 1974 (ERISA) was a response to these problems. ERISA does not require employers to establish or fund pension plans and does not set benefit levels. Instead, it tries to check abuses and to protect employees' expectations that promised pension benefits will be paid.

ERISA imposes *fiduciary duties* on pension fund managers. For example, it requires that managers diversify the plan's investments to minimize the risk of large losses, unless this is clearly imprudent. ERISA also imposes *record-keeping, reporting,* and *disclosure* requirements. For instance, it requires that covered plans provide annual reports to their participants and specifies the contents of those reports. In addition, the act has a provision restricting an employer's ability to *delay an employee's participation* in the plan. For example, certain employees who complete one year of service with an employer cannot be denied plan participation. Furthermore, ERISA contains *funding* and *plan termination insurance* requirements for protecting plan participants against loss of pension income. Finally, ERISA contains complex *vesting* requirements that determine when an employee's right to receive pension benefits becomes nonforfeitable. These requirements help prevent employers from using a late vesting date to avoid pension obligations to employees who change jobs or are fired before that date. ERISA's remedies include civil suits by plan participants and beneficiaries, equitable relief, and criminal penalties.

## Labor Law

Early in the 19th century, some courts treated labor unions as illegal criminal conspiracies. After this restriction disappeared around mid-century, organized labor began its rise to power. One common explanation for the emergence of unions is that workers had to combine to counter the increasing size and power of their corporate employers. Another is the unfortunate working conditions many 19th-century workers confronted. During the late 19th and early 20th centuries, labor's growing political power and the increasing number of wage earners in the electorate led to the passage of many laws protecting workers. These included statutes outlawing "yellow dog" contracts (under which employees agreed not to join or remain a union member), minimum wage and maximum hours legislation, laws regulating the employment of women and children, factory safety measures, and workers' compensation. Courts, however, tended to represent business interests during this period. Thus, some pro-labor measures were struck down on constitutional grounds. Also, some courts were quick to issue temporary and permanent injunctions to restrain union picketing and boycotts and help quell strikes.

**The National Labor Relations Act**    Despite the holding actions just mentioned, organized labor's power continued to grow during the first part of the 20th century. In 1926, Congress passed the Railway Labor Act, which regulates labor relations in the railroad industry and which later came to include airlines. This was followed by the Norris-LaGuardia Act of 1932, which limited the circumstances in which federal courts could enjoin strikes and picketing in labor disputes, and also prohibited federal court enforcement of yellow-dog contracts.

The most important 20th-century American labor statute, however, was the National Labor Relations Act of 1935 (the NLRA or Wagner Act). The act gave employees the *right to organize* by enabling them to form, join, and assist labor organizations. It also allowed them to *bargain collectively* through their own representatives and to engage in other activities that would promote collective bargaining. In addition, the Wagner Act prohibited certain *unfair labor practices* that were believed to discourage collective bargaining. These forbidden employer practices include: (1) interfering with employees' exercise of their rights to form, join, and assist labor unions; (2) dominating or interfering with the formation or administration of a labor union, or giving a union financial or other support; (3) discriminating against employees in hiring, tenure, or any term of employment due to their union membership; (4) discriminating against employees because they have filed charges or given testimony under the NLRA; and (5) refusing to bargain collectively with any duly designated employee representative.

The NLRA also established the National Labor Relations Board (NLRB). The NLRB's main functions are: (1) handling representation cases (which involve the process by which a union becomes the certified employee representative within a bargaining unit), and (2) deciding whether challenged employer or union activity is an unfair labor practice.

**The Labor Management Relations Act**   In 1947, Congress amended the NLRA by passing the Labor Management Relations Act (LMRA or Taft-Hartley Act). In part, the Taft-Hartley Act reflected the post–World War II period's revival of business power and its more conservative political climate. It also reflected public concern over frequent strikes, the alleged excessive power of union bosses, and various perceived unfair practices by unions.

Thus, the Taft-Hartley Act declared that certain acts by *unions* are unfair labor practices. These include: (1) restraining or coercing employees in the exercise of their guaranteed bargaining rights (e.g., their right to refrain from joining a union); (2) causing an employer to discriminate against an employee who is not a union member; (3) refusing to bargain collectively with an employer; (4) conducting a secondary strike or a secondary boycott for a specified illegal purpose;[4] (5) requiring employees covered by union-shop contracts to pay

excessive or discriminatory initiation fees or dues; and (6) featherbedding (forcing an employer to pay for work not actually performed).

The LMRA also established an 80-day cooling off period for strikes that the president finds likely to endanger national safety or health. In addition, it created a Federal Mediation and Conciliation Service to assist employers and unions in settling labor disputes.

**The Labor Management Reporting and Disclosure Act**   Congressional investigations during the 1950s uncovered corruption in internal union affairs and also revealed that the internal procedures of many unions were undemocratic. In response to these findings, Congress enacted the Labor Management Reporting and Disclosure Act (or Landrum-Griffin Act) in 1959. The act established a "bill of rights" for union members and attempted to make internal union affairs more democratic. It also amended the NLRA by adding to the LMRA's list of unfair union labor practices.

## The Fair Labor Standards Act

Although federal labor law regulates several aspects of labor-management relations, it still permits many terms of employment to be determined by private bargaining. Nonetheless, sometimes the law directly regulates such key terms of employment as wages and hours worked. The most important example is the Fair Labor Standards Act (FLSA) of 1938.

The FLSA regulates *wages and hours* by entitling covered employees to: (1) a specified minimum wage whose amount changes over time, and (2) a time-and-a-half rate for work exceeding 40 hours per week. These provisions basically apply to employees who are engaged in interstate commerce or the production of goods for such commerce, or who are employed by an enterprise that does the same and that has annual gross sales of sufficient size. State and local employees are also covered. The many exemptions from the FLSA's wages-and-hours provisions include executive, administrative, professional, and outside sales personnel.

The FLSA also forbids "oppressive" *child labor* by any employer engaged in interstate commerce or in the production of goods for such commerce, and also forbids the interstate shipment of goods produced in an establishment where oppressive child labor occurs. Oppressive child labor includes:

---

[4]These are strikes or boycotts aimed at a third party with which the union has no real dispute. Their purpose is to coerce that party not to deal with an employer with which the union *does* have a dispute, and thus to gain some leverage over the employer.

(1) most employment of children below the age of 14; (2) employment of children aged 14 to 15, unless they work in an occupation specifically approved by the Department of Labor; and (3) employment of children aged 16 to 17 who work in occupations declared particularly hazardous by the Labor Department. These provisions do not apply to most agricultural employment.

Both affected employees and the Labor Department can recover any unpaid minimum wages or overtime, plus an additional equal amount as liquidated damages, from an employer that has violated the FLSA's wages-and-hours provisions. A suit by the Labor Department terminates an employee's right to sue, but the department pays the amounts it recovers to the employee. Violations of the act's child labor provisions may result in civil penalties. Other FLSA remedies include injunctive relief and criminal liability for willful violations.

## The Family and Medical Leave Act

After concluding that proper child-raising, family stability, and job security require that employees get reasonable work leave for family and medical reasons, Congress passed the Family and Medical Leave Act (FMLA) in 1993. In general, the act covers those employed for at least 12 months, and for 1,250 hours during those 12 months, by an employer employing 50 or more employees. In addition to private employers, the act includes federal, state, and local government agencies.

Under the FMLA, covered employees are entitled to a total of 12 workweeks of leave during any 12-month period for one or more of the following reasons: (1) the birth of a child and the need to care for that child; (2) placement of a child with the employee for adoption or foster care; (3) the need to care for a spouse, child, or parent with a serious health condition; and (4) the employee's own serious health condition. Usually, the leave may be without pay. Upon the employee's return from leave, the employer ordinarily must restore her to the position she held when the leave began or to an equivalent position, and not deny her any benefits accrued before the leave began.

Employers who deny any of an employee's FMLA rights are civilly liable to the affected employee for resulting lost wages or, if no wages were lost, for any other resulting monetary losses not exceeding 12 weeks' wages. Employees may also

recover an additional equal amount as liquidated damages unless the employer acted in good faith and had reasonable grounds for believing that it was not violating the act. Like the FLSA, the FMLA permits civil actions by the secretary of labor, with any sums recovered distributed to affected employees. Employees may also obtain equitable relief, including reinstatement and promotion.

## The Equal Pay Act

The Equal Pay Act (EPA), which forbids *sex* discrimination regarding *pay,* was a 1963 amendment to the FLSA. Its coverage resembles the coverage of the FLSA's minimum wage provisions. Unlike the FLSA, however, the EPA covers executive, administrative, and professional employees.

The Equal Pay Act forbids gender-based pay discrimination against men. But the typical EPA case involves a woman who claims that she has received lower pay than a male employee performing substantially equal work for the same employer. The requirement of substantially equal work is met if the plaintiff's job and the higher-paid male employee's job involve *each* of the following: (1) equal effort, (2) equal skill, (3) equal responsibility, and (4) similar working conditions.

*Effort* basically means physical or mental exertion. *Skill* refers to the experience, training, education, and ability required for the positions being compared. Here, the issue is not whether the employees being compared have equal skills, but whether *their jobs require or utilize* substantially the same skills. *Responsibility* (or accountability) involves such factors as the degree of supervision each job requires and the importance of each job to the employer. For instance, a retail sales position in which an employee may not approve customer checks is probably not equal to a sales position in which an employee has this authority. *Working conditions* refer to such factors as temperature, weather, fumes, ventilation, toxic conditions, and risk of injury. These need only be *similar,* not equal. As the *Grove* case (which follows shortly) suggests, many courts do not discuss the four equal-work criteria individually.

If the two jobs are substantially equal but they are paid unequally, an employer must prove one of the EPA's four defenses or it will lose the case. To do so, the employer must show that the pay disparity is based on: (1) seniority, (2) merit, (3) quality or quantity of production (e.g., a piecework system), or (4) any factor other than sex. As *Grove* emphasizes in the case of merit, the first three defenses usually require an employer to show some organized, systematic, structured, and communicated rating system with predetermined criteria that apply equally to employees of each sex. The any-factor-other-than-sex defense is a catchall category that may include shift differentials, bonuses paid because the job is part of a training program, and differences in the profitability of the products or services on which employees work.

The EPA's remedial scheme resembles the FLSA's scheme. Under the EPA, however, employee suits are for the amount of *back pay* lost because of an employer's discrimination, not for unpaid minimum wages or overtime. An employee may also recover an equal sum as liquidated damages. The EPA is enforced by the Equal Employment Opportunity Commission (EEOC) rather than the Labor Department.[5] Unlike some of the employment discrimination statutes described later, however, the EPA does not require that private plaintiffs submit their complaints to the EEOC or a state agency before mounting suit.

---

[5]The EEOC is an independent federal agency with a sizable staff and many regional offices. Its functions include: (1) enforcing most of the employment discrimination laws discussed in this chapter through lawsuits that it initiates or in which it intervenes, (2) conciliating employment discrimination charges (e.g., by encouraging their negotiated settlement), (3) investigating discrimination-related matters, and (4) interpreting the statutes it enforces through regulations and guidelines.

---

## GROVE V. FROSTBURG STATE BANK
### 549 F. Supp. 922 (D. Md. 1982)

Sheila Grove and David Klink were hired as loan tellers by the Frostburg National Bank in 1967. Both were high school graduates at the time, and neither had prior work experience. Each was paid the same yearly starting salary in 1967. Klink was drafted into the army late in 1967, and he returned to the bank in 1969. From that time until 1976, he basically performed a loan teller's duties, although he also took on various miscellaneous tasks. Grove also basically performed loan teller duties during the period 1969 to 76. Throughout that period, Klink's yearly salary exceeded Grove's. Salary and raise determinations were made by David P. Willetts, the bank's vice president, who based these determinations primarily on his own observations of employees. Grove sued the bank in federal district court under the Equal Pay Act.

---

**Jones, District Judge** The burden is on the plaintiff to make a prima facie showing that the employer pays different wages to males and females for equal work requiring equal skill, effort, and responsibility under similar working conditions. Once that showing is made, the employer has the burden of showing that the pay differential is justified under one of the four statutory exceptions. Only substantial equality of work need be proved; the jobs need not be identical. A wage differential is justified by extra tasks only if they create significant variations in skill, effort, and responsibility. If the purported extra tasks are not done; if females also have extra tasks of equal skill, effort, and responsibility; if females are not given the opportunity to do the extra tasks; or if the extra tasks only involve minimal time and are of peripheral importance, they do not justify a wage differential.

Sheila Grove performed work substantially equal to that of David Klink from 1969 through September, 1976. As loan tellers, [each] had basically the same duties. Klink had some extra tasks from time to time. He set up the drive-in branch in 1970. He reviewed the safe deposit box rent records and noted some delinquencies and increases in 1971. After 1971, he arranged for drilling the boxes. Some time in the 1970s, he began shredding paper.

Setting up the drive-in branch was a one-time task, involving taking supplies and equipment to the drive-in installation. To the extent that it involved any different skills or effort than the normal work of the loan tellers, they were largely physical. Moreover, no female loan teller had an opportunity to perform this task, because it was done at the request of Willetts. Although Klink's initiative in bringing the box rents up to date is commendable, the work did not consume a significant amount of time, as compared with his other duties. It was a one-time project. To the extent that he performed extra tasks thereafter in arranging for the drilling, no significant amount of time was involved. Shredding paper is a task involving less skill, effort, and responsibility than the regular work of loan tellers. It did not involve a significant amount of time, only occasional afternoons or Saturdays.

Grove has sustained her burden of demonstrating that her work as loan teller was substantially equal to that of Klink. The bank tried to justify Klink's higher salary on two grounds. It stated that Klink was paid a higher salary when he returned to the bank in 1969, which was perpetuated through yearly increases, as a reward for his patriotism in serving in the Army. The bank also claimed that Klink received higher pay because he was more responsible, conscientious, and harder-working: that is, on merit.

The bank has failed to show that Klink's 1969 salary was based on a factor other than sex. Even assuming that military service could be a proper reason for a wage differential, Klink was drafted into the service. No female worker could have been.

The bank has also failed to show that the wage differential was based on a legitimate merit system. A merit system need not be in writing to be recognized; it must, however, be an organized and structured procedure with systematic evaluations under predetermined criteria. If it is not in writing, employees must be aware of it. The system used by Willetts does not meet this test. It was not organized or structured; Willetts did not recall, for example, whether he had consulted with department supervisors at the end of each year concerning individual employees. A systematic evaluation, using predetermined criteria, was not made. Although Willetts cited a number of factors that influenced his pay decisions, these were not applied uniformly, and he eventually admitted that the primary criterion was his "gut feeling" about the employee. Finally, employees were not aware of the existence of any merit system.

**Judgment for Grove.**

# Title VII

Unlike the other laws discussed in the previous section, the EPA is an *employment discrimination* provision. Employment discrimination might be defined as employer behavior that penalizes certain individuals because of personal traits that they cannot control and/or that bear no relation to effective job performance. Such discrimination was common before the law began to attack it during the 1960s and 1970s. Today, however, employers confront a maze of legal rules forbidding various kinds of employment discrimination.

Of the many employment discrimination laws in force today, the most important is Title VII of the 1964 Civil Rights Act. Unlike the Equal Pay Act, which merely forbids sex discrimination regarding pay, Title VII is a wide-ranging employment discrimination provision. It prohibits discrimination based on *race, color, religion, sex,* and *national origin* in hiring, firing, job assignments, pay, access to training and apprenticeship programs, and most other employment decisions.

## Basic Features of Title VII

In discussing Title VII,[6] we first examine some general rules that govern all the kinds of discrimination it forbids. Then we examine each forbidden basis of discrimination in detail.

**Covered Entities**    Title VII covers all employers employing 15 or more employees and engaging in an industry affecting interstate commerce. Employers include individuals, partnerships, corporations, colleges and universities, labor unions and employment agencies (with respect to their own employees),

---

[6]This discussion reflects the state of the law at the conclusion of 1993.

and state and local governments.[7] Also, *referrals* by employment agencies are covered, no matter what the size of the agency, if an employer serviced by the agency has 15 or more employees. In addition, Title VII covers certain unions—mainly those with 15 or more members—in their capacity as *employee representatives.*

**Procedures**    Although the EEOC sometimes sues to enforce Title VII, the usual Title VII suit is a private claim. The complicated procedures governing private Title VII suits are beyond the scope of this text, but a few points should be kept in mind. Private parties with a Title VII claim have no automatic right to sue. Instead, they first must file a *charge* with the EEOC, or with a state agency in states having suitable fair employment laws and enforcement schemes. This allows the EEOC or the state agency to investigate the claim, attempt conciliation if the claim has substance, or sue the employer itself. If a plaintiff files with a state agency and the state fails to act, the plaintiff can still file a charge with the EEOC. Even if the EEOC fails to act on the claim, a plaintiff may still mount her own suit. Here, the EEOC issues a "right-to-sue letter" enabling the plaintiff to sue.

**Proving Discrimination**    The permissible methods for *proving* a Title VII violation are critical to its effectiveness against employment discrimination. For this reason, they have been a major political battleground in recent years. Proof of discrimination is easy in cases such as the *Johnson Controls* decision later in the chapter, where the employer had an **express policy** disfavoring one of Title VII's protected classes. **Direct evidence** of a discriminatory motive such as testimony or written evidence is obviously useful to plaintiffs as well. However, employers can discriminate without leaving such obvious tracks. Thus, the courts have devised other methods of proving a Title VII violation. As of late 1993, two such methods predominated. Both are difficult, controversial, and critical in determining Title VII's practical impact. Because each method's many details are beyond the scope of this text, and because each may have changed by the time you read this section, we merely outline them here.

Title VII **disparate treatment** suits usually involve an individual plaintiff who alleges some specific instance or instances of discrimination. In such suits, the plaintiff first must show a *prima facie case*—a case strong enough to create a presumption of discrimination and to require a counterargument from the defendant. The proof needed for a prima facie case varies with the nature of the challenged employment decision (e.g., hiring or promotion), but ordinarily it gives plaintiffs few difficulties. Once the plaintiff establishes a prima facie case, the employer must *produce evidence* that the challenged employment decision was taken for *legitimate, nondiscriminatory reasons* or it will lose the lawsuit. In a hiring case, for example, an employer might produce evidence that it rejected the plaintiff because she did not meet its criteria for the position in question. If the employer produces satisfactory reasons, the plaintiff then must *show that discrimination actually occurred.* She might do so by showing that the employer's alleged nondiscriminatory reasons were a *pretext* for a decision that really involved discrimination. For example, she might show that the employer's alleged hiring criteria were not applied to similarly situated male job applicants.

Title VII's **disparate impact** (or adverse impact) proof method is most often used when the alleged discrimination affects many employees. Here, the plaintiffs ordinarily maintain that the employer uses a *particular employment practice* that causes a *disparate impact* on the basis of race, color, religion, sex, or national origin. Often, the practice is an employer rule that is neutral on its face but has a disproportionate adverse effect on one of Title VII's protected groups—for example, a height, weight, or high school diploma requirement for hiring, or a written test for hiring or promotion. If the plaintiffs show a disparate impact, the employer loses unless it demonstrates that the challenged practice is *job-related for the position in question and consistent with business necessity.* For example, the employer might show that its promotion test really predicts effective job performance, and that effective performance in the relevant job is necessary for its operations. Even if the employer makes this demonstration, the plaintiffs have another option—to show that the employer's legitimate business needs can be advanced by an *alternative employment practice* that is *less discriminatory than the challenged practice.* For example, the plaintiffs might show that the

---

[7]Employment discrimination within the federal government is beyond the scope of this text.

employer's legitimate needs can be met by a different promotion test that has less adverse impact on the protected group. If the employer refuses to adopt this practice, the plaintiffs prevail.

**Defenses** Even if a plaintiff proves a Title VII violation, the employer still prevails if it can establish one of Title VII's defenses. The most important such defenses are:

**1.** *Seniority.* Title VII is not violated if the employer treats employees differently pursuant to a *bona fide seniority system.* To be bona fide, such a system at least must treat all employees equally on its face, not have been created for discriminatory reasons, and not operate in a discriminatory fashion.

**2.** *The various "merit" defenses.* An employer also escapes Title VII liability if it acts pursuant to: a *bona fide merit system,* a system basing earnings on *quantity or quality of production,* or the results of a *professionally developed ability test.* Presumably, such systems and tests at least must meet the general standards for seniority systems stated above. Also, the EEOC has promulgated lengthy *Uniform Guidelines on Employee Selection Procedures* that speak to these and other matters.

**3.** *The BFOQ defense.* Finally, Title VII allows employers to discriminate on the bases of sex, religion, or national origin where one of those traits is a *bona fide occupational qualification (BFOQ) that is reasonably necessary to the business in question.* This BFOQ defense does not protect race or color discrimination. As the following *Johnson Controls* case makes clear, moreover, the defense is a narrow one even where it applies. Generally, it is available only where a certain gender, religion, or national origin is necessary for effective job performance. For example, a BFOQ probably would exist where a female is employed to model women's clothing or to fit women's undergarments, or a French restaurant hires a French chef. But the BFOQ defense is usually unavailable where the discrimination is based on stereotypes (e.g., that women are less aggressive than men) or on the preferences of co-workers or customers (e.g., the preference of airline travelers for female rather than male flight attendants). As *Johnson Controls* suggests, the defense is also unavailable where the employer's discriminatory practice promotes goals such as fetal protection that do not concern effective job performance.

---

## AUTO WORKERS V. JOHNSON CONTROLS, INC.
### 499 U.S. 187 (U.S. Sup. Ct. 1991)

Johnson Controls, Inc. manufactures batteries. Lead is a primary ingredient in that manufacturing process. A female employee's occupational exposure to lead involves a risk of harm to any fetus she carries. For this reason, Johnson Controls excluded women who are pregnant or who are capable of bearing children from jobs that involve exposure to lead. Numerous plaintiffs, including a woman who had chosen to be sterilized to avoid losing her job, entered a federal district court class action alleging that Johnson Controls' policy constituted illegal sex discrimination under Title VII. The district court entered a summary judgment for Johnson Controls and the court of appeals affirmed. The plaintiffs appealed to the U.S. Supreme Court.

---

**Blackmun, Justice** Johnson Controls' fetal-protection policy explicitly discriminates against women on the basis of their sex. The policy excludes women with childbearing capacity from lead-exposed jobs and so creates a facial classification based on gender. [But] an employer may discriminate on the basis of "religion, sex, or national origin in those certain instances where religion, sex, or national ori-

gin is a bona fide occupational qualification reasonably necessary to the normal operation of that particular business or enterprise." The BFOQ defense is written narrowly, and this Court has read it narrowly.

Johnson Controls argues that its fetal-protection policy falls within the so-called safety exception [of] the BFOQ. Discrimination on the basis of sex because of safety concerns is allowed only in narrow circumstances. In *Dothard v. Rawlinson* (1977), we allowed the employer to hire only male guards in contact areas of maximum-security male penitentiaries only because more was at stake than the individual woman's decision to weigh and accept the risks of employment. We found sex to be a BFOQ inasmuch as the employment of a female guard would create real risks of safety to others if [rape-related] violence broke out because the guard was a woman. Sex discrimination was tolerated because sex was related to the guard's ability to do the job—maintaining prison security. Similarly, some courts have approved airlines' layoffs of pregnant flight attendants on the ground that the employer's policy was necessary to ensure the safety of passengers. In two of these cases, the courts pointedly indicated that fetal, as opposed to passenger, safety was best left to the mother.

Therefore, the safety exception is limited to instances in which sex or pregnancy actually interferes with the employee's ability to perform the job. ... [Thus,] Johnson Controls cannot establish a BFOQ. Fertile women, as far as appears in the record, manufacture batteries as efficiently as anyone else. Johnson Controls' professed moral and ethical concerns about the next generation do not suffice to establish a BFOQ of female sterility. Decisions about the welfare of future children must be left to the parents who conceive, bear, support, and raise them rather than to the employers who hire those parents.

**Judgment in favor of Johnson Controls reversed; case returned to the lower courts for further proceedings consistent with the Supreme Court's opinion.**

---

**Remedies**    Various remedies are possible once private plaintiffs or the EEOC win a Title VII suit. If intentional discrimination has caused lost wages, employees can obtain **back pay** accruing from a date two years before the filing of the charge. At the court's discretion, successful private plaintiffs may also recover reasonable **attorney's fees.** Victims of intentional discrimination can also recover **compensatory damages** for harms such as emotional distress, sickness, loss of reputation, or denial of credit. Victims of intentional discrimination can also recover **punitive damages** where the defendant discriminated with malice or with reckless indifference to the plaintiff's rights. However, the sum of the plaintiff's compensatory and punitive damages cannot exceed certain amounts that vary with the size of the employer. For example, they cannot total more than $300,000 for an employer with more than 500 employees.

Intentional discrimination may also entitle successful plaintiffs to **equitable relief.** Examples include orders compelling hiring, reinstatement, or retroactive seniority. On occasion, moreover, the courts have ordered quotalike racial preferences in Title VII cases.[8] After determining that an employer has engaged in a longstanding pattern of hiring discrimi-

nation against racial minorities, for example, a court might order that whites and minorities be hired on a 50–50 basis until minority representation in the employer's work force reaches some specified percentage. Generally speaking, such orders are permissible if: (1) an employer has engaged in severe, widespread, or longstanding discrimination; (2) the order does not unduly restrict the employment interests of white people; and (3) it does not force an employer to hire unqualified workers. Minority preferences may also appear in the **consent decrees** courts issue when approving the terms on which the parties have settled a Title VII case.

## Race or Color Discrimination

At this point, we consider each of Title VII's prohibited bases of discrimination in more detail. *Race or color* discrimination includes discrimination against blacks, other racial minorities, Eskimos, and Native Americans, among others. Title VII also prohibits racial discrimination against whites. Nonetheless, voluntary racial preferences that favor minorities survive a Title VII attack if they: (1) are intended to correct a "manifest imbalance" reflecting underrepresentation of minorities in "traditionally segregated job categories," (2) do not "unnecessarily trammel" the rights of white employees or

---

[8]Occasionally, such preferential relief has been awarded in sex discrimination cases as well.

create an absolute bar to their advancement, and (3) are only temporary.[9] Note that here our concern is not the use of minority preferences as a *remedy* for a Title VII violation, but whether such preferences *themselves violate* Title VII when voluntarily established by an employer.

## National Origin Discrimination

*National origin* discrimination includes discrimination based on: (1) the country of one's or one's ancestors' origin; or (2) one's possession of physical, cultural, or linguistic characteristics identified with people of a particular nation. Thus, plaintiffs in national origin discrimination cases need not have been born in the country at issue. In fact, if the discrimination is based on physical, cultural, or linguistic traits identified with a particular nation, even the plaintiff's ancestors need not have been born there. Thus, a person of pure French ancestry may have a Title VII case if she suffers discrimination because she looks like, acts like, or talks like a German.

Certain formally neutral employment practices can also constitute national origin discrimination. Employers who hire only U.S. citizens may violate Title VII if their policy has the purpose or effect of discriminating against one or more national origin groups. This could happen where the employer is located in an area where aliens of a particular nationality are heavily concentrated. Also, employment criteria such as height, weight, and fluency in English may violate Title VII if they have a disparate impact on a national origin group and are not job-related.

## Religious Discrimination

For Title VII purposes, the term *religion* is broadly defined. Although all courts may not agree, the EEOC says that it includes any set of moral beliefs that are sincerely held with the same strength as traditional religious views. In fact, Title VII forbids religious discrimination against atheists. It also forbids discrimination based on religious *observances or practices*—for example, grooming, clothing, or

the refusal to work on the Sabbath. But such discrimination is permissible if an employer cannot reasonably accommodate the religious practice without undue hardship. Undue hardship exists when the accommodation imposes more than a minimal cost on an employer.

## Sex Discrimination

Title VII's ban on sex discrimination aims at *gender-based* discrimination and does not forbid discrimination on the basis of homosexuality or transsexuality. Just as clearly, it applies to gender discrimination against *both men and women.* Still, voluntary employer programs favoring women in hiring or promotion survive a Title VII attack if they meet the previous tests for voluntary racial preferences (reformulated in terms of gender). Title VII also forbids discrimination on the bases of *pregnancy and childbirth*, and requires employers to treat these conditions like any other condition similarly affecting working ability in their sick leave programs, medical benefit and disability plans, and so forth. Finally, *sexual stereotyping* violates Title VII. This is employer behavior that either: (1) denies a woman employment opportunities by assuming that she must have traditionally "female" traits (e.g., unaggressiveness), or (2) penalizes her for lacking such traits (e.g., for acting aggressively).

**Sexual Harassment**    Unwelcome sexual advances, requests for sexual favors, and other verbal or physical conduct of a sexual nature can violate Title VII under two different theories.[10] The first, called **quid pro quo** sexual harassment, involves some express or implied linkage between an employee's submission to sexually oriented behavior and tangible job consequences. Quid pro quo cases usually arise when, due to an employee's refusal to submit, she suffers a *tangible job detriment* of an economic nature; indeed, courts generally require such a detriment for recovery. For example, suppose that a supervisor fires a secretary because she

---

[9]*United Steelworkers v. Weber*, 443 U.S. 193 (1979).

---

[10]The principles stated in this discussion also apply to race, color, religious, and national origin harassment. In addition, men can sue for sexual harassment by women. A few courts have allowed recoveries for homosexually oriented sexual harassment. A few also have allowed recoveries by employees who are passed over for some job benefit in favor of a co-employee who submits to sexual behavior.

refuses to have sexual relations with him or refuses to submit to other sex-related behavior. Such conduct would violate Title VII whether or not the supervisor expressly told the secretary that she would be fired for refusing to submit. Title VII is also violated if a supervisor denies a subordinate a deserved promotion or other job benefit for refusing to submit.

However, no quid pro quo and no tangible job detriment are required when an employee is subjected to **work environment** sexual harassment. As stated in the *Harris* case below, this is unwelcome sex-related behavior that is sufficiently severe or pervasive to change the conditions of the victim's employment and create an abusive working environment. Work environment sexual harassment can be inflicted by both supervisors and co-workers; *Harris* is an example of the former. Because such behavior must be *unwelcome,* however, an em-

ployee may have trouble recovering if she instigated or contributed to the sex-related behavior. Also, the offending behavior must be sufficiently *severe or pervasive* to create an environment that a *reasonable person* would find hostile or abusive. Finally, the victim must *subjectively perceive* the environment as hostile or abusive.

When is an *employer* liable for sexual harassment committed by its employees? Courts try to use agency law to resolve this question.[11] They usually conclude that: (1) employers are strictly liable for quid pro quo harassment, and (2) employers are liable for work environment harassment if they knew or should have known of the harassment and failed to take appropriate corrective action.

---

[11] It is unclear *which* agency law rules courts should apply in sexual harassment cases. Chapter 28 provides some possibilities.

---

## HARRIS V. FORKLIFT SYSTEMS, INC.
### 114 S. Ct. 367 (U.S. Sup. Ct. 1993)

In April 1985, Theresa Harris started work as a manager for Forklift Systems, Inc. (Forklift). During Harris's two and one-half years with Forklift, she was subjected to gender-based insults and unwanted sexual innuendos from Charles Hardy, the firm's president. Several times, for example, Hardy told Harris: "You're a woman, what do you know?" and "We need a man as the rental manager." Once, he suggested that he and Harris negotiate her raise at the Holiday Inn. Hardy would also ask Harris and other female employees to get coins from his front pants pocket and to pick up objects that he threw on the ground. Most of these incidents occurred with other employees present.

After Harris complained to Hardy in August 1987, he apologized and promised to stop his offensive behavior. In early September, however, he inquired whether Harris had promised sex to a customer with whom she had concluded a deal on Forklift's behalf. On October 1, Harris quit. She then sued Forklift for work environment sexual harassment in federal district court. Although it considered Harris's claim "a close case," the court found for Forklift. It did so in part because it concluded that Hardy's actions were not sufficiently severe to seriously affect Harris's psychological well-being. After the court of appeals affirmed, Harris appealed to the U.S. Supreme Court.

---

**O'Connor, Justice**    Title VII makes it "an unlawful employment practice for an employer . . . to discriminate against any individual with respect to his compensation, terms, conditions, or privileges of employment, because of such individual's race, color, religion, sex, or national origin." . . . The phrase "terms, conditions, or privileges of employment" evinces a Congressional intent to strike at the entire spectrum of disparate treatment of men and women in employment, which includes requiring people to work in a discriminatorily hostile or abusive environment. When the workplace is permeated with discriminatory intimidation, ridicule, and insult that is sufficiently severe or pervasive to alter the conditions of the victim's employment and create an abusive working environment, Title VII is violated.

This standard . . . takes a middle path between making actionable any conduct that is merely offensive and requiring the conduct to cause a tangible psychological injury. . . . Conduct that is not severe or pervasive enough to create an environment that a reasonable person would find hostile or abusive is beyond Title VII's purview. Likewise, if the victim does not subjectively perceive the environment to be abusive, there is no Title VII violation.

But Title VII comes into play before the harassing conduct leads to a nervous breakdown. A discriminatorily abusive work environment, even one that does not seriously affect employees' psychological well-being, can and often will detract from employees' job performance, discourage employees from remaining on the job, or keep them from advancing in their careers. We therefore believe the district court erred in relying on whether the conduct seriously affected plaintiff's psychological well-being or led her to suffer injury. Such an inquiry may needlessly focus the fact-finder's attention on concrete psychological harm, an element Title VII does not require. Certainly Title VII bars conduct that would seriously affect a reasonable person's psychological well-being, but the statute is not limited to such conduct. So long as the environment would reasonably be perceived, and is perceived, as hostile or abusive, there is no need for it also to be psychologically injurious.

This is not, and by its nature cannot be, a mathematically precise test. . . . Whether an environment is "hostile" or "abusive" can be determined only by looking at all the circumstances. These may include the frequency of the discriminatory conduct; its severity; whether it is physically threatening or humiliating, or a mere offensive utterance; and whether it unreasonably interferes with an employee's work performance.

**Court of appeals decision in Forklift's favor reversed. Case returned to the district court for proceedings consistent with the Supreme Court's opinion.**

## OTHER IMPORTANT EMPLOYMENT DISCRIMINATION PROVISIONS

### Section 1981

Where it applies, a post–Civil War civil rights statute called section 1981 sets employment discrimination standards resembling those of Title VII. Section 1981 apparently applies to public and private employment discrimination against blacks, people of certain racially characterized national origins such as Mexicans, and ethnic groups such as gypsies and Jews. Due to a 1991 amendment, section 1981 now applies to most of the contexts in which an employer might discriminate against an employee.

Section 1981 is important because it gives covered plaintiffs certain advantages that Title VII does not provide. Although courts often use Title VII's methods of proof in section 1981 cases, Title VII's limitations on covered employers and its complex procedural requirements do not apply. Also, damages are apt to be greater under section 1981; in particular, Title VII's limits on compensatory and punitive damages are inapplicable. For these rea- sons, covered plaintiffs often include a section 1981 claim along with a Title VII claim in their complaint.

### Age Discrimination in Employment Act

The 1967 Age Discrimination in Employment Act (ADEA) prohibits age-based employment discrimination against employees who are *at least 40 years of age*. People within this age group are protected against age discrimination in favor of both younger and older individuals, including favored individuals inside the protected age group.

**Coverage**   The ADEA covers individuals, partnerships, labor organizations and employment agencies (as to their employees), and corporations that: (1) engage in an industry affecting interstate commerce, and (2) employ at least 20 persons. The act also controls state and local governments.[12] *Referrals*

---

[12]Age discrimination in the federal government is beyond the scope of this text.

by an employment agency to a covered employer are within the ADEA's scope regardless of the agency's size. In addition, the ADEA reaches labor union practices affecting *union members;* usually, unions with 25 or more members are covered. The ADEA protects against age discrimination in many employment contexts, including hiring, firing, pay, job assignment, and fringe benefits.

**Procedural Requirements**   The complex procedural requirements for an ADEA suit are beyond the scope of this text. Before she can sue in her own right, a private plaintiff must file a charge with the EEOC or with an appropriate state agency. The EEOC may also sue to enforce the ADEA; such a suit precludes private suits arising from the same alleged violation. For both government and private suits, the statute of limitations is three years from the date of an alleged *willful* violation and two years from the date of an alleged *nonwillful* violation.

**Proof**   Proving age discrimination is no problem where an employer uses an explicit age classification, and may be easy where there is direct evidence of discrimination such as testimony or incriminating documents. However, many ADEA cases, such as the following *Biggins* decision, are brought under the Title VII disparate treatment theory discussed earlier. A few courts have used Title VII's disparate impact theory in ADEA cases.

**Defenses**   The ADEA allows employers to discharge or otherwise discipline an employee for *good cause,* and to use *reasonable factors other than age* in their employment decisions. It also allows employers to observe the terms of a *bona fide seniority system,* except where such a system is used to require or permit the involuntary retirement of anyone 40 or over.

In addition, the ADEA has a bona fide occupational qualification (BFOQ) defense. In general, an employer seeking to use this defense must show that its age classification is reasonably necessary to the proper performance—usually the safe performance—of the job in question. Specifically, the employer must show *either*: (1) that it was reasonable to believe that all or most employees of a certain age cannot perform the job safely, or (2) that it is impossible or highly impractical to test employees on an individualized basis. For example, an employer that refuses to hire anyone over 60 as a helicopter pilot should have a BFOQ defense if it has a reasonable basis for concluding that 60-and-over helicopter pilots pose significant safety risks, or that it is not feasible to test older pilots individually.

**Remedies**   Remedies available after a successful ADEA suit include unpaid back wages and overtime pay resulting from the discrimination; an additional equal award of liquidated damages where the employer acted willfully; attorney's fees; and equitable relief, including hiring, reinstatement, and promotion. Most courts do not allow punitive damages and recoveries for pain, suffering, mental distress, and so forth.

---

## HAZEN PAPER CO. V. BIGGINS
### 113 S. Ct. 1701 (U.S. Sup. Ct. 1993)

Walter F. Biggins worked as a technical director for the Hazen Paper Company. In 1986, when Biggins was 62, Hazen fired him. Its justification was that Biggins had been doing business with Hazen's competitors. At the time of the firing, Biggins was within a few weeks of completing the 10-year vesting period for his employer-provided pension. There was also evidence that Hazen offered to retain Biggins as a consultant to the company, in which case he would not have been entitled to pension benefits.

After Biggins sued Hazen under the ADEA, a federal district court jury found in his favor. The court of appeals affirmed, and Hazen appealed to the U.S. Supreme Court.

**O'Connor, Justice**   The courts of appeals repeatedly have faced the question whether an employer violates the ADEA by acting on the basis of a factor, such as an employee's pension status or seniority, that is empirically correlated with age. We now clarify that there is no disparate treatment under the ADEA when the factor motivating the employer is some feature other than the employee's age.

We have long distinguished between disparate treatment and disparate impact theories of employment discrimination. The disparate treatment theory is available under the ADEA. By contrast, we have never decided whether a disparate impact theory of liability is available under the ADEA, and we need not do so here. Biggins claims only that he received disparate treatment.

In a disparate treatment case, liability depends on whether the protected trait (under the ADEA, age) actually motivated the employer's decision. It is the very essence of age discrimination for an older employee to be fired because the employer believes that productivity and competence decline with old age. The employer cannot rely on age as a proxy for an employee's remaining characteristics, such as productivity, but must instead focus on those factors directly.

When the employer's decision *is* wholly motivated by factors other than age, the problem of inaccurate and stigmatizing stereotypes disappears. This is true even if the motivating factor is correlated with age, as pension status typically is. Pension plans typically provide that an employee's accrued benefits will become nonforfeitable, or "vested," once the employee completes a certain number of years of service with the employer. On average, an older employee has had more years in the work force than a younger employee, and thus may well have accumulated more years of service with a particular employer. Yet an employee's age is analytically distinct from his years of service. An employee who is younger than 40, and therefore outside the class of older workers as defined by the ADEA, may have worked for a particular employer his entire career, while an older worker may have been newly hired. Because age and years of service are analytically distinct, an employer can take account of one while ignoring the other, and thus it is incorrect to say that a decision based on years of service is necessarily age-based.

We do not mean to suggest that an employer *lawfully* could fire an employee in order to prevent his pension benefits from vesting. Such conduct is actionable under [ERISA]. But it would not, without more, violate the ADEA.

Besides the evidence of pension interference, the court of appeals cited some additional evidentiary support for ADEA liability. Biggins was asked to sign a confidentiality agreement, even though no other employee had been required to do so, and his replacement was a younger man who was given a less onerous agreement. In the ordinary ADEA case, indirect evidence of this kind may well suffice to support liability if the plaintiff also shows that the employer's explanation for its decision—here, that Biggins had been disloyal to Hazen by doing business with its competitors—is unworthy of credence. But inferring age-motivation from the implausibility of the employer's explanation may be problematic in cases where other unsavory motives, such as pension interference, were present. We therefore remand the case for the court of appeals to reconsider whether the jury had sufficient evidence to find an ADEA violation.

**Judgment reversed. Case returned to the court of appeals to consider whether, under the standards outlined in its opinion, there was sufficient evidence to find Hazen liable for age discrimination.**

## Americans with Disabilities Act

Until recently, federal regulation of employment discrimination against handicapped people was mainly limited to certain federal contractors and recipients of federal financial assistance. By passing Title I of the Americans with Disabilities Act of 1990 (ADA), however, Congress addressed this problem comprehensively. This portion of the ADA is primarily enforced by the EEOC, and its procedures and remedies are the same as for Title VII.

**Covered Entities**     After mid-1994, Title I of the ADA covers employers who have 15 or more employees and who are engaged in an industry affecting interstate commerce. Employers include individuals, partnerships, corporations, colleges and universities, labor unions and employment agencies (regarding their own employees), and state and local governments. The act also covers certain labor unions in their capacity as employee representatives, as well as employment agencies' treatment of their clients.

**Substantive Protections**     The ADA forbids covered entities from discriminating against qualified individuals with a disability because of that disability. It covers disability-related discrimination regarding hiring, firing, promotion, pay, and innumerable other employment decisions. The act defines a *disability* as: (1) a physical or mental impairment that substantially limits one or more of an individual's major life activities, (2) a record of such an impairment, or (3) one's being regarded as having such an impairment. (The last two categories protect, among others, those who have previously been misdiagnosed or who have recovered from earlier impairments.) Not protected, however, are those who suffer discrimination for currently engaging in the illegal use of drugs. Furthermore, homosexuality, bisexuality, transvestism, transsexualism, and various other sex-related traits or conditions are not considered disabilities.

A *qualified individual with a disability* is a person who can perform the essential functions of the relevant job either: (1) without reasonable accommodation, or (2) with such accommodation. Thus, the ADA protects both individuals who can perform their job despite their handicap, and individuals who could perform their job if reasonable accommodation is provided. In the latter case, employers illegally discriminate if they do not provide such accommodation. *Reasonable accommodation* includes: making existing facilities readily accessible and usable, acquiring new equipment, restructuring jobs, modifying work schedules, and reassigning workers to vacant positions, among other options. In the following *Harmer* case, the employer provided the employee with reasonable accommodation because it did enough to allow him to perform the essential functions of his job.

In addition, employers need not make reasonable accommodation—and thus can discriminate against handicapped individuals—where such accommodation would cause them to suffer *undue hardship*. Undue hardship is an act requiring significant difficulty or expense. Among the factors used to determine its existence are the cost of the accommodation, the covered entity's overall financial resources, and the accommodation's effect on the covered entity's activities. The ADA also protects employers whose allegedly discriminatory decisions are based on *job-related criteria and business necessity,* so long as proper job performance cannot be accomplished by reasonable accommodation.

---

## HARMER V. VIRGINIA ELECTRIC & POWER CO.

**831 F. Supp. 1300 (E.D. Va. 1993)**

Robert Harmer was a buyer in the purchasing department at the headquarters of Virginia Electric & Power Company. He worked in an unenclosed cubicle. Harmer suffered from bronchial asthma, and that condition was aggravated by tobacco smoke from nearby workers. Nonetheless, he always received satisfactory performance evaluations for his work.

As early as 1989, Harmer and other workers requested that Virginia Electric eliminate the smoke-filled air in Harmer's working environment. Virginia Electric took various steps to deal with the problem, culminating in a virtual ban on smoking in all its facilities effective August 1, 1993. Nonetheless, Harmer sued Virginia Electric under the ADA for an injunction against all smoking in its facilities (on the theory that the utility could always revoke its new policy). He also sought alleged lost wages, compensatory damages, punitive damages, attorney's fees and costs. Virginia Electric moved for summary judgment.

---

**Williams, District Judge**    The ADA forbids discrimination by covered employers against a qualified individual with a disability. Virginia Power, as an employer engaged in an industry affecting commerce who has [15] or more employees, qualifies as a covered employer. Discrimination includes failure to provide reasonable accommodations for the physical and mental limitations of an otherwise qualified individual with a disability, unless the accommodation would impose an undue hardship on the operation of the employer's business. The act defines a qualified individual with a disability as a disabled individual who, with or without reasonable accommodation, can perform the essential functions of his position. [It] defines a disability as a physical or mental impairment that substantially limits one or more of an individual's major life activities, a record of such an impairment, or being regarded as having such an impairment. The court assumes for purposes of Virginia Electric's summary judgment motion that Harmer has a disability as defined by the act.

Therefore, the ADA protects Harmer from discrimination due to his disability. But Harmer still must show that he is entitled to a complete smoking ban as a reasonable accommodation to his disability, and he is unable to do so. The purpose of reasonable accommodation is to allow a disabled employee to perform the essential functions of his job. Harmer is not entitled to absolute accommodation because he can perform the essential functions of his position with the reasonable accommodations made by Virginia Electric, as [is] evidenced by his job performance appraisals, which indicate that he consistently met his job requirements. . . . Therefore, because the evidence established that Harmer could at all times adequately perform his employment duties, Harmer is not entitled to further accommodation under the ADA.

**Virginia Electric's motion for summary judgment granted.**

---

## Executive Order 11246

Executive Order 11246, issued in 1965 and later amended, forbids race, color, national origin, religion, and sex discrimination by certain federal contractors. The order is enforced by the Labor Department's Office of Federal Contract Compliance Programs (OFCCP). Under the order, each federal contracting agency must insert an "equal opportunity clause" in most of its private-sector contracts for more than $10,000. Among other things, this clause requires that the contractor not discriminate on the grounds mentioned above and that it undertake affirmative action to prevent such discrimination.

## State Antidiscrimination Laws

Most states have statutes that parallel Title VII, the EPA, the ADEA, and the ADA. These statutes sometimes provide more extensive protection than their federal counterparts. In addition, some states prohibit forms of discrimination not barred by federal law. Examples include discrimination on the bases of one's marital status, physical appearance, sexual orientation, political affiliation, AIDS infection, and off-the-job smoking.

Finally, some states and localities have adopted laws that adopt the employment discrimination theory called **comparable worth.** These laws, which typically apply only to public employees, sometimes say that state governments should not discriminate in pay between female-dominated jobs and male-dominated jobs of comparable overall worth to the employer. The worth of different jobs is often determined by giving each job a point rating under factors such as skill, responsibility, effort, and working conditions; adding the ratings; and comparing the totals. It was once believed that comparable worth claims might find favor under Title VII, but that possibility has receded over the years.

---

**CONCEPT REVIEW**

## The Employment Discrimination Laws Compared

| | Protected Traits | Covered Employer Decisions | Need to File Charge in Private Suit? |
|---|---|---|---|
| **Equal Pay Act** | Sex only | Pay only | No |
| **Title VII** | Race, color, national origin, religion, sex | Wide range | Yes |
| **Section 1981** | Race, racially characterized national origin, perhaps alienage | Wide range | No |
| **Age Discrimination in Employment Act** | Age, if victim 40 or over | Wide range | Yes |
| **Americans with Disabilities Act** | Existence of disability, if person qualified to perform job with or without reasonable accommodation | Wide range | Yes |
| **Executive Order 11246** | Race, color, religion, national origin, sex | Wide range | Not applicable; enforced by OFCCP |

---

## Employee Privacy

The term *employee privacy* describes several employment-related issues that have assumed increasing importance recently. Uniting these issues is a concern with protecting employees' personal dignity and increasing their freedom from intrusions, surveillance, and the revelation of personal matters.

### Polygraph Testing

Over the years, employers have made increasing use of polygraph and other lie detector tests—most often, to screen job applicants and to investigate employee thefts. This has led to concerns about the accuracy of such tests; the personal questions examiners sometimes ask; and the tests' impact on workers' job prospects, job security, and personal privacy. Besides provoking various state restrictions on polygraph testing, such worries led Congress to pass the Employee Polygraph Protection Act in 1988.

The Employee Polygraph Protection Act mainly regulates lie detector tests, which include polygraph tests and certain other devices for assessing a person's honesty. Under the act, employers may not: (1) require, suggest, request, or cause employees or prospective employees to take any lie detector test; (2) use, accept, refer to, or inquire about the results of any lie detector test administered to employees or prospective employees; and (3) take or threaten to take almost any unfavorable employment-related action against employees or prospective employees because of the results of any lie detector test, or because such parties failed or refused to take such a test.

However, certain employers and tests are exempt from these provisions. They include: (1) federal, state, and local government employers; (2) certain national defense and security-related tests by the federal government; (3) certain tests by security service firms; and (4) certain tests by firms manufacturing and distributing controlled substances. The act also contains a limited exemption for private employers that use polygraph tests when investigating economic losses caused by theft, embezzlement, industrial espionage, and so forth. Finally, the act restricts the disclosure of test results by examiners and by most employers.

The Polygraph Protection Act is enforced by the Labor Department, which has issued regulations in furtherance of that mission. It does not preempt state laws that prohibit lie detector tests or that set standards stricter than those imposed by federal law. Violations of the act or its regulations can result in civil penalties, suits for equitable relief by the Labor Department, and private suits for damages and equitable relief. Workers and job applicants who succeed in a private suit can obtain employment, reinstatement, promotion, and payment of lost wages and benefits.

## Drug and Alcohol Testing

Due to their impact on employees' safe and effective job performance, employers have become increasingly concerned about both on-the-job and off-the-job drug and alcohol use. Thus, employers increasingly require employees and job applicants to undergo urine tests for drugs and/or alcohol. Because those who test positive may be either disciplined or induced to undergo treatment, and because the tests themselves can raise privacy concerns, some legal checks on their use have emerged.

Drug and alcohol testing by *public* employers can be attacked under the Fourth Amendment's search-and-seizure provisions. However, such tests generally are constitutional where there is a reasonable basis for suspecting that an employee is using drugs or alcohol, or drug use in a particular job could threaten the public interest or public safety. Due to the government action requirement discussed in Chapter 3, *private-sector* employees generally have no federal constitutional protection against drug and alcohol testing. Some state constitutions, however, lack a government action requirement. In addition, several states now regulate private drug and/or alcohol testing by statute. Tort suits for invasion of privacy or infliction of emotional distress may also be possible in some cases.

Despite these protections, however, federal law *requires* private-sector drug testing in certain situations.[13] Under a 1988 Defense Department rule, for example, employers who contract with the department must agree to establish a drug-testing program under which employees who work in sensitive positions may sometimes be tested. Also, 1988 Transportation Department regulations require random testing of public and private employees occupying safety-sensitive or security-related positions in industries such as aviation, trucking, railroads, mass transit, and others.

## Employer Searches

Employers concerned about thefts, drug use, and other misbehavior by their employees sometimes conduct searches of those employees' offices, desks, lockers, files, briefcases, packages, vehicles, and even bodies to confirm their suspicions. In 1987, the Supreme Court held that public employees sometimes have a reasonable expectation of privacy in areas such as their offices, desks, or files. But it also held that searches of those areas are constitutional under the Fourth Amendment when they are reasonable under the circumstances. Determining reasonableness generally means balancing the employee's legitimate privacy expectations against the government's need for supervision and control of the workplace, with more intrusive searches demanding a higher degree of justification. Finally, the Court also said that neither probable cause nor a warrant is necessary for such searches to proceed.

As noted above, the U.S. Constitution ordinarily does not apply to private employment. Nonetheless, both private and public employees can mount common law invasion of privacy suits against employers who conduct searches. In such cases, courts usually try to weigh the intrusiveness of the search against the purposes justifying it, and consider the availability of less intrusive alternatives that still would satisfy the employer's legitimate needs.

## Employer Monitoring

Although employers have always monitored their employees' work, recent technological advances enable such monitoring to occur without those employees' knowledge. Examples include closed-circuit television, video monitoring, telephone

---

[13]The ADA, however, is neutral on the subject, saying that nothing in the act should be construed to encourage, prohibit, or authorize drug testing or the making of employment decisions on that basis.

monitoring, the monitoring of computer worksta-tions (e.g., by counting keystrokes), and metal de-tectors at plant entrances. Such monitoring has encountered objections because employees are often unaware that it exists, or may suffer stress when they do know or suspect its existence. Employers counter these objections by stressing that monitor-ing is highly useful in evaluating employee perfor-mance, improving efficiency, and reducing theft.

Telephone monitoring has occasionally been found illegal under federal wiretapping law. Al-though such claims have been uncommon, invasion of privacy suits may succeed in situations where an employer's need for surveillance is slight and it is conducted in areas, such as restrooms and lounges, in which employees have a reasonable expectation of privacy. Despite various state and federal bills proposing statutes regulating various forms of monitoring, little such legislation had passed as of late 1993.

## Records and References

Many states allow both public and private employees at least some access to personnel files maintained by their employers. Also, some states limit third-party access to such records. In addition, employers who transmit such data to third parties may be civilly liable for defamation or invasion of privacy. However, truth is a defense in defamation cases, and in both defamation and invasion of privacy suits the employer's actions may be privileged. These defenses can protect employers who are sued for truthful, good faith statements made in references for former employ-ees.

## Wrongful Discharge

### The Doctrine of Employment at Will

The traditional employment-at-will rule, which first appeared around 1870, says that either party can terminate an employment contract for an indefinite time period. Indefinite-time contracts include those for "steady," "regular," or "permanent" employ-ment. The termination can occur at any time; and can be for good, bad, or no cause. However, em-ployees may recover for work actually done.

## The Common Law Exceptions

Because it gives employers the ability to discharge indefinite-term employees with virtual impunity, employment at will has long been regarded as a boon to business and a threat to workers' interests. Although the doctrine remains important today, it has been eroded by many of the developments described in this chapter. For example, the NLRA forbids dismissal for union affiliation, and labor contracts frequently bar termination without just cause. Also, Title VII prohibits firings based on certain personal traits, the ADEA blocks discharges on the basis of age, and the ADA forbids termina-tions for covered personal disabilities.

Over the past 20 years, courts have been carving out further exceptions to employment at will. The three most important such exceptions are discussed below. Although a few states have refused to do so, most recognize one or more of these exceptions. In such states, a terminated employee can recover against her employer for **wrongful discharge** or **unjust dismissal**. The remedies in successful wrongful discharge suits depend heavily on whether the plaintiff's suit is a contract or a tort claim, with tort remedies being more advantageous for plain-tiffs.

**The Public Policy Exception**   The *public policy* exception to employment at will, which has been recognized by over three fourths of the states, is the most common basis for a wrongful discharge suit. As the *Peterson* case (which follows shortly) suggests, it is usually a tort claim. In public policy cases, the terminated employee argues that his discharge was unlawful because it violated the state's public policy. As *Peterson* makes clear, there is some disagreement about the permissible *sources* of state public policies. Perhaps the most common pattern is to limit public policy to the policies furthered by *existing laws* such as constitutional provisions and statutes. For this reason, employees often fail to recover where they are fired for *ethical* objections to job assignments or employer prac-tices.

Successful suits under the public policy excep-tion usually involve firings motivated by an employee's: (1) refusal to commit an unlawful act (e.g., committing perjury or violating the antitrust laws), (2) performance of an important public obligation (e.g., jury duty or whistle-blowing),[14] or (3) exercise of a legal right or privilege (e.g., making a workers' compensation claim or refusing to take an illegal polygraph test). In each case, the act (or refusal to act) that caused the firing is consistent with some public policy; for this reason, the firing tends to frustrate the policy. For example, firing an employee for filing a workers' compensation claim undermines the public policies underlying state workers' compensation statutes.

### The Implied Covenant of Good Faith and Fair Dealing

A wrongful discharge suit based on the *implied covenant of good faith and fair dealing* is usually a contract claim. Here, the employee argues that her discharge was unlawful because it was not made in good faith or did not amount to fair dealing, thus violating the implied contract term. Only about

---

[14]Whistle-blowers are employees who publicly disclose dangerous, illegal, or improper employer behavior. A few states have passed statutes protecting the employment rights of certain whistle-blowers.

25 percent of the states have recognized this exception to employment at will, and most of these give it a narrow scope.

**Promises by Employers**   Using various legal theories, courts have increasingly made employers liable for breaking *promises* to their employees regarding termination policy. Such promises typically are express statements made by employers during hiring or employee orientation, or in their employee manuals, handbooks, personnel policies, and benefit plans. Occasionally, such promises are implied from business custom and usage as well. If such sources state the reasons for which employees will be fired or the procedures accompanying employee terminations, and if the employer fails to follow those promises, it is liable for breach of contract. At least two thirds of the states recognize this exception to employment at will. As the following *Progress Printing* case suggests, however, employers often succeed in disclaiming liability for their own promises.

---

## PETERSON v. BROWNING

### 832 P.2d 1280 (Utah Sup. Ct. 1992)

Vern Peterson was a customs officer with Browning, a Utah corporation. After being terminated from that position, Peterson sued Browning in federal district court, alleging that he was fired for refusing to falsify tax documents in violation of Utah and Missouri law and to falsify customs documents in violation of federal law. The district court then certified two questions to the Utah Supreme Court: (1) whether the Utah public policy exception to employment at will includes violations of federal law and the law of states other than Utah; and (2) whether the Utah public policy exception is a tort claim or a contract claim.

---

**Durham, Justice**   The public policy exception to employment at will restricts an employer's right to terminate an employee for any reason. Under the exception, the at-will doctrine will not insulate an employer from liability where an employee is fired in a manner or for a reason that contravenes a clear and substantial public policy. Actions falling within the public policy exception typically involve termination of employment for: (1) refusing to commit an illegal or wrongful act, (2) performing a public obligation, or (3) exercising a legal right or privi-

lege. Here, Peterson alleges that he was terminated for refusing to commit an unlawful act.

How a court defines "public policy" is a determining factor in whether it will invoke the public policy exception. Declarations of public policy can be found in our statutes and constitutions. This does not mean that all statements made in a statute are expressions of public policy. Many statutes impose requirements whose fulfillment does not implicate fundamental public policy concerns. A number of courts have refused to recognize a cause of action unless the public policy allegedly violated is clear or substantial. This court will narrowly construe the public policies on which a wrongful termination action may be based. It is not the purpose of the exception to eliminate employer discretion in discharging at-will employees, or to impose a requirement of good cause for discharge. We hold that the public policy exception applies in this state when the statutory language expressing the public conscience is clear and when the affected interests of society are substantial.

We turn to the question whether the public policy exception in this state includes violations of federal law and the laws of other states in addition to Utah law. A number of state courts have recognized that certain federal laws may properly form the basis for a wrongful termination action under a state's public policy exception. We are not prepared to hold, however, that a violation of any federal or other state's law automatically provides the basis for a wrongful termination action based on the Utah public policy exception. Many ancient, anachronistic, and unenforced criminal sanctions remain on the books of local, state, and national governments. Violations of such laws would not necessarily violate Utah public policy. A violation of a state or federal law must contravene the clear and substantial public policy of the state of Utah. A plaintiff must establish the connection between the law violated and the public policies of Utah. That has been done here.

In the present case, it is alleged that the employer discharged the employee because he would not falsify tax and customs documents. Such falsification involves serious misconduct and is in all likelihood a felony. To hold that one's continued employment could be made contingent upon his commission of a felonious act at the instance of his employer would be to encourage criminal conduct [by] both the employee and the employer and would

contaminate the honest administration of public affairs. Persons who are terminated from their employment because they refuse to engage in illegal activities that implicate clear and substantial Utah public policy considerations should be protected regardless of whether the applicable law is that of Utah, the federal government, or another state.

The second issue is whether the public policy exception sounds in tort or in contract. Characterizing a case as tort or contract orients the parties to the requisite elements of proof, permits anticipation of potential defenses, and defines the remedies available. Of those courts recognizing the public policy exception, the overwhelming majority adopt the tort theory. We agree with the majority and hold that the exception sounds in tort.

The duty at issue in actions for wrongful termination in violation of public policy does not arise out of the employment contract. It is imposed by law, and thus is properly conceptualized as a tort. Significant consequences flow from this conceptual approach, one of which is the type of damages available. When a contract theory is applied, compensation may be limited to economic losses such as back pay. In contrast, a tort theory will permit a plaintiff [to] recover punitive damages. Potential punitive damages will exert a valuable deterrent effect on employers who might otherwise subject their employees to a choice between violating the law and losing their jobs.

**The Utah Supreme Court held that: (1) the Utah public policy exception includes violations of federal law and the laws of other states if those violations contravene the clear and substantial public policies of Utah; and (2) the public policy exception is a tort claim rather than a contract claim.**

---

## PROGRESS PRINTING CO. v. NICHOLS
### 421 S.E.2d 428 (Va. Sup. Ct. 1992)

On January 20, 1987, William H. Nichols began work as a pressman for the Progress Printing Company. At that time, Nichols was provided with a copy of the company's Employees' Handbook. The handbook stated that Progress would not discharge or suspend an employee "without just cause" and that the company "shall give at least one warning notice in writing" before termination, except under certain circumstances not relevant here.

On February 2, 1987, however, the firm's personnel director gave Nichols a form that stated in part:

I have received a copy of the Progress Printing Employee Handbook. I recognize that an uderstanding [sic] of this information is important to a successful relationship between Progress Printing and myself. I agree to follow the procedures and guidelines it contains. Any questions concerning Progress Printing's polices will be directed to the Personnel Director.

The employment relationship between Progress Printing and the employee is *at will and may be terminated by either party at any time* [emphasis in original].

Nichols and the personnel director both signed the form.

On March 8, 1989, Nichols became upset over Progress's failure to correct a recurring defect in a print job, and he refused to complete that job assignment as a result. Nichols was fired on the following day, without the prior written notice promised by the Employee Handbook.

Nichols then sued for wrongful discharge in a Virginia trial court. After that court ruled in his favor and awarded him $9,000 in damages, Progress appealed.

---

**Lacy, Justice** In Virginia, as in a majority of jurisdictions, the employment relationship is presumed to be "at will," which means that the employment term extends for an indefinite period and may be terminated for any reason. This presumption may be rebutted if sufficient evidence is produced to show that the employment is for a definite, rather than an indefinite, term. Progress argues that Nichols failed to rebut the presumption because the handbook did not constitute an enforceable employment contract and, even if it did, the subsequent execution of the acknowledgement form created an at-will employment relationship.

A number of jurisdictions have held that the employer can be bound by termination-for-cause provisions contained in employee handbooks where those provisions are communicated to the employee in a sufficiently specific manner. We have held that an employment condition which allows termination only for cause sets a definite term for the duration of the employment. We nevertheless agree with Progress that the acknowledgement form specifically superseded and replaced that [just cause] provision with the agreement that the employment relationship was at will. We base this holding on a number of grounds.

The termination-for-cause language of the handbook and the employment-at-will relationship agreed to in the subsequent acknowledgement form are in direct conflict and cannot be reconciled in any reasonable way. If the documents are considered a single contract, this conflict fails to provide sufficient evidence to rebut the presumption of employment at will.

[In any event,] the acknowledgement form was not a part of the handbook and was executed thirteen days after Nichols began work. Under these circumstances, the form reflects an understanding between the parties separate from that contained in the handbook. Execution of the form memorialized reciprocal commitments that satisfy the requisites of a contract—there was an offer of employment at will; the employee continued service, which constituted the consideration; and the employee accepted by performance.

We conclude that the employment relationship between Nichols and Progress was at-will employment which either party could terminate at any time. Therefore, Progress did not breach the employment contract when it terminated Nichols.

**Trial court decision on Nichols's employment-at-will claim reversed in favor of Progress.**

---

### PROBLEMS AND PROBLEM CASES

**1.** A class of male employees sued the American Cast Iron Pipe Company (ACIPCO) under the Equal Pay Act. One of the plaintiffs, James Dollar, argued that the act was violated because he was paid less than certain female employees despite having greater skills and responsibility. Dollar had worked for ACIPCO as a production machinist, radial drill operator, and machinist apprentice. The female employees to whom Dollar compared himself included data entry operators, receptionists, estimators, stenographer-clerks, and a truckload-carload coordinator. Did Dollar's EPA claim succeed?

**2.** Dianne Rawlinson, a rejected female applicant for employment as a prison guard in the Alabama prison system, challenged certain state rules restricting her employment prospects under Title VII. They were: (1) requirements that all prison employees be at least 5 feet 2 inches tall and weigh at least 120 pounds, and (2) a rule expressly prohibiting women from assuming close-contact prison guard positions in maximum-security prisons (most of which were all-male). What method of proving a Title VII case should Rawlinson use in attacking the height and weight requirements? Does she need to use one of these methods to attack the second rule? What argument should the state use if Rawlinson establishes a prima facie case against the height and weight requirements? What Title VII defense might the state have for the second rule? With regard to the second rule, assume that at this time Alabama's maximum security prisons housed their male prisoners dormitory-style rather than putting them in cells, and that they did not separate sex offenders from other prisoners.

**3.** The American Cast Iron Pipe Company (ACIPCO) limits the medical and dental benefits it provides to its employees' dependents. In order for the children of an employee to qualify for coverage, the company requires that the children reside full time with their employee-parent. Because men comprised 397 of the 400 ACIPCO employees who were negatively affected by this policy, a male employee named Ray Beavers mounted a Title VII class action suit against the firm for sex discrimination. Can a male employee like Beavers sue for sex discrimination under Title VII? In any event, what Title VII proof method would Beavers's suit have to involve?

**4.** Farah Manufacturing Company had a long-standing policy against employing aliens. Cecilia Espinoza, a lawful alien married to an American citizen, applied for employment as a seamstress at Farah. She was rejected, and she sued Farah under Title VII for national origin discrimination. Did Farah's decision violate Title VII? Assume that Espinoza's suit attacks the policy just described and

that she is not making either a disparate treatment or a disparate impact argument.

**5.** Jesse Cook, a Seventh Day Adventist, worked at a Chrysler Corporation plant. Because he lacked sufficient seniority in his job, Cook was assigned to the evening shift, which required him to work on Friday nights. Cook's religion prohibited him from working from sundown Friday until sundown Saturday. Cook was informed that under the relevant collective bargaining agreement, his shift could not be changed. Eventually, Cook was fired for his continuing Friday night absences from work. Accommodating Cook probably would have required Chrysler to make Cook a part-time employee while paying him full-time benefits. Also, it probably would have required Chrysler to use a temporary part-time employee (or floater) to replace Cook every Friday night. This would have meant that Chrysler either had to forgo using a floater elsewhere or hire another floater. Also, more repairs and lower efficiency are likely when a floater is used on the line.

Cook sued Chrysler and the union for religious discrimination under Title VII. Will the defendants succeed if they argue that they were not discriminating against Cook's *religion* as such, but rather against his refusal to work on Friday nights? In any event, what other argument might they use? Will it work here?

**6.** Ann Hopkins, a senior manager at the accounting firm of Price Waterhouse, was denied partnership in the firm. A persistent theme in existing partners' written comments on Hopkins's candidacy was the belief that Hopkins acted in ways inappropriate for a woman to act. Thus, one partner described her as "macho," another wrote that she "overcompensated for being a woman," yet another advised that she take "a course at charm school," and still others objected to her use of profanity. Also, a partner who tried to help Hopkins through the process told her that to improve her chances, she should walk more femininely, dress more femininely, wear makeup, have her hair styled, and wear jewelry. Assuming that these opinions were the only reason for Hopkins's failure to make partner, was that denial illegal sex discrimination under Title VII?

**7.** Mechelle Vinson alleged that during her four years with the Meritor Savings Bank, her supervisor Sidney Taylor repeatedly demanded sexual favors from her, and that she had sexual intercourse with him on 40 to 50 separate occasions. She also contended that Taylor fondled her in front of other employees, followed her into the women's restroom, exposed himself to her, and forcibly raped her on several occasions. Despite these allegations, however, Vinson apparently was well treated by her employer in other respects. She received three promotions during her time with the bank, and it was undisputed that her advancement was based solely on merit. Assuming that Vinson's allegations are true and that Taylor's behavior was unwelcome to her, can she recover against the bank for quid pro quo sexual harassment? Can she recover for work environment sexual harassment? Assume that the bank would be liable for Taylor's behavior.

**8.** William Guthrie managed a J. C. Penney Company store in Meridian, Mississippi. J. C. Penney originally had a policy that all store managers retire at age 60, but this policy was changed after passage of the ADEA. In 1979, just before Guthrie's 60th birthday, various Penney employees made "friendly" inquiries about his retirement plans. Guthrie, however, continued to manage the Meridian store, receiving satisfactory performance ratings and making decent profits for J. C. Penney. In 1982, however, Guthrie's new Penney supervisor reprimanded Guthrie before other store employees, overrode several decisions ordinarily made by Guthrie, lowered Guthrie's performance ratings, and gave him some difficult new performance objectives. Feeling that his discharge was inevitable, Guthrie resigned. Under the younger store manager who succeeded him, the Meridian store did less well in sales and profits, but the new manager received satisfactory performance ratings and was allowed to run the store without interference.

Guthrie sued Penney for constructive discharge under the ADEA. What method of proof would his suit involve? Can that method be used under the ADEA?

**9.** At the age of 66, Fleming Tullis was discharged from his job as a school bus driver with a private school. He sued the school under the Age Discrimination in Employment Act. Did the school have a BFOQ defense here? Assume that tests for determining the driving ability of individual people are available and reliable. Also, assume that the school failed to produce any evidence showing that people in their 60s cannot safely operate school buses.

**10.** Catherine Sue Wagenseller was fired from her job as paramedic coordinator in the Scottsdale Memorial Hospital's emergency department. She sued the hospital for wrongful discharge under the public policy exception to the employment-at-will doctrine, alleging that she was fired because of animosity resulting from her refusal to participate in an off-the-job group parody of the song *Moon River* in which group members mooned the audience. A state statute provided that: "A person commits indecent exposure if he or she exposes his or her genitals or anus . . . and another person is present, and the defendant is reckless about whether such other person, as a reasonable person, would be offended or alarmed by the act." Assuming that the audience to the parody enjoyed watching the mooning, would Wagenseller have been criminally liable if she had participated? Does this necessarily defeat her civil claim for wrongful discharge under the public policy exception?

**11.** 📼    *Video Case.* See "How Safe is Too Safe?" Mike, a factory worker at XYZ Manufacturing, suffers injury to his fingers while working for XYZ. The injury occurs while Mike is operating a table saw built by ABCO Assembly. The saw was designed with a detachable blade guard assembly. The blade guard assembly would have prevented Mike's injury had it been in place while he was using the saw, but it was detached at that time. Assuming for the sake of argument that Mike was contributorily negligent or that he assumed the risk of the injury he suffered, can XYZ use either of these defenses to prevent Mike from recovering under workers' compensation for his injuries? Suppose that Mike wants to mount a product liability suit against ABCO. Would workers' compensation block such a suit?

---

## CAPSTONE QUESTIONS

Ed Blemish is the new personnel manager for the Idex Corporation. Some problems with legal implications now are crowding Ed's once-neat desk. They are:

**1.** *The case of the injured employees.* Six Idex employees have been injured in a work-related industrial accident. The injuries were partially due to Idex's negligent supervision of a work project and partially due to the employees' own carelessness. The employees want to sue Idex in negligence for their injuries, and their claims for pain, suffering, and medical expenses are likely to be huge. From a business law course taken long ago, Ed vaguely remembers a concept called comparative negligence that is taking over tort law. More and more states, he recalls, are saying that in cases like this one, where both parties are negligent, the plaintiff's recovery should equal the plaintiff's damages times the defendant's percentage share of the negligence causing those damages. This compromise replaces the old rule under which any degree of employee contributory negligence, however slight, was a complete defense for the employer. Ed figures that while the old rule would be better for his firm, comparative negligence still will assist it here.

**Required:**

Answer the following and give reasons for your conclusion.

Is Ed right about the applicability of comparative negligence? Assume that workers' compensation applies.

**2.** *The weekend work dilemma.* For a long time, Idex has been paying hourly employees an extra 10 percent (110 percent) of their hourly wage for working on a Saturday or a Sunday. Ed thinks that this is less than federal law requires and that the firm must pay such workers at a time-and-a-half rate once they exceed 40 hours per week.

**Required:**

Answer the following and give reasons for your conclusion.

Is Ed right?

**3.** *The matching taxes conundrum.* Finally, Ed is having trouble deciding what to do about federal social security taxes and federal unemployment compensation taxes. He's figured out the wage bases for each tax—the amount of employee compensation to which each tax applies. But he can't recall whether each tax requires that both the employer and the employee pay a certain percentage rate on that wage base. Ed tells a subordinate to have the firm pay the relevant percentage rate on the applicable wage base for both taxes and to deduct the same amounts from each employee's paycheck.

**Required:**

Answer the following and give reasons for your conclusion.

Has Ed done the right thing?

# GLOSSARY OF LEGAL TERMS AND DEFINITIONS

**A**

**Abandonment**   To intentionally give up possession or claim to property with the intent of relinquishment of any ownership or claim.

**Abatement**   An action of stopping or removing.

**Ab Initio**   From the beginning. A contract that is void ab initio is void from its inception.

**Abstract of Title**   A summary of the conveyances, transfers, and other facts relied on as evidence of title, together with all such facts appearing of record that may impair its validity. It should contain a brief but complete history of the title.

**Abuse of Process**   An intentional tort designed to protect against the initiation of legal proceedings for a primary purpose other than the one for which such proceedings were designed.

**Acceleration**   The shortening of the time for the performance of a contract or the payment of a note by the operation of some provision in the contract or note itself.

**Acceptance**   The actual or implied receipt and retention of that which is tendered or offered.

**Accession**   The acquisition of property by its incorporation or union with other property.

**Accommodation Paper**   A negotiable instrument signed without consideration by a party as acceptor, drawer, or indorser for the purpose of enabling the payee to obtain credit.

**Accommodation Party**   A person who signs a negotiable instrument for the purpose of adding his name and liability to another party to the instrument.

**Accord and Satisfaction**   A legally binding agreement to settle a disputed claim for a definite amount.

**Account Stated**   An account that has been rendered by one to another and which purports to state the true balance due and that balance is either expressly or impliedly admitted to be due by the debtor.

**Acquit**   To set free or judicially to discharge from an accusation; to release from a debt, duty, obligation, charge, or suspicion of guilt.

**Actionable**   Capable of being remedied by a legal action or claim.

**Act of God**   An occurrence resulting exclusively from natural forces that could not have been prevented or whose effect could not have been avoided by care or foresight.

**Act of State Doctrine**   A doctrine of international law that no nation is permitted to judge the act of another nation committed within its own boundaries.

**Adjudge**   To give judgment; to decide; to sentence.

**Adjudicate**   To adjudge; to settle by judicial decree, as a court.

**Ad Litem**   During the pendency of the action or proceeding.

**Administrator**   The personal representative appointed by a probate court to settle the estate of a deceased person who died intestate (without leaving a valid will).

**Adoption**   In corporation law, a corporation's acceptance of a preincorporation contract by action of its board of directors, by which the corporation becomes liable on the contract.

**Advance Directive**   A written document such as a living will or durable power of attorney that directs others how future health care decisions should be made in the event that the individual becomes incapacitated.

**Adverse Possession**   Open and notorious possession of real property over a given length of time that denies ownership in any other claimant.

**Advised Letter of Credit**   See *Letter of Credit, Advised.*

**Affidavit**   A signed writing containing statements of fact to whose accuracy the signing party has sworn. Used in a variety of judicial proceedings, including the motion for summary judgment.

**Affirm**   To confirm or uphold a former judgment or order of a court. Appellate courts, for instance, may affirm the decisions of lower courts.

**After-Acquired Property**   Property of the debtor that is obtained after a security interest in the debtor's property has been created.

**Agency**   A legal relationship in which an agent acts under the direction of a principal for the principal's benefit. Also used to refer to government regulatory bodies of all kinds.

**Agent**   One who acts under the direction of a principal for the principal's benefit in a legal relationship known as agency. See *Principal*.

**Aggregate Theory**   In partnership law, the view that there is no distinction between a partnership and the partners who own it. See *Entity Theory*.

**Aggrieved**   One whose legal rights have been invaded by the act of another is said to be aggrieved. Also, one whose pecuniary interest is directly affected by a judgment, or whose right of property may be divested by an action.

**Alienation**   The voluntary act or acts by which one person transfers his or her own property to another.

**Alien Corporation**   A corporation incorporated in one country that is doing business in another country. See *Foreign Corporation*.

**Allegation**   A statement of a party to an action in a declaration or pleading of what the party intends to prove.

**Allege**   To make a statement of fact; to plead.

**Alteration**   An addition or change in a document.

**Alter Ego**   Other self. In corporation law, a doctrine that permits a court to pierce a corporation's veil and to hold a shareholder liable for the actions of a corporation dominated by the shareholder.

**Alternative Dispute Resolution (ADR)**   A general name applied to the many nonjudicial means of settling private disputes.

**Amortize**   To provide for the payment of a debt by creating a sinking fund or paying in installments.

**Ancillary**   Auxiliary to. An ancillary receiver is a receiver who has been appointed in aid of, and in subordination to, the primary receiver.

**Ancillary Covenant Not to Compete**   A promise that is ancillary to (part of) a valid contract whereby one party to a contract agrees not to compete with the other party for a specified time and within a specified location. Also called *non-competition clause*.

**Answer**   The pleading of a defendant in which he or she may deny any or all the facts set out in the plaintiff's declaration or complaint.

**Anticipatory Breach**   A contracting party's indication before the time for performance that he cannot or will not perform the contract.

**Appearance**   The first act of the defendant in court.

**Appellant**   The party making an appeal.

**Appellate Jurisdiction**   Jurisdiction to revise or correct the work of a subordinate court.

**Appellee**   A party against whom a favorable court decision is appealed. May be called the *respondent* in some jurisdictions.

**Applicant**   A petitioner; one who files a petition or application.

**Appraisal, Right of**   A shareholder's right to receive the fair value of her shares from her corporation when she objects to a corporate transaction that significantly alters her rights in the corporation.

**Appurtenance**   An accessory; something that belongs to another thing.

**Arbitrate**   To submit some disputed matter to selected persons and to accept their decision or award as a substitute for the decision of a judicial tribunal.

**Argument**   The discussion by counsel for the respective parties of their contentions on the law and the facts of the case being tried in order to aid the jury in arriving at a correct and just conclusion.

**Articles of Incorporation**   A document that must be filed with a secretary of state to create a corporation. Usually, it includes the basic rights and responsibilities of the corporation and the shareholders.

**Articles of Partnership**   A formal written contract between the partners of a partnership that states the rights and the responsibilities of the partners.

**Artisan's Lien**   A common law possessory security interest arising out of the improvement of property by one skilled in some mechanical art or craft; the lien entitles the improver of the property to retain possession in order to secure the agreed-on price or the value of the work performed.

**Assault**   An intentional tort that prohibits any attempt or offer to cause harmful or offensive contact with another if it results in a well-grounded apprehension of imminent battery in the mind of the threatened person.

**Assent**   To give or express one's concurrence or approval of something done.

**Assignable**   Capable of being lawfully assigned or transferred; transferable; negotiable. Also, capable of being specified or pointed out as an assignable error.

**Assignee**   A person to whom an assignment is made.

**Assignment**   A transfer of property or some right or interest.

**Assignment of Partnership Interest**   A partner's voluntary transfer of her partnership interest to the partner's personal creditor, giving the creditor the right to receive the partner's share of partnership profits.

**Assignor**   The maker of an assignment.

**Assumption of Risk**   A traditional defense to negligence liability based on the argument that the plaintiff voluntarily exposed himself to a known danger created by the defendant's negligence.

**Assurance**   To provide confidence or to inform positively.

**Attachment**   In general, the process of taking a person's property under an appropriate judicial order by an appropriate officer of the court. Used for a variety of purposes, including the acquisition of jurisdiction over the property seized and the securing of property that may be used to satisfy a debt.

**Attest**   To bear witness to; to affirm; to be true or genuine.

**Attorney-in-Fact**   An agent who is given express, written authorization by his principal to do a particular act or series of acts on behalf of the principal.

**At Will**   See *Employment at Will.*

**Audit Committee**   In corporation law, a committee of the board that recommends and supervises the public accountant who audits the corporation's financial records.

**Authentication**   Such official attestation of a written instrument as will render it legally admissible in evidence.

**Authority**   In agency law, an agent's ability to affect his principal's legal relations with third parties. Also used to refer to an actor's legal power or ability to do something. In addition, sometimes used to refer to a statute, case, or other legal source that justifies a particular result.

**Authorized Shares**   Shares that a corporation is empowered to issue by its articles of incorporation.

**Automatic Stay**   Under the Bankruptcy Act, the suspension of all litigation against the debtor and his property, which is triggered by the filing of a bankruptcy petition.

**Averment**   A positive statement of fact made in a pleading.

**Avoid**   To nullify a contractual obligation.

**B**

**Bad Faith**   A person's actual intent to mislead or deceive another; an intent to take an unfair and unethical advantage of another.

**Bailee**   The person to whom a bailment is made.

**Bailment**   The transfer of personal property by its owner to another person with the understanding that the property will be returned to the owner in the future.

**Bailor**   The owner of bailed property; the one who delivers personal property to another to be held in bailment.

**Bankruptcy**   The state of a person who is unable to pay his or her debts without respect to time; one whose liabilities exceed his or her assets.

**Bar**   As a collective noun, those persons who are admitted to practice law, members of the bar. The court itself. A plea or defense asserted by a defendant that is sufficient to destroy a plaintiff's action.

**Battery**   An intentional tort that prohibits the harmful or offensive touching of another without his consent.

**Bearer**   A person in possession of a negotiable instrument that is payable to him, his order, or to whoever is in possession of the instrument.

**Bench**   Generally used as a synonym for the term *court* or the judges of a court.

**Beneficiary**   The person for whose benefit an insurance policy, trust, will, or contract is established. In the case of a contract, the beneficiary is called a *third party beneficiary.*

**Bequest**   In a will, a gift of personal property or money. Also called a *legacy.*

**Bid**   To make an offer at an auction or at a judicial sale. As a noun, an offer.

**Bilateral Contract**   A contract in which the promise of one of the parties forms the consideration for the promise of the other; a contract formed by an offer requiring a reciprocal promise.

**Bill of Exchange**   An unconditional order in writing by one person to another, signed by the person giving it, requiring the person to whom it is addressed to pay on demand or at a fixed or determinable future time a sum certain in money to order or to bearer.

**Bill of Lading**   A written acknowledgment of the receipt of goods to be transported to a designated place and delivery to a named person or to his or her order.

**Bill of Sale**   A written agreement by which one person assigns or transfers interests or rights in personal property to another.

**Binder**   Also called a *binding slip.* A brief memorandum or agreement issued by an insurer as a temporary policy for the convenience of all the parties, constituting a present insurance in the amount specified, to continue in force until the execution of a formal policy.

**Blue Sky Laws**   The popular name for state statutes that regulate securities transactions.

**Bona Fide**   Made honestly and in good faith; genuine.

**Bona Fide Purchaser**   An innocent buyer for valuable consideration who purchases goods without notice of any defects in the title of the goods acquired.

**Bond**   A long-term debt security that is secured by collateral.

**Bonus Shares**   Also called *bonus stock.* Shares issued for no lawful consideration. See *Discount Shares* and *Watered Shares.*

**Breaking Bulk**   The division or separation of the contents of a package or container.

**Brief**   A statement of a party's case or legal arguments, usually prepared by an attorney. Often used to support some of the motions described in Chapter 2, and also used to make legal arguments before appellate courts. Also, an abridgement of a reported case.

**Broker**   An agent who bargains or carries on negotiations in behalf of the principal as an intermediary between the latter and third persons in transacting business relative to the acquisition of contractual rights, or to the sale or purchase of property the custody of which is not intrusted to him or her for the purpose of discharging the agency.

**Bulk Transfer**   The sale or transfer of a major part of the stock of goods of a merchant at one time and not in the ordinary course of business.

**Burden of Proof**   Used to refer both to the necessity or obligation of proving the facts needed to support a party's claim, and the persuasiveness of the evidence used to do so. Regarding the second sense of the term, the usual burden of proof in a civil case is a preponderance of the evidence; in a criminal case, it is proof beyond a reasonable doubt.

**Business Judgment Rule**   A rule protecting business managers from liability for making bad decisions when they have acted prudently and in good faith.

**Buy-and-Sell Agreement**   A share transfer restriction compelling a shareholder to sell his shares to the other shareholders or the corporation and obligating the other shareholders or the corporation to buy the shareholder's shares.

**Buyer in Ordinary Course of Business**   A person who, in good faith and without knowledge that the sale to him is in violation of a third party's ownership rights or security interest in the goods, buys in ordinary course from a person who is in the business of selling goods of that kind.

**Bylaws**   In corporation law, a document that supplements the articles of incorporation and contains less important rights, powers, and responsibilities of a corporation and its shareholders, officers, and directors.

## C

**C&F**   The price of the goods includes the cost of the goods plus the freight to the named destination.

**Call**   See *Redemption.* Also, a type of option permitting a person to buy a fixed number of securities at a fixed price at a specified time. See *Put.*

**Canceled Shares**   Previously outstanding shares repurchased by a corporation and canceled by it; such shares no longer exist.

**Cancellation**   The act of crossing out a writing. The operation of destroying a written instrument.

**Capacity**   The ability to incur legal obligations and acquire legal rights.

**Capital**   Contributions of money and other property to a business made by the owners of the business.

**Capital Stock**   See *Stated Capital.*

**Capital Surplus**   Also called *additional paid capital.* A balance sheet account; the portion of shareholders' contributions exceeding the par or stated value of shares.

**Case Law**   The law extracted from decided cases.

**Cashier's Check**   A draft (including a check) drawn by a bank on itself and accepted by the act of issuance.

**Causa Mortis**   In contemplation of approaching death.

**Cause of Action**   A legal rule giving the plaintiff the right to obtain some legal relief once certain factual elements are proven. Often used synonymously with the terms *claim* or *theory of recovery.*

**Caveat Emptor**   Let the buyer beware.

**Caveat Venditor**   Let the seller beware.

**Certificate of Deposit**   An acknowledgment by a bank of the receipt of money with an engagement to pay it back.

**Certificate of Limited Partnership**   A document that must be filed with a secretary of state to create a limited partnership.

**Certification**   The return of a writ; a formal attestation of a matter of fact; the appropriate marking of a certified check.

**Certified Check**   A check that has been accepted by the drawee bank and has been so marked or certified that it indicates such acceptance.

**Chancellor**   A judge of a court of chancery.

**Chancery**   Equity or a court of equity.

**Charge**   The legal instructions that a judge gives a jury before the jury begins its deliberations. In the prosecution of a crime, to formally accuse the offender or charge him with the crime.

**Charging Order**   A court's order granting rights in a partner's partnership interest to a personal creditor of the partner; a creditor with a charging order is entitled to the partner's share of partnership profits.

**Charter**   An instrument or authority from the sovereign power bestowing the right or power to do business under the corporate form of organization. Also, the organic law of a city or town, and representing a portion of the statute law of the state.

**Chattel**   An article of tangible property other than land.

**Chattel Mortgage**   An instrument whereby the owner of chattels transfers the title to such property to another as security for the performance of an obligation subject to be defeated on the performance of the obligation. Under the UCC, called merely a *security interest.*

**Chattel Paper**   Written documents that evidence both an obligation to pay money and a security interest in particular goods.

**Check**   A written order on a bank or banker payable on demand to the person named or his order or bearer and drawn by virtue of credits due the drawer from the bank created by money deposited with the bank.

**Chose in Action**   A personal right not reduced to possession but recoverable by a suit at law.

**CIF**   An abbreviation for cost, freight, and insurance, used in mercantile transactions, especially in import transactions.

**Citation of Authorities**   The reference to legal authorities such as reported cases or treatises to support propositions advanced.

**Civil Action**   An action brought to enforce a civil right; in contrast to a criminal action.

**Civil Law**   The body of law applicable to lawsuits involving two private parties.

**Class Action**   An action brought on behalf of the plaintiff and others similarly situated.

**Close Corporation**   A corporation with few shareholders generally having a close personal relationship to each other and participating in the management of the business.

**COD**   Cash on delivery. When goods are delivered to a carrier for a cash on delivery shipment, the carrier must not deliver without receiving payment of the amount due.

**Code**   A system of law; a systematic and complete body of law.

**Codicil**   Some addition to or qualification of one's last will and testament.

**Collateral**   Property put up to secure the performance of a promise, so that if the promisor fails to perform as promised, the creditor may look to the property to make him whole.

**Collateral Attack**   An attempt to impeach a decree, a judgment, or other official act in a proceeding that has not been instituted for the express purpose of correcting or annulling or modifying the decree, judgment, or official act.

**Collateral Contract**   A contract in which one person agrees to pay the debt of another if the principal debtor fails to pay. See *Guaranty.*

**Comaker**   A person who with another or others signs a negotiable instrument on its face and thereby becomes primarily liable for its payment.

**Commercial Impracticability**   The standards used by the UCC, replacing the common law doctrine of impossibility, to define when a party is relieved of his or her contract obligations because of the occurrence of unforeseeable, external events beyond his or her control.

**Commercial Law**   The law that relates to the rights of property and persons engaged in trade or commerce.

**Commercial Paper**   Negotiable paper such as promissory notes, drafts, and checks that provides for the payment of money and can readily be transferred to other parties.

**Commercial Unit**   Under the UCC, any unit of goods that is treated by commercial usage as a single whole. It may, for example, be a single article or a set of articles such as a dozen, bale, gross, or carload.

**Common Area**   In landlord-tenant law, an area over which the landlord retains control but which is often used by or for the benefit of tenants. For example, hallways in an apartment building.

**Common Carrier**   One who undertakes, for hire or reward, to transport the goods of such of the public as choose to employ him.

**Common Law**   The law that is made and applied by judges in cases not governed by other forms of positive law.

**Common Shareholders**   Shareholders who claim the residual profits and assets of a corporation, and usually have the exclusive power and right to elect the directors of the corporation.

**Comparative Fault**   Often used synonymously with *comparative negligence.* But also sometimes used to refer to a defense that operates like comparative negligence but considers the plaintiff's and the defendant's overall fault rather than either's negligence alone.

**Comparative Negligence**   The contemporary replacement for the traditional doctrine of contributory negligence. The basic idea is that damages are apportioned between the parties to a negligence action in proportion to their relative fault. The details vary from state to state.

**Compensatory Damages**   See *Damages, Compensatory.*

**Complaint**   The pleading in a civil case in which the plaintiff states his claim and requests relief.

**Composition with Creditors**   An agreement between creditors and their common debtor and between themselves whereby the creditors agree to accept the sum or security stipulated in full payment of their claims.

**Concealment**   In contract law, taking active steps to prevent another from learning the truth.

**Concurrent**   Running with; simultaneously with. The word is used in different senses. In contracts, concurrent conditions are conditions that must be performed simultaneously by the mutual acts required by each of the parties.

**Condemn**   To appropriate land for public use. To adjudge a person guilty; to pass sentence on a person convicted of a crime.

**Condition**   In contract law, a future, uncertain event that creates or extinguishes a duty of performance; a provision or clause in a contract that operates to suspend or rescind a party's duty to perform.

**Conditional Acceptance**   An acceptance of a bill of exchange containing some qualification limiting or altering the acceptor's liability on the bill.

**Conditional Gift**   A gift that does not become absolute or complete until the occurrence of some express or implied condition.

**Conditional Sale**   The term is most frequently applied to a sale in which the seller reserves the title to the goods, although the possession is delivered to the buyer, until the purchase price is paid in full.

**Condition Precedent**   A condition that operates to give rise to a contracting party's duty to perform.

**Condition Subsequent**   A condition that operates to relieve or discharge one from his obligation under a contract.

**Confession of Judgment**   An entry of judgment on the admission or confession of the debtor without the formality, time, or expense involved in an ordinary proceeding.

**Confirmed Letter of Credit**   See *Letter of Credit, Confirmed.*

**Confusion**   The inseparable intermixture of property belonging to different owners.

**Consent Decree** or **Consent Order**   Used to refer to the order courts or administrative agencies issue when approving the settlement of a lawsuit or administrative action against some party.

**Consent Restraint**   A security transfer restriction requiring a shareholder to obtain the consent of the corporation or its shareholders prior to the shareholder's sale of her shares.

**Consequential Damages**   See *Damages, Consequential.*

**Conservator** (of an incompetent person)   A person appointed by a court to take care of and oversee the person and estate of an incompetent person.

**Consideration**   In contract law, a basic requirement for an enforceable agreement under traditional contract principles, defined in this text as legal value, bargained for and given in exchange for an act or promise. In corporation law, cash or property contributed to a corporation in exchange for shares, or a promise to contribute such cash or property.

**Consignee**   A person to whom goods are consigned, shipped, or otherwise transmitted, either for sale or for safekeeping.

**Consignment**   A bailment for sale. The consignee does not undertake the absolute obligation to sell or pay for the goods.

**Consignor**   One who sends goods to another on consignment. A shipper or transmitter of goods.

**Conspicuous**   Noticeable by a reasonable person, such as a term or clause in a contract that is in bold print, in capitals, or a contrasting color or type style.

**Constructive Eviction**   In landlord-tenant law, a breach of duty by the landlord that makes the premises uninhabitable or otherwise deprives the tenant of the benefit of the lease and gives rise to the tenant's right to vacate the property and terminate the lease.

**Construe**   To read a statute or document for the purpose of ascertaining its meaning and effect, but in doing so the law must be regarded.

**Contempt**   Conduct in the presence of a legislative or judicial body tending to disturb its proceedings or impair the respect due to its authority, or a disobedience to the rules or orders of such a body, which interferes with the due administration of law.

**Continuation Statement**   A document, usually a multicopy form, filed in a public office to indicate the continuing viability of a financing statement. See *Financing Statement.*

**Contra**   Otherwise; disagreeing with; contrary to.

**Contract**   A legally enforceable promise or set of promises.

**Contract of Adhesion**   A contract in which a stronger party is able to dictate terms to a weaker party, leaving the weaker party no practical choice but to adhere to the terms. If the stronger party has exploited its bargaining power to achieve unfair terms, the contract is against public policy.

**Contribution**    In business organization law, the cash or property contributed to a business by its owners.

**Contributory Negligence**    A traditional defense to negligence liability based on the plaintiff's failure to exercise reasonable care for his own safety.

**Conversion**    Any distinct act of dominion wrongfully exerted over another's personal property in denial of or inconsistent with his rights therein. That tort committed by a person who deals with chattels not belonging to him in a manner that is inconsistent with the ownership of the lawful owner.

**Convertible Securities**    Securities giving their holders the power to exchange those securities for other securities without paying any additional consideration.

**Conveyance**    A written instrument transferring the title to land or some interest therein from one person to another.

**Copartnership**    A partnership.

**Copyright**    A set of exclusive rights, protected by federal law, pertaining to certain creative works such as books, musical compositions, computer programs, works of art, and so forth. The rights are: (1) to reproduce the work in question, (2) to prepare derivative works based on it, (3) to sell or otherwise distribute it, and (4) to perform or display it publicly.

**Corporation**    A form of business organization that is owned by owners, called shareholders, who have no inherent right to manage the business, and is managed by a board of directors that is elected by the shareholders.

**Corporation by Estoppel**    A doctrine that prevents persons from denying that a corporation exists when the persons hold themselves out as representing a corporation or believe themselves to be dealing with a corporation.

**Corporeal**    Possessing physical substance; tangible; perceptible to the senses.

**Counterclaim**    A legal claim made in response to the plaintiff's initial claim in a civil suit. Unlike a defense, the counterclaim is the defendant's affirmative attempt to obtain legal relief; in effect, it states a cause of action entitling the defendant to such relief. Often, the counterclaim must arise out of the occurrence that forms the basis for the plaintiff's claim.

**Counteroffer**    A cross-offer made by the offeree to the offeror.

**Countertrade**    A buyer's purchase of the seller's goods in exchange for the seller's agreement to purchase goods of the buyer or other person; usually required as a condition to selling goods to a foreign trade corporation.

**Course of Dealing**    A sequence of previous conduct between the parties to a transaction that is fairly to be regarded as establishing a common basis for interpreting their contract.

**Covenant**    A contract; a promise.

**Cover**    To obtain substitute or equivalent goods.

**Credible**    As applied to a witness, competent.

**Creditor**    A person to whom a debt or legal obligation is owed, and who has the right to enforce payment of that debt or obligation.

**Crime**    An act prohibited by the state; a public wrong.

**Criminal Law**    The body of law setting out public wrongs that the government attempts to correct by prosecuting wrongdoers.

**Culpable**    Blameworthy; denotes breach of legal duty but not necessarily criminal conduct.

**Cumulative Voting**    A procedure for voting for directors that permits a shareholder to multiply the number of shares he owns by the number of directors to be elected and to cast the resulting total of votes for one or more directors. See *Straight Voting*.

**Curtesy**    At common law, a husband's right in property owned by his wife during her life.

**Custody**    The bare control or care of a thing as distinguished from the possession of it.

**Cy Pres**    As near as possible. In the law of trusts, a doctrine applied to prevent a charitable trust from failing when the application of trust property to the charitable beneficiary designated by the settlor becomes illegal or impossible to carry out; in such a case, cy pres allows the court to redirect the distribution of trust property for some purpose that is as near as possible to the settlor's general charitable intent.

## D

**Damages**    The sum of money recoverable by a plaintiff who has received a judgment in a civil case.

  **Compensatory**    Damages that will compensate a party for direct losses due to an injury suffered.

  **Consequential**    Damages that do not flow directly and immediately from an act but rather flow from the results of the act; damages that are indirect consequences of a breach of contract or certain other legal wrongs. Examples include personal injury, damage to property, and lost profits.

  **Incidental**    Collateral damages that result from a breach of contract, including all reasonable expenses that are incurred because of the breach; damages that compensate a person injured by a breach of contract for reasonable costs he incurs in an attempt to avoid further loss.

**Liquidated**  Damages made certain by the prior agreement of the parties.

**Nominal**  Damages that are recoverable when a legal right is to be vindicated against an invasion that has produced no actual present loss.

**Punitive**  Damages designed to punish flagrant wrongdoers and to deter them and others from engaging in similar conduct in the future.

**Special**  Actual damages that would not necessarily but because of special circumstances do in fact flow from an injury.

**Treble**  Three times provable damages, as may be granted to private parties bringing an action under the antitrust laws.

**Date of Issue**  As applied to notes, bonds, and so on of a series, the arbitrary date fixed as the beginning of the term for which they run, without reference to the precise time when convenience or the state of the market may permit their sale or delivery.

**D/B/A**  Doing business as; indicates the use of a trade name.

**Deal**  To engage in transactions of any kind, to do business with.

**Debenture**  A long-term, unsecured debt security.

**Debtor**  A person who is under a legal obligation to pay a sum of money to another (the creditor).

**Decedent**  A person who has died.

**Deceit**  A tort involving intentional misrepresentation or cheating by means of some device.

**Decision**  The judgment of a court; the opinion merely represents the reasons for that judgment.

**Declaratory Judgment**  One that expresses the opinion of a court on a question of law without ordering anything to be done.

**Decree**  An order or sentence of a court of equity determining some right or adjudicating some matter affecting the merits of the cause.

**Deed**  A writing, sealed and delivered by the parties; an instrument conveying real property.

**Deed of Trust**  A three-party instrument used to create a security interest in real property in which the legal title to the real property is placed in one or more trustees to secure the repayment of a sum of money or the performance of other conditions.

**De Facto**  In fact, actual. Often used in contrast to *de jure* to refer to a real state of affairs.

**De Facto Corporation**  A corporation that has complied substantially with the mandatory conditions precedent to incorporation, taken as a whole.

**Defalcation**  The word includes both embezzlement and misappropriation and is a broader term than either.

**Defamation**  An intentional tort that prohibits the publication of false and defamatory statements concerning another.

**Default**  Fault; neglect; omission; the failure of a party to an action to appear when properly served with process; the failure to perform a duty or obligation; the failure of a person to pay money when due or when lawfully demanded.

**Defeasible**  Regarding title to property, capable of being defeated. A title to property that is open to attack or that may be defeated by the performance of some act.

**Defend**  To oppose a claim or action; to plead in defense of an action; to contest an action suit or proceeding.

**Defendant**  The party who is sued in a civil case, or the party who is prosecuted in a criminal case.

**Defendant in Error**  Any of the parties in whose favor a judgment was rendered that the losing party seeks to have reversed or modified by writ of error and whom he names as adverse parties.

**Defense**  A rule of law entitling the defendant to a judgment in his favor even if the plaintiff proves all elements of his claim or cause of action.

**Deficiency**  That part of a debt that a mortgage was made to secure, not realized by the liquidation of the mortgaged property. Something which is lacking.

**Defraud**  To deprive another of a right by deception or artifice.

**De Jure**  According to the law; legitimate; by legal right.

**De Jure Corporation**  A corporation that has complied substantially with each of the mandatory conditions precedent to incorporation.

**Delegation**  In constitutional law and administrative law, a process whereby a legislature effectively hands over some of its legislative power to an administrative agency that it has created, thus giving the agency power to make law within the limits set by the legislature. In contract law, a transaction whereby a person who owes a legal duty to perform under a contract appoints someone else to carry out his performance.

**Deliver**  To surrender property to another person.

**Demand**  A claim; a legal obligation; a request to perform an alleged obligation; a written statement of a claim. In corporation law, a request that the board of directors sue a person who has harmed the corporation; a prerequisite to a shareholder derivative suit.

**Demurrer**   A civil motion that attacks the plaintiff's complaint by assuming the truth of the facts stated in the complaint for purposes of the motion, and by arguing that even if these facts are true, there is no rule of law entitling the plaintiff to recovery. Roughly similar to the motion to dismiss for failure to state a claim on which relief can be granted.

**De Novo**   Anew; over again; a second time. A trial de novo, for example, is a new trial in which the entire case is retried.

**Deposition**   A form of discovery consisting of the oral examination of a party or a party's witness by the other party's attorney.

**Deputy**   A person subordinate to a public officer whose business and object is to perform the duties of the principal.

**Derivative Suit**   Also called *derivative action*. A suit to enforce a corporate right of action brought on behalf of a corporation by one or more of its shareholders.

**Descent**   Hereditary succession. It is the title whereby, upon the death of an ancestor, the heir acquires the ancestor's estate under state law.

**Detriment**   Any act or forbearance by a promisee. A loss or harm suffered in person or property.

**Devise**   In a will, a gift of real property.

**Dictum**   Language in a judicial opinion that is not necessary for the decision of the case and that, while perhaps persuasive, does not bind subsequent courts. Distinguished from *holding*.

**Directed Verdict**   A verdict issued by a judge who has, in effect, taken the case away from the jury by directing a verdict for one party. Usually, the motion for a directed verdict is made at trial by one party after the other party has finished presenting his evidence.

**Disaffirm**   In contract law, a party's exercise of his power to avoid a contract entered before the party reached the age of majority; a minor's cancellation of his contract.

**Discharge**   Release from liability.

**Discharge in Bankruptcy**   An order or decree rendered by a court in bankruptcy proceedings, the effect of which is to satisfy all debts provable against the estate of the bankrupt as of the time when the bankruptcy proceedings were initiated.

**Disclaimer**   A term in a contract whereby a party attempts to relieve itself of some potential liability associated with the contract. The most common example is the seller's attempt to disclaim liability for defects in goods that it sells.

**Discount**   A loan on an evidence of debt, where the compensation for the use of the money until the maturity of the debt is deducted from the principal and retained by the lender at the time of making the loan.

**Discount Shares**   Also called *discount stock*. Shares issued for less than their par value or stated value. See *Bonus Shares* and *Watered Shares*.

**Discovery**   A process of information-gathering that takes place before a civil trial. See *Deposition* and *Interrogatory*.

**Dishonor**   The failure to pay or accept a negotiable instrument that has been properly presented.

**Dismiss**   To order a cause, motion, or prosecution to be discontinued or quashed.

**Dissolution**   In partnership law, the change in the relation of the partners caused by any partner ceasing to be associated with the carrying on of the business.

**Distribution**   In business organization law, a business's gratuitous transfer of its assets to the owners of the business. Includes cash and property dividends and redemptions.

**Divided Court**   A court is so described when there has been a division of opinion between its members on a matter that has been submitted to it for decision.

**Dividends, Cash or Property**   A corporation's distribution of a portion of its assets to its shareholders, usually corresponding to current or historical corporate profits; unlike a redemption, it is not accompanied by a repurchase of shares.

**Dividends, Share**   Also called *stock dividends*. A corporation's pro rata issuance of shares to existing shareholders for no consideration.

**Documents of Title**   A classification of personal property that includes bills of lading, warehouse receipts, dock warrants, and dock receipts.

**Domain**   The ownership of land; immediate or absolute ownership. The public lands of a state are frequently termed the *public domain*.

**Domicile**   A place where a person lives or has his home; in a strict legal sense, the place where he has his true, fixed, permanent home and principal establishment, and to which place he has, whenever he is absent, the intention of returning.

**Donee**   A person to whom a gift is made.

**Donor**   A person who makes a gift.

**Double Jeopardy Clause**   A constitutional provision designed to protect criminal defendants from multiple prosecutions for the same offense.

**Dower**   The legal right or interest that a wife has in her husband's real estate by virtue of their marriage.

**Draft**    A written order drawn on one person by another, requesting him to pay money to a designated third person.

**Drawee**    A person on whom a draft is drawn by the drawer.

**Drawer**    The maker of a draft.

**Due Bill**    An acknowledgment of a debt in writing, not made payable to order.

**Dummy**    One posing or represented as acting for himself, but in reality acting for another. A tool or "straw man" for the real parties in interest.

**Dumping**    The selling of goods by a seller in a foreign nation at unfairly low prices.

**Durable Power of Attorney**    A power of attorney that is not affected by the principal's incapacity. See *Power of Attorney* and *Attorney-in-Fact*.

**Durable Power of Attorney for Health Care**    A durable power of attorney in which the principal specifically gives the attorney-in-fact the authority to make health care decisions for her in the event that the principal should become incompetent. Also called *health care representative*.

**Duress**    Overpowering of the will of a person by force or fear.

### E

**Earned Surplus**    Also called *retained earnings*. A balance sheet account; a corporation's profits that have not been distributed to shareholders.

**Earnest Money**    Something given as part of the purchase price to bind the bargain.

**Easement**    The right to make certain uses of another person's property or to prevent another person from making certain uses of his own property.

**Edict**    A command or prohibition promulgated by a sovereign and having the effect of law.

**E.g.**    For example.

**Ejectment**    By statute in some states, an action to recover the immediate possession of real property.

**Eleemosynary Corporation**    A corporation created for a charitable purpose or for charitable purposes.

**Emancipate**    To release; to set free. In contract law, a parent's waiver of his rights to control and receive the services of his minor child.

**Embezzlement**    A statutory offense consisting of the fraudulent conversion of another's personal property by one to whom it has been intrusted, with the intention of depriving the owner thereof, the gist of the offense being usually the violation of relations of a fiduciary character.

**Eminent Domain**    A governmental power whereby the government can take or condemn private property for a public purpose on the payment of just compensation.

**Employment at Will**    A rule stating that if an employment is not for a definite time period, either party may terminate the employment without liability at any time and for any reason.

**Enabling Legislation**    The statute by which a legislative body creates an administrative agency.

**En Banc (in Banc)**    By all the judges of a court, with all the judges of a court sitting.

**Encumbrance**    A right in a third person that diminishes the value of the land but is consistent with the passing of ownership of the land by deed.

**Endorsement**    See *Indorsement*.

**Entity Theory**    In partnership law, the view that a partnership is a legal entity distinct from the partners who own it. See *Aggregate Theory*.

**Entry**    Recordation; noting in a record; going on land; taking actual possession of land.

**Environmental Impact Statement**    A document that the National Environmental Policy Act requires federal agencies to prepare in connection with any legislative proposals or proposed actions that will significantly affect the environment.

**Equity**    A system of justice that developed in England separate from the common law courts. Few states in the United States still maintain separate equity courts, though most apply equity principles and procedures when remedies derived from the equity courts are sought. A broader meaning denotes fairness and justice. In business organization law, the capital contributions of owners plus profits that have not been distributed to the owners; stated capital plus capital surplus plus earned surplus.

**Equity of Redemption**    The right of a mortgagee to discharge the mortgage when due and to have title to the mortgaged property free and clear of the mortgage debt.

**Error**    A mistake of law or fact; a mistake of the court in the trial of an action.

**Escheat**    The reversion of land to the state in the event that a decedent dies leaving no heirs.

**Estate**    An interest in land. Property owned by a decedent at the time of his death.

**Estop**    To bar or stop.

**Estoppel**    That state of affairs that arises when one is forbidden by law from alleging or denying a fact because of his previous action or inaction.

**Et Al.**    And another or and others. An abbreviation for the Latin *et alius,* meaning and another; also of *et alii,* meaning and others.

**Eviction**   Depriving the tenant of the possession of leased premises.

**Evidence**   That which makes clear or ascertains the truth of the fact or point in issue either on the one side or the other; those rules of law whereby we determine what testimony is to be admitted and what rejected in each case and what is the weight to be given to the testimony admitted.

**Exception**   An objection; a reservation; a contradiction.

**Exclusionary Rule**   The rule that bars the admissibility in criminal proceedings of evidence seized in violation of the Fourth Amendment's prohibition against unreasonable searches and seizures.

**Exculpatory Clause**   A clause in a contract or trust instrument that excuses a party from some duty.

**Executed**   When applied to written instruments, synonymous with the word *signed*; more frequently, it means everything has been done to complete the transaction; that is, the instrument has been signed, sealed, and delivered. An executed contract is one in which the object of the contract is performed.

**Execution**   A process of enforcing a judgment, usually by having an appropriate officer seize property of the defendant and sell it at a judicial sale. The final consummation of a contract or other instrument, including completion of all the formalities needed to make it binding.

**Executive Order**   A legal rule issued by a chief executive (e.g., the president or a state governor), usually pursuant to a delegation of power from the legislature.

**Executor**   The personal representative appointed to administer the estate of a person who died leaving a valid will.

**Executory**   Not yet executed; not yet fully performed, completed, fulfilled, or carried out; to be performed wholly or in part.

**Exemption**   A release from some burden, duty, or obligation; a grace; a favor; an immunity; taken out from under the general rule, not to be like others who are not exempt.

**Exhibit**   A copy of a written instrument on which a pleading is founded, annexed to the pleading and by reference made a part of it. Any paper or thing offered in evidence and marked for identification.

**Ex Post Facto**   After the fact. The U.S. Constitution prohibits ex post facto criminal laws, meaning those that criminalize behavior that was legal when committed.

**Express Warranty**   A warranty made in words, either oral or written.

**Expropriation**   A government's taking of a business's assets, such as a manufacturing facility, usually without just compensation.

**Ex Ship**   A shipping term that does not specify a particular ship for transportation of goods but does not place the expense and risk of transportation on the seller until the goods are unloaded from whatever ship is used.

**F**

**Face Value**   The nominal or par value of an instrument as expressed on its face; in the case of a bond, this is the amount really due, including interest.

**Factor**   An agent who is employed to sell goods for a principal, usually in his own name, and who is given possession of the goods.

**False Imprisonment**   An intentional tort that prohibits the unlawful confinement of another for an appreciable time without his consent.

**FAS**   An abbreviation for the expression free alongside steamer.

**Federal Supremacy**   The ability of federal laws to defeat inconsistent state laws in case they conflict.

**Fee Simple Absolute**   The highest form of land ownership, which gives the owner the right to possess and use the land for an unlimited period of time, subject only to governmental or private restrictions, and unconditional power to dispose of the property during his lifetime or upon his death.

**Felony**   As a general rule, all crimes punishable by death or by imprisonment in a state prison.

**Fiction**   An assumption made by the law that something is true that is or may be false.

**Fiduciary**   One who holds goods in trust for another or one who holds a position of trust and confidence.

**Field Warehousing**   A method of protecting a security interest in the inventory of a debtor whereby the creditor or his agent retains the physical custody of the debtor's inventory, which is released to the debtor as he complies with the underlying security agreement.

**Financing Statement**   A document, usually a multicopy form, filed in a public office serving as constructive notice to the world that a creditor claims a security interest in collateral that belongs to a certain named debtor.

**Firm Offer**   Under the Uniform Commercial Code, a signed, written offer by a merchant containing assurances that it will be held open, and which is not revocable for the time stated in the offer, or for a reasonable time if no such time is stated.

**Fixture**   A thing that was originally personal property and that has been actually or constructively affixed to the soil itself or to some structure legally a part of the land.

**FOB**   An abbreviation of free on board.

**Force Majeure Clause**   A contract provision, commonly encountered in international agreements for the sale of goods, that excuses nonperformance that results from conditions beyond the parties' control.

**Foreclosure**   To terminate the rights of the mortgagor/owner of property.

**Foreign Corporation**   A corporation incorporated in one state doing business in another state. See *Alien Corporation.*

**Foreign Trade Corporation**   A corporation in a NME nation that is empowered by the government to conduct the whole business of exporting or importing a particular product.

**Forwarder**   A person who, having no interest in goods and no ownership or interest in the means of their carriage, undertakes, for hire, to forward them by a safe carrier to their destination.

**Franchise**   A special privilege conferred by government on individuals, and which does not belong to the citizens of a country generally, of common right. Also a contractual relationship establishing a means of marketing goods or services giving certain elements of control to the supplier (franchisor) in return for the right of the franchisee to use the supplier's tradename or trademark, usually in a specific marketing area.

**Fraud**   Misrepresentation made with knowledge of its falsity and intent to deceive. See *Misrepresentation.*

**Freeze-Out**   In corporation law, a type of oppression by which only minority shareholders are forced to sell their shares.

**Fungible Goods**   Goods any unit of which is from its nature or by mercantile custom treated as the equivalent of any other unit.

**Future Advances**   Money or other value provided to a debtor by a creditor subsequent to the time a security interest in the debtor's collateral is taken by that creditor.

**Futures**   Contracts for the sale and future delivery of stocks or commodities, wherein either party may waive delivery, and receive or pay, as the case may be, the difference in market price at the time set for delivery.

## G

**Garnishee**   Used as a noun, the third party who is subjected to the process of garnishment. Used as a verb, to institute garnishment proceedings; to cause a garnishment to be levied on the garnishee.

**Garnishment**   A statutory proceeding whereby money, property, wages, or credits of the defendant that are in the hands of a third party are seized to satisfy a judgment or legally valid claim that the plaintiff has against the defendant.

**General Partnership**   See *Partnership.*

**Gift**   A voluntary transfer of property for which the donor receives no consideration in return.

**Good Faith**   Honesty in fact; an honest intention to abstain from taking an unfair advantage of another.

**Goodwill**   The value of a business due to expected continued public patronage of the business.

**Grantee**   A person to whom a grant is made.

**Grantor**   A person who makes a grant.

**Gravamen**   The gist, essence, or central point of a legal claim or argument.

**Grey Market Goods**   Goods lawfully bearing trademarks or using patented or copyrighted material, but imported into a foreign market without the authorization of the owner of the trademark, patent, or copyright.

**Guarantor**   A person who promises to perform the same obligation as another person (called the *principal*), upon the principal's default.

**Guaranty**   An undertaking by one person to be answerable for the payment of some debt, or the due performance of some contract or duty by another person, who remains liable to pay or perform the same.

**Guardian**   A person (in some rare cases, a corporation) to whom the law has entrusted the custody and control of the person, or estate, or both, of an incompetent person.

## H

**Habeas Corpus**   Any of several common law writs having as their object to bring a party before the court or judge. The only issue it presents is whether the prisoner is restrained of his liberty by due process.

**Hearing**   The supporting of one's contentions by argument and if need be, by proof.

**Hedging**   A market transaction in which a party buys a certain quantity of a given commodity at the price current on the date of the purchase and sells an equal quantity of the same commodity for future delivery for the purpose of getting protection against loss due to fluctuation in the market.

**Heirs**   Those persons appointed by law to succeed to the estate of a decedent who has died without leaving a valid will.

**Holder**   A person in possession of a document of title or an instrument payable or indorsed to him, his order, or to bearer.

**Holder in Due Course**   A person who is a holder of a negotiable instrument who took the instrument for value, in good faith, without notice that it is overdue or has been dishonored or that there is any uncured default with respect to payment of another instrument issued as part of the same series, without notice that the instrument contains an unauthorized signature or has been altered, without notice of any claim of a property or possessory interest in it, and without notice that any party has any defense against it or claim in recoupment to it.

**Holding**   Language in a judicial opinion that is necessary for the decision the court reached and that is said to be binding on subsequent courts. Distinguished from *dictum.*

**Holding Company**   A corporation whose purpose or function is to own or otherwise hold the shares of other corporations either for investment or control.

**Holographic Will**   A will written in the handwriting of the testator.

**Homestead**   In a legal sense, the real estate occupied as a home and also the right to have it exempt from levy and forced sale. It is the land, not exceeding a prescribed amount, upon which the owner and his family reside, including the house in which they reside as an indispensable part.

**I**

**I.e.**   That is.

**Illusory**   Deceiving or intending to deceive, as by false appearances; fallacious. An illusory promise is a promise that appears to be binding but that in fact does not bind the promisor.

**Immunity**   A personal favor granted by law, contrary to the general rule.

**Impanel**   To place the names of the jurors on a panel; to make a list of the names of those persons who have been selected for jury duty; to go through the process of selecting a jury that is to try a cause.

**Implied Warranty**   A warranty created by operation of law.

**Implied Warranty of Habitability**   Implied warranty arising in lease or sale of residential real estate that the property will be fit for human habitation.

**Impossibility**   A doctrine under which a party to a contract is relieved of his or her duty to perform when that performance has become impossible because of the occurrence of an event unforeseen at the time of contracting.

**Inalienable**   Incapable of being alienated, transferred, or conveyed; nontransferable.

**In Camera**   In the judge's chambers; in private.

**Incapacity**   A legal disability, such as infancy or want of authority.

**Inception**   Initial stage. The word does not refer to a state of actual existence but to a condition of things or circumstances from which the thing may develop.

**Inchoate**   Imperfect; incipient; not completely formed.

**Incidental Damages**   See *Damages, Incidental.*

**Independent Contractor**   A person who contracts with a principal to perform some task according to his own methods, and who is not under the principal's control regarding the physical details of the work. Under the *Restatement (Second) of Agency,* an independent contractor may or may not be an agent.

**Indictment**   A finding by a grand jury that there is probable cause to believe an accused committed a crime.

**Indorsement**   Writing on the back of an instrument; the contract whereby the holder of an instrument (such as a draft, check, or note) or a document (such as a warehouse receipt or bill of lading) transfers to another person his right to such instrument and incurs the liabilities incident to the transfer.

**Infant**   See *Minor.*

**Information**   A written accusation of crime brought by a public prosecuting officer to a court without the intervention of a grand jury.

**Injunction**   An equitable remedy whereby the defendant is ordered to perform certain acts or to desist from certain acts.

**In Pari Delicto**   Equally at fault in tort or crime; in equal fault or guilt.

**In Personam**   Against a person. For example, in personam jurisdiction.

**In Re**   In the matter of.

**In Rem**   Against a thing and not against a person; concerning the condition or status of a thing; for example, in rem jurisdiction.

**Inside Information**   Confidential information possessed by a person due to his relationship with a business.

**Insolvency**   In corporation law, the inability of a business to pay its currently maturing obligations.

**Instrument**   Formal or legal documents in writing, such as contracts, deeds, wills, bonds, leases, and mortgages.

**Insurable Interest**   Any interest in property such that the owner would experience a benefit from the continued existence of the property or a loss from its destruction.

**Inter Alia**   Among other things.

**Interlocutory**   Something not final but deciding only some subsidiary matter raised while a lawsuit is pending.

**Interpleader**    An equitable remedy applicable where one fears injury from conflicting claims. Where a person does not know which of two or more persons claiming certain property held by him has a right to it, filing a bill of interpleader forces the claimants to litigate the title between themselves.

**Interrogatory**    Written questions directed to a party, answered in writing, and signed under oath.

**Inter Se**    Between or among themselves.

**Interstate**    Between or among two or more states.

**Intervening Cause**    An intervening force that plays so substantial a role in causing a particular plaintiff's injury that it relieves a negligent defendant of any responsibility for that injury. Also called *superseding cause.*

**Intervention**    A proceeding by which one not originally made a party to an action or suit is permitted, on his own application, to appear therein and join one of the original parties in maintaining his cause of action or defense, or to assert some cause of action against some or all of the parties to the proceeding as originally instituted.

**Inter Vivos**    A transaction between living persons.

**Intestate**    Having died without leaving a valid will.

**In Toto**    Wholly, completely.

**Intrastate**    Within a particular state.

**Investment Contract**    In securities law, a type of security encompassing any contract by which an investor invests in a common enterprise with an expectation of profits solely from the efforts of persons other than the investor.

**Invitee**    A person who is on private premises for a purpose connected with the business interests of the possessor of those premises, or a member of the public who is lawfully on land open to the public.

**Ipso Facto**    By the fact itself; by the very fact.

**Irrevocable Letter of Credit**    See *Letter of Credit, Irrevocable.*

**Issue**    Lineal descendants such as children and grandchildren. This category of persons includes adopted children.

**Issued Shares**    A corporation's shares that a corporation has sold to its shareholders. Includes shares repurchased by the corporation and retained as treasury shares, but not shares canceled or returned to unissued status.

**Issuer**    In securities law, a person who issues or proposes to issue a security; the person whose obligation is represented by a security.

**J**

**Joint and Several Liability**    Liability of a group of persons in which the plaintiff may sue any member of the group individually and get a judgment against that person, or may sue all members of the group collectively.

**Joint Bank Account**    A bank account of two persons so fixed that they shall be joint owners thereof during their mutual lives, and the survivor shall take the whole on the death of other.

**Joint Liability**    Liability of a group of persons in which, if one of these persons is sued, he can insist that the other liable parties be joined to the suit as codefendants, so that all must be sued collectively.

**Jointly**    Acting together or in concert or cooperating; holding in common or interdependently, not separately. Persons are jointly bound in a bond or note when both or all must be sued in one action for its enforcement, not either one at the election of the creditor.

**Joint Tenancy**    An estate held by two or more jointly, with an equal right in all to share in the enjoyments of the land during their lives. An incident of joint tenancy is the right of survivorship.

**Joint Venture**    A form of business organization identical to a partnership, except that it is engaged in a single project, not carrying on a business.

**Judgment**    A court's final resolution of a lawsuit or other proceeding submitted to it for decision.

**Judgment Lien**    The statutory lien on the real property of a judgment debtor that is created by the judgment itself. At common law, a judgment imposes no lien on the real property of the judgment debtor, and to subject the property of the debtor to the judgment, it was necessary to take out a writ called an *elegit.*

**Judgment notwithstanding the Verdict**    A judgment made by a judge contrary to a prior jury verdict whereby the judge effectively overrules the jury's verdict. Also called the *j.n.o.v.* or the *judgment non obstante veredicto.* Similar to the directed verdict, except that it occurs after the jury has issued its verdict.

**Judicial Review**    The courts' power to declare the actions of the other branches of government unconstitutional.

**Jurisdiction**    The power of a court to hear and decide a case.

**Jurisprudence**    The philosophy of law. Also sometimes used to refer to the collected positive law of some jurisdiction.

**Jury**    A body of lay persons, selected by lot, or by some other fair and impartial means, to ascertain, under the guidance of the judge, the truth in questions of fact arising either in civil litigation or a criminal process.

## K

**Kite**   To secure the temporary use of money by issuing or negotiating worthless paper and then redeeming such paper with the proceeds of similar paper. The word is also used as a noun, meaning the worthless paper thus employed.

## L

**Laches**   The established doctrine of equity that, apart from any question of statutory limitation, its courts will discourage delay and sloth in the enforcement of rights. Equity demands conscience, good faith, and reasonable diligence.

**Land Contract**   A conditional agreement for the sale and purchase of real estate in which the legal title to the property is retained by the seller until the purchaser has fulfilled the agreement, usually by completing the payment of the agreed-on purchase price.

**Larceny**   The unlawful taking and carrying away of personal property with the intent to deprive the owner of his property permanently.

**Last Clear Chance**   Under traditional tort principles, a doctrine that allowed a contributorily negligent plaintiff to recover despite his failure to exercise reasonable care for his own safety by arguing that the defendant had the superior opportunity (last clear chance) to avoid the harm.

**Law Merchant**   The custom of merchants, or lex mercatorio, that grew out of the necessity and convenience of business, and that, although different from the general rules of the common law, was engrafted into it and became a part of it. It was founded on the custom and usage of merchants.

**Leading Case**   The most significant and authoritative case regarded as having settled and determined a point of law. Often, the first case to have done so in a definitive and complete fashion.

**Leading Questions**   Questions that suggest to the witness the answer desired or those that assume a fact to be proved that is not proved, or that, embodying a material fact, allow the witness to answer by a simple negative or affirmative.

**Lease**   A contract for the possession and use of land or other property, including goods, on one side, and a recompense of rent or other income on the other; a conveyance to a person for life, or years, or at will in consideration of a return of rent or other recompense.

**Legacy**   A bequest; a testamentary gift of personal property. Sometimes incorrectly applied to a testamentary gift of real property.

**Legal**   According to the principles of law; according to the method required by statute; by means of judicial proceedings; not equitable.

**Letter of Credit**   An instrument containing a request (general or special) to pay to the bearer or person named money, or sell him or her some commodity on credit or give something of value and look to the drawer of the letter for recompense.

  **Advised**   The seller's bank acts as the seller's agent to collect against the letter of credit issued by the buyer's bank.

  **Confirmed**   The seller's bank agrees to assume liability on the letter of credit issued by the buyer's bank.

  **Irrevocable**   The issuing bank may not revoke the letter of credit issued by the buyer's bank.

  **Standby**   The seller's bank promises to pay the buyer if the seller defaults on his contract to deliver conforming goods.

**Levy**   At common law, a levy on goods consisted of an officer's entering the premises where they were and either leaving an assistant in charge of them or removing them after taking an inventory. Today, courts differ as to what is a valid levy, but by the weight of authority there must be an actual or constructive seizure of the goods. In most states, a levy on land must be made by some unequivocal act of the officer indicating the intention of singling out certain real estate for the satisfaction of the debt.

**Libel**   The defamation action appropriate to printed or written defamations, or to those that have a physical form.

**License**   A personal privilege to do some act or series of acts on the land of another, without possessing any ownership interest in the land. A permit or authorization to do something that, without a license, would be unlawful.

**Licensee**   A person lawfully on land in possession of another for purposes unconnected with the business interests of the possessor.

**Lien**   In its most extensive meaning, it is a charge on property for the payment or discharge of a debt or duty; a qualified right; a proprietary interest that, in a given case, may be exercised over the property of another.

**Life Estate**   A property interest that gives a person the right to possess and use property for a time that is measured by his lifetime or that of another person.

**Limited Partner**   An owner of a limited partnership who has no right to manage the business but who possesses liability limited to his capital contribution to the business.

**Limited Partnership**  A form of business organization that has one or more general partners who manage the business and have unlimited liability for the obligations of the business and one or more limited partners who do not manage and have limited liability.

**Liquidated Damages**  The stipulation by the parties to a contract of the sum of money to be recovered by the aggrieved party in the event of a breach of the contract by the other party.

**Liquidated Debt**  A debt that is due and certain. That is, one that is not the subject of a bona fide dispute either as to its existence or the amount that is owed.

**Lis Pendens**  A pending suit. As applied to the doctrine of lis pendens, it is the jurisdiction, power, or control that courts acquire over property involved in a suit, pending the continuance of the action, and until its final judgment.

**Listing Contract**  A so-called contract whereby an owner of real property employs a broker to procure a purchaser without giving the broker an exclusive right to sell. Under such an agreement, it is generally held that the employment may be terminated by the owner at will, and that a sale of the property by the owner terminates the employment.

**Litigant**  A party to a lawsuit.

**Living Will**  A document executed with specific legal formalities stating a person's preference that heroic life support measures should not be used if there is no hope of the person's recovery.

**Long-Arm Statute**  A state statute that grants to a state's courts broad authority to exercise jurisdiction over out-of-state persons who have contacts with the state.

**Looting**  In corporation law, the transfer of a corporation's assets to its managers or controlling shareholders at less than fair value.

## M

**Magistrate**  A word commonly applied to the lower judicial officers such as justices of the peace, police judges, town recorders, and other local judicial functionaries. In a broader sense, a magistrate is a public civil officer invested with some part of the legislative, executive, or judicial power given by the Constitution. The president of the United States is the chief magistrate of the nation.

**Maker**  A person who makes or executes an instrument. The signer of an instrument.

**Malfeasance**  The doing of an act that a person ought not to do at all. It is to be distinguished from misfeas-ance—the improper doing of an act that a person might lawfully do.

**Malicious Prosecution**  An intentional tort designed to protect against the wrongful initiation of criminal proceedings.

**Mandamus**  We command. It is a command issuing from a competent jurisdiction, in the name of the state or sovereign, directed to some inferior court, officer, corporation, or person, requiring the performance of a particular duty therein specified, which duty results from the official station of the party to whom it is directed, or from operation of law.

**Margin**  A deposit by a buyer in stocks with a seller or a stockbroker, as security to cover fluctuations in the market in reference to stocks that the buyer has purchased, but for which he has not paid. Commodities are also traded on margin.

**Marshals**  Ministerial officers belonging to the executive department of the federal government, who with their deputies have the same powers of executing the laws of the United States in each state as the sheriffs and their deputies in such state may have in executing the laws of that state.

**Material**  Important. In securities law, a fact is material if a reasonable person would consider it important in his decision to purchase shares or to vote shares.

**Materialman's Lien**  A claim created by law for the purpose of securing a priority of payment of the price or value of materials furnished in erecting or repairing a building or other structure.

**Mechanic's Lien**  A claim created by law for the purpose of securing a priority of payment of the price or value of work performed and materials furnished in erecting or repairing a building or other structure; as such, it attaches to the land as well as to the buildings erected therein.

**Memorandum**  A writing.

**Mens Rea**  A guilty mind; criminal intent.

**Merchant**  Under the Uniform Commercial Code, one who regularly deals in goods of the kind sold in the contract at issue, or holds himself out as having special knowledge or skill relevant to such goods, or who makes the sale through an agent who regularly deals in such goods or claims such knowledge or skill.

**Merchantable**  Of good quality and salable, but not necessarily the best. As applied to articles sold, the word requires that the article shall be such as is usually sold in the market, of medium quality, and bringing the average price.

**Merger**  In corporation law, traditionally, a transaction by which one corporation acquires another corporation, with the acquiring corporation being owned by the shareholders of both corporations and the acquired corporation going out of existence. Today, loosely applied to any negotiated acquisition of one corporation by another.

**Merger Clause**   A contract clause providing that the written contract is the complete expression of the parties' agreement. Also called *integration clause.*

**Mining Partnership**   A form of business organization used for mining and drilling mineral resources that is identical to a partnership, except that mining partnership interests are freely transferable and the death or bankruptcy of a mining partner does not cause a dissolution.

**Minor**   A person who has not reached the age at which the law recognizes a general contractual capacity (called *majority*), which is 18 in most states.

**Misdemeanor**   Any crime that is punishable neither by death nor by imprisonment in a state prison.

**Misrepresentation**   The assertion of a fact that is not in accord with the truth. A contract can be rescinded on the ground of misrepresentation when the assertion relates to a material fact or is made fraudulently and the other party actually and justifiably relies on the assertion.

**Mistrial**   An invalid trial due to lack of jurisdiction, error in selection of jurors, or some other fundamental requirement.

**Mitigation of Damages**   A reduction in the amount of damages due to extenuating circumstances.

**Mortgage**   A conveyance of property to secure the performance of some obligation, the conveyance to be void on the due performance thereof.

**Mortgagee**   The creditor to whom property has been mortgaged to secure the performance of an obligation.

**Mortgagor**   The owner of the property that has been mortgaged or pledged as security for a debt.

**Motion to Dismiss**   A motion made by the defendant in a civil case to defeat the plaintiff's case, usually after the complaint or all the pleadings have been completed. The most common form of motion to dismiss is the motion to dismiss for failure to state a claim on which relief can be granted, which attacks the legal sufficiency of the plaintiff's complaint. See *Demurrer.*

**Motive**   The cause or reason that induced a person to commit a crime.

**Mutuality**   Reciprocal obligations of the parties required to make a contract binding on either party.

### N

**National Ambient Air Quality Standards**   Federally established air pollution standards designed to protect the public health and welfare.

**Natural Law**   A body of allegedly existing ethical rules or principles that is morally superior to positive law and that prevails over positive law in case of a clash between it and the natural law. See *Positive Law.*

**Necessaries**   That which is reasonably necessary for a minor's proper and suitable maintenance, in view of the income level and social position of the minor's family.

**Negligence**   The omission to do something that a reasonable person, guided by those considerations that ordinarily regulate human affairs, would do, or doing something that a prudent and reasonable person would not do.

**Negligence Per Se**   The doctrine that provides that a conclusive presumption of breach of duty arises when a defendant has violated a statute and thereby caused a harm the statute was designed to prevent to a person the statute was designed to protect.

**Negotiable**   Capable of being transferred by indorsement or delivery so as to give the holder a right to sue in his or her own name and to avoid certain defenses against the payee.

**Negotiable Instrument**   An instrument that may be transferred or negotiated, so that the holder may maintain an action thereon in his own name.

**Negotiation**   The transfer of an instrument in such form that the transferee becomes a holder.

**NME**   A nonmarket economy; a socialist economy in which a central government owns and controls all significant means of production, thereby setting prices and the levels of production.

**Nolo Contendere**   A no contest plea by the defendant in a criminal case that has much the same effect as a guilty plea but that cannot be used as an admission of guilt in other legal proceedings.

**Nominal Damages**   See *Damages, Nominal.*

**Non Compos Mentis**   Mentally incompetent.

**Nonfeasance**   In the law of agency, the total omission or failure of an agent to enter on the performance of some distinct duty or undertaking that he or she has agreed with the principal to do.

**Non Obstante Veredicto**   Notwithstanding the verdict. J.n.o.v. See *Judgment notwithstanding the Verdict.*

**No-Par Value Stock**   Stock of a corporation having no face or par value.

**Novation**   A mutual agreement, between all parties concerned, for the discharge of a valid existing obligation by the substitution of a new valid obligation on the part of the debtor or another, or a like agreement for the discharge of a debtor to his creditor by the substitution of a new creditor.

**Nudum Pactum**    A naked promise, a promise for which there is no consideration.

**Nuisance**    That which endangers life or health, gives offense to the senses, violates the laws of decency, or obstructs the reasonable and comfortable use of property.

**Nuncupative Will**    An oral will. Such wills are valid in some states, but only under limited circumstances and to a limited extent.

**O**

**Oath**    Any form of attestation by which a person signifies that he is bound in conscience to perform an act faithfully and truthfully.

**Obiter Dictum**    That which is said in passing; a rule of law set forth in a court's opinion but not necessary to decide the case. See *Dictum.*

**Objection**    In the trial of a case the formal remonstrance made by counsel to something that has been said or done, in order to obtain the court's ruling thereon.

**Obligee**    A person to whom another is bound by a promise or other obligation; a promisee.

**Obligor**    A person who is bound by a promise or other obligation; a promisor.

**Offer**    A proposal by one person to another that is intended to create legal relations on acceptance by the person to whom it is made.

**Offeree**    A person to whom an offer is made.

**Offeror**    A person who makes an offer.

**Opinion**    The opinion of the court represents merely the reasons for its judgment, while the decision of the court is the judgment itself.

**Oppression**    The officers, directors, or controlling shareholder's isolation of one group of shareholders for disadvantageous treatment to the benefit of another group of shareholders.

**Option**    A separate contract in which an offeror agrees not to revoke her offer for a stated period of time in exchange for some valuable consideration.

**Option Agreement**    A share transfer restriction granting a corporation or its shareholders an option to buy a selling shareholder's shares at a price determined by the agreement.

**Ordinance**    A legislative enactment of a county or an incorporated city or town.

**Original Jurisdiction**    The power to decide a case as a trial court.

**Outstanding Shares**    A corporation's shares currently held by shareholders.

**Overdraft**    The withdrawal from a bank by a depositor of money in excess of the amount of money he or she has on deposit there.

**Overdue**    When an instrument is not paid when due or at maturity.

**Overplus**    That which remains; a balance left over.

**Owner's Risk**    A term employed by common carriers in bills of lading and shipping receipts to signify that the carrier does not assume responsibility for the safety of the goods.

**P**

**Par**    Par means equal, and par value means a value equal to the face of a bond or a stock certificate.

**Parent Corporation**    A corporation that owns a controlling interest of another corporation, called a *subsidiary corporation.*

**Parol**    Oral; verbal; by word of mouth.

**Parol Evidence**    Where a written contract exists, evidence about promises or statements made prior to or during the execution of the writing that are not contained in the written contract.

**Parties**    All persons who are interested in the subject matter of an action and who have a right to make defense, control the proceedings, examine and cross-examine witnesses, and appeal from the judgment.

**Partition**    A proceeding the object of which is to enable those who own property as joint tenants or tenants in common to put an end to the tenancy so as to vest in each a sole estate in specific property or an allotment of the lands and tenements. If a division of the estate is impracticable, the estate ought to be sold and the proceeds divided.

**Partners**    The owners of a partnership.

**Partnership**    A form of business organization; specifically, an association of two or more persons to carry on as co-owners of a business for profit.

**Partnership by Estoppel**    The appearance of partnership when there is no partnership; it arises when a person misleads a second person into believing that the first person is a partner of a third person; a theory that allows the second person to recover from the first person all reasonable damages the second person has suffered due to his reliance on the appearance of partnership.

**Partnership Interest**    A partner's ownership interest in a partnership.

**Party to Be Charged**    The person against whom enforcement of a contract is sought; the person who is asserting the statute of frauds as a defense.

**Par Value**   An arbitrary dollar amount assigned to shares by the articles of incorporation, representing the minimum amount of consideration for which the corporation may issue the shares and the portion of consideration that must be allocated to the stated capital amount.

**Patent**   A patent for land is a conveyance of title to government lands by the government; a patent of an invention is the right of monopoly secured by statute to those who invent or discover new and useful devices and processes.

**Patentee**   The holder of a patent.

**Pawn**   A pledge; a bailment of personal property as security for some debt or engagement, redeemable on certain terms, and with an implied power of sale on default.

**Payee**   A person to whom a payment is made or is made payable.

**Pecuniary**   Financial; pertaining or relating to money.

**Pendente Lite**   During the litigation.

**Per Capita**   A distribution of property in which each member of a group shares equally.

**Per Curiam**   By the court as a whole, without an opinion signed by a particular judge.

**Peremptory Challenge**   A challenge to a proposed juror that a defendant may make as an absolute right, and that cannot be questioned by either opposing counsel or the court.

**Perfection**   The process or method by which a secured party obtains a priority in certain collateral belonging to a debtor against creditors or claimants of a debtor; it usually entails giving notice of the security interest, such as by taking possession or filing a financial statement.

**Performance**   The fulfillment of a contractual duty.

**Periodic Tenancy**   The tenancy that exists when the landlord and tenant agree that rent will be paid in regular successive intervals until notice to terminate is given but do not agree on a specific duration of the lease. A typical periodic tenancy is a tenancy from month to month.

**Perjury**   The willful and corrupt false swearing or affirming, after an oath lawfully administered, in the course of a judicial or quasi-judicial proceeding, as to some matter material to the issue or point in question.

**Per Se**   In itself or as such.

**Personal Property**   All objects and rights, other than real property, that can be owned. See *Real Property*.

**Per Stirpes**   A distribution in which each surviving descendant divides the share that his or her parent would have taken if the parent had survived. Also called *by right of representation*.

**Petition**   In equity pleading, a petition is in the nature of a pleading (at least when filed by a stranger to the suit) and forms a basis for independent action.

**Petition (Bankruptcy)**   The document filed with the appropriate federal court that initiates a bankruptcy proceeding. It may be either a voluntary petition (i.e., filed by the debtor) or an involuntary petition (i.e., filed by creditors).

**Piercing the Corporate Veil**   Holding a shareholder responsible for acts of a corporation due to a shareholder's domination and improper use of the corporation.

**Plaintiff**   The party who sues in a civil case.

**Plaintiff in Error**   The unsuccessful party to the action who prosecutes a writ of error in a higher court.

**Plea**   A plea is an answer to a declaration or complaint or any material allegation of fact therein that, if untrue, would defeat the action. In criminal procedure, a plea is the matter that the accused, on his arraignment, alleges in answer to the charge against him.

**Pleadings**   The documents the parties file with the court when they state their claims and counterarguments early in a civil case. Examples include the complaint and the answer.

**Pledge**   A pawn; a bailment of personal property as security for some debt or engagement, redeemable on certain terms, and with an implied power of sale on default.

**Pledgee**   A person to whom personal property is pledged by a pledgor.

**Pledgor**   A person who makes a pledge of personal property to a pledgee.

**Police Power**   The states' power to regulate to promote the public health, safety, morals, and welfare.

**Positive Law**   Laws actually and specifically enacted or adopted by proper authority for the government of a jural society as distinguished from principles of morality or laws of honor.

**Possession**   Respecting real property, exclusive dominion and control such as owners of like property usually exercise over it. Manual control of personal property either as owner or as one having a qualified right in it.

**Postdated Check**   A check dated with a date later than its date of issue.

**Power of Attorney**   A written authorization by a principal to an agent to perform specified acts on behalf of the principal. See *Attorney-in-Fact*.

**Precedent**   A past judicial decision relied on as authority in a present case.

**Preemptive Right** A shareholder's option to purchase new issuances of shares in proportion to the shareholder's current ownership of the corporation.

**Preference** The act of a debtor in paying or securing one or more of his creditors in a manner more favorable to them than to other creditors or to the exclusion of such other creditors. In the absence of statute, a preference is perfectly good, but to be legal it must be bona fide, and not a mere subterfuge of the debtor to secure a future benefit to himself or to prevent the application of his property to his debts.

**Preferential** Having priority.

**Preferred Shareholders** Shareholders who have dividend and liquidation preferences over other classes of shareholders, usually common shareholders.

**Prenuptial Contract** A contract between prospective marriage partners respecting matters such as property ownership and division.

**Preponderance** Most; majority; more probable than not.

**Prerogative** A special power, privilege, or immunity, usually used in reference to an official or his office.

**Presentment** A demand for acceptance or payment of a negotiable instrument made on the maker, acceptor, drawee, or other payor by or on behalf of the holder.

**Presumption** A term used to signify that which may be assumed without proof, or taken for granted. It is asserted as a self-evident result of human reason and experience.

**Pretermitted** In the law of wills, an heir born after the execution of the testator's will.

**Prima Facie** At first sight; a fact that is presumed to be true unless disproved by contrary evidence.

**Prima Facie Case** A case sufficiently strong that, unless rebutted by the defendant in some fashion, it entitles the plaintiff to recover against the defendant.

**Principal** In agency law, one under whose direction an agent acts and for whose benefit that agent acts.

**Priority** Having precedence or the better right.

**Privilege** Generally, a legal right to engage in conduct that would otherwise result in legal liability. Privileges are commonly classified as absolute (unqualified) or conditional (qualified). Occasionally, privilege is also used to denote a legal right to refrain from particular behavior (e.g., the constitutional privilege against self-incrimination).

**Privity of Contract** The existence of a direct contractual relation between two parties.

**Probate** A term used to include all matters of which probate courts have jurisdiction, which in many states are the estates of deceased persons and of persons under guardianship.

**Procedural Law** The body of law controlling public bodies such as courts, as they create and enforce rules of substantive law. See *Substantive Law.*

**Proceeds** Whatever is received on the sale, exchange, collection, or other disposition of collateral.

**Process** Generally, the summons or notice of beginning of suit.

**Proffer** To offer for acceptance or to make a tender of.

**Profit** An interest in land giving a person the right to enter land owned by another and remove natural resources (e.g., timber) from the land. Also called *profit à prendre.*

**Promisee** The person to whom a promise is made.

**Promisor** A person who makes a promise to another; a person who promises.

**Promissory Estoppel** An equitable doctrine that protects those who foreseeably and reasonably rely on the promises of others by enforcing such promises when enforcement is necessary to avoid injustice, even though one or more of the elements normally required for an enforceable agreement is absent.

**Promissory Note** Commercial paper or instrument in which the maker promises to pay a specific sum of money to another person, to his order, or to bearer.

**Promoter** A person who incorporates a business, organizes its initial management, and raises its initial capital.

**Property** Something that is capable of being owned. A right or interest associated with something that gives the owner the ability to exercise dominion over it.

**Pro Rata** Proportionate; in proportion.

**Prospectus** In securities law, a document given to prospective purchasers of a security that contains information about an issuer of securities and the securities being issued.

**Pro Tanto** For so much; to such an extent.

**Proximate Cause** A legal limitation on a negligent wrongdoer's liability for the actual consequences of his actions. Such wrongdoers are said to be relieved of responsibility for consequences that are too remote or not the proximate result of their actions. Various tests for proximate cause are employed by the courts.

**Proxy** A person who is authorized to vote the shares of another person. Also, the written authorization empowering a person to vote the shares of another person.

**Pseudoforeign Corporation** A corporation incorporated under the laws of a state but doing most of its business in one other state.

**Publicly Held Corporation**    A corporation owned by a large number of widely dispersed shareholders.

**Punitive Damages**    See *Damages, Punitive.*

**Purchase Money Security Interest**    A security interest that is (1) taken or retained by the seller of collateral to secure all or part of its purchase price or (2) taken by a debtor to acquire rights in or the use of the collateral if the value is so used.

**Put**    A type of option permitting a person to sell a fixed number of securities at a fixed price at a specified time. See *Call.*

## Q

**Qualified Acceptance**    A conditional or modified acceptance. In order to create a contract, an acceptance must accept the offer substantially as made; hence, a qualified acceptance is no acceptance at all, is treated by the courts as a rejection of the offer made, and is in effect an offer by the offeree, which the offeror may, if he chooses, accept and thus create a contract.

**Quantum Meruit**    As much as is deserved. A part of a common law action in assumpsit for the value of services rendered.

**Quash**    To vacate or make void.

**Quasi-Contract**    The doctrine by which courts imply, as a matter of law, a promise to pay the reasonable value of goods or services when the party receiving such goods or services has knowingly done so under circumstances that make it unfair to retain them without paying for them.

**Quasi-Judicial**    Acts of public officers involving investigation of facts and drawing conclusions from them as a basis of official action.

**Quiet Title, Action to**    An action to establish a claimant's title in land by requiring adverse claimants to come into court to prove their claim or to be barred from asserting it later.

**Quitclaim Deed**    A deed conveying only the right, title, and interest of the grantor in the property described, as distinguished from a deed conveying the property itself.

**Quorum**    That number of persons, shares represented, or officers who may lawfully transact the business of a meeting called for that purpose.

**Quo Warranto**    By what authority. The name of a writ (and also of the whole pleading) by which the government commences an action to recover an office or franchise from the person or corporation in possession of it.

## R

**Ratification**    The adoption or affirmance by a person of a prior act that did not bind him.

**Real Property**    The earth's crust and all things firmly attached to it.

**Rebuttal**    Testimony addressed to evidence produced by the opposite party; rebutting evidence.

**Receiver**    One appointed by a court to take charge of a business or the property of another during litigation to preserve it and/or to dispose of it as directed by the court.

**Recklessness**    Behavior that indicates a conscious disregard for a known high risk of probable harm to others.

**Recognizance**    At common law, an obligation entered into before some court of record or magistrate duly authorized, with a condition to do some particular act, usually to appear and answer to a criminal accusation. Being taken in open court and entered on the order book, it was valid without the signature or seal of any of the obligors.

**Recorder**    A public officer of a town or county charged with the duty of keeping the record books required by law to be kept in his or her office and of receiving and causing to be copied in such books such instruments as by law are entitled to be recorded.

**Redemption**    The buying back of one's property after it has been sold. The right to redeem property sold under an order or decree of court is purely a privilege conferred by, and does not exist independently of, statute.

**Redemption Right**    Also called a call. In corporation law, the right of a corporation to repurchase shares held by existing shareholders.

**Redress**    Remedy; indemnity; reparation.

**Reformation**    An equitable remedy in which a court effectively rewrites the terms of a contract.

**Rejection**    In contract law, an express or implied manifestation of an offeree's unwillingness to contract on the terms of an offer. In sales law, a buyer's refusal to accept goods because they are defective or nonconforming.

**Release**    The giving up or abandoning of a claim or right to a person against whom the claim exists or the right is to be enforced or exercised. It is the discharge of a debt by the act of the party, in distinction from an extinguishment that is a discharge by operation of law.

**Remainderman**    One who is entitled to the remainder of the estate after a particular estate carved out of it has expired.

**Remand**    A process whereby an appellate court returns the case to a lower court (usually a trial court) for proceedings not inconsistent with the appellate court's decision.

**Remedy**    The appropriate legal form of relief by which a remediable right may be enforced.

**Remittitur**    The certificate of reversal issued by an appellate court upon reversing the order or judgment appealed from.

**Repatriation**    An investor's removal to the investor's nation of profits from his investment in a foreign nation.

**Replevin**    A common law action by which the owner recovers possession of his own goods.

**Repudiation**    Indicating to another party to a contract that the party does not intend to perform his obligations.

**Res**    The thing; the subject matter of a suit; the property involved in the litigation; a matter; property; the business; the affair; the transaction.

**Rescind**    As the word is applied to contracts, to terminate the contract as to future transactions or to annul the contract from the beginning.

**Rescission**    The rescinding or cancellation of a contract or transaction. In general, its effect is to restore the parties to their original precontractual position.

**Residue**    Residuary; all that portion of the estate of a testator of which no effectual disposition has been made by his will otherwise than in the residuary clause.

**Res Ipsa Loquitur**    Literally, the thing speaks for itself. A doctrine that, in some circumstances, gives rise to an inference that a defendant was negligent and that his negligence was the cause of the plaintiff's injury.

**Res Judicata**    A matter that has been adjudicated; that which is definitely settled by a judicial decision.

**Respondeat Superior**    A legal doctrine making an employer (or master) liable for the torts of an employee (servant) that are committed within the scope of the employee's employment.

**Respondent**    A term often used to describe the party charged in an administrative proceeding. The party adverse to the appellant in a case appealed to a higher court. In this sense, often synonymous with *appellee.*

**Restatement(s)**    Collections of legal rules produced by the American Law Institute, covering certain subject matter areas. Although *Restatements* are often persuasive to courts, they are not legally binding unless adopted by the highest court of a particular state.

**Restitution**    A remedy whereby one is able to obtain the return of that which he has given the other party, or an amount of money equivalent to that which he has given the other party.

**Restrictive Covenant**    An agreement restricting the use of real property.

**Reverse**    To reject or overturn a judgment or order of a court. An appellate court, for example, may reverse the decision of a trial court. See *Affirm.*

**Revocation**    In general, the recalling or voiding of a prior action. In contract law, the withdrawal of an offer by the offeror prior to effective acceptance by the offeree.

**Right**    An interest given and protected by law. In corporation law, an option to purchase shares given to existing shareholders, permitting them to buy quantities of newly issued securities in proportion to their current ownership.

**Right of Appraisal**    See *Appraisal, Right of.*

**Right of First Refusal**    In corporation law, a share transfer restriction granting a corporation or its shareholders an option to match the offer that a selling shareholder receives for her shares. See also *Option Agreement.*

**Right of Survivorship**    A feature of some types of co-ownership of property causing a co-owner's interest in property to be transferred on his death immediately and by operation of law to his surviving co-owner(s). See *Tenancy by the Entirety, Tenant in Partnership,* and *Joint Tenancy.*

**Riparian**    Pertaining to or situated on the bank of a river.

## S

**Sale of Goods**    The transfer of ownership to tangible personal property in exchange for money, other goods, or the performance of service.

**Sale on Approval**    A conditional sale that is to become final only in case the buyer, after a trial, approves or is satisfied with the article sold.

**Sale or Return**    A contract in which the seller delivers a quantity of goods to the buyer on the understanding that if the buyer desires to retain, use, or sell any portion of the goods, he will consider such part as having been sold to him, and that he will return the balance or hold it as bailee for the seller.

**Sanction**    The penalty that will be incurred by a wrongdoer for the violation of a law.

**Satisfaction**    A performance of the terms of an accord. If such terms require a payment of a sum of money, then satisfaction means that such payment has been made.

**Scienter**    In cases of fraud and deceit, the word means knowledge on the part of the person making the representations, at the time when they are made, that they are false. In an action for deceit, scienter must be proved.

**S Corporation**    Also called *Subchapter S corporation.* A close corporation whose shareholders have elected to be taxed essentially like partners are taxed under federal income tax law.

**Seal** At common law, a seal is an impression on wax or some other tenacious material, but in modern practice the letters *l.s.* (locus sigilli) or the word *seal* enclosed in a scroll, either written, or printed, and acknowledged in the body of the instrument to be a seal, are often used as substitutes.

**Security** An instrument commonly dealt with in the securities markets or commonly recognized as a medium of investment and evidencing an obligation of an issuer or a share, participation, or other interest in an enterprise.

**Security Agreement** An agreement that creates or provides a security interest or lien on personal property. A term used in the UCC including a wide range of transactions in the nature of chattel mortgages, conditional sales, and so on.

**Security Interest** A lien given by a debtor to his creditor to secure payment or performance of a debt or obligation.

**Service** As applied to a process of courts, the word ordinarily implies something in the nature of an act or proceeding adverse to the party served, or of a notice to him.

**Set off** That right that exists between two parties, each of whom, under an independent contract, owes an ascertained amount to the other, to calculate their respective debts by way of mutual deduction, so that, in any action brought for the larger debt, the residue only, after such deduction, shall be recovered.

**Settlor** A person who creates a trust. Also called *trustor.*

**Severable Contract** A contract that is not entire or indivisible. If the consideration is single, the contract is entire; but if it is expressly or by necessary implication apportioned, the contract is severable. The question is ordinarily determined by inquiring whether the contract embraces one or more subject matters, whether the obligation is due at the same time to the same person, and whether the consideration is entire or apportioned.

**Share** An equity security, representing a shareholder's ownership of a corporation.

**Share Dividend** See *Dividends, Share.*

**Shareholder** Also called *stockholder.* An owner of a corporation, who has no inherent right to manage the corporation but has liability limited to his capital contribution.

**Share Split** Also called *stock split.* Traditionally, a corporation's dividing existing shares into two or more shares, thereby increasing the number of authorized, issued, and outstanding shares and reducing their par value. In modern corporation law, treated like a share dividend.

**Sight** A term signifying the date of the acceptance or that of protest for the nonacceptance of a bill of exchange; for example, 10 days after sight.

**Sinking Fund** A fund established by an issuer of securities to accumulate funds to repurchase the issuer's securities.

**Situs** Location; local position; the place where a person or thing is, is his situs. Intangible property has no actual situs, but it may have a legal situs, and for the purpose of taxation, its legal situs is at the place where it is owned and not at the place where it is owed.

**Slander** The defamation action appropriate to oral defamation.

**Sole Proprietor** The owner of a sole proprietorship.

**Sole Proprietorship** A form of business under which one person owns and controls the business.

**Sovereign Immunity** Generally, the idea that the sovereign (or state) may not be sued unless it consents to be sued. In antitrust law, the statutory immunity from antitrust liability for governmental actions that foreign governments enjoy under the Foreign Sovereign Immunities Act of 1976.

**Special Damages** See *Damages, Special.*

**Specific Performance** A contract remedy whereby the defendant is ordered to perform according to the terms of his contract.

**Stale Check** A check more than six months past its date of issue.

**Standby Letter of Credit** See *Letter of Credit, Standby.*

**Standing** The legal requirement that anyone seeking to challenge a particular action in court must demonstrate that such action substantially affects his legitimate interests before he will be entitled to bring suit.

**Stare Decisis** A doctrine whereby a court is said to be bound to follow past cases that are like the present case on the facts and on the legal issues it presents, and that are issued by an authoritative court.

**Stated Capital** Also called *capital stock.* A balance sheet account; shareholders' capital contributions representing the par value of par shares or stated value of no-par shares.

**Stated Value** An arbitrary dollar amount assigned to shares by the board of directors, representing the minimum amount of consideration for which the corporation may issue the shares and the portion of consideration that must be allocated to the stated capital account.

**State Implementation Plan**   A document prepared by states in which the emissions to the air from individual sources are limited legally so that the area will meet the national ambient air quality standards.

**Status Quo**   The existing state of things. In contract law, returning a party to status quo or status quo ante means putting him in the position he was in before entering the contract.

**Statute of Frauds**   A statute that provides that no lawsuit may be brought to enforce certain classes of contracts unless there is a written note or memorandum signed by the party against whom enforcement is sought or by his agent.

**Statute of Limitations**   A statute that requires that certain classes of lawsuits must be brought within defined limits of time after the right to begin them accrued or the right to bring the lawsuit is lost.

**Stipulation**   An agreement between opposing counsel in a pending action, usually required to be made in open court and entered on the minutes of the court, or else to be in writing and filed in the action, ordinarily entered into for the purpose of avoiding delay, trouble, or expense in the conduct of the action.

**Stock**   A business's inventory. Also, as used in corporation and securities law, see *Share*.

**Stock Dividend**   See *Dividends, Share*.

**Stockholder**   See *Shareholder*.

**Stock Split**   See *Share Split*.

**Stoppage in Transitu**   A right that the vendor of goods on credit has to recall them, or retake them, on the discovery of the insolvency of the vendee. It continues so long as the carrier remains in the possession and control of the goods or until there has been an actual or constructive delivery to the vendee, or some third person has acquired a bona fide right in them.

**Stop-Payment Order**   A request made by the drawer of a check to the drawee asking that the order to pay not be followed.

**Straight Voting**   A form of voting for directors that ordinarily permits a shareholder to cast a number of votes equal to the number of shares he owns for as many nominees as there are directors to be elected. See *Cumulative Voting*.

**Strict Liability**   Legal responsibility placed on an individual for the results of his actions irrespective of whether he was culpable or at fault.

**Strike Suit**   In corporation law, a derivative suit motivated primarily by an intent to gain an out-of-court settlement for the suing shareholder personally or to earn large attorney's fees for lawyers, rather than to obtain a recovery for the corporation.

**Subchapter S Corporation**   See *S Corporation*.

**Sub Judice**   Before a court.

**Sublease**   A transfer of some but not all of a tenant's remaining right to possess property under a lease.

**Sub Nom.**   Under the name of.

**Subpoena**   A process for compelling a witness to appear before a court and give testimony.

**Subrogation**   The substitution of one person in the place of another with reference to a lawful claim or right, frequently referred to as the doctrine of substitution. It is a device adopted or invented by equity to compel the ultimate discharge of a debt or obligation by the person who in good conscience ought to pay it.

**Subscription**   In corporation law, a promise by a person to purchase from a corporation a specified number of shares at a specified price.

**Subsidiary Corporation**   A corporation owned and controlled by another corporation, called a *parent corporation*.

**Substantive Law**   The body of law setting out rights and duties that affect how people behave in organized social life. See *Procedural Law*.

**Sui Generis**   Of its own kind, unique, peculiar to itself.

**Summary Judgment**   A method of reaching a judgment in a civil case before trial. The standard for granting a motion for summary judgment is that there be no significant issue of material fact and that the moving party be entitled to judgment as a matter of law.

**Summary Proceedings**   Proceedings, usually statutory, in the course of which many formalities are dispensed with. But such proceedings are not concluded without proper investigation of the facts, or without notice, or an opportunity to be heard by the person alleged to have committed the act, or whose property is sought to be affected.

**Summons**   A writ or process issued and served on a defendant in a civil action for the purpose of securing his appearance in the action.

**Superseding Cause**   See *Intervening Cause*.

**Supra**   Above; above mentioned; in addition to.

**Surety**   A person who promises to perform the same obligation as another person (the principal) and who is jointly liable along with the principal for that obligation's performance. See *Guarantor*.

**T**

**T/A**   Trading as, indicating the use of a trade name.

**Tacking**   The adding together of successive periods of adverse possession of persons in privity with each other, in order to constitute one continuous adverse possession for the time required by the statute, to establish title.

**Takeover**　A tender offer; also applied generally to any acquisition of one business by another business.

**Tangible**　Having a physical existence; real; substantial; evident.

**Tariff**　A tax or duty imposed on goods by a nation when the goods are imported into that nation.

**Tax Haven**　A nation that has no or minimal taxation of personal, business, and investment income.

**Tenancy**　General term indicating a possessory interest in property. In landlord-tenant law, a property owner's conveyance to another person of the right to possess the property exclusively for a period of time.

**Tenancy at Sufferance**　The leasehold interest that occurs when a tenant remains in possession of property after the expiration of a lease.

**Tenancy at Will**　A leasehold interest that occurs when property is leased for an indefinite period of time and is terminable at the will of either landlord or tenant.

**Tenancy by the Entirety**　A form of co-ownership of property by a married couple that gives the owners a right of survivorship and cannot be severed during life by the act of only one of the parties.

**Tenancy for a Term**　A leasehold interest that results when the landlord and tenant agree on a specific duration for a lease and fix the date on which the tenancy will terminate.

**Tenancy in Common**　A form of co-ownership of property that is freely disposable both during life and at death, and in which the co-owners have undivided interests in the property and equal rights to possess the property.

**Tenancy in Partnership**　The manner in which partners co-own partnership property, much like a tenancy in common, except that partners have a right of survivorship.

**Tender**　An unconditional offer of payment, consisting in the actual production in money or legal tender of a sum not less than the amount due.

**Tender Offer**　A public offer by a bidder to purchase a subject company's shares directly from its shareholders at a specified price for a fixed period of time.

**Testament**　A will; the disposition of one's property to take effect after death.

**Testator**　A deceased person who died leaving a will.

**Testimony**　In some contexts, the word bears the same import as the word *evidence,* but in most connections it has a much narrower meaning. Testimony is the words heard from the witness in court, and evidence is what the jury considers it worth.

**Thin Capitalization**　In corporation law, a ground for piercing the corporate veil due to the shareholders' contributing too little capital to the corporation in relation to its needs.

**Third Party Beneficiary**　A person who is not a party to a contract but who has the right to enforce it because the parties to the contract made the contract with the intent to benefit him.

**Title**　Legal ownership; also, a document evidencing legal rights to real or personal property.

**Tombstone Advertisement**　A brief newspaper advertisement alerting prospective shareholders that an issuer is offering to sell the securities described in the advertisement.

**Tort**　A private (civil) wrong against a person or his property.

**Tortfeasor**　A person who commits a tort; a wrongdoer.

**Tortious**　Partaking of the nature of a tort; wrongful; injurious.

**Trade Fixtures**　Articles of personal property that have been annexed to real property leased by a tenant during the term of the lease and that are necessary to the carrying on of a trade.

**Trademark**　A distinctive word, name, symbol, device, or combination thereof, which enables consumers to identify favored products or services and which may find protection under state or federal law.

**Trade Secret**　A secret formula, pattern, process, program, device, method, technique, or compilation of information that is used in its owner's business and affords that owner a competitive advantage. Trade secrets are protected by state law.

**Transcript**　A copy of a writing.

**Transferee**　A person to whom a transfer is made.

**Transferor**　A person who makes a transfer.

**Treasury Shares**　Previously outstanding shares repurchased by a corporation that are not canceled or restored to unissued status.

**Treble Damages**　See *Damages, Treble.*

**Trespass**　An unauthorized entry on another's property.

**Trial**　An examination before a competent tribunal, according to the law of the land, of the facts or law put in issue in a cause, for the purpose of determining such issue. When the court hears and determines any issue of fact or law for the purpose of determining the rights of the parties, it may be considered a trial.

**Trust**　A legal relationship in which a person who has legal title to property has the duty to hold it for the use or benefit of another person. The term is also used in a general sense to mean confidence reposed in one person by another.

**Trustee**    A person in whom property is vested in trust for another.

**Trustee in Bankruptcy**    The federal bankruptcy act defines the term as an officer, and he is an officer of the courts in a certain restricted sense, but not in any such sense as a receiver. He takes the legal title to the property of the bankrupt and in respect to suits stands in the same general position as a trustee of an express trust or an executor. His duties are fixed by statute. He is to collect and reduce to money the property of the estate of the bankrupt.

## U

**Ultra Vires**    Beyond the powers. In administrative law, it describes an act that is beyond the authority granted to an administrative agency by its enabling legislation. In corporation law, it describes a corporation's performing an act beyond the limits of its purposes as stated in its articles of incorporation.

**Unconscionable**    In contract law, a contract that is grossly unfair or one-sided; one that "shocks the conscience of the court." The Uniform Commercial Code expressly gives courts the broad discretionary powers to deal with such contracts.

**Unilateral Contract**    A contract formed by an offer or a promise on one side for an act to be done on the other, and a doing of the act by the other by way of acceptance of the offer or promise; that is, a contract wherein the only acceptance of the offer that is necessary is the performance of the act.

**Unliquidated**    Undetermined in amount.

**Usage of Trade**    Customs and practices generally known by people in the business and usually assumed by parties to a contract for goods of that type.

**Usurpation**    In corporation law, an officer, director, or shareholder's taking to himself a business opportunity that belongs to his corporation.

**Usury**    The taking of more than the law allows on a loan or for forbearance of a debt. Illegal interest; interest in excess of the rate allowed by law.

## V

**Valid**    Effective; operative; not void; subsisting; sufficient in law.

**Value**    Under the Code (except for negotiable instruments and bank collections), generally any consideration sufficient to support a simple contract.

**Vendee**    A purchaser of property. The word is more commonly applied to a purchaser of real property, the word *buyer* being more commonly applied to the purchaser of personal property.

**Vendor**    A person who sells property to a vendee. The words *vendor* and *vendee* are more commonly applied to the seller and purchaser of real estate, and the words *seller* and *buyer* are more commonly applied to the seller and purchaser of personal property.

**Venire**    The name of a writ by which a jury is summoned.

**Venue**    A requirement distinct from jurisdiction that the court be geographically situated so that it is the most appropriate and convenient court to try the case.

**Verdict**    Usually, the decision made by a jury and reported to the judge on the matters or questions submitted to it at trial. In some situations, however, the judge may be the party issuing a verdict, as, for example, in the motion for a directed verdict. See *Directed Verdict*.

**Versus**    Against.

**Vest**    To give an immediate fixed right of present or future enjoyment.

**Vicarious Liability**    The imposition of liability on one party for the wrongs of another. Also called *imputed liability*. For example, the civil liability of a principal for the wrongs his agent commits when acting within the scope of his employment. See *Respondeat Superior*. Such liability is also occasionally encountered in the criminal context (e.g., the criminal liability that some regulatory statutes impose on managers for the actions of employees under their supervision).

**Void**    That which is entirely null. A void act is one that is not binding on either party and that is not susceptible of ratification.

**Voidable**    Capable of being made void; not utterly null, but annullable, and hence that may be either voided or confirmed. See *Avoid*.

**Voidable Title**    A title that is capable of, or subject to, being judged invalid or void.

**Voting Trust**    A type of shareholder voting arrangement by which shareholders transfer their voting rights to a voting trustee.

## W

**Waive**    To throw away; to relinquish voluntarily, as a right that one may enforce, if he chooses.

**Waiver**    The intentional relinquishment of a known right. It is a voluntary act and implies an election by the party to dispense with something of value, or to forgo some advantage that he or she might have demanded and insisted on.

**Warehouse Receipt**   A receipt issued by a person engaged in the business of storing goods for hire.

**Warrant**   An order authorizing a payment of money by another person to a third person. Also, an option to purchase a security. As a verb, the word means to defend; to guarantee; to enter into an obligation of warranty.

**Warrant of Arrest**   A legal process issued by competent authority, usually directed to regular officers of the law, but occasionally issued to private persons named in it, directing the arrest of a person or persons on grounds stated therein.

**Warranty**   An undertaking relating to characteristics of a thing being sold; a guaranty.

**Waste**   The material alteration, abuse, or destructive use of property by one in rightful possession of it that results in injury to one having an underlying interest in it.

**Watered Shares**   Also called *watered stock*. Shares issued in exchange for property that has been overvalued. See *Bonus Shares* and *Discount Shares*.

**Will**   A document executed with specific legal formalities that contains a person's instructions about the disposition of his property at his death.

**Winding Up**   In partnership and corporation law, the orderly liquidation of the business's assets.

**Writ**   A commandment of a court given for the purpose of compelling certain action from the defendant, and usually executed by a sheriff or other judicial officer.

**Writ of Certiorari**   An order of a court to an inferior court to forward the record of a case for reexamination by the superior court.

**Wrongful Use of Civil Proceedings**   An intentional tort designed to protect against the wrongful initiation of civil proceedings.

# INDEX